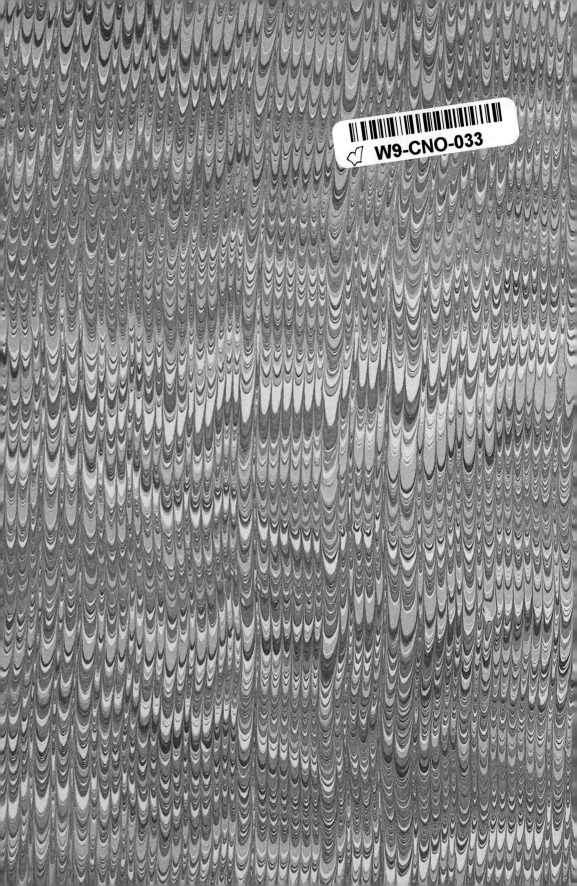

WILLIAM SHAKESPEARE

WILLIAM SHAKESPEARE

THE TRAGEDIES
THE POEMS

The Cambridge text established by
JOHN DOVER WILSON
for the
CAMBRIDGE UNIVERSITY PRESS

This volume first published in Great Britain in 1986 by

Octopus Books Limited
59 Grosvenor Street
London W1

Copyright © The Cambridge text of the Complete Works of
William Shakespeare, Cambridge University Press
1921, 1922, 1923, 1924, 1926, 1928, 1929, 1930,
1931, 1934, 1936, 1939, 1946, 1947, 1949, 1950,
1952, 1954, 1955, 1956, 1957, 1960, 1962, 1966

Copyright © 1986 arrangement Octopus Books Limited

ISBN 0 7064 2743 2

Printed in the United States of America
by R. R. Donnelley and Sons Company

Contents

Not marble, nor the gilded monuments
Of princes shall outlive this powerful rhyme.

Sonnet 55

Troilus and Cressida

The scene: Troy, and the Greek camp

CHARACTERS IN THE PLAY

PRIAM, *king of Troy*
HECTOR
TROILUS
PARIS } *his sons*
DEIPHOBUS
HELENUS
MARGARELON, *a bastard son of Priam*
ÆNEAS
ANTENOR } *Trojan commanders*
CALCHAS, *a Trojan Priest, taking part with the Greeks*
PANDARUS, *uncle to Cressida*
AGAMEMNON, *the Greek general*
MENELAUS, *his brother*
ACHILLES
AJAX
ULYSSES
NESTOR } *Greek commanders*
DIOMEDES
PATROCLUS

THERSITES, *a deformed and scurrilous Greek*
ALEXANDER, *servant to Cressida*
Servant to Troilus
Servant to Paris
Servant to Diomedes
The Prologue
HELEN, *wife to Menelaus*
ANDROMACHE, *wife to Hector*
CASSANDRA, *daughter to Priam; a prophetess*
CRESSIDA, *daughter to Calchas*
Trojan and Greek Soldiers, and Attendants

Troilus and Cressida

PROLOGUE

PROLOGUE. In Troy there lies the scene. From isles
of Greece
The princes orgulous, their high blood chafed,
Have to the port of Athens sent their ships,
Fraught with the ministers and instruments
Of cruel war; sixty and nine, that wore
Their crownets regal, from th'Athenian bay
Put forth toward Phrygia, and their vow is made
To ransack Troy, within whose strong immures
The ravished Helen, Menelaus' queen,
With wanton Paris sleeps—and that's the quarrel. 10
To Tenedos they come,
And the deep-drawing barks to there disgorge
Their warlike fraughtage; now on Dardan plains
The fresh and yet unbruisèd Greeks do pitch
Their brave pavilions: Priam's six-gated city,
Dardan, and Timbria, Helias, Chetas, Troien,
And Antenorides, with massy staples
And correspronsive and fulfilling bolts,
Sperr up the sons of Troy.
Now expectation, tickling skittish spirits 20
On one and other side, Trojan and Greek,
Sets all on hazard—and hither am I come
A Prologue armed, but not in confidence
Of author's pen or actor's voice, but suited
In like condition as our argument,
To tell you, fair beholders, that our play
Leaps o'er the vaunt and firstlings of those broils,
Beginning in the middle; starting thence away
To what may be digested in a play.
Like or find fault; do as your pleasures are: 30
Now good or bad, 'tis but the chance of war.

Goes

ACT 1
Scene 1: *Troy. Before Priam's palace*

Enter Pandarus and Troilus in armour

TROILUS. Call here my varlet; I'll unarm again:
Why should I war without the walls of Troy
That find such cruel battle here within?
Each Trojan that is master of his heart,
Let him to field; Troilus, alas, hath none!
PANDARUS. Will this gear ne'er be mended?
TROILUS. The Greeks are strong, and skilful to
their strength,
Fierce to their skill, and to their fierceness valiant,
But I am weaker than a woman's tear,
Tamer than sleep, fonder than ignorance, 10
Less valiant than the virgin in the night,
And skilless as unpractised infancy.
PANDARUS. Well, I have told you enough of this; for
my part, I'll not meddle nor make no farther. He
that will have a cake out of the wheat must tarry
the grinding.
TROILUS. Have I not tarried?
PANDARUS. Ay, the grinding; but you must tarry the
bolting.

TROILUS. Have I not tarried? 20
PANDARUS. Ay, the bolting; but you must tarry the
leavening.
TROILUS. Still have I tarried.
PANDARUS. Ay, to the leavening; but there's yet in the
word hereafter, the kneading, the making of the
cake, the heating of the oven, and the baking; nay,
you must stay the cooling too, or you may chance
to burn your lips.
TROILUS. Patience herself, what goddess e'er she be,
Doth lesser blench at sufferance than I do; 30
At Priam's royal table do I sit,
And when fair Cressid comes into my thoughts—
So, traitor! 'When she comes!'—When is she
thence?
PANDARUS. Well, she looked yesternight fairer than
ever I saw her look, or any woman else.
TROILUS. I was about to tell thee—when my heart,
As wedgèd with a sigh, would rive in twain,
Lest Hector or my father should perceive me,
I have, as when the sun doth light a storm,
Buried this sigh in wrinkle of a smile: 40
But sorrow that is couched in seeming gladness
Is like that mirth fate turns to sudden sadness.
PANDARUS. An her hair were not somewhat darker
than Helen's—well, go to—there were no more
comparison between the women. But, for my part,
she is my kinswoman; I would not, as they term it,
praise her, but I would somebody had heard her
talk yesterday, as I did. I will not dispraise your
sister Cassandra's wit, but—
TROILUS. O Pandarus! I tell thee, Pandarus— 50
When I do tell thee there my hopes lie drowned,
Reply not in how many fathoms deep
They lie indrenched. I tell thee I am mad
In Cressid's love. Thou answer'st she is fair;
Pour'st in the open ulcer of my heart
Her eyes, her hair, her cheek, her gait, her voice;
Handlest in thy discourse—O, that her hand,
In whose comparison all whites are ink
Writing their own reproach, to whose soft seizure
The cygnet's down is harsh, and spirit of sense 60
Hard as the palm of ploughman! this thou tell'st me,
As true thou tell'st me, when I say I love her;
But saying thus, instead of oil and balm,
Thou lay'st in every gash that love hath given me
The knife that made it.
PANDARUS. I speak no more than truth.
TROILUS. Thou dost not speak so much.
PANDARUS. Faith, I'll not meddle in 't. Let her be as
she is. If she be fair, 'tis the better for her; an she
be not, she has the mends in her own hands. 70
TROILUS. Good Pandarus, how now, Pandarus!
PANDARUS. I have had my labour for my travail:
ill thought on of her, and ill thought on of you;
gone between and between, but small thanks for my
labour.
TROILUS. What, art thou angry, Pandarus? what,
with me?
PANDARUS. Because she's kin to me, therefore she's not

so fair as Helen; an she were not kin to me, she
would be as fair o' Friday as Helen is o' Sunday. But
what care I? I care not an she were a blackamoor; 80
'tis all one to me.

TROILUS. Say I she is not fair?

PANDARUS. I do not care whether you do or no.
She's a fool to stay behind her father. Let her to the
Greeks, and so I'll tell her the next time I see her.
For my part, I'll meddle nor make no more i'th'
matter.

TROILUS. Pandarus—

PANDARUS. Not I.

TROILUS. Sweet Pandarus—   90

PANDARUS. Pray you, speak no more to me: I will
leave all as I found it, and there an end.
                                          Goes; alarum

TROILUS. Peace, you ungracious clamours! peace,
rude sounds!
Fools on both sides! Helen must needs be fair,
When with your blood you daily paint her thus.
I cannot fight upon this argument;
It is too starved a subject for my sword.
But Pandarus—O gods, how do you plague me!
I cannot come to Cressid but by Pandar,   100
And he's as tetchy to be wooed to woo
As she is stubborn-chaste against all suit.
Tell me, Apollo, for thy Daphne's love,
What Cressid is, what Pandar, and what we?
Her bed is India; there she lies, a pearl;
Between our Ilium and where she resides
Let it be called the wild and wandering flood;
Ourself the merchant, and this sailing Pandar,
Out doubtful hope, our convoy and our bark.

Alarum. Enter Æneas

ÆNEAS. How now, Prince Troilus! Wherefore
not afield?

TROILUS. Because not there; this woman's answer
sorts,   110
For womanish it is to be from thence.
What news, Æneas, from the field today?

ÆNEAS. That Paris is returnéd home, and hurt.

TROILUS. By whom, Æneas?

ÆNEAS.   Troilus, by Menelaus.

TROILUS. Let Paris bleed: 'tis but a scar to scorn;
Paris is gored with Menelaus' horn.   *Alarum*

ÆNEAS. Hark what good sport is out of town today!

TROILUS. Better at home, if 'would I might' were
'may'.
But to the sport abroad: are you bound thither?

ÆNEAS. In all swift haste.

TROILUS.   Come, go we then together. 120
                                          They go

Scene 2: *The same. A street*

Enter Cressida and Alexander, her man

CRESSIDA. Who were those went by?

ALEXANDER.   Queen Hecuba and Helen.

CRESSIDA. And whither go they?

ALEXANDER.   Up to the eastern tower,
Whose height commands as subject all the vale,
To see the battle. Hector, whose patience
Is as a virtue fixed, today was moved:
He chid Andromache and struck his armourer;
And, like as there were husbandry in war,

Before the sun rose he was harnessed light,
And to the field goes he; where every flower
Did, as a prophet, weep what it foresaw   10
In Hector's wrath.

CRESSIDA.   What was his cause of anger?

ALEXANDER. The noise goes this: there is among
the Greeks
A lord of Trojan blood, nephew to Hector;
They call him Ajax.

CRESSIDA.   Good; and what of him?

ALEXANDER. They say he is a very man per se,
And stands alone.

CRESSIDA. So do all men, unless they are drunk, sick,
or have no legs.

ALEXANDER. This man, lady, hath robbed many beasts
of their particular additions: he is as valiant as the 20
lion, churlish as the bear, slow as the elephant—a
man into whom nature hath so crowded humours
that his valour is crushed into folly, his folly forced
with discretion. There is no man hath a virtue that
he hath not a glimpse of, nor any man an attaint
but he carries some stain of it; he is melancholy
without cause and merry against the hair; he hath
the joints of everything, but everything so out of
joint that he is a gouty Briareus, many hands and
no use, or a purblind Argus, all eyes and no sight. 30

CRESSIDA. But how should this man, that makes me
smile, make Hector angry?

ALEXANDER. They say he yesterday coped Hector in
the battle and struck him down, the disdain and
shame whereof hath ever since kept Hector fasting
and waking.

CRESSIDA. Who comes here?

ALEXANDER. Madam, your uncle Pandarus.

Enter Pandarus

CRESSIDA. Hector's a gallant man.

ALEXANDER. As may be in the world, lady.   40

PANDARUS. What's that? what's that?

CRESSIDA. Good morrow, uncle Pandarus.

PANDARUS. Good morrow, cousin Cressid. What do
you talk of? Good morrow, Alexander. How do
you, cousin? When were you at Ilium?

CRESSIDA. This morning, uncle.

PANDARUS. What were you talking of when I came?
Was Hector armed and gone ere you came to Ilium?
Helen was not up, was she?

CRESSIDA. Hector was gone; but Helen was not up. 50

PANDARUS. E'en so: Hector was stirring early.

CRESSIDA. That were we talking of, and of his anger.

PANDARUS. Was he angry?

CRESSIDA. So he says here.

PANDARUS. True, he was so; I know the cause too;
he'll lay about him today, I can tell them that. And
there's Troilus will not come far behind him; let
them take heed of Troilus, I can tell them that too.

CRESSIDA. What, is he angry too?

PANDARUS. Who, Troilus? Troilus is the better man 60
of the two.

CRESSIDA. O Jupiter! there's no comparison.

PANDARUS. What, not between Troilus and Hector?
Do you know a man if you see him?

CRESSIDA. Ay, if I ever saw him before and knew him.

PANDARUS. Well, I say Troilus is Troilus.

CRESSIDA. Then you say as I say; for I am sure he is
not Hector.

PANDARUS. No, nor Hector is not Troilus in some degrees. 70

CRESSIDA. 'Tis just to each of them; he is himself.

PANDARUS. Himself! Alas, poor Troilus! I would he were—

CRESSIDA. So he is.

PANDARUS. Condition I had gone barefoot to India.

CRESSIDA. He is not Hector.

PANDARUS. Himself! no, he's not himself. Would 'a were himself! Well, the gods are above; time must friend or end. Well, Troilus, well, I would my heart were in her body! No, Hector is not a better 80 man than Troilus.

CRESSIDA. Excuse me.

PANDARUS. He is elder.

CRESSIDA. Pardon me, pardon me.

PANDARUS. Th'other's not come to't. You shall tell me another tale when th'other's come to't. Hector shall not have his wit this year.

CRESSIDA. He shall not need it, if he have his own.

PANDARUS. Nor his qualities.

CRESSIDA. No matter. 90

PANDARUS. Nor his beauty.

CRESSIDA. 'Twould not become him; his own's better.

PANDARUS. You have no judgement, niece. Helen herself swore th'other day that Troilus for a brown favour, for so 'tis, I must confess—not brown neither—

CRESSIDA. No, but brown.

PANDARUS. Faith, to say the truth, brown and not brown.

CRESSIDA. To say the truth, true and not true. 100

PANDARUS. She praised his complexion above Paris.

CRESSIDA. Why, Paris hath colour enough.

PANDARUS. So he has.

CRESSIDA. Then Troilus should have too much: if she praised him above, his complexion is higher than his; he having colour enough, and the other higher, is too flaming a praise for a good complexion. I had as lief Helen's golden tongue had commended Troilus for a copper nose.

PANDARUS. I swear to you, I think Helen loves him 110 better than Paris.

CRESSIDA. Then she's a merry Greek indeed.

PANDARUS. Nay, I am sure she does. She came to him th'other day into the compassed window—and, you know, he has not past three or four hairs on his chin—

CRESSIDA. Indeed, a tapster's arithmetic may soon bring his particulars therein to a total.

PANDARUS. Why, he is very young; and yet will he within three pound lift as much as his brother 120 Hector.

CRESSIDA. Is he so young a man and so old a lifter?

PANDARUS. But to prove to you that Helen loves him: she came and puts me her white hand to his cloven chin—

CRESSIDA. Juno have mercy! how came it cloven?

PANDARUS. Why, you know, 'tis dimpled. I think his smiling becomes him better than any man in all Phrygia.

CRESSIDA. O, he smiles valiantly. 130

PANDARUS. Does he not?

CRESSIDA. O yes, an 'twere a cloud in autumn.

PANDARUS. Why, go to, then! But to prove to you that Helen loves Troilus—

CRESSIDA. Troilus will stand to the proof, if you'll prove it so.

PANDARUS. Troilus! Why, he esteems her no more than I esteem an addle egg.

CRESSIDA. If you love an addle egg as well as you love an idle head, you would eat chickens i'th'shell. 140

PANDARUS. I cannot choose but laugh to think how she tickled his chin; indeed, she has a marvellous white hand, I must needs confess—

CRESSIDA. Without the rack.

PANDARUS. And she takes upon her to spy a white hair on his chin.

CRESSIDA. Alas, poor chin! many a wart is richer.

PANDARUS. But there was such laughing! Queen Hecuba laughed, that her eyes ran o'er.

CRESSIDA. With millstones. 150

PANDARUS. And Cassandra laughed.

CRESSIDA. But there was a more temperate fire under the pot of her eyes. Did her eyes run o'er too?

PANDARUS. And Hector laughed.

CRESSIDA. At what was all this laughing?

PANDARUS. Marry, at the white hair that Helen spied on Troilus' chin.

CRESSIDA. An't had been a green hair, I should have laughed too.

PANDARUS. They laughed not so much at the hair as at 160 his pretty answer.

CRESSIDA. What was his answer?

PANDARUS. Quoth she, 'Here's but two and fifty hairs on your chin, and one of them is white'.

CRESSIDA. This is her question.

PANDARUS. That's true; make no question of that. 'Two and fifty hairs', quoth he, 'and one white; that white hair is my father, and all the rest are his sons.' 'Jupiter!' quoth she, 'which of these hairs is Paris my husband?' 'The forked one,' quoth he; 'pluck't out, 170 and give it him.' But there was such laughing, and Helen so blushed, and Paris so chafed, and all the rest so laughed, that it passed!

CRESSIDA. So let it now; for it has been a great while going by.

PANDARUS. Well, cousin, I told you a thing yesterday; think on't.

CRESSIDA. So I do.

PANDARUS. I'll be sworn 'tis true; he will weep you an 'twere a man born in April. 180

CRESSIDA. And I'll spring up in his tears an 'twere a nettle against May.   *Retreat sounded*

PANDARUS. Hark! they are coming from the field. Shall we stand up here and see them as they pass toward Ilion? Good niece, do, sweet niece Cressida.

CRESSIDA. At your pleasure.

PANDARUS. Here, here, here's an excellent place; here we may see most bravely. I'll tell you them all by their names as they pass by. But mark Troilus above the rest. 190

CRESSIDA. Speak not so loud.

Æneas passes

PANDARUS. That's Æneas. Is not that a brave man? He's one of the flowers of Troy, I can tell you. But mark Troilus; you shall see Troilus anon.

Antenor passes

CRESSIDA. Who's that?

PANDARUS. That's Antenor. He has a shrewd wit, I can

tell you, and he's a man good enough: he's one
o'th' soundest judgements in Troy whosoever, and a
proper man of person. When comes Troilus? I'll
show you Troilus anon. If he see me, you shall see   200
him nod at me.
CRESSIDA. Will he give you the nod?
PANDARUS. You shall see.
CRESSIDA. If he do, the rich shall have more.

Hector passes

PANDARUS. That's Hector, that, that, look you, that;
there's a fellow! Go thy way, Hector! There's a
brave man, niece. O brave Hector! Look how he
looks! There's a countenance! Is't not a brave man?
CRESSIDA. O, a brave man!
PANDARUS. Is 'a not? It does a man's heart good. Look   210
you what hacks are on his helmet! Look you yonder,
do you see? look you there: there's no jesting;
there's laying on, take't off who will, as they say;
there be hacks!
CRESSIDA. Be those with swords?
PANDARUS. Swords! anything, he cares not; an the
devil come to him, it's all one. By God's lid, it does
one's heart good. Yonder comes Paris, yonder
comes Paris.

Paris passes

Look ye yonder, niece; is't not a gallant man too, is't   220
not? Why, this is brave now. Who said he came
home hurt today? He's not hurt. Why, this will do
Helen's heart good now, ha! Would I could see
Troilus now! You shall see Troilus anon.

Helenus passes

CRESSIDA. Who's that?
PANDARUS. That's Helenus. I marvel where Troilus is.
That's Helenus. I think he went not forth today.
That's Helenus.
CRESSIDA. Can Helenus fight, uncle?
PANDARUS. Helenus! no—yes, he'll fight indifferent   230
well. I marvel where Troilus is. Hark! do you not
hear the people cry 'Troilus'? Helenus is a priest.
CRESSIDA. What sneaking fellow comes yonder?

Troilus passes

PANDARUS. Where? yonder? that's Deiphobus. 'Tis
Troilus! there's a man, niece! Hem! Brave Troilus!
the prince of chivalry!
CRESSIDA. Peace, for shame, peace!
PANDARUS. Mark him; note him. O brave Troilus!
Look well upon him, niece; look you how his sword
is bloodied, and his helm more hacked than Hec-   240
tor's, and how he looks, and how he goes! O
admirable youth! he ne'er saw three and twenty. Go
thy way, Troilus, go thy way! Had I a sister were
a grace, or a daughter a goddess, he should take
his choice. O admirable man! Paris? Paris is dirt to
him; and, I warrant, Helen, to change, would give
an eye to boot.

Common Soldiers pass

CRESSIDA. Here come more.
PANDARUS. Asses, fools, dolts! chaff and bran, chaff and
bran! porridge after meat! I could live and die i' th'   250
eyes of Troilus. Ne'er look, ne'er look; the eagles
are gone: crows and daws, crows and daws! I had

rather be such a man as Troilus than Agamemnon
and all Greece.
CRESSIDA. There is among the Greeks Achilles, a
better man than Troilus.
PANDARUS. Achilles! a drayman, a porter, a very
camel.
CRESSIDA. Well, well.
PANDARUS. Well, well! Why, have you any discretion?   260
have you any eyes? do you know what a man is?
Is not birth, beauty, good shape, discourse, manhood, learning, gentleness, virtue, youth, liberality,
and such like, the spice and salt that season a man?
CRESSIDA. Ay, a minced man; and then to be baked
with no date in the pie, for then the man's date is
out.
PANDARUS. You are such another woman, a man
knows not at what ward you lie.
CRESSIDA. Upon my back, to defend my belly; upon   270
my wit, to defend my wiles; upon my secrecy, to
defend mine honesty; my mask, to defend my
beauty; and you, to defend all these: and at all these
wards I lie, at a thousand watches.
PANDARUS. Say one of your watches.
CRESSIDA. Nay, I'll watch you for that; and that's one
of the chiefest of them too: if I cannot ward what I
would not have hit, I can watch you for telling how
I took the blow; unless it swell past hiding, and then
it's past watching.   280
PANDARUS. You are such another!

Enter Troilus' Boy

BOY. Sir, my lord would instantly speak with you.
PANDARUS. Where?
BOY. At your own house; there he unarms him.
PANDARUS. Good boy, tell him I come.   *Boy goes*
I doubt he be hurt. Fare ye well, good niece.
CRESSIDA. Adieu, uncle.
PANDARUS. I'll be with you, niece, by and by.
CRESSIDA. To bring, uncle?
PANDARUS. Ay, a token from Troilus.   290
CRESSIDA. By the same token, you are a bawd.

Pandarus goes

Words, vows, gifts, tears, and love's full sacrifice,
He offers in another's enterprise;
But more in Troilus thousandfold I see
Than in the glass of Pandar's praise may be.
Yet hold I off: women are angels, wooing;
Things won are done—joy's soul lies in the doing.
That she beloved knows nought that knows not this:
Men prize the thing ungained more than it is.
That she was never yet that ever knew   300
Love got so sweet as when desire did sue.
Therefore this maxim out of love I teach:
'Achievement is command; ungained, beseech.'
Then though my heart's content firm love doth
  bear,
Nothing of that shall from mine eyes appear.
                                                    They go

Scene 3: *The Greek Camp. Before Agamemnon's tent*

*Sennet. Enter Agamemnon, Nestor, Ulysses, Menelaus,
with others*

AGAMEMNON. Princes,
What grief hath set this jaundice on your cheeks?
The ample proposition that hope makes

In all designs begun on earth below
Fails in the promised largeness: checks
   and disasters
Grow in the veins of actions highest reared,
As knots, by the conflux of meeting sap,
Infect the sound pine and divert his grain
Tortive and errant from his course of growth
Nor, princes, is it matter new to us   10
That we come short of our suppose so far
That after seven years' siege yet Troy walls stand;
Sith every action that hath gone before
Whereof we have record, trial did draw
Bias and thwart, not answering the aim
And that unbodied figure of the thought
That gave't surmisèd shape. Why then, you princes,
Do you with cheeks abashed behold our works,
And call them shames, which are indeed nought else
But the protractive trials of great Jove   20
To find persistive constancy in men?
The fineness of which metal is not found
In fortune's love: for then the bold and coward,
The wise and fool, the artist and unread,
The hard and soft, seem all affined and kin;
But, in the wind and tempest of her frown,
Distinction with a broad and powerful fan,
Puffing at all, winnows the light away,
And what hath mass or matter, by itself
Lies rich in virtue and unminglèd.   30
NESTOR. With due observance of thy godlike seat,
Great Agamemnon, Nestor shall apply
Thy latest words. In the reproof of chance
Lies the true proof of men: the sea being smooth,
How many shallow bauble boats dare sail
Upon her patient breast, making their way
With those of nobler bulk!
But let the ruffian Boreas once enrage
The gentle Thetis, and anon behold
The strong-ribbed bark through liquid mountains
   cut,   40
Bounding between the two moist elements
Like Perseus' horse; where's then the saucy boat
Whose weak untimbered sides but even now
Co-rivalled greatness?—either to harbour fled,
Or made a toast for Neptune. Even so
Doth valour's show and valour's worth divide
In storms of fortune: for in her ray and brightness
The herd hath more annoyance by the breese
Than by the tiger; but when the splitting wind
Makes flexible the knees of knotted oaks   50
And flies flee under shade, why then the thing
   of courage,
As roused with rage, with rage doth sympathize,
And with an accent tuned in selfsame key
Retorts to chiding fortune.
ULYSSES.   Agamemnon,
Thou great commander, nerve and bone of Greece,
Heart of our numbers, soul and only spirit,
In whom the tempers and the minds of all
Should be shut up, hear what Ulysses speaks.
Besides th'applause and approbation
The which, [to Agamemnon] most mighty for thy
   place and sway,   60
[to Nestor] And thou most reverend for thy
   stretched-out life,
I give to both your speeches, which were such
As, Agamemnon, all the hands of Greece

Should hold up high in brass, and such again
As, venerable Nestor, hatched in silver,
Should with a bond of air, strong as the axletree
On which heaven rides, knit all the Greekish ears
To his experienced tongue—yet let it please both,
Thou great, and wise, to hear Ulysses speak.
AGAMEMNON. Speak, Prince of Ithaca; and be't of
   less expect   70
That matter needless, of importless burden,
Divide thy lips than we are confident,
When rank Thersites opes his mastic jaws,
We shall hear music, wit and oracle.
ULYSSES. Troy, yet upon his basis, had been down,
And the great Hector's sword had lacked a master,
But for these instances:
The specialty of rule hath been neglected;
And look how many Grecian tents do stand
Hollow upon this plain, so many hollow factions. 80
When that the general is not like the hive
To whom the foragers shall all repair,
What honey is expected? Degree being vizarded,
Th'unworthiest shows as fairly in the mask.
The heavens themselves, the planets, and this centre,
Observe degree, priority, and place,
Insisture, course, proportion, season, form,
Office, and custom, in all line of order;
And therefore is the glorious planet Sol
In noble eminence enthroned and sphered   90
Amidst the other; whose medicinable eye
Corrects the influence of evil planets,
And posts, like the commandment of a king,
Sans check to good and bad. But when the planets
In evil mixture to disorder wander,
What plagues and what portents, what mutiny,
What raging of the sea, shaking of earth,
Commotion in the winds, frights, changes, horrors,
Divert and crack, rend and deracinate
The unity and married calm of states   100
Quite from their fixure! O, when degree is shaked,
Which is the ladder of all high designs,
The enterprise is sick! How could communities,
Degrees in schools, and brotherhoods in cities,
Peaceful commerce from dividable shores,
The primogenitive and due of birth,
Prerogative of age, crowns, sceptres, laurels,
But by degree, stand in authentic place?
Take but degree away, untune that string,
And hark what discord follows! each thing meets 110
In mere oppugnancy: the bounded waters
Should lift their bosoms higher than the shores,
And make a sop of all this solid globe;
Strength should be lord of imbecility,
And the rude son should strike his father dead;
Force should be right; or rather, right and wrong,
Between whose endless jar justice resides,
Should lose their names, and so should justice too.
Then everything includes itself in power,
Power into will, will into appetite;   120
And appetite, an universal wolf,
So doubly seconded with will and power,
Must make perforce an universal prey,
And last eat up himself. Great Agamemnon,
This chaos, when degree is suffocate,
Follows the choking.
And this neglection of degree it is
That by a pace goes backward, with a purpose

It hath to climb. The general's disdained
By him one step below, he by the next,   130
That next by him beneath; so every step,
Exampled by the first pace that is sick
Of his superior, grows to an envious fever
Of pale and bloodless emulation—
And 'tis this fever that keeps Troy on foot,
Not her own sinews: to end a tale of length,
Troy in our weakness stands, not in her strength.
NESTOR. Most wisely hath Ulysses here discovered
The fever whereof all our power is sick.
AGAMEMNON. The nature of the sickness found,
    Ulysses,   140
    What is the remedy?
ULYSSES. The great Achilles, whom opinion crowns
The sinew and the forehand of our host,
Having his ear full of his airy fame,
Grows dainty of his worth, and in his tent
Lies mocking our designs. With him, Patroclus,
Upon a lazy bed, the livelong day
Breaks scurril jests,
And with ridiculous and awkward action,
Which, slanderer, he imitation calls,   150
He pageants us. Sometime, great Agamemnon,
Thy topless deputation he puts on,
And, like a strutting player whose conceit
Lies in his hamstring, and doth think it rich
To hear the wooden dialogue and sound
'Twixt his stretched footing and the scaffoldage,
Such to-be-pitied and o'er-wrested seeming
He acts thy greatness in; and, when he speaks,
'Tis like a chime a-mending; with terms unsquared,
Which, from the tongue of roaring Typhon
    dropped,   160
Would seem hyperboles. At this fusty stuff,
The large Achilles, on his pressed bed lolling,
From his deep chest laughs out a loud applause,
Cries 'Excellent! 'tis Agamemnon right!
Now play me Nestor: hem, and stroke thy beard,
As be being dressed to some oration.'
That's done—as near as the extremest ends
Of parallels, as like as Vulcan and his wife.
Yet god Achilles still cries 'Excellent!
'Tis Nestor right! Now play him me, Patroclus,   170
Arming to answer in a night alarm.'
And then, forsooth, the faint defects of age
Must be the scene of mirth: to cough and spit,
And, with a palsy fumbling on his gorget,
Shake in and out the rivet. And at this sport
Sir Valour dies; cries 'O, enough, Patroclus,
Or give me ribs of steel! I shall split all
In pleasure of my spleen!' And in this fashion,
All our abilities, gifts, natures, shapes,
Severals and generals of grace exact,   180
Achievements, plots, orders, preventions,
Excitements to the field or speech for truce,
Success or loss, what is or is not, serves
As stuff for these two to make paradoxes.
NESTOR. And in the imitation of these twain,
Who, as Ulysses says, opinion crowns
With an imperial voice, many are infect.
Ajax is grown self-willed and bears his head
In such a rein, in full as proud a place
As broad Achilles; keeps his tent like him;   190
Makes factious feasts; rails on our state of war
Bold as an oracle; and sets Thersites,

A slave whose gall coins slanders like a mint,
To match us in comparisons with dirt,
To weaken and discredit our exposure,
How rank soever rounded in with danger.
ULYSSES. They tax our policy and call it cowardice,
Count wisdom as no member of the war,
Forestall prescience, and esteem no act
But that of hand; the still and mental parts   200
That do contrive how many hands shall strike
When fitness calls them on, and know by measure
Of their observant toil the enemy's weight—
Why, this hath not a finger's dignity:
They call this bed-work, mappery, closet-war;
So that the ram that batters down the wall,
For the great swing and rudeness of his poise,
They place before his hand that made the engine
Or those that with the fineness of their souls
By reason guide his execution.   210
NESTOR. Let this be granted, and Achilles' horse
Makes many Thetis' sons.   Tucket
AGAMEMNON. What trumpet? look, Menelaus.
MENELAUS. From Troy.

Enter Æneas

AGAMEMNON. What would you 'fore our tent?
ÆNEAS. Is this great Agamemnon's tent, I pray you?
AGAMEMNON. Even this.
ÆNEAS. May one that is a herald and a prince
Do a fair message to his kingly eyes?
AGAMEMNON. With surety stronger than Achilles'
    arms   220
'Fore all the Greekish heads, which with one voice
Call Agamemnon head and general.
ÆNEAS. Fair leave and large security. How may
A stranger to those most imperial looks
Know them from eyes of other mortals?
AGAMEMNON.   How?
ÆNEAS. Ay:
I ask, that I might waken reverence,
And bid the cheek be ready with a blush
Modest as morning when she coldly eyes
The youthful Phoebus.   230
Which is that god in office, guiding men?
Which is the high and mighty Agamemnon?
AGAMEMNON. This Trojan scorns us, or the men
    of Troy
Are ceremonious courtiers.
ÆNEAS. Courtiers as free, as debonair, unarmed,
As bending angels: that's their fame in peace.
But when they would seem soldiers, they have galls,
Good arms, strong joints, true swords, and—
    Jove's accord—
Nothing so full of heart. But peace, Æneas,
Peace, Trojan; lay thy finger on thy lips!   240
The worthiness of praise distains his worth,
If that the praised himself bring the praise forth:
But what the repining enemy commends,
That breath fame blows; that praise, sole
    pure, transcends.
AGAMEMNON. Sir you of Troy, call you
    yourself Æneas?
ÆNEAS. Ay, Greek, that is my name.
AGAMEMNON. What's your affair, I pray you?
ÆNEAS. Sir, pardon: 'tis for Agamemnon's ears.
AGAMEMNON. He hears nought privately that comes
    from Troy.

ÆNEAS. Nor I from Troy come not to whisper him; 250
  I bring a trumpet to awake his ear,
  To set his sense on the attentive bent,
  And then to speak.
AGAMEMNON.   Speak frankly as the wind;
  It is not Agamemnon's sleeping hour.
  That thou shalt know, Trojan, he is awake,
  He tells thee so himself.
ÆNEAS.   Trumpet, blow loud,
  Send thy brass voice through all these lazy tents;
  And every Greek of mettle, let him know,
  What Troy means fairly shall be spoke aloud.
                    Trumpet sounds
  We have, great Agamemnon, here in Troy 260
  A prince called Hector—Priam is his father—
  Who in this dull and long-continued truce
  Is resty grown. He bade me take a trumpet,
  And to this purpose speak: kings, princes, lords!
  If there be one among the fair'st of Greece,
  That holds his honour higher than his ease,
  That seeks his praise more than he fears his peril,
  That knows his valour and knows not his fear,
  That loves his mistress more than in confession
  With truant vows to her own lips he loves, 270
  And dare avow her beauty and her worth
  In other arms than hers—to him this challenge!
  Hector, in view of Trojans and of Greeks,
  Shall make it good, or do his best to do it,
  He hath a lady, wiser, fairer, truer,
  Than ever Greek did couple in his arms;
  And will tomorrow with his trumpet call
  Midway between your tents and walls of Troy,
  To rouse a Grecian that is true in love.
  If any come, Hector shall honour him; 280
  If none, he'll say in Troy when he retires,
  The Grecian dames are sunburnt and not worth
  The splinter of a lance. Even so much.
AGAMEMNON. This shall be told our lovers, Lord
  Æneas.
  If none of them have soul in such a kind,
  We left them all at home. But we are soldiers;
  And may that soldier a mere recreant prove,
  That means not, hath not, or is not in love!
  If then one is, or hath, or means to be,
  That one meets Hector; if none else, I am he. 290
NESTOR. Tell him of Nestor, one that was a man
  When Hector's grandsire sucked. He is old now;
  But if there be not in our Grecian host
  One noble man that hath one spark of fire,
  To answer for his love, tell him from me
  I'll hide my silver beard in a gold beaver
  And in my vantbrace put this withered brawn,
  And, meeting him, will tell him that my lady
  Was fairer than his grandam and as chaste
  As may be in the world: his youth in flood,
  I'll prove this truth with my three drops of blood. 300
ÆNEAS. Now heavens forfend such scarcity of youth!
ULYSSES. Amen.
AGAMEMNON. Fair Lord Æneas, let me touch
  your hand;
  To our pavilion shall I lead you first.
  Achilles shall have word of this intent;
  So shall each lord of Greece, from tent to tent.
  Yourself shall feast with us before you go,
  And find the welcome of a noble foe.
            They go; Ulysses detains Nestor

ULYSSES. Nestor! 310
NESTOR. What says Ulysses?
ULYSSES. I have a young conception in my brain;
  Be you my time to bring it to some shape.
NESTOR. What is't?
ULYSSES. This 'tis:
  Blunt wedges rive hard knots; the seeded pride
  That hath to this maturity blown up
  In rank Achilles must or now be cropped,
  Or, shedding, breed a nursery of like evil
  To overbulk us all.
NESTOR.   Well, and how? 320
ULYSSES. This challenge that the gallant Hector sends,
  However it is spread in general name,
  Relates in purpose only to Achilles.
NESTOR. True: the purpose is perspicuous
    as substance,
  Whose grossness little characters sum up;
  And, in the publication, make no strain
  But that Achilles, were his brain as barren
  As banks of Libya—though, Apollo knows,
  'Tis dry enough—will, with great speed of
    judgement,
  Ay, with celerity, find Hector's purpose 330
  Pointing on him.
ULYSSES. And wake him to the answer, think you?
NESTOR. Why, 'tis most meet. Who may you
    else oppose
  That can from Hector bring his honour off,
  If not Achilles? Though't be a sportful combat,
  Yet in this trial much opinion dwells:
  For here the Trojans taste our dear'st repute
  With their fin'st palate—and trust to me, Ulysses,
  Our imputation shall be oddly poised
  In this wild action; for the success, 340
  Although particular, shall give a scantling
  Of good or bad unto the general;
  And in such indexes, although small pricks
  To their subsequent volumes, there is seen
  The baby figure of the giant mass
  Of things to come at large. It is supposed
  He that meets Hector issues from our choice;
  And choice, being mutual act of all our souls,
  Makes merit her election, and doth boil,
  As 'twere from forth us all, a man distilled 350
  Out of our virtues; who miscarrying,
  What heart receives from hence a conquering part,
  To steel a strong opinion to themselves?
  Which entertained, limbs are his instruments,
  E'en no less working than are swords and bows
  Directive by the limbs.
ULYSSES. Give pardon to my speech: therefore 'tis meet
  Achilles meet not Hector. Let us, like merchants,
  First show foul wares, and think perchance they'll
    sell.
  If not, the lustre of the better shall exceed 360
  By showing the worse first. Do not consent
  That ever Hector and Achilles meet;
  For both our honour and our shame in this
  Are dogged with two strange followers.
NESTOR. I see them not with my old eyes: what
  are they?
ULYSSES. What glory our Achilles shares
    from Hector,
  Were he not proud, we all should share with him.
  But he already is too insolent;

And we were better parch in Afric sun
Than in the pride and salt scorn of his eyes,   370
Should he scape Hector fair: if he were foiled,
Why, then we did our main opinion crush
In taint of our best man. No, make a lottery,
And by device let blockish Ajax draw
The sort to fight with Hector; 'mong ourselves
Give him allowance as the better man;
For that will physic the great Myrmidon,
Who broils in loud applause, and make him fall
His crest that prouder than blue Iris bends.
If the dull brainless Ajax come safe off,   380
We'll dress him up in voices; if he fail,
Yet go we under our opinion still
That we have better men. But, hit or miss,
Our project's life this shape of sense assumes—
Ajax employed plucks down Achilles' plumes.
NESTOR. Ulysses,
Now I begin to relish thy advice,
And I will give a taste thereof forthwith
To Agamemnon. Go we to him straight.
Two curs shall tame each other: pride alone   390
Must tarre the mastiffs on, as 'twere their bone.

          They go

ACT 2
Scene 1: *The Greek camp*

Enter Ajax and Thersites

AJAX. Thersites!
THERSITES. Agamemnon—how if he had boils, full, all
    over, generally?
AJAX. Thersites!
THERSITES. And those boils did run? Say so: did not
    the general run then? were not that a botchy core?
AJAX. Dog!
THERSITES. Then would come some matter from him;
    I see none now.
AJAX. Thou bitch-wolf's son, canst thou not hear?   10
    Feel, then.   *Strikes him*
THERSITES. The plague of Greece upon thee, thou
    mongrel beef-witted lord!
AJAX. Speak then, thou vinewed'st leaven, speak! I
    will beat thee into handsomeness!
THERSITES. I shall sooner rail thee into wit and holiness;
    but I think thy horse will sooner con an oration than
    thou learn a prayer without book. Thou canst strike,
    canst thou? A red murrain o' thy jade's tricks!
AJAX. Toadstool, learn me the proclamation.   20
THERSITES. Dost thou think I have no sense, thou
    strikest me thus?
AJAX. The proclamation!
THERSITES. Thou art proclaimed a fool, I think.
AJAX. Do not, porpentine, do not; my fingers itch.
THERSITES. I would thou didst itch from head to foot
    and I had the scratching of thee; I would make thee
    the loathsomest scab in Greece. When thou art forth
    in the incursions, thou strikest as slow as another.
AJAX. I say, the proclamation!   30
THERSITES. Thou grumblest and railest every hour on
    Achilles, and thou art as full of envy at his greatness
    as Cerberus is at Proserpina's beauty, ay, that thou
    barkest at him.
AJAX. Mistress Thersites!
THERSITES. Thou shouldst strike him.

AJAX. Cobloaf!
THERSITES. He would pun thee into shivers with his
    fist, as a sailor breaks a biscuit.
AJAX. You whoreson cur!   *Strikes him*   40
THERSITES. Do, do, thou stool for a witch! ay, do, do,
    thou sodden-witted lord! Thou hast no more brain
    in thy head than I have in mine elbows; an assinego
    may tutor thee. Thou scurvy-valiant ass! thou art
    here but to thrash Trojans; and thou art bought and
    sold among those of any wit, like a barbarian slave.
    If thou use to beat me, I will begin at thy heel and
    tell what thou art by inches, thou thing of no
    bowels, thou!
AJAX. You dog!   50
THERSITES. You scurvy lord!
AJAX. You cur!   *Strikes him*
THERSITES. Mars his idiot! do, rudeness; do, camel,
    do, do.

Enter Achilles and Patroclus

ACHILLES. Why, how now, Ajax! Wherefore do you
    thus? How now, Thersites! What's the matter, man?
THERSITES. You see him there, do you?
ACHILLES. Ay; what's the matter?
THERSITES. Nay, look upon him.
ACHILLES. So I do; what's the matter?   60
THERSITES. Nay, but regard him well.
ACHILLES. 'Well!'—why, so I do.
THERSITES. But yet you look not well upon him: for
    whosoever you take him to be, he is Ajax.
ACHILLES. I know that, fool.
THERSITES. Ay, but that fool knows not himself.
AJAX. Therefore I beat thee.
THERSITES. Lo, lo, lo, lo, what modicums of wit he
    utters! His evasions have ears thus long. I have
    bobbed his brain more than he has beat my bones.   70
    I will buy nine sparrows for a penny, and his pia
    mater is not worth the ninth part of a sparrow.
    This lord, Achilles—Ajax, who wears his wit in his
    belly and his guts in his head—I'll tell you what I
    say of him.
ACHILLES. What?
THERSITES. I say this Ajax—   *Ajax offers to strike him*
ACHILLES. Nay, good Ajax.
THERSITES. Has not so much wit—
ACHILLES. Nay, I must hold you.   80
THERSITES. As will stop the eye of Helen's needle, for
    whom he comes to fight.
ACHILLES. Peace, fool!
THERSITES. I would have peace and quietness, but the
    fool will not—he there; that he; look you there!
AJAX. O thou damned cur! I shall—
ACHILLES. Will you set your wit to a fool's?
THERSITES. No, I warrant you; for the fool's will
    shame it.
PATROCLUS. Good words, Thersites.   90
ACHILLES. What's the quarrel?
AJAX. I bade the vile owl go learn me the tenour of
    the proclamation, and he rails upon me.
THERSITES. I serve thee not.
AJAX. Well, go to, go to.
THERSITES. I serve here voluntary.
ACHILLES. Your last service was sufferance, 'twas not
    voluntary. No man is beaten voluntary. Ajax was
    here the voluntary, and you as under an impress.
THERSITES. E'en so; a great deal of your wit too lies in   100

your sinews, or else there be liars. Hector shall have
a great catch an 'a knock out either of your brains:
'a were as good crack a fusty nut with no kernel.

ACHILLES. What, with me too, Thersites?

THERSITES. There's Ulysses and old Nestor, whose wit
was mouldy ere your grandsires had nails on their
toes, yoke you like draught-oxen, and make you
plough up the wars.

ACHILLES. What? what?

THERSITES. Yes, good sooth: to, Achilles! to, Ajax, to! 110

AJAX. I shall cut out your tongue.

THERSITES. 'Tis no matter; I shall speak as much wit
as thou afterwards.

PATROCLUS. No more words, Thersites; peace!

THERSITES. I will hold my peace when Achilles' brach
bids me, shall I?

ACHILLES. There's for you, Patroclus.

THERSITES. I will see you hanged, like clotpolls, ere
I come any more to your tents. I will keep where
there is wit stirring, and leave the faction of fools. 120
                                             Goes

PATROCLUS. A good riddance.

ACHILLES. Marry, this, sir, is proclaimed through all
    our host:
That Hector, by the fifth hour of the sun,
Will with a trumpet 'twixt our tents and Troy
Tomorrow morning call some knight to arms
That hath a stomach, and such a one that dare
Maintain—I know not what; 'tis trash. Farewell.

AJAX. Farewell. Who shall answer him?

ACHILLES. I know not. 'Tis put to lottery; otherwise
He knew his man.   130

AJAX. O, meaning you. I'll go learn more of it.
                                           They go

Scene 2: *Troy. Priam's palace*

Enter Priam, Hector, Troilus, Paris, and Helenus

PRIAM. After so many hours, lives, speeches spent,
Thus once again says Nestor from the Greeks:
'Deliver Helen, and all damage else—
As honour, loss of time, travail, expense,
Wounds, friends, and what else dear that
    is consumed
In hot digestion of this cormorant war—
Shall be struck off.' Hector, what say you to't?

HECTOR. Though no man lesser fears the Greeks
    than I
As far as toucheth my particular,
Yet dread Priam,   10
There is no lady of more softer bowels,
More spongy to suck in the sense of fear,
More ready to cry out 'Who knows what follows?'
Than Hector is. The wound of peace is surety,
Surety secure; but modest doubt is called
The beacon of the wise, the tent that searches
To th'bottom of the worst. Let Helen go.
Since the first sword was drawn about this question,
Every tithe-soul 'mongst many thousand dismes
Hath been as dear as Helen—I mean, of ours.   20
If we have lost so many tenths of ours
To guard a thing not ours, nor worth to us—
Had it our name—the value of one ten,
What merit's in that reason which denies
The yielding of her up?

TROILUS.   Fie, fie, my brother!

Weigh you the worth and honour of a king
So great as our dread father in a scale
Of common ounces? Will you with counters sum
The past-proportion of his infinite,
And buckle in a waist most fathomless   30
With spans and inches so diminutive
As fears and reasons? Fie, for godly shame!

HELENUS. No marvel though you bite so sharp
    at reasons,
You are so empty of them. Shall not our father
Bear the great sway of his affairs with reasons,
Because your speech hath none that tells him so?

TROILUS. You are for dreams and slumbers,
    brother priest.
You fur your gloves with reasons. Here are
    your reasons:
You know an enemy intends you harm;
You know a sword employed is perilous,   40
And reason flies the object of all harm;
Who marvels then, when Helenus beholds
A Grecian and his sword, if he do set
The very wings of reason to his heels
And fly, like chidden Mercury from Jove
Or like a star disorbed? Nay, if we talk of reason,
Let's shut our gates and sleep. Manhood
    and honour
Should have hare hearts, would they but fat
    their thoughts
With this crammed reason; reason and respect
Make livers pale and lustihood deject.   50

HECTOR. Brother, she is not worth what she doth cost
    The keeping.

TROILUS.   What's aught, but as 'tis valued?

HECTOR. But value dwells not in particular will:
It holds his estimate and dignity
As well wherein 'tis precious of itself
As in the prizer. 'Tis mad idolatry
To make the service greater than the god;
And the will dotes that is attributive
To what infectiously itself affects,
Without some image of th'affected merit.   60

TROILUS. I take today a wife, and my election
Is led on in the conduct of my will;
My will enkindled by mine eyes and ears—
Two traded pilots 'twixt the dangerous shores
Of will and judgement—how may I avoid,
Although my will distaste what it elected,
The wife I chose? There can be no evasion
To blench from this and to stand firm by honour.
We turn not back the silks upon the merchant
When we have soiled them; nor the remainder
    viands   70
We do not throw in unrespective sieve
Because we now are full. It was thought meet
Paris should do some vengeance on the Greeks;
Your breath of full consent bellied his sails;
The seas and winds, old wranglers, took a truce,
And did him service; he touched the ports desired;
And for an old aunt whom the Greeks held captive
He brought a Grecian queen, whose youth
    and freshness
Wrinkles Apollo's and makes pale the morning.
Why keep we her?—the Grecians keep our aunt;   80
Is she worth keeping?—why, she is a pearl
Whose price hath launched above a thousand ships
And turned crowned kings to merchants.

If you'll avouch 'twas wisdom Paris went—
As you must needs, for you all cried 'Go, go';
If you'll confess he brought home worthy prize—
As you must needs, for you all clapped your hands
And cried 'Inestimable!'; why do you now
The issue of your proper wisdoms rate,
And do a deed that Fortune never did,   90
Beggar the estimation which you prized
Richer than sea and land? O, theft most base,
That we have stolen what we do fear to keep!
But thieves unworthy of a thing so stolen,
That in their country did them that disgrace
We fear to warrant in our native place!
CASSANDRA [within]. Cry, Trojans, cry!
PRIAM.   What noise, what shriek is this?
TROILUS. 'Tis our mad sister, I do know her voice.
CASSANDRA [within]. Cry, Trojans!
HECTOR. It is Cassandra.   100

Enter Cassandra, raving, with her hair about her ears

CASSANDRA. Cry, Trojans, cry! lend me ten
    thousand eyes,
And I will fill them with prophetic tears.
HECTOR. Peace, sister, peace!
CASSANDRA. Virgins and boys, mid-age and
    wrinkled eld,
Soft infancy, that nothing canst but cry,
Add to my clamours! Let us pay betimes
A moiety of that mass of moan to come.
Cry, Trojans, cry! Practise your eyes with tears!
Troy must not be, nor goodly Ilion stand;
Our firebrand brother, Paris, burns us all.   110
Cry, Trojans, cry! a Helen and a woe:
Cry, cry! Troy burns, or else let Helen go.   *Goes*
HECTOR. Now youthful Troilus, do not these
    high strains
Of divination in our sister work
Some touches of remorse, or is your blood
So madly hot that no discourse of reason,
Nor fear of bad success in a bad cause,
Can qualify the same?
TROILUS.   Why, brother Hector,
We may not think the justness of each act
Such and no other than event doth form it,   120
Nor once deject the courage of our minds
Because Cassandra's mad. Her brainsick raptures
Cannot distaste the goodness of a quarrel
Which hath our several honours all engaged
To make it gracious. For my private part,
I am no more touched than all Priam's sons;
And Jove forbid there should be done amongst us
Such things as might offend the weakest spleen
To fight for and maintain!
PARIS. Else might the world convince of levity   130
As well my undertakings as your counsels;
But I attest the gods, your full consent
Gave wings to my propension and cut off
All fears attending on so dire a project.
For what, alas, can these my single arms?
What propugnation is in one man's valour
To stand the push and enmity of those
This quarrel would excite? Yet, I protest,
Were I alone to pass the difficulties
And had as ample power as I have will,   140
Paris should ne'er retract what he hath done,
Nor faint in the pursuit.

PRIAM.   Paris, you speak
Like one besotted on your sweet delights;
You have the honey still, but these the gall:
So to be valiant is no praise at all.
PARIS. Sir, I propose not merely to myself
The pleasures such a beauty brings with it,
But I would have the soil of her fair rape
Wiped off in honourable keeping her.
What treason were it to the ransacked queen,   150
Disgrace to your great worths, and shame to me.
Now to deliver her possession up
On terms of base compulsion! Can it be
That so degenerate a strain as this
Should once set footing in your generous bosoms?
There's not the meanest spirit on our party
Without a heart to dare or sword to draw
When Helen is defended; nor none so noble
Whose life were ill bestowed or death unfamed
Where Helen is the subject. Then, I say,   160
Well may we fight for her whom we know well
The world's large spaces cannot parallel.
HECTOR. Paris and Troilus, you have both said well,
And on the cause and question now in hand
Have glozed—but superficially; not much
Unlike young men, whom Aristotle thought
Unfit to hear moral philosophy.
The reasons you allege do more conduce
To the hot passion of distempered blood
Than to make up a free determination   170
'Twixt right and wrong: for pleasure and revenge
Have ears more deaf than adders to the voice
Of any true decision. Nature craves
All dues be rendered to their owners: now,
What nearer debt in all humanity
Than wife is to the husband? If this law
Of nature be corrupted through affection,
And that great minds, of partial indulgence
To their benumbéd wills, resist the same,
There is a law in each well-ordered nation   180
To curb those raging appetites that are
Most disobedient and refractory.
If Helen then be wife to Sparta's king,
And it is known she is, these moral laws
Of nature and of nations speak aloud
To have her back returned. Thus to persist
In doing wrong extenuates not wrong,
But makes it much more heavy. Hector's opinion
Is this in way of truth. Yet, ne'ertheless,
My sprightly brethren, I propend to you   190
In resolution to keep Helen still;
For 'tis a cause that hath no mean dependence
Upon our joint and several dignities.
TROILUS. Why, there you touched the life of
    our design:
Were it not glory that we more affected
Than the performance of our heaving spleens,
I would not wish a drop of Trojan blood
Spent more in her defence. But, worthy Hector,
She is a theme of honour and renown,
A spur to valiant and magnanimous deeds,   200
Whose present courage may beat down our foes,
And fame in time to come canonize us;
For I presume brave Hector would not lose
So rich advantage of a promised glory
As smiles upon the forehead of this action
For the wide world's revenue.

HECTOR.   I am yours,
You valiant offspring of great Priamus.
I have a roisting challenge sent amongst
The dull and factious nobles of the Greeks
Will strike amazement to their drowsy spirits.   210
I was advertised their great general slept,
Whilst emulation in the army crept:
This, I presume, will wake him.   *They go*

Scene 3: *The Greek camp. Before the tent of Achilles*

Enter Thersites, solus

THERSITES. How now, Thersites! What, lost in the
labyrinth of thy fury! Shall the elephant Ajax carry
it thus? He beats me, and I rail at him. O worthy
satisfaction! Would it were otherwise: that I could
beat him, whilst he railed at me. 'Sfoot, I'll learn to
conjure and raise devils but I'll see some issue of my
spiteful execrations. Then there's Achilles—a rare
enginer. If Troy be not taken till these two under-
mine it, the walls will stand till they fall of themselves. O thou great thunder-darter of Olympus,   10
forget that thou art Jove, the king of gods, and,
Mercury, lose all the serpentine craft of thy cadu-
ceus, if ye take not that little little less than little wit
from them that they have! which short-armed
ignorance itself knows is so abundant scarce, it will
not in circumvention deliver a fly from a spider
without drawing their massy irons and cutting the
web. After this, the vengeance on the whole camp!
or, rather, the Neapolitan bone-ache? for that,
methinks, is the curse dependent on those that war   20
for a placket. I have said my prayers; and devil Envy
say 'Amen'. What ho! my Lord Achilles!
PATROCLUS [*within*]. Who's there? Thersites? Good
Thersites, come in and rail.
THERSITES. If I could a' remembered a gilt counterfeit,
thou wouldst not have slipped out of my contemplation; but it is no matter—thyself upon thyself!
The common curse of mankind, folly and ignorance, be thine in great revenue! Heaven bless thee
from a tutor, and discipline come not near thee!   30
Let thy blood be thy direction till thy death! Then
if she that lays thee out says thou art a fair corpse,
I'll be sworn and sworn upon't she never shrouded
any but lazars. Amen.

Enter Patroclus

     Where's Achilles?
PATROCLUS. What, art thou devout? Wast thou in
prayer?
THERSITES. Ay; the heavens hear me!
PATROCLUS. Amen.
ACHILLES [*within*]. Who's there?   40
PATROCLUS. Thersites, my lord.

Enter Achilles

ACHILLES. Where, where? O where? Art thou come?
Why, my cheese, my digestion, why hast thou not
served thyself in to my table so many meals? Come,
what's Agamemnon?
THERSITES. Thy commander, Achilles; then tell me,
Patroclus, what's Achilles?
PATROCLUS. Thy lord, Thersites; then tell me, I pray
thee, what's thyself?

THERSITES. Thy knower, Patroclus; then tell me,   50
Patroclus, what art thou?
PATROCLUS. Thou mayst tell that knowest.
ACHILLES. O tell, tell.
THERSITES. I'll decline the whole question. Agamem-
non commands Achilles; Achilles is my lord; I am
Patroclus' knower, and Patroclus is a fool.
PATROCLUS. You rascal!
THERSITES. Peace, fool! I have not done.
ACHILLES. He is a privileged man. Proceed, Thersites.
THERSITES. Agamemnon is a fool; Achilles is a fool;   60
Thersites is a fool, and, as aforesaid, Patroclus is a
fool.
ACHILLES. Derive this; come.
THERSITES. Agamemnon is a fool to offer to command
Achilles; Achilles is a fool to be commanded of
Agamemnon; Thersites is a fool to serve such a
fool; and Patroclus is a fool positive.
PATROCLUS. Why am I a fool?
THERSITES. Make that demand of the Creator. It
suffices me thou art. Look you, who comes here?   70
ACHILLES. Patroclus, I'll speak with nobody. Come in
with me, Thersites.   *Enters his tent*
THERSITES. Here is such patchery, such juggling and
such knavery! All the argument is a whore and a
cuckold—a good quarrel to draw emulous factions
and bleed to death upon. Now, the dry serpigo on
the subject, and war and lechery confound all!
          Enters the tent

Enter Agamemnon, Ulysses, Nestor, Diomedes, and Ajax

AGAMEMNON. Where is Achilles?
PATROCLUS. Within his tent; but ill-disposed, my lord.
AGAMEMNON. Let it be known to him that we are here.   80
We sent our messengers, and we lay by
Our appertainments, visiting of him.
Let him be told so, lest perchance he think
We dare not move the question of our place,
Or know not what we are.
PATROCLUS.   I shall say so to him.   *Goes in*
ULYSSES. We saw him at the opening of his tent:
He is not sick.
AJAX. Yes, lion-sick, sick of proud heart. You may
call it melancholy, if you will favour the man; but,
by my head, 'tis pride. But why, why? Let him show   90
us the cause. A word, my lord.
          Takes Agamemnon aside
NESTOR. What moves Ajax thus to bay at him?
ULYSSES. Achilles hath inveigled his fool from him.
NESTOR. Who, Thersites?
ULYSSES. He.
NESTOR. Then will Ajax lack matter, if he have lost
his argument.
ULYSSES. No, you see, he is his argument that has his
argument—Achilles.
NESTOR. All the better: their fraction is more our wish   100
than their faction. But it was a strong composure
a fool could disunite.
ULYSSES. The amity that wisdom knits not, folly may
easily untie.

Re-enter Patroclus

     Here comes Patroclus.
NESTOR. No Achilles with him.
ULYSSES. The elephant hath joints, but none for

courtesy: his legs are legs for necessity, not for
flexure.
PATROCLUS. Achilles bids me say he is much sorry   110
If anything more than your sport and pleasure
Did move your greatness and this noble state
To call upon him; he hopes it is no other
But for your health and your digestion's sake,
An after-dinner's breath.
AGAMEMNON.   Hear you, Patroclus:
We are too well acquainted with these answers;
But his evasion, winged thus swift with scorn,
Cannot outfly our apprehensions.
Much attribute he hath, and much the reason
Why we ascribe it to him; yet all his virtues,   120
Not virtuously on his own part beheld,
Do in our eyes begin to lose their gloss,
Yea, like fair fruit in an unwholesome dish,
Are like to rot untasted. Go and tell him
We come to speak with him; and you shall not sin
If you do say we think him over-proud
And under-honest, in self-assumption greater
Than in the note of judgement; and worthier
than himself
Here tend the savage strangeness he puts on,
Disguise the holy strength of their command,   130
And underwrite in an observing kind
His humorous predominance; yea, watch
His pettish lunes, his ebbs and flows, as if
The passage and whole carriage of this action
Rode on his tide. Go tell him this, and add
That if he overhold his price so much
We'll none of him but let him, like an engine
Not portable, lie under this report:
'Bring action hither; this cannot go to war:
A stirring dwarf we do allowance give   140
Before a sleeping giant.' Tell him so.
PATROCLUS. I shall; and bring his answer presently.

Enters the tent

AGAMEMNON. In second voice we'll not be satisfied;
We come to speak with him. Ulysses, enter you.

Ulysses follows

AJAX. What is he more than another?
AGAMEMNON. No more than what he thinks he is.
AJAX. Is he so much? Do you not think he thinks
himself a better man than I am?
AGAMEMNON. No question.
AJAX. Will you subscribe his thought and say he is?   150
AGAMEMNON. No, noble Ajax; you are as strong, as
valiant, as wise, no less noble, much more gentle,
and altogether more tractable.
AJAX. Why should a man be proud? How doth pride
grow? I know not what pride is.
AGAMEMNON. Your mind is the clearer, Ajax, and your
virtues the fairer. He that is proud eats up himself:
pride is his own glass, his own trumpet, his own
chronicle; and whatever praises itself but in the deed,
devours the deed in the praise.   160
AJAX. I do hate a proud man as I do hate the
engendering of toads.
NESTOR. And yet he loves himself: is it not strange?

Re-enter Ulysses

ULYSSES. Achilles will not to the field tomorrow.
AGAMEMNON. What's his excuse?
ULYSSES.   He doth rely on none,
But carries on the stream of his dispose

Without observance or respect of any,
In will peculiar and in self-admission.
AGAMEMNON. Why will he not, upon our fair request,
Untent his person and share th'air with us?   170
ULYSSES. Things small as nothing, for request's
sake only,
He makes important; possessed he is with greatness,
And speaks not to himself but with a pride
That quarrels at self-breath: imagined worth
Holds in his blood such swollen and hot discourse
That 'twixt his mental and his active parts
Kingdomed Achilles in commotion rages
And batters down himself. What should I say?
He is so plaguey proud that the death-tokens of it
Cry 'No recovery'.
AGAMEMNON.   Let Ajax go to him.   180
Dear lord, go you and greet him in his tent.
'Tis said he holds you well, and will be led,
At your request, a little from himself.
ULYSSES. O Agamemnon, let it not be so!
We'll consecrate the steps that Ajax makes
When they go from Achilles. Shall the proud lord
That bastes his arrogance with his own seam
And never suffers matter of the world
Enter his thoughts, save such as doth revolve
And ruminate himself, shall he be worshipped   190
Of that we hold an idol more than he?
No, this thrice-worthy and right valiant lord
Must not so stale his palm, nobly acquired,
Nor, by my will, assubjugate his merit—
As amply titled as Achilles is—
By going to Achilles:
That were to enlard his fat-already pride,
And add more coals to Cancer when he burns
With entertaining great Hyperion.
This lord go to him! Jupiter forbid,   200
And say in thunder 'Achilles go to him'.
NESTOR [aside]. O, this is well; he rubs the vein of him.
DIOMEDES [aside]. And how his silence drinks up
this applause!
AJAX. If I go to him, with my arméd fist
I'll pash him o'er the face.
AGAMEMNON. O, no, you shall not go.
AJAX. An 'a be proud with me, I'll feeze his pride:
Let me go to him.
ULYSSES. Not for the worth that hangs upon
our quarrel.
AJAX. A paltry, insolent fellow!   210
NESTOR [aside]. How he describes himself!
AJAX. Can he not be sociable?
ULYSSES [aside]. The raven chides blackness.
AJAX. I'll let his humour's blood.
AGAMEMNON [aside]. He will be the physician that
should be the patient.
AJAX. An all men were o' my mind—
ULYSSES [aside]. Wit would be out of fashion.
AJAX. 'A should not bear it so; 'a should eat swords
first. Shall pride carry it?   220
NESTOR [aside]. An 'twould, you'ld carry half.
ULYSSES [aside]. 'A would have ten shares.
AJAX. I'll knead him, I'll make him supple.
NESTOR [aside]. He's not yet through warm. Force him
with praises: pour in, pour in; his ambition is dry.
ULYSSES [to Agamemnon]. My lord, you feed too much
on this dislike.
NESTOR. Our noble general, do not do so.

DIOMEDES. You must prepare to fight
  without Achilles.
ULYSSES. Why, 'tis this naming of him does him harm.
  Here is a man—but 'tis before his face: 230
  I will be silent.
NESTOR.   Wherefore should you so?
  He is not emulous, as Achilles is.
ULYSSES. Know the whole world, he is as valiant.
AJAX. A whoreson dog, that shall palter thus
  with us!
  Would he were a Trojan!
NESTOR. What a vice were it in Ajax now—
ULYSSES. If he were proud—
DIOMEDES. Or covetous of praise—
ULYSSES. Ay, or surly borne—
DIOMEDES. Or strange, or self-affected! 240
ULYSSES. Thank the heavens, lord, thou art of
  sweet composure;
  Praise him that got thee, she that gave thee suck;
  Famed be thy tutor, and thy parts of nature
  Thrice-famed beyond, beyond all erudition:
  But he that disciplined thine arms to fight,
  Let Mars divide eternity in twain,
  And give him half; and, for thy vigour,
  Bull-bearing Milo his addition yield
  To sinewy Ajax. I will not praise thy wisdom,
  Which, like a bourn, a pale, a shore, confines 250
  Thy spacious and dilated parts. Here's Nestor,
  Instructed by the antiquary times;
  He must, he is, he cannot but be wise:
  But pardon, father Nestor, were your days
  As green as Ajax', and your brain so tempered,
  You should not have the eminence of him,
  But be as Ajax.
AJAX.   Shall I call you father?
NESTOR. Ay, my good son.
DIOMEDES.   Be ruled by him, Lord Ajax.
ULYSSES. There is no tarrying here: the
  hart Achilles
  Keeps thicket. Please it our great general 260
  To call together all his state of war:
  Fresh kings are come to Troy; tomorrow
  We must with all our main of power stand fast;
  And here's a lord, come knights from east to west,
  And cull their flower, Ajax shall cope the best.
AGAMEMNON. Go we to council. Let Achilles sleep:
  Light boats sail swift, though greater hulks draw
  deep.   *They go*

ACT 3

Scene 1: *Troy. Priam's palace*

Enter Pandarus and a Servant

PANDARUS. Friend, you, pray you, a word: do you not
  follow the young Lord Paris?
SERVANT. Ay sir, when he goes before me.
PANDARUS. You depend upon him, I mean?
SERVANT. Sir, I do depend upon the Lord.
PANDARUS. You depend upon a noble gentleman;
  I must needs praise him.
SERVANT. The Lord be praised!
PANDARUS. You know me, do you not?
SERVANT. Faith, sir, superficially. 10
PANDARUS. Friend, know me better: I am the Lord
  Pandarus.

SERVANT. I hope I shall know your honour better.
PANDARUS. I do desire it.
SERVANT. You are in the state of grace.
PANDARUS. Grace! not so, friend: honour and lordship
  are my titles. [*music within*] What music is this?
SERVANT. I do but partly know, sir: it is music in
  parts.
PANDARUS. Know you the musicians? 20
SERVANT. Wholly, sir.
PANDARUS. Who play they to?
SERVANT. To the hearers, sir.
PANDARUS. At whose pleasure, friend?
SERVANT. At mine, sir, and theirs that love music.
PANDARUS. Command, I mean, friend.
SERVANT. Who shall I command, sir?
PANDARUS. Friend, we understand not one another:
  I am too courtly, and thou art too cunning. At
  whose request do these men play? 30
SERVANT. That's to't, indeed, sir: marry, sir, at the
  request of Paris my lord, who is there in person;
  with him, the mortal Venus, the heart-blood of
  beauty, love's indivisible soul.
PANDARUS. Who, my cousin Cressida?
SERVANT. No, sir, Helen. Could you not find out that
  by her attributes?
PANDARUS. It should seem, fellow, that thou hast not
  seen the Lady Cressida. I come to speak with Paris
  from the Prince Troilus; I will make a complimental 40
  assault upon him, for my business seethes.
SERVANT. Sodden business! There's a stewed phrase
  indeed!

Enter Paris and Helen, attended

PANDARUS. Fair be to you, my lord, and to all this fair
  company! Fair desires, in all fair measure, fairly
  guide them! Especially to you, fair queen, fair
  thoughts be your fair pillow!
HELEN. Dear lord, you are full of fair words.
PANDARUS. You speak your fair pleasure, sweet queen.
  Fair prince, here is good broken music. 50
PARIS. You have broke it, cousin; and, by my life,
  you shall make it whole again: you shall piece it out
  with a piece of your performance. Nell, he is full of
  harmony.
PANDARUS. Truly, lady, no.
HELEN. O, sir—
PANDARUS. Rude, in sooth; in good sooth, very rude.
PARIS. Well said, my lord! well, you say so in fits.
PANDARUS. I have business to my lord, dear queen.
  My lord, will you vouchsafe me a word? 60
HELEN. Nay, this shall not hedge us out; we'll hear
  you sing, certainly.
PANDARUS. Well, sweet queen, you are pleasant with
  me.—But, marry, thus, my lord: my dear lord, and
  most esteemed friend, your brother Troilus—
HELEN. My Lord Pandarus; honey-sweet lord—
PANDARUS. Go to, sweet queen, go to—commends
  himself most affectionately to you—
HELEN. You shall not bob us out of our melody. If
  you do, our melancholy upon your head! 70
PANDARUS. Sweet queen, sweet queen; that's a sweet
  queen, i'faith.
HELEN. And to make a sweet lady sad is a sour offence.
PANDARUS. Nay, that shall not serve your turn; that
  shall it not, in truth, la. Nay, I care not for such
  words; no, no.—And, my lord, he desires you, that

if the king call for him at supper you will make his
excuse.

HELEN. My Lord Pandarus—

PANDARUS. What says my sweet queen, my very very 80
sweet queen?

PARIS. What exploit's in hand? where sups he tonight?

HELEN. Nay, but, my lord—

PANDARUS. What says my sweet queen?—My cousin
will fall out with you. You must not know where
he sups.

PARIS. I'll lay my life, with my disposer Cressida.

PANDARUS. No, no, no such matter; you are wide:
come, your disposer is sick.

PARIS. Well, I'll make's excuse.   90

PANDARUS. Ay, good my lord. Why should you say
Cressida? no, your poor disposer's sick.

PARIS. I spy.

PANDARUS. You spy! What do you spy? Come, give
me an instrument. Now, sweet queen.

HELEN. Why, this is kindly done.

PANDARUS. My niece is horribly in love with a thing
you have, sweet queen.

HELEN. She shall have it, my lord, if it be not my
lord Paris.   100

PANDARUS. He! no, she'll none of him; they two are
twain.

HELEN. Falling in, after falling out, may make them
three.

PANDARUS. Come, come, I'll hear no more of this.
I'll sing you a song now.

HELEN. Ay, ay, prithee now. By my troth, sweet lord,
thou hast a fine forehead.

PANDARUS. Ay, you may, you may.

HELEN. Let thy song be love; this love will undo us all. 110
O Cupid, Cupid, Cupid!

PANDARUS. Love! ay, that it shall, i'faith.

PARIS. Ay, good now, love, love, nothing but love

PANDARUS. In good troth, it begins so.   Sings

Love, love, nothing but love, still love, still more!
    For, O, Love's bow
    Shoots buck and doe;
    The shaft confounds
    Not that it wounds,
But tickles still the sore.   120
These lovers cry Oh, oh, they die!
    Yet that which seems the wound to kill,
Doth turn oh! oh! to ha! ha! he!
    So dying love lives still.
Oh! oh! a while, but ha! ha! ha!
Oh! oh! groans out for ha! ha! ha!

Heigh-ho!

HELEN. In love, i'faith, to the very tip of the nose.

PARIS. He eats nothing but doves, love, and that
breeds hot blood, and hot blood begets hot 130
thoughts, and hot thoughts beget hot deeds, and hot
deeds is love.

PANDARUS. Is this the generation of love?—hot blood,
hot thoughts, and hot deeds? Why, they are vipers.
Is love a generation of vipers? Sweet lord, who's
afield today?

PARIS. Hector, Deiphobus, Helenus, Antenor, and all
the gallantry of Troy. I would fain have armed
today, but my Nell would not have it so. How
chance my brother Troilus went not?   140

HELEN. He hangs the lip at something; you know all,
Lord Pandarus.

PANDARUS. Not I, honey-sweet queen. I long to hear
how they sped today.—You'll remember your
brother's excuse?

PARIS. To a hair.

PANDARUS. Farewell, sweet queen.

HELEN. Commend me to your niece.

PANDARUS. I will, sweet queen.   Goes
                                      Retreat sounded

PARIS. They're come from th'field: let us to
    Priam's hall,   150
To greet the warriors. Sweet Helen, I must woo you
To help unarm our Hector. His stubborn buckles,
With these your white enchanting fingers touched,
Shall more obey than to the edge of steel
Or force of Greekish sinews. You shall do more
Than all the island kings—disarm great Hector.

HELEN. 'Twill make us proud to be his
    servant, Paris;
Yea, what he shall receive of us in duty
Gives us more palm in beauty than we have,
Yea, overshines ourself.   160

PARIS. Sweet, above thought I love thee.   They go

Scene 2: *The same. Pandarus' orchard*

Enter Pandarus and Troilus' Boy, meeting

PANDARUS. How now! Where's thy master? At my
cousin Cressida's?

BOY. No, sir; he stays for you to conduct him thither.

PANDARUS. O, here he comes.

Enter Troilus

How now, how now!

TROILUS. Sirrah, walk off.   Boy goes

PANDARUS. Have you seen my cousin?

TROILUS. No, Pandarus; I stalk about her door,
Like a strange soul upon the Stygian banks
Staying for waftage. O, be thou my Charon,   10
And give me swift transportance to those fields
Where I may wallow in the lily beds
Proposed for the deserver! O gentle Pandar,
From Cupid's shoulder pluck his painted wings,
And fly with me to Cressid!

PANDARUS. Walk here i'th'orchard; I'll bring her
straight.   Goes

TROILUS. I am giddy: expectation whirls me round.
Th'imaginary relish is so sweet
That it enchants my sense. What will it be   20
When that the watery palate tastes indeed
Love's thrice repuréd nectar?—death, I fear me,
Swooning distraction, or some joy too fine,
Too subtle-potent, tuned too sharp in sweetness,
For the capacity of my ruder powers;
I fear it much, and I do fear besides
That I shall lose distinction in my joys,
As doth a battle, when they charge on heaps
The enemy flying.

Re-enter Pandarus

PANDARUS. She's making her ready; she'll come 30
straight. You must be witty now: she does so blush,
and fetches her wind so short as if she were frayed
with a sprite. I'll fetch her. It is the prettiest villain;
she fetches her breath as short as a new-ta'en
sparrow.   Goes

TROILUS. Even such a passion doth embrace my
  bosom:
My heart beats thicker than a feverous pulse;
And all my powers do their bestowing lose,
Like vassalage at unawares encountering
The eye of majesty.   40

Re-enter Pandarus and Cressida

PANDARUS. Come, come, what need you blush?
  Shame's a baby. Here she is now. Swear the oaths
  now to her that you have sworn to me. What, are
  you gone again? You must be watched ere you be
  made tame, must you? Come your ways, come your
  ways; an you draw backward, we'll put you i'th'
  fills. Why do you not speak to her? Come, draw
  this curtain, and let's see your picture. Alas the
  day, how loath you are to offend daylight! An
  'twere dark, you'ld close sooner. So, so; rub on, and 50
  kiss the mistress. How now! a kiss in fee-farm!—
  build there, carpenter; the air is sweet. Nay, you shall
  fight your hearts out ere I part you—the falcon as
  the tercel, for all the ducks i'th'river. Go to, go to.
TROILUS. You have bereft me of all words, lady.
PANDARUS. Words pay no debts, give her deeds; but
  she'll bereave you o'th'deeds too, if she call your
  activity in question. What, billing again? Here's 'In
  witness whereof the parties interchangeably'—
  Come in, come in; I'll go get a fire.   *Goes* 60
CRESSIDA. Will you walk in, my lord?
TROILUS. O Cressida, how often have I wished me
  thus!
CRESSIDA. Wished, my lord?—The gods grant—O,
  my lord!
TROILUS. What should they grant? What makes this
  pretty abruption? What too curious dreg espies my
  sweet lady in the fountain of our love?
CRESSIDA. More dregs than water, if my fears have
  eyes.   70
TROILUS. Fears make devils of cherubins; they never
  see truly.
CRESSIDA. Blind fear, that seeing reason leads, finds
  safer footing than blind reason stumbling without
  fear: to fear the worst oft cures the worse.
TROILUS. O, let my lady apprehend no fear: in all
  Cupid's pageant there is presented no monster.
CRESSIDA. Nor nothing monstrous neither?
TROILUS. Nothing but our undertakings, when we
  vow to weep seas, live in fire, eat rocks, tame tigers; 80
  thinking it harder for our mistress to devise imposition enough than for us to undergo any difficulty
  imposed. This is the monstruosity in love, lady—
  that the will is infinite and the execution confined;
  that the desire is boundless and the act a slave to
  limit.
CRESSIDA. They say all lovers swear more performance
  than they are able, and yet reserve an ability that
  they never perform; vowing more than the perfection of ten, and discharging less than the tenth part 90
  of one. They that have the voice of lions and the
  act of hares, are they not monsters?
TROILUS. Are there such? Such are not we. Praise us
  as we are tasted, allow us as we prove. Our head
  shall go bare till merit crown it: no perfection in
  reversion shall have a praise in present. We will
  not name desert before his birth; and, being born,
  his addition shall be humble. Few words to fair

faith: Troilus shall be such to Cressid as what envy
can say worst shall be a mock for his truth; and 100
what truth can speak truest, not truer than Troilus.
CRESSIDA. Will you walk in, my lord?

Re-enter Pandarus

PANDARUS. What, blushing still? Have you not done
  talking yet?
CRESSIDA. Well, uncle, what folly I commit, I dedicate
  to you.
PANDARUS. I thank you for that: if my lord get a boy
  of you, you'll give him me. Be true to my lord; if
  he flinch, chide me for it.
TROILUS. You know now your hostages: your uncle's 110
  word and my firm faith.
PANDARUS. Nay, I'll give my word for her too. Our
  kindred, though they be long ere they are wooed,
  they are constant being won. They are burs, I can
  tell you; they'll stick where they are thrown.
CRESSIDA. Boldness comes to me now and brings
    me heart:
Prince Troilus, I have loved you night and day
For many weary months.
TROILUS. Why was my Cressid then so hard to win?
CRESSIDA. Hard to seem won; but I was won,
    my lord,   120
With the first glance that ever—pardon me;
If I confess much, you will play the tyrant.
I love you now; but not, till now, so much
But I might master it. In faith, I lie!
My thoughts were like unbridled children, grown
Too headstrong for their mother. See, we fools!
Why have I blabbed? Who shall be true to us,
When we are so unsecret to ourselves?
But, though I loved you well, I wooed you not;
And yet, good faith, I wished myself a man,   130
Or that we women had men's privilege
Of speaking first. Sweet, bid me hold my tongue;
For in this rapture I shall surely speak
The thing I shall repent. See, see, your silence,
Cunning in dumbness, from my weakness draws
My very soul of counsel! Stop my mouth.
TROILUS. And shall, albeit sweet music issues thence.
                                            Kisses her
PANDARUS. Pretty, i'faith.
CRESSIDA. My lord, I do beseech you, pardon me:
'Twas not my purpose thus to beg a kiss.   140
I am ashamed. O heavens! what have I done?
For this time will I take my leave, my lord.
TROILUS. Your leave, sweet Cressid?
PANDARUS. Leave! An you take leave till tomorrow
  morning—
CRESSIDA. Pray you, content you.
TROILUS. What offends you, lady?
CRESSIDA. Sir, mine own company.
TROILUS. You cannot shun yourself.
CRESSIDA. Let me go and try.   150
I have a kind of self resides with you,
But an unkind self that itself will leave
To be another's fool. I would be gone.
Where is my wit? I know not what I speak.
TROILUS. Well know they what they speak that speak
  so wisely.
CRESSIDA. Perchance, my lord, I show more craft
    than love,
And fell so roundly to a large confession

To angle for your thoughts; but you are wise,
Or else you love not: for to be wise and love
Exceeds man's might; that dwells with gods above. 160
TROILUS. O that I thought it could be in a woman—
As, if it can, I will presume in you—
To feed for aye her lamp and flame of love;
To keep her constancy in plight and youth,
Outliving beauties outward, with a mind
That doth renew swifter than blood decays!
Or that persuasion could but thus convince me
That my integrity and truth to you
Might be affronted with the match and weight
Of such a winnowed purity in love— 170
How were I then uplifted! But, alas,
I am as true as truth's simplicity,
And simpler than the infancy of truth!
CRESSIDA. In that I'll war with you.
TROILUS.   O virtuous fight,
When right with right wars who shall be most right!
True swains in love shall in the world to come
Approve their truths by Troilus. When their
     rhymes,
Full of protest, of oath, and big compare,
Want similes, truth tired with iteration—
'As true as steel, as plantage to the moon, 180
As sun to day, as turtle to her mate,
As iron to adamant, as earth to th'centre'—
Yet, after all comparisons of truth,
As truth's authentic author to be cited,
'As true as Troilus' shall crown up the verse
And sanctify the numbers.
CRESSIDA.   Prophet may you be!
If I be false, or swerve a hair from truth,
When time is old and hath forgot itself,
When waterdrops have worn the stones of Troy,
And blind oblivion swallowed cities up, 190
And mighty states characterless are grated
To dusty nothing, yet let memory,
From false to false, among false maids in love,
Upbraid my falsehood! When they've said 'as false
As air, as water, wind or sandy earth,
As fox to lamb, or wolf to heifer's calf,
Pard to the hind, or stepdame to her son',
Yea let them say, to stick the heart of falsehood,
'As false as Cressid'.
PANDARUS. Go to, a bargain made. Seal it, seal it. 200
I'll be the witness. Here I hold your hand; here my
cousin's. If ever you prove false one to another,
since I have taken such pains to bring you together,
let all pitiful goers-between be called to the world's
end after my name—call them all Pandars: let all
constant men be Troiluses, all false women Cressids,
and all brokers-between Pandars! Say 'amen'.
TROILUS. Amen.
CRESSIDA. Amen.
PANDARUS. Amen. Whereupon I will show you a 210
chamber with a bed; which bed, because it shall not
speak of your pretty encounters, press it to death.
Away!   *They go*
And Cupid grant all tongue-tied maidens here
Bed, chamber, pandar, to provide this gear! *Goes*

Scene 3: *The Greek camp*

*Flourish. Enter Agamemnon, Ulysses, Diomedes, Nestor,
Ajax, Menelaus, and Calchas*

CALCHAS. Now, princes, for the service I have done,
Th'advantage of the time prompts me aloud
To call for recompense. Appear it to your minds
That, through the sight I bear in things to come,
I have abandoned Troy, left my possession,
Incurred a traitor's name, exposed myself,
From certain and possessed conveniences,
To doubtful fortunes; sequestering from me all
That time, acquaintance, custom and condition
Made tame and most familiar to my nature;   10
And here, to do you service, am become
As new into the world, strange, unacquainted.
I do beseech you, as in way of taste,
To give me now a little benefit
Out of those many registered in promise,
Which, you say, live to come in my behalf.
AGAMEMNON. What wouldst thou of us, Trojan?
     Make demand.
CALCHAS. You have a Trojan prisoner
     called Antenor,
Yesterday took; Troy holds him very dear.
Oft have you—often have you thanks therefore— 20
Desired my Cressid in right great exchange,
Whom Troy hath still denied; but this Antenor
I know is such a wrest in their affairs,
That their negotiations all must slack,
Wanting his manage; and they will almost
Give us a prince of blood, a son of Priam,
In change of him. Let him be sent, great princes,
And he shall buy my daughter; and her presence
Shall quite strike off all service I have done
In most accepted pain.
AGAMEMNON.   Let Diomed bear him, 30
And bring us Cressid hither; Calchas shall have
What he requests of us. Good Diomed,
Furnish you fairly for this interchange;
Withal, bring word if Hector will tomorrow
Be answered in his challenge: Ajax is ready.
DIOMEDES. This shall I undertake, and 'tis a burden
Which I am proud to bear.
                              Diomedes and Calchas go

Enter Achilles and Patroclus, before their tent

ULYSSES. Achilles stands i'th'entrance of his tent:
Please it our general pass strangely by him,
As if he were forgot; and, princes all,   40
Lay negligent and loose regard upon him.
I will come last. 'Tis like he'll question me
Why such unplausive eyes are bent on him.
If so, I have derision medicinable
To use between your strangeness and his pride,
Which his own will shall have desire to drink..
It may do good: pride hath no other glass
To show itself but pride; for supple knees
Feed arrogance and are the proud man's fees.
AGAMEMNON. We'll execute your purpose and put on 50
A form of strangeness as we pass along;
So do each lord, and either greet him not
Or else disdainfully, which shall shake him more
Than if not looked on. I will lead the way.
                                        They go
ACHILLES. What, comes the general to speak with me?
You know my mind: I'll fight no more 'gainst Troy.
AGAMEMNON. What says Achilles? Would he aught
     with us?
NESTOR. Would you, my lord, aught with the general?

ACHILLES. No.
NESTOR. Nothing, my lord.   60
AGAMEMNON. The better.   *Agamemnon and Nestor go*
ACHILLES. Good day, good day.
MENELAUS. How do you? how do you?   *Goes*
ACHILLES. What, does the cuckold scorn me?
AJAX. How now, Patroclus!
ACHILLES. Good morrow, Ajax.
AJAX. Ha?
ACHILLES. Good morrow.
AJAX. Ay, and good next day too.   *Goes*
ACHILLES. What mean these fellows? Know they
   not Achilles?   70
PATROCLUS. They pass by strangely. They were used
   to bend,
  To send their smiles before them to Achilles,
  To come as humbly as they use to creep
  To holy altars.
ACHILLES.   What, am I poor of late?
  'Tis certain, greatness, once fallen out with fortune,
  Must fall out with men too. What the declined is
  He shall as soon read in the eyes of others
  As feel in his own fall; for men, like butterflies,
  Show not their mealy wings but to the summer,
  And not a man, for being simply man,   80
  Hath any honour but honour for those honours
  That are without him—as place, riches, and favour,
  Prizes of accident as oft as merit;
  Which, when they fall, as being slippery standers,
  The love that leaned on them as slippery too,
  Doth one pluck down another and together
  Die in the fall. But 'tis not so with me:
  Fortune and I are friends; I do enjoy
  At ample point all that I did possess,
  Save these men's looks; who do, methinks, find out 90
  Something not worth in me such rich beholding
  As they have often given. Here is Ulysses;
  I'll interrupt his reading.
  How now, Ulysses!
ULYSSES.   Now, great Thetis' son!
ACHILLES. What are you reading?
ULYSSES.   A strange fellow here
  Writes me that man, how dearly ever parted,
  How much in having, or without or in,
  Cannot make boast to have that which he hath,
  Nor feels not what he owes, but by reflection;
  As when his virtues, shining upon others,   100
  Heat them and they retort that heat again
  To the first giver.
ACHILLES.   This is not strange, Ulysses.
  The beauty that is borne here in the face
  The bearer knows not, but commends itself
  To others' eyes; nor doth the eye itself,
  That most pure spirit of sense, behold itself,
  Not going from itself; but eye to eye opposed
  Salutes each other with each other's form:
  For speculation turns not to itself
  Till it hath travelled and is mirrored there   110
  Where it may see itself. This is not strange at all.
ULYSSES. I do not strain at the position—
  It is familiar—but at the author's drift;
  Who in his circumstance expressly proves
  That no man is the lord of anything,
  Though in and of him there be much consisting,
  Till he communicate his parts to others;
  Nor doth he of himself know them for aught

Till he behold them forméd in th'applause
Where they're extended; who, like an
  arch, reverberate   120
The voice again; or, like a gate of steel
Fronting the sun, receives and renders back
His figure and his heat. I was much rapt in this,
And apprehended here immediately
The unknown Ajax.
Heavens! what a man is there! a very horse,
That has he knows not what. Nature, what things
  there are
Most abject in regard and dear in use!
What things again most dear in the esteem
And poor in worth! Now shall we see tomorrow— 130
An act that very chance doth throw upon him—
Ajax renowned. O heavens, what some men do,
While some men leave to do!
How some men creep in skittish Fortune's hall,
While others play the idiots in her eyes!
How one man eats into another's pride,
While pride is fasting in his wantonness!
To see these Grecian lords!—why, even already
They clap the lubber Ajax on the shoulder,
As if his foot were on brave Hector's breast   140
And great Troy shrinking.
ACHILLES. I do believe it; for they passed by me
  As misers do by beggars, neither gave to me
  Good word nor look. What, are my deeds forgot?
ULYSSES. Time hath, my lord, a wallet at his back
  Wherein he puts alms for oblivion,
  A great-sized monster of ingratitude.
  Those scraps are good deeds past, which are
   devoured
  As fast as they are made, forgot as soon
  As done. Perseverance, dear my lord,   150
  Keeps honour bright: to have done, is to hang
  Quite out of fashion, like a rusty mail
  In monumental mockery. Take the instant way;
  For honour travels in a strait so narrow
  Where one but goes abreast. Keep then the path;
  For emulation hath a thousand sons
  That one by one pursue. If you give way,
  Or hedge aside from the direct forthright,
  Like to an entered tide they all rush by
  And leave you hindmost;   160
  Or, like a gallant horse fallen in first rank,
  Lie there for pavement to the abject rear,
  O'er-run and trampled on. Then what they do
  in present,
  Though less than yours in past, must o'ertop yours;
  For Time is like a fashionable host
  That slightly shakes his parting guest by th'hand
  And, with his arms outstretched as he would fly,
  Grasps in the comer: welcome ever smiles,
  And farewell goes out sighing. O, let not virtue seek
  Remuneration for the thing it was;   170
  For beauty, wit,
  High birth, vigour of bone, desert in service,
  Love, friendship, charity, are subject all
  To envious and calumniating Time.
  One touch of nature makes the whole world kin,
  That all with one consent praise new-born gawds,
  Though they are made and moulded of things past,
  And give to dust that is a little gilt
  More laud than gilt o'er-dusted.
  The present eye praises the present object: 180

Then marvel not, thou great and complete man,
That all the Greeks begin to worship Ajax;
Since things in motion sooner catch the eye
Than what not stirs. The cry went once on thee,
And still it might, and yet it may again,
If thou wouldst not entomb thyself alive
And case thy reputation in thy tent,
Whose glorious deeds but in these fields of late
Made emulous missions 'mongst the gods
    themselves,
And drave great Mars to faction.

ACHILLES.   Of this my privacy   190
I have strong reasons.

ULYSSES.   But 'gainst your privacy
The reasons are more potent and heroical.
'Tis known, Achilles, that you are in love
With one of Priam's daughters.

ACHILLES.   Ha! known?

ULYSSES. Is that a wonder?
The providence that's in a watchful state
Knows almost every grain of Pluto's gold,
Finds bottom in th'uncomprehensive deeps,
Keeps place with thought and almost like the gods
Does thoughts unveil in their dumb cradles.   200
There is a mystery, with whom relation
Durst never meddle, in the soul of state,
Which hath an operation more divine
Than breath or pen give expressure to.
All the commerce that you have had with Troy
As perfectly is ours as yours, my lord;
And better would it fit Achilles much
To throw down Hector than Polyxena.
But it must grieve young Pyrrhus now at home,
When fame shall in our islands sound her trump,   210
And all the Greekish girls shall tripping sing
'Great Hector's sister did Achilles win,
But our great Ajax bravely beat down him'.
Farewell, my lord. I as your lover speak:
The fool slides o'er the ice that you should break.
                                        Goes

PATROCLUS. To this effect, Achilles, have I
    moved you.
A woman impudent and mannish grown
Is not more loathed than an effeminate man
In time of action. I stand condemned for this:
They think my little stomach to the war   220
And your great love to me restrains you thus.
Sweet, rouse yourself, and the weak wanton Cupid
Shall from your neck unloose his amorous fold
And, like a dew-drop from the lion's mane,
Be shook to air.

ACHILLES.   Shall Ajax fight with Hector?

PATROCLUS. Ay, and perhaps receive much honour
    by him.

ACHILLES. I see my reputation is at stake;
My fame is shrewdly gored.

PATROCLUS.   O, then, beware:
Those wounds heal ill that men do give themselves:
Omission to do what is necessary   230
Seals a commission to a blank of danger;
And danger, like an ague, subtly taints
Even then when we sit idly in the sun.

ACHILLES. Go call Thersites hither, sweet Patroclus;
I'll send the fool to Ajax and desire him
T'invite the Trojan lords after the combat
To see us here unarmed. I have a woman's longing,

An appetite that I am sick withal,
To see great Hector in his weeds of peace,
To talk with him, and to behold his visage,   240
Even to my full of view.

Enter Thersites

                    A labour saved!

THERSITES. A wonder!

ACHILLES. What?

THERSITES. Ajax goes up and down the field, asking
for himself.

ACHILLES. How so?

THERSITES. He must fight singly tomorrow with
Hector, and is so prophetically proud of an heroical
cudgelling that he raves in saying nothing.

ACHILLES. How can that be?   250

THERSITES. Why, 'a stalks up and down like a peacock—a stride and a stand; ruminates like an hostess
that hath no arithmetic but her brain to set down her
reckoning; bites his lip with a politic regard, as who
should say 'There were wit in this head, an 'twould
out'—and so there is; but it lies as coldly in him as
fire in a flint, which will not show without knocking. The man's undone for ever, for if Hector break
not his neck i'th' combat, he'll break't himself in
vainglory. He knows not me. I said 'Good morrow,   260
Ajax', and he replies 'Thanks, Agamemnon'. What
think you of this man, that takes me for the general?
He's grown a very landfish, languageless, a monster.
A plague of opinion!—a man may wear it on both
sides, like a leather jerkin.

ACHILLES. Thou must be my ambassador to him,
Thersites.

THERSITES. Who, I? Why, he'll answer nobody. He
professes not answering. Speaking is for beggars; he
wears his tongue in's arms. I will put on his presence.   270
Let Patroclus make demands to me, you shall see the
pageant of Ajax.

ACHILLES. To him, Patroclus. Tell him I humbly
desire the valiant Ajax to invite the most valorous
Hector to come unarmed to my tent, and to procure
safe-conduct for his person of the magnanimous
and most illustrious six-or-seven-times honoured
captain-general of the Grecian army, Agamemnon,
et cetera. Do this.

PATROCLUS. Jove bless great Ajax!   280

THERSITES. Hum!

PATROCLUS. I come from the worthy Achilles—

THERSITES. Ha!

PATROCLUS. Who most humbly desires you to invite
Hector to his tent—

THERSITES. Hum!

PATROCLUS. And to procure safe-conduct from
Agamemnon.

THERSITES. Agamemnon?

PATROCLUS. Ay, my lord.   290

THERSITES. Ha!

PATROCLUS. What say you to't?

THERSITES. God bu'y you, with all my heart.

PATROCLUS. Your answer, sir.

THERSITES. If tomorrow be a fair day, by eleven
o'clock it will go one way or other. Howsoever, he
shall pay for me ere he has me.

PATROCLUS. Your answer, sir.

THERSITES. Fare you well, with all my heart.

ACHILLES. Why, but he is not in this tune, is he?   300

THERSITES. No, but he's out o' tune thus. What music
will be in him when Hector has knocked out his
brains, I know not; but, I am sure, none, unless the
fiddler Apollo gets his sinews to make catlings on.

ACHILLES. Come, thou shalt bear a letter to him
straight.

THERSITES. Let me carry another to his horse; for that's
the more capable creature.

ACHILLES. My mind is troubled like a fountain stirred,
And I myself see not the bottom of it.   310

Achilles and Patroclus go in

THERSITES. Would the fountain of your mind were
clear again, that I might water an ass at it! I had
rather be a tick in a sheep than such a valiant
ingorance.   *Goes*

ACT 4

Scene 1: *Troy. A street*

*Enter, at one side, Æneas, and Servant with a torch;
at the other, Paris, Deiphobus, Antenor, Diomedes, and
others, with torches*

PARIS. See, ho! who is that there?

DEIPHOBUS. It is the Lord Æneas.

ÆNEAS. Is the prince there in person?
Had I so good occasion to lie long
As you, Prince Paris, nothing but heavenly business
Should rob my bed-mate of my company.

DIOMEDES. That's my mind too. Good morrow,
Lord Æneas.

PARIS. A valiant Greek, Æneas—take his hand—
Witness the process of your speech, wherein
You told how Diomed, a whole week by days,   10
Did haunt you in the field.

ÆNEAS. Health to you, valiant sir,
During all question of the gentle truce;
But when I meet you armed, as black defiance
As heart can think or courage execute.

DIOMEDES. The one and other Diomed embraces
Our bloods are now in calm; and so long, health!
But when contention and occasion meet,
By Jove, I'll play the hunter for thy life
With all my force, pursuit, and policy.   20

ÆNEAS. And thou shalt hunt a lion, that will fly
With his face backward. In humane gentleness,
Welcome to Troy! now, by Anchises' life,
Welcome indeed! By Venus' hand I swear
No man alive can love in such a sort
The thing he means to kill more excellently.

DIOMEDES. We sympathise. Jove, let Æneas live,
If to my sword his fate be not the glory,
A thousand complete courses of the sun!
But, in mine emulous honour, let him die   30
With every joint a wound, and that tomorrow.

ÆNEAS. We know each other well.

DIOMEDES. We do; and long to know each other
worse.

PARIS. This is the most despiteful-gentle greeting,
The noblest-hateful love, that e'er I heard of.
What business, lord, so early?

ÆNEAS. I was sent for to the king; but why,
I know not.

PARIS. His purpose meets you: 'twas to bring this
Greek
To Calchas' house, and there to render him,

For the enfreed Antenor, the fair Cressid.   40
Let's have your company, or, if you please,
Haste there before us. I constantly do think—
Or rather, call my thought a certain knowledge—
My brother Troilus lodges there tonight;
Rouse him and give him note of our approach,
With the whole quality wherefore; I fear
We shall be much unwelcome.

ÆNEAS.   That I assure you,
Troilus had rather Troy were borne to Greece
Than Cressid borne from Troy.

PARIS.   There is no help;
The bitter disposition of the time   50
Will have it so. On, lord; we'll follow you.

ÆNEAS. Good morrow all.   *Goes, with Servant*

PARIS. And tell me, noble Diomed, faith, tell me true,
Even in the soul of sound good-fellowship,
Who, in your thoughts, merits fair Helen most,
Myself or Menelaus?

DIOMEDES.   Both alike:
He merits well to have her that doth seek her,
Not making any scruple of her soilure,
With such a hell of pain and world of charge;
And you as well to keep her that defend her,   60
Not palating the taste of her dishonour,
With such a costly loss of wealth and friends.
He, like a puling cuckold, would drink up
The lees and dregs of a flat taméd piece;
You, like a lecher, out of whorish loins
Are pleased to breed out your inheritors;
Both merits poised, each weighs nor less nor more;
But he as he, the heavier for a whore.

PARIS. You are too bitter to your countrywoman.

DIOMEDES. She's bitter to her country. Hear me, Paris: 70
For every false drop in her bawdy veins
A Grecian's life hath sunk; for every scruple
Of her contaminated carrion weight
A Trojan hath been slain; since she could speak,
She hath not given so many good words breath
As for her Greeks and Trojans suffered death.

PARIS. Fair Diomed, you do as chapmen do,
Dispraise the thing that you desire to buy;
But we in silence hold this virtue well,
We'll but commend what we intend to sell.   80
Here lies our way.   *They go*

Scene 2: *The same. The court of Pandarus' house*

Enter Troilus and Cressida

TROILUS. Dear, trouble not yourself; the morn is cold.

CRESSIDA. Then, sweet my lord, I'll call mine
uncle down;
He shall unbolt the gates.

TROILUS.   Trouble him not;
To bed, to bed! sleep lull those pretty eyes,
And give as soft attachment to thy senses
As infants empty of all thought!

CRESSIDA.   Good morrow, then.

TROILUS. I prithee now, to bed!

CRESSIDA.   Are you aweary of me?

TROILUS. O Cressida! but that the busy day,
Waked by the lark, hath roused the ribald crows,
And dreaming night will hide our joys no longer,   10
I would not from thee.

CRESSIDA.   Night hath been too brief.

TROILUS. Beshrew the witch! with venomous wights
   she stays
   As tediously as hell, but flies the grasps of love
   With wings more momentary-swift than thought.
   You will catch cold, and curse me.
CRESSIDA.   Prithee, tarry.
   You men will never tarry.
   O foolish Cressid! I might have still held off,
   And then you would have tarried. Hark! there's
   one up.
PANDARUS [within]. What's all the doors open here?
TROILUS. It is your uncle.   20
CRESSIDA. A pestilence on him! now will he
   be mocking;
   I shall have such a life!

Enter Pandarus

PANDARUS. How now, how now! how go maiden-
   heads? Here, you maid! where's my cousin Cressid?
CRESSIDA. Go hang yourself, you naughty
   mocking uncle!
   You bring me to do—and then you flout me too.
PANDARUS. To do what? to do what? let her say what!
   What have I brought you to do?
CRESSIDA. Come, come, beshrew your heart! you'll
   ne'er be good,
   Nor suffer others.   30
PANDARUS. Ha, ha! Alas, poor wretch! a poor
   capocchia! Has't not slept tonight? Would he not,
   a naughty man, let it sleep? A bugbear take him!
CRESSIDA. Did not I tell you? Would he were
   knocked i'th' head!   *Knocking*
   Who's that at door? Good uncle, go and see.
   My lord, come you again into my chamber.
   You smile and mock me, as if I meant naughtily.
TROILUS. Ha, ha!
CRESSIDA. Come, you're deceived, I think of no
   such thing.   *Knocking*
   How earnestly they knock! Pray you, come in;   40
   I would not for half Troy have you seen here.
                 Troilus and Cressida go
PANDARUS. Who's there? what's the matter? will you
   beat down the door? How now! what's the matter?

Enter Æneas

ÆNEAS. Good morrow, lord, good morrow.
PANDARUS. Who's there? my Lord Æneas! By my
   troth, I knew you not. What news with you so
   early?
ÆNEAS. Is not prince Troilus here?
PANDARUS. Here! what should he do here?
ÆNEAS. Come, he is here, my lord. Do not deny him;   50
   It doth import him much to speak with me.
PANDARUS. Is he here, say you? 'Tis more than I know,
   I'll be sworn; for my own part, I came in late. What
   should he do here?
ÆNEAS. Ho! nay, then; come, come, you'll do him
   wrong ere you're ware; you'll be so true to him,
   to be false to him. Do not you know of him, but
   yet go fetch him hither; go.

Re-enter Troilus

TROILUS. How now! what's the matter?
ÆNEAS. My lord, I scarce have leisure to salute you,   60
   My matter is so rash: there is at hand
   Paris your brother and Deiphobus,

The Grecian Diomed, and our Antenor
Delivered to us; and for him forthwith,
Ere the first sacrifice, within this hour,
We must give up to Diomedes' hand
The Lady Cressida.
TROILUS.   Is it so concluded?
ÆNEAS. By Priam and the general state of Troy.
   They are at hand and ready to effect it.
TROILUS. How my achievements mock me!   70
   I will go meet them; and, my Lord Æneas,
   We met by chance: you did not find me here.
ÆNEAS. Good, good, my lord; the secrets of
   neighbour Pandar
   Have not more gift in taciturnity.
                Troilus and Æneas go
PANDARUS. Is't possible? no sooner got but lost? The
   devil take Antenor! The young prince will go mad.
   A plague upon Antenor! I would they had broke's
   neck!

Re-enter Cressida

CRESSIDA. How now! what's the matter? who was
   here?   80
PANDARUS. Ah, ah!
CRESSIDA. Why sigh you so profoundly? Where's
   my lord? Gone? Tell me, sweet uncle, what's the matter?
PANDARUS. Would I were as deep under the earth as
   I am above!
CRESSIDA. O the gods! What's the matter?
PANDARUS. Prithee, get thee in. Would thou hadst
   ne'er been born! I knew thou wouldst be his death.
   O, poor gentleman! A plague upon Antenor!
CRESSIDA. Good uncle, I beseech you, on my knees   90
   I beseech you, what's the matter?
PANDARUS. Thou must be gone, wench, thou must be
   gone; thou art changed for Antenor; thou must to
   thy father, and be gone from Troilus: 'twill be his
   death; 'twill be his bane; he cannot bear it.
CRESSIDA. O you immortal gods! I will not go.
PANDARUS. Thou must.
CRESSIDA. I will not, uncle. I have forgot my father;
   I know no touch of consanguinity;
   No kin, no love, no blood, no soul so near me   100
   As the sweet Troilus. O you gods divine!
   Make Cressid's name the very crown of falsehood,
   If ever she leave Troilus! Time, force, and death,
   Do to this body what extremes you can;
   But the strong base and building of my love
   Is as the very centre of the earth,
   Drawing all things to it. I'll go in and weep
PANDARUS. Do, do.
CRESSIDA. Tear my bright hair and scratch my
   praiséd cheeks,
   Crack my clear voice with sobs and break my heart   110
   With sounding Troilus. I will not go from Troy.
                      They go

Scene 3: The same. A street before Pandarus' house

Enter Paris, Troilus, followed by Æneas, Deiphobus,
Antenor, and Diomedes

PARIS. It is great morning, and the hour prefixed
   For her delivery to this valiant Greek
   Comes fast upon us. Good my brother Troilus,
   Tell you the lady what she is to do
   And haste her to the purpose.

TROILUS.   Walk into her house;
    I'll bring her to the Grecian presently;
    And to his hand when I deliver her,
    Think it an altar, and thy brother Troilus
    A priest, there offering to it his own heart.   *Goes*
PARIS. I know what 'tis to love,   10
    And would, as I shall pity, I could help!
    Please you walk in, my lords.   *They go*

        Scene 4: *The same. Pandarus' house*

Enter Pandarus and Cressida

PANDARUS. Be moderate, be moderate.
CRESSIDA. Why tell you me of moderation?
    The grief is fine, full, perfect, that I taste,
    And violenteth in a sense as strong
    As that which causeth it. How can I moderate it?
    If I could temporise with my affection,
    Or brew it to a weak and colder palate,
    The like allayment could I give my grief.
    My love admits no qualifying dross;
    No more my grief, in such a precious loss.   10

Enter Troilus

PANDARUS. Here, here, here he comes. Ah sweet
    ducks!
CRESSIDA. O Troilus! Troilus!   *Embracing him*
PANDARUS. What a pair of spectacles is here! Let me
    embrace too. 'O heart,' as the goodly saying is,
        O heart, O heavy heart,
        Why sigh'st thou without breaking?
    where he answers again,
        Because thou canst not ease thy smart
        By friendship nor by speaking.   20
    There was never a truer rhyme. Let us cast away
    nothing, for we may live to have need of such a
    verse. We see it, we see it. How now, lambs!
TROILUS. Cressid, I love thee in so strained a purity,
    That the blest gods, as angry with my fancy,
    More bright in zeal than the devotion which
    Cold lips blow to their deities, take thee from me.
CRESSIDA. Have the gods envy?
PANDARUS. Ay, ay, ay, ay; 'tis too plain a case.
CRESSIDA. And is it true that I must go from Troy?   30
TROILUS. A hateful truth.
CRESSIDA.   What, and from Troilus too?
TROILUS. From Troy and Troilus.
CRESSIDA.   Is it possible?
TROILUS. And suddenly; where injury of chance
    Puts back leave-taking, jostles roughly by
    All time of pause, rudely beguiles our lips
    Of all rejoindure, forcibly prevents
    Our locked embraces, strangles our dear vows
    Even in the birth of our own labouring breath.
    We two, that with so many thousand sighs
    Did buy each other, must poorly sell ourselves   40
    With the rude brevity and discharge of one.
    Injurious Time now with a robber's haste
    Crams his rich thievery up, he knows not how:
    As many farewells as be stars in heaven,
    With distinct breath and consigned kisses to them,
    He fumbles up into a loose adieu,
    And scants us with a single famished kiss,
    Distasted with the salt of broken tears.
ÆNEAS [*within*]. My lord, is the lady ready?
TROILUS. Hark! you are called. Some say the Genius so   50

Cries 'Come!' to him that instantly must die.
    Bid them have patience; she shall come anon.
PANDARUS. Where are my tears? Rain, to lay this
    wind, or my heart will be blown up by th'root!
                                   Goes
CRESSIDA. I must then to the Grecians?
TROILUS.   No remedy.
CRESSIDA. A woeful Cressid 'mongst the merry
    Greeks!
    When shall we see again?
TROILUS. Hear me, my love: be thou but true
    of heart—
CRESSIDA. I true! how now! what wicked deem
    is this?
TROILUS. Nay, we must use expostulation kindly,   60
    For it is parting from us.
    I speak not 'be thou true', as fearing thee,
    For I will throw my glove to Death himself
    That there's no maculation in thy heart;
    But 'be thou true' say I, to fashion in
    My sequent protestation: be thou true,
    And I will see thee.
CRESSIDA. O, you shall be exposed, my lord, to
    dangers
    As infinite as imminent! But I'll be true.
TROILUS. And I'll grow friend with danger. Wear
    this sleeve.   70
CRESSIDA. And you this glove. When shall I see you?
TROILUS. I will corrupt the Grecian sentinels,
    To give thee nightly visitation.
    But yet, be true.
CRESSIDA.   O heavens! 'Be true' again!
TROILUS. Hear why I speak it, love:
    The Grecian youths are full of quality;
    Their loving well composed with gifts of nature,
    And flowing e'er with arts and exercise.
    How novelties may move and parts with person—
    Alas, a kind of godly jealousy,   80
    Which, I beseech you, call a virtuous sin—
    Makes me afeard.
CRESSIDA.   O heavens! you love me not.
TROILUS. Die I a villain then!
    In this I do not call your faith in question
    So mainly as my merit: I cannot sing,
    Nor heel the high lavolt, nor sweeten talk,
    Nor play at subtle games—fair virtues all,
    To which the Grecians are most prompt and
    pregnant;
    But I can tell that in each grace of these
    There lurks a still and dumb-discoursive devil   90
    That tempts most cunningly. But be not tempted.
CRESSIDA. Do you think I will?
TROILUS. No;
    But something may be done that we will not,
    And sometimes we are devils to ourselves,
    When we will tempt the frailty of our powers,
    Presuming on their changeful potency.
ÆNEAS [*within*]. Nay, good my lord!
TROILUS.   Come, kiss; and let us part.
PARIS [*within*]. Brother Troilus!
TROILUS.   Good brother, come
    you hither;
    And bring Æneas and the Grecian with you.   100
CRESSIDA. My lord, will you be true?
TROILUS. Who, I? alas, it is my vice, my fault!
    Whiles others fish with craft for great opinion,

I with great truth catch mere simplicity;
Whilst some with cunning gild their copper crowns,
With truth and plainness I do wear mine bare.
Fear not my truth: the moral of my wit
Is 'plain and true'; there's all the reach of it.

Enter Æneas, Paris, Antenor, Deiphobus, and Diomedes

Welcome, Sir Diomed! Here is the lady
Which for Antenor we deliver you.   110
At the port, lord, I'll give her to thy hand,
And by the way possess thee what she is.
Entreat her fair; and, by my soul, fair Greek,
If e'er thou stand at mercy of my sword,
Name Cressid, and thy life shall be as safe
As Priam is in Ilion.

DIOMEDES.   Fair Lady Cressid,
So please you, save the thanks this prince expects.
The lustre in your eye, heaven in your cheek,
Pleads your fair usage; and to Diomed
You shall be mistress, and command him wholly.   120

TROILUS. Grecian, thou dost not use me courteously,
To shame the zeal of my petition to thee
In praising her. I tell thee, lord of Greece,
She is as far high-soaring o'er thy praises
As thou unworthy to be called her servant.
I charge thee use her well, even for my charge;
For, by the dreadful Pluto, if thou dost not,
Though the great bulk Achilles be thy guard,
I'll cut thy throat.

DIOMEDES.   O, be not moved, Prince Troilus.
Let me be privileged by my place and message   13c
To be a speaker free. When I am hence,
I'll answer to my lust; and know you, lord,
I'll nothing do on charge: to her own worth
She shall be prized; but that you say 'Be't so',
I'll speak it in my spirit and honour 'No!'

TROILUS. Come, to the port. I'll tell thee, Diomed,
This brave shall oft make thee to hide thy head.
Lady, give me your hand; and, as we walk,
To our own selves bend we our needful talk.

             Troilus, Cressida, and Diomedes go;
                              trumpet sounds

PARIS. Hark! Hector's trumpet.

ÆNEAS.   How have we spent
   this morning!   140
The prince must think me tardy and remiss,
That swore to ride before him to the field.

PARIS. 'Tis Troilus' fault; come, come, to field
   with him.

DEIPHOBUS. Let us make ready straight.

ÆNEAS. Yea, with a bridegroom's fresh alacrity,
Let us address to tend on Hector's heels.
The glory of our Troy doth this day lie
On his fair worth and single chivalry.   *They go*

             Scene 5: The Greek camp. Lists set out

Enter Ajax, armed; Agamemnon, Achilles, Patroclus,
Menelaus, Ulysses, Nestor, and others

AGAMEMNON. Here art thou in appointment fresh
   and fair,
Anticipating time with starting courage.
Give with thy trumpet a loud note to Troy,
Thou dreadful Ajax, that the appalled air
May pierce the head of the great combatant
And hale him hither.

AJAX.   Thou trumpet, there's my purse.
Now crack thy lungs, and split thy brazen pipe;
Blow, villain, till thy spherèd bias cheek
Outswell the choller of puffed Aquilon.
Come, stretch thy chest, and let thy eyes spout
   blood;   10
Thou blow'st for Hector.   *Trumpet sounds*

ULYSSES. No trumpet answers.

ACHILLES.   'Tis but early days.

AGAMEMNON. Is not yon Diomed, with
   Calchas' daughter?

ULYSSES. 'Tis he, I ken the manner of his gait:
He rises on the toe; that spirit of his
In aspiration lifts him from the earth.

Enter Diomedes, with Cressida

AGAMEMNON. Is this the Lady Cressid?

DIOMEDES.   Even she.

AGAMEMNON. Most dearly welcome to the Greeks,
   sweet lady.   *Kisses her*

NESTOR. Our general doth salute you with a kiss.

ULYSSES. Yet is the kindness but particular;   20
'Twere better she were kissed in general.

NESTOR. And very courtly counsel. I'll begin.
So much for Nestor.   *Kisses her*

ACHILLES. I'll take that winter from your lips, fair lady.
Achilles bids you welcome.   *Kisses her*

MENELAUS. I had good argument for kissing once.

PATROCLUS. But that's no argument for kissing now;
For thus popped Paris in his hardiment,
And parted thus you and your argument.
                                         Kisses her

ULYSSES. O deadly gall, and theme of all our scorns!   30
For which we lose our heads to gild his horns.

PATROCLUS. The first was Menelaus' kiss; this, mine—
Patroclus kisses you.   *Kisses her again*

MENELAUS.   O, this is trim!

PATROCLUS. Paris and I kiss evermore for him.

MENELAUS. I'll have my kiss, sir. Lady, by your leave.

CRESSIDA. In kissing, do you render or receive?

MENELAUS. Both take and give.

CRESSIDA.   I'll make my match
   to live,
The kiss you take is better than you give;
Therefore no kiss.

MENELAUS. I'll give you boot, I'll give you three
   for one.   40

CRESSIDA. You're an odd man; give even, or
   give none.

MENELAUS. An odd man, lady! every man is odd.

CRESSIDA. No, Paris is not; for you know 'tis true
That you are odd, and he is even with you.

MENELAUS. You fillip me o'th' head.

CRESSIDA.   No, I'll be sworn.

ULYSSES. It were no match, your nail against his horn.
May I, sweet lady, beg a kiss of you?

CRESSIDA. You may.

ULYSSES.   I do desire it.

CRESSIDA.   Why, beg too.

ULYSSES. Why then, for Venus' sake, give me a kiss
When Helen is a maid again, and his.   50

CRESSIDA. I am your debtor; claim it when 'tis due.

ULYSSES. Never's my day, and then a kiss of you.

DIOMEDES. Lady, a word; I'll bring you to
   your father.   *Goes, with Cressida*

NESTOR. A woman of quick sense.

ULYSSES.   Fie, fie upon her!
There's language in her eye, her cheek, her lip,
Nay, her foot speaks; her wanton spirits look out
At every joint and motive of her body.
O, these encounterers, so glib of tongue,
That give accosting welcome ere it comes,
And wide unclasp the tables of their thoughts   60
To every tickling reader!—set them down
For sluttish spoils of opportunity
And daughters of the game.   *Trumpet within*
ALL. The Trojans' trumpet.
AGAMEMNON.   Yonder comes the troop.

Flourish. Enter Hector, armed; Æneas, Troilus, and other
Trojans, with Attendants

ÆNEAS. Hail, all the state of Greece! What shall be done
To him that victory commands? Or do you purpose
A victor shall be known? Will you the knights
Shall to the edge of all extremity
Pursue each other, or shall they be divided
By any voice or order of the field?   70
Hector bade ask.
AGAMEMNON.   Which way would Hector have it?
ÆNEAS. He cares not; he'll obey conditions.
AGAMEMNON. 'Tis done like Hector.
ACHILLES.   But securely done,
A little proudly, and great deal misprizing
The knight opposed.
ÆNEAS.   If not Achilles, sir.
What is your name?
ACHILLES.   If not Achilles, nothing.
ÆNEAS. Therefore Achilles. But whate'er, know this:
In the extremity of great and little,
Valour and pride excel themselves in Hector;
The one almost as infinite as all,   80
The other blank as nothing. Weigh him well,
And that which looks like pride is courtesy.
This Ajax is half made of Hector's blood,
In love whereof, half Hector stays at home;
Half heart, half hand, half Hector comes to seek
This blended knight, half Trojan and half Greek.
ACHILLES. A maiden battle then? O, I perceive you.

Re-enter Diomedes

AGAMEMNON. Here is Sir Diomed, Go, gentle knight,
Stand by our Ajax. As you and Lord Æneas
Consent upon the order of their fight,   90
So be it; either to the uttermost,
Or else a breath. The combatants being kin
Half stints their strife before their strokes begin.
                    Ajax and Hector enter the lists
ULYSSES. They are opposed already.
AGAMEMNON. What Trojan is that same that looks
    so heavy?
ULYSSES. The youngest son of Priam, a true knight;
Not yet mature, yet matchless-firm of word;
Speaking in deeds and deedless in his tongue;
Not soon provoked nor, being provoked, soon
    calmed;
His heart and hand both open and both free;   100
For what he has he gives, what thinks he shows;
Yet gives he not till judgement guide his bounty,
Nor dignifies an impair thought with breath;
Manly as Hector, but more dangerous;
For Hector in his blaze of wrath subscribes
To tender objects, but he in heat of action

Is more vindicative than jealous love;
They call him Troilus, and on him erect
A second hope, as fairly built as Hector:
Thus says Æneas, one that knows the youth   110
Even to his inches, and with private soul
Did in great Ilion thus translate him to me.
                    Alarum; Hector and Ajax fight
AGAMEMNON. They are in action.
NESTOR. Now, Ajax, hold thine own!
TROILUS.   Hector, thou sleep'st;
Awake thee!
AGAMEMNON. His blows are well disposed.
    There, Ajax!   *Trumpets cease*
DIOMEDES. You must no more.
ÆNEAS.   Princes, enough, so please you.
AJAX. I am not warm yet; let us fight again.
DIOMEDES. As Hector pleases.
HECTOR.   Why, then will I no more:
Thou art, great lord, my father's sister's son,   120
A cousin-german to great Priam's seed;
The obligation of our blood forbids
A gory emulation 'twixt us twain.
Were thy commixtion Greek and Trojan so,
That thou couldst say 'This hand is Grecian all,
And this is Trojan; the sinews of this leg
All Greek, and this all Troy; my mother's blood
Runs on the dexter cheek, and this sinister
Bounds in my father's', by Jove multipotent,
Thou shouldst not bear from me a Greekish member   130
Wherein my sword had not impressure made
Of our rank feud; but the just gods gainsay
That any drop thou borrow'dst from thy mother,
My sacred aunt, should by my mortal sword
Be drainéd! Let me embrace thee, Ajax.
By him that thunders, thou hast lusty arms;
Hector would have them fall upon him thus.
Cousin, all honour to thee!
AJAX.   I thank thee, Hector.
Thou art too gentle and too free a man.
I came to kill thee, cousin, and bear hence   140
A great addition earnéd in thy death.
HECTOR. Not Neoptolemus so mirable,
On whose bright crest Fame with her loud'st oyez
Cries 'This is he', could promise to himself
A thought of added honour torn from Hector.
ÆNEAS. There is expectance here from both
    the sides
What further you will do.
HECTOR.   We'll answer it:
The issue is embracement; Ajax, farewell.
AJAX. If I might in entreaties find success,
As seld I have the chance, I would desire   150
My famous cousin to our Grecian tents.
DIOMEDES. 'Tis Agamemnon's wish; and great
    Achilles
Doth long to see unarmed the valiant Hector.
HECTOR. Æneas, call my brother Troilus to me,
And signify this loving interview
To the expecters of our Trojan part;
Desire them home. Give me thy hand, my cousin;
I will go eat with thee, and see your knights.
AJAX. Great Agamemnon comes to meet us here.
HECTOR. The worthiest of them tell me name
    by name;   160
But for Achilles, my own searching eyes
Shall find him by his large and portly size.

AGAMEMNON. Worthy of arms! as welcome as to one
　That would be rid of such an enemy—
　But that's no welcome; understand more clear,
　What's past and what's to come is strewed with
　　husks
　And formless ruin of oblivion;
　But in this extant moment, faith and troth,
　Strained purely from all hollow bias-drawing,
　Bids thee, with most divine integrity,　　　　　170
　From heart of very heart, great Hector, welcome.
HECTOR. I thank thee, most imperious Agamemnon.
AGAMEMNON [to Troilus]. My well-famed lord of
　Troy, no less to you.
MENELAUS. Let me confirm my princely brother's
　greeting;
　You brace of warlike brothers, welcome hither.
HECTOR. Who must we answer?
ÆNEAS.　　　　　　　　　　　The noble Menelaus.
HECTOR. O, you, my lord! by Mars his gauntlet,
　thanks!
　Mock not that I affect th'untraded oath;
　Your quondam wife swears still by Venus' glove.
　She's well, but bade me not commend her to you.　180
MENELAUS. Name her not now, sir; she's a deadly
　theme.
HECTOR. O, pardon; I offend.
NESTOR. I have, thou gallant Trojan, seen thee oft,
　Labouring for destiny, make cruel way
　Through ranks of Greekish youth; and I have
　　seen thee,
　As hot as Perseus, spur thy Phrygian steed,
　And seen thee scorning forfeits and subduements
　When thou hast hung thy advanced sword i'th'air,
　Not letting it decline on the declined,
　That I have said to some my standers-by　　　190
　'Lo, Jupiter is yonder, dealing life!'
　And I have seen thee pause and take thy breath
　When that a ring of Greeks have hemmed thee in,
　Like an Olympian wrestling. This have I seen,
　But this thy countenance, still locked in steel,
　I never saw till now. I knew thy grandsire,
　And once fought with him. He was a soldier good;
　But, by great Mars the captain of us all,
　Never like thee. O, let an old man embrace thee;
　And, worthy warrior, welcome to our tents.　　200
ÆNEAS. 'Tis the old Nestor.
HECTOR. Let me embrace thee, good old chronicle,
　That hast so long walked hand in hand with time;
　Most reverend Nestor, I am glad to clasp thee.
NESTOR. I would my arms could match thee in
　contention,
　As they contend with thee in courtesy.
HECTOR. I would they could.
NESTOR. Ha!
　By this white beard, I'ld fight with thee tomorrow.
　Well, welcome, welcome! I have seen the time.　210
ULYSSES. I wonder now how yonder city stands
　When we have here her base and pillar by us.
HECTOR. I know your favour, Lord Ulysses, well.
　Ah, sir, there's many a Greek and Trojan dead,
　Since first I saw yourself and Diomed
　In Ilion, on your Greekish embassy.
ULYSSES. Sir, I foretold you then what would ensue.
　My prophecy is but half his journey yet;
　For yonder walls, that pertly front your town,
　Yon towers, whose wanton tops do buss the clouds,　220

Must kiss their own feet.
HECTOR.　　　　　　　I must not believe you.
　There they stand yet; and modestly I think
　The fall of every Phrygian stone will cost
　A drop of Grecian blood. The end crowns all;
　And that old common arbitrator, Time,
　Will one day end it.
ULYSSES.　　　　　　So to him we leave it.
　Most gentle and most valiant Hector, welcome.
　After the general, I beseech you next
　To feast with me and see me at my tent.
ACHILLES. I shall forestall thee, Lord Ulysses, thou!　230
　Now Hector, I have fed mine eyes on thee;
　I have with exact view perused thee, Hector,
　And quoted joint by joint.
HECTOR.　　　　　　　Is this Achilles?
ACHILLES. I am Achilles.
HECTOR. Stand fair, I pray thee; let me look on thee.
ACHILLES. Behold thy fill.
HECTOR.　　　　　　Nay, I have done already.
ACHILLES. Thou art too brief. I will the second time,
　As I would buy thee, view thee limb by limb.
HECTOR. O, like a book of sport thou'lt read me o'er;
　But there's more in me than thou understand'st.　240
　Why dost thou so oppress me with thine eye?
ACHILLES. Tell me, you heavens, in which part of
　his body
　Shall I destroy him?—whether there, or there, or
　there?—
　That I may give the local wound a name,
　And make distinct the very breach whereout
　Hector's great spirit flew. Answer me, heavens!
HECTOR. It would discredit the blest gods, proud man,
　To answer such a question. Stand again;
　Think'st thou to catch my life so pleasantly
　As to prenominate in nice conjecture　　　　250
　Where thou wilt hit me dead?
ACHILLES.　　　　　　　I tell thee yea.
HECTOR. Wert thou an oracle to tell me so,
　I'ld not believe thee. Henceforth guard thee well;
　For I'll not kill thee there, nor there, nor there;
　But, by the forge that stithied Mars his helm,
　I'll kill thee everywhere, yea, o'er and o'er.
　You wisest Grecians, pardon me this brag:
　His insolence draws folly from my lips;
　But I'll endeavour deeds to match these words,
　Or may I never—
AJAX.　　　　　　Do not chafe thee, cousin;　260
　And you, Achilles, let these threats alone
　Till accident or purpose bring you to't.
　You may have every day enough of Hector,
　If you have stomach. The general state, I fear,
　Can scarce entreat you to be odd with him.
HECTOR. I pray you, let us see you in the field;
　We have had pelting wars since you refused
　The Grecians' cause.
ACHILLES.　　　　　Dost thou entreat me, Hector?
　Tomorrow do I meet thee, fell as death;
　Tonight all friends.
HECTOR.　　　　　Thy hand upon that match.　270
AGAMEMNON. First, all you peers of Greece, go to
　my tent;
　There in the full convive we. Afterwards,
　As Hector's leisure and your bounties shall
　Concur together, severally entreat him.
　Beat loud the taborins, let the trumpets blow,

That this great soldier may his welcome know.
    Flourish; all go but Troilus and Ulysses
TROILUS. My Lord Ulysses, tell me, I beseech you,
In what place of the field doth Calchas keep?
ULYSSES. At Menelaus' tent, most princely Troilus.
There Diomed doth feast with him tonight; 280
Who neither looks upon the heaven nor earth,
But gives all gaze and bent of amorous view
On the fair Cressid.
TROILUS. Shall I, sweet lord, be bound to you
 so much,
After we part from Agamemnon's tent,
To bring me thither?
ULYSSES.   You shall command me, sir.
As gentle tell me, of what honour was
This Cressida in Troy? Had she no lover there
That wails her absence?
TROILUS. O, sir, to such as boasting show their scars, 290
A mock is due. Will you walk on, my lord?
She was beloved, she loved; she is, and doth;
But still sweet love is food for fortune's tooth.
        They go

ACT 5
Scene 1: *The same. Before Achilles' tent*

Enter Achilles and Patroclus

ACHILLES. I'll heat his blood with Greekish wine
 tonight,
Which with my scimitar I'll cool tomorrow.
Patroclus, let us feast him to the height.
PATROCLUS. Here comes Thersites.

Enter Thersites

ACHILLES.   How now, thou core of envy!
Thou crusty botch of nature, what's the news?
THERSITES. Why, thou picture of what thou seemest,
and idol of idiot-worshippers, here's a letter for thee.
ACHILLES. From whence, fragment?
THERSITES. Why, thou full dish of fool, from Troy.
PATROCLUS. Who keeps the tent now? 10
THERSITES. The surgeon's box, or the patient's wound.
PATROCLUS. Well said, adversity! and what need these
 tricks!
THERSITES. Prithee, be silent, boy; I profit not by thy
talk; thou art thought to be Achilles' male varlet.
PATROCLUS. Male varlet, you rogue! what's that?
THERSITES. Why, his masculine whore. Now, the
rotten diseases of the south, the guts-griping,
ruptures, catarrhs, loads o' gravel i'th'back, lethar-
gies, cold palsies, raw eyes, dirt-rotten livers, wheez- 20
ing lungs, bladders full of impostume, sciaticas,
limekilns i'th'palm, incurable bone-ache, and the
rivelled fee-simple of the tetter, take and take again
such preposterous discoveries!
PATROCLUS. Why, thou damnable box of envy, thou;
what mean'st thou to curse thus?
THERSITES. Do I curse thee?
PATROCLUS. Why, no, you ruinous butt; you whoreson indistinguishable cur, no.
THERSITES. No! Why art thou then exasperate, thou 30
idle immaterial skein of sleave-silk, thou green
sarsenet flap for a sore eye, thou tassel of a prodigal's
purse, thou? Ah, how the poor world is pestered
with such waterflies, diminutives of nature!

PATROCLUS. Out, gall!
THERSITES. Finch-egg!
ACHILLES. My sweet Patroclus, I am thwarted quite
From my great purpose in tomorrow's battle.
Here is a letter from Queen Hecuba,
A token from her daughter, my fair love, 40
Both taxing me and gaging me to keep
An oath that I have sworn. I will not break it:
Fall Greeks; fail fame; honour or go or stay;
My major vow lies here; this I'll obey.
Come, come, Thersites, help to trim my tent;
This night in banqueting must all be spent.
Away Patroclus! *Achilles and Patroclus go in*
THERSITES. With too much blood and too little brain,
these two may run mad; but if with too much brain
and too little blood they do, I'll be a curer of 50
madmen. Here's Agamemnon, an honest fellow
enough and one that loves quails, but he has not so
much brain as earwax; and the goodly transformation of Jupiter there, his brother, the bull, the
primitive statue and oblique memorial of cuckolds,
a thrifty shoeing-horn in a chain, hanging at his
brother's leg—to what form but that he is, should
wit larded with malice and malice forced with wit
turn him to? To an ass, were nothing: he is both ass
and ox; to an ox, were nothing: he is both ox and 60
ass. To be a dog, a mule, a cat, a fitchew, a toad,
a lizard, an owl, a puttock, or a herring without a
roe, I would not care; but to be Menelaus, I would
conspire against destiny! Ask me not what I would
be, if I were not Thersites; for I care not to be the
louse of a lazar, so I were not Menelaus. Hoy-day!
spirits and fires!

*Enter Hector, Troilus, Ajax, Agamemnon, Ulysses,
Nestor, Menelaus, and Diomedes, with lights*

AGAMEMNON. We go wrong, we go wrong.
AJAX.   No, yonder 'tis;
There, where we see the lights.
HECTOR.   I trouble you.
AJAX. No, not a whit.

Re-enter Achilles

ULYSSES.   Here comes himself to guide you. 70
ACHILLES. Welcome, brave Hector; welcome,
 princes all.
AGAMEMNON. So now, fair Prince of Troy, I bid
 good night.
Ajax commands the guard to tend on you.
HECTOR. Thanks and good night to the Greeks'
 general.
MENELAUS. Good night, my lord.
HECTOR.   Good night, sweet Lord Menelaus.
THERSITES. Sweet draught: sweet, quoth 'a! sweet sink,
sweet sewer.
ACHILLES. Good night and welcome, both at once,
 to those
That go or tarry.
AGAMEMNON. Good night.   80
        Agamemnon and Menelaus go
ACHILLES. Old Nestor tarries; and you too, Diomed,
Keep Hector company an hour or two.
DIOMEDES. I cannot, lord; I have important business,
The tide whereof is now. Good night, great Hector.
HECTOR. Give me your hand.

ULYSSES [*aside to Troilus*]. Follow his torch; he goes
  to Calchas' tent.
  I'll keep you company.
TROILUS.   Sweet sir, you honour me.
HECTOR. And so, good night.
                              Diomedes goes; Ulysses and
                                    Troilus following
ACHILLES. Come, come, enter my tent.
                              Achilles, Hector, Ajax and Nestor go in
THERSITES. That same Diomed's a false-hearted rogue,   90
  a most unjust knave; I will no more trust him when
  he leers than I will a serpent when he hisses; he
  will spend his mouth and promise, like Babbler the
  hound; but when he performs, astronomers foretell
  it; it is prodigious, there will come some change;
  the sun borrows of the moon when Diomed keeps
  his word. I will rather leave to see Hector than not
  to dog him. They say he keeps a Trojan drab and
  uses the traitor Calchas' tent; I'll after. Nothing but
  lechery! all incontinent varlets!   *Goes*   100

          Scene 2: *The same. Before Calchas' tent*

Enter Diomedes

DIOMEDES. What, are you up here, ho? speak.
CALCHAS [*within*]. Who calls?
DIOMEDES. Diomed. Calchas, I think. Where's your
  daughter?
CALCHAS [*within*]. She comes to you.

*Enter Troilus and Ulysses, at a distance; after them
Thersites*

ULYSSES. Stand where the torch may not discover us.

Enter Cressida

TROILUS. Cressid comes forth to him.
DIOMEDES.   How now, my charge!
CRESSIDA. Now, my sweet guardian! Hark, a word
  with you.   *Whispers*
TROILUS. Yea, so familiar!
ULYSSES. She will sing any man at first sight.   10
THERSITES. And any man may sing her, if he can take
  her clef; she's noted.
DIOMEDES. Will you remember?
CRESSIDA. Remember? Yes.
DIOMEDES. Nay, but do then;
  And let your mind be coupled with your words.
TROILUS. What should she remember?
ULYSSES. List.
CRESSIDA. Sweet honey Greek, tempt me no more
  to folly.
THERSITES. Roguery!   20
DIOMEDES. Nay, then—
CRESSIDA. I'll tell you what—
DIOMEDES. Foh, foh! come, tell a pin; you are
  forsworn.
CRESSIDA. In faith, I cannot. What would you have
  me do?
THERSITES. A juggling trick—to be secretly open.
DIOMEDES. What did you swear you would bestow
  on me?
CRESSIDA. I prithee, do not hold me to mine oath;
  Bid me do anything but that, sweet Greek.
DIOMEDES. Good night.
TROILUS. Hold, patience!
ULYSSES. How now, Trojan!   30

CRESSIDA. Diomed—
DIOMEDES. No no, good night; I'll be your fool
  no more.
TROILUS. Thy better must.
CRESSIDA. Hark, one work in your ear.
TROILUS. O plague and madness!
ULYSSES. You are moved, prince; let us depart,
    I pray you,
  Lest your displeasure should enlarge itself
  To wrathful terms. This place is dangerous;
  The time right deadly; I beseech you, go.   40
TROILUS. Behold, I pray you!
ULYSSES.   Nay, good my lord. go off;
  You flow to great distraction; come, my lord.
TROILUS. I pray thee, stay.
ULYSSES.   You have not patience; come.
TROILUS. I pray you, stay; by hell and all hell's
    torments,
  I will not speak a word.
DIOMEDES.   And so, good night.
CRESSIDA. Nay, but you part in anger.
TROILUS.   Doth that grieve thee?
  O withered truth!
ULYSSES.   Why, how now, lord!
TROILUS.   By Jove,
  I will be patient.
CRESSIDA.   Guardian! Why, Greek!
DIOMEDES. Foh, foh! adieu; you palter.
CRESSIDA. In faith, I do not; come hither once again.   50
ULYSSES. You shake, my lord, at something; will
    you go?
  You will break out.
TROILUS   She strokes his cheek!
ULYSSES.   Come, come.
TROILUS. Nay, stay; by Jove, I will not speak a word:
  There is between my will and all offences
  A guard of patience. Stay a little while.
THERSITES. How the devil luxury, with his fat rump
  and potato-finger, tickles these together! Fry,
  lechery, fry!
DIOMEDES. But will you then?
CRESSIDA. In faith, I will, la; never trust me else.   60
DIOMEDES. Give me some token for the surety of it.
CRESSIDA. I'll fetch you one.   *Goes*
ULYSSES. You have sworn patience.
TROILUS.   Fear me not, sweet lord;
  I will not be myself, nor have cognition
  Of what I feel. I am all patience.

Re-enter Cressida

THERSITES. Now the pledge; now, now, now!
CRESSIDA. Here, Diomed, keep this sleeve.
TROILUS. O beauty! where is thy faith?
ULYSSES.   My lord—
TROILUS. I will be patient; outwardly I will.
CRESSIDA. You look upon that sleeve; behold it well.   70
  He loved me—O false wench!—Give't me again.
DIOMEDES. Whose was't?
CRESSIDA. It is no matter, now I have't again.
  I will not meet with you tomorrow night.
  I prithee, Diomed, visit me no more.
THERSITES. Now she sharpens; well said, whetstone!
DIOMEDES. I shall have it.
CRESSIDA.   What, this?
DIOMEDES.   Ay, that.
CRESSIDA. O, all you gods! O pretty, pretty pledge!

Thy master now lies thinking in his bed
Of thee and me, and sighs, and takes my glove,   80
And gives memorial dainty kisses to it,
As I kiss thee. Nay, do not snatch it from me;
He that takes that doth take my heart withal.

DIOMEDES. I had your heart before; this follows it.

TROILUS. I did swear patience.

CRESSIDA. You shall not have it, Diomed; faith, you
shall not;
I'll give you something else.

DIOMEDES. I will have this. Whose was it?

CRESSIDA.   It is no matter.

DIOMEDES. Come, tell me whose it was.

CRESSIDA. 'Twas one's that loved me better than
you will.   90
But now you have it, take it.

DIOMEDES.   Whose was it?

CRESSIDA. By all Diana's waiting-women yond,
And by herself, I will not tell you whose.

DIOMEDES. Tomorrow will I wear it on my helm,
And grieve his spirit that dares not challenge it.

TROILUS. Wert thou the devil, and wor'st it on thy
horn,
It should be challenged.

CRESSIDA. Well, well, 'tis done, 'tis past—and yet it
is not;
I will not keep my word.

DIOMEDES.   Why then, farewell;
Thou never shalt mock Diomed again.   100

CRESSIDA. You shall not go; one cannot speak a word,
But it straight starts you.

DIOMEDES.   I do not like this fooling.

TROILUS. Nor I, by Pluto; but that that likes not you
Pleases me best.

DIOMEDES.   What, shall I come? the hour?

CRESSIDA. Ay, come. O Jove! do come; I shall be
plagued.

DIOMEDES. Farewell till then.

CRESSIDA.   Good night; I prithee, come.

Diomedes goes

Troilus, farewell! One eye yet looks on thee,
But with my heart the other eye doth see.
Ah, poor our sex! this fault in us I find,
The error of our eye directs our mind;   110
What error leads must err—O, then conclude
Minds swayed by eyes are full of turpitude.   *Goes*

THERSITES. A proof of strength she could not publish
more,
Unless she said 'My mind is now turned whore'.

ULYSSES. All's done, my lord.

TROILUS.   It is.

ULYSSES.   Why stay we then?

TROILUS. To make a recordation to my soul
Of every syllable that here was spoke.
But if I tell how these two did co-act,
Shall I not lie in publishing a truth?
Sith yet there is a credence in my heart,   120
An esperance so obstinately strong,
That doth invert th'attest of eyes and tears;
And if those organs had deceptious functions,
Created only to calumniate.
Was Cressid here?

ULYSSES.   I cannot conjure, Trojan.

TROILUS. She was not, sure.

ULYSSES.   Most sure she was.

TROILUS. Why, my negation hath no taste of madness.

ULYSSES. Nor mine, my lord; Cressid was here but
now.

TROILUS. Let it not be believed for womanhood!
Think we had mothers. Do not give advantage   130
To stubborn critics, apt without a theme
For depravation, to square the general sex   .
By Cressid's rule; rather think this not Cressid.

ULYSSES. What hath she done, prince, that can soil
our mothers?

TROILUS. Nothing at all, unless that this were she.

THERSITES. Will 'a swagger himself out on's own eyes?

TROILUS. This she? No; this is Diomed's Cressida.
If beauty have a soul, this is not she;
If souls guide vows, if vows be sanctimonies,
If sanctimony be the gods' delight,   140
If there be rule in unity itself,
This is not she. O madness of discourse,
That cause sets up with and against itself!
Bifold authority! where reason can revolt
Without perdition, and loss assume all reason
Without revolt. This is, and is not, Cressid!
Within my soul there doth conduce a fight
Of this strange nature, that a thing inseparate
Divides more wider than the sky and earth;
And yet the spacious breadth of this division   150
Admits no orifex for a point as subtle
As Ariachne's broken woof to enter.
Instance, O instance! strong as Pluto's gates:
Cressid is mine, tied with the bonds of heaven.
Instance, O instance! strong as heaven itself:
The bonds of heaven are slipped, dissolved and
loosed,
And with another knot, five-finger-tied,
The fractions of her faith, orts of her love,
The fragments, scraps, the bits and greasy relics
Of her o'ereaten faith are given to Diomed.   160

ULYSSES. May worthy Troilus be but half attached
With that which here his passion doth express?

TROILUS. Ay, Greek; and that shall be divulgéd well
In characters as red as Mars his heart
Inflamed with Venus. Never did young man fancy
With so eternal and so fixed a soul.
Hark, Greek: as much as I do Cressid love,
So much by weight hate I her Diomed.
That sleeve is mine that he'll bear on his helm.
Were it a casque composed by Vulcan's skill,   170
My sword should bite it. Not the dreadful spout
Which shipmen do the hurricano call,
Constringed in mass by the almighty sun,
Shall dizzy with more clamour Neptune's ear
In his descent, than shall my prompted sword
Falling on Diomed.

THERSITES. He'll tickle it for his concupy.

TROILUS. O Cressid! O false Cressid! false, false, false!
Let all untruths stand by thy stainéd name,
And they'll seem glorious.

ULYSSES.   O, contain yourself;   180
Your passion draws ears hither.

Enter Æneas

ÆNEAS. I have been seeking you this hour, my lord.
Hector by this is arming him in Troy;
Ajax your guard stays to conduct you home.

TROILUS. Have with you, prince. My courteous
lord, adieu.
Farewell, revolted fair! and, Diomed,

Stand fast, and wear a castle on thy head!
ULYSSES. I'll bring you to the gates.
TROILUS. Accept distracted thanks.

Troilus, Æneas, and Ulysses go

THERSITES. Would I could meet that rogue Diomed! I 190
would croak like a raven; I would bode, I would
bode. Patroclus will give me anything for the
intelligence of this whore; the parrot will not do
more for an almond than he for a commodious
drab. Lechery, lechery! Still wars and lechery!
Nothing else holds fashion. A burning devil take
them!   *Goes*

Scene 3: *Troy. Before Priam's palace*

Enter Hector and Andromache

ANDROMACHE. When was my lord so much urgently
tempered,
To stop his ears against admonishment?
Unarm, unarm, and do not fight today.
HECTOR. You train me to offend you; get you in.
By all the everlasting gods, I'll go!
ANDROMACHE. My dreams will sure prove ominous
to the day.
HECTOR. No more, I say.

Enter Cassandra

CASSANDRA.   Where is my brother Hector?
ANDROMACHE. Here, sister; armed, and bloody in
intent.
Consort with me in loud and dear petition;
Pursue we him on knees; for I have dreamed   10
Of bloody turbulence, and this whole night
Hath nothing been but shapes and forms of
slaughter.
CASSANDRA. O, 'tis true.
HECTOR.   Ho! bid my trumpet sound!
CASSANDRA. No notes of sally, for the heavens,
sweet brother.
HECTOR. Be gone, I say. The gods have heard me
swear.
CASSANDRA. The gods are deaf to hot and peevish
vows:
They are polluted offerings, more abhorred
Than spotted livers in the sacrifice.
ANDROMACHE. O, be persuaded! Do not count it holy
To hurt by being just; it is as lawful,   20
For we would give much, to use violent thefts
And rob in the behalf of charity.
CASSANDRA. It is the purpose that makes strong the
vow;
But vows to every purpose must not hold.
Unarm, sweet Hector.
HECTOR.   Hold you still, I say;
Mine honour keeps the weather of my fate.
Life every man holds dear; but the dear man
Holds honour far more precious-dear than life.

Enter Troilus

How now, young man! Mean'st thou to fight
today?
ANDROMACHE. Cassandra, call my father to persuade.   30
Cassandra goes
HECTOR. No, faith, young Troilus; doff thy harness,
youth;
I am today i'th'vein of chivalry.

Let grow thy sinews till their knots be strong,
And tempt not yet the brushes of the war.
Unarm thee, go; and doubt thou not, brave boy,
I'll stand today for thee and me and Troy.
TROILUS. Brother, you have a vice of mercy in you,
Which better fits a lion than a man.
HECTOR. What vice is that? Good Troilus, chide me
for it.
TROILUS. When many times the captive Grecian falls,   40
Even in the fan and wind of your fair sword,
You bid them rise and live.
HECTOR. O, 'tis fair play.
TROILUS.   Fool's play, by heaven, Hector.
HECTOR. How now! How now!
TROILUS.   For th'love of all the gods,
Let's leave the hermit pity with our mother;
And when we have our armours buckled on,
The venomed vengeance ride upon our swords,
Spur them to ruthful work, rein them from ruth!
HECTOR. Fie, savage, fie!
TROILUS.   Hector, then 'tis wars.
HECTOR. Troilus, I would not have you fight today.   50
TROILUS. Who should withhold me?
Not fate, obedience, nor the hand of Mars
Beckoning with fiery truncheon my retire;
Not Priamus and Hecuba on knees,
Their eyes o'ergallèd with recourse of tears;
Nor you, my brother, with your true sword drawn,
Opposed to hinder me, should stop my way,
But by my ruin.

Re-enter Cassandra, with Priam

CASSANDRA. Lay hold upon him, Priam, hold him fast;
He is thy crutch; now if thou lose thy stay,   60
Thou on him leaning, and all Troy on thee,
Fall all together.
PRIAM.   Come, Hector, come, go back.
Thy wife hath dreamed; thy mother hath had
visions;
Cassandra doth foresee; and I myself
Am like a prophet suddenly enrapt,
To tell thee that this day is ominous;
Therefore, come back.
HECTOR.   Æneas is afield;
And I do stand engaged to many Greeks,
Even in the faith of valour, to appear
This morning to them.
PRIAM.   Ay, but thou shalt not go.   70
HECTOR. I must not break my faith.
You know me dutiful; therefore, dear sir,
Let me not shame respect, but give me leave
To take that course by your consent and voice
Which you do here forbid me, royal Priam.
CASSANDRA. O Priam, yield not to him!
ANDROMACHE.   Do not, dear father.
HECTOR. Andromache, I am offended with you;
Upon the love you bear me, get you in.   *She goes*
TROILUS. This foolish, dreaming, superstitious girl
Makes all these bodements.
CASSANDRA.   O, farewell, dear Hector!   80
Look how thou diest! look how thy eye turns pale!
Look how thy wounds do bleed at many vents!
Hark how Troy roars! how Hecuba cries out!
How poor Andromache shrills her dolours forth!
Behold, distraction, frenzy, and amazement,
Like witless antics, one another meet,

And all cry 'Hector! Hector's dead! O Hector!'
TROILUS. Away! away!
CASSANDRA. Farewell—yet soft! Hector, I take
my leave;
Thou dost thyself and all our Troy deceive. *Goes* 90
HECTOR. You are amazed, my liege, at her exclaims.
Go in and cheer the town; we'll forth and fight,
Do deeds worth praise and tell you them at night.
PRIAM. Farewell. The gods with safety stand about
thee!   *Priam and Hector go severally;*
                                                alarum
TROILUS. They are at it, hark! Proud Diomed, believe,
I come to lose my arm, or win my sleeve.

Enter Pandarus

PANDARUS. Do you hear, my lord? do you hear?
TROILUS. What now?
PANDARUS. Here's a letter from yon poor girl.
TROILUS. Let me read.   100
PANDARUS. A whoreson tisick, a whoreson rascally
tisick so troubles me, and the foolish fortune of this
girl; and what one thing, what another, that I shall
leave you one o'these days. And I have a rheum in
mine eyes too, and such an ache in my bones that,
unless a man were cursed, I cannot tell what to think
on't. What says she there?
TROILUS. Words, words, mere words; no matter
from the heart;
Th'effect doth operate another way.
                                              Tearing the letter
Go, wind, to wind! there turn and change together. 110
My love with words and errors still she feeds,
But edifies another with her deeds.
                                      They go severally

Scene 4: *The field between Troy and the Greek camp*

Alarums. Excursions. Enter Thersites

THERSITES. Now they are clapper-clawing one another; I'll go look on. That dissembling abominable
varlet, Diomed, has got that same scurvy doting
foolish young knave's sleeve of Troy there in his
helm. I would fain see them meet; that that same
young Trojan ass, that loves the whore there, might
send that Greekish whore-masterly villain with the
sleeve back to the dissembling luxurious drab of a
sleeveless errand. O't'other side, the policy of those
crafty-swearing rascals, that stale old mouse-eaten 10
dry cheese, Nestor, and that same dog-fox, Ulysses,
is proved not worth a blackberry. They set me up
in policy that mongrel cur, Ajax, against that dog of
as bad a kind, Achilles; and now is the cur Ajax
prouder than the cur Achilles, and will not arm
today; whereupon the Grecians begin to proclaim
barbarism, and policy grows into an ill opinion.
Soft! here comes sleeve, and t'other.

Enter Diomedes, Troilus following

TROILUS. Fly not; for shouldst thou take the river Styx,
I would swim after.
DIOMEDES.   Thou dost miscall retire; 20
I do not fly; but advantageous care
Withdrew me from the odds of multitude.
Have at thee!
THERSITES. Hold thy whore, Grecian! Now for thy
whore, Trojan! Now the sleeve, now the sleeve!
                        Troilus and Diomedes go off fighting

Enter Hector

HECTOR. What art thou, Greek? Art thou for
Hector's match?
Art thou of blood and honour?
THERSITES. No, no; I am a rascal; a scurvy railing
knave; a very filthy rogue.
HECTOR. I do believe thee. Live   *Goes* 30
THERSITES. God-a-mercy, that thou wilt believe me;
but a plague break thy neck for frighting me! What's
become of the wenching rogues! I think they have
swallowed one another. I would laugh at that
miracle; yet in a sort lechery eats itself. I'll seek
them.   *Goes*

Scene 5: *Another part of the field*

Enter Diomedes and Servant

DIOMEDES. Go, go, my servant, take thou Troilus'
horse;
Present the fair steed to my lady Cressid.
Fellow, commend my service to her beauty;
Tell her I have chastised the amorous Trojan,
And am her knight by proof.
SERVANT.   I go, my lord. *Goes*

Enter Agamemnon

AGAMEMNON. Renew, renew! The fierce Polydamas
Hath beat down Menon; bastard Margarelon
Hath Doreus prisoner,
And stands colossus-wise, waving his beam,
Upon the pashéd corpses of the kings   10
Epistrophus and Cedius; Polyxenes is slain;
Amphimachus and Thoas deadly hurt;
Patroclus ta'en or slain; and Palamedes
Sore hurt and bruised; the dreadful sagittary
Appals our numbers; haste we, Diomed,
To reinforcement, or we perish all.   *Goes*

Enter Nestor and other Greeks

NESTOR. Go, bear Patroclus' body to Achilles,
And bid the snail-paced Ajax arm for shame.
                                              Some go
There is a thousand Hectors in the field:
Now here he fights on Galathe his horse,   20
And there lacks work; anon he's there afoot,
And there they fly or die, like scaléd sculls
Before the belching whale; then is he yonder,
And there the strawy Greeks, ripe for his edge,
Fall down before him, like a mower's swath;
Here, there and everywhere he leaves and takes,
Dexterity so obeying appetite
That what he will he does, and does so much
That proof is called impossibility.

Enter Ulysses

ULYSSES. O, courage, courage, princes! great Achilles 30
Is arming, weeping, cursing, vowing vengeance;
Patroclus' wounds have roused his drowsy blood,
Together with his mangled Myrmidons,
That noseless, handless, hacked and chipped, come
to him,
Crying on Hector. Ajax hath lost a friend,
And foams at mouth, and he is armed and at it,
Roaring for Troilus; who hath done today
Mad and fantastic execution,

Engaging and redeeming of himself
With such a careless force and forceless care   40
As if that luck, in very spite of cunning,
Bade him win all.

Enter Ajax

AJAX. Troilus! thou coward Troilus!   *Goes*
DIOMEDES.   Ay, there, there.   *Follows*
NESTOR. So, so, we draw together.

Enter Achilles

ACHILLES.   Where is this Hector?
Come, come, thou boy-queller, show me thy face;
Know what it is to meet Achilles angry;
Hector! where's Hector? I will none but Hector.
                                        They go

Scene 6: *Another part of the field*

Enter Ajax

AJAX. Troilus, thou coward Troilus, show thy head!

Enter Diomedes

DIOMEDES. Troilus, I say! where's Troilus?
AJAX: What wouldst thou?
DIOMEDES. I would correct him.
AJAX. Were I the general, thou shouldst have my
    office
Ere that correction. Troilus, I say! what, Troilus!

Enter Troilus

TROILUS. O traitor Diomed! Turn thy false face,
    thou traitor,
And pay the life thou ow'st me for my horse.
DIOMEDES. Ha! art thou there?
AJAX. I'll fight with him alone; stand, Diomed.
DIOMEDES. He is my prize; I will not look upon.   10
TROILUS. Come both you cogging Greeks; have at
    you both!   *They go, fighting*

Enter Hector

HECTOR. Yea, Troilus? O, well fought, my youngest
    brother!

Enter Achilles

ACHILLES. Now do I see thee; ha! have at thee,
    Hector!   *They fight*
HECTOR. Pause, if thou wilt.
ACHILLES. I do disdain thy courtesy, proud Trojan.
Be happy that my arms are out of use;
My rest and negligence befriends thee now,
But thou anon shalt hear of me again;
Till when, go seek thy fortune.   *Goes*
HECTOR.   Fare thee well.
I would have been much more a fresher man,   20
Had I expected thee.

Re-enter Troilus

                    How now, my brother!
TROILUS. Ajax hath ta'en Æneas. Shall it be?
No, by the flame of yonder glorious heaven,
He shall not carry him; I'll be ta'en too,
Or bring him off. Fate, hear me what I say!
I reck not though thou end my life today.   *Goes*

Enter one in sumptuous armour

HECTOR. Stand, stand, thou Greek; thou art a
    goodly mark.
No! wilt thou not? I like thy armour well;
I'll frush it and unlock the rivets all,
But I'll be master of it. [*the Greek goes*] Wilt
    thou not, beast, abide?   30
Why then, fly on; I'll hunt thee for thy hide.
                                        Goes after

Scene 7: *Another part of the field*

Enter Achilles, with Myrmidons

ACHILLES. Come here about me, you my Myrmidons;
Mark what I say. Attend me where I wheel;
Strike not a stroke, but keep yourselves in breath,
And when I have the bloody Hector found
Empale him with your weapons round about;
In fellest manner execute your arms.
Follow me, sirs, and my proceedings eye;
It is decreed Hector the great must die.   *They go*

Enter Menelaus and Paris, fighting; then Thersites

THERSITES. The cuckold and the cuckold-maker are at
it. Now, bull! now, dog! 'Loo, Paris, 'loo! now, my   10
double-horned Spartan! 'loo, Paris, 'loo! The bull
has the game. Ware horns, ho!
                    Paris and Menelaus go

Enter Margarelon

MARGARELON. Turn, slave, and fight.
THERSITES. What art thou?
MARGARELON. A bastard son of Priam's.
THERSITES. I am a bastard too; I love bastards. I am
a bastard begot, bastard instructed, bastard in mind,
bastard in valour, in everything illegitimate. One
bear will not bite another, and wherefore should
one bastard? Take heed; the quarrel's most ominous   20
to us; if the son of a whore fight for a whore, he
tempts judgement. Farewell, bastard.   *Goes*
MARGARELON. The devil take thee, coward!   *Goes*

Scene 8: *Another part of the field*

Enter Hector

HECTOR. Most putrefied core, so fair without,
Thy goodly armour thus hath cost thy life.
Now is my day's work done. I'll take good breath.
Rest, sword; thou hast thy fill of blood and death.
                                        Disarms

Enter Achilles and Myrmidons

ACHILLES. Look, Hector, how the sun begins to set,
How ugly night comes breathing at his heels;
Even with the vail and darking of the sun,
To close the day up, Hector's life is done.
HECTOR. I am unarmed; forego this vantage, Greek.
ACHILLES. Strike, fellows, strike; this is the man
    I seek.   *Hector falls*   10
So, Ilion, fall thou next! now, Troy, sink down!
Here lies thy heart, thy sinews, and thy bone.
On, Myrmidons, and cry you all amain
'Achilles hath the mighty Hector slain'.
                                        Retreat sounded
Hark! a retire upon our Grecian part.
MYRMIDON. The Trojan trumpets sound the like,
    my lord.

ACHILLES. The dragon wing of night o'erspreads
  the earth,
And stickler-like the armies separates.
My half-supped sword that frankly would have fed,
Pleased with this dainty bait, thus goes to bed.   20
                        Sheathes his sword
Come, tie his body to my horse's tail;
Along the field I will the Trojan trail.
              They go; retreat sounded

Scene 9: *Another part of the field*

Enter Agamemnon, Ajax, Menelaus, Nestor, Diomedes,
and the rest, marching. Shouts within

AGAMEMNON. Hark! hark! what shout is that?
NESTOR. Peace, drums!
SOLDIERS [*within*]. Achilles! Achilles! Hector's slain!
  Achilles!
DIOMEDES. The bruit is Hector's slain, and by
  Achilles.
AJAX. If it be so, yet bragless let it be;
  Great Hector was as good a man as he.
AGAMEMNON. March patiently along. Let one be sent
  To pray Achilles see us at our tent.
  If in his death gods have us befriended,
  Great Troy is ours, and our sharp wars are ended. 10
              They march off

Scene 10: *Another part of the field*

Enter Æneas, Paris, Antenor, and Deiphobus

ÆNEAS. Stand, ho! yet are we masters of the field.
  Never go home; here starve we out the night.

Enter Troilus

TROILUS. Hector is slain.
ALL.   Hector! The gods forbid!
TROILUS. He's dead; and at the murderer's horse's tail
  In beastly sort dragged through the shameful field.
  Frown on, you heavens, effect your rage with speed!
  Sit, gods, upon your thrones and smite at Troy!
  I say, at once let your brief plagues be mercy,
  And linger not our sure destructions on!
ÆNEAS. My lord, you do discomfort all the host.   10
TROILUS. You understand me not that tell me so;
  I dare not speak of flight, of fear, of death,
  But dare all imminence that gods and men

Address their dangers in. Hector is gone:
Who shall tell Priam so, or Hecuba?
Let him that will a screech-owl aye be called:
Go in to Troy and say there 'Hector's dead',
There is a word will Priam turn to stone,
Make wells and Niobes of the maids and wives,
Cold statues of the youth, and, in a word,   20
Scare Troy out of itself. But march away.
Hector is dead; there is no more to say.
Stay yet. You vile abominable tents,
Thus proudly pight upon our Phrygian plains
Let Titan rise as early as he dare,
I'll through and through you! and thou great-
  sized coward,
No space of earth shall sunder our two hates;
I'll haunt thee like a wicked conscience still,
That mouldeth goblins swift as frenzy's thoughts.
Strike a free march to Troy! with comfort go: 30
Hope of revenge shall hide our inward woe.
              Æneas and Trojans go

Enter Pandarus

PANDARUS. But hear you, hear you!
TROILUS. Hence, broker-lackey! ignomy and shame
  Pursue thy life, and live aye with thy name! *Goes*
PANDARUS. A goodly medicine for my aching bones!
O world! world! world! thus is the poor agent
despised! O traders and bawds, how earnestly are
you set a-work, and how ill requited! Why should
our endeavour be so desired and the performance
so loathed? What verse for it? what instance for it? 40
Let me see:
  Full merrily the humble-bee doth sing
  Till he hath lost his honey and his sting;
  And being once subdued in arméd tail,
  Sweet honey and sweet notes together fail.
Good traders in the flesh, set this in your painted
  cloths:
As many as be here of Pandar's hall,
Your eyes, half out, weep out at Pandar's fall;
Or if you cannot weep, yet give some groans,
Though not for me, yet for your aching bones.   50
Brethren and sisters of the hold-door trade,
Some two months hence my will shall here be made.
It should be now, but that my fear is this,
Some galléd goose of Winchester would hiss.
Till then I'll sweat and seek about for eases,
And at that time bequeath you my diseases. *Goes*

Coriolanus

The scene: Rome and the neighbourhood; Corioli
and the neighbourhood; Antium

CHARACTERS IN THE PLAY

CAIUS MARCIUS, *afterwards* CAIUS MARCIUS CORIOLANUS
TITUS LARTIUS, } *generals against the Volscians*
COMINIUS,
MENENIUS AGRIPPA, *friend to Coriolanus*
SICINIUS VELUTUS, } *Tribunes of the people*
JUNIUS BRUTUS,
YOUNG MARCIUS, *son to Coriolanus*
A Roman Herald
NICANOR, *a Roman*
TULLUS AUFIDIUS, *general of the Volscians*
Lieutenant to Aufidius
Conspirators with Aufidius

ADRIAN, *a Volscian*
A Citizen of Antium
Two Volscian Guards
VOLUMNIA, *mother to Coriolanus*
VIRGILIA, *wife to Coriolanus*
VALERIA, *friend to Virgilia*
Gentlewoman attending on Virgilia
Usher attending on Valeria
Roman and Volscian Senators, Patricians, Ædiles,
    Lictors, Soldiers, Citizens, Messengers, Servants to
    Aufidius, and other Attendants

Coriolanus

ACT 1
Scene 1: *Rome. A street*

Enter a company of mutinous Citizens, with staves, clubs, and other weapons

1 CITIZEN. Before we proceed any further, hear me speak.

ALL. Speak, speak.

1 CITIZEN. You are all resolved rather to die than to famish?

ALL. Resolved, resolved.

1 CITIZEN. First, you know Caius Marcius is chief enemy to the people.

ALL. We know't, we know't.

1 CITIZEN. Let us kill him, and we'll have corn at our 10 own price. Is't a verdict?

ALL. No more talking on't; let it be done. Away, away!

2 CITIZEN. One word, good citizens.

1 CITIZEN. We are accounted poor citizens, the patricians good. What authority surfeits on would relieve us. If they would yield us but the superfluity while it were wholesome, we might guess they relieved us humanely; but they think we are too dear: the leanness that afflicts us, the object of our 20 misery, is as an inventory to particularize their abundance; our sufferance is a gain to them. Let us revenge this with our pikes ere we become rakes; for the gods know I speak this in hunger for bread, not in thirst for revenge.

2 CITIZEN. Would you proceed especially against Caius Marcius?

1 CITIZEN. Against him first: he's a very dog to the commonalty.

2 CITIZEN. Consider you what services he has done for 30 his country?

1 CITIZEN. Very well, and could be content to give him good report for't, but that he pays himself with being proud.

2 CITIZEN. Nay, but speak not maliciously.

1 CITIZEN. I say unto you, what he hath done famously he did it to that end; though soft-conscienced men can be content to say it was for his country, he did it partly to please his mother and to be proud, which he is, even to the altitude of his virtue. 40

2 CITIZEN. What he cannot help in his nature you account a vice in him. You must in no way say he is covetous.

1 CITIZEN. If I must not, I need not be barren of accusations; he hath faults (with surplus) to tire in repetition. [*shouts*]. What shouts are these? The other side o' the city is risen: why stay we prating here? To th' Capitol!

ALL. Come, come.

1 CITIZEN. Soft! who comes here? 50

Enter Menenius Agrippa

2 CITIZEN. Worthy Menenius Agrippa, one that hath always loved the people.

1 CITIZEN. He's one honest enough; would all the rest were so!

MENENIUS. What work's, my countrymen, in hand? Where go you
With bats and clubs? The matter? Speak, I pray you.

1 CITIZEN. Our business is not unknown to th' Senate; they have had inkling this fortnight what we intend to do, which now we'll show 'em in deeds. They say poor suitors have strong breaths: they shall know we have strong arms too. 60

MENENIUS. Why, masters, my good friends, mine honest neighbours,
Will you undo yourselves?

1 CITIZEN. We cannot, sir; we are undone already.

MENENIUS. I tell you, friends, most charitable care
Have the patricians of you. For your wants,
Your suffering in this dearth, you may as well
Strike at the heaven with your staves as lift them
Against the Roman state, whose course will on
The way it takes; cracking ten thousand curbs 70
Of more strong link asunder than can ever
Appear in your impediment. For the dearth,
The gods, not the patricians, make it, and
Your knees to them (not arms) must help. Alack,
You are transported by calamity
Thither where more attends you; and you slander
The helms o' th' state, who care for you like fathers,
When you curse them as enemies.

1 CITIZEN. Care for us! True, indeed! They ne'er cared for us yet. Suffer us to famish, and their storehouses 80 crammed with grain; make edicts for usury, to support usurers; repeal daily any wholesome act established against the rich, and provide more piercing statutes daily to chain up and restrain the poor. If the wars eat us not up, they will; and there's all the love they bear us.

MENENIUS. Either you must
Confess yourselves wondrous malicious,
Or be accused of folly. I shall tell you
A pretty tale: it may be you have heard it; 90
But, since it serves my purpose, I will venture
To stale't a little more.

1 CITIZEN. Well, I'll hear it, sir: yet you must not think to fob off our disgrace with a tale: but, an't please you, deliver.

MENENIUS. There was a time when all the body's members
Rebelled against the Belly; thus accused it:
That only like a gulf it did remain
I' th' midst o' th' body, idle and unactive,
Still cupboarding the viand, never bearing 100
Like labour with the rest; where th' other instruments
Did see and hear, devise, instruct, walk, feel,
And, mutually participate, did minister
Unto the appetite and affection common
Of the whole body. The Belly answered—

1 CITIZEN. Well, sir, what answer made the Belly?

MENENIUS. Sir, I shall tell you. With a kind of smile,
Which ne'er came from the lungs, but even thus—

For, look you, I may make the Belly smile
As well as speak—it tauntingly replied
To th' discontented members, the mutinous parts
That envied his receipt; even so most fitly
As you malign our senators for that
They are not such as you.

1 CITIZEN.   Your Belly's answer—What?
The kingly crownéd head, the vigilant eye,
The counsellor heart, the arm our soldier,
Our steed the leg, the tongue our trumpeter,
With other muniments and petty helps
In this our fabric, if that they—

MENENIUS.   What then?
'Fore me, this fellow speaks! what then? what then? 120

1 CITIZEN. Should by the cormorant Belly be
restrained,
Who is the sink o' th' body,—

MENENIUS.   Well, what then?

1 CITIZEN. The former agents, if they did complain,
What could the Belly answer?

MENENIUS.   I will tell you;
If you'll bestow a small (of what you have little)
Patience awhile, you'st hear the belly's answer.

1 CITIZEN. You're long about it.

MENENIUS.   Note me this, good friend;
Your most grave Belly was deliberate,
Not rash like his accusers, and thus answered:
'True is it, my incorporate friends,' quoth he, 130
'That I receive the general food at first,
Which you do live upon; and fit it is,
Because I am the storehouse and the shop
Of the whole body. But, if you do remember,
I send it through the rivers of your blood,
Even to the court, the heart, to th'seat o' th' brain;
And, through the cranks and offices of man,
The strongest nerves and small inferior veins
From me receive that natural competency
Whereby they live: and though that all at once, 140
You, my good friends'—this says the Belly, mark
me—

1 CITIZEN. Ay, sir; well, well.

MENENIUS.   'Though all at once cannot
See what I do deliver out to each,
Yet I can make my audit up, that all
From me do back receive the flour of all,
And leave me but the bran.' What say you to't?

1 CITIZEN. It was an answer. How apply you this?

MENENIUS. The senators of Rome are this good Belly,
And you the mutinous members: for examine
Their counsels and their cares, digest things rightly 150
Touching the weal o'th' common, you shall find
No public benefit which you receive
But it proceeds or comes from them to you,
And no way from yourselves. What do you think,
You, the great toe of this assembly?

1 CITIZEN. I the great toe! why the great toe?

MENENIUS. For that, being one o'th' lowest, basest,
poorest,
Of this most wise rebellion, thou goest foremost.
Thou rascal, that art worst in blood to run,
Lead'st first to win some vantage. 160
But make you ready your stiff bats and clubs:
Rome and her rats are at the point of battle;
The one side must have bale.

Enter Caius Marcius

                    Hail, noble Marcius!

MARCIUS. Thanks. What's the matter, you dissentious 110
rogues
That, rubbing the poor itch of your opinion,
Make yourselves scabs?

1 CITIZEN.   We have ever your good word.

MARCIUS. He that will give good words to thee will
flatter
Beneath abhorring. What would you have, you
curs,
That like nor peace nor war? the one affrights you,
The other makes you proud. He that trusts to you, 170
Where he should find you lions, finds you hares;
Where foxes, geese: you are no surer, no,
Than is the coal of fire upon the ice,
Or hailstone in the sun. Your virtue is
To make him worthy whose offence subdues him
And curse that justice did it. Who deserves greatness
Deserves your hate. And your affections are
A sick man's appetite, who desires most that
Which would increase his evil. He that depends
Upon your favours swims with fins of lead 180
And hews down oaks with rushes. Hang ye! Trust
ye?
With every minute you do change a mind,
And call him noble that was now your hate,
Him vile that was your garland. What's the matter
That in these several places of the city
You cry against the noble Senate, who
(Under the gods) keep you in awe, which else
Would feed on one another? What's their seeking?

MENENIUS. For corn at their own rates, whereof they
say
The city is well stored.

MARCIUS.   Hang 'em! They say! 190
They'll sit by th'fire, and presume to know
What's done i'th' Capitol: who's like to rise,
Who thrives and who declines; side factions and
give out
Conjectural marriages, making parties strong,
And feebling such as stand not in their liking
Below their cobbled shoes. They say there's grain
enough!
Would the nobility lay aside their ruth,
And let me use my sword, I'd make a quarry
With thousands of these quartered slaves, as high
As I could pick my lance. 200

MENENIUS. Nay, these are all most thoroughly
persuaded;
For though abundantly they lack discretion,
Yet are they passing cowardly. But, I beseech you,
What says the other troop?

MARCIUS.   They are dissolved: hang 'em!
They said they were an-hungry; sighed forth
proverbs—
That hunger broke stone walls, that dogs must eat,
That meat was made for mouths, that the gods sent
not
Corn for the rich men only: with these shreds
They vented their complainings; which being
answered,
And a petition granted them—a strange one, 210
To break the heart of generosity
And make bold power look pale—they threw their
caps
As they would hang them on the horns o'th' moon,

Shouting their emulation.
MENENIUS.　　　　　　　　　What is granted them?
MARCIUS. Five tribunes to defend their vulgar
　wisdoms,
Of their own choice. One's Junius Brutus, one
Sicinius Velutus, and—I know not. 'Sdeath!
The rabble should have first unroofed the city,
Ere so prevailed with me: it will in time
Win upon power and throw forth greater themes 220
For insurrection's arguing.
MENENIUS.　　　　　　　　This is strange.
MARCIUS. Go, get you home, you fragments!

Enter a Messenger, hastily

MESSENGER. Where's Caius Marcius?
MARCIUS.　　　　　　Here: what's the matter?
MESSENGER. The news is, sir, the Volsces are in arms.
MARCIUS. I am glad on 't: then we shall ha' means to
　vent
Our musty superfluity. See, our best elders.

Enter Cominius, Titus Lartius, and other Senators;
Junius Brutus and Sicinius Velutus

1 SENATOR. Marcius, 'tis true that you have lately told
　us;
The Volsces are in arms.
MARCIUS.　　　　　　　　They have a leader,
Tullus Aufidius, that will put you to 't.
I sin in envying his nobility;　　　　　　　　230
And were I anything but what I am,
I would wish me only he.
COMINIUS.　　　　　　You have fought together.
MARCIUS. Were half to half the world by th' ears, and
　he
Upon my party, I'd revolt, to make
Only my wars with him. He is a lion
That I am proud to hunt.
1 SENATOR.　　　　　　Then, worthy Marcius,
Attend upon Cominius to these wars.
COMINIUS. It is your former promise.
MARCIUS.　　　　　　　　Sir, it is,
And I am constant. Titus Lartius, thou
Shalt see me once more strike at Tullus' face.　240
What, art thou stiff? stand'st out?
TITUS.　　　　　　　No, Caius Marcius;
I'll lean upon one crutch and fight with t'other
Ere stay behind this business.
MENENIUS.　　　　　　　O, true-bred!
1 SENATOR. Your company to th' Capitol; where
　I know
Our greatest friends attend us.
TITUS [*to Cominius*].　　　　Lead you on.
[*to Marcius*] Follow Cominius; we must follow you;
　Right worthy you priority.
COMINIUS.　　　　　　Noble Marcius!
1 SENATOR [*to the citizens*]. Hence to your homes; be
　gone!
MARCIUS.　　　　　　Nay, let them follow.
The Volsces have much corn; take these rats thither
To gnaw their garners [*citizens steal away*];
　Worshipful mutineers,　　　　　　　　　　250
Your valour puts well forth. Pray, follow.
　　　　　　　　　All go but Sicinius and Brutus
SICINIUS. Was ever man so proud as is this Marcius?
BRUTUS. He has no equal.

SICINIUS. When we were chosen tribunes for the
　people—
BRUTUS. Marked you his lip and eyes?
SICINIUS.　　　　　　　Nay, but his taunts.
BRUTUS. Being moved, he will not spare to gird the
　gods.
SICINIUS. Bemock the modest moon.
BRUTUS. The present wars devour him! He is grown
Too proud to be so valiant.
SICINIUS.　　　　　　　Such a nature,
Tickled with good success, disdains the shadow　260
Which he treads on at noon. But I do wonder
His insolence can brook to be commanded
Under Cominius.
BRUTUS.　　　　　　Fame, at the which he aims,
In whom already he's well graced, can not
Better be held, nor more attained, than by
A place below the first: for what miscarries
Shall be the general's fault, though he perform
To th' utmost of a man; and giddy censure
Will then cry out of Marcius 'O, if he
Had borne the business!'
SICINIUS.　　　　　　Besides, if things go well, 270
Opinion, that so sticks on Marcius, shall
Of his demerits rob Cominius.
BRUTUS.　　　　　　　Come:
Half all Cominius' honours are to Marcius,
Though Marcius earned them not; and all his faults
To Marcius shall be honours, though indeed
In aught he merit not.
SICINIUS.　　　　　　Let's hence, and hear
How the dispatch is made; and in what fashion,
More than his singularity, he goes
Upon this present action.
BRUTUS.　　　　　Let's along.　　*They go*

Scene 2: *Corioli. The Senate-House*

Enter Tullus Aufidius, with Senators of Corioli

1 SENATOR. So, your opinion is, Aufidius,
That they of Rome are ent'red in our counsels,
And know how we proceed.
AUFIDIUS.　　　　　　Is it not yours?
What ever hath been thought on in this state
That could be brought to bodily act ere Rome
Had circumvention? 'Tis not four days gone
Since I heard thence: these are the words: I think
I have the letter here: yes, here it is:
[*reads*] 'They have pressed a power, but it is not
　known
Whether for east or west. The dearth is great; 10
The people mutinous: and it is rumoured,
Cominius, Marcius your old enemy
(Who is of Rome worse hated than of you),
And Titus Lartius, a most valiant Roman,
These three lead on this preparation
Whither 'tis bent: most likely 'tis for you:
Consider of it.'
1 SENATOR.　　　　Our army's in the field:
We never yet made doubt but Rome was ready
To answer us.
AUFIDIUS.　　　Nor did you think it folly
To keep your great pretences veiled till when　20
They needs must show themselves; which in the
　hatching,
It seemed, appeared to Rome. By the discovery

We shall be short'ned in our aim, which was
To take in many towns ere almost Rome
Should know we were afoot.
2 SENATOR.   Noble Aufidius,
Take your commission; hie you to your bands:
Let us alone to guard Corioli.
If they set down before 's, for the remove
Bring up your army; but I think you'll find
They've not prepared for us.
AUFIDIUS.   O, doubt not that;   30
I speak from certainties. Nay, more,
Some parcels of their power are forth already,
And only hitherward. I leave your honours.
If we and Caius Marcius chance to meet,
'Tis sworn between us we shall ever strike
Till one can do no more.
ALL.   The gods assist you!
AUFIDIUS. And keep your honours safe!
1 SENATOR.   Farewell.
2 SENATOR.   Farewell.
ALL. Farewell.   *They go*

Scene 3: *Rome. A room in Marcius' house*

*Enter Volumnia and Virgilia, mother and wife to Marcius:
they set them down on two low stools, and sew*

VOLUMNIA. I pray you, daughter, sing, or express
yourself in a more comfortable sort: if my son were
my husband, I should freelier rejoice in that absence
wherein he won honour than in the embracements
of his bed where he would show most love. When
yet he was but tender-bodied, and the only son of
my womb; when youth with comeliness plucked all
gaze his way; when, for a day of kings' entreaties,
a mother should not sell him an hour from her
beholding; I, considering how honour would be-   10
come such a person—that it was no better than
picture-like to hang by th'wall, if renown made it
not stir—was pleased to let him seek danger where
he was like to find fame. To a cruel war I sent
him, from whence he returned his brows bound
with oak. I tell thee, daughter, I sprang not more in
joy at first hearing he was a man-child than now in
first seeing he had proved himself a man.
VIRGILIA. But had he died in the business, madam,
how then?   20
VOLUMNIA. Then his good report should have been
my son; I therein would have found issue. Hear me
profess sincerely: had I a dozen sons, each in my love
alike, and none less dear than thine and my good
Marcius, I had rather had eleven die nobly for their
country than one voluptuously surfeit out of action.

Enter a Gentlewoman

GENTLEWOMAN. Madam, the Lady Valeria is come to
visit you.
VIRGILIA. Beseech you give me leave to retire myself.
VOLUMNIA. Indeed, you shall not.   30
Methinks I hear hither your husband's drum;
See him pluck Aufidius down by th' hair;
As children from a bear, the Volsces shunning him.
Methinks I see him stamp thus, and call thus:
'Come on, you cowards! you were got in fear,
Though you were born in Rome.' His bloody brow
With his mailed hand then wiping, forth he goes,
Like to a harvest-man that's tasked to mow
Or all or lose his hire.

VIRGILIA. His bloody brow? O Jupiter, no blood!   40
VOLUMNIA. Away, you fool! It more becomes a man
Than gilt his trophy. The breasts of Hecuba,
When she did suckle Hector, looked not lovelier
Than Hector's forehead when it spit forth blood
At Grecian sword, contemning. Tell Valeria
We are fit to bid her welcome.
                    Gentlewoman goes
VIRGILIA. Heavens bless my lord from fell Aufidius!
VOLUMNIA. He'll beat Aufidius' head below his knee,
And tread upon his neck.

Re-enter Gentlewoman with Valeria and her Usher

VALERIA. My ladies both, good day to you.   50
VOLUMNIA. Sweet madam!
VIRGILIA. I am glad to see your ladyship.
VALERIA. How do you both? you are manifest house-
keepers. What are you sewing here? A fine spot, in
good faith. How does your little son?
VIRGILIA. I thank your ladyship; well, good madam.
VOLUMNIA. He had rather see the swords and hear a
drum than look upon his schoolmaster.
VALERIA. O' my word, the father's son: I'll swear 'tis
a very pretty boy. O' my troth, I looked upon him   60
o' Wednesday half an hour together: has such a confirmed countenance! I saw him run after a gilded
butterfly; and when he caught it, he let it go again;
and after it again; and over and over he comes, and
up again; catched it again: or whether his fall
enraged him, or how 'twas, he did so set his teeth,
and tear it; O, I warrant, how he mammocked it!
VOLUMNIA. One on's father's moods.
VALERIA. Indeed, la, 'tis a noble child.
VIRGILIA. A crack, madam.   70
VALERIA. Come, lay aside your stitchery; I must have
you play the idle huswife with me this afternoon.
VIRGILIA. No, good madam; I will not out of doors.
VALERIA. Not out of doors!
VOLUMNIA. She shall, she shall.
VIRGILIA. Indeed, no, by your patience; I'll not over
the threshold till my lord return from the wars.
VALERIA. Fie, you confine yourself most unreasonably;
come, you must go visit the good lady that lies in.
VIRGILIA. I will wish her speedy strength, and visit her   80
with my prayers; but I cannot go thither.
VOLUMNIA. Why I pray you?
VIRGILIA. 'Tis not to save labour, nor that I want love.
VALERIA. You would be another Penelope; yet, they
say, all the yarn she spun in Ulysses' absence did but
fill Ithaca full of moths. Come; I would your
cambric were sensible as your finger, that you might
leave pricking it for pity. Come, you shall go with
us.
VIRGILIA. No, good madam, pardon me; indeed, I will   90
not forth.
VALERIA. In truth, la, go with me, and I'll tell you
excellent news of your husband.
VIRGILIA. O, good madam, there can be none yet.
VALERIA. Verily, I do not jest with you; there came
news from him last night.
VIRGILIA. Indeed, madam?
VALERIA. In earnest, it's true; I heard a senator speak
it. Thus it is: the Volsces have an army forth; against
whom Cominius the general is gone, with one part   100
of our Roman power: your lord and Titus Lartius
are set down before their city Corioli; they nothing

doubt prevailing, and to make it brief wars. This is true, on mine honour; and so, I pray, go with us.

VIRGILIA. Give me excuse, good madam; I will obey you in every thing hereafter.

VOLUMNIA. Let her alone, lady; as she is now, she will but disease our better mirth.

VALERIA. In troth, I think she would. Fare you well, then. Come, good sweet lady. Prithee, Virgilia, turn 110 they solemness out o' door, and go along with us.

VIRGILIA. No, at a word, madam; indeed, I must not. I wish you much mirth.

VALERIA. Well then, farewell.   *They go*

Scene 4: *Before the gates of Corioli*

Enter Marcius, Titus Lartius, Captains and Soldiers, with drum, trumpet, and colours. To them a Messenger

MARCIUS. Yonder comes news: a wager they have met.

LARTIUS. My horse to yours, no.

MARCIUS.   'Tis done.

LARTIUS.   Agreed.

MARCIUS. Say, has our general met the enemy?

MESSENGER. They lie in view, but have not spoke as yet.

LARTIUS. So, the good horse is mine.

MARCIUS.   I'll buy him of you.

LARTIUS. No, I'll nor sell nor give him: lend you him I will
For half a hundred years. [*to the trumpeter*] Summon the town.

MARCIUS. How far off lie these armies?

MESSENGER.   Within this mile and half.

MARCIUS. Then shall we hear their 'larum, and they ours.
Now, Mars, I prithee, make us quick in work,   10
That we with smoking swords may march from hence
To help our fielded friends! Come, blow thy blast.

They sound a parley. Enter two Senators with others, on the walls

Tullus Aufidius, is he within your walls?

I SENATOR. No, nor a man that fears you less than he;
That's lesser than a little. [*drum afar off*] Hark, our drums
Are bringing forth our youth. We'll break our walls
Rather than they shall pound us up: our gates,
Which yet seem shut, we have but pinned with rushes;
They'll open of themselves. [*alarum far off*] Hark you, far off!
There is Aufidius. List what work he makes   20
Amongst your cloven army.

MARCIUS.   O, they are at it!

LARTIUS. Their noise be our instruction. Ladders, ho!

The gates open and the Volsces enter

MARCIUS. They fear us not, but issue forth their city.
Now put your shields before your hearts, and fight
With hearts more proof than shields. Advance, brave Titus.
They do disdain us much beyond our thoughts,
Which makes me sweat with wrath. Come on, my fellows.
He that retires, I'll take him for a Volsce,

And he shall feel mine edge.

Alarum. The Romans are beat back to their trenches. Enter Marcius, cursing

MARCIUS. All the contagion of the south light on you, 30
You shames of Rome! you herd of—Boils and plagues
Plaster you o'er, that you may be abhorred
Farther than seen, and one infect another
Against the wind a mile! You souls of geese
That bear the shapes of men, how have you run
From slaves that apes would beat! Pluto and hell!
All hurt behind! backs red, and faces pale
With flight and agued fear! Mend and charge home,
Or, by the fires of heaven, I'll leave the foe,
And make my wars on you. Look to't. Come on;   40
If you'll stand fast, we'll beat them to their wives,
As they us to our trenches.

Another alarum. The Volsces fly, and Marcius follows them to the gates

So, now the gates are ope: now prove good seconds:
'Tis for the followers Fortune widens them,
Not for the fliers. Mark me, and do the like.
                                Enters the gates

1 SOLDIER. Fool-hardiness; not I.

2 SOLDIER. Nor I.   *Marcius is shut in*

1 SOLDIER. See, they have shut him in.

ALL.   To th' pot, I warrant him.
                                Alarum continues

Enter Titus Lartius

LARTIUS. What is become of Marcius?

ALL.   Slain, sir, doubtless.

1 SOLDIER. Following the fliers at the very heels,   50
With them he enters; who, upon the sudden,
Clapped to their gates. He is himself alone,
To answer all the city.

LARTIUS.   O noble fellow!
Who sensibly outdares his senseless sword,
And when it bows stand'st up! Thou art lost, Marcius!
A carbuncle entire, as big as thou art,
Were not so rich a jewel. Thou wast a soldier
Even to Cato's wish, not fierce and terrible
Only in strokes; but with thy grim looks and
The thunder-like percussion of thy sounds   60
Thou mad'st thine enemies shake, as if the world
Were feverous and did tremble.

The gates re-open, and Marcius, bleeding, assaulted by the enemy is seen within

1 SOLDIER.   Look, sir.

LARTIUS.   O, 'tis Marcius!
Let's fetch him off, or make remain alike.
                    They fight, and all enter the city

Scene 5

Certain Romans, with spoils come running from the city

1 ROMAN. This will I carry to Rome.

2 ROMAN. And I this.

3 ROMAN. A murrain on't! I took this for silver.
                    Sounds of the distant battle still heard

Enter Marcius and Titus Lartius with a trumpeter

MARCIUS. See here these movers that do prize their
  honours
At a cracked drachma! Cushions, leaden spoons,
Irons of a doit, doublets that hangmen would
Bury with those that wore them, these base slaves,
Ere yet the fight be done, pack up. Down with
  them!
And hark, what noise the general makes! To him!
There is the man of my soul's hate, Aufidius,   10
Piercing our Romans: then, valiant Titus, take
Convenient numbers to make good the city;
Whilst I, with those that have the spirit, will haste
To help Cominius.
LARTIUS.   Worthy sir, thou bleed'st;
Thy exercise hath been too violent
For a second course of fight.
MARCIUS.   Sir, praise me not;
My work hath yet not warmed me. Fare you well:
The blood I drop is rather physical
Than dangerous to me. To Aufidius thus
I will appear, and fight.
LARTIUS.   Now the fair goddess, Fortune, 20
Fall deep in love with thee; and her great charms
Misguide thy opposers' swords! Bold gentleman,
Prosperity be thy page!
MARCIUS.   Thy friend no less
Than those she placeth highest! So farewell.
LARTIUS. Thou worthiest Marcius!   *Marcius goes*
Go, sound thy trumpet in the market-place;
Call thither all the officers o'th' town,
Where they shall know our mind. Away!
                                        They go

Scene 6: *Near the Roman camp*

Enter Cominius, as it were in retire, with soldiers

COMINIUS. Breathe you, my friends: well fought; we
  are come off
Like Romans, neither foolish in our stands
Nor cowardly in retire. Believe me, sirs,
We shall be charged again. Whiles we have struck,
By interims and conveying gusts we have heard
The charges of our friends. The Roman gods,
Lead their successes as we wish our own,
That both our powers, with smiling fronts
  encount'ring,
May give you thankful sacrifice!

Enter a Messenger

                                        Thy news?
MESSENGER. The citizens of Corioli have issued,   10
And given to Lartius and to Marcius battle:
I saw our party to their trenches driven,
And then I came away.
COMINIUS.   Though thou speak'st truth,
Methinks thou speak'st not well. How long is't
  since?
MESSENGER. Above an hour, my lord.
COMINIUS. 'Tis not a mile; briefly we heard their
  drums.
How couldst thou in a mile confound an hour,
And bring thy news so late?
MESSENGER.   Spies of the Volsces
Held me in chase, that I was forced to wheel
Three or four miles about; else had I, sir,   20
Half an hour since brought my report.

Marcius approaches

COMINIUS.   Who's yonder
That does appear as he were flayed? O gods!
He has the stamp of Marcius, and I have
Before-time seen him thus.
MARCIUS.   Come I too late?
COMINIUS. The shepherd knows not thunder from a
  tabor
More than I know the sound of Marcius' tongue
From every meaner man.
MARCIUS.   Come I too late?
COMINIUS. Ay, if you come not in the blood of others,
But mantled in your own.
MARCIUS.   O, let me clip ye
In arms as sound as when I wooed; in heart   30
As merry as when our nuptial day was done,
And tapers burned to bedward!
COMINIUS.   Flower of warriors!—
How is't with Titus Lartius?
MARCIUS. As with a man busied about decrees:
Condemning some to death and some to exile;
Ransoming him or pitying, threat'ning th' other;
Holding Corioli in the name of Rome,
Even like a fawning greyhound in the leash,
To let him slip at will.
COMINIUS.   Where is that slave
Which told me they had beat you to your trenches? 40
Where is he? call him hither.
MARCIUS.   Let him alone;
He did inform the truth. But for our gentlemen,
The common file—a plague! tribunes for them!—
The mouse ne'er shunned the cat as they did budge
From rascals worse than they.
COMINIUS.   But how prevailed you?
MARCIUS. Will the time serve to tell? I do not think.
Where is the enemy? Are you lords o' th' field?
If not, why cease you till you are so?
COMINIUS.   Marcius,
We have at disadvantage fought and did
Retire to win our purpose.   50
MARCIUS. How lies their battle? know you on which
  side
They have placed their men of trust?
COMINIUS.   As I guess, Marcius,
Their bands i' th' vaward are the Antiates,
Of their best trust; o'er them Aufidius,
Their very heart of hope.
MARCIUS.   I do beseech you,
By all the battles wherein we have fought,
By th' blood we have shed together, by th' vows
We have made to endure friends, that you directly
Set me against Aufidius and his Antiates;
And that you not delay the present, but,   60
Filling the air with swords advanced and darts,
We prove this very hour.
COMINIUS.   Though I could wish
You were conducted to a gentle bath,
And balms applied to you, yet dare I never
Deny your asking: take your choice of those
That best can aid your action.
MARCIUS.   Those are they
That most are willing. If any such be here—
As it were sin to doubt—that love this painting
Wherein you see me smeared; if any fear
Lesser his person than an ill report;   70

If any think brave death outweighs bad life,
And that his country's dearer than himself;
Let him alone, or so many so minded,
Wave thus, to express his disposition,
And follow Marcius.

> *They all shout, and wave their*
> *swords; take him up in their*
> *arms, and cast up their caps*

O me, alone! Make you a sword of me?
If these shows be not outward, which of you
But is four Volsces? none of you but is
Able to bear against the great Aufidius
A shield as hard as his. A certain number,   80
Though thanks to all, must I select from all: the rest
Shall bear the business in some other fight,
As cause will be obeyed. Please you to march;
And I shall quickly draw out my command,
Which men are best inclined.

COMINIUS.   March on, my fellows:
Make good this ostentation, and you shall
Divide in all with us.   *They go*

Scene 7: *Before the gates of Corioli*

Titus Lartius, having set a guard upon Corioli, going
with drum and trumpet toward Cominius and Caius
Marcius, enters with a Lieutenant, other Soldiers, and a
Scout

LARTIUS. So, let the ports be guarded: keep your
    duties
As I have set them down. If I do send, dispatch
Those centuries to our aid; the rest will serve
For a short holding. If we lose the field,
We cannot keep the town.

LIEUTENANT.   Fear not our care, sir.

LARTIUS. Hence, and shut your gates upon 's.
Our guider, come; to th' Roman camp conduct us.
                                                    They go

Scene 8: *Near the Roman camp*

Alarum as in battle. Enter Marcius and Aufidius, from
opposite sides

MARCIUS. I'll fight with none but thee, for I do hate
    thee
Worse than a promise-breaker.

AUFIDIUS.   We hate alike:
Not Afric owns a serpent I abhor
More than thy fame and envy. Fix thy foot.

MARCIUS. Let the first budger die the other's slave,
And the gods doom him after!

AUFIDIUS.   If I fly, Marcius,
Holloa me like a hare.

MARCIUS.   Within these three hours, Tullus,
Alone I fought in your Corioli walls,
And made what work I pleased. 'Tis not my blood
Wherein thou seest me masked. For thy revenge   10
Wrench up thy power to th' highest.

AUFIDIUS.   Wert thou the Hector
That was the whip of your bragged progeny,
Thou shouldst not scape me here.

Here they fight, and certain Volsces come in the aid of
Aufidius

Officious, and not valiant, you have shamed me
In your condemnèd seconds.

Marcius fights till they be driven away breathless

Scene 9

Flourish. Alarum. A retreat is sounded. Enter, from one
side, Cominius with the Romans; from the other side,
Marcius, with his arm in a scarf

COMINIUS. If I should tell thee o'er this thy day's work,
Thou't not believe thy deeds: but I'll report it
Where senators shall mingle tears with smiles;
Where great patricians shall attend, and shrug,
I' th' end admire; where ladies shall be frighted,
And, gladly quaked, hear more; where the dull
    tribunes,
That with the fusty plebeians hate thine honours,
Shall say against their hearts 'We thank the gods
Our Rome hath such a soldier.'
Yet cam'st thou to a morsel of this feast,   10
Having fully dined before.

Enter Titus Lartius, with his power, from the pursuit

LARTIUS.   O general,
Here is the steed, we the caparison!
Hadst thou beheld—

MARCIUS.   Pray now, no more: my mother,
Who has a charter to extol her blood,
When she does praise me grieves me. I have done
As you have done—that's what I can: induced
As you have been—that's for my country:
He that has but effected his good will
Hath overta'en mine act.

COMINIUS.   You shall not be
The grave of your deserving; Rome must know   20
The value of her own: 'twere a concealment
Worse than a theft, no less than a traducement,
To hide your doings; and to silence that
Which, to the spire and top of praises vouched,
Would seem but modest: therefore, I beseech you,
In sign of what you are, not to reward
What you have done, before our army hear me.

MARCIUS. I have some wounds upon me, and they
    smart
To hear themselves rememb'red.

COMINIUS.   Should they not,
Well might they fester 'gainst ingratitude,   30
And tent themselves with death. Of all the horses—
Whereof we have ta'en good, and good store—of
    all
The treasure in this field achieved and city,
We render you the tenth; to be ta'en forth
Before the common distribution at
Your only choice.

MARCIUS.   I thank you, general;
But cannot make my heart consent to take
A bribe to pay my sword: I do refuse it,
And stand upon my common part with those
That have upheld the doing.   40

> *A long flourish. They all cry Marcius!*
> *Marcius! cast up their caps and lances:*
> *Cominius and Lartius stand bare*

MARCIUS. May these same instruments which you
    profane
Never sound more! When drums and trumpets shall
I' th' field prove flatterers, let courts and cities be
Made all of false-faced soothing!
When steel grows soft as the parasite's silk,
Let him be made a coverture for th' wars!
No more, I say! For that I have not washed

My nose that bled, or foiled some debile wretch,
Which without note here's many else have done,
You shout me forth   50
In acclamations hyperbolical;
As if I loved my little should be dieted
In praises sauced with lies.
COMINIUS.   Too modest are you;
More cruel to your good report than grateful
To us that give you truly. By your patience,
If 'gainst yourself you be incensed, we'll put you
(Like one that means his proper harm) in manacles,
Then reason safely with you. Therefore, be it
   known,
As to us, to all the world, that Caius Marcius
Wears this war's garland: in token of the which,   60
My noble steed, known to the camp, I give him,
With all his trim belonging; and from this time,
For what he did before Corioli, call him,
With all th' applause and clamour of the host,
CAIUS MARCIUS CORIOLANUS.
Bear th' addition nobly ever!
                  Flourish; trumpets sound, and drums
ALL. Caius Marcius Coriolanus!
CORIOLANUS. I will go wash;
And when my face is fair, you shall perceive
Whether I blush, or no. Howbeit, I thank you: 70
I mean to stride your steed, and at all times
To undercrest your good addition
To th' fairness of my power.
COMINIUS.   So, to our tent;
Where, ere we do repose us, we will write
To Rome of our success. You, Titus Lartius,
Must to Corioli back: send us to Rome
The best, with whom we may articulate
For their own good and ours.
LARTIUS.   I shall, my lord.
CORIOLANUS. The gods begin to mock me. I, that now
Refused most princely gifts, am bound to beg   80
Of my lord general.
COMINIUS.   Take't; 'tis yours. What is't?
CORIOLANUS. I sometime lay here in Corioli
And at a poor man's house; he used me kindly.
He cried to me; I saw him prisoner;
But then Aufidius was within my view,
And wrath o'erwhelmed my pity. I request you
To give my poor host freedom.
COMINIUS.   O, well begged!
Were he the butcher of my son, he should
Be free as is the wind. Deliver him, Titus.
LARTIUS. Marcius, his name?
CORIOLANUS.   By Jupiter, forgot!   90
I am weary; yea, my memory is tired.
Have we no wine here?
COMINIUS.   Go we to our tent:
The blood upon your visage dries; 'tis time
It should be looked to: come.   *They go*

Scene 10: *The camp of the Volsces*

*A flourish. Cornets. Enter Tullus Aufidius bloody, with
two or three soldiers*

AUFIDIUS. The town is ta'en!
1 SOLDIER. 'Twill be delivered back on good
   condition.
AUFIDIUS. Condition!
I would I were a Roman; for I cannot,

Being a Volsce, be that I am. Condition!
What good condition can a treaty find
I' th' part that is at mercy? Five times, Marcius,
I have fought with thee; so often hast thou beat me;
And wouldst do so, I think, should we encounter
As often as we eat. By th' elements,   10
If e'er again I meet him beard to beard,
He's mine or I am his. Mine emulation
Hath not that honour in't it had; for where
I thought to crush him in an equal force,
True sword to sword, I'll potch at him some way,
Or wrath or craft may get him.
1 SOLDIER.   He's the devil.
AUFIDIUS. Bolder, though not so subtle. My valour's
   poisoned
With only suff'ring stain by him; for him
Shall fly out of itself. Nor sleep nor sanctuary,
Being naked, sick, nor fane nor Capitol,   20
The prayers of priests nor times of sacrifice,
Embarquements all of fury, shall lift up
Their rotten privilege and custom 'gainst
My hate to Marcius. Where I find him, were it
At home, upon my brother's guard, even there,
Against the hospitable canon, would I
Wash my fierce hand in's heart. Go you to th' city;
Learn how 'tis held, and what they are that must
Be hostages for Rome.
1 SOLDIER.   Will not you go?
AUFIDIUS. I am attended at the cypress grove: I pray
   you—   30
'Tis south the city mills—bring me word thither
How the world goes, that to the pace of it
I may spur on my journey.
1 SOLDIER.   I shall, sir.   *They go*

ACT 2

Scene 1: *Rome. A public place*

*Enter Menenius, with the two Tribunes of the people,
Sicinius, and Brutus*

MENENIUS. The augurer tells me we shall have news
   to-night.
BRUTUS. Good or bad?
MENENIUS. Not according to the prayer of the people,
   for they love not Marcius.
SICINIUS. Nature teaches beasts to know their friends.
MENENIUS. Pray you, who does the wolf love?
SICINIUS. The lamb.
MENENIUS. Ay, to devour him, as the hungry plebeians
   would the noble Marcius.   10
BRUTUS. He's a lamb indeed, that baas like a bear.
MENENIUS. He's a bear indeed, that lives like a lamb.
   You two are old men: tell me one thing that I shall
   ask you.
BOTH. Well, sir.
MENENIUS. In what enormity is Marcius poor in, that
   you two have not in abundance?
BRUTUS. He's poor in no one fault, but stored with all.
SICINIUS. Especially in pride.
BRUTUS. And topping all others in boasting.   20
MENENIUS. This is strange now. Do you two know
   how you are censured here in the city—I mean of
   us o'th' right-hand file? do you?
BOTH. Why, how are we censured?

MENENIUS. Because you talk of pride now—will you not be angry?

BOTH. Well, well, sir, well.

MENENIUS. Why, 'tis no great matter; for a very little thief of occasion will rob you of a great deal of patience. Give your dispositions the reins, and be 30 angry at your pleasures; at the least, if you take it as a pleasure to you in being so. You blame Marcius for being proud?

BRUTUS. We do it not alone, sir.

MENENIUS. I know you can do very little alone; for your helps are many, or else your actions would grow wondrous single: your abilities are too infantlike for doing much alone. You talk of pride. O that you could turn your eyes toward the napes of your necks, and make but an interior survey of your good 40 selves! O that you could!

BOTH. What then, sir?

MENENIUS. Why, then you should discover a brace of unmeriting, proud, violent, testy magistrates (alias fools) as any in Rome.

SICINIUS. Menenius, you are known well enough too.

MENENIUS. I am known to be a humorous patrician, and one that loves a cup of hot wine with not a drop of allaying Tiber in't; said to be something imperfect in favouring the first complaint, hasty and tinder- 50 like upon too trivial motion; one that converses more with the buttock of the night than with the forehead of the morning. What I think I utter, and spend my malice in my breath. Meeting two such wealsmen as you are—I cannot call you Lycurguses —if the drink you give me touch my palate adversely, I make a crooked face at it. I cannot say your worships have delivered the matter well, when I find the ass in compound with the major part of your syllables; and though I must be content to bear 60 with those that say you are reverend grave men, yet they lie deadly that tell you you have good faces. If you see this in the map of my microcosm, follows it that I am known well enough too? what harm can your bisson conspectuities glean out of this character, if I be known well enough too?

BRUTUS. Come, sir, come, we know you well enough.

MENENIUS. You know neither me, yourselves, nor any thing. You are ambitious for poor knaves' caps and legs: you wear out a good wholesome forenoon in 70 hearing a cause between an orange-wife and a faucet-seller, and then rejourn the controversy of three-pence to a second day of audience. When you are hearing a matter between party and party, if you chance to be pinched with the colic, you make faces like mummers, set up the bloody flag against all patience, and, in roaring for a chamber-pot, dismiss the controversy bleeding, the more entangled by your hearing. All the peace you make in their cause is calling both the parties knaves. You are a pair of 80 strange ones.

BRUTUS. Come, come, you are well understood to be a perfecter giber for the table than a necessary bencher in the Capitol.

MENENIUS. Our very priests must become mockers, if they shall encounter such ridiculous subjects as you are. When you speak best unto the purpose, it is not worth the wagging of your beards; and your beards deserve not so honourable a grave as to stuff a botcher's cushion or to be entombed in an ass's pack- 90

saddle. Yet you must be saying Marcius is proud; who, in a cheap estimation, is worth all your predecessors since Deucalion; though peradventure some of the best of 'em were hereditary hangmen. God-den to your worships: more of your conversation would infect my brain, being the herdsmen of the beastly plebeians. I will be bold to take my leave of you. *Brutus and Sicinius stand aside*

Enter Volumnia, Virgilia, and Valeria

How now, my as fair as noble ladies—and the moon, were she earthly, no nobler—whither do you 100 follow your eyes so fast?

VOLUMNIA. Honourable Menenius, my boy Marcius approaches; for the love of Juno, let's go.

MENENIUS. Ha? Marcius coming home!

VOLUMNIA. Ay, worthy Menenius; and with most prosperous approbation.

MENENIUS. Take my cap, Jupiter, and I thank thee. Hoo! Marcius coming home!

VIRGILIA. }
VALERIA. }   Nay, 'tis true.

VOLUMNIA. Look, here's a letter from him: the state 110 hath another, his wife another; and, I think, there's one at home for you.

MENENIUS. I will make my very house reel to-night. A letter for me?

VIRGILIA. Yes, certain, there's a letter for you; I saw 't.

MENENIUS. A letter for me! it gives me an estate of seven years' health; in which time I will make a lip at the physician: the most sovereign prescription in Galen is but empiricutic, and, to this preservative, of no better report than a horse-drench. Is he not 120 wounded? he was wont to come home wounded.

VIRGILIA. O, no, no, no.

VOLUMNIA. O, he is wounded; I thank the gods for't.

MENENIUS. So do I too, if it be not too much. Brings a' victory in his pocket, the wounds become him.

VOLUMNIA. On's brows, Menenius. He comes the third time home with the oaken garland.

MENENIUS. Has he disciplined Aufidius soundly?

VOLUMNIA. Titus Lartius writes they fought together, but Aufidius got off. 130

MENENIUS. And 'twas time for him too, I'll warrant him that: an he had stayed by him, I would not have been so fidiused for all the chests in Corioli, and the gold that's in them. Is the Senate possessed of this?

VOLUMNIA. Good ladies, let's go. Yes, yes, yes: the Senate has letters from the General, wherein he gives my son the whole name of the war: he hath in this action outdone his former deeds doubly.

VALERIA. In troth, there's wondrous things spoke of 140 him.

MENENIUS. Wondrous! ay, I warrant you, and not without his true purchasing.

VIRGILIA. The gods grant them true!

VOLUMNIA. True! pooh-pooh!

MENENIUS. True! I'll be sworn they are true. Where is he wounded?—[observing the tribunes] God save your good worships! Marcius is coming home: he has more cause to be proud.—Where is he wounded? 150

VOLUMNIA. I' th' shoulder and i' th' left arm: there will be large cicatrices to show the people, when he

shall stand for his place. He received in the repulse
of Tarquin seven hurts i' th' body.

MENENIUS. One i' th' neck, and two i' th' thigh—
there's nine that I know.

VOLUMNIA. He had before this last expedition twenty-
five wounds upon him.

MENENIUS. Now it's twenty-seven: every gash was an
enemy's grave. [*A shout and flourish*] Hark! the 160
trumpets.

VOLUMNIA. These are the ushers of Marcius. Before
him he carries noise, and behind him he leaves tears:
Death, that dark spirit, in's nervy arm doth lie,
Which, being advanced, declines, and then men die.

*A sennet. Trumpets sound. Enter Cominius the general
and Titus Lartius; between them, Coriolanus, crowned
with an oaken garland; with Captains and Soldiers, and
a Herald*

HERALD. Know, Rome, that all alone Marcius did
 fight
Within Corioli gates, where he hath won,
With fame, a name to Caius Marcius; these
In honour follows Coriolanus.
Welcome to Rome, renownéd Coriolanus! 170
           Flourish

ALL. Welcome to Rome, renownéd Coriolanus!

CORIOLANUS. No more of this, it does offend my heart;
Pray now, no more.

COMINIUS.   Look, sir, your mother!

CORIOLANUS.   O, *Kneels*
You have, I know, petitioned all the gods
For my prosperity!

VOLUMNIA.   Nay, my good soldier, up;
My gentle Marcius, worthy Caius, and
By deed-achieving honour newly named—
What is it?—Coriolanus must I call thee?—
But, O, thy wife!

CORIOLANUS.   My gracious silence, hail!
Wouldst thou have laughed had I come coffined
 home, 180
That weep'st to see me triumph? Ah, my dear,
Such eyes the widows in Corioli wear,
And mothers that lack sons.

MENENIUS.   Now, the gods crown thee!

CORIOLANUS. And live you yet? [*sees Valeria*] O my
 sweet lady, pardon.

VOLUMNIA. I know not where to turn: O, welcome
 home!
And welcome, General: and you're welcome all.

MENENIUS. A hundred thousand welcomes. I could
 weep
And I could laugh, I am light and heavy. Welcome!
A curse begnaw the very root on's heart
That is not glad to see thee! You are three 190
That Rome should dote on: yet, by the faith of
 men,
We have some old crab-trees here at home that will
 not
Be grafted to your relish. Yet welcome, warriors:
We call a nettle but a nettle, and
The faults of fools but folly.

COMINIUS.   Ever right.

CORIOLANUS. Menenius, ever, ever.

HERALD. Give way there, and go on.

CORIOLANUS [*to wife and mother*]. Your hand, and
 yours!

Ere in our own house I do shade my head,
The good patricians must be visited; 200
From whom I have received not only greetings,
But with them change of honours.

VOLUMNIA.   I have lived
To see inherited my very wishes
And the buildings of my fancy: only
There's one thing wanting, which I doubt not but
Our Rome will cast upon thee.

CORIOLANUS.   Know, good mother,
I had rather be their servant in my way
Than away with them in theirs.

COMINIUS.   On, to the Capitol!
  Flourish; cornets. Exeunt in state, as before.
    Brutus and Sicinius come forward

BRUTUS. All tongues speak of him, and the bleared
 sights
Are spectacled to see him. Your prattling nurse 210
Into a rapture lets her baby cry
While she chats him: the kitchen malkin pins
Her richest lockram 'bout her reechy neck,
Clamb'ring the walls to eye him: stalls, bulks,
 windows,
Are smothered up, leads filled and ridges horsed
With variable complexions, all agreeing
In earnestness to see him: seld-shown flamens
Do press among the popular throngs, and puff
To win a vulgar station: our veiled dames
Commit the war of white and damask in 220
Their nicely-guarded cheeks to th' wanton spoil
Of Phœbus' burning kisses: such a pother,
As if that whatsoever god who leads him
Were slily crept into his human powers,
And gave him graceful posture.

SICINIUS.   On the sudden,
I warrant him consul.

BRUTUS.   Then our office may
During his power go sleep.

SICINIUS. He cannot temp'rately transport his honours
From where he should begin and end, but will
Lose those he hath won.

BRUTUS.   In that there's comfort.

SICINIUS.   Doubt not 230
The commoners, for whom we stand, but they
Upon their ancient malice will forget
With the least cause these his new honours; which
That he will give make I as little question
As he is proud to do't.

BRUTUS.   I heard him swear,
Were he to stand for consul, never would he
Appear i' th' market-place, nor on him put
The napless vesture of humility;
Nor, showing, as the manner is, his wounds
To' th' people, beg their stinking breaths.

SICINIUS.   'Tis right. 240

BRUTUS. It was his word. O, he would miss it rather
Than carry it but by the suit of the gentry to him
And the desire of the nobles.

SICINIUS.   I wish no better
Than have him hold that purpose and to put it
In execution.

BRUTUS. 'Tis most like he will.

SICINIUS. It shall be to him then as our good wills:
A sure destruction.

BRUTUS.   So it must fall out
To him or our authorities. For an end,

We must suggest the people in what hatred
He still hath held them; that to's power he would   240
Have made them mules, silenced their pleaders and
Dispropertied their freedoms; holding them,
In human action and capacity,
Of no more soul nor fitness for the world
Than camels in the war, who have their provand
Only for bearing burthens, and sore blows
For sinking under them.
SICINIUS.   This, as you say, suggested
At some time when his soaring insolence
Shall touch the people—which time shall not want,
If he be put upon't, and that's as easy   250
As to set dogs on sheep—will be the fire
To kindle their dry stubble; and their blaze
Shall darken him for ever.

Enter a Messenger

BRUTUS.   What's the matter?
MESSENGER. You are sent for to the Capitol. 'Tis
     thought
That Marcius shall be consul.
I have seen the dumb men throng to see him and
The blind to hear him speak; matrons flung gloves,
Ladies and maids their scarfs and handkerchers,
Upon him as he passed; the nobles bended,
As to Jove's statue, and the commons made   260
A shower and thunder with their caps and shouts.
I never saw the like.
BRUTUS.   Let's to the Capitol,
And carry with us ears and eyes for th' time,
But hearts for the event.
SICINIUS.   Have with you.
                                        They go

Scene 2: *Rome. The Senate House at the Capitol*

Enter two Officers, to lay cushions

1 OFFICER. Come, come, they are almost here. How
     many stand for consulships?
2 OFFICER. Three, they say: but 'tis thought of every
     one Coriolanus will carry it.
1 OFFICER. That's a brave fellow; but he's vengeance
     proud, and loves not the common people.
2 OFFICER. Faith, there hath been many great men that
     have flattered the people, who ne'er loved them; and
     there be many that they have loved, they know not
     wherefore: so that, if they love they know not why,   10
     they hate upon no better a ground. Therefore, for
     Coriolanus neither to care whether they love or hate
     him manifests the true knowledge he has in their
     disposition; and out of his noble carelessness lets
     them plainly see't.
1 OFFICER. If he did not care whether he had their love
     or no, he waved indifferently 'twixt doing them
     neither good nor harm. But he seeks their hate with
     greater devotion than they can render it him, and
     leaves nothing undone that may fully discover him   20
     their opposite. Now, to seem to affect the malice
     and displeasure of the people is as bad as that which
     he dislikes, to flatter them for their love.
2 OFFICER. He hath deserved worthily of his country;
     and his ascent is not by such easy degrees as those
     who, having been supple and courteous to the
     people, bonneted, without any further deed to have
     them at all, into their estimation and report. But he

hath so planted his honours in their eyes and his
actions in their hearts that for their tongues to be   30
silent and not confess so much were a kind of
ingrateful injury; to report otherwise were a malice
that, giving itself the lie, would pluck reproof and
rebuke from every ear that heard it.
1 OFFICER. No more of him; he's a worthy man. Make
     way, they are coming.

*A sennet. Enter the Patricians and the Tribunes of the
People, Lictors before them; Coriolanus, Menenius,
Cominius the Consul. Siginius and Brutus take their
places by themselves*

MENENIUS. Having determined of the Volsces, and
     To send for Titus Lartius, it remains,
     As the main point of this our after-meeting,
     To gratify his noble service that   40
     Hath thus stood for his country: therefore, please
        you
     Most reverend and grave elders, to desire
     The present consul, and last general
     In our well-found successes, to report
     A little of that worthy work performed
     By Caius Marcius Coriolanus; whom
     We met here both to thank and to remember
     With honours like himself.
1 SENATOR.   Speak, good Cominius:
     Leave nothing out for length, and make us think
     Rather our state's defective for requital   50
     Than we to stretch it out. [*to the Tribunes*] Masters
        o' th' people,
     We do request your kindest ears; and, after,
     Your loving motion toward the common body,
     To yield what passes here.
SICINIUS.   We are convented
     Upon a pleasing treaty, and have hearts
     Inclinable to honour and advance
     The theme of our assembly.
BRUTUS.   Which the rather
     We shall be blessed to do, if he remember
     A kinder value of the people than
     He hath hereto prized them at.
MENENIUS.   That's off, that's off;   60
     I would you rather had been silent. Please you
     To hear Cominius speak?
BRUTUS.   Most willingly:
     But yet my caution was more pertinent
     Than the rebuke you give it.
MENENIUS.   He loves your people;
     But tie him not to be their bedfellow.
     Worthy Cominius, speak.
                    Coriolanus rises and offers to go away
                              Nay, keep your place.
1 SENATOR. Sit, Coriolanus; never shame to hear
     What you have nobly done.
CORIOLANUS.   Your Honours' pardon:
     I had rather have my wounds to heal again
     Than hear say how I got them.
BRUTUS.   Sir, I hope   70
     My words disbenched you not.
CORIOLANUS.   No, sir: yet oft,
     When blows have made me stay, I fled from words.
     You soothed not, therefore hurt not: but your
        people,
     I love them as they weigh—
MENENIUS.   Pray now, sit down.

CORIOLANUS. I had rather have one scratch my head i'
 th' sun
 When the alarum were struck than idly sit
 To hear my nothings monstered. *He goes*
MENENIUS. Masters of the people,
 Your multiplying spawn how can he flatter—
 That's thousand to one good one—when you now
 see
 He had rather venture all his limbs for honour   80
 Than one on's ears to hear it? Proceed, Cominius.
COMINIUS. I shall lack voice: the deeds of Coriolanus
 Should not be uttered feebly. It is held
 That valour is the chiefest virtue and
 Most dignifies the haver: if it be,
 The man I speak of cannot in the world
 Be singly counterpoised. At sixteen years,
 When Tarquin made a head for Rome, he fought
 Beyond the mark of others: our then dictator,
 Whom with all praise I point at, saw him fight,   90
 When with his Amazonian chin he drove
 The bristled lips before him: he bestrid
 An o'erpressed Roman, and i' th' consul's view
 Slew three opposers: Tarquin's self he met,
 And struck him on his knee: in that day's feats,
 When he might act the woman in the scene,
 He proved best man i' th' field, and for his meed
 Was brow-bound with the oak. His pupil age
 Man-ent'red thus, he waxéd like a sea;
 And, in the brunt of seventeen battles since,   100
 He lurched all swords of the garland. For this
 last,
 Before and in Corioli, let me say,
 I cannot speak him home. He stopped the fliers,
 And by his rare example made the coward
 Turn terror into sport: as weeds before
 A vessel under sail, so men obeyed,
 And fell below his stem. His sword, death's stamp,
 Where it did mark, it took; from face to foot
 He was a thing of blood, whose every motion
 Was timed with dying cries. Alone he ent'red   110
 The mortal gate of th' city, which he painted
 With shunless destiny; aidless came off,
 And with a sudden re-enforcement struck
 Corioli like a planet. Now all's his,
 When by and by the din of war 'gan pierce
 His ready sense, then straight his doubled spirit
 Re-quickened what in flesh was fatigate,
 And to the battle came he; where he did
 Run reeking o'er the lives of men, as if
 'Twere a perpetual spoil: and till we called   120
 Both field and city ours, he never stood
 To ease his breast with panting.
MENENIUS. Worthy man!
I SENATOR. He cannot but with measure fit the
 honours
 Which we devise him.
COMINIUS. Our spoils he kicked at,
 And looked upon things precious as they were
 The common muck of the world: he covets less
 Than misery itself would give, rewards
 His deeds with doing them, and is content
 To spend the time to end it.
MENENIUS. He's right noble:
 Let him be called for.
I SENATOR. Call Coriolanus.
OFFICER. He doth appear.   130

Coriolanus returns

MENENIUS. The Senate, Coriolanus, are well pleased
 To make thee consul.
CORIOLANUS. I do owe them still
 My life and services.
MENENIUS. It then remains
 That you do speak to the people.
CORIOLANUS. I do beseech you
 Let me o'erleap that custom, for I cannot
 Put on the gown, stand naked, and entreat them,
 For my wounds' sake, to give their suffrage: please
 you
 That I may pass this doing.
SICINIUS. Sir, the people
 Must have their voices; neither will they bate   140
 One jot of ceremony.
MENENIUS. Put them not to't.
 Pray you, go fit you to the custom, and
 Take to you, as your predecessors have,
 Your honour with your form.
CORIOLANUS. It is a part
 That I shall blush in acting, and might well
 Be taken from the people.
BRUTUS. Mark you that.
CORIOLANUS. To brag unto them, 'Thus I did, and
 thus!'
 Show them th' unaching scars which I should hide,
 As if I had received them for the hire
 Of their breath only!
MENENIUS. Do not stand upon't.   150
 [*aloud*] We recommend to you, tribunes of the
 people,
 Our purpose to them: and to our noble consul
 Wish we all joy and honour.
SENATORS. To Coriolanus come all joy and honour!
 *Flourish of cornets; all leave the Senate
 House but Sicinius and Brutus*
BRUTUS. You see how he intends to use the people.
SICINIUS. May they perceive's intent! He will require
 them,
 As if he did contemn what he requested
 Should be in them to give.
BRUTUS. Come, we'll inform them
 Of our proceedings here. On th' market-place,
 I know, they do attend us. *They follow* 160

Scene 3: *Rome. The Forum*

Enter seven or eight Citizens

I CITIZEN. Once, if he do require our voices, we ought
 not to deny him.
2 CITIZEN. We may, sir, if we will.
3 CITIZEN. We have power in ourselves to do it, but it
 is a power that we have no power to do: for if he
 show us his wounds and tell us his deeds, we are to
 put our tongues into those wounds and speak for
 them; so, if he tell us his noble deeds, we must also
 tell him our noble acceptance of them. Ingratitude
 is monstrous: and for the multitude to be ingrateful, 10
 were to make a monster of the multitude; of the
 which we being members, should bring ourselves to
 be monstrous members.
I CITIZEN. And to make us no better thought of, a
 little help will serve; for once we stood up about the

corn, he himself stuck not to call us the many-headed multitude.

3 CITIZEN. We have been called so of many; not that our heads are some brown, some black, some abram, some bald, but that our wits are so diversely 20 coloured: and truly I think, if all our wits were to issue out of one skull, they would fly east, west, north, south, and their consent of one direct way should be at once to all the points o' th' compass.

2 CITIZEN. Think you so? Which way do you judge my wit would fly?

3 CITIZEN. Nay, your wit will not so soon out as another man's will; 'tis strongly wedged up in a blockhead; but if it were at liberty, 'twould, sure, southward. 30

2 CITIZEN. Why that way?

3 CITIZEN. To lose itself in a fog; where being three parts melted away with rotten dews, the fourth would return for conscience sake, to help to get thee a wife.

2 CITIZEN. You are never without your tricks: you may, you may.

3 CITIZEN. Are you all resolved to give your voices? But that's no matter, the greater part carries it. I say, if he would incline to the people, there was 40 never a worthier man.

Enter Coriolanus in a gown of humility, with Menenius

Here he comes, and in the gown of humility: mark his behaviour. We are not to stay all together, but to come by him where he stands, by ones, by twos, and by threes. He's to make his requests by particulars; wherein every one of us has a single honour, in giving him our own voices with our own tongues: therefore follow me, and I'll direct you how you shall go by him.

ALL. Content, content. *They go* 50

MENENIUS. O sir, you are not right: have you not known
The worthiest men have done 't?

CORIOLANUS. What must I say?—
'I pray, sir'—Plague upon't! I cannot bring
My tongue to such a pace. 'Look, sir, my wounds!
I got them in my country's service, when
Some certain of your brethren roared and ran
From th' noise of our own drums.'

MENENIUS. O me, the gods!
You must not speak of that: you must desire them
To think upon you.

CORIOLANUS. Think upon me! hang 'em!
I would they would forget me, like the virtues 60
Which our divines lose by 'em.

MENENIUS. You'll mar all.
I'll leave you. Pray you, speak to 'em, I pray you,
In wholesome manner. *He goes*

Re-enter Second and Third Citizens

CORIOLANUS. Bid them wash their faces,
And keep their teeth clean. So, here comes a brace.
You know the cause, sir, of my standing here.

3 CITIZEN. We do, sir; tell us what hath brought you to't.

CORIOLANUS. Mine own desert.

2 CITIZEN. Your own desert?

CORIOLANUS. Ay, not mine own desire. 70

3 CITIZEN. How not your own desire?

CORIOLANUS. No, sir, 'twas never my desire yet to trouble the poor with begging.

3 CITIZEN. You must think, if we give you any thing, we hope to gain by you.

CORIOLANUS. Well then, I pray, your price o' th' consulship?

3 CITIZEN. The price is, to ask it kindly.

CORIOLANUS. Kindly, sir, I pray let me ha't: I have wounds to show you, which shall be yours in 80 private. [*to the Second Citizen*] Your good voice, sir; what say you?

2 CITIZEN. You shall ha' it, worthy sir.

CORIOLANUS. A match, sir. There's in all two worthy voices begged. I have your alms: adieu.

3 CITIZEN. But this is something odd.

2 CITIZEN. An 'twere to give again—but 'tis no matter. *They go*

Enter two other Citizens

CORIOLANUS. Pray you now, if it may stand with the tune of your voices that I may be consul, I have 90 here the customary gown.

4 CITIZEN. You have deserved nobly of your country, and you have not deserved nobly.

CORIOLANUS. Your enigma?

4 CITIZEN. You have been a scourge to her enemies, you have been a rod to her friends. You have not indeed loved the common people.

CORIOLANUS. You should account me the more virtuous, that I have not been common in my love. I will, sir, flatter my sworn brother, the people, to 100 earn a dearer estimation of them; 'tis a condition they account gentle: and since the wisdom of their choice is rather to have my hat than my heart, I will practise the insinuating nod, and be off to them most counterfeitly; that is, sir, I will counterfeit the bewitchment of some popular man, and give it bountiful to the desirers. Therefore, beseech you I may be consul.

5 CITIZEN. We hope to find you our friend; and therefore give you our voices heartily. 110

4 CITIZEN. You have received many wounds for your country.

CORIOLANUS. I will not seal your knowledge with showing them. I will make much of your voices and so trouble you no farther.

BOTH CITIZENS. The gods give you joy, sir, heartily! *They go*

CORIOLANUS. Most sweet voices!
Better it is to die, better to starve,
Than crave the hire which first we do deserve.
Why in this woolvish toge should I stand here, 120
To beg of Hob and Dick that do appear
Their needless vouches? Custom calls me to't.
What custom wills, in all things should we do't,
The dust on antique time would lie unswept,
And mountainous error be too highly heaped
For truth to o'erpeer. Rather than fool it so,
Let the high office and the honour go
To one that would do thus. I am half through:
The one part suffered, the other will I do.

Enter three Citizens more

Here come moe voices. 130
Your voices! For your voices I have fought;
Watched for your voices; for your voices bear

Of wounds two dozen odd; battles thrice six
I have seen, and heard of; for your voices have
Done many things, some less, some more. Your voices!
Indeed, I would be consul.

5 CITIZEN. He has done nobly, and cannot go without any honest man's voice.

6 CITIZEN. Therefore let him be consul: the gods give him joy, and make him good friend to the people! 140

ALL. Amen, amen. God save thee, noble consul!

They go

CORIOLANUS. Worthy voices!

Enter Menenius, with Brutus and Sicinius

MENENIUS. You have stood your limitation; and the tribunes
Endue you with the people's voice. Remains
That in th' official marks invested you
Anon do meet the Senate.

CORIOLANUS. Is this done?

SICINIUS. The custom of request you have discharged:
The people do admit you, and are summoned
To meet anon upon your approbation.

CORIOLANUS. Where? at the Senate House?

SICINIUS. There, Coriolanus. 150

CORIOLANUS. May I change these garments?

SICINIUS. You may, sir.

CORIOLANUS. That I'll straight do, and, knowing myself again,
Repair to th' Senate House.

MENENIUS. I'll keep you company. Will you along?

BRUTUS. We stay here for the people.

SICINIUS. Fare you well.

Coriolanus and Menenius depart

He has it now; and, by his looks, methinks
'Tis warm at's heart.

BRUTUS. With a proud heart he wore
His humble weeds. Will you dismiss the people?

Citizens return

SICINIUS. How now, my masters! have you chose this man?

1 CITIZEN. He has our voices, sir.

BRUTUS. We pray the gods he may deserve your loves. 160

2 CITIZEN. Amen, sir: to my poor unworthy notice,
He mocked us when he begged our voices.

3 CITIZEN. Certainly;
He flouted us downright.

1 CITIZEN. No, 'tis his kind of speech—he did not mock us.

2 CITIZEN. Not one amongst us, save yourself, but says
He used us scornfully: he should have showed us
His marks of merit, wounds received for's country.

SICINIUS. Why, so he did, I am sure. 170

ALL. No, no; no man saw 'em.

3 CITIZEN. He said he had wounds which he could show in private;
And with his hat, thus waving it in scorn,
'I would be consul,' says he: 'agèd custom,
But by your voices, will not so permit me;
Your voices therefore.' When we granted that,
Here was 'I thank you for your voices. Thank you,
Your most sweet voices. Now you have left your voices,
I have no further with you.' Was not this mockery?

SICINIUS. Why either were you ignorant to see't, 180

Or, seeing it, of such childish friendliness
To yield your voices?

BRUTUS. Could you not have told him—
As you were lessoned—when he had no power,
But was a petty servant to the state,
He was your enemy, ever spake against
Your liberties and the charters that you bear
I' th' body of the weal: and now, arriving
A place of potency and sway o' th' state,
If he should still malignantly remain
Fast foe to th' plebeii, your voices might 190
Be curses to yourselves? You should have said
That as his worthy deeds did claim no less
Than what he stood for, so his gracious nature
Would think upon you for your voices, and
Translate his malice towards you into love,
Standing your friendly lord.

SICINIUS. Thus to have said,
As you were fore-advised, had touched his spirit
And tried his inclination; from him plucked
Either his gracious promise, which you might,
As cause had called you up, have held him to; 200
Or else it would have galled his surly nature,
Which easily endures not article
Tying him to aught: so, putting him to rage,
You should have ta'en th' advantage of his choler.
And passed him unelected.

BRUTUS. Did you perceive
He did solicit you in free contempt
When he did need your loves; and do you think
That his contempt shall not be bruising to you
When he hath power to crush? Why, had your bodies
No heat among you? or had you tongues to cry 210
Against the rectorship of judgement?

SICINIUS. Have you
Ere now denied the asker, and now again,
Of him that did not ask but mock, bestow
Your sued-for tongues?

3 CITIZEN. He's not confirmed; we may deny him yet.

2 CITIZEN. And will deny him:
I'll have five hundred voices of that sound.

1 CITIZEN. I twice five hundred, and their friends to piece 'em.

BRUTUS. Get you hence instantly, and tell those friends 220
They have chose a consul that will from them take
Their liberties, make them of no more voice
Than dogs that are as often beat for barking
As therefore kept to do so.

SICINIUS. Let them assemble;
And, on a safer judgement, all revoke
Your ignorant election. Enforce his pride
And his old hate unto you: besides, forget not
With what contempt he wore the humble weed,
How in his suit he scorned you: but your loves,
Thinking upon his services, took from you 230
Th' apprehension of his present portance,
Which, gibingly, ungravely, he did fashion
After the inveterate hate he bears you.

BRUTUS. Lay
A fault on us, your tribunes, that we laboured,
No impediment between, but that you must
Cast your election on him.

SICINIUS. Say you chose him
More after our commandment than as guided

By your own true affections; and that your minds,
Pre-occupied with what you rather must do
Than what you should, made you against the grain 240
To voice him consul. Lay the fault on us.
BRUTUS. Ay, spare us not. Say we read lectures to you,
How youngly he began to serve his country,
How long continued; and what stock he springs of,
The noble house o' th' Marcians, from whence
    came
That Ancus Marcius, Numa's daughter's son,
Who after great Hostilius here was king;
Of the same house Publius and Quintus were,
That our best water brought by conduits hither;
[And Censorinus that was so surnamed]   250
And nobly naméd so, twice being censor,
Was his great ancestor.
SICINIUS.   One thus descended,
That hath beside well in his person wrought
To be set high in place, we did commend
To your remembrances: but you have found,
Scaling his present bearing with his past,
That he's your fixéd enemy, and revoke
Your sudden approbation.
BRUTUS.   Say you ne'er had done't—
Harp on that still—but by our putting on:
And presently, when you have drawn your   260
    number,
Repair to th' Capitol.
CITIZENS.   We will so: almost all
Repent in their election.   *They go*
BRUTUS.   Let them go on;
This mutiny were better put in hazard
Than stay, past doubt, for greater:
If, as his nature is, he fall in rage
With their refusal, both observe and answer
The vantage of his anger.
SICINIUS.   To th' Capitol, come:
We will be there before the stream o' th' people;
And this shall seem, as partly 'tis, their own,
Which we have goaded onward.   *They go* 270

ACT 3
Scene 1: *Rome. A street*

*Cornets. Enter Coriolanus, Menenius, all the Gentry,
Cominius, Titus Lartius, and other Senators*

CORIOLANUS. Tullus Aufidius then had made new
    head?
LARTIUS. He had, my lord; and that it was which
    caused
Our swifter composition.
CORIOLANUS. So then the Volsces stand but as at first;
Ready, when time shall prompt them, to make
    road
Upon's again.
COMINIUS.   They are worn, Lord Consul, so
That we shall hardly in our ages see
Their banners wave again.
CORIOLANUS.   Saw you Aufidius?
LARTIUS. On safeguard he came to me; and did curse
Against the Volsces, for they had so vilely   10
Yielded the town: he is retired to Antium.
CORIOLANUS. Spoke he of me?
LARTIUS.   He did, my lord.
CORIOLANUS.   How? what?

LARTIUS. How often he had met you, sword to
    sword;
That of all things upon the earth he hated
Your person most; that he would pawn his fortunes
To hopeless restitution, so he might
Be called your vanquisher.
CORIOLANUS.   At Antium lives he?
LARTIUS. At Antium.
CORIOLANUS. I wish I had a cause to seek him there,
To oppose his hatred fully. Welcome home.   20

Enter Sicinius and Brutus

Behold, these are the tribunes of the people,
The tongues o' th' common mouth. I do despise
    them;
For they do prank them in authority,
Against all noble sufferance.
SICINIUS.   Pass no further.
CORIOLANUS. Ha? what is that?
BRUTUS. It will be dangerous to go on—no further.
CORIOLANUS. What makes this change?
MENENIUS.   The matter?
COMINIUS. Hath he not passed the noble and the
    common?
BRUTUS. Cominius, no.
CORIOLANUS.   Have I had children's voices? 30
I SENATOR. Tribunes, give way; he shall to th'
    market-place.
BRUTUS. The people are incensed against him.
SICINIUS.   Stop,
Or all will fall in broil.
CORIOLANUS.   Are these your herd?
Must these have voices, that can yield them now,
And straight disclaim their tongues? What are your
    offices?
You being their mouths, why rule you not their
    teeth?
Have you not set them on?
MENENIUS.   Be calm, be calm.
CORIOLANUS. It is a purposed thing, and grows by
    plot,
To curb the will of the nobility:
Suffer't, and live with such as cannot rule,   40
Nor ever will be ruled.
BRUTUS.   Call't not a plot:
The people cry you mocked them; and of late,
When corn was given them gratis, you repined,
Scandaled the suppliants for the people, called them
Time-pleasers, flatterers, foes to nobleness.
CORIOLANUS. Why, this was known before.
BRUTUS.   Not to them all.
CORIOLANUS. Have you informed them sithence?
BRUTUS.   How! I inform them!
CORIOLANUS. You are like to do such business.
BRUTUS.   Not unlike
Each way to better yours.
CORIOLANUS. Why then should I be consul? By yond
    clouds,   50
Let me deserve so ill as you, and make me
Your fellow tribune.
SICINIUS.   You show too much of that
For which the people stir: if you will pass
To where you are bound, you must inquire your
    way,
Which you are out of, with a gentler spirit,
Or never be so noble as a consul,

Nor yoke with him for tribune.
MENENIUS.   Let's be calm.
COMINIUS. The people are abused; set on. This
    palt'ring
Becomes not Rome; nor has Coriolanus
Deserved this so dishonoured rub, laid falsely   60
I' th' plain way of his merit.
CORIOLANUS.   Tell me of corn!
This was my speech, and I will speak't again—
MENENIUS. Not now, not now.
I SENATOR.   Not in this heat, sir, now.
CORIOLANUS. Now, as I live, I will.
My nobler friends, I crave their pardons. For
The mutable, rank-scented meiny, let them
Regard me as I do not flatter, and
Therein behold themselves. I say again,
In soothing them, we nourish 'gainst our Senate
The cockle of rebellion, insolence, sedition,   70
Which we ourselves have ploughed for, sowed, and
    scattered,
By mingling them with us, the honoured number;
Who lack not virtue, no, nor power, but that
Which they have given to beggars.
MENENIUS.   Well, no more.
I SENATOR. No more words, we beseech you.
CORIOLANUS.   How! no more!
As for my country I have shed my blood,
Not fearing outward force, so shall my lungs
Coin words till their decay against those measles,
Which we disdain should tetter us, yet sought
The very way to catch them.
BRUTUS.   You speak o' th' people,   80
As if you were a god, to punish; not
A man of their infirmity.
SICINIUS.   'Twere well
We let the people know't.
MENENIUS.   What, what? his choler?
CORIOLANUS. Choler!
Were I as patient as the midnight sleep,
By Jove, 'twould be my mind!
SICINIUS.   It is a mind
That shall remain a poison where it is,
Not poison any further.
CORIOLANUS.   Shall remain!
Hear you this Triton of the minnows? mark you
His absolute 'shall'?
COMINIUS.   'Twas from the canon.
CORIOLANUS.   'Shall'!   90
O good but most unwise patricians! Why,
You grave but reckless senators, have you thus
Given Hydra here to choose an officer,
That with his peremptory 'shall,' being but
The horn and noise o' th' monster's, wants not
    spirit
To say he'll turn your current in a ditch,
And make your channel his? If he have power,
Then vail your ignorance; if none, awake
Your dangerous lenity. If you are learned,
Be not as common fools; if you are not,   100
Let them have cushions by you. You are plebeians,
If they be senators; and they no less,
When, both your voices blended, the great'st taste
Most palates theirs. They choose their magistrate;
And such a one as he, who puts his 'shall,'
His popular 'shall', against a graver bench
Than ever frowned in Greece. By Jove himself,

It makes the consuls base! and my soul aches
To know, when two authorities are up,
Neither supreme, how soon confusion   110
May enter 'twixt the gap of both and take
The one by th' other.
COMINIUS.   Well, on to th' market-place.
CORIOLANUS. Whoever gave that counsel to give forth
The corn o' th' storehouse gratis, as 'twas used
Sometime in Greece—
MENENIUS.   Well, well, no more of that.
CORIOLANUS. Though there the people had more
    absolute power,
I say they nourished disobedience, fed
The ruin of the state.
BRUTUS.   Why shall the people give
One that speaks thus their voice?
CORIOLANUS.   I'll give my reasons,
More worthier than their voices. They know the
    corn   120
Was not our recompense, resting well assured
They ne'er did service for't. Being pressed to th'
    war,
Even when the navel of the state was touched,
They would not thread the gates; this kind of
    service
Did not deserve corn gratis. Being i' th' war,
Their mutinies and revolts, wherein they showed
Most valour, spoke not for them. Th' accusation
Which they have often made against the Senate,
All cause unborn, could never be the native
Of our so frank donation. Well, what then?   130
How shall this bosom multiplied digest
The Senate's courtesy? Let deeds express
What's like to be their words: 'We did request it;
We are the greater poll, and in true fear
They gave us our demands.' Thus we debase
The nature of our seats, and make the rabble
Call our cares fears; which will in time
Break ope the locks o' th' Senate and bring in
The crows to peck the eagles.
MENENIUS.   Come, enough.
BRUTUS. Enough, with over measure.
CORIOLANUS.   No, take more.   140
What may be sworn by, both divine and human,
Seal what I end withal! This double worship,
Where one part does disdain with cause, the other
Insult without all reason; where gentry, title,
    wisdom,
Cannot conclude but by the yea and no
Of general ignorance—it must omit
Real necessities, and give way the while
To unstable slightness. Purpose so barred, it follows
Nothing is done to purpose. Therefore, beseech
    you—
You that will be less fearful than discreet;   150
That love the fundamental part of state
More than you doubt the change on 't; that prefer
A noble life before a long, and wish
To jump a body with a dangerous physic
That's sure of death without it—at once pluck out
The multitudinous tongue; let them not lick
The sweet which is their poison. Your dishonour
Mangles true judgement, and bereaves the state
Of that integrity which should become't;
Not having the power to do the good it would,   160
For th' ill which doth control 't.

BRUTUS.   Has said enough.
SICINIUS. Has spoken like a traitor and shall answer
  As traitors do.
CORIOLANUS. Thou wretch, despite o'erwhelm thee!
  What should the people do with these bald tribunes,
  On whom depending, their obedience fails
  To th' greater bench? In a rebellion,
  When what's not meet, but what must be, was law,
  Then were they chosen: in a better hour
  Let what is meet be said it must be meet,
  And throw their power i' th' dust.   170
BRUTUS. Manifest treason!
SICINIUS.   This a consul? No.
BRUTUS. The ædiles, ho!

Enter an Ædile

              Let him be apprehended.
SICINIUS. Go, call the people: [*Ædile goes*] in whose
  name myself
  Attach thee as a traitorous innovator,
  A foe to th' public weal. Obey, I charge thee,
  And follow to thine answer.
CORIOLANUS.   Hence, old goat!
SENATORS, & C. We'll surety him.
COMINIUS.   Agéd sir, hands off.
CORIOLANUS. Hence, rotten thing! or I shall shake thy
  bones
  Out of thy garments.
SICINIUS.   Help, ye citizens!

Enter a rabble of Plebeians with the Ædiles

MENENIUS. On both sides more respect.   180
SICINIUS. Here's he that would take from you all your
  power.
BRUTUS. Seize him, ædiles!
CITIZENS. Down with him! down with him!
2 SENATOR. Weapons, weapons, weapons!
        They all bustle about Coriolanus
CRIES. 'Tribunes!' 'Patricians!' 'Citizens!' 'What, ho!'
  'Sicinius!' 'Brutus!' 'Coriolanus!' 'Citizens!'
  'Peace, peace, peace!' 'Stay! hold! peace!'
MENENIUS. What is about to be? I am out of breath.
  Confusion's near. I cannot speak. You, tribunes
  To th' people! Coriolanus, patience!   190
  Speak, good Sicinius.
SICINIUS.   Hear me, people; peace!
CITIZENS. Let's hear our tribune: peace!—Speak,
  speak, speak.
SICINIUS. You are at point to lose your liberties:
  Marcius would have all from you; Marcius,
  Whom late you have named for consul.
MENENIUS.   Fie, fie, fie!
  This is the way to kindle, not to quench.
1 SENATOR. To unbuild the city, and to lay all flat.
SICINIUS. What is the city but the people?
CITIZENS.   True,
  The people are the city.
BRUTUS. By the consent of all, we were established   200
  The people's magistrates.
CITIZENS.   You so remain.
MENENIUS. And so are like to do.
COMINIUS. That is the way to lay the city flat,
  To bring the roof to the foundation,
  And bury all which yet distinctly ranges,
  In heaps and piles of ruin.
SICINIUS.   This deserves death.

BRUTUS. Or let us stand to our authority,
  Or let us lose it. We do here pronounce,
  Upon the part o' th' people, in whose power
  We were elected theirs, Marcius is worthy   210
  Of present death.
SICINIUS.   Therefore lay hold of him;
  Bear him to th' rock Tarpeian, and from thence
  Into destruction cast him.
BRUTUS.   Ædiles, seize him!
CITIZENS. Yield, Marcius, yield!
MENENIUS.   Hear me one word;
  Beseech you, tribunes, hear me but a word.
ÆDILES. Peace, peace!
MENENIUS. [*to Brutus*]. Be that you seem, truly your
  country's friend,
  And temp'rately proceed to what you would
  Thus violently redress.
BRUTUS.   Sir, those cold ways,
  That seem like prudent helps, are very poisonous   220
  Where the disease is violent. Lay hands upon him,
  And bear him to the rock.
CORIOLANUS [*draws his sword*]. No, I'll die here.
  There's some among you have beheld me fighting:
  Come, try upon yourselves what you have seen me.
MENENIUS. Down with that sword! Tribunes,
  withdraw awhile.
BRUTUS. Lay hands upon him.
MENENIUS.   Help Marcius, help,
  You that be noble; help him, young and old!
CITIZENS. Down with him, down with him!

*In this mutiny, the Tribunes, the Ædiles, and the people,
are beat in*

MENENIUS. Go, get you to your house; be gone, away!
  All will be naught else.
2 SENATOR.   Get you gone.
CORIOLANUS.   Stand fast; 230
  We have as many friends as enemies.
MENENIUS. Shall it be put to that?
1 SENATOR.   The gods forbid!
  I prithee, noble friend, home to thy house;
  Leave us to cure this cause.
MENENIUS.   For 'tis a sore upon us
  You cannot tent yourself: be gone, beseech you.
COMINIUS. Come, sir, along with us.
CORIOLANUS. I would they were barbarians, as they
  are,
  Though in Rome littered; not Romans, as they are
  not,
  Though calved i' th' porch o' th' Capitol.
MENENIUS.   Be gone.
  Put not your worthy rage into your tongue: 240
  One time will owe another.
CORIOLANUS.   On fair ground
  I could beat forty of them.
MENENIUS.   I could myself
  Take up a brace o' th' best of them; yea, the two
  tribunes.
COMINIUS. But now 'tis odds beyond arithmetic;
  And manhood is called foolery when it stands
  Against a falling fabric. Will you hence
  Before the tag return? whose rage doth rend
  Like interrupted waters, and o'erbear
  What they are used to bear.
MENENIUS.   Pray you, be gone.
  I'll try whether my old wit be in request   250

With those that have but little: this must be patched
With cloth of any colour.
COMINIUS [to Coriolanus].   Nay, come away
                    Coriolanus and Cominius depart
1 PATRICIAN. This man has marred his fortune.
MENENIUS. His nature is too noble for the world:
He would not flatter Neptune for his trident,
Or Jove for's power to thunder. His heart's his
    mouth:
What his breast forges, that his tongue must vent;
And, being angry, does forget that ever
He heard the name of death.
                    Noise of the people returning
Here's goodly work!
2 PATRICIAN.   I would they were a-bed!   260
MENENIUS. I would they were in Tiber! What the
    vengeance,
Could he not speak 'em fair?

Enter Brutus and Sicinius, with the rabble again

SICINIUS.   Where is this viper
That would depopulate the city and
Be every man himself?
MENENIUS.   You worthy tribunes—
SICINIUS. He shall be thrown down the Tarpeian rock
With rigorous hands: he hath resisted law,
And therefore law shall scorn him further trial
Than the severity of the public power,
Which he so sets at nought.
1 CITIZEN.   He shall well know
The noble tribunes are the people's mouths,   270
And we their hands.
ALL THE CITIZENS. He shall, sure on't.
MENENIUS.   Sir, sir—
SICINIUS. Peace!
MENENIUS. Do not cry havoc, where you should but
    hunt
With modest warrant.
SICINIUS.   Sir, how comes't that you
Have holp to make this rescue?
MENENIUS.   Hear me speak:
As I do know the consul's worthiness,
So can I name his faults.
SICINIUS.   Consul! what consul?
MENENIUS. The consul Coriolanus.
BRUTUS.   He consul!
ALL THE CITIZENS. No, no, no, no, no.
MENENIUS. If, by the tribunes' leave, and yours, good
    people,   280
I may be heard, I would crave a word or two;
The which shall turn you to no further harm
Than so much loss of time.
SICINIUS.   Speak briefly then;
For we are peremptory to dispatch
This viperous traitor: to eject him hence
Were but our danger, and to keep him here
Our certain death: therefore it is decreed
He dies to-night.
MENENIUS.   Now the good gods forbid
That our renownéd Rome, whose gratitude
Towards her deservéd children is enrolled   290
In Jove's own book, like an unnatural dam
Should now eat up her own!
SICINIUS. He's a disease that must be cut away.
MENENIUS. O, he's a limb that has but a disease;
Mortal, to cut it off; to cure it, easy.

What has he done to Rome that's worthy death?
Killing our enemies, the blood he hath lost—
Which I dare vouch is more than that he hath
By many an ounce—he dropped it for his country;
And what is left, to lose it by his country   300
Were to us all that do't and suffer it
A brand to th' end o' th' world.
SICINIUS.   This is clean kam.
BRUTUS. Merely awry: when he did love his country,
It honoured him.
SICINIUS.   The service of the foot
Being once gangrened, is not then respected
For what before it was.
BRUTUS.   We'll hear no more.
Pursue him to his house and pluck him thence,
Lest his infection, being of catching nature,
Spread further.
MENENIUS.   One word more, one word!
This tiger-footed rage, when it shall find   310
The harm of unscanned swiftness, will, too late,
Tie leaden pounds to's heels. Proceed by process;
Lest parties—as he is beloved—break out,
And sack great Rome with Romans.
BRUTUS.   If it were so—
SICINIUS. What do ye talk?
Have we not had a taste of his obedience?
Our aediles smote? ourselves resisted? Come!
MENENIUS. Consider this: he has been bred i' th' wars
Since a' could draw a sword, and is ill schooled
In bolted language; meal and bran together   320
He throws without distinction. Give me leave,
I'll go to him, and undertake to bring him
Where he shall answer, by a lawful form,
In peace, to his utmost peril.
1 SENATOR.   Noble tribunes,
It is the human way: the other course
Will prove too bloody; and the end of it
Unknown to the beginning.
SICINIUS.   Noble Menenius,
Be you then as the people's officer.
Masters, lay down your weapons.
BRUTUS.   Go not home.
SICINIUS. Meet on the market-place. We'll attend you
    there: 330
Where, if you bring not Marcius, we'll proceed
In our first way.
MENENIUS.   I'll bring him to you.
[to the Senators] Let me desire your company: he
    must come,
Or what is worst will follow.
SENATORS.   Pray you, let's to him.
                                            They go

Scene 2: Rome. The house of Coriolanus

Enter Coriolanus with Nobles

CORIOLANUS. Let them pull all about mine ears;
    present me
Death on the wheel or at wild horses' heels;
Or pile ten hills on the Tarpeian rock,
That the precipitation might down stretch
Below the beam of sight; yet will I still
Be thus to them.
A NOBLE.   You do the nobler.
CORIOLANUS. I muse my mother
Does not approve me further, who was wont

To call them woollen vassals, things created
To buy and sell with groats; to show bare heads 10
In congregations, to yawn, be still and wonder,
When one but of my ordinance stood up
To speak of peace or war.

Enter Volumnia

                        I talk of you:
Why did you wish me milder? would you have me
False to my nature? Rather say I play
The man I am.
VOLUMNIA.   O, sir, sir, sir,
I would have had you put your power well on,
Before you had worn it out.
CORIOLANUS.   Let go.
VOLUMNIA. You might have been enough the man
  you are,
With striving less to be so: lesser had been 20
The thwartings of your dispositions, if
You had not showed them how ye were
  disposed
Ere they lacked power to cross you.
CORIOLANUS.   Let them hang.
VOLUMNIA. Ay, and burn too.

Enter Menenius with the Senators

MENENIUS. Come, come, you have been too rough,
  something too rough;
You must return and mend it.
SENATOR.   There's no remedy,
Unless, by not so doing, our good city
Cleave in the midst and perish.
VOLUMNIA.   Pray be counselled:
I have a heart as little apt as yours,
But yet a brain that leads my use of anger 30
To better vantage.
MENENIUS.   Well said, noble woman!
Before he should thus stoop to th' herd—but that
The violent fit o' th' time craves it as physic
For the whole state—I would put mine armour on,
Which I can scarcely bear.
CORIOLANUS.   What must I do?
MENENIUS. Return to th' tribunes.
CORIOLANUS.   Well, what then? what then?
MENENIUS. Repent what you have spoke.
CORIOLANUS. For them! I cannot do it to the gods;
Must I then do't to them?
VOLUMNIA.   You are too absolute;
Though therein you can never be too noble 40
But when extremities speak. I have heard you say,
Honour and policy, like unsevered friends,
I' th' war do grow together: grant that, and tell me
In peace what each of them by th' other lose
That they combine not there.
CORIOLANUS.   Tush, tush!
MENENIUS.   A good demand.
VOLUMNIA. If it be honour in your wars to seem
The same you are not, which for your best ends
You adopt your policy, how is it less or worse
That it shall hold companionship in peace
With honour as in war; since that to both 50
It stands in like request?
CORIOLANUS.   Why force you this?
VOLUMNIA. Because that now it lies you on to speak
To th' people, not by your own instruction,
Nor by th' matter which your heart prompts you,

But with such words that are but roted in
Your tongue, though but bastards and syllables
Of no allowance to your bosom's truth.
Now, this no more dishonours you at all
Than to take in a town with gentle words,
Which else would put you to your fortune and 60
The hazard of much blood.
I would dissemble with my nature, where
My fortunes and my friends at stake required
I should do so in honour. I am in this,
Your wife, your son, these senators, the nobles;
And you will rather show our general louts
How you can frown than spend a fawn upon 'em
For the inheritance of their loves and safeguard
Of what that want might ruin.
MENENIUS.   Noble lady!
Come, go with us; speak fair: you may salve so, 70
Not what is dangerous present, but the loss
Of what is past.
VOLUMNIA.   I prithee now, my son,
Go to them with this bonnet in thy hand;
And thus far having stretched it, here be with them,
Thy knee bussing the stones—[*curtseys*] for in such
  business
Action is eloquence, and the eyes of th' ignorant
More learnèd than the ears. Waving thy head,
With often thus correcting thy stout heart
(Now humble as the ripest mulberry
That will not hold the handling), say to them, 80
Thou art their soldier, and being bred in broils
Hast not the soft way which, thou dost confess,
Were fit for thee to use, as they to claim,
In asking their good loves; but thou wilt frame
Thyself, forsooth, hereafter theirs, so far
As thou hast power and person.
MENENIUS.   This but done,
Even as she speaks, why, their hearts were yours;
For they have pardons, being asked, as free
As words to little purpose.
VOLUMNIA.   Prithee now,
Go, and be ruled: although I know thou hadst
  rather 90
Follow thine enemy in a fiery gulf
Than flatter him in a bower.

Enter Cominius

                        Here is Cominius.
COMINIUS. I have been i' th' market-place; and, sir,
  'tis fit
You make strong party, or defend yourself
By calmness or by absence: all's in anger.
MENENIUS. Only fair speech.
COMINIUS.   I think 'twill serve, if he
Can thereto frame his spirit.
VOLUMNIA.   He must, and will.
Prithee now, say you will, and go about it.
CORIOLANUS. Must I go show them my unbarbed
  sconce?
With my base tongue give to my noble heart 100
A lie that it must bear? Well, I will do't:
Yet, were there but this single plot to lose,
This mould of Marcius, they to dust should grind it,
And throw't against the wind. To th' market-place!
You have put me now to such a part which never
I shall discharge to th' life.
COMINIUS.   Come, come, we'll prompt you.

VOLUMNIA. I prithee now, sweet son, as thou hast said
My praises made thee first a soldier, so,
To have my praise for this, perform a part
Thou hast not done before.
CORIOLANUS.   Well, I must do't.   110
Away, my disposition, and possess me
Some harlot's spirit! My throat of war be turned,
Which choiréd with my drum, into a pipe
Small as an eunuch or the virgin voice
That babies lulls asleep! The smiles of knaves
Tent in my cheeks, and schoolboys' tears take up
The glasses of my sight! A beggar's tongue
Make motion through my lips, and my armed
    knees,
Who bowed but in my stirrup, bend like his
That hath received an alms! I will not do't;   120
Lest I surcease to honour mine own truth,
And by my body's action teach my mind
A most inherent baseness.
VOLUMNIA.   At thy choice then.
To beg of thee, it is my more dishonour
Than thou of them. Come all to ruin: let
Thy mother rather feel thy pride than fear
Thy dangerous stoutness, for I mock at death
With as big heart as thou. Do as thou list.
Thy valiantness was mine, thou suck'dst it from me,
But owe thy pride thyself.
CORIOLANUS.   Pray, be content: 130
Mother, I am going to the market-place;
Chide me no more. I'll mountebank their loves,
Cog their hearts from them, and come home
    beloved
Of all the trades in Rome. Look, I am going:
Commend me to my wife. I'll return consul;
Or never trust to what my tongue can do
I' th' way of flattery further.
VOLUMNIA.   Do your will.
                                        She goes
COMINIUS. Away! the tribunes do attend you. Arm
    yourself
To answer mildly; for they are prepared
With accusations, as I hear, more strong   140
Than are upon you yet.
CORIOLANUS. The word is 'mildly.' Pray you, let us
    go.
Let them accuse me by invention, I
Will answer in mine honour.
MENENIUS.   Ay, but mildly.
CORIOLANUS. Well, mildly be it then—mildly.
                                        They go

Scene 3: *Rome. The Forum*

Enter Sicinius and Brutus

BRUTUS. In this point charge him home, that he
    affects
Tyrannical power. If he evade us there,
Enforce him with his envy to the people,
And that the spoil got on the Antiates
Was ne'er distributed.

Enter an Ædile

                     What, will he come?
ÆDILE. He's coming.
BRUTUS.   How accompanied?

ÆDILE. With old Menenius and those senators
That always favoured him.
SICINIUS.   Have you a catalogue
Of all the voices that we have procured,
Set down by th' poll?
ÆDILE.   I have; 'tis ready.   10
SICINIUS. Have you collected them by tribes?
ÆDILE.   I have.
SICINIUS. Assemble presently the people hither:
And when they hear me say 'It shall be so
I' th' right and strength o' th' commons,' be it
    either
For death, for fine, or banishment, then let them,
If I say 'Fine', cry 'Fine!' if 'Death', cry 'Death!'
Insisting on the old prerogative
And power i' th' truth o' th' cause.
ÆDILE.   I shall inform them.
BRUTUS. And when such time they have begun to cry,
Let them not cease, but with a din confused   20
Enforce the present execution
Of what we chance to sentence.
ÆDILE.   Very well.
SICINIUS. Make them be strong, and ready for this
    hint,
When we shall hap to give't them.
BRUTUS.   Go about it.   *The Ædile goes*
Put him to choler straight. He hath been used
Ever to conquer and to have his worth
Of contradiction: being once chafed, he cannot
Be reined again to temperance; then he speaks
What's in his heart; and that is there which looks
With us to break his neck.
SICINIUS.   Well, here he comes.   30

*Enter Coriolanus, Menenius, and Cominius, with
Senators and Patricians*

MENENIUS. Calmly, I do beseech you.
CORIOLANUS. Ay, as an ostler, that for th' poorest
    piece
Will bear the knave by th' volume. [*aloud*] Th'
    honoured gods
Keep Rome in safety, and the chairs of justice
Supplied with worthy men! plant love among 's!
Throng our large temples with the shows of peace,
And not our streets with war!
I SENATOR.   Amen, amen.
MENENIUS. A noble wish.

Enter the Ædile, with the Plebeians

SICINIUS. Draw near, ye people.
ÆDILE. List to your tribunes. Audience! peace, I say!   40
CORIOLANUS. First, hear me speak.
BOTH TRIBUNES.   Well, say. Peace, ho!
CORIOLANUS. Shall I be charged no further than this
    present?
Must all determine here?
SICINIUS.   I do demand,
If you submit you to the people's voices,
Allow their officers, and are content
To suffer lawful censure for such faults
As shall be proved upon you?
CORIOLANUS.   I am content.
MENENIUS. Lo, citizens, he says he is content.
The warlike service he has done, consider; think
Upon the wounds his body bears, which show   50
Like graves i' th' holy churchyard.

CORIOLANUS. Scratches with briers,
Scars to move laughter only.
MENENIUS. Consider further,
That when he speaks not like a citizen,
You find him like a soldier: do not take
His rougher accents for malicious sounds,
But, as I say, such as become a soldier
Rather than envy you.
COMINIUS. Well, well, no more.
CORIOLANUS. What is the matter
That, being passed for consul with full voice,
I am so dishonoured that the very hour 60
You take it off again?
SICINIUS. Answer to us.
CORIOLANUS. Say, then: 'tis true, I ought so.
SICINIUS. We charge you, that you have contrived to
take
From Rome all seasoned office, and to wind
Yourself into a power tyrannical;
For which you are a traitor to the people.
CORIOLANUS. How! traitor!
MENENIUS. Nay, temperately! your promise.
CORIOLANUS. The fires i' th' lowest hell fold in the
people!
Call me their traitor! Thou injurious tribune!
Within thine eyes sat twenty thousand deaths, 70
In thy hands clutched as many millions, in
Thy lying tongue both numbers, I would say
'Thou liest' unto thee with a voice as free
As I do pray the gods.
SICINIUS. Mark you this, people?
CITIZENS. To th' rock, to th' rock with him!
SICINIUS. Peace!
We need not put new matter to his charge,
What you have seen him do and heard him speak,
Beating your officers, cursing yourselves,
Opposing laws with strokes, and here defying
Those whose great power must try him—even this, 80
So criminal and in such capital kind,
Deserves th' extremest death.
BRUTUS. But since he hath
Served well for Rome—
CORIOLANUS. What do you prate of service?
BRUTUS. I talk of that that know it.
CORIOLANUS. You!
MENENIUS. Is this the promise that you made your
mother?
COMINIUS. Know, I pray you—
CORIOLANUS. I'll know no further.
Let them pronounce the steep Tarpeian death,
Vagabond exile, flaying, pent to linger
But with a grain a day, I would not buy 90
Their mercy at the price of one fair word,
Nor check my courage for what they can give,
To have't with saying 'Good morrow.'
SICINIUS. For that he has
(As much as in him lies) from time to time
Envied against the people, seeking means
To pluck away their power, as now at last
Given hostile strokes, and that not in the presence
Of dreaded justice, but on the ministers
That do distribute it—in the name o' th' people,
And in the power of us the tribunes, we, 100
Even from this instant, banish him our city,
In peril of precipitation
From off the rock Tarpeian, never more

To enter our Rome gates. I' th' people's name,
I say it shall be so.
CITIZENS. It shall be so, it shall be so! Let him away!
He's banished, and it shall be so.
COMINIUS. Hear me, my masters and my common
friends—
SICINIUS. He's sentenced; no more hearing.
COMINIUS. Let me speak.
I have been consul, and can show for Rome 110
Her enemies' marks upon me. I do love
My country's good with a respect more tender,
More holy and profound, than mine own life,
My dear wife's estimate, her womb's increase
And treasure of my loins; then if I would
Speak that—
SICINIUS. We know your drift. Speak what?
BRUTUS. There's no more to be said, but he is
banished
As enemy to the people and his country.
It shall be so.
CITIZENS. It shall be so, it shall be so.
CORIOLANUS. You common cry of curs! whose breath
I hate 120
As reek o' th' rotten fens, whose loves I prize
As the dead carcasses of unburied men
That do corrupt my air—I banish you.
And here remain with your uncertainty!
Let every feeble rumour shake your hearts!
Your enemies, with nodding of their plumes,
Fan you into despair! Have the power still
To banish your defenders, till at length
Your ignorance—which finds not till it feels,
Making but reservation of yourselves, 130
Still your own foes—deliver you as most
Abated captives to some nation
That won you without blows! Despising
For you the city, thus I turn my back:
There is a world elsewhere.
He goes, followed by Cominius,
Menenius, Senators and Patricians
ÆDILE. The people's enemy is gone, is gone!
CITIZENS. Our enemy is banished! he is gone!
Hoo—oo! *They all shout, and throw up*
their caps
SICINIUS. Go see him out at gates, and follow him,
As he hath followed you, with all despite;
Give him deserved vexation. Let a guard 140
Attend us through the city.
CITIZENS. Come, come, let's see him out at gates;
come!
The gods preserve our noble tribunes! Come.
They go

ACT 4
Scene 1: *Rome. Before a gate of the city*

Enter Coriolanus, Volumnia, Virgilia, Menenius,
Cominius, with the young Nobility of Rome

CORIOLANUS. Come, leave your tears; a brief farewell!
The beast
With many heads butts me away. Nay, mother,
Where is your ancient courage? you were used
To say extremity was the trier of spirits;
That common chances common men could bear;
That when the sea was calm all boats alike

Showed mastership in floating; fortune's blows,
When most struck home, being gentle wounded,
        craves
A noble cunning. You were used to load me
With precepts that would make invincible   10
The heart that conned them.
VIRGILIA. O heavens! O heavens!
CORIOLANUS.   Nay, I prithee, woman—
VOLUMNIA. Now the red pestilence strike all trades in
        Rome,
And occupations perish!
CORIOLANUS.   What, what, what!
I shall be loved when I am lacked. Nay, mother,
Resume that spirit when you were wont to say,
If you had been the wife of Hercules,
Six of his labours you'ld have done, and saved
Your husband so much sweat. Cominius,
Droop not; adieu. Farewell, my wife, my mother: 20
I'll do well yet. Thou old and true Menenius,
Thy tears are salter than a younger man's,
And venomous to thine eyes. My sometime
        general,
I have seen thee stern, and thou hast oft beheld
Heart-hard'ning spectacles; tell these sad women
'Tis fond to wail inevitable strokes,
As 'tis to laugh at 'em. Mother, you wot well
My hazards still have been your solace: and
Believe't not lightly—though I go alone,
Like to a lonely dragon that his fen   30
Makes feared and talked of more than seen—your
        son
Will or exceed the common or be caught
With cautelous baits and practice.
VOLUMNIA.   My first son,
Whither wilt thou go? Take good Cominius.
With thee awhile: determine on some course
More than a wild exposure to each chance
That starts i' th' way before thee.
VIRGILIA.   O the gods!
COMINIUS. I'll follow thee a month, devise with thee
Where thou shalt rest, that thou mayst hear of us
And we of thee: so, if the time thrust forth   40
A cause for thy repeal, we shall not send
O'er the vast world to seek a single man,
And lose advantage, which doth ever cool
I' th' absence of the needer.
CORIOLANUS.   Fare ye well:
Thou hast years upon thee; and thou art too full
Of the wars' surfeits to go rove with one
That's yet unbruised: bring me but out at gate.
Come, my sweet wife, my dearest mother, and
My friends of noble touch; when I am forth,
Bid me farewell, and smile. I pray you, come.   50
While I remain above the ground you shall
Hear from me still, and never of me aught
But what is like me formerly.
MENENIUS.   That's worthily
As any ear can hear. Come, let's not weep.
If I could shake off but one seven years
From these old arms and legs, by the good gods,
I'ld with thee every foot.
CORIOLANUS.   Give me thy hand.
Come.   *They go*

Scene 2: *Rome. A street near the gate*

*Enter the two Tribunes, Sicinius and Brutus, with the
Ædile*

SICINIUS. Bid them all home; he's gone, and we'll no
        further.
The nobility are vexed, whom we see have sided
In his behalf.
BRUTUS.   Now we have shown our power,
Let us seem humbler after it is done
Than when it was a-doing.
SICINIUS.   Bid them home:
Say their great enemy is gone, and they
Stand in their ancient strength.
BRUTUS.   Dismiss them home.
                                    The Ædile goes
Here comes his mother.

Enter Volumnia, Virgilia, and Menenius

SICINIUS.   Let's not meet her.
BRUTUS.   Why?
SICINIUS. They say she's mad.
BRUTUS. They have ta'en note of us: keep on your
        way.   10
VOLUMNIA. O, you're well met: th' hoarded plague o'
        th' gods
Requite your love!
MENENIUS.   Peace, peace, be not so loud.
VOLUMNIA. If that I could for weeping, you should
        hear—
Nay, and you shall hear some. [*to Brutus*] Will you
        be gone?
VIRGILIA [*to Sicinius*]. You shall stay too. I would I had
        the power
To say so to my husband,
SICINIUS.   Are you mankind?
VOLUMNIA. Ay, fool; is that a shame? Note but this,
        fool.
Was not a man my father? Hadst thou foxship
To banish him that struck more blows for Rome
Than thou hast spoken words?
SICINIUS.   O blessed heavens!   20
VOLUMNIA. Moe noble blows than ever thou wise
        words;
And for Rome's good. I'll tell thee what—yet go!
Nay, but thou shalt stay too. I would my son
Were in Arabia, and thy tribe before him,
His good sword in his hand.
SICINIUS.   What then?
VIRGILIA.   What then!
He'ld make an end of thy posterity.
VOLUMNIA. Bastards and all.
Good man, the wounds that he does bear for
        Rome!
MENENIUS. Come, come, peace.
SICINIUS. I would he had continued to his country   30
As he began, and not unknit himself
The noble knot he made.
BRUTUS.   I would he had.
VOLUMNIA. 'I would he had!' 'Twas you incensed the
        rabble;
Cats, that can judge as fitly of his worth
As I can of those mysteries which heaven
Will not have earth to know.
BRUTUS.   Pray, let's go.
VOLUMNIA. Now, pray, sir, get you gone;

You have done a brave deed. Ere you go, hear this:
As far as doth the Capitol exceed
The meanest house in Rome, so far my son—   40
This lady's husband here, this, do you see?
Whom you have banished—does exceed you all.

BRUTUS. Well, well, we'll leave you.

SICINIUS.   Why stay we to be baited
With one that wants her wits?

VOLUMNIA.   Take my prayers with you.
                                   Tribunes go
I would the gods had nothing else to do
But to confirm my curses! Could I meet 'em
But once a day, it would unclog my heart
Of what lies heavy to't.

MENENIUS.   You have told them home,
And by my troth you have cause. You'll sup with
me?

VOLUMNIA. Anger's my meat; I sup upon myself,   50
And so shall starve with feeding. Come, let's go:
Leave this faint puling, and lament as I do,
In anger, Juno-like. Come, come, come.
                            Volumnia and Virgilia depart

MENENIUS. Fie, fie, fie!   *He follows*

Scene 3: *A highway between Rome and Antium*

Enter a Roman and a Volsce, meeting

ROMAN. I know you well, sir, and you know me: your
name, I think, is Adrian.

VOLSCE. It is so, sir: truly, I have forgot you.

ROMAN. I am a Roman; and my services are, as you
are, against 'em. Know you me yet?

VOLSCE. Nicanor? no.

ROMAN. The same, sir.

VOLSCE. You had more beard when I last saw you; but
your favour is well approved by your tongue.
What's the news in Rome? I have a note from the   10
Volscian state to find you out there: you have well
saved me a day's journey.

ROMAN. There hath been in Rome strange insurrec-
tions; the people against the senators, patricians, and
nobles.

VOLSCE. Hath been! is it ended then? Our state thinks
not so: they are in a most warlike preparation, and
hope to come upon them in the heat of their
division.

ROMAN. The main blaze of it is past, but a small thing   20
would make it flame again; for the nobles receive so
to heart the banishment of that worthy Coriolanus,
that they are in a ripe aptness to take all power from
the people and to pluck from them their tribunes
for ever. This lies glowing, I can tell you, and is
almost mature for the violent breaking out.

VOLSCE. Coriolanus banished!

ROMAN. Banished, sir.

VOLSCE. You will be welcome with this intelligence,
Nicanor.   30

ROMAN. The day serves well for them now. I have
heard it said the fittest time to corrupt a man's wife
is when she's fall'n out with her husband. Your
noble Tullus Aufidius will appear well in these wars,
his great opposer, Coriolanus, being now in no
request of his country.

VOLSCE. He cannot choose. I am most fortunate thus
accidentally to encounter you: you have ended my
business, and I will merrily accompany you home.

ROMAN. I shall, between this and supper, tell you most   40
strange things from Rome; all tending to the good
of their adversaries. Have you an army ready, say
you?

VOLSCE. A most royal one; the centurions and their
charges, distinctly billeted, already in th' entertainment, and to be on foot at an hour's warning.

ROMAN. I am joyful to hear of their readiness, and am
the man, I think, that shall set them in present action.
So, sir, heartily well met, and most glad of your
company.   50

VOLSCE. You take my part from me, sir; I have the
most cause to be glad of yours.

ROMAN. Well, let us go together.   *They go*

Scene 4: *Antium. Before Aufidius's house*

Enter Coriolanus in mean apparel, disguised and muffled

CORIOLANUS. A goodly city is this Antium. City,
'Tis I that made thy widows: many an heir
Of these fair edifices 'fore my wars
Have I heard groan and drop. Then know me not,
Lest that thy wives with spits and boys with stones
In puny battle slay me.

Enter a Citizen

                            Save you, sir.

CITIZEN. And you.

CORIOLANUS.   Direct me, if it be your will,
Where great Aufidius lies. Is he in Antium?

CITIZEN. He is, and feasts the nobles of the state
At his house this night.

CORIOLANUS.   Which is his house, beseech you?   10

CITIZEN. This here before you.

CORIOLANUS.   Thank you, sir: farewell.
                                   Citizen goes
O world, thy slippery turns! Friends now fast
sworn,
Whose double bosoms seem to wear one heart,
Whose hours, whose bed, whose meal and exercise
Are still together, who twin, as 'twere, in love
Unseparable, shall within this hour,
On a dissension of a doit, break out
To bitterest enmity: so fellest foes,
Whose passions and whose plots have broke their
sleep
To take the one the other, by some chance,   20
Some trick not worth an egg, shall grow dear
friends
And interjoin their issues. So with me:
My birth-place hate I, and my love's upon
This enemy town. I'll enter: if he slay me,
He does fair justice; if he give me way,
I'll do his country service.   *He enters the house*

Scene 5: *Antium. A hall in Aufidius's house*

Music plays. Enter a Servingman

1 SERVINGMAN. Wine, wine, wine! What service is
there!
I think our fellows are asleep.   *Goes*

Enter another Servingman from the chamber

2 SERVINGMAN. Where's Cotus? my master calls for
him. Cotus!   *Returns*

Enter Coriolanus from without

CORIOLANUS. A goodly house. The feast smells well,
but I
Appear not like a guest.

Re-enter 1 Servingman

1 SERVINGMAN. What would you have, friend? whence
are you? Here's no place for you: pray go to the
door! *Goes*
CORIOLANUS. I have deserved no better entertainment,
In being Coriolanus. 10

Re-enter 2 Servingman

2 SERVINGMAN. Whence are you, sir? Has the porter
his eyes in his head that he gives entrance to such
companions? Pray get you out.
CORIOLANUS. Away!
2 SERVINGMAN. 'Away!' Get you away.
CORIOLANUS. Now thou'rt troublesome.
2 SERVINGMAN. Are you so brave? I'll have you talked
with anon.

Enter 3 Servingman with 1 Servingman

3 SERVINGMAN. What fellow's this?
1 SERVINGMAN. A strange one as ever I looked on! 20
I cannot get him out o' th' house. Prithee call my
master to him.
3 SERVINGMAN. What have you to do here, fellow?
Pray you avoid the house.
CORIOLANUS. Let me but stand; I will not hurt your
hearth.
3 SERVINGMAN. What are you?
CORIOLANUS. A gentleman.
3 SERVINGMAN. A marv'llous poor one.
CORIOLANUS. True, so I am. 30
3 SERVINGMAN. Pray you, poor gentleman, take up
some other station; here's no place for you. Pray you
avoid. Come.
CORIOLANUS. Follow your function, go and batten on
cold bits. *Pushes him away from him*
3 SERVINGMAN. What, you will not? Prithee, tell my
master what a strange guest he has here.
2 SERVINGMAN. And I shall. *Goes*
3 SERVINGMAN. Where dwell'st thou?
CORIOLANUS. Under the canopy. 40
3 SERVINGMAN. Under the canopy!
CORIOLANUS. Ay.
3 SERVINGMAN. Where's that?
CORIOLANUS. I' th' city of kites and crows.
3 SERVINGMAN. I' th' city of kites and crows! What
an ass it is! then thou dwell'st with daws too?
CORIOLANUS. No, I serve not thy master.
3 SERVINGMAN. How, sir! do you meddle with my
master?
CORIOLANUS. Ay; 'tis an honester service than to 50
meddle with thy mistress. Thou prat'st, and prat'st;
serve with thy trencher. Hence!
Beats him from the room

Enter Aufidius with 2 Servingman

AUFIDIUS. Where is this fellow?
2 SERVINGMAN. Here, sir. I'ld have beaten him like a
dog, but for disturbing the lords within. *Returns*
AUFIDIUS. Whence com'st thou? What wouldst thou?
Thy name?
Why speak'st not? Speak, man. What's thy name?
CORIOLANUS [*unmuffling*]. If, Tullus,

Not yet thou know'st me, and, seeing me, dost not
Think me for the man I am, necessity
Commands me name myself.
AUFIDIUS. What is thy name? 60
CORIOLANUS. A name unmusical to the Volscians' ears,
And harsh in sound to thine.
AUFIDIUS. Say, what's thy name?
Thou hast a grim appearance, and thy face
Bears a command in't; though thy tackle's torn,
Thou show'st a noble vessel. What's thy name?
CORIOLANUS. Prepare thy brow to frown—know'st
thou me yet?
AUFIDIUS. I know thee not. Thy name!
CORIOLANUS. My name is Caius Marcius, who hath
done
To thee particularly, and to all the Volsces,
Great hurt and mischief; thereto witness may 70
My surname, Coriolanus. The painful service,
The extreme dangers, and the drops of blood
Shed for my thankless country, are requited
But with that surname—a good memory
And witness of the malice and displeasure
Which thou shouldst bear me. Only that name
remains:
The cruelty and envy of the people,
Permitted by our dastard nobles, who
Have all forsook me, hath devoured the rest;
And suffered me by th' voice of slaves to be 80
Whooped out of Rome. Now, this extremity
Hath brought me to thy hearth: not out of hope—
Mistake me not—to save my life; for if
I had feared death, of all the men i' th' world
I would have 'voided thee; but in mere spite,
To be full quit of those my banishers,
Stand I before thee here. Then if thou hast
A heart of wreak in thee, that wilt revenge
Thine own particular wrongs and stop those maims
Of shame seen through thy country, speed thee
straight 90
And make my misery serve thy turn. So use it
That my revengeful services may prove
As benefits to thee; for I will fight
Against my cank'red country with the spleen
Of all the under fiends. But if so be
Thou dar'st not this and that to prove more fortunes
Thou'rt tired, then, in a word, I also am
Longer to live most weary, and present
My throat to thee and to thy ancient malice;
Which not to cut would show thee but a fool, 100
Since I have ever followed thee with hate,
Drawn tuns of blood out of thy country's breast,
And cannot live but to thy shame, unless
It be to do thee service.
AUFIDIUS. O Marcius, Marcius!
Each word thou hast spoke hath weeded from my
heart
A root of ancient envy. If Jupiter
Should from yond cloud speak divine things,
And say 'Tis true', I'ld not believe them more
Than thee, all noble Marcius. Let me twine
Mine arms about that body, where against 110
My grainéd ash an hundred times hath broke
And scarred the moon with splinters: here I clip
The anvil of my sword, and do contest
As hotly and as nobly with thy love
As ever in ambitious strength I did

Contend against thy valour. Know thou first,
I loved the maid I married; never man
Sighed truer breath; but that I see thee here,
Thou noble thing, more dances my rapt heart
Than when I first my wedded mistress saw   120
Bestride my threshold. Why, thou Mars, I tell thee,
We have a power on foot, and I had purpose
Once more to hew thy target from thy brawn,
Or lose mine arm for't. Thou hast beat me out
Twelve several times, and I have nightly since
Dreamt of encounters 'twixt thyself and me;
We have been down together in my sleep,
Unbuckling helms, fisting each other's throat;
And waked half dead with nothing. Worthy
      Marcius,
Had we no quarrel else to Rome but that   130
Thou art thence banished, we would muster all
From twelve to seventy, and pouring war
Into the bowels of ungrateful Rome,
Like a bold flood o'erbear't. O, come, go in,
And take our friendly senators by th' hands,
Who now are here, taking their leaves of me
Who am prepared against your territories,
Though not for Rome itself.
CORIOLANUS.   You bless me, gods!
AUFIDIUS. Therefore, most absolute sir, if thou wilt
      have
The leading of thine own revenges, take   140
Th' one half of my commission, and set down—
As best thou art experienced, since thou know'st
Thy country's strength and weakness—thine own
      ways,
Whether to knock against the gates of Rome,
Or rudely visit them in parts remote
To fright them ere destroy. But come in:
Let me commend thee first to those that shall
Say yea to thy desires. A thousand welcomes!
And more a friend than e'er an enemy;
Yet, Marcius, that was much. Your hand: most
      welcome!   *Coriolanus and Aufidius go* 150

Enter two of the Servingmen

1 SERVINGMAN. Here's a strange alteration!
2 SERVINGMAN. By my hand, I had thought to have
    strucken him with a cudgel; and yet my mind gave
    me his clothes made a false report of him.
1 SERVINGMAN. What an arm he has! he turned me
    about with his finger and his thumb, as one would
    set up a top.
2 SERVINGMAN. Nay, I knew by his face that there
    was something in him; he had, sir, a kind of face,
    methought—I cannot tell how to term it.   160
1 SERVINGMAN. He had so, looking as it were—Would
    I were hanged, but I thought there was more in him
    than I could think.
2 SERVINGMAN. So did I, I'll be sworn: he is simply
    the rarest man i' th' world.
1 SERVINGMAN. I think he is; but a greater soldier than
    he, you wot one.
2 SERVINGMAN. Who, my master?
1 SERVINGMAN. Nay, it's no matter for that.
2 SERVINGMAN. Worth six on him.   170
1 SERVINGMAN. Nay, not so neither: but I take him to
    be the greater soldier.
2 SERVINGMAN. Faith, look you, one cannot tell how to

say that: for the defence of a town our general is
excellent.
1 SERVINGMAN. Ay, and for an assault too.

Enter the third Servingman   120

3 SERVINGMAN. O slaves, I can tell you news—news,
    you rascals!
1, 2 SERVINGMEN. What, what, what? Let's partake.
3 SERVINGMAN. I would not be a Roman, of all nations;   180
    I had as lief be a condemned man.
1, 2 SERVINGMEN. Wherefore? wherefore?
3 SERVINGMAN. Why, here's he that was wont to
    thwack our general—Caius Marcius.
1 SERVINGMAN. Why do you say 'thwack our general'?
3 SERVINGMAN. I do not say 'thwack our general', but
    he was always good enough for him.
2 SERVINGMAN. Come, we are fellows and friends. He
    was ever too hard for him; I have heard him say so
    himself.   190
1 SERVINGMAN. He was too hard for him directly. To
    say the troth on't, before Corioli he scotched him
    and notched him like a carbonado.
2 SERVINGMAN. An he had been cannibally given, he
    might have broiled and eaten him too.
1 SERVINGMAN. But more of thy news?
3 SERVINGMAN. Why, he is so made on here within as
    if he were son and heir to Mars; set at upper end
    o' th' table; no question asked him by any of the
    senators but they stand bald before him. Our general   200
    himself makes a mistress of him; sanctifies himself
    with's hand, and turns up the white o' th' eye to his
    discourse. But the bottom of the news is, our general
    is cut i' th' middle and but one half of what he was
    yesterday, for the other has half by the entreaty and
    grant of the whole table. He'll go, he says, and sowl
    the porter of Rome gates by th' ears; he will mow
    all down before him, and leave his passage polled.
2 SERVINGMAN. And he's as like to do't as any man I can
    imagine.   210
3 SERVINGMAN. Do't! he will do't; for look you, sir, he
    has as many friends as enemies; which friends, sir,
    as it were, durst not—look you, sir—show them-
    selves, as we term it, his friends whilst he's in
    dejectitude.
1 SERVINGMAN. Dejectitude! what's that?
3 SERVINGMAN. But when they shall see, sir, his crest
    up again and the man in blood, they will out of their
    burrows, like conies after rain, and revel all with
    him.   220
1 SERVINGMAN. But when goes this forward?
3 SERVINGMAN. To-morrow, to-day, presently. You
    shall have the drum struck up this afternoon; 'tis as
    it were a parcel of their feast, and to be executed
    ere they wipe their lips.
2 SERVINGMAN. Why, then we shall have a stirring
    world again. This peace is nothing but to rust iron,
    increase tailors, and breed ballad-makers.
1 SERVINGMAN. Let me have war, say I; it exceeds peace
    as far as day does night; it's sprightly, waking,   230
    audible, and full of vent. Peace is a very apoplexy,
    lethargy; mulled, deaf, sleepy, insensible; a getter of
    more bastard children than war's a destroyer of men.
2 SERVINGMAN. 'Tis so: and as war in some sort may be
    said to be a ravisher, so it cannot be denied but peace
    is a great maker of cuckolds.

1 SERVINGMAN. Ay, and it makes men hate one
another.
3 SERVINGMAN. Reason: because they then less need
one another. The wars for my money. I hope to see 240
Romans as cheap as Volscians. They are rising, they
are rising.
1, 2 SERVINGMEN. In, in, in, in!   *They go*

Scene 6: *Rome. A public place*

Enter the two Tribunes, Sicinius and Brutus

SICINIUS. We hear not of him, neither need we fear
  him.
  His remedies are tame. The present peace
  And quietness of tne people, which before
  Were in wild hurry, here do make his friends
  Blush that the world goes well; who rather had,
  Though they themselves did suffer by't, behold
  Dissentious numbers pest'ring streets than see
  Our tradesmen singing in their shops, and going
  About their functions friendly.
BRUTUS. We stood to't in good time.

Enter Menenius

                                  Is this Menenius? 10
SICINIUS. 'Tis he, 'tis he. O, he is grown most kind
  Of late. Hail, sir!
MENENIUS.   Hail to you both!
SICINIUS. Your Coriolanus is not much missed
  But with his friends. The commonwealth doth
    stand,
  And so would do, were he more angry at it.
MENENIUS. All's well; and might have been much
    better, if
  He could have temporized.
SICINIUS.   Where is he, hear you?
MENENIUS. Nay, I hear nothing: his mother and his
    wife
  Hear nothing from him.

Enter three or four Citizens

CITIZENS. The gods preserve you both!
SICINIUS.   God-den, our neighbours. 20
BRUTUS. God-den to you all, god-den to you all.
1 CITIZEN. Ourselves, our wives, and children, on our
    knees,
  Are bound to pray for you both.
SICINIUS.   Live, and thrive!
BRUTUS. Farewell, kind neighbours: we wished
    Coriolanus
  Had loved you as we did.
CITIZENS.   Now the gods keep you!
BOTH TRIBUNES. Farewell, farewell. *Citizens pass on*
SICINIUS. This is a happier and more comely time
  Than when these fellows ran about the streets
  Crying confusion.
BRUTUS.   Caius Marcius was
  A worthy officer i' th' war, but insolent,   30
  O'ercome with pride, ambitious past all thinking,
  Self-loving—
SICINIUS.   And affecting one sole throne,
  Without assistance.
MENENIUS.   I think not so.
SICINIUS. We should by this, to all our lamentation,
  If he had gone forth consul, found it so.

BRUTUS. The gods have well prevented it, and Rome
  Sits safe and still without him.

Enter an Ædile

ÆDILE.   Worthy tribunes,
  There is a slave, whom we have put in prison,
  Reports the Volsces with two several powers
  Are ent'red in the Roman territories,   40
  And with the deepest malice of the war
  Destroy what lies before 'em.
MENENIUS.   'Tis Aufidius,
  Who, hearing of our Marcius' banishment,
  Thrusts forth his horns again into the world,
  Which were inshelled when Marcius stood for
    Rome,
  And durst not once peep out.
SICINIUS.   Come, what talk you
  Of Marcius?
BRUTUS. Go see this rumourer whipped. It cannot be
  The Volsces dare break with us.
MENENIUS.   Cannot be!
  We have record that very well it can;   50
  And three examples of the like hath been
  Within my age. But reason with the fellow,
  Before you punish him, where he heard this,
  Lest you shall chance to whip your information
  And beat the messenger who bids beware
  Of what is to be dreaded.
SICINIUS.   Tell not me:
  I know this cannot be.
BRUTUS.   Not possible.

Enter a Messenger

MESSENGER. The nobles in great earnestness are going
  All to the Senate House: some news is come
  That turns their countenances.
SICINIUS.   'Tis this slave—   60
  Go whip him 'fore the people's eyes—his raising,
  Nothing but his report.
MESSENGER.   Yes, worthy sir,
  The slave's report is seconded; and more,
  More fearful, is delivered.
SICINIUS.   What more fearful?
MESSENGER. It is spoke freely out of many mouths—
  How probable I do not know—that Marcius,
  Joined with Aufidius, leads a power 'gainst Rome,
  And vows revenge as spacious as between
  The young'st and oldest thing
SICINIUS.   This is most likely!
BRUTUS. Raised only that the weaker sort may wish 70
  Good Marcius home again.
SICINIUS.   The very trick on't.
MENENIUS. This is unlikely:
  He and Aufidius can no more atone
  Than violent'st contrarieties.

Enter a second Messenger

2 MESSENGER. You are sent for to the Senate.
  A fearful army, led by Caius Marcius
  Associated with Aufidius, rages
  Upon our territories, and have already
  O'erborne their way, consumed with fire, and took
  What lay before them.   80

Enter Cominius

COMINIUS. O, you have made good work!

MENENIUS.   What news? what news?
COMINIUS. You have holp to ravish your own
    daughters and
    To melt the city leads upon your pates,
    To see your wives dishonoured to your noses—
MENENIUS. What's the news? what's the news?
COMINIUS. Your temples burnéd in their cement, and
    Your franchises, whereon you stood, confined
    Into an auger's bore.
MENENIUS.   Pray now, your news?—
    You have made fair work, I fear me.—Pray, your
     news?—
    If Marcius should be joined wi' th' Volscians—
COMINIUS.   If! 90
    He is their god; he leads them like a thing
    Made by some other deity than Nature,
    That shapes man better; and they follow him
    Against us brats with no less confidence
    Than boys pursuing summer butterflies,
    Or butchers killing flies.
MENENIUS.   You have made good work,
    You and your apron-men; you that stood so much
    Upon the voice of occupation and
    The breath of garlic-eaters!
COMINIUS.   He will shake
    Your Rome about your ears.
MENENIUS.   As Hercules   100
    Did shake down mellow fruit. You have made
     fair work!
BRUTUS. But is this true, sir?
COMINIUS.   Ay; and you'll look pale
    Before you find it other. All the regions
    Do smilingly revolt, and who resist
    Are mocked for valiant ignorance,
    And perish constant fools. Who is't can blame him?
    Your enemies and his find something in him.
MENENIUS. We are all undone, unless
    The noble man have mercy.
COMINIUS.   Who shall ask it?
    The tribunes cannot do't for shame; the people   110
    Deserve such pity of him as the wolf
    Does of the shepherds; for his best friends, if they
    Should say 'Be good to Rome,' they charged him
     even
    As those should do that had deserved his hate,
    And therein showed like enemies.
MENENIUS.   'Tis true:
    If he were putting to my house the brand
    That should consume it, I have not the face
    To say 'Beseech you, cease.' You have made fair
     hands,
    You and your crafts! you have crafted fair!
COMINIUS.   You have brought
    A trembling upon Rome, such as was never   120
    S' incapable of help.
BOTH TRIBUNES.   Say not we brought it.
MENENIUS. How! Was't we? We loved him, but, like
     beasts
    And cowardly nobles, gave way unto your clusters,
    Who did hoot him out o' th' city.
COMINIUS.   But I fear
    They'll roar him in again. Tullus Aufidius,
    The second name of men, obeys his points
    As if he were his officer. Desperation
    Is all the policy, strength, and defence,
    That Rome can make against them.

Enter a troop of Citizens

MENENIUS.   Here come the clusters.
    And is Aufidius with him? You are they   130
    That made the air unwholesome when you cast
    Your stinking greasy caps in hooting at
    Coriolanus' exile. Now he's coming,
    And not a hair upon a soldier's head
    Which will not prove a whip; as many coxcombs
    As you threw caps up will he tumble down,
    And pay you for your voices. 'Tis no matter;
    If he could burn us all into one coal,
    We have deserved it.
CITIZENS. Faith, we hear fearful news.
1 CITIZEN.   For mine own part, 140
    When I said banish him, I said 'twas pity.
2 CITIZEN. And so did I.
3 CITIZEN. And so did I; and, to say the truth, so did
    very many of us. That we did, we did for the best;
    and though we willingly consented to his banish-
    ment, yet it was against our will.
COMINIUS. You're goodly things, you voices!
MENENIUS.   You have made
    Good work, you and your cry! Shall's to the
     Capitol?
COMINIUS. O, ay, what else?
                  Cominius and Menenius go
SICINIUS. Go masters, get you home; be not dismayed; 150
    These are a side that would be glad to have
    This true which they so seem to fear. Go home,
    And show no sign of fear.
1 CITIZEN. The gods be good to us! Come, masters,
    let's home. I ever said we were i'th' wrong when
    we banished him.
2 CITIZEN. So did we all. But come, let's home.
                         Citizens go
BRUTUS. I do not like this news.
SICINIUS. Nor I.
BRUTUS. Let's to the Capitol. Would half my wealth 160
    Would buy this for a lie!
SICINIUS.   Pray, let us go.
                            They go

Scene 7: *A camp at a small distance from Rome*

Enter Aufidius with his Lieutenant

AUFIDIUS. Do they still fly to th' Roman?
LIEUTENANT. I do not know what witchcraft's in him,
    but
    Your soldiers use him as the grace fore meat,
    Their talk at table and their thanks at end;
    And you are dark'ned in this action sir,
    Even by your own.
AUFIDIUS.   I cannot help it now,
    Unless by using means I lame the foot
    Of our design. He bears himself more proudlier,
    Even to my person, than I thought he would
    When first I did embrace him; yet his nature   10
    In that's no changeling, and I must excuse
    What cannot be amended.
LIEUTENANT.   Yet I wish, sir—
    I mean for your particular—you had not
    Joined in commission with him, but either
    Had borne the action of yourself, or else
    To him had left it solely.
AUFIDIUS. I understand thee well; and be thou sure,

When he shall come to his account, he knows not
What I can urge against him. Although it seems,
And so he thinks, and is no less apparent   20
To th' vulgar eye, that he bears all things fairly
And shows good husbandry for the Volscian state,
Fights dragon-like, and does achieve as soon
As draw his sword; yet he hath left undone
That which shall break his neck or hazard mine,
Whene'er we come to our account.

LIEUTENANT. Sir, I beseech you, think you he'll carry
    Rome?

AUFIDIUS. All places yield to him ere he sits down,
And the nobility of Rome are his;
The senators and patricians love him too.   30
The tribunes are no soldiers, and their people
Will be as rash in the repeal, as hasty
To expel him thence. I think he'll be to Rome
As is the osprey to the fish, who takes it
By sovereignty of nature. First he was
A noble servant to them, but he could not
Carry his honours even. Whether 'twas pride,
Which out of daily fortune ever taints
The happy man; whether defect of judgement,
To fail in the disposing of those chances   40
Which he was lord of; or whether nature,
Not to be other than one thing, not moving
From th' casque to th' cushion, but commanding
    peace
Even with the same austerity and garb
As he controlled the war; but one of these—
As he hath spices of them all—not all,
For I dare so far free him—made him feared,
So hated, and so banished: but he has a merit
To choke it in the utt'rance. So our virtues
Lie in th' interpretation of the time;   50
And power, unto itself most commendable,
Hath not a tomb so evident as a chair
T' extol what it hath done.
One fire drives out one fire; one nail, one nail;
Rights by rights falter, strengths by strengths do
    fail.
Come, let's away. When, Caius, Rome is thine,
Thou art poor'st of all; then shortly art thou mine.
                                        They go

ACT 5
Scene 1: *Rome. A public place*

*Enter Menenius, Cominius, Sicinius, Brutus, the two
Tribunes, with others*

MENENIUS. No, I'll not go: you hear what he hath said
Which was sometime his general, who loved him
In a most dear particular. He called me father;
But what o' that? Go you that banished him,
A mile before his tent fall down, and knee
The way into his mercy. Nay, if he coyed
To hear Cominius speak, I'll keep at home.

COMINIUS. He would not seem to know me.

MENENIUS.   Do you hear?

COMINIUS. Yet one time he did call me by my name.
I urged our old acquaintance, and the drops   10
That we have bled together. 'Coriolanus'
He would not answer to; forbad all names;
He was a kind of nothing, titleless,
Till he had forged himself a name i' th' fire

Of burning Rome.

MENENIUS.   Why, so! You have made good work!
A pair of tribunes that have wrecked fair Rome
To make coals cheap—a noble memory!

COMINIUS. I minded him how royal 'twas to pardon
When it was less expected; he replied,
It was a bare petition of a state   20
To one whom they had punished.

MENENIUS.   Very well.
Could he say less?

COMINIUS. I offered to awaken his regard
For 's private friends: his answer to me was,
He could not stay to pick them in a pile
Of noisome musty chaff. He said 'twas folly,
For one poor grain or two, to leave unburnt
And still to nose th' offence.

MENENIUS.   For one poor grain or two!
I am one of those; his mother, wife, his child,
And this brave fellow too, we are the grains: 30
You are the musty chaff, and you are smelt
Above the moon. We must be burnt for you.

SICINIUS. Nay, pray, be patient: if you refuse your aid
In this so never-needed help, yet do not
Upbraid's with our distress. But, sure, if you
Would be your country's pleader, your good
    tongue,
More than the instant army we can make,
Might stop our countryman.

MENENIUS.   No, I'll not meddle.

SICINIUS. Pray you, go to him.

MENENIUS.   What should I do?

BRUTUS. Only make trial what your love can do   40
For Rome, towards Marcius.

MENENIUS.   Well, and say that Marcius
Return me, as Cominius is returned,
Unheard—what then?
But as a discontented friend, grief-shot
With his unkindness? Say 't be so?

SICINIUS.   Yet your good will
Must have that thanks from Rome after the
    measure
As you intended well.

MENENIUS.   I'll undertake 't:
I think he'll hear me. Yet to bite his lip
And hum at good Cominius much unhearts me.
He was not taken well; he had not dined: 50
The veins unfilled, our blood is cold, and then
We pout upon the morning, are unapt
To give or to forgive; but when we have stuffed
These pipes and these conveyances of our blood
With wine and feeding, we have suppler souls
Than in our priest-like fasts: therefore I'll watch him
Till he be dieted to my request,
And then I'll set upon him.

BRUTUS. You know the very road into his kindness,
And cannot lose your way.

MENENIUS.   Good faith, I'll prove him, 60
Speed how it will. I shall ere long have knowledge
Of my success.   *Goes*

COMINIUS.   He'll never hear him.

SICINIUS.   Not?

COMINIUS. I tell you he does sit in gold, his eye
Red as 'twould burn Rome, and his injury
The gaoler to his pity. I kneeled before him;
'Twas very faintly he said 'Rise;' dismissed me
Thus with his speechless hand. What he would do

He sent in writing after me; what he would not,
Bound with an oath to yield to his conditions:
So that all hope is vain,   70
Unless his noble mother, and his wife—
Who, as I hear, mean to solicit him
For mercy to his country. Therefore, let's hence,
And with our fair entreaties haste them on.

They go

Scene 2: *Entrance of the Volscian camp before Rome*

Enter Menenius to the Watch on Guard

1 WATCH. Stay. Whence are you?
2 WATCH.   Stand, and go back.
MENENIUS. You guard like men, 'tis well; but, by your
     leave,
I am an officer of state, and come
To speak with Coriolanus.
1 WATCH.   From whence?
MENENIUS.   From Rome.
1 WATCH. You may not pass, you must return: our
     general
Will no more hear from thence.
2 WATCH. You'll see your Rome embraced with fire,
     before
You'll speak with Coriolanus.
MENENIUS.   Good my friends,
If you have heard your general talk of Rome
And of his friends there, it is lots to blanks   10
My name hath touched your ears: it is Menenius.
1 WATCH. Be it so; go back. The virtue of your name
Is not here passable.
MENENIUS.   I tell thee, fellow,
Thy general is my lover. I have been
The book of his good acts whence men have read
His fame unparalleled—haply amplified;
For I have ever varnishéd my friends
(Of whom he's chief) with all the size that verity
Would without lapsing suffer: nay, sometimes,
Like to a bowl upon a subtle ground,   20
I have tumbled past the throw, and in his praise
Have almost stamped the leasing: therefore, fellow,
I must have leave to pass.
1 WATCH. Faith, sir, if you had told as many lies in his
behalf as you have uttered words in your own, you
should not pass here; no, though it were as virtuous
to lie as to live chastely. Therefore go back.
MENENIUS. Prithee, fellow, remember my name is
Menenius, always factionary on the party of your
general.   30
2 WATCH. Howsoever you have been his liar, as you
say you have, I am one that, telling true under him,
must say you cannot pass. Therefore go back.
MENENIUS. Has he dined, canst thou tell? For I would
not speak with him till after dinner.
1 WATCH. You are a Roman, are you?
MENENIUS. I am, as thy general is.
1 WATCH. Then you should hate Rome, as he does.
Can you, when you have pushed out your gates the
very defender of them, and in a violent popular   40
ignorance given your enemy your shield, think to
front his revenges with the easy groans of old
women, the virginal palms of your daughters, or
with the palsied intercession of such a decayed
dotant as you seem to be? Can you think to blow
out the intended fire your city is ready to flame in,

with such weak breath as this? No, you are deceived;
therefore, back to Rome, and prepare for your
execution. You are condemned; our general has
sworn you out of reprieve and pardon.   50
MENENIUS. Sirrah, if thy captain knew I were here, he
would use me with estimation.
2 WATCH. Come, my captain knows you not.
MENENIUS. I mean, thy general.
1 WATCH. My general cares not for you. Back, I say;
go, lest I let forth your half-pint of blood. Back—
that's the utmost of your having. Back.
MENENIUS. Nay, but, fellow, fellow—

Enter Coriolanus with Aufidius

CORIOLANUS. What's the matter?
MENENIUS. Now, you companion, I'll say an errand   60
for you; you shall know now that I am in estimation;
you shall perceive that a Jack guardant cannot office
me from my son Coriolanus. Guess but by me entertainment with him if thou stand'st not i' th' state of
hanging, or of some death more long in spectator-
ship and crueller in suffering; behold now presently,
and swoon for what's to come upon thee. [*to
Coriolanus*] The glorious gods sit in hourly synod
about thy particular prosperity, and love thee no
worse than thy old father Menenius does! O my   70
son, my son! thou art preparing fire for us; look
thee, here's water to quench it. I was hardly moved
to come to thee; but being assured none but myself
could move thee, I have been blown out of your
gates with sighs; and conjure thee to pardon Rome
and thy petitionary countrymen. The good gods
assuage thy wrath, and turn the dregs of it upon
this varlet here; this, who, like a block, hath denied
my access to thee.
CORIOLANUS. Away!   80
MENENIUS. How! away!
CORIOLANUS. Wife, mother, child, I know not. My
     affairs
Are servanted to others. Though I owe
My revenge properly, my remission lies
In Volscian breasts. That we have been familiar,
Ingrate forgetfulness shall poison rather
Than pity note how much. Therefore be gone.
Mine ears against your suits are stronger than
Your gates against my force. Yet, for I loved thee,
Take this along; I writ it for thy sake,   90
And would have sent it. [*gives him a letter*] Another
     word, Menenius,
I will not hear thee speak. This man, Aufidius,
Was my beloved in Rome: yet thou behold'st.
AUFIDIUS. You keep a constant temper.

Coriolanus and Aufidius go

1 WATCH. Now, sir, is your name Menenius?
2 WATCH. 'Tis a spell, you see, of much power. You
know the way home again.
1 WATCH. Do you hear how we are shent for keeping
your greatness back?
2 WATCH. What cause, do you think, I have to swoon? 100
MENENIUS. I neither care for th' world nor your
general: for such things as you, I can scarce think
there's any, you're so slight. He that hath a will to
die by himself fears it not from another. Let your
general do his worst. For you, be that you are, long;
and your misery increase with your age! I say to you,
as I was said to, Away!   *Goes*

1 WATCH. A noble fellow, I warrant him.
2 WATCH. The worthy fellow is our general: he's the
rock, the oak not to be wind-shaken.   *They go* 110

Scene 3: *The tent of Coriolanus*

Enter Coriolanus with Aufidius and others

CORIOLANUS. We will before the walls of Rome
to-morrow
Set down our host. My partner in this action,
You must report to th' Volscian lords how plainly
I have borne this business.
AUFIDIUS.   Only their ends
You have respected; stopped your ears against
The general suit of Rome; never admitted
A private whisper—no, not with such friends
That thought them sure of you.
CORIOLANUS.   This last old man,
Whom with a cracked heart I have sent to Rome,
Loved me above the measure of a father,   10
Nay, godded me indeed. Their latest refuge
Was to send him; for whose old love I have—
Though I showed sourly to him—once more
offered
The first conditions, which they did refuse
And cannot now accept; to grace him only
That thought he could do more, a very little
I have yielded to. Fresh embassies and suits,
Nor from the state nor private friends, hereafter
Will I lend ear to. [*shouting heard*] Ha! what shout
is this?
Shall I be tempted to infringe my vow   20
In the same time 'tis made? I will not.

*Enter, in mourning habits, Virgilia, Volumnia, Valeria,
young Marcius, with Attendants*

[*Aside*] My wife comes foremost; then the
honoured mould
Wherein this trunk was framed, and in her hand
The grandchild to her blood. But out, affection!
All bond and privilege of nature, break!
Let it be virtuous to be obstinate.
What is that curtsy worth? or those doves' eyes,
Which can make gods forsworn? I melt, and am not
Of stronger earth than others. My mother bows;
As if Olympus to a molehill should   30
In supplication nod: and my young boy
Hath an aspect of intercession which
Great Nature cries 'Deny not.' Let the Volsces
Plough Rome, and harrow Italy: I'll never
Be such a gosling to obey instinct, but stand
As if a man were author of himself
And knew no other kin.
VIRGILIA.   My lord and husband!
CORIOLANUS. These eyes are not the same I wore in
Rome.
VIRGILIA. The sorrow that delivers us thus changed
Makes you think so.
CORIOLANUS.   Like a dull actor now   40
I have forgot my part and I am out,
Even to a full disgrace. Best of my flesh,
Forgive my tyranny; but do not say,
For that, 'Forgive our Romans.' O, a kiss
Long as my exile, sweet as my revenge!
Now, by the jealous queen of heaven, that kiss
I carried from thee, dear, and my true lip

Hath virgined it e'er since. You gods! I prate,
And the most noble mother of the world
Leave unsaluted. Sink, my knee, i' th' earth;   50
                                              Kneels
Of thy deep duty more impression show
Than that of common sons.
VOLUMNIA.   O, stand up blest!
Whilst with no softer cushion than the flint
I kneel before thee, and unproperly
Show duty, as mistaken all this while
Between the child and parent.   *Kneels*
CORIOLANUS.   What's this?
Your knees to me? to your corrected son?
                                      Raises her
Then let the pebbles on the hungry beach
Fillip the stars; then let the mutinous winds
Strike the proud cedars 'gainst the fiery sun,   60
Murd'ring impossibility, to make
What cannot be, slight work.
VOLUMNIA.   Thou art my warrior;
I holp to frame thee. Do you know this lady?
CORIOLANUS. The noble sister of Publicola,
The moon of Rome, chaste as the icicle
That's curdied by the frost from purest snow
And hangs on Dian's temple—dear Valeria!
VOLUMNIA [*showing young Marcius*]. This is a poor
epitome of yours,
Which by th' interpretation of full time
May show like all yourself.
CORIOLANUS.   The god of soldiers,   70
With the consent of supreme Jove, inform
Thy thoughts with nobleness, that thou mayst
prove
To shame unvulnerable, and stick i' th' wars
Like a great sea-mark, standing every flaw,
And saving those that eye thee!
VOLUMNIA.   Your knee, sirrah.
CORIOLANUS. That's my brave boy!
VOLUMNIA. Even he, your wife, this lady, and myself
Are suitors to you.
CORIOLANUS.   I beseech you, peace!
Or, if you'ld ask, remember this before:
The thing I have forsworn to grant may never   80
Be held by you denials. Do not bid me
Dismiss my soldiers, or capitulate
Again with Rome's mechanics. Tell me not
Wherein I seem unnatural; desire not
T' allay my rages and revenges with
Your colder reasons.
VOLUMNIA.   O, no more, no more!
You have said you will not grant us any thing;
For we have nothing else to ask but that
Which you deny already. Yet we will ask,
That, if you fail in our request, the blame   90
May hang upon your hardness: therefore hear us.
CORIOLANUS. Aufidius, and you Volsces, mark; for
we'll
Hear nought from Rome in private. [*sits*]
Your request?
VOLUMNIA. Should we be silent and not speak, our
raiment
And state of bodies would bewray what life
We have led since thy exile. Think with thyself
How more unfortunate than all living women
Are we come hither; since that thy sight, which
should

Make our eyes flow with joy, hearts dance with
  comforts,
Constrains them weep and shake with fear and
  sorrow,   100
Making the mother, wife, and child, to see
The son, the husband, and the father, tearing
His country's bowels out. And to poor we
Thine enmity's most capital: thou barr'st us
Our prayers to the gods, which is a comfort
That all but we enjoy. For how can we,
Alas, how can we for our country pray,
Whereto we are bound, together with thy victory,
Whereto we are bound? Alack, or we must lose
The country, our dear nurse, or else thy person,   110
Our comfort in the country. We must find
An evident calamity, though we had
Our wish, which side should win; for either thou
Must as a foreign recreant be led
With manacles thorough our streets, or else
Triumphantly tread on thy country's ruin,
And bear the palm for having bravely shed
Thy wife and children's blood. For myself, son,
I purpose not to wait on fortune till
These wars determine: if I can not persuade thee   120
Rather to show a noble grace to both parts
Than seek the end of one, thou shalt no sooner
March to assault thy country than to tread—
Trust to't, thou shalt not—on thy mother's womb,
That brought thee to this world.

VIRGILIA.   Ay, and mine,
That brought you forth this boy, to keep your name
Living to time.

BOY.   A' shall not tread on me;
I'll run away till I am bigger, but then I'll fight.

CORIOLANUS. Not of a woman's tenderness to be,
Requires nor child nor woman's face to see.   130
I have sat too long.   *Rising*

VOLUMNIA.   Nay, go not from us thus.
If it were so that our request did tend
To save the Romans, thereby to destroy
The Volsces whom you serve, you might
  condemn us,
As poisonous of your honour: no; our suit
Is, that you reconcile them: while the Volsces
May say 'This mercy we have showed,' the
  Romans,
'This we received;' and each in either side
Give the all-hail to thee, and cry 'Be blest
For making up this peace!' Thou know'st, great son, 140
The end of war's uncertain; but this certain,
That, if thou conquer Rome, the benefit
Which thou shalt thereby reap is such a name
Whose repetition will be dogged with curses;
Whose chronicle thus writ: 'The man was noble,
But with his last attempt he wiped it out,
Destroyed his country, and his name remains
To th' ensuing age abhorred.' Speak to me, son:
Thou hast affected the fine strains of honour,
To imitate the graces of the gods;   150
To tear with thunder the wide cheeks o' th' air,
And yet to charge thy sulphur with a bolt
That should but rive an oak. Why dost not speak?
Think'st thou it honourable for a noble man
Still to remember wrongs? Daughter, speak you:
He cares not for your weeping. Speak thou, boy:
Perhaps thy childishness will move him more

Than can our reasons. There's no man in the world
More bound to 's mother, yet here he lets me prate
Like one i' th' stocks. Thou hast never in thy life 160
Showed thy dear mother any courtesy,
When she, poor hen, fond of no second brood,
Has clucked thee to the wars, and safely home
Loaden with honour. Say my request's unjust,
And spurn me back; but if it be not so,
Thou art not honest, and the gods will plague thee,
That thou restrain'st from me the duty which
To a mother's part belongs. He turns away:
Down, ladies; let us shame him with our knees.
To his surname Coriolanus 'longs more pride   170
Than pity to our prayers. Down: an end;
This is the last: so we will home to Rome,
And die among our neighbours. Nay, behold's!
This boy, that cannot tell what he would have,
But kneels and holds up hands for fellowship,
Does reason our petition with more strength
Than thou hast to deny 't. Come, let us go:
This fellow had a Volscian to his mother;
His wife is in Corioli, and his child
Like him by chance. Yet give us our dispatch.   180
I am hushed until our city be a-fire,
And then I'll speak a little.

CORIOLANUS [*Holds her by the hand, silent*].
                          O mother, mother!
What have you done? Behold, the heavens do ope,
The gods look down, and this unnatural scene
They laugh at. O my mother, mother! O!
You have won a happy victory to Rome;
But, for your son—believe it, O, believe it—
Most dangerously you have with him prevailed,
If not most mortal to him. But let it come.
Aufidius, though I cannot make true wars,   190
I'll frame convenient peace. Now, good Aufidius,
Were you in my stead, would you have heard
A mother less? or granted less, Aufidius?

AUFIDIUS. I was moved withal.

CORIOLANUS.   I dare be sworn you were!
And, sir, it is no little thing to make
Mine eyes to sweat compassion. But, good sir,
What peace you'll make, advise me: for my part,
I'll not to Rome, I'll back with you; and pray you
Stand to me in this cause. O mother! wife!
                          Speaks with them apart

AUFIDIUS [*aside*]. I am glad thou hast set thy mercy
  and thy honour   200
At difference in thee. Out of that I'll work
Myself a former fortune.

CORIOLANUS [*coming forward with Volumnia and
  Virgilia*].   Ay, by and by;
But we will drink together; and you shall bear
A better witness back than words, which we
On like conditions will have counter-sealed.
Come, enter with us. Ladies, you deserve
To have a temple built you. All the swords
In Italy, and her confederate arms,
Could not have made this peace.   *They go*

Scene 4: *Rome. A street near the gate*

Enter Menenius and Sicinius

MENENIUS. See you yond coign o' th' Capitol, yond
  cornerstone?

SICINIUS. Why, what of that?

MENENIUS. If it be possible for you to displace it with
your little finger, there is some hope the ladies of
Rome, especially his mother, may prevail with him.
But I say there is no hope in't: our throats are
sentenced, and stay upon execution.

SICINIUS. Is't possible that so short a time can alter the
condition of a man?   10

MENENIUS. There is differency between a grub and a
butterfly; yet your butterfly was a grub. This
Marcius is grown from man to dragon: he has
wings; he's more than a creeping thing.

SICINIUS. He loved his mother dearly.

MENENIUS. So did he me: and he no more remembers
his mother now than an eight-year-old horse. The
tartness of his face sours ripe grapes; when he walks,
he moves like an engine and the ground shrinks
before his treading. He is able to pierce a corslet 20
with his eye, talks like a knell, and his hum is a
battery. He sits in his state as a thing made for
Alexander. What he bids be done is finished with
his bidding. He wants nothing of a god but eternity
and a heaven to throne in.

SICINIUS. Yes, mercy, if you report him truly.

MENENIUS. I paint him in the character. Mark what
mercy his mother shall bring from him: there is no
more mercy in him than there is milk in a male
tiger; that shall our poor city find. And all this is 30
'long of you.

SICINIUS. The gods be good unto us!

MENENIUS. No, in such a case the gods will not be
good unto us. When we banished him, we respected
not them; and, he returning to break our necks, they
respect not us.

Enter a Messenger

MESSENGER. Sir, if you'ld save your life, fly to your
house:
The plebeians have got your fellow-tribune,
And hale him up and down; all swearing if
The Roman ladies bring not comfort home   40
They'll give him death by inches.

Enter another Messenger

SICINIUS.   What's the news?

2 MESSENGER. Good news, good news! The ladies have
prevailed,
The Volscians are dislodged, and Marcius gone.
A merrier day did never yet greet Rome,
No, not th' expulsion of the Tarquins.

SICINIUS.   Friend,
Art thou certain this is true? Is't most certain?

2 MESSENGER. As certain as I know the sun is fire.
Where have you lurked, that you make doubt of it?
Ne'er through an arch so hurried the blown tide,
As the recomforted through the gates. Why, hark
you!   50

Trumpets, hautboys, drums, beat, all together

The trumpets, sackbuts, psalteries, and fifes,
Tabors and cymbals, and the shouting Romans,
Make the sun dance. [*a shout*] Hark you!

MENENIUS.   This is good news.
I will go meet the ladies. This Volumnia
Is worth of consuls, senators, patricians,
A city full; of tribunes such as you,

A sea and land full. You have prayed well to-day:
This morning for ten thousand of your throats
I'ld not have given a doit. [*shouts, trumpets, etc.
heard louder*] Hark, how they joy!

SICINIUS. First, the gods bless you for your tidings;
next,   60
Accept my thankfulness.

2 MESSENGER.   Sir, we have all
Great cause to give great thanks.

SICINIUS.   They are near the city!

2 MESSENGER. Almost at point to enter.

SICINIUS.   We will meet them,
And help the joy.   *They go towards the gate*

Scene 5

*Enter in procession the Ladies with a great press of
Senators, Patricians and People*

1 SENATOR. Behold our patroness, the life of Rome!
Call all your tribes together, praise the gods,
And make triumphant fires; strew flowers before
them.
Unshout the noise that banished Marcius,
Repeal him with the welcome of his mother;
Cry 'Welcome, ladies, welcome!'

ALL.   Welcome, ladies,
Welcome!

                              *They pass on; a flourish with
                                     drums and trumpets*

Scene 6: *Corioli. A public place*

Enter Tullus Aufidius, with Attendants

AUFIDIUS. Go tell the lords o' th' city I am here:
Deliver them this paper: having read it,
Bid them repair to th' market-place, where I,
Even in theirs and in the commons' ears,
Will vouch the truth of it. Him I accuse
The city ports by this hath entered, and
Intends t' appear before the people, hoping
To purge himself with words. Dispatch.

                                        Attendants go

Enter three or four Conspirators of Aufidius' faction

Most welcome!

1 CONSPIRATOR. How it is with our general?

AUFIDIUS.   Even so
As with a man by his own alms empoisoned,   10
And with his charity slain.

2 CONSPIRATOR.   Most noble sir,
If you do hold the same intent wherein
You wished us parties, we'll deliver you
Of your great danger.

AUFIDIUS.   Sir, I cannot tell;
We must proceed as we do find the people.

3 CONSPIRATOR. The people will remain uncertain
whilst
'Twixt you there's difference; but the fall of either
Makes the survivor heir of all.

AUFIDIUS.   I know it,
And my pretext to strike at him admits
A good construction. I raised him, and I pawned 20
Mine honour for his truth; who being so
heightened,
He watered his new plants with dews of flattery,
Seducing so my friends; and, to this end,
He bowed his nature, never known before

But to be rough, unswayable, and free.
3 CONSPIRATOR.   Sir, his stoutness
When he did stand for consul, which he lost
By lack of stooping—
AUFIDIUS.   That I would have spoke of.
Being banished for't, he came unto my hearth;
Presented to my knife his throat: I took him,   30
Made him joint-servant with me; gave him way
In all his own desires; nay, let him choose
Out of my files, his projects to accomplish,
My best and freshest men; served his designments
In mine own person; holp to reap the fame
Which he did end all his; and took some pride
To do myself this wrong: till at the last
I seemed his follower, not partner; and
He waged me with his countenance, as if
I had been mercenary.
I CONSPIRATOR.   So he did, my lord: 40
The army marvelled at it; and, in the last,
When he had carried Rome and that we looked
For no less spoil than glory—
AUFIDIUS.   There was it;
For which my sinews shall be stretched upon him.
At a few drops of women's rheum, which are
As cheap as lies, he sold the blood and labour
Of our great action: therefore shall he die,
And I'll renew me in his fall. But hark!

Drums and trumpets sound, with great shouts of the people

I CONSPIRATOR. Your native town you entered like a
   post,
And had no welcomes home; but he returns,   50
Splitting the air with noise.
I CONSPIRATOR.   And patient fools,
Whose children he hath slain, their base throats tear
With giving him glory.
3 CONSPIRATOR.   Therefore, at your vantage,
Ere he express himself or move the people
With what he would say, let him feel your sword,
Which we will second. When he lies along,
After your way his tale pronounced shall bury
His reasons with his body.
AUFIDIUS.   Say no more:
Here come the lords.

Enter the Lords of the city

LORDS. You are most welcome home.
AUFIDIUS.   I have not deserved it. 60
But, worthy lords, have you with heed perused
What I have written to you?
LORDS.   We have.
I LORD.   And grieve to hear 't.
What faults he made before the last, I think
Might have found easy fines; but there to end
Where he was to begin, and give away
The benefit of our levies, answering us
With our own charge, making a treaty where
There was a yielding—this admits no excuse.
AUFIDIUS. He approaches: you shall hear him.

*Enter Coriolanus, marching with drum and colours; the
commoners being with him*

CORIOLANUS. Hail, lords! I am returned your soldier; 70
No more infected with my country's love
Than when I parted hence, but still subsisting
Under your great command. You are to know

That prosperously I have attempted, and
With bloody passage led your wars even to
The gates of Rome. Our spoils we have brought
   home
Doth more than counterpoise a full third part
The charges of the action. We have made peace
With no less honour to the Antiates
Than shame to th' Romans; and we here deliver, 80
Subscribed by th' consuls and patricians,
Together with the seal o' th' senate, what
We have compounded on.
AUFIDIUS.   Read it not, noble lords;
But tell the traitor in the highest degree
He hath abused your powers.
CORIOLANUS. Traitor! how now!
AUFIDIUS.   Ay, traitor, Marcius!
CORIOLANUS.   Marcius!
AUFIDIUS. Ay, Marcius, Caius Marcius! Dost thou
   think
I'll grace thee with that robbery, thy stol'n name
Coriolanus, in Corioli?
You lords and heads o' th' state, perfidiously   90
He has betrayed your business and given up,
For certain drops of salt, your city Rome,
I say 'your city', to his wife and mother;
Breaking his oath and resolution, like
A twist of rotten silk; never admitting
Counsel o' th' war; but at his nurse's tears
He whined and roared away your victory;
That pages blushed at him and men of heart
Looked wond'ring each at other.
CORIOLANUS.   Hear'st thou, Mars?
AUFIDIUS. Name not the god, thou boy of tears!
CORIOLANUS.   Ha! 100
AUFIDIUS. No more.
CORIOLANUS. Measureless liar, thou hast made my
   heart
Too great for what contains it. 'Boy!' O slave!
Pardon me, lords, 'tis the first time that ever
I was forced to scold. Your judgements, my grave
   lords,
Must give this cur the lie: and his own notion—
Who wears my stripes impressed upon him; that
Must bear my beating to his grave—shall join
To thrust the lie unto him.
I LORD. Peace, both, and hear me speak.   110
CORIOLANUS. Cut me to pieces, Volsces; men and lads,
Stain all your edges on me. 'Boy'! False hound!
If you have writ your annals true, 'tis there,
That, like an eagle in a dove-cote, I
Fluttered your Volscians in Corioli.
Alone I did it. 'Boy!'
AUFIDIUS.   Why, noble lords,
Will you be put in mind of his blind fortune,
Which was your shame, by this unholy braggart,
'Fore your own eyes and ears?
THE CONSPIRATORS.   Let him die for't.
THE PEOPLE. 'Tear him to pieces.' 'Do it presently.' 120
'He killed my son.' 'My daughter.' 'He killed my
cousin Marcus.' 'He killed my father.'
2 LORD. Peace, ho! no outrage: peace!
The man is noble, and his fame folds in
This orb o' th' earth. His last offences to us
Shall have judicious hearing. Stand, Aufidius,
And trouble not the peace.
CORIOLANUS.   O that I had him,

With six Aufidiuses or more—his tribe,
To use my lawful sword!
AUFIDIUS.   Insolent villain!
THE CONSPIRATORS. Kill, kill, kill, kill, kill him!

The Conspirators draw, and kill Coriolanus: Aufidius
stands on his body

LORDS.   Hold, hold, hold, hold! 130
AUFIDIUS. My noble masters, hear me speak.
1 LORD.   O Tullus!
2 LORD. Thou has done a deed whereat valour will
  weep.
3 LORD. Tread not upon him. Masters all, be quiet;
  Put up your swords.
AUFIDIUS. My lords, when you shall know—as in this
  rage
  Provoked by him, you cannot—the great danger
  Which this man's life did owe you, you'll rejoice
  That he is thus cut off. Please it your honours
  To call me to your senate, I'll deliver

Myself your loyal servant, or endure   140
Your heaviest censure.
1 LORD.   Bear from hence his body,
And mourn you for him. Let him be regarded
As the most noble corse that ever herald
Did follow to his urn.
2 LORD.   His own impatience
Takes from Aufidius a great part of blame.
Let's make the best of it.
AUFIDIUS.   My rage is gone,
And I am struck with sorrow. Take him up:
Help, three o' th' chiefest soldiers; I'll be one.
Beat thou the drum, that it speak mournfully:
Trail your steel pikes. Though in this city he·   150
Hath widowed and unchilded many a one,
Which to this hour bewail the injury,
Yet he shall have a noble memory.
Assist.

Exeunt bearing away the body of Coriolanus;
a dead march sounded

Titus
Andronicus

The scene: Rome, and the country near by

CHARACTERS IN THE PLAY

SATURNINUS, *son to the late Emperor of Rome, afterwards Emperor*
BASSIANUS, *brother to Saturninus*
TITUS ANDRONICUS, *a noble Roman*
MARCUS ANDRONICUS, *tribune of the people, and brother to Titus*
LUCIUS
QUINTUS
MARTIUS } *sons to Titus Andronicus*
MUTIUS
Young LUCIUS, *a boy, son to Lucius*
PUBLIUS, *son to Marcus Andronicus*

ÆMILIUS, *a noble Roman*
ALARBUS
DEMETRIUS } *sons to Tamora*
CHIRON
AARON, *a Moor, beloved by Tamora*
A Captain, Tribune, Messenger, and Clown; Romans and Goths
TAMORA, *Queen of the Goths*
LAVINIA, *daughter to Titus Andronicus*
Nurse, and a blackamoor Child
Kinsmen of Titus, Senators, Tribunes, Officers, Soldiers, and Attendants

Titus Andronicus

ACT 1

Scene 1: *Rome, before the Capitol, beside which there stands the monument of the Andronici. Through a window opening on to the balcony of an upper chamber in the Capitol may be seen the Senate in session. Drums and trumpets are heard*

Saturninus and his followers march into the square on one side; Bassianus and his followers on the other

SATURNINUS. Noble patricians, patrons of my right,
Defend the justice of my cause with arms;
And, countrymen, my loving followers,
Plead my successive title with your swords:
I am his first-born son, that was the last
That ware the imperial diadem of Rome;
Then let my father's honours live in me,
Nor wrong mine age with this indignity.

BASSIANUS. Romans, friends, followers, favourers of
    my right,
If ever Bassianus, Cæsar's son,   10
Were gracious in the eyes of royal Rome,
Keep then this passage to the Capitol,
And suffer not dishonour to approach
The imperial seat, to virtue consecrate,
To justice, continence, and nobility:
But let desert in pure election shine,
And, Romans, fight for freedom in your choice.

Marcus Andronicus comes forward on to the balcony bearing a crown in his hands

MARCUS. Princes, that strive by factions and by friends
Ambitiously for rule and empery,
Know that the people of Rome, for whom we stand   20
A special party, have by common voice,
In election for the Roman empery,
Chosen Andronicus, surnaméd Pius
For many good and great deserts to Rome.
A noble man, a braver warrior,
Lives not this day within the city walls.
He by the senate is accited home
From weary wars against the barbarous Goths;
That with his sons, a terror to our foes,
Hath yoked a nation strong, trained up in arms.   30
Ten years are spent since first he undertook
This cause of Rome, and chastiséd with arms
Our enemies' pride: five times he hath returned
Bleeding to Rome, bearing his valiant sons
In coffins from the field [and as this day
To the monument of the Andronici
Done sacrifice of expiation,
And slain the noblest prisoner of the Goths.]
And now at last, laden with honour's spoils,
Returns the good Andronicus to Rome,   40
Renownéd Titus, flourishing in arms.
Let us entreat, by honour of his name,
Whom worthily you would have now succeed,
And in the Capitol and senate's right,
Whom you pretend to honour and adore,
That you withdraw you and abate your strength,
Dismiss your followers, and, as suitors should,
Plead your deserts in peace and humbleness.

SATURNINUS. How fair the tribune speaks to calm my
    thoughts!

BASSIANUS. Marcus Andronicus, so I do affy   50
In thy uprightness and integrity,
And so I love and honour thee and thine,
Thy nobler brother Titus and his sons,
And her to whom my thoughts are humbled all,
Gracious Lavinia, Rome's rich ornament,
That I will here dismiss my loving friends;
And to my fortune's and the people's favour
Commit my cause in balance to be weighed.

                    His followers disperse

SATURNINUS. Friends, that have been thus forward in
    my right,
I thank you all, and here dismiss you all,   60
And to the love and favour of my country
Commit myself, my person, and the cause.

                    His followers disperse

Rome, be as just and gracious unto me,
As I am confident and kind to thee.
Open the gates and let me in.

BASSIANUS. Tribunes, and me, a poor competitor.

                They go up into the Senate-house

Enter a Captain

CAPTAIN. Romans, make way! the good Andronicus,
Patron of virtue, Rome's best champion,
Successful in the battles that he fights,
With honour and with fortune is returned,   70
From where he circumscribéd with his sword,
And brought to yoke, the enemies of Rome.

A sound of drums and trumpets. Then enter in procession Mutius and Martius, two soldiers bearing a coffin covered with black, Quintus and Lucius, and Titus Andronicus, followed by his prisoners Tamora Queen of the Goths, her sons Alarbus, Chiron, and Demetrius, Aaron the Moor, and others. The soldiers set down the coffin, and Titus speaks

TITUS. Hail, Rome, victorious in thy mourning
    weeds!
Lo, as the bark that hath discharged his fraught
Returns with precious lading to the bay
From whence at first she weighed her anchorage,
Cometh Andronicus, bound with laurel boughs,
To re-salute his country with his tears,
Tears of true joy for his return to Rome.
Thou great defender of this Capitol,   80
Stand gracious to the rites that we intend!
Romans, of five and twenty valiant sons,
Half of the number that King Priam had,
Behold the poor remains, alive and dead!
These that survive let Rome reward with love;
These that I bring unto their latest home,
With burial amongst their ancestors.
Here Goths have given me leave to sheathe my
    sword.
Titus, unkind and careless of thine own,
Why suffer'st thou thy sons, unburied yet,   90
To hover on the dreadful shore of Styx?

Make way to lay them by their bretheren.
They open the tomb
There greet in silence, as the dead are wont,
And sleep in peace, slain in your country's wars!
O sacred receptacle of my joys,
Sweet cell of virtue and nobility,
How many sons hast thou of mine in store,
That thou wilt never render to me more!

LUCIUS. Give us the proudest prisoner of the Goths,
That we may hew his limbs, and on a pile   100
'Ad manes fratrum' sacrifice his flesh,
Before this earthy prison of their bones,
That so the shadows be not unappeased,
Nor we disturbed with prodigies on earth.

TITUS. I give him you, the noblest that survives,
The eldest son of this distressèd queen.

TAMORA. Stay, Roman brethren! Gracious conqueror,
Victorious Titus, rue the tears I shed,
A mother's tears in passion for her son:
And if thy sons were ever dear to thee,   110
O, think my son to be as dear to me!
Sufficeth not that we are brought to Rome,
To beautify thy triumphs and return,
Captive to thee and to thy Roman yoke;
But must my sons be slaughtered in the streets,
For valiant doings in their country's cause?
O, if to fight for king and commonweal
Were piety in thine, it is in these:
Andronicus, stain not thy tomb with blood.
Wilt thou draw near the nature of the gods?   120
Draw near them then in being merciful:
Sweet mercy is nobility's true badge;
Thrice-noble Titus, spare my first-born son.

TITUS. Patient yourself, madam, and pardon me.
These are their brethren, whom your Goths beheld
Alive and dead, and for their brethren slain
Religiously they ask a sacrifice:
To this your son is marked, and die he must,
T' appease their groaning shadows that are gone.

LUCIUS. Away with him! and make a fire straight, 130
And with our swords, upon a pile of wood,
Let's hew his limbs till they be clean consumed.
The sons of Titus bring out Alarbus

TAMORA. O cruel, irreligious piety!

CHIRON. Was never Scythia half so barbarous.

DEMETRIUS. Oppose not Scythia to ambitious Rome.
Alarbus goes to rest, and we survive
To tremble under Titus' threat'ning look.
Then, madam, stand resolved, but hope withal
The self-same gods that armed the Queen of Troy
With opportunity of sharp revenge   140
Upon the Thracian tyrant in her tent
May favour Tamora, the Queen of Goths,
(When Goths were Goths and Tamora was queen)
To quit the bloody wrongs upon her foes.

Enter the sons of Andronicus again, with their swords bloody

LUCIUS. See, lord and father, how we have performed
Our Roman rites! Alarbus' limbs are lopped,
And entrails feed the sacrificing fire,
Whose smoke like incense doth perfume the sky.
Remaineth naught but to inter our brethren,
And with loud 'larums welcome them to Rome.   150

TITUS. Let it be so, and let Andronicus
Make this his latest farewell to their souls.

*Trumpets sounded and the coffin
laid in the tomb*
In peace and honour rest you here, my sons,
Rome's readiest champions, repose you here in rest,
Secure from worldly chances and mishaps!
Here lurks no treason, here no envy swells,
Here grow no damnèd drugs, here are no storms,
No noise, but silence and eternal sleep:

Enter Lavinia

In peace and honour rest you here, my sons!

LAVINIA. In peace and honour live Lord Titus long,   160
My noble lord and father, live in fame!
Lo, at this tomb my tributary tears
I render for my brethren's obsequies,
And at thy feet I kneel, with tears of joy
Shed on this earth for thy return to Rome.
O, bless me here with thy victorious hand,
Whose fortunes Rome's best citizens applaud.

TITUS. Kind Rome, that hast thus lovingly reserved
The cordial of mine age to glad my heart!
Lavinia, live, outlive thy father's days,   170
And fame's eternal date, for virtue's praise!

Enter above Marcus Andronicus, Saturninus, Bassianus, and others

MARCUS. Long live Lord Titus, my belovèd brother,
Gracious triumpher in the eyes of Rome!

TITUS. Thanks, gentle tribune, noble brother Marcus.

MARCUS. And welcome, nephews, from successful
wars,
You that survive, and you that sleep in fame!
Fair lords, your fortunes are alike in all,
That in your country's service drew your swords,
But safer triumph is this funeral pomp,
That hath aspired to Solon's happiness,   180
And triumphs over chance in honour's bed.
Titus Andronicus, the people of Rome,
Whose friend in justice thou hast ever been,
Send thee by me, their tribune and their trust,
This palliament of white and spotless hue,
And name thee in election for the empire
With these our late-deceasèd emperor's sons:
Be 'candidatus' then, and put it on,
And help to set a head on headless Rome.

TITUS. A better head her glorious body fits   190
Than his that shakes for age and feebleness:
What should I don this robe and trouble you?
Be chosen with proclamations to-day,
To-morrow yield up rule, resign my life,
And set abroad new business for you all?
Rome, I have been thy soldier forty years,
And led my country's strength successfully,
And buried one and twenty valiant sons,
Knighted in field, slain manfully in arms,
In right and service of their noble country: 200
Give me a staff of honour for mine age,
But not a sceptre to control the world.
Upright he held it, lords, that held it last.

MARCUS. Titus, thou shalt obtain and ask the empery.

SATURNINUS. Proud and ambitious tribune, canst thou
tell?

TITUS. Patience, Prince Saturninus.

SATURNINUS.   Romans, do me right.
Patricians, draw your swords and sheathe them not
Till Saturninus be Rome's emperor:

Andronicus, would thou were shipped to hell,
Rather than rob me of the people's hearts.   210
LUCIUS. Proud Saturnine, interrupter of the good
That noble-minded Titus means to thee!
TITUS. Content thee, prince, I will restore to thee
The people's hearts, and wean them from
themselves.
BASSIANUS. Andronicus, I do not flatter thee,
But honour thee, and will do till I die;
My faction if thou strengthen with thy friends,
I will most thankful be, and thanks to men
Of noble minds is honourable meed.
TITUS. People of Rome, and people's tribunes here,   220
I ask your voices and your suffrages.
Will ye bestow them friendly on Andronicus?
TRIBUNE. To gratify the good Andronicus,
And gratulate his safe return to Rome,
The people will accept whom he admits.
TITUS. Tribunes, I thank you, and this suit I make,
That you create our emperor's eldest son,
Lord Saturnine; whose virtues I hope
Reflect on Rome as Titan's rays on earth,
And ripen justice in this commonweal: 230
Then if you will elect by my advice,
Crown him, and say, 'Long live our emperor!'
MARCUS. With voices and applause of every sort,
Patricians and plebians, we create
Lord Saturninus Rome's great emperor,
And say 'Long live our Emperor Saturnine!'
          A long flourish till they come down
SATURNINUS. Titus Andronicus, for thy favours done
To us in our election this day,
I give thee thanks in part of thy deserts,
And will with deeds requite thy gentleness: 240
And for an onset, Titus, to advance
Thy name and honourable family,
Lavinia will I make my emperess,
Rome's royal mistress, mistress of my heart,
And in the sacred Pantheon her espouse:
Tell me, Andronicus, doth this motion please thee?
TITUS. It doth, my worthy lord, and in this match
I hold me highly honoured of your grace,
And here in sight of Rome to Saturnine,
King and commander of our commonweal,   250
The wide world's emperor, do I consecrate
My sword, my chariot, and my prisoners,
Presents well worthy Rome's imperious lord:
Receive them then, the tribute that I owe,
Mine honour's ensigns humbled at thy feet.
SATURNINUS. Thanks, noble Titus, father of my life!
How proud I am of thee and of thy gifts
Rome shall record, and when I do forget
The least of these unspeakable deserts,
Romans, forget your fealty to me.   260
TITUS [*to Tamora*]. Now, madam, are you prisoner to
an emperor,
To him that, for your honour and your state,
Will use you nobly and your followers.
SATURNINUS. A goodly lady, trust me! Of the hue
That I would choose, were I to choose anew.
[*aloud*] Clear up, fair queen, that cloudy
countenance.
Though chance of war hath wrought this change
of cheer,
Thou com'st not to be made a scorn in Rome.
Princely shall be thy usage every way.

Rest on my word, and let not discontent   270
Daunt all your hopes. Madam, he comforts you
Can make you greater than the Queen of Goths.
Lavinia, you are not displeased with this?
LAVINIA. Not I, my lord, sith true nobility
Warrants these words in princely courtesy.
SATURNINUS. Thanks, sweet Lavinia. Romans, let us
go.
Ransomless here we set our prisoners free.
Proclaim our honours, lords, with trump and drum.
          *Flourish. Saturninus courts Tamora
                                in dumb show*
BASSIANUS [*seizing Lavinia*]. Lord Titus, by your leave,
this maid is mine.
TITUS. How, sir! are you in earnest then, my lord?   280
BASSIANUS. Ay, noble Titus, and resolved withal
To do myself this reason and this right.
MARCUS. 'Suum cuique' is our Roman justice.
This prince in justice seizeth but his own.
LUCIUS. And that he will, and shall, if Lucius live.
TITUS. Traitors, avaunt! Where is the
emperor's guard?
Treason, my lord! Lavinia is surprised!
SATURNINUS. Surprised! by whom?
BASSIANUS.   By him that justly may
Bear his betrothed from all the world away.
MUTIUS. Brothers, help to convey her hence away,   290
And with my sword I'll keep this door safe.

*Marcus, Bassianus and the brothers Lucius, Quintus, and
Martius leave with Lavinia*

TITUS. Follow, my lord, and I'll soon bring her back.

*Saturninus, Tamora, and her sons go up into the Capitol
with Aaron*

MUTIUS. My lord, you pass not here.
TITUS.   What, villain boy!
Barr'st me my way in Rome?   *They fight*
MUTIUS [*falling*].   Help, Lucius, help!

Lucius returns

LUCIUS. My lord, you are unjust; and more than so,
In wrongful quarrel you have slain your son.
TITUS. Nor thou, nor he, are any sons of mine:
My sons would never so dishonour me.
Traitor, restore Lavinia to the emperor.
LUCIUS. Dead if you will, but not to be his wife,   300
That is another's lawful promised love.   *He goes*

*Enter aloft the Emperor with Tamora and her two sons and
Aaron the Moor*

SATURNINUS. No, Titus, no, the emperor needs her
not,
Not her, nor thee, nor any of thy stock:
I'll trust by leisure him that mocks me once,
Thee never, nor thy traitorous haughty sons,
Confederates all thus to dishonour me.
Was none in Rome to make a stale
But Saturnine? Full well, Andronicus,
Agree the deeds with that proud brag of thine,
That saidst, I begged the empire at thy hands.   310
TITUS. O monstrous! what reproachful words are
these?
SATURNINUS. But go thy ways, go, give that changing
piece
To him that flourished for her with his sword:

A valiant son-in-law thou shalt enjoy,
One fit to bandy with thy lawless sons,
To ruffle in the commonwealth of Rome.
TITUS. These words are razors to my wounded heart.
SATURNINUS. And therefore, lovely Tamora, Queen of
    Goths,
    That like the stately Phœbe 'mongst her nymphs
    Dost overshine the gallant'st dames of Rome,   320
    If thou be pleased with this my sudden choice,
    Behold, I choose thee, Tamora, for my bride,
    And will create thee emperess of Rome.
    Speak, Queen of Goths, dost thou applaud my
    choice?
    And here I swear by all the Roman Gods,
    Sith priest and holy water are so near,
    And tapers burn so bright, and every thing
    In readiness for Hymenæus stand,
    I will not re-salute the streets of Rome,
    Or climb my palace, till from forth this place   330
    I lead espoused my bride along with me.
TAMORA. And here in sight of heaven to Rome I
    swear,
    If Saturnine advance the Queen of Goths,
    She will a handmaid be to his desires,
    A loving nurse, a mother to his youth.
SATURNINUS. Ascend, fair queen, Pantheon. Lords,
    accompany
    Your noble emperor and his lovely bride,
    Sent by the heavens for Prince Saturnine,
    Whose wisdom hath her fortune conqueréd.
    There shall we consummate our spousal rites.   340
                    They go within
TITUS. I am not bid to wait upon this bride.
    Titus, when wert thou wont to walk alone,
    Dishonoured thus and challengéd of wrongs?

Re-enter Marcus, Lucius, Quintus, and Martius

MARTIUS. O Titus, see, O, see, what thou hast done!
    In a bad quarrel slain a virtuous son.
TITUS. No, foolish tribune, no; no son of mine,
    Nor thou, nor these, confederates in the deed
    That hath dishonoured all our family,
    Unworthy brother, and unworthy sons!
LUCIUS. But let us give him burial as becomes;   350
    Give Mutius burial with our bretheren.
TITUS. Traitors, away! he rests not in this tomb:
    This monument five hundred years hath stood,
    Which I have sumptuously re-edified:
    Here none but soldiers and Rome's servitors
    Repose in fame; none basely slain in brawls.
    Bury him where you can, he comes not here.
MARCUS. My lord, this is impiety in you.
    My nephew Mutius' deeds do plead for him,
    He must be buried with his bretheren.   360
QUINTUS, MARTIUS. And shall, or him we will
    accompany.
TITUS. And shall? what villain was it spake that word?
QUINTUS. He that would vouch it in any place but
    here.
TITUS. What, would you bury him in my despite?
MARCUS. No, noble Titus, but entreat of thee
    To pardon Mutius and to bury him.
TITUS. Marcus, even thou hast struck upon my crest,
    And with these boys mine honour thou hast
    wounded.
    My foes I do repute you every one,

So trouble me no more, but get you gone.   370
MARTIUS. He is not with himself, let us withdraw.
QUINTUS. Not I, till Mutius' bones be buried.
              The brother and the sons kneel
MARCUS. Brother, for in that name doth nature
    plead,—
QUINTUS. Father, and in that name doth nature
    speak,—
TITUS. Speak thou no more, if all the rest will speed.
MARCUS. Renownéd Titus, more than half my soul
LUCIUS. Dear father, soul and substance of us all—
MARCUS. Suffer thy brother Marcus to inter
    His noble nephew here in virtue's nest,
    That died in honour and Lavinia's cause.   380
    Thou art a Roman, be not barbarous:
    The Greeks upon advice did bury Ajax
    That slew himself; and wise Laertes' son
    Did graciously plead for his funerals:
    Let not young Mutius then, that was thy joy,
    Be barred his entrance here.
TITUS.   Rise, Marcus, rise.
    The dismal'st day is this that e'er I saw,
    To be dishonoured by my sons in Rome!
    Well, bury him, and bury me the next.

They put him in the tomb

LUCIUS. There lie thy bones, sweet Mutius, with thy
    friends,   390
    Till we with trophies do adorn thy tomb.

They all kneel and say

ALL. No man shed tears for noble Mutius,
    He lives in fame that died in virtue's cause.
MARCUS. My lord, to step out of these dreary dumps,
    How comes it that the subtle Queen of Goths
    Is of a sudden thus advanced in Rome?
TITUS. I know not, Marcus, but I know it is,
    (Whether by device or no, the heavens can tell.)
    Is she not then beholding to the man
    That brought her for this high good turn so far?   400
    Yes, and will nobly him remunerate.

*Re-enter, from one side, Saturninus attended, Tamora,
Demetrius, Chiron, and Aaron; from the other, Bassianus,
Lavinia, with others*

SATURNINUS. So Bassianus, you have played your
    prize:
    God give you joy, sir, of your gallant bride!
BASSIANUS. And you of yours, my lord! I say no more,
    Nor wish no less, and so I take my leave.
SATURNINUS. Traitor, if Rome have law, or we have
    power,
    Thou and thy faction shall repent this rape.
BASSIANUS. Rape, call you it, my lord, to seize my
    own,
    My true-betrothéd love, and now my wife?
    But let the laws of Rome determine all,   410
    Meanwhile am I possessed of that is mine.
SATURNINUS. 'Tis good, sir; you are very short with us,
    But if we live we'll be as sharp with you.
BASSIANUS. My lord, what I have done, as best I may
    Answer I must, and shall do with my life.
    Only thus much I give your grace to know—
    By all the duties that I owe to Rome,
    This noble gentleman, Lord Titus here,
    Is in opinion and in honour wronged;

That in the rescue of Lavinia
With his own hand did slay his youngest son,
In zeal to you and highly moved to wrath
To be controlled in that he frankly gave.
Receive him then to favour, Saturnine,
That hath expressed himself in all his deeds
A father and a friend to thee and Rome.
TITUS. Prince Bassianus, leave to plead my deeds,
'Tis thou and those that have dishonoured me.
Rome and the righteous heavens be my judge,
How I have loved and honoured Saturnine!   430
TAMORA. My worthy lord, if ever Tamora
Were gracious in those princely eyes of thine,
Then hear me speak indifferently for all;
And at my suit, sweet, pardon what is past.
SATURNINUS. What, madam! be dishonoured openly,
And basely put it up without revenge?
TAMORA. Not so, my lord, the gods of Rome forfend
I should be author to dishonour you!
But on mine honour dare I undertake
For good Lord Titus' innocence in all,   440
Whose fury not dissembled speaks his griefs:
Then at my suit look graciously on him,
Lose not so noble a friend on vain suppose,
Nor with sour looks afflict his gentle heart.
[Aside] My lord, be ruled by me, be won at last,
Dissemble all your griefs and discontents—
You are but newly planted in your throne—
Lest then the people, and patricians too,
Upon a just survey, take Titus' part,
And so supplant you for ingratitude,   450
Which Rome reputes to be a heinous sin.
Yield at entreats: and then let me alone,
I'll find a day to massacre them all,
And raze their faction and their family,
The cruel father and his traitorous sons,
To whom I suéd for my dear son's life;
And make them know what 'tis to let a queen
Kneel in the streets and beg for grace in vain.
[Aloud] Come, come, sweet emperor—come,
    Andronicus—
Take up this good old man, and cheer the heart   460
That dies in tempest of thy angry frown.
SATURNINUS. Rise, Titus, rise, my empress hath
    prevailed.
TITUS. I thank your majesty, and her, my lord.
These words, these looks, infuse new life in me.
TAMORA. Titus, I am incorporate in Rome,
A Roman now adopted happily,
And must advise the emperor for his good.
This day all quarrels die, Andronicus.
And let it be mine honour, good my lord,
That I have reconciled your friends and you.
For you, Prince Bassianus, I have passed   470
My word and promise to the emperor,
That you will be more mild and tractable.
And fear not, lords, and you, Lavinia;
By my advice, all humbled on your knees,
                                            They kneel
You shall ask pardon of his majesty.
LUCIUS. We do, and vow to heaven, and to his
    highness,
That what we did was mildly as we might,
Tend'ring our sister's honour and our own.
MARCUS. That on mine honour here do I protest.   480
SATURNINUS. Away, and talk not, trouble us no more.

TAMORA. Nay, nay, sweet emperor, we must all be
    friends.
The tribune and his nephews kneel for grace.
I will not be denied. Sweet heart, look back.
SATURNINUS. Marcus, for thy sake, and thy brother's
    here,
And at my lovely Tamora's entreats,
I do remit these young men's heinous faults.
Stand up.
Lavinia, though you left me like a churl,
I found a friend, and sure as death I swore   490
I would not part a bachelor from the priest.
Come, if the emperor's court can feast two brides,
You are my guest, Lavinia, and your friends.
This day shall be a love-day, Tamora.
TITUS. To-morrow, an it please your majesty,
To hunt the panther and the hart with me,
With horn and hound we'll give your grace
    bonjour.
SATURNINUS. Be it so, Titus, and gramercy too.
                    They go with trumpets blowing.
                                        Aaron remains

ACT 2
Scene 1

AARON. Now climbeth Tamora Olympus' top,
Safe out of fortune's shot, and sits aloft,
Secure of thunder's crack or lightning flash,
Advanced above pale envy's threat'ning reach.
As when the golden sun salutes the morn,
And having gilt the ocean with his beams,
Gallops the zodiac in his glistering coach,
And overlooks the highest-peering hills;
So Tamora.
Upon her wit doth earthly honour wait,   10
And virtue stoops and trembles at her frown.
Then, Aaron, arm thy heart, and fit thy thoughts,
To mount aloft with thy imperial mistress,
And mount her pitch, whom thou in triumph long
Hast prisoner held, fettered in amorous chains,
And faster bound to Aaron's charming eyes,
Than is Prometheus tied to Caucasus.
Away with slavish weeds and servile thoughts!
I will be bright, and shine in pearl and gold,
To wait upon this new-made emperess.   20
To wait, said I? to wanton with this queen,
This goddess, this Semiramis, this nymph,
This siren, that will charm Rome's Saturnine,
And see his shipwreck and his commonweal's.
Holloa! what storm is this?   He steps aside

Enter Chiron and Demetrius, braving

DEMETRIUS. Chiron, thy years want wit, thy wits want
    edge,
And manners, to intrude where I am graced,
And may for aught thou know'st affected be.
CHIRON. Demetrius, thou dost overween in all,
And so in this, to bear me down with braves.   30
'Tis not the difference of a year or two
Makes me less gracious, or thee more fortunate;
I am as able and as fit as thou
To serve, and to deserve my mistress' grace,
And that my sword upon thee shall approve,
And plead my passions for Lavinia's love.

AARON [aside]. Clubs, clubs! these lovers will not keep
    the peace.
DEMETRIUS. Why, boy, although our mother,
    unadvised,
Gave you a dancing-rapier by your side,
Are you so desperate grown, to threat your friends? 40
Go to; have your lath glued within your sheath,
Till you know better how to handle it.
CHIRON. Meanwhile, sir, with the little skill I have,
Full well shalt thou perceive how much I dare.
DEMETRIUS. Ay, boy, grow ye so brave? They draw
AARON [comes forward].   Why, how now, lords!
So near the emperor's palace dare ye draw,
And maintain such a quarrel openly?
Full well I wot the ground of all this grudge.
I would not for a million of gold
The cause were known to them it most concerns, 50
Nor would your noble mother for much more
Be so dishonoured in the court of Rome.
For shame, put up.
DEMETRIUS.   Not I, till I have sheathed
My rapier in his bosom, and withal
Thrust those reproachful speeches down his throat,
That he hath breathed in my dishonour here.
CHIRON. For that I am prepared and full resolved,
Foul-spoken coward, that thund'rest with thy
    tongue
And with thy weapon nothing dar'st perform.
AARON. Away, I say!   60
Now, by the gods that warlike Goths adore,
This petty brabble will undo us all.
Why, lords, and think you not how dangerous
It is to jet upon a prince's right?
What, is Lavinia then become so loose,
Or Bassianus so degenerate,
That for her love such quarrels may be broached
Without controlment, justice, or revenge?
Young lords, beware! an should the empress know
This discord's ground, the music would not please. 70
CHIRON. I care not, I, knew she and all the world:
I love Lavinia more than all the world.
DEMETRIUS. Youngling, learn thou to make some
    meaner choice.
Lavinia is thine elder brother's hope.
AARON. Why, are ye mad? or know ye not, in Rome
How furious and impatient they be,
And cannot brook competitors in love?
I tell you, lords, you do but plot your deaths
By this device.
CHIRON.   Aaron, a thousand deaths
Would I propose to achieve her whom I love.   80
AARON. To achieve her how?
DEMETRIUS.   Why mak'st thou it so strange?
She is a woman, therefore may be wooed;
She is a woman, therefore may be won;
She is Lavinia, therefore must be loved.
What, man! more water glideth by the mill
Than wots the miller of, and easy it is
Of a cut loaf to steal a shive, we know:
Though Bassianus be the emperor's brother,
Better than he have worn Vulcan's badge.
AARON [aside]. Ay, and as good as Saturninus may. 90
DEMETRIUS. Then why should he despair that knows
    to court it
With words, fair looks, and liberality?
What, hast thou not full often struck a doe,

And borne her cleanly by the keeper's nose?
AARON. Why then, it seems, some certain snatch or so
Would serve your turns.
CHIRON.   Ay, so the turn were served.
DEMETRIUS. Aaron, thou hast hit it.
AARON.   Would you had hit it too,
Then should not we be tired with this ado.
Why, hark ye, hark ye! and are you such fools
To square for this? would it offend you then   100
That both should speed?
CHIRON.   Faith, not me.
DEMETRIUS. Nor me, so I were one.
AARON. For shame, be friends, and join for that you
    jar.
'Tis policy and stratagem must do
That you affect, and so must you resolve,
That what you cannot as you would achieve,
You must perforce accomplish as you may.
Take this of me, Lucrece was not more chaste
Than this Lavinia, Bassianus' love.
A speedier course than ling'ring languishment   110
Must we pursue, and I have found the path.
My lords, a solemn hunting is in hand,
There will the lovely Roman ladies troop:
The forest walks are wide and spacious,
And many unfrequented plots there are
Fitted by kind for rape and villainy:
Single you thither then this dainty doe,
And strike her home by force, if not by words:
This way, or not at all, stand you in hope.
Come, come, our empress, with her sacred wit   120
To villainy and vengeance consecrate,
Will we acquaint with all that we intend,
And she shall file our engines with advice,
That will not suffer you to square yourselves,
But to your wishes' height advance you both.
The emperor's court is like the House of Fame,
The palace full of tongues, of eyes, and ears:
The woods are ruthless, dreadful, deaf, and dull;
There speak, and strike, brave boys, and take your
    turns,
There serve your lust shadowed from heaven's eye, 130
And revel in Lavinia's treasury.
CHIRON. Thy counsel, lad, smells of no cowardice.
DEMETRIUS. 'Sit fas aut nefas', till I find the stream
To cool this heat, a charm to calm these fits,
'Per Styga, per manes vehor'.   They go

Scene 2: A glade in a forest near Rome

Enter Titus Andronicus with his three sons and Marcus,
making a noise with hounds and horns

TITUS. The hunt is up, the morn is bright and grey,
The fields are fragrant, and the woods are green:
Uncouple here, and let us make a bay,
And wake the emperor and his lovely bride,
And rouse the prince, and ring a hunter's peal,
That all the court may echo with the noise.
Sons, let it be your charge, as it is ours,
To attend the emperor's person carefully:
I have been troubled in my sleep this night,
But dawning day new comfort hath inspired.   10

Here a cry of hounds, and wind horns in a peal: then enter
Saturninus, Tamora, Bassianus, Lavinia, Chiron, Demetrius, and their attendants

Many good morrows to your majesty!
Madam, to you as many and as good!
I promiséd your grace a hunter's peal.
SATURNINUS. And you have rung it lustily, my lords,
Somewhat too early for new-married ladies.
BASSIANUS. Lavinia, how say you?
LAVINIA.   I say, no;
I have been broad awake two hours and more.
SATURNINUS. Come on then, horse and chariots let us
    have,
And to our sport. [to Tamora] Madam, now shall ye
    see
Our Roman hunting.
MARCUS.   I have dogs, my lord,   20
Will rouse the proudest panther in the chase,
And climb the highest promontory top.
TITUS. And I have horse will follow where the game
Makes way and run like swallows o'er the plain.
DEMETRIUS. Chiron, we hunt not, we, with horse nor
    hound,
But hope to pluck a dainty doe to ground.
                                          They go

                    Scene 3

Enter Aaron alone, with a bag of gold

AARON. He that had wit would think that I had none,
To bury so much gold under a tree,
And never after to inherit it.
Let him that thinks of me so abjectly
Know that this gold must coin a stratagem,
Which, cunningly effected, will beget
A very excellent piece of villainy:
And so repose, sweet gold, for their unrest,
That have their alms out of the empress' chest.
                                      Hides the gold

Enter Tamora alone to the Moor

TAMORA. My lovely Aaron, wherefore look'st thou
    sad,   10
When every thing doth make a gleeful boast?
The birds chaunt melody on every bush,
The snake lies rolléd in the cheerful sun,
The green leaves quiver with the cooling wind,
And make a chequered shadow on the ground:
Under their sweet shade, Aaron, let us sit,
And whilst the babbling echo mocks the hounds,
Replying shrilly to the well-tuned horns,
As if a double hunt were heard at once,
Let us sit down and mark their yellowing noise: 20
And after conflict such as was supposed
The wandering prince and Dido once enjoyed,
When with a happy storm they were surprised,
And curtained with a counsel-keeping cave,
We may, each wreathéd in the other's arms,
(Our pastimes done) possess a golden slumber,
Whiles hounds and horns and sweet melodious birds
Be unto us as is a nurse's song
Of lullaby to bring her babe asleep.
AARON. Madam, though Venus govern your desires,   30
Saturn is dominator over mine:
What signifies my deadly-standing eye,
My silence and my cloudy melancholy,
My fleece of woolly hair that now uncurls
Even as an adder when she doth unroll
To do some fatal execution?

No, madam, these are no venereal signs:
Vengeance is in my heart, death in my hand,
Blood and revenge are hammering in my head.
Hark, Tamora, the empress of my soul,   40
Which never hopes more heaven than rests in thee,
This is the day of doom for Bassianus:
His Philomel must lose her tongue to-day,
Thy sons make pillage of her chastity,
And wash their hands in Bassianus' blood.
Seest thou this letter? take it up, I pray thee,
And give the king this fatal-plotted scroll.
Now question me no more; we are espied;
Here comes a parcel of our hopeful booty,
Which dreads not yet their lives' destruction.   50

Enter Bassianus and Lavinia

TAMORA. Ah, my sweet Moor, sweeter to me than life!
AARON. No more, great empress, Bassianus comes.
Be cross with him, and I'll go fetch thy sons
To back thy quarrels whatsoe'er they be.
                                          He goes
BASSIANUS. Who have we here? Rome's royal
    emperess,
Unfurnished of her well-beseeming troop?
Or is it Dian, habited like her,
Who hath abandonéd her holy groves
To see the general hunting in this forest?
TAMORA. Saucy controller of my private steps!   60
Had I the power that some say Dian had,
Thy temples should be planted presently
With horns, as was Actæon's, and the hounds
Should drive upon thy new-transforméd limbs,
Unmannerly intruder as thou art!
LAVINIA. Under your patience, gentle emperess,
'Tis thought you have a goodly gift in horning,
And to be doubted that your Moor and you
Are singled forth to try experiments:
Jove shield your husband from his hounds to-day!   70
'Tis pity they should take him for a stag.
BASSIANUS. Believe me, queen, your swarth
    Cimmerian
Doth make your honour of his body's hue,
Spotted, detested, and abominable.
Why are you séquest'réd from all your train,
Dismounted from your snow-white goodly steed,
And wandered hither to an obscure plot,
Accompanied but with a barbarous Moor,
If foul desire had not conducted you?
LAVINIA. And, being intercepted in your sport,   80
Great reason that my noble lord be rated
For sauciness. I pray you, let us hence,
And let her joy her raven-coloured love,
This valley fits the purpose passing well.
BASSIANUS. The king my brother shall have note of
    this.
LAVINIA. Ay, for these slips have made him noted long.
Good king, to be so mightily abused!
TAMORA. Why have I patience to endure all this?

Enter Chiron and Demetrius

DEMETRIUS. How now, dear sovereign, and our
    gracious mother,
Why doth your highness look so pale and wan?   90
TAMORA. Have I not reason, think you, to look pale?
These two have ticed me hither to this place,
A barren detested vale, you see it is;

The trees, though summer, yet forlorn and lean,
O'ercome with moss and baleful mistletoe:
Here never shines the sun; here nothing breeds,
Unless the nightly owl or fatal raven:
And when they showed me this abhorréd pit,
They told me, here, at dead time of the night
A thousand fiends, a thousand hissing snakes,   100
Ten thousand swelling toads, as many urchins,
Would make such fearful and confuséd cries,
As any mortal body hearing it
Should straight fall mad, or else die suddenly.
No sooner had they told this hellish tale,
But straight they told me they would bind me here
Unto the body of a dismal yew,
And leave me to this miserable death.
And then they called me foul adulteress,
Lascivious Goth, and all the bitterest terms   110
That ever ear did hear to such effect.
And, had you not by wondrous fortune come,
This vengeance on me had they executed:
Revenge it, as you love your mother's life,
Or be ye not henceforth my children called.

DEMETRIUS. This is a witness that I am thy son.
                                        Stabs Bassianus

CHIRON. And this for me, struck home to show my
    strength.   *Stabbing him likewise*

LAVINIA. Ay come, Semiramis, nay, barbarous
    Tamora!
For no name fits thy nature but thy own!

TAMORA. Give me the poniard! you shall know, my
    boys,   120
Your mother's hand shall right your mother's
    wrong.

DEMETRIUS. Stay, madam, here is more belongs to her.
First thrash the corn, then after burn the straw:
This minion stood upon her chastity,
Upon her nuptial vow, her loyalty,
And with that painted hope she braves your
    mightiness:
And shall she carry this unto her grave?

CHIRON. An if she do, I would I were an eunuch.
Drag hence her husband to some secret hole,
And make his dead trunk pillow to our lust.   130

TAMORA. But when ye have the honey ye desire,
Let not this wasp outlive, us both to sting.

CHIRON. I warrant you, madam, we will make that
    sure:
Come, mistress, now perforce we will enjoy
That nice-preservéd honesty of yours.

LAVINIA. O Tamora! thou bear'st a woman's face—

TAMORA. I will not hear her speak, away with her.

LAVINIA. Sweet lords, entreat her hear me but a word.

DEMETRIUS. Listen, fair madam, let it be your glory
To see her tears, but be your heart to them   140
As unrelenting flint to drops of rain.

LAVINIA. When did the tiger's young ones teach the
    dam?
O, do not learn her wrath; she taught it thee.
The milk thou suck'dst from her did turn to marble,
Even at thy teat thou hadst thy tyranny.
Yet every mother breeds not sons alike,
                                        To Chiron
Do thou entreat her show a woman's pity.

CHIRON. What! wouldst thou have me prove myself
    a bastard?

LAVINIA. 'Tis true; the raven doth not hatch a lark:

Yet I have heard—O could I find it now!—   150
The lion, moved with pity, did endure
To have his princely paws pared all away:
Some say that ravens foster forlorn children,
The whilst their own birds famish in their nests:
O, be to me, though thy hard heart say no,
Nothing so kind but something pitiful!

TAMORA. I know not what it means, away with her!

LAVINIA. O, let me teach thee for my father's sake,
That gave thee life when well he might have slain
    thee.
Be not obdurate, open thy deaf ears.   160

TAMORA. Hadst thou in person ne'er offended me,
Even for his sake am I pitiless.
Remember, boys, I poured forth tears in vain
To save your brother from the sacrifice,
But fierce Andronicus would not relent.
Therefore away with her, and use her as you will;
The worse to her, the better loved of me.

LAVINIA. O Tamora, be called a gentle queen,
And with thine own hands kill me in this place!
For 'tis not life that I have begged so long,   170
Poor I was slain when Bassianus died.

TAMORA. What begg'st thou then? fond woman, let
    me go.

LAVINIA. 'Tis present death I beg, and one thing more
That womanhood denies my tongue to tell.
O, keep me from their worse than killing lust,
And tumble me into some loathsome pit,
Where never man's eye may behold my body
Do this, and be a charitable murderer.

TAMORA. So should I rob my sweet sons of their fee.
No, let them satisfy their lust on her.   180

DEMETRIUS. Away! for thou hast staid us here too long.

LAVINIA. No grace? no womanhood? Ah beastly
    creature!
The blot and enemy to our general name!
Confusion fall——

CHIRON. Nay, then I'll stop your mouth. Bring thou
    her husband.
This is the hole where Aaron bid us hide him.

*Demetrius heaves the corpse into a pit; the two then go off
dragging Lavinia between them*

TAMORA. Farewell, my sons, see that you make her
    sure.
Ne'er let my heart know merry cheer indeed
Till all the Andronici be made away.
Now will I hence to seek my lovely Moor,
And let my spleenful sons this trull deflower.   190
                                        She goes

Enter Aaron with Quintus and Martius

AARON. Come on, my lords, the better foot before!
Straight will I bring you to the loathsome pit
Where I espied the panther fast asleep.

QUINTUS. My sight is very dull, whate'er it bodes.

MARTIUS. And mine, I promise you: were it not for
    shame,
Well could I leave our sport to sleep awhile.
                                        He falls into the pit

QUINTUS. What, art thou fallen? What subtle hole is
    this,
Whose mouth is covered with rude-growing briers,
Upon whose leaves are drops of new-shed blood   200
As fresh as morning dew distilled on flowers?

A very fatal place it seems to me.
Speak, brother, hast thou hurt thee with the fall?
MARTIUS. O, brother, with the dismall'st object hurt
That ever eye with sight made heart lament.
AARON [aside]. Now will I fetch the king to find them
here,
That he thereby may have a likely guess,
How these were they that made away his brother.
                                          He goes
MARTIUS. Why dost not comfort me, and help me out
From this unhallowed and blood-stained hole?   210
QUINTUS. I am surprised with an uncouth fear,
A chilling sweat o'er-runs my trembling joints,
My heart suspects more than mine eye can see.
MARTIUS. To prove thou hast a true-divining heart,
Aaron and thou look down into this den,
And see a fearful sight of blood and death.
QUINTUS. Aaron is gone, and my compassionate heart
Will not permit mine eyes once to behold
The thing whereat it trembles by surmise:
O, tell me who it is, for ne'er till now   220
Was I a child to fear I know not what.
MARTIUS. Lord Bassianus lies berayed in blood,
All on a heap, like to a slaughtered lamb,
In this detested, dark, blood-drinking pit.
QUINTUS. If it be dark, how dost thou know 'tis he?
MARTIUS. Upon his bloody finger he doth wear
A precious ring, that lightens all this hole,
Which, like a taper in some monument,
Doth shine upon the dead man's earthy cheeks,
And shows the ragged entrails of this pit: 230
So pale did shine the moon on Pyramus,
When he by night lay bathed in maiden blood.
O brother, help me with thy fainting hand—
If fear hath made thee faint, as me it hath—
Out of this fell devouring receptacle,
As hateful as Cocytus' misty mouth.
QUINTUS. Reach me thy hand, that I may help thee
out;
Or, wanting strength to do thee so much good,
I may be plucked into the swallowing womb
Of this deep pit, poor Bassianus' grave.   240
I have no strength to pluck thee to the brink.
MARTIUS. Nor I no strength to climb without thy help.
QUINTUS. Thy hand once more, I will not loose again,
Till thou art here aloft or I below:
Thou canst not come to me, I come to thee.
                                          He falls in

Enter the Emperor and Aaron the Moor

SATURNINUS. Along with me! I'll see what hole is here,
And what he is that now is leaped into it.
Say, who art thou, that lately didst descend
Into this gaping hollow of the earth?
MARTIUS. The unhappy sons of old Andronicus,   250
Brought hither in a most unlucky hour,
To find thy brother Bassianus dead.
SATURNINUS. My brother dead! I know thou dost but
jest;
He and his lady both are at the lodge,
Upon the north side of this pleasant chase;
'Tis not an hour since I left them there.
MARTIUS. We know not where you left them all alive,
But, out alas! here have we found him dead.

Enter Tamora, Andronicus, and Lucius

TAMORA. Where is my lord the king?
SATURNINUS. Here, Tamora, though griped with
killing grief.   260
TAMORA. Where is thy brother, Bassianus?
SATURNINUS. Now to the bottom dost thou search my
wound;
Poor Bassianus here lies murderéd.
TAMORA. Then all too late I bring this fatal writ,
The complot of this timeless tragedy;
And wonder greatly that man's face can fold
In pleasing smiles such murderous tyranny.
                          She giveth Saturnine a letter
SATURNINUS [reads]. 'An if we miss to meet him
handsomely—
Sweet huntsman, Bassianus 'tis we mean—
Do thou so much as dig the grave for him.   270
Thou know'st our meaning. Look for thy reward
Among the nettles at the elder tree,
Which overshades the mouth of that same pit
Where we decreed to bury Bassianus.
Do this and purchase us thy lasting friends.'
O, Tamora! was ever heard the like?
This is the pit, and this the elder-tree.
Look, sirs, if you can find the huntsman out
That should have murdered Bassianus here.
AARON. My gracious lord, here is the bag of gold.   280
SATURNINUS [to Titus]. Two of thy whelps, fell curs
of bloody kind,
Have here bereft my brother of his life.
Sirs, drag them from the pit unto the prison,
There let them bide until we have devised
Some never-heard-of torturing pain for them.
TAMORA. What, are they in this pit? O wondrous
thing!
How easily murder is discovered!
TITUS. High emperor, upon my feeble knee
I beg this boon, with tears not lightly shed,
That this fell fault of my accurséd sons,   290
Acccurséd, if the fault be proved in them—
SATURNINUS. If it be proved! you see, it is apparent.
Who found this letter? Tamora, was it you?
TAMORA. Andronicus himself did take it up.
TITUS. I did, my lord, yet let me be their bail,
For by my father's reverend tomb I vow
They shall be ready at your highness' will,
To answer their suspicion with their lives.
SATURNINUS. Thou shalt not bail them, see thou follow
me.
Some bring the murdered body, some the
murderers,   300
Let them not speak a word, the guilt is plain,
For by my soul were there worse end than death,
That end upon them should be executed.
TAMORA. Andronicus, I will entreat the king,
Fear not thy sons, they shall do well enough.
TITUS. Come, Lucius, come, stay not to talk with
them.   *They go*

Scene 4

*Enter the Empress' sons with Lavinia, her hands cut off,
and her tongue cut out, and ravished*

DEMETRIUS. So, now go tell, an if thy tongue can
speak,
Who 'twas that cut thy tongue and ravished thee.

CHIRON. Write down thy mind, bewray thy meaning
    so,
  And, if thy stumps will let thee, play the scribe.
DEMETRIUS. See, how with signs and tokens she can
    scrowl.
CHIRON. Go home, call for sweet water, wash thy
    hands.
DEMETRIUS. She hath no tongue to call nor hands to
    wash,
  And so let's leave her to her silent walks.
CHIRON. An 'twere my cause, I should go hang myself.
DEMETRIUS. If thou hadst hands to help thee knit the
    cord.   *They go* 10

Enter Marcus from hunting

MARCUS. Who is this? my niece, that flies away so fast!
  Cousin, a word, where is your husband?
  If I do dream, would all my wealth would wake me!
  If I do wake, some planet strike me down,
  That I may slumber an eternal sleep!
  Speak, gentle niece, what stern ungentle hands
  Hath lopped and hewed and made thy body bare
  Of her two branches? those sweet ornaments,
  Whose circling shadows kings have sought to sleep
    in,
  And might not gain so great a happiness   20
  As half thy love? Why dost not speak to me?
  Alas, a crimson river of warm blood,
  Like to a bubbling fountain stirred with wind,
  Doth rise and fall between thy roséd lips,
  Coming and going with thy honey breath.
  But, sure, some Tereus hath deflowered thee,
  And, lest thou shouldst detect him, cut thy tongue.
  Ah, now thou turn'st away thy face for shame!
  And, notwithstanding all this loss of blood,
  As from a conduit with three issuing spouts,   30
  Yet do thy cheeks look red as Titan's face
  Blushing to be encountered with a cloud.
  Shall I speak for thee? shall I say 'tis so?
  O, that I knew thy heart, and knew the beast,
  That I might rail at him to ease my mind!
  Sorrow concealéd, like an oven stopped,
  Doth burn the heart to cinders where it is.
  Fair Philomel, why she but lost her tongue,
  And in a tedious sampler sewed her mind:
  But lovely niece, that mean is cut from thee;   40
  A craftier Tereus, cousin, hast thou met,
  And he hath cut those pretty fingers off,
  That could have better sewed than Philomel.
  O, had the monster seen those lily hands
  Tremble like aspen leaves upon a lute,
  And make the silken strings delight to kiss them,
  He would not then have touched them for his life!
  Or, had he heard the heavenly harmony
  Which that sweet tongue hath made,
  He would have dropped his knife, and fell asleep 50
  As Cerberus at the Thracian poet's feet.
  Come, let us go and make thy father blind,
  For such a sight will blind a father's eye.
  One hour's storm will drown the fragrant meads,
  What will whole months of tears thy father's eyes?
  Do not draw back, for we will mourn with thee:
  O, could our mourning ease thy misery!
                            They go

ACT 3
Scene 1

Enter the Judges and Senators with Titus' two sons bound,
passing on to the palace of execution, and Titus going before,
pleading

TITUS. Hear me, grave fathers! noble tribunes, stay!
  For pity of mine age, whose youth was spent
  In dangerous wars, whilst you securely slept;
  For all my blood in Rome's great quarrel shed,
  For all the frosty nights that I have watched,
  And for these bitter tears, which now you see
  Filling the agéd wrinkles in my cheeks,
  Be pitiful to my condemnéd sons,
  Whose souls are not corrupted as 'tis thought.
  For two and twenty sons I never wept,   10
  Because they died in honour's lofty bed;

Andronicus lieth down and the Judges pass by him

  For these, tribunes, in the dust I write
  My heart's deep languor and my soul's sad tears:
  Let my tears stanch the earth's dry appetite;
  My sons' sweet blood will make it shame and blush.
  O earth, I will befriend thee more with rain,
  That shall distil from these two ancient urns,
  Than youthful April shall with all his showers:
  In summer's drought I'll drop upon thee still,
  In winter with warm tears I'll melt the snow,   20
  And keep eternal spring-time on thy face,
  So thou refuse to drink my dear sons' blood.

Enter Lucius, with his weapon drawn

  O reverend tribunes! O gentle agéd men!
  Unbind my sons, reverse the doom of death,
  And let me say, that never wept before,
  My tears are now prevailing orators.
LUCIUS. O noble father, you lament in vain,
  The tribunes hear you not, no man is by,
  And you recount your sorrows to a stone.
TITUS. Ah, Lucius, for thy brothers let me plead.   30
  Grave tribunes, once more I entreat of you.
LUCIUS. My gracious lord, no tribune hears you speak.
TITUS. Why, 'tis no matter, man, if they did hear
  They would not mark me, if they did mark
  They would not pity me, yet plead I must,
  And bootless unto them . . .
  Therefore I tell my sorrows to the stones,
  Who though they cannot answer my distress,
  Yet in some sort they are better than the tribunes,
  For that they will not intercept my tale: 40
  When I do weep, they humbly at my feet
  Receive my tears, and seem to weep with me;
  And were they but attiréd in grave weeds,
  Rome could afford no tribunes like to these.
  A stone is soft as wax, tribunes' more hard than
    stones:
  A stone is silent and offendeth not,
  And tribunes with their tongues doom men to
    death.   *Rises*
  But wherefore stand'st thou with thy weapon
    drawn?
LUCIUS. To rescue my two brothers from their death:
  For which attempt the judges have pronounced 50
  My everlasting doom of banishment.
TITUS. O happy man! they have befriended thee:
  Why foolish Lucius, dost thou not perceive

That Rome is but a wilderness of tigers?
Tigers must prey, and Rome affords no prey
But me and mine. How happy art thou then,
From these devourers to be banishéd!
But who comes with our brother Marcus here?

Enter Marcus with Lavinia

MARCUS. Titus, prepare thy agéd eyes to weep,
  Or if not so, thy noble heart to break: 60
I bring consuming sorrow to thine age.
TITUS. Will it consume me? let me see it then.
MARCUS. This was thy daughter.
TITUS.   Why, Marcus, so she is.
LUCIUS. Ah me! this object kills me!
TITUS. Faint-hearted boy, arise, and look upon her.
  Speak, Lavinia, what accurséd hand
Hath made thee handless in thy father's sight?
What fool hath added water to the sea,
Or brought a faggot to bright-burning Troy?
My grief was at the height before thou cam'st,   70
And now like Nilus it disdaineth bounds.
Give me a sword, I'll chop off my hands too,
For they have fought for Rome, and all in vain;
And they have nursed this woe, in feeding life;
In bootless prayer have they been held up,
And they have served me to effectless use.
Now all the service I require of them
Is, that the one will help to cut the other.
'Tis well, Lavinia, that thou hast no hands,
For hands to do Rome service is but vain.   80
LUCIUS. Speak, gentle sister, who hath martyred thee?
MARCUS. O, that delightful engine of her thoughts,
  That blabbed them with such pleasing eloquence,
Is torn from forth that pretty hollow cage,
Where like a sweet melodious bird it sung
Sweet varied notes, enchanting every ear!
LUCIUS. O, say thou for her, who hath done this
  deed?
MARCUS. O, thus I found her, straying in the park,
  Seeking to hide herself, as doth the deer
That hath received some unrecuring wound.   90
TITUS. It was my dear, and he that wounded her
  Hath hurt me more than had he killed me dead:
For now I stand as one upon a rock,
Environed with a wilderness of sea,
Who marks the waxing tide grow wave by wave,
Expecting ever when some envious surge
Will in his brinish bowels swallow him.
This way to death my wretched sons are gone,
Here stands my other son, a banished man,
And here my brother weeping at my woes: 100
But that which gives my soul the greatest
Is dear Lavinia, dearer than my soul.
Had I but seen thy picture in this plight,
It would have madded me: what shall I do
Now I behold thy lively body so?
Thou hast no hands to wipe away thy tears,
Nor tongue to tell me who hath martyred thee:
Thy husband he is dead, and for his death
Thy brothers are condemned, and dead by this.
Look, Marcus! ah, son Lucius, look on her!   110
When I did name her brothers, then fresh tears
Stood on her cheeks, as doth the honey-dew
Upon a gathered lily almost withered.
MARCUS. Perchance she weeps because they killed her
  husband,

Perchance because she knows them innocent.
TITUS. If they did kill thy husband, then be
  joyful,
Because the law hath ta'en revenge on them.
No, no, they would not do so foul a deed,
Witness the sorrow that their sister makes.
Gentle Lavinia, let me kiss thy lips,   120
Or make some sign how I may do thee ease:
Shall thy good uncle, and thy brother Lucius,
And thou, and I, sit round about some fountain,
Looking all downwards, to behold our cheeks
How they are stained, like meadows yet not dry
With miry slime left on them by a flood?
And in the fountain shall we gaze so long
Till the fresh taste be taken from that clearness,
And made a brine-pit with our bitter tears?
Or shall we cut away our hands, like thine?   130
Or shall we bite our tongues, and in dumb shows
Pass the remainder of our hateful days?
What shall we do? let us, that have our tongues,
Plot some device of further misery,
To make us wondered at in time to come.
LUCIUS. Sweet father, cease your tears, for at your grief
  See how my wretched sister sobs and weeps.
MARCUS. Patience, dear niece. Good Titus, dry thine
  eyes.
TITUS. Ah, Marcus, Marcus! brother, well I wot
  Thy napkin cannot drink a tear of mine,   140
For thou, poor man, hast drowned it with thine
  own.
LUCIUS. Ah, my Lavinia, I will wipe thy cheeks.
TITUS. Mark, Marcus, mark! I understand her signs:
  Had she a tongue to speak, now would she say
That to her brother which I said to thee:
His napkin, with his true tears all bewet,
Can do no service on her sorrowful cheeks.
O, what a sympathy of woe is this!
As far from help as Limbo is from bliss!

Enter Aaron the Moor alone

AARON. Titus Andronicus, my lord the emperor   150
  Sends thee this word, that, if thou love thy sons,
Let Marcus, Lucius, or thyself, old Titus,
Or any one of you, chop off your hand,
And send it to the king: he for the same
Will send thee hither both thy sons alive,
And that shall be the ransom for their fault.
TITUS. O, gracious emperor! O, gentle Aaron!
  Did ever raven sing so like a lark,
That gives sweet tidings of the sun's uprise?
With all my heart, I'll send the emperor   160
My hand;
Good Aaron, wilt thou help to chop it off?
LUCIUS. Stay, father! for that noble hand of thine,
  That hath thrown down so many enemies,
Shall not be sent: my hand will serve the turn.
My youth can better spare my blood than you,
And therefore mine shall save my brothers' lives.
MARCUS. Which of your hands hath not defended
  Rome,
And reared aloft the bloody battle-axe,
Writing destruction on the enemy's castle?   170
O, none of both but are of high desert:
My hand hath been but idle, let it serve
To ransom my two nephews from their death,
Then have I kept it to a worthy end.

AARON. Nay, come, agree whose hand shall go along,
  For fear they die before their pardon come.
MARCUS. My hand shall go.
LUCIUS.   By heaven, it shall not go.
TITUS. Sirs, strive no more; such withered herbs
      as these
  Are meet for plucking up, and therefore mine.
LUCIUS. Sweet father, if I shall be thought thy son,   180
  Let me redeem my brothers both from death.
MARCUS. And, for our father's sake and mother's care,
  Now let me show a brother's love to thee.
TITUS. Agree between you, I will spare my hand.
LUCIUS. Then I'll go fetch an axe.
MARCUS. But I will use the axe.
                          Lucius and Marcus go
TITUS. Come hither, Aaron. I'll deceive them both;
  Lend me thy hand, and I will give thee mine.
AARON. If that be called deceit, I will be honest,
  And never whilst I live deceive men so: 190
  But I'll deceive you in another sort,
  And that you'll say, ere half an hour pass.
                          He cuts off Titus' hand

Enter Lucius and Marcus again

TITUS. Now stay your strife, what shall be is
      dispatched.
  Good Aaron, give his majesty my hand,
  Tell him it was a hand that warded him
  From thousand dangers, bid him bury it—
  More hath it merited, that let it have:
  As for my sons, say I account of them
  As jewels purchased at an easy price,
  And yet dear too because I bought mine own.   200
AARON. I go, Andronicus, and for thy hand
  Look by and by to have thy sons with thee.
  [*Aside*] Their heads, I mean. O, how this villainy
  Doth fat me with the very thoughts of it!
  Let fools do good, and fair men call for grace,
  Aaron will have his soul black like his face.
                          He goes
TITUS. O, here I lift this one hand up to heaven,
  And bow this feeble ruin to the earth.
  If any power pities wretched tears,
  To that I call! [*to Lavinia*] What, wouldst thou
      kneel with me?   210
  Do then, dear heart, for heaven shall hear our
      prayers,
  Or with our sighs we'll breathe the welkin dim,
  And stain the sun with fog, as sometime clouds
  When they do hug him in their melting bosoms.
MARCUS. O brother, speak with possibility,
  And do not break into these deep extremes.
TITUS. Is not my sorrow deep, having no bottom?
  Then be my passions bottomless with them.
MARCUS. But yet let reason govern thy lament.
TITUS. If there were reason for these miseries,   220
  Then into limits could I bind my woes:
  When heaven doth weep, doth not the earth
      o'erflow?
  If the winds rage, doth not the sea wax mad,
  Threat'ning the welkin with his big-swoln face?
  And wilt thou have a reason for this coil?
  I am the sea; hark, how her sighs doth blow!
  She is the weeping welkin, I the earth:
  Then must my sea be movéd with her sighs,
  Then must my earth with her continual tears

Become a deluge, overflowed and drowned: 230
  For why? my bowels cannot hide her woes,
  But like a drunkard must I vomit them.
  Then give me leave, for losers will have leave
  To ease their stomachs with their bitter tongues.

Enter a Messenger, with two heads and a hand

MESSENGER. Worthy Andronicus, ill art thou repaid
  For that good hand thou sent'st the emperor:
  Here are the heads of thy two noble sons,
  And here's thy hand in scorn to thee sent back,
  Thy griefs their sports, thy resolution mocked:
  That woe is me to think upon thy woes,   240
  More than remembrance of my father's death.
                          He goes
MARCUS. Now let hot Ætna cool in Sicily,
  And be my heart an ever-burning hell!
  These miseries are more than may be borne!
  To weep with them that weep doth ease some deal,
  But sorrow flouted at is double death.
LUCIUS. Ah, that this sight should make so deep a
      wound,
  And yet detested life not shrink thereat!
  That ever death should let life bear his name,
  Where life hath no more interest but to breathe!   250
                          Lavinia kisses Titus
MARCUS. Alas, poor heart, that kiss is comfortless
  As frozen water to a starvéd snake.
TITUS. When will this fearful slumber have an end?
MARCUS. Now, farewell, flattery, die Andronicus,
  Thou dost not slumber, see thy two sons' heads,
  Thy warlike hand, thy mangled daughter here,
  Thy other banished son with this dear sight
  Struck pale and bloodless, and thy brother, I,
  Even like a stony image cold and numb.
  Ah! now no more will I control thy griefs: 260
  Rend off thy silver hair, thy other hand
  Gnawing with thy teeth, and be this dismal sight
  The closing up of our most wretched eyes:
  Now is a time to storm, why art thou still?
TITUS. Ha, ha, ha!
MARCUS. Why dost thou laugh? it fits not with this
      hour.
TITUS. Why, I have not another tear to shed;
  Besides, this sorrow is an enemy,
  And would usurp upon my wat'ry eyes,
  And make them blind with tributary tears;   270
  Then which way shall I find Revenge's Cave?
  For these two heads do seem to speak to me,
  And threat me I shall never come to bliss
  Till all these mischiefs be returned again,
  Even in their throats that hath committed them.
  Come, let me see what task I have to do.
  You heavy people, circle me about,
  That I may turn me to each one of you,
  And swear unto my soul to right your wrongs.
  The vow is made. Come, brother, take a head;   280
  And in this hand the other will I bear.
  And Lavinia, thou shalt be employed in this;
  Bear thou my hand, sweet wench, between thy
      teeth:
  As for thee, boy, go, get thee from my sight.
  Thou art an exile, and thou must not stay.
  Hie to the Goths, and raise an army there,
  And, if ye love me, as I think you do,
  Let's kiss and part, for we have much to do.

Titus departs with Marcus and Lavinia

LUCIUS. Farewell, Andronicus, my noble father,
The woefull'st man that ever lived in Rome! 290
Farewell, proud Rome! till Lucius come again,
He leaves his pledges dearer than his life:
Farewell, Lavinia, my noble sister,
O, would thou wert as thou tofore hast been!
But now nor Lucius nor Lavinia lives
But in oblivion and hateful griefs.
If Lucius live, he will requite your wrongs,
And make proud Saturnine and his empress
Beg at the gates, like Tarquin and his queen.
Now will I to the Goths and raise a power, 300
To be revenged on Rome and Saturnine.

He goes

Scene 2: *A room in Titus' house. A banquet set out*

Enter Titus, Marcus, Lavinia, and young Lucius

TITUS. So, so, now sit, and look you eat no more
Than will preserve just so much strength in us
As will revenge these bitter woes of ours.
Marcus, unknit that sorrow-wreathen knot:
Thy niece and I, poor creatures, want our hands,
And cannot passionate our tenfold grief
With folded arms. This poor right hand of mine
Is left to tyrannize upon my breast;
Who, when my heart all mad with misery
Beats in this hollow prison of my flesh, 10
Then thus I thump it down.
[*To Lavinia*] Thou map of woe, that thus dost talk
in signs,
When thy poor heart beats with outrageous beating,
Thou canst not strike it thus to make it still.
Wound it with sighing, girl, kill it with groans;
Or get some little knife between thy teeth,
And just against thy heart make thou a hole,
That all the tears that thy poor eyes let fall
May run into that sink, and soaking in
Drown the lamenting fool in sea-salt tears. 20
MARCUS. Fie, brother, fie! teach her not thus to lay
Such violent hands upon her tender life.
TITUS. How now! has sorrow made thee dote already?
Why, Marcus, no man should be mad but I.
What violent hands can she lay on her life!
Ah, wherefore dost thou urge the name of hands,
To bid Æneas tell the tale twice o'er,
How Troy was burnt and he made miserable?
O, handle not the theme, to talk of hands,
Lest we remember still that we have none. 30
Fie, fie, how franticly I square my talk,
As if we should forget we had no hands,
If Marcus did not name the word of hands!
Come, let's fall to; and, gentle girl, eat thou.
Here is no drink? Hark, Marcus, what she says—
I can interpret all her martyred signs—
She says she drinks no other drink but tears,
Brewed with her sorrows, meshed upon her cheeks.
Speechless complainer, I will learn thy thought;
In thy dumb action will I be as perfect 40
As begging hermits in their holy prayers:
Thou shalt not sigh, nor hold thy stumps to heaven,
Nor wink, nor nod, nor kneel, nor make a sign,
But I of these will wrest an alphabet,
And by still practice learn to know thy meaning.
BOY. Good grandsire, leave these bitter deep laments.

Make my aunt merry with some pleasing tale.
MARCUS. Alas, the tender boy, in passion moved,
Doth weep to see his grandsire's heaviness.
TITUS. Peace, tender sapling, thou art made of tears, 50
And tears will quickly melt thy life away.
Marcus strikes the dish with a knife
What dost thou strike at, Marcus, with thy knife?
MARCUS. At that that I have killed, my lord,—a fly.
TITUS. Out on thee, murderer! thou kill'st my heart;
Mine eyes are cloyed with view of tyranny:
A deed of death done on the innocent
Becomes not Titus' brother: get thee gone;
I see thou art not for my company.
MARCUS. Alas, my lord, I have but killed a fly.
TITUS. 'But!' How, if that fly had a father and mother? 60
How would he hang his slender gilded wings,
And buzz lamenting doings in the air!
Poor harmless fly,
That, with his pretty buzzing melody,
Came here to make us merry! and thou hast killed
him.
MARCUS. Pardon me, sir; it was a black ill-favoured fly,
Like to the empress' Moor. Therefore I killed him.
TITUS. O, O, O,
Then pardon me for reprehending thee,
For thou hast done a charitable deed. 70
Give me thy knife, I will insult on him,
Flattering myself, as if it were the Moor,
Come hither purposely to poison me.
There's for thyself, and that's for Tamora.
Ah, sirrah!
Yet I think we are not brought so low,
But that between us we can kill a fly
That comes in likeness of a coal-black Moor.
MARCUS. Alas, poor man! grief has so wrought on him,
He takes false shadows for true substances. 80
TITUS. Come, take away. Lavinia, go with me:
I'll to thy closet, and go read with thee
Sad stories chancéd in the times of old.
Come, boy, and go with me: thy sight is young,
And thou shalt read when mine begins to dazzle.

They go

ACT 4

Scene 1: *Before Titus' house*

*Enter Lucius' son and Lavinia running after him; and the
boy flies from her with his books under his arm. Then enter
Titus and Marcus*

BOY. Help, grandsire, help! my aunt Lavinia
Follows me everywhere, I know not why.
Good uncle Marcus, see how swift she comes.
Alas, sweet aunt, I know not what you mean.
MARCUS. Stand by me, Lucius, do not fear thine aunt.
TITUS. She loves thee, boy, too well to do thee harm.
BOY. Ay, when my father was in Rome she did.
MARCUS. What means my niece Lavinia by these signs?
TITUS. Fear her not, Lucius. Somewhat doth she mean.
See, Lucius, see, how much she makes of thee: 10
Somewhither would she have thee go with her.
Ah, boy, Cornelia never with more care
Read to her sons than she hath read to thee
Sweet poetry and Tully's Orator.
Canst thou not guess wherefore she plies thee thus?

BOY. My lord, I know not, I, nor can I guess,
Unless some fit or frenzy do possess her:
For I have heard my grandsire say full oft,
Extremity of griefs would make men mad;
And I have read that Hecuba of Troy   20
Ran mad for sorrow. That made me to fear,
Although, my lord, I know my noble aunt
Loves me as dear as e'er my mother did,
And would not, but in fury, fright my youth:
Which made me down to throw my books and fly,
Causeless perhaps. But pardon me, sweet aunt:
And, madam, if my uncle Marcus go,
I will most willingly attend your ladyship.
MARCUS. Lucius, I will.
       Lavinia with her stumps turns over
       the books which Lucius has let fall
TITUS. How now, Lavinia? Marcus, what means this? 30
Some book there is that she desires to see:
Which is it, girl, of these? Open them, boy.
But thou art deeper read, and better skilled:
Come, and take choice of all my library,
And so beguile thy sorrow, till the heavens
Reveal the damned contriver of this deed.
Why lifts she up her arms in sequence thus?
MARCUS. I think she means that there were more than
    one
Confederate in the fact. Ay, more there was;
Or else to heaven she heaves them for revenge. 40
TITUS. Lucius, what book is that she tosseth so?
BOY. Grandsire, 'tis Ovid's Metamorphoses;
My mother gave it me.
MARCUS.   For love of her that's gone,
Perhaps she culled it from among the rest.
TITUS. Soft! so busily she turns the leaves!
Help her!
What would she find? Lavinia, shall I read?
This is the tragic tale of Philomel,
And treats of Tereus' treason and his rape;
And rape, I fear, was root of thy annoy. 50
MARCUS. See, brother, see, note how she quotes the
    leaves.
TITUS. Lavinia, wert thou thus surprised, sweet girl,
Ravished and wronged, as Philomela was,
Forced in the ruthless, vast, and gloomy woods?
See, see!
Ay, such a place there is, where we did hunt,—
O, had we never, never hunted there!—
Patterned by that the poet here describes,
By nature made for murders and for rapes.
MARCUS. O, why should nature build so foul a den, 60
Unless the gods delight in tragedies?
TITUS. Give signs, sweet girl, for here are none but
friends,
What Roman lord it was durst do the deed:
Or slunk not Saturnine, as Tarquin erst,
That left the camp to sin in Lucrece' bed?
MARCUS. Sit down, sweet niece: brother, sit down by
me.
Apollo, Pallas, Jove, or Mercury,
Inspire me, that I may this treason find!
My lord, look here: look here, Lavinia:
       He writes his name with his
       staff, and guides it with
       feet and mouth.
This sandy plot is plain; guide, if thou canst, 70
This after me. I have writ my name

Without the help of any hand at all.
Cursed be that heart that forced us to this shift!
Write thou, good niece, and here display at last
What God will have discovered for revenge:
Heaven guide thy pen to print thy sorrows plain,
That we may know the traitors and the truth!
       She takes the staff in her mouth,
       and guides it with her stumps
       and writes
TITUS. O, do ye read, my lord, what she hath writ?
'Stuprum. Chiron. Demetrius.'
MARCUS. What, what! the lustful sons of Tamora   80
Performers of this heinous, bloody deed?
TITUS. Magni Dominator poli,
Tam lentus audis scelera? tam lentus vides?
MARCUS. O, calm thee, gentle lord! although I know
There is enough written upon this earth
To stir a mutiny in the mildest thoughts,
And arm the minds of infants to exclaims.
My lord, kneel down with me; Lavinia, kneel;
And kneel, sweet boy, the Roman Hector's hope;
And swear with me, as, with the woful fere   90
And father of that chaste dishonoured dame,
Lord Junius Brutus sware for Lucrece' rape,
That we will prosecute by good advice
Mortal revenge upon these traitorous Goths,
And see their blood, or die with this reproach.
TITUS. 'Tis sure enough, an you knew how,
But if you hurt these bear-whelps, then beware:
The dam will wake; and if she wind ye once,
She's with the lion deeply still in league,
And lulls him whilst she playeth on her back,   100
And when he sleeps will she do what she list.
You are a young huntsman, Marcus, let alone;
And, come, I will go get a leaf of brass,
And with a gad of steel will write these words,
And lay it by: the angry northern wind
Will blow these sands like Sibyl's leaves abroad,
And where's our lesson then? Boy, what say you?
BOY. I say, my lord, that if I were a man,
Their mother's bed-chamber should not be safe
For these base bondmen to the yoke of Rome.   110
MARCUS. Ay, that's my boy! thy father hath full oft
For his ungrateful country done the like.
BOY. And, uncle, so will I, an if I live.
TITUS. Come, go with me into mine armoury:
Lucius, I'll fit thee, and withal my boy
Shall carry from me to the empress' sons
Presents that I intend to send them both:
Come, come; thou'lt do my message, wilt thou not?
BOY. Ay, with my dagger in their bosoms, grandsire.
TITUS. No, boy, not so; I'll teach thee another course. 120
Lavinia, come. Marcus, look to my house.
Lucius and I'll go brave it at the court;
Ah, marry, will we, sir; and we'll be waited on.
      He goes; Lavinia and young Lucius
      follow
MARCUS. O heavens, can you hear a good man groan,
And not relent, or not compassion him?
Marcus, attend him in his ecstasy,
That hath more scars of sorrow in his heart,
Than foe-men's marks upon his battered shield,
But yet so just that he will not revenge.
Revenge the heavens for old Andronicus!   130
      He goes

Scene 2: *A room in the palace*

Enter Aaron, Chiron, and Demetrius, at one door: at another door, young Lucius and another, with a bundle of weapons and verses writ upon them

CHIRON. Demetrius, here's the son of Lucius,
　He hath some message to deliver us.
AARON. Ay, some mad message from his mad
　grandfather.
BOY. My lords, with all the humbleness I may,
　I greet your honours from Andronicus.
　[*Aside*] And pray the Roman gods confound you
　both.
DEMETRIUS. Gramercy, lovely Lucius, what's the
　news?
BOY [*aside*]. That you are both deciphered, that's the
　news,
　For villains marked with rape. [*aloud*] May it
　please you,
　My grandsire, well-advised, hath sent by me　　10
　The goodliest weapons of his armoury
　To gratify your honourable youth,
　The hope of Rome; for so he bade me say;
　And so I do, and with his gifts present
　Your lordships, that whenever you have need,
　You may be arméd and appointed well.
　And so I leave you both ... [*aside*] like bloody
　villains.　　　　　　　　　　　　　　　*He goes*
DEMETRIUS. What's here? a scroll, and written round
　about?
　Let's see:
　'Integer vitæ, scelerisque purus,　　　　　　20
　Non eget Mauri jaculis, nec arcu.'
CHIRON. O, 'tis a verse in Horace; I know it well:
　I read it in the grammar long ago.
AARON. Ay, just; a verse in Horace; right, you have it.
　[*Aside*] Now, what a thing it is to be an ass!
　Here's no sound jest! the old man hath found their
　guilt,
　And sends them weapons wrapped about with lines
　That wound, beyond their feeling, to the quick.
　But were our witty empress well afoot,
　She would applaud Andronicus' conceit.　　30
　But let her rest in her unrest awhile.
　[*Aloud*] And now, young lords, was't not a happy
　star
　Led us to Rome, strangers, and more than so,
　Captives, to be advancéd to this height?
　It did me good, before the palace gate
　To brave the tribune in his brother's hearing.
DEMETRIUS. But me more good, to see so great a lord
　Basely insinuate and send us gifts.
AARON. Had he not reason, lord Demetrius?
　Did you not use his daughter very friendly?　　40
DEMETRIUS. I would we had a thousand Roman dames
　At such a bay, by turn to serve our lust.
CHIRON. A charitable wish and full of love.
AARON. Here lacks but your mother for to say amen.
CHIRON. And that would she for twenty thousand
　more.
DEMETRIUS. Come, let us go, and pray to all the gods
　For our belovéd mother in her pains.
AARON [*aside*]. Pray to the devils, the gods have given
　us over.　　　　　　　　　　　　　*Trumpets sound*
DEMETRIUS. Why do the emperor's trumpets flourish
　thus?

CHIRON. Belike, for joy the emperor hath a son.　　50
DEMETRIUS. Soft! who comes here?

Enter Nurse with a blackamoor child

NURSE.　　　　　　　　　　Good morrow, lords.
　O, tell me, did you see Aaron the Moor?
AARON. Well, more or less, or ne'er a whit at all,
　Here Aaron is; and what with Aaron now?
NURSE. O gentle Aaron, we are all undone!
　Now help, or woe betide thee evermore!
AARON. Why, what a caterwauling dost thou keep!
　What dost thou wrap and fumble in thy arms?
NURSE. O, that which I would hide from heaven's eye,
　Our empress' shame and stately Rome's disgrace!　60
　She is delivered, lords, she is delivered.
AARON. To whom?
NURSE.　　　　　　I mean, she is brought a-bed.
AARON. Well, God give her good rest! What hath he
　sent her?
NURSE. A devil.
AARON.　　　　　Why, then she is the devil's dam;
　A joyful issue.
NURSE. A joyless, dismal, black, and sorrowful issue!
　Here is the babe, as loathsome as a toad
　Amongst the fair-faced breeders of our clime.
　The empress sends it thee, thy stamp, thy seal,
　And bids thee christen it with thy dagger's point.　70
AARON. Zounds, ye whore! is black so base a hue?
　Sweet blowse, you are a beauteous blossom, sure.
DEMETRIUS. Villain, what hast thou done?
AARON. That which thou canst not undo.
CHIRON. Thou hast undone our mother.
AARON. Villain, I have done thy mother.
DEMETRIUS. And therein, hellish dog, thou hast
　undone her.
　Woe to her chance, and damned her loathéd choice!
　Accursed the offspring of so foul a fiend!
CHIRON. It shall not live.　　　　　　　　　　80
AARON. It shall not die.
NURSE. Aaron, it must; the mother wills it so.
AARON. What, must it, nurse? then let no man but I
　Do execution on my flesh and blood.
DEMETRIUS. I'll broach the tadpole on my rapier's
　point:
　Nurse, give it me; my sword shall soon dispatch it.
AARON. Sooner this sword shall plough thy bowels up.
　　　　　　　　Takes the child from the nurse, and draws
　Stay, murderous villains! will you kill your brother?
　Now, by the burning tapers of the sky,
　That shone so brightly when this boy was got,　　90
　He dies upon my scimitar's sharp point
　That touches this my first-born son and heir!
　I tell you, younglings, not Enceladus,
　With all his threat'ning band of Typhon's brood,
　Nor great Alcides, nor the god of war,
　Shall seize this prey out of his father's hands.
　What, what, ye sanguine, shallow-hearted boys!
　Ye white-limed walls! ye alehouse painted signs!
　Coal-black is better than another hue,
　In that it scorns to bear another hue;　　　　100
　For all the water in the ocean
　Can never turn the swan's black legs to white,
　Although she lave them hourly in the flood.
　Tell the empress from me, I am of age
　To keep mine own, excuse it how she can.
DEMETRIUS. Wilt thou betray thy noble mistress thus?

AARON. My mistress is my mistress, this my self,
The vigour and the picture of my youth:
This before all the world do I prefer;
This maugre all the world will I keep safe,   110
Or some of you shall smoke for it in Rome.
DEMETRIUS. By this our mother is for ever shamed.
CHIRON. Rome will despise her for this foul escape.
NURSE. The emperor in his rage will doom her death.
CHIRON. I blush to think upon this ignomy.
AARON. Why, there's the privilege your beauty bears:
Fie, treacherous hue! that will betray with blushing
The close enacts and counsels of thy heart!
Here's a young lad framed of another leer:
Look, how the black slave smiles upon the father,   120
As who should say, 'Old lad, I am thine own'.
He is your brother, lords, sensibly fed
Of that self blood that first gave life to you,
And from that womb where you imprisoned were
He is enfranchised and come to light;
Nay, he's your brother by the surer side,
Although my seal be stampéd in his face.
NURSE. Aaron, what shall I say unto the empress?
DEMETRIUS. Advise thee, Aaron, what is to be done,
And we will all subscribe to thy advice: 130
Save thou the child, so we may all be safe.
AARON. Then sit we down and let us all consult.
My son and I will have the wind of you:
Keep there: now talk at pleasure of your safety.
                                      They sit
DEMETRIUS. How many women saw this child of his?
AARON. Why, so, brave lords! when we join in league,
I am a lamb: but if you brave the Moor,
The chaféd boar, the mountain lioness,
The ocean swells not so as Aaron storms.
But say again, how many saw the child?   140
NURSE. Cornelia the midwife, and myself,
And no one else but the delivered empress.
AARON. The emperess, the midwife, and yourself:
Two may keep counsel when the third's away:
Go to the empress, tell her this I said.
                                      He kills her
Wheak, wheak!
So cries a pig prepared to the spit.
DEMETRIUS. What mean'st thou, Aaron? wherefore
didst thou this?
AARON. O, lord, sir, 'tis a deed of policy!
Shall she live to betray this guilt of ours?   150
A long-tongued babbling gossip? no, lords, no.
And now be it known to you my full intent.
Not far one Muly lives, my countryman,
His wife but yesternight was brought to bed;
His child is like to her, fair as you are:
Go pack with him, and give the mother gold,
And tell them both the circumstance of all,
And how by this their child shall be advanced,
And be received for the emperor's heir,
And substituted in the place of mine,   160
To calm this tempest whirling in the court;
And let the emperor dandle him for his own.
Hark ye, lords; you see I have given her physic,
                              Points to the body
And you must needs bestow her funeral;
The fields are near, and you are gallant grooms.
This done, see that you take no longer days,
But send the midwife presently to me.
The midwife and the nurse well made away,

Then let the ladies tattle what they please.
CHIRON. Aaron, I see, thou wilt not trust the air   170
With secrets.
DEMETRIUS.   For this care of Tamora,
Herself and hers are highly bound to thee.
                              They bear off the Nurse
AARON. Now to the Goths, as swift as swallow flies,
There to dispose this treasure in mine arms,
And secretly to greet the empress' friends.
Come on, you thick-lipped slave, I'll bear you
hence;
For it is you that puts us to our shifts:
I'll make you feed on berries and on roots,
And feed on curds and whey, and suck the goat,
And cabin in a cave, and bring you up   180
To be a warrior and command a camp.   *He goes*

Scene 3: *Before the palace in Rome*

*Enter Titus, old Marcus, his son Publius, young Lucius,
and other gentlemen, with bows; and Titus bears arrows
with letters on the ends of them*

TITUS. Come, Marcus, come; kinsmen, this is the way.
Sir boy, let me see your archery;
Look ye draw home enough, and 'tis there straight.
'Terras Astræa reliquit',
Be you remembered, Marcus: she's gone, she's fled.
Sirs, take you to your tools. You, cousins, shall
Go sound the ocean, and cast your nets;
Haply you may catch her in the sea;
Yet there's as little justice as at land:
No, Publius and Sempronius, you must do it;   10
'Tis you must dig with mattock and with spade,
And pierce the inmost centre of the earth:
Then, when you come to Pluto's region,
I pray you deliver him this petition:
Tell him, it is for justice and for aid,
And that it comes from old Andronicus,
Shaken with sorrows in ungrateful Rome.
Ah, Rome! Well, well; I made thee miserable
What time I threw the people's suffrages
On him that thus doth tyrannize o'er me.   20
Go, get you gone, and pray be careful all,
And leave you not a man of war unsearched:
This wicked emperor may have shipped her hence,
And, kinsmen, then we may go pipe for justice.
MARCUS. O, Publius, is not this a heavy case,
To see thy noble uncle thus distract?
PUBLIUS. Therefore, my lord, it highly us concerns
By day and night t'attend him carefully,
And feed his humour kindly as we may,
Till time beget some careful remedy.
MARCUS. Kinsmen, his sorrows are past remedy.   30
Join with the Goths, and with revengeful war
Take wreak on Rome for this ingratitude,
And vengeance on the traitor Saturnine.
TITUS. Publius, how now! how now, my masters!
What, have you met with her?
PUBLIUS. No, my good lord, but Pluto sends you
word,
If you will have revenge from hell, you shall:
Marry, for Justice, she is so employed,
He thinks, with Jove in heaven, or somewhere else,   40
So that perforce you must needs stay a time.
TITUS. He doth me wrong to feed me with delays.
I'll dive into the burning lake below,

And pull her out of Acheron by the heels.
Marcus, we are but shrubs, no cedars we,
No big-boned men framed of the Cyclops' size;
But metal, Marcus, steel to the very back,
Yet wrung with wrongs more than our backs can
      bear:
And sith there's no justice in earth nor hell,
We will solicit heaven, and move the gods   50
To send down Justice for to wreak our wrongs.
Come, to this gear. You are a good archer, Marcus.
                  He gives them the arrows
'Ad Jovem', that's for you: here, 'Ad Apollinem':
'Ad Martem', that's for myself:
Here, boy, to Pallas: here, to Mercury:
To Saturn, Caius, not to Saturnine;
You were as good to shoot against the wind.
To it, boy! Marcus, loose when I bid.
Of my word, I have written to effect;
There's not a god left unsolicited.   60
MARCUS. Kinsmen, shoot all your shafts into the
      court:
We will afflict the emperor in his pride.
TITUS. Now, masters, draw. [*they shoot*] O, well said,
      Lucius!
Good boy, in Virgo's lap; give it Pallas.
MARCUS. My lord, I aimed a mile beyond the moon;
Your letter is with Jupiter by this.
TITUS. Ha, ha!
Publius, Publius, what hast thou done!
See, see, thou hast shot off one of Taurus' horns.
MARCUS. This was the sport, my lord: when
      Publius shot,   70
The bull being galled, gave Aries such a knock
That down fell both the Ram's horns in the court,
And who should find them but the empress' villain?
She laughed, and told the Moor he should not
      choose
But give them to his master for a present.
TITUS. Why, there it goes! God give his lordship
      joy!

Enter a Clown, with a basket and two pigeons in it

News, news from heaven! Marcus, the post is come.
Sirrah, what tidings? have you any letters?
Shall I have justice? what says Jupiter?
CLOWN. O, the gibbet-maker! he says that he hath 80
taken them down again, for the man must not be
hanged till the next week.
TITUS. But what says Jupiter, I ask thee?
CLOWN. Alas, sir, I know not Jubiter; I never drank
with him in all my life.
TITUS. Why, villain, art not thou the carrier?
CLOWN. Ay, of my pigeons, sir, nothing else.
TITUS. Why, didst thou not come from heaven?
CLOWN. From heaven? alas, sir, I never came there!
God forbid, I should be so bold to press to heaven in 90
my young days. Why, I am going with my pigeons
to the tribunal plebs, to take up a matter of brawl
betwixt my uncle and one of the emperal's men.
MARCUS. Why, sir, that is as fit as can be to serve for
your oration; and let him deliver the pigeons to the
emperor from you.
TITUS. Tell me, can you deliver an oration to the
emperor with a grace?
CLOWN. Nay, truly, sir, I could never say grace in all
my life.   100

TITUS. Sirrah, come hither: make no more ado,
But give your pigeons to the emperor:
By me thou shalt have justice at his hands.
Hold, hold, meanwhile, here's money for thy
      charges.
Give me a pen and ink.
Sirrah, can you with a grace deliver a supplication?
CLOWN. Ay, sir.
TITUS. Then here is a supplication for you. And when
you come to him, at the first approach you must
kneel, then kiss his foot, then deliver up your   110
pigeons, and then look for your reward. I'll be at
hand, sir! See you do it bravely.
CLOWN. I warrant you, sir, let me alone.
TITUS. Sirrah, hast thou a knife? come, let me see it.
Here, Marcus, fold it in the oration,
For thou hast made it like an humble suppliant.
And when thou hast given it to the emperor,
Knock at my door, and tell me what he says.
CLOWN. God be with you, sir; I will.   *He goes*
TITUS. Come, Marcus, let us go. Publius, follow me. 120
                                          They go

Scene 4

*Enter Emperor and Empress and her two sons, with lords,
etc. The Emperor brings the arrows in his hand that Titus
shot at him*

SATURNINUS. Why, lords, what wrongs are these!
      Was ever seen
An emperor in Rome thus overborne,
Troubled, confronted thus, and for the extent
Of egal justice used in such contempt?
My lords, you know, as know the mightful gods,
However these disturbers of our peace
Buzz in the people's ears, there naught hath passed
But even with law against the wilful sons
Of old Andronicus. And what an if
His sorrows have so overwhelmed his wits,   10
Shall we be thus afflicted in his wreaks,
His fits, his frenzy, and his bitterness?
And now he writes to heaven for his redress!
See, here's to Jove, and this to Mercury,
This to Apollo, this to the god of war:
Sweet scrolls to fly about the streets of Rome!
What's this but libelling against the senate,
And blazoning our unjustice every where?
A goodly humour, is it not, my lords?
As who would say, in Rome no justice were.   20
But if I live, his feignéd ecstasies
Shall be no shelter to these outrages,
But he and his shall know that justice lives
In Saturninus' health; whom, if she sleep,
He'll so awake, as he in fury shall
Cut off the proud'st conspirator that lives.
TAMORA. My gracious lord, my lovely Saturnine,
Lord of my life, commander of my thoughts,
Calm thee, and bear the faults of Titus' age,
Th'effects of sorrow for his valiant sons,   30
Whose loss hath pierced him deep and scarred his
      heart;
And rather comfort his distresséd plight
Than prosecute the meanest or the best
For these contempts. [*aside*] Why, thus it shall
      become
High-witted Tamora to gloze with all.

But, Titus, I have touched thee to the quick,
Thy life-blood out: if Aaron now be wise,
Then is all safe, the anchor in the port.—

Enter Clown

How now, good fellow? wouldst thou speak with
us?
CLOWN. Yea, forsooth, an your mistress-ship be
emperial. 40
TAMORA. Empress I am, but yonder sits the emperor.
CLOWN. 'Tis he. God and Saint Stephen give you
godden. I have brought you a letter and a couple of
pigeons here. *Saturninus reads the letter*
SATURNINUS. Go, take him away, and hang him
presently.
CLOWN. How much money must I have?
TAMORA. Come, sirrah, you must be hanged.
CLOWN. Hanged! by'r lady, then I have brought up
a neck to a fair end. *Guards lead him away*
SATURNINUS. Despiteful and intolerable wrongs! 50
Shall I endure this monstrous villainy?
I know from whence this same device proceeds.
May this be borne? As if his traitorous sons,
That died by law for murder of our brother,
Have by my means been butchered wrongfully.
Go, drag the villain hither by the hair;
Nor age nor honour shall shape privilege:
For this proud mock I'll be thy slaughterman—
Sly frantic wretch, that holp'st to make me great,
In hope thyself should govern Rome and me. 60

Enter Æmilius, a messenger

What news with thee, Æmilius?
ÆMILIUS. Arm, arm, my lord! Rome never had more
cause.
The Goths have gathered head, and with a power
Of high-resolvéd men, bent to the spoil,
They hither march amain, under condúct
Of Lucius, son to old Andronicus;
Who threats, in course of this revenge, to do
As much as ever Coriolanus did.
SATURNINUS. Is warlike Lucius general of the Goths?
These tidings nip me, and I hang the head 70
As flowers with frost or grass beat down with
storms.
Ay, now begin our sorrows to approach:
'Tis he the common people love so much;
Myself hath often heard them say,
When I have walkéd like a private man,
That Lucius' banishment was wrongfully,
And they have wished that Lucius were their
emperor.
TAMORA. Why should you fear? is not your city
strong?
SATURNINUS. Ay, but the citizens favour Lucius,
And will revolt from me to succour him. 80
TAMORA. King, be thy thoughts imperious, like thy
name.
Is the sun dimmed, that gnats do fly in it?
The eagle suffers little birds to sing,
And is not careful what they mean thereby,
Knowing that with the shadow of his wings
He can at pleasure stint their melody:
Even so mayst thou the giddy men of Rome.
Then cheer thy spirit: for know, thou emperor,
I will enchant the old Andronicus

With words more sweet, and yet more dangerous, 90
Than baits to fish, or honey-stalks to sheep;
Whenas the one is wounded with the bait,
The other rotted with delicious feed.
SATURNINUS. But he will not entreat his son for us.
TAMORA. If Tamora entreat him, then he will:
For I can smooth, and fill his agéd ears
With golden promises, that, were his heart
Almost impregnable, his old ears deaf,
Yet should both ear and heart obey my tongue.
[*To Æmilius*] Go thou before, be our ambassador: 100
Say that the emperor requests a parley
Of warlike Lucius, and appoint the meeting
Even at his father's house, the old Andronicus.
SATURNINUS. Æmilius, do this message honourably,
And if he stand on hostage for his safety,
Bid him demand what pledge will please him best.
ÆMILIUS. Your bidding shall I do effectually.
He goes
TAMORA. Now will I to that old Andronicus,
And temper him with all the art I have,
To pluck proud Lucius from the warlike Goths. 110
And now, sweet emperor, be blithe again,
And bury all thy fear in my devices.
SATURNINUS. Then go successantly, and plead to
him. *They go*

ACT 5
Scene 1: *Plains near Rome*

Enter Lucius, with an army of Goths. Drums and colours

LUCIUS. Approvéd warriors, and my faithful friends,
I have receivéd letters from great Rome,
Which signifies what hate they bear their emperor,
And how desirous of our sight they are.
Therefore, great lords, be as your titles witness
Imperious, and impatient of your wrongs;
And wherein Rome hath done you any scath,
Let him make treble satisfaction.
1 GOTH. Brave slip, sprung from the great Andronicus,
Whose name was once our terror, now our comfort, 10
Whose high exploits and honourable deeds
Ingrateful Rome requites with foul contempt,
Be bold in us: we'll follow where thou lead'st,
Like stinging bees in hottest summer's day,
Led by their master to the flow'réd fields,
And be avenged on curséd Tamora.
THE OTHER GOTHS. And as he saith, so say we all
with him.
LUCIUS. I humbly thank him, and I thank you all.
But who comes here, led by a lusty Goth?

Enter a Goth, leading Aaron with his child in his arms

2 GOTH. Renownéd Lucius, from our troops I strayed 20
To gaze upon a ruinous monastery,
And, as I earnestly did fix mine eye
Upon the wasted building, suddenly
I heard a child cry underneath a wall.
I made unto the noise, when soon I heard
The crying babe controlled with this discourse:
'Peace, tawny slave, half me and half thy dam!
Did not thy hue bewray whose brat thou art,
Had nature lent thee but thy mother's look,
Villain, thou mightst have been an emperor: 30
But where the bull and cow are both milk-white,

They never do beget a coal-black calf.
Peace, villain, peace!'—even thus he rates the babe—
'For I must bear thee to a trusty Goth,
Who, when he knows thou art the empress' babe,
Will hold thee dearly for thy mother's sake.'
With this, my weapon drawn, I rushed upon him,
Surprised him suddenly, and brought him hither,
To use as you think needful of the man.

LUCIUS. O worthy Goth, this is the incarnate devil   40
That robbed Andronicus of his good hand.
This is the pearl that pleased your empress' eye,
And here's the base fruit of her burning lust.
Say, wall-eyed slave, whither wouldst thou convey
This growing image of thy fiend-like face?
Why dost not speak? What, deaf? not a word?
A halter, soldiers! hang him on this tree,
And by his side his fruit of bastardy.

AARON. Touch not the boy, he is of royal blood.

LUCIUS. Too like the sire for ever being good.   50
First hang the child, that he may see it sprawl—
A sight to vex the father's soul withal.
Get me a ladder.

A ladder brought, and Aaron
forced to ascend

AARON.   Lucius, save the child;
And bear it from me to the emperess.
If thou do this, I'll show thee wondrous things,
That highly may advantage thee to hear:
If thou wilt not, befall what may befall,
I'll speak no more but 'Vengeance rot you all!'

LUCIUS. Say on, and if it please me which thou
  speak'st,
Thy child shall live, and I will see it nourished.   60

AARON. And if it please thee! why, assure thee, Lucius,
'Twill vex thy soul to hear what I shall speak;
For I must talk of murders, rapes, and massacres,
Acts of black night, abominable deeds,
Complots of mischief, treason, villainies
Ruthful to hear, yet piteously performed:
And this shall all be buried in my death,
Unless thou swear to me my child shall live.

LUCIUS. Tell on thy mind, I say thy child shall live.

AARON. Swear that he shall, and then I will begin.   70

LUCIUS. Who should I swear by? thou believest no
  god:
That granted, how canst thou believe an oath?

AARON. What if I do not? as indeed I do not;
Yet, for I know thou art religious,
And hast a thing within thee callèd conscience,
With twenty popish tricks and ceremonies,
Which I have seen thee careful to observe,
Therefore I urge thy oath; for that I know
An idiot holds his bauble for a god,
And keeps the oath which by that god he swears,   80
To that I'll urge him: therefore thou shalt vow
By that same god, what god soe'er it be,
That thou adorest and hast in reverence,
To save my boy, to nourish and bring him up;
Or else I will discover naught to thee.

LUCIUS. Even by my god I swear to thee I will.

AARON. First know thou, I begot him on the empress.

LUCIUS. O most insatiate and luxurious woman!

AARON. Tut, Lucius, this was but a deed of charity
To that which thou shalt hear of me anon.   90
'Twas her two sons that murdered Bassianus;
They cut thy sister's tongue, and ravished her,

And cut her hands, and trimmed her as thou sawest.

LUCIUS. O detestable villain! call'st thou that
  trimming?

AARON. Why, she was washed, and cut, and trimmed!
  and 'twas
Trim sport for them which had the doing of it.

LUCIUS. O barbarous, beastly villains, like thyself!

AARON. Indeed, I was their tutor to instruct them.
That codding spirit had they from their mother,
As sure a card as ever won the set;   100
That bloody mind, I think, they learned of me,
As true a dog as ever fought at head.
Well, let my deeds be witness of my worth.
I trained thy brethren to that guileful hole,
Where the dead corpse of Bassianus lay:
I wrote the letter that thy father found,
And hid the gold within that letter mentioned,
Confederate with the queen and her two sons:
And what not done, that thou hast cause to rue,
Wherein I had no stroke of mischief in it?   110
I played the cheater for thy father's hand,
And when I had it drew myself apart,
And almost broke my heart with extreme laughter.
I pried me through the crevice of a wall,
When for his hand he had his two sons' heads;
Beheld his tears and laughed so heartily,
That both mine eyes were rainy like to his:
And when I told the empress of this sport,
She swounded almost at my pleasing tale,
And for my tidings gave me twenty kisses.   120

GOTH. What, canst thou say all this, and never blush?

AARON. Ay, like a black dog, as the saying is.

LUCIUS. Art thou not sorry for these heinous deeds?

AARON. Ay, that I had not done a thousand more.
Even now I curse the day—and yet, I think,
Few come within the compass of my curse—
Wherein I did not some notorious ill:
As kill a man or else devise his death,
Ravish a maid or plot the way to do it,
Accuse some innocent and forswear myself,   130
Set deadly enmity between two friends,
Make poor men's cattle break their necks,
Set fire on barns and hay-stacks in the night,
And bid the owners quench them with their tears.
Oft have I digged up dead men from their graves,
And set them upright at their dear friends' door,
Even when their sorrow almost was forgot,
And on their skins, as on the bark of trees,
Have with my knife carvèd in Roman letters
'Let not your sorrow die, though I am dead.'   140
Tut, I have done a thousand dreadful things
As willingly as one would kill a fly,
And nothing grieves me heartily indeed,
But that I cannot do ten thousand more.

LUCIUS. Bring down the devil, for he must not die
So sweet a death as hanging presently.

AARON. If there be devils, would I were a devil,
To live and burn in everlasting fire,
So I might have your company in hell,
But to torment you with my bitter tongue!   150

LUCIUS. Sirs, stop his mouth, and let him speak no
  more.

A Goth comes up

GOTH. My lord, there is a messenger from Rome
Desires to be admitted to your presence.

LUCIUS. Let him come near.

Æmilius is brought forward

Welcome, Æmilius, what's the news from Rome?
ÆMILIUS. Lord Lucius, and you princes of the Goths,
The Roman emperor greets you all by me;
And, for he understands you are in arms,
He craves a parley at your father's house,
Willing you to demand your hostages,   160
And they shall be immediately delivered.
1 GOTH. What says our general?
LUCIUS. Æmilius, let the emperor give his pledges
Unto my father and my uncle Marcus,
And we will come. March away.   *They go*

Scene 2: *Court of Titus' house*

Enter Tamora and her two sons, disguised as Revenge attended by Rape and Murder

TAMORA. Thus, in this strange and sad habiliment,
I will encounter with Andronicus,
And say I am Revenge, sent from below
To join with him and right his heinous wrongs.
Knock at his study, where, they say, he keeps
To ruminate strange plots of dire revenge;
Tell him Revenge is come to join with him,
And work confusion on his enemies.   *They knock*

Titus opens a window above

TITUS. Who doth molest my contemplation?
Is it your trick to make me ope the door,   10
That so my sad decrees may fly away,
And all my study be to no effect?
You are deceived: for what I mean to do
See here in bloody lines I have set down.
And what is written shall be executed.
TAMORA. Titus, I am come to talk with thee.
TITUS. No, not a word. How can I grace my talk,
Wanting a hand to give it action?
Thou hast the odds of me, therefore no more.
TAMORA. If thou didst know me, thou wouldst talk
with me.   20
TITUS. I am not mad, I know thee well enough.
Witness this wretched stump, witness these crimson
lines,
Witness these trenches made by grief and care,
Witness the tiring day and heavy night,
Witness all sorrow, that I know thee well
For our proud empress, mighty Tamora:
Is not thy coming for my other hand?
TAMORA. Know thou, sad man, I am not Tamora;
She is thy enemy, and I thy friend.
I am Revenge, sent from th'infernal kingdom   30
To ease the gnawing vulture of thy mind,
By working wreakful vengeance on thy foes.
Come down and welcome me to this world's light;
Confer with me of murder and of death:
There's not a hollow cave or lurking-place,
No vast obscurity or misty vale,
Where bloody murder or detested rape
Can couch for fear, but I will find them out,
And in their ears tell them my dreadful name,
Revenge, which makes the foul offender quake.   40
TITUS. Art thou Revenge? and art thou sent to me,
To be a torment to mine enemies?

TAMORA. I am, therefore come down and welcome
me.
TITUS. Do me some service ere I come to thee.
Lo, by thy side where Rape and Murder stands;
Now give some surance that thou art Revenge,
Stab them, or tear them on thy chariot wheels;
And then I'll come and be thy waggoner,
And whirl along with thee about the globe.
Provide two proper palfreys, black as jet,   50
To hale thy vengeful waggon swift away,
And find out murderers in their guilty caves:
And when thy car is loaden with their heads,
I will dismount, and by thy waggon-wheel
Trot like a servile footman all day long,
Even from Hyperion's rising in the east,
Until his very downfall in the sea.
And day by day I'll do this heavy task,
So thou destroy Rapine and Murder there.
TAMORA. These are my ministers and come with me.   60
TITUS. Are these thy ministers? what are they called?
TAMORA. Rape and Murder; therefore called so,
'Cause they take vengeance of such kind of men.
TITUS. Good Lord, how like the empress' sons they
are!
And you the empress! but we worldly men
Have miserable, mad, mistaking eyes.
O sweet Revenge, now do I come to thee:
And, if one arm's embracement will content thee,
I will embrace thee in it by and by.
                         He shuts the window
TAMORA. This closing with him fits his lunacy.   70
Whate'er I forge to feed his brain-sick humours,
Do you uphold and maintain in your speeches,
For now he firmly takes me for Revenge,
And, being credulous in this mad thought,
I'll make him send for Lucius his son;
And, whilst I at a banquet hold him sure,
I'll find some cunning practice out of hand,
To scatter and disperse the giddy Goths,
Or at the least make them his enemies.
See, here he comes, and I must ply my theme.   80

Titus comes from the house

TITUS. Long have I been forlorn, and all for thee.
Welcome, dread Fury, to my woful house:
Rapine and Murder, you are welcome too:
How like the empress and her sons you are!
Well are you fitted, had you but a Moor:
Could not all hell afford you such a devil?
For well I wot the empress never wags
But in her company there is a Moor;
And, would you represent our queen aright,
It were convenient you had such a devil: 90
But welcome, as you are. What shall we do?
TAMORA. What wouldst thou have us do, Andronicus?
DEMETRIUS. Show me a murderer, I'll deal with him.
CHIRON. Show me a villain that hath done a rape,
And I am sent to be revenged on him.
TAMORA. Show me a thousand that hath done thee
wrong,
And I will be revengéd on them all.
TITUS. Look round about the wicked streets of Rome,
And when thou find'st a man that's like thyself,
Good Murder, stab him; he's a murderer.   100
Go thou with him, and when it is thy hap
To find another that is like to thee,

Good Rapine, stab him; he's a ravisher.
Go thou with them, and in the emperor's court
There is a queen attended by a Moor;
Well shalt thou know her by thine own proportion,
For up and down she doth resemble thee;
I pray thee, do on them some violent death;
They have been violent to me and mine.
TAMORA. Well hast thou lessoned us: this shall we do.   110
But would it please thee, good Andronicus,
To send for Lucius, thy thrice valiant son,
Who leads towards Rome a band of warlike Goths,
And bid him come and banquet at thy house:
When he is here, even at thy solemn feast,
I will bring in the empress and her sons,
The emperor himself, and all thy foes,
And at thy mercy shall they stoop and kneel,
And on them shalt thou ease thy angry heart.
What says Andronicus to this device?   120
TITUS. Marcus, my brother! 'tis sad Titus calls.

Marcus comes forth

Go, gentle Marcus, to thy nephew Lucius;
Thou shalt enquire him out among the Goths:
Bid him repair to me and bring with him
Some of the chiefest princes of the Goths:
Bid him encamp his soldiers where they are:
Tell him the emperor and the empress too
Feast at my house, and he shall feast with them.
This do thou for my love, and so let him,
As he regards his agéd father's life.   130
MARCUS. This will I do, and soon return again.
                                                        He goes
TAMORA. Now will I hence about thy business,
And take my ministers along with me.
TITUS. Nay, nay, let Rape and Murder stay with me,
Or else I'll call my brother back again,
And cleave to no revenge but Lucius.
TAMORA [*aside*]. What say you, boys? will you abide
    with him,
Whiles I go tell my lord the emperor
How I have governed our determined jest?
Yield to his humour, smooth and speak him fair,   140
And tarry with him till I turn again.
TITUS [*aside*]. I knew them all, though they supposed
    me mad;
And will o'er-reach them in their own devices,
A pair of curséd hell-hounds and their dam.
DEMETRIUS. Madam, depart at pleasure, leave us here.
TAMORA. Farewell, Andronicus: Revenge now goes
To lay a complot to betray thy foes.
TITUS. I know thou dost; and, sweet Revenge,
    farewell.   *She goes*
CHIRON. Tell us, old man, how shall we be employed?
TITUS. Tut, I have work enough for you to do.   150
Publius, come hither, Caius, and Valentine!

Publius and others come from the house

PUBLIUS. What is your will?
TITUS. Know you these two?
PUBLIUS. The empress' sons, I take them, Chiron and
    Demetrius.
TITUS. Fie, Publius, fie! thou art too much deceived;
The one is Murder, and Rape is the other's name:
And therefore bind them, gentle Publius:
Caius and Valentine, lay hands on them:
Oft have you heard me wish for such an hour,   160

And now I find it: therefore bind them sure;
And stop their mouths, if they begin to cry.
                                                        He goes in
                                        Publius, etc. lay hold on Chiron
                                                    and Demetrius
CHIRON. Villains, forbear! we are the empress' sons.
PUBLIUS. And therefore do we what we are
    commanded.
Stop close their mouths, let them not speak a word:
Is he sure bound? look that you bind them fast.

*Enter Titus Andronicus with a knife, and Lavinia with
a basin*

TITUS. Come, come, Lavinia; look, thy foes are
    bound.
Sirs, stop their mouths, let them not speak to me,
But let them hear what fearful words I utter.
O villains, Chiron and Demetrius!   170
Here stands the spring whom you have stained with
    mud,
This goodly summer with your winter mixed.
You killed her husband, and, for that vile fault
Two of her brothers were condemned to death,
My hand cut off and made a merry jest:
Both her sweet hands, her tongue, and that more
    dear
Than hands or tongue, her spotless chastity,
Inhuman traitors, you constrained and forced.
What would you say, if I should let you speak?
Villains, for shame you could not beg for grace.   180
Hark, wretches, how I mean to martyr you.
This one hand yet is left to cut your throats,
Whiles that Lavinia 'tween her stumps doth hold
The basin that receives your guilty blood.
You know your mother means to feast with me,
And calls herself Revenge, and thinks me mad:
Hark, villains, I will grind your bones to dust,
And with your blood and it I'll make a paste,
And of the paste a coffin I will rear,
And make two pasties of your shameful heads,   190
And bid that strumpet, your unhallowed dam,
Like to the earth, swallow her own increase.
This is the feast that I have bid her to,
And this the banquet she shall surfeit on;
For worse than Philomel you used my daughter,
And worse than Progne I will be revenged.
And now prepare your throats. Lavinia, come,
Receive the blood; and when that they are dead,
Let me go grind their bones to powder small,
And with this hateful liquor temper it,   200
And in that paste let their vile heads be baked.
Come, come, be every one officious
To make this banquet, which I wish may prove
More stern and bloody than the Centaurs' feast.
                                            He cuts their throats
So, now bring them in, for I'll play the cook,
And see them ready against their mother comes.
                                    They bear the bodies into the house

Scene 3

*Enter Lucius, Marcus, and the Goths, with Aaron a
prisoner, and the child in the arms of an attendant*

LUCIUS. Uncle Marcus, since 'tis my father's mind
    That I repair to Rome, I am content.
1 GOTH. And ours with thine, befall what fortune will.

LUCIUS. Good uncle, take you in this barbarous Moor,
This ravenous tiger, this accursèd devil;
Let him receive no sustenance, fetter him,
Till he be brought unto the empress' face,
For testimony of her foul proceedings:
And see the ambush of our friends be strong;
I fear the emperor means no good to us.　　　　　10
AARON. Some devil whisper curses in my ear,
And prompt me, that my tongue may utter forth
The venomous malice of my swelling heart!
LUCIUS. Away, inhuman dog! unhallowed slave!
Sirs, help our uncle to convey him in.
　　　　　　　　Goths lead Aaron in. Trumpets
　　　　　　　　　　　　　　　　　sound
The trumpets show the emperor is at hand.

Enter Emperor and Empress, with Tribunes and others

SATURNINUS. What, hath the firmament mo suns than
　one?
LUCIUS. What boots it thee to call thyself a sun?
MARCUS. Rome's emperor, and nephew, break the
　parle;
These quarrels must be quietly debated.　　　　20
The feast is ready, which the careful Titus
Hath ordained to an honourable end,
For peace, for love, for league, and good to Rome.
Please you, therefore, draw nigh, and take your
　places.
SATURNINUS. Marcus, we will.

*Servants bring forth a table. Trumpets sounding, enter
Titus, like a cook, placing the dishes, and Lavinia with a
veil over her face, young Lucius, and others*

TITUS. Welcome, my lord; welcome, dread queen;
Welcome, ye warlike Goths; welcome, Lucius;
And welcome, all: although the cheer be poor,
'Twill fill your stomachs; please you eat of it.
SATURNINUS. Why art thou thus attired, Andronicus?　30
TITUS. Because I would be sure to have all well,
To entertain your highness and your empress.
TAMORA. We are beholding to you, good Andronicus.
TITUS. An if your highness knew my heart, you were.
My lord the emperor, resolve me this:
Was it well done of rash Virginius
To slay his daughter with his own right hand,
Because she was enforced, stained, and deflowered?
SATURNINUS. It was, Andronicus.
TITUS. Your reason, mighty lord!　　　　　　40
SATURNINUS. Because the girl should not survive her
　shame,
And by her presence still renew his sorrows.
TITUS. A reason mighty, strong, and effectual,
A pattern, precedent, and lively warrant,
For me, most wretched, to perform the like.
Die, die, Lavinia, and thy shame with thee,
And with thy shame thy father's sorrow die!
　　　　　　　　　　　　He kills her
SATURNINUS. What hast thou done, unnatural and
　unkind?
TITUS. Killed her for whom my tears have made me
　blind.
I am as woful as Virginius was,　　　　　　50
And have a thousand times more cause than he
To do this outrage, and it now is done.
SATURNINUS. What, was she ravished? tell who did the
　deed.
TITUS. Will't please you eat? will't please your
　highness feed?
TAMORA. Why hast thou slain thine only daughter
　thus?
TITUS. Not I; 'twas Chiron and Demetrius:
They ravished her and cut away her tongue;
And they, 'twas they, that did her all this wrong.
SATURNINUS. Go, fetch them hither to us presently.
TITUS. Why, there they are both, bakèd in this pie,　60
Whereof their mother daintily hath fed,
Eating the flesh that she herself hath bred.
'Tis true, 'tis true; witness my knife's sharp point.
　　　　　　　　　　　He stabs the empress
SATURNINUS. Die, frantic wretch, for this accursèd
　deed.　　　　　　　　　　　*Kills Titus*
LUCIUS. Can the son's eye behold his father bleed?
There's meed for meed, death for a deadly deed.

*He kills Saturninus. A great tumult. Lucius, Marcus, and
others go up into the balcony*

MARCUS. You sad-faced men, people and sons of
　Rome,
By uproars severed, as a flight of fowl
Scattered by winds and high tempestuous gusts,
O, let me teach you how to knit again　　　　70
This scattered corn into one mutual sheaf,
These broken limbs again into one body;
Lest Rome herself be bane unto herself,
And she whom mighty kingdoms curt'sy to,
Like a forlorn and desperate castaway,
Do shameful execution on herself.
But if my frosty signs and chaps of age,
Grave witnesses of true experience,
Cannot induce you to attend my words,—
[*to Lucius*] Speak, Rome's dear friend, as erst our
　ancestor,　　　　　　　　　　　　80
When with his solemn tongue he did discourse
To love-sick Dido's sad attending ear
The story of that baleful burning night,
When subtle Greeks surprised King Priam's Troy;
Tell us what Sinon hath bewitched our ears,
Or who hath brought the fatal engine in
That gives our Troy, our Rome, the civil wound.
My heart is not compact of flint nor steel;
Nor can I utter all our bitter grief,
But floods of tears will drown my oratory,　　90
And break my utt'rance, even in the time
When it should move ye to attend me most,
And force you to commiseration.
Here's Rome's young captain, let him tell the tale,
While I stand by and weep to hear him speak.
LUCIUS. Then, gracious auditory, be it known to you,
That Chiron and the damned Demetrius
Were they that murderèd our emperor's brother;
And they it were that ravishèd our sister.
For their fell faults our brothers were beheaded,　100
Our father's tears despised, and basely cozened
Of that true hand that fought Rome's quarrel out
And sent her enemies unto the grave.
Lastly, myself unkindly banishèd,
The gates shut on me, and turned weeping out,
To beg relief among Rome's enemies;
Who drowned their enmity in my true tears,
And oped their arms to embrace me as a friend:
I am the turned-forth, be it known to you,
That have preserved her welfare in my blood,　110

And from her bosom took the enemy's point,
Sheathing the steel in my advent'rous body.
Alas, you know I am no vaunter, I;
My scars can witness, dumb although they are,
That my report is just and full of truth.
But, soft! methinks, I do digress too much,
Citing my worthless praise. O, pardon me,
For when no friends are by, men praise themselves.
MARCUS. Now is my turn to speak. Behold the child:

Points

Of this was Tamora deliveréd,　　　　　　　　　120
The issue of an irreligious Moor,
Chief architect and plotter of these woes:
The villain is alive in Titus' house,
Damned as he is, to witness this is true.
Now judge what cause had Titus to revenge
These wrongs, unspeakable, past patience,
Or more than any living man could bear.
Now have you heard the truth. What say you,
　　Romans?
Have we done aught amiss, show us wherein,
And, from the place where you behold us pleading　130
The poor remainder of Andronici
Will, hand in hand, all headlong hurl ourselves
And on the ragged stones beat forth our souls,
And make a mutual closure of our house.
Speak, Romans, speak, and if you say we shall,
Lo, hand in hand, Lucius and I will fall.
ÆMILIUS. Come, come, thou reverend man of Rome,
And bring our emperor gently in thy hand,
Lucius our emperor; for well I know
The common voice do cry it shall be so.　　　　140
ALL. Lucius, all hail, Rome's royal emperor!
MARCUS [*to soldiers*]. Go, go into old Titus' sorrowful
　　house,
And hither hale that misbelieving Moor,
To be adjudged some direful slaught'ring death,
As punishment for his most wicked life.

Lucius, Marcus, and the others descend

ALL. Lucius, all hail, Rome's gracious governor!
LUCIUS. Thanks, gentle Romans: may I govern so,
To heal Rome's harms and wipe away her woe!
But, gentle people, give me aim awhile,
For nature puts me to a heavy task.　　　　　　150
Stand all aloof; but, uncle, draw you near,
To shed obsequious tears upon this trunk.

He kisses the dead Titus

O, take this warm kiss on thy pale cold lips,
These sorrowful drops upon thy blood-stained face,
The last true duties of thy noble son!
MARCUS. Tear for tear and loving kiss for kiss

Thy brother Marcus tenders on thy lips:
O, were the sum of these that I should pay
Countless and infinite, yet would I pay them!
LUCIUS. Come hither, boy; come, come, and learn of
　　us　　　　　　　　　　　　　　　　　160
To melt in showers: thy grandsire loved thee well:
Many a time he danced thee on his knee,
Sung thee asleep, his loving breast thy pillow;
Many a story hath he told to thee,
And bid thee bear his pretty tales in mind,
And talk of them when he was dead and gone.
MARCUS. How many thousand times hath these poor
　　lips,
When they were living, warmed themselves on
　　thine!
O, now, sweet boy, give them their latest kiss,
Bid him farewell; commit him to the grave;　　170
Do him that kindness, and take leave of him.
BOY. O, grandsire, grandsire! even with all my heart
Would I were dead, so you did live again!—
O Lord, I cannot speak to him for weeping,
My tears will choke me, if I ope my mouth.

Soldiers return with Aaron

ROMAN. You sad Andronici, have done with woes;
Give sentence on this execrable wretch,
That hath been breeder of these dire events.
LUCIUS. Set him breast-deep in earth, and famish him;
There let him stand and rave and cry for food:　180
If any one relieves or pities him,
For the offence he dies. This is our doom.
Some stay, to see him fastened in the earth.
AARON. Ah, why should wrath be mute, and fury
　　dumb?
I am no baby, I, that with base prayers
I should repent the evils I have done:
Ten thousand worse than ever yet I did
Would I perform, if I might have my will:
If one good deed in all my life I did,
I do repent it from my very soul.　　　　　　190
LUCIUS. Some loving friends convey the emperor
　　hence,
And give him burial in his father's grave:
My father and Lavinia shall forthwith
Be closéd in our household's monument.
As for that ravenous tiger, Tamora,
No funeral rite, nor man in mourning weed,
No mournful bell shall ring her burial;
But throw her forth to beasts and birds of prey.
Her life was beastly and devoid of pity,
And being dead, let birds on her take pity.　　200

They go

Romeo and Juliet

The scene: Verona and Mantua

CHARACTERS IN THE PLAY

ESCALUS, *prince of Verona*
PARIS, *a young nobleman, kinsman to the prince*
MONTAGUE } *heads of two houses at enmity with each*
CAPULET } *other*
An old man, kinsman to Capulet
ROMEO, *son to Montague*
MERCUTIO, *kinsman to the prince, and friend to Romeo*
BENVOLIO, *nephew to Montague, and friend to Romeo*
TYBALT, *nephew to Lady Capulet*
FRIAR LAWRENCE, *a Franciscan*
FRIAR JOHN, *of the same order*
BALTHASAR, *servant to Romeo*
SAMPSON } *servants to Capulet*
GREGORY }

PETER, *servant to Juliet's Nurse*
ABRAHAM, *servant to Montague*
An Apothecary
Three Musicians
Page to Paris, another Page, an Officer
LADY MONTAGUE, *wife to Montague*
LADY CAPULET, *wife to Capulet*
JULIET, *daughter to Capulet*
Nurse to Juliet
Citizens, Kinsfolk of both houses, Guards, Watchmen,
  Servants and Attendants
CHORUS

Romeo and Juliet

THE PROLOGUE

Enter Chorus

CHORUS.
Two households, both alike in dignity,
    In fair Verona, where we lay our scene,
From ancient grudge break to new mutiny,
    Where civil blood makes civil hands unclean.
From forth the fatal loins of these two foes
    A pair of star-crossed lovers take their life
Whose misadventured piteous overthrows
    Doth with their death bury their parents'
    strife.
The fearful passage of their death-marked
    love,   10
    And the continuance of their parents' rage,
Which, but their children's end, nought
    could remove,
    Is now the two hours' traffic of our stage;
The which if you with patient ears attend,
What here shall miss, our toil shall strive to
    mend.

                                                Exit

ACT 1
Scene 1: *Verona. A public place*

*Enter Sampson and Gregory of the house of Capulet,
with swords and bucklers*

SAMPSON. Gregory, on my word we'll not carry coals.
GREGORY. No, for then we should be colliers.
SAMPSON. I mean, an we be in choler we'll draw.
GREGORY. Ay, while you live draw your neck out of
    collar.
SAMPSON. I strike quickly, being moved.
GREGORY. But thou art not quickly moved to strike.
SAMPSON. A dog of the house of Montague moves me.
GREGORY. To move is to stir, and to be valiant is to
    stand: therefore if thou art moved thou runn'st   10
    away.
SAMPSON. A dog of that house shall move me to stand:
    I will take the wall of any man or maid of
    Montague's.
GREGORY. That shows thee a weak slave, for the
    weakest goes to the wall.
SAMPSON. 'Tis true, and therefore women, being the
    weaker vessels, are ever thrust to the wall: therefore
    I will push Montague's men from the wall, and
    thrust his maids to the wall.   20
GREGORY. The quarrel is between our masters, and us
    their men.
SAMPSON. 'Tis all one; I will show myself a tyrant:
    when I have fought with the men, I will be cruel
    with the maids: I will cut off their heads.
GREGORY. The heads of the maids?
SAMPSON. Ay, the heads of the maids, or their maiden-
    heads; take it in what sense thou wilt.

GREGORY. They must take it in sense that feel it.
SAMPSON. Me they shall feel while I am able to stand, 30
    and 'tis known I am a pretty piece of flesh.
GREGORY. 'Tis well thou art not fish; if thou hadst,
    thou hadst been poor John. Draw thy tool; here
    comes two of the house of Montagues.

Enter Abraham and another serving man

SAMPSON. My naked weapon is out: quarrel; I will
    back thee.
GREGORY. How? Turn thy back and run?
SAMPSON. Fear me not.
GREGORY. No, marry; I fear thee!
SAMPSON. Let us take the law of our sides; let them   40
    begin.
GREGORY. I will frown as I pass by, and let them take it
    as they list.
SAMPSON. Nay, as they dare. I will bite my thumb at
    them, which is disgrace to them if they bear it.
ABRAHAM. Do you bite your thumb at us, sir?
SAMPSON. I do bite my thumb, sir.
ABRAHAM. Do you bite your thumb at us, sir?
SAMPSON [*aside*]. Is the law of our side if I say ay?
GREGORY [*aside*]. No.   50
SAMPSON. No, sir, I do not bite my thumb at you, sir,
    but I bite my thumb, sir.
GREGORY. Do you quarrel, sir?
ABRAHAM. Quarrel, sir? No, sir.
SAMPSON. But if you do, sir, I am for you: I serve as
    good a man as you.
ABRAHAM. No better.
SAMPSON. Well, sir.

Enter Benvolio on one side, Tybalt on the other

GREGORY [*seeing Tybalt*]. Say 'better': here comes one
    of my master's kinsmen.   60
SAMPSON. Yes, better, sir.
ABRAHAM. You lie.
SAMPSON. Draw, if you be men. Gregory, remember
    thy washing blow.   *They fight*
BENVOLIO [*intervening from behind*]. Part, fools!
    Put up your swords; you know not what you do.

Tybalt comes up

TYBALT. What, art thou drawn among these heartless
    hinds?
    Turn thee, Benvolio; look upon thy death.
BENVOLIO. I do but keep the peace: put up thy sword,
    Or manage it to part these men with me.   70
TYBALT. What, drawn, and talk of peace? I hate the
    word,
    As I hate hell, all Montagues, and thee:
    Have at thee, coward.   *They fight*

*Enter three or four Citizens with clubs or partisans, and an
Officer*

OFFICER. Clubs, bills, and partisans! Strike, beat them
    down.
    Down with the Capulets, down with the
    Montagues!

Enter old Capulet in his gown, and his wife

CAPULET. What noise is this? Give me my long
    sword, ho!
LADY CAPULET. A crutch, a crutch! Why call you for
    a sword?
CAPULET. My sword, I say! Old Montague is come,
    And flourishes his blade in spite of me.

Enter old Montague and his wife

MONTAGUE. Thou villain Capulet!—Hold me not, let
    me go.
LADY MONTAGUE. Thou shalt not stir one foot to seek   80
    a foe.

Enter Prince Escalus, with his train

PRINCE. Rebellious subjects, enemies to peace,
    Profaners of this neighbour-stainéd steel,—
    Will they not hear? What ho! you men, you beasts,
    That quench the fire of your pernicious rage
    With purple fountains issuing from your veins,
    On pain of torture, from those bloody hands
    Throw your mistempered weapons to the
        ground,
    And hear the sentence of your movéd prince.
    Three civil brawls, bred of an airy word
    By thee, old Capulet, and Montague,   90
    Have thrice disturbed the quiet of our streets,
    And made Verona's ancient citizens
    Cast by their grave beseeming ornaments
    To wield old partisans, in hands as old,
    Cankered with peace, to part your cankered hate:
    If ever you disturb our streets again,
    Your lives shall pay the forfeit of the peace.
    For this time, all the rest depart away:
    You, Capulet, shall go along with me;
    And, Montague, come you this afternoon,   100
    To know our farther pleasure in this case,
    To old Freetown, our common judgement-place.
    Once more, on pain of death, all men depart.
            All but Montague, Lady Montague,
                      and Benvolio depart
MONTAGUE. Who set this ancient quarrel new
    abroach?
    Speak, nephew, were you by when it began?
BENVOLIO. Here were the servants of your adversary
    And yours, close fighting ere I did approach:
    I drew to part them; in the instant came
    The fiery Tybalt, with his sword prepared,   110
    Which, as he breathed defiance to my ears,
    He swung about his head, and cut the winds,
    Who, nothing hurt withal, hissed him in scorn:
    While we were interchanging thrusts and blows,
    Came more and more, and fought on part and part,
    Till the prince came, who parted either part.
LADY MONTAGUE. O where is Romeo? Saw you him
    today?
    Right glad I am he was not at this fray.
BENVOLIO. Madam, an hour before the worshipped
    sun
    Peered forth the golden window of the east,   120
    A troubled mind drave me to walk abroad,
    Where, underneath the grove of sycamore
    That westward rooteth from this city's side,
    So early walking did I see your son:
    Towards him I made, but he was ware of me,

    And stole into the covert of the wood:
    I, measuring his affections by my own,
    Which then most sought where most might not
      be found,
    Being one too many by my weary self,
    Pursued my humour, not pursuing his,   130
    And gladly shunned who gladly fled from me.
MONTAGUE. Many a morning hath he there been seen,
    With tears augmenting the fresh morning's dew,
    Adding to clouds more clouds with his deep sighs;
    But all so soon as the all-cheering sun
    Should in the farthest east begin to draw
    The shady curtains from Aurora's bed,
    Away from light steals home my heavy son,
    And private in his chamber pens himself,
    Shuts up his windows, locks fair daylight out,   140
    And makes himself an artificial night:
    Black and portentous must this humour prove,
    Unless good counsel may the cause remove.
BENVOLIO. My noble uncle, do you know the cause?
MONTAGUE. I neither know it, nor can learn of him
BENVOLIO. Have you importuned him by any
    means?
MONTAGUE. Both by myself and many other friends:
    But he, his own affections' counsellor,
    Is to himself—I will not say how true—
    But to himself so secret and so close,   150
    So far from sounding and discovery,
    As is the bud bit with an envious worm,
    Ere he can spread his sweet leaves to the air,
    Or dedicate his beauty to the sun.
    Could we but learn from whence his sorrows grow,
    We would as willingly give cure as know.

Enter Romeo

BENVOLIO. See where he comes: so please you,
    step aside;
    I'll know his grievance or be much denied.
MONTAGUE. I would thou wert so happy by thy stay
    To hear true shrift. Come, madam, let's away.   160
              Montague and his wife depart
BENVOLIO. Good morrow, cousin.
ROMEO.   Is the day so young?
BENVOLIO. But new struck nine.
ROMEO.   Ay me, sad hours seem long.
    Was that my father that went hence so fast?
BENVOLIO. It was. What sadness lengthens Romeo's
    hours?
ROMEO. Not having that which, having, makes them
    short.
BENVOLIO. In love?
ROMEO. Out—
BENVOLIO. Of love?
ROMEO. Out of her favour where I am in love.
BENVOLIO. Alas that Love, so gentle in his view,   170
    Should be so tyrannous and rough in proof!
ROMEO. Alas that Love, whose view is muffled still,
    Should without eyes see pathways to his will!
    Where shall we dine?—O me! What fray was here?
    Yet tell me not, for I have heard it all:
    Here's much to do with hate, but more with love:
    Why, then, O brawling love, O loving hate,
    O anything of nothing first create!
    O heavy lightness, serious vanity,
    Misshapen chaos of well-seeming forms,   180

Feather of lead, bright smoke, cold fire, sick health,
Still-waking sleep, that is not what it is!
This love feel I, that feel no love in this.
Dost thou not laugh?

BENVOLIO.   No, coz, I rather weep.
ROMEO. Good heart, at what?
BENVOLIO.   At thy good heart's oppression.
ROMEO. Why, such is love's transgression.
    Griefs of mine own lie heavy in my breast,
    Which thou wilt propagate, to have it pressed
    With more of thine. This love that thou hast shown
    Doth add more grief to too much of mine own.   190
    Love is a smoke made with the fume of sighs;
    Being purged, a fire sparkling in lovers' eyes;
    Being vexed, a sea nourished with lovers' tears.
    What is it else? A madness most discreet,
    A choking gall and a preserving sweet.
    Farewell, my coz.
BENVOLIO.   Soft, I will go along:
    And if you leave me so, you do me wrong.
ROMEO. Tut, I have lost myself, I am not here,
    This is not Romeo, he's some other where.
BENVOLIO. Tell me in sadness, who is that you love?   200
ROMEO. What, shall I groan and tell thee?
BENVOLIO.   Groan? Why no:
    But sadly tell me, who?
ROMEO. Bid a sick man in sadness make his will—
    A word ill urged to one that is so ill.
    In sadness, cousin, I do love a woman.
BENVOLIO. I aimed so near when I supposed you
    loved.
ROMEO. A right good markman! And she's fair I love.
BENVOLIO. A right fair mark, fair coz, is soonest hit.
ROMEO. Well, in that hit you miss. She'll not be hit
    With Cupid's arrow: she hath Dian's wit,   210
    And, in strong proof of chastity well armed,
    From Love's weak childish bow she lives unharmed.
    She will not stay the siege of loving terms,
    Nor bide th'encounter of assailing eyes,
    Nor ope her lap to saint-seducing gold.
    O, she is rich in beauty, only poor
    That, when she dies, with beauty dies her store.
BENVOLIO. Then she hath sworn that she will still live
    chaste?
ROMEO. She hath, and in that sparing makes huge
    waste:
    For beauty, starved with her severity,   220
    Cuts beauty off from all posterity.
    She is too fair, too wise, wisely too fair.
    To merit bliss by making me despair:
    She hath forsworn to love, and in that vow
    Do I live dead, that live to tell it now.
BENVOLIO. Be ruled by me; forget to think of her.
ROMEO. O, teach me how I should forget to think.
BENVOLIO. By giving liberty unto thine eyes;
    Examine other beauties.
ROMEO.   'Tis the way
    To call hers (exquisite) in question more.   230
    These happy masks that kiss fair ladies' brows,
    Being black, puts us in mind they hide the fair.
    He that is strucken blind cannot forget
    The precious treasure of his eyesight lost.
    Show me a mistress that is passing fair:
    What doth her beauty serve but as a note
    Where I may read who passed that passing fair?
    Farewell, thou canst not teach me to forget.

BENVOLIO. I'll pay that doctrine, or else die in debt.
                                        They go

                Scene 2: *The same*

*Enter Capulet, County Paris, and the Clown, servant to
Capulet*

CAPULET. But Montague is bound as well as I,
    In penalty alike; and 'tis not hard, I think,
    For men so old as we to keep the peace.
PARIS. Of honourable reckoning are you both,
    And pity 'tis you lived at odds so long.
    But now, my lord, what say you to my suit?
CAPULET. But saying o'er what I have said before:
    My child is yet a stranger in the world;
    She hath not seen the change of fourteen years:
    Let two more summers wither in their pride   10
    Ere we may think her ripe to be a bride.
PARIS. Younger than she are happy mothers made.
CAPULET. And too soon marred are those so early
    made.
    Earth hath swallowed all my hopes but she;
    She is the hopeful lady of my earth.
    But woo her, gentle Paris, get her heart;
    My will to her consent is but a part:
    And, she agreed, within her scope of choice
    Lies my consent and fair according voice.
    This night I hold an old accustomed feast,   20
    Whereto I have invited many a guest,
    Such as I love; and you among the store,
    One more most welcome, makes my number more.
    At my poor house look to behold this night
    Earth-treading stars that make dark heaven light.
    Such comfort as do lusty young men feel
    When well-apparelled April on the heel
    Of limping winter treads, even such delight
    Among fresh female buds shall you this night
    Inherit at my house: hear all, all see,   30
    And like her most whose merit most shall be:
    Which on more view, of many mine being one
    May stand in number, though in reckoning none.
    Come, go with me. [*to the Clown*] Go, sirrah,
    trudge about
    Through fair Verona; find those persons out
    Whose names are written there, [*giving him a paper*]
    and to them say
    My house and welcome on their pleasure stay.
                            Capulet and Paris go
CLOWN. Find them out whose names are written here!
    It is written that the shoemaker should meddle with 40
    his yard and the tailor with his last, the fisher with
    his pencil and the painter with his nets. But I am sent
    to find those persons whose names are here writ,
    and can never find what names the writing person
    hath here writ. I must to the learned. In good time!

Enter Benvolio and Romeo

BENVOLIO. Tut, man, one fire burns out another's
    burning,
    One pain is lessened by another's anguish;
    Turn giddy, and be holp by backward turning;
    One desperate grief cures with another's languish;
    Take thou some new infection to thy eye,
    And the rank poison of the old will die.   50
ROMEO. Your plantain leaf is excellent for that.
BENVOLIO. For what, I pray thee?

ROMEO.   For your broken shin.
BENVOLIO. Why, Romeo, art thou mad?
ROMEO. Not mad, but bound more than a madman is:
     Shut up in prison, kept without my food,
     Whipped and tormented, and—God-den, good
     fellow.
CLOWN. God gi' god-den. I pray, sir, can you read?
ROMEO. Ay, mine own fortune in my misery.
CLOWN. Perhaps you have learned it without book:
     but, I pray, can you read anything you see?   60
ROMEO. Ay, if I know the letters and the language.
CLOWN. Ye say honestly: rest you merry.
ROMEO. Stay, fellow; I can read.   *He reads the list*
     'Signior Martino and his wife and daughters,
     County Anselmo and his beauteous sisters,
     The lady widow of Vitruvio,
     Signior Placentio and his lovely nieces,
     Mercutio and his brother Valentine,
     Mine uncle Capulet, his wife and daughters,
     My fair niece Rosaline and Livia,   70
     Signior Valentio and his cousin Tybalt,
     Lucio and the lively Helena.'
     A fair assembly: whither should they come?
CLOWN. Up.
ROMEO. Whither?
CLOWN. To supper; to our house.
ROMEO. Whose house?
CLOWN. My master's.
ROMEO. Indeed I should have asked thee that before.
CLOWN. Now I'll tell you without asking. My master   80
     is the great rich Capulet; and, if you be not of the
     house of Montagues, I pray come and crush a cup
     of wine. Rest you merry.   *Goes*
BENVOLIO. At this same ancient feast of Capulet's
     Sups the fair Rosaline whom thou so loves,
     With all the admiréd beauties of Verona:
     Go thither, and with unattainted eye
     Compare her face with some that I shall show,
     And I will make thee think thy swan a crow.
ROMEO. When the devout religion of mine eye   90
     Maintains such falsehood, then turn tears to fires:
     And these who, often drowned, could never die,
     Transparent heretics, be burnt for liars.
     One fairer than my love! The all-seeing sun
     Ne'er saw her match since first the world begun.
BENVOLIO. Tut, you saw her fair, none else being by,
     Herself poised with herself in either eye:
     But in that crystal scales let there be weighed
     Your lady's love against some other maid
     That I will show you shining at this feast,   100
     And she shall scant show well that now seems best.
ROMEO. I'll go along, no such sight to be shown,
     But to rejoice in splendour of mine own.   *They go*

Scene 3: *Within Capulet's house*

Enter Capulet's Wife, and Nurse

LADY CAPULET. Nurse, where's my daughter? Call her
     forth to me.
NURSE. Now, by my maidenhead at twelve year old,
     I bade her come. What, lamb! What, lady-bird!
     God forbid! Where's this girl? What, Juliet!

Enter Juliet

JULIET. How now, who calls?
NURSE. Your mother.

JULIET. Madam, I am here. What is your will?
LADY CAPULET. This is the matter. Nurse, give leave
     awhile:
     We must talk in secret. Nurse, come back again:
     I have remembered me; thou's hear our counsel.   10
     Thou knowest my daughter's of a pretty age.
NURSE. Faith, I can tell her age unto an hour.
LADY CAPULET. She's not fourteen.
NURSE.   I'll lay fourteen of my teeth—
     And yet, to my teen be it spoken, I have but four—
     She's not fourteen. How long is it now
     To Lammas-tide?
LADY CAPULET.   A fortnight and odd days.
NURSE. Even or odd, of all days in the year,
     Come Lammas-Eve at night shall she be fourteen.
     Susan and she—God rest all Christian souls—
     Were of an age. Well, Susan is with God;   20
     She was too good for me. But, as I said,
     On Lammas-Eve at night shall she be fourteen:
     That shall she, marry; I remember it well.
     'Tis since the earthquake now eleven years,
     And she was weaned—I never shall forget it—
     Of all the days of the year, upon that day:
     For I had then laid wormwood to my dug,
     Sitting in the sun under the dove-house wall.
     My lord and you were then at Mantua—
     Nay, I do bear a brain! But, as I said,   30
     When it did taste the wormwood on the nipple
     Of my dug, and felt it bitter, pretty fool,
     To see it tetchy and fall out with the dug!
     'Shake,' quoth the dove-house: 'twas no need, I
     trow,
     To bid me trudge.
     And since that time it is eleven years:
     For then she could stand high-lone; nay, by th' rood,
     She could have run and waddled all about:
     For even the day before, she broke her brow,
     And then my husband—God be with his soul,   40
     'A was a merry man—took up the child:
     'Yea,' quoth he, 'dost thou fall upon thy face?
     Thou wilt fall backward when thou hast more wit;
     Wilt thou not, Jule?' And, by my holidame,
     The pretty wretch left crying, and said 'Ay'.
     To see now how a jest shall come about!
     I warrant, an I should live a thousand years,
     I never should forget it: 'Wilt thou, Jule?'
     quoth he;
     And, pretty fool, it stinted, and said 'Ay'.
LADY CAPULET. Enough of this; I pray thee hold thy
     peace.   50
NURSE. Yes, madam, yet I cannot choose but laugh,
     To think it should leave crying, and say 'Ay':
     And yet, I warrant, it had upon it brow
     A bump as big as a young cockerel's stone,
     A perilous knock: and it cried bitterly.
     'Yea', quoth my husband, 'fallst upon thy face?
     Thou wilt fall backward when thou comest to age;
     Wilt thou not, Jule?' It stinted, and said 'Ay'.
JULIET. And stint thou too, I pray thee, Nurse, say I.
NURSE. Peace, I have done. God mark thee to his
     grace!   60
     Thou wast the prettiest babe that e'er I nursed:
     An I might live to see thee married once,
     I have my wish.
LADY CAPULET. Marry, that 'marry' is the very theme
     I came to talk of. Tell me, daughter Juliet,

How stands your dispositions to be married?
JULIET. It is an honour that I dream not of.
NURSE. An honour! Were not I thine only nurse,
    I would say thou hadst sucked wisdom from thy
    teat.
LADY CAPULET. Well, think of marriage now; younger
    than you   70
    Here in Verona, ladies of esteem,
    Are made already mothers. By my count,
    I was your mother much upon these years
    That you are now a maid. Thus then in brief:
    The valiant Paris seeks you for his love.
NURSE. A man, young lady! Lady, such a man
    As all the world—Why, he's a man of wax.
LADY CAPULET. Verona's summer hath not such a
    flower.
NURSE. Nay, he's a flower; in faith, a very flower.
LADY CAPULET. What say you? Can you love the
    gentleman?   80
    This night you shall behold him at our feast:
    Read o'er the volume of young Paris' face,
    And find delight writ there with beauty's pen;
    Examine every married lineament,
    And see how one another lends content;
    And what obscured in this fair volume lies
    Find written in the margent of his eyes.
    This precious book of love, this unbound lover,
    To beautify him, only lacks a cover.
    The fish lives in the sea; and 'tis much pride   90
    For fair without the fair within to hide.
    That book in many's eyes doth share the glory,
    That in gold clasps locks in the golden story:
    So shall you share all that he doth possess,
    By having him making yourself no less.
NURSE. No less! Nay, bigger women grow by men!
LADY CAPULET. Speak briefly, can you like of Paris'
    love?
JULIET. I'll look to like, if looking liking move;
    But no more deep will I endart mine eye
    Than your consent gives strength to make it fly.   100

Enter Servingman

SERVINGMAN. Madam, the guests are come, supper
    served up, you called, my young lady asked for, the
    nurse cursed in the pantry, and everything in ex-
    tremity. I must hence to wait; I beseech you follow
    straight.
LADY CAPULET. We follow thee. Juliet, the County
    stays.
NURSE. Go, girl, seek happy night to happy days.
                                                    They go

Scene 4: *Without Capulet's house*

*Enter Romeo, Mercutio, Benvolio, with five or six other
masquers; torch-bearers*

ROMEO. What, shall this speech be spoke for our
    excuse?
    Or shall we on without apology?
BENVOLIO. The date is out of such prolixity:
    We'll have no Cupid hoodwinked with a scarf,
    Bearing a Tartar's painted bow of lath,
    Scaring the ladies like a crow-keeper:
    Nor no without-book prologue, faintly spoke
    After the prompter, for our entrance:
    But, let them measure us by what they will,

We'll measure them a measure and be gone.   10
ROMEO. Give me a torch: I am not for this ambling;
    Being but heavy, I will bear the light.
MERCUTIO. Nay, gentle Romeo, we must have you
    dance.
ROMEO. Not I, believe me: you have dancing shoes
    With nimble soles; I have a soul of lead
    So stakes me to the ground I cannot move.
MERCUTIO. You are a lover: borrow Cupid's wings,
    And soar with them above a common bound.
ROMEO. I am too sore enpiercéd with his shaft
    To soar with his light feathers and so bound;   20
    I cannot bound a pitch above dull woe:
    Under love's heavy burden do I sink.
MERCUTIO. And, to sink in it, should you burden
    love—
    Too great oppression for a tender thing.
ROMEO. Is love a tender thing? It is too rough,
    Too rude, too boisterous, and it pricks like thorn.
MERCUTIO. If love be rough with you, be rough with
    love;
    Prick love for pricking, and you beat love down.
    Give me a case to put my visage in:
    A visor for a visor! What care I   30
    What curious eye doth quote deformities?
    Here are the beetle-brows shall blush for me.
                                        Putting on a mask
BENVOLIO. Come, knock and enter, and no sooner in
    But every man betake him to his legs.
ROMEO. A torch for me; let wantons light of heart
    Tickle the senseless rushes with their heels.
    For I am proverbed with a grandsire phrase,
    I'll be a candle-holder, and look on.
    The game was ne'er so fair, and I am done.
MERCUTIO. Tut, dun's the mouse, the constable's own
    word: 40
    If thou art Dun, we'll draw thee from the mire,
    Or save-your-reverence love, wherein thou stickest
    Up to the ears. Come, we burn daylight, ho.
ROMEO. Nay, that's not so.
MERCUTIO.   I mean, sir, in delay
    We waste our lights in vain, like lights by day.
    Take our good meaning, for our judgement sits
    Five times in that ere once in our five wits.
ROMEO. And we mean well in going to this masque,
    But 'tis no wit to go.
MERCUTIO.   Why, may one ask?
ROMEO. I dreamt a dream tonight.
MERCUTIO.   And so did I.   50
ROMEO. Well, what was yours?
MERCUTIO.   That dreamers often lie.
ROMEO. In bed asleep while they do dream things true.
MERCUTIO. O then I see Queen Mab hath been with
    you.
    She is the fairies' midwife, and she comes
    In shape no bigger than an agate-stone
    On the fore-finger of an alderman,
    Drawn with a team of little atomi
    Over men's noses as they lie asleep.
    Her chariot is an empty hazel-nut,
    Made by the joiner squirrel or old grub   60
    Time out o' mind the fairies' coachmakers:
    Her waggon-spokes made of long spinners' legs,
    The cover of the wings of grasshoppers,
    Her traces of the smallest spider-web,
    Her collars of the moonshine's watery beams,

Her ship of cricket's bone, the lash of film;
Her waggoner a small grey-coated gnat,
Not half so big as a round little worm
Pricked from the lazy finger of a maid.
And in this state she gallops night by night   70
Through lovers' brains, and then they dream of
love;
O'er courtiers' knees, that dream on curtsies
straight;
O'er lawyers' fingers who straight dream on fees;
O'er ladies' lips, who straight on kisses dream,
Which oft the angry Mab with blisters plagues
Because their breaths with sweetmeats tainted are
Sometimes she gallops o'er a courtier's nose,
And then dreams he of smelling out a suit:
And sometime comes she with a tithe-pig's tail
Tickling a parson's nose as 'a lies asleep,   80
Then dreams he of another benefice.
Sometimes she driveth o'er a soldier's neck,
And then dreams he of cutting foreign throats,
Of breaches, ambuscadoes, Spanish blades,
Of healths five fathom deep; and then anon
Drums in his ear, at which he starts and wakes,
And being thus frighted swears a prayer or two,
And sleeps again. This is that very Mab
That plats the manes of horses in the night,
And bakes the elf-locks in foul sluttish hairs,   90
Which once untangled much misfortune bodes:
This is the hag, when maids lie on their backs,
That presses them and learns them first to bear,
Making them women of good carriage:
This is she—
ROMEO.   Peace, peace Mercutio, peace!
Thou talkst of nothing.
MERCUTIO.   True, I talk of dreams,
Which are the children of an idle brain,
Begot of nothing but vain fantasy,
Which is as thin of substance as the air,
And more inconstant than the wind, who woos   100
Even now the frozen bosom of the north,
And, being angered, puffs away from thence,
Turning his side to the dew-dropping south.
BENVOLIO. This wind you talk of blows us from
ourselves:
Supper is done, and we shall come too late.
ROMEO. I fear, too early: for my mind misgives
Some consequence, yet hanging in the stars,
Shall bitterly begin his fearful date
With this night's revels, and expire the term
Of a despised life closed in my breast,   110
By some vile forfeit of untimely death.
But He that hath the steerage of my course
Direct my sail! On, lusty gentlemen.
BENVOLIO. Strike, drum.   *They march into the house*

Scene 5: *The hall in Capulet's house; musicians waiting*

*Enter the masquers, march round the hall, and stand aside.
Servingmen come forth with napkins*

FIRST SERVINGMAN. Where's Potpan, that he helps not
to take away? He shift a trencher! He scrape a
trencher!
SECOND SERVINGMAN. When good manners shall lie all
in one or two men's hands, and they unwashed too,
'tis a foul thing.
FIRST SERVINGMAN. Away with the joined-stools,

remove the court-cupboard, look to the plate—
Good thou, save me a piece of marchpane; and, as
thou loves me, let the porter let in Susan Grindstone 10
and Nell—Antony and Potpan!
THIRD SERVINGMAN. Ay, boy, ready.
FIRST SERVINGMAN. You are looked for and called for,
asked for and sought for, in the great chamber.
FOURTH SERVINGMAN. We cannot be here and there
too. Cheerly, boys; be brisk a while, and the longer
liver take all.   *Servingmen withdraw*

*Enter Capulet, and Juliet, with all the guests and
gentlewomen to the masquers*

CAPULET. Welcome, gentlemen! Ladies that have their
toes
Unplagued with corns will walk a bout with you.
Ah, my mistresses, which of you all   20
Will now deny to dance? She that makes dainty,
She I'll swear hath corns: am I come near ye now?
Welcome, gentlemen! I have seen the day
That I have worn a visor and could tell
A whispering tale in a fair lady's ear,
Such as would please: 'tis gone, 'tis gone, 'tis gone.
You are welcome, gentlemen! Come, musicians,
play.
A hall, a hall! Give room. And foot it, girls.
                        Music plays and they dance
More light, you knaves, and turn the tables up,
And quench the fire—the room is grown too hot. 30
Ah, sirrah, this unlooked-for sport comes well.—
Nay sit, nay sit, good cousin Capulet,
For you and I are past our dancing days.
How long is't now since last yourself and I
Were in a masque?
SECOND CAPULET.   By'r Lady, thirty years.
CAPULET. What, man! 'tis not so much, 'tis not so
much:
'Tis since the nuptial of Lucentio,
Come Pentecost as quickly as it will,
Some five and twenty years, and then we masqued.
SECOND CAPULET. 'Tis more, 'tis more; his son is elder,
sir: 40
His son is thirty.
CAPULET.   Will you tell me that?
His son was but a ward two years ago.
ROMEO [*to a servingman*]. What lady's that which doth
enrich the hand
Of yonder knight?
SERVINGMAN.   I know not, sir.
ROMEO. O she doth teach the torches to burn bright!
It seems she hangs upon the cheek of night
As a rich jewel in an Ethiop's ear—
Beauty too rich for use, for earth too dear!
So shows a snowy dove trooping with crows,
As yonder lady o'er her fellows shows.   50
The measure done, I'll watch her place of stand,
And, touching hers, make blessèd my rude hand,
Did my heart love till now? Forswear it, sight!
For I ne'er saw true beauty till this night.
TYBALT. This, by his voice, should be a Montague.
Fetch me my rapier, boy. What dare the slave
Come hither, covered with an antic face,
To fleer and scorn at our solemnity?
Now, by the stock and honour of my kin,
To strike him dead I hold it not a sin.   60

CAPULET. Why, how now, kinsman! wherefore storm
  you so?
TYBALT. Uncle, this is a Montague, our foe:
  A villain that is hither come in spite,
  To scorn at our solemnity this night.
CAPULET. Young Romeo is it?
TYBALT.   'Tis he, that villain Romeo.
CAPULET. Content thee, gentle coz, let him alone,
  'A bears him like a portly gentleman:
  And, to say truth, Verona brags of him
  To be a virtuous and well-governed youth.
  I would not for the wealth of all this town   70
  Here in my house do him disparagement:
  Therefore be patient, take no note of him.
  It is my will, the which if thou respect,
  Show a fair presence and put off these frowns,
  An ill-beseeming semblance for a feast.
TYBALT. It fits when such a villain is a guest:
  I'll not endure him.
CAPULET.   He shall be endured.
  What, goodman boy? I say he shall. Go to,
  Am I the master here, or you? Go to,
  You'll not endure him? God shall mend my soul!   80
  You'll make a mutiny among my guests!
  You will set cock-a-hoop! You'll be the man!
TYBALT. Why, uncle, 'tis a shame.
CAPULET.   Go to, go to,
  You are a saucy boy. Is't so indeed?
  This trick may chance to scathe you, I know what.
  You must contrary me! Marry, 'tis time—
  Well said, my hearts!—You are a princox: go,
  Be quiet, or—More light, more light, for shame!—
  I'll make you quiet.—What, cheerly, my hearts!
TYBALT. Patience perforce with wilful choler meeting   90
  Makes my flesh tremble in their different greeting.
  I will withdraw, but this intrusion shall,
  Now seeming sweet, convert to bitterest gall.
                        Goes
ROMEO [*takes Juliet's hand*]. If I profane with my
  unworthiest hand
  This holy shrine, the gentle sin is this:
  My lips, two blushing pilgrims, ready stand
  To smooth that rough touch with a tender kiss.
JULIET. Good pilgrim, you do wrong your hand too
  much,
  Which mannerly devotion shows in this:
  For saints have hands that pilgrims' hands do touch,   100
  And palm to palm is holy palmers' kiss.
ROMEO. Have not saints lips, and holy palmers too?
JULIET. Ay, pilgrim, lips that they must use in
  prayer.
ROMEO. O then, dear saint, let lips do what hands do,
  They pray: grant thou, lest faith turn to despair.
JULIET. Saints do not move, though grant for prayers'
  sake.
ROMEO. Then move not, while my prayer's effect I
  take.
  Thus from my lips by thine my sin is purged.
                    Kissing her
JULIET. Then have my lips the sin that they have took.
ROMEO. Sin from my lips? O trespass sweetly urged!   110
  Give me my sin again.   *Kissing her*
JULIET.   You kiss by th' book.
NURSE. Madam, your mother craves a word with you.
ROMEO. What is her mother?
NURSE.   Marry, bachelor,

Her mother is the lady of the house,
And a good lady, and a wise and virtuous.
I nursed her daughter that you talked withal.
I tell you, he that can lay hold of her
Shall have the chinks.
ROMEO.   Is she a Capulet?
O dear account! My life is my foe's debt.
BENVOLIO. Away be gone; the sport is at the best.   120
ROMEO. Ay, so I fear; the more is my unrest.
CAPULET. Nay, gentlemen, prepare not to be gone;
  We have a trifling foolish banquet towards.

The masquers excuse themselves, whispering in his ear

Is it e'en so? Why, then, I thank you all:
I thank you, honest gentlemen; good night.
More torches here; come on! then let's to bed.
Ah, sirrah, by my fay, it waxes late:
I'll to my rest.   *All leave but Juliet and Nurse*
JULIET. Come hither, nurse. What is yond gentleman?
NURSE. The son and heir of old Tiberio.   130
JULIET. What's he that now is going out of door?
NURSE. Marry, that I think be young Petruchio.
JULIET. What's he that follows there, that would not
  dance?
NURSE. I know not.
JULIET. Go ask his name.—If he be married,
  My grave is like to be my wedding bed.
NURSE. His name is Romeo, and a Montague,
  The only son of your great enemy.
JULIET. My only love sprung from my only hate!
  Too early seen unknown, and known too late!   140
  Prodigious birth of love it is to me,
  That I must love a loathéd enemy.
NURSE. What's this, what's this?
JULIET.   A rhyme I learned even now
  Of one I danced withal.

One calls within, Juliet

NURSE.   Anon, anon!
Come, let's away; the strangers all are gone.
                    They go

ACT 2
Prologue

Enter Chorus

CHORUS.
  Now old desire doth in his deathbed lie,
    And young affection gapes to be his heir;
  That fair for which love groaned for and
    would die,
    With tender Juliet matched, is now not fair.
  Now Romeo is beloved and loves again,
    Alike bewitchéd by the charm of looks,
  But to his foe supposed he must complain,
    And she steal love's sweet bait from
    fearful hooks:
  Being held a foe, he may not have access
    To breathe such vows as lovers use to swear;   10
  And she as much in love, her means much less
    To meet her new belovéd anywhere:
  But passion lends them power, time means,
    to meet,
  Tempering extremities with extreme sweet.
                    Exit

Scene 1: *Capulet's orchard*

Enter Romeo alone in the lane by the orchard wall

ROMEO. Can I go forward when my heart is here?
  Turn back, dull earth, and find thy centre out.
            He climbs the wall and leaps into
                      the orchard

*Enter Benvolio with Mercutio in the lane. Romeo listens
behind the wall.*

BENVOLIO. Romeo, my cousin Romeo!
MERCUTIO.   He is wise,
  And on my life hath stolen him home to bed.
BENVOLIO. He ran this way and leapt this orchard wall.
  Call, good Mercutio.
MERCUTIO.   Nay, I'll conjure too.
  Romeo, humours, madman, passion, lover!
  Appear thou in the likeness of a sigh;
  Speak but one rhyme and I am satisfied:
  Cry but 'Ay me!', pronounce but 'love' and 'dove'; 10
  Speak to my gossip Venus one fair word,
  One nickname for her purblind son and heir,
  Young Abraham Cupid, he that shot so trim
  When King Cophetua loved the beggar maid.
  He heareth not, he stirreth not, he moveth not;
  The ape is dead, and I must conjure him.
  I conjure thee by Rosaline's bright eyes,
  By her high forehead and her scarlet lip,
  By her fine foot, straight leg, and quivering thigh,
  And the demesnes that there adjacent lie,   20
  That in thy likeness thou appear to us.
BENVOLIO. An if he hear thee, thou wilt anger him.
MERCUTIO. This cannot anger him. 'Twould anger
  him
  To raise a spirit in his mistress' circle
  Of some strange nature, letting it there stand
  Till she had laid it and conjured it down;
  That were some spite. My invocation
  Is fair and honest; in his mistress' name
  I conjure only but to raise up him.
BENVOLIO. Come! He hath hid himself among these
  trees   30
  To be consorted with the humorous night:
  Blind is his love and best befits the dark.
MERCUTIO. If love be blind, love cannot hit the mark.
  Now will he sit under a medlar tree,
  And wish his mistress were that kind of fruit
  As maids call medlars when they laugh alone.
  O Romeo, that she were, O that she were
  An open-arse and thou a poperin pear!
  Romeo, goodnight. I'll to my truckle-bed;
  This field-bed is too cold for me to sleep.   40
  Come, shall we go?
BENVOLIO.   Go then, for 'tis in vain
  To seek him here that means not to be found.
                       They go

Scene 2

ROMEO. He jests at scars that never felt a wound.

Juliet appears aloft at the window

  But soft! What light through yonder window
    breaks?
  It is the east, and Juliet is the sun.
  Arise, fair sun, and kill the envious moon,

Who is already sick and pale with grief
That thou, her maid, art far more fair than she.
Be not her maid, since she is envious.
Her vestal livery is but sick and green,
And none but fools do wear it: cast it off.
It is my lady, O it is my love;   10
O that she knew she were.
She speaks, yet she says nothing. What of that?
Her eye discourses: I will answer it.
I am too bold: 'tis not to me she speaks.
Two of the fairest stars in all the heaven,
Having some business, do entreat her eyes
To twinkle in their spheres till they return.
What if her eyes were there, they in her head?
The brightness of her cheek would shame those stars
As daylight doth a lamp; her eyes in heaven   20
Would through the airy region stream so bright
That birds would sing and think it were not night.
See how she leans her cheek upon her hand!
O that I were a glove upon that hand,
That I might touch that cheek.
JULIET.   Ay me!
ROMEO.   She speaks.
  O speak again, bright angel, for thou art
  As glorious to this night, being o'er my head,
  As is a wingèd messenger of heaven
  Unto the white-upturnèd wondering eyes
  Of mortals that fall back to gaze on him   30
  When he bestrides the lazy-passing clouds
  And sails upon the bosom of the air.
JULIET. O Romeo, Romeo! Wherefore art thou
  Romeo?
  Deny thy father and refuse thy name:
  Or, if thou wilt not, be but sworn my love,
  And I'll no longer be a Capulet.
ROMEO [*aside*]. Shall I hear more, or shall I speak at this?
JULIET. 'Tis but thy name that is my enemy.
  Thou art thy self, though not a Montague.
  O be some other name! What's Montague?   40
  It is nor hand, nor foot, nor arm, nor face,
  Nor any part belonging to a man.
  What's in a name? That which we call a rose
  By any other name would smell as sweet.
  So Romeo would, were he not Romeo called,
  Retain that dear perfection which he owes,
  Without that title. Romeo, doff thy name;
  And for thy name, which is no part of thee,
  Take all myself.
ROMEO.   I take thee at thy word.
  Call me but love, and I'll be new baptized;   50
  Henceforth I never will be Romeo.
JULIET. What man art thou that, thus bescreened in
  night,
  So stumblest on my counsel?
ROMEO.   By a name
  I know not how to tell thee who I am.
  My name, dear saint, is hateful to myself
  Because it is an enemy to thee.
  Had I it written, I would tear the word.
JULIET. My ears have yet not drunk a hundred words
  Of thy tongue's uttering, yet I know the sound.
  Art thou not Romeo, and a Montague?   60
ROMEO. Neither, fair maid, if either thee dislike.
JULIET. How camest thou hither, tell me, and
  wherefore?
  The orchard walls are high and hard to climb,

And the place death, considering who thou art,
If any of my kinsmen find thee here.
ROMEO. With love's light wings did I o'erperch these
  walls;
For stony limits cannot hold love out,
And what love can do, that dares love attempt:
Therefore thy kinsmen are no stop to me.
JULIET. If they do see thee, they will murther thee.   70
ROMEO. Alack, there lies more peril in thine eye
  Than twenty of their swords. Look thou but sweet,
  And I am proof against their enmity.
JULIET. I would not for the world they saw thee here.
ROMEO. I have night's cloak to hide me from their
  eyes;
And but thou love me, let them find me here:
My life were better ended by their hate
Than death prorogued, wanting of thy love.
JULIET. By whose direction foundst thou out this
  place?
ROMEO. By love, that first did prompt me to enquire.   80
He lent me counsel, and I lent him eyes.
I am no pilot; yet, wert thou as far
As that vast shore washed with the farthest sea,
I should adventure for such merchandise.
JULIET. Thou knowest the mask of night is on my
  face;
Else would a maiden blush bepaint my cheek,
For that which thou hast heard me speak tonight.
Fain would I dwell on form; fain, fain deny
What I have spoke: but farewell compliment!
Dost thou love me? I know thou wilt say 'Ay',   90
And I will take thy word. Yet, if thou swearst,
Thou mayst prove false. At lovers' perjuries
They say Jove laughs. O gentle Romeo,
If thou dost love, pronounce it faithfully.
Or, if thou think'st I am too quickly won,
I'll frown and be perverse and say thee nay,
So thou wilt woo; but else, not for the world.
In truth, fair Montague, I am too fond,
And therefore thou mayst think my haviour light;
But trust me, gentleman, I'll prove more true   100
Than those that have more cunning to be strange.
I should have been more strange, I must confess,
But that thou overheardst, ere I was ware,
My true-love passion. Therefore pardon me,
And not impute this yielding to light love,
Which the dark night hath so discovered.
ROMEO. Lady, by yonder blessèd moon I vow,
That tips with silver all these fruit tree tops—
JULIET. O swear not by the moon, th'inconstant
  moon,
That monthly changes in her circled orb,   110
Lest that thy love prove likewise variable.
ROMEO. What shall I swear by?
JULIET.   Do not swear at all:
Or, if thou wilt, swear by thy gracious self,
Which is the god of my idolatry,
And I'll believe thee.
ROMEO.   If my heart's dear love—
JULIET. Well, do not swear. Although I joy in thee,
I have no joy of this contract tonight:
It is too rash, too unadvised, too sudden,
Too like the lightning, which doth cease to be
Ere one can say 'It lightens'. Sweet, goodnight: 120
This bud of love, by summer's ripening breath,
May prove a beauteous flower when next we meet.

Goodnight, goodnight! As sweet repose and rest
Come to thy heart as that within my breast.
ROMEO. O wilt thou leave me so unsatisfied?
JULIET. What satisfaction canst thou have tonight?
ROMEO. Th'exchange of thy love's faithful vow for
  mine.
JULIET. I gave thee mine before thou didst request it:
And yet I would it were to give again.
ROMEO. Would'st thou withdraw it? For what
  purpose, love?   130
JULIET. But to be frank and give it thee again:
And yet I wish but for the thing I have.
My bounty is as boundless as the sea,
My love as deep: the more I give to thee,
The more I have: for both are infinite.
I hear some noise within. Dear love, adieu—
                                    Nurse calls within
Anon, good nurse!—sweet Montague, be true.
Stay but a little; I will come again.   *Juliet goes in*
ROMEO. O blessed, blessed night! I am afeared,
Being in night, all this is but a dream,   140
Too flattering sweet to be substantial.

Juliet reappears at the window

JULIET. Three words, dear Romeo, and good night
  indeed.
If that thy bent of love be honourable,
Thy purpose marriage, send me word tomorrow,
By one that I'll procure to come to thee,
Where and what time thou wilt perform the rite;
And all my fortunes at thy foot I'll lay,
And follow thee my lord throughout the world.
NURSE [*within*]. Madam!
JULIET. I come, anon.—But if thou meanest not well,   150
  I do beseech thee—
NURSE [*within*].   Madam!
JULIET.   By and by I come—
To cease thy suit, and leave me to my grief.
Tomorrow will I send.
ROMEO. So thrive my soul—
JULIET.   A thousand times good night!
                                         She goes in
ROMEO. A thousand times the worse, to want thy
  light!
Love goes toward love as schoolboys from their
  books,
But love from love, toward school with heavy
  looks.

Juliet returns to the window

JULIET. Hist, Romeo, hist! O for a falconer's voice
To lure this tassel-gentle back again!
Bondage is hoarse and may not speak aloud,   160
Else would I tear the cave where Echo lies,
And make her airy tongue more hoarse than mine
With repetition of my "Romeo!"
ROMEO. It is my soul that calls upon my name.
How silver-sweet sound lovers' tongues by night,
Like softest music to attending ears!
JULIET. Romeo!
ROMEO.   My nièss!
JULIET.   What o'clock tomorrow
Shall I send to thee?
ROMEO.   By the hour of nine.
JULIET. I will not fail. 'Tis twenty year till then.
I have forgot why I did call thee back.   170

ROMEO. Let me stand here till thou remember it.
JULIET. I shall forget, to have thee still stand there,
  Rememb'ring how I love thy company.
ROMEO. And I'll still stay, to have thee still forget,
  Forgetting any other home but this.
JULIET. 'Tis almost morning. I would have thee gone,
  And yet no farther than a wanton's bird,
  That lets it hop a little from her hand,
  Like a poor prisoner in his twisted gyves,
  And with a silk thread plucks it back again,   180
  So loving-jealous of his liberty.
ROMEO. I would I were thy bird.
JULIET.   Sweet, so would I;
  Yet I should kill thee with much cherishing.
  Goodnight, goodnight! Parting is such sweet
    sorrow,
  That I shall say goodnight till it be morrow.
ROMEO. Sleep dwell upon thine eyes, peace in thy
    breast!
  Would I were sleep and peace, so sweet to rest!
                                    She goes in
  Hence will I to my ghostly sire's close cell,
  His help to crave, and my dear hap to tell.   *He goes*

Scene 3: *Friar Lawrence's cell*

Enter Friar alone with a basket

FRIAR. The grey-eyed morn smiles on the frowning
    night,
  Check'ring the eastern clouds with streaks of light:
  And darkness fleckéd like a drunkard reels
  From forth day's pathway, made by Titan's wheels:
  Now ere the sun advance his burning eye,
  The day to cheer and night's dank dew to dry,
  I must upfill this osier cage of ours,
  With baleful weeds and precious-juicéd flowers.
  The earth that's nature's mother is her tomb;
  What is her burying grave, that is her womb;   10
  And from her womb children of divers kind
  We sucking on her natural bosom find:
  Many for many virtues excellent,
  None but for some, and yet all different.
  O mickle is the powerful grace that lies
  In plants, herbs, stones, and their true qualities:
  For nought so vile that on the earth doth live
  But to the earth some special good doth give;
  Nor aught so good but, strained from that fair use,
  Revolts from true birth, stumbling on abuse.   20
  Virtue itself turns vice, being misapplied,
  And vice something by action dignified.

Romeo approaches

  Within the infant rind of this weak flower
  Poison hath residence, and medicine power:
  For this, being smelt, with that part cheers each part;
  Being tasted, stays all senses with the heart.
  Two such opposéd kings encamp them still
  In man as well as herbs—grace and rude will:
  And where the worser is predominant,
  Full soon the canker death eats up that plant.   30
ROMEO. Good morrow, father.
FRIAR.   Benedicite!
  What early tongue so sweet saluteth me?
  Young son, it argues a distempered head,
  So soon to bid goodmorrow to thy bed.
  Care keeps his watch in every old man's eye,

And where care lodges sleep will never lie:
  But where unbruiséd youth with unstuffed brain
  Doth couch his limbs, there golden sleep doth reign.
  Therefore thy earliness doth me assure
  Thou art uprouséd with some distemperature: 40
  Or if not so, then here I hit it right—
  Our Romeo hath not been in bed tonight.
ROMEO. That last is true—the sweeter rest was mine
FRIAR. God pardon sin! Wast thou with Rosaline?
ROMEO. With Rosaline? My ghostly father, no;
  I have forgot that name, and that name's woe.
FRIAR. That's my good son! But where hast thou been
    then?
ROMEO. I'll tell thee ere thou ask it me again.
  I have been feasting with mine enemy,
  Where on a sudden one hath wounded me   50
  That's by me wounded. Both our remedies
  Within thy help and holy physic lies.
  I bear no hatred, blessed man, for lo,
  My intercession likewise steads my foe.
FRIAR. Be plain, good son, and homely in thy drift.
  Riddling confession finds but riddling shrift.
ROMEO. Then plainly know my heart's dear love is set
  On the fair daughter of rich Capulet:
  As mine on hers, so hers is set on mine,
  And all combined save what thou must combine   60
  By holy marriage: when and where and how
  We met, we wooed, and made exchange of vow
  I'll tell thee as we pass; but this I pray,
  That thou consent to marry us today.
FRIAR. Holy Saint Francis, what a change is here!
  Is Rosaline, that thou didst love so dear,
  So soon forsaken? Young men's love then lies
  Not truly in their hearts but in their eyes.
  Jesu Maria, what a deal of brine
  Hath washed thy sallow cheeks for Rosaline!   70
  How much salt water thrown away in waste
  To season love, that of it doth not taste!
  The sun not yet thy sighs from heaven clears,
  Thy old groans ring yet in mine ancient ears;
  Lo, here upon thy cheek the stain doth sit
  Of an old tear that is not washed off yet.
  If e'er thou wast thyself, and these woes thine,
  Thou and these woes were all for Rosaline.
  And art thou changed? Pronounce this sentence,
    then—
  Women may fall, when there's no strength in men.   80
ROMEO. Thou chid'st me oft for loving Rosaline.
FRIAR. For doting, not for loving, pupil mine.
ROMEO. And bad'st me bury love.
FRIAR.   Not in a grave
  To lay one in, another out to have.
ROMEO. I pray thee chide me not. Her I love now
  Doth grace for grace and love for love allow:
  The other did not so.
FRIAR.   O, she knew well
  Thy love did read by rote, that could not spell.
  But come, young waverer, come go with me;
  In one respect I'll thy assistant be: 90
  For this alliance may so happy prove
  To turn your households' rancour to pure love.
ROMEO. O let us hence! I stand on sudden haste.
FRIAR. Wisely and slow. They stumble that run fast.
                                          They go

Scene 4: *A public place*

Enter Benvolio and Mercutio

MERCUTIO. Where the devil should this Romeo be?
Came he not home tonight?

BENVOLIO. Not to his father's; I spoke with his
man.

MERCUTIO. Why, that same pale hard-hearted wench,
that Rosaline,
Torments him so, that he will sure run mad.

BENVOLIO. Tybalt, the kinsman to old Capulet,
Hath sent a letter to his father's house.

MERCUTIO. A challenge, on my life.

BENVOLIO. Romeo will answer it.

MERCUTIO. Any man that can write may answer a
letter.   10

BENVOLIO. Nay, he will answer the letter's master,
how he dares being dared.

MERCUTIO. Alas, poor Romeo, he is already dead—
stabbed with a white wench's black eye, run
through the ear with a love-song, the very pin of
his heart cleft with the blind bow-boy's butt-shaft;
and is he a man to encounter Tybalt?

BENVOLIO. Why, what is Tybalt?

MERCUTIO. More than Prince of Cats. O, he's the
courageous captain of compliments. He fights as   20
you sing pricksong—keeps time, distance, and proportion; he rests his minim rests—one, two, and the
third in your bosom. The very butcher of a silk
button, a duellist, a duellist, a gentleman of the very
first house, of the first and second cause! Ah, the
immortal passado, the punto reverso, the hai!

BENVOLIO. The what?

MERCUTIO. The pox of such antic, lisping, affecting
fantasticoes, these new tuners of accent! 'By Jesu, a
very good blade! a very tall man! a very good   30
whore!' Why, is not this a lamentable thing, grandsire, that we should be thus afflicted with these
strange flies, these fashion-mongers, these pardon-
me's, who stand so much on the new form that they
cannot sit at ease on the old bench? O, their bones,
their bones!

Enter Romeo

BENVOLIO. Here comes Romeo, here comes Romeo!

MERCUTIO. Without his roe, like a dried herring. O
flesh, flesh, how art thou fishified! Now is he for the
numbers that Petrarch flowed in. Laura to his lady   40
was a kitchen wench—marry, she had a better love
to be-rhyme her!—Dido a dowdy, Cleopatra a
gipsy, Helen and Hero hildings and harlots, Thisbe
a gray eye or so, but not to the purpose. Signior
Romeo, bon jour! There's a French salutation to
your French slop. You gave us the counterfeit fairly
last night.

ROMEO. Good morrow to you both. What counterfeit
did I give you?

MERCUTIO. The slip, sir, the slip. Can you not con-   50
ceive?

ROMEO. Pardon, good Mercutio. My business was
great, and in such a case as mine a man may strain
courtesy.

MERCUTIO. That's as much as to say, such a case as
yours constrains a man to bow in the hams.

ROMEO. Meaning to curtsy?

MERCUTIO. Thou hast most kindly hit it.

ROMEO. A most courteous exposition.

MERCUTIO. Nay, I am the very pink of courtesy.   60

ROMEO. Pink for flower?

MERCUTIO. Right.

ROMEO. Why, then is my pump well flowered.

MERCUTIO. Sure wit! Follow me this jest now till thou
hast worn out thy pump, that, when the single sole
of it is worn, the jest may remain, after the wearing,
solely singular.

ROMEO. O single-soled jest, solely singular for the
singleness!

MERCUTIO. Come between us, good Benvolio; my   70
wits faints.

ROMEO. Switch and spurs, switch and spurs; or I'll
cry a match.

MERCUTIO. Nay, if our wits run the wild-goose chase,
I am done: for thou hast more of the wild goose in
one of thy wits than, I am sure, I have in my whole
five. Was I with you there for the goose?

ROMEO. Thou wast never with me for anything when
thou wast not there for the goose.

MERCUTIO. I will bite thee by the ear for that jest.   80

ROMEO. Nay, good goose, bite not.

MERCUTIO. Thy wit is a very bitter sweeting; it is a
most sharp sauce.

ROMEO. And is it not then well served in to a sweet
goose?

MERCUTIO. O, here's a wit of cheveril, that stretches
from an inch narrow to an ell broad.

ROMEO. I stretch it out for that word 'broad', which,
added to the goose, proves thee far and wide a broad
goose.   90

MERCUTIO. Why, is not this better now than groaning
for love? Now art thou sociable, now art thou
Romeo: now art thou what thou art, by art as well
as by nature. For this drivelling love is like a great
natural that runs lolling up and down to hide his
bauble in a hole.

BENVOLIO. Stop there, stop there!

MERCUTIO. Thou desirest me to stop in my tale, against
the hair?

BENVOLIO. Thou wouldst else have made thy tale large.   100

MERCUTIO. O, thou art deceived! I would have made it
short, for I was come to the whole depth of my tale,
and meant indeed to occupy the argument no
longer.

Enter the Nurse with her man Peter

ROMEO. Here's goodly gear! A sail, a sail!

MERCUTIO. Two, two! a shirt and a smock.

NURSE. Peter!

PETER. Anon.

NURSE. My fan, Peter.

MERCUTIO. Good Peter, to hide her face; for her fan's   110
the fairer face.

NURSE. God ye good morrow, gentlemen.

MERCUTIO. God ye good-den, fair gentlewoman.

NURSE. Is it good-den?

MERCUTIO. 'Tis no less, I tell ye; for the bawdy hand of
the dial is now upon the prick of noon.

NURSE. Out upon you! What a man are you?

ROMEO. One, gentlewoman, that God hath made,
himself to mar.

NURSE. By my troth, it is well said. 'For himself to   120

mar,' quoth 'a? Gentlemen, can any of you tell me
where I may find the young Romeo?
ROMEO. I can tell you; but young Romeo will be older
when you have found him than he was when you
sought him. I am the youngest of that name, for
fault of a worse.
NURSE. You say well.
MERCUTIO. Yea, is the worst well? Very well took,
i' faith! Wisely, wisely!
NURSE. If you be he, sir, I desire some confidence with   130
you.
BENVOLIO. She will indite him to some supper.
MERCUTIO. A bawd, a bawd, a bawd! So ho!
ROMEO. What, hast thou found?
MERCUTIO. No hare, sir; unless a hare, sir, in a lenten
pie, that is something stale and hoar ere it be spent.

He walks by them and sings

> An old hare hoar
> And an old hare hoar
> Is very good meat in Lent.
> But a hare that is hoar   140
> Is too much for a score
> When it hoars ere it be spent.

Romeo, will you come to your father's? We'll to
dinner thither.
ROMEO. I will follow you.
MERCUTIO. Farewell, ancient lady; farewell, [*singing*]
'lady, lady, lady'.   *Mercutio and Benvolio go*
NURSE. I pray you, sir, what saucy merchant was this
that was so full of his ropery?
ROMEO. A gentleman, Nurse, that loves to hear him-   150
self talk, and will speak more in a minute than he
will stand to in a month.
NURSE. And 'a speak anything against me, I'll take
him down and 'a were lustier than he is, and
twenty such Jacks: and if I cannot, I'll find those
that shall. Scurvy knave! I am none of his flirt-gills,
I am none of his skains-mates. [*to Peter*] And thou
must stand by too, and suffer every knave to use
me at his pleasure!
PETER. I saw no man use you at his pleasure. If I had,   160
my weapon should quickly have been out. I warrant
you I dare draw as soon as another man, if I see
occasion in a good quarrel, and the law on my side.
NURSE. Now afore God, I am so vexed that every part
about me quivers. Scurvy knave! Pray you, sir, a
word. And as I told you, my young lady bid me
enquire you out. What she bid me say I will keep
to myself: but first let me tell ye, if ye should lead
her in a fool's paradise, as they say, it were a very
gross kind of behaviour, as they say: for the gentle-   170
woman is young; and therefore, if you should deal
double with her, truly it were an ill thing to be
offered to any gentlewoman, and very weak
dealing.
ROMEO. Nurse, commend me to thy lady and mistress.
I protest unto thee—
NURSE. Good heart! and i' faith I will tell her as much.
Lord, Lord! she will be a joyful woman.
ROMEO. What wilt thou tell her, Nurse? Thou dost not
mark me!   180
NURSE. I will tell her, sir, that you do protest, which,
as I take it, is a gentlemanlike offer.
ROMEO. Bid her devise

Some means to come to shrift this afternoon,
And there she shall at Friar Lawrence' cell
Be shrived and married. Here is for thy pains.
NURSE. No, truly, sir; not a penny.
ROMEO. Go to, I say you shall.
NURSE. This afternoon, sir; well, she shall be there.
ROMEO. And stay, good Nurse, behind the abbey wall.   190
Within this hour my man shall be with thee
And bring thee cords made like a tackled stair,
Which to the high topgallant of my joy
Must be my convoy in the secret night.
Farewell. Be trusty, and I'll quit thy pains.
Farewell. Commend me to thy mistress.
NURSE. Now God in heaven bless thee! Hark you, sir.
ROMEO. What sayst thou, my dear Nurse?
NURSE. Is your man secret? Did you ne'er hear say,
'Two may keep counsel, putting one away'?   200
ROMEO. I warrant thee my man's as true as steel.
NURSE. Well, sir, my mistress is the sweetest lady.
Lord, Lord! when 'twas a little prating thing—O,
there is a nobleman in town, one Paris, that would
fain lay knife aboard: but she, good soul, had as lief
see a toad, a very toad, as see him. I anger her sometimes, and tell her that Paris is the properer man;
but I'll warrant you, when I say so, she looks as
pale as any clout in the versal world. Doth not
rosemary and Romeo begin both with a letter?   210
ROMEO. Ay, Nurse; what of that? Both with an R.
NURSE. Ah, mocker, that's the dog-name; R is for
the—No; I know it begins with some other letter;
and she hath the prettiest sententious of it, of you
and rosemary, that it would do you good to hear it.
ROMEO. Commend me to thy lady.
NURSE. Ay, a thousand times. [*Romeo goes*] Peter!
PETER. Anon.
NURSE. Before and apace.   *They go*

Scene 5: *Capulet's orchard*

Enter Juliet

JULIET. The clock struck nine when I did send
the Nurse;
In half an hour she promised to return.
Perchance she cannot meet him. That's not so.
O, she is lame! Love's heralds should be thoughts,
Which ten times faster glides than the sun's beams
Driving back shadows over louring hills.
Therefore do nimble-pinioned doves draw Love,
And therefore hath the wind-swift Cupid wings.
Now is the sun upon the highmost hill
Of this day's journey, and from nine till twelve   10
Is three long hours; yet she is not come.
Had she affections and warm youthful blood,
She would be swift in motion as a ball;
My words would bandy her to my sweet love,
And his to me.
But old folks, many feign as they were dead—
Unwieldy, slow, heavy, and pale as lead.

Enter Nurse, with Peter

O God, she comes! O honey Nurse, what news?
Hast thou met with him? Send thy man away.
NURSE. Peter, stay at the gate.   *Peter withdraws* 20
JULIET. Now good sweet Nurse—O Lord, why
look'st thou sad?
Though news be sad, yet tell them merrily;

If good, thou shamest the music of sweet news
By playing it to me with so sour a face.
NURSE. I am aweary, give me leave a while.
Fie, how my bones ache! What a jaunce have I!
JULIET. I would thou hadst my bones, and I thy
news:
Nay, come, I pray thee speak; good, good Nurse,
speak.
NURSE. Jesu, what haste! Can you not stay awhile?
Do you not see that I am out of breath?   30
JULIET. How art thou out of breath when thou hast
breath
To say to me that thou art out of breath?
The excuse that thou dost make in this delay
Is longer than the tale thou dost excuse.
Is thy news good or bad? Answer to that.
Say either, and I'll stay the circumstance.
Let me be satisfied; is't good or bad?
NURSE. Well, you have made a simple choice; you
know not how to choose a man. Romeo? No, not
he. Though his face be better than any man's, yet   40
his leg excels all men's; and for a hand and a foot
and a body, though they be not to be talked on,
yet they are past compare. He is not the flower of
courtesy, but, I'll warrant him, as gentle as a lamb.
Go thy ways, wench; serve God. What, have you
dined at home?
JULIET. No, no. But all this did I know before.
What says he of our marriage, what of that?
NURSE. Lord, how my head aches! what a head have I!
It beats as it would fall in twenty pieces.   50
My back o' t'other side; ah, my back, my back!
Beshrew your heart for sending me about
To catch my death with jauncing up and down.
JULIET. I' faith, I am sorry that thou art not well.
Sweet, sweet, sweet Nurse, tell me, what says my
love?
NURSE. 'Your love says, like an honest gentleman, and
a courteous, and a kind, and a handsome, and, I
warrant, a virtuous—Where is your mother?
JULIET. Where is my mother? Why, she is within.
Where should she be? How oddly thou repliest: 60
'Your love says, like an honest gentleman,
"Where is your mother?"'
NURSE.   O god's Lady dear!
Are you so hot? Marry come up, I trow!
Is this the poultice for my aching bones?
Henceforward do your messages yourself.
JULIET. Here's such a coil! Come, what says Romeo?
NURSE. Have you got leave to go to shrift today?
JULIET. I have.
NURSE. Then hie you hence to Friar Lawrence' cell;
There stays a husband to make you a wife.   70
Now comes the wanton blood up in your cheeks;
They'll be in scarlet straight at any news.
Hie you to church; I must another way,
To fetch a ladder, by the which your love
Must climb a bird's nest soon when it is dark.
I am the drudge, and toil in your delight:
But you shall bear the burden soon at night.
Go; I'll to dinner; hie you to the cell.
JULIET. Hie to high fortune! Honest Nurse, farewell.
                                        They go

Scene 6: *Friar Lawrence's cell*

Enter Friar and Romeo

FRIAR. So smile the heavens upon this holy act
That after-hours with sorrow chide us not.
ROMEO. Amen, amen. But come what sorrow can,
It cannot countervail the exchange of joy
That one short minute gives me in her sight.
Do thou but close our hands with holy words,
Then love-devouring death do what he dare;
It is enough I may but call her mine.
FRIAR. These violent delights have violent ends,
And in their triumph die like fire and powder   10
Which, as they kiss, consume. The sweetest honey
Is loathsome in his own deliciousness,
And in the taste confounds the appetite.
Therefore love moderately; long love doth so:
Too swift arrives as tardy as too slow.
Here comes the lady.

Enter Juliet

                        O, so light a foot
Will ne'er wear out the everlasting flint!
A lover may bestride the gossamers
That idles in the wanton summer air,
And yet not fall; so light is vanity.   20
JULIET. Good even to my ghostly confessor.
FRIAR. Romeo shall thank thee, daughter, for us both.
JULIET. As much to him, else is his thanks too much.
ROMEO. Ah, Juliet, if the measure of thy joy
Be heaped like mine, and that thy skill be more
To blazon it, then sweeten with thy breath
This neighbour air, and let rich music's tongue
Unfold the imagined happiness that both
Receive in either by this dear encounter.
JULIET. Conceit, more rich in matter than in words, 30
Brags of his substance, not of ornament.
They are but beggars that can count their worth;
But my true love is grown to such excess
I cannot sum up sum of half my wealth.
FRIAR. Come, come with me, and we will make short
work;
For, by your leaves, you shall not stay alone
Till Holy Church incorporate two in one.
                                        They go

ACT 3
Scene 1: *A public place*

Enter Mercutio, Benvolio, and their men

BENVOLIO. I pray thee, good Mercutio, let's retire;
The day is hot, the Capels are abroad:
And if we meet we shall not scape a brawl,
For now, these hot days, is the mad blood stirring.
MERCUTIO. Thou art like one of these fellows that,
when he enters the confines of a tavern, claps me
his sword upon the table and says 'God send me no
need of thee'; and, by the operation of the second
cup, draws him on the drawer, when indeed there
is no need.   10
BENVOLIO. Am I like such a fellow?
MERCUTIO. Come, come, thou art as hot a Jack in thy
mood as any in Italy; and as soon moved to be
moody, and as soon moody to be moved.
BENVOLIO. And what to?

MERCUTIO. Nay, an there were two such, we should
have none shortly, for one would kill the other.
Thou? Why, thou wilt quarrel with a man that hath
a hair more or a hair less in his beard than thou
hast. Thou wilt quarrel with a man for cracking 20
nuts, having no other reason but because thou hast
hazel eyes. What eye but such an eye would spy
out such a quarrel? Thy head is as full of quarrels
as an egg is full of meat, and yet thy head hath been
beaten as addle as an egg for quarrelling. Thou hast
quarrelled with a man for coughing in the street,
because he hath wakened thy dog that hath lain
asleep in the sun. Didst thou not fall out with a tailor
for wearing his new doublet before Easter? With
another for tying his new shoes with old riband? 30
And yet thou wilt tutor me from quarrelling?
BENVOLIO. An I were so apt to quarrel as thou art,
any man should buy the fee-simple of my life for an
hour and a quarter.
MERCUTIO. The fee-simple? O simple!

Enter Tybalt, and others

BENVOLIO. By my head, here comes the Capulets.
MERCUTIO. By my heel, I care not.
TYBALT. Follow me close, for I will speak to them.
Gentlemen, good-den: a word with one of you.
MERCUTIO. And but one word with one of us? Couple 40
it with something; make it a word and a blow.
TYBALT. You shall find me apt enough to that, sir, an
you will give me occasion.
MERCUTIO. Could you not take some occasion without
giving?
TYBALT. Mercutio, thou consort'st with Romeo—
MERCUTIO. Consort? What, dost thou make us min-
strels? An thou make minstrels of us, look to hear
nothing but discords. Here's my fiddlestick; here's
that shall make you dance. Zounds, consort!   50
BENVOLIO. We talk here in the public haunt of men.
Either withdraw unto some private place
And reason coldly of your grievances,
Or else depart: here all eyes gaze on us.
MERCUTIO. Men's eyes were made to look, and let
them gaze.
I will not budge for no man's pleasure, I.

Enter Romeo

TYBALT. Well, peace be with you, sir; here comes my
man.
MERCUTIO. But I'll be hanged, sir, if he wears your
livery.
Marry, go before to field, he'll be your follower!
Your worship in that sense may call him man.   60
TYBALT. Romeo, the love I bear thee can afford
No better term than this: thou art a villain.
ROMEO. Tybalt, the reason that I have to love thee
Doth much excuse the appertaining rage
To such a greeting. Villain am I none—
Therefore farewell; I see thou knowest me not.
TYBALT. Boy, this shall not excuse the injuries
That thou hast done me; therefore turn and draw.
ROMEO. I do protest I never injured thee,
But love thee better than thou canst devise   70
Till thou shalt know the reason of my love:
And so, good Capulet, which name I tender
As dearly as mine own, be satisfied.
MERCUTIO. O calm, dishonourable, vile submission!

'Alla stoccata' carries it away.   *Draws*
Tybalt, you rat-catcher, will you walk?
TYBALT. What wouldst thou have with me?
MERCUTIO. Good King of Cats, nothing but one of
your nine lives that I mean to make bold withal and,
as you shall use me hereafter, dry-beat the rest of the 80
eight. Will you pluck your sword out of his pilcher
by the ears? Make haste, lest mine be about your
ears ere it be out.
TYBALT. I am for you.   *Draws*
ROMEO. Gentle Mercutio, put thy rapier up.
MERCUTIO. Come, sir, your passado.   *They fight*
ROMEO. Draw, Benvolio; beat down their weapons.
Gentlemen, for shame forbear this outrage.
Tybalt, Mercutio, the prince expressly hath
Forbid this bandying in Verona streets.   90
Hold, Tybalt! good Mercutio!

Tybalt under Romeo's arm thrusts Mercutio in and flies

MERCUTIO.   I am hurt.
A plague o' both your houses! I am sped.
Is he gone and hath nothing?
BENVOLIO.   What, art thou hurt?
MERCUTIO. Ay, ay, a scratch, a scratch; marry, 'tis
enough.
Where is my page? Go, villain, fetch a surgeon.
                                      Page goes
ROMEO. Courage, man; the hurt cannot be much.
MERCUTIO. No, 'tis not so deep as a well, nor so wide
as a church door, but 'tis enough, 'twill serve. Ask
for me tomorrow and you shall find me a grave
man. I am peppered, I warrant, for this world. A 100
plague o' both your houses! Zounds! A dog, a rat,
a mouse, a cat, to scratch a man to death! A braggart,
a rogue, a villain, that fights by the book of
arithmetic! Why the devil came you between us?
I was hurt under your arm.
ROMEO. I thought all for the best.
MERCUTIO. Help me into some house, Benvolio,
Or I shall faint. A plague o' both your houses!
They have made worms' meat of me. I have it,
And soundly too. Your houses!   110
                          Benvolio helps him away
ROMEO. This gentleman, the prince's near ally,
My very friend, hath got this mortal hurt
In my behalf, my reputation stained
With Tybalt's slander—Tybalt that an hour
Hath been my cousin. O sweet Juliet,
Thy beauty hath made me effeminate,
And in my temper softened valour's steel!

Benvolio returns

BENVOLIO. O Romeo, Romeo, brave Mercutio's
dead.
That gallant spirit hath aspired the clouds,
Which too untimely here did scorn the earth.   120
ROMEO. This day's black fate on moe days doth
depend;
This but begins the woe others must end.

Tybalt returns

BENVOLIO. Here comes the furious Tybalt back again.
ROMEO. Again! in triumph, and Mercutio slain!
Away to heaven, respective lenity,
And fire-eyed fury be my conduct now!
Now, Tybalt, take the 'villain' back again

That late thou gavest me, for Mercutio's soul
Is but a little way above our heads,
Staying for thine to keep him company.   130
Either thou or I, or both, must go with him.
TYBALT. Thou wretched boy that didst consort him
    here
Shalt with him hence.
ROMEO.   This shall determine that.
              They fight, Tybalt falls
BENVOLIO. Romeo, away, be gone!
The citizens are up, and Tybalt slain.
Stand not amazed. The prince will doom thee death
If thou art taken. Hence, be gone, away!
ROMEO. O, I am Fortune's fool.
BENVOLIO.   Why dost thou stay?
                          Romeo goes

Enter Citizens

A CITIZEN. Which way ran he that killed Mercutio?
Tybalt, that murderer, which way ran he?   140
BENVOLIO. There lies that Tybalt.
A CITIZEN.   Up, sir, go with me:
I charge thee in the prince's name obey.

Enter Prince, old Montague, Capulet, their wives and all

PRINCE. Where are the vile beginners of this fray?
BENVOLIO. O noble Prince, I can discover all
The unlucky manage of this fatal brawl.
There lies the man, slain by young Romeo,
That slew thy kinsman, brave Mercutio.
LADY CAPULET. Tybalt, my cousin, O my
    brother's child!
O prince! O husband! O, the blood is spilled
Of my dear kinsman. Prince, as thou art true,   150
For blood of ours shed blood of Montague.
O cousin, cousin!
PRINCE. Benvolio, who began this bloody fray?
BENVOLIO. Tybalt, here slain, whom Romeo's hand
    did slay.
Romeo, that spoke him fair, bid him bethink
How nice the quarrel was, and urged withal
Your high displeasure. All this—utteréd
With gentle breath, calm look, knees humbly
    bowed—
Could not take truce with the unruly spleen
Of Tybalt deaf to peace, but that he tilts   160
With piercing steel at bold Mercutio's breast,
Who, all as hot, turns deadly point to point,
And, with a martial scorn, with one hand beats
Cold death aside and with the other sends
It back to Tybalt, whose dexterity
Retorts it. Romeo he cries aloud,
'Hold, friends! friends, part!' and, swifter than
    his tongue,
His agile arm beats down their fatal points,
And 'twixt them rushes; underneath whose arm
An envious thrust from Tybalt hit the life   170
Of stout Mercutio, and then Tybalt fled,
But by and by comes back to Romeo
Who had but newly entertained revenge,
And to 't they go like lightning; for, ere I
Could draw to part them, was stout Tybalt slain,
And, as he fell, did Romeo turn and fly:
This is the truth, or let Benvolio die.
LADY CAPULET. He is a kinsman to the Montague;
Affection makes him false, he speaks not true.

Some twenty of them fought in this black strife,   180
And all those twenty could but kill one life.
I beg for justice, which thou, Prince, must give:
Romeo slew Tybalt; Romeo must not live.
PRINCE. Romeo slew him; he slew Mercutio.
Who now the price of his dear blood doth owe?
MONTAGUE. Not Romeo, Prince; he was
    Mercutio's friend;
His fault concludes but what the law should end—
The life of Tybalt.
PRINCE.   And for that offence
Immediately we do exile him hence.
I have an interest in your hearts' proceeding: 190
My blood for your rude brawls doth lie a-bleeding.
But I'll amerce you with so strong a fine
That you shall all repent the loss of mine.
I will be deaf to pleading and excuses;
Nor tears nor prayers shall purchase out abuses.
Therefore use none. Let Romeo hence in haste,
Else, when he is found, that hour is his last.
Bear hence this body, and attend our will.
Mercy but murders, pardoning those that kill.
                          They go

Scene 2: *Capulet's house*

Enter Juliet alone

JULIET. Gallop apace, you fiery-footed steeds,
Towards Phoebus' lodging! Such a waggoner
As Phaëton would whip you to the west
And bring in cloudy night immediately.
Spread thy close curtain, love-performing night,
That runaways' eyes may wink, and Romeo
Leap to these arms untalked of and unseen.
Lovers can see to do their amorous rites
By their own beauties; or, if love be blind,
It best agrees with night. Come, civil Night,   10
Thou sober-suited matron all in black,
And learn me how to lose a winning match,
Played for a pair of stainless maidenhoods.
Hood my unmanned blood, bating in my cheeks,
With thy black mantle till strange love, grown bold,
Think true love acted simple modesty.
Come, Night! Come, Romeo! Come, thou day in
    night;
For thou wilt lie upon the wings of night
Whiter than snow upon a raven's back.
Come, gentle Night; come, loving, black-browed
    Night: 20
Give me my Romeo; and, when he shall die,
Take him and cut him out in little stars,
And he will make the face of heaven so fine
That all the world will be in love with night
And pay no worship to the garish sun.
O, I have bought the mansion of a love,
But not possessed it; and though I am sold,
Not yet enjoyed. So tedious is this day
As is the night before some festival
To an impatient child that hath new robes   30
And may not wear them. O, here comes my nurse,

Enter Nurse with cords

And she brings news; and every tongue that speaks
But Romeo's name speaks heavenly eloquence.
Now, Nurse, what news? What hast thou there?
    The cords

That Romeo bid thee fetch?
NURSE.   Ay, ay, the cords.
                          Throws them down
JULIET. Ay me, what news? Why dost thou wring thy
  hands?
NURSE. Ah, weraday! He's dead, he's dead, he's dead!
  We are undone, lady, we are undone.
  Alack the day, he's gone, he's killed, he's dead!
JULIET. Can heaven be so envious?
NURSE.   Romeo can,   40
  Though heaven cannot. O Romeo, Romeo!
  Who ever would have thought it? Romeo!
JULIET. What devil art thou that dost torment me
  thus?
  This torture should be roared in dismal hell.
  Hath Romeo slain himself? Say thou but 'ay',
  And that bare vowel 'I' shall poison more
  Than the death-darting eye of cockatrice.
  I am not I if there be such an 'I',
  Or those eyes shut that makes thee answer 'ay'.
  If he be slain, say 'ay', or, if not, 'no'.   50
  Brief sounds determine of my weal or woe.
NURSE. I saw the wound, I saw it with mine eyes,
  (God save the mark!) here on his manly breast.
  A piteous corse, a bloody piteous corse,
  Pale, pale as ashes, all bedaubed in blood,
  All in gore blood; I swounded at the sight.
JULIET. O break, my heart! Poor bankrout, break at
  once!
  To prison, eyes; ne'er look on liberty.
  Vile earth, to earth resign, end motion here,
  And thou and Romeo press one heavy bier!   60
NURSE. O Tybalt, Tybalt, the best friend I had!
  O courteous Tybalt, honest gentleman,
  That ever I should live to see thee dead!
JULIET. What storm is this that blows so contrary?
  Is Romeo slaught'red? and is Tybalt dead?
  My dearest cousin, and my dearer lord?
  Then, dreadful trumpet, sound the general doom;
  For who is living if those two are gone?
NURSE. Tybalt is gone and Romeo banishèd;
  Romeo that killed him, he is banishèd.   70
JULIET. O God! did Romeo's hand shed Tybalt's
  blood?
NURSE. It did, it did! alas the day, it did!
JULIET. O serpent heart, hid with a flowering face!
  Did ever dragon keep so fair a cave?
  Beautiful tyrant, fiend angelical,
  Dove-feathered raven, wolvish-ravening lamb!
  Despisèd substance of divinest show,
  Just opposite to what thou justly seemst—
  A damnèd saint, an honourable villain!
  O nature, what hadst thou to do in hell   80
  When thou didst bower the spirit of a fiend
  In mortal paradise of such sweet flesh?
  Was ever book containing such vile matter
  So fairly bound? O that deceit should dwell
  In such a gorgeous palace!
NURSE.   There's no trust,
  No faith, no honesty in men; all perjured,
  All forsworn, all naught, all dissemblers.
  Ah, where's my man? Give me sone aqua vitae.
  These griefs, these woes, these sorrows make me old.
  Shame come to Romeo!
JULIET.   Blistered be thy tongue   90
  For such a wish! He was not born to shame.

Upon his brow shame is ashamed to sit:
For 'tis a throne where honour may be crowned
Sole monarch of the universal earth.
O what a beast was I to chide at him!
NURSE. Will you speak well of him that killed your
  cousin?
JULIET. Shall I speak ill of him that is my husband?
  Ah, poor my lord, what tongue shall smooth thy
  name
  When I, thy three-hours wife, have mangled it?
  But wherefore, villain, didst thou kill my cousin?   100
  That villain cousin would have killed my husband.
  Back, foolish tears, back to your native spring!
  Your tributary drops belong to woe
  Which you, mistaking, offer up to joy.
  My husband lives, that Tybalt would have slain,
  And Tybalt's dead that would have slain my
  husband:
  All this is comfort; wherefore weep I then?
  Some word there was, worser than Tybalt's death,
  That murd'red me. I would forget it fain,
  But oh, it presses to my memory   110
  Like damnèd guilty deeds to sinners' minds—
  'Tybalt is dead and Romeo banishèd'.
  That 'banishèd', that one word 'banishèd',
  Hath slain ten thousand Tybalts. Tybalt's death
  Was woe enough if it had ended there:
  Or, if sour woe delights in fellowship
  And needly will be ranked with other griefs,
  Why followed not, when she said 'Tybalt's dead',
  'Thy father', or 'thy mother', nay, or both,
  Which modern lamentation might have moved?   120
  But, with a rearward following Tybalt's death,
  'Romeo is banishèd'! To speak that word
  Is father, mother, Tybalt, Romeo, Juliet,
  All slain, all dead: 'Romeo is banishèd'!
  There is no end, no limit, measure, bound,
  In that word's death; no words can that woe
  sound.
  Where is my father and my mother, Nurse?
NURSE. Weeping and wailing over Tybalt's corse.
  Will you go to them? I will bring you thither.
JULIET. Wash they his wounds with tears? Mine shall
  be spent,   130
  When theirs are dry, for Romeo's banishment.
  Take up those cords. Poor ropes, you are beguiled,
  Both you and I, for Romeo is exiled.
  He made you for a highway to my bed,
  But I, a maid, die maiden-widowèd.
  Come, cords; come, Nurse: I'll to my wedding bed,
  And death, not Romeo, take my maidenhead!
NURSE. Hie to your chamber. I'll find Romeo
  To comfort you: I wot well where he is.
  Hark ye, your Romeo will be here at night: 140
  I'll to him; he is hid at Lawrence' cell.
JULIET. O find him! Give this ring to my true knight
  And bid him come to take his last farewell.
                          They go

Scene 3: *Friar Lawrence's cell*

Enter Friar

FRIAR. Romeo, come forth; come forth, thou fearful
  man.
  Affliction is enamoured of thy parts,

And thou art wedded to calamity.

Enter Romeo

ROMEO. Father, what news? What is the prince's
    doom?
    What sorrow craves acquaintance at my hand
    That I yet know not?
FRIAR.   Too familiar
    Is my dear son with such sour company!
    I bring thee tidings of the prince's doom.
ROMEO. What less than doomsday is the prince's
    doom?
FRIAR. A gentler judgement vanished from his lips; 10
    Not body's death, but body's banishment.
ROMEO. Ha, banishment? Be merciful, say 'death':
    For exile hath more terror in his look,
    Much more than death: do not say 'banishment'.
FRIAR. Hence from Verona art thou banishéd.
    Be patient, for the world is broad and wide.
ROMEO. There is no world without Verona walls,
    But purgatory, torture, hell itself:
    Hence banishéd is banished from the world,
    And world's exile is death. Then 'banishéd' 20
    Is death mis-termed. Calling death 'banishéd',
    Thou cut'st my head off with a golden axe,
    And smilest upon the stroke that murders me.
FRIAR. O deadly sin! O rude unthankfulness!
    Thy fault our law calls death, but the kind Prince,
    Taking thy part, hath rushed aside the law,
    And turned that black word 'death' to 'banishment'.
    This is dear mercy, and thou seest it not.
ROMEO. 'Tis torture and not mercy. Heaven is here
    Where Juliet lives, and every cat and dog 30
    And little mouse, every unworthy thing,
    Live here in heaven and may look on her,
    But Romeo may not. More validity,
    More honourable state, more courtship, lives
    In carrion flies than Romeo: they may seize
    On the white wonder of dear Juliet's hand,
    And steal immortal blessing from her lips,
    Who even in pure and vestal modesty
    Still blush, as thinking their own kisses sin;
    This may flies do, when I from this must fly; 40
    And say'st thou yet that exile is not death?
    [But Romeo may not—he is banishéd.
    Flies may do this, but I from this must fly:
    They are free men, but I am banishéd.]
    Hadst thou no poison mixed, no sharp-ground
      knife,
    No sudden mean of death, though ne'er so mean,
    But 'banishéd' to kill me? 'Banishéd'!
    O friar, the damnéd use that word in hell:
    Howling attends it. How hast thou the heart,
    Being a divine, a ghostly confessor, 50
    A sin-absolver, and my friend professed,
    To mangle me with that word 'banishéd'?
FRIAR. Thou fond mad man, hear me a little speak.
ROMEO. O thou wilt speak again of banishment.
FRIAR. I'll give thee armour to keep off that word—
    Adversity's sweet milk, philosophy,
    To comfort thee though thou art banishéd.
ROMEO. Yet 'banishéd'? Hang up philosophy!
    Unless philosophy can make a Juliet,
    Displant a town, reverse a prince's doom, 60
    It helps not, it prevails not; talk no more.
FRIAR. O then I see that madmen have no ears.

ROMEO. How should they, when that wise men have
    no eyes?
FRIAR. Let me dispute with thee of thy estate.
ROMEO. Thou canst not speak of that thou dost not
    feel.
    Wert thou as young as I, Juliet thy love,
    An hour but married, Tybalt murderéd,
    Doting like me, and like me banishéd,
    Then mightst thou speak, then mightst thou tear
      thy hair,
    And fall upon the ground as I do now, 70
    Taking the measure of an unmade grave.
                    Knocking without
FRIAR. Arise; one knocks. Good Romeo, hide thyself.
ROMEO. Not I, unless the breath of heartsick groans
    Mist-like infold me from the search of eyes.
                    Knocking again
FRIAR. Hark, how they knock!—Who's there?—
    Romeo, arisè;
    Thou wilt be taken.—Stay awhile!—Stand up;
                    Louder knocking
    Run to my study.—By and by!—God's will,
    What simpleness is this?—I come, I come?
                  Knocking yet again
    Who knocks so hard? Whence come you? What's
    your will?
NURSE [*from without*]. Let me come in and you shall
    know my errand: 80
    I come from Lady Juliet.
FRIAR.   Welcome then.

Enter Nurse

NURSE. O holy friar, O tell me, holy friar,
    Where is my lady's lord? Where's Romeo?
FRIAR. There on the ground, with his own tears made
    drunk.
NURSE. O he is even in my mistress' case,
    Just in her case.
FRIAR.   O woeful sympathy;
    Piteous predicament!
NURSE.   Even so lies she,
    Blubbering and weeping, weeping and blubbering.
    Stand up, stand up! Stand an you be a man;
    For Juliet's sake, for her sake rise and stand; 90
    Why should you fall into so deep an O?
ROMEO [*rising*]. Nurse!
NURSE.   Ah sir, ah sir, death's the end of all.
ROMEO. Spakest thou of Juliet? How is it with her?
    Doth not she think me an old murderer,
    Now I have stained the childhood of our joy
    With blood removed but little from her own?
    Where is she? and how doth she? and what says
    My concealed lady to our cancelled love?
NURSE. O she says nothing, sir, but weeps and weeps,
    And now falls on her bed, and then starts up, 100
    And Tybalt calls, and then on Romeo cries,
    And then down falls again.
ROMEO.   As if that name,
    Shot from the deadly level of a gun,
    Did murder her, as that name's curséd hand
    Murdered her kinsman. O tell me, friar, tell me,
    In what vile part of this anatomy
    Doth my name lodge? Tell me, that I may sack
    The hateful mansion.
          He offers to stab himself, and Nurse
          snatches the dagger away

FRIAR.   Hold thy desperate hand!
Art thou a man? Thy form cries out thou art:
Thy tears are womanish, thy wild acts denote   110
The unreasonable fury of a beast.
Unseemly woman in a seeming man,
And ill-beseeming beast in seeming both!
Thou hast amazed me. By my holy order,
I thought thy disposition better tempered.
Hast thou slain Tybalt? Wilt thou slay thyself?
And slay thy lady, that in thy life lives,
By doing damnéd hate upon thyself?
Why rail'st thou on thy birth, the heaven, and
    earth,
Since birth, and heaven, and earth, all three do meet   120
In thee at once, which thou at once wouldst lose?
Fie, fie! thou sham'st thy shape, thy love, thy wit,
Which like a usurer abound'st in all,
And usest none in that true use indeed
Which should bedeck thy shape, thy love, thy wit.
Thy noble shape is but a form of wax,
Digressing from the valour of a man;
Thy dear love sworn but hollow perjury,
Killing that love which thou hast vowed to cherish;
Thy wit, that ornament to shape and love,   130
Misshapen in the conduct of them both,
Like powder in a skilless soldier's flask
Is set afire by thine own ignorance,
And thou dismembered with thine own defence.
What, rouse thee, man! Thy Juliet is alive,
For whose dear sake thou wast but lately dead.
There art thou happy. Tybalt would kill thee,
But thou slewest Tybalt. There art thou happy.
The law that threatened death becomes thy friend,
And turns it to exile. There art thou happy too.   140
A pack of blessings light upon thy back;
Happiness courts thee in her best array;
But, like a misbehaved and sullen wench,
Thou pouts upon thy fortune and thy love.
Take heed, take heed, for such die miserable.
Go get thee to thy love, as was decreed;
Ascend her chamber; hence and comfort her.
But look thou stay not till the watch be set,
For then thou canst not pass to Mantua,
Where thou shalt live till we can find a time   150
To blaze your marriage, reconcile your friends,
Beg pardon of the prince, and call thee back
With twenty hundred thousand times more joy
Than thou wentst forth in lamentation.
Go before, Nurse. Commend me to thy lady,
And bid her hasten all the house to bed,
Which heavy sorrow makes them apt unto.
Romeo is coming.
NURSE. O Lord, I could have stayed here all the night
To hear good counsel; O what learning is!   160
My lord, I'll tell my lady you will come.
ROMEO. Do so, and bid my sweet prepare to chide.

Nurse offers to go in and turns again

NURSE. Here, sir, a ring she bid me give you, sir.
Hie you, make haste, for it grows very late.
                                  She goes
ROMEO. How well my comfort is revived by this.
FRIAR. Go hence; goodnight; and here stands all your
    state:
Either be gone before the watch be set,
Or by the break of day disguised from hence.

Sojourn in Mantua. I'll find out your man,
And he shall signify from time to time   170
Every good hap to you that chances here.
Give me thy hand. 'Tis late; farewell, goodnight.
ROMEO. But that a joy past joy calls out on me,
It were a grief so brief to part with thee.
Farewell.   *They go*

Scene 4: *Capulet's house*

Enter old Capulet, his wife, and Paris

CAPULET. Things have fall'n out, sir, so unluckily
That we have had no time to move our daughter.
Look you, she loved her kinsman Tybalt dearly,
And so did I. Well, we were born to die.
'Tis very late; she'll not come down tonight.
I promise you, but for your company,
I would have been abed an hour ago.
PARIS. These times of woe afford no times to woo.
Madam, goodnight; commend me to your
    daughter.
LADY CAPULET. I will, and know her mind early
    tomorrow;   10
Tonight she's mewed up to her heaviness.

Paris offers to go; Capulet calls him again

CAPULET. Sir Paris, I will make a desperate tender
Of my child's love: I think she will be ruled
In all respects by me: nay more, I doubt it not.
Wife, go you to her ere you go to bed;
Acquaint her ear of my son Paris' love,
And bid her, mark you me, on Wednesday next—
But soft, what day is this?
PARIS.   Monday, my lord.
CAPULET. Monday, ha, ha; well, Wednesday is too
    soon;
O' Thursday let it be—O' Thursday, tell her,   20
She shall be married to this noble earl—
Will you be ready? Do you like this haste?
We'll keep no great ado; a friend or two:
For hark you, Tybalt being slain so late,
It may be thought we held him carelessly,
Being our kinsman, if we revel much:
Therefore we'll have some half a dozen friends,
And there an end. But what say you to Thursday?
PARIS. My lord, I would that Thursday were
    tomorrow.
CAPULET. Well, get you gone. O' Thursday be it then. 30
Go you to Juliet ere you go to bed;
Prepare her, wife, against this wedding day.
Farewell, my lord. Light to my chamber, ho!
Afore me, 'tis so very late, that we
May call it early by and by. Goodnight.   *They go*

Scene 5: *Juliet's bedroom: to one side the window above the Orchard; to the other a door*

Romeo and Juliet stand by the window

JULIET. Wilt thou be gone? It is not yet near day.
It was the nightingale, and not the lark,
That pierced the fearful hollow of thine ear.
Nightly she sings on yond pomegranate tree.
Believe me, love, it was the nightingale.
ROMEO. It was the lark, the herald of the morn;
No nightingale. Look, love, what envious streaks
Do lace the severing clouds in yonder east.
Night's candles are burnt out, and jocund day

Stands tiptoe on the misty mountain tops.   10
I must be gone and live, or stay and die.
JULIET. Yond light is not daylight; I know it, I:
  It is some meteor that the sun exhaled
  To be to thee this night a torchbearer
  And light thee on thy way to Mantua.
  Therefore stay yet; thou needst not to be gone.
ROMEO. Let me be ta'en, let me be put to
    death;
  I am content, so thou wilt have it so.
  I'll say yon gray is not the morning's eye,
  'Tis but the pale reflex of Cynthia's brow;   20
  Nor that is not the lark whose notes do beat
  The vaulty heaven so high above our heads.
  I have more care to stay than will to go:
  Come, death, and welcome! Juliet wills it so.
  How is't, my soul? Let's talk; it is not day.
JULIET. It is, it is! Hie hence, be gone, away!
  It is the lark that sings so out of tune,
  Straining harsh discords and unpleasing sharps.
  Some say the lark makes sweet division:
  This doth not so, for she divideth us.   30
  Some say the lark and loathéd toad changed eyes;
  O now I would they had changed voices too,
  Since arm from arm that voice doth us affray,
  Hunting thee hence with hunt's-up to the day.
  O now be gone! More light and light it grows.
ROMEO. More light and light, more dark and dark
    our woes.

Enter Nurse hastily

NURSE. Madam!
JULIET. Nurse?
NURSE. Your lady mother is coming to your chamber.
  The day is broke; be wary, look about.   *She goes* 40
JULIET. Then, window, let day in and let life out.
ROMEO. Farewell, farewell; one kiss, and I'll descend.
        He lowers the ladder and descends
JULIET. Art thou gone so, love, lord, ay husband,
    friend?
  I must hear from thee every day in the hour,
  For in a minute there are many days.
  O, by this count I shall be much in years
  Ere I again behold my Romeo.
ROMEO [*from the orchard*]. Farewell!
  I will omit no opportunity
  That may convey my greetings, love, to thee.   50
JULIET. O, think'st thou we shall ever meet again?
ROMEO. I doubt it not; and all these woes shall serve
  For sweet discourses in our times to come.
JULIET. O God, I have an ill-divining soul!
  Methinks I see thee, now thou art so low,
  As one dead in the bottom of a tomb.
  Either my eyesight fails or thou look'st pale.
ROMEO. And trust me, love, in my eye so do you.
  Dry sorrow drinks our blood. Adieu, adieu!
        He goes
JULIET. O Fortune, Fortune, all men call thee fickle; 60
  If thou art fickle, what dost thou with him
  That is renowned for faith? Be fickle, Fortune:
  For then I hope thou wilt not keep him long,
  But send him back.
LADY CAPULET [*without the door*]. Ho, daughter, are
    you up?
JULIET. Who is't that calls? It is my lady mother.
  Is she not down so late, or up so early?

What unaccustomed cause procures her hither?

Enter Lady Capulet

LADY CAPULET. Why, how now, Juliet?
JULIET.   Madam, I am not well.
LADY CAPULET. Evermore weeping for your cousin's
    death?
  What, wilt thou wash him from his grave with
    tears?   70
  An if thou couldst, thou couldst not make him live:
  Therefore have done—some grief shows much of
    love,
  But much of grief shows still some want of wit.
JULIET. Yet let me weep for such a feeling loss.
LADY CAPULET. So shall you feel the loss, but not the
    friend
  Which you weep for.
JULIET.   Feeling so the loss,
  I cannot choose but ever weep the friend.
LADY CAPULET. Well, girl, thou weep'st not so much
    for his death,
  As that the villain lives which slaughtered him.
JULIET. What villain, madam?
LADY CAPULET.   That same villain Romeo. 80
JULIET [*aside*]. Villain and he be many miles asunder.
  [*aloud*] God pardon him; I do, with all my heart:
  And yet no man like he doth grieve my heart.
LADY CAPULET. That is because the traitor murderer
    lives.
JULIET. Ay, madam, from the reach of these my hands.
  Would none but I might venge my cousin's death!
LADY CAPULET. We will have vengeance for it, fear
    thou not.
  Then weep no more. I'll send to one in Mantua,
  Where that same banished runagate doth live,
  Shall give him such an unaccustomed dram   90
  That he shall soon keep Tybalt company;
  And then I hope thou wilt be satisfied.
JULIET. Indeed I never shall be satisfied
  With Romeo till I behold him—dead—
  Is my poor heart so for a kinsman vexed.
  Madam, if you could find out but a man
  To bear a poison, I would temper it
  That Romeo should upon receipt thereof
  Soon sleep in quiet. O how my heart abhors
  To hear him named and cannot come to him   100
  To wreak the love I bore my cousin
  Upon his body that hath slaughtered him.
LADY CAPULET. Find thou the means and I'll find such
    a man.
  But now I'll tell thee joyful tidings, girl.
JULIET. And joy comes well in such a needy time.
  What are they, I beseech your ladyship?
LADY CAPULET. Well, well, thou hast a careful father,
    child;
  One who, to put thee from thy heaviness,
  Hath sorted out a sudden day of joy
  That thou expects not, nor I looked not for.   110
JULIET. Madam, in happy time! What day is that?
LADY CAPULET. Marry, my child, early next Thursday
    morn
  The gallant, young, and noble gentleman,
  The County Paris, at Saint Peter's Church
  Shall happily make thee there a joyful bride.
JULIET. Now by Saint Peter's Church, and Peter too,

He shall not make me there a joyful bride.
I wonder at this haste, that I must wed
Ere he that should be husband comes to woo.
I pray you tell my lord and father, madam, 120
I will not marry yet; and when I do, I swear
It shall be Romeo, whom you know I hate,
Rather than Paris. These are news indeed!
LADY CAPULET. Here comes your father; tell him so
yourself,
And see how he will take it at your hands.

Enter Capulet and Nurse

CAPULET. When the sun sets, the air doth drizzle dew;
But for the sunset of my brother's son
It rains downright.
How now, a conduit, girl? What, still in tears?
Evermore showering? In one little body 130
Thou conterfeits a bark, a sea, a wind:
For still thy eyes, which I may call the sea,
Do ebb and flow with tears; the bark thy body is,
Sailing in this salt flood; the winds thy sighs,
Who raging with thy tears, and they with them,
Without a sudden calm will overset
Thy tempest-tosséd body. How now, wife?
Have you delivered to her our decree?
LADY CAPULET. Ay, sir; but she will none, she gives
you thanks.
I would the fool were married to her grave! 140
CAPULET. Soft, take me with you, take me with you,
wife.
How? Will she none? Doth she not give us thanks?
Is she not proud? Doth she not count her blest,
Unworthy as she is, that we have wrought
So worthy a gentleman to be her bride?
JULIET. Not proud you have, but thankful that you
have.
Proud can I never be of what I hate,
But thankful even for hate that is meant love.
CAPULET. How how! how how, chop-logic! what is
this?
'Proud', and 'I thank you', and 'I thank you not', 150
And yet 'not proud', mistress minion you?
Thank me no thankings nor proud me no prouds,
But fettle your fine joints 'gainst Thursday next
To go with Paris to Saint Peter's Church,
Or I will drag thee on a hurdle thither.
Out, you green-sickness carrion! out, you baggage!
You tallow-face!
LADY CAPULET. Fie, fie! what, are you mad?
JULIET [*kneeling*]. Good father, I beseech you on
my knees,
Hear me with patience but to speak a word.
CAPULET. Hang thee, young baggage! disobedient
wretch! 160
I tell thee what; get thee to church o' Thursday,
Or never after look me in the face.
Speak not, reply not, do not answer me!
My fingers itch. Wife, we scarce thought us
blest
That God had lent us but this only child;
But now I see this one is one too much,
And that we have a curse in having her.
Out on her, hilding!
NURSE. God in heaven bless her!
You are to blame, my lord, to rate her so.

CAPULET. And why, my Lady Wisdom? Hold your
tongue, 170
Good Prudence. Smatter with your gossips, go!
NURSE. I speak no treason.
CAPULET. O Godigoden!
NURSE. May not one speak?
CAPULET. Peace, you mumbling fool!
Utter your gravity o'er a gossip's bowl,
For here we need it not.
LADY CAPULET. You are too hot.
CAPULET. God's bread! it makes me mad. Day, night,
work, play,
Alone, in company, still my care hath been
To have her matched; and having now provided
A gentleman of noble parentage,
Of fair demesnes, youthful and nobly trained, 180
Stuffed, as they say, with honourable parts,
Proportioned as one's thought would wish a man—
And then to have a wretched puling fool,
A whining mammet, in her fortune's tender,
To answer 'I'll not wed, I cannot love;
I am too young, I pray you pardon me'.
But, an you will not wed, I'll pardon you—
Graze where you will; you shall not house with me.
Look to't, think on't; I do not use to jest.
Thursday is near. Lay hand on heart; advise. 190
An you be mine, I'll give you to my friend;
An you be not, hang, beg, starve, die in the streets,
For by my soul I'll ne'er acknowledge thee,
Nor what is mine shall never do thee good:
Trust to 't; bethink you; I'll not be forsworn.
He goes
JULIET. Is there no pity sitting in the clouds
That sees into the bottom of my grief?
O sweet my mother, cast me not away!
Delay this marriage for a month, a week;
Or, if you do not, make the bridal bed 200
In that dim monument where Tybalt lies.
LADY CAPULET. Talk not to me, for I'll not speak a
word;
Do as thou wilt, for I have done with thee.
She goes
JULIET. O God!—O nurse, how shall this be
prevented?
My husband is on earth, my faith in heaven;
How shall that faith return again to earth,
Unless that husband send it me from heaven
By leaving earth? Comfort me, counsel me.
Alack, alack, that heaven should practise stratagems
Upon so soft a subject as myself! 210
What sayst thou? Hast thou not a word of joy?
Some comfort, nurse.
NURSE. Faith, here it is. Romeo
Is banishéd; and all the world to nothing
That he dares ne'er come back to challenge you;
Or, if he do, it needs must be by stealth.
Then, since the case so stands as now it doth,
I think it best you married with the County.
O, he's a lovely gentleman!
Romeo's a dishclout to him. An eagle, madam,
Hath not so green, so quick, so fair an eye 220
As Paris hath. Beshrew my very heart,
I think you are happy in this second match,
For it excels your first; or, if it did not,
Your first is dead—or 'twere as good he were
As living here and you no use of him.

JULIET. Speakst thou from thy heart?

NURSE. And from my soul too; else beshrew them
both.

JULIET. Amen!

NURSE. What?

JULIET. Well, thou hast comforted me marvellous
much.   230
Go in and tell my lady I am gone,
Having displeased my father, to Lawrence' cell
To make confession and to be absolved.

NURSE. Marry, I will; and this is wisely done.
She goes

JULIET. Ancient damnation! O most wicked fiend!
Is it more sin to wish me thus forsworn,
Or to dispraise my lord with that same tongue
Which she hath praised him with above compare
So many thousand times? Go, counsellor!
Thou and my bosom henceforth shall be twain.   240
I'll to the friar to know his remedy.
If all else fail, myself have power to die.   *She goes*

ACT 4
Scene 1: *Friar Lawrence's cell*

Enter Friar and County Paris

FRIAR. On Thursday, sir? The time is very short.

PARIS. My father Capulet will have it so,
And I am nothing slow to slack his haste.

FRIAR. You say you do not know the lady's mind?
Uneven is the course; I like it not.

PARIS. Immoderately she weeps for Tybalt's death,
And therefore have I little talked of love,
For Venus smiles not in a house of tears.
Now, sir, her father counts it dangerous
That she do give her sorrow so much sway,   10
And in his wisdom hastes our marriage
To stop the inundation of her tears,
Which, too much minded by herself alone,
May be put from her by society.
Now do you know the reason of this haste.

FRIAR [*aside*]. I would I knew not why it should be
slowed—
Look, sir, here comes the lady toward my cell.

Enter Juliet

PARIS. Happily met, my lady and my wife!

JULIET. That may be, sir, when I may be a wife.

PARIS. That 'may be' must be, love, on Thursday
next.   20

JULIET. What must be shall be.

FRIAR.   That's a certain text.

PARIS. Come you to make confession to this father?

JULIET. To answer that, I should confess to you.

PARIS. Do not deny to him that you love me.

JULIET. I will confess to you that I love him.

PARIS. So will ye, I am sure, that you love me.

JULIET. If I do so, it will be of more price,
Being spoke behind your back, than to your face.

PARIS. Poor soul, thy face is much abused with tears.

JULIET. The tears have got small victory by that,   30
For it was bad enough before their spite.

PARIS. Thou wrong'st it more than tears with that
report.

JULIET. That is no slander, sir, which is a truth;
And what I spake, I spake it to my face.

PARIS. Thy face is mine, and thou hast sland'red it.

JULIET. It may be so, for it is not mine own.—
Are you at leisure, holy father, now,
Or shall I come to you at evening mass?

FRIAR. My leisure serves me, pensive daughter, now.
My lord, we must entreat the time alone.   40

PARIS. God shield I should disturb devotion!
Juliet, on Thursday early will I rouse ye;
Till then adieu, and keep this holy kiss.   *Goes*

JULIET. O shut the door, and, when thou hast done so,
Come weep with me—past hope, past cure, past
help.

FRIAR. O Juliet, I already know thy grief;
It strains me past the compass of my wits.
I hear thou must, and nothing may prorogue it,
On Thursday next be married to this County.

JULIET. Tell me not, friar, that thou hearest of this,   50
Unless thou tell me how I may prevent it.
If in thy wisdom thou canst give no help,
Do thou but call my resolution wise
And with this knife I'll help it presently.
God joined my heart and Romeo's, thou our hands;
And ere this hand, by thee to Romeo's sealed,
Shall be the label to another deed,
Or my true heart with treacherous revolt
Turn to another, this shall slay them both:
Therefore, out of thy long-experienced time,   60
Give me some present counsel; or, behold,
'Twixt my extremes and me this bloody knife
Shall play the umpire, arbitrating that
Which the commission of thy years and art
Could to no issue of true honour bring.
Be not so long to speak: I long to die
If what thou speak'st speak not of remedy.

FRIAR. Hold, daughter. I do spy a kind of hope,
Which craves as desperate an execution
As that is desperate which we would prevent.   70
If, rather than to marry County Paris,
Thou hast the strength of will to slay thyself,
Then is it likely thou wilt undertake
A thing like death to chide away this shame,
That copest with death himself to scape from it;
And, if thou darest, I'll give thee remedy.

JULIET. O bid me leap, rather than marry Paris,
From off the battlements of any tower,
Or walk in thievish ways, or bid me lurk
Where serpents are; chain me with roaring bears,   80
Or hide me nightly in a charnel house,
O'ercovered quite with dead men's rattling bones,
With reeky shanks and yellow chapless skulls;
Or bid me go into a new-made grave
And lay me with a dead man in his shroud—
Things that, to hear them told, have made me
tremble—
And I will do it without fear of doubt,
To live an unstained wife to my sweet love.

FRIAR. Hold, then. Go home, be merry, give consent
To marry Paris. Wednesday is tomorrow.   90
Tomorrow night look that thou lie alone;
Let not the nurse lie with thee in thy chamber.
Take thou this vial, being then in bed,
And this distilléd liquor drink thou off,
When presently through all thy veins shall run
A cold and drowsy humour, for no pulse
Shall keep his native progress, but surcease;
No warmth, no breath, shall testify thou livest;

The roses in thy lips and cheeks shall fade
To wanny ashes, thy eyes' windows fall
Like death when he shuts up the day of life.
Each part, deprived of supple government,
Shall stiff and stark and cold appear like death;
And in this borrowed likeness of shrunk death
Thou shalt continue two and forty hours,
And then awake as from a pleasant sleep.
Now, when the bridegroom in the morning comes
To rouse thee from thy bed, there art thou dead.
Then, as the manner of our country is,
In thy best robes, uncovered on the bier, 110
Thou shalt be borne to that same ancient vault
Where all the kindred of the Capulets lie.
In the meantime, against thou shalt awake,
Shall Romeo by my letters know our drift,
And hither shall he come; and he and I
Will watch thy waking, and that very night
Shall Romeo bear thee hence to Mantua.
And this shall free thee from this present shame,
If no inconstant toy nor womanish fear
Abate thy valour in the acting it. 120
JULIET. Give me, give me! O tell not me of fear!
FRIAR. Hold, get you gone! Be strong and
    prosperous
In this resolve. I'll send a friar with speed
To Mantua with my letters to thy lord.
JULIET. Love give me strength! and strength shall help
    afford.
Farewell, dear father. *They go*

Scene 2: *Capulet's house*

*Enter Capulet, Lady Capulet, Nurse and two or three
Servingmen*

CAPULET. So many guests invite as here are writ.
                               Servingman goes
[*to another*] Sirrah, go hire me twenty cunning
cooks.
SERVINGMAN. You shall have none ill, sir; for I'll try
if they can lick their fingers.
CAPULET. How canst thou try them so?
SERVINGMAN. Marry, sir, 'tis an ill cook that cannot
lick his own fingers: therefore he that cannot lick
his fingers goes not with me.
CAPULET. Go, be gone.   *He goes* 10
We shall be much unfurnished for this time.
What, is my daughter gone to Friar Lawrence?
NURSE. Ay, forsooth.
CAPULET. Well, he may chance to do some good on
her.
A peevish self-willed harlotry it is.

Enter Juliet

NURSE. See where she comes from shrift with merry
look.
CAPULET. How now, my headstrong? Where have
you been gadding?
JULIET. Where I have learned me to repent the sin
Of disobedient opposition
To you and your behests, and am enjoined 20
By holy Lawrence to fall prostrate here
To beg your pardon. [*abasing herself*] Pardon, I
beseech you!
Henceforward I am ever ruled by you.
CAPULET. Send for the County: go tell him of this.

I'll have this knot knit up tomorrow morning.
JULIET. I met the youthful lord at Lawrence' cell 100
And gave him what becoméd love I might,
Not stepping o'er the bounds of modesty.
CAPULET. Why, I am glad on't; this is well.
    Stand up.
This is as 't should be. Let me see, the County: 30
Ay, marry, go, I say, and fetch him hither.
Now, afore God, this reverend holy friar,
All our whole city is much bound to him.
JULIET. Nurse, will you go with me into my closet
To help me sort such needful ornaments
As you think fit to furnish me tomorrow?
LADY CAPULET. No, not till Thursday; there is
    time enough.
CAPULET. Go, nurse, go with her; we'll to church
    tomorrow.   *Nurse departs with Juliet*
LADY CAPULET. We shall be short in our provision;
'Tis now near night.
CAPULET.   Tush, I will stir about, 40
And all things shall be well, I warrant thee, wife.
Go thou to Juliet; help to deck up her.
I'll not to bed tonight. Let me alone;
I'll play the housewife for this once. What, ho!
They are all forth; well, I will walk myself
To County Paris, to prepare up him
Against tomorrow. My heart is wondrous light
Since this same wayward girl is so reclaimed.
                                        They go

Scene 3: *Juliet's chamber*

Enter Juliet and Nurse

JULIET. Ay, those attires are best. But, gentle nurse,
I pray thee leave me to myself tonight:
For I have need of many orisons
To move the heavens to smile upon my state,
Which well thou knowest is cross and full of sin.

Enter Lady Capulet

LADY CAPULET. What, are you busy, ho? Need you
    my help?
JULIET. No, madam, we have culled such necessaries
As are behoveful for our state tomorrow.
So please you, let me now be left alone,
And let the nurse this night sit up with you, 10
For I am sure you have your hands full all
In this so sudden business.
LADY CAPULET.   Good night.
Get thee to bed and rest, for thou hast need.
                         She departs with the Nurse
JULIET. Farewell! God knows when we shall meet
    again.
I have a faint cold fear thrills through my veins
That almost freezes up the heat of life.
I'll call them back again to comfort me.
Nurse!—What should she do here?
My dismal scene I needs must act alone.
Come, vial! 20
What if this mixture do not work at all?
Shall I be married then tomorrow morning?
No, no! This shall forbid it. Lie thou there.
                         Laying down her knife
What if it be a poison which the friar
Subtly hath minist'red to have me dead,
Lest in this marriage he should be dishonoured

Because he married me before to Romeo?
I fear it is; and yet methinks it should not,
For he hath still been tried a holy man.
How if, when I am laid into the tomb,   30
I wake before the time that Romeo
Come to redeem me? There's a fearful point!
Shall I not then be stifled in the vault,
To whose foul mouth no healthsome air breathes in,
And there die strangled ere my Romeo comes?
Or, if I live, is it not very like
The horrible conceit of death and night,
Together with the terror of the place—
As in a vault, an ancient receptacle
Where for this many hundred years the bones   40
Of all my buried ancestors are packed;
Where bloody Tybalt, yet but green in earth,
Lies festering in his shroud; where, as they say,
At some hours in the night spirits resort—
Alack, alack, is it not like that I,
So early waking—what with loathsome smells,
And shrieks like mandrakes' torn out of the earth,
That living mortals, hearing them, run mad—
O, if I wake, shall I not be distraught,
Environèd with all these hideous fears,   50
And madly play with my forefathers' joints,
And pluck the mangled Tybalt from his shroud,
And, in this rage, with some great kinsman's bone,
As with a club, dash out my desp'rate brains?
O, look! Methinks I see my cousin's ghost
Seeking out Romeo, that did spit his body
Upon a rapier's point. Stay, Tybalt, stay!
Romeo, I come! this do I drink to thee.
                    She falls upon her bed within the curtains

           Scene 4: *Hall in Capulet's house*

Enter Lady Capulet and Nurse with herbs

LADY CAPULET. Hold, take these keys and fetch more
        spices, nurse.
NURSE. They call for dates and quinces in the pastry.

Enter old Capulet

CAPULET. Come, stir, stir, stir! The second cock hath
        crowed:
        The curfew bell hath rung, 'tis three o'clock.
        Look to the baked meats, good Angelica;
        Spare not for cost.
NURSE.   Go, you cot-quean, go,
        Get you to bed. Faith, you'll be sick tomorrow
        For this night's watching.
CAPULET. No, not a whit. What, I have watched ere
        now
        All night for lesser cause, and ne'er been sick.   10
LADY CAPULET. Ay, you have been a mouse-hunt in
        your time,
        But I will watch you from such watching now.
                              She goes out with Nurse
CAPULET. A jealous hood, a jealous hood!

Enter three or four with spits and logs and baskets

                    Now, fellow, what is there?
FIRST SERVINGMAN. Things for the cook, sir; but I
        know not what.
CAPULET. Make haste, make haste. [*1 servingman goes*]
                    Sirrah, fetch drier logs.
        Call Peter; he will show thee where they are.

SECOND SERVINGMAN. I have a head, sir, that will find
        out logs
        And never trouble Peter for the matter.
CAPULET. Mass, and well said; a merry whoreson, ha!
        Thou shalt be loggerhead.   [*2 servingman goes*]
        Good faith, 'tis day!   20
        The County will be here with music straight,
        For so he said he would. [*music*] I hear him near.
        Nurse! Wife! What, ho! What, nurse, I say!

Enter Nurse

        Go waken Juliet; go and trim her up.
        I'll go and chat with Paris. Hie, make haste,
        Make haste! The bridegroom he is come already:
        Make haste, I say.   *They go*

           Scene 5: *Juliet's chamber*

Enter Nurse

NURSE. Mistress! what, mistress! Juliet! Fast, I warrant
        her, she.
        Why, lamb! why, lady! Fie, you slug-a-bed!
        Why, love, I say! madam! sweetheart! why, bride!
        What, not a word? You take your pennyworths
        now!
        Sleep for a week; for the next night, I warrant,
        The County Paris hath set up his rest
        That you shall rest but little. God forgive me!
        Marry, and amen! How sound is she asleep!
        I needs must wake her. Madam, madam, madam!
        Ay, let the County take you in your bed,   10
        He'll fright you up, i'faith! Will it not be?
                              Draws back the curtains
        What, dressed, and in your clothes, and down again?
        I must needs wake you. Lady, lady, lady!
        Alas, alas! Help, help! My lady's dead!
        O weraday that ever I was born!
        Some aqua-vitae, ho! My lord! my lady!

Enter Lady Capulet

LADY CAPULET. What noise is here?
NURSE.   O lamentable day!
LADY CAPULET. What is the matter?
NURSE.   Look, look! O heavy day!
LADY CAPULET. O me, O me! My child, my only life!
        Revive, look up, or I will die with thee!   20
        Help, help! Call help.

Enter Capulet

CAPULET. For shame, bring Juliet forth; her lord is
        come.
NURSE. She's dead, deceased: she's dead, alack the day!
LADY CAPULET. Alack the day, she's dead, she's dead,
        she's dead!
CAPULET. Ha, let me see her. Out, alas! She's cold,
        Her blood is settled, and her joints are stiff:
        Life and these lips have long been separated;
        Death lies on her like an untimely frost
        Upon the sweetest flower of all the field.
NURSE. O lamentable day!
LADY CAPULET.   O woeful time!   30
CAPULET. Death, that hath ta'en her hence to make
        me wail,
        Ties up my tongue and will not let me speak.

Enter Friar and the County with Musicians

FRIAR. Come, is the bride ready to go to church?

CAPULET. Ready to go, but never to return.
  O son, the night before thy wedding day
  Hath Death lain with thy wife. There she lies,
  Flower as she was, defloweréd by him.
  Death is my son-in-law, Death is my heir;
  My daughter he hath wedded! I will die
  And leave him all; life, living, all is Death's.   40
PARIS. Have I thought long to see this morning's face,
  And doth it give me such a sight as this?
LADY CAPULET. Accursed, unhappy, wretched, hateful
    day!
  Most miserable hour that e'er time saw
  In lasting labour of his pilgrimage!
  But one, poor one, one poor and loving child,
  But one thing to rejoice and solace in,
  And cruel Death hath catched it from my sight!
NURSE. O woe! O woeful, woeful, woeful day!
  Most lamentable day, most woeful day   50
  That ever, ever I did yet behold!
  O day, O day, O day, O hateful day!
  Never was seen so black a day as this.
  O woeful day, O woeful day!
PARIS. Beguiled, divorcéd, wrongéd, spited, slain!
  Most detestable Death, by thee beguiled,
  By cruel, cruel thee quite overthrown!
  O love! O life! Not life, but love in death!
CAPULET. Despised, distresséd, hated, martyred, killed!
  Uncomfortable time, why cam'st thou now   60
  To murder, murder our solemnity?
  O child, O child! my soul, and not my child!
  Dead art thou. Alack, my child is dead,
  And with my child my joys are buriéd!
FRIAR. Peace, ho, for shame! Confusion's cure lives not
  In these confusions. Heaven and yourself
  Had part in this fair maid; now heaven hath all,
  And all the better is it for the maid.
  Your part in her you could not keep from death,
  But heaven keeps his part in eternal life.   70
  The most you sought was her promotion,
  For 'twas your heaven she should be advanced;
  And weep ye now, seeing she is advanced
  Above the clouds as high as heaven itself?
  O, in this love you love your child so ill
  That you run mad, seeing that she is well.
  She's not well married that lives married long,
  But she's best married that dies married young.
  Dry up your tears and stick your rosemary
  On this fair corse, and as the custom is,   80
  All in her best array, bear her to church:
  For though fond nature bids us all lament,
  Yet nature's tears are reason's merriment.
CAPULET. All things that we ordainéd festival
  Turn from their office to black funeral,
  Our instruments to melancholy bells,
  Our wedding cheer to a sad burial feast;
  Our solemn hymns to sullen dirges change,
  Our bridal flowers serve for a buried corse,
  And all things change them to the contrary.   90
FRIAR. Sir, go you in; and, madam, go with him;
  And go, Sir Paris. Everyone prepare
  To follow this fair corse unto her grave.
  The heavens do lour upon you for some ill;
  Move them no more by crossing their high will.
          *All but the Nurse and the Musicians go
          forth, casting rosemary upon her
          and shutting the curtains*

1 MUSICIAN. Faith, we may put up our pipes and be
    gone.
NURSE. Honest good fellows, ah, put up, put up!
  For well you know this is a pitiful case.
1 MUSICIAN. Ay, by my troth, the case may be
    amended.   *Nurse goes*

Enter Peter

PETER. Musicians, O musicians, 'Heart's ease', 'Heart's   100
  ease'! O, an you will have me live, play 'Heart's
  ease'.
1 MUSICIAN. Why 'Heart's ease'?
PETER. O musicians, because my heart itself plays 'My
  heart is full of woe'. O play me some merry dump
  to comfort me.
1 MUSICIAN. Not a dump we! 'Tis no time to play now.
PETER. You will not then?
1 MUSICIAN. No.
PETER. I will then give it you soundly.   110
1 MUSICIAN. What will you give us?
PETER. No money, on my faith, but the gleek. I will
  give you the minstrel.
1 MUSICIAN. Then will I give you the serving-creature.
PETER. Then will I lay the serving-creature's dagger on
  your pate. I will carry no crotchets. I'll re you, I'll
  fa you. Do you note me?
1 MUSICIAN. An you re us and fa us, you note us.
2 MUSICIAN. Pray you put up your dagger, and put
  out your wit.   120
PETER. Then have at you with my wit! I will dry-beat
  you with an iron wit, and put up my iron dagger.
  Answer me like men:
    'When griping grief the heart doth wound,
      And doleful dumps the mind oppress,
      Then music with her silver sound—'
  Why 'silver sound'? Why 'music with her silver
  sound'? What say you, Simon Catling?
1 MUSICIAN. Marry, sir, because silver hath a sweet
  sound.   130
PETER. Pretty! What say you, Hugh Rebeck?
2 MUSICIAN. I say 'silver sound', because musicians
  sound for silver.
PETER. Pretty too! What say you, James Soundpost?
3 MUSICIAN. Faith, I know not what to say.
PETER. O, I cry you mercy! You are the singer. I will
  say for you. It is 'music with her silver sound',
  because musicians have no gold for sounding.
    'Then music with her silver sound
      With speedy help doth lend redress.'   140
                                    He goes
1 MUSICIAN. What a pestilent knave is this same!
2 MUSICIAN. Hang him, Jack! Come, we'll in here,
  tarry for the mourners, and stay dinner.
                                    They go

                        ACT 5
              Scene 1: *Mantua. A street*

Enter Romeo

ROMEO. If I may trust the flattering truth of sleep,
  My dreams presage some joyful news at hand.
  My bosom's lord sits lightly in his throne,
  And all this day an unaccustomed spirit
  Lifts me above the ground with cheerful thoughts.
  I dreamt my lady came and found me dead—

Strange dream that gives a dead man leave to
    think!—
And breathed such life with kisses in my lips
That I revived and was an emperor.
Ah me! how sweet is love itself possessed,   10
When but love's shadows are so rich in joy!

Enter Balthasar, Romeo's man, booted

News from Verona! How now, Balthasar?
Dost thou not bring me letters from the friar?
How doth my lady? Is my father well?
How fares my Juliet? That I ask again,
For nothing can be ill if she be well.
BALTHASAR. Then she is well, and nothing can be ill.
Her body sleeps in Capel's monument,
And her immortal part with angels lives.
I saw her laid low in her kindred's vault,   20
And presently took post to tell it you.
O pardon me for bringing these ill news,
Since you did leave it for my office, sir.
ROMEO. Is it e'en so? Then I defy you, stars!
Thou know'st my lodging. Get me ink and paper,
And hire post-horses; I will hence tonight.
BALTHASAR. I do beseech you, sir, have patience.
Your looks are pale and wild and do import
Some misadventure.
ROMEO.   Tush, thou art deceived.
Leave me, and do the thing I bid thee do.   30
Hast thou no letters to me from the friar?
BALTHASAR. No, my good lord.
ROMEO.   No matter. Get thee gone,
And hire those horses; I'll be with thee straight.
                                      Balthasar goes
Well, Juliet, I will lie with thee tonight.
Let's see for means. O mischief, thou art swift
To enter in the thoughts of desperate men!
I do remember an apothecary,
And hereabouts 'a dwells, which late I noted
In tatt'red weeds, with overwhelming brows,
Culling of simples. Meagre were his looks;   40
Sharp misery had worn him to the bones:
And in his needy shop a tortoise hung,
An alligator stuffed, and other skins
Of ill-shaped fishes; and about his shelves
A beggarly account of empty boxes,
Green earthen pots, bladders, and musty seeds,
Remnants of packthread, and old cakes of roses
Were thinly scattered, to make up a show.
Noting this penury, to myself I said,
'An if a man did need a poison now,   50
Whose sale is present death in Mantua,
Here lives a caitiff wretch would sell it him'.
O, this same thought did but forerun my need,
And this same needy man must sell it me.
As I remember, this should be the house.
Being holiday, the beggar's shop is shut.
What ho, apothecary!

Enter Apothecary

APOTHECARY.   Who calls so loud?
ROMEO. Come hither, man. I see that thou art poor.
Hold, there is forty ducats; let me have
A dram of poison, such soon-speeding gear   60
As will disperse itself through all the veins
That the life-weary taker may fall dead,
And that the trunk may be discharged of breath

As violently as hasty powder fired
Doth hurry from the fatal cannon's womb.
APOTHECARY. Such mortal drugs I have, but Mantua's
    law
Is death to any he that utters them.
ROMEO. Art thou so bare and full of wretchedness
And fear'st to die? Famine is in thy cheeks,
Need and oppression starveth in thy eyes,   70
Contempt and beggary hangs upon thy back:
The world is not thy friend, nor the world's law;
The world affords no law to make thee rich:
Then be not poor, but break it and take this.
APOTHECARY. My poverty but not my will consents.
ROMEO. I pay thy poverty and not thy will.
APOTHECARY. Put this in any liquid thing you will
And drink it off, and if you had the strength
Of twenty men it would dispatch you straight.
ROMEO. There is thy gold—worse poison to men's   80
    souls,
Doing more murder in this loathsome world,
Than these poor compounds that thou mayst not
    sell.
I sell thee poison; thou hast sold me none.
Farewell; buy food and get thyself in flesh.
                                   Apothecary goes
Come, cordial and not poison, go with me
To Juliet's grave, for there must I use thee.
                                      He passes on

Scene 2: *Verona. Friar Lawrence's cell*

Enter Friar John

FRIAR JOHN. Holy Franciscan friar, brother, ho!

Enter Friar Lawrence

FRIAR LAWRENCE. This same should be the voice of
    Friar John.
Welcome from Mantua. What says Romeo?
Or, if his mind be writ, give me his letter.
FRIAR JOHN. Going to find a barefoot brother out,
One of our order, to associate me,
Here in this city visiting the sick,
And finding him, the searchers of the town,
Suspecting that we both were in a house
Where the infectious pestilence did reign,   10
Sealed up the doors, and would not let us forth,
So that my speed to Mantua there was stayed.
FRIAR LAWRENCE. Who bare my letter then to Romeo?
FRIAR JOHN. I could not send it—here it is again—
Nor get a messenger to bring it thee,
So fearful were they of infection.
FRIAR LAWRENCE. Unhappy fortune! By my
    brotherhood,
The letter was not nice, but full of charge,
Of dear import; and the neglecting it
May do much danger. Friar John, go hence,   20
Get me an iron crow and bring it straight
Unto my cell.
FRIAR JOHN. Brother, I'll go and bring it thee.   *Goes*
FRIAR LAWRENCE. Now must I to the monument alone.
Within this three hours will fair Juliet wake.
She will beshrew me much that Romeo
Hath had no notice of these accidents;
But I will write again to Mantua,
And keep her at my cell till Romeo come.

Poor living corse, closed in a dead man's tomb!   30

He goes

Scene 3: *Verona. A churchyard; in it the monument of
the Capulets*

Enter Paris and his Page, bearing flowers and a torch

PARIS. Give me thy torch, boy. Hence, and stand aloof.
Yet put it out, for I would not be seen.
Under yond yew-trees lay thee all along,
Holding thine ear close to the hollow ground;
So shall no foot upon the churchyard tread,
Being loose, unfirm with digging up of graves,
But thou shalt hear it. Whistle then to me
As signal that thou hear'st some thing approach.
Give me those flowers. Do as I bid thee; go.

PAGE [*aside*]. I am almost afraid to stand alone   10
Here in the churchyard, yet I will adventure.

Retires

PARIS. Sweet flower, with flowers thy bridal bed
I strew—
O woe, thy canopy is dust and stones!—
Which with sweet water nightly I will dew,
Or, wanting that, with tears distilled by moans.
The obsequies that I for thee will keep
Nightly shall be to strew thy grave and weep.

Page whistles

The boy gives warning something doth approach.
What cursed foot wanders this way tonight
To cross my obsequies and true love's rite?   20
What, with a torch? Muffle me, night, awhile.

Retires

*Enter Romeo and Balthasar, with a torch, a mattock,
and a crow of iron*

ROMEO. Give me that mattock and the wrenching
iron.
Hold, take this letter. Early in the morning
See thou deliver it to my lord and father.
Give me the light. Upon thy life I charge thee,
Whate'er thou hear'st or seest, stand all aloof
And do not interrupt me in my course.
Why I descend into this bed of death
Is partly to behold my lady's face,
But chiefly to take thence from her dead finger   30
A precious ring, a ring that I must use
In dear employment. Therefore hence, be gone.
But if thou, jealous, dost return to pry
In what I farther shall intend to do,
By heaven, I will tear thee joint by joint
And strew this hungry churchyard with thy limbs.
The time and my intents are savage-wild,
More fierce and more inexorable far
Than empty tigers or the roaring sea.

BALTHASAR. I will be gone, sir, and not trouble ye.   40

ROMEO. So shalt thou show me friendship. Take thou
that;
Live and be prosperous; and farewell, good fellow.

BALTHASAR. [*aside*]. For all this same, I'll hide me
hereabout.
His looks I fear, and his intents I doubt.   *Retires*

ROMEO. Thou detestable maw, thou womb of death,
Gorged with the dearest morsel of the earth,
Thus I enforce thy rotten jaws to open,

Begins to open the tomb

And in despite I'll cram thee with more food.

PARIS. This is that banished haughty Montague
That murd'red my love's cousin—with which grief   50
It is supposed the fair creature died—
And here is come to do some villainous shame
To the dead bodies: I will apprehend him.—

Comes forward

Stop thy unhallowed toil, vile Montague!
Can vengeance be pursued further than death?
Condemnéd villain, I do apprehend thee.
Obey, and go with me, for thou must die.

ROMEO. I must indeed, and therefore came I hither.
Good gentle youth, tempt not a desp'rate man.
Fly hence and leave me. Think upon these gone;   60
Let them affright thee. I beseech thee, youth,
Put not another sin upon my head
By urging me to fury. O be gone!
By heaven, I love thee better than myself,
For I come hither armed against myself.
Stay not, be gone. Live, and hereafter say
A madman's mercy bid thee run away.

PARIS. I do defy thy conjuration,
And apprehend thee for a felon here.

ROMEO. Wilt thou provoke me? Then have at
thee, boy!   *They fight*   70

PAGE. O Lord, they fight! I will go call the watch.

Goes

PARIS. O, I am slain! [*falls*] If thou be merciful,
Open the tomb, lay me with Juliet.   *Dies*

ROMEO. In faith, I will. Let me peruse this face.
Mercutio's kinsman, noble County Paris!
What said my man when my betosséd soul
Did not attend him as we rode? I think
He told me Paris should have married Juliet.
Said he not so? Or did I dream it so?
Or am I mad, hearing him talk of Juliet,   80
To think it was so? O give me thy hand,
One writ with me in sour misfortune's book!
I'll bury thee in a triumphant grave.
A grave? O no!—a lanthorn, slaught'red youth:
For here lies Juliet, and her beauty makes
This vault a feasting presence full of light.
Dead, lie thou there, by a dead man interred.

Lays Paris within the tomb

How oft when men are at the point of death
Have they been merry, which their keepers call
A light'ning before death! O how may I   90
Call this a light'ning? O my love, my wife!
Death, that hath sucked the honey of thy breath,
Hath had no power yet upon thy beauty.
Thou art not conquered; beauty's ensign yet
Is crimson in thy lips and in thy cheeks,
And death's pale flag is not advancéd there.
Tybalt, liest thou there in thy bloody sheet?
O, what more favour can I do to thee
Than with that hand that cut thy youth in twain
To sunder his that was thine enemy?   100
Forgive me, cousin! Ah, dear Juliet,
Why art thou yet so fair? Shall I believe
That unsubstantial Death is amorous,
And that the lean abhorréd monster keeps
Thee here in dark to be his paramour?
For fear of that I still will stay with thee,
And never from this palace of dim night
Depart again. Here, here will I remain
With worms that are thy chambermaids. O, here
Will I set up my everlasting rest,   110

And shake the yoke of inauspicious stars
From this world-wearied flesh. Eyes, look your last!
Arms, take your last embrace! and lips, O you,
The doors of breath, seal with a righteous kiss
A dateless bargain to engrossing Death!
Come, bitter conduct; come, unsavoury guide!
Thou desperate pilot, now at once run on
The dashing rocks thy seasick weary bark!
Here's to my love! [*drinks*] O true apothecary!
Thy drugs are quick. Thus with a kiss I die.   *Dies* 120

Enter Friar Lawrence with lanthorn, crow, and spade

FRIAR. Saint Francis be my speed! how oft tonight
  Have my old feet stumbled at graves! Who's there?
BALTHASAR. Here's one, a friend, and one that knows
  you well.
FRIAR. Bliss be upon you! Tell me, good my friend,
  What torch is yond that vainly lends his light
  To grubs and eyeless skulls? As I discern,
  It burneth in the Capels' monument.
BALTHASAR. It doth so, holy sir; and there's my master,
  One that you love.
FRIAR.   Who is it?
BALTHASAR.   Romeo.
FRIAR. How long hath he been there?
BALTHASAR.   Full half an hour. 130
FRIAR. Go with me to the vault.
BALTHASAR.   I dare not, sir.
  My master knows not but I am gone hence,
  And fearfully did menace me with death
  If I did stay to look on his intents.
FRIAR. Stay then; I'll go alone. Fear comes upon me.
  O, much I fear some ill unthrifty things.
BALTHASAR. As I did sleep under this yew-tree here,
  I dreamt my master and another fought,
  And that my master slew him.
FRIAR.   Romeo! *Advances*
  Alack, alack, what blood is this which stains   140
  The stony entrance of this sepulchre?
  What mean these masterless and gory swords
  To lie discoloured by this place of peace?
                              Enters the tomb
  Romeo! O, pale! Who else? What, Paris too?
  And steeped in blood? Ah, what an unkind hour
  Is guilty of this lamentable chance!
  The lady stirs.   *Juliet wakes*
JULIET. O comfortable friar, where is my lord?
  I do remember well where I should be,
  And there I am. Where is my Romeo?   150
                              Voices afar off
FRIAR. I hear some noise, lady. Come from that nest
  Of death, contagion, and unnatural sleep.
  A greater power than we can contradict
  Hath thwarted our intents. Come, come away.
  Thy husband in thy bosom there lies dead:
  And Paris too. Come, I'll dispose of thee
  Among a sisterhood of holy nuns.
  Stay not to question, for the watch is coming.
  Come, go, good Juliet; I dare no longer stay.
JULIET. Go, get thee hence, for I will not away.   160
                              He goes
  What's here? A cup, closed in my true love's hand?
  Poison, I see, hath been his timeless end,
  O churl! drunk all, and left no friendly drop
  To help me after? I will kiss thy lips.
  Haply some poison yet doth hang on them

To make me die with a restorative.   *Kisses him*
  Thy lips are warm!

The Page of Paris enters the graveyard with Watch

1 WATCHMAN. Lead, boy. Which way?
JULIET. Yea, noise? Then I'll be brief. O happy dagger,
                              Snatching Romeo's dagger
  This is thy sheath [*stabs herself*]; there rest, and let
  me die.   *Falls on Romeo's body and dies* 170
PAGE. This is the place, there where the torch doth
  burn.
1 WATCHMAN. The ground is bloody. Search about
  the churchyard.
  Go, some of you; whoe'er you find attach.
                              Some Watchmen depart
  Pitiful sight! Here lies the County slain:
  And Juliet bleeding, warm and newly dead,
  Who here hath lain this two days buried.
  Go tell the Prince; run to the Capulets;
  Raise up the Montagues; some others search.
                              Other Watchmen depart
  We see the ground whereon these woes do lie,
  But the true ground of all these piteous woes   180
  We cannot without circumstance descry.

Re-enter some of the Watch, with Balthasar

2 WATCHMAN. Here's Romeo's man; we found him in
  the churchyard.
1 WATCHMAN. Hold him in safety till the Prince come
  hither.

Re-enter another Watchman, with Friar Lawrence

3 WATCHMAN. Here is a friar that trembles, sighs, and
  weeps.
  We took this mattock and this spade from him
  As he was coming from this churchyard's side.
1 WATCHMAN. A great suspicion! Stay the friar too.

Enter the Prince and attendants

PRINCE. What misadventure is so early up,
  That calls our person from our morning rest?

Enter Capulet and his wife

CAPULET. What should it be that is so shrieked abroad? 190
LADY CAPULET. O, the people in the street cry
  'Romeo',
  Some 'Juliet', and some 'Paris', and all run
  With open outcry toward our monument.
PRINCE. What fear is this which startles in our ears?
1 WATCHMAN. Sovereign, here lies the County Paris
  slain;
  And Romeo dead; and Juliet, dead before,
  Warm and new killed.
PRINCE. Search, seek, and know how this foul murder
  comes.
1 WATCHMAN. Here is a friar, and slaughtered
  Romeo's man,
  With instruments upon them fit to open   200
  These dead men's tombs.
CAPULET. O heaven! O wife, look how our daughter
  bleeds!
  This dagger hath mista'en, for, lo, his house
  Is empty on the back of Montague,
  And it mis-sheathed in my daughter's bosom.
LADY CAPULET. O me! this sight of death is as a bell
  That warns my old age to a sepulchre.

Enter Montague

PRINCE. Come Montague; for thou art early up
  To see thy son and heir more early down.
MONTAGUE. Alas, my liege, my wife is dead tonight; 210
  Grief of my son's exile hath stopped her breath.
  What further woe conspires against mine age?
PRINCE. Look and thou shalt see.
MONTAGUE. O thou untaught! what manners is in this,
  To press before thy father to a grave?
PRINCE. Seal up the mouth of outrage for a while,
  Till we can clear these ambiguities,
  And know their spring, their head, their true
    descent;
  And then will I be general of your woes,
  And lead you even to death. Meantime forbear, 220
  And let mischance be slave to patience.
  Bring forth the parties of suspicion.

Watchmen bring forward Friar Lawrence and Balthasar

FRIAR. I am the greatest; able to do least,
  Yet most suspected, as the time and place
  Doth make against me, of this direful murder:
  And here I stand both to impeach and purge
  Myself condemnèd and myself excused.
PRINCE. Then say at once what thou dost know in this.
FRIAR. I will be brief, for my short date of breath
  Is not so long as is a tedious tale. 230
  Romeo there dead was husband to that Juliet;
  And she, there dead, that Romeo's faithful wife.
  I married them; and their stol'n marriage day
  Was Tybalt's doomsday, whose untimely death
  Banished the new-made bridegroom from this city;
  For whom, and not for Tybalt, Juliet pined.
  You, to remove that siege of grief from her,
  Betrothed and would have married her perforce
  To County Paris. Then comes she to me,
  And with wild looks bid me devise some mean 240
  To rid her from this second marriage,
  Or in my cell there would she kill herself.
  Then gave I her (so tutored by my art)
  A sleeping potion; which so took effect
  As I intended, for it wrought on her
  The form of death. Meantime I writ to Romeo
  That he should hither come as this dire night
  To help to take her from her borrowed grave,
  Being the time the potion's force should cease.
  But he which bore my letter, Friar John, 250
  Was stayed by accident, and yesternight
  Returned my letter back. Then all alone
  At the prefixèd hour of her waking
  Came I to take her from her kindred's vault,
  Meaning to keep her closely at my cell
  Till I conveniently could send to Romeo.
  But when I came, some minute ere the time
  Of her awakening, here untimely lay

  The noble Paris and true Romeo dead.
  She wakes; and I entreated her come forth, 260
  And bear this work of heaven with patience;
  But then a noise did scare me from the tomb,
  And she, too desperate, would not go with me,
  But, as it seems, did violence on herself.
  All this I know; and to the marriage
  Her nurse is privy: and if aught in this
  Miscarried by my fault, let my old life
  Be sacrificed, some hour before his time,
  Unto the rigour of severest law.
PRINCE. We still have known thee for a holy man. 270
  Where's Romeo's man? What can he say to this?
BALTHASAR. I brought my master news of Juliet's
    death,
  And then in post he came from Mantua
  To this same place, to this same monument.
  This letter he early bid me give his father,
  And threat'ned me with death, going in the vault,
  If I departed not and left him there.
PRINCE. Give me the letter; I will look on it.
  Where is the County's page, that raised the watch?
                             Page comes forward
  Sirrah, what made your master in this place? 280
PAGE. He came with flowers to strew his lady's grave,
  And bid me stand aloof, and so I did.
  Anon comes one with light to ope the tomb,
  And by and by my master drew on him,
  And then I ran away to call the watch.
PRINCE. This letter doth make good the friar's words,
  Their course of love, the tidings of her death;
  And here he writes that he did buy a poison
  Of a poor pothecary, and therewithal
  Came to this vault to die, and lie with Juliet. 290
  Where be these enemies? Capulet, Montague?
  See what a scourge is laid upon your hate,
  That heaven finds means to kill your joys with love!
  And I, for winking at your discords too,
  Have lost a brace of kinsmen. All are punished.
CAPULET. O brother Montague, give me thy hand.
  This is my daughter's jointure, for no more
  Can I demand.
MONTAGUE.   But I can give thee more;
  For I will raise her statue in pure gold,
  That, whiles Verona by that name is known, 300
  There shall no figure at such rate be set
  As that of true and faithful Juliet.
CAPULET. As rich shall Romeo's by his lady's lie—
  Poor sacrifices of our enmity!
PRINCE. A glooming peace this morning with it
    brings;
  The sun for sorrow will not show his head.
  Go hence, to have more talk of these sad things.
  Some shall be pardoned, and some punishèd;
  For never was a story of more woe
  Than this of Juliet and her Romeo.   *They go* 310

The Life of Timon of Athens

The scene: Athens and neighbourhood

CHARACTERS IN THE PLAY

TIMON, *a noble Athenian*
LUCIUS
LUCULLUS } *flattering lords*
SEMPRONIUS
VENTIDIUS, *one of Timon's false friends*
ALCIBIADES, *an Athenian captain*
APEMANTUS, *a churlish philosopher*
FLAVIUS, *steward to Timon*
Poet, Painter, Jeweller, *and* Merchant
An old Athenian
FLAMINIUS
LUCILIUS } *servants to Timon*
SERVILIUS

CAPHIS
PHILOTUS
TITUS } *servants to Timon's creditors and to the*
HORTENSIUS   *Lords*
And others
A Page.   A Fool.   Three Strangers
PHRYNIA
TIMANDRA } *mistresses to Alcibiades*
Cupid *and* Amazons *in the masque*
Other Lords, Senators, Officers, Banditti, *and* Attendants

The Life of Timon of Athens

Scene 1: *Athens. A hall in Timon's house*

Enter Poet, Painter, Jeweller, Merchant, and others, at several doors

POET. Good day, sir.
PAINTER.   I am glad you're well.
POET. I have not seen you long; how goes the world?
PAINTER. It wears, sir, as it grows.
POET.   Ay, that's well known.
But what particular rarity? what strange,
Which manifold record not matches? See,
Magic of bounty, all these spirits thy power
Hath conjured to attend. I know the merchant.
PAINTER. I know them both; th'other's a jeweller.
MERCHANT. O, 'tis a worthy lord!
JEWELLER.   Nay, that's most fixed.
MERCHANT. A most incomparable man, breathed, as it
were,   10
To an untirable and continuate goodness.
He passes.
JEWELLER. I have a jewel here.
MERCHANT. O, pray, let's see't. For the Lord Timon,
sir?
JEWELLER. If he will touch the estimate. But for that—
POET [*reciting to himself*]. 'When we for recompense
have praised the vile,
It stains the glory in that happy verse
Which aptly sings the good.'
MERCHANT. 'Tis a good form.
JEWELLER. And rich. Here is a water, look ye.   20
PAINTER. You are rapt, sir, in some work, some
dedication
To the great lord.
POET.   A thing slipped idly from me.
Our poesy is as a gum which oozes
From whence 'tis nourished. The fire i'th'flint
Shows not till it be struck: our gentle flame
Provokes itself, and like the current flies
Each bound it chafes. What have you there?
PAINTER. A picture, sir. When comes your book forth?
POET. Upon the heels of my presentment, sir.
Let's see your piece.   30
PAINTER. 'Tis a good piece.
POET. So 'tis; this comes off well and excellent.
PAINTER. Indifferent.
POET.   Admirable. How this grace
Speaks his own standing! what a mental power
This eye shoots forth! how big imagination
Moves in this lip! to th'dumbness of the gesture
One might interpret.
PAINTER. It is a pretty mocking of the life.
Here is a touch; is't good?
POET.   I will say of it,
It tutors nature; artificial strife   40
Lives in these touches, livelier than life.

Enter certain Senators, and pass by

PAINTER. How this lord is followed!
POET. The senators of Athens—happy man!

PAINTER. Look, moe!
POET. You see this confluence, this great flood of
visitors:
I have in this rough work shaped out a man
Whom this beneath world doth embrace and hug
With amplest entertainment. My free drift
Halts not particularly, but moves itself
In a wide sea of wax; no levelled malice   50
Infects one comma in the course I hold,
But flies an eagle flight, bold and forth on,
Leaving no tract behind.
PAINTER. How shall I understand you?
POET.   I will unbolt to you.
You see how all conditions, how all minds,
As well of glib and slipp'ry creatures as
Of grave and austere quality, tender down
Their services to Lord Timon. His large fortune,
Upon his good and gracious nature hanging,
Subdues and properties to his love and tendance   60
All sorts of hearts; yea, from the glass-faced flatterer
To Apemantus, that few things loves better
Than to abhor himself; even he drops down
The knee before him, and returns in peace
Most rich in Timon's nod.
PAINTER.   I saw them speak together.
POET. Sir, I have upon a high and pleasant hill
Feigned Fortune to be throned. The base
o'th'mount
Is ranked with all deserts, all kind of natures,
That labour on the bosom of this sphere
To propagate their states; amongst them all   70
Whose eyes are on this sovereign lady fixed
One do I personate of Lord Timon's frame,
Whom Fortune with her ivory hand wafts to her,
Whose present grace to present slaves and servants
Translates his rivals.
PAINTER.   'Tis conceived to scope.
This throne, this Fortune, and this hill, methinks,
With one man beckoned from the rest below,
Bowing his head against the steepy mount
To climb his happiness, would be well expressed
In our condition.
POET.   Nay, sir, but hear me on.   80
All those which were his fellows but of late,
Some better than his value, on the moment
Follow his strides, his lobbies fill with tendance,
Rain sacrificial whisperings in his ear,
Make sacred even his stirrup, and through him
Drink the free air.
PAINTER.   Ay, marry, what of these?
POET. When Fortune in her shift and change of mood
Spurns down her late beloved, all his dependants,
Which laboured after him to the mountain's top
Even on their knees and hands, let him slip down,   90
Not one accompanying his declining foot.
PAINTER. 'Tis common:
A thousand moral paintings I can show,
That shall demonstrate these quick blows of
Fortune's
More pregnantly than words. Yet you do well

To show Lord Timon that mean eyes have seen
The foot above the head.

*Trumpets sound. Enter Lord Timon, addressing himself
courteously to every suitor; a Messenger from Ventidius
talking with him; Lucilius and other servants following*

TIMON.   Imprisoned is he, say you?
MESSENGER. Ay, my good lord; five talents is his debt,
His means most short, his creditors most strait.
Your honourable letter he desires   100
To those have shut him up, which failing
Periods his comfort.
TIMON.   Noble Ventidius! Well.
I am not of that feather to shake off
My friend when he must need me. I do know him
A gentleman that well deserves a help,
Which he shall have. I'll pay the debt and free him.
MESSENGER. Your lordship ever binds him.
TIMON. Commend me to him; I will send his ransom;
And, being enfranchiséd, bid him come to me.
'Tis not enough to help the feeble up,   110
But to support him after. Fare you well.
MESSENGER. All happiness to your honour!   *Goes*

Enter an old Athenian

ATHENIAN. Lord Timon, hear me speak.
TIMON.   Freely, good father.
ATHENIAN. Thou hast a servant named Lucilius.
TIMON. I have so; what of him?
ATHENIAN. Most noble Timon, call the man before
thee.
TIMON. Attends he here, or no? Lucilius!
LUCILIUS. Here, at your lordship's service.
ATHENIAN. This fellow here, Lord Timon, this thy
creature,
By night frequents my house. I am a man   120
That from my first have been inclined to thrift,
And my estate deserves an heir more raised
Than one which holds a trencher.
TIMON.   Well; what further?
ATHENIAN. One only daughter have I, no kin else,
On whom I may confer what I have got.
The maid is fair, o'th'youngest for a bride,
And I have bred her at my dearest cost
In qualities of the best. This man of thine
Attempts her love; I prithee, noble lord,
Join with me to forbid him her resort;   130
Myself have spoke in vain.
TIMON.   The man is honest.
ATHENIAN. Therefore he will be, Timon.
His honesty rewards him in itself;
It must not bear my daughter.
TIMON.   Does she love him?
ATHENIAN. She is young and apt.
Our own precedent passions do instruct us
What levity's in youth.
TIMON [*to Lucilius*].   Love you the maid?
LUCILIUS. Ay, my good lord, and she accepts of it.
ATHENIAN. If in her marriage my consent be missing,
I call the gods to witness, I will choose   140
Mine heir from forth the beggars of the world,
And dispossess her all.
TIMON.   How shall she be endowéd,
If she be mated with an equal husband?
ATHENIAN. Three talents on the present; in future, all.
TIMON. This gentleman of mine hath served me long;

To build his fortune I will strain a little,
For 'tis a bond in men. Give him thy daughter:
What you bestow, in him I'll counterpoise,
And make him weigh with her.
ATHENIAN.   Most noble lord,
Pawn me to this your honour, she is his.   150
TIMON. My hand to thee; mine honour on my
promise.
LUCILIUS. Humbly I thank your lordship; never may
That state or fortune fall into my keeping
Which is not owed to you!   .
                              Lucilius and Old Athenian go
POET. Vouchsafe my labour, and long live your
lordship!
TIMON. I thank you; you shall hear from me anon.
Go not away. What have you there, my friend?
PAINTER. A piece of painting, which I do beseech
Your lordship to accept.
TIMON.   Painting is welcome.
The painting is almost the natural man;   160
For since dishonour traffics with man's nature,
He is but outside; these pencilled figures are
Even such as they give out. I like your work,
And you shall find I like it; wait attendance
Till you hear further from me.
PAINTER.   The gods preserve ye!
TIMON. Well fare you, gentleman. Give me your
hand;
We must needs dine together. Sir, your jewel
Hath sufferéd under praise.
JEWELLER.   What, my lord, dispraise?
TIMON. A mere satiety of commendations.
If I should pay you for't as 'tis extolled,   170
It would unclew me quite.
JEWELLER.   My lord, 'tis rated
As those which sell would give; but you well know,
Things of like value, differing in the owners,
Are prized by their masters. Believe't, dear lord,
You mend the jewel by the wearing it.
TIMON. Well mocked.
MERCHANT. No, my good lord; he speaks the common
tongue
Which all men speak with him.
TIMON. Look who comes here; will you be chid?

Enter Apemantus

JEWELLER. We'll bear, with your lordship.
MERCHANT.   He'll spare none. 180
TIMON. Good morrow to thee, gentle Apemantus.
APEMANTUS. Till I be gentle, stay thou for thy good
morrow;
When thou art Timon's dog, and these knaves
honest.
TIMON. Why dost thou call them knaves? thou
know'st them not.
APEMANTUS. Are they not Athenians?
TIMON. Yes.
APEMANTUS. Then I repent not.
JEWELLER. You know me, Apemantus?
APEMANTUS. Thou know'st I do; I called thee by thy
name.
TIMON. Thou art proud, Apemantus.   190
APEMANTUS. Of nothing so much as that I am not like
Timon.
TIMON. Whither art going?

APEMANTUS. To knock out an honest Athenian's
brains.
TIMON. That's a deed thou'lt die for.
APEMANTUS. Right, if doing nothing be death by
th'law.
TIMON. How lik'st thou this picture, Apemantus?
APEMANTUS. The best, for the innocence.
TIMON. Wrought he not well that painted it?
APEMANTUS. He wrought better that made the painter;
and yet he's but a filthy piece of work.   200
PAINTER. You're a dog.
APEMANTUS. Thy mother's of my generation; what's
she, if I be a dog?
TIMON. Wilt dine with me, Apemantus?
APEMANTUS. No; I eat not lords.
TIMON. An thou shouldst, thou'ldst anger ladies.
APEMANTUS. O, they eat lords; so they come by great
bellies.
TIMON. That's a lascivious apprehension.
APEMANTUS. So thou apprehend'st it; take it for thy   210
labour.
TIMON. How dost thou like this jewel, Apemantus?
APEMANTUS. Not so well as plain-dealing, which will
not cost a man a doit.
TIMON. What dost thou think 'tis worth?
APEMANTUS. Not worth my thinking. How now,
poet!
POET. How now, philosopher!
APEMANTUS. Thou liest.
POET. Art not one?   220
APEMANTUS. Yes.
POET. Then I lie not.
APEMANTUS. Art not a poet?
POET. Yes.
APEMANTUS. Then thou liest. Look in thy last work,
where thou hast feigned him a worthy fellow.
POET. That's not feigned; he is so.
APEMANTUS. Yes, he is worthy of thee, and to pay thee
for thy labour. He that loves to be flattered is
worthy o'th'flatterer. Heavens, that I were a lord! 230
TIMON. What wouldst do then, Apemantus?
APEMANTUS. E'en as Apemantus does now: hate a lord
with my heart.
TIMON. What, thyself?
APEMANTUS. Ay.
TIMON. Wherefore?
APEMANTUS. That I had no angry wit to be a lord.
Art not thou a merchant?
MERCHANT. Ay, Apemantus.
APEMANTUS. Traffic confound thee, if the gods will   240
not!
MERCHANT. If traffic do it, the gods do it.
APEMANTUS. Traffic's thy god, and thy god confound
thee!

Trumpet sounds. Enter a Messenger

TIMON. What trumpet's that?
MESSENGER. 'Tis Alcibiades, and some twenty horse,
All of companionship.
TIMON. Pray, entertain them; give them guide to us.
                         Some attendants go
You must needs dine with me. Go not you hence
Till I have thanked you. When dinner's done,
Show me this piece. I am joyful of your sights.   250

Enter Alcibiades, with the rest

Most welcome, sir!
APEMANTUS.   So, so, there!
Achës contract and starve your supple joints!
That there should be small love amongst these sweet
knaves,
And all this courtesy! The strain of man's bred out
Into baboon and monkey.
ALCIBIADES. Sir, you have saved my longing, and I
feed
Most hungerly on your sight.
TIMON.   Right welcome, sir!
Ere we depart, we'll share a bounteous time
In different pleasures. Pray you, let us in.
                         All but Apemantus go

Enter two Lords

I LORD. What time o' day is't, Apemantus?   260
APEMANTUS. Time to be honest.
I LORD. That time serves still.
APEMANTUS. The more accursèd thou that still omit'st
it.
2 LORD. Thou art going to Lord Timon's feast?
APEMANTUS. Ay, to see meat fill knaves and wine heat
fools.
2 LORD. Fare thee well, fare thee well.
APEMANTUS. Thou art a fool to bid me farewell twice.
2 LORD. Why, Apemantus?
APEMANTUS. Shouldst have kept one to thyself, for I
mean to give thee none.   270
I LORD. Hang thyself.
APEMANTUS. No, I will do nothing at thy bidding;
make thy requests to thy friend.
2 LORD. Away, unpeaceable dog, or I'll spurn thee
hence.
APEMANTUS. I will fly, like a dog, the heels o'th'ass.
                         Goes
I LORD. He's opposite to humanity.
Come, shall we in,
And taste Lord Timon's bounty? he outgoes
The very heart of kindness.   280
2 LORD. He pours it out. Plutus, the god of gold,
Is but his steward; no meed, but he repays
Sevenfold above itself; no gift to him
But breeds the giver a return exceeding
All use of quittance.
I LORD.   The noblest mind he carries
That ever governed man.
2 LORD. Long may he live in fortunes! Shall we in?
I LORD. I'll keep you company.   *They go*

Scene 2: A banqueting-room in Timon's house

*Hautboys playing loud music. A great banquet served in;
Flavius and others attending; and then enter Lord Timon,
Alcibiades, Lords, Senators, and Ventidius. Then comes,
dropping after all, Apemantus, discontentedly, like himself*

VENTIDIUS. Most honourèd Timon,
It hath pleased the gods to remember my father's
age,
And call him to long peace.
He is gone happy, and has left me rich.
Then, as in grateful virtue I am bound
To your free heart, I do return those talents,
Doubled with thanks and service, from whose help
I derived liberty.
TIMON.   O, by no means,

Honest Ventidius; you mistake my love;
I gave it freely ever, and there's none   10
Can truly say he gives, if he receives.
If our betters play at that game, we must not dare
To imitate them; faults that are rich are fair.
VENTIDIUS. A noble spirit!
TIMON. Nay, my lords, ceremony was but devised at
    first
To set a gloss on faint deeds, hollow welcomes,
Recanting goodness, sorry ere 'tis shown;
But where there is true friendship, there needs none.
Pray, sit; more welcome are ye to my fortunes
Than my fortunes to me.   *They sit* 20
1 LORD. My lord, we always have confessed it.
APEMANTUS. Ho, ho, confessed it? hanged it, have you
    not?
TIMON. O, Apemantus, you are welcome.
APEMANTUS.   No;
You shall not make me welcome.
I come to have thee thrust me out of doors.
TIMON. Fie, thou'rt a churl; ye've got a humour there
Does not become a man; 'tis much to blame.
They say, my lords, 'ira furor brevis est'; but yond
man is ever angry. Go, let him have a table by   30
himself; for he does neither affect company, nor is
he fit for't indeed.
APEMANTUS. Let me stay at thine apperil, Timon.
I come to observe, I give thee warning on't.
TIMON. I take no heed of thee; thou'rt an Athenian,
therefore welcome; I myself would have no power
—prithee let my meat make thee silent.
APEMANTUS. I scorn thy meat; 'twould choke me, for
I should ne'er flatter thee. O you gods, what a
number of men eats Timon, and he sees 'em not! It
grieves me to see so many dip their meat in one   40
man's blood; and all the madness is, he cheers them
up too.
I wonder men dare trust themselves with men.
Methinks they should invite them without knives:
Good for their meat, and safer for their lives.
There's much example for't; the fellow that sits next
him, now parts bread with him, pledges the breath
of him in a divided draught, is the readiest man to
kill him:'t has been proved. If I were a huge man, I
should fear to drink at meals,   50
Lest they should spy my windpipe's dangerous
    notes.
Great men should drink with harness on their
    throats.
TIMON. My lord, in heart; and let the health go round.
2 LORD. Let it flow this way, my good lord.
APEMANTUS. Flow this way? A brave fellow. He keeps
his tides well. Those healths will make thee and thy
state look ill, Timon.
Here's that which is too weak to be a sinner,
Honest water, which ne'er left man i'th'mire.
This and my food are equals; there's no odds.   60
Feasts are too proud to give thanks to the gods.
        APEMANTUS' GRACE
Immortal gods, I crave no pelf;
I pray for no man but myself;
Grant I may never prove so fond
To trust man on his oath or bond,
Or a harlot for her weeping,
Or a dog that seems a-sleeping,
Or a keeper with my freedom,

Or my friends if I should need 'em.
Amen. So fall to't: 70
Rich men sin, and I eat root.
                                        Eats and drinks
Much good dich thy good heart, Apemantus!
TIMON. Captain Alcibiades, your heart's in the field
now.
ALCIBIADES. My heart is ever at your service, my lord.
TIMON. You had rather be at a breakfast of enemies
than a dinner of friends.
ALCIBIADES. So they were bleeding-new, my lord;
there's no meat like 'em; I could wish my best friend
at such a feast.   80
APEMANTUS. Would all those flatterers were thine
enemies, then, that then thou mightst kill 'em—and
bid me to 'em!
1 LORD. Might we but have that happiness, my lord,
that you would once use our hearts, whereby we
might express some part of our zeals, we should
think ourselves for ever perfect.
TIMON. O, no doubt, my good friends, but the gods
themselves have provided that I shall have much
help from you: how had you been my friends else?   90
Why have you that charitable title from thousands,
did not you chiefly belong to my heart? I have told
more of you to myself than you can with modesty
speak in your own behalf; and thus far I confirm
you. O you gods, think I, what need we have any
friends, if we should ne'er have need of 'em? they
were the most needless creatures living, should we
ne'er have use for 'em; and would most resemble
sweet instruments hung up in cases, that keeps their
sounds to themselves. Why, I have often wished   100
myself poorer, that I might come nearer to you. We
are born to do benefits; and what better or properer
can we call our own than the riches of our friends?
O, what a precious comfort 'tis to have so many
like brothers commanding one another's fortunes!
O joy, e'en made away ere't can be born! Mine
eyes cannot hold out water, methinks. To forget
their faults, I drink to you.
APEMANTUS. Thou weep'st to make them drink,
Timon.   110
2 LORD. Joy had the like conception in our eyes,
And at that instant like a babe sprung up.
APEMANTUS. Ho, ho! I laugh to think that babe a
bastard.
3 LORD. I promise you, my lord, you moved me much.
APEMANTUS. Much!   *Tucket heard*
TIMON. What means that trump?

Enter a Servant

                                        How now?
SERVANT. Please you, my lord, there are certain ladies
most desirous of admittance.
TIMON. Ladies? what are their wills?
SERVANT. There comes with them a forerunner, my   120
lord, which bears that office to signify their
pleasures.
TIMON. I pray let them be admitted.

Enter Cupid

CUPID. Hail to thee, worthy Timon, and to all
That of his bounties taste! The five best senses
Acknowledge thee their patron, and come freely
To gratulate thy plenteous bosom. Th'ear,

Taste, touch, smell, all pleased from thy table rise;
They only now come but to feast thine eyes.
TIMON. They're welcome all; let 'em have kind
admittance. 130
Music make their welcome! *Cupid goes*
I LORD. You see, my lord, how ample you're beloved.

Music. Re-enter Cupid, with a masque of Ladies as
Amazons, with lutes in their hands, dancing and playing

APEMANTUS. Hoy-day, what a sweep of vanity comes
this way!
They dance? they are madwomen.
Like madness is the glory of this life
As this pomp shows to a little oil and root.
We make ourselves fools, to disport ourselves,
And spend our flatteries to drink those men
Upon whose age we void it up again
With poisonous spite and envy. 140
Who lives that's not depravéd or depraves?
Who dies that bears not one spurn to their graves
Of their friends' gift?
I should fear those that dance before me now
Would one day stamp upon me. 'T has been done;
Men shut their doors against a setting sun.

The Lords rise from table, with much adoring of Timon,
and to show their loves, each single out an Amazon, and
all dance, men with women, a lofty strain or two to the
hautboys, and cease

TIMON. You have done our pleasures much grace, fair
ladies,
Set a fair fashion on our entertainment,
Which was not half so beautiful and kind;
You have added worth unto't and lustre, 150
And entertained me with mine own device.
I am to thank you for't.
I LADY. My lord, you take us even at the best.
APEMANTUS. Faith, for the worst is filthy, and would
not hold taking, I doubt me.
TIMON. Ladies, there is an idle banquet attends you,
Please you to dispose yourselves.
ALL LADIES. Most thankfully, my lord.
Cupid and Ladies go
TIMON. Flavius!
FLAVIUS. My lord?
TIMON. The little casket bring me hither. 160
FLAVIUS. Yes, my lord. [*aside*] More jewels yet!
There is no crossing him in's humour,
Else I should tell him well, i' faith I should;
When all's spent, he'ld be crossed then, an he could.
'Tis pity bounty had not eyes behind,
That man might ne'er be wretched for his mind.
Goes
I LORD. Where be our men?
SERVANT. Here, my lord, in readiness.
2 LORD. Our horses!

Re-enter Flavius, with the casket

TIMON. O my friends, 170
I have one word to say to you. Look you, my good
lord,
I must entreat you honour me so much
As to advance this jewel; accept it and wear it,
Kind my lord.
I LORD. I am so far already in your gifts.
ALL. So are we all.

Enter a Servant

SERVANT. My lord, there are certain nobles of the
senate newly alighted and come to visit you.
TIMON. They are fairly welcome.
FLAVIUS. I beseech your honour, vouchsafe me a word; 180
it does concern you near.
TIMON. Near? why, then, another time I'll hear thee.
I prithee let's be provided to show them enter-
tainment.
FLAVIUS [*aside*]. I scarce know how.

Enter another Servant

2 SERVANT. May it please your honour, Lord Lucius,
Out of his free love, hath presented to you
Four milk-white horses, trapped in silver.
TIMON. I shall accept them fairly. Let the presents
Be worthily entertained.

Enter a third Servant

How now? what news? 190
3 SERVANT. Please you, my lord, that honourable
gentleman. Lord Lucullus, entreats your company
to-morrow to hunt with him, and has sent your
honour two brace of greyhounds.
TIMON. I'll hunt with him; and let them be received,
Not without fair reward.
FLAVIUS [*aside*]. What will this come to?
He commands us to provide and give great gifts,
And all out of an empty coffer;
Nor will he know his purse, or yield me this,
To show him what a beggar his heart is, 200
Being of no power to make his wishes good.
His promises fly so beyond his state
That what he speaks is all in debt, he owes
For every word. He is so kind that he now
Pays interest for't; his land's put to their books.
Well, would I were gently put out of office,
Before I were forced out!
Happier is he that has no friend to feed
Than such that do e'en enemies exceed.
I bleed inwardly for my lord. *Goes* 210
TIMON. You do yourselves much wrong.
You bate too much of your own merits.
Here, my lord, a trifle of our love.
2 LORD. With more than common thanks I will
receive it.
3 LORD. O, he's the very soul of bounty!
TIMON. And now I remember, my lord, you gave
good words the other day of a bay courser I rode
on. 'Tis yours because you liked it.
3 LORD. O, I beseech you pardon me, my lord, in that.
TIMON. You may take my word, my lord; I know no 220
man can justly praise but what he does affect. I
weigh my friend's affection with mine own. I'll tell
you true, I'll call to you.
ALL LORDS. O, none so welcome.
TIMON. I take all and your several visitations
So kind to heart, 'tis not enough to give;
Methinks I could deal kingdoms to my friends,
And ne'er be weary. Alcibiades,
Thou art a soldier, therefore seldom rich.
It comes in charity to thee; for all thy living 230
Is 'mongst the dead, and all the lands thou hast
Lie in a pitched field.
ALCIBIADES. Ay, defiled land, my lord.

1 LORD. We are so virtuously bound—
TIMON. And so am I to you.
2 LORD. So infinitely endeared—
TIMON. All to you. Lights, more lights!
1 LORD. The best of happiness, honour and fortunes,
   Keep with you, Lord Timon!
TIMON. Ready for his friends.
                    All leave but Apemantus and Timon
APEMANTUS.   What a coil's here! 240
   Serving of becks and jutting-out of bums!
   I doubt whether their legs be worth the sums
   That are given for 'em. Friendship's full of dregs:
   Methinks false hearts should never have sound legs.
   Thus honest fools lay out their wealth on curtsies.
TIMON. Now, Apemantus, if thou wert not sullen,
   I would be good to thee.
APEMANTUS. No, I'll nothing; for if I should be bribed
   too, there would be none left to rail upon thee, and
   then thou wouldst sin the faster. Thou giv'st so long, 250
   Timon, I fear me thou wilt give away thyself in
   paper shortly. What needs these feasts, pomps and
   vainglories?
TIMON. Nay, an you begin to rail on society once, I
   am sworn not to give regard to you. Farewell, and
   come with better music.   *Goes*
APEMANTUS. So. Thou wilt not hear me now; thou
   shalt not then. I'll lock thy heaven from thee.
   O, that men's ears should be
   To counsel deaf, but not to flattery!   *Goes* 260

ACT 2

Scene 1: *A Senator's house*

Enter a Senator, with papers in his hand

SENATOR. And late five thousand; to Varro and to
      Isidore
   He owes nine thousand, besides my former sum,
   Which makes it five and twenty. Still in motion
   Of raging waste? It cannot hold; it will not.
   If I want gold, steal but a beggar's dog
   And give it Timon, why, the dog coins gold.
   If I would sell my horse and buy twenty moe
   Better than he, why, give my horse to Timon,
   Ask nothing, give it him, it foals me straight,
   And able horses. No porter at his gate,   10
   But rather one that smiles, and still invites
   All that pass by. It cannot hold; no reason
   Can sound his state in safety. Caphis, ho!
   Caphis, I say!

Enter Caphis

CAPHIS.   Here, sir; what is your pleasure?
SENATOR. Get on your cloak, and haste you to Lord
      Timon;
   Importune him for my moneys; be not ceased
   With slight denial; nor then silenced when
   'Commend me to your master' and the cap
   Plays in the right hand, thus; but tell him
   My uses cry to me, I must serve my turn   20
   Out of mine own; his days and times are past,
   And my reliances on his fracted dates
   Have smit my credit. I love and honour him,
   But must not break my back to heal his finger.
   Immediate are my needs, and my relief
   Must not be tossed and turned to me in words,

But find supply immediate. Get you gone;
   Put on a most importunate aspect,
   A visage of demand; for I do fear,
   When every feather sticks in his own wing,   30
   Lord Timon will be left a naked gull,
   Which flashes now a phoenix. Get you gone.
CAPHIS. I go, sir.
SENATOR.   Take the bonds along with you,
   And have the dates in compt.
CAPHIS.   I will, sir.
SENATOR.   Go.
                                              They go

Scene 2: *Before Timon's house*

Enter Flavius, with many bills in his hand

FLAVIUS. No care, no stop, so senseless of expense
   That he will neither know how to maintain it,
   Nor cease his flow of riot; takes no account
   How things go from him, nor resumes no care
   Of what is to continue; never mind
   Was to be so unwise to be so kind.
   What shall be done? he will not hear till feel.
   I must be round with him, now he comes from
      hunting.
   Fie, fie, fie, fie!

Enter Caphis, with the Servants of Isidore and Varro

CAPHIS. Good even, Varro. What, you come for
      money?   10
VARRO'S SERVANT. Is't not your business too?
CAPHIS. It is; and yours too, Isidore?
ISIDORE'S SERVANT. It is so.
CAPHIS. Would we were all discharged!
VARRO'S SERVANT. I fear it.
CAPHIS. Here comes the lord.

Enter Timon and his Train, with Alcibiades

TIMON. So soon as dinner's done, we'll forth again,
   My Alcibiades. With me? What is your will?
CAPHIS. My lord, here is a note of certain dues.
TIMON. Dues? Whence are you?
CAPHIS.   Of Athens here, my lord. 20
TIMON. Go to my steward.
CAPHIS. Please it your lordship, he hath put me off
   To the succession of new days this month.
   My master is awaked by great occasion
   To call upon his own, and humbly prays you
   That with your other noble parts you'll suit
   In giving him his right.
TIMON.   Mine honest friend,
   I prithee but repair to me next morning.
CAPHIS. Nay, good my lord—
TIMON.   Contain thyself, good friend.
VARRO'S SERVANT. One Varro's servant, my good 30
   lord—
ISIDORE'S SERVANT. From Isidore; he humbly prays
   your speedy payment.
CAPHIS. If you did know, my lord, my master's
   wants,—
VARRO'S SERVANT. 'Twas due on forfeiture, my lord,
   six weeks and past.
ISIDORE'S SERVANT. Your steward puts me off, my
   lord, and I
   Am sent expressly to your lordship.
TIMON. Give me breath.

I do beseech you, good my lords, keep on;   40
I'll wait upon you instantly.
                    Alcibiades, Lords and others go
                    [to Flavius] Come hither. Pray you,
How goes the world, that I am thus encount'red
With clamorous demands of broken bonds,
And the detention of long-since-due debts
Against my honour?
FLAVIUS.   Please you, gentlemen,
The time is unagreeable to this business.
Your importunacy cease till after dinner,
That I may make his lordship understand
Wherefore you are not paid.
TIMON. Do so, my friends. See them well entertained. 50
                                        He goes
FLAVIUS. Pray draw near.   *He goes*

Enter Apemantus and Fool

CAPHIS. Stay, stay, here comes the fool with Apeman-
    tus. Let's ha' some sport with 'em.
VARRO'S SERVANT. Hang him, he'll abuse us.
ISIDORE'S SERVANT. A plague upon him, dog!
VARRO'S SERVANT. How dost, fool?
APEMANTUS. Dost dialogue with thy shadow?
VARRO'S SERVANT. I speak not to thee.
APEMANTUS. No, 'tis to thy self *[to the Fool]* Come
    away.
ISIDORE'S SERVANT. There's the fool hangs on your 60
    back already.
APEMANTUS. No, thou stand'st single, thou'rt not on
    him yet.
CAPHIS. Where's the fool now?
APEMANTUS. He last asked the question. Poor rogues,
    and usurers' men, bawds between gold and want!
ALL SERVANTS. What are we, Apemantus?
APEMANTUS. Asses.
ALL SERVANTS. Why?
APEMANTUS. That you ask me what you are, and do 70
    not know yourselves. Speak to 'em, fool.
FOOL. How do you, gentlemen?
ALL SERVANTS. Gramercies, good fool. How does your
    mistress?
FOOL. She's e'en setting on water to scald such chickens
    as you are. Would we could see you at Corinth!
APEMANTUS. Good, gramercy.

Enter Page

FOOL. Look you, here comes my mistress' page.
PAGE *[to the Fool]*. Why, how now, captain? what do
    you in this wise company? How dost thou, 80
    Apemantus?
APEMANTUS. Would I had a rod in my mouth, that I
    might answer thee profitably.
PAGE. Prithee, Apemantus, read me the superscription
    of these letters. I know not which is which.
APEMANTUS. Canst not read?
PAGE. No.
APEMANTUS. There will little learning die then, that
    day thou art hanged. This is to Lord Timon; this
    to Alcibiades. Go, thou wast born a bastard, and 90
    thou'lt die a bawd.
PAGE. Thou wast whelped a dog, and thou shalt famish
    a dog's death. Answer not, I am gone.   *Goes*
APEMANTUS. E'en so thou outrun'st grace. Fool, I will
    go with you to Lord Timon's.
FOOL. Will you leave me there?

APEMANTUS. If Timon stay at home. You three serve
    three usurers?
ALL SERVANTS. Ay; would they served us!
APEMANTUS. So would I—as good a trick as ever hang- 100
    man served thief.
FOOL. Are you three usurers' men?
ALL SERVANTS. Ay, fool.
FOOL. I think no usurer but has a fool to his servant.
    My mistress is one, and I am her fool. When men
    come to borrow of your masters, they approach
    sadly and go away merry; but they enter my
    mistress' house merrily and go away sadly. The
    reason of this?
VARRO'S SERVANT. I could render one.   110
APEMANTUS. Do it then, that we may account thee a
    whoremaster and a knave; which notwithstanding,
    thou shalt be no less esteemed.
VARRO'S SERVANT. What is a whoremaster, fool?
FOOL. A fool in good clothes, and something like thee.
    'Tis a spirit. Sometime 't appears like a lord, some-
    time like a lawyer, sometime like a philosopher,
    with two stones moe than 's artificial one. He is very
    often like a knight; and generally, in all shapes that
    man goes up and down in, from fourscore to 120
    thirteen, this spirit walks in.
VARRO'S SERVANT. Thou art not altogether a fool.
FOOL. Nor thou altogether a wise man: as much
    foolery as I have, so much wit thou lack'st.
APEMANTUS. That answer might have become Ape-
    mantus.
ALL SERVANTS. Aside, aside; here comes Lord Timon.

Re-enter Timon and Flavius

APEMANTUS. Come with me, fool, come.
FOOL. I do not always follow lover, elder brother,
    and woman; sometime the philosopher.   *They go* 130
FLAVIUS. Pray you, walk near: I'll speak with you
    anon.   *Servants withdraw*
TIMON. You make me marvel wherefore ere this time
    Had you not fully laid my state before me,
    That I might so have rated my expense
    As I had leave of means.
FLAVIUS.   You would not hear me.
    At many leisures I proposed—
TIMON.   Go to.
    Perchance some single vantages you took
    When my indisposition put you back,
    And that unaptness made your minister
    Thus to excuse yourself.
FLAVIUS.   O my good lord,   140
    At many times I brought in my accounts,
    Laid them before you; you would throw them off,
    And say you found them in mine honesty.
    When for some trifling present you have bid me
    Return so much, I have shook my head and wept;
    Yea, 'gainst th'authority of manners prayed you
    To hold your hand more close. I did endure
    Not seldom, nor no slight checks, when I have
    Prompted you in the ebb of your estate
    And your great flow of debts. My loved lord—   150
    Though you hear now too late, yet now's a time—
    The greatest of your having lacks a half
    To pay your present debts.
TIMON.   Let all my land be sold.
FLAVIUS. 'Tis all engaged, some forfeited and gone,
    And what remains will hardly stop the mouth

Of present dues. The future comes apace;
What shall defend the interim? and at length
How goes our reck'ning?
TIMON. To Lacedæmon did my land extend.
FLAVIUS. O my good lord, the world is but a word; 160
Were it all yours to give it in a breath,
How quickly were it gone!
TIMON.   You tell me true.
FLAVIUS. If you suspect my husbandry or falsehood,
Call me before th'exactest auditors,
And set me on the proof. So the gods bless me,
When all our offices have been oppressed
With riotous feeders, when our vaults have wept
With drunken spilth of wine, when every room
Hath blazed with lights and brayed with minstrelsy,
I have retired me to a wasteful cock,   170
And set mine eyes at flow.
TIMON.   Prithee no more.
FLAVIUS. Heavens, have I said, the bounty of this lord!
How many prodigal bits have slaves and peasants
This night englutted! Who is not Timon's?
What heart, head, sword, force, means, but is Lord
Timon's?
Great Timon, noble, worthy, royal Timon!
Ah, when the means are gone that buy this praise,
The breath is gone whereof this praise is made.
Feast-won, fast-lost; one cloud of winter showers,
These flies are couched.
TIMON.   Come, sermon me no further. 180
No villainous bounty yet hath passed my heart;
Unwisely, not ignobly, have I given.
Why dost thou weep? Canst thou the conscience
lack
To think I shall lack friends? Secure thy heart;
If I would broach the vessels of my love,
And try the argument of hearts, by borrowing,
Men and men's fortunes could I frankly use
As I can bid thee speak.
FLAVIUS.   Assurance bless your thoughts!
TIMON. And in some sort these wants of mine are
crowned,
That I account them blessings; for by these   190
Shall I try friends:
You shall perceive how you mistake my fortunes;
I am wealthy in my friends.
Within there! Flaminius! Servilius!

Enter Flaminius, Servilius, and another Servant

SERVANTS. My lord, my lord?
TIMON. I will dispatch you severally. You to Lord
Lucius, to Lord Lucullus you—I hunted with his
honour to-day—you to Sempronius, commend me
to their loves; and I am proud, say, that my occasions
have found time to use 'em toward a supply of 200
money. Let the request be fifty talents.
FLAMINIUS. As you have said, my Lord.
FLAVIUS. Lord Lucius and Lucullus? hum!
TIMON. Go you, sir, to the senators,
Of whom, even to the state's best health, I have
Deserved this hearing; bid 'em send o'th'instant
A thousand talents to me.
FLAVIUS.   I have been bold,
For that I knew it the most general way,
To them to use your signet and your name;
But they do shake their heads, and I am here   210
No richer in return.

TIMON.   Is't true? can't be?
FLAVIUS. They answer, in a joint and corporate voice,
That now they are at fall, want treasure, cannot
Do what they would; are sorry—you are
honourable—
But yet they could have wished—they know not—
Something hath been amiss—a noble nature
May catch a wrench—would all were well—'tis
pity;
And so, intending other serious matters,
After distasteful looks, and these hard fractions,
With certain half-caps and cold-moving nods   220
They froze me into silence.
TIMON.   You gods, reward them!
Prithee, man, look cheerly. These old fellows
Have their ingratitude in them hereditary.
Their blood is caked, 'tis cold, it seldom flows;
'Tis lack of kindly warmth they are not kind;
And nature, as it grows again toward earth,
Is fashioned for the journey, dull and heavy.
Go to Ventidius. Prithee, be not sad;
Thou art true and honest; ingeniously I speak,
No blame belongs to thee. Ventidius lately   230
Buried his father, by whose death he's stepped
Into a great estate. When he was poor,
Imprisoned, and in scarcity of friends,
I cleared him with five talents. Greet him from me;
Bid him suppose some good necessity
Touches his friend, which craves to be rememb'red
With those five talents. That had, give't these
fellows
To whom 'tis instant due. Ne'er speak or think
That Timon's fortunes 'mong his friends can sink.
FLAVIUS. I would I could not think it.   240
That thought is bounty's foe;
Being free itself, it thinks all others so.   *They go*

ACT 3
Scene 1: *A room in Lucullus's house*

*Flaminius waiting to speak with Lucullus from his master,
enters a Servant to him*

SERVANT. I have told my lord of you; he is coming
down to you.
FLAMINIUS. I thank you, sir.

Enter Lucullus

SERVANT. Here's my lord.
LUCULLUS [*aside*]. One of Lord Timon's men? a gift, I
warrant. Why, this hits right; I dreamt of a silver
basin and ewer to-night. [*aloud*] Flaminius, honest
Flaminius, you are very respectively welcome, sir.
Fill me some wine. [*Servant goes*] And how does
that honourable, complete, free-hearted gentleman 10
of Athens, thy very bountiful good lord and master?
FLAMINIUS. His health is well, sir.
LUCULLUS. I am right glad that his health is well, sir.
And what hast thou there under thy cloak, pretty
Flaminius?
FLAMINIUS. Faith, nothing but an empty box, sir,
which in my lord's behalf I come to entreat your
honour to supply; who, having great and instant
occasion to use fifty talents, hath sent to your lordship to furnish him, nothing doubting your present 20
assistance therein.

LUCULLUS. La, la, la, la! 'Nothing doubting', says he?
  Alas, good lord! a noble gentleman 'tis, if he would
  not keep so good a house. Many a time and often
  I ha' dined with him, and told him on't, and come
  again to supper to him of purpose to have him spend
  less, and yet he would embrace no counsel, take no
  warning by my coming. Every man has his fault,
  and honesty is his. I ha' told him on't, but I could
  ne'er get him from't.   30

Re-enter Servant, with wine

SERVANT. Please your lordship, here is the wine.
LUCULLUS. Flaminius, I have noted thee always wise.
  Here's to thee.
FLAMINIUS. Your lordship speaks your pleasure.
LUCULLUS. I have observed thee always for a towardly
  prompt spirit, give thee thy due, and one that knows
  what belongs to reason; and canst use the time well,
  if the time use thee well. Good parts in thee. [*to
  Servant*] Get you gone, sirrah. [*Servant goes*] Draw
  nearer, honest Flaminius. Thy lord's a bountiful   40
  gentleman; but thou art wise, and thou know'st well
  enough, although thou com'st to me, that this is no
  time to lend money, especially upon bare friendship
  without security. Here's three solidares for thee.
  Good boy, wink at me, and say thou saw'st me not.
  Fare thee well.
FLAMINIUS. Is't possible the world should so much
    differ,
  And we alive that lived? Fly, damnéd baseness,
  To him that worships thee!
                              Throwing back the money
LUCULLUS. Ha! now I see thou art a fool, and fit for 50
  thy master.   *Goes*
FLAMINIUS. May these add to the number that may
    scald thee!
  Let molten coin be thy damnation,
  Thou disease of a friend, and not himself!
  Has friendship such a faint and milky heart,
  It turns in less than two nights? O you gods,
  I feel my master's passion! this slave,
  Unto this hour, has my lord's meat in him;
  Why should it thrive and turn to nutriment,
  When he is turn'd to poison?   60
  O, may diseases only work upon't!
  And when he's sick to death, let not that part of
    nature
  Which my lord paid for be of any power
  To expel sickness, but prolong his hour!   *Goes*

Scene 2: *A public place*

Enter Lucius, with three Strangers

LUCIUS. Who, the Lord Timon? he is my very good
  friend, and an honourable gentleman.
1 STRANGER. We know him for no less, though we are
  but strangers to him. But I can tell you one thing,
  my lord, and which I hear from common rumours:
  now Lord Timon's happy hours are done and past,
  and his estate shrinks from him.
LUCIUS. Fie, no, do not believe it; he cannot want
  for money.
2 STRANGER. But believe you this, my lord, that not 10
  long ago one of his men was with the Lord Lucullus
  to borrow so many talents; nay, urged extremely

for't, and showed what necessity belonged to't, and
  yet was denied.
LUCIUS. How?
2 STRANGER. I tell you, denied, my lord.
LUCIUS. What a strange case was that! now, before the
  gods, I am ashamed on't. Denied that honourable
  man? there was very little honour showed in't. For
  my own part, I must needs confess, I have received   20
  some small kindnesses from him, as money, plate,
  jewels, and such-like trifles, nothing comparing to
  his; yet, had he mistook him and sent to me, I should
  ne'er have denied his occasion so many talents.

Enter Servilius

SERVILIUS. See, by good hap, yonder's my lord; I have
  sweat to see his honour. My honoured lord!
LUCIUS. Servilius? you are kindly met, sir. Fare thee
  well; commend me to thy honourable virtuous lord,
  my very exquisite friend.
SERVILIUS. May it please your honour, my lord hath   30
  sent—
LUCIUS. Ha! what has he sent? I am so much endeared
  to that lord; he's ever sending. How shall I thank
  him, think'st thou? And what has he sent now?
SERVILIUS. Has only sent his present occasion now, my
  lord; requesting your lordship to supply his instant
  use with so many talents.
LUCIUS. I know his lordship is but merry with me;
  He cannot want fifty five hundred talents.
SERVILIUS. But in the mean time he wants less, my
  lord.   40
  If his occasion were not virtuous,
  I should not urge it half so faithfully.
LUCIUS. Dost thou speak seriously, Servilius?
SERVILIUS. Upon my soul, 'tis true, sir.
LUCIUS. What a wicked beast was I to disfurnish
  myself against such a good time, when I might ha'
  shown myself honourable! how unluckily it
  happ'ned that I should purchase the day before for
  a little part, and undo a great deal of honour!
  Servilius, now before the gods, I am not able to   50
  do—the more beast, I say—I was sending to use
  Lord Timon myself, these gentlemen can witness;
  but I would not, for the wealth of Athens, I had
  done't now. Commend me bountifully to his good
  lordship, and I hope his honour will conceive the
  fairest of me, because I have no power to be kind.
  And tell him this from me, I count it one of my
  greatest afflictions, say, that I cannot pleasure such
  an honourable gentleman. Good Servilius, will you
  befriend me so far as to use mine own words to him?   60
SERVILIUS. Yes, sir, I shall.
LUCIUS. I'll look you out a good turn, Servilius.
                                       Servilius goes
  True, as you said, Timon is shrunk indeed,
  And he that's once denied will hardly speed.
                                                  Goes
1 STRANGER. Do you observe this, Hostilius?
2 STRANGER.   Ay, too well.
1 STRANGER. Why, this is the world's soul; and just of
    the same piece
  Is every flatterer's spirit. Who can call him his friend
  That dips in the same dish? for, in my knowing,
  Timon has been this lord's father,
  And kept his credit with his purse;   70
  Supported his estate; nay, Timon's money

Has paid his men their wages. He ne'er drinks
But Timon's silver treads upon his lip;
And yet—O, see the monstrousness of man
When he looks out in an ungrateful shape—
He does deny him, in respect of his,
What charitable men afford to beggars.
3 STRANGER. Religion groans at it.
1 STRANGER.   For mine own part,
I never tasted Timon in my life,
Nor came any of his bounties over me,   80
To mark me for his friend. Yet I protest,
For his right noble mind, illustrious virtue,
And honourable carriage,
Had his necessity made use of me,
I would have put my wealth into donation,
And the best half should have returned to him,
So much I love his heart. But I perceive,
Men must learn now with pity to dispense,
For policy sits above conscience.   *They go*

Scene 3: *A room in Sempronius's house*

Enter Sempronius, and a Servant of Timon's

SEMPRONIUS. Must he needs trouble me in't—hum!
—'bove all others?
He might have tried Lord Lucius or Lucullus;
And now Ventidius is wealthy too,
Whom he redeemed from prison. All these
Owe their estates unto him.
SERVANT.   My lord,
They have all been touched and found base metal,
for
They have all denied him.
SEMPRONIUS.   How? have they denied him?
Has Ventidius and Lucullus denied him,
And does he send to me? Three? hum!
It shows but little love or judgement in him.   10
Must I be his last refuge? His friends, like physicians,
Thrice give him over: must I take th'cure upon me?
Has much disgraced me in't; I'm angry at him,
That might have known my place. I see no sense
for't,
But his occasions might have wooed me first;
For, in my conscience, I was the first man
That e'er receivéd gift from him.
And does he think so backwardly of me now,
That I'll requite it last? No;
So it may prove an argument of laughter   20
To th'rest, and I 'mongst lords be thought a fool.
I'd rather than the worth of thrice the sum
Had sent to me first, but for my mind's sake;
I'd such a courage to do him good. But now return,
And with their faint reply this answer join:
Who bates mine honour shall not know my coin.
                                                                Goes
SERVANT. Excellent. Your lordship's a goodly villain.
The devil knew not what he did when he made man
politic; he crossed himself by't; and I cannot think
but in the end the villainies of man will set him clear.   30
How fairly this lord strives to appear foul! takes
virtuous copies to be wicked; like those that under
hot ardent zeal would set whole realms on fire:
Of such a nature is his politic love.
This was my lord's best hope; now all are fled,
Save only the gods. Now his friends are dead,
Doors that were ne'er acquainted with their wards

Many a bounteous year must be employed
Now to guard sure their master.
And this is all a liberal course allows;   40
Who cannot keep his wealth must keep his house.
                                                                Goes

Scene 4: *A hall in Timon's house*

*Enter two Servants of Varro, and the Servant of Lucius,
meeting Titus, Hortensius, and other Servants of Timon's
creditors, waiting his coming out*

1 VARRO'S SERVANT. Well met; good morrow, Titus
and Hortensius.
TITUS. The like to you, kind Varro.
HORTENSIUS.   Lucius;
What, do we meet together?
LUCIUS'S SERVANT.   Ay, and I think
One business does command us all;
For mine is money.
TITUS.   So is theirs and ours.

Enter Philotus

LUCIUS'S SERVANT. And Sir Philotus too!
PHILOTUS.   Good day at once.
LUCIUS'S SERVANT. Welcome, good brother. What do
you think the hour?
PHILOTUS. Labouring for nine.
LUCIUS'S SERVANT. So much?
PHILOTUS.   Is not my lord seen yet?
LUCIUS'S SERVANT.   Not yet.
PHILOTUS. I wonder on't; he was wont to shine at
seven.   10
LUCIUS'S SERVANT. Ay, but the days are waxed shorter
with him;
You must consider that a prodigal course
Is like the sun's, but not, like his, recoverable.
I fear
'Tis deepest winter in Lord Timon's purse;
That is,
One may reach deep enough and yet find little.
PHILOTUS. I am of your fear for that.
TITUS. I'll show you how t'observe a strange event
Your lord sends now for money?
HORTENSIUS.   Most true, he does.   20
TITUS. And he wears jewels now of Timon's gift,
For which I wait for money.
HORTENSIUS. It is against my heart.
LUCIUS'S SERVANT.   Mark, how strange it shows
Timon in this should pay more than he owes;
And e'en as if your lord should wear rich jewels
And send for money for 'em.
HORTENSIUS. I'm weary of this charge, the gods can
witness;
I know my lord hath spent of Timon's wealth,
And now ingratitude makes it worse than stealth.
1 VARRO'S SERVANT. Yes, mine's three thousand
crowns; what's yours?   30
LUCIUS'S SERVANT. Five thousand mine.
1 VARRO'S SERVANT. 'Tis much deep; and it should
seem by th'sum
Your master's confidence was above mine,
Else, surely, his had equalled.

Enter Flaminius

TITUS. One of Lord Timon's men.

LUCIUS'S SERVANT. Flaminius? Sir, a word. Pray, is my
   lord ready to come forth?
FLAMINIUS. No, indeed he is not.
TITUS. We attend his lordship; pray signify so much.
FLAMINIUS. I need not tell him that; he knows you are 40
   too diligent.   *Goes*

Enter Flavius in a cloak, muffled

LUCIUS'S SERVANT. Ha, is not that his steward muffled
   so?
   He goes away in a cloud. Call him, call him.
TITUS. Do you hear, sir?
2 VARRO'S SERVANT. By your leave, sir.
FLAVIUS. What do ye ask of me, my friend?
TITUS. We wait for certain money here, sir.
FLAVIUS.   Ay,
   If money were as certain as your waiting,
   'Twere sure enough.
   Why then preferred you not your sums and bills, 50
   When your false masters ate of my lord's meat?
   Then they could smile and fawn upon his debts,
   And take down th'interest into their glutt'nous
   maws.
   You do yourselves but wrong to stir me up;
   Let me pass quietly.
   Believe't, my lord and I have made an end;
   I have no more to reckon, he to spend.
LUCIUS'S SERVANT. Ay, but this answer will not serve.
FLAVIUS. If 'twill not serve, 'tis not so base as you,
   For you serve knaves.   *Goes* 60
1 VARRO'S SERVANT. How? what does his cashiered
   worship mutter?
2 VARRO'S SERVANT. No matter what; he's poor, and
   that's revenge enough. Who can speak broader than
   he that has no house to put his head in? such may
   rail against great buildings.

Enter Servilius

TITUS. O, here's Servilius; now we shall know some
   answer.
SERVILIUS. If I might beseech you, gentlemen, to repair
   some other hour, I should derive much from't; for, 70
   take't of my soul, my lord leans wondrously to
   discontent. His comfortable temper has forsook
   him; he's much out of health and keeps his chamber.
LUCIUS'S SERVANT. Many do keep their chambers are
   not sick;
   And if it be so far beyond his health,
   Methinks he should the sooner pay his debts,
   And make a clear way to the gods.
SERVILIUS.   Good gods!
TITUS. We cannot take this for an answer, sir.
FLAMINIUS [*within*]. Servilius, help! My lord, my lord!

Enter Timon, in a rage, Flaminius following

TIMON. What, are my doors opposed against my
   passage?   80
   Have I been ever free, and must my house
   Be my retentive enemy, my gaol?
   The place which I have feasted, does it now,
   Like all mankind, show me an iron heart?
LUCIUS'S SERVANT. Put in now, Titus.
TITUS. My lord, here is my bill.
LUCIUS'S SERVANT. Here's mine.
HORTENSIUS. And mine, my lord.
BOTH VARRO'S SERVANTS. And ours, my lord.

PHILOTUS. All our bills.   90
TIMON. Knock me down with 'em; cleave me to the
   girdle.
LUCIUS'S SERVANT. Alas, my lord—
TIMON. Cut my heart in sums.
TITUS. Mine, fifty talents.
TIMON. Tell out my blood.
LUCIUS'S SERVANT. Five thousand crowns, my lord.
TIMON. Five thousand drops pays that. What yours?
   and yours?
1 VARRO'S SERVANT. My lord—
2 VARRO'S SERVANT. My lord—
TIMON. Tear me, take me, and the gods fall upon you!| 100
                                       Goes
HORTENSIUS. Faith, I perceive our masters may throw
   their caps at their money; these debts may well be
   called desperate ones, for a madman owes 'em.
                                   They go

Re-enter Timon and Flavius

TIMON. They have e'en put my breath from me, the
   slaves.
   Creditors? devils!
FLAVIUS. My dear lord—
TIMON. What if it should be so?
FLAVIUS. My lord—
TIMON. I'll have it so. My steward!
FLAVIUS. Here, my lord.   110
TIMON. So fitly! Go, bid all my friends again,
   Lucius, Lucullus, and Sempronius—all.
   I'll once more feast the rascals.
FLAVIUS.   O my lord,
   You only speak from your distracted soul;
   There is not so much left, to furnish out
   A moderate table.
TIMON.   Be it not in thy care;
   Go,
   I charge thee, invite them all: let in the tide
   Of knaves once more; my cook and I'll provide.
                                    They go

Scene 5: The Senate-house

Enter three Senators; Alcibiades, attended, at the door

1 SENATOR. My lord, you have my voice to't; the
   fault's bloody;
   'Tis necessary he should die:
   Nothing emboldens sin so much as mercy.
2 SENATOR. Most true; the law shall bruise him.

Alcibiades is brought forward

ALCIBIADES. Honour, health, and compassion to the
   senate!
1 SENATOR. Now, captain?
ALCIBIADES. I am an humble suitor to your virtues;
   For pity is the virtue of the law,
   And none but tyrants use it cruelly.
   It pleases time and fortune to lie heavy   10
   Upon a friend of mine, who in hot blood
   Hath stepped into the law, which is past depth
   To those that without heed do plunge into't.
   He is a man, setting this fault aside,
   Of comely virtues;
   Nor did he soil the fact with cowardice—
   An honour in him which buys out his fault—
   But with a noble fury and fair spirit,

Seeing his reputation touched to death,
He did oppose his foe;   20
And with such sober and unnoted passion
He did behove his anger, ere 'twas spent,
As if he had but proved an argument.
1 SENATOR. You undergo too strict a paradox,
Striving to make an ugly deed look fair;
Your words have took such pains as if they laboured
To bring manslaughter into form, and set
    quarrelling
Upon the head of valour; which indeed
Is valour misbegot, and came into the world
When sects and factions were newly born.   30
He's truly valiant that can wisely suffer
The worst that man can breathe,
And make his wrongs his outsides,
To wear them like his raiment, carelessly,
And ne'er prefer his injuries to his heart,
To bring it into danger.
If wrongs be evils and enforce us kill,
What folly 'tis to hazard life for ill!
ALCIBIADES. My lord—
1 SENATOR.   You cannot make gross sins look clear:
To revenge is no valour, but to bear.   40
ALCIBIADES. My lords, then, under favour, pardon me
If I speak like a captain.
Why do fond men expose themselves to battle,
And not endure all threats? sleep upon't,
And let the foes quietly cut their throats,
Without repugnancy? If there be
Such valour in the bearing, what make we
Abroad? why then women are more valiant
That stay at home, if bearing carry it,
And the ass more captain than the lion,   50
The felon loaden with irons wiser than the judge,
If wisdom be in suffering. O my lords,
As you are great, be pitifully good.
Who cannot condemn rashness in cold blood?
To kill, I grant, is sin's extremest gust;
But in defence, by Mercy, 'tis most just.
To be in anger is impiety;
But who is man that is not angry?
Weigh but the crime with this.
2 SENATOR. You breathe in vain.
ALCIBIADES.   In vain? His service done 60
At Lacedæmon and Byzantium
Were a sufficient briber for his life.
1 SENATOR. What's that?
ALCIBIADES.   Why, I say, my lords, has done
    fair service,
And slain in fight many of your enemies;
How full of valour did he bear himself
In the last conflict, and made plenteous wounds!
2 SENATOR. He has made too much plenty with 'em.
He's a sworn rioter; he has a sin
That often drowns him and takes his valour
    prisoner.
If there were no foes, that were enough   70
To overcome him. In that beastly fury
He has been known to commit outrages
And cherish factions. 'Tis inferred to us,
His days are foul and his drink dangerous.
1 SEN. He dies.
ALCIBIADES.   Hard fate! he might have died in war.
My lords, if not for any parts in him—
Though his right arm might purchase his own time

And be in debt to none—yet, more to move you,
Take my deserts to his and join 'em both;
And, for I know   80
Your reverend ages love security,
I'll pawn my victories, all my honour to you,
Upon his good returns.
If by this crime he owes the law his life,
Why, let the war receive't in valiant gore,
For law is strict, and war is nothing more.
1 SENATOR. We are for law: he dies; urge it no more,
On height of our displeasure. Friend or brother,
He forfeits his own blood that spills another.
ALCIBIADES. Must it be so? it must not be. My lords, 90
I do beseech you, know me.
2 SENATOR. How?
ALCIBIADES. Call me to your remembrances.
3 SENATOR. What?
ALCIBIADES. I cannot think but your age has forgot
    me;
It could not else be I should prove so base
To sue and be denied such common grace.
My wounds ache at you.
1 SENATOR.   Do you dare our anger?
'Tis in few words, but spacious in effect:
We banish thee for ever.
ALCIBIADES.   Banish me?   100
Banish your dotage, banish usury,
That makes the senate ugly.
1 SENATOR. If, after two days' shine, Athens contain
    thee,
Attend our weightier judgement. And, not to swell
    our spirit,
He shall be executed presently.   Senators go
ALCIBIADES. Now the gods keep you old enough, that
    you may live
Only in bone, that none may look on you!
I'm worse than mad; I have kept back their foes,
While they have told their money and let out
Their coin upon large interest, I myself   110
Rich only in large hurts. All those for this?
Is this the balsam that the usuring senate
Pours into captains' wounds? Banishment!
It comes not ill; I hate not to be banished;
It is a cause worthy my spleen and fury,
That I may strike at Athens. I'll cheer up
My discontented troops, and lay for hearts.
'Tis honour with most lands to be at odds;
Soldiers should brook as little wrongs as gods.
                                                                            Goes

Scene 6: *A banqueting-room in Timon's house*

Music. Tables set out; Servants attending. Enter divers
Lords, Senators and others, at several doors

1 LORD. The good time of day to you, sir.
2 LORD. I also wish it to you. I think this honourable
    lord did but try us this other day.
1 LORD. Upon that were my thoughts tiring when we
    encount'red. I hope it is not so low with him as he
    made it seem in the trial of his several friends.
2 LORD. It should not be, by the persuasion of his new
    feasting.
1 LORD. I should think so. He hath sent me an earnest
    inviting, which many my near occasions did urge 10
    me to put off; but he hath conjured me beyond
    them, and I must needs appear.

2 LORD. In like manner was I in debt to my importunate business, but he would not hear my excuse. I am sorry, when he sent to borrow of me, that my provision was out.

I LORD. I am sick of that grief too, as I understand how all things go.

2 LORD. Every man here's so. What would he have borrowed of you?   20

I LORD. A thousand pieces.

2 LORD. A thousand pieces?

I LORD. What of you?

2 LORD. He sent to me, sir—Here he comes.

Enter Timon and Attendants

TIMON. With all my heart, gentlemen both; and how fare you?

I LORD. Ever at the best, hearing well of your lordship.

2 LORD. The swallow follows not summer more willing than we your lordship.

TIMON. Nor more willingly leaves winter; such sum-   30
mer birds are men. [*aloud*] Gentlemen, our dinner will not recompense this long stay; feast your ears with the music awhile, if they will fare so harshly o'th'trumpet's sound; we shall to't presently.

I LORD. I hope it remains not unkindly with your lordship, that I returned you an empty messenger.

TIMON. O, sir, let it not trouble you.

2 LORD. My noble lord,—

TIMON. Ah, my good friend, what cheer?

2 LORD. My most honourable lord, I am e'en sick of   40
shame that when your lordship this other day sent to me I was so unfortunate a beggar.

TIMON. Think not on't, sir.

2 LORD. If you had sent but two hours before—

TIMON. Let it not cumber your better remembrance. [*the banquet brought in*] Come, bring in all together.

2 LORD. All covered dishes.

I LORD. Royal cheer, I warrant you.

3 LORD. Doubt not that, if money and the season can yield it.   50

I LORD. How do you? What's the news?

3 LORD. Alcibiades is banished. Hear you of it?

I AND 2 LORDS. Alcibiades banished?

3 LORD. 'Tis so, be sure of it.

I LORD. How? how?

2 LORD. I pray you, upon what?

TIMON. My worthy friends, will you draw near?

3 LORD. I'll tell you more anon. Here's a noble feast toward.

2 LORD. This is the old man still.   60

3 LORD. Will't hold? will't hold?

2 LORD. It does; but time will—and so—

3 LORD. I do conceive.

TIMON. Each man to his stool, with that spur as he would to the lip of his mistress; your diet shall be in all places alike. Make not a city feast of it, to let the meat cool ere we can agree upon the first place. Sit, sit. The gods require our thanks.

You great benefactors, sprinkle our society with thankfulness. For your own gifts, make yourselves   70
praised; but reserve still to give, lest your deities be despised. Lend to each man enough, that one need not lend to another; for, were your godheads to borrow of men, men would forsake the gods. Make the meat be beloved more than the man that gives it. Let no assembly of twenty be without a score of

villains. If there sit twelve women at the table, let a dozen of them be—as they are. The rest of your fees, O gods—the senators of Athens, together with the common lag of people—what is amiss in them,   80
you gods, make suitable for destruction. For these my present friends, as they are to me nothing, so in nothing bless them, and to nothing are they welcome.

Uncover, dogs, and lap.

The dishes are uncovered and seen to be full of warm water and stones

SOME SPEAK. What does his lordship mean?

SOME OTHER. I know not.

TIMON. May you a better feast never behold,
You knot of mouth-friends! smoke and lukewarm water
Is your perfection. This is Timon's last,   90
Who, stuck and spangled with your flatteries,
Washes it off, and sprinkles in your faces
Your reeking villainy. [*throwing the water in their faces*] Live loathed and long,
Most smiling, smooth, detested parasites,
Courteous destroyers, affable wolves, meek bears,
You fools of fortune, trencher-friends, time's flies,
Cap-and-knee slaves, vapours, and minute-jacks!
Of man and beast the infinite malady
Crust you quite o'er! What, dost thou go?
Soft, take thy physic first; thou too, and thou.   100
Stay, I will lend thee money, borrow none.

Throws the stones at them, and drives them out

What, all in motion? Henceforth be no feast,
Whereat a villain's not a welcome guest.
Burn house! sink Athens! henceforth hated be
Of Timon man and all humanity!   *Goes*

Re-enter the Lords, Senators, etc.

I LORD. How now, my lords!

2 LORD. Know you the quality of Lord Timon's fury?

3 LORD. Push! did you see my cap?

4 LORD. I have lost my gown.

I LORD. He's but a mad lord, and nought but humours   110
sways him. He gave me a jewel th'other day, and now he has beat it out of my hat. Did you see my jewel?

3 LORD. Did you see my cap?

2 LORD. Here 'tis.

4 LORD. Here lies my gown.

I LORD. Let's make no stay.

2 LORD. Lord Timon's mad.

3 LORD.   I feel't upon my bones.

4 LORD. One day he gives us diamonds, next day stones.   *They go*

ACT 4
Scene 1: *Without the walls of Athens*

Enter Timon

TIMON. Let me look back upon thee. O thou wall
That girdles in those wolves, dive in the earth,
And fence not Athens. Matrons, turn incontinent.
Obedience fail in children. Slaves and fools
Pluck the grave wrinkled senate from the bench,
And minister in their steads. To general filths
Convert o'th'instant, green virginity.
Do't in your parents' eyes. Bankrupts, hold fast;

Rather than render back, out with your knives,
And cut your trusters' throats. Bound servants, steal: 10
Large-handed robbers your grave masters are,
And pill by law. Maid, to thy master's bed:
Thy mistress is o'th'brothel. Son of sixteen,
Pluck the lined crutch from thy old limping sire,
With it beat out his brains. Piety and fear,
Religion to the gods, peace, justice, truth,
Domestic awe, night-rest, and neighbourhood,
Instruction, manners, mysteries and trades,
Degrees, observances, customs and laws,
Decline to your confounding contraries, 20
And yet confusion live. Plagues incident to men,
Your potent and infectious fevers heap
On Athens, ripe for stroke. Thou cold sciatica,
Cripple our senators, that their limbs may halt
As lamely as their manners. Lust and liberty
Creep in the minds and marrows of our youth,
That 'gainst the stream of virtue they may strive,
And drown themselves in riot. Itches, blains,
Sow all th'Athenian bosoms, and their crop
Be general leprosy! Breath infect breath, 30
That their society, as their friendship, may
Be merely poison! Nothing I'll bear from thee
But nakedness, thou destestable town;
Take thou that too, with multiplying bans.
Timon will to the woods, where he shall find
Th'unkindest beast more kinder than mankind.
The gods confound—hear me, you good gods all—
Th'Athenians both within and out that wall.
And grant, as Timon grows, his hate may grow
To the whole race of mankind, high and low. 40
Amen.   *Goes*

Scene 2: *Athens. Timon's house*

Enter Flavius, with two or three Servants

1 SERVANT. Hear you, master steward, where's our
    master?
  Are we undone? cast off? nothing remaining?
FLAVIUS. Alack, my fellows, what should I say to you?
  Let me be recorded by the righteous gods,
  I am as poor as you.
1 SERVANT.   Such a house broke?
  So noble a master fall'n; all gone, and not
  One friend to take his fortune by the arm,
  And go along with him?
2 SERVANT.   As we do turn our backs
  From our companion thrown into his grave,
  So his familiars to his buried fortunes 10
  Slink all away; leave their false vows with him,
  Like empty purses picked; and his poor self.
  A dedicated beggar to the air,
  With his disease of all-shunned poverty,
  Walks like contempt alone. More of our fellows.

Enter other Servants

FLAVIUS. All broken implements of a ruined house.
3 SERVANT. Yet do our hearts wear Timon's livery,
  That see I by our faces; we are fellows still,
  Serving alike in sorrow. Leaked is our bark,
  And we, poor mates, stand on the dying deck, 20
  Hearing the surges threat; we must all part
  Into this sea of air.
FLAVIUS.   Good fellows all,
  The latest of my wealth I'll share amongst you.

Wherever we shall meet, for Timon's sake
Let's yet be fellows; let's shake our heads, and say,
As 'twere a knell unto our master's fortunes,
'We have seen better days'. Let each take some.
Nay, put out all your hands. Not one word more:
Thus part we rich in sorrow, parting poor.
      Servants embrace, and part several ways
O the fierce wretchedness that glory brings us! 30
Who would not wish to be from wealth exempt,
Since riches point to misery and contempt?
Who would be so mocked with glory, or to live
But in a dream of friendship,
To have his pomp and all what state compounds
But only painted, like his varnished friends?
Poor honest lord, brought low by his own heart,
Undone by goodness: strange, unusual blood,
When man's worst sin is, he does too much good.
Who then dares to be half so kind again? 40
For bounty, that makes gods, does still mar men.
My dearest lord, blest to be most accursed,
Rich only to be wretched, thy great fortunes
Are made thy chief afflictions. Alas, kind lord,
He's flung in rage from this ingrateful seat
Of monstrous friends;
Nor has he with him to supply his life,
Or that which can command it.
I'll follow, and inquire him out.
I'll ever serve his mind with my best will; 50
Whilst I have gold, I'll be his steward still.   *Goes*

Scene 3: *Woods and cave, near the sea-shore*

Enter Timon, from the cave

TIMON. O blessed breeding sun, draw from the earth
  Rotten humidity; below thy sister's orb
  Infect the air. Twinned brothers of one womb,
  Whose procreation, residence, and birth,
  Scarce is dividant, touch them with several
    fortunes,
  The greater scorns the lesser. Not nature,
  To whom all sores lay siege, can bear great fortune
  But by contempt of nature.
  Raise me this beggar and deject that lord,
  The senator shall bear contempt hereditary, 10
  The beggar native honour.
  It is the pasture lards the wether's dies,
  The want that makes him lean. Who dares, who
    dares,
  In purity of manhood stand upright,
  And say, 'This man's a flatterer'? If one be,
  So are they all; for every grise of fortune
  Is smoothed by that below. The learnéd pate
  Ducks to the golden fool. All's obliquy;
  There's nothing level in our curséd natures
  But direct villainy. Therefore be abhorred 20
  All feasts, societies and throngs of men.
  His semblable, yea, himself, Timon disdains;
  Destruction fang mankind. Earth, yield me roots.
                   Digging
  Who seeks for better of thee; sauce his palate
  With thy most operant poison. What is here?
  Gold? yellow, glittering, precious gold?
  No, gods, I am no idle votarist:
  Roots, you clear heavens! thus much of this will
    make

Black white, foul fair, wrong right,
Base noble, old young, coward valiant.   30
Ha, you gods! why this? what this, you gods? Why,
    this
Will lug your priests and servants from your sides,
Pluck stout men's pillows from below their heads.
This yellow slave
Will knit and break religions; bless th'accursed;
Make the hoar leprosy adored; place thieves,
And give them title, knee and approbation
With senators on the bench. This is it
That makes the wappered widow wed again;
She whom the spital-house and ulcerous sores   40
Would cast the gorge at, this embalms and spices
To th'April day again. Come, damnéd earth,
Thou common whore of mankind, that puts odds
Among the rout of nations, I will make thee
Do thy right nature. [march afar off] Ha, a drum?
    Thou'rt quick,
But yet I'll bury thee. Thou'lt go, strong thief,
When gouty keepers of thee cannot stand.
Nay, stay thou out for earnest.

                                        Keeping some gold

*Enter Alcibiades, with drum and fife, in warlike manner;
and Phrynia and Timandra*

ALCIBIADES.   What art thou there? speak.
TIMON. A beast, as thou art. The canker gnaw thy
    heart
For showing me again the eyes of man!   50
ALCIBIADES. What is thy name? Is man so hateful to
    thee,
That art thyself a man?
TIMON. I am Misanthropos, and hate mankind.
For thy part, I do wish thou wert a dog,
That I might love thee something.
ALCIBIADES.   I know thee well;
But in thy fortunes am unlearned and strange.
TIMON. I know thee too, and more than that I know
    thee
I not desire to know. Follow thy drum;
With man's blood paint the ground, gules, gules.
Religious canons, civil laws are cruel;   60
Then what should war be? This fell whore of thine
Hath in her more destruction than thy sword,
For all her cherubin look.
PHRYNIA.   Thy lips rot off!
TIMON. I will not kiss thee; then the rot returns
To thine own lips again.
ALCIBIADES. How came the noble Timon to this
    change?
TIMON. As the moon does, by wanting light to give.
But then renew I could not like the moon;
There were no suns to borrow of.
ALCIBIADES. Noble Timon, what friendship may I do
    thee?   70
TIMON. None, but to maintain my opinion.
ALCIBIADES. What is it, Timon?
TIMON. Promise me friendship, but perform none. If
    thou wilt not promise, the gods plague thee, for
    thou art a man! If thou dost perform, confound thee,
    for thou art a man!
ALCIBIADES. I have heard in some sort of thy miseries.
TIMON. Thou saw'st them when I had prosperity.
ALCIBIADES. I see them now; then was a blessed time.

TIMON. As thine is now, held with a brace of harlots. 80
TIMANDRA. Is this th'Athenian minion whom the
    world
Voiced so regardfully?
TIMON.   Art thou Timandra?
TIMANDRA. Yes.
TIMON. Be a whore still; they love thee not that use
    thee;
Give them diseases, leaving with thee their lust.
Make use of thy salt hours. Season the slaves
For tubs and baths; bring down rose-cheeked youth
To the tub-fast and the diet.
TIMANDRA.   Hang thee, monster!
ALCIBIADES. Pardon him, sweet Timandra, for his wits
Are drowned and lost in his calamities.   90
I have but little gold of late, brave Timon,
The want whereof doth daily make revolt
In my penurious band. I have heard, and grieved,
How curséd Athens, mindless of thy worth,
Forgetting thy great deeds, when neighbour states,
But for thy sword and fortune, trod upon them—
TIMON. I prithee beat thy drum and get thee gone.
ALCIBIADES. I am thy friend, and pity thee, dear
    Timon.
TIMON. How dost thou pity him whom thou dost
    trouble?
I had rather be alone.
ALCIBIADES.   Why, fare thee well; 100
Here is some gold for thee.
TIMON.   Keep it, I cannot eat it.
ALCIBIADES. When I have laid proud Athens on a
    heap—
TIMON. Warr'st thou 'gainst Athens?
ALCIBIADES.   Ay, Timon, and have cause.
TIMON. The gods confound them all in thy conquest,
And thee after, when thou hast conquered!
ALCIBIADES. Why me, Timon?
TIMON.   That by killing of villains
Thou wast born to conquer my country.
Put up thy gold. Go on, here's gold, go on;
Be as a planetary plague, when Jove
Will o'er some high-viced city hang his poison   110
In the sick air: let not thy sword skip one;
Pity not honoured age for his white beard;
He is an usurer. Strike me the counterfeit matron:
It is her habit only that is honest,
Herself's a bawd. Let not the virgin's cheek
Make soft thy trenchant sword; for those milk-paps
That through the window-bars bore at men's eyes
Are not within the leaf of pity writ,
But set them down horrible traitors. Spare not the
    babe
Whose dimpled smiles from fools exhaust their
    mercy;   120
Think it a bastard whom the oracle
Hath doubtfully pronounced thy throat shall cut,
And mince it sans remorse. Swear against objects;
Put armour on thine ears and on thine eyes,
Whose proof nor yells of mothers, maids, nor babes,
Nor sight of priests in holy vestments bleeding,
Shall pierce a jot. There's gold to pay thy soldiers;
Make large confusion; and, thy fury spent,
Confounded be thyself. Speak not, be gone.
ALCIBIADES. Hast thou gold yet? I'll take the gold thou
    givest me,   130
Not all thy counsel.

TIMON. Dost thou or dost thou not, heaven's curse
    upon thee!
PHRYNIA AND TIMANDRA. Give us some gold, good
    Timon; hast thou more?
TIMON. Enough to make a whore forswear her trade,
    And to make whores, a bawd. Hold up, you sluts,
    Your aprons mountant; you are not oathable,
    Although, I know, you'll swear, terribly swear,
    Into strong shudders and to heavenly agues,
    Th'immortal gods that hear you. Spare your oaths;
    I'll trust to your conditions. Be whores still;   140
    And he whose pious breath seeks to convert you,
    Be strong in whore, allure him, burn him up;
    Let your close fire predominate his smoke,
    And be no turncoats. Yet may your pains six months
    Be quite contrary: and thatch
    Your poor thin roofs with burdens of the dead—
    Some that were hanged, no matter:
    Wear them, betray with them; whore still;
    Paint till a horse may mire upon your face.
    A pox of wrinkles!
PHRYNIA AND TIMANDRA. Well, more gold. What
    then?   150
    Believe't that we'll do any thing for gold.
TIMON. Consumptions sow
    In hollow bones of man; strike their sharp shins,
    And mar men's spurring. Crack the lawyer's voice,
    That he may never more false title plead,
    Nor sound his quillets shrilly. Hoar the flamen,
    That scolds against the quality of flesh
    And not believes himself. Down with the nose,
    Down with it flat, take the bridge quite away
    Of him that his particular to foresee   160
    Smells from the general weal. Make curled-pate
        ruffians bald;
    And let the unscarred braggarts of the war
    Derive some pain from you. Plague all,
    That your activity may defeat and quell
    The source of all erection. There's more gold.
    Do you damn others, and let this damn you,
    And ditches grave you all!
PHRYNIA AND TIMANDRA. More counsel with more
    money, bounteous Timon.
TIMON. More whore, more mischief first; I have given
    you earnest.
ALCIBIADES. Strike up the drum towards Athens.
    Farewell, Timon;   170
    If I thrive well, I'll visit thee again.
TIMON. If I hope well, I'll never see thee more.
ALCIBIADES. I never did thee harm.
TIMON. Yes, thou spok'st well of me.
ALCIBIADES.   Call'st thou that harm?
TIMON. Men daily find it. Get thee away, and take
    Thy beagles with thee.
ALCIBIADES.   We but offend him. Strike!
    Drum beats. Alcibiades, Phrynia,
                            and Timandra go
TIMON. That nature, being sick of man's unkindness,
    Should yet be hungry! Common mother, thou,
                                            Digging
    Whose womb unmeasurable and infinite breast
    Teems, and feeds all; whose selfsame mettle,   180
    Whereof thy proud child, arrogant man, is puffed,
    Engenders the black toad and adder blue,
    The gilded newt and eyeless venomed worm,
    With all th'abhorréd births below crisp heaven

Whereon Hyperion's quick'ning fire doth shine;
Yield him, who all thy human sons doth hate,
From forth thy plenteous bosom, one poor root.
Ensear thy fertile and conceptious womb;
Let it no more bring out ingrateful man.
Go great with tigers, dragons, wolves and bears,   190
Teem with new monsters, whom thy upward face
Hath to the marbléd mansion all above
Never presented. O, a root, dear thanks!
Dry up thy marrows, vines and plough-torn leas,
Whereof ingrateful man with liquorish draughts
And morsels unctuous greases his pure mind,
That from it all consideration slips!

Enter Apemantus

    More man? plague, plague!
APEMANTUS. I was directed hither. Men report
    Thou dost affect my manners, and dost use them.   200
TIMON. 'Tis, then, because thou dost not keep a dog,
    Whom I would imitate. Consumption catch thee!
APEMANTUS. This is in thee a nature but infected,
    A poor unmanly melancholy sprung
    From change of fortune. Why this spade? this place?
    This slave-like habit and these looks of care?
    Thy flatterers yet wear silk, drink wine, lie soft,
    Hug their diseased perfumes, and have forgot
    That ever Timon was. Shame not these woods
    By putting on the cunning of a carper.   210
    Be thou a flatterer now, and seek to thrive
    By that which has undone thee; hinge thy knee
    And let his very breath whom thou'lt observe
    Blow off thy cap; praise his most vicious strain
    And call it excellent. Thou wast told thus;
    Thou gav'st thine ears like tapsters that bade
        welcome
    To knaves and all approachers. 'Tis most just
    That thou turn rascal; hadst thou wealth again,
    Rascals should have't. Do not assume my likeness.
TIMON. Were I like thee, I'd throw away myself.   220
APEMANTUS. Thou hast cast away thyself, being like
        thyself;
    A madman so long, now a fool. What, think'st
    That the bleak air, thy boisterous chamberlain,
    Will put thy shirt on warm? will these mossed trees,
    That have outlived the eagle, page thy heels,
    And skip where thou point'st out? will the cold
        brook,
    Candied with ice, caudle thy morning taste,
    To cure thy o'ernight's surfeit? Call the creatures
    Whose naked natures live in all the spite
    Of wreakful heaven, whose bare unhouséd trunks,   230
    To the conflicting elements exposed,
    Answer mere nature; bid them flatter thee;
    O, thou shalt find—
TIMON.   A fool of thee. Depart.
APEMANTUS. I love thee better now than e'er I did.
TIMON. I hate thee worse.
APEMANTUS.   Why?
TIMON.   Thou flatter'st misery.
APEMANTUS. I flatter not, but say thou art a caitiff.
TIMON. Why dost thou seek me out?
APEMANTUS.   To vex thee.
TIMON. Always a villain's office or a fool's.
    Dost please thyself in't?
APEMANTUS.   Ay.
TIMON.   What, a knave too?

APEMANTUS. If thou didst put this sour, cold habit on 240
    To castigate thy pride, 'twere well; but thou
    Dost it enforcedly. Thou'ldst courtier be again,
    Wert thou not beggar. Willing misery
    Outlives incertain pomp, is crowned before;
    The one is filling still, never complete,
    The other at high wish; best state, contentless,
    Hath a distracted and most wretched being,
    Worse than the worst, content.
    Thou shouldst desire to die, being miserable.
TIMON. Not by his breath that is more miserable. 250
    Thou art a slave whom Fortune's tender arm
    With favour never clasped, but bred a dog.
    Hadst thou like us from our first swath proceeded
    The sweet degrees that this brief world affords
    To such as may the passive drugs of it
    Freely command, thou wouldst have plunged
      thyself
    In general riot, melted down thy youth
    In different beds of lust, and never learned
    The icy precepts of respect, but followed
    The sug'red game before thee. But myself, 260
    Who had the world as my confectionary,
    The mouths, the tongues, the eyes and hearts of men
    At duty, more than I could frame employment;
    That numberless upon me stuck, as leaves
    Do on the oak, have with one winter's brush
    Fell from their boughs, and left me open, bare
    For every storm that blows—I to bear this,
    That never knew but better, is some burden.
    Thy nature did commence in sufferance, time
    Hath made thee hard in't. Why shouldst thou hate
      men? 270
    They never flattered thee. What hast thou given?
    If thou wilt curse, thy father, that poor rag,
    Must be thy subject; who in spite put stuff
    To some she-beggar and compounded thee
    Poor rogue hereditary. Hence, be gone.
    If thou hadst not been born the worst of men,
    Thou hadst been a knave and flatterer.
APEMANTUS. Art thou proud yet?
TIMON.   Ay, that I am not thee.
APEMANTUS. I, that I was no prodigal.
TIMON. I, that I am one now. 280
    Were all the wealth I have shut up in thee,
    I'ld give thee leave to hang it. Get thee gone.
    That the whole life of Athens were in this!
    Thus would I eat it.   *Eating a root*
APEMANTUS.   Here, I will mend thy feast.
                       Offering him another
TIMON. First mend my company; take away thyself.
APEMANTUS. So I shall mend mine own, by th'lack of
    thine.
TIMON. 'Tis not well mended so, it is but botched;
    If not, I would it were.
APEMANTUS. What wouldst thou have to Athens?
TIMON. Thee thither in a whirlwind. If thou wilt, 290
    Tell them there I have gold; look, so I have.
APEMANTUS. Here is no use for gold.
TIMON.   The best and truest;
    For here it sleeps, and does no hiréd harm.
APEMANTUS. Where liest a-nights, Timon?
TIMON. Under that's above me.
    Where feed'st thou a-days, Apemantus?
APEMANTUS. Where my stomach finds meat; or,
    rather, where I eat it.

TIMON. Would poison were obedient, and knew my
    mind! 300
APEMANTUS. Where wouldst thou send it?
TIMON. To sauce thy dishes.
APEMANTUS. The middle of humanity thou never
    knewest, but the extremity of both ends. When
    thou wast in thy gilt and thy perfume, they mocked
    thee for too much curiosity; in thy rags thou
    know'st none, but art despised for the contrary.
    There's a medlar for thee; eat it.
TIMON. On what I hate I feed not.
APEMANTUS. Dost hate a medlar? 310
TIMON. Ay, though it look like thee.
APEMANTUS. An thou'dst hated meddlers sooner, thou
    shouldst have loved thyself better now. What man
    didst thou ever know unthrift that was beloved after
    his means?
TIMON. Who, without those means thou talk'st of,
    didst thou ever know beloved?
APEMANTUS. Myself.
TIMON. I understand thee; thou hadst some means to
    keep a dog. 320
APEMANTUS. What things in the world canst thou
    nearest compare to thy flatterers?
TIMON. Women nearest; but men—men are the things
    themselves. What wouldst thou do with the world,
    Apemantus, if it lay in thy power?
APEMANTUS. Give it the beasts, to be rid of the men.
TIMON. Wouldst thou have thyself fall in the con-
    fusion of men, and remain a beast with the beasts?
APEMANTUS. Ay, Timon.
TIMON. A beastly ambition, which the gods grant thee 330
    t'attain to! If thou wert the lion, the fox would
    beguile thee; if thou wert the lamb, the fox would
    eat thee; if thou wert the fox, the lion would suspect
    thee when peradventure thou wert accused by the
    ass; if thou wert the ass, thy dulness would torment
    thee, and still thou livedst but as a breakfast to the
    wolf; if thou wert the wolf, thy greediness would
    afflict thee, and oft thou shouldst hazard thy life for
    thy dinner; wert thou the unicorn, pride and wrath
    would confound thee and make thine own self the 340
    conquest of thy fury; wert thou a bear, thou wouldst
    be killed by the horse; wert thou a horse, thou
    wouldst be seized by the leopard; wert thou a
    leopard, thou wert german to the lion, and the spots
    of thy kindred were jurors on thy life; all thy safety
    were remotion, and thy defence absence. What beast
    couldst thou be that were not subject to a beast? and
    what a beast art thou already, that seest not thy loss
    in transformation!
APEMANTUS. If thou couldst please me with speaking 350
    to me, thou mightst have hit upon it here. The
    commonwealth of Athens is become a forest of
    beasts.
TIMON. How has the ass broke the wall, that thou art
    out of the city?
APEMANTUS. Yonder comes a poet and a painter; the
    plague of company light upon thee! I will fear to
    catch it, and give way. When I know not what else
    to do, I'll see thee again.
TIMON. When there is nothing living but thee, thou 360
    shalt be welcome. I had rather be a beggar's dog than
    Apemantus.
APEMANTUS. Thou art the cap of all the fools alive.
TIMON. Would thou wert clean enough to spit upon!

APEMANTUS. A plague on thee! thou art too bad to
  curse.

TIMON. All villains that do stand by thee are pure.

APEMANTUS. There is no leprosy but what thou
  speak'st.

TIMON. If I name thee.   370
  I'ld beat thee, but I should infect my hands.

APEMANTUS. I would my tongue could rot them off.

TIMON. Away, thou issue of a mangy dog!
  Choler does kill me that thou art alive;
  I swoon to see thee.

APEMANTUS. Would thou wouldst burst!

TIMON.   Away, thou tedious rogue!
  I am sorry I shall lose a stone by thee.

                              Throws a stone at him

APEMANTUS. Beast!

TIMON. Slave!

APEMANTUS. Toad!   380

TIMON. Rogue, rogue, rogue!
  I am sick of this false world, and will love nought
  But even the mere necessities upon't.
  Then, Timon, presently prepare thy grave;
  Lie where the light foam of the sea may beat
  Thy grave-stone daily; make thine epitaph,
  That death in me at others' lives may laugh.
  [*To the gold*] O thou sweet king-killer, and dear
    divorce
  'Twixt natural son and sire, thou bright defiler
  Of Hymen's purest bed, thou valiant Mars,   390
  Thou ever young, fresh, loved, and delicate wooer,
  Whose blush doth thaw the consecrated snow
  That lies on Dian's lap, thou visible god,
  That sold'rest close impossibilities,
  And mak'st them kiss; that speak'st with every
    tongue,
  To every purpose! O thou touch of hearts!
  Think thy slave man rebels; and by thy virtue
  Set them into confounding odds, that beasts
  May have the world in empire.

APEMANTUS.   Would 'twere so,
  But not till I am dead. I'll say thou'st gold.   400
  Thou wilt be thronged to shortly.

TIMON.   Thronged to?

APEMANTUS.   Ay.

TIMON. Thy back, I prithee.

APEMANTUS.   Live, and love thy misery.

TIMON. Long live so, and so die. [*Apemantus goes*] I am
  quit.
  Moe things like men? Eat, Timon, and abhor them.

Enter three Bandits

I BANDIT. Where should he have this gold? It is some
  poor fragment, some slender ort of his remainder.
  The mere want of gold, and the falling-from of his
  friends, drove him into this melancholy.

2 BANDIT. It is noised he hath a mass of treasure.

3 BANDIT. Let us make the assay upon him; if he care   410
  not for't, he will supply us easily; if he covetously
  reserve it, how shall's get it?

2 BANDIT. True; for he bears it not about him; 'tis hid.

I BANDIT. Is not this he?

3 BANDIT. Where?

2 BANDIT. 'Tis his description.

3 BANDIT. He? I know him.

BANDITS. Save thee, Timon.

TIMON. Now, thieves?

BANDITS. Soldiers, not thieves.   420

TIMON. Both two, and women's sons.

BANDITS. We are not thieves, but men that much do
  want.

TIMON. Your greatest want is, you want much of
  meat.
  Why should you want? Behold, the earth hath roots;
  Within this mile break forth a hundred springs;
  The oaks bear mast, the briers scarlet hips;
  The bounteous housewife Nature on each bush
  Lays her full mess before you. Want? why want?

I BANDIT. We cannot live on grass, on berries, water,
  As beasts and birds and fishes.   430

TIMON. Nor on the beasts themselves, the birds and
  fishes;
  You must eat men. Yet thanks I must you con
  That you are thieves professed, that you work not
  In holier shapes; for there is boundless theft
  In limited professions. Rascal thieves,
  Here's gold. Go, suck the subtle blood o'th'grape,
  Till the high fever seethe your blood to froth,
  And so 'scape hanging. Trust not the physician;
  His antidotes are poison, and he slays
  Moe than you rob, takes wealth and lives together.   440
  Do villainy, do, since you protest to do't,
  Like workmen. I'll example you with thievery:
  The sun's a thief, and with his great attraction
  Robs the vast sea; the moon's an arrant thief,
  And her pale fire she snatches from the sun;
  The sea's a thief, whose liquid surge resolves
  The moon into salt tears; the earth's a thief,
  That feeds and breeds by a composture stol'n
  From gen'ral excrement—each thing's a thief.
  The laws, your curb and whip, in their rough
    power   450
  Has unchecked theft. Love not yourselves; away,
  Rob one another. There's more gold. Cut throats;
  All that you meet are thieves; to Athens go,
  Break open shops; nothing can you steal,
  But thieves do lose it; steal less for this I give you,
  And gold confound you howsoe'er. Amen.

3 BANDIT. Has almost charmed me from my profession by persuading me to it.

I BANDIT. 'Tis in the malice of mankind that he thus
  advises us, not to have us thrive in our mystery.   460

2 BANDIT. I'll believe him as an enemy, and give other
  my trade.

I BANDIT. Let us first see peace in Athens; there is no
  time so miserable but a man may be true.

                                                Bandits go

Enter Flavius

FLAVIUS. O you gods!
  Is yond despised and ruinous man my lord?
  Full of decay and failing? O monument
  And wonder of good deeds evilly bestowed!
  What an alteration of honour has desp'rate want
    made!
  What viler thing upon the earth than friends,   470
  Who can bring noblest minds to basest ends!
  How rarely does it meet with this time's guise,
  When man was wished to love his enemies!
  Grant I may ever love, and rather woo
  Those that would mischief me than those that do!
  Has caught me in his eye;
  I will present my honest grief unto him,

And as my lord still serve him with my life.
  My dearest master!
TIMON. Away! what art thou?
FLAVIUS.   Have you forgot me, sir? 480
TIMON. Why dost ask that? I have forgot all men.
  Then, if thou grant'st thou'rt a man, I have forgot
  thee.
FLAVIUS. An honest poor servant of yours.
TIMON. Then I know thee not;
  I never had honest man about me, I; all
  I kept were knaves, to serve in meat to villains.
FLAVIUS. The gods are witness,
  Ne'er did poor steward wear a truer grief
  For his undone lord than mine eyes for you.
TIMON. What, dost thou weep? come nearer; then I
  love thee,   490
  Because thou art a woman, and disclaim'st
  Flinty mankind, whose eyes do never give
  But thorough lust and laughter. Pity's sleeping.
  Strange times, that weep with laughing, not with
  weeping!
FLAVIUS. I beg of you to know me, good my lord,
  T'accept my grief, and whilst this poor wealth lasts
  To entertain me as your steward still.
TIMON. Had I a steward
  So true, so just, and now so comfortable?
  It almost turns my dangerous nature mild.   500
  Let me behold thy face. Surely this man
  Was born of woman.
  Forgive my general and exceptless rashness,
  You perpetual-sober gods! I do proclaim
  One honest man—mistake me not, but one;
  No more, I pray—and he's a steward
  How fain would I have hated all mankind,
  And thou redeem'st thyself. But all save thee
  I fell with curses.
  Methinks thou art more honest now than wise;   510
  For, by oppressing and betraying me,
  Thou mightst have sooner got another service;
  For many so arrive at second masters,
  Upon their first lord's neck. But tell me true—
  For I must ever doubt, though ne'er so sure—
  Is not thy kindness subtle-covetous,
  A usuring kindness, as rich men deal gifts,
  Expecting in return twenty for one?
FLAVIUS. No, my most worthy master, in whose
  breast
  Doubt and suspect, alas, are placed too late.   520
  You should have feared false times when you did
  feast:
  Suspect still comes where an estate is least.
  That which I show, heaven knows, is merely love,
  Duty and zeal to your unmatchéd mind,
  Care of your food and living; and believe it,
  My most honoured lord,
  For any benefit that points to me,
  Either in hope or present, I'ld exchange
  For this one wish, that you had power and wealth
  To requite me by making rich yourself.   530
TIMON. Look thee, 'tis so. Thou singly honest man,
  Here, take. The gods, out of my misery,
  Have sent thee treasure. Go, live rich and happy,
  But thus conditioned: thou shalt build from men,
  Hate all, curse all, show charity to none,
  But let the famished flesh slide from the bone
  Ere thou relieve the beggar. Give to dogs

What thou deniest to men. Let prisons swallow 'em,
  Debts wither 'em to nothing; be men like blasted
  woods,
  And may diseases lick up their false bloods!   540
  And so farewell, and thrive.
FLAVIUS. O, let me stay and comfort you, my master.
TIMON. If thou hat'st curses
  Stay not; fly, whilst thou art blest and free;
  Ne'er see thou man, and let me ne'er see thee.
                                    They depart severally

ACT 5

Scene 1: *The woods. Before Timon's cave*

Enter Poet and Painter; Timon listens from his cave, unseen

PAINTER. As I took note of the place, it cannot be far
  where he abides.
POET. What's to be thought of him? does the rumour
  hold for true, that he's so full of gold?
PAINTER. Certain. Alcibiades reports it; Phrynia and
  Timandra had gold of him. He likewise enriched
  poor straggling soldiers with great quantity. 'Tis
  said he gave unto his steward a mighty sum.
POET. Then this breaking of his has been but a try for
  his friends.   10
PAINTER. Nothing else. You shall see him a palm in
  Athens again, and flourish with the highest. Therefore 'tis not amiss we tender our loves to him in this
  supposed distress of his; it will show honestly in us,
  and is very likely to load our purposes with what
  they travail for, if it be a just and true report that
  goes of his having.
POET. What have you now to present unto him?
PAINTER. Nothing at this time but my visitation; only
  I will promise him an excellent piece.   20
POET. I must serve him so too, tell him of an intent
  that's coming toward him.
PAINTER. Good as the best. Promising is the very air
  o'th'time; it opens the eyes of expectation. Performance is ever the duller for his act, and but in the
  plainer and simpler kind of people the deed of saying
  is quite out of use. To promise is most courtly and
  fashionable; performance is a kind of will or
  testament which argues a great sickness in his judgement that makes it.   30
TIMON [*aside*]. Excellent workman! thou canst not
  paint a man so bad as is thyself.
POET. I am thinking what I shall say I have provided
  for him. It must be a personating of himself; a satire
  against the softness of prosperity, with a discovery of
  the infinite flatteries that follow youth and
  opulency.
TIMON [*aside*]. Must thou needs stand for a villain in
  thine own work? wilt thou whip thine own faults
  in other men? Do so, I have gold for thee.   40
POET. Nay, let's seek him.
  Then do we sin against our own estate,
  When we may profit meet, and come too late.
PAINTER. True.
  When the day serves, before black-cornered night,
  Find what thou want'st by free and offered light.
  Come.
TIMON [*aside*]. I'll meet you at the turn. What a god's
  gold,
  That he is worshipped in a baser temple

Than where swine feed!   50
'Tis thou that rigg'st the bark and plough'st the
    foam,
Settlest admiréd reverence in a slave.
To thee be worship, and thy saints for aye
Be crowned with plagues, that thee alone obey!
Fit I meet them.   *Coming forward*
POET. Hail, worthy Timon!
PAINTER.   Our late noble master!
TIMON. Have I once lived to see two honest men?
POET. Sir,
Having often of your open bounty tasted,
Hearing you were retired, your friends fall'n off,   60
Whose thankless natures—O abhorréd spirits!—
Not all the whips of heaven are large enough—
What, to you,
Whose star-like nobleness gave life and influence
To their whole being! I am rapt, and cannot cover
The monstrous bulk of this ingratitude
With any size of words.
TIMON. Let it go naked, men may see't the better.
You that are honest, by being what you are,
Make them best seen and known.
PAINTER.   He and myself   70
Have travelled in the great shower of your gifts,
And sweetly felt it.
TIMON.   Ay, you are honest men.
PAINTER. We are hither come to offer you our service.
TIMON. Most honest men. Why, how shall I requite
    you?
Can you eat roots, and drink cold water? no?
BOTH. What we can do, we'll do, to do you service.
TIMON. Ye're honest men: ye've heard that I have
    gold;
I am sure you have. Speak truth; ye're honest men.
PAINTER. So it is said, my noble lord, but therefore
Came not my friend nor I.   80
TIMON. Good honest men. Thou draw'st a counterfeit
Best in all Athens; thou'rt indeed the best;
Thou counterfeit'st most lively.
PAINTER.   So so, my lord.
TIMON. E'en so, sir, as I say. And for thy fiction,
Why, thy verse swells with stuff so fine and smooth
That thou art even natural in thine art.
But for all this, my honest-natured friends,
I must needs say you have a little fault;
Marry, 'tis not monstrous in you, neither wish I
You take much pains to mend.
BOTH.   Beseech your honour   90
To make it known to us.
TIMON.   You'll take it ill.
BOTH. Most thankfully, my lord.
TIMON.   Will you indeed?
BOTH. Doubt it not, worthy lord.
TIMON. There's never a one of you but trusts a knave
That mightily deceives you.
BOTH.   Do we, my lord?
TIMON. Ay, and you hear him cog, see him dissemble,
Know his gross patchery, love him, feed him,
Keep in your bosom; yet remain assured
That he's a made-up villain.
PAINTER. I know none such, my lord.
POET.   Nor I.   100
TIMON. Look you, I love you well; I'll give you gold,
Rid me these villains from your companies.
Hang them or stab them, drown them in a draught,

Confound them by some course, and come to me,
I'll give you gold enough.
BOTH. Name them, my lord, let's know them.
TIMON. You that way, and you this—but two in
    company—
Each man apart, all single and alone,
Yet an arch-villain keeps him company.
If, where thou art, two villains shall not be,   110
Come not near him. If thou wouldst not reside
But where one villain is, then him abandon.
Hence, pack, there's gold; you came for gold, ye
    slaves.
[*to Painter*] You have work for me; there's payment.
    Hence!
[*to Poet*] You are an alchemist, make gold of that.
Out, rascal dogs!   *He beats them out, and retires*
                                              into his cave

Enter Flavius and two Senators

FLAVIUS. It is in vain that you would speak with
    Timon;
For he is set so only to himself
That nothing but himself which looks like man
Is friendly with him.
1 SENATOR.   Bring us to his cave: 120
It is our part and promise to th'Athenians
To speak with Timon.
2 SENATOR.   At all times alike
Men are not still the same; 'twas time and griefs
That framed him thus. Time, with his fairer hand,
Offering the fortunes of his former days,
The former man may make him. Bring us to him,
And chance it as it may.
FLAVIUS.   Here is his cave.
Peace and content be here! Lord Timon, Timon,
Look out, and speak to friends. Th'Athenians
By two of their most reverend senate greet thee.   130
Speak to them, noble Timon.

Timon comes from his cave

TIMON. Thou sun, that comforts, burn! Speak and be
    hanged.
For each true word a blister, and each false
Be as a cantherizing to the root o'th'tongue,
Consuming it with speaking!
1 SENATOR.   Worthy Timon—
TIMON. Of none but such as you, and you of Timon.
1 SENATOR. The senators of Athens greet thee, Timon.
TIMON. I thank them, and would send them back the
    plague,
Could I but catch it for them.
1 SENATOR.   O, forget
What we are sorry for ourselves in thee.   140
The senators with one consent of love
Entreat thee back to Athens, who have thought
On special dignities, which vacant lie
For thy best use and wearing.
2 SENATOR.   They confess
Toward thee forgetfulness too general-gross;
Which now the public body, which doth seldom
Play the recanter, feeling in itself
A lack of Timon's aid, hath sense withal
Of it own fail, restraining aid to Timon;
And send forth us, to make their sorrowéd render,   150
Together with a recompense more fruitful
Than their offence can weigh down by the dram;

Ay, even such heaps and sums of love and wealth
As shall to thee blot out what wrongs were theirs,
And write in thee the figures of their love,
Ever to read them thine.

TIMON.   You witch me in it;
Surprise me to the very brink of tears.
Lend me a fool's heart and a woman's eyes,
And I'll beweep these comforts, worthy senators.

1 SENATOR. Therefore so please thee to return with us, 160
And of our Athens, thine and ours, to take
The captainship, thou shalt be met with thanks,
Allowed with absolute power, and thy good name
Live with authority: so soon we shall drive back
Of Alcibiades th'approaches wild,
Who like a boar too savage doth root up
His country's peace.

2 SENATOR.   And shakes his threat'ning sword
Against the walls of Athens.

1 SENATOR.   Therefore, Timon—

TIMON. Well, sir, I will—therefore I will, sir, thus:
If Alcibiades kill my countrymen,   170
Let Alcibiades know this of Timon,
That Timon cares not. But if he sack fair Athens,
And take our goodly agèd men by th'beards,
Giving our holy virgins to the stain
Of contumelious, beastly, mad-brained war;
Then let him know, and tell him Timon speaks it,
In pity of our agèd and our youth,
I cannot choose but tell him that I care not,
And let him take't at worst; for their knives care not,
While you have throats to answer; for myself,   180
There's not a whittle in th'unruly camp
But I do prize it at my love before
The reverend'st throat in Athens. So I leave you
To the protection of the prosperous gods,
As thieves to keepers.

FLAVIUS.   Stay not, all's in vain.

TIMON. Why, I was writing of my epitaph;
It will be seen to-morrow. My long sickness
Of health and living now begins to mend,
And nothing brings me all things. Go, live still;
Be Alcibiades your plague, you his,   190
And last so long enough!

1 SENATOR.   We speak in vain.

TIMON. But yet I love my country, and am not
One that rejoices in the common wreck,
As common bruit doth put it.

1 SENATOR.   That's well spoke.

TIMON. Commend me to my loving countrymen—

1 SENATOR. These words become your lips as they pass
through them.

2 SENATOR. And enter in our ears like great triumphers
In their applauding gates.

TIMON.   Commend me to them,
And tell them that, to ease them of their griefs,
Their fears of hostile strokes, their achës, losses, 200
Their pangs of love, with other incident throes
That nature's fragile vessel doth sustain
In life's uncertain voyage, I will some kindness do
them;
I'll teach them to prevent wild Alcibiades' wrath.

1 SENATOR. I like this well; he will return again.

TIMON. I have a tree, which grows here in my close,
That mine own use invites me to cut down,
And shortly must I fell it. Tell my friends,
Tell Athens, in the sequence of degree

From high to low throughout, that whoso please 210
To stop affliction, let him take his haste,
Come hither ere my tree hath felt the axe,
And hang himself. I pray you do my greeting.

FLAVIUS. Trouble him no further; thus you still shall
find him.

TIMON. Come not to me again, but say to Athens,
Timon hath made his everlasting mansion
Upon the beachèd verge of the salt flood,
Who once a day with his embossèd froth
The turbulent surge shall cover; thither come,
And let my grave-stone be your oracle.   220
Lips, let four words go by, and language end:
What is amiss, plague and infection mend!
Graves only be men's works, and death their gain!
Sun, hide thy beams; Timon hath done his reign.
                              Retires to his cave

1 SENATOR. His discontents are unremovably
Coupled to nature.

2 SENATOR. Our hope in him is dead. Let us return,
And strain what other means is left unto us
In our dear peril.

1 SENATOR.   It requires swift foot.
                              They go

Scene 2: *Before the walls of Athens*

Enter two other Senators, with a Messenger

3 SENATOR. Thou hast painfully discovered; are his
files
As full as thy report?

MESSENGER.   I have spoke the least.
Besides, his expedition promises
Present approach.

4 SENATOR. We stand much hazard if they bring not
Timon.

MESSENGER. I met a courier, one mine ancient friend,
Whom, though in general part we were opposed,
Yet our old love made a particular force,
And made us speak like friends. This man was riding
From Alcibiades to Timon's cave   10
With letters of entreaty, which imported
His fellowship i'th'cause against your city,
In part for his sake moved.

3 SENATOR.   Here come our brothers.

Enter the other Senators from Timon.

1 SENATOR. No talk of Timon, nothing of him expect.
The enemy's drum is heard, and fearful scouring
Doth choke the air with dust: in, and prepare.
Ours is the fall, I fear, our foe's the snare.
                              They go

Scene 3: *The woods. Timon's cave, and a rude tomb seen*

Enter a Soldier, seeking Timon

SOLDIER. By all description this should be the place.
Who's here? speak, ho! No answer? What is this?
[*reads*] 'Timon is dead, who hath outstretched his
span;
Some beast read this; there does not live a man.'
Dead, sure, and this his grave. What's on this tomb
I cannot read; the character I'll take with wax;
Our captain hath in every figure skill,
An aged interpreter, though young in days;

Before proud Athens he's set down by this,
Whose fall the mark of his ambition is.   *He goes* 10

Scene 4: Before the walls of Athens

Trumpets sound. Enter Alcibiades with his powers

ALCIBIADES. Sound to this coward and lascivious town
Our terrible approach.   *Sounds a parley*

The Senators appear upon the walls

Till now you have gone on and filled the time
With all licentious measure, making your wills
The scope of justice. Till now, myself and such
As stepped within the shadow of your power
Have wandered with our traversed arms and
    breathed
Our sufferance vainly; now the time is flush,
When crouching marrow in the bearer strong
Cries of itself 'No more'; now breathless wrong   10
Shall sit and pant in your great chairs of ease,
And pursy insolence shall break his wind
With fear and horrid flight.
1 SENATOR.   Noble and young,
When thy first griefs were but a mere conceit,
Ere thou hadst power or we had cause of fear,
We sent to thee, to give thy rages balm,
To wipe out our ingratitude with loves
Above their quantity.
2 SENATOR.   So did we woo
Transforméd Timon to our city's love
By humble message and by promised means;   20
We were not all unkind, nor all deserve
The common stroke of war.
1 SENATOR.   These walls of ours
Were not erected by their hands from whom
You have received your griefs; nor are they such
That these great towers, trophies, and schools
    should fall
For private faults in them.
2 SENATOR.   Nor are they living
Who were the motives that you first went out;
Shame, that they wanted cunning, in excess
Hath broke their hearts. March, noble lord,
Into our city with thy banners spread;   30
By decimation and a tithéd death,
If thy revenges hunger for that food
Which nature loathes, take thou the destined tenth,
And by the hazard of the spotted die
Let die the spotted.
1 SENATOR.   All have not offended;
For those that were, it is not square to take,
On those that are, revenges; crimes like lands
Are not inherited. Then, dear countryman,
Bring in thy ranks, but leave without thy rage;
Spare thy Athenian cradle and those kin   40
Which, in the bluster of thy wrath, must fall

With those that have offended. Like a shepherd
Approach the fold and cull th'infected forth,
But kill not all together.
2 SENATOR.   What thou wilt,
Thou rather shalt enforce it with thy smile
Than hew to't with thy sword.
1 SENATOR.   Set but thy foot
Against our rampired gates, and they shall ope;
So thou wilt send thy gentle heart before,
To say thou'lt enter friendly.
2 SENATOR.   Throw thy glove,
Or any token of thine honour else,   50
That thou wilt use the wars as thy redress
And not as our confusion, all thy powers
Shall make their harbour in our town, till we
Have sealed thy full desire.
ALCIBIADES.   Then there's my glove;
Descend, and open your uncharged ports;
Those enemies of Timon's, and mine own,
Whom you yourselves shall set out for reproof,
Fall, and no more; and, to atone your fears
With my more noble meaning, not a man
Shall pass his quarter, or offend the stream   60
Of regular justice in your city's bounds,
But shall be rendered to your public laws
At heaviest answer.
BOTH.   'Tis most nobly spoken.
ALCIBIADES. Descend, and keep your words.
          The Senators descend, and open the gates

Enter Soldier

SOLDIER. My noble general, Timon is dead,
Entombed upon the very hem o'th'sea,
And on his grave-stone this insculpture, which
With wax I brought away, whose soft impression
Interprets for my poor ignorance.
ALCIBIADES [*reads*]. 'Here lies a wretched corse, of
    wretched soul bereft;   70
Seek not my name: a plague consume you wicked
    caitiffs left!
Here lie I, Timon, who alive all living men did hate;
Pass by and curse thy fill, but pass, and stay not here
    thy gait.'
These well express in thee thy latter spirits.
Though thou abhorredst in us our human griefs,
Scornedst our brain's flow, and those our droplets
    which
From niggard nature fall, yet rich conceit
Taught thee to make vast Neptune weep for aye
On thy low grave, on faults forgiven. Dead
Is noble Timon, of whose memory   80
Hereafter more. Bring me into your city,
And I will use the olive with my sword,
Make war breed peace, make peace stint war, make
    each
Prescribe to other, as each other's leech.
Let our drums strike.   *They go*

Julius Caesar

The scene: Rome; the neighbourhood of Sardis;
the neighbourhood of Philippi

CHARACTERS IN THE PLAY

JULIUS CÆSAR
OCTAVIUS CÆSAR ⎫
MARCUS ANTONIUS ⎬ *triumvirs after the death of*
M. ÆMILIUS LEPIDUS ⎭ *Julius Cæsar*

CICERO ⎫
PUBLIUS ⎬ *senators*
POPILIUS LENA ⎭

MARCUS BRUTUS
CASSIUS
CASCA
TREBONIUS ⎫ *conspirators against Julius*
LIGARIUS ⎬ *Cæsar*
DECIUS BRUTUS
METELLUS CIMBER
CINNA ⎭

FLAVIUS *and* MARULLUS, *tribunes*
ARTEMIDORUS *of Cnidos, a teacher of Rhetoric*
A Soothsayer
CINNA, *a poet*

Another poet
LUCILIUS
TITINIUS
MESSALA ⎫ *friends to Brutus and Cassius*
YOUNG CATO
VOLUMNIUS

VARRO
CLITUS
CLAUDIUS
STRATO ⎬ *servants to Brutus or his officers*
LUCIUS
DARDANIUS
LABEO
FLAVIUS ⎭

PINDARUS, *bondman to Cassius*
CALPHURNIA, *wife to Cæsar*
PORTIA, *wife to Brutus*
Senators, Citizens, Officers, Attendants, etc.

Julius Caesar

ACT 1
Scene 1: *Rome. A street*

Flavius, Marullus, and certain commoners

FLAVIUS. Hence! home, you idle creatures, get you
  home:
  Is this a holiday? what! know you not,
  Being mechanical, you ought not walk
  Upon a labouring day without the sign
  Of your profession? Speak, what trade art thou?
1 COMMONER. Why, sir, a carpenter.
MARULLUS. Where is thy leather apron and thy rule?
  What dost thou with thy best apparel on?
  You, sir, what trade are you?
2 COMMONER. Truly, sir, in respect of a fine workman, 10
  I am but as you would say a cobbler.
MARULLUS. But what trade art thou? answer me
  directly.
2 COMMONER. A trade, sir, that I hope I may use with
  a safe conscience, which is indeed, sir, a mender of
  bad soles.
MARULLUS. What trade, thou knave? thou naughty
  knave, what trade?
2 COMMONER. Nay, I beseech you, sir, be not out with
  me: yet if you be out, sir, I can mend you. 20
MARULLUS. What mean'st thou by that? mend me,
  thou saucy fellow!
2 COMMONER. Why, sir, cobble you.
FLAVIUS. Thou art a cobbler, are thou?
2 COMMONER. Truly, sir, all that I live by is with the
  awl: I meddle with no tradesman's matters, nor
  women's matters; but withal I am indeed, sir, a
  surgeon to old shoes; when they are in great danger,
  I recover them. As proper men as ever trod upon
  neat's leather have gone upon my handiwork. 30
FLAVIUS. But wherefore art not in thy shop to-day?
  Why dost thou lead these men about the streets?
2 COMMONER. Truly, sir, to wear out their shoes, to
  get myself into more work. But indeed, sir, we
  make holiday, to see Cæsar and to rejoice in his
  triumph.
MARULLUS. Wherefore rejoice? What conquest brings
  he home?
  What tributaries follow him to Rome,
  To grace in captive bonds his chariot-wheels?
  You blocks, you stones, you worse than senseless
    things! 40
  O you hard hearts, you cruel men of Rome,
  Knew you not Pompey? Many a time and oft
  Have you climbed up to walls and battlements,
  To towers and windows, yea, to chimney-tops,
  Your infants in your arms, and there have sat
  The live-long day with patient expectation
  To see great Pompey pass the streets of Rome:
  And when you saw his chariot but appear,
  Have you not made an universal shout,
  That Tiber trembled underneath her banks 50
  To hear the replication of your sounds
  Made in her concave shores?
  And do you now put on your best attire?

And do you now cull out a holiday?
And do you now strew flowers in his way
That comes in triumph over Pompey's blood?
Be gone!
Run to your houses, fall upon your knees,
Pray to the gods to intermit the plague
That needs must light on this ingratitude. 60
FLAVIUS. Go, go, good countrymen, and for this fault
  Assemble all the poor men of your sort;
  Draw them to Tiber banks and weep your tears
  Into the channel, till the lowest stream
  Do kiss the most exalted shores of all.
                   The crowd goes
  See, whe'r their basest mettle be not moved;
  They vanish tongue-tied in their guiltiness.
  Go you down that way towards the Capitol;
  This way will I: disrobe the images,
  If you do find them decked with ceremonies. 70
MARULLUS. May we do so?
  You know it is the feast of Lupercal.
FLAVIUS. It is no matter; let no images
  Be hung with Cæsar's trophies. I'll about,
  And drive away the vulgar from the streets:
  So do you too, where you perceive them thick.
  These growing feathers plucked from Cæsar's wing
  Will make him fly an ordinary pitch,
  Who else would soar above the view of men
  And keep us all in servile fearfulness. *They go*

Scene 2

*Enter Cæsar, Antony, stripped for the course, Calphurnia,
Portia, Decius, Cicero, Brutus, Cassius, Casca, a
Soothsayer, and after them Marullus and Flavius, with a
great crowd following*

CÆSAR. Calphurnia!
CASCA.   Peace, ho! Cæsar speaks.
CÆSAR.   Calphurnia!
CALPHURNIA. Here, my lord.
CÆSAR. Stand you directly in Antonius' way,
  When he doth run his course. Antonius!
ANTONY. Cæsar, my lord?
CÆSAR. Forget not, in your speed, Antonius,
  To touch Calphurnia; for our elders say,
  The barren, touchéd in this holy chase,
  Shake off their sterile curse.
ANTONY.   I shall remember:
  When Cæsar says 'do this,' it is performed. 10
CÆSAR. Set on, and leave no ceremony out.
                             Music
SOOTHSAYER. Cæsar!
CÆSAR. Ha! who calls?
CASCA. Bid every noise be still: peace yet again!
CÆSAR. Who is it in the press that calls on me?
  I hear a tongue, shriller than all the music,
  Cry 'Cæsar.' Speak, Cæsar is turned to hear.
SOOTHSAYER. Beware the ides of March.
CÆSAR.   What man is that?
BRUTUS. A soothsayer bids you beware the ides
  of March.

CÆSAR. Set him before me, let me see his face. 20
CASSIUS. Fellow, come from the throng, look
    upon Cæsar.
CÆSAR. What say'st thou to me now? speak once
    again.
SOOTHSAYER. Beware the ides of March.
CÆSAR. He is a dreamer, let us leave him: pass.
                 Sennet; the procession goes
CASSIUS. Will you go see the order of the course?
BRUTUS. Not I.
CASSIUS. I pray you, do.
BRUTUS. I am not gamesome: I do lack some part
    Of that quick spirit that is in Antony.
    Let me not hinder, Cassius, your desires; 30
    I'll leave you.
CASSIUS. Brutus, I do observe you now of late:
    I have not from your eyes that gentleness
    And show of love as I was wont to have:
    You bear too stubborn and too strange a hand
    Over your friend that loves you.
BRUTUS.   Cassius,
    Be not deceived: if I have veiled my look,
    I turn the trouble of my countenance
    Merely upon myself. Vexéd I am
    Of late with passions of some difference, 40
    Conceptions only proper to myself,
    Which give some soil perhaps to my behaviours;
    But let not therefore my good friends be grieved
    (Among which number, Cassius, be you one),
    Nor construe any further my neglect
    Than that poor Brutus with himself at war
    Forgets the shows of love to other men.
CASSIUS. Then, Brutus, I have much mistook your
    passion,
    By means whereof this breast of mine hath buried
    Thoughts of great value, worthy cogitations. 50
    Tell me, good Brutus, can you see your face?
BRUTUS. No, Cassius; for the eye sees not itself
    But by reflection, by some other things.
CASSIUS. 'Tis just,
    And it is very much lamented, Brutus,
    That you have no such mirrors as will turn
    Your hidden worthiness into your eye,
    That you might see your shadow. I have heard
    Where many of the best respect in Rome
    (Except immortal Cæsar), speaking of Brutus, 60
    And groaning underneath this age's yoke,
    Have wished that noble Brutus had his eyes.
BRUTUS. Into what dangers would you lead me,
    Cassius,
    That you would have me seek into myself
    For that which is not in me?
CASSIUS. Therefore, good Brutus, be prepared to hear:
    And since you know you cannot see yourself
    So well as by reflection, I your glass
    Will modestly discover to yourself
    That of yourself which you yet know not of. 70
    And be not jealous on me, gentle Brutus:
    Were I a common laughter, or did use
    To stale with ordinary oaths my love
    To every new protester; if you know
    That I do fawn on men and hug them hard,
    And after scandal them; or if you know
    That I profess myself in banqueting
    To all the rout, then hold me dangerous.
                 Flourish and shout

BRUTUS. What means this shouting? I do fear, the 20
    people
    Choose Cæsar for their king.
CASSIUS.   Ay, do you fear it? 80
    Then must I think you would not have it so.
BRUTUS. I would not, Cassius, yet I love him well ...
    But wherefore do you hold me here so long?
    What is it that you would impart to me?
    If it be aught toward the general good,
    Set honour in one eye and death i'th'other,
    And I will look on both indifferently:
    For let the gods so speed me as I love
    The name of honour more than I fear death.
CASSIUS. I know that virtue to be in you, Brutus, 90
    As well as I do know your outward favour.
    Well, honour is the subject of my story ...
    I cannot tell what you and other men
    Think of this life; but, for my single self,
    I had as lief not be as live to be
    In awe of such a thing as I myself.
    I was born free as Cæsar, so were you;
    We both have fed as well, and we can both
    Endure the winter's cold as well as he.
    For once, upon a raw and gusty day, 100
    The troubled Tiber chafing with her shores,
    Cæsar said to me 'Dar'st thou, Cassius, now
    Leap in with me into this angry flood,
    And swim to yonder point?' Upon the word,
    Accoutréd as I was, I plungéd in
    And bade him follow: so indeed he did.
    The torrent roared, and we did buffet it
    With lusty sinews, throwing it aside
    And stemming it with hearts of controversy.
    But ere we could arrive the point proposed, 110
    Cæsar cried 'Help me, Cassius, or I sink!'
    I, as Æneas our great ancestor
    Did from the flames of Troy upon his shoulder
    The old Anchises bear, so from the waves of Tiber
    Did I the tired Cæsar: and this man
    Is now become a god, and Cassius is
    A wretched creature, and must bend his body
    If Cæsar carelessly but nod on him.
    He had a fever when he was in Spain,
    And when the fit was on him, I did mark 120
    How he did shake: 'tis true, this god did shake;
    His coward lips did from their colour fly,
    And that same eye whose bend doth awe the world
    Did lose his lustre: I did hear him groan:
    Ay, and that tongue of his that bade the Romans
    Mark him and write his speeches in their books,
    Alas, it cried, 'Give me some drink, Titinius,'
    As a sick girl ... Ye gods! it doth amaze me
    A man of such a feeble temper should
    So get the start of the majestic world, 130
    And bear the palm alone.   *Shout; flourish*
BRUTUS. Another general shout!
    I do believe that these applauses are
    For some new honours that are heaped on Cæsar.
CASSIUS. Why, man, he doth bestride the narrow
    world
    Like a Colossus, and we petty men
    Walk under his huge legs and peep about
    To find ourselves dishonourable graves.
    Men at some time are masters of their fates:
    The fault, dear Brutus, is not in our stars, 140
    But in ourselves, that we are underlings.

Brutus and Cæsar: what should be in that 'Cæsar'?
Why should that name be sounded more than
     yours?
Write them together, yours is as fair a name;
Sound them, it doth become the mouth as well;
Weigh them, it is as heavy; conjure with 'em,
Brutus will start a spirit as soon as Cæsar.
Now, in the names of all the gods at once,
Upon what meat doth this our Cæsar feed,
That he is grown so great? Age, thou art shamed! 150
Rome, thou hast lost the breed of noble bloods!
When went there by an age, since the great flood,
But it was famed with more than with one man?
When could they say, till now, that talked of Rome
That her wide walls encompassed but one man?
Now is it Rome indeed, and room enough,
When there is in it but one only man.
O, you and I have heard our fathers say
There was a Brutus once that would have brooked
Th'eternal devil to keep his state in Rome 160
As easily as a king.
BRUTUS. That you do love me, I am nothing jealous;
What you would work me to, I have some aim:
How I have thought of this and of these times,
I shall recount hereafter; for this present,
I would not (so with love I might entreat you)
Be any further moved. What you have said
I will consider; what you have to say
I will with patience hear, and find a time
Both meet to hear and answer such high things. 170
Till then, my noble friend, chew upon this:
Brutus had rather be a villager
Than to repute himself a son of Rome
Under these hard conditions as this time
Is like to lay upon us.
CASSIUS. I am glad that my weak words
Have struck but thus much show of fire from
     Brutus.

Re-enter Cæsar and his train

BRUTUS. The games are done, and Cæsar is returning.
CASSIUS. As they pass by, pluck Casca by the sleeve,
And he will (after his sour fashion) tell you 180
What hath proceeded worthy note to-day.
BRUTUS. I will do so: but, look you, Cassius
The angry spot doth glow on Cæsar's brow,
And all the rest look like a chidden train:
Calphurnia's cheek is pale, and Cicero
Looks with such ferret and such fiery eyes
As we have seen him in the Capitol,
Being crossed in conference by some senator.
CASSIUS. Casca will tell us what the matter is.
CÆSAR. Antonius! 190
ANTONY. Cæsar?
CÆSAR. Let me have men about me that are fat,
Sleek-headed men, and such as sleep a-nights:
Yond Cassius has a lean and hungry look;
He thinks too much: such men are dangerous.
ANTONY. Fear him not, Cæsar; he's not dangerous;
He is a noble Roman, and well given.
CÆSAR. Would he were fatter! but I fear him not
Yet if my name were liable to fear,
I do not know the man I should avoid 200
So soon as that spare Cassius. He reads much;
He is a great observer, and he looks
Quite through the deeds of men; he loves no plays,

As thou dost, Antony; he hears no music;
Seldom he smiles, and smiles in such a sort
As if he mocked himself and scorned his spirit
That could be moved to smile at any thing.
Such men as he be never at heart's ease
Whiles they behold a greater than themselves,
And therefore are they very dangerous. 210
I rather tell thee what is to be feared
Than what I fear; for always I am Cæsar.
Come on my right hand, for this ear is deaf,
And tell me truly what thou think'st of him.
          Sennet. Cæsar and his train pass on
CASCA. You pulled me by the cloak, would you speak
with me?
BRUTUS. Ay, Casca, tell us what hath chanced to-day,
That Cæsar looks so sad.
CASCA. Why, you were with him, were you not?
BRUTUS. I should not then ask Casca what had
chanced. 220
CASCA. Why, there was a crown offered him: and
being offered him, he put it by with the back of his
hand, thus: and then the people fell a-shouting.
BRUTUS. What was the second noise for?
CASCA. Why, for that too.
CASSIUS. They shouted thrice: what was the last cry
for?
CASCA. Why, for that too.
BRUTUS. Was the crown offered him thrice?
CASCA. Ay, marry, was't, and he put it by thrice, every 230
time gentler than other; and at every putting-by
mine honest neighbours shouted.
CASSIUS. Who offered him the crown?
CASCA. Why, Antony.
BRUTUS. Tell us the manner of it, gentle Casca.
CASCA. I can as well be hanged as tell the manner of
it: it was mere foolery, I did not mark it. I saw Mark
Antony offer him a crown, yet 'twas not a crown
neither, 'twas one of these coronets: and, as I told
you, he put it by once: but for all that, to my think- 240
ing, he would fain have had it. Then he offered it
to him again; then he put it by again: but, to my
thinking, he was very loath to lay his fingers off
it. And then he offered it the third time; he put it
the third time by: and still as he refused it, the rabble-
ment hooted and clapped their chopped hands and
threw up their sweaty night-caps and uttered such a
deal of stinking breath because Cæsar refused the
crown, that it had almost choked Cæsar; for he
swooned and fell down at it: and for mine own part, 250
I durst not laugh, for fear of opening my lips and
receiving the bad air.
CASSIUS. But, soft, I pray you: what, did Cæsar swoon?
CASCA. He fell down in the market-place and foamed
at mouth and was speechless.
BRUTUS. 'Tis very like: he hath the falling-sickness.
CASSIUS. No, Cæsar hath it not; but you, and I,
And honest Casca, we have the falling-sickness.
CASCA. I know not what you mean by that, but I am
sure Cæsar fell down. If the tag-rag people did not 260
clap him and hiss him according as he pleased and
displeased them, as they use to do the players in the
theatre, I am no true man.
BRUTUS. What said he when he came unto himself?
CASCA. Marry, before he fell down, when he perceived the common herd was glad he refused the
crown, he plucked me ope his doublet and offered

them his throat to cut. An I had been a man of any
occupation, if I would not have taken him at a word,
I would I might go to hell among the rogues. And 270
so he fell. When he came to himself again, he said,
if he had done or said any thing amiss, he desired their
worships to think it was his infirmity. Three or four
wenches, where I stood, cried 'Alas, good soul!' and
forgave him with all their hearts: but there's no heed
to be taken of them; if Cæsar had stabbed their
mothers, they would have done no less.

BRUTUS. And after that, he came, thus sad, away?

CASCA. Ay.

CASSIUS. Did Cicero say any thing?   280

CASCA. Ay, he spoke Greek.

CASSIUS. To what effect?

CASCA. Nay, an I tell you that, I'll ne'er look you i'
th'face again: but those that understood him smiled
at one another and shook their heads; but for mine
own part, it was Greek to me. I could tell you more
news too: Marullus and Flavius, for pulling scarfs
off Cæsar's images, are put to silence. Fare you well.
There was more foolery yet, if I could remember it.

CASSIUS. Will you sup with me to-night, Casca?   290

CASCA. No, I am promised forth.

CASSIUS. Will you dine with me to-morrow?

CASCA. Ay, if I be alive, and your mind hold, and your
dinner worth the eating.

CASSIUS. Good; I will expect you.

CASCA. Do so: farewell, both.   *He goes*

BRUTUS. What a blunt fellow is this grown to be!
He was quick mettle when he went to school.

CASSIUS. So is he now in execution
Of any bold or noble enterprise,   300
However he puts on this tardy form.
This rudeness is a sauce to his good wit,
Which gives men stomach to digest his words
With better appetite.

BRUTUS. And so it is.... For this time I will leave you:
To-morrow, if you please to speak with me,
I will come home to you; or, if you will,
Come home to me and I will wait for you.

CASSIUS. I will do so: till then, think of the world.

                       Brutus goes

Well, Brutus, thou art noble; yet I see   310
Thy honourable metal may be wrought
From that it is disposed: therefore it is meet
That noble minds keep ever with their likes;
For who so firm that cannot be seduced?
Cæsar doth bear me hard, but he loves Brutus:
If I were Brutus now and he were Cassius,
He should not humour me. I will this night,
In several hands, in at his windows throw,
As if they came from several citizens,
Writings, all tending to the great opinion   320
That Rome holds of his name, wherein obscurely
Cæsar's ambition shall be glancéd at:
And after this let Cæsar seat him sure;
For we will shake him, or worse days endure.

                       He goes

Scene 3: *The same*

*Thunder and lightning. Enter, from opposite sides, Casca,
with his sword drawn, and Cicero*

CICERO. Good even, Casca: brought you Cæsar home?
Why are you breathless? and why stare you so?

CASCA. Are not you moved, when all the sway of
    earth
Shapes like a thing unfirm? O Cicero,
I have seen tempests, when the scolding winds
Have rived the knotty oaks, and I have seen
Th'ambitious ocean swell and rage and foam,
To be exalted with the threat'ning clouds;
But never till to-night, never till now,
Did I go through a tempest dropping fire.   10
Either there is a civil strife in heaven,
Or else the world too saucy with the gods
Incenses them to send destruction.

CICERO. Why, saw you anything more wonderful?

CASCA. A common slave—you know him well by
    sight—
Held up his left hand, which did flame and burn
Like twenty torches joined, and yet his hand
Not sensible of fire remained unscorched.
Besides—I ha' not since put up my sword—
Against the Capitol I met a lion,   20
Who glazed upon me and went surly by
Without annoying me: and there were drawn
Upon a heap a hundred ghastly women
Transforméd with their fear, who swore they saw
Men all in fire walk up and down the streets.
And yesterday the bird of night did sit
Even at noon-day upon the market-place,
Hooting and shrieking. When these prodigies
Do so conjointly meet, let not men say
'These are their reasons: they are natural:'   30
For, I believe, they are portentous things
Unto the climate that they point upon.

CICERO. Indeed, it is a strange-disposéd time:
But men may construe things, after their fashion,
Clean from the purpose of the things themselves.
Comes Cæsar to the Capitol to-morrow?

CASCA. He doth; for he did bid Antonius
Send word to you he would be there to-morrow.

CICERO. Good night then, Casca: this disturbéd sky
Is not to walk in.

CASCA.   Farewell, Cicero.   *Cicero goes* 40

Cassius enters

CASSIUS. Who's there?

CASCA.   A Roman.

CASSIUS.   Casca, by your voice.

CASCA. Your ear is good. Cassius, what night is this!

CASSIUS. A very pleasing night to honest men.

CASCA. Who ever knew the heavens menace so?

CASSIUS. Those that have known the earth so full of
    faults.
For my part, I have walked about the streets,
Submitting me unto the perilous night,
And thus unbracéd, Casca, as you see,
Have bared my bosom to the thunder-stone;
And when the cross blue lightning seemed to open 50
The breast of heaven, I did present myself
Even in the aim and very flash of it.

CASCA. But wherefore did you so much tempt the
    heavens?
It is the part of men to fear and tremble
When the most mighty gods by tokens send
Such dreadful heralds to astonish us.

CASSIUS. You are dull, Casca, and those sparks of life
That should be in a Roman you do want,
Or else you use not. You look pale and gaze

And put on fear and cast yourself in wonder,   60
To see the strange impatience of the heavens:
But if you would consider the true cause
Why all these fires, why all these gliding ghosts,
Why birds and beasts from quality and kind,
Why old men, fools, and children calculate,
Why all these things change from their ordinance,
Their natures and preforméd faculties,
To monstrous quality, why, you shall find
That heaven hath infused them with these spirits
To make them instruments of fear and warning   70
Unto some monstrous state.
Now could I, Casca, name to thee a man
Most like this dreadful night,
That thunders, lightens, opens graves, and roars
As doth the lion in the Capitol;
A man no mightier than thyself or me
In personal action, yet prodigious grown
And fearful, as these strange eruptions are.

CASCA. 'Tis Cæsar that you mean; is it not, Cassius?
CASSIUS. Let it be who it is: for Romans now   80
Have thews and limbs like to their ancestors;
But, woe the while! our fathers' minds are dead,
And we are governed with our mothers' spirits;
Our yoke and sufferance show us womanish.
CASCA. Indeed they say the senators to-morrow
Mean to establish Cæsar as a king;
And he shall wear his crown by sea and land,
In every place save here in Italy.
CASSIUS. I know where I will wear this dagger then:
Cassius from bondage will deliver Cassius.   90
Therein, ye gods, you make the weak most strong;
Therein, ye gods, you tyrants do defeat.
Nor stony tower, nor walls of beaten brass,
Nor airless dungeon, nor strong links of iron,
Can be retentive to the strength of spirit;
But life, being weary of these worldly bars,
Never lacks power to dismiss itself.
If I know this, know all the world besides,
That part of tyranny that I do bear
I can shake off at pleasure.   *Thunder still*
CASCA.   So can I: 100
So every bondman in his own hand bears
The power to cancel his captivity.
CASSIUS. And why should Cæsar be a tyrant then?
Poor man! I know he would not be a wolf
But that he sees the Romans are but sheep:
He were no lion were not Romans hinds.
Those that with haste will make a mighty fire
Begin it with weak straws: what trash is Rome,
What rubbish and what offal, when it serves
For the base matter to illuminate   110
So vile a thing as Cæsar! But, O grief,
Where hast thou led me? I perhaps speak this
Before a willing bondman; then I know
My answer must be made. But I am armed,
And dangers are to me indifferent.
CASCA. You speak to Casca, and to such a man
That is no fleering tell-tale. Hold, my hand:
Be factious for redress of all these griefs,
And I will set this foot of mine as far
As who goes farthest.
CASSIUS.   There's a bargain made.   120
Now know you, Casca, I have moved already
Some certain of the noblest-minded Romans
To undergo with me an enterprise

Of honourable-dangerous consequence;
And I do know, by this they stay for me
In Pompey's porch: for now, this fearful night,
There is no stir or walking in the streets,
And the complexion of the element
In favour's like the work we have in hand,
Most bloody-fiery and most terrible.   130

Cinna approaches

CASCA. Stand close awhile, for here comes one in haste.
CASSIUS. 'Tis Cinna; I do know him by his gait;
He is a friend. Cinna, where haste you so?
CINNA. To find out you. Who's that? Metellus
Cimber?
CASSIUS. No, it is Casca, one incorporate
To our attempts. Am I not stayed for, Cinna?
CINNA. I am glad on't. What a fearful night is this!
There's two or three of us have seen strange sights.
CASSIUS. Am I not stayed for? tell me.
CINNA.   Yes, you are.
O Cassius, if you could   140
But win the noble Brutus to our party—
CASSIUS. Be you content. Good Cinna, take this paper,
And look you lay it in the prætor's chair,
Where Brutus may but find it; and throw this
In at his window; set this up with wax
Upon old Brutus' statue: all this done,
Repair to Pompey's porch, where you shall find us.
Is Decius Brutus and Trebonius there?
CINNA. All but Metellus Cimber; and he's gone
To seek you at your house. Well, I will hie,   150
And so bestow these papers as you bade me.
CASSIUS. That done, repair to Pompeys' theatre.
                        Cinna goes
Come, Casca, you and I will yet ere day
See Brutus at his house: three parts of him
Is ours already, and the man entire
Upon the next encounter yields him ours.
CASCA. O, he sits high in all the people's hearts;
And that which would appear offence in us
His countenance, like richest alchemy,
Will change to virtue and to worthiness.   160
CASSIUS. Him and his worth and our great need of him
You have right well conceited. Let us go,
For it is after midnight, and ere day
We will awake him and be sure of him.   *They go*

ACT 2

Scene 1: *An orchard beside the house of Brutus*

Enter Brutus

BRUTUS. What, Lucius, ho!
I cannot, by the progress of the stars,
Give guess how near to day. Lucius, I say!
I would it were my fault to sleep so soundly.
When, Lucius, when? awake, I say! what, Lucius!

Lucius appears

LUCIUS. Called you, my lord?
BRUTUS. Get me a taper in my study, Lucius:
When it is lighted, come and call me here.
LUCIUS. I will, my lord.   *Goes in*
BRUTUS. It must be by his death: and, for my part,   10
I know no personal cause to spurn at him,
But for the general—he would be crowned:

How that might change his nature, there's the
  question.
It is the bright day that brings forth the adder;
And that craves wary walking ... Crown him!—
  that!
And then, I grant, we put a sting in him,
That at his will he may do danger with.
Th'abuse of greatness is when it disjoins
Remorse from power: and, to speak truth of Cæsar,
I have not known when his affections swayed   20
More than his reason. But 'tis a common proof,
That lowliness is young ambition's ladder,
Whereto the climber-upward turns his face;
But when he once attains the upmost round,
He then unto the ladder turns his back,
Looks in the clouds, scorning the base degrees
By which he did ascend: so Cæsar may;
Then, lest he may, prevent. And, since the quarrel
Will bear no colour for the thing he is,
Fashion it thus: that what he is, augmented,   30
Would run to these and these extremities:
And therefore think him as a serpent's egg
Which hatched would as his kind grow
  mischievous,
And kill him in the shell.

Lucius returns

LUCIUS. The taper burneth in your colsed, sir.
  Searching the window for a flint I found
  This paper thus sealed up, and I am sure
  It did not lie there when I went to bed.
                    Gives him the letter
BRUTUS. Get you to bed again, it is not day.
  Is not to-morrow, boy, the ides of March?   40
LUCIUS. I know not, sir.
BRUTUS. Look in the calendar and bring me word.
LUCIUS. I will, sir.   *Goes in*
BRUTUS. The exhalations whizzing in the air
  Gives so much light that I may read by them.
             Opens the letter and reads
  'Brutus, thou sleep'st: awake and see thyself.
  Shall Rome, etc. Speak, strike, redress....'
  'Brutus, thou sleep'st: awake.'
  Such instigations have been often dropped
  Where I have took them up.   50
  'Shall Rome, etc.' Thus must I piece it out:
  Shall Rome stand under one man's awe? What,
    Rome?
  My ancestors did from the streets of Rome
  The Tarquin drive, when he was called a king.
  'Speak, strike, redress.' Am I entreated
  To speak and strike? O Rome, I make thee promise,
  If the redress will follow, thou receivest
  Thy full petition at the hand of Brutus!

Lucius returns

LUCIUS. Sir, March is wasted fifteen days.   *Knocking*
BRUTUS. 'Tis good. Go to the gate; somebody knocks. 60
                    Lucius obeys
  Since Cassius first did whet me against Cæsar
  I have not slept.
  Between the acting of a dreadful thing
  And the first motion all the interim is
  Like a phantasma or a hideous dream:
  The Genius and the mortal instruments
  Are then in council, and the state of man

Like to a little kingdom suffers then
The nature of an insurrection.

Lucius returns

LUCIUS. Sir, 'tis your brother Cassius at the door,   70
  Who doth desire to see you.
BRUTUS.   Is he alone?
LUCIUS. No, sir, there are mo with him.
BRUTUS.   Do you know them?
LUCIUS. No, sir, their hats are plucked about their ears,
  And half their faces buried in their cloaks,
  That by no means I may discover them
  By any mark of favour.
BRUTUS.   Let 'em enter. *Lucius goes*
  They are the faction. O conspiracy,
  Sham'st thou to show thy dang'rous brow by night,
  When evils are most free? O, then, by day
  Where wilt thou find a cavern dark enough   80
  To mask thy monstrous visage? Seek none,
    conspiracy;
  Hide it in smiles and affability:
  For if thou path, thy native semblance on,
  Not Erebus itself were dim enough
  To hide thee from prevention.

*Enter the conspirators, Cassius, Casca, Decius, Cinna,
Metellus, and Trebonius*

CASSIUS. I think we are too bold upon your rest:
  Good morrow, Brutus, do we trouble you?
BRUTUS. I have been up this hour, awake all night.
  Know I these men that come along with you?
CASSIUS. Yes, every man of them; and no man here 90
  But honours you; and every one doth wish
  You had but that opinion of yourself
  Which every noble Roman bears of you.
  This is Trebonius.
BRUTUS.   He is welcome hither.
CASSIUS. This, Decius Brutus.
BRUTUS.   He is welcome too.
CASSIUS. This, Casca; this, Cinna; and this, Metellus
  Cimber.
BRUTUS. They are all welcome.
  What watchful cares do interpose themselves
  Betwixt your eyes and night?
CASSIUS. Shall I entreat a word?   *They whisper* 100
DECIUS. Here lies the east: doth not the day break here?
CASCA. No.
CINNA. O, pardon, sir, it doth, and yon grey lines
  That fret the clouds are messengers of day.
CASCA. You shall confess that you are both deceived.
  Here, as I point my sword, the sun arises;
  Which is a great way growing on the south,
  Weighing the youthful season of the year.
  Some two months hence up higher toward the
    north
  He first presents his fire, and the high east   110
  Stands as the Capitol, directly here.
BRUTUS. Give me your hands all over, one by one.
CASSIUS. And let us swear our resolution.
BRUTUS. No, not an oath: if not the face of men,
  The sufferance of our souls, the time's abuse—
  If these be motives weak, break off betimes,
  And every man hence to his idle bed;
  So let high-sighted tyranny range on
  Till each man drop by lottery. But if these,
  As I am sure they do, bear fire enough   120

To kindle cowards and to steel with valour
The melting spirits of women, then, countrymen,
What need we any spur but our own cause
To prick us to redress? what other bond
Than secret Romans that have spoke the word,
And will not palter? and what other oath
Than honesty to honesty engaged
That this shall be or we will fall for it?
Swear priests and cowards and men cautelous,
Old feeble carrions and such suffering souls   130
That welcome wrongs; unto bad causes swear
Such creatures as men doubt: but do not stain
The even virtue of our enterprise,
Nor th'insuppressive mettle of our spirits,
To think that or our cause or our performance
Did need an oath; when every drop of blood
That every Roman bears, and nobly bears,
Is guilty of a several bastardy
If he do break the smallest particle
Of any promise that hath passed from him.   140
CASSIUS. But what of Cicero? shall we sound him?
I think he will stand very strong with us.
CASCA. Let us not leave him out.
CINNA.   No, by no means.
METELLUS. O, let us have him, for his silver hairs
Will purchase us a good opinion
And buy men's voices to commend our deeds:
It shall be said his judgement ruled our hands;
Our youths and wildness shall no whit appear,
But all be buried in his gravity.
BRUTUS. O, name him not: let us not break with him, 150
For he will never follow anything
That other men begin.
CASSIUS.   Then leave him out.
CASCA. Indeed he is not fit.
DECIUS. Shall no man else be touched but only Cæsar?
CASSIUS. Decius, well urged: I think it is not meet
Mark Antony, so well beloved of Cæsar,
Should outlive Cæsar: we shall find of him
A shrewd contriver; and you know his means,
If he improve them, may well stretch so far
As to annoy us all: which to prevent,   160
Let Antony and Cæsar fall together.
BRUTUS. Our course will seem too bloody, Caius
Cassius,
To cut the head off and then hack the limbs,
Like wrath in death and envy afterwards;
For Antony is but a limb of Cæsar:
Let us be sacrificers, but not butchers, Caius.
We all stand up against the spirit of Cæsar,
And in the spirit of men there is no blood:
O, that we then could come by Cæsar's spirit,
And not dismember Cæsar! But, alas,   170
Cæsar must bleed for it! And, gentle friends,
Let's kill him boldly, but not wrathfully;
Let's carve him as a dish fit for the gods,
Not hew him as a carcass fit for hounds:
And let our hearts, as subtle masters do,
Stir up their servants to an act of rage
And after seem to chide 'em. This shall make
Our purpose necessary and not envious:
Which so appearing to the common eyes,
We shall be called purgers, not murderers.   180
And for Mark Antony, think not of him;
For he can do no more than Cæsar's arm
When Cæsar's head is off.

CASSIUS.   Yet I fear him,
For in the ingrafted love he bears to Cæsar—
BRUTUS. Alas, good Cassius, do not think of him:
If he love Cæsar, all that he can do
Is to himself, take thought and die for Cæsar:
And that were much he should, for he is given
To sports, to wildness and much company.
TREBONIUS. There is no fear in him; let him not die; 190
For he will live and laugh at this hereafter.
                                        Clock strikes
BRUTUS. Peace! count the clock.
CASSIUS.   The clock hath stricken three.
TREBONIUS. 'Tis time to part.
CASSIUS.   But it is doubtful yet
Whether Cæsar will come forth to-day or no;
For he is superstitious grown of late,
Quite from the main opinion he held once
Of fantasy, of dreams and ceremonies:
It may be these apparent prodigies,
The unaccustomed terror of this night,
And the persuasion of his augurers   200
May hold him from the Capitol to-day.
DECIUS. Never fear that: if he be so resolved,
I can o'ersway him; for he loves to hear
That unicorns may be betrayed with trees
And bears with glasses, elephants with holes,
Lions with toils and men with flatterers:
But when I tell him he hates flatterers,
He says he does, being then most flatteréd.
Let me work;
For I can give his humour the true bent,   210
And I will bring him to the Capitol.
CASSIUS. Nay, we will all of us be there to fetch him.
BRUTUS. By the eighth hour: is that the uttermost?
CINNA. Be that the uttermost, and fail not then.
METELLUS. Caius Ligarius doth bear Cæsar hard,
Who rated him for speaking well of Pompey:
I wonder none of you have thought of him.
BRUTUS. Now, good Metellus, go along by him:
He loves me well, and I have given him reasons;
Send him but hither, and I'll fashion him.   220
CASSIUS. The morning comes upon's: we'll leave you,
Brutus:
And, friends, disperse yourselves: but all remember
What you have said and show yourselves true
Romans.
BRUTUS. Good gentlemen, look fresh and merrily;
Let not our looks put on our purposes;
But bear it as our Roman actors do,
With untired spirits and formal constancy:
And so, good morrow to you every one.
                                All but Brutus depart
Boy! Lucius! Fast asleep! It is no matter;
Enjoy the honey-heavy dew of slumber: 230
Thou hast no figures nor no fantasies,
Which busy care draws in the brains of men;
Therefore thou sleep'st so sound.

Portia enters

PORTIA.   Brutus, my lord!
BRUTUS. Portia, what mean you? wherefore rise
you now?
It is not for your health thus to commit
Your weak condition to the raw cold morning.
PORTIA. Nor for yours neither. You've ungently,
Brutus,

Stole from my bed: and yesternight at supper
You suddenly arose and walked about,
Musing and sighing, with your arms across; 240
And when I asked you what the matter was,
You stared upon me with ungentle looks:
I urged you further; then you scratched your head
And too impatiently stamped with your foot:
Yet I insisted, yet you answered not,
But with an angry wafture of your hand
Gave sign for me to leave you: so I did,
Fearing to strengthen that impatience
Which seemed too much enkindled, and withal
Hoping it was but an effect of humour, 250
Which sometime hath his hour with every man.
It will not let you eat, nor talk, nor sleep,
And, could it work so much upon your shape
As it hath much prevailed on your condition,
I should not know you Brutus. Dear my lord,
Make me acquainted with your cause of grief.
BRUTUS. I am not well in health, and that is all.
PORTIA. Brutus is wise, and, were he not in health,
He would embrace the means to come by it.
BRUTUS. Why, so I do: good Portia, go to bed. 260
PORTIA. Is Brutus sick, and is it physical
To walk unbracéd and suck up the humours
Of the dank morning? What, is Brutus sick,
And will he steal out of his wholesome bed,
To dare the vile contagion of the night
And tempt the rheumy and unpurgéd air
To add unto his sickness? No, my Brutus;
You have some sick offence within your mind,
Which by the right and virtue of my place
I ought to know of: and, upon my knees, 270
I charm you, by my once commended beauty,
By all your vows of love and that great vow
Which did incorporate and make us one,
That you unfold to me, your self, your half,
Why you are heavy—and what men to-night
Have had resort to you; for here have been
Some six or seven, who did hide their faces
Even from darkness.
BRUTUS.   Kneel not, gentle Portia.
PORTIA. I should not need, if you were gentle Brutus.
Within the bond of marriage, tell me, Brutus, 280
Is it excepted I should know no secrets
That appertain to you? Am I your self
But, as it were, in sort or limitation,
To keep with you at meals, comfort your bed,
And talk to you sometimes? Dwell I but in the
    suburbs
Of your good pleasure? If it be no more,
Portia is Brutus' harlot, not his wife.
BRUTUS. You are my true and honourable wife,
As dear to me as are the ruddy drops
That visit my sad heart. 290
PORTIA. If this were true, then should I know this
    secret.
I grant I am a woman, but withal
A woman that Lord Brutus took to wife:
I grant I am a woman, but withal
A woman well reputed, Cato's daughter.
Think you I am no stronger than my sex,
Being so fathered and so husbanded?
Tell me your counsels, I will not disclose 'em:
I have made strong proof of my constancy,
Giving myself a voluntary wound 300

Here in the thigh: can I bear that with patience
And not my husband's secrets?
BRUTUS.   O ye gods,
Render me worthy of this noble wife!   *Knocking*
Hark, hark! one knocks: Portia, go in awhile;
And by and by thy bosom shall partake
The secrets of my heart:
All my engagements I will construe to thee,
All the charactery of my sad brows.
Leave me with haste. [*she goes*] Lucius, who's that
    knocks?

Lucius enters, followed by Ligarius

LUCIUS. Here is a sick man that would speak with you. 310
BRUTUS. Caius Ligarius, that Metellus spake of.
    Boy, stand aside. Caius Ligarius! how?
LIGARIUS. Vouchsafe good-morrow from a feeble
    tongue.
BRUTUS. O, what a time have you chose out, brave
    Caius,
To wear a kerchief! Would you were not sick!
LIGARIUS. I am not sick, if Brutus have in hand
Any exploit worthy the name of honour.
BRUTUS. Such an exploit have I in hand, Ligarius,
Had you a healthful ear to hear of it.
LIGARIUS. By all the gods that Romans bow before, 320
I here discard my sickness! Soul of Rome!
Brave son, derived from honourable loins!
Thou, like an exorcist, hast conjured up
My mortifiéd spirit. Now bid me run,
And I will strive with things impossible,
Yea, get the better of them. What's to do?
BRUTUS. A piece of work that will make sick men
    whole.
LIGARIUS. But are not some whole that we must make
    sick?
BRUTUS. That must we also. What it is, my Caius,
I shall unfold to thee, as we are going 330
To whom it must be done.
LIGARIUS.   Set on your foot,
And with a heart new-fired I follow you,
To do I know not what: but it sufficeth
That Brutus leads me on.
BRUTUS.   Follow me then.
                                   They go

Scene 2: *Cæsar's house*

*Thunder and lightning. Enter Julius Cæsar, in his
night-gown*

CÆSAR. Nor heaven nor earth have been at peace
    to-night:
Thrice hath Calphurnia in her sleep cried out,
'Help, ho! they murder Cæsar!' Who's within?

A servant appears

SERVANT. My lord?
CÆSAR. Go bid the priests do present sacrifice,
And bring me their opinions of success.
SERVANT. I will, my lord.   *Goes*

Enter Calphurnia

CALPHURNIA. What mean you, Cæsar? think you to
    walk forth?
You shall not stir out of your house to-day.
CÆSAR. Cæsar shall forth: the things that threatened me 10

Ne'er looked but on my back; when they shall see
The face of Cæsar, they are vanishéd.
CALPHURNIA. Cæsar, I never stood on ceremonies,
Yet now they fright me. There is one within,
Besides the things that we have heard and seen,
Recounts most horrid sights seen by the watch.
A lioness hath whelpéd in the streets;
And graves have yawned and yielded up their dead;
Fierce fiery warriors fought upon the clouds,
In ranks and squadrons and right form of war,   20
Which drizzled blood upon the Capitol;
The noise of battle hurtled in the air,
Horses did neigh and dying men did groan,
And ghosts did shriek and squeal about the streets.
O Cæsar! these things are beyond all use,
And I do fear them.
CÆSAR.   What can be avoided
Whose end is purposed by the mighty gods?
Yet Cæsar shall go forth; for these predictions
Are to the world in general as to Cæsar.
CALPHURNIA. When beggars die, there are no
comets seen;   30
The heavens themselves blaze forth the death of
princes.
CÆSAR. Cowards die many times before their deaths;
The valiant never taste of death but once.
Of all the wonders that I yet have heard,
It seems to me most strange that men should fear,
Seeing that death, a necessary end,
Will come when it will come.

The servant returns

                              What say the augurers?
SERVANT. They would not have you to stir forth
to-day.
Plucking the entrails of an offering forth,
They could not find a heart within the beast.   40
CÆSAR. The gods do this in shame of cowardice:
Cæsar should be a beast without a heart
If he should stay at home to-day for fear.
No, Cæsar shall not: Danger knows full well
That Cæsar is more dangerous than he:
We are two lions littered in one day,
And I the elder and more terrible:
And Cæsar shall go forth.
CALPHURNIA.   Alas, my lord,
Your wisdom is consumed in confidence.
Do not go forth to-day: call it my fear   50
That keeps you in the house and not your own.
We'll send Mark Antony to the Senate House,
And he shall say you are not well to-day:
Let me, upon my knee, prevail in this.
CÆSAR. Mark Antony shall say I am not well,
And, for thy humour, I will stay at home.

Enter Decius

Here's Decius Brutus, he shall tell them so.
DECIUS. Cæsar, all hail! good morrow, worthy Cæsar:
I come to fetch you to the Senate House.
CÆSAR. And you are come in very happy time,   60
To bear my greeting to the senators
And tell them that I will not come to-day:
Cannot, is false, and that I dare not, falser:
I will not come to-day: tell them so, Decius.
CALPHURNIA. Say he is sick.
CÆSAR.   Shall Cæsar send a lie?

Have I in conquest stretched mine arm so far,
To be afeard to tell graybeards the truth?
Decius, go tell them Cæsar will not come.
DECIUS. Most mighty Cæsar, let me know some
cause,
Lest I be laughed at when I tell them so.   70
CÆSAR. The cause is in my will: I will not come;
That is enough to satisfy the senate.
But, for your private satisfaction,
Because I love you, I will let you know.
Calphurnia here, my wife, stays me at home:
She dreamt to-night she saw my statua,
Which like a fountain with an hundred spouts
Did run pure blood, and many lusty Romans
Came smiling and did bathe their hands in it:
And these does she apply for warnings and portents   80
And evils imminent; and on her knee
Hath begged that I will stay at home to-day.
DECIUS. This dream is all amiss interpreted;
It was a vision fair and fortunate:
Your statue spouting blood in many pipes,
In which so many smiling Romans bathed,
Signifies that from you great Rome shall suck
Reviving blood, and that great men shall press
For tinctures, stains, relics, and cognizance.
This by Calphurnia's dream is signified.   90
CÆSAR. And this way have you well expounded it.
DECIUS. I have, when you have heard what I can say:
And know it now: the senate have concluded
To give this day a crown to mighty Cæsar.
If you shall send them word you will not come,
Their minds may change. Besides, it were a mock
Apt to be rendered, for some one to say
'Break up the senate till another time,
When Cæsar's wife shall meet with better dreams.'
If Cæsar hide himself, shall they not whisper   100
'Lo, Cæsar is afraid'?
Pardon me, Cæsar, for my dear dear love
To your proceeding bids me tell you this,
And reason to my love is liable.
CÆSAR. How foolish do your fears seem now,
Calphurnia!
I am ashaméd I did yield to them.
Give me my robe, for I will go.

Enter Publius, Brutus, Ligarius, Metellus, Casca,
Trebonius, and Cinna

And look where Publius is come to fetch me.
PUBLIUS. Good morrow, Cæsar.
CÆSAR.   Welcome, Publius.
What, Brutus, are you stirred so early too?   110
Good morrow, Casca. Caius Ligarius,
Cæsar was ne'er so much your enemy
As that same ague which hath made you lean.
What is't o'clock?
BRUTUS.   Cæsar, 'tis strucken eight.
CÆSAR. I thank you for your pains and courtesy.

Enter Antony

See! Antony, that revels long a-nights,
Is notwithstanding up. Good morrow, Antony.
ANTONY. So to most noble Cæsar.
CÆSAR [*to Calphurnia*].   Bid them
prepare within: *She goes*
I am to blame to be thus waited for.
Now, Cinna: now, Metellus: what, Trebonius!   120

I have an hour's talk in store for you;
Remember that you call on me to-day:
Be near me, that I may remember you.
TREBONIUS. Cæsar, I will. [aside] And so near will I be,
    That your best friends shall wish I had been further.
CÆSAR. Good friends, go in and taste some wine with
    me;
And we like friends will straightway go together.
BRUTUS [aside]. That every like is not the same,
    O Cæsar,
The heart of Brutus earns to think upon!   *They go*

Scene 3: *A street near the Capitol, before the house
of Brutus*

Enter Artemidorus, reading a paper

ARTEMIDORUS. 'Cæsar, beware of Brutus; take heed of
Cassius; come not near Casca; have an eye to Cinna;
trust not Trebonius; mark well Metellus Cimber:
Decius Brutus loves thee not: thou hast wronged
Caius Ligarius. There is but one mind in all these
men, and it is bent against Cæsar. If thou beest not
immortal, look about you: security gives way to
conspiracy. The mighty gods defend thee!
          Thy lover, ARTEMIDORUS.'
Here will I stand till Cæsar pass along,   10
And as a suitor will I give him this.
My heart laments that virtue cannot live
Out of the teeth of emulation.
If thou read this, O Cæsar, thou mayst live;
If not, the Fates with traitors do contrive.
                He stand aside

Scene 4

Portia and Lucius come from the house

PORTIA. I prithee, boy, run to the Senate House;
Stay not to answer me, but get thee gone.
Why dost thou stay?
LUCIUS.   To know my errand, madam.
PORTIUS. I would have had thee there and here again,
Ere I can tell thee what thou shouldst do there.
O constancy, be strong upon my side!
Set a huge mountain 'tween my heart and tongue!
I have a man's mind, but a woman's might.
How hard it is for women to keep counsel!
Art thou here yet?
LUCIUS.   Madam, what should I do?   10
Run to the Capitol, and nothing else?
And so return to you, and nothing else?
PORTIA. Yes, bring me word, boy, if thy lord look
    well,
For he went sickly forth: and take good note
What Cæsar doth, what suitors press to him.
Hark, boy! what noise is that?
LUCIUS. I hear none, madam.
PORTIA.   Prithee, listen well:
I heard a bustling rumour like a fray,
And the wind brings it from the Capitol.
LUCIUS. Sooth, madam, I hear nothing.

Enter the Soothsayer

PORTIA.   Come hither, fellow: 20
Which way hast thou been?
SOOTHSAYER.   At mine own house, good lady.
PORTIA. What is't o'clock?

SOOTHSAYER.   About the ninth hour, lady.
PORTIA. Is Cæsar yet gone to the Capitol?
SOOTHSAYER. Madam, not yet: I go to take my stand,
    To see him pass on to the Capitol.
PORTIA. Thou hast some suit to Cæsar, hast thou not?
SOOTHSAYER. That I have, lady: if it will please Cæsar
    To be so good to Cæsar as to hear me,
I shall beseech him to befriend himself.
PORTIA. Why, know'st thou any harm's intended
    towards him?   30
SOOTHSAYER. None that I know will be, much that I
    fear may chance.
Good morrow to you. Here the street is narrow:
The throng that follows Cæsar at the heels,
Of senators, of prætors, common suitors,
Will crowd a feeble man almost to death:
I'll get me to a place more void and there
Speak to great Cæsar as he comes along.
                     He passes on
PORTIA. I must go in.... Ay me, how weak a thing
The heart of woman is! O Brutus,
The heavens speed thee in thine enterprise!   40
Sure, the boy heard me. Brutus hath a suit
That Cæsar will not grant. O, I grow faint.
Run, Lucius, and commend me to my lord;
Say I am merry: come to me again,
And bring me word what he doth say to thee.
         Lucius goes forward: she turns home

ACT 3

Scene 1: *Before the Senate House; Senators in session seen
through open doors*

*A crowd of people stand waiting; among them Artemidorus
and the Soothsayer. Flourish. Enter Cæsar, Brutus,
Cassius, Casca, Decius, Metellus, Trebonius, Cinna,
Antony, Lepidus, Popilius, Publius, and others*

CÆSAR [to the Soothsayer]. The ides of March are come.
SOOTHSAYER. Ay, Cæsar; but not gone.
ARTEMIDORUS. Hail, Cæsar! read this schedule.
DECIUS. Trebonius doth desire you to o'er-read,
    At your best leisure, this his humble suit.
ARTEMIDORUS. O Cæsar, read mine first; for mine's a
    suit
That touches Cæsar nearer: read it, great Cæsar.
CÆSAR. What touches us ourself shall be last served.
ARTEMIDORUS. Delay not, Cæsar, read it instantly.
CÆSAR. What, is the fellow mad?
PUBLIUS.   Sirrah, give place. 10
CASSIUS. What, urge you your petitions in the street?
    Come to the Capitol.

Cæsar enters the Senate House, the rest following

POPILIUS. I wish your enterprise to-day may thrive.
CASSIUS. What enterprise, Popilius?
POPILIUS.   Fare you well.
      Advances to Cæsar, and they speak together
BRUTUS. What said Popilius Lena?
CASSIUS. He wished to-day our enterprise might
    thrive.
I fear our purpose is discoveréd.
BRUTUS. Look, how he makes to Cæsar: mark him.
CASSIUS.   Casca,
Be sudden, for we fear prevention.

Brutus, what shall be done? If this be known,   20
Cassius or Cæsar never shall turn back,
For I will slay myself.
BRUTUS.   Cassius, be constant:
Popilius Lena speaks not of our purposes;
For, look, he smiles, and Cæsar doth not change.
CASSIUS. Trebonius knows his time; for, look you,
    Brutus,
He draws Mark Antony out of the way.
                    Antony and Trebonius depart
DECIUS. Where is Metellus Cimber? Let him go,
And presently prefer his suit to Cæsar.
BRUTUS. He is addressed: press near and second him.
CINNA. Casca, you are the first that rears your hand.   30
CÆSAR. Are we all ready? What is now amiss
That Cæsar and his senate must redress?
METELLUS [*kneels*]. Most high, most mighty, and
    most puissant Cæsar,
Metellus Comber throws before thy seat
An humble heart—
CÆSAR.   I must prevent thee, Cimber.
These couchings and these lowly courtesies
Might fire the blood of ordinary men,
And turn pre-ordinance and first decree
Into the law of children. Be not fond
To think that Cæsar bears such rebel blood   40
That will be thawed from the true quality
With that which melteth fools, I mean, sweet words,
Low-crookéd curtsies and base spaniel-fawning.
Thy brother by decree is banishéd:
If thou dost bend and pray and fawn for him,
I spurn thee like a cur out of my way.
Know, Cæsar doth not wrong, nor without cause
Will he be satisfied.
METELLUS. Is there no voice more worthy than my
    own,
To sound more sweetly in great Cæsar's ear   50
For the repealing of my banished brother?
BRUTUS. I kiss thy hand, but not in flattery, Cæsar;
Desiring thee that Publius Cimber may
Have an immediate freedom of repeal.
CÆSAR. What, Brutus!
CASSIUS.   Pardon, Cæsar; Cæsar, pardon:
As low as to thy foot doth Cassius fall,
To beg enfranchisement for Publius Cimber.
CÆSAR. I could be well moved, if I were as you;
If I could pray to move, prayers would move me:
But I am constant as the northern star,   60
Of whose true-fixed and resting quality
There is no fellow in the firmament.
The skies are painted with unnumbered sparks;
They are all fire and every one doth shine;
But there's but one in all doth hold his place:
So in the world; 'tis furnished well with men,
And men are flesh and blood, and apprehensive;
Yet in the number I do know but one
That unassailable holds on his rank,
Unshaked of motion: and that I am he,   70
Let me a little show it, even in this:
That I was constant Cimber should be banished,
And constant do remain to keep him so.
CINNA. O Cæsar—
CÆSAR.   Hence! wilt thou lift up Olympus?
DECIUS. Great Cæsar—
CÆSAR.   Doth not Brutus bootless kneel?
CASCA. Speak, hands, for me!

*Strikes him from behind; the conspirators
                    and Brutus hack at him*
CÆSAR. Et tu, Brute? Then fall, Cæsar!   *Dies*
CINNA. Liberty! freedom! Tyranny is dead!
Run hence, proclaim, cry it about the streets.
CASSIUS. Some to the common pulpits, and cry out   80
'Liberty, freedom and enfranchisement!'
BRUTUS. People, and senators, be not affrighted;
Fly not; stand still: ambition's debt is paid.
CASCA. Go to the pulpit, Brutus.
DECIUS. And Cassius too.
BRUTUS. Where's Publius?
CINNA. Here, quite confounded with this mutiny.
METELLUS. Stand fast together, lest some friend of
    Cæsar's
Should chance—
BRUTUS. Talk not of standing. Publius, good cheer;   90
There is no harm intended to your person,
Nor to no Roman else: so tell them, Publius.
CASSIUS. And leave us, Publius, lest that the people
Rushing on us should do your age some mischief.
BRUTUS. Do so: and let no man abide this deed
But we the doers.

Trebonius returns

CASSIUS. Where is Antony?
TREBONIUS.   Fled to his house amazed:
Men, wives and children stare, cry out and run
As it were doomsday.
BRUTUS.   Fates, we will know your pleasures:
That we shall die, we know; 'tis but the time,   100
And drawing days out, that men stand upon.
CASCA. Why, he that cuts off twenty years of life
Cuts off so many years of fearing death.
BRUTUS. Grant that, and then is death a benefit:
So are we Cæsar's friends, that have abridged
His time of fearing death. Stoop, Romans, stoop,
And let us bathe our hands in Cæsar's blood
Up to the elbows, and besmear our swords:
Then walk we forth, even to the market-place,
And waving our red weapons o'er our heads,   110
Let's all cry 'Peace, freedom and liberty!'
CASSIUS. Stoop then, and wash. How many ages
    hence
Shall this our lofty scene be acted over
In states unborn and accents yet unknown!
BRUTUS. How many times shall Cæsar bleed in sport,
That now on Pompey's basis lies along
No worthier than the dust!
CASSIUS.   So oft as that shall be,
So often shall the knot of us be called
The men that gave their country liberty.
DECIUS. What, shall we forth?
CASSIUS.   Ay, every man away: 120
Brutus shall lead, and we will grace his heels
With the most boldest and best hearts of Rome.

A servant enters

BRUTUS. Soft! who comes here? A friend of Antony's.
SERVANT. Thus, Brutus, did my master bid me kneel;
Thus did Mark Antony bid me fall down;
And, being prostrate, thus he bade me say:
Brutus is noble, wise, valiant and honest;
Cæsar was mighty, bold, royal and loving:
Say I love Brutus and I honour him;
Say I feared Cæsar, honoured him and loved him.   130

If Brutus will vouchsafe that Antony
May safely come to him and be resolved
How Cæsar hath deserved to lie in death,
Mark Antony shall not love Cæsar dead
So well as Brutus living, but will follow
The fortunes and affairs of noble Brutus
Thorough the hazards of this untrod state
With all true faith. So says my master Antony.
BRUTUS. Thy master is a wise and valiant Roman;   140
  I never thought him worse.
  Tell him, so please him come unto this place,
  He shall be satisfied; and, by my honour,
  Depart untouched.
SERVANT.   I'll fetch him presently.   Goes
BRUTUS. I know that we shall have him well to friend.
CASSIUS. I wish we may: but yet have I a mind
  That fears him much, and my misgiving still
  Falls shrewdly to the purpose.

Enter Antony

BRUTUS. But here comes Antony. Welcome, Mark
  Antony.
ANTONY. O mighty Cæsar! dost thou lie so low?
  Are all thy conquests, glories, triumphs, spoils,   150
  Shrunk to this little measure? Fare thee well.
  I know not, gentlemen, what you intend,
  Who else must be let blood, who else is rank:
  If I myself, there is no hour so fit
  As Cæsar's death hour, nor no instrument
  Of half that worth as those your swords, made rich
  With the most noble blood of all this world.
  I do beseech ye, if you bear me hard,
  Now, whilst your purpled hands do reek and
    smoke,
  Fulfil your pleasure. Live a thousand years,   160
  I shall not find myself so apt to die:
  No place will please me so, no mean of death,
  As here by Cæsar, and by you cut off,
  The choice and master spirits of this age.
BRUTUS. O Antony, beg not your death of us.
  Though now we must appear bloody and cruel,
  As, by our hands and this our present act,
  You see we do; yet see you but our hands
  And this the bleeding business they have done:
  Our hearts you see not; they are pitiful;   170
  And pity to the general wrong of Rome—
  As fire drives our fire, so pity pity—
  Hath done this deed on Cæsar. For your part,
  To you our swords have leaden points, Mark
    Antony:
  Our arms in strength of malice, and our hearts
  Of brothers' temper, do receive you in
  With all kind love, good thoughts and reverence.
CASSIUS. Your voice shall be as strong as any man's
  In the disposing of new dignities.
BRUTUS. Only be patient till we have appeased   180
  The multitude, beside themselves with fear,
  And then we will deliver you the cause
  Why I, that did love Cæsar when I struck him,
  Have thus proceeded.
ANTONY.   I doubt not of your wisdom.
  Let each man render me his bloody hand:
  First, Marcus Brutus, will I shake with you;
  Next, Caius Cassius, do I take your hand;
  Now, Decius Brutus, yours; now yours, Metellus;
  Yours, Cinna; and, my valiant Casca, yours;

Though last, not least in love, yours, good
  Trebonius.   190
Gentlemen all . . . alas, what shall I say?
My credit now stands on such slippery ground,
That one of two bad ways you must conceit me,
Either a coward or a flatterer.
That I did love thee, Cæsar, O, 'tis true:
If then thy spirit look upon us now,
Shall it not grieve thee deárer than thy death,
To see thy Antony making his peace,
Shaking the bloody fingers of thy foes,
Most noble! in the presence of thy corse?   200
Had I as many eyes as thou hast wounds,
Weeping as fast as they stream forth thy blood,
It would become me better than to close
In terms of friendship with thine enemies.
Pardon me, Julius! Here wast thou bayed, brave
  hart,
Here didst thou fall, and here thy hunters stand,
Signed in thy spoil and crimsoned in thy lethe.
O world, thou wast the forest to this hart;
And this, indeed, O world, the heart of thee.
How like a deer strucken by many princes   210
Dost thou here lie!
CASSIUS. Mark Antony—
ANTONY.   Pardon me, Caius Cassius:
  The enemies of Cæsar shall say this;
  Then, in a friend, it is cold modesty.
CASSIUS. I blame you not for praising Cæsar so,
  But what compact mean you to have with us?
  Will you be pricked in number of our friends,
  Or shall we on, and not depend on you?
ANTONY. Therefore I took your hands, but was indeed
  Swayed from the point by looking down on Cæsar. 220
  Friends am I with you all and love you all,
  Upon this hope that you shall give me reasons
  Why and wherein Cæsar was dangerous.
BRUTUS. Or else were this a savage spectacle:
  Our reasons are so full of good regard
  That were you, Antony, the son of Cæsar,
  You should be satisfied.
ANTONY.   That's all I seek,
  And am moreover suitor that I may
  Produce his body to the market-place,
  And in the pulpit as becomes a friend   230
  Speak in the order of his funeral.
BRUTUS. You shall, Mark Antony.
CASSIUS [*aside*].   Brutus, a word with you.
  You know not what you do: do not consent
  That Antony speak in his funeral:
  Know you how much the people may be moved
  By that which he will utter?
BRUTUS.   By your pardon:
  I will myself into the pulpit first,
  And show the reason of our Cæsar's death:
  What Antony shall speak, I will protest
  He speaks by leave and by permission,   240
  And that we are contented Cæsar shall
  Have all true rites and lawful ceremonies.
  It shall advantage more than do us wrong.
CASSIUS. I know not what may fall; I like it not.
BRUTUS. Mark Antony, here, take you Cæsar's body.
  You shall not in your funeral speech blame us,
  But speak all good you can devise of Cæsar;
  And say you do 't by our permission;
  Else shall you not have any hand at all

About his funeral. And you shall speak   250
In the same pulpit whereto I am going,
After my speech is ended.
ANTONY.   Be it so;
I do desire no more.
BRUTUS. Prepare the body then, and follow us.
                                        They go;
                                Antony remains
ANTONY. O, pardon me, thou bleeding piece of earth,
That I am meek and gentle with these butchers!
Thou art the ruins of the noblest man
That ever livéd in the tide of times.
Woe to the hands that shed this costly blood!
Over thy wounds now do I prophesy   260
(Which like dumb mouths do ope their ruby lips
To beg the voice and utterance of my tongue),
A curse shall light upon the limbs of men;
Domestic fury and fierce civil strife
Shall cumber all the parts of Italy;
Blood and destruction shall be so in use,
And dreadful objects so familiar,
That mothers shall but smile when they behold
Their infants quartered with the hands of war;
All pity choked with custom of fell deeds: 270
And Cæsar's spirit ranging for revenge,
With Até by his side come hot from hell,
Shall in these confines with a monarch's voice
Cry 'Havoc,' and let slip the dogs of war;
That this foul deed shall smell above the earth
With carrion men, groaning for burial.

Enter a servant

You serve Octavius Cæsar, do you not?
SERVANT. I do, Mark Antony.
ANTONY. Cæsar did write for him to come to Rome.
SERVANT. He did receive his letters and is coming,   280
And bid me say to you by word of mouth—
O Cæsar!   *Seeing the body*
ANTONY. Thy heart is big; get thee apart and weep:
Passion I see is catching, for mine eyes,
Seeing those beads of sorrow stand in thine,
Began to water. Is thy master coming?
SERVANT. He lies to-night within seven leagues of
Rome.
ANTONY. Post back with speed, and tell him what hath
chanced:
Here is a mourning Rome, a dangerous Rome,
No Rome of safety for Octavius yet;   290
Hie hence, and tell him so. Yet stay awhile;
Thou shalt not back till I have borne this corse
Into the market-place: there shall I try,
In my oration, how the people take
The cruel issue of these bloody men;
According to the which, thou shalt discourse
To young Octavius of the state of things.
Lend me you hand.   *They bear away the body*

Scene 2: *The Forum*

Enter Brutus and Cassius, and a throng of plebeians

PLEBEIANS. We will be satisfied; let us be satisfied.
BRUTUS. Then follow me, and give me audience,
friends.
Cassius, go you into the other street,
And part the numbers.
Those that will hear me speak, let 'em stay here;

Those that will follow Cassius, go with him;
And public reasons shall be renderéd
Of Cæsar's death.
1 PLEBEIAN.   I will hear Brutus speak.
2 PLEBEIAN. I will hear Cassius; and compare their
reasons,
When severally we hear them renderéd.   10
            Cassius departs with some of the plebeians.
                    Brutus goes up into the pulpit
3 PLEBEIAN. The noble Brutus is ascended: silence!
BRUTUS. Be patient till the last.
Romans, countrymen, and lovers! hear me for my
cause, and be silent, that you may hear: believe me
for mine honour, and have respect to mine honour,
that you may believe: censure me in your wisdom,
and awake your senses, that you may the better
judge. If there be any in this assembly, any dear
friend of Cæsar's, to him I say that Brutus' love to
Cæsar was no less than his. If then that friend   20
demand why Brutus rose against Cæsar, this is my
answer: not that I loved Cæsar less, but that I loved
Rome more. Had you rather Cæsar were living, and
die all slaves, than that Cæsar were dead, to live all
free men? As Cæsar loved me, I weep for him; as
he was fortunate, I rejoice at it; as he was valiant,
I honour him; but as he was ambitious, I slew him.
There is tears for his love; joy for his fortune; honour for his valour; and death for his ambition. Who
is here so base that would be a bondman? If any,   30
speak; for him have I offended. Who is here so rude
that would not be a Roman? If any, speak; for him
have I offended. Who is here so vile that will not
love his country? If any, speak; for him have I
offended. I pause for a reply.
ALL. None, Brutus, none.
BRUTUS. Then none have I offended. I have done no
more to Cæsar than you shall do to Brutus. The
question of his death is enrolled in the Capitol; his
glory not extenuated, wherein he was worthy, nor   40
his offences enforced, for which he suffered death.

Antony enters, with bearers carrying Cæsar's body

Here comes his body, mourned by Mark Antony,
who, though he had no hand in his death, shall
receive the benefit of his dying, a place in the
commonwealth; as which of you shall not? With
this I depart—that, as I slew my best lover for the
good of Rome, I have the same dagger for myself,
when it shall please my country to need my death.
ALL. Live, Brutus! live, live!
1 PLEBEIAN. Bring him with triumph home unto his
house.   50
2 PLEBEIAN. Give him a statue with his ancestors.
3 PLEBEIAN. Let him be Cæsar.
4 PLEBEIAN.   Cæsar's better parts
Shall be crowned in Brutus.
1 PLEBEIAN. We'll bring him to his house with shouts
and clamours.
BRUTUS. My countrymen—
2 PLEBEIAN.   Peace! silence! Brutus speaks.
1 PLEBEIAN. Peace, ho!
BRUTUS. Good countrymen, let me depart alone,
And, for my sake, stay here with Antony:
Do grace to Cæsar's corpse, and grace his speech
Tending to Cæsar's glories, which Mark Antony   60
By our permission is allowed to make.

'I do entreat you, not a man depart,
Save I alone, till Antony have spoke.   *He goes*
1 PLEBEIAN. Stay, ho! and let us hear Mark Antony.
3 PLEBEIAN. Let him go up into the public chair;
We'll hear him. Noble Antony, go up.
ANTONY. For Brutus' sake, I am beholding to you.
                              Goes into the pulpit
4 PLEBEIAN. What does he say of Brutus?
3 PLEBEIAN.   He says, for Brutus' sake,
He finds himself beholding to us all.
4 PLEBEIAN. 'Twere best he speak no harm of Brutus
here.   70
1 PLEBEIAN. This Cæsar was a tyrant.
3 PLEBEIAN.   Nay, that's certain:
We are blest that Rome is rid of him.
2 PLEBEIAN. Peace! let us hear what Antony can say.
ANTONY. You gentle Romans—
ALL.   Peace, ho! let us hear him.
ANTONY. Friends, Romans, countrymen, lend me
    your ears;
I come to bury Cæsar, not to praise him;
The evil that men do lives after them,
The good is oft interréd with their bones,
So let it be with Cæsar.... The noble Brutus
Hath told you Cæsar was ambitious: 80
If it were so, it was a grievous fault,
And grievously hath Cæsar answered it....
Here, under leave of Brutus and the rest,
(For Brutus is an honourable man;
So are they all; all honourable men)
Come I to speak in Cæsar's funeral....
He was my friend, faithful and just to me:
But Brutus says he was ambitious;
And Brutus is an honourable man....
He hath brought many captives home to Rome,   90
Whose ransoms did the general coffers fill:
Did this in Cæsar seem ambitious?
When that the poor have cried, Cæsar hath wept:
Ambition should be made of sterner stuff:
Yet Brutus says he was ambitious;
And Brutus is an honourable man.
You all did see that on the Lupercal
I thrice presented him a kingly crown,
Which he did thrice refuse: was this ambition?
Yet Brutus says he was ambitious;   100
And, sure, he is an honourable man.
I speak not to disprove what Brutus spoke,
But here I am to speak what I do know.
You all did love him once, not without cause:
What cause withholds you then to mourn for him?
O judgement! thou art fled to brutish beasts,
And men have lost their reason.... Bear with me;
My heart is in the coffin there with Cæsar,
And I must pause till it come back to me.
1 PLEBEIAN. Methinks there is much reason in his
sayings.   110
2 PLEBEIAN. If thou consider rightly of the matter,
Cæsar has had great wrong.
3 PLEBEIAN.   Has he, masters?
I fear there will a worse come in his place.
4 PLEBEIAN. Marked ye his words? He would not take
the crown;
Therefore 'tis certain he was not ambitious.
1 PLEBEIAN. If it be found so, some will dear abide it.
2 PLEBEIAN. Poor soul! his eyes are red as fire with
weeping.

3 PLEBEIAN. There's not a nobler man in Rome than
Antony.
4 PLEBEIAN. Now mark him, he begins again to speak.
ANTONY. But yesterday the word of Cæsar might   120
Have stood against the world: now lies he there,
And none so poor to do him reverence.
O masters, if I were disposed to stir
Your hearts and minds to mutiny and rage,
I should do Brutus wrong and Cassius wrong,
Who, you all know, are honourable men:
I will not do them wrong; I rather choose
To wrong the dead, to wrong myself and you,
Than I will wrong such honourable men.
But here's a parchment with the seal of Cæsar;   130
I found it in his closet; 'tis his will:
Let but the commons hear this testament—
Which, pardon me, I do not mean to read—
And they would go and kiss dead Cæsar's wounds,
And dip their napkins in his sacred blood,
Yea, beg a hair of him for memory,
And, dying, mention it within their wills,
Bequeathing it as a rich legacy
Unto their issue.
4 PLEBEIAN. We'll hear the will: read it, Mark Antony. 140
ALL. The will, the will! we will hear Cæsar's will.
ANTONY. Have patience, gentle friends, I must not
    read it;
It is not meet you know how Cæsar loved you.
You are not wood, you are not stones, but men;
And, being men, hearing the will of Cæsar,
It will inflame you, it will make you mad:
'Tis good you know not that you are his heirs;
For if you should, O, what would come of it!
4 PLEBEIAN. Read the will; we'll hear it, Antony;
You shall read us the will, Cæsar's will.   150
ANTONY. Will you be patient? will you stay awhile?
I have o'ershot myself to tell you of it:
I fear I wrong the honourable men
Whose daggers have stabbed Cæsar; I do fear it.
4 PLEBEIAN. They were traitors: honourable men!
ALL. The will! the testament!
2 PLEBEIAN. They were villains, murderers: the will!
read the will!
ANTONY. You will compel me then to read the will?
Then make a ring about the corpse of Cæsar,   160
And let me show you him that made the will.
Shall I descend? and will you give me leave?
ALL. Come down.
2 PLEBEIAN. Descend.   *Antony comes down*
3 PLEBEIAN. You shall have leave.
4 PLEBEIAN. A ring; stand round.
1 PLEBEIAN. Stand from the hearse, stand from the
body.
2 PLEBEIAN. Room for Antony, most noble Antony.
ANTONY. Nay, press not so upon me; stand far off.
ALL. Stand back. Room! Bear back.   170
ANTONY. If you have tears, prepare to shed them now.
You all do know this mantle: I remember
The first time ever Cæsar put it on;
'Twas on a summer's evening, in his tent,
That day he overcame the Nervii:
Look, in this place ran Cassius' dagger through:
See what a rent the envious Casca made:
Through this the well-belovéd Brutus stabbed;
And as he plucked his curséd steel away,
Mark how the blood of Cæsar followed it,   180

As rushing out of doors, to be resolved
If Brutus so unkindly knocked, or no:
For Brutus, as you know, was Cæsar's angel:
Judge, O you gods, how dearly Cæsar loved him!
This was the most unkindest cut of all;
For when the noble Cæsar saw him stab,
Ingratitude, more strong than traitors' arms,
Quite vanquished him: then burst his mighty heart;
And, in his mantle muffling up his face,
Even at the base of Pompey's statua   190
(Which all the while ran blood), great Cæsar fell.
O, what a fall was there, my countrymen!
Then I, and you, and all of us fell down,
Whilst bloody Treason flourished over us.
O, now you weep, and I perceive you feel
The dint of pity: these are gracious drops.
Kind souls, what weep you when you but behold
Our Cæsar's vesture wounded? Look you here,
Here is himself, marred, as you see, with traitors.
                                      He lifts the mantle

1 PLEBEIAN. O piteous spectacle!   200
2 PLEBEIAN. O noble Cæsar!
3 PLEBEIAN. O woful day!
4 PLEBEIAN. O traitors, villains!
1 PLEBEIAN. O most bloody sight!
2 PLEBEIAN. We will be revenged.
ALL. Revenge! About! Seek! Burn! Fire! Kill! Slay!
    Let not a traitor live!
ANTONY. Stay, countrymen.
1 PLEBEIAN. Peace there! hear the noble Antony.
2 PLEBEIAN. We'll hear him, we'll follow him, we'll   210
    die with him.
ANTONY. Good friends, sweet friends, let me not stir
    you up
To such a sudden flood of mutiny:
They that have done this deed are honourable.
What private griefs they have, alas, I know not,
That made them do it: they are wise and
    honourable,
And will, no doubt, with reasons answer you.
I come not, friends, to steal away your hearts:
I am no orator, as Brutus is;
But, as you know me all, a plain blunt man,   220
That love my friend; and that they know full well
That gave me public leave to speak of him:
For I have neither wit, nor words, nor worth,
Action, nor utterance, nor the power of speech
To stir men's blood: I only speak right on;
I tell you that which you yourselves do know;
Show you sweet Cæsar's wounds, poor poor dumb
    mouths,
And bid them speak for me: but were I Brutus,
And Brutus Antony, there were an Antony
Would ruffle up your spirits, and put a tongue   230
In every wound of Cæsar, that should move
The stones of Rome to rise and mutiny.
ALL. We'll mutiny.
1 PLEBEIAN. We'll burn the house of Brutus.
3 PLEBEIAN. Away, then! come, seek the conspirators.
ANTONY. Yet hear me, countrymen; yet hear me
    speak.
ALL. Peace, ho! Hear Antony! Most noble Antony!
ANTONY. Why, friends, you go to do you know not
    what:
Wherein hath Cæsar thus deserved your loves?
Alas, you know not; I must tell you then: 240

You have forgot the will I told you of.
ALL. Most true: the will! Let's stay and hear the will.
ANTONY. Here is the will, and under Cæsar's seal.
To every Roman citizen he gives,
To every several man, seventy five drachmas.
2 PLEBEIAN. Most noble Cæsar! we'll revenge his death.
3 PLEBEIAN. O royal Cæsar!
ANTONY. Hear me with patience.
ALL. Peace, ho!
ANTONY. Moreover, he hath left you all his walks,   250
His private arbours and new-planted orchards,
On this side Tiber; he hath left them you,
And to your heirs for ever; common pleasures,
To walk abroad and recreate yourselves.
Here was a Cæsar! when comes such another?
1 PLEBEIAN. Never, never. Come, away, away!
We'll burn his body in the holy place,
And with the brands fire the traitors' houses.
Take up the body.
2 PLEBEIAN. Go fetch fire.   260
3 PLEBEIAN. Pluck down benches.
4 PLEBEIAN. Pluck down forms, windows, anything.
        They go; the bearers follow with the body
ANTONY. Now let it work. Mischief, thou art afoot,
Take thou what course thou wilt.

Octavius's servant enters

                          How now, fellow!
SERVANT. Sir, Octavius is already come to Rome.
ANTONY. Where is he?
SERVANT. He and Lepidus are at Cæsar's house.
ANTONY. And thither will I straight to visit him:
He comes upon a wish. Fortune is merry,
And in this mood will give us anything.   270
SERVANT. I heard him say, Brutus and Cassius
Are rid like madmen through the gates of Rome.
ANTONY. Belike they had some notice of the people,
How I had moved them. Bring me to Octavius.
                                      They go

Scene 3

Enter Cinna the poet, with plebeians behind him

CINNA. I dreamt to-night that I did feast with Cæsar,
And things unluckily charge my fantasy:
I have no will to wander forth of doors,
Yet something leads me forth.

Plebeians surround him

1 PLEBEIAN. What is your name?
2 PLEBEIAN. Whither are you going?
3 PLEBEIAN. Where do you dwell?
4 PLEBEIAN. Are you a married man or a bachelor?
2 PLEBEIAN. Answer every man directly.
1 PLEBEIAN. Ay, and briefly.   10
4 PLEBEIAN. Ay, and wisely.
3 PLEBEIAN. Ay, and truly, you were best.
CINNA. What is my name? Whither am I going?
Where do I dwell? Am I a married man or a
bachelor? Then, to answer every man directly and
briefly, wisely and truly: wisely I say, I am a
bachelor.
2 PLEBEIAN. That's as much as to say, they are fools
that marry: you'll bear me a bang for that, I fear.
Proceed; directly.   20
CINNA. Directly, I am going to Cæsar's funeral.

1 PLEBEIAN. As a friend or an enemy?
CINNA. As a friend.
2 PLEBEIAN. That matter is answered directly.
4 PLEBEIAN. For your dwelling, briefly.
CINNA. Briefly, I dwell by the Capitol.
3 PLEBEIAN. Your name, sir, truly.
CINNA. Truly, my name is Cinna.
1 PLEBEIAN. Tear him to pieces, he's a conspirator.
CINNA. I am Cinna the poet, I am Cinna the poet.　30
4 PLEBEIAN. Tear him for his bad verses, tear him for
　his bad verses.
CINNA. I am not Cinna the conspirator.
4 PLEBEIAN. It is no matter, his name's Cinna; pluck
　but his name out of his heart, and turn him going.
3 PLEBEIAN. Tear him, tear him! [they set upon him]
　Come, brands, ho! fire-brands: to Brutus', to
　Cassius', burn all: some to Decius' house, and some
　to Casca's; away, go!

　　　　　　　　They go, dragging the body of
　　　　　　　　　　　　　Cinna after them

ACT 4

Scene 1: A room in Antony's house

Antony, Octavius, and Lepidus, seated at a table

ANTONY. These many then shall die; their names are
　pricked.
OCTAVIUS. Your brother too must die; consent you,
　Lepidus?
LEPIDUS. I do consent—
OCTAVIUS.　　　　　　Prick him down, Antony.
LEPIDUS. Upon condition Publius shall not live,
Who is your sister's son, Mark Antony.
ANTONY. He shall not live; look, with a spot I damn
　him.
But, Lepidus, go you to Cæsar's house;
Fetch the will hither, and we shall determine
How to cut off some charge in legacies.
LEPIDUS. What, shall I find you here?　　　　10
OCTAVIUS. Or here, or at the Capitol.　*Lepidus goes*
ANTONY. This is a slight unmeritable man,
Meet to be sent on errands: is it fit,
The three-fold world divided, he should stand
One of the three to share it?
OCTAVIUS.　　　　　　So you thought him,
And took his voice who should be pricked to die
In our black sentence and proscription.
ANTONY. Octavius, I have seen more days than you:
And though we lay these honours on this man,
To ease ourselves of divers sland'rous loads,　　20
He shall but bear them as the ass bears gold,
To groan and sweat under the business,
Either led or driven, as we point the way;
And having brought our treasure where we will,
Then take we down his load and turn him off,
Like to the empty ass, to shake his ears
And graze in commons.
OCTAVIUS.　　　　　　You may do your will:
But he's a tried and valiant soldier.
ANTONY. So is my horse, Octavius, and for that
I do appoint him store of provender:　　　　30
It is a creature that I teach to fight,
To wind, to stop, to run directly on,
His corporal motion governed by my spirit.
And in some taste is Lepidus but so;

He must be taught, and trained, and bid go forth;
A barren-spirited fellow; one that feeds
On objects, arts, and imitations
Which, out of use and staled by other men,
Begin his fashion: do not talk of him
But as a property. And now, Octavius,　　　　40
Listen great things: Brutus and Cassius
Are levying powers: we must straight make head:
Therefore let our alliance be combined,
Our best friends made, our means stretched;
And let us presently go sit in council,
How covert matters may be best disclosed,
And open perils surest answeréd.
OCTAVIUS. Let us do so: for we are at the stake,
And bayed about with many enemies;
And some that smile have in their hearts, I fear,　50
Millions of mischiefs.　　　　　　　*They go*

Scene 2: Before Brutus's tent in the camp near Sardis

*Drum. Enter Lucilius with troops and Pindarus, the
bondman of Cassius. Brutus comes from the tent with
Lucius in attendance*

BRUTUS. Stand, ho!
LUCILIUS. Give the word, ho! and stand!
BRUTUS. What now, Lucilius! is Cassius near?
LUCILIUS. He is at hand, and Pindarus is come
To do you salutation from his master.
BRUTUS. He greets me well. Your master, Pindarus,
In his own change, or by ill officers,
Hath given me some worthy cause to wish
Things done undone: but if he be at hand,
I shall be satisfied.
PINDARUS.　　　　I do not doubt　　　　10
But that my noble master will appear
Such as he is, full of regard and honour.
BRUTUS. He is not doubted. A word, Lucilius;
How he received you, let me be resolved.
LUCILIUS. With courtesy and with respect enough,
But not with such familiar instances,
Nor with such free and friendly conference,
As he hath used of old.
BRUTUS.　　　　　　Thou hast described
A hot friend cooling: ever note, Lucilius,
When love begins to sicken and decay,　　　　20
It useth an enforcéd ceremony.
There are no tricks in plain and simple faith:
But hollow men, like horses hot at hand,
Make gallant show and promise of their mettle,
But when they should endure the bloody spur,
They fall their crests and like deceitful jades
Sink in the trial. Comes his army on?
LUCILIUS. They mean this night in Sardis to be
　quartered;
The greater part, the horse in general,
Are come with Cassius.　　　　　*Drums heard*
BRUTUS.　　　　　　Hark, he is arrived:　　30
March gently on to meet him.

Cassius approaches with Titinius and his powers

CASSIUS. Stand, ho!
BRUTUS. Stand, ho! Speak the word along.
1 OFFICER. Stand!
2 OFFICER. Stand!
3 OFFICER. Stand!

CASSIUS. Most noble brother, you have done me
　　wrong.
BRUTUS. Judge me, you gods; wrong I mine enemies?
　　And, if not so, how should I wrong a brother?
CASSIUS. Brutus, this sober form of yours hides
　　wrongs,　　　　　　　　　　　　　　　　　　40
　　And when you do them—
BRUTUS.　　　　　　　　　　Cassius, be content,
　　Speak your griefs softly, I do know you well.
　　Before the eyes of both our armies here,
　　Which should perceive nothing but love from us,
　　Let us not wrangle. Bid them move away;
　　Then in my tent, Cassius, enlarge your griefs,
　　And I will give you audience.
CASSIUS.　　　　　　　　　　Pindarus,
　　Bid our commanders lead their charges off
　　A little from this ground.
BRUTUS. Lucius, do you the like, and let no man　　50
　　Come to our tent till we have done our conference.
　　Lucilius and Titinius guard our door.

Scene 3

The armies march away; Brutus and Cassius enter the tent;
Lucilius and Titinius stand guard without

CASSIUS. That you have wronged me doth appear in
　　this:
　　You have condemned and noted Lucius Pella
　　For taking bribes here of the Sardians;
　　Wherein my letters, praying on his side,
　　Because I knew the man, was slighted off.
BRUTUS. You wronged yourself to write in such a case.
CASSIUS. In such a time as this it is not meet
　　That every nice offence should bear his comment.
BRUTUS. Let me tell you, Cassius, you yourself
　　Are much condemned to have an itching palm,　　10
　　To sell and mart your offices for gold
　　To undeservers.
CASSIUS.　　　　　　I an itching palm!
　　You know that you are Brutus that speaks this,
　　Or, by the gods, this speech were else your last.
BRUTUS. The name of Cassius honours this corruption,
　　And chastisement doth therefore hide his head.
CASSIUS. Chastisement!
BRUTUS. Remember March, the ides of March
　　remember!
　　Did not great Julius bleed for justice' sake?
　　What villain touched his body, that did stab,　　20
　　And not for justice? What, shall one of us,
　　That struck the foremost man of all this world
　　But for supporting robbers, shall we now
　　Contaminate our fingers with base bribes,
　　And sell the mighty space of our large honours
　　For so much trash as may be graspéd thus?
　　I had rather be a dog, and bay the moon,
　　Than such a Roman.
CASSIUS.　　　　　　Brutus, bay not me,
　　I'll not endure it: you forget yourself,
　　To hedge me in; I am a soldier, I,　　　　　　30
　　Older in practice, abler than yourself
　　To make conditions.
BRUTUS.　　　　　　Go to; you are not, Cassius.
CASSIUS. I am.
BRUTUS. I say you are not.
CASSIUS. Urge me no more, I shall forget myself;

Have mind upon your health; tempt me no farther.
BRUTUS. Away, slight man!
CASSIUS. Is't possible?
BRUTUS.　　　　　　Hear me, for I will speak.
　　Must I give way and room to your rash choler?
　　Shall I be frighted when a madman stares?　　40
CASSIUS. O ye gods, ye gods! must I endure all this?
BRUTUS. All this! ay, more: fret till your proud heart
　　break;
　　Go show your slaves how choleric you are,
　　And make your bondmen tremble. Must I budge?
　　Must I observe you? must I stand and crouch
　　Under your testy humour? By the gods,
　　You shall digest the venom of your spleen,
　　Though it do split you; for, from this day forth,
　　I'll use you for my mirth, yea, for my laughter,
　　When you are waspish.
CASSIUS.　　　　　　　Is it come to this?　　50
BRUTUS. You say you are a better soldier:
　　Let it appear so; make your vaunting true,
　　And it shall please me well: for mine own part,
　　I shall be glad to learn of noble men.
CASSIUS. You wrong me every way; you wrong me,
　　Brutus;
　　I said, an elder soldier, not a better:
　　Did I say, better?
BRUTUS.　　　　　If you did, I care not.
CASSIUS. When Cæsar lived, he durst not thus have
　　moved me.
BRUTUS. Peace, peace! you durst not so have tempted
　　him.
CASSIUS. I durst not?　　　　　　　　　　　　60
BRUTUS. No.
CASSIUS. What, durst not tempt him?
BRUTUS.　　　　　　　For your life you durst not.
CASSIUS. Do not presume too much upon my love,
　　I may do that I shall be sorry for.
BRUTUS. You have done that you should be sorry for.
　　There is no terror, Cassius, in your threats;
　　For I am armed so strong in honesty
　　That they pass by me as the idle wind
　　Which I respect not. I did send to you
　　For certain sums of gold, which you denied me:　　70
　　For I can raise no money by vile means:
　　By heaven, I had rather coin my heart,
　　And drop my blood for drachmas, than to wring
　　From the hard hands of peasants their vile trash
　　By any indirection. I did send
　　To you for gold to pay my legions,
　　Which you denied me: was that done like Cassius?
　　Should I have answered Caius Cassius so?
　　When Marcus Brutus grows so covetous,
　　To lock such rascal counters from his friends,　　80
　　Be ready, gods, with all your thunderbolts,
　　Dash him to pieces!
CASSIUS.　　　　　　I denied you not.
BRUTUS. You did.
CASSIUS.　　　　　I did not: he was but a fool
　　That brought my answer back. Brutus hath rived
　　my heart:
　　A friend should bear his friend's infirmities,
　　But Brutus makes mine greater than they are.
BRUTUS. I do not, till you practise them on me.
CASSIUS. You love me not.
BRUTUS.　　　　　　I do not like your faults.
CASSIUS. A friendly eye could never see such faults.

BRUTUS. A flatterer's would not, though they do
　appear　　　　　　　　　　　　　　　　　　90
　As huge as high Olympus.
CASSIUS. Come, Antony, and young Octavius, come,
　Revenge yourselves alone on Cassius,
　For Cassius is aweary of the world;
　Hated by one he loves; braved by his brother;
　Checked like a bondman; all his faults observed,
　Set in a note-book, learned and conned by rote,
　To cast into my teeth. O, I could weep
　My spirit from mine eyes! There is my dagger,
　And here my naked breast; within, a heart　　100
　Dearer than Pluto's mine, richer than gold:
　If that thou be'st a Roman, take it forth;
　I, that denied thee gold, will give my heart:
　Strike, as thou didst at Cæsar; for I know,
　When thou didst hate him worst, thou lovedst him
　　better
　Than ever thou lovedst Cassius.
BRUTUS.　　　　　　　　　Sheathe your dagger:
　Be angry when you will, it shall have scope;
　Do what you will, dishonour shall be humour.
　O Cassius, you are yokéd with a lamb,
　That carries anger as the flint bears fire,　　110
　Who, much enforcéd, shows a hasty spark
　And straight is cold again.
CASSIUS.　　　　　　　　　Hath Cassius lived
　To be but 'mirth' and 'laughter' to his Brutus,
　When grief and blood ill-tempered vexeth him?
BRUTUS. When I spoke that, I was ill-tempered too.
CASSIUS. Do you confess so much? Give me your hand.
BRUTUS. And my heart too.
CASSIUS.　　　　　　　　　O Brutus!
BRUTUS.　　　　　　　　　What's the matter?
CASSIUS. Have not you love enough to bear with me,
　When that rash humour which my mother gave me
　Makes me forgetful?
BRUTUS.　　　　　　Yes, Cassius, and from henceforth, 120
　When you are over-earnest with your Brutus,
　He'll think your mother chides, and leave you so.
A VOICE WITHOUT. Let me go in to see the generals;
　There is some grudge between 'em; 'tis not meet
　They be alone.
LUCILIUS [without]. You shall not come to them.
VOICE WITHOUT. Nothing but death shall stay me.

Enter a poet, followed by Lucilius, Titinius, and Lucius

CASSIUS. How now! what's the matter?
POET. For shame, you generals! what do you mean?
　Love and be friends, as two such men should be;
　For I have seen more years, I'm sure, than ye.　130
CASSIUS. Ha, ha! how vilely doth this cynic rhyme!
BRUTUS. Get you hence, sirrah; saucy fellow, hence!
CASSIUS. Bear with him, Brutus; 'tis his fashion.
BRUTUS. I'll know his humour when he knows his
　time:
　What should the wars do with these jigging fools?
　Companion, hence!
CASSIUS.　　　　　　Away, away, be-gone!
　　　　　　　　　　　　　　They drive him out
BRUTUS. Lucilius and Titinius, bid the commanders
　Prepare to lodge their companies to-night.
CASSIUS. And come yourselves, and bring Messala
　with you
　Immediately to us.　　*Lucilius and Titinius depart*

BRUTUS.　　　　　　　　Lucius, a bowl of wine!　140
　　　　　　　　　　　　　　　　Lucius goes
CASSIUS. I did not think you could have been so angry.
BRUTUS. O Cassius, I am sick of many griefs.
CASSIUS. Of your philosophy you make no use,
　If you give place to accidental evils.
BRUTUS. No man bears sorrow better: Portia is dead.
CASSIUS. Ha! Portia!
BRUTUS. She is dead.
CASSIUS. How scaped I killing when I crossed you so?
　O insupportable and touching loss!
　Upon what sickness?
BRUTUS.　　　　　　Impatient of my absence,　150
　And grief that young Octavius with Mark Antony
　Have made themselves so strong: for with her death
　That tidings came: with this she fell distract,
　And, her attendants absent, swallowed fire.
CASSIUS. And died so?
BRUTUS.　　　　　　Even so.
CASSIUS.　　　　　　　　O ye immortal gods!

Lucius brings wine and tapers

BRUTUS. Speak no more of her. Give me a bowl of
　wine.
　In this I bury all unkindness, Cassius.　　*Drinks*
CASSIUS. My heart is thirsty for that noble pledge.
　Fill, Lucius, till the wine o'erswell the cup;
　I cannot drink too much of Brutus' love.　　160
　　　　　　　　　　　　　Drinks; Lucius goes

Enter Titinius, with Messala

BRUTUS. Come in, Titinius! Welcome, good Messala.
　Now sit we close about this taper here,
　And call in question our necessities.
CASSIUS. Portia, art thou gone?
BRUTUS.　　　　　　　　No more, I pray you.
　Messala, I have here receivéd letters,
　That young Octavius and Mark Antony
　Come down upon us with a mighty power,
　Bending their expedition toward Philippi.
MESSALA. Myself have letters of the selfsame tenour.
BRUTUS. With what addition?　　　　　　170
MESSALA. That by proscription and bills of outlawry
　Octavius, Antony, and Lepidus
　Have put to death an hundred senators.
BRUTUS. Therein our letters do not well agree;
　Mine speak of seventy senators that died
　By their proscriptions, Cicero being one.
CASSIUS. Cicero one!
MESSALA.　　　　　　Cicero is dead,
　And by that order of proscription.
　Had you your letters from your wife, my lord?
BRUTUS. No, Messala.　　　　　　　　180
MESSALA. Nor nothing in your letters writ of her?
BRUTUS. Nothing, Messala.
MESSALA.　　　　　　That, methinks, is strange.
BRUTUS. Why ask you? hear you aught of her in yours?
MESSALA. No, my lord.
BRUTUS. Now, as you are a Roman, tell me true.
MESSALA. Then like a Roman bear the truth I tell:
　For certain she is dead, and by strange manner.
BRUTUS. Why, farewell, Portia. We must die, Messala:
　With meditating that she must die once
　I have the patience to endure it now.　　190
MESSALA. Even so great men great losses should
　endure.

CASSIUS. I have as much of this in art as you,
But yet my nature could bear it so.
BRUTUS. Well, to our work alive. What do you think
of marching to Philippi presently?
CASSIUS. I do not think it good.
BRUTUS.   Your reason?
CASSIUS.   This it is:
'Tis better that the enemy seek us:
So shall he waste his means, weary his soldiers,
Doing himself offence; whilst we lying still
Are full of rest, defence and nimbleness.   200
BRUTUS. Good reasons must of force give place to
better.
The people 'twixt Philippi and this ground
Do stand but in a forced affection,
For they have grudged us contribution:
The enemy, marching along by them,
By them shall make a fuller number up,
Come on refreshed, new-added and encouraged;
From which advantage shall we cut him off
If at Philippi we do face him there,
These people at our back.
CASSIUS.   Hear me, good brother. 210
BRUTUS. Under your pardon. You must note beside
That we have tried the utmost of our friends,
Our legions are brim-full, our cause is ripe:
The enemy increaseth every day;
We, at the height, are ready to decline.
There is a tide in the affairs of men
Which taken at the flood leads on to fortune;
Omitted, all the voyage of their life
Is bound in shallows and in miseries.
On such a full sea are we now afloat,   220
And we must take the current when it serves,
Or lose our ventures.
CASSIUS.   Then, with your will, go on;
We'll along ourselves and meet them at Philippi.
BRUTUS. The deep of night is crept upon our talk,
And nature must obey necessity;
Which we will niggard with a little rest.
There is no more to say?
CASSIUS.   No more. Good night:
Early to-morrow will we rise and hence.
BRUTUS. Lucius! [Lucius re-enters] My gown. Farewell,
good Messala.   Lucius goes
Good night, Titinius: noble, noble Cassius,   230
Good night, and good repose.
CASSIUS.   O my dear brother!
This was an ill beginning of the night:
Never come such division 'tween our souls!
Let it not, Brutus.
BRUTUS.   Everything is well.
CASSIUS. Good night, my lord.
BRUTUS.   Good night, good brother.
TITINIUS, MESSALA. Good night, Lord Brutus.
BRUTUS.   Farewell, every one.
                                                  They go

Re-enter Lucius, with the gown

Give me the gown. Where is thy instrument?
LUCIUS. Here in the tent.
BRUTUS.   What, thou speak'st drowsily?
Poor knave, I blame thee not; thou art o'erwatched.
Call Claudius and some other of my men;   240
I'll have them sleep on cushions in my tent.
LUCIUS. Varro and Claudius!

Varro and Claudius enter

VARRO. Calls my lord?
BRUTUS. I pray you, sirs, lie in my tent and sleep;
It may be I shall raise you by and by
On business to my brother Cassius.
VARRO. So please you, we will stand and watch your
pleasure.
BRUTUS. I will not have it so: lie down, good sirs;
It may be I shall otherwise bethink me.
Look, Lucius, here's the book I sought for so;   250
I put it in the pocket of my gown.
                              Varro and Claudius lie down
LUCIUS. I was sure your lordship did not give it me.
BRUTUS. Bear with me, good boy, I am much
forgetful.
Canst thou hold up thy heavy eyes awhile,
And touch thy instrument a strain or two?
LUCIUS. Ay, my lord, an't please you.
BRUTUS.   It dies, my boy:
I trouble thee too much, but thou art willing.
LUCIUS. It is my duty, sir.
BRUTUS. I should not urge thy duty past thy might;
I know young bloods look for a time of rest.   260
LUCIUS. I have slept, my lord, already.
BRUTUS. It was well done; and thou shalt sleep again;
I will not hold thee long: if I do live,
I will be good to thee.   *Music and a song*
This is a sleepy tune. O murd'rous slumber,
Layest thou thy leaden mace upon my boy,
That plays thee music? Gentle knave, good night;
I will not do thee so much wrong to wake thee:
If thou dost nod, thou break'st thy instrument;
I'll take it from thee; and, good boy, good night. 270
Let me see, let me see; is not the leaf turned down
Where I left reading? Here it is, I think.

Enter the Ghost of Cæsar

How ill this taper burns! Ha! who comes here?
I think it is the weakness of mine eyes
That shapes this monstrous apparition.
It comes upon me. Art thou any thing?
Art thou some god, some angel, or some devil,
That mak'st my blood cold, and my hair to stare?
Speak to me what thou art.
GHOST. Thy evil spirit, Brutus.
BRUTUS.   Why com'st thou?   280
GHOST. To tell thee thou shalt see me at Philippi.
BRUTUS. Well; then I shall see thee again?
GHOST. Ay, at Philippi.
BRUTUS. Why, I will see thee at Philippi then.
                              The Ghost disappears
Now I have taken heart thou vanishest.
Ill spirit, I would hold more talk with thee.
Boy, Lucius! Varro! Claudius! Sirs, awake!
Claudius!
LUCIUS. The strings, my lord, are false.
BRUTUS. He thinks he still is at his instrument.   290
Lucius, awake!
LUCIUS. My lord?
BRUTUS. Didst thou dream, Lucius, that thou so criedst
out?
LUCIUS. My lord, I do not know that I did cry.
BRUTUS. Yes, that thou didst: didst thou see any thing?
LUCIUS. Nothing, my lord.

BRUTUS. Sleep again, Lucius. Sirrah Claudius!
　[to Varro] Fellow thou, awake!
VARRO. My lord?
CLAUDIUS. My lord?   300
BRUTUS. Why did you so cry out, sirs, in your sleep?
VARRO, CLAUDIUS. Did we, my lord?
BRUTUS.　　　　　　　　　Ay: saw you any thing?
VARRO. No, my lord, I saw nothing.
CLAUDIUS.　　　　　　　　　　　　　Nor I, my lord.
BRUTUS. Go and commend me to my brother Cassius;
　Bid him set on his powers betimes before,
　And we will follow.
VARRO, CLAUDIUS.　　　　　It shall be done, my lord.
　　　　　　　　　　　　　　　　　　　　　　　　　They go

ACT 5
Scene 1: The plains of Philippi

Enter Octavius, Antony, and their army

OCTAVIUS. Now, Antony, our hopes are answeréd:
　You said the enemy would not come down,
　But keep the hills and upper regions:
　It proves not so: their battles are at hand;
　They mean to warn us at Philippi here,
　Answering before we do demand of them.
ANTONY. Tut, I am in their bosoms, and I know
　Wherefore they do it: they could be content
　To visit other places; and come down
　With fearful bravery, thinking by this face   10
　To fasten in our thoughts that they have courage;
　But 'tis not so.

A messenger comes up

MESSENGER.　　　Prepare you, generals:
　The enemy comes on in gallant show;
　Their bloody sign of battle is hung out,
　And something to be done immediately.
ANTONY. Octavius, lead your battle softly on,
　Upon the left hand of the even field.
OCTAVIUS. Upon the right hand I; keep thou the left.
ANTONY. Why do you cross me in this exigent?
OCTAVIUS. I do not cross you; but I will do so.   20

Drum. Enter Brutus, Cassius, and their army; Lucilius,
Titinius, Messala, and others

BRUTUS. They stand, and would have parley.
CASSIUS. Stand fast, Titinius: we must out and talk.
OCTAVIUS. Mark Antony, shall we give sign of battle?
ANTONY. No, Cæsar, we will answer on their charge.
　Make forth; the generals would have some words.
OCTAVIUS. Stir not until the signal.
BRUTUS. Words before blows: is it so, countrymen?
OCTAVIUS. Not that we love words better, as you do.
BRUTUS. Good words are better than bad strokes,
　Octavius.
ANTONY. In your bad strokes, Brutus, you give good
　words: 30
　Witness the hole you made in Cæsar's heart,
　Crying 'Long live! hail, Cæsar!
CASSIUS.　　　　　　　　　　　　Antony,
　The posture of your blows are yet unknown;
　But for your words, they rob the Hybla bees,
　And leave them honeyless.
ANTONY.　　　　　　　　　Not stingless too?
BRUTUS. O, yes, and soundless too;
　For you have stol'n their buzzing, Antony,

And very wisely threat before you sting.
ANTONY. Villains, you did not so, when your vile
　daggers
　Hacked one another in the sides of Cæsar: 40
　You showed your teeth like apes, and fawned like
　hounds,
　And bowed like bondmen, kissing Cæsar's feet;
　Whilst damnéd Casca, like a cur, behind
　Struck Cæsar on the neck. O you flatterers!
CASSIUS. Flatterers! Now, Brutus, thank yourself:
　This tongue had not offended so to-day,
　If Cassius might have ruled.
OCTAVIUS. Come, come, the cause: if arguing make us
　sweat,
　The proof of it will turn to redder drops.
　Look;   50
　I draw my sword against conspirators;
　When think you that the sword goes up again?
　Never, till Cæsar's three and thirty wounds
　Be well avenged, or till another Cæsar
　Have added slaughter to the sword of traitors.
BRUTUS. Cæsar, thou canst not die by traitors' hands,
　Unless thou bring'st them with thee.
OCTAVIUS.　　　　　　　　　　　　So I hope;
　I was not born to die on Brutus' sword.
BRUTUS. O, if thou wert the noblest of thy strain,
　Young man, thou couldst not die more honourable.   60
CASSIUS. A peevish schoolboy, worthless of such
　honour,
　Joined with a masker and a reveller!
ANTONY. Old Cassius still!
OCTAVIUS.　　　　　　　　　Come, Antony; away!
　Defiance, traitors, hurl we in your teeth;
　If you dare fight to-day, come to the field:
　If not, when you have stomachs.
　　　　　　　　　　　　Octavius, Antony, and their
　　　　　　　　　　　　　　army march away
CASSIUS. Why, now, blow wind, swell billow and
　swim bark!
　The storm is up, and all is on the hazard.
BRUTUS. Ho, Lucilius! hark, a word with you.
LUCILIUS [standing forth].　　My lord?　They talk apart
CASSIUS. Messala!
MESSALA. [standing forth]. What says my general?
CASSIUS.　　　　　　　　　　　　　　　　Messala,   70
　This is my birth-day; as this very day
　Was Cassius born. Give me thy hand, Messala:
　Be thou my witness that, against my will,
　(As Pompey was) am I compelled to set
　Upon one battle all our liberties.
　You know that I held Epicurus strong,
　And his opinion: now I change my mind,
　And partly credit things that do presage.
　Coming from Sardis, on our former ensign
　Two mighty eagles fell, and there they perched,   80
　Gorging and feeding from our soldiers' hands;
　Who to Philippi here consorted us:
　This morning are they fled away and gone,
　And in their steads do ravens, crows, and kites
　Fly o'er our heads and downward look on us,
　As we were sickly prey: their shadows seem
　A canopy most fatal, under which
　Our army lies, ready to give up the ghost.
MESSALA. Believe not so.
CASSIUS.　　　　　　　　　I but believe it partly,
　For I am fresh of spirit and resolved   90

To meet all perils very constantly.
BRUTUS. Even so, Lucilius.
CASSIUS.   Now, most noble Brutus,
The gods to-day stand friendly, that we may,
Lovers in peace, lead on our days to age!
But, since the affairs of men rest still incertain,
Let's reason with the worst that may befall.
If we do lose this battle, then is this
The very last time we shall speak together:
What are you then determinèd to do?
BRUTUS. Even by the rule of that philosophy   100
By which I did blame Cato for the death
Which he did give himself, I know not how
But I do find it cowardly and vile,
For fear of what might fall, so to prevent
The time of life; arming myself with patience
To stay the providence of some high powers
That govern us below.
CASSIUS.   Then, if we lose this battle,
You are contented to be led in triumph
Thorough the streets of Rome?
BRUTUS. No, Cassius, no! think not, thou noble
    Roman,   110
That ever Brutus will go bound to Rome;
He bears too great a mind. But this same day
Must end that work the ides of March begun;
And whether we shall meet again I know not.
Therefore our everlasting farewell take.
For ever, and for ever, farewell, Cassius!
If we do meet again, why, we shall smile;
If not, why then this parting was well made.
CASSIUS. For ever, and for ever farewell, Brutus!
If we do meet again, we'll smile indeed;   120
If not, 'tis true this parting was well made.
BRUTUS. Why then, lead on. O, that a man might
    know
The end of this day's business ere it come!
But it sufficeth that the day will end,
And then the end is known. Come, ho! away!
                                         They go

Scene 2

The noise of battle is heard. Brutus enters with Messala

BRUTUS. Ride, ride, Messala, ride, and give these bills
Unto the legions on the other side:
Let them set on at once; for I perceive
But cold demeanour in Octavius' wing,
And sudden push gives them the overthrow.
Ride, ride, Messala: let them all come down.
                                         They go

Scene 3

Alarums. Enter Cassius and after him Titinius

CASSIUS. O, look, Titinius, look, the villains fly!
Myself have to mine own turned enemy:
This ensign here of mine was turning back;
I slew the coward, and did take it from him.
TITINIUS. O Cassius, Brutus gave the word too early;
Who, having some advantage on Octavius,
Took it too eagerly: his soldiers fell to spoil,
Whilst we by Antony are all enclosed.

Pindarus enters

PINDARUS. Fly further off, my lord, fly further off;

Mark Antony is in your tents, my lord: 10
Fly, therefore, noble Cassius, fly far off.
CASSIUS. This hill is far enough. Look, look, Titinius;
Are those my tents where I perceive the fire?
TITINIUS. They are, my lord.
CASSIUS.   Titinius, if thou lovest me,
Mount thou my horse and hide thy spurs in him,
Till he have brought thee up to yonder troops
And here again; that I may rest assured
Whether yond troops are friend or enemy.
TITINIUS. I will be here again, even with a thought.
                                         He goes
CASSIUS. Go, Pindarus, get higher on that hill;   20
My sight was ever thick; regard Titinius,
And tell me what thou not'st about the field.
                                 Pindarus ascends
This day I breathèd first! time is come round,
And where I did begin, there shall I end;
My life is run his compass. Sirrah, what news?
PINDARUS [*above*]. O my lord!
CASSIUS. What news?
PINDARUS [*above*]. Titinius is enclosèd round about
With horsemen that make to him on the spur;
Yet he spurs on. Now they are almost on him.   30
Now, Titinius! Now some light. O, he lights too.
He's ta'en. [*a shout*] And, hark! they shout for joy.
CASSIUS. Come down, behold no more.
O, coward that I am, to live so long,
To see my best friend ta'en before my face!

Pindarus descends

Come hither, sirrah:
In Parthia did I take thee prisoner;
And then I swore thee, saving of thy life,
That whatsoever I did bid thee do,
Thou shouldst attempt it. Come now, keep thine
    oath!   40
Now be a freeman, and with this good sword
That ran through Cæsar's bowels search this bosom.
Stand not to answer: here, take thou the hilts,
And when my face is covered, as 'tis now,
Guide thou the sword. [*Pindarus thrusts him through*]
    Cæsar, thou art revenged,
Even with the sword that killed thee.   *Dies*
PINDARUS. So, I am free, yet would not so have been,
Durst I have done my will. O Cassius!
Far from this country Pindarus shall run,
Where never Roman shall take note of him.   50
                                         He goes

Titinius returns with Messala

MESSALA. It is but change, Titinius; for Octavius
Is overthrown by noble Brutus' power,
As Cassius' legions are by Antony.
TITINIUS. These tidings will well comfort Cassius.
MESSALA. Where did you leave him?
TITINIUS.   All disconsolate,
With Pindarus his bondman, on this hill.
MESSALA. Is not that he that lies upon the ground?
TITINIUS. He lies not like the living. O my heart!
MESSALA. Is not that he?
TITINIUS.   No, this was he, Messala,
But Cassius is no more. O setting sun,   60
As in thy red rays thou dost sink to night,
So in his red blood Cassius' day is set,
The sun of Rome is set! Our day is gone;

Clouds, dews and dangers come; our deeds are done!
Mistrust of my success hath done this deed.
MESSALA. Mistrust of good success hath done this deed.
O hateful error, melancholy's child,
Why dost thou show to the apt thoughts of men
The things that are not? O error, soon conceived,
Thou never com'st unto a happy birth,   70
But kill'st the mother that engend'red thee!
TITINIUS. What, Pindarus! where art thou, Pindarus?
MESSALA. Seek him, Titinius, whilst I go to meet
The noble Brutus, thrusting this report
Into his ears: I may say 'thrusting' it,
For piercing steel and darts envenoméd
Shall be as welcome to the ears of Brutus
As tiding of this sight.
TITINIUS.   Hie you, Messala,
And I will seek for Pindarus the while.
                                        Messala goes
Why didst thou send me forth, brave Cassius?   80
Did I not meet thy friends? and did not they
Put on my brows this wreath of victory,
And bid me give it thee? Didst thou not hear their
        shouts?
Alas, thou hast misconstrued everything!
But, hold thee, take this garland on thy brow;
Thy Brutus bid me give it thee, and I
Will do his bidding. Brutus, come apace,
And see how I regarded Caius Cassius.
By your leave, gods: this is a Roman's part:
Come, Cassius' sword, and find Titinius' heart.   90
                                        Kills himself

*The noise of battle dies away; then re-enter Messala, with
Brutus, young Cato, Lucilius, Labeo, Flavius, and others*

BRUTUS. Where, where, Messala, doth his body lie?
MESSALA. Lo, yonder, and Titinius mourning it.
BRUTUS. Titinius' face is upward.
CATO.   He is slain.
BRUTUS. O Julius Cæsar, thou art mighty yet!
Thy spirit walks abroad, and turns our swords
In our own proper entrails.
CATO.   Brave Titinius!
Look, whe'r he have not crowned dead Cassius!
BRUTUS. Are yet two Romans living such as these?
The last of all the Romans, fare thee well!
It is impossible that ever Rome   100
Should breed thy fellow. Friends, I owe mo tears
To this dead man than you shall see me pay.
I shall find time, Cassius, I shall find time.
Come therefore, and to Thasos send his body:
His funerals shall not be in our camp,
Lest it discomfort us. Lucilius, come,
And come, young Cato: let us to the field.
Labeo and Flavius, set our battles on.
'Tis three o'clock; and, Romans, yet ere night
We shall try fortune in a second fight.   110
        They pass on, soldiers bearing off the bodies

*Scene 4: The battle resumes. Presently re-enter Brutus,
Messala, young Cato, Lucilius, and their army, yielding
ground to the opposing force*

BRUTUS. Yet, countrymen! O, yet hold up your heads!
                *He charges, followed out by
                        Messala, and others*
CATO. What bastard doth not? Who will go with me?

I will proclaim my name about the field.
I am the son of Marcus Cato, ho!
A foe to tyrants, and my country's friend;
I am the son of Marcus Cato, ho!
LUCILIUS. And I am Brutus, Marcus Brutus, I;
Brutus, my country's friend; know me for Brutus!
                        *They charge in turn;
                                young Cato is slain*
O young and noble Cato, art thou down?
Why, now thou diest as bravely as Titinius,   10
And mayst be honoured, being Cato's son.
1 SOLDIER. Yield, or thou diest.
LUCILIUS.   Only I yield to die:
There is so much that thou wilt kill me straight:
Kill Brutus, and be honoured in his death.
1 SOLDIER. We must not: a noble prisoner.
2 SOLDIER. Room, ho! Tell Antony, Brutus is ta'en.
1 SOLDIER. I'll tell the news. Here comes the general.

Enter Antony

Brutus is ta'en, Brutus is ta'en, my lord.
ANTONY. Where is he?
LUCILIUS. Safe, Antony; Brutus is safe enough: 20
I dare assure thee that no enemy
Shall ever take alive the noble Brutus:
The gods defend him from so great a shame!
When you do find him, or alive or dead,
He will be found like Brutus, like himself.
ANTONY. This is not Brutus, friend, but, I assure you,
A prize no less in worth: keep this man safe,
Give him all kindness: I had rather have
Such men my friends than enemies. Go on,
And see whe'r Brutus be alive or dead,   30
And bring us word unto Octavius' tent
How everything is chanced.   *They go*

Scene 5

*Enter Brutus, Dardanius, Clitus, Strato,
and Volumnius*

BRUTUS. Come, poor remains of friends, rest on this
        rock.
CLITUS. Statilius showed the torch-light, but, my lord,
He came not back: he is or ta'en or slain.
BRUTUS. Sit thee down, Clitus: slaying is the word;
It is a deed in fashion. Hark thee, Clitus.   *Whispers*
CLITUS. What, I, my lord? No, not for all the world.
BRUTUS. Peace then, no words.
CLITUS.   I'll rather kill myself.
BRUTUS. Hark thee, Dardanius.   *Whispers*
DARDANIUS.   Shall I do such a deed?
CLITUS. O Dardanius!
DARDANIUS. O Clitus!   10
CLITUS. What ill request did Brutus make to thee?
DARDANIUS. To kill him, Clitus. Look, he meditates.
CLITUS. Now is that noble vessel full of grief,
That it runs over even at his eyes.
BRUTUS. Come hither, good Volumnius; list a word.
VOLUMNIUS. What says my lord?
BRUTUS.   Why, this, Volumnius:
The ghost of Cæsar hath appeared to me
Two several times by night: at Sardis once,
And this last night here in Philippi fields:
I know my hour is come.
VOLUMNIUS.   Not so, my lord.   20
BRUTUS. Nay, I am sure it is, Volumnius.

Thou seest the world, Volumnius, how it goes;
Our enemies have beat us to the pit:
                              Fighting heard at a distance
It is more worthy to leap in ourselves
Than tarry till they push us. Good Volumnius,
Thou know'st that we two went to school together:
Even for that our love of old, I prithee,
Hold thou my sword-hilts, whilst I run on it.
VOLUMNIUS. That's not an office for a friend my lord.
                              The sound draws near
CLITUS. Fly, fly, my lord, there is no tarrying here.   30
BRUTUS. Farewell to you; and you; and you
          Volumnius.
     Strato, thou hast been all this while asleep;
     Farewell to thee too, Strato. Countrymen,
     My heart doth joy that yet in all my life
     I found no man but he was true to me.
     I shall have glory by this losing day,
     More than Octavius and Mark Antony
     By this vile conquest shall attain unto.
     So, fare you well at once; for Brutus' tongue
     Hath almost ended his life's history: 40
     Night hangs upon mine eyes; my bones would rest,
     That have but laboured to attain this hour.
                    Loud alarum and cries of 'Fly, fly, fly!' *heard*
CLITUS. Fly, my lord, fly.
BRUTUS.   Hence! I will follow
                    Clitus, Dardanius, and Volumnius go
     I prithee, Strato, stay thou by thy lord:
     Thou art a fellow of a good respect;
     Thy life hath had some smatch of honour in it:
     Hold then my sword, and turn away thy face,
     While I do run upon it. Wilt thou, Strato?
STRATO. Give me your hand first: fare you well, my
          lord.
BRUTUS. Farewell, good Strato. [*runs on his sword*]
          Cæsar, now be still: 50
     I killed not thee with half so good a will.   *Dies*

Enter the army of Antony, pursuing the remnant of
Brutus' forces, and later sounding the retreat. Then
enter Octavius and Antony, with Messala, Lucilius,
as prisoners

OCTAVIUS. What man is that?
MESSALA. My master's man. Strato, where is thy
          master?
STRATO. Free from the bondage you are in, Messala:
     The conquerors can but make a fire of him;
     For Brutus only overcame himself,
     And no man else hath honour by his death.
LUCILIUS. So Brutus should be found. I thank thee,
          Brutus,
     That thou hast proved Lucilius' saying true.
OCTAVIUS. All that served Brutus, I will entertain
          them.   60
     Fellow, wilt thou bestow thy time with me?
STRATO. Ay, if Messala will prefer me to you.
OCTAVIUS. Do so, good Messala.
MESSALA. How died my master, Strato?
STRATO. I held the sword, and he did run on it.
MESSALA. Octavius, then take him to follow thee,
     That did the latest service to my master.
ANTONY. This was the noblest Roman of them all:
     All the conspirators save only he
     Did that they did in envy of great Cæsar;   70
     He only, in a general honest thought
     And common good to all, made one of them.
     His life was gentle, and the elements
     So mixed in him that Nature might stand up
     And say to all the world 'This was a man!'
OCTAVIUS. According to his virtue let us use him,
     With all respect and rites of burial.
     Within my tent his bones to-night shall lie,
     Most like a soldier, ordered honourably.
     So call the field to rest, and let's away,   80
     To part the glories of this happy day.
                              They march on

Macbeth

The scene: Scotland and (in 4.3) England

CHARACTERS IN THE PLAY

DUNCAN, *King of Scotland*
MALCOLM } *his sons*
DONALBAIN
MACBETH, *at first a general, later King of Scotland*
BANQUO, *a general*
MACDUFF
LENNOX
ROSS
MENTEITH } *noblemen of Scotland*
ANGUS
CAITHNESS
FLEANCE, *son to Banquo*
SIWARD, *Earl of Northumberland, general of the English forces*
YOUNG SIWARD, *his son*
SETON, *armour-bearer to Macbeth*

A Boy, son to Macduff
A Captain
A Porter
An Old Man
An English Doctor
A Scotch Doctor
Three Murderers
LADY MACBETH
LADY MACDUFF
A Gentlewoman attending on Lady Macbeth
The Weird Sisters
HECATE
Apparitions
Lords, Gentlemen, Officers, Soldiers, Attendants, and Messengers

Macbeth

ACT 1
Scene 1

Thunder and lightning. Enter three Witches

1 WITCH. When shall we three meet again
   In thunder, lightning, or in rain?
2 WITCH. When the hurlyburly's done,
   When the battle's lost and won.
3 WITCH. That will be ere the set of sun.
1 WITCH. Where the place?
2 WITCH.   Upon the heath.
3 WITCH. There to meet with Macbeth.
1 WITCH. I come, Graymalkin!
2 WITCH. Paddock calls.
3 WITCH. Anon!   10
ALL. Fair is foul, and foul is fair:
   Hover through the fog and filthy air.   *They go*

Scene 2: *A camp*

*Alarum. Enter King Duncan, Malcolm, Donalbain,
Lennox, with attendants, meeting a bleeding Captain*

DUNCAN. What bloody man is that? He can report,
   As seemeth by his plight, of the revolt
   The newest state.
MALCOLM.   This is the sergeant,
   Who like a good and hardy soldier fought
   'Gainst my captivity ... Hail, brave friend!
   Say to the king the knowledge of the broil
   As thou didst leave it.
CAPTAIN   Doubtful it stood,
   As two spent swimmers that do cling together
   And choke their art ... The merciless Macdonwald
   (Worthy to be a rebel, for to that   10
   The multiplying villainies of nature
   Do swarm upon him) from the Western Isles
   Of kerns and gallowglasses is supplied,
   And Fortune, on his damnéd quarrel smiling,
   Showed like a rebel's whore: but all's too weak:
   For brave Macbeth (well he deserves that name)
   Disdaining fortune, with his brandished steel,
   Which smoked with bloody execution,
   Like Valour's minion carvéd out his passage,
   Till he faced the slave;   20
   Which ne'er shook hands, nor bade farewell to him,
   Till he unseamed him from the nave to th' chops,
   And fixed his head upon our battlements.
DUNCAN. O, valiant cousin! worthy gentleman!
CAPTAIN. As whence the sun 'gins his reflection
   Shipwracking storms and direful thunders break;
   So from that spring whence comfort seemed to
     come
   Discomfort swells: mark, king of Scotland, mark!
   No sooner justice had, with valour armed,
   Compelled these skipping kerns to trust their heels, 30
   But the Norweyan lord, surveying vantage,
   With furbished arms and new supplies of men,
   Began a fresh assault.
DUNCAN.   Dismayed not this
   Our captains, Macbeth and Banquo?
CAPTAIN.   Yes;
   As sparrows, eagles; or the hare, the lion.
   If I say sooth, I must report they were
   As cannons overcharged with double cracks;
   So they
   Doubly redoubled strokes upon the foe:
   Except they meant to bathe in reeking wounds,   40
   Or memorize another Golgotha,
   I cannot tell:
   But I am faint, my gashes cry for help.
DUNCAN. So well thy words become thee as thy
     wounds,
   They smack of honour both: Go get him surgeons.
                          Attendants help him thence
   Who comes here?

Enter Ross and Angus

MALCOLM.   The worthy thane of Ross.
LENNOX. What a haste looks through his eyes! So
   should he look
   That seems to speak things strange.
ROSS.   God save the king!
DUNCAN. Whence cam'st thou, worthy thane?
ROSS.   From Fife, great king,
   Where the Norweyan banners flout the sky,   50
   And fan our people cold.
   Norway himself, with terrible numbers,
   Assisted by that most disloyal traitor
   The thane of Cawdor, began a dismal conflict,
   Till that Bellona's bridegroom, lapped in proof,
   Confronted him with self-comparisons,
   Point against point, rebellious arm 'gainst arm,
   Curbing his lavish spirit: and, to conclude,
   The victory fell on us.
DUNCAN.   Great happiness!
ROSS. That now   60
   Sweno, the Norways' king, craves composition;
   Nor would we deign him burial of his men
   Till he disburséd, at Saint Colme's Inch,
   Ten thousand dollars to our general use.
DUNCAN. No more that thane of Cawdor shall deceive
   Our bosom interest: go pronounce his present death,
   And with his former title greet Macbeth.
ROSS. I'll see it done.
DUNCAN. What he hath lost, noble Macbeth hath won.
                                          They go

Scene 3: *A barren heath*

Thunder. Enter the three Witches

1 WITCH. Where hast thou been, sister?
2 WITCH. Killing swine.
3 WITCH. Sister, where thou?
1 WITCH. A sailor's wife had chestnuts in her lap,
   And munched, and munched, and munched: 'Give
     me', quoth I.
   'Aroint thee, witch!' the rump-fed ronyon cries.
   Her husband's to Aleppo gone, master o'th' Tiger:
   But in a sieve I'll thither sail,
   And, like a rat without a tail,

I'll do, I'll do, and I'll do.   10
2 WITCH. I'll give thee a wind.
1 WITCH. Th'art kind.
3 WITCH. And I another.
1 WITCH. I myself have all the other,
  And the very ports they blow,
  All the quarters that they know
  I'th' shipman's card.
  I will drain him dry as hay:
  Sleep shall, neither night nor day
  Hang upon his pent-house lid;   20
  He shall live a man forbid:
  Weary sev'nights nine times nine
  Shall he dwindle, peak, and pine:
  Though his bark cannot be lost,
  Yet it shall be tempest-tost.
  Look what I have.
2 WITCH. Show me, show me.
1 WITCH. Here I have a pilot's thumb,
  Wrecked as homeward he did come   *Drum within*
3 WITCH. A drum, a drum!   30
  Macbeth doth come.
ALL. The Weïrd Sisters, hand in hand,
  Posters of the sea and land,
  Thus do go, about, about,
  Thrice to thine, and thrice to mine,
  And thrice again, to make up nine.
  Peace! the charm's wound up.

Enter Macbeth and Banquo

MACBETH. So foul and fair a day I have not seen.
BANQUO. How far is't called to Forres? What are these,
  So withered, and so wild in their attire,   40
  That look not like th'inhabitants o'th'earth,
  And yet are on't? Live you? or are you aught
  That man may question? You seem to understand
    me,
  By each at once her choppy finger laying
  Upon her skinny lips: you should be women,
  And yet your beards forbid me to interpret
  That you are so.
MACBETH.   Speak, if you can: what are you?
1 WITCH. All hail, Macbeth! hail to thee, thane of
  Glamis!
2 WITCH. All hail, Macbeth! hail to thee, thane of
  Cawdor!
3 WITCH. All hail, Macbeth! that shalt be king
  hereafter.   50
BANQUO. Good sir, why do you start, and seem to
  fear
  Things that do sound so fair? I'th' name of truth,
  Are ye fantastical, or that indeed
  Which outwardly ye show? My noble partner
  You greet with present grace and great prediction
  Of noble having and of royal hope,
  That he seems rapt withal: to me you speak not.
  If you can look into the seeds of time,
  And say which grain will grow and which will not,
  Speak then to me, who neither beg nor fear   60
  Your favours nor your hate.
1 WITCH. Hail!
2 WITCH. Hail!
3 WITCH. Hail!
1 WITCH. Lesser than Macbeth, and greater.
2 WITCH. Not so happy, yet much happier.

3 WITCH. Thou shalt get kings, though thou be none:
  So all hail, Macbeth and Banquo!
1 WITCH. Banquo and Macbeth, all hail!
MACBETH. Stay, you imperfect speakers, tell me more: 70
  By Sinel's death I know I am thane of Glamis,
  But how of Cawdor? the thane of Cawdor lives
  A prosperous gentleman; and to be king
  Stands not within the prospect of belief,
  No more than to be Cawdor. Say from whence
  You owe this strange intelligence, or why
  Upon this blasted heath you stop our way
  With such prophetic greeting. Speak, I charge you.
                                        They disappear
BANQUO. The earth hath bubbles, as the water has,
  And these are of them: whither are they vanished? 80
MACBETH. Into the air; and what seemed corporal,
    melted,
  As breath into the wind. Would they had stayed!
BANQUO. Were such things here as we do speak about?
  Or have we eaten on the insane root
  That takes the reason prisoner?
MACBETH. Your children shall be kings.
BANQUO.   You shall be king.
MACBETH. And thane of Cawdor too: went it not so?
BANQUO. To th' selfsame tune and words. Who's here?

Enter Ross and Angus

ROSS. The king hath happily received, Macbeth,
  The news of thy success: and when he reads   90
  Thy personal venture in the rebels' fight,
  His wonders and his praises do contend
  Which should be thine or his: silenced with that,
  In viewing o'er the rest o'th' self-same day,
  He finds thee in the stout Norweyan ranks,
  Nothing afeard of what thyself didst make
  Strange images of death. As thick as hail
  Came post with post, and every one did bear
  Thy praises in his kingdom's great defence,
  And poured them down before him.
ANGUS.   We are sent 100
  To give thee from our royal master thanks,
  Only to herald thee into his sight,
  Not pay thee.
ROSS. And for an earnest of a greater honour,
  He bade me, from him, call thee thane of Cawdor:
  In which addition, hail, most worthy thane,
  For it is thine.
BANQUO.   What, can the devil speak true?
MACBETH. The thane of Cawdor lives: why do you
    dress me
  In borrowed robes?
ANGUS.   Who was the thane lives yet,
  But under heavy judgment bears that life   110
  Which he deserves to lose. Whether he was
    combined
  With those of Norway, or did line the rebel
  With hidden help and vantage, or that with both
  He laboured in his country's wreck, I know not;
  But treasons capital, confessed, and proved,
  Have overthrown him.
MACBETH. [*aside*].   Glamis, and thane of
    Cawdor:
  The greatest is behind.—[*aloud*] Thanks for your
    pains—
  [*aside to Banquo*] Do you not hope your children shall
    be kings,

When those that gave the thane of Cawdor to me
Promised no less to them?
BANQUO.   That, trusted home,   120
Might yet enkindle you unto the crown,
Besides the thane of Cawdor. But 'tis strange:
And oftentimes, to win us to our harm,
The instruments of darkness tell us truths,
Win us with honest trifles, to betray's
In deepest consequence.
Cousins, a word, I pray you.
MACBETH [aside].   Two truths are told,
As happy prologues to the swelling act
Of the imperial theme. [aloud] I thank you, gentle-
men.
[aside] This supernatural soliciting   130
Cannot be ill; cannot be good. If ill,
Why hath it given me earnest of success,
Commencing in a truth? I am thane of Cawdor.
If good, why do I yield to that suggestion
Whose horrid image doth unfix my hair,
And make my seated heart knock at my ribs,
Against the use of nature? Present fears
Are less than horrible imaginings:
My thought, whose murder yet is but fantastical,
Shales so my single state of man that function   140
Is smothered in surmise, and nothing is
But what is not.
BANQUO.   Look how our partner's rapt.
MACBETH [aside]. If chance will have me king, why,
chance may crown me,
Without my stir.
BANQUO.   New honours come upon him,
Like our strange garments, cleave not to their mould
But with the aid of use.
MACBETH [aside].   Come what come may,
Time and the hour runs through the roughest day.
BANQUO. Worthy Macbeth, we stay upon your
leisure.
MACBETH. Give me your favour: my dull brain was
wrought
With things forgotten. Kind gentlemen, your pains   150
Are registered where every day I turn
The leaf to read them.... Let us toward the king.
                                    Aside to Banquo
Think upon what hath chanced; and at more time,
The interim having weighed it, let us speak
Our free hearts each to other.
BANQUO.   Very gladly.
MACBETH. Till then, enough.... Come, friends.
                                    They go

Scene 4: Forres. The Palace

Flourish. Enter King Duncan, Malcolm, Donalbain,
Lennox, and Attendants

DUNCAN. Is execution done on Cawdor? Are not
Those in commission yet returned?
MALCOLM.   My liege,
They are not yet come back. But I have spoke
With one that saw him die: who did report
That very frankly he confessed his treasons,
Implored your highness' pardon, and set forth
A deep repentance: nothing in his life
Became him like the leaving it; he died
As one that had been studied in his death,
To throw away the dearest thing he owed   10

As 'twere a careless trifle.
DUNCAN.   There's no art
To find the mind's construction in the face:
He was a gentleman on whom I built
An absolute trust.

Enter Macbeth, Banquo, Ross, and Angus

                              O worthiest cousin!
The sin of my ingratitude even now
Was heavy on me. Thou art so far before,
That swiftest wing of recompense is slow
To overtake thee. Would thou hadst less deserved,
That the proportion both of thanks and payment
Might have been mine! only I have left to say,   20
More is thy due than more than all can pay.
MACBETH. The service and the loyalty I owe,
In doing it, pays itself. Your highness' part
Is to receive our duties: and our duties
Are to your throne and state children and servants;
Which do but what they should, by doing every
thing
Safe toward your love and honour.
DUNCAN.   Welcome hither:
I have begun to plant thee, and will labour
To make thee full of growing. Noble Banquo,
That hast no less deserved, nor must be known   30
No less to have done so: let me infold thee,
And hold thee to my heart.
BANQUO.   There if I grow,
The harvest is your own.
DUNCAN.   My plenteous joys,
Wanton in fulness, seek to hide themselves
In drops of sorrow.... Sons, kinsmen, thanes,
And you whose places are the nearest, know,
We will establish our estate upon
Our eldest, Malcolm, whom we name hereafter
The Prince of Cumberland: which honour must
Not unaccompanied invest him only,   40
But signs of nobleness, like stars, shall shine
On all deservers.... From hence to Inverness,
And bind us further to you.
MACBETH. The rest is labour, which is not used for
you:
I'll be myself the harbinger, and make joyful
The hearing of my wife with your approach;
So humbly take my leave.
DUNCAN.   My worthy Cawdor!
MACBETH. The Prince of Cumberland! that is a step
On which I must fall down, or else o'er-leap,
For in my way it lies. Stars, hide your fires!   50
Let not light see my black and deep desires:
The eye wink at the hand; yet let that be
Which the eye fears, when it is done, to see.
                                    He goes
DUNCAN. True, worthy Banquo; he is full so valiant,
And in his commendations I am fed;
It is a banquet to me. Let's after him,
Whose care is gone before to bid us welcome:
It is a peerless kinsman.   Flourish. They go

Scene 5: Inverness. Macbeth's castle

Enter Macbeth's wife alone, with a letter

LADY M. [reads] 'They met me in the day of success;
and I have learned by the perfect'st report, they have
more in them than mortal knowledge. When I

burned in desire to question them further, they
made themselves air, into which they vanished.
Whiles I stood rapt in the wonder of it, came
missives from the king, who all-hailed me, 'Thane
of Cawdor', by which title, before, these Weïrd
Sisters saluted me, and referred me to the coming
on of time, with 'Hail, king that shalt be!' This 10
have I thought good to deliver thee (my dearest
partner of greatness) that thou mightst not lose the
dues of rejoicing, by being ignorant of what great-
ness is promised thee. Lay it to thy heart, and fare-
well.'
  Glamis thou art, and Cawdor, and shalt be
What thou art promised: yet do I fear thy nature,
It is too full o'th' milk of human kindness
To catch the nearest way: thou wouldst be great,
Art not without ambition, but without   20
The illness should attend it: what thou wouldst
  highly,
That wouldst thou holily; wouldst not play false,
And yet wouldst wrongly win: thou'ldst have, great
  Glamis,
That which cries 'Thus thou must do', if thou
  have it,
And that which rather thou dost fear to do
Than wishest should be undone. Hie thee hither,
That I may pour my spirits in thine ear,
And chastise with the valour of my tongue
All that impedes thee from the golden round,
Which fate and metaphysical aid doth seem   30
To have thee crowned withal.

An attendant enters

                                  What is your tidings?
ATTENDANT. The king comes here to-night.
LADY M.   Thou'rt mad to say it!
  Is not thy master with him? who, were't so,
  Would have informed for preparation.
ATTENDANT. So please you, it is true: our thane is
  coming:
  One of my fellows had the speed of him;
  Who, almost dead for breath, had scarcely more
  Than would make up his message.
LADY M.   Give him tending,
  He brings great news. [*attendant goes*] The raven
    himself is hoarse
  That croaks the fatal entrance of Duncan   40
  Under my battlements.... Come, you spirits
  That tend on mortal thoughts, unsex me here,
  And fill me, from the crown to the toe, top-full
  Of direst cruelty! make thick my blood,
  Stop up th'access and passage to remorse,
  That no compunctious visitings of nature
  Shake my fell purpose, nor keep peace between
  Th'effect and it! Come to my woman's breasts,
  And take my milk for gall, you murd'ring ministers,
  Wherever in your sightless substances   50
  You wait on nature's mischief! Come, thick night,
  And pall thee in the dunnest smoke of hell,
  That my keen knife see not the wound it makes,
  Nor heaven peep through the blanket of the dark,
  To cry 'Hold, hold!'

Enter Macbeth

                          Great Glamis! worthy Cawdor!
  Greater than both, by the all-hail hereafter!

Thy letters have transported me beyond
This ignorant present, and I feel now
The future in the instant.
MACBETH   My dearest love,
  Duncan comes here to-night.
LADY M.   And when goes hence? 60
MACBETH. To-morrow, as he purposes.
LADY M.   O, never
  Shall sun that morrow see!
  Your face, my thane, is as a book, where men
  May read strange matters. To beguile the time,
  Look like the time, bear welcome in your eye,
  Your hand, your tongue: look like th'innocent
    flower,
  But be the serpent under't. He that's coming
  Must be provided for: and you shall put
  This night's great business into my dispatch,
  Which shall to all our nights and days to come   70
  Give solely sovereign sway and masterdom.
MACBETH. We will speak further.
LADY M.   Only look up clear:
  To alter favour ever is to fear:
  Leave all the rest to me.   *They go*

Scene 6

*Hautboys. Enter King Duncan, Malcolm, Donalbain,
Banquo, Lennox, Macduff, Ross, Angus, and attendants*

DUNCAN. This castle hath a pleasant seat; the air
  Nimbly and sweetly recommends itself
  Unto our gentle senses.
BANQUO.   This guest of summer,
  The temple-haunting martlet, does approve,
  By his loved mansionry, that the heaven's breath
  Smells wooingly here: no jutty, frieze,
  Buttress, nor coign of vantage, but this bird
  Hath made his pendent bed and procreant cradle:
  Where they most breed and haunt, I have observed
  The air is delicate.

Enter Lady Macbeth

DUNCAN.   See, see! our honoured hostess! 10
  The love that follows us sometime is our trouble,
  Which still we thank as love. Herein I teach you
  How you shall bid God 'ield us for your pains,
  And thank us for your trouble.
LADY M.   All our service
  In every point twice done, and then done double,
  Were poor and single business to contend
  Against those honours deep and broad, wherewith
  Your majesty loads our house: for those of old,
  And the late dignities heaped up to them,
  We rest your hermits.
DUNCAN.   Where's the thane of Cawdor? 20
  We coursed him at the heels, and had a purpose
  To be his purveyor: but he rides well,
  And his great love (sharp as his spur) hath holp him
  To his home before us. Fair and noble hostess,
  We are your guest to-night.
LADY M.   Your servants ever
  Have theirs, themselves, and what is theirs, in
    compt,
  To make their audit at your highness' pleasure,
  Still to return your own.
DUNCAN.   Give me your hand:
  Conduct me to mine host; we love him highly,

And shall continue our graces towards him.   30
By your leave, hostess.   *They go*

Scene 7: *A court in Macbeth's castle*

Hautboys. Torches. Enter a sewer directing divers servants
who pass with dishes and service across the court. Then
enter Macbeth.

MACBETH. If it were done, when 'tis done, then 'twere
    well
It were done quickly: if th'assassination
Could trammel up the consequence, and catch,
With his surcease, success; that but this blow
Might be the be-all and the end-all.... here,
But here, upon this bank and shoal of time,
We'ld jump the life to come. But in these cases
We still have judgement here—that we but teach
Bloody instructions, which being taught return
To plague th'inventor: this even-handed justice   10
Commends th'ingredience of our poisoned chalice
To our own lips. He's here in double trust:
First, as I am his kinsman and his subject,
Strong both against the deed; then, as his host,
Who should against his murderer shut the door,
Not bear the knife myself. Besides, this Duncan
Hath borne his faculties so meek, hath been
So clear in his great office, that his virtues
Will plead like angels, trumpet-tongued, against
The deep damnation of his taking-off;   20
And pity, like a naked new-born babe,
Striding the blast, or Heaven's cherubin, horsed
Upon the sightless couriers of the air,
Shall blow the horrid deed in every eye,
That tears shall drown the wind. I have no spur
To prick the sides of my intent, but only
Vaulting ambition, which o'erleaps itself,
And falls on th'other—

Enter Lady Macbeth

                    How now, what news?
LADY M. He has almost supped: why have you left
    the chamber?
MACBETH. Hath he asked for me?
LADY M.   Know you not he has?   30
MACBETH. We will proceed no further in this business:
He hath honoured me of late, and I have bought
Golden opinions from all sorts of people,
Which would be worn now in their newest gloss,
Not cast aside so soon.
LADY M.   Was the hope drunk
Wherein you dressed yourself? hath it slept since?
And wakes it now, to look so green and pale
At what it did so freely? From this time
Such I account thy love. Art thou afeard
To be the same in thine own act and valour   40
As thou art in desire? Wouldst thou have that
Which thou esteem'st the ornament of life,
And live a coward in thine own esteem,
Letting 'I dare not' wait upon 'I would',
Like the poor cat i'th'adage?
MACBETH.   Prithee, peace:
I dare do all that may become a man;
Who dares do more, is none.
LADY M.   What beast was't then
That made you break this enterprise to me?
When you durst do it, then you were a man;

And, to be more than what you were, you would   50
Be so much more the man. Nor time nor place
Did then adhere, and yet you would make both:
They have made themselves, and that their fitness
    now
Does unmake you. I have given suck, and know
How tender 'tis to love the babe that milks me—
I would, while it was smiling in my face,
Have plucked my nipple from his boneless gums,
And dashed the brains out, had I so sworn as you
Have done to this.
MACBETH.   If we should fail?
LADY M.   We fail?
But screw your courage to the sticking place,   60
And we'll not fail. When Duncan is asleep
(Whereto the rather shall his day's hard journey
Soundly invite him) his two chamberlains
Will I with wine and wassail so convince,
That memory, the warder of the brain,
Shall be a fume, and the receipt of reason
A limbec only: when in swinish sleep
Their drenchéd natures lie as in a death,
What cannot you and I perform upon
Th'unguarded Duncan? what not put upon   70
His spongy officers, who shall bear the guilt
Of our great quell?
MACBETH.   Bring forth men-children only!
For thy undaunted mettle should compose
Nothing but males. Will it not be received,
When we have marked with blood those sleepy two
Of his own chamber, and used their very daggers,
That they have done't?
LADY M.   Who dares receive it other,
As we shall make our griefs and clamour roar
Upon his death?
MACBETH.   I am settled, and bend up
Each corporal agent to this terrible feat.   80
Away, and mock the time with fairest show:
False face must hide what the false heart doth know.
                                          They go

ACT 2
Scene 1: *The same*

Enter Banquo, and Fleance with a torch before him

BANQUO. How goes the night, boy?
FLEANCE. The moon is down; I have not heard the
    clock.
BANQUO. And she goes down at twelve.
FLEANCE.   I take't, 'tis later, sir.
BANQUO. Hold, take my sword.... There's husbandry
    in heaven,
Their candles are all out....
                    Unclasps his belt with its dagger
                    Take thee that too.
A heavy summons lies like lead upon me,
And yet I would not sleep. Merciful powers,
Restrain in me the curséd thoughts that nature
Gives way to in repose! Give me my sword,

Enter Macbeth, and a servant with a torch

Who's there?   10
MACBETH. A friend.
BANQUO. What, sir, not yet at rest? The king's a-bed.
He hath been in unusual pleasure, and
Sent forth great largess to your offices.

This diamond he greets your wife withal,
By the name of most kind hostess; and shut up
In measureless content.
MACBETH.   Being unprepared.
Our will became the servant to defect,
Which else should free have wrought.
BANQUO.   All's well.
I dreamt last night of the three Wierd Sisters: 20
To you they have showed some truth.
MACBETH.   I think not of them:
Yet, when we can entreat an hour to serve,
We would spend it in some words upon that
     business,
If you would grant the time.
BANQUO.   At your kind'st leisure.
MACBETH. If you shall cleave to my consent, when 'tis,
It shall make honour for you.
BANQUO.   So I lose none
In seeking to augment it, but still keep
My bosom franchised and allegiance clear,
I shall be counselled.
MACBETH.   Good repose the while!
BANQUO. Thanks, sir: the like to you!   30
          Banquo and Fleance go
MACBETH. Go bid thy mistress, when my drink is
     ready,
She strike upon the bell. Get thee to bed.
          The servant goes
Is this a dagger which I see before me,
The handle toward my hand? Come, let me clutch
     there:
I have thee not, and yet I see thee still.
Art thou not, fatal vision, sensible
To feeling as to sight? or art thou but
A dagger of the mind, a false creation,
Proceeding from the heat-oppressèd brain?
I see thee yet, in form as palpable   40
As this which now I draw.
Thou marshall'st me the way that I way going,
And such an instrument I was to use!
Mine eyes are made the fools o'th'other senses,
Or else worth all the rest: I see thee still;
And on thy blade and dudgeon gouts of blood,
Which was not so before. There's no such thing:
It is the bloody business which informs
Thus to mine eyes.... Now o'er the one half-world
Nature seems dead, and wicked dreams abuse   50
The curtained sleep; Witchcraft celebrates
Pale Hecate's off'ring; and withered Murder,
Alarumed by his sentinel, the wolf,
Whose howl's his watch, thus with his stealthy pace,
With Tarquin's ravishing strides, towards his design
Moves like a ghost. Thou sure and firm-set earth,
Hear not my steps, which way they walk, for fear
Thy very stones prate of my whereabout,
And take the present horror from the time,
Which now suits with it. Whiles I threat, he lives: 60
Words to the heat of deeds too cold breath gives.
          A bell rings
I go, and it is done: the bell invites me.
Hear it not, Duncan, for it is a knell
That summons thee to heaven, or to hell.
          He goes

Scene 2

Lady Macbeth enters

LADY M. That which hath made them drunk hath
     made me bold:
What hath quenched them hath given me fire. Hark!
     Peace:
It was the owl that shrieked, the fatal bellman,
Which gives the stern'st good-night. He is about it:
The doors are open; and the surfeited grooms
Do mock their charge with snores: I have drugged
     their possets,
That death and nature do contend about them,
Whether they live or die.
MACBETH [*within*].   Who's there? what, ho!
LADY M. Alack! I am afraid they have awaked,
And 'tis not done: th'attempt and not the deed   10
Confounds us. Hark! I laid their daggers ready,
He could not miss 'em. Had he not resembled
My father as he slept, I had done't.

Macbeth enters

          My husband!
MACBETH. I have done the deed.... Didst thou not
     hear a noise?
LADY M. I heard the owl scream, and the crickets cry.
Did not you speak?
MACBETH.   When?
LADY M.   Now.
MACBETH.   As I descended?
LADY M. Ay.
MACBETH. Hark!
Who lies i'th' second chamber?
LADY M.   Donalbain.
MACBETH. This is a sorry sight.   20
          Stretching forth his right hand
LADY M. A foolish thought, to say a sorry sight.
MACBETH. There's one did laugh in's sleep, and one
     cried 'Murder!'
That they did wake each other: I stood and heard
     them:
But they did say their prayers, and addressed them
Again to sleep.
LADY M.   There are two lodged together.
MACBETH. One cried 'God bless us!' and 'Amen' the
     other,
As they had seen me with these hangman's hands:
List'ning their fear, I could not say 'Amen',
When they did say 'God bless us'.
LADY M. Consider it not so deeply.   30
MACBETH. But wherefore could not I pronounce
     'Amen'?
I had most need of blessing, and 'Amen'
Stuck in my throat.
LADY M.   These deeds must not be thought
After these ways; so, it will make us mad.
MACBETH. Methought I heard a voice cry 'Sleep no
     more!
Macbeth does murder sleep'—the innocent sleep,
Sleep that knits up the ravelled sleave of care,
The death of each day's life, sore labour's bath,
Balm of hurt minds, great Nature's second course,
Chief nourisher in life's feast,—
LADY M.   What do you mean?   40
MACBETH. Still it cried 'Sleep no more!' to all the
     house:
'Glamis hath murdered sleep, and therefore Cawdor

Shall sleep no more: Macbeth shall sleep no more!'

LADY M. Who was it that thus cried? Why, worthy
    thane,
You do unbend your noble strength, to think
So brainsickly of things. Go get some water,
And wash this filthy witness from your hand.
Why did you bring these daggers from the place?
They must lie there: go carry them, and smear
The sleepy grooms with blood.

MACBETH.   I'll go no more: 50
I am afraid to think what I have done;
Look on't again I dare not.

LADY M.   Infirm of purpose!
Give me the daggers: the sleeping and the dead
Are but as pictures: 'tis the eye of childhood
That fears a painted devil. If he do bleed,
I'll gild the faces of the grooms withal,
For it must seem their guilt.
              She goes up. A knocking heard.

MACBETH.   Whence is that knocking?
How is't with me, when every noise appals me?
What hands are here? ha! they pluck out mine eyes!
Will all great Neptune's ocean wash this blood   60
Clean from my hand? No; this my hand will rather
The multitudinous seas incarnadine,
Making the green—one red.

Lady Macbeth returns

LADY M. My hands are of your colour; but I shame
To wear a heart so white. [*knocking*] I hear a
    knocking
At the south entry: retire we to our chamber:
A little water clears us of this deed:
How easy is it then! Your constancy
Hath left you unattended. [*knocking*] Hark! more
    knocking.
Get on your nightgown, lest occasion call us   70
And show us to be watchers: be not lost
So poorly in your thoughts.

MACBETH. To know my deed, 'twere best not know
    myself.   *Knocking*
Wake Duncan with thy knocking! I would thou
    couldst!   *They go*

Scene 3

*The knocking grows louder; a drunken Porter enters
the court*

PORTER. Here's a knocking indeed! If a man were
porter of hell-gate, he should have old turning the
key.[*knocking*] Knock, knock, knock! Who's there,
i'th' name of Beelzebub? Here's a farmer, that
hanged himself on th'expectation of plenty: come
in, time-server; have napkins enow about you, here
you'll sweat for't. [*knocking*] Knock, knock! Who's
there, in th'other devil's name? Faith, here's an
equivocator, that could swear in both the scales
against either scale, who committed treason enough   10
for God's sake, yet could not equivocate to heaven:
O, come in, equivocator. [*knocking*] Knock, knock,
knock! Who's there? Faith, here's an English tailor
come hither, for stealing out of a French hose: come
in, tailor, here you may roast your goose. [*knocking*]
Knock, knock! never at quiet! What are you? But
this place is too cold for hell. I'll devil-porter it no
further: I had thought to have let in some of all

professions, that go the primrose way to th'everlasting bonfire. [*knocking*] Anon, anon! I pray you,   20
remember the porter.   *Opens the gate*

Enter Macduff and Lennox

MACDUFF. Was it so late, friend, ere you went to bed,
That you do lie so late?

PORTER. Faith, sir, we were carousing till the second
cock: and drink, sir, is a great provoker of three
things.

MACDUFF. What three things does drink especially
provoke?

PORTER. Marry, sir, nose-painting, sleep, and urine.
Lechery, sir, it provokes and unprovokes: it pro-   30
vokes the desire, but it takes away the performance.
Therefore, much drink may be said to be an
equivocator with lechery: it makes him, and it mars
him; it sets him on, and it takes him off; it persuades
him, and disheartens him; makes him stand to, and
not stand to: in conclusion, equivocates him in a
sleep, and giving him the lie, leaves him.

MACDUFF. I believe drink gave thee the lie last night.

PORTER. That it did, sir, i'the very throat on me: but
I requited him for his lie, and, I think, being too   40
strong for him, though he took up my legs sometime, yet I made a shift to cast him.

MACDUFF. Is thy master stirring?

Macbeth returns

Our knocking has awaked him; here he comes.

LENNOX. Good-morrow, noble sir.

MACBETH.   Good-morrow, both.

MACDUFF. Is the king stirring, worthy thane?

MACBETH.   Not yet.

MACDUFF. He did command me to call timely on him;
I have almost slipped the hour.

MACBETH.   I'll bring you to him.

MACDUFF. I know this is a joyful trouble to you;
But yet 'tis one.   50

MACBETH. The labour we delight in physics pain.
This is the door.

MACDUFF.   I'll make so bold to call,
For 'tis my limited service.   *He goes in*

LENNOX. Goes the king hence to-day?

MACBETH. He does: he did appoint so.

LENNOX. The night has been unruly: where we lay,
Our chimneys were blown down, and, as they say,
Lamentings heard i'th'air, strange screams of death,
And prophesying with accents terrible
Of dire combustion and confused events   60
New hatched to th' woeful time. The obscure bird
Clamoured the livelong night: some say, the earth
Was feverous and did shake.

MACBETH.   'Twas a rough night.

LENNOX. My young remembrance cannot parallel
A fellow to it.

Macduff returns

MACDUFF. O horror! horror! horror! Tongue, nor
    heart,
Cannot conceive nor name thee!

MACBETH, LENNOX.   What's the matter?

MACDUFF. Confusion now hath made his masterpiece!
Most sacrilegious murder hath broke ope
The Lord's anointed temple, and stole thence   70
The life o'th' building.

MACBETH. What is't you say? the life?
LENNOX. Mean you his majesty?
MACDUFF. Approach the chamber, and destroy your sight
With a new Gorgon: do not bid me speak;
See, and then speak yourselves.
Macbeth and Lennox go
Awake! awake!
Ring the alarum bell! Murder and treason!
Banquo and Donalbain! Malcolm, awake!
Shake off this downy sleep, death's counterfeit,
And look on death itself! up, up, and see
The great doom's image! Malcolm! Banquo!   80
As from your graves rise up, and walk like sprites,
To countenance this horror!   *Bell rings*

Enter Lady Macbeth

LADY M. What's the business,
That such a hideous trumpet calls to parley
The sleepers of the house? speak, speak!
MACDUFF. O, gentle lady,
'Tis not for you to hear what I can speak:
The repetition, in a woman's ear,
Would murder as it fell.

Enter Banquo

O Banquo! Banquo!
Our royal master's murdered!
LADY M. Woe, alas!
What, in our house?
BANQUO. Too cruel, any where.
Dear Duff, I prithee, contradict thyself,   90
And say it is not so.

Macbeth and Lennox return

MACBETH. Had I but died an hour before this chance,
I had lived a blessèd time; for from this instant
There's nothing serious in mortality:
All is but toys: renown and grace is dead,
The wine of life is drawn, and the mere lees
Is left this vault to brag of.

Enter Malcolm and Donalbain

DONALBAIN. What is amiss?
MACBETH. You are, and do not know't:
The spring, the head, the fountain of your blood
Is stopped—the very source of it is stopped.   100
MACDUFF. Your royal father's murdered.
MALCOLM. O, by whom?
LENNOX. Those of his chamber, as it seemed, had done't:
Their hands and faces were all badged with blood,
So were their daggers, which unwiped we found
Upon their pillows:
They stared and were distracted, no man's life
Was to be trusted with them.
MACBETH. O, yet I do repent me of my fury,
That I did kill them.
MACDUFF. Wherefore did you so?
MACBETH. Who can be wise, amazed, temp'rate and furious,   110
Loyal and neutral, in a moment? no man:
Th'expedition of my violent love
Outrun the pauser, reason. Here lay Duncan,
His silver skin laced with his golden blood,
And his gashed stabs looked like a breach in nature

For ruin's wasteful entrance: there, the murderers,
Steeped in the colours of their trade, their daggers
Unmannerly breeched with gore: who could refrain,
That had a heart to love, and in that heart
Courage to make's love known?
LADY M. Help me hence, ho!   120
MACDUFF. Look to the lady.
MALCOLM [*aside*]. Why do we hold our tongues,
That most may claim this argument for ours?
DONALBAIN [*aside*]. What should be spoken here, where our fate,
Hid in an auger-hole, may rush and seize us?
Let's away.
Our tears are not yet brewed.
MALCOLM [*aside*]. Nor our strong sorrow
Upon the foot of motion.   *Enter waiting-women*
BANQUO. Look to the lady ...
They lead her out
And when we have our naked frailties hid,
That suffer in exposure, let us meet,
And question this most bloody piece of work,   130
To know it further. Fears and scruples shake us:
In the great hand of God I stand, and thence
Against the undivulged pretence I fight
Of treasonous malice.
MACDUFF. And so do I.
ALL. So all.
MACBETH. Let's briefly put on manly readiness,
And meet i'th'hall together.
ALL. Well contented.
All go but Malcolm and Donalbain
MALCOLM. What will you do? Let's not consort with them:
To show an unfelt sorrow is an office
Which the false man does easy. I'll to England.
DONALBAIN. To Ireland, I: our separated fortune   140
Shall keep us both the safer: where we are
There's daggers in men's smiles: the near in blood,
The nearer bloody.
MALCOLM. This murderous shaft that's shot
Hath not yet lighted, and our safest way
Is to avoid the aim. Therefore to horse,
And let us not be dainty of leave-taking,
But shift away: there's warrant in that theft
Which steals itself when there's no mercy left.
They go

Scene 4: *Before Macbeth's castle*

Enter Ross with an Old Man

OLD MAN. Threescore and ten I can remember well,
Within the volume of which time I have seen
Hours dreadful and things strange; but this sore night
Hath trifled former knowings.
ROSS. Ha, good father,
Thou seest the heavens, as troubled with man's act,
Threatens his bloody stage: by th' clock 'tis day,
And yet dark night strangles the travelling lamp:
Is't night's predominance, or the day's shame,
That darkness does the face of earth entomb,
When living light should kiss it?
OLD MAN. 'Tis unnatural,   10
Even like the deed that's done. On Tuesday last
A falcon towering in her pride of place

Was by a mousing owl hawked at and killed.
ROSS. And Duncan's horses—a thing most strange and
　　certain—
Beauteous and swift, the minions of their race,
Turned wild in nature, broke their stalls, flung out,
Contending 'gainst obedience, as they would make
War with mankind.
OLD MAN. 　　　　　　　'Tis said they eat each other.
ROSS. They did so, to th'amazement of mine eyes,
That looked upon't.

Macduff enters

　　　　　　　Here comes the good Macduff. 20
How goes the world, sir, now?
MACDUFF. 　　　　　　　Why, see you not?
ROSS. Is't known who did this more than bloody deed?
MACDUFF. Those that Macbeth hath slain.
ROSS. 　　　　　　　　Alas, the day!
What good could they pretend?
MACDUFF. 　　　　　　　They were suborned.
Malcolm and Donalbain, the king's two sons,
Are stol'n away and fled, which puts upon them
Suspicion of the deed.
ROSS. 　　　　　　　'Gainst nature still!
Thriftless ambition, that wilt ravin up
Thine own life's means! Then 'tis most like
The sovereignty will fall upon Macbeth. 　　30
MACDUFF. He is already named, and gone to Scone
To be invested.
ROSS. 　　　　　　Where is Duncan's body?
MACDUFF. Carried to Colme kill,
The sacred storehouse of his predecessors,
And guardian of their bones.
ROSS. 　　　　　　　Will you to Scone?
MACDUFF. No cousin, I'll to Fife.
　　　　　　　　Well, I will thither.
MACDUFF. Well, may you see things well done there;
　　adieu!
Lest our old robes sit easier than our new!
ROSS. Farewell, father.
OLD MAN. God's benison go with you, and with those 40
That would make good of bad and friends of foes!
　　　　　　　　　　　They go

ACT 3
Scene 1: *The palace at Forres*

Banquo enters

BANQUO. Thou hast it now, King, Cawdor, Glamis,
　　all,
As the weïrd women promised, and I fear
Thou play'dst most foully for't: yet it was said
It should not stand in thy posterity,
But that myself should be the root and father
Of many kings. If there come truth from them—
As upon thee, Macbeth, their speeches shine—
Why, by the verities on thee made good,
May they not be my oracles as well,
And set me up in hope? But hush, no more. 　　10

*Sennet sounded. Enter Macbeth, as King, Lady Macbeth,
as Queen, Lennox, Ross, Lords, and attendants*

MACBETH. Here's our chief guest.
LADY M. 　　　　　　If he had been forgotten,
It had been as a gap in our great feast,
And all-thing unbecoming.

MACBETH. To-night we hold a solemn supper, sir,
And I'll request your presence.
BANQUO. 　　　　　　　Let your highness
Command upon me, to the which my duties
Are with a most indissoluble tie
For ever knit.
MACBETH. Ride you this afternoon?
BANQUO. 　　　　　　　　Ay, my good lord.
MACBETH. We should have else desired your good
　　advice 　　　　　　　　　　　　　　　20
(Which still hath been both grave and prosperous)
In this day's council; but we'll take to-morrow.
Is't far you ride?
BANQUO. As far, my lord, as will fill up the time
'Twixt this and supper. Go not my horse the better,
I must become a borrower of the night
For a dark hour or twain.
MACBETH. 　　　　　　Fail not our feast.
BANQUO. My lord, I will not.
MACBETH. We hear our bloody cousins are bestowed
In England and in Ireland, not confessing 　　30
Their cruel parricide, filling their hearers
With strange invention: but of that to-morrow,
When therewithal we shall have cause of state
Craving us jointly. Hie you to horse: adieu,
Till you return at night. Goes Fleance with you?
BANQUO. Ay, my good lord: our time does call upon's.
MACBETH. I wish your horses swift and sure of foot;
And so I do commend you to their backs.
Farewell. 　　　　　　　　　　*Banquo goes*
Let every man be master of his time 　　　　40
Till seven at night; to make society
The sweeter welcome, we will keep ourself
Till supper-time alone: while then, God be with
　　you!
　　　　　All depart but Macbeth and a servant
Sirrah, a word with you: attend those men
Our pleasure?
ATTENDANT. They are, my lord, without the palace
　　gate.
MACBETH. Bring them before us. 　　*The servant goes*
　　　　　　　　　　　To be thus is nothing,
But to be safely thus: our fears in Banquo
Stick deep, and in his royalty of nature
Reigns that which would be feared. 'Tis much he
　　dares, 　　　　　　　　　　　　　　50
And, to that dauntless temper of his mind,
He hath a wisdom that doth guide his valour
To act in safety. There is none but he
Whose being I do fear: and under him
My Genius is rebuked, as it is said
Mark Antony's was by Cæsar. He chid the Sisters,
When first they put the name of king upon me,
And bade them speak to him; then prophet-like
They hailed him father to a line of kings:
Upon my head they placed a fruitless crown, 　　60
And put a barren sceptre in my gripe,
Thence to be wrenched with an unlineal hand,
No son of mine succeeding. If't be so,
For Banquo's issue have I filed my mind,
For them the gracious Duncan have I murdered,
Put rancours in the vessel of my peace
Only for them, and mine eternal jewel
Given to the common enemy of man,
To make them kings, the seed of Banquo kings!
Rather than so, come Fate into the list, 　　70

And champion me to th'utterance. Who's there?

The servant returns with two murderers

Now go to the door, and stay there till we call.
Servant goes
Was it not yesterday we spoke together?
1 MURDERER. It was, so please your highness.
MACBETH. Well then, now
Have you considered of my speeches? Know
That it was he in the times past which held you
So under fortune, which you thought had been
Our innocent self: this I made good to you
In our last conference; passed in probation with you,
How you were borne in hand, how crossed, the instruments, 80
Who wrought with them, and all things else that might
To half a soul and to a notion crazed
Say 'Thus did Banquo'.
1 MURDERER. You made it known to us.
MACBETH. I did so; and went further, which is now
Our point of second meeting. Do you find
Your patience so predominant in your nature,
That you can let this go? Are you so gospelled,
To pray for this good man, and for his issue,
Whose heavy hand hath bowed you to the grave
And beggared yours for ever?
1 MURDERER. We are men, my liege. 90
MACBETH. Ay, in the catalogue ye go for men,
As hounds and greyhounds, mongrels, spaniels, curs,
Shoughs, water-rugs, and demi-wolves, are clept
All by the name of dogs: the valued file
Distinguishes the swift, the slow, the subtle,
The housekeeper, the hunter, every one
According to the gift which bounteous nature
Hath in him closed, whereby he does receive
Particular addition, from the bill
That writes them all alike: and so of men. 100
Now, if you have a station in the file,
Not i'th' worst rank of manhood, say't,
And I will put that business in your bosoms,
Whose execution takes your enemy off,
Grapples you to the heart and love of us,
Who wear our health but sickly in his life,
Which in his death were perfect.
2 MURDERER. I am one, my liege,
Whom the vile blows and buffets of the world
Hath so incensed that I am reckless what
I do to spite the world.
1 MURDERER. And I another 110
So weary with disasters, tugged with fortune,
That I would set my life on any chance,
To mend it, or be rid on't.
MACBETH. Both of you
Know Banquo war your enemy.
BOTH MURDERERS. True, my lord.
MACBETH. So is he mine: and in such bloody distance,
That every minute of his being thrusts
Against my near'st of life: and though I could
With barefaced power sweep him from my sight,
And bid my will avouch it, yet I must not,
For certain friends that are both his and mine, 120
Whose loves I may not drop, but wail his fall
Who I myself struck down: and thence it is
That I to your assistance do make love,
Masking the business from the common eye,

For sundry weighty reasons.
2 MURDERER. We shall, my lord,
Perform what you command us.
1 MURDERER. Though our lives—
MACBETH. Your spirits shine through you. Within this hour at most
I will advise you where to plant yourselves,
Acquaint you with the perfect spy o'th' time,
The moment on't, for't must be done to-night, 130
And something from the palace; always thought
That I require a clearness: and with him
To leave no rubs nor botches in the work—
Fleance his son, that keeps him company,
Whose absence is no less material to me
Than is his father's, must embrace the fate
Of that dark hour. Resolve yourselves apart;
I'll come to you anon.
BOTH MURDERERS. We are resolved, my lord.
MACBETH. I'll call upon you straight; abide within.
They go
It is concluded: Banquo, thy soul's flight, 140
If it find heaven, must find it out to-night.
He leaves by another door

Scene 2

Lady Macbeth enters with a servant

LADY M. Is Banquo gone from court?
SERVANT. Ay, madam, but returns again to-night.
LADY M. Say to the king, I would attend his leisure
For a few words.
SERVANT. Madam, I will. *He goes*
LADY M. Nought's had, all's spent,
Where our desire is got without content:
'Tis safer to be that which we destroy
Than by destruction dwell in doubtful joy.

Macbeth enters

How now, my lord! why do you keep alone,
Of sorriest fancies your companions making,
Using those thought which should indeed have died 10
With them they think on? Things without all remedy
Should be without regard: what's done, is done.
MACBETH. We have scorched the snake, not killed it:
She'll close and be herself, whilst our poor malice
Remains in danger of her former tooth.
But let the frame of things disjoint, both the worlds suffer,
Ere we will eat our meal in fear, and sleep
In the affliction of these terrible dreams
That shake us nightly: better be with the dead,
Whom we, to gain our peace, have sent to peace, 20
Than on the torture of the mind to lie
In restless ecstasy. Duncan is in his grave;
After life's fitful fever he sleeps well;
Treason has done his worst: nor steel, nor poison,
Malice domestic, foreign levy, nothing,
Can touch him further.
LADY M. Come on;
Gentle my lord, sleek o'er your rugged looks,
Be bright and jovial among your guests to-night.
MACBETH. So shall I, love, and so I pray be you:
Let your remembrance apply to Banquo; 30
Present him eminence, both with eye and tongue:
Unsafe the while, that we

Must lave our honours in these flattering streams,
And make our faces vizards to our hearts,
Disguising what they are.
LADY M.   You must leave this.
MACBETH. O, full of scorpions is my mind, dear
    wife!
Thou know'st that Banquo and his Fleance lives.
LADY M. But in them nature's copy's not eterne.
MACBETH. There's comfort yet, they are assailable,
Then be thou jocund: ere the bat hath flown   40
His cloistered flight, ere to black Hecate's summons
The shard-borne beetle with his drowsy hums
Hath rung night's yawning peal, there shall be done
A deed of dreadful note.
LADY M.   What's to be done?
MACBETH. Be innocent of the knowledge, dearest
    chuck,
Till thou applaud the deed ... Come, seeling night,
Scarf up the tender eye of pitiful day,
And with thy bloody and invisible hand
Cancel and tear to pieces that great bond
Which keeps me paled! Light thickens, and the crow 50
Makes wing to th' rooky wood:
Good things of day begin to droop and drowse,
Whiles night's black agents to their preys do rouse.
Thou marvell'st at my words: but hold thee still;
Things bad begun make strong themselves by ill:
So, prithee, go with me.   They go

Scene 3: The royal park, some way from the palace.

The two murderers enter, with a third

1 MURDERER. But who did bid thee join with us?
3 MURDERER.   Macbeth.
2 MURDERER. He needs not our mistrust, since he
    delivers
Our offices and what we have to do,
To the direction just.
1 MURDERER.   Then stand with us.
The west yet glimmers with some streaks of day:
Now spurs the lated traveller apace
To gain the timely inn, and near approaches
The subject of our watch.
3 MURDERER.   Hark! I hear horses.
BANQUO [at a distance]. Give us a light there, ho!
2 MURDERER.   Then 'tis he; the rest
That are within the note of expectation   10
Already are i'th' court.
1 MURDERER.   His horses go about.
3 MURDERER. Almost a mile: but he does usually—
So all men do—from hence to th' palace gate
Make it their walk.

Enter Banquo and Fleance with a torch

2 MURDERER.   A light, a light!
3 MURDERER.   'Tis he.
1 MURDERER. Stand to't.
BANQUO. It will be rain to-night.
1 MURDERER.   Let it come down.
                          They set upon Banquo
BANQUO. O, treachery! Fly, good Fleance, fly, fly, fly!
Thou mayst revenge. O slave!
                          He dies; Fleance escapes
3 MURDERER. Who did strike out the light?
1 MURDERER.   Was't not the way?
3 MURDERER. There's but one down; the son is fled.

2 MURDERER.   We have lost   20
Best half of our affair.
1 MURDERER. Well, let's away, and say how much is
    done.   They go

Scene 4: The hall of the palace.

A banquet prepared. Enter Macbeth, Lady Macbeth, Ross,
Lennox, lords, and attendants

MACBETH. You know your own degrees, sit down at
    first
And last, the hearty welcome.
LORDS.   Thanks to your majesty.
MACBETH. Ourself will mingle with society,
And play the humble host:
Our hostess keeps her state, but in best time
We will require her welcome.
LADY M. Pronounce it for me, sir, to all our friends,
For my heart speaks they are welcome.

1 Murderer appears at the door

MACBETH. See, they encounter thee with their hearts'
    thanks.
Both sides are even: here I'll sit i'th' midst.   10
Be large in mirth, anon we'll drink a measure
The table round.
[turns to the door] There's blood upon thy face.
MURDERER. 'Tis Banquo's then.
MACBETH. 'Tis better thee without than he within.
Is he dispatched?
MURDERER. My lord, his throat is cut, that I did for
    him.
MACBETH. Thou art the best o'th' cut-throats! Yet
    he's good
That did the like for Fleance: if thou didst it,
Thou art the nonpareil.
MURDERER.   Most royal sir,
Fleance is 'scaped.   20
MACBETH. Then comes my fit again: I had else been
    perfect;
Whole as the marble, founded as the rock,
As broad and general as the casing air:
But now I am cabined, cribbed, confined, bound in
To saucy doubts and fears. But Banquo's safe?
MURDERER. Ay, my good lord: safe in a ditch he bides,
With twenty trenchéd gashes on his head;
The least a death to nature.
MACBETH.   Thanks for that:
There the grown serpent lies; the worm that's fled
Hath nature that in time will venom breed,   30
No teeth for th' present. Get thee gone; to-morrow
We'll hear ourselves again.   Murderer goes
LADY M.   My royal lord,
You do not give the cheer. The feast is sold
That is not often vouched, while 'tis a-making,
'Tis given with welcome: to feed were best at home;
From thence the sauce to meat is ceremony;
Meeting were bare without it.

The Ghost of Banquo appears, and sits in Macbeth's place

MACBETH.   Sweet remembrancer!
Now good digestion wait on appetite,
And health on both!
LENNOX.   May't please your highness sit?
MACBETH. Here had we now our country's honour
    roofed,   40

Were the graced person of our Banquo present;
Who may I rather challenge for unkindness
Than pity for mischance!

ROSS.   His absence, sir,
Lays blame upon his promise. Please't your highness
To grace us with your royal company?

MACBETH. The table's full.

LENNOX.   Here is a place reserved, sir.

MACBETH. Where?

LENNOX. Here, my good lord.... What is't that moves
your highness?

MACBETH. Which of you have done this?

LORDS.   What, my good lord?

MACBETH. Thou canst not say I did it: never shake   50
Thy gory locks at me.

ROSS. Gentlemen, rise, his highness is not well.

LADY M. Sit, worthy friends: my lord is often thus,
And hath been from his youth: pray you, keep seat,
The fit is momentary, upon a thought
He will again be well: if much you note him,
You shall offend him and extend his passion:
Feed, and regard him not. [aside] Are you a man?

MACBETH. Ay, and a bold one, that dare look on that
Which might appal the devil.

LADY M.   O proper stuff!   60
This is the very painting of your fear:
This is the air-drawn dagger which, you said,
Led you to Duncan. O, these flaws and starts
(Imposter to true fear) would well become
A woman's story at a winter's fire,
Authorized by her grandam.... Shame itself!
Why do you make such faces? When all's done,
You look but on a stool.

MACBETH. Prithee, see there! behold! look! lo! how say
you?
Why what care I? If thou canst nod, speak too.   70
If charnel-houses and our graves must send
Those that we bury back, our monuments
Shall be the maws of kites.   *The Ghost vanishes*

LADY M.   What! quite unmanned in folly?

MACBETH. If I stand here, I saw him.

LADY M.   Fie, for shame!

MACBETH. Blood hath been shed ere now, i'th'olden
time,
Ere humane statute purged the gentle weal;
Ay, and since too, murders have been performed
Too terrible for the ear: the time has been,
That, when the brains were out, the man would die,
And there an end: but now they rise again,   80
With twenty mortal murders on their crowns,
And push us from our stools.... This is more strange
Than such a murder is.

LADY M.   My worthy lord,
Your noble friends do lack you.

MACBETH.   I do forget ...
Do not muse at me, my most worthy friends;
I have a strange infirmity, which is nothing
To those that know me. Come, love and health
to all;
Then I'll sit down. Give me some wine, fill full.
                 The Ghost reappears
I drink to th' general joy o'th' whole table,
And to our dear friend Banquo, whom we miss;   90
Would he were here! to all, and him we thirst,
And all to all!

LORDS.   Our duties, and the pledge.

MACBETH. Avaunt! and quit my sight! let the earth
hide thee!
Thy bones are marrowless, thy blood is cold;
Thou hast no speculation in those eyes
Which thou dost glare with!

LADY M.   Think of this, good peers,
But as a thing of custom: 'tis no other;
Only it spoils the pleasure of the time.

MACBETH. What man dare, I dare:
Approach thou like the ruggéd Russian bear,   100
The armed rhinoceros, or th'Hyrcan tiger,
Take any shape but that, and my firm nerves
Shall never tremble: or be alive again,
And dare me to the desert with thy sword;
If trembling I inhabit then, protest me
The baby of a girl. Hence, horrible shadow!
Unreal mock'ry, hence!   *The Ghost vanishes*
                 Why, so; being gone,
I am a man again. Pray you, sit still.

LADY M. You have displaced the mirth, broke the good
meeting,
With most admired disorder.

MACBETH.   Can such things be,   110
And overcome us like a summer's cloud,
Without our special wonder? You make me strange
Even to the disposition that I owe,
When now I think you can behold such sights,
And keep the natural ruby of your cheeks,
When mine is blanched with fear.

ROSS.   What sights, my lord?

LADY M. I pray you, speak not; he grows worse and
worse;
Question enrages him: at once, good night.
Stand not upon the order of your going,
But go at once.

LENNOX.   Good night, and better health   120
Attend his majesty!

LADY M.   A kind good night to all!
                          They leave

MACBETH. It will have blood; they say, blood will have
blood:
Stones have been known to move and trees to speak;
Augures and understood relations have
By maggot-pies and choughs and rooks brought
forth
The secret'st man of blood.... What is the night?

LADY M. Almost at odds with morning, which is
which

MACBETH. How say'st thou, that Macduff denies his
person
At our great bidding?

LADY M.   Did you send to him, sir?

MACBETH. I hear it by the way; but I will send: 130
There's not a one of them but in his house
I keep a servant fee'd.... I will to-morrow
(And betimes I will) to the Weïrd Sisters:
More shall they speak; for now I am bent to know,
By the worst means, and worst. For mine own good
All causes shall give way: I am in blood
Stepped in so far that, should I wade no more,
Returning were as tedious as go o'er:
Strange things I have in head that will to hand,
Which must be acted ere they may be scanned.   140

LADY M. You lack the season of all natures, sleep.

MACBETH. Come, we'll to sleep. My strange and
self-abuse

Is the initiate fear that wants hard use:
We are yet but young in deed.   *They go*

Scene 5: *A heath*

Thunder. Enter the three Witches, meeting Hecate

1 WITCH. Why, how now, Hecat, you look angerly.
HECATE. Have I not reason, beldams as you are,
Saucy and overbold? How did you dare
To trade and traffic with Macbeth
In riddles and affairs of death;
And I, the mistress of your charms,
The close contriver of all harms,
Was never called to bear my part,
Or show the glory of our art?
And, which is worse, all you have done   10
Hath been but for a wayward son,
Spiteful and wrathful, who (as others do)
Loves for his own ends, not for you.
But make amends now: get you gone,
And at the pit of Acheron
Meet me i'th' morning: thither he
Will come to know his destiny.
Your vessels and your spells provide,
Your charms and every thing beside.
I am for th'air; this night I'll spend   20
Unto a dismal and a fatal end.
Great business must be wrought ere noon:
Upon the corner of the moon
There hangs a vap'rous drop profound;
I'll catch it ere it come to ground:
And that distilled by magic sleights
Shall raise such artificial sprites
As by the strength of their illusion
Shall draw him on to his confusion.
He shall spurn fate, scorn death, and bear   30
His hopes 'bove wisdom, grace, and fear:
And you all know security
Is mortals' chiefest enemy.

Music and a song: 'Come away, come away' etc.

Hark, I am called: my little spirit, see,
Sits in a foggy cloud, and stays for me.   *She goes*
1 WITCH. Come, let's make haste; she'll soon be back
again.   *They vanish*

Scene 6: *A castle in Scotland*

Enter Lennox and another Lord

LENNOX. My former speeches have but hit your
thoughts,
Which can interpret farther: only I say
Things have been strangely borne. The gracious
Duncan
Was pitied of Macbeth: marry, he was dead:
And the right valiant Banquo walked too late—
Whom you may say (if't please you) Fleance killed,
For Fleance fled: men must not walk too late.
Who cannot want the thought, how monstrous
It was for Malcolm and for Donalbain
To kill their gracious father? damnéd fact!   10
How it did grieve Macbeth! did he not straight,
In pious rage, the two delinquents tear,
That were the slaves of drink and thralls of sleep?
Was not that nobly done? Ay, and wisely too;
For 'twould have angered any heart alive

To hear the men deny't. So that, I say,
He has borne all things well: and I do think
That, had he Duncan's sons under his key
(As, an't please heaven, he shall not) they should find
What 'twere to kill a father; so should Fleance.   20
But, peace! for from broad words, and 'cause he
failed
His presence at the tyrant's feast, I hear,
Macduff lives in disgrace. Sir, can you tell
Where he bestows himself?
LORD.   The son of Duncan
(From whom this tyrant holds the due of birth)
Lives in the English court, and is received
Of the most pious Edward with such grace
That the malevolence of fortune nothing
Takes from his high respect. Thither Macduff
Is gone to pray the holy king, upon his aid   30
To wake Northumberland and warlike
Siward,
That by the help of these (with Him above
To ratify the work) we may again
Give to our tables meat, sleep to our nights;
Free from our feasts and banquets bloody knives;
Do faithful homage and receive free honours:
All which we pine for now. And this report
Hath so exasperate the king that he
Prepares for some attempt of war.
LENNOX.   Sent he to Macduff?
LORD. He did: and with an absolute 'Sir, not I',   40
The cloudy messenger turns me his back,
And hums, as who should say, 'You'll rue the time
That clogs me with this answer'.
LENNOX.   And that well might
Advise him to a caution, t'hold what distance
His wisdom can provide. Some holy angel
Fly to the court of England and unfold
His message ere he come, that a swift blessing
May soon return to this our suffering country
Under a hand accursed!
LORD.   I'll send my prayers with him.
                                           They go

ACT 4

Scene 1: *A cavern and in the midst a boiling cauldron*

Thunder. Enter the Weird Sisters

1 WITCH. Thrice the brinded cat hath mewed.
2 WITCH. Thrice and once the hedge-pig whined.
3 WITCH. Harpier cries:—'Tis time, 'tis time.
1 WITCH. Round about the cauldron go:
In the poisoned entrails throw.
Toad, that under cold stone
Days and nights has thirty-one
Sweltered venom sleeping got,
Boil thou first i'th' charméd pot!
ALL. Double, double toil and trouble;   10
Fire burn and cauldron bubble.
2 WITCH. Fillet of a fenny snake,
In the cauldron boil and bake:
Eye of newt and toe of frog,
Wool of bat and tongue of dog,
Adder's fork and blind-worm's sting,
Lizard's leg and howlet's wing,
For a charm of powerful trouble,
Like a hell-broth boil and bubble.

ALL. Double, double toil and trouble;
    Fire burn and cauldron bubble.
3 WITCH. Scale of dragon, tooth of wolf,
    Witch's mummy, maw and gulf
    Of the ravined salt-sea shark,
    Root of hemlock digged i'th' dark,
    Liver of blaspheming Jew,
    Gall of goat and slips of yew
    Slivered in the moon's eclipse,
    Nose of Turk and Tartar's lips,
    Finger of birth-strangled babe   30
    Ditch-delivered by a drab,
    Make the gruel thick and slab:
    Add thereto a tiger's chaudron,
    For th'ingredience of our cauldron.
ALL. Double, double toil and trouble;
    Fire burn and cauldron bubble.
2 WITCH. Cool it with a baboon's blood,
    Then the charm is firm and good.

Enter Hecate and the other three Witches.

HECATE. O, well done! I commend your pains,
    And every one shall share i'th' gains: 40
    And now about the cauldron sing,
    Like elves and fairies in a ring,
    Enchanting all that you put in.

Music and a song: Black spirits, etc. Hecate goes

2 WITCH. By the pricking of my thumbs,
    Something wicked this way comes:
    Open, locks,
    Whoever knocks!

Macbeth enters

MACBETH. How now, you secret, black, and midnight
    hags!
    What is't you do?
ALL.   A deed without a name.
MACBETH. I conjure you, by that which you profess   50
    (Howe'er you come to know it) answer me:
    Though you untie the winds and let them fight
    Against the churches; though the yesty waves
    Confound and swallow navigation up;
    Though bladed corn be lodged and trees blown
    down;
    Though castles topple on their warders' heads;
    Though palaces and pyramids do slope
    Their heads to their foundations; though the
    treasure
    Of Nature's germens tumble all together,
    Even till destruction sicken; answer me   60
    To what I ask you.
1 WITCH.   Speak.
2 WITCH.   Demand.
3 WITCH.   We'll answer.
1 WITCH. Say if th'hadst rather hear it from our
    mouths,
    Or from our masters.
MACBETH.   Call 'em, let me see 'em!
1 WITCH. Pour in sow's blood, that hath eaten
    Her nine farrow; grease that's sweaten
    From the murderer's gibbet throw
    Into the flame.
ALL.   Come, high or low;
    Thyself and office deftly show.

Thunder. First Apparition, an armed head

MACBETH. Tell me, thou unknown power—   20
1 WITCH.   He knows thy thought:
    Hear his speech, but say thou nought.   70
1 APPARITION. Macbeth! Macbeth! Macbeth! beware
    Macduff.
    Beware the thane of Fife. Dismiss me. Enough.
                                   Descends
MACBETH. Whate'er thou art, for thy good caution
    thanks;
    Thou hast harped my fear aright. But one word
    more—
1 WITCH. He will not be commanded: here's another,
    More potent than the first.

Thunder. Second Apparition, a bloody child

2 APPARITION. Macbeth! Macbeth! Macbeth!
MACBETH. Had I three ears, I'ld hear thee.
2 APPARITION. Be bloody, bold, and resolute: laugh to
    scorn
    The power of man; for none of woman born   80
    Shall harm Macbeth.   *Descends*
MACBETH. Then live, Macduff: what need I fear of
    thee?
    But yet I'll make assurance double sure,
    And take a bond of fate: thou shalt not live,
    That I may tell pale-hearted fear it lies,
    And sleep in spite of thunder.

*Thunder. Third Apparition, a child crowned, with a tree
in his hand*

                                 What is this,
    That rises like the issue of a king,
    And wears upon his baby-brow the round
    And top of sovereignty?
ALL.   Listen, but speak not to't.
3 APPARITION. Be lion-mettled, proud, and take no
    care   90
    Who chafes, who frets, or where conspirers are:
    Macbeth shall never vanquished be until
    Great Birnam wood to high Dunsinane hill
    Shall come against him.   *Descends*
MACBETH.   That will never be;
    Who can impress the forest, bid the tree
    Unfix his earth-bound root? Sweet bodements!
    good.
    Rebellious dead, rise never, till the wood
    Of Birnam rise, and our high-placed Macbeth
    Shall live the lease of nature, pay his breath
    To time and mortal custom. Yet my heart   100
    Throbs to know one thing; tell me, if your art
    Can tell so much: shall Banquo's issue ever
    Reign in this kingdom?
ALL.   Seek to know no more.
MACBETH. I will be satisfied: deny me this,
    And an eternal curse fall on you! Let me know....

Hautboys

    Why sinks that cauldron? and what noise is this?
1 WITCH. Show!
2 WITCH. Show!
3 WITCH. Show!
ALL. Show his eyes, and grieve his heart;   110
    Come like shadows, so depart.

*A show of eight kings, the last with a glass in his hand;
Banquo's Ghost following*

MACBETH. Thou art too like the spirit of Banquo:
   down!
Thy crown does sear mine eye-balls. And thy hair,
Thou other gold-bound brow, is like the first.
A third is like the former. Filthy hags!
Why do you show me this?—A fourth? Start, eyes!
What, will the line stretch out to th' crack of doom?
Another yet? A seventh? I'll see no more:
And yet the eighth appears, who bears a glass
Which shows me many more; and some I see   120
That two-fold balls and treble sceptres carry.
Horrible sight! ... Now I see 'tis true,
For the blood-boltered Banquo smiles upon me,
And points at them for his. What, is this so?
1 WITCH. Ay, sir, all this is so. But why
Stands Macbeth thus amazedly?
Come, sisters, cheer we up his sprites,
And show the best of our delights.
I'll charm the air to give a sound,
While you perform your antic round: 130
That this great king may kindly say
Our duties did his welcome pay.

Music. The Witches dance, and vanish

MACBETH. Where are they? Gone? Let this pernicious
   hour
Stand aye accurséd in the calendar
Come in, without there!

Enter Lennox

LENNOX.   What's your grace's will?
MACBETH. Saw you the Weïrd Sisters?
LENNOX.   No, my lord.
MACBETH. Came they not by you?
LENNOX.   No indeed, my lord.
MACBETH. Infected be the air whereon they ride,
And damned all those that trust them! I did hear
The galloping of horse. Who was't came by?   140
LENNOX. 'Tis two or three, my lord, that bring you
   word
Macduff is fled to England.
MACBETH.   Fled to England!
LENNOX. Ay, my good lord.
MACBETH [*aside*]. Time, thou anticipat'st my dread
   exploits:
The flighty purpose never is o'ertook
Unless the deed go with it. From this moment
The very firstlings of my heart shall be
The firstlings of my hand. And even now
To crown my thoughts with acts, be it thought and
   done:
The castle of Macduff I will surprise,   150
Seize upon Fife, give to th'edge o'th' sword
His wife, his babes, and all unfortunate souls
That trace him in his line. No boasting like a fool;
This deed I'll do before this purpose cool.
But no more sights! [*aloud*] Where are these
   gentlemen?
Come, bring me where they are.   *They go*

Scene 2: *Fife. Macduff's castle*

Enter Macduff's Wife, her Son, and Ross

L. MACDUFF. What had he done, to make him fly the
   land?

ROSS. You must have patience, madam.
L. MACDUFF.   He had none:
His flight was madness: when our actions do not,
Our fears do make us traitors.
ROSS.   You know not
Whether it was his wisdom or his fear.
L. MACDUFF. Wisdom! to leave his wife, to leave his
   babes,
His mansion and his titles, in a place
From whence himself does fly? He loves us not;
He wants the natural touch: for the poor wren,
The most diminutive of birds, will fight,   10
Her young ones in her nest, against the owl.
All is the fear and nothing is the love;
As little is the wisdom, where the flight
So runs against all reason.
ROSS.   My dearest coz,
I pray you, school yourself. But, for your husband,
He is noble, wise, judicious, and best knows
The fits o'th' season. I dare not speak much further,
But cruel are the times, when we are traitors
And do not know ourselves; when we hold rumour
From what we fear, yet know not what we fear,   20
But float upon a wild and violent sea,
Each way and none. I take my leave of you:
Shall not be long but I'll be here again:
Things at the worst will cease, or else climb upward
To what they were before. My pretty cousin,
Blessing upon you!
L. MACDUFF. Fathered he is, and yet he's fatherless.
ROSS. I am so much a fool, should I stay longer
It would be my disgrace and your discomfort.
I take my leave at once.   *He goes*
L. MACDUFF.   Sirrah, your father's dead,   30
And what will you do now? How will you live?
SON. As birds do, mother.
L. MACDUFF.   What, with worms and flies?
SON. With what I get, I mean, and so do they.
L. MACDUFF. Poor bird! thou'ldst never fear the net
   nor lime,
The pitfall nor the gin.
SON. Why should I, mother? Poor birds they are not
   set for.
My father is not dead, for all your saying.
L. MACDUFF. Yes, he is dead: how wilt thou do for a
   father?
SON. Nay, how will you do for a husband?
L. MACDUFF. Why, I can buy me twenty at any market. 40
SON. Then you'll buy 'em to sell again.
L. MACDUFF. Thou speak'st with all thy wit, and yet
   i'faith
With wit enough for thee.
SON. Was my father a traitor, mother?
L. MACDUFF. Ay, that he was.
SON. What is a traitor?
L. MACDUFF. Why, one that swears and lies.
SON. And be all traitors that do so?
L. MACDUFF. Every one that does so is a traitor, and
   must be hanged.
SON. And must they all be hanged that swear and lie? 50
L. MACDUFF. Every one.
SON. Who must hang them?
L. MACDUFF. Why, the honest men.
SON. Then the liars and swearers are fools; for there
   are liars and swearers enow to beat the honest men
   and hang up them.

L. MACDUFF. Now God help thee, poor monkey! But
  how wilt thou do for a father?
SON. If he were dead, you'ld weep for him: if you
  would not, it were a good sign that I should quickly   60
  have a new father.
L. MACDUFF. Poor prattler, how thou talk'st!

Enter a Messenger

MESSENGER. Bless you, fair dame! I am not to you
    known,
  Though in your state of honour I am perfect.
  I doubt some danger does approach you nearly.
  If you will take a homely man's advice,
  Be not found here; hence, with your little ones.
  To fright you thus, methinks I am too savage;
  To do worse to you were fell cruelty,
  Which is too nigh your person. Heaven preserve
      you!
  I dare abide no longer.   *He goes*   70
L. MACDUFF.   Whither should I fly?
  I have done no harm. But I remember now
  I am in this earthly world; where to do harm
  Is often laudable, to do good sometime
  Accounted dangerous folly: why then, alas,
  Do I put up that womanly defence,
  To say I have done no harm?

Enter Murderers

                            What are these faces?
MURDERER. Where is your husband?
L. MACDUFF. I hope in no place so unsanctified
  Where such as thou mayst find him.
MURDERER.   He's a traitor.   80
SON. Thou liest, thou shag-haired villain.
MURDERER.   What, you egg!   *Stabs him*
  Young fry of treachery!
SON.   He has killed me, mother:
  Run away, I pray you.   *Dies*
              *Lady Macduff goes, crying murder
              and pursued by the Murderers*

Scene 3: *England. Before the palace of King Edward the
            Confessor*

Enter Malcolm and Macduff

MALCOLM. Let us seek out some desolate shade, and
    there
  Weep our sad bosoms empty.
MACDUFF.   Let us rather
  Hold fast the mortal sword, and like good men
  Bestride our down-fall'n birthdom: each new morn
  New widows howl, new orphans cry, new sorrows
  Strike heaven on the face, that it resounds
  As if it felt with Scotland and yelled out
  Like syllable of dolour.
MALCOLM.   What I believe, I'll wail;
  What know, believe; and what I can redress,
  As I shall find the time to friend, I will.   10
  What you have spoke, it may be so perchance.
  This tyrant, whose sole name blisters our tongues,
  Was once thought honest: you have loved him well;
  He hath not touched you yet. I am young, but
    something
  You may deserve of him through me; and wisdom
  To offer up a weak, poor, innocent lamb,
  T'appease an angry god.
MACDUFF. I am not treacherous.

MALCOLM.   But Macbeth is.
  A good and virtuous nature may recoil
  In an imperial charge. But I shall crave your pardon;   20
  That which you are, my thoughts cannot transpose:
  Angels are bright still, though the brightest fell:
  Though all things foul would wear the brows of
      grace,
  Yet grace must still look so.
MACDUFF.   I have lost my hopes.
MALCOLM. Perchance even there where I did find my
    doubts.
  Why in that rawness left you wife and child,
  Those precious motives, those strong knots of love,
  Without leave-taking? I pray you,
  Let not my jealousies be your dishonours,
  But mine own safeties: you may be rightly just,   30
  Whatever I shall think.
MACDUFF.   Bleed, bleed, poor country!
  Great tyranny, lay thou thy basis sure,
  For goodness dares not check thee: wear thou thy
      wrongs,
  The title is affeered! Fare thee well, lord:
  I would not be the villain that thou think'st
  For the whole space that's in the tyrant's grasp,
  And the rich East to boot.
MALCOLM.   Be not offended:
  I speak not as in absolute fear of you:
  I think our country sinks beneath the yoke,
  It weeps, it bleeds, and each new day a gash   40
  Is added to her wounds. I think withal
  There would be hands uplifted in my right;
  And here from gracious England have I offer
  Of goodly thousands. But for all this,
  When I shall tread upon the tyrant's head,
  Or wear it on my sword, yet my poor country
  Shall have more vices than it had before,
  More suffer and more sundry ways than ever,
  By him that shall succeed.
MACDUFF.   What should he be?
MALCOLM. It is myself I mean: in whom I know   50
  All the particulars of vice so grafted
  That, when they shall be opened, black Macbeth
  Will seem as pure as snow, and the poor state
  Esteem him as a lamb, being compared
  With my confineless harms.
MACDUFF.   Not in the legions
  Of horrid hell can come a devil more damned
  In evils to top Macbeth.
MALCOLM.   I grant him bloody,
  Luxurious, avaricious, false, deceitful,
  Sudden, malicious, smacking of every sin
  That has a name: but there's no bottom, none,   60
  In my voluptuousness: your wives, your daughters,
  Your matrons and your maids, could not fill up
  The cistern of my lust, and my desire
  All continent impediments would o'erbear
  That did oppose my will. Better Macbeth,
  Than such an one to reign.
MACDUFF.   Boundless intemperance
  In nature is a tyranny; it hath been
  Th'untimely emptying of the happy throne,
  And fall of many kings. But fear not yet
  To take upon you what is yours: you may   70
  Convey your pleasures in a spacious plenty,
  And yet seem cold, the time you may so hoodwink:
  We have willing dames enough; there cannot be

That vulture in you, to devour so many
As will to greatness dedicate themselves,
Finding it so inclined.
MALCOLM.   With this there grows
In my most ill-composed affection such
A stanchless avarice that, were I king,
I should cut off the nobles for their lands,
Desire his jewels and this other's house,   80
And my more-having would be as a sauce
To make me hunger more, that I should forge
Quarrels unjust against the good and loyal,
Destroying them for wealth.
MACDUFF.   This avarice
Sticks deeper; grows with more pernicious root
Than summer-seeming lust: and it hath been
The sword of our slain kings: yet do not fear;
Scotland hath foisons to fill up your will
Of your mere own. All these are portable,
With other graces weighed.   90
MALCOLM. But I have none. The king-becoming
      graces,
As justice, verity, temp'rance, stableness,
Bounty, perseverance, mercy, lowliness,
Devotion, patience, courage, fortitude,
I have no relish of them, but abound
In the division of each several crime,
Acting it many ways. Nay, had I power, I should
Pour the sweet milk of concord into hell,
Uproot the universal peace, confound
All unity on earth.
MACDUFF.   O Scotland! Scotland!   100
MALCOLM. If such a one be fit to govern, speak:
I am as I have spoken.
MACDUFF.   Fit to govern!
No, not to live. O nation miserable!
With an untitled tyrant bloody-sceptred,
When shalt thou see thy wholesome days again,
Since that the truest issue of thy throne
By his own interdiction stands accurst,
And does blaspheme his breed? Thy royal father
Was a most sainted king; the queen that bore thee
Oft'ner upon her knees than on her feet,   110
Died every day she lived. Fare thee well!
These evils thou repeat'st upon thyself
Hath banished me from Scotland. O my breast,
Thy hope ends here!
MALCOLM.   Macduff, this noble passion,
Child of integrity, hath from my soul
Wiped the black scruples, reconciled my thoughts
To thy good truth and honour. Devilish Macbeth
By many of these trains hath sought to win me
Into his power; and modest wisdom plucks me
From over-credulous haste: but God above   120
Deal between thee and me! for even now
I put myself to thy direction, and
Unspeak mine own detraction; here abjure
The taints and blames I laid upon myself,
For strangers to my nature. I am yet
Unknown to woman, never was forsworn,
Scarcely have coveted what was mine own,
At no time broke my faith, would not betray
The devil to his fellow, and delight
No less in truth than life: my first false speaking   130
Was this upon myself: what I am truly
Is thine and my poor country's to command:
Whither indeed, before thy here-approach,

Old Siward, with ten thousand warlike men,
Already at a point, was setting forth:
Now we'll together, and the chance of goodness
Be like our warranted quarrel! Why are you silent?
MACDUFF. Such welcome and unwelcome things at
      once
'Tis hard to reconcile.

A Doctor enters

MALCOLM. Well, more anon. Comes the king forth,
      I pray you?   140
DOCTOR. Ay, sir: there are a crew of wretched souls
That stay his cure: their malady convinces
The great assay of art; but at his touch,
Such sanctity hath heaven given his hand,
They presently amend.
MALCOLM.   I thank you, doctor.   *The Doctor goes*
MACDUFF. What's the disease he means?
MALCOLM.   'Tis called the evil:
A most miraculous work in this good king,
Which often, since my here-remain in England,
I have seen him do. How he solicits heaven,
Himself best knows: but strangely-visited people,   150
All swoln and ulcerous, pitiful to the eye,
The mere despair of surgery, he cures,
Hanging a golden stamp about their necks,
Put on with holy prayers: and 'tis spoken,
To the succeeding royalty he leaves
The healing benediction. With this strange virtue
He hath a heavenly gift of prophecy,
And sundry blessings hang about his throne
That speak him full of grace.

Ross approaches

MACDUFF.   See who comes here.
MALCOLM. My countryman; but yet I know him not.   160
MACDUFF. My ever gentle cousin, welcome hither.
MALCOLM. I know him now: good God, betimes
      remove
The means that makes us strangers!
ROSS.   Sir, amen.
MACDUFF. Stands Scotland where it did?
ROSS.   Alas, poor country,
Almost afraid to know itself! It cannot
Be called our mother, but our grave; where nothing,
But who knows nothing, is once seen to smile;
Where sighs and groans and shrieks that rend the
      air,
Are made, not marked; where violent sorrow seems
A modern ecstasy: the dead man's knell   170
Is there scarce asked for who, and good men's lives
Expire before the flowers in their caps,
Dying or ere they sicken.
MACDUFF.   O, relation
Too nice, and yet too true!
MALCOLM.   What's the newest grief?
ROSS. That of an hour's age doth hiss the speaker;
Each minute teems a new one.
MACDUFF.   How does my wife?
ROSS. Why, well.
MACDUFF.   And all my children?
ROSS.   Well too.
MACDUFF. The tyrant has not battered at their peace?
ROSS. No, they were well at peace, when I did leave
      'em.

MACDUFF. Be not a niggard of your speech: how
    goes't? 180
ROSS. When I came hither to transport the tidings
    Which I have heavily borne, there ran a rumour
    Of many worthy fellows that were out;
    Which was to my belief witnessed the rather,
    For that I saw the tyrant's power a-foot.
    Now is the time of help: your eye in Scotland
    Would create soldiers, make our women fight,
    To doff their dire distresses.
MALCOLM.   Be't their comfort
    We are coming thither: gracious England hath
    Lent us good Siward and ten thousand men; 190
    An older and a better soldier none
    That Christendom gives out.
ROSS.   Would I could answer
    This comfort with the like! But I have words,
    That would be howled out in the desert air,
    Where hearing should not latch them.
MACDUFF.   What concern they?
    The general cause? or is it a fee-grief
    Due to some single breast?
ROSS.   No mind that's honest
    But in it shares some woe, though the main part
    Pertains to you alone.
MACDUFF.   If it be mine,
    Keep it not from me, quickly let me have it. 200
ROSS. Let not your ears despise my tongue for ever.
    Which shall possess them with the heaviest sound
    That ever yet they heard.
MACDUFF.   Humh! I guess at it.
ROSS. Your castle is surprised; your wife and babes
    Savagely slaughtered: to relate the manner,
    Were, on the quarry of these murdered deer,
    To add the death of you.
MALCOLM.   Merciful heaven!
    What, man! ne'er pull your hat upon your brows;
    Give sorrow words: the grief that does not speak
    Whispers the o'er-fraught heart and bids it break. 210
MACDUFF. My children too?
ROSS.   Wife, children, servants, all
    That could be found.
MACDUFF.   And I must be from thence!
    My wife killed too?
ROSS.   I have said.
MALCOLM.   Be comforted:
    Let's make us med'cines of our great revenge,
    To cure this deadly grief.
MACDUFF. He has no children. All my pretty ones?
    Did you say all? O, hell-kite! All?
    What, all my pretty chickens and their dam
    At one fell swoop?
MALCOLM. Dispute it like a man.
MACDUFF.   I shall do so; 220
    But I must also feel it as a man:
    I cannot but remember such things were,
    That were most precious to me. Did heaven look on,
    And would not take their part? Sinful Macduff,
    They were all struck for thee! naught that I am,
    Not for their own demerits, but for mine,
    Fell slaughter on their souls: heaven rest them now!
MALCOLM. Be this the whetstone of your sword:
    let grief
    Convert to anger; blunt not the heart, enrage it.
MACDUFF. O, I could play the woman with mine eyes, 230
    And braggart with my tongue! But, gentle heavens,

Cut short all intermission; front to front
Bring thou this fiend of Scotland and myself;
Within my sword's length set him; if he 'scape,
Heaven forgive him too!
MALCOLM.   This tune goes manly.
Come, go we to the king, our power is ready,
Our lack is nothing but our leave. Macbeth
Is ripe for shaking, and the Powers above
Put on their instruments. Receive what cheer you
    may;
The night is long that never finds the day. 240
                        They go

ACT 5
Scene 1: Dunsinane. A room in the castle

Enter a Doctor of Physic, and a Waiting Gentlewoman

DOCTOR. I have two nights watched with you, but can
perceive no truth in your report. When was it she
last walked?
GENTLEWOMAN. Since his majesty went into the field,
I have seen her rise from her bed, throw her night-
gown upon her, unlock her closet, take forth paper,
fold it, write upon't, read it, afterwards seal it, and
again return to bed; yet all this while in a most fast
sleep.
DOCTOR. A great perturbation in nature, to receive at 10
once the benefit of sleep and do the effects of
watching! In this slumbry agitation, besedes her
walking and other actual performances, what, at any
time, have you heard her say?
GENTLEWOMAN. That, sir, which I will not report after
her.
DOCTOR. You may to me, and 'tis most meet you
should.
GENTLEWOMAN. Neither to you nor any one, having
no witness to confirm my speech. 20

Enter Lady Macbeth, with a taper

Lo you, here she comes! This is her very guise, and
upon my life fast asleep. Observe her, stand close.
DOCTOR. How came she by that light?
GENTLEWOMAN. Why, it stood by her: she has light by
her continually, 'tis her command.
DOCTOR. You see, her eyes are open.
GENTLEWOMAN. Ay, but their sense are shut.
DOCTOR. What is it she does now? Look, how she
rubs her hands.
GENTLEWOMAN. It is an accustomed action with her, to 30
seem thus washing her hands: I have known her
continue in this a quarter of an hour.
LADY. M. Yet here's a spot.
DOCTOR. Hark, she speaks! I will set down what comes
from her, to satisfy my remembrance the more
strongly.
LADY M. Out, damnéd spot! out, I say! One: two:
why, then 'tis time to do't. Hell is murky! Fie, my
lord, fie! a soldier, and afeard? What need we fear
who knows it, when none can call our power to 40
accompt? Yet who would have thought the old man
to have had so much blood in him?
DOCTOR. Do you mark that?
LADY M. The Thane of Fife had a wife; where is she
now? What, will these hands ne'er be clean? No
more o'that, my lord, no more o'that: you mar all
with this starting.

DOCTOR. Go to, go to; you have known what you
should not.

GENTLEWOMAN. She has spoke what she should not, I   50
am sure of that: heaven knows what she has known.

LADY M. Here's the smell of the blood still: all the
perfumes of Arabia will not sweeten this little hand.
Oh! oh! oh!

DOCTOR. What a sigh is there! The heart is sorely
charged.

GENTLEWOMAN. I would not have such a heart in my
bosom, for the dignity of the whole body.

DOCTOR. Well, well, well,—

GENTLEWOMAN. Pray God it be, sir.   60

DOCTOR. This disease is beyond my practice: yet I have
known those which have walked in their sleep who
have died holily in their beds.

LADY M. Wash your hands, put on your night-gown,
look not so pale: I tell you yet again, Banquo's
buried; he cannot come out on's grave.

DOCTOR. Even so?

LADY M. To bed, to bed: there's knocking at the gate:
come, come, come, come, give me your hand:
what's done, cannot be undone: to bed, to bed, to   70
bed.   *She goes*

DOCTOR. Will she go now to bed?

GENTLEWOMAN. Directly.

DOCTOR. Foul whisp'rings are abroad: unnatural deeds
Do breed unnatural troubles: infected minds
To their deaf pillows will discharge their secrets:
More needs she the divine than the physician.
God, God forgive us all! Look after her,
Remove from her the means of all annoyance,
And still keep eyes upon her. So, good night: 80
My mind she has mated and amazed my sight:
I think, but dare not speak.

GENTLEWOMAN.   Good night, good doctor.
                                              They go

Scene 2: *The country near Dunsinane. Drum and Colours*

Enter Menteith, Caithness, Angus, Lennox, Soldiers

MENTEITH. The English power is near, led on by
Malcolm,
His uncle Siward and the good Macduff.
Revenges burn in them: for their dear causes
Would to the bleeding and the grim alarm
Excite the mortified man.

ANGUS.   Near Birnam wood
Shall we well meet them, that way are they coming.

CAITHNESS. Who knows if Donalbain be with his
brother?

LENNOX. For certain, sir, he is not: I have a file
Of all the gentry: there is Siward's son,
And many unrough youths, that even now   10
Protest their first of manhood.

MENTEITH.   What does the tyrant?

CAITHNESS. Great Dunsinane he strongly fortifies:
Some say he's mad; others, that lesser hate him,
Do call it valiant fury: but, for certain,
He cannot buckle his distempered cause
Within the belt of rule.

ANGUS.   Now does he feel
His secret murders sticking on his hands;
Now minutely revolts upbraid his faith-breach;
Those he commands move only in command,
Nothing in love: now does he feel his title   20

Hang loose about him, like a giant's robe
Upon a dwarfish thief.

MENTEITH.   Who then shall blame
His pestered senses to recoil and start,
When all that is within him does condemn
Itself for being there?

CAITHNESS.   Well, march we on,
To give obedience where 'tis truly owed:
Meet we the med'cine of the sickly weal,
And with him pour we, in our country's purge,
Each drop of us.

LENNOX.   Or so much as it needs
To dew the sovereign flower and drown the weeds.   30
Make we our march towards Birnam.

                                          Exeunt, marching

Scene 3: *Dunsinane. A court in the castle*

Enter Macbeth, Doctor, and Attendants

MACBETH. Bring me no more reports, let them fly all:
Till Birnam wood remove to Dunsinane
I cannot taint with fear. What's the boy Malcolm?
Was he not born of woman? The spirits that know
All mortal consequences have pronounced me thus:
'Fear not, Macbeth, no man that's born of a woman
Shall e'er have power upon thee'. Then fly, false
thanes,
And mingle with the English epicures:
The mind I sway by and the heart I bear
Shall never sag with doubt nor shake with fear.   10

A servant enters

The devil damn thee black, thou cream-faced loon!
Where got'st thou that goose look?

SERVANT. There is ten thousand—

MACBETH.   Geese, villain?

SERVANT.   Soldiers, sir.

MACBETH. Go prick thy face and over-red thy fear,
Thou lily-livered boy. What soldiers, patch?
Death of thy soul! those linen cheeks of thine
Are counsellors to fear. What soldiers, whey-face?

SERVANT. The English force, so please you.

MACBETH. Take thy face hence.   *Servant goes*
                    Seton!—I am sick at heart,
When I behold—Seton, I say!—This push   20
Will cheer me ever, or disseat me now.
I have lived long enough: my way of life
Is fall'n into the sere, the yellow leaf,
And that which should accompany old age,
As honour, love, obedience, troops of friends,
I must not look to have; but, in their stead,
Curses, not loud but deep, mouth-honour, breath
Which the poor heart would fain deny and dare not.
Seton!

Seton enters

SETON. What's your gracious pleasure?

MACBETH.   What news more?   30

SETON. All is confirmed, my lord, which was reported.

MACBETH. I'll fight, till from my bones my flesh be
hacked.
Give me my armour.

SETON.   'Tis not needed yet.

MACBETH. I'll put it on.
Send out moe horses, skirr the country round,

Hang those that talk of fear. Give me mine
    armour....   *Seton goes*
How does your patient, doctor?
DOCTOR.   Not so sick, my lord,
As she is troubled with thick-coming fancies,
That keep her from her rest.
MACBETH.   Cure her of that:
Canst thou not minister to a mind diseased,   40
Pluck from the memory a rooted sorrow,
Raze out the written troubles of the brain,
And with some sweet oblivious antidote
Cleanse the stuffed bosom of that perilous stuff
Which weighs upon the heart?
DOCTOR.   Therein the patient
Must minister to himself.
MACBETH. Throw physic to the dogs, I'll none of it.
Come, put mine armour on; give me my staff;
Seton, send out; doctor, the thanes fly from me;
Come, sir, dispatch.—If thou couldst, doctor, cast   50
The water of my land, find her disease,
And purge it to a sound and pristine health,
I would applaud thee to the very echo,
That should applaud again.—Pull't off, I say.—
What rhubarb, senna, or what purgative drug,
Would scour these English hence? Hear'st thou of
    them?
DOCTOR. Ay, my good lord; your royal preparation
Makes us hear something.
MACBETH.   Bring it after me.
I will not be afraid of death and bane
Till Birnam forest come to Dunsinane.   *He goes*   60
DOCTOR. Were I from Dunsinane away and clear,
Profit again should hardly draw me here.
                           He goes

Scene 4: Country near Birnam. Drum and Colours

*Enter Malcolm, Siward, Macduff, Siward's Son, Menteith,
Caithness, Angus, Lennox, Ross, and Soldiers, marching*

MALCOLM. Cousins, I hope, the days are near at hand
That chambers will be safe.
MENTEITH.   We doubt it nothing.
SIWARD. What wood is this before us?
MENTEITH.   The wood of Birnam.
MALCOLM. Let every soldier hew him down a bough,
And bear't before him: thereby shall we shadow
The number of our host, and make discovery
Err in report of us.
SOLDIER.   It shall be done.
SIWARD. We learn no other but the confident tyrant
Keeps still in Dunsinane, and will endure
Our setting down before't.
MALCOLM.   'Tis his main hope: 10
For where there is advantage to be gone,
Both more and less have given him the revolt,
And none serve with him but constrainéd things
Whose hearts are absent too.
MACDUFF.   Let our just censures
Attend the true event, and put we on
Industrious soldiership.
SIWARD.   The time approaches,
That will with due decision make us know
What we shall say we have and what we owe.
Thoughts speculative their unsure hopes relate,
But certain issue strokes must arbitrate: 20

Towards which advance the war.
                       Exeunt, marching

Scene 5: Dunsinane. The court of the castle as before

Enter Macbeth, Seton, and Soldiers with Drum and Colours

MACBETH. Hang out our banners on the outward
    walls;
The cry is still 'They come': our castle's strength
Will laugh a siege to scorn: here let them lie
Till famine and the ague eat them up:
Were they not forced with those that should be ours,
We might have met them dareful, beard to beard,
And beat them backward home.
                   A cry within of women
                     What is that noise?
SETON. It is the cry of women, my good lord.   *Goes*
MACBETH. I have almost forgot the taste of fears:
The time has been, my senses would have cooled   10
To hear a night-shriek, and my fell of hair
Would at a dismal treatise rouse and stir
As life were in't: I have supped full with horrors;
Direness, familiar to my slaughterous thoughts,
Cannot once start me.
Seton returns
                   Wherefore was that cry?
SETON. The queen, my lord, is dead.
MACBETH. She should have died hereafter;
There would have been a time for such a word.
To-morrow, and to-morrow, and to-morrow,
Creeps in this petty pace from day to day,   20
To the last syllable of recorded time;
And all our yesterdays have lighted fools
The way to dusty death. Out, out, brief candle!
Life's but a walking shadow, a poor player
That struts and frets his hour upon the stage,
And then is heard no more: it is a tale
Told by an idiot, full of sound and fury,
Signifying nothing.

Enter a messenger

Thou com'st to use thy tongue; thy story quickly.
MESSENGER. Gracious my lord,   30
I should report that which I say I saw,
But know not how to do't.
MACBETH.   Well, say, sir.
MESSENGER. As I did stand my watch upon the hill,
I looked toward Birnam, and anon methought
The wood began to move.
MACBETH.   Liar and slave!
MESSENGER. Let me endure your wrath, if't be not so:
Within this three mile may you see it coming.
I say, a moving grove.
MACBETH.   If thou speak'st false,
Upon the next tree shalt thou hang alive,
Till famine cling thee: if thy speech be sooth,   40
I care not if thou dost for me as much.
I pall in resolution, and begin
To doubt th'equivocation of the fiend
That lies like truth: 'Fear not, till Birnam wood
Do come to Dunsinane'; and now a wood
Comes toward Dunsinane. Arm, arm, and out!
If this which he avouches does appear,
There is nor flying hence nor tarrying here.
I 'gin to be aweary of the sun,
And wish th'estate o'th' world were now undone.   50

Ring the alarum bell! Blow, wind! come, wrack!
At least we'll die with harness on our back.
They go

Scene 6: *Dunsinane. Before the castle gate. Drum*
and Colours

Enter Malcolm, Siward, Macduff, and their army,
with boughs

MALCOLM. Now near enough: your leavy screens
    throw down,
And show like those you are. You, worthy uncle,
Shall with my cousin your right noble son
Lead our first battle: worthy Macduff and we
Shall take upon's what else remains to do,
According to our order.
SIWARD.   Fare you well.
Do we but find the tyrant's power to-night,
Let us be beaten, if we cannot fight.
MACDUFF. Make all our trumpets speak; give them all
    breath,
Those clamorous harbingers of blood and death.   10

        They go forward, their trumpets sounding

Scene 7

Enter Macbeth

MACBETH. They have tied me to a stake; I cannot fly,
But bear-like I must fight the course. What's he
That was not born of woman? Such a one
Am I to fear, or none.

Young Siward comes up

YOUNG SIWARD. What is thy name?
MACBETH.   Thou'lt be afraid to hear it.
YOUNG SIWARD. No; though thou call'st thyself a
    hotter name
Than any is in hell.
MACBETH.   My name's Macbeth.
YOUNG SIWARD. The devil himself could not
    pronounce a title
More hateful to mine ear.
MACBETH.   No, nor more fearful.
YOUNG SIWARD. Thou liest, abhorréd tyrant, with my
    sword   10
I'll prove the lie thou speak'st.
        They fight, and young Siward is slain
MACBETH.   Thou wast born of woman.
But swords I smile at, weapons laugh to scorn,
Brandished by man that's of a woman born.

He passes on. Macduff comes up

MACDUFF. That way the noise is. Tyrant, show thy
    face!
If thou beest slain and with no stroke of mine,
My wife and children's ghosts will haunt me still.
I cannot strike at wretched kerns, whose arms
Are hired to bear their staves; either thou, Macbeth,
Or else my sword with an unbattered edge
I sheathe again undeeded. There thou shouldst be;   20
By this great clatter, one of greatest note
Seems bruited. Let me find him, fortune!
And more I beg not. *He follows Macbeth. Alarums*

Malcolm and old Siward come up

SIWARD. This way, my lord; the castle's gently
    rendered:
The tyrant's people on both sides do fight,
The noble thanes do bravely in the war,
The day almost itself professes yours,
And little is to do.
MALCOLM.   We have met with foes
That strike beside us.
SIWARD.   Enter, sir, the castle
                                    They go. Alarum

Scene 8

Macbeth returns

MACBETH. Why should I play the Roman fool, and die
On mine own sword? whiles I see lives, the gashes
Do better upon them.

Macduff returns, following him

MACDUFF.   Turn, hell hound, turn.
MACBETH. Fall men else I have avoided thee:
But get thee back, my soul is too much charged
With blood of thine already.
MACDUFF.   I have no words:
My voice is my sword, thou bloodier villain
Than terms can give thee out! *They fight. Alarum*
MACBETH.   Thou losest labour.
As easy mayst thou the intrenchant air
With thy keen sword impress as make me bleed: 10
Let fall thy blade on vulnerable crests,
I bear a charméd life, which must not yield
To one of woman born.
MACDUFF.   Despair thy charm,
And let the angel whom thou still hast served
Tell thee, Macduff was from his mother's womb
Untimely ripped.
MACBETH. Acccurséd be that tongue that tells me so,
For it hath cowed my better part of man!
And be these juggling fiends no more believed,
That palter with us in a double sense,   20
That keep the word of promise to our ear,
And break it to our hope. I'll not fight with thee.
MACDUFF. Then yield thee, coward,
And live to be the show and gaze o'th' time.
We'll have thee, as our rarer monsters are,
Painted upon a pole, and underwrit,
'Here may you see the tyrant'.
MACBETH.   I will not yield,
To kiss the ground before young Malcolm's feet,
And to be baited with the rabble's curse.
Though Birnam wood be come to Dunsinane,   30
And thou opposed, being of no woman born,
Yet I will try the last. Before my body
I throw my warlike shield: lay on, Macduff,
And damned be him that first cries 'Hold, enough'.
        They fight until Macbeth is slain

Scene 9: *Within the castle*

Retreat and flourish. Enter, with Drum and Colours,
Malcolm, Siward, Ross, Thanes and Soldiers

MALCOLM. I would the friends we miss were safe
    arrived.
SIWARD. Some must go off: and yet, by these I see,
So great a day as this is cheaply bought.
MALCOLM. Macduff is missing, and your noble son.

ROSS. Your son, my lord, has paid a soldier's debt:
He only lived but till he was a man,
The which no sooner had his prowess confirmed
In the unshrinking station where he fought,
But like a man he died.
SIWARD.   Then he is dead?
ROSS. Ay, and brought off the field: your cause of
    sorrow   10
Must not be measured by his worth, for then
It hath no end.
SIWARD.   Had he his hurts before?
ROSS. Ay, on the front.
SIWARD.   Why then, God's soldier be he!
Had I as many sons as I have hairs,
I would not wish them to a fairer death:
And so his knell is knolled.
MALCOLM.   He's worth more sorrow,
And that I'll spend for him.
SIWARD.   He's worth no more.
They say he parted well and paid his score:
And so God be with him! Here comes newer
    comfort.

Enter Macduff, with Macbeth's head

MACDUFF. Hail, king! for so thou art. Behold, where
    stands   20
Th'usurper's cursèd head: the time is free:
I see thee compassed with thy kingdom's pearl,
That speak my salutation in their minds;
Whose voices I desire aloud with mine:
Hail, king of Scotland!
ALL.   Hail, King of Scotland! *Flourish*
MALCOLM. We shall not spend a large expense of time
Before we reckon with your several loves,
And make us even with you. My thanes and
    kinsmen,
Henceforth be earls, the first that ever Scotland
In such an honour named. What's more to do,   30
Which would be planted newly with the time,
As calling home our exiled friends abroad
That fled the snares of watchful tyranny,
Producing forth the cruel ministers
Of this dead butcher and his fiend-like queen,
Who, as 'tis thought, by self and violent hands
Took off her life; this, and what needful else
That calls upon us, by the grace of Grace
We will perform in measure, time, and place:
So thanks to all at once, and to each one,   40
Whom we invite to see us crowned at Scone.
                        Flourish. They go

The Tragedy of Hamlet, Prince of Denmark

The scene: Denmark

CHARACTERS IN THE PLAY

CLAUDIUS, *King of Denmark*
HAMLET, *Prince of Denmark, son to the late, and nephew
  to the present king*
POLONIUS, *Principal Secretary of State*
HORATIO, *friend to Hamlet*
LAERTES, *son to Polonius*
VALTEMAND } *ambassadors to Norway*
CORNELIUS
ROSENCRANTZ } *formerly fellow-students with Hamlet*
GUILDENSTERN
OSRIC, *a fantastic fop*
A gentleman
A Doctor of Divinity

MARCELLUS }
BARNARDO } *Gentlemen of the Guard*
FRANCISCO
REYNALDO, *servant to Polonius*
Four or five Players
Two grave-diggers
FORTINBRAS, *Prince of Norway*
A Norwegian Captain
English Ambassadors
GERTRUDE, *Queen of Denmark, mother to Hamlet*
OPHELIA, *daughter to Polonius*
*Lords, Ladies, Soldiers, Sailors, Messenger, and
  Attendants*
The GHOST *of Hamlet's father*

The Tragedy of Hamlet, Prince of Denmark

ACT 1

Scene 1: *The castle at Elsinore. A narrow platform upon
the battlements*

Francisco, a sentinel. Enter Barnardo, another sentinel

BARNARDO. Who's there?

FRANCISCO. Nay, answer me. Stand and unfold
yourself.

BARNARDO. Long live the king!

FRANCISCO. Barnardo?

BARNARDO. He.

FRANCISCO. You come most carefully upon your hour.

BARNARDO. 'Tis now struck twelve, get thee to bed,
Francisco.

FRANCISCO. For this relief much thanks, 'tis bitter cold,
And I am sick at heart.

BARNARDO. Have you had quiet guard?

FRANCISCO.   Not a mouse stirring. 10

BARNARDO. Well, good night:
If you do meet Horatio and Marcellus,
The rivals of my watch, bid them make haste.

Horatio and Marcellus enter

FRANCISCO. I think I hear them. Stand ho, who is
there?

HORATIO. Friends to this ground.

MARCELLUS.   And liegemen to the Dane.

FRANCISCO. Give you good night.

MARCELLUS.   O, farewell honest soldier,
Who hath relieved you?

FRANCISCO.   Barnardo hath my place;
Give you good night.   *Francisco goes*

MARCELLUS.   Holla, Barnado!

BARNARDO.   Say,
What, is Horatio there?

HORATIO.   A piece of him.

BARNARDO. Welcome Horatio, welcome good
Marcellus.   20

HORATIO. What, has this thing appeared again
to-night?

BARNARDO. I have seen nothing.

MARCELLUS. Horatio says 'tis but our fantasy,
And will not let belief take hold of him
Touching this dreaded sight twice seen of us,
Therefore I have entreated him along
With us to watch the minutes of this night,
That if again this apparition come,
He may approve our eyes and speak to it.

HORATIO. Tush, tush, 'twill not appear.

BARNARDO.   Sit down awhile, 30
And let us once again assail your ears,
That are so fortified against our story,
What we have two nights seen.

HORATIO.   Well, sit we down,
And let us hear Barnardo speak of this.

BARNARDO. Last night of all,
When yon same star that's westward from the pole
Had made his course t'illume that part of heaven
Where now i burns, Marcellus and myself,
The bell then beating one——

A Ghost appears

MARCELLUS. Peace, break thee off, look where it comes
again!   40

BARNARDO. In the same figure like the king that's
dead.

MARCELLUS. Thou art a scholar, speak to it, Horatio.

BARNARDO. Looks a' not like the king? mark it,
Horatio.

HORATIO. Most like, it harrows me with fear and
wonder.

BARNARDO. It would be spoke to.

MARCELLUS.   Question it, Horatio.

HORATIO. What art thou that usurp'st this time of
night,
Together with that fair and warlike form
In which the majesty of buried Denmark
Did sometimes march? by heaven I charge thee
speak.

MARCELLUS. It is offended.

BARNARDO.   See, it stalks away.   50

HORATIO. Stay, speak, speak, I charge thee speak.
         The Ghost vanishes

MARCELLUS. 'Tis gone and will not answer.

BARNARDO. How now Horatio, you tremble and look
pale,
Is not this something more than fantasy?
What think you on't?

HORATIO. Before my God, I might not this believe
Without the sensible and true avouch
Of mine own eyes.

MARCELLUS.   Is it not like the king?

HORATIO. As thou art to thyself.
Such was the very armour he had on,   60
When he the ambitious Norway combated,
So frowned he once, when in an angry parle
He smote the sledded Polacks on the ice.
'Tis strange.

MARCELLUS. Thus twice before, and jump at this dead
hour,
With martial stalk hath he gone by our watch.

HORATIO. In what particular thought to work I know
not,
But in the gross and scope of mine opinion,
This bodes some strange eruption to our state.

MARCELLUS. Good now sit down, and tell me he that
knows,   70
Why this same strict and most observant watch
So nightly toils the subject of the land,
And why such daily cast of brazen cannon
And foreign mart for implements of war,
Why such impress of shipwrights, whose sore task
Does not divide the Sunday from the week,
What might be toward that this sweaty haste
Doth make the night joint-labourer with the day,
Who is't that can inform me?

HORATIO.   That can I,
At least the whisper goes so; our last king,   80
Whose image even but now appeared to us,
Was as you know by Fortinbras of Norway,

Thereto pricked on by a most emulate pride,
Dared to the combat; in which our valiant Hamlet
(For so this side of our known world esteeméd him)
Did slay this Fortinbras, who by a sealed compact,
Well ratified by law and heraldy,
Did forfeit (with his life) all those his lands
Which he stood seized of, to the conqueror,
Against the which a moiety competent   90
Was gagéd by our king, which had returned
To the inheritance of Fortinbras,
Had he been vanquisher; as by the same co-mart,
And carriage of the article designed,
His fell to Hamlet; now sir, young Fortinbras,
Of unimprovéd mettle hot and full,
Hath in the skirts of Norway here and there
Sharked up a list of lawless resolutes
For food and diet to some enterprise
That hath a stomach in't, which is no other,   100
As it doth well appear unto our state,
But to recover of us by strong hand
And terms compulsatory, those foresaid lands
So by his father lost; and this, I take it,
Is the main motive of our preparations,
The source of this our watch, and the chief head
Of this post-haste and romage in the land.
BARNARDO. I think it be no other but e'en so;
Well may it sort that this portentous figure
Comes arméd through our watch so like the king   110
That was and is the question of these wars.
HORATIO. A mote it is to trouble the mind's eye:
In the most high and palmy state of Rome,
A little ere the mightiest Julius fell,
The graves stood tenantless, and the sheeted dead
Did squeak and gibber in the Roman streets,
And even the like precurse of fierce events,
As harbingers preceding still the fates
And prologue to the omen coming on,
Have heaven and earth together demonstrated   120
Unto our climatures and countrymen,
As stars with trains of fire and dews of blood,
Disasters in the sun; and the moist star,
Upon whose influence Neptune's empire stands,
Was sick almost to doomsday with eclipse.

The Ghost reappears

But soft, behold, lo where it comes again!
I'll cross it though it blast me . . .
                    He spreads his arms
                    Stay, illusion!
If thou hast any sound or use of voice,
Speak to me.
If there be any good thing to be done   130
That may to thee do ease, and grace to me,
Speak to me.
If thou art privy to thy country's fate
Which happily foreknowing may avoid,
O, speak!
Or if thou hast uphoarded in thy life
Extorted treasure in the womb of earth,
For which they say you spirits oft walk in death,
                    A cock crows
Speak of it—stay and speak—stop it, Marcellus!
MARCELLUS. Shall I strike at it with my partisan?   140
HORATIO. Do if it will not stand.
BARNARDO.   'Tis here!
HORATIO.   'Tis here!

MARCELLUS. 'Tis gone!   *The Ghost vanishes*
We do it wrong being so majestical
To offer it the show of violence,
For it is as the air, invulnerable,
And our vain blows malicious mockery.
BARNARDO. It was about to speak when the cock crew.
HORATIO. And then it started like a guilty thing,
Upon a fearful summons; I have heard
The cock that is the trumpet to the morn   150
Doth with his lofty and shrill-sounding throat
Awake the god of day, and at his warning
Whether in sea or fire, in earth or air,
Th'extravagant and erring spirit hies
To his confine, and of the truth herein
This present object made probation.
MARCELLUS. It faded on the crowing of the cock.
Some say that ever 'gainst that season comes
Wherein our Saviour's birth is celebrated
This bird of dawning singeth all night long,   160
And then they say no spirit dare stir abroad,
The nights are wholesome, then no planets strike,
No fairy takes, nor witch hath power to charm,
So hallowed, and so gracious is that time.
HORATIO. So have I heard and do in part believe it.
But look, the morn in russet mantle clad
Walks o'er the dew of yon high eastward hill.
Break we our watch up and by my advice
Let us impart what we have seen to-night
Unto young Hamlet, for upon my life   170
This spirit dumb to us, will speak to him:
Do you consent we shall acquaint him with it,
As needful in our loves, fitting our duty?
MARCELLUS. Let's do't, I pray, and I this morning know
Where we shall find him most convenient.
                                        They go

Scene 2: *The Council Chamber in the castle*

*A flourish of trumpets. Enter Claudius King of Denmark,
Gertrude the Queen, Councillors, Polonius and his son
Laertes, Valtemand and Cornelius; and last of all Prince
Hamlet*

KING. Though yet of Hamlet our dear brother's death
The memory be green, and that it us befitted
To bear our hearts in grief, and our whole kingdom
To be contracted in one brow of woe,
Yet so far hath discretion fought with nature,
That we with wisest sorrow think on him
Together with remembrance of ourselves:
Therefore our sometime sister, now our queen,
Th'imperial jointress to this warlike state,
Have we as 'twere with a defeated joy,   10
With an auspicious, and a dropping eye,
With mirth in funeral, and with dirge in marriage,
In equal scale weighing delight and dole,
Taken to wife: nor have we herein barred
Your better wisdoms, which have freely gone
With this affair along—for all, our thanks.
Now follows that you know, young Fortinbras,
Holding a weak supposal of our worth,
Or thinking by our late dear brother's death
Our state to be disjoint and out of frame,   20
Colleaguéd with this dream of his advantage,
He hath not failed to pester us with message
Importing the surrender of those lands
Lost by his father, with all bands of law,

To our most valiant brother—so much for him:
Now for ourself, and for this time of meeting,
Thus much the business is. We have here writ
To Norway, uncle of young Fortinbras—
Who impotent and bed-rid scarcely hears
Of this his nephew's purpose—to suppress 30
His further gait herein, in that the levies,
The lists, and full proportions, are all made
Out of his subject. And we here dispatch
You good Cornelius, and you Valtemand,
For bearers of this greeting to old Norway,
Giving to you no further personal power
To business with the king, more than the scope
Of these delated articles allow:
Farewell, and let your haste commend your duty.
CORNELIUS, VALTEMAND. In that, and all things, will we
    show our duty. 40
KING. We doubt it nothing, heartily farewell.
           Valtemand and Cornelius depart
And now, Laertes, what's the news with you?
You told us of some suit, what is't, Laertes?
You cannot speak of reason to the Dane,
And lose your voice; what wouldst thou beg,
    Laertes,
That shall not be my offer, not thy asking?
The head is not more native to the heart,
The hand more instrumental to the mouth,
Than is the throne of Denmark to thy father.
What wouldst thou have, Laertes?
LAERTES.   My dread lord, 50
Your leave and favour to return to France,
From whence though willingly I came to Denmark,
To show my duty in your coronation;
Yet now I must confess, that duty done,
My thoughts and wishes bend again toward France,
And bow them to your gracious leave and pardon.
KING. Have you your father's leave? what says
    Polonius?
POLONIUS. He hath, my lord, wrung from me my
    slow leave
By laboursome petition, and at last
Upon his will I sealed my hard consent. 60
I do beseech you give him leave to go.
KING. Take thy fair hour, Laertes, time be thine,
And thy best graces spend it at thy will ...
But now my cousin Hamlet, and my son—
HAMLET [*aside*]. A little more than kin, and less than
    kind.
KING. How is it that the clouds still hang on you?
HAMLET. Not so, my lord, I am too much in the 'son.'
QUEEN. Good Hamlet, cast thy nighted colour off,
    And let thine eye look like a friend on Denmark,
Do not for ever with thy vailéd lids 70
Seek for thy noble father in the dust,
Thou know'st 'tis common, all that lives must die,
Passing through nature to eternity.
HAMLET. Ay, madam, it is common.
QUEEN.   If it be,
Why seems it so particular with thee?
HAMLET. Seems, madam! nay it is, I know not 'seems.'
'Tis not alone my inky cloak, good mother,
Nor customary suits of solemn black,
Nor windy suspiration of forced breath,
No, nor the fruitful river in the eye, 80
Nor the dejected haviour of the visage,
Together with all forms, modes, shapes of grief,

That can denote me truly. These indeed seem,
For they are actions that a man might play,
But I have that within which passes show,
These but the trappings and the suits of woe.
KING. 'Tis sweet and commendable in your nature,
    Hamlet,
To give these mourning duties to your father,
But you must know your father lost a father,
That father lost, lost his, and the survivor bound 90
In filial obligation for some term
To do obsequious sorrow. But to persever
In obstinate condolement is a course
Of impious stubbornness, 'tis unmanly grief,
It shows a will most incorrect to heaven,
A heart unfortified, a mind impatient,
An understanding simple and unschooled.
For what we know must be and is as common
As any the most vulgar thing to sense,
Why should we in our peevish opposition 100
Take it to heart? fie, 'tis a fault to heaven,
A fault against the dead, a fault to nature,
To reason most absurd, whose common theme
Is death of fathers, and who still hath cried,
From the first corse till he that died to-day,
'This must be so' ... We pray you throw to earth
This unprevailing woe, and think of us
As of a father, for let the world take note
You are the most immediate to our throne,
And with no less nobility of love 110
Than that which dearest father bears his son,
Do I impart toward you ... For your intent
In going back to school in Wittenberg,
It is most retrograde to our desire,
And we beseech you, bend you to remain
Here in the cheer and comfort of our eye,
Our chiefest courtier, cousin, and our son.
QUEEN. Let not thy mother lose her prayers, Hamlet,
I pray thee stay with us, go not to Wittenberg.
HAMLET. I shall in all my best obey you, madam. 120
KING. Why, 'tis a loving and a fair reply,
Be as ourself in Denmark. Madam, come.
This gentle and unforced accord of Hamlet
Sits smiling to my heart, in grace whereof,
No jocund health that Denmark drinks to-day,
But the great cannon to the clouds shall tell,
And the king's rouse the heaven shall bruit again,
Re-speaking earthly thunder; come away.
          Flourish. Exeunt all but Hamlet
HAMLET. O, that this too too sullied flesh would melt,
Thaw and resolve itself into a dew, 130
Or that the Everlasting had not fixed
His canon 'gainst self-slaughter. O God, God,
How weary, stale, flat, and unprofitable
Seem to me all the uses of this world!
Fie on't, ah fie, 'tis an unweeded garden
That grows to seed, things rank and gross in nature
Possess it merely. That it should come to this,
But two months dead, nay not so much, not two,
So excellent a king, that was to this
Hyperion to a satyr, so loving to my mother, 140
That he might not beteem the winds of heaven
Visit her face too roughly—heaven and earth
Must I remember? why, she would hang on him
As if increase of appetite had grown
By what it fed on, and yet within a month,
Let me not think on't ... frailty thy name is woman!

A little month or ere those shoes were old
With which she followed my poor father's body
Like Niobe all tears, why she, even she—
O God, a beast that wants discourse of reason   150
Would have mourned longer—married with my
  uncle,
My father's brother, but no more like my father
Than I to Hercules, within a month,
Ere yet the salt of most unrighteous tears
Had left the flushing in her gallèd eyes
She married. O most wicked speed . . . to post
With such dexterity to incestuous sheets!
It is not, nor it cannot come to good,
But break my heart, for I must hold my tongue.

Horatio, Marcellus and Barnardo enter

HORATIO. Hail to your lordship!
HAMLET.   I am glad to see you well;   160
Horatio—or I do forget my self!
HORATIO. The same, my lord, and your poor servant
  ever.
HAMLET. Sir, my good friend, I'll change that name
  with you.
And what make you from Wittenberg, Horatio?
Marcellus.
MARCELLUS. My good lord!
HAMLET. I am very glad to see you—good even, sir.
                              To Barnardo
But what in faith make you from Wittenberg?
HORATIO. A truant disposition, good my lord.
HAMLET. I would not hear your enemy say so,   170
Nor shall you do mine ear that violence
To make it truster of your own report
Against yourself. I know you are no truant,
But what is your affair in Elsinore?
We'll teach you to drink deep ere you depart.
HORATIO. My lord, I came to see your father's funeral.
HAMLET. I prithee thee do not mock me
  fellow-student;
I think it was to see my mother's wedding.
HORATIO. Indeed, my lord, it followed hard upon.
HAMLET. Thrift, thrift, Horatio, the funeral baked
  meats   180
Did coldly furnish forth the marriage tables.
Would I had met my dearest foe in heaven
Or ever I had seen that day, Horatio—
My father, methinks I see my father.
HORATIO. Where, my lord?
HAMLET.   In my mind's eye, Horatio.
HORATIO. I saw him once, a' was a goodly king—
HAMLET. A' was a man, take him for all in all,
I shall not look upon his like again.
HORATIO. My lord, I think I saw him yesternight.
HAMLET. Saw, who?   190
HORATIO. My lord, the king your father.
HAMLET.   The king my father!
HORATIO. Season your admiration for a while
With an attent ear till I may deliver
Upon the witness of these gentlemen
This marvel to you.
HAMLET.   For God's love let me hear!
HORATIO. Two nights together had these gentlemen,
Marcellus and Barnardo, on their watch
In the dead waste and middle of the night,
Been thus encountered. A figure like your father
Armèd at point exactly, cap-a-pe,   200

Appears before them, and with solemn march,
Goes slow and stately by them; thrice he walked
By their oppressed and fear-surprisèd eyes
Within his truncheon's length, whilst they distilled
Almost to jelly with the act of fear,
Stand dumb and speak not to him; this to me
In dreadful secrecy impart they did,
And I with them the third night kept the watch,
Where, as they had delivered, both in time,
Form of the thing, each word made true and good,   210
The apparition comes: I knew your father,
These hands are not more like.
HAMLET.   But where was this?
MARCELLUS. My lord, upon the platform where we
  watch.
HAMLET. Did you not speak to it?
HORATIO.   My lord, I did,
But answer made it none, yet once methought
It lifted up it head, and did address
Itself to motion like as it would speak:
But even then the morning cock crew loud,
And at the sound it shrunk in haste away
And vanished from our sight.
HAMLET.   'Tis very strange.   220
HORATIO. As I do live my honoured lord 'tis true,
And we did think it writ down in our duty
To let you know of it.
HAMLET. Indeed, indeed, sirs, but this troubles me.
Hold you the watch to-night?
ALL.   We do, my lord.
HAMLET. Armed, say you?
ALL. Armed, my lord.
HAMLET. From top to toe?
ALL.   My lord, from head to foot.
HAMLET. Then saw you not his face.
HORATIO. O yes, my lord, he wore his beaver up.   230
HAMLET. What, looked he frowningly?
HORATIO. A countenance more in sorrow than in
  anger.
HAMLET. Pale, or red?
HORATIO. Nay, very pale.
HAMLET.   And fixed his eyes upon you?
HORATIO. Most constantly.
HAMLET.   I would I had been there.
HORATIO. It would have much amazed you.
HAMLET. Very like, very like, stayed it long?
HORATIO. While one with moderate haste might tell a
  hundred.
MARCELLUS, BARNARDO. Longer, longer.
HORATIO. Not when I saw't.
HAMLET.   His beard was grizzled, no?   240
HORATIO. It was as I have seen it in his life,
A sable silvered.
HAMLET.   I will watch to-night,
Perchance 'twill walk again.
HORATIO.   I war'nt it will.
HAMLET. If it assume my noble father's person,
I'll speak to it though hell itself should gape
And bid me hold my peace; I pray you all
If you have hitherto concealed this sight
Let it be tenable in your silence still,
And whatsomever else shall hap to-night,
Give it an understanding but no tongue.   250
I will requite your loves, so fare you well:
Upon the platform 'twixt eleven and twelve
I'll visit you.

ALL. Our duty to your honour.
HAMLET. Your loves, as mine to you. Farewell.
They depart
My father's spirit (in arms!) all is not well,
I doubt some foul play, would the night were come,
Till then sit still my soul, foul deeds will rise,
Though all the earth o'erwhelm them, to men's
eyes. *He goes*

Scene 3: *A room in the house of Polonius*

Enter Laertes and Ophelia his sister

LAERTES. My necessaries are embarked, farewell,
And sister, as the winds give benefit
And convoy is assistant, do not sleep,
But let me hear from you.
OPHELIA. Do you doubt that?
LAERTES. For Hamlet, and the trifling of his favour,
Hold it a fashion, and a toy in blood,
A violet in the youth of primy nature,
Forward, not permanent, sweet, not lasting,
The perfume and suppliance of a minute,
No more.
OPHELIA. No more but so?
LAERTES. Think it no more. 10
For nature crescent does not grow alone
In thews and bulk, but as this temple waxes
The inward service of the mind and soul
Grows wide withal. Perhaps he loves you now,
And now no soil nor cautel doth besmirch
The virtue of his will. But you must fear,
His greatness weighed, his will is not his own,
For he himself is subject to his birth.
He may not, as unvalued persons do,
Carve for himself, for on his choice depends 20
The sanity and health of this whole state,
And therefore must his choice be circumscribed
Unto the voice and yielding of that body
Whereof he is the head. Then if he says he loves you,
It fits your wisdom so far to believe it
As he in his particular act and place
May give his saying deed, which is no further
Than the main voice of Denmark goes withal.
Then weigh what loss your honour may sustain
If with too credent ear you list his songs, 30
Or lose your heart, or your chaste treasure open
To his unmast'red importunity.
Fear it Ophelia, fear it my dear sister,
And keep you in the rear of your affection,
Out of the shot and danger of desire.
"The chariest maid is prodigal enough
"If she unmask her beauty to the moon."
"Virtue itself 'scapes not calumnious strokes."
"The canker galls the infants of the spring
"Too oft before their buttons be disclosed, 40
"And in the morn and liquid dew of youth
"Contagious blastments are most imminent."
Be wary then—best safety lies in fear,
Youth to itself rebels, though none else near.
OPHELIA. I shall the effect of this good lesson keep
As watchman to my heart. But good my brother
Do not, as some ungracious pastors do,
Show me the steep and thorny way to heaven,
Whiles like a puffed and reckless libertine
Himself the primrose path of dalliance treads, 50
And recks not his own rede.

Polonius enters

LAERTES. O fear me not,
I stay too long—but here my father comes.
A double blessing is a double grace,
Occasion smiles upon a second leave.
POLONIUS. Yet here Laertes? aboard, aboard for
shame!
The wind sits in the shoulder of your sail,
And you are stayed for. There—my blessing with
thee, *He lays his hand on Laertes' head*
And these few precepts in thy memory
Look thou character. Give thy thoughts no tongue,
Nor any unproportioned thought his act. 60
Be thou familiar, but by no means vulgar,
Those friends thou hast, and their adoption tried,
Grapple them unto thy soul with hoops of steel,
But do not dull thy palm with entertainment
Of each new-hatched unfledged courage. Beware
Of entrance to a quarrel, but being in,
Bear't that th'opposéd may beware of thee.
Give every man thy ear, but few thy voice,
Take each man's censure, but reserve thy
judgement.
Costly thy habit as thy purse can buy, 70
But not expressed in fancy; rich not gaudy.
For the apparel oft proclaims the man,
And they in France of the best rank and station,
Or of a most select and generous, chief in that:
Neither a borrower nor a lender be,
For loan oft loses both itself and friend,
And borrowing dulls the edge of husbandry;
This above all, to thine own self be true
And it must follow as the night the day
Thou canst not then be false to any man ... 80
Farewell—my blessing season this in thee.
LAERTES. Most humbly do I take my leave, my lord.
POLONIUS. The time invites you, go, your servants
tend.
LAERTES. Farewell, Ophelia, and remember well
What I have said to you.
OPHELIA. 'Tis in my memory locked,
And you yourself shall keep the key of it.
LAERTES. Farewell. *He goes*
POLONIUS. What is't, Ophelia, he hath said to you?
OPHELIA. So please you, something touching the Lord
Hamlet.
POLONIUS. Marry, well bethought. 90
'Tis told me he hath very oft of late
Given private time to you, and you yourself
Have of your audience been most free and
bounteous.
If it be so—as so 'tis put on me,
And that in way of caution—I must tell you,
You do not understand yourself so clearly
As it behoves my daughter and your honour.
What is between you? give me up the truth.
OPHELIA. He hath, my lord, of late made many tenders
Of his affection to me. 100
POLONIUS. Affection, pooh! you speak like a green girl
Unsifted in such perilous circumstance.
Do you believe his tenders as you call them?
OPHELIA. I do not know, my lord, what I should
think.
POLONIUS. Marry, I will teach you—think yourself a
baby

That you have ta'en these tenders for true pay
Which are not sterling. Tender yourself more
  dearly,
Or (not to crack the wind of the poor phrase,
Running it thus) you'll tender me a fool.
OPHELIA. My lord, he hath importuned me with love 110
In honourable fashion.
POLONIUS. Ay, fashion you may call it, go to, go to.
OPHELIA. And hath given countenance to his speech,
  my lord,
With almost all the holy vows of heaven.
POLONIUS. Ay, springes to catch woodcocks. I do
  know
When the blood burns, how prodigal the soul
Lends the tongue vows. These blazes daughter,
Giving more light than heat, extinct in both,
Even in their promise, as it is a-making,
You must not take for fire. From this time 120
Be something scanter of your maiden presence,
Set your entreatments at a higher rate
Than a command to parle; for Lord Hamlet,
Believe so much in him that he is young,
And with a larger tether may he walk
Than may be given you: in few Ophelia,
Do not believe his vows, for they are brokers
Not of that dye which their investments show,
But mere implorators of unholy suits,
Breathing like sanctified and pious bonds 130
The better to beguile ... This is for all,
I would not in plain terms from this time forth
Have you so slander any moment leisure
As to give words or talk with the Lord Hamlet.
Look to't I charge you, come your ways.
OPHELIA. I shall obey, my lord. *They go*

    Scene 4: *The platform on the battlements*

Enter Hamlet, Horatio and Marcellus

HAMLET. The air bites shrewdly, it is very cold.
HORATIO. It is a nipping and an eager air.
HAMLET. What hour now?
HORATIO.   I think it lacks of twelve.
MARCELLUS. No, it is struck.
HORATIO. Indeed? I heard it not—it then draws near
  the season,
Wherein the spirit held his wont to walk.
    A flourish of trumpets, and ordnance shot off
What does this mean, my lord?
HAMLET. The king doth wake to-night and takes his
  rouse,
Keeps wassail and the swagg'ring upspring reels:
And as he drains his draughts of Rhenish down, 10
The kettle-drum and trumpet thus bray out
The triumph of his pledge.
HORATIO.   Is it a custom?
HAMLET. Ay marry is't,
But to my mind, though I am native here
And to the manner born, it is a custom
More honoured in the breach than the observance.
This heavy-headed revel east and west
Makes us traduced and taxed of other nations.
They clepe us drunkards, and with swinish phrase
Soil our addition, and indeed it takes 20
From our achievements, though performed at
  height,
The pith and marrow of our attribute.

So, oft it chances in particular men,
That for some vicious mole of nature in them,
As in their birth, wherein they are not guilty
(Since nature cannot choose his origin),
By the o'ergrowth of some complexion,
Oft breaking down the pales and forts of reason,
Or by some habit, that too much o'er-leavens
The form of plausive manners—that these men, 30
Carrying I say the stamp of one defect,
Being nature's livery, or fortune's star,
His virtues else be they as pure as grace,
As infinite as man may undergo,
Shall in the general censure take corruption
From that particular fault: the dram of evil
Doth all the noble substance of a doubt,
To his own scandal.

The Ghost appears

HORATIO.   Look, my lord, it comes!
HAMLET. Angels and ministers of grace defend us!
Be thou a spirit of health, or goblin damned, 40
Bring with thee airs from heaven, or blasts from
  hell,
Be thy intents wicked, or charitable,
Thou com'st in such a questionable shape,
That I will speak to thee. I'll call thee Hamlet,
King, father, royal Dane. O, answer me!
Let me not burst in ignorance, but tell
Why thy canonized bones hearsèd in death
Have burst their cerements? why the sepulchre,
Wherein we saw thee quietly inurned,
Hath oped his ponderous and marble jaws 50
To cast thee up again? what may this mean
That thou, dead corse, again in complete steel
Revisits thus the glimpses of the moon,
Making night hideous, and we fools of nature
So horridly to shake our disposition
With thoughts beyond the reaches of our souls?
Say why is this? wherefore? what should we do?
                The Ghost beckons
HORATIO. It beckons you to go away with it,
As if it some impartment did desire
To you alone.
MARCELLUS.   Look with what courteous action 60
It waves you to a more removèd ground,
But do not go with it.
HORATIO.   No, by no means.
HAMLET. It will not speak, then I will follow it.
HORATIO. Do not my lord.
HAMLET.   Why, what should be the fear?
I do not set my life at a pin's fee,
And for my soul, what can it do to that
Being a thing immortal as itself;
It waves me forth again, I'll follow it.
HORATIO. What if it tempt you toward the flood, my
  lord,
Or to the dreadful summit of the cliff 70
That beetles o'er his base into the sea,
And there assume some other horrible form,
Which might deprive your sovereignty of reason,
And draw you into madness? think of it—
The very place puts toys of desperation,
Without more motive, into every brain
That looks so many fathoms to the sea
And hears it roar beneath.

HAMLET.   It waves me still.
  Go on, I'll follow thee.
MARCELLUS. You shall not go, my lord.
HAMLET.   Hold off your hands. 80
HORATIO. Be ruled, you shall not go.
HAMLET.   My fate cries out,
  And makes each petty artere in this body
  As hardy as the Nemean lion's nerve;
  Still am I called, unhand me gentlemen,
  By heaven I'll make a ghost of him that lets me!
  I say, away! go on, I'll follow thee.
             The Ghost goes, Hamlet following
HORATIO. He waxes desperate with imagination.
MARCELLUS. Let's follow, 'tis not fit thus to obey him.
HORATIO. Have after—to what issue will this come?
MARCELLUS. Something is rotten in the state of
  Denmark.   90
HORATIO. Heaven will direct it.
MARCELLUS.   Nay, let's follow him.
                    They follow

      Scene 5: At the foot of the castle wall

Enter the Ghost, and Hamlet after

HAMLET. Whither wilt thou lead me? speak, I'll go no
  further.
GHOST. Mark me.
HAMLET.   I will.
GHOST.   My hour is almost come,
  When I to sulph'rous and tormenting flames
  Must render up myself.
HAMLET.   Alas poor ghost!
GHOST. Pity me not, but lend thy serious hearing
  To what I shall unfold.
HAMLET.   Speak, I am bound to hear.
GHOST. So art thou to revenge, when thou shalt hear.
HAMLET. What?
GHOST. I am thy father's spirit,
  Doomed for a certain term to walk the night,   10
  And for the day confined to fast in fires,
  Till the foul crimes done in my days of nature
  Are burnt and purged away: but that I am forbid
  To tell the secrets of my prison-house,
  I could a tale unfold whose lightest word
  Would harrow up thy soul, freeze thy young blood,
  Make thy two eyes like stars start from their spheres,
  Thy knotted and combinéd locks to part,
  And each particular hair to stand an end,
  Like quills upon the fretful porpentine.   20
  But this eternal blazon must not be
  To ears of flesh and blood. List, list, O list!
  If thou didst ever thy dear father love——
HAMLET. O God!
GHOST. Revenge his foul and most unnatural murder.
HAMLET. Murder!
GHOST. Murder most foul, as in the best it is,
  But this most foul, strange and unnatural.
HAMLET. Haste me to know't, that I with wings as
  swift
  As meditation or the thoughts of love,   30
  May sweep to my revenge.
GHOST.   I find thee apt,
  And duller shouldst thou be than the fat weed
  That rots itself in ease on Lethe wharf,
  Wouldst thou not stir in this; now Hamlet hear,
  'Tis given out, that sleeping in my orchard,

A serpent stung me, so the whole ear of Denmark
Is by a forgéd process of my death
Rankly abused: but know, thou noble youth,
The serpent that did sting thy father's life
Now wears his crown.
HAMLET.   O, my prophetic soul!   40
  My uncle?
GHOST. Ay, that incestuous, that adulterate beast,
  With witchcraft of his wit, with traitorous gifts,
  O wicked wit and gifts, that have the power
  So to seduce; won to his shameful lust
  The will of my most seeming-virtuous queen;
  O Hamlet, what a falling-off was there!
  From me whose love was of that dignity,
  That it went hand in hand even with the vow
  I made to her in marriage, and to decline   50
  Upon a wretch whose natural gifts were poor
  To those of mine;
  But virtue, as it never will be moved,
  Though lewdness court it in a shape of heaven,
  So lust, though to a radiant angel linked,
  Will sate itself in a celestial bed
  And prey on garbage.
  But soft, methinks I scent the morning air,
  Brief let me be; sleeping within my orchard,
  My custom always of the afternoon,   60
  Upon my secure hour thy uncle stole
  With juice of cursed hebona in a vial,
  And in the porches of my ears did pour
  The leperous distilment, whose effect
  Holds such an enmity with blood of man,
  That swift as quicksilver it courses through
  The natural gates and alleys of the body,
  And with a sudden vigour it doth posset
  And curd, like eager droppings into milk,
  The thin and wholesome blood; so did it mine,   70
  And a most instant tetter barked about
  Most lazar-like with vile and loathsome crust
  All my smooth body....
  Thus was I sleeping by a brother's hand,
  Of life, of crown, of queen at once dispatched,
  Cut off even in the blossoms of my sin,
  Unhouseled, disappointed, unaneled,
  No reck'ning made, but sent to my account
  With all my imperfections on my head.
  O, horrible! O, horrible! most horrible!   80
  If thou hast nature in thee bear it not,
  Let not the royal bed of Denmark be
  A couch for luxury and damnéd incest....
  But howsomever thou pursues this act,
  Taint not thy mind, nor let thy soul contrive
  Against thy mother aught—leave her to heaven,
  And to those thorns that in her bosom lodge
  To prick and sting her. Fare thee well at once,
  The glow-worm shows the matin to be near,
  And 'gins to pale his uneffectual fire.   90
  Adieu, adieu, adieu, remember me.
               The Ghost vanishes
HAMLET. O all you host of heaven! O earth! what else?
  And shall I couple hell? O fie! Hold, hold, my heart,
  And you, my sinews, grow not instant old,
  But bear me stiffly up ... Remember thee?
  Ay thou poor ghost whiles memory holds a seat
  In this distracted globe. Remember thee?
  Yea, from the table of my memory
  I'll wipe away all trivial fond records,

All saws of books, all forms, all pressures past 100
That youth and observation copied there,
And thy commandment all alone shall live
Within the book and volume of my brain,
Unmixed with baser matter—yes by heaven!
O most pernicious woman!
O villain, villain, smiling, damnéd villain!
My tables, meet it is I set it down   *He writes*
That one may smile, and smile, and be a villain,
At least I am sure it may be so in Denmark ...
So, uncle, there you are. Now, to my Word, 110
It is 'Adieu, adieu, remember me.'...
I have sworn't.

Enter Horatio and Marcellus

HORATIO. My lord, my lord!
MARCELLUS.   Lord Hamlet!
HORATIO.   Heaven secure him!
HAMLET. So be it!
MARCELLUS. Illo, ho, ho, my lord!
HAMLET. Hillo, ho, ho, boy! come, bird, come.
MARCELLUS. How is't, my noble lord?
HORATIO.   What news, my lord?
HAMLET. O, wonderful!
HORATIO.   Good my lord, tell it.
HAMLET. No, you will reveal it.
HORATIO. Not I, my lord, by heaven.
MARCELLUS.   Nor I, my lord. 120
HAMLET. How say you then, would heart of man once
   think it?
   But you'll be secret?
HORATIO, MARCELLUS. Ay, by heaven, my lord.
HAMLET. There's ne'er a villain dwelling in all
   Denmark
   But he's an arrant knave.
HORATIO. There needs no ghost, my lord, come from
   the grave,
   To tell us this.
HAMLET.   Why right, you are in the right,
   And so without more circumstance at all
   I hold it fit that we shake hands and part,
   You, as your business and desire shall point you,
   For every man hath business and desire 130
   Such as it is, and for my own poor part,
   Look you, I will go pray.
HORATIO. These are but wild and whirling words, my
   lord.
HAMLET. I am sorry they offend you, heartily,
   Yes, faith, heartily.
HORATIO.   There's no offence, my lord.
HAMLET. Yes, by Saint Patrick, but there is, Horatio,
   And much offence too—touching this vision here,
   It is an honest ghost that let me tell you—
   For your desire to know what is between us,
   O'ermaster't as you may. And now, good friends, 140
   As you are friends, scholars, and soldiers,
   Give me one poor request.
HORATIO. What is't, my lord? we will.
HAMLET. Never make known what you have seen
   to-night.
BOTH. My lord, we will not.
HAMLET.   Nay, but swear't.
HORATIO.   In faith,
   My lord, not I.
MARCELLUS. Nor I, my lord, in faith.
HAMLET. Upon my sword.

MARCELLUS.   We have sworn, my lord, already.
HAMLET. Indeed, upon my sword, indeed.
GHOST [*beneath*]. Swear.
HAMLET. Ha, ha, boy! say'st thou so? art thou there,
   truepenny? 150
   Come on, you hear this fellow in the cellarage,
   Consent to swear.
HORATIO.   Propose the oath, my lord.
HAMLET. Never to speak of this that you have seen,
   Swear by my sword.
GHOST [*beneath*]. Swear.
HAMLET. Hic et ubique? then we'll shift our ground:
   Come hither gentlemen,
   And lay your hands again upon my sword.
   Swear by my sword,
   Never to speak of this that you have heard. 160
GHOST [*beneath*]. Swear by his sword.
HAMLET. Well said, old mole! canst work i'th'earth so
   fast?
   A worthy pioner! Once more remove, good
   friends.
HORATIO. O day and night, but this is wondrous
   strange!
HAMLET. And therefore as a stranger give it welcome.
   There are more things in heaven and earth, Horatio,
   Than are dreamt of in your philosophy.
   But come—
   Here as before, never, so help you mercy
   (How strange or odd some'er I bear myself, 170
   As I perchance hereafter shall think meet
   To put an antic disposition on)
   That you at such times seeing me, never shall
   With arms encumbered thus, or this head-shake,
   Or by pronouncing of some doubtful phrase,
   As 'Well, well, we know,' or 'We could an if we
      would,'
   Or 'If we list to speak,' or 'There be an if they
      might,'
   Or such ambiguous giving out, to note
   That you know aught of me—this do swear,
   So grace and mercy at your most need help you! 180
GHOST [*beneath*]. Swear.
HAMLET. Rest, rest, perturbéd spirit! [*they swear*] So,
   gentlemen,
   With all my love I do commend me to you,
   And what so poor a man as Hamlet is
   May do t'express his love and friending to you
   God willing shall not lack. Let us go in together,
   And still your fingers on your lips I pray.
   The time is out of joint, O cursed spite,
   That ever I was born to set it right!
   Nay come, let's go together.   *They go* 190

ACT 2

Scene 1: *A room in the house of Polonius*

Polonius and Reynaldo

POLONIUS. Give him this money, and these notes,
   Reynaldo,
REYNALDO. I will, my lord.
POLONIUS. You shall do marvellous wisely, good
   Reynaldo,
   Before you visit him, to make inquire
   Of his behaviour.
REYNALDO.   My lord, I did intend it.

POLONIUS. Marry, well said, very well said; look you
  sir,
Inquire me first what Danskers are in Paris,
And how, and who, what means, and where they
  keep,
What company, at what expense, and finding
By this encompassment and drift of question   10
That they do know my son, come you more nearer
Than your particular demands will touch it,
Take you as 'twere some distant knowledge of him,
As thus, 'I know his father, and his friends.
And in part him'—do you mark this, Reynaldo?
REYNALDO. Ay, very well, my lord.
POLONIUS. 'And in part him, but,' you may say, 'not
  well,
But if't be he I mean, he's very wild,
Addicted so and so.' And there put on him
What forgeries you please, marry none so rank   20
As may dishonour him, take heed of that,
But sir such wanton, wild, and usual slips,
As are companions noted and most known
To youth and liberty.
REYNALDO.   As gaming, my lord.
POLONIUS. Ay, or drinking, fencing, swearing,
  quarrelling,
Drabbing—you may go so far.
REYNALDO. My lord, that would dishonour him.
POLONIUS. Faith no, as you may season it in the
  charge.
You must not put another scandal on him,
That he is open to incontinency,   30
That's not my meaning, but breathe his faults so
  quaintly
That they may seem the taints of liberty,
The flash and outbreak of a fiery mind,
A savageness in unreclaiméd blood,
Of general assault.
REYNALDO.   But, my good lord——
POLONIUS. Wherefore should you do this?
REYNALDO.   Ay my lord,
I would know that.
POLONIUS.   Marry sir, here's my drift,
And I believe it is a fetch of warrant,
You laying these slight sullies on my son,
As 'twere a thing a little soiled i'th' working,   40
Mark you, your party in converse, him you would
  sound,
Having ever seen in the prenominate crimes
The youth you breathe of guilty, be assured
He closes with you in this consequence,
'Good sir,' or so, or 'friend,' or 'gentleman,'
According to the phrase, or the addition
Of man and country.
REYNALDO.   Very good, my lord.
POLONIUS. And then sir, does a' this, a' does, what was
  I about to say?
By the mass I was about to say something.
Where did I leave?
REYNALDO.   At 'closes in the consequence,'   50
At 'friend, or so, and gentleman.'
POLONIUS. At 'closes in the consequence.' ay marry—
He closes thus, 'I know the gentleman,
I saw him yesterday, or th'other day,
Or then, or then, with such or such, and as you say,
There was a' gaming, there o'ertook in's rouse,
There falling out at tennis,' or perchance,

'I saw him enter such a house of sale,'
Videlicet, a brothel, or so forth. See you now,
Your bait of falsehood takes this carp of truth,   60
And thus do we of wisdom, and of reach,
With windlasses, and with assays of bias,
By indirections find directions out,
So by my former lecture and advice
Shall you my son; you have me, have you not?
REYNALDO. My lord, I have.
POLONIUS.   God bye ye, fare ye well.
REYNALDO. Good, my lord.
POLONIUS. Observe his inclination in yourself.
REYNALDO. I shall, my lord.
POLONIUS. And let him ply his music.
REYNALDO.   Well, my lord.   *He goes* 70
POLONIUS. Farewell.

Ophelia enters

         How now Ophelia, what's the matter?
OPHELIA. O my lord, my lord, I have been so
  affrighted!
POLONIUS. With what, i'th'name of God?
OPHELIA. My lord, as I was sewing in my closet,
Lord Hamlet with his doublet all unbraced,
No hat upon his head, his stockings fouled,
Ungart'red, and down-gyvéd to his ankle,
Pale as his shirt, his knees knocking each other,
And with a look so piteous in purport
As if he had been looséd out of hell   80
To speak of horrors—he comes before me.
POLONIUS. Mad for thy love?
OPHELIA.   My lord, I do not know,
But truly I do fear it.
POLONIUS.   What said he?
OPHELIA. He took me by the wrist, and held me hard,
Then goes he to the length of all his arm,
And with his other hand thus o'er his brow,
He falls to such perusal of my face
As a' would draw it. Long stayed he so,
At last, a little shaking of mine arm,
And thrice his head thus waving up and down,   90
He raised a sigh so piteous and profound
As it did seem to shatter all his bulk,
And end his being; that done, he lets me go,
And with his head over his shoulder turned
He seemed to find his way without his eyes,
For out adoors he went without their helps,
And to the last bended their light on me.
POLONIUS. Come, go with me. I will go seek the king.
This is the very ecstasy of love,
Whose violent property fordoes itself,   100
And leads the will to desperate undertakings,
As oft as any passion under heaven
That does afflict our natures: I am sorry—
What, have you given him any hard words of late?
OPHELIA. No, my good lord, but as you did command
I did repel his letters, and denied
His access to me.
POLONIUS.   That hath made him mad.
I am sorry that with better heed and judgement
I had not quoted him. I feared he did but trifle
And meant to wreck thee, but beshrew my jealousy: 110
By heaven it is as proper to our age
To cast beyond ourselves in our opinions,
As it is common for the younger sort
To lack discretion; come, go we to the king.

This must be known, which, being kept close,
  might move
More grief to hide, than hate to utter love.
Come.   *They go*

Scene 2: *An audience chamber in the castle*

A flourish of trumpets. The King and Queen enter followed
by Rosencrantz, Guildenstern and attendants

KING. Welcome, dear Rosencrantz and Guildenstern!
  Moreover that we much did long to see you,
  The need we have to use you did provoke
  Our hasty sending. Something have you heard
  Of Hamlet's transformation—so call it,
  Sith nor th'exterior nor the inward man
  Resembles that it was. What it should be,
  More than his father's death, that thus hath put him
  So much from th'understanding of himself,
  I cannot dream of: I entreat you both,   10
  That being of so young days brought up with him,
  And sith so neighboured to his youth and haviour,
  That you vouchsafe your rest here in our court
  Some little time, so by your companies
  To draw him on to pleasures, and to gather
  So much as from occasion you may glean
  Whether aught to us unknown afflicts him thus,
  That opened lies within our remedy.
QUEEN. Good gentlemen, he hath much talked of you,
  And sure I am two men there are not living   20
  To whom he more adheres. If it will please you
  To show us so much gentry and good will
  As to expend your time with us awhile,
  For the supply and profit of our hope,
  Your visitation shall receive such thanks
  As fits a king's remembrance.
ROSENCRANTZ.   Both your majesties
  Might by the sovereign power you have of us,
  Put your dread pleasures more into command
  Than to entreaty.
GUILDENSTERN.   But we both obey,
  And here give up ourselves in the full bent,   30
  To lay our service freely at your feet
  To be commanded.
KING. Thanks Rosencrantz, and gentle Guildenstern.
QUEEN. Thanks Guildenstern, and gentle Rosencrantz,
  And I beseech you instantly to visit
  My too much changéd son. Go some of you
  And bring these gentlemen where Hamlet is.
GUILDENSTERN. Heavens make our presence and our
  practices
  Pleasant and helpful to him!
QUEEN.   Ay, amen!
           Rosencrantz and Guildenstern depart

Polonius enters

POLONIUS. The ambassadors from Norway, my good
  lord,
  Are joyfully returned.   40
KING. Thou still hast been the father of good news.
POLONIUS. Have I, my lord? Assure you, my good
  liege,
  I hold my duty as I hold my soul,
  Both to my God and to my gracious king;
  And I do think, or else this brain of mine
  Hunts not the trail of policy so sure
  As it hath used to do, that I have found

The very cause of Hamlet's lunacy.
KING. O speak of that, that do I long to hear.   50
POLONIUS. Give first admittance to th'ambassadors.
  My news shall be the fruit to that great feast.
KING. Thyself do grace to them, and bring them in.
                                        Polonius goes
  He tells me, my dear Gertrude, he hath found
  The head and source of all your son's distemper.
QUEEN. I doubt it is no other but the main,
  His father's death and our o'erhasty marriage.
KING. Well, we shall sift him.

Polonius returns with Valtemand and Cornelius

                                Welcome, my good friends!
  Say Valtemand, what from our brother Norway?
VALTEMAND. Most fair return of greetings and desires; 60
  Upon our first, he sent out to suppress
  His nephew's levies, which to him appeared
  To be a preparation 'gainst the Polack,
  But better looked into, he truly found
  It was against your highness, whereat grieved
  That so his sickness, age and impotence
  Was falsely borne in hand, sends out arrests
  On Fortinbras, which he in brief obeys,
  Receives rebuke from Norway, and in fine,
  Makes vow before his uncle never more   70
  To give th'assay of arms against your majesty:
  Whereon old Norway, overcome with joy,
  Gives him threescore thousand crowns in annual
    fee,
  And his commission to employ those soldiers,
  So levied, as before, against the Polack,
  With an entreaty, herein further shown,
  That it might please you to give quiet pass
  Through your dominions for this enterprise,
  On such regards of safety and allowance
  As therein are set down.   *He proffers a paper*
KING.   It likes us well,   80
  And at our more considered time, we'll read,
  Answer, and think upon this business:
  Meantime, we thank you for your well-took
    labour.
  Go to your rest, at night we'll feast together.
  Most welcome home!
                    Valtemand and Cornelius depart
POLONIUS.   This business is well ended....
  My liege and madam, to expostulate
  What majesty should be, what duty is,
  Why day is day, night night, and time is time,
  Were nothing but to waste night, day and time.
  Therefore since brevity is the soul of wit,   90
  And tediousness the limbs and outward flourishes,
  I will be brief—your noble son is mad:
  Mad call I it, for to define true madness,
  What is't but to be nothing else but mad?
  But let that go.
QUEEN.   More matter, with less art.
POLONIUS. Madam, I swear I use no art at all.
  That he is mad 'tis true, 'tis true, 'tis pity,
  And pity 'tis 'tis true—a foolish figure,
  But farewell it, for I will use no art.
  Mad let us grant him then, and now remains   100
  That we find out the cause of this effect,
  Or rather say, the cause of this defect,
  For this effect defective comes by cause:
  Thus it remains, and the remainder thus.

Perpend.
I have a daughter, have while she is mine,
Who in her duty and obedience, mark,
Hath given me this, now gather and surmise.
[he reads] 'To the celestial, and my soul's idol, the
most beautified Ophelia,'—   110
That's an ill phrase, a vile phrase, 'beautified' is a vile
phrase, but you shall hear. Thus: *He reads*
'In her excellent white bosom, these, etc.'—
QUEEN. Came this from Hamlet to her?
POLONIUS. Good madam stay awhile, I will be
  faithful—   *He reads*
   'Doubt thou the stars are fire,
    Doubt that the sun doth move,
   Doubt truth to be a liar,
    But never doubt I love.
O dear Ophelia, I am ill at these numbers, I have 120
not art to reckon my groans, but that I love thee
best, O most best, believe it. Adieu.
   Thine evermore, most dear lady, whilst
    this machine is to him, HAMLET.'
This in obedience hath my daughter shown me,
And more above hath his solicitings,
As they fell out by time, by means, and place,
All given to mine ear.
KING.   But how hath she
Received his love?
POLONIUS.   What do you think of me?
KING. As of a man faithful and honourable. 130
POLONIUS. I would fain prove so. But what might you
  think
When I had seen this hot love on the wing,
As I perceived it (I must tell you that)
Before my daughter told me, what might you,
Or my dear majesty your queen here think,
If I had played the desk or table-book,
Or given my heart a working mute and dumb,
Or looked upon this love with idle sight,
What might you think? no, I went round to work,
And my young mistress thus I did bespeak— 140
'Lord Hamlet is a prince out of thy star,
This must not be': and then I prescripts gave her
That she should lock herself from his resort,
Admit no messengers, receive no tokens.
Which done, she took the fruits of my advice:
And he repelléd, a short tale to make,
Fell into a sadness, then into a fast,
Thence to a watch, thence into a weakness,
Thence to a lightness, and by this declension,
Into the madness wherein now he raves, 150
And all we mourn for.
KING.   Do you think 'tis this?
QUEEN. It may be, very like.
POLONIUS. Hath there been such a time, I would fain
  know that,
That I have positively said ''Tis so,'
When it proved otherwise?
KING.   Not that I know.
POLONIUS. Take this from this, if this be otherwise;
     He points to his head and shoulder
If circumstances lead me, I will find
Where truth is hid, though it were hid indeed
Within the Centre.

Hamlet, reading a book, enters at the back; he pauses a
moment, unobserved

KING.   How may we try it further?
POLONIUS. You know sometimes he walks four hours
  together   150
Here in the lobby.
QUEEN.   So he does, indeed.
POLONIUS. At such a time I'll loose my daughter to
  him.
Be you and I behind an arras then,
Mark the encounter, if he love her not,
And be not from his reason fall'n thereon,
Let me be no assistant for a state,
But keep a farm and carters.
KING.   We will try it.

Hamlet comes forward, his eyes on the book

QUEEN. But look where sadly the poor wretch comes
  reading.
POLONIUS. Away, I do beseech you both away,
  I'll board him presently, O give me leave. 170
       The King and Queen go
How does my good Lord Hamlet?
HAMLET. Well, God-a-mercy.
POLONIUS. Do you know me, my lord?
HAMLET. Excellent well, you are a fishmonger.
POLONIUS. Not I, my lord.
HAMLET. Then I would you were so honest a man.
POLONIUS. Honest, my lord?
HAMLET. Ay sir, to be honest as this world goes, is to
  be one man picked out of ten thousand.
POLONIUS. That's very true, my lord.   180
HAMLET. For if the sun breed maggots in a dead dog,
  being a good kissing carrion.... have you a
  daughter?
POLONIUS. I have, my lord.
HAMLET. Let her not walk i'th'sun. Conception is a
  blessing, but as your daughter may conceive, friend
  look to't.
POLONIUS [aside]. How say you by that? still harping
  on my daughter, yet he knew me not at first, a' said
  I was a fishmonger. A' is far gone, far gone, and 190
  truly in my youth I suffered much extremity for
  love, very near this.... I'll speak to him again....
  What do you read, my lord?
HAMLET. Words, words, words.
POLONIUS. What is the matter, my lord?
HAMLET. Between who?
POLONIUS. I mean the matter that you read, my lord.
HAMLET. Slanders, sir; for the satirical rogue says here
  that old men have grey beards, that their faces are
  wrinkled, their eyes purging thick amber and plum- 200
  tree gum, and that they have a plentiful lack of wit,
  together with most weak hams—all which, sir,
  though I most powerfully and potently believe, yet
  I hold it not honesty to have it thus set down, for
  yourself, sir, shall grow old as I am ... if like a crab
  you could go backward.
POLONIUS [aside]. Though this be madness, yet there is
  method in't.
Will you walk out of the air, my lord?
HAMLET. Into my grave.   210
POLONIUS [aside]. Indeed, that's out of the air; how
  pregnant sometimes his replies are! a happiness that
  often madness hits on, which reason and sanity could
  not so prosperously be delivered of. I will leave him,
  and suddenly contrive the means of meeting
  between him and my daughter.

My honourable lord, I will most humbly take my
leave of you.

HAMLET. You cannot, sir, take from me any thing that
I will more willingly part withal: except my life, 220
except my life, except my life.

POLONIUS. Fare you well, my lord.

HAMLET. These tedious old fools!

Rosencrantz and Guildenstern enter

POLONIUS. You go to seek the Lord Hamlet, there he
is.

ROSENCRANTZ [*to Polonius*]. God save you, sir!
                                              Polonius goes

GUILDENSTERN. My honoured lord!

ROSENCRANTZ. My most dear lord!

HAMLET. My excellent good friends! How dost thou,
Guildenstern?
Ah, Rosencrantz! Good lads, how do you both? 230

ROSENCRANTZ. As the indifferent children of the earth.

GUILDENSTERN. Happy, in that we are not over-happy,
On Fortune's cap we are not the very button.

HAMLET. Nor the soles of her shoe?

ROSENCRANTZ. Neither, my lord.

HAMLET. Then you live about her waist, or in the
middle of her favours?

GUILDENSTERN. Faith, her privates we.

HAMLET. In the secret parts of fortune? O most true,
she is a strumpet. What's the news? 240

ROSENCRANTZ. None, my lord, but that the world's
grown honest.

HAMLET. Then is doomsday near. But your news is not
true. Let me question more in particular: what have
you, my good friends, deserved at the hands of
Fortune, that she sends you to prison hither?

GUILDENSTERN. Prison, my lord!

HAMLET. Denmark's a prison.

ROSENCRANTZ. Then is the world one.

HAMLET. A goodly one, in which there are many con- 250
fines, wards and dungeons; Denmark being one
o'th'worst.

ROSENCRANTZ. We think not so, my lord.

HAMLET. Why, then 'tis none to you; for there is
nothing either good or bad, but thinking makes it
so: to me it is a prison.

ROSENCRANTZ. Why, then your ambition makes it
one: 'tis too narrow for your mind.

HAMLET. O God! I could be bounded in a nut-shell,
and count myself a king of infinite space; were it 260
not that I have bad dreams.

GUILDENSTERN. Which dreams, indeed, are ambition:
for the very substance of the ambitious is merely the
shadow of a dream.

HAMLET. A dream itself is but a shadow.

ROSENCRANTZ. Truly, and I hold ambition of so airy
and light a quality, that it is but a shadow's shadow.

HAMLET. Then are our beggars bodies, and our monarchs and outstretched heroes the beggars' shadows
... Shall we to th' court? for, by my fay, I cannot 270
reason.

ROSENCRANTZ, GUILDENSTERN. We'll wait upon you.

HAMLET. No such matter: I will not sort you with the
rest of my servants; for to speak to you like an
honest man, I am most dreadfully attended.... But,
in the beaten way of friendship, what make you at
Elsinore?

ROSENCRANTZ. To visit you, my lord, no other occasion.

HAMLET. Beggar that I am, I am even poor in thanks, 280
but I thank you—and sure, dear friends, my thanks
are too dear a halfpenny: were you not sent for? is
it your own inclining? is it a free visitation? come,
come, deal justly with me, come, come, nay speak.

GUILDENSTERN. What should we say, my lord?

HAMLET. Why, any thing but to th'purpose ... You
were sent for, and there is a kind of confession in
your looks, which your modesties have not craft
enough to colour—I know the good king and queer
have sent for you. 290

ROSENCRANTZ. To what end, my lord?

HAMLET. That you must teach me: but let me conjure
you, by the rights of our fellowship, by the consonancy of our youth, by the obligation of our ever-
preserved love, and by what more dear a better
proposer can charge you withal, be even and direct
with me whether you were sent for or no?

ROSENCRANTZ [*aside to Guildenstern*]. What say you?

HAMLET [*aside*]. Nay then, I have an eye of you!
[*aloud*] If you love me, hold not off. 300

GUILDENSTERN. My lord, we were sent for.

HAMLET. I will tell you why, so shall my anticipation
prevent your discovery, and your secrecy to the
king and queen moult no feather. I have of late, but
wherefore I know not, lost all my mirth, forgone all
custom of exercises: and indeed it goes so heavily
with my disposition, that this goodly frame the
earth, seems to me a sterile promontory, this most
excellent canopy the air, look you, this brave
o'erhanging firmament, this majestical roof fretted 310
with golden fire, why it appeareth nothing to me
but a foul and pestilent congregation of vapours....
What a piece of work is a man, how noble in
reason, how infinite in faculties, in form and
moving, how express and admirable in action, how
like an angel in apprehension, how like a god: the
beauty of the world; the paragon of animals; and yet
to me, what is this quintessence of dust? man delights
not me, no, nor woman neither, though by your
smiling you seem to say so. 320

ROSENCRANTZ. My lord, there was no such stuff in my
thoughts.

HAMLET. Why did ye laugh then, when I said 'man
delights not me'?

ROSENCRANTZ. To think, my lord, if you delight not
in man, what lenten entertainment the players shall
receive from you. We coted them on the way, and
hither are they coming to offer you service.

HAMLET. He that plays the King shall be welcome, his
majesty shall have tribute on me, the adventurous 330
Knight shall use his foil and target, the Lover shall
not sigh gratis, the Humorous Man shall end his part
in peace, the Clown shall make those laugh whose
lungs are tickle o'th'sere, and the Lady shall say her
mind freely ... or the blank verse shall halt for't.
What players are they?

ROSENCRANTZ. Even those you were wont to take such
delight in, the tragedians of the city.

HAMLET. How chances it they travel? their residence
both in reputation and profit was better both ways. 340

ROSENCRANTZ. I think their inhibition comes by the
means of the late innovation.

HAMLET. Do they hold the same estimation they did

when I was in the city; are they so followed?
ROSENCRANTZ. No, indeed, are they not.
HAMLET. How comes it? do they grow rusty?
ROSENCRANTZ. Nay, their endeavour keeps in the
wonted pace; but there is, sir, an aery of children,
little eyases, that cry out on the top of question,
and are most tyrannically clapped for't: these are 350
now the fashion, and so berattle the common stages
(so they call them) that many wearing rapiers are
afraid of goose-quills, and dare scarce come thither.
HAMLET. What, are they children? who maintains 'em?
how are they escoted? Will they pursue the quality
no longer than they can sing? will they not say
afterwards if they should grow themselves to
common players (as it is like most will if their
means are not better) their writers do them wrong,
to make them exclaim against their own succession? 360
ROSENCRANTZ. Faith, there has been much to-do on
both sides: and the nation holds it no sin to tarre
them to controversy. There was, for a while, no
money bid for argument, unless the Poet and the
Player went to cuffs in the question.
HAMLET. Is't possible?
GUILDENSTERN. O, there has been much throwing
about of brains.
HAMLET. Do the boys carry it away?
ROSENCRANTZ. Ay, that they do my lord, Hercules and 370
his load too.
HAMLET. It is not very strange, for my uncle is king
of Denmark, and those that would make mows at
him while my father lived, give twenty, forty, fifty,
a hundred ducats apiece for his picture in little.
'Sblood, there is something in this more than
natural, if philosophy could find it out.
                                    A flourish of trumpets heard
GUILDENSTERN. There are the players.
HAMLET. Gentlemen, you are welcome to Elsinore [*he
bows*]. Your hands? come then, th'appurtenance of 380
welcome is fashion and ceremony; let me comply
with you in this garb ... lest my extent to the
players, which I tell you must show fairly outwards,
should more appear like entertainment than yours
... You are welcome: but my uncle-father, and
aunt-mother, are deceived.
GUILDENSTERN. In what, my dear lord?
HAMLET. I am but mad north-north-west; when the
wind is southerly, I know a hawk from a handsaw.

Polonius enters

POLONIUS. Well be with you, gentlemen!   390
HAMLET [*aside*]. Hark you Guildenstern, and you too,
at each ear a hearer—that great baby you see there
is not yet out of his swaddling-clouts.
ROSENCRANTZ. Happily he is the second time come to
them, for they say an old man is twice a child.
HAMLET. I will prophesy, he comes to tell me of the
players, mark it.
[*raises his voice*] You say right sir, a Monday morn-
ing, 'twas then indeed.
POLONIUS. My lord, I have news to tell you.   400
HAMLET. My lord, I have news to tell you ... When
Roscius was an actor in Rome—
POLONIUS. The actors are come hither, my lord.
HAMLET. Buz, buz!
POLONIUS. Upon my honour—
HAMLET. 'Then came each actor on his ass'—

POLONIUS. The best actors in the world, either for
tragedy, comedy, history, pastoral, pastoral-
comical, historical-pastoral, tragical-historical, tra-
gical-comical-historical-pastoral, scene individable, 410
or poem unlimited. Seneca cannot be too heavy nor
Plautus too light for the law of writ and the liberty,
these are the only men.
HAMLET. O Jephthah, judge of Israel, what a treasure
hadst thou!
POLONIUS. What a treasure had he, my lord?
HAMLET. Why
    'One fair daughter, and no more,
        The which he lovéd passing well.'
POLONIUS [*aside*]. Still on my daughter.   420
HAMLET. Am I not i'th' right, old Jephthah?
POLONIUS. If you call me Jephthah, my lord, I have a
daughter that I love passing well.
HAMLET. Nay, that follows not.
POLONIUS. What follows then, my lord?
HAMLET. Why,
            'As by lot, God wot,'
and then you know
            'It came to pass, as most like it was ...'
the first row of the pious chanson will show you 430
more, for look where my abridgement comes.

Enter four or five Players

You are welcome masters, welcome all—I am glad
to see thee well—Welcome, good friends—O, my
old friend! why, thy face is valanced since I saw thee
last, com'st thou to beard me in Denmark?—What,
my young lady and mistress! by'r lady, your ladyship is nearer to heaven than when I saw you last
by the altitude of a chopine. Pray God your voice,
like a piece of uncurrent gold, be not cracked within
the ring ... Masters, you are all welcome. We'll e'en 440
to't like French falconers, fly at any thing we see,
we'll have a speech straight. Come give us a taste
of your quality, come a passionate speech.
I PLAYER. What speech, my good lord?
HAMLET. I heard thee speak me a speech once, but it
was never acted, or if it was, not above once, for the
play I remember pleased not the million, 'twas
caviary to the general, but it was—as I received it,
and others, whose judgements in such matters cried
in the top of mine—an excellent play, well digested 450
in the scenes, set down with as much modesty as
cunning.... I remember one said there were no
sallets in the lines, to make the matter savoury, nor
no matter in the phrase that might indict the author
of affection, but called it an honest method, as
wholesome as sweet, and by very much more handsome than fine: one speech in't I chiefly loved, 'twas
Æneas' tale to Dido, and thereabout of it especially
where he speaks of Priam's slaughter. If it live in
your memory begin at this line, let me see, let me 460
see—
    'The rugged Pyrrhus, like th'Hyrcanian beast'—
'tis not so, it begins with Pyrrhus—
'The rugged Pyrrhus, he whose sable arms,
Black as his purpose, did the night resemble
When he lay couchéd in th'ominous horse,
Hath now this dread and black complexion
    smeared
With heraldy more dismal: head to foot

Now is he total gules, horridly tricked
With blood of fathers, mothers, daughters, sons,   470
Baked and impasted with the parching streets,
That lend a tyrannous and a damnéd light
To their lord's murder. Roasted in wrath and fire,
And thus o'er-sizéd with coagulate gore,
With eyes like carbuncles, the hellish Pyrrhus
Old grandsire Priam seeks' ...
So proceed you.

POLONIUS. Fore God, my lord, well spoken, with
good accent and good discretion.

I PLAYER.   'Anon he finds him   480
Striking too short at Greeks, his antique sword,
Rebellious to his arm, lies where it falls,
Repugnant to command; unequal matched,
Pyrrhus at Priam drives, in rage strikes wide,
But with the whiff and wind of his fell sword
Th'unnervéd father falls: then senseless Ilium,
Seeming to feel this blow, with flaming top
Stoops to his base; and with a hideous crash
Takes prisoner Pyrrhus' ear. For lo! his sword,
Which was declining on the milky head   490
Of reverend Priam, seemed i'th'air to stick,
So as a painted tyrant Pyrrhus stood,
And like a neutral to his will and matter,
Did nothing:
But as we often see, against some storm,
A silence in the heavens, the rack stand still,
The bold winds speechless, and the orb below
As hush as death, anon the dreadful thunder
Doth rend the region, so after Pyrrhus' pause,
A rouséd vengeance sets him new awork,   500
And never did the Cyclops' hammers fall
On Mars's armour, forged for proof eterne,
With less remorse than Pyrrhus' bleeding sword
Now falls on Priam.
Out, out, thou strumpet Fortune! All you gods,
In general synod take away her power,
Break all the spokes and fellies from her wheel,
And bowl the round nave down the hill of heaven
As low as to the fiends.'

POLONIUS. This is too long.   510

HAMLET. It shall to the barber's with your beard;
prithee say on—he's for a jig, or a tale of bawdry, or
he sleeps—say on, come to Hecuba.

I PLAYER. 'But who, ah woe! had seen the mobled
queen—'

HAMLET. 'The mobled queen'?

POLONIUS. That's good, 'mobled queen' is good.

I PLAYER. 'Run barefoot up and down, threat'ning
the flames
With bisson rheum, a clout upon that head
Where late the diadem stood, and for a robe,
About her lank and all o'er-teeméd loins,   520
A blanket in the alarm of fear caught up—
Who this had seen, with tongue in venom steeped,
'Gainst Fortune's state would treason have
pronounced;
But if the gods themselves did see her then,
When she saw Pyrrhus make malicious sport
In mincing with his sword her husband's limbs,
The instant burst of clamour that she made,
Unless things mortal move them not at all,
Would have made milch the burning eyes of
heaven,
And passion in the gods.'   530

POLONIUS. Look whe'r he has not turned his colour,
and has tears in's eyes—prithee no more.

HAMLET. 'Tis well, I'll have thee speak out the rest of
this soon. Good my lord, will you see the players
well bestowed; do you hear, let them be well used,
for they are the abstracts and brief chronicles of the
time; after your death you were better have a bad
epitaph than their ill report while you live.

POLONIUS. My lord, I will use them according to their
desert.   540

HAMLET. God's bodkin, man, much better! use every
man after his desert, and who shall 'scape whipping?
Use them after your own honour and dignity—the
less they deserve the more merit is in your bounty.
Take them in.

POLONIUS. Come, sirs.

HAMLET. Follow him, friends, we'll hear a play to-
morrow; [he stops the First Player] dost thou hear me,
old friend, can you play The Murder of Gonzago?

I PLAYER. Ay, my lord.   550

HAMLET. We'll ha't to-morrow night. You could for a
need study a speech of some dozen or sixteen lines,
which I would set down and insert in't, could you
not?

I PLAYER. Ay, my lord.

                              Polonius and the Players go out

HAMLET. Very well. Follow that lord, and look you
mock him not.   First Player goes
[to Rosencrantz and Guildenstern] My good friends,
I'll leave you till night. You are welcome to
Elsinore.   560

ROSENCRANTZ. Good my lord.   They go

HAMLET. Ay, so, God bye to you! now I am alone.
O, what a rogue and peasant slave am I!
Is it not monstrous that this player here,
But in a fiction, in a dream of passion,
Could force his soul so to his own conceit
That from her working all his visage wanned,
Tears in his eyes, distraction in his aspect,
A broken voice, and his whole function suiting
With forms to his conceit; and all for nothing!   570
For Hecuba!
What's Hecuba to him, or he to Hecuba,
That he should weep for her? what would he do,
Had he the motive and the cue for passion
That I have? he would drown the stage with tears.
And cleave the general ear with horrid speech,
Make mad the guilty and appal the free,
Confound the ignorant, and amaze indeed
The very faculties of eyes and ears; yet I,
A dull and muddy-mettled rascal, peak   580
Like John-a-dreams, unpregnant of my cause,
And can say nothing; no, not for a king,
Upon whose property and most dear life
A damned defeat was made: am I a coward?
Who calls me villain, breaks my pate across,
Plucks off my beard and blows it in my face,
Tweaks me by the nose, gives me the lie i'th'throat
As deep as to the lungs? who does me this?
Ha, 'swounds, I should take it: for it cannot be
But I am pigeon-livered, and lack gall   590
To make oppression bitter, or ere this
I should ha' fatted all the region kites
With this slave's offal. Bloody, bawdy villain!
Remorseless, treacherous, lecherous, kindless
villain!

O, vengeance!
Why, what an ass am I. This is most brave,
That I, the son of a dear father murdered,
Prompted to my revenge by heaven and hell,
Must like a whore unpack my heart with words,
And fall a-cursing like a very drab;   600
A stallion! fie upon't! foh!
About, my brains; hum, I have heard
That guilty creatures sitting at a play
Have by the very cunning of the scene
Been struck so to the soul, that presently
They have proclaimed their malefactions:
For murder, though it have no tongue, will speak
With most miraculous organ: I'll have these players
Play something like the murder of my father
Before mine uncle, I'll observe his looks,   610
I'll tent him to the quick, if a' do blench
I know my course.... The spirit that I have seen
May be a devil, and the devil hath power
T'assume a pleasing shape, yea, and perhaps
Out of my weakness and my melancholy,
As he is very potent with such spirits,
Abuses me to damn me; I'll have grounds
More relative than this—the play's the thing
Wherein I'll catch the conscience of the king.

He goes

ACT 3

Scene 1: *The lobby of the audience chamber*

The King and the Queen enter with Polonius, Rosencrantz,
and Guildenstern; Ophelia follows a little behind

KING. And can you by no drift of conference
    Get from him why he puts on this confusion,
    Grating so harshly all his days of quiet
    With turbulent and dangerous lunacy?
ROSENCRANTZ. He does confess he feels himself
        distracted,
    But from what cause a' will by no means speak.
GUILDENSTERN. Nor do we find him forward to be
        sounded,
    But with a crafty madness keeps aloof
    When we would bring him on to some confession
    Of his true state.
QUEEN.   Did he receive you well?   10
ROSENCRANTZ. Most like a gentleman.
GUILDENSTERN. But with much forcing of his
    disposition.
ROSENCRANTZ. Niggard of question, but of our
        demands
    Most free in his reply.
QUEEN.   Did you assay him
    To any pastime?
ROSENCRANTZ. Madam, it so fell out that certain
        players
    We o'er-raught on the way. Of these we told him,
    And there did seem in him a kind of joy
    To hear of it: they are here about the court,
    And as I think, they have already order   20
    This night to play before him.
POLONIUS.   'Tis most true,
    And he beseeched me to entreat your majesties
    To hear and see the matter.
KING. With all my heart, and it doth much content me
    To hear him so inclined.

Good gentlemen, give him a further edge,
And drive his purpose into these delights.
ROSENCRANTZ. We shall, my lord.
            Rosencrantz and Guildenstern go
KING.   Sweet Gertrude, leave us too,
    For we have closely sent for Hamlet hither,
    That he, as 'twere by accident, may here   30
    Affront Ophelia;
    Her father and myself, lawful espials,
    Will so bestow ourselves, that seeing unseen,
    We may of their encounter frankly judge,
    And gather by him as he is behaved,
    If't be th'affliction of his love or no
    That thus he suffers for.
QUEEN.   I shall obey you—
    And for your part, Ophelia, I do wish
    That your good beauties be the happy cause
    Of Hamlet's wildness, so shall I hope your virtues 40
    Will bring him to his wonted way again,
    To both your honours.
OPHELIA.   Madam, I wish it may.
                    The Queen goes
POLONIUS. Ophelia, walk you here. Gracious, so please
        you,
    We will bestow ourselves ... Read on this book,
    That show of such an exercise may colour
    Your loneliness; we are oft to blame in this,
    'Tis too much proved, that with devotion's visage
    And pious action we do sugar o'er
    The devil himself.
KING [*aside*].   O, 'tis too true,
    How smart a lash that speech doth give my
        conscience.   50
    The harlot's cheek, beautied with plast'ring art,
    Is not more ugly to the thing that helps it,
    Than is my deed to my most painted word:
    O heavy burden!
POLONIUS. I hear him coming, let's withdraw, my
        lord.   *They do so*

Hamlet enters

HAMLET. To be, or not to be, that is the question,
    Whether 'tis nobler in the mind to suffer
    The slings and arrows of outrageous fortune,
    Or to take arms against a sea of troubles,
    And by opposing, end them. To die, to sleep—   60
    No more, and by a sleep to say we end
    The heart-ache, and the thousand natural shocks
    That flesh is heir to; 'tis a consummation
    Devoutly to be wished to die to sleep!
    To sleep, perchance to dream, ay there's the rub,
    For in that sleep of death what dreams may come
    When we have shuffled off this mortal coil
    Must give us pause—there's the respect
    That makes calamity of so long life:
    For who would bear the whips and scorns of time, 70
    Th'oppressor's wrong, the proud man's contumely,
    The pangs of disprized love, the law's delay,
    The insolence of office, and the spurns
    That patient merit of th'unworthy takes,
    When he himself might his quietus make
    With a bare bodkin; who would fardels bear,
    To grunt and sweat under a weary life,
    But that the dread of something after death,
    The undiscovered country, from whose bourn
    No traveller returns, puzzles the will,   80

And makes us rather bear those ills we have,
Than fly to others that we know not of?
Thus conscience does make cowards of us all,
And thus the native hue of resolution
Is sicklied o'er with the pale cast of thought,
And enterprises of great pitch and moment
With this regard their currents turn awry,
And lose the name of action.... Soft you now,
The fair Ophelia—Nymph, in thy orisons
Be all my sins remembered.

OPHELIA   Good my lord,   90
How does your honour for this many a day?

HAMLET. I humbly thank you, well, well, well.

OPHELIA. My lord, I have remembrances of yours,
That I have longed long to re-deliver.
I pray you now receive them.

HAMLET.   No, not I,
I never gave you aught.

OPHELIA. My honoured lord, you know right well
    you did,
And with them words of so sweet breath composed
As made the things more rich. Their perfume lost,
Take these again, for to the noble mind   100
Rich gifts wax poor when givers prove unkind.
There, my lord.

HAMLET.   Ha, ha! are you honest?

OPHELIA. My lord?

HAMLET. Are you fair?

OPHELIA. What means your lordship?

HAMLET. That if you be honest and fair, your honesty
should admit no discourse to your beauty.

OPHELIA. Could beauty, my lord, have better commerce than with honesty?

HAMLET. Ay truly, for the power of beauty will sooner 110
transform honesty from what it is to a bawd, than
the force of honesty can translate beauty into his
likeness. This was sometime a paradox, but now the
time gives it proof. I did love you once.

OPHELIA. Indeed, my lord, you made me believe so.

HAMLET. You should not have believed me, for virtue
cannot so inoculate our old stock, but we shall relish
of it—I loved you not.

OPHELIA. I was the more deceived.

HAMLET. Get thee to a nunnery, why wouldst thou be 120
a breeder of sinners? I am myself indifferent honest,
but yet I could accuse me of such things, that it
were better my mother had not borne me: I am very
proud, revengeful, ambitious, with more offences at
my beck, than I have thoughts to put them in,
imagination to give them shape, or time to act them
in: what should such fellows as I do crawling
between earth and heaven? we are arrant knaves all,
believe none of us—go thy ways to a nunnery....
Where's your father?   130

OPHELIA. At home, my lord.

HAMLET. Let the doors be shut upon him, that he may
play the fool no where but in's own house. Farewell.

OPHELIA. O help him, you sweet heavens!

HAMLET. If thou dost marry, I'll give thee this plague
for thy dowry—be thou as chaste as ice, as pure as
snow, thou shalt not escape calumny; get thee to a
nunnery, go, farewell.... Or if thou wilt needs
marry, marry a fool, for wise men know well
enough what monsters you make of them: to a   140
nunnery, go, and quickly too, farewell.

OPHELIA. O heavenly powers, restore him!

HAMLET. I have heard of your paintings too, well
enough. God hath given you one face and you make
yourselves another, you jig, you amble, and you
lisp, you nickname God's creatures, and make your
wantonness your ignorance; go to, I'll no more on't,
it hath made me mad. I say we will have no mo
marriage—those that are married already, all but
one, shall live, the rest shall keep as they are: to a 150
nunnery, go.   He departs

OPHELIA. O, what a noble mind is here o'erthrown!
The courtier's, soldier's, scholar's, eye, tongue,
    sword,
Th'expectancy and rose of the fair state,
The glass of fashion, and the mould of form,
Th'observed of all observers, quite quite down,
And I of ladies most deject and wretched,
That sucked the honey of his music vows,
Now see that noble and most sovereign reason
Like sweet bells jangled, out of tune and harsh,   160
That unmatched form and feature of blown youth,
Blasted with ecstasy! O, woe is me!
T'have seen what I have seen, see what I see!
                                        She prays

The King and Polonius come forward

KING. Love! his affections do not that way tend,
Nor what he spake, though it lacked form a little,
Was not like madness—there's something in his
    soul,
O'er which his melancholy sits on brood,
And I do doubt the hatch and the disclose
Will be some danger; which for to prevent,
I have in quick determination   170
Thus set it down: he shall with speed to England,
For the demand of our neglected tribute.
Haply the seas, and countries different,
With variable objects, shall expel
This something-settled matter in his heart,
Whereon his brains still beating puts him thus
From fashion of himself. What think you on't?
                            Ophelia comes forward

POLONIUS. It shall do well. But yet do I believe
The origin and commencement of his grief
Sprung from neglected love ... How now,
    Ophelia?   180
You need not tell us what Lord Hamlet said,
We heard it all ... My lord, do as you please,
But if you hold it fit, after the play,
Let his queen-mother all alone entreat him
To show his grief, let her be round with him,
And I'll be placed (so please you) in the ear
Of all their conference. If she find him not,
To England send him; or confine him where
Your wisdom best shall think.

KING.   It shall be so,
Madness in great ones must not unwatched go.   190
                                        They depart

Scene 2: *The hall of the castle*

Enter Hamlet, and three of the Players

HAMLET. Speak the speech I pray you as I pronounced
it to you, trippingly on the tongue, but if you mouth
it as many of your players do, I had as lief the
town-crier spoke my lines. Nor do not saw the air
too much with your hand thus, but use all gently, for

in the very torrent, tempest, and as I may say whirlwind of your passion, you must acquire and beget a
temperance that may give it smoothness. O, it
offends me to the soul, to hear a robustious periwig-
pated fellow tear a passion to tatters, to very rags,   10
to split the ears of the groundlings, who for the most
part are capable of nothing but inexplicable dumb-
shows and noise: I would have such a fellow
whipped for o'erdoing Termagant, it out-herods
Herod, pray you avoid it.

1 PLAYER. I warrant your honour.

HAMLET. Be not too tame neither, but let your own
discretion be your tutor, suit the action to the word,
the word to the action, with this special observance,
that you o'erstep not the modesty of nature: for any   20
thing so o'erdone is from the purpose of playing,
whose end both at the first, and now, was and is,
to hold as 'twere the mirror up to nature, to show
virtue her own feature, scorn her own image, and
the very age and body of the time his form and
pressure ... Now this overdone, or come tardy off,
though it make the unskilful laugh, cannot but make
the judicious grieve, the censure of the which one
must in your allowance o'erweigh a whole theatre
of others. O there be players that I have seen play—   30
and heard others praise, and that highly—not to
speak it profanely, that neither having th'accent of
Christians, nor the gait of Christian, pagan, nor
man, have so strutted and bellowed, that I have
thought some of nature's journeymen had made
men, and not made them well, they imitated
humanity so abominably.

1 PLAYER. I hope we have reformed that indifferently
with us, sir.

HAMLET. O reform it altogether, and let those that play   40
your clowns speak no more than is set down for
them, for there be of them that will themselves
laugh, to set on some quantity of barren spectators
to laugh too, though in the mean time some
necessary question of the play be then to be considered. That's villanous, and shows a most pitiful
ambition in the fool that uses it ... Go, make you
ready.   *The Players go*

Polonius enters with Rosencrantz and Guildenstern

How now, my lord? will the king hear this piece of
work?

POLONIUS. And the queen too, and that presently.   50

HAMLET. Bid the players make haste.
                                    Polonius departs
Will you two help to hasten them?

ROSENCRANTZ. Ay, my lord.
                    Rosencrantz and Guildenstern follow Polonius

HAMLET. What, ho! Horatio!

Horatio comes in

HORATIO. Here, sweet lord, at your service.

HAMLET. Horatio, thou art e'en as just a man
As e'er my conversation coped withal.

HORATIO. O, my dear lord,—

HAMLET.   Nay, do not think I flatter,
For what advancement may I hope from thee,
That no revenue hast but thy good spirits   60
To feed and clothe thee? why should the poor be
flattered?
No, let the candied tongue lick absurd pomp,

And crook the pregnant hinges of the knee
Where thrift may follow fawning ... Dost thou
    hear?
Since my dear soul was mistress of her choice,
And could of men distinguish her election,
Sh'hath sealed thee for herself, for thou hast been
As one in suff'ring all that suffers nothing,
A man that Fortune's buffets and rewards
Hast ta'en with equal thanks; and blest are those   70
Whose blood and judgement are so well co-medled,
That they are not a pipe for Fortune's finger
To sound what stop she please: give me that man
That is not passion's slave, and I will wear him
In my heart's core, ay in my heart of heart,
As I do thee. Something too much of this—
There is a play to-night before the king,
One scene of it comes near the circumstance
Which I have told thee of my father's death.
I prithee when thou seest that act afoot,   80
Even with the very comment of thy soul
Observe my uncle--if his occulted guilt
Do not itself unkennel in one speech,
It is a damnéd ghost that we have seen,
And my imaginations are as foul
As Vulcan's stithy; give him heedful note,
For I mine eyes will rivet to his face,
And after we will both our judgements join
In censure of his seeming.

HORATIO.   Well, my lord,
If a' steal aught the whilst this play is playing,   90
And 'scape detecting, I will pay the theft.
                    Trumpets and kettle-drums heard

HAMLET. They are coming to the play. I must be idle.
Get you a place.

*The King and Queen enter, followed by Polonius, Ophelia,
Rosencrantz, Guildenstern, and other courtiers*

KING. How fares our cousin Hamlet?

HAMLET. Excellent i'faith, of the chameleon's dish, I
eat the air, promise-crammed—you cannot feed
capons so.

KING. I have nothing with this answer, Hamlet. These
words are not mine.

HAMLET. No, nor mine now. [*to Polonius*] My lord,   100
you played once i'th'university, you say?

POLONIUS. That did I, my lord, and was accounted a
good actor.

HAMLET. What did you enact?

POLONIUS. I did enact Julius Cæsar. I was killed i'th'
Capitol, Brutus killed me.

HAMLET. It was a brute part of him to kill so capital a
calf there. Be the players ready?

ROSENCRANTZ. Ay, my lord, they stay upon your
patience.   110

QUEEN. Come hither, my dear Hamlet, sit by me.

HAMLET. No, good mother, here's metal more attract-
ive.

POLONIUS [*to the King*]. O ho! do you mark that?

HAMLET. Lady, shall I lie in your lap?

OPHELIA. No, my lord.

HAMLET. I mean, my head upon your lap?

OPHELIA. Ay, my lord.   *He lies at her feet*

HAMLET. Do you think I meant country matters?

OPHELIA. I think nothing, my lord.   120

HAMLET. That's a fair thought to lie between maids'
legs.

OPHELIA. What is, my lord?

HAMLET. Nothing.

OPHELIA. You are merry, my lord.

HAMLET. Who, I?

OPHELIA. Ay, my lord.

HAMLET. O God, your only jig-maker. What should a man do but be merry, for look you how cheerfully my mother looks, and my father died within's two hours. 130

OPHELIA. Nay, 'tis twice two months, my lord.

HAMLET. So long? nay then let the devil wear black, for I'll have a suit of sables; O heavens, die two months ago, and not forgotten yet? then there's hope a great man's memory may outlive his life half a year, but by'r lady a' must build churches then, or else shall a' suffer not thinking on, with the hobby-horse, whose epitaph is 'For O! for O! the hobby-horse is forgot.' 140

The trumpets sound, and a Dumb-Show follows

The Dumb-Show

Enter a King and a Queen, very lovingly, the Queen embracing him and he her, she kneels and makes show of protestation unto him, he takes her up and declines his head upon her neck, he lies him down upon a bank of flowers, she seeing him asleep leaves him: anon comes in another man, takes off his crown, kisses it, and pours poison in the sleeper's ears and leaves him: the Queen returns, finds the King dead, and makes passionate action: the poisoner with some three or four mutes comes in again, seeming to condole with her: the dead body is carried away: the poisoner wooes the Queen with gifts, she seems harsh awhile, but in the end accepts his love   *They go*

OPHELIA. What means this, my lord?

HAMLET. Marry, this is miching mallecho, it means mischief.

OPHELIA. Belike this show imports the argument of the play.

Enter a player

HAMLET. We shall know by this fellow. The players cannot keep counsel, they'll tell all.

OPHELIA. Will a' tell us what this show meant?

HAMLET. Ay, or any show that you will show him— be not you ashamed to show, he'll not shame to tell you what it means. 150

OPHELIA. You are naught, you are naught, I'll mark the play.

PLAYER.   For us and for our tragedy,
          Here stooping to your clemency,
          We beg your hearing patiently.   *Exit*

HAMLET. Is this a prologue, or the posy of a ring?

OPHELIA. 'Tis brief, my lord.

HAMLET. As woman's love.

Enter two Players, a King and a Queen

PLAYER KING. Full thirty times hath Phœbus' cart gone round 160
   Neptune's salt wash, and Tellus' orbéd ground,
   And thirty dozen moons with borrowed sheen
   About the world have times twelve thirties been,
   Since love our hearts and Hymen did our hands
   Unite commutual in most sacred bands.

PLAYER QUEEN. So many journeys may the sun and moon

Make us again count o'er ere love be done!
But woe is me, you are so sick of late,
So far from cheer, and from your former state,
That I distrust you. Yet though I distrust, 170
Discomfort you, my lord, it nothing must.
For women fear too much, even as they love,
And women's fear and love hold quantity,
In neither aught, or in extremity.
Now what my love is proof hath made you know,
And as my love is sized, my fear is so.
Where love is great, the littlest doubts are fear,
Where little fears grow great, great love grows there.

PLAYER KING. Faith, I must leave thee, love, and shortly too.
My operant powers their functions leave to do, 180
And thou shalt live in this fair world behind,
Honoured, beloved, and haply one as kind
For husband shalt thou—

PLAYER QUEEN.   O, confound the rest!
Such love must needs be treason in my breast,
In second husband let me be accurst,
None wed the second, but who killed the first.

HAMLET. That's wormwood, wormwood.

PLAYER QUEEN. The instances that second marriage move
Are base respects of thrift, but none of love.
A second time I kill my husband dead, 190
When second husband kisses me in bed.

PLAYER KING. I do believe you think what now you speak,
But what we do determine, oft we break.
Purpose is but the slave to memory,
Of violent birth but poor validity,
Which now like fruit unripe sticks on the tree,
But fall unshaken when they mellow be.
Most necessary 'tis that we forget
To pay ourselves what to ourselves is debt.
What to ourselves in passion we propose, 200
The passion ending, doth the purpose lose,
The violence of either grief or joy
Their own enactures with themselves destroy,
Where joy most revels, grief doth most lament,
Grief joys, joy grieves, on slender accident.
This world is not for aye, nor 'tis not strange
That even our loves should with our fortunes change:
For 'tis a question left us yet to prove,
Whether love lead fortune, or else fortune love.
The great man down, you mark his favourite flies, 210
The poor advanced makes friends of enemies,
And hitherto doth love on fortune tend,
For who not needs shall never lack a friend,
And who in want a hollow friend doth try,
Directly seasons him his enemy.
But orderly to end where I begun,
Our wills and fates do so contrary run,
That our devices still are overthrown,
Our thoughts are ours, their ends none of our own—
So think thou wilt no second husband wed, 220
But die thy thoughts when thy first lord is dead.

PLAYER QUEEN. Nor earth to me give food nor heaven light,
Sport and repose lock from me day and night,
To desperation turn my trust and hope,

An anchor's cheere in prison be my scope,
Each opposite that blanks the face of joy
Meet what I would have well and it destroy,
Both here and hence pursue me lasting strife,
If once a widow, ever I be wife!
HAMLET. If she should break it now!　　　　　　　　230
PLAYER KING. 'Tis deeply sworn. Sweet leave me here
　awhile,
My spirits grow dull, and fain I would beguile
The tedious day with sleep.　　　　　　　*He sleeps*
PLAYER QUEEN.　　　　　　　　　Sleep rock thy brain,
And never come mischance between us twain!
　　　　　　　　　　　　　　　　　　Exit
HAMLET. Madam, how like you this play?
QUEEN. The lady doth protest too much methinks.
HAMLET. O, but she'll keep her word.
KING. Have you heard the argument? is there no
　offence in't?
HAMLET. No, no, they do but jest, poison in jest, no　240
　offence i'th'world.
KING. What do you call the play?
HAMLET. The Mouse-trap. Marry, how?—tropically.
　This play is the image of a murder done in Vienna.
　Gonzago is the duke's name, his wife Baptista, you
　shall see anon, 'tis a knavish piece of work, but what
　of that? your majesty, and we that have free souls,
　it touches us not—let the galled jade wince, our
　withers are unwrung....

Enter First Player for Lucianus

This is one Lucianus, nephew to the king.　　　　250
OPHELIA. You are as good as a chorus, my lord.
HAMLET. I could interpret between you and your love,
　if I could see the puppets dallying.
OPHELIA. You are keen, my lord, you are keen.
HAMLET. It would cost you a groaning to take off mine
　edge.
OPHELIA. Still better and worse.
HAMLET. So you mis-take your husbands.... Begin,
　murderer. Pox! leave thy damnable faces and begin!
　Come——'the croaking raven doth bellow for　260
　revenge.'
LUCIANUS. Thoughts black, hands apt, drugs fit, and
　time agreeing,
Confederate season, else no creature seeing,
Thou mixture rank, of midnight weeds collected,
With Hecate's ban thrice blasted, thrice infected,
Thy natural magic and dire property
On wholesome life usurps immediately.
　　　　　　　Pours the poison in his ears
HAMLET. A' poisons him i'th'garden for's estate, his
　name's Gonzago, the story is extant, and written in
　very choice Italian, you shall see anon how the　270
　murderer gets the love of Gonzago's wife.
OPHELIA. The king rises.
HAMLET. What, frighted with false fire!
QUEEN. How fares my lord?
POLONIUS. Give o'er the play.
KING. Give me some light—away!　　　　　*He goes*
POLONIUS. Lights, lights, lights!
　　　　　All but Hamlet and Horatio depart
HAMLET.
　Why, let the stricken deer go weep,
　　The hart ungalled play,
　For some must watch while some must sleep,　280
　　Thus runs the world away.

Would not this, sir, and a forest of feathers, if the
rest of my fortunes turn Turk with me, with two
Provincial roses on my razed shoes, get me a fellow-
ship in a cry of players, sir?
HORATIO. Half a share.
HAMLET. A whole one, I.
　For thou dost know, O Damon dear,
　　This realm dismantled was
　Of Jove himself, and now reigns here　　　　290
　　A very, very—peacock.
HORATIO. You might have rhymed.
HAMLET. O good Horatio, I'll take the ghost's word
　for a thousand pound.... Didst perceive?
HORATIO. Very well, my lord.
HAMLET. Upon the talk of the poisoning?
HORATIO. I did very well note him.

Rosencrantz and Guildenstern return

HAMLET. Ah, ha! Come, some music! come, the
　recorders!
　For if the king like not the comedy,　　　　300
　　Why then, belike,—he likes it not, perdy.
Come, some music!
GUILDENSTERN. Good my lord, vouchsafe me a word
　with you.
HAMLET. Sir, a whole history.
GUILDENSTERN. The king, sir,—
HAMLET. Ay, sir, what of him?
GUILDENSTERN. Is in his retirement marvellous dis-
　tempered.
HAMLET. With drink, sir?　　　　　　　　310
GUILDENSTERN. No, my lord, rather with choler.
HAMLET. Your wisdom should show itself more richer
　to signify this to the doctor. For, for me to put him
　to his purgation, would perhaps plunge him into
　more choler.
GUILDENSTERN. Good my lord, put your discourse into
　some frame, and start not so wildly from my affair.
HAMLET. I am tame, sir—pronounce.
GUILDENSTERN. The queen your mother, in most great
　affliction of spirit, hath sent me to you.　　　320
HAMLET. You are welcome.
GUILDENSTERN. Nay, good my lord, this courtesy is
　not of the right breed. If it shall please you to make
　me a wholesome answer, I will do your mother's
　commandment. If not, your pardon and my return
　shall be the end of my business.
HAMLET. Sir, I cannot.
ROSENCRANTZ. What, my lord?
HAMLET. Make you a wholesome answer—my wit's
　diseased. But, sir, such answer as I can make, you　330
　shall command, or rather as you say, my mother.
　Therefore no more, but to the matter—my mother,
　you say—
ROSENCRANTZ. Then thus she says, your behaviour
　hath struck her into amazement and admiration.
HAMLET. O wonderful son that can so stonish a
　mother! but is there no sequel at the heels of this
　mother's admiration? impart.
ROSENCRANTZ. She desires to speak with you in her
　closet ere you go to bed.　　　　　　　340
HAMLET. We shall obey, were she ten times our
　mother. Have you any further trade with us?
ROSENCRANTZ. My lord, you once did love me.
HAMLET. And do still, by these pickers and stealers.
ROSENCRANTZ. Good my lord, what is your cause of

distemper? you do surely bar the door upon your own liberty, if you deny your griefs to your friend.

HAMLET. Sir, I lack advancement.

ROSENCRANTZ. How can that be, when you have the voice of the king himself for your succession in 350 Denmark?

HAMLET. Ay, sir, but 'While the grass grows'—the proverb is something musty.

Players bring in recorders

O, the recorders, let me see one. To withdraw with you, why do you go about to recover the wind of me, as if you would drive me into a toil?

GUILDENSTERN. O, my lord, if my duty be too bold, my love is too unmannerly.

HAMLET. I do not well understand that—will you play upon this pipe?   360

GUILDENSTERN. My lord, I cannot.

HAMLET. I pray you.

GUILDENSTERN. Believe me, I cannot.

HAMLET. I do beseech you.'

GUILDENSTERN. I know no touch of it, my lord.

HAMLET. It is as easy as lying; govern these ventages with your fingers and thumb, give it breath with your mouth, and it will discourse most eloquent music—look you, these are the stops.

GUILDENSTERN. But these cannot I command to any 370 utt'rance of harmony, I have not the skill.

HAMLET. Why, look you now, how unworthy a thing you make of me! you would play upon me, you would seem to know my stops, you would pluck out the heart of my mystery, you would sound me from my lowest note to the top of my compass— and there is much music, excellent voice, in this little organ, yet cannot you make it speak. 'Sblood, do you think I am easier to be played on than a pipe? call me what instrument you will, though you can 380 fret me, you cannot play upon me.

Polonius enters

God bless you, sir!

POLONIUS. My lord, the queen would speak with you, and presently.

HAMLET. Do you see yonder cloud that's almost in shape of a camel?

POLONIUS. By th'mass and 'tis, like a camel indeed.

HAMLET. Methinks it is like a weasel.

POLONIUS. It is backed like a weasel.

HAMLET. Or, like a whale?   390

POLONIUS. Very like a whale.

HAMLET. Then I will come to my mother by and by. [*aside*] They fool me to the top of my bent— I will come by and by.

POLONIUS. I will say so.
                    Polonius, Rosencrantz and Guildenstern depart

HAMLET. 'By and by' is easily said.   *The rest go*
Leave me, friends.
'Tis now the very witching time of night,
When churchyards yawn, and hell itself breathes out
Contagion to this world: now could I drink hot blood,   400
And do such bitter business as the day
Would quake to look on: soft, now to my mother—
O heart, lose not thy nature, let not ever
The soul of Nero enter this firm bosom,
Let me be cruel not unnatural.

I will speak daggers to her, but use none.
My tongue and soul in this be hypocrites,
How in my words somever she be shent,
To give them seals never, my soul, consent!
                                            He goes

Scene 3: *The lobby; the audience chamber without*

Enter the King, Rosencrantz and Guildenstern

KING. I like him not, nor stands it safe with us
To let his madness range. Therefore prepare you,
I your commission will forthwith dispatch,
And he to England shall along with you.
The terms of our estate may not endure
Hazard so near's as doth hourly grow
Out of his brows.

GUILDENSTERN.   We will ourselves provide.
Most holy and religious fear it is
To keep those many many bodies safe
That live and feed upon your majesty.   10

ROSENCRANTZ. The single and peculiar life is bound
With all the strength and armour of the mind
To keep itself from noyance, but much more
That spirit upon whose weal depends and rests
The lives of many. The cess of majesty
Dies not alone; but like a gulf doth draw
What's near it with it. O, 'tis a massy wheel
Fixed on the summit of the highest mount,
To whose huge spokes ten thousand lesser things
Are mortised and adjoined, which when it falls,   20
Each small annexment, petty consequence,
Attends the boist'rous ruin. Never alone
Did the king sigh, but with a general groan.

KING. Arm you, I pray you, to this speedy voyage,
For we will fetters put about this fear,
Which now goes too free-footed.

ROSENCRANTZ.   We will haste us.
                                            They go

Polonius enters

POLONIUS. My lord, he's going to his mother's closet—
Behind the arras I'll convey myself
To hear the process—I'll warrant she'll tax him home,
And as you said, and wisely was it said,   30
'Tis meet that some more audience than a mother,
Since nature makes them partial, should o'erhear
The speech of vantage; fare you well, my liege,
I'll call upon you ere you go to bed,
And tell you what I know.

KING.   Thanks, dear my lord....
                                        Polonius goes
O, my offence is rank, it smells to heaven,
It hath the primal eldest curse upon't,
A brother's murder! Pray can I not,
Though inclination be as sharp as will.
My stronger guilt defeats my strong intent,   40
And like a man to double business bound,
I stand in pause where I shall first begin,
And both neglect. What if this cursed hand
Were thicker than itself with brother's blood,
Is there not rain enough in the sweet heavens
To wash it white as snow? whereto serves mercy
But to confront the visage of offence?
And what's in prayer but this two-fold force,

To be forestalléd ere we come to fall,
Or pardoned being down? then I'll look up.... 50
My fault is past, but O, what form of prayer
Can serve my turn? 'Forgive me my foul murder'?
That cannot be since I am still possessed
Of those effects for which I did the murder;
My crown, mine own ambition, and my queen;
May one be pardoned and retain th'offence?
In the corrupted currents of this world
Offence's gilded hand may shove by justice,
And oft 'tis seen the wicked prize itself
Buys out the law. But 'tis not so above, 60
There is no shuffling, there the action lies
In his true nature, and we ourselves compelled
Even to the teeth and forehead of our faults
To give in evidence. What then? what rests?
Try what repentance can—what can it not?
Yet what can it, when one can not repent?
O wretched state! O bosom black as death!
O liméd soul, that struggling to be free,
Art more engaged; help, angels! Make assay,
Bow stubborn knees, and heart, with strings of steel, 70
Be soft as sinews of the new-born babe—
All may be well. *He kneels*

Hamlet enters

HAMLET. Now might I do it pat, now a'is a-praying—
And now I'll do't, and so a' goes to heaven,
And so am I revenged. That would be scanned:
A villain kills my father, and for that
I his sole son do this same villain send
To heaven....
Why, this is bait and salary, not revenge.
A' took my father grossly, full of bread, 80
With all his crimes broad blown, as flush as May,
And how his audit stands who knows save heaven?
But in our circumstance and course of thought,
'Tis heavy with him: and am I then revenged
To take him in the purging of his soul,
When he is fit and seasoned for his passage?
No.
Up, sword, and know thou a more horrid hent,
When he is drunk asleep, or in his rage,
Or in th'incestuous pleasure of his bed, 90
At game, a-swearing, or about some act
That has no relish of salvation in't,
Then trip him that his heels may kick at heaven,
And that his soul may be as damned and black
As hell whereto it goes; my mother stays,
This physic but prolongs thy sickly days.
He passes on

KING [*rises*]. My words fly up, my thoughts remain
below.
Words without thoughts never to heaven go.
He goes

Scene 4: *The Queen's closet*

Enter the Queen and Polonius

POLONIUS. A' will come straight. Look you lay home
to him,
Tell him his pranks have been too broad to bear
with,
And that your grace hath screened and stood
between
Much heat and him. I'll silence me even here—

Pray you be round with him.
HAMLET [*without*]. Mother, mother, mother!
QUEEN. I'll war'nt you,
Fear me not. Withdraw, I hear him coming.
Polonius hides behind the arras

Hamlet enters

HAMLET. Now, mother, what's the matter?
QUEEN. Hamlet, thou hast thy father much offended.
HAMLET. Mother, you have my father much offended. 10
QUEEN. Come, come, you answer with an idle tongue.
HAMLET. Go, go, you question with a wicked tongue.
QUEEN. Why, how now, Hamlet?
HAMLET. What's the matter now?
QUEEN. Have you forgot me?
HAMLET. No, by the rood not so,
You are the queen, your husband's brother's wife,
And would it were not so, you are my mother.
QUEEN. Nay then, I'll set those to you that can speak.
HAMLET. Come, come, and sit you down, you shall
not budge,
You go not till I set you up a glass
Where you may see the inmost part of you. 20
QUEEN. What wilt thou do? thou wilt not murder me?
Help, help, ho!
POLONIUS [*behind the arras*]. What, ho! help, help, help!
HAMLET [*draws*]. How now! a rat? dead, for a ducat,
dead. *He makes a pass through the arras*
POLONIUS [*falls*]. O, I am slain!
QUEEN. O me, what hast thou done?
HAMLET. Nay, I know no.
Is it the king?
He lifts up the arras and discovers Polonius, dead
QUEEN. O what a rash and bloody deed is this!
HAMLET. A bloody deed—almost as bad, good
mother,
As kill a king, and marry with his brother.
QUEEN. As kill a king!
HAMLET. Ay, lady, it was my word.... 30
[*to Polonius*] Thou wretched, rash, intruding fool,
farewell!
I took thee for thy better, take thy fortune,
Thou find'st to be too busy is some danger.
Leave wringing of your hands, peace, sit you down,
And let me wring your heart, for so I shall
If it be made of penetrable stuff,
If damnéd custom have not brassed it so,
That it be proof and bulwark against sense.
QUEEN. What have I done, that thou dar'st wag thy
tongue
In noise so rude against me?
HAMLET. Such an act 40
That blurs the grace and blush of modesty,
Calls virtue hypocrite, takes off the rose
From the fair forehead of an innocent love
And sets a blister there, makes marriage vows
As false as dicers' oaths, O such a deed
As from the body of contraction plucks
The very soul, and sweet religion makes
A rhapsody of words; heaven's face does glow,
And this solidity and compound mass
With heated visage, as against the doom, 50
Is thought-sick at the act.
QUEEN. Ay me, what act,
That roars so loud, and thunders in the index?
HAMLET. Look here, upon this picture, and on this,

The counterfeit presentment of two brothers.
See what a grace was seated on this brow—
Hyperion's curls, the front of Jove himself,
An eye like Mars to threaten and command,
A station like the herald Mercury,
New-lighted on a heaven-kissing hill,   60
A combination and a form indeed,
Where every god did seem to set his seal
To give the world assurance of a man.
This was your husband—Look you now what
    follows.
Here is your husband, like a mildewed ear,
Blasting his wholesome brother. Have you eyes?
Could you on this fair mountain leave to feed,
And batten on this moor? ha! have you eyes?
You cannot call it love, for at your age
The hey-day in the blood is tame, it's humble,
And waits upon the judgement, and what
    judgement   70
Would step from this to this? Sense sure you have
Else could you not have motion, but sure that sense
Is apoplexed, for madness would not err,
Nor sense to ecstasy was ne'er so thralled,
But it reserved some quantity of choice
To serve in such a difference. What devil was't
That thus hath cozened you at hoodman-blind?
Eyes without feeling, feeling without sight,
Ears without hands or eyes, smelling sans all,
Or but a sickly part of one true sense   80
Could not so mope: O shame, where is thy blush?
Rebellious hell,
If thou canst mutine in a matron's bones,
To flaming youth let virtue be as wax
And melt in her own fire. Proclaim no shame
When the compulsive ardour gives the charge,
Since frost itself as actively doth burn,
And reason pandars will.
QUEEN.   O Hamlet, speak no more.
Thou turn'st my eyes into my very soul,
And there I see such black and grainéd spots   90
As will not leave their tinct.
HAMLET.   Nay, but to live
In the rank sweat of an enseaméd bed
Stewed in corruption, honeying, and making love
Over the nasty sty—
QUEEN.   O speak to me no more,
These words like daggers enter in mine ears,
No more, sweet Hamlet.
HAMLET.   A murderer and a villain,
A slave that is not twentieth part the tithe
Of your precedent lord, a vice of kings,
A cutpurse of the empire and the rule,
That from a shelf the precious diadem stole   100
And put it in his pocket—
QUEEN.   No more.
HAMLET. A king of shreds and patches—

Enter the Ghost in his night-gown

Save me and hover o'er me with your wings,
You heavenly guards!—What would your gracious
    figure?
QUEEN. Alas, he's mad.
HAMLET. Do you not come your tardy son to chide,
That lapsed in time and passion lets go by
Th'important acting of your dread command?
O, say!

GHOST. Do not forget! this visitation   110
Is but to whet thy almost blunted purpose—
But look, amazement on thy mother sits,
O step between her and her fighting soul,
Conceit in weakest bodies strongest works,
Speak to her, Hamlet.
HAMLET.   How is it with you, lady?
QUEEN. Alas, how is't with you,
That you do bend your eye on vacancy,
And with th'incorporal air do hold discourse?
Forth at your eyes your spirits wildly peep,
And as the sleeping soldiers in th'alarm,   120
Your bedded hairs like life in excrements
Start up and stand an end. O gentle son,
Upon the heat and flame of thy distemper
Sprinkle cool patience. Whereon do you look?
HAMLET. On him! on him! Look you, how pale he
    glares!
His form and cause conjoined, preaching to stones,
Would make them capable. Do not look upon me,
Lest with this piteous action you convert
My stern effects, then what I have to do
Will want true colour, tears perchance for blood.   130
QUEEN. To whom do you speak this?
HAMLET.   Do you see nothing there?
QUEEN. Nothing at all, yet all that is I see.
HAMLET. Nor did you nothing hear?
QUEEN.   No, nothing but ourselves.
HAMLET. Why, look you there! look how it steals
    away!
My father in his habit as he lived,
Look where he goes, even now, out at the portal.
                                             The Ghost vanishes
QUEEN. This is the very coinage of your brain!
This bodiless creation ecstasy
Is very cunning in.
HAMLET.   Ecstasy!
My pulse as yours doth temperately keep time,   140
And makes as healthful music—it is not madness
That I have uttered, bring me to the test
And I the matter will re-word, which madness
Would gambol from. Mother, for love of grace,
Lay not that flattering unction to your soul,
That not your trespass but my madness speaks,
It will but skin and film the ulcerous place,
Whiles rank corruption mining all within
Infects unseen. Confess yourself to heaven,
Repent what's past, avoid what is to come,   150
And do not spread the compost on the weeds
To make them ranker. Forgive me this my virtue,
For in the fatness of these pursy times
Virtue itself of vice must pardon beg,
Yea curb and woo for leave to do him good.
QUEEN. O Hamlet, thou hast cleft my heart in twain.
HAMLET. O throw away the worser part of it,
And live the purer with the other half.
Good night, but go not to my uncle's bed,
Assume a virtue if you have it not.   160
That monster custom, who all sense doth eat
Of habits evil, is angel yet in this,
That to the use of actions fair and good
He likewise gives a frock or livery
That aptly is put on. Refrain to-night,
And that shall lend a kind of easiness
To the next abstinence, the next more easy:
For use almost can change the stamp of nature,

And either ... the devil, or throw him out,
With wondrous potency: once more, good night, 170
And when you are desirous to be blessed,
I'll blessing beg of you. For this same lord,
                                    Pointing to Polonius
I do repent; but heaven hath pleased it so,
To punish me with this, and this with me,
That I must be their scourge and minister.
I will bestow him and will answer well
The death I gave him; so, again, good night.
I must be cruel only to be kind.
This bad begins, and worse remains behind....
One word more, good lady.
QUEEN.   What shall I do? 180
HAMLET. Not this by no means that I bid you do—
Let the bloat king tempt you again to bed,
Pinch wanton on your cheek, call you his mouse,
And let him for a pair of reechy kisses,
Or paddling in your neck with his damned fingers,
Make you to ravel all this matter out
That I essentially am not in madness,
But mad in craft. 'Twere good you let him know,
For who that's but a queen, fair, sober, wise,
Would from a paddock, from a bat, a gib, 190
Such dear concernings hide? who would do so?
No, in despite of sense and secrecy,
Unpeg the basket on the house's top,
Let the birds fly, and like the famous ape,
To try conclusions in the basket creep,
And break your own neck down.
QUEEN. Be thou assured, if words be made of breath,
And breath of life, I have no life to breathe
What thou hast said to me.
HAMLET. I must to England, you know that?
QUEEN.   Alack, 200
I had forgot, 'tis so concluded on.
HAMLET. There's letters sealed, and my two
     school-fellows,
Whom I will trust as I will adders fanged,
They bear the mandate—they must sweep my way
And marshal me to knavery: let it work,
For 'tis the sport to have the enginer
Hoist with his own petar, and't shall go hard
But I will delve one yard below their mines,
And blow them at the moon: O, 'tis most sweet
When in one line two crafts directly meet. 210
This man shall set me packing,
I'll lug the guts into the neighbour room;
Mother, good night indeed. This counsellor
Is now most still, most secret, and most grave,
Who was in life a foolish prating knave....
Come, sir, to draw toward an end with you....
Good night, mother.
             He drags the body from the room

ACT 4
Scene 1

The King enters with Rosencrantz and Guildenstern

KING. There's matter in these sighs, these profound
     heaves,
  You must translate, 'tis fit we understand them.
  Where is your son?
QUEEN. Bestow this place on us a little while....
             Rosencrantz and Guildenstern depart

Ah, mine own lord, what have I seen to-night!
KING. What, Gertrude? how does Hamlet?
QUEEN. Mad as the sea and wind when both contend
  Which is the mightier—in his lawless fit,
  Behind the arras hearing something stir,
  Whips out his rapier, cries 'A rat, a rat!' 10
  And in this brainish apprehension kills
  The unseen good old man.
KING.   O heavy deed!
  It had been so with us had we been there.
  His liberty is full of threats to all,
  To you yourself, to us, to every one.
  Alas, how shall this bloody deed be answered?
  It will be laid to us, whose providence
  Should have kept short, restrained, and out of haunt
  This mad young man; but so much was our love,
  We would not understand what was most fit, 20
  But like the owner of a foul disease,
  To keep it from divulging, let it feed
  Even on the pith of life: where is he gone?
QUEEN. To draw apart the body he hath killed,
  O'er whom his very madness, like some ore
  Among a mineral of metals base,
  Shows itself pure—a' weeps for what is done.
KING. O, Gertrude, come away!
  The sun no sooner shall the mountains touch,
  But we will ship him hence, and this vile deed 30
  We must with all our majesty and skill
  Both countenance and excuse. Ho! Guildenstern!

Rosencrantz and Guildenstern return

  Friends both, go join you with some further aid—
  Hamlet in madness hath Polonius slain,
  And from his mother's closet hath he dragged
     him—
  Go, seek him out, speak fair, and bring the body
  Into the chapel; I pray you, haste in this.
                                        They go
  Come, Gertrude, we'll call up our wisest friends,
  And let them know both what we mean to do
  And what's untimely done: [so haply slander,] 40
  Whose whisper o'er the world's diameter,
  As level as the cannon to his blank
  Transports his poisoned shot, may miss our name,
  And hit the woundless air. O, come away!
  My soul is full of discord and dismay.   *They go*

Scene 2: *Another room of the castle*

Hamlet enters

HAMLET. Safely stowed.
CALLING WITHOUT. Hamlet! Lord Hamlet!
HAMLET. But soft, what noise, who calls on Hamlet?
  O, here they come!

Rosencrantz and Guildenstern enter

ROSENCRANTZ. What have you done, my lord, with
     the dead body?
HAMLET. Compounded it with dust whereto 'tis kin.
ROSENCRANTZ. Tell us where 'tis that we may take it
     thence,
  And bear it to the chapel.
HAMLET. Do not believe it.
ROSENCRANTZ. Believe what? 10
HAMLET. That I can keep your counsel and not mine

own. Besides, to be demanded of a sponge, what replication should be made by the son of a king?

ROSENCRANTZ. Take you me for a sponge, my lord?

HAMLET. Ay, sir, that soaks up the king's countenance, his rewards, his authorities. But such officers do the king best service in the end, he keeps them like an apple in the corner of his jaw, first mouthed to be last swallowed—when he needs what you have gleaned, it is but squeezing you, and, sponge, you 20 shall be dry again.

ROSENCRANTZ. I understand you not, my lord.

HAMLET. I am glad of it—a knavish speech sleeps in a foolish ear.

ROSENCRANTZ. My lord, you must tell us where the body is, and go with us to the king.

HAMLET. The body is with the king, but the king is not with the body. The king is a thing——

GUILDENSTERN. A thing, my lord!

HAMLET. Of nothing, bring me to him. Hide fox, and 30 all after.   *He goes; they pursue*

Scene 3: *The hall of the castle, as before*

Enter the King with two or three councillors of state

KING. I have sent to seek him, and to find the body. How dangerous is it that this man goes loose! Yet must not we put the strong law on him, He's loved of the distracted multitude, Who like not in their judgement but their eyes, And where 'tis so, th'offender's scourge is weighed But never the offence: to bear all smooth and even, This sudden sending him away must seem Deliberate pause. Diseases desperate grown By desperate appliance are relieved,   10 Or not at all.

Rosencrantz, Guildenstern and others enter

                        How now! what hath befallen?

ROSENCRANTZ. Where the dead body is bestowed, my lord, We cannot get from him.

KING.   But where is he?

ROSENCRANTZ. Without, my lord, guarded, to know your pleasure.

KING. Bring him before us.

ROSENCRANTZ.   Ho! bring in the lord.

Hamlet enters guarded by soldiers

KING. Now, Hamlet, where's Polonius?

HAMLET. At supper.

KING. At supper? where?

HAMLET. Not where he eats, but where a' is eaten— a certain convocation of politic worms are e'en at 20 him: your worm is your only emperor for diet, we fat all creatures else to fat us, and we fat ourselves for maggots. Your fat king and your lean beggar is but variable service, two dishes, but to one table— that's the end.

KING. Alas, alas!

HAMLET. A man may fish with the worm that hath eat of a king, and eat of the fish that hath fed of that worm.

KING. What dost thou mean by this?   30

HAMLET. Nothing, but to show you how a king may go a progress through the guts of a beggar.

KING. Where is Polonius?

HAMLET. In heaven—send thither to see, if your messenger find him not there, seek him i'th'other place yourself. But if indeed you find him not within this month, you shall nose him as you go up the stairs into the lobby.

KING [*to attendants*]. Go seek him there.

HAMLET. A' will stay till you come.   *They depart* 40

KING. Hamlet, this deed, for thine especial safety, Which we do tender, as we dearly grieve For that which thou hast done, must send thee hence With fiery quickness. Therefore prepare thyself, The bark is ready, and the wind at help, Th'associates tend, and every thing is bent For England.

HAMLET.   For England.

KING.   Ay. Hamlet.

HAMLET.   Good.

KING. So is it if thou knew'st our purposes.

HAMLET. I see a cherub that sees them. But, come, for England! Farewell, dear mother.   50

KING. Thy loving father, Hamlet.

HAMLET. My mother—father and mother is man and wife, man and wife is one flesh, and so my mother: come, for England!   *They go*

KING [*to Rosencrantz and Guildenstern*]. Follow him at foot, tempt him with speed aboard, Delay it not, I'll have him hence to-night. Away! for every thing is sealed and done That else leans on th'affair—pray you, make haste....

                        All depart save the King

And, England, if my love thou hold'st at aught— As my great power thereof may give thee sense,   60 Since yet thy cicatrice looks raw and red After the Danish sword, and thy free awe Pays homage to us—thou mayst not coldly set Our sovereign process, which imports at full By letters congruing to that effect, The present death of Hamlet. Do it, England, For like the hectic in my blood he rages, And thou must cure me; till I know 'tis done, Howe'er my haps, my joys were ne'er begun.

                        He goes

Scene 4: *A plain near to a port in Denmark*

Prince Fortinbras, with his army on the march

FORTINBRAS. Go, captain, from me greet the Danish king, Tell him that by his license Fortinbras Craves the conveyance of a promised march Over his kingdom. You know the rendezvous. If that his majesty would aught with us, We shall express our duty in his eye, And let him know so.

CAPTAIN.   I will do't, my lord.

FORTINBRAS [*to the troops*]. Go softly on.

                        Fortinbras and the army go

The Captain meets Hamlet, Rosencrantz, Guildenstern and the guard

HAMLET. Good sir, whose powers are these?

CAPTAIN. They are of Norway, sir.   10

HAMLET. How purposed, sir, I pray you?

CAPTAIN. Against some part of Poland.

HAMLET. Who commands them, sir?

CAPTAIN. The nephew to old Norway, Fortinbras.
HAMLET. Goes it against the main of Poland, sir,
Or for some frontier?
CAPTAIN. Truly to speak, and with no addition,
We go to gain a little patch of ground
That hath in it no profit but the name.
To pay five ducats, five, I would not farm it; 20
Nor will it yield to Norway or the Pole
A ranker rate should it be sold in fee.
HAMLET. Why, then the Polack never will defend it.
CAPTAIN. Yes, 'tis already garrisoned.
HAMLET. Two thousand souls and twenty thousand
ducats
Will not debate the question of this straw!
This is th'imposthume of much wealth and peace,
That inward breaks, and shows no cause without
Why the man dies.... I humbly thank you, sir.
CAPTAIN. God bye you, sir.   *He goes*
ROSENCRANTZ.   Will't please you go, my lord? 30
HAMLET. I'll be with you straight, go a little before....
            Rosencrantz, Guildenstern and the rest pass on
How all occasions do inform against me,
And spur my dull revenge! What is a man,
If his chief good and market of his time
Be but to sleep and feed? a beast, no more:
Sure he that made us with such large discourse,
Looking before and after, gave us not
That capability and god-like reason
To fust in us unused. Now, whether it be
Bestial oblivion, or some craven scruple   40
Of thinking too precisely on th'event—
A thought which quartered hath but one part
wisdom,
And ever three parts coward—I do not know
Why yet I live to say 'This thing's to do,'
Sith I have cause, and will, and strength, and means,
To do't ... Examples gross as earth exhort me.
Witness this army of such mass and charge,
Led by a delicate and tender prince,
Whose spirit with divine ambition puffed
Makes mouths at the invisible event,   50
Exposing what is mortal and unsure
To all that fortune, death and danger dare,
Even for an egg-shell.... Rightly to be great
Is not to stir without great argument,
But greatly to find quarrel in a straw
When honour's at the stake. How stand I then,
That have a father killed, a mother stained,
Excitements of my reason and my blood,
And let all sleep? while to my shame I see
The imminent death of twenty thousand men,   60
That for a fantasy and trick of fame
Go to their graves like beds, fight for a plot
Whereon the numbers cannot try the cause,
Which is not tomb enough and continent
To hide the slain? O, from this time forth,
My thoughts be bloody, or be nothing worth!
                              He follows on

Scene 5: *A room in the castle of Elsinore*

The Queen with her ladies, Horatio and a gentleman

QUEEN. I will not speak with her.
GENTLEMAN. She is importunate, indeed distract,
Her mood will needs be pitied.
QUEEN.   What would she have?

GENTLEMAN. She speaks much of her father, says she
hears
There's tricks i'th'world, and hems, and beats her
heart,
Spurns enviously at straws, speaks things in doubt
That carry but half sense. Her speech is nothing,
Yet the unshapéd use of it doth move
The hearers to collection—they aim at it,
And botch the words up fit to their own thoughts, 10
Which as her winks and nods and gestures yield
them,
Indeed would make one think there might be
thought,
Though nothing sure, yet much unhappily.
HORATIO. 'Twere good she were spoken with, for she
may strew
Dangerous conjectures in ill-breeding minds.
QUEEN. Let her come in.   *The gentleman goes out*
[*aside*] "To my sick soul, as sin's true nature is,
Each toy seems prologue to some great amiss,
So full of artless jealousy is guilt,
It spills itself, in fearing to be spilt."   20

*The gentleman returns with Ophelia, distracted, a lute in
her hands and her hair about her shoulders*

OPHELIA. Where is the beauteous majesty of
Denmark?
QUEEN. How now, Ophelia?
OPHELIA [*sings*].
         How should I your true love know
              From another one?
         By his cockle hat and staff,
              And his sandal shoon.
QUEEN. Alas, sweet lady, what imports this song?
OPHELIA. Say you? nay, pray you mark.
[*sings*]   He is dead and gone, lady,
              He is dead and gone,   30
         At his head a grass-green turf,
              At his heels a stone.
O, ho!
QUEEN.   Nay, but Ophelia—
OPHELIA.   Pray you mark.
[*sings*] White his shroud as the mountain snow—

The King enters

QUEEN. Alas, look here, my lord.
OPHELIA [*sings*].
         Larded all with sweet flowers,
         Which bewept to the grave did not go,
              With true-love showers.
KING. How do you, pretty lady?
OPHELIA. Well, God dild you! they say the owl was a 40
baker's daughter. Lord, we know what we are, but
know not what we may be.... God be at your
table!
KING. Conceit upon her father.
OPHELIA. Pray you let's have no words of this, but
when they ask you what it means, say you this....
[*sings*] To-morrow is Saint Valentine's day,
              All in the morning betime,
         And I a maid at your window
              To be your Valentine.   50
         Then up he rose, and donned his clo'es,
              And dupped the chamber door,
         Let in the maid, that out a maid
              Never departed more.

KING. Pretty Ophelia!

OPHELIA. Indeed, la, without an oath, I'll make an
end on't—
[sings] By Gis and by Saint Charity,
Alack and fie for shame!
Young men will do't, if they come to't, 60
By Cock, they are to blame.
Quoth she, Before you tumbled me,
You promised me to wed.
(He answers.)
So would I ha' done, by yonder sun,
An thou hadst not come to my bed.

KING. How long hath she been thus?

OPHELIA. I hope all will be well. We must be patient,
but I cannot choose but weep to think they would
lay him i'th'cold ground. My brother shall know of 70
it, and so I thank you for your good counsel. Come,
my coach! Good night, ladies, good night. Sweet
ladies, good night, good night.   *She goes*

KING. Follow her close, give her good watch, I pray
you.   *Horatio and the gentleman follow her*
O, this is the poison of deep grief, it springs
All from her father's death—and now behold!
O Gertrude, Gertrude,
When sorrows come, they come not single spies,
But in battalions: first her father slain,
Next your son gone, and he most violent author 80
Of his own just remove, the people muddied,
Thick and unwholesome in their thoughts and
whispers
For good Polonius' death—and we have done but
greenly,
In hugger-mugger to inter him—poor Ophelia
Divided from herself and her fair judgement,
Without the which we are pictures or mere beasts,
Last, and as much containing as all these,
Her brother is in secret come from France,
Feeds on his wonder, keeps himself in clouds,
And wants not buzzers to infect his ear 90
With pestilent speeches of his father's death,
Wherein necessity, of matter beggared,
Will nothing stick our person to arraign
In ear and ear: O my dear Gertrude, this
Like to a murdering-piece in many places
Gives me superfluous death!   *A tumult without*

QUEEN.   Alack! what noise is this?

KING [calls]. Attend!   *An attendant enters*
Where are my Switzers? let them guard the door.
What is the matter?

ATTENDANT.   Save yourself, my lord!
The ocean, overpeering of his list, 100
Eats not the flats with more impiteous haste
Than young Laertes in a riotous head
O'erbears your officers: the rabble call him lord,
And as the world were now but to begin,
Antiquity forgot, custom not known,
The ratifiers and props of every word,
They cry 'Choose we, Laertes shall be king!'
Caps, hands, and tongues applaud it to the clouds,
'Laertes shall be king, Laertes king!'
The shouts grow louder

QUEEN. How cheerfully on the false trail they cry! 110
O, this is counter, you false Danish dogs!

KING. The doors are broke.

Enter Laertes, armed, with Danes following

LAERTES. Where is this king? Sirs, stand you all
without.

DANES. No, let's come in.

LAERTES.   I pray you, give me leave.

DANES. We will, we will.
They retire without the door

LAERTES. I thank you, keep the door. O thou vile king,
Give me my father.

QUEEN.   Calmly, good Laertes.

LAERTES. That drop of blood that's calm proclaims me
bastard,
Cries cuckold to my father, brands the harlot,
Even here, between the chaste unsmirchéd brows 120
Of my true mother.

KING.   What is the cause, Laertes,
That thy rebellion looks so giant-like?
Let him go Gertrude, do not fear our person,
There's such divinity doth hedge a king,
That treason can but peep to what it would,
Acts little of his will. Tell me, Laertes,
Why thou art thus incensed—let him go,
Gertrude—
Speak, man.

LAERTES. Where is my father?

KING.   Dead.

QUEEN.   But not by him.

KING. Let him demand his fill. 130

LAERTES. How came he dead? I'll not be juggled with
To hell allegiance, vows to the blackest devil,
Conscience and grace to the profoundest pit!
I dare damnation. To this point I stand,
That both the worlds I give to negligence,
Let come what comes, only I'll be revenged
Most throughly for my father.

KING.   Who shall stay you?

LAERTES. My will, not all the world's:
And for my means, I'll husband them so well,
They shall go far with little.

KING.   Good Laertes, 140
If you desire to know the certainty
Of your dear father, is't writ in your revenge,
That, sweepstake, you will draw both friend and
foe,
Winner and loser?

LAERTES. None but his enemies.

KING.   Will you know them then?

LAERTES. To his good friends thus wide I'll ope my
arms,
And like the kind life-rend'ring pelican,
Repast them with my blood.

KING.   Why, now you speak
Like a good child and a true gentleman.
That I am guiltless of your father's death, 150
And am most sensibly in grief for it,
It shall as level to your judgement 'pear,
As day does to your eye.

SHOUTING WITHOUT.   Let her come in.

LAERTES. How now! what noise is that?

Ophelia re-enters

O heat, dry up my brains, tears seven times salt,
Burn out the sense and virtue of mine eye!
By heaven, thy madness shall be paid with weight,
Till our scale turn the beam. O rose of May,
Dear maid, kind sister, sweet Ophelia!
O heavens, is't possible a young maid's wits 160

Should be as mortal as an old man's life?
Nature is fine in love, and where 'tis fine,
It sends some precious instance of itself
After the thing it loves.
OPHELIA [*sings*].
    They bore him barefaced on the bier,
    Hey non nonny, nonny, hey nonny,
    And in his grave rained many a tear—
Fare you well, my dove!
LAERTES. Hadst thou thy wits, and didst persuade
    revenge,
It could not move thus.   170
OPHELIA. You must sing, 'Adown adown,' an you call
him adown-a. O, how the wheel becomes it! It is
the false steward that stole his master's daughter.
LAERTES. This nothing's more than matter.
OPHELIA [*to Laertes*]. There's rosemary, that's for remembrance—pray you, love, remember—and
there is pansies, that's for thoughts.
LAERTES. A document in madness, thoughts and remembrance fitted.
OPHELIA [*to the King*]. There's fennel for you, and   180
columbines. [*to the Queen*] There's rue for you, and
here's some for me, we may call it herb of grace
o'Sundays—O, you must wear your rue with a
difference. There's a daisy. I would give you some
violets, but they withered all, when my father
died—they say a' made a good end——
[*sings*]   For bonny sweet Robin is all my joy—
LAERTES. Thought and affliction, passion, hell itself,
She turns to favour and to prettiness.
OPHELIA [*sings*].
    And will a' not come again?   190
    And will a' not come again?
      No, no, he is dead,
      Go to thy death-bed,
    He never will come again.
    His beard was as white as snow,
    All flaxen was his poll,
      He is gone, he is gone,
      And we cast away moan,
    God ha' mercy on his soul!—
And of all Christian souls I pray God. God bye you.   200
                          She goes
LAERTES. Do you see this, O God?
KING. Laertes, I must commune with your grief,
Or you deny me right. Go but apart,
Make choice of whom your wisest friends you will,
And they shall hear and judge 'twixt you and me.
If by direct or by collateral hand
They find us touched, we will our kingdom give,
Our crown, our life, and all that we call ours,
To you in satisfaction; but if not,
Be you content to lend your patience to us,   210
And we shall jointly labour with your soul
To give it due content.
LAERTES.   Let this be so.
His means of death, his obscure funeral,
No trophy, sword, nor hatchment o'er his bones,
No noble rite, nor formal ostentation,
Cry to be heard as 'twere from heaven to earth,
That I must call't in question.
KING.   So you shall,
And where th'offence is let the great axe fall.
I pray you, go with me.   *They go*

Scene 6

Horatio and others enter

HORATIO. What are they that would speak with me?
GENTLEMAN. Seafaring men, sir. They say they have
letters for you.
HORATIO. Let them come in.   *An attendant goes out*
[*aside*] I do not know from what part of the world
I should be greeted, if not from Lord Hamlet.

The attendant brings in sailors

1 SAILOR. God bless you, sir.
HORATIO. Let him bless thee too.
1 SAILOR. A' shall, sir, an't please him. There's a letter
for you, sir, it came from th'ambassador that was   10
bound for England, if your name be Horatio, as I
am let to know it is.
HORATIO [*turns aside and reads*]. 'Horatio, when thou
shalt have overlooked this, give these fellows some
means to the king, they have letters for him ... Ere
we were two days old at sea, a pirate of very warlike appointment gave us chase. Finding ourselves
too slow of sail, we put on a compelled valour, and
in the grapple I boarded them. On the instant they
got clear of our ship, so I alone became their   20
prisoner. They have dealt with me like thieves of
mercy, but they knew what they did. I am to do a
good turn for them. Let the king have the letters I
have sent, and repair thou to me with as much speed
as thou wouldest fly death. I have words to speak
in thine ear will make thee dumb, yet are they much
too light for the bore of the matter. These good
fellows will bring thee where I am. Rosencrantz
and Guildenstern hold their course for England—of
them I have much to tell thee. Farewell.   30
          He that thou knowest thine, HAMLET.'
Come, I will give you way for these your letters,
And do't the speedier that you may direct me
To him from whom you brought them.
                              They go

Scene 7

The King and Laertes return

KING. Now must your conscience my acquittance seal,
And you must put me in your heart for friend,
Sith you have heard and with a knowing ear
That he which hath your noble father slain
Pursued my life.
LAERTES.   It well appears: but tell me,
Why you proceeded not against these feats,
So crimeful and so capital in nature,
As by your safety, greatness, wisdom, all things else,
You mainly were stirred up.
KING.   O, for two special reasons,
Which may to you perhaps seem much unsinewed,   10
But yet to me they're strong. The queen his mother
Lives almost by his looks, and for myself,
My virtue or my plague, be it either which,
She is so conjunctive to my life and soul,
That as the star moves not but in his sphere
I could not but by her. The other motive,
Why to a public count I might not go,
Is the great love the general gender bear him,
Who dipping all his faults in their affection,
Would like the spring that turneth wood to stone,   20

Convert his gyves to graces, so that my arrows,
Too slightly timbered for so loud a wind,
Would have reverted to my bow again,
And not where I had aimed them.
LAERTES. And so have I a noble father lost,
A sister driven into desperate terms,
Whose worth, if praises may go back again,
Stood challenger on mount of all the age
For her perfections. But my revenge will come.
KING. Break not your sleeps for that, you must not
think   30
That we are made of stuff so flat and dull,
That we can let our beard be shook with danger
And think it pastime. You shortly shall hear more.
I loved your father, and we love ourself,
And that I hope will teach you to imagine—

Enter a Messenger with letters

How now! what news?
MESSENGER.   Letters, my lord, from Hamlet.
These to your majesty, these to the queen.
KING. From Hamlet! who brought them?
MESSENGER. Sailors, my lord, they say, I saw them not.
They were given me by Claudio, he received them 40
Of him that brought them.
KING.   Laertes, you shall hear them ...
Leave us.   *The Messenger goes*
[*reads*] 'High and mighty, you shall know I am set
naked on your kingdom. To-morrow shall I beg
leave to see your kingly eyes, when I shall, first
asking your pardon thereunto, recount the occasion
of my sudden and more strange return. HAMLET.'
What should this mean? are all the rest come back?
Or is it some abuse, and no such thing?
LAERTES. Know you the hand?
KING.   'Tis Hamlet's character.... 'Naked'— 50
And in a postscript here he says 'alone.'
Can you devise me?
LAERTES. I am lost in it, my lord, but let him come!
It warms the very sickness in my heart
That I shall live and tell him to his teeth
'Thus diddest thou.'
KING.   If it be so, Laertes,—
As how should it be so? how otherwise?—
Will you be ruled by me?
LAERTES.   Ay, my lord,
So you will not o'errule me to a peace.
KING. To thine own peace. If he be now returned, 60
As checking at his voyage, and that he means
No more to undertake it, I will work him
To an exploit, now ripe in my device,
Under the which he shall not choose but fall:
And for his death no wind of blame shall breathe,
But even his mother shall uncharge the practice,
And call it accident.
LAERTES.   My lord, I will be ruled,
The rather if you could devise it so
That I might be the organ.
KING.   It falls right.
You have been talked of since your travel much, 70
And that in Hamlet's hearing, for a quality
Wherein they say you shine. Your sum of parts
Did not together pluck such envy from him,
As did that one, and that in my regard
Of the unworthiest siege.
LAERTES.   What part is that, my lord?

KING. A very riband in the cap of youth,
Yet needful too, for youth no less becomes
The light and careless livery that it wears,
Than settled age his sables and his weeds
Importing health and graveness; two months since, 80
Here was a gentleman of Normandy—
I have seen myself, and served against, the French,
And they can well on horseback—but this gallant
Had witchcraft in't, he grew unto his seat,
And to such wondrous doing brought his horse,
As had he been incorpsed and demi-natured
With the brave beast. So far he topped my thought,
That I in forgery of shapes and tricks
Come short of what he did.
LAERTES.   A Norman, was't?
KING. A Norman.   90
LAERTES. Upon my life, Lamord.
KING.   The very same.
LAERTES. I know him well, he is the brooch indeed
And gem of all the nation.
KING. He made confession of you,
And gave you such a masterly report
For art and exercise in your defence,
And for your rapier most especial,
That he cried out 'twould be a sight indeed
If one could match you; the scrimers of their nation
He swore had neither motion, guard, nor eye, 100
If you opposed them; sir, this report of his
Did Hamlet so envenom with his envy,
That he could nothing do but wish and beg
Your sudden coming o'er to play with him.
Now, out of this—
LAERTES.   What out of this, my lord?
KING. Laertes, was your father dear to you?
Or are you like the painting of a sorrow,
A face without a heart?
LAERTES.   Why ask you this?
KING. Not that I think you did not love your father,
But that I know love is begun by time, 110
And that I see in passages of proof
Time qualifies the spark and fire of it.
There lives within the very flame of love
A kind of wick or snuff that will abate it,
And nothing is at a like goodness still,
For goodness, growing to a plurisy,
Dies in his own too-much. That we would do
We should do when we would: for this 'would'
changes,
And hath abatements and delays as many
As there are tongues, are hands, are accidents, 120
And then this 'should' is like a spendthrift sigh,
That hurts by easing; but to the quick o'th'ulcer—
Hamlet comes back, what would you undertake
To show yourself your father's son in deed
More than in words?
LAERTES.   To cut his throat i'th'church.
KING. No place indeed should murder sanctuarize,
Revenge should have no bounds: but, good Laertes,
Will you do this, keep close within your chamber.
Hamlet returned shall know you are come home.
We'll put on those shall praise your excellence, 130
And set a double varnish on the fame
The Frenchman gave you, bring you in fine
together,
And wager on your heads; he being remiss,
Most generous, and free from all contriving,

Will not peruse the foils, so that with ease,
Or with a little shuffling, you may choose
A sword unbated, and in a pass of practice
Requite him for your father.
LAERTES.   I will do't,
And, for the purpose, I'll anoint my sword.
I bought an unction of a mountebank,   140
So mortal, that but dip a knife in it,
Where it draws blood, no cataplasm so rare,
Collected from all simples that have virtue
Under the moon, can save the thing from death
That is but scratched withal. I'll touch my point
With this contagion, that if I gall him slightly,
It may be death.
KING.   Let's further think of this,
Weigh what convenience both of time and means
May fit us to our shape. If this should fail,
And that our drift look through our bad
    performance,   150
'Twere better not assayed. Therefore this project
Should have a back or second that might hold,
If this did blast in proof; soft, let me see,
We'll make a solemn wager on your cunnings—
I ha't!
When in your motion you are hot and dry,
As make your bouts more violent to that end,
And that he calls for drink, I'll have preferred him
A chalice for the nonce, whereon but sipping,
If he by chance escape your venomed stuck,   160
Our purpose may hold there ... But stay, what
    noise?

The Queen enters

QUEEN. One woe doth tread upon another's heel,
So fast they follow; your sister's drowned, Laertes.
LAERTES. Drowned! O, where?
QUEEN. There is a willow grows askant the brook,
That shows his hoar leaves in the glassy stream,
Therewith fantastic garlands did she make
Of crow-flowers, nettles, daisies, and long purples
That liberal shepherds give a grosser name,
But our cold maids do dead men's fingers call them.   170
There on the pendent boughs her crownet weeds
Clamb'ring to hang, an envious sliver broke,
When down her weedy trophies and herself
Fell in the weeping brook. Her clothes spread wide,
And mermaid-like awhile they bore her up,
Which time she chanted snatches of old lauds,
As one incapable of her own distress,
Or like a creature native and indued
Unto that element. But long it could not be
Till that her garments, heavy with their drink,   180
Pulled the poor wretch from her melodious lay
To muddy death.
LAERTES.   Alas then, she is drowned?
QUEEN. Drowned, drowned.
LAERTES. Too much of water hast thou, poor Ophelia,
And therefore I forbid my tears; but yet
It is our trick, nature her custom holds,
Let shame say what it will—when these are gone,
The woman will be out ... Adieu, my lord!
I have a speech o' fire that fain would blaze,
But that this folly douts it.   *He goes*
KING.   Let's follow, Gertrude.   190
How much I had to do to calm his rage!

Now fear I this will give it start again,
Therefore let's follow.   *They follow*

ACT 5
Scene 1: *A graveyard*

*Enter two clowns (a sexton and his mate) with spades and
mattocks*

1 CLOWN. Is she to be buried in Christian burial when
she wilfully seeks her own salvation?
2 CLOWN. I tell thee she is, therefore make her grave
straight. The crowner hath sat on her, and finds it
Christian burial.
1 CLOWN. How can that be, unless she drowned herself
in her own defence?
2 CLOWN. Why, 'tis found so.
1 CLOWN. It must be 'se offendendo,' it cannot be else.
For here lies the point, if I drown myself wittingly,   10
it argues an act, and an act hath three branches, it is
to act, to do, and to perform—argal, she drowned
herself wittingly.
2 CLOWN. Nay, but hear you, goodman delver.
1 CLOWN. Give me leave. Here lies the water—good.
Here stands the man—good. If the man go to this
water and drown himself, it is, will he nill he, he
goes, mark you that. But if the water come to him,
and drown him, he drowns not himself—argal, he
that is not guilty of his own death, shortens not his   20
own life.
2 CLOWN. But is this law?
1 CLOWN. Ay, marry is't, crowner's quest law.
2 CLOWN. Will you ha' the truth an't? if this had not
been a gentlewoman, she should have been buried
out a Christian burial.
1 CLOWN. Why, there thou say'st, and the more pity
that great folk should have countenance in this
world to drown or hang themselves more than their
even-Christen ... Come, my spade! there is no   30
ancient gentlemen but gardeners, ditchers and
grave-makers—they hold up Adam's profession.
2 CLOWN. Was he a gentleman?
1 CLOWN. A' was the first that ever bore arms.
2 CLOWN. Why, he had none.
1 CLOWN. What, art a heathen? how dost thou understand the Scripture? the Scripture says Adam
digged; could he dig without arms? I'll put another
question to thee. If thou answerest me not to the
purpose, confess thyself—   40
2 CLOWN. Go to.
1 CLOWN. What is he that builds stronger than either
the mason, the shipwright, or the carpenter?
2 CLOWN. The gallows-maker, for that frame outlives
a thousand tenants.
1 CLOWN. I like thy wit well in good faith, the gallows
does well—but how does it well? it does well to
those that do ill. Now thou dost ill to say the gallows
is built stronger than the church—argal, the gallows
may do well to thee. To't again, come.   50
2 CLOWN. 'Who builds stronger than a mason, a shipwright, or a carpenter?'
1 CLOWN. Ay, tell me that, and unyoke.
2 CLOWN. Marry, now I can tell.
1 CLOWN. To't.
2 CLOWN. Mass, I cannot tell.
1 CLOWN. Cudgel thy brains no more about it, for

your dull ass will not mend his pace with beating. And when you are asked this question next, say 'a grave-maker.' The houses he makes lasts till dooms- 60 day. Go, get thee to Yaughan, and fetch me a stoup of liquor.   *Second Clown goes*

Hamlet and Horatio are seen entering the graveyard

First Clown digs and sings

> In youth when I did love, did love,
>   Methought it was very sweet,
> To contract o' the time for a my behove,
>   O, methought there a was nothing a meet.

HAMLET. Has this fellow no feeling of his business that a' sings in grave-making?

HORATIO. Custom hath made it in him a property of easiness.   70

HAMLET. 'Tis e'en so, the hand of little employment hath the daintier sense.

1 CLOWN [*sings*].

> But age with his stealing steps
>   Hath clawed me in his clutch,
> And hath shipped me intil the land,
>   As if I had never been such.

He throws up a skull

HAMLET. That skull had a tongue in it, and could sing once! how the knave jowls it to the ground, as if 'twere Cain's jaw-bone, that did the first murder! This might be the pate of a politician, which this ass 80 now o'er-reaches; one that would circumvent God, might it not?

HORATIO. It might, my lord.

HAMLET. Or of a courtier, which could say 'Good morrow, sweet lord! how dost thou, good lord?' This might be my lord such-a-one, that praised my lord such-a-one's horse, when a' meant to beg it, might it not?

HORATIO. It might, my lord.

HAMLET. Why, e'en so, and now my Lady Worm's, 90 chopless and knocked about the mazzard with a sexton's spade; here's fine revolution an we had the trick to see't! did these bones cost no more the breeding, but to play at loggats with them? mine ache to think on't.

1 CLOWN [*sings*].

> A pick-axe, and a spade, a spade,
>   For and a shrouding sheet,
> O, a pit of clay for to be made
>   For such a guest is meet.

He throws up a second skull

HAMLET. There's another. Why may not that be the 100 skull of a lawyer? Where be his quiddities now, his quillities, his cases, his tenures, and his tricks? why does he suffer this rude knave now to knock him about the sconce with a dirty shovel, and will not tell him of his action of battery? Hum! this fellow might be in's time a great buyer of land, with his statutes, his recognizances, his fines, his double vouchers, his recoveries: is this the fine of his fines, and the recovery of his recoveries, to have his fine pate full of fine dirt? will his vouchers vouch him no 110 more of his purchases, and double ones too, than the length and breadth of a pair of indentures? the very conveyances of his lands will scarcely lie in this box, and must th'inheritor himself have no more, ha?

HORATIO. Not a jot more, my lord.

HAMLET. Is not parchment made of sheep-skins?

HORATIO. Ay, my lord, and of calves'-skins too.

HAMLET. They are sheep and calves which seek out assurance in that. I will speak to this fellow.... [*they go forward*] Whose grave's this, sirrah?   120

1 CLOWN. Mine, sir—

[*sings*]   O, a pit of clay for to be made
>   For such a guest is meet.

HAMLET. I think it be thine, indeed, for thou liest in't.

1 CLOWN. You lie out on't sir, and therefore 'tis not yours; for my part I do not lie in't, and yet it is mine.

HAMLET. Thou dost lie in't, to be in't and say it is thine. 'Tis for the dead, not for the quick—therefore thou liest.   130

1 CLOWN. 'Tis a quick lie, sir, 'twill away again from me to you.

HAMLET. What man dost thou dig it for?

1 CLOWN. For no man, sir.

HAMLET. What woman then?

1 CLOWN. For none neither.

HAMLET. Who is to be buried in't?

1 CLOWN. One that was a woman, sir, but rest her soul she's dead.

HAMLET. How absolute the knave is! we must speak 140 by the card or equivocation will undo us. By the Lord, Horatio, this three years I have took note of it, the age is grown so picked, that the toe of the peasant comes so near the heel of the courtier he galls his kibe.... How long hast thou been grave-maker?

1 CLOWN. Of all the days i'th'year I came to't that day that our last king Hamlet overcame Fortinbras.

HAMLET. How long is that since?

1 CLOWN. Cannot you tell that? every fool can tell that. It was that very day that young Hamlet was 150 born: he that is mad and sent into England.

HAMLET. Ay, marry, why was he sent into England?

1 CLOWN. Why, because a' was mad: a' shall recover his wits there, or if a' do not, 'tis no great matter there.

HAMLET. Why?

1 CLOWN. 'Twill not be seen in him there, there the men are as mad as he.

HAMLET. How came he mad?

1 CLOWN. Very strangely, they say.   160

HAMLET. How strangely?

1 CLOWN. Faith, e'en with losing his wits.

HAMLET. Upon what ground?

1 CLOWN. Why, here in Denmark: I have been sexton here man and boy thirty years.

HAMLET. How long will a man lie i'th'earth ere he rot?

1 CLOWN. Faith, if a' be not rotten before a' die, as we have many pocky corses now-a-days that will scarce hold the laying in, a' will last you some eight year, or nine year. A tanner will last you nine year.   170

HAMLET. Why he more than another?

1 CLOWN. Why sir, his hide is so tanned with his trade, that a' will keep out water a great while; and your water is a sore decayer of your whoreson dead body. Here's a skull now: this skull hath lien you i'th'earth three-and-twenty years.

HAMLET. Whose was it?

1 CLOWN. A whoreson mad fellow's it was, whose do you think it was?

HAMLET. Nay, I know not.   180

1 CLOWN. A pestilence on him for a mad rogue! a'

poured a flagon of Rhenish on my head once; this
same skull, sir, was, sir, Yorick's skull, the king's
jester.
HAMLET. This?
I CLOWN. E'en that.
HAMLET. Let me see. [*he takes the skull*] Alas, poor
Yorick! I knew him, Horatio—a fellow of infinite
jest, of most excellent fancy. He hath borne me on
his back a thousand times, and now how abhorred   190
in my imagination it is! my gorge rises at it.... Here
hung those lips that I have kissed I know not how
oft. Where be your gibes now? your gambols, your
songs, your flashes of merriment, that were wont to
set the table on a roar? not one now to mock your
own grinning? quite chopfallen? Now get you to
my lady's chamber, and tell her, let her paint an
inch thick, to this favour she must come. Make her
laugh at that.... Prithee, Horatio, tell me one thing.
HORATIO. What's that, my lord.   200
HAMLET. Dost thou think Alexander looked o' this
fashion i'th'earth?
HORATIO. E'en so.
HAMLET. And smelt so? pah!   *He sets down the skull*
HORATIO. E'en so, my lord.
HAMLET. To what base uses we may return, Horatio!
Why may not imagination trace the noble dust of
Alexander, till a' find it stopping a bung-hole?
HORATIO. 'Twere to consider too curiously, to con-
sider so.   210
HAMLET. No, faith, not a jot, but to follow him thither
with modesty enough, and likelihood to lead it; as
thus—Alexander died, Alexander was buried, Alex-
ander returneth to dust, the dust is earth, of earth
we make loam, and why of that loam whereto he
was converted might they not stop a beer-barrel?
Imperious Cæsar, dead and turned to clay,
Might stop a hole to keep the wind away.
O, that that earth, which kept the world in awe,
Should patch a wall t'expel the winter's flaw!   220
But soft, but soft, awhile—here comes the king,
The queen, the courtiers.

*A procession enters the graveyard: the corpse of Ophelia,
with Laertes, the King, the Queen, courtiers and a Doctor
of Divinity following*

                              Who is this they follow?
And with such maimèd rites? This doth betoken
The corse they follow did with desp'rate hand
Fordo it own life. 'Twas of some estate.
Couch we awhile, and mark.   *They retire*
LAERTES. What ceremony else?
HAMLET.   That is Laertes,
A very noble youth—mark.
LAERTES. What ceremony else?
DOCTOR. Her obsequies have been as far enlarged   230
As we have warranty. Her death was doubtful,
And but that great command o'ersways the order,
She should in ground unsanctified have lodged
Till the last trumpet: for charitable prayers,
Shards, flints and pebbles should be thrown on her:
Yet here she is allowed her virgin crants,
Her maiden strewments, and the bringing home
Of bell and burial.
LAERTES. Must there no more be done?
DOCTOR.   No more be done!
We should profane the service of the dead   240

To sing sage requiem and such rest to her
As to peace-parted souls.
LAERTES.   Lay her i'th'earth,
And from her fair and unpolluted flesh
May violets spring! I tell thee, churlish priest,
A minist'ring angel shall my sister be,
When thou liest howling.
HAMLET.   What, the fair Ophelia!
QUEEN [*scattering flowers*]. Sweets to the sweet.
     Farewell!
I hoped thou shouldst have been my Hamlet's wife:
I thought thy bride-bed to have decked, sweet maid,
And not have strewed thy grave.
LAERTES.   O, treble woe   250
Fall ten times treble on that cursèd head
Whose wicked deed thy most ingenious sense
Deprived thee of! Hold off the earth awhile,
Till I have caught her once more in mine arms;
                              Leaps in the grave
Now pile your dust upon the quick and dead,
Till of this flat a mountain you have made
T'o'ertop old Pelion, or the skyish head
Of blue Olympus.
HAMLET [*comes forward*]. What is he whose grief
Bears such an emphasis? whose phrase of sorrow
Conjures the wand'ring stars, and makes them stand 260
Like wonder-wounded hearers? This is I,
Hamlet the Dane.   *Leaps in after Laertes*
LAERTES [*grappling with him*]. The devil take thy soul
HAMLET. Thou pray'st not well.
I prithee take thy fingers from my throat,
For though I am not splenitive and rash,
Yet have I in me something dangerous,
Which let thy wiseness fear; hold off thy hand.
KING. Pluck them asunder.
QUEEN.   Hamlet, Hamlet!
ALL. Gentlemen!
HORATIO.   Good my lord, be quiet.
     *Attendants part them, and they come
                         up out of the grave*
HAMLET. Why, I will fight with him upon this theme 270
Until my eyelids will no longer wag.
QUEEN. O my son, what theme?
HAMLET. I loved Ophelia, forty thousand brothers
Could not with all their quantity of love
Make up my sum.... What wilt thou do for her?
KING. O, he is mad, Laertes.
QUEEN. For love of God, forbear him.
HAMLET. 'Swounds, show me what thou't do:
Woo't weep? woo't fight? woo't fast? woo't tear
     thyself?
Woo't drink up eisel? eat a crocodile?   280
I'll do't. Dost thou come here to whine?
To outface me with leaping in her grave?
Be buried quick with her, and so will I.
And if thou prate of mountains, let them throw
Millions of acres on us, till our ground,
Singeing his pate against the burning zone,
Make Ossa like a wart! nay, an thou'lt mouth,
I'll rant as well as thou.
QUEEN.   This is mere madness,
And thus awhile the fit will work on him.
Anon as patient as the female dove   290
When that her golden couplets are disclosed
His silence will sit drooping.
HAMLET.   Hear you, sir,

What is the reason that you use me thus?
I loved you ever, but it is no matter,
Let Hercules himself do what he may,
The cat will mew, and dog will have his day.

                                    He goes

KING. I pray thee, good Horatio, wait upon him....

                           Horatio follows

[*to Laertes*] Strengthen your patience in our last
    night's speech,
We'll put the matter to the present push....
Good Gertrude, set some watch over your son.   300
This grave shall have a living monument.
An hour of quiet shortly shall we see,
Till then, in patience our proceeding be.

                                     They go

        Scene 2: *The hall of the castle*

Hamlet and Horatio enter

HAMLET. So much for this, sir, now shall you see the
    other—
    You do remember all the circumstance?
HORATIO. Remember it, my lord!
HAMLET. Sir, in my heart there was a kind of fighting
That would not let me sleep—methought I lay
Worse than the mutines in the bilboes. Rashly,
And praised be rashness for it.... let us know
Our indiscretion sometime serves us well,
When our deep plots do pall, and that should learn
    us
There's a divinity that shapes our ends,   10
Rough-hew them how we will—
HORATIO.   That is most certain.
HAMLET. Up from my cabin,
My sea-gown scarfed about me, in the dark
Groped I to find out them, had my desire,
Fingered their packet, and in fine withdrew
To mine own room again, making so bold,
My fears forgetting manners, to unseal
Their grand commission; where I found, Horatio—
Ah, royal knavery!—an exact command,
Larded with many several sorts of reasons,   20
Importing Denmark's health and England's too,
With, ho! such bugs and goblins in my life,
That on the supervise, no leisure bated,
No, not to stay the grinding of the axe,
My head should be struck off.
HORATIO.   Is't possible?
HAMLET. Here's the commission, read it at more
    leisure.
But wilt thou hear now how I did proceed?
HORATIO. I beseech you.
HAMLET. Being thus be-netted round with villanies—
Or I could make a prologue to my brains   30
They had begun the play. I sat me down,
Devised a new commission, wrote it fair—
I once did hold it, as our statists do,
A baseness to write fair, and laboured much
How to forget that learning, but, sir, now
It did me yeoman's service. Wilt thou know
Th'effect of what I wrote?
HORATIO.   Ay, good my lord.
HAMLET. An earnest conjuration from the king,
As England was his faithful tributary,
As love between them like the palm might flourish,   40
As peace should still her wheaten garland wear

And stand a comma 'tween their amities,
And many such like 'as'es' of great charge,
That on the view and knowing of these contents,
Without debatement further, more or less,
He should those bearers put to sudden death,
Not shriving-time allowed.
HORATIO.   How was this sealed?
HAMLET. Why, even in that was heaven ordinant,
I had my father's signet in my purse,
Which was the model of that Danish seal,   50
Folded the writ up in the form of th'other,
Subscribed it, gave't th'impression, placed it safely,
The changeling never known: now, the next day
Was our sea-fight, and what to this was sequent
Thou knowest already.
HORATIO. So Guildenstern and Rosencrantz go to't.
HAMLET. Why, man, they did make love to this
    employment,
They are not near my conscience, their defeat
Does by their own insinuation grow.
'Tis dangerous when the baser nature comes   60
Between the pass and fell incensed points
Of mighty opposites.
HORATIO.   Why, what a king is this!
HAMLET. Does it not, think thee, stand me now
    upon—
He that hath killed my king, and whored my
    mother,
Popped in between th'election and my hopes,
Thrown out his angle for my proper life,
And with such cozenage—is't not perfect conscience
To quit him with this arm? and is't not to be
    damned,
To let this canker of our nature come
In further evil?   70
HORATIO. It must be shortly known to him from
    England
What is the issue of the business there.
HAMLET. It will be short, the interim is mine,
And a man's life's no more than to say 'One' ...
But I am very sorry, good Horatio,
That to Laertes I forgot myself;
For by the image of my cause I see
The portraiture of his; I'll court his favours:
But sure the bravery of his grief did put me
Into a towering passion.
HORATIO.   Peace, who comes here?   80

Enter Osric, a courtier

OSRIC. Your lordship is right welcome back to
Denmark.
HAMLET. I humbly thank you, sir.... Dost know this
water-fly?
HORATIO. No, my good lord.
HAMLET. Thy state is the more gracious, for 'tis a vice
to know him. He hath much land, and fertile: let a
beast be lord of beasts, and his crib shall stand at the
king's mess. 'Tis a chough, but, as I say, spacious in
the possession of dirt.   90
OSRIC. Sweet lord, if your lordship were at leisure, I
should impart a thing to you from his majesty.
HAMLET. I will receive it, sir, with all diligence of spirit.
Put your bonnet to his right use, 'tis for the head.
OSRIC. I thank your lordship, it is very hot.
HAMLET. No, believe me, 'tis very cold, the wind is
northerly.

OSRIC. It is indifferent cold, my lord, indeed.

HAMLET. But yet, methinks, it is very sultry and hot for
my complexion.   100

OSRIC. Exceedingly, my lord, it is very sultry—as
'twere—I cannot tell how ... But, my lord, his
majesty bade me signify to you that a' has laid a great
wager on your head. Sir, this is the matter,—

HAMLET [moves him to put on his hat]. I beseech you
remember—

OSRIC. Nay, good my lord, for mine ease, in good
faith. Sir, here is newly come to court Laertes—
believe me, an absolute gentleman, full of most
excellent differences, of very soft society, and great   110
showing: indeed, to speak sellingly of him, he is the
card or calendar of gentry; for you shall find in him
the continent of what parts a gentleman would see.

HAMLET. Sir, his definement suffers no perdition in
you, though I know to divide him inventorially
would dizzy th'arithmetic of memory, and yet but
yaw neither in respect of his quick sail, but in the
verity of extolment I take him to be a soul of great
article, and his infusion of such dearth and rareness,
as to make true diction of him, his semblable is his   120
mirror, and who else would trace him?—his um-
brage, nothing more.

OSRIC. Your lordship speaks most infallibly of him.

HAMLET. The concernancy, sir? why do we wrap the
gentleman in our more rawer breath?

OSRIC. Sir?

HORATIO. Is't not possible to understand in another
tongue? You will to't, sir, really.

HAMLET. What imports the nomination of this gentle-
man?   130

OSRIC. Of Laertes?

HORATIO. His purse is empty already, all's golden
words are spent.

HAMLET. Of him, sir.

OSRIC. I know you are not ignorant—

HAMLET. I would you did, sir, yet in faith if you did,
it would not much approve me. Well, sir?

OSRIC. You are not ignorant of what excellence
Laertes is—

HAMLET. I dare not confess that, lest I should compare   140
with him in excellence, but to know a man well
were to know himself.

OSRIC. I mean, sir, for his weapon, but in the imputation laid on him by them in his meed, he's un-
fellowed.

HAMLET. What's his weapon?

OSRIC. Rapier and dagger.

HAMLET. That's two of his weapons—but, well.

OSRIC. The king, sir, hath wagered with him six
Barbary horses, against the which he has impawned,   150
as I take it, six French rapiers and poniards, with
their assigns, as girdle, hangers, and so. Three of the
carriages in faith are very dear to fancy, very
responsive to the hilts, most delicate carriages, and of
very liberal conceit.

HAMLET. What call you the carriages?

HORATIO. I knew you must be edified by the margent
ere you had done.

OSRIC. The carriages, sir, are the hangers.

HAMLET. The phrase would be more germane to the   160
matter, if we could carry a cannon by our sides—I
would it might be hangers till then. But on! six
Barbary horses against six French swords, their

assigns, and three liberal-conceited carriages—that's
the French bet against the Danish. Why is this all
'impawned' as you call it?

OSRIC. The king, sir, hath laid, sir, that in a dozen
passes between yourself and him he shall not exceed
you three hits. He hath laid on twelve for nine. And
it would come to immediate trial, if your lordship   170
would vouchsafe the answer.

HAMLET. How if I answer 'no'?

OSRIC. I mean, my lord, the opposition of your person
in trial.

HAMLET. Sir, I will walk here in the hall, if it please his
majesty. It is the breathing time of day with me. Let
the foils be brought, the gentleman willing, and the
king hold his purpose, I will win for him an I can, if
not I will gain nothing but my shame and the odd
hits.   180

OSRIC. Shall I re-deliver you e'en so?

HAMLET. To this effect, sir,—after what flourish your
nature will.

OSRIC. I commend my duty to your lordship.

HAMLET. Yours, yours.   Osric goes
He does well to commend it himself, there are no
tongues else for's turn.

HORATIO. This lapwing runs away with the shell on
his head.

HAMLET. A' did comply, sir, with his dug before a'   190
sucked it. Thus has he—and many more of the same
bevy that I know the drossy age dotes on—only got
the tune of the time and, out of an habit of
encounter, a kind of yeasty collection, which carries
them through and through the most profound and
winnowed opinions, and do but blow them to their
trial, the bubbles are out.

A lord enters

LORD. My lord, his majesty commended him to you
by young Osric, who brings back to him that you
attend him in the hall. He sends to know if your   200
pleasure hold to play with Laertes, or that you will
take longer time.

HAMLET. I am constant to my purposes, they follow
the king's pleasure. If his fitness speaks, mine is
ready; now or whensoever, provided I be so able as
now.

LORD. The king, and queen, and all are coming down.

HAMLET. In happy time.

LORD. The queen desires you to use some gentle entertainment to Laertes before you fall to play.   210

HAMLET. She well instructs me.   The lord departs

HORATIO. You will lose this wager, my lord.

HAMLET. I do not think so. Since he went into France,
I have been in continual practice. I shall win at the
odds; but thou wouldst not think how ill all's here
about my heart—but it is no matter.

HORATIO. Nay, good my lord—

HAMLET. It is but foolery, but it is such a kind of gain-
giving as would perhaps trouble a woman.

HORATIO. If your mind dislike any thing, obey it. I will   220
forestall their repair hither, and say you are not fit.

HAMLET. Not a whit, we defy augury. There is special
providence in the fall of a sparrow. If it be now, 'tis
not to come—if it be not to come, it will be now—
if it be not now, yet it will come—the readiness is all.
Since no man, of aught he leaves, knows what is't
to leave betimes, let be.

Attendants enter to set benches and carry in cushions for the
spectators; next follow trumpeters and drummers with kettle-
drums, the King, the Queen and all the court, Osric and
another lord, as judges, bearing foils and daggers which are
placed upon a table near the wall, and last of all Laertes
dressed for the fence

KING. Come, Hamlet, come and take this hand from
     me.

                    He puts the hand of Laertes into
                              the hand of Hamlet
HAMLET. Give me your pardon, sir. I have done you
     wrong,
     But pardon't, as you are a gentleman.   230
     This presence knows, and you must needs have
         heard,
     How I am punished with a sore distraction.
     What I have done
     That might your nature, honour and exception
     Roughly awake, I here proclaim was madness.
     Was't Hamlet wronged Laertes? never Hamlet.
     If Hamlet from himself be ta'en away,
     And when he's not himself does wrong Laertes,
     Then Hamlet does it not, Hamlet denies it.
     Who does it then? his madness. If't be so,   240
     Hamlet is of the faction that is wronged,
     His madness is poor Hamlet's enemy.
     Sir, in this audience,
     Let my disclaiming from a purposed evil
     Free me so far in your most generous thoughts,
     That I have shot my arrow o'er the house,
     And hurt my brother.
LAERTES.   I am satisfied in nature,
     Whose motive in this case should stir me most
     To my revenge, but in my terms of honour
     I stand aloof, and will no reconcilement,   250
     Till by some elder masters of known honour
     I have a voice and precedent of peace,
     To keep my name ungored: but till that time,
     I do receive your offered love like love,
     And will not wrong it.
HAMLET.   I embrace it freely,
     And will this brother's wager frankly play....
     Give us the foils, come on.
LAERTES.   Come. one for me.
HAMLET. I'll be your foil, Laertes. In mine ignorance
     Your skill shall like a star i'th'darkest night
     Stick fiery off indeed.
LAERTES.   You mock me, sir.   260
HAMLET. No, by this hand.
KING. Give them the foils, young Osric. Cousin
     Hamlet,
     You know the wager?
HAMLET.   Very well, my lord.
     Your grace has laid the odds o'th'weaker side.
KING. I do not fear it, I have seen you both—
     But since he is bettered, we have therefore odds.
LAERTES. This is too heavy: let me see another.
HAMLET. This likes me well. These foils have all a
     length?
OSRIC. Ay, my good lord.

Hamlet makes ready; servants bear in flagons of wine with
cups

KING. Set me the stoups of wine upon that table.   270
     If Hamlet give the first or second hit,

Or quit in answer of the third exchange,
Let all the battlements their ordnance fire.
The king shall drink to Hamlet's better breath,
And in the cup an union shall he throw,
Richer than that which four successive kings
In Denmark's crown have worn: give me the cups,
And let the kettle to the trumpet speak,
The trumpet to the cannoneer without,
The cannons to the heavens, the heaven to earth,   280
'Now the king drinks to Hamlet.' Come, begin,
And you, the judges, bear a wary eye.

Trumpets sound; Hamlet and Laertes take their stations

HAMLET. Come on, sir.
LAERTES.   Come, my lord.

They play

HAMLET.   One!
LAERTES.   No.
HAMLET.   Judgement?
OSRIC. A hit, a very palpable hit.
                    The kettle-drum sounds, the trumpets blow,
                              and a cannon-shot is heard without
LAERTES.   Well, again.
KING. Stay, give me drink. Hamlet, this pearl is thine.
     Here's to thy health! Give him the cup.
HAMLET. I'll play this bout first, set it by a while.
     Come. [*they play again*] Another hit! What say you?
LAERTES. A touch, a touch, I do confess't.
KING. Our son shall win.
QUEEN.   He's fat, and scant of breath. 290
     Here, Hamlet, take my napkin, rub thy brows.
     The queen carouses to thy fortune, Hamlet.
HAMLET. Good madam!
KING.   Gertrude, do not drink.
QUEEN. I will, my lord, I pray you pardon me.
KING [*aside*]. It is the poisoned cup, it is too late!
HAMLET. I dare not drink yet, madam—by and by.
QUEEN. Come, let me wipe thy face.
LAERTES. My lord, I'll hit him now.
KING.   I do not think't.
LAERTES. And yet 'tis almost 'gainst my conscience.
HAMLET. Come, for the third, Laertes. You do but
     dally,   300
     I pray you pass with your best violence.
     I am afeard you make a wanton of me.
LAERTES. Say you so? come on.

They play the third bout

OSRIC. Nothing neither way.
LAERTES. Have at you now!
                    He wounds Hamlet slightly; in
                              scuffling they change rapiers
KING.   Part them, they are incensed.
HAMLET. Nay, come again.   *The Queen falls*
OSRIC.   Look to the queen there, ho!
                    Hamlet wounds Laertes deeply
HORATIO. They bleed on both sides!—how is it, my
     lord?   *Laertes falls*
OSRIC. How is't, Laertes?
LAERTES. Why, as a woodcock to my own springe,
     Osric!
     I am justly killed with mine own treachery.   310
HAMLET. How does the queen?
KING.   She swoons to see them bleed.

QUEEN. No, no, the drink, the drink—O my dear
    Hamlet—
  The drink, the drink! I am poisoned!   *She dies*
HAMLET. O villainy! ho! let the door be locked—
  Treachery! seek it out.
LAERTES. It is here, Hamlet. Hamlet, thou art slain,
  No medicine in the world can do thee good,
  In thee there is not half an hour of life,
  The treacherous instrument is in thy hand,
  Unbated and envenomed. The foul practice   320
  Hath turned itself on me, lo, here I lie,
  Never to rise again—thy mother's poisoned—
  I can no more—the king, the king's to blame.
HAMLET. The point envenomed too!—
  Then, venom, to thy work.   *He stabs the King*
ALL. Treason! treason!
KING. O, yet defend me, friends, I am but hurt.
HAMLET. Here, thou incestuous, murderous, damnéd
  Dane,
  Drink off this potion. Is thy union here?
  Follow my mother.   *The King dies*
LAERTES.   He is justly served,   330
  It is a poison tempered by himself.
  Exchange forgiveness with me, noble Hamlet,
  Mine and my father's death come not upon thee,
  Nor thine on me!   *He dies*
HAMLET. Heaven make thee free of it! I follow thee ...
                          He falls
  I am dead, Horatio. Wretched queen, adieu!
  You that look pale and tremble at this chance,
  That are but mutes or audience to this act,
  Had I but time, as this fell sergeant, Death,
  Is strict in his arrest, O, I could tell you—   340
  But let it be; Horatio, I am dead,
  Thou livest, report me and my cause aright
  To the unsatisfied.
HORATIO.   Never believe it;
  I am more an antique Roman than a Dane—
  Here's yet some liquor left.
HAMLET.   As thou'rt a man,
  Give me the cup, let go, by heaven I'll ha't!
  O God, Horatio, what a wounded name,
  Things standing thus unknown, shall live behind
  me!
  If thou didst ever hold me in thy heart,
  Absent thee from felicity awhile,   350
  And in this harsh world draw thy breath in pain,
  To tell my story ...
      The tread of soldiers marching heard afar off,
          and later a shot; Osric goes out
          What warlike noise is this?
OSRIC [*returning*]. Young Fortinbras, with conquest
  come from Poland,
  To th'ambassadors of England gives
  This warlike volley.
HAMLET.   O, I die, Horatio,
  The potent poison quite o'er-crows my spirit,
  I cannot live to hear the news from England,
  But I do prophesy th'election lights
  On Fortinbras, he has my dying voice.

So tell him, with th'occurrents more and less   360
  Which have solicited—the rest is silence.   *He dies*
HORATIO. Now cracks a noble heart. Good night,
  sweet prince;
  And flights of angels sing thee to thy rest!
  Why does the drum come hither?

Prince Fortinbras, the English ambassadors, and others enter

FORTINBRAS. Where is this sight?
HORATIO.   What is it you would see?
  If aught of woe or wonder cease your search.
FORTINBRAS. This quarry cries on havoc. O proud
  death,
  What feast is toward in thine eternal cell,
  That thou so many princes at a shot
  So bloodily hast struck?
I AMBASSADOR.   The sight is dismal,   370
  And our affairs from England come too late.
  The ears are senseless that should give us hearing,
  To tell him his commandment is fulfilled,
  That Rosencrantz and Guildenstern are dead.
  Where should we have our thanks?
HORATIO.   Not from his mouth,
  Had it th'ability of life to thank you;
  He never gave commandment for their death;
  But since, so jump upon this bloody question,
  You from the Polack wars, and you from England,
  Are here arrived, give order that these bodies   380
  High on a stage be placéd to the view,
  And let me speak to th'yet unknowing world
  How these things came about; so shall you hear
  Of carnal, bloody and unnatural acts,
  Of accidental judgements, casual slaughters,
  Of deaths put on by cunning and forced cause,
  And, in this upshot, purposes mistook
  Fall'n on th'inventors' heads: all this can I
  Truly deliver.
FORTINBRAS.   Let us haste to hear it,
  And call the noblest to the audience.   390
  For me, with sorrow I embrace my fortune.
  I have some rights of memory in this kingdom,
  Which now to claim my vantage doth invite me.
HORATIO. Of that I shall have also cause to speak,
  And from his mouth whose voice will draw on
  more.
  But let this same be presently performed,
  Even while men's minds are wild, lest more
  mischance
  On plots and errors happen.
FORTINBRAS.   Let four captains
  Bear Hamlet like a soldier to the stage,
  For he was likely, had he been put on,   400
  To have proved most royal; and for his passage,
  The soldiers' music and the rite of war
  Speak loudly for him:
  Take up the bodies—such a sight as this
  Becomes the field, but here shows much amiss.
  Go, bid the soldiers shoot.

*The soldiers bear away the bodies, the while a dead march
is heard; after the which a peal of ordnance is shot off*

King Lear

The scene: Britain

CHARACTERS IN THE PLAY

LEAR, *king of Britain*
KING OF FRANCE
DUKE OF BURGUNDY
DUKE OF CORNWALL, *husband to Regan*
DUKE OF ALBANY, *husband to Goneril*
EARL OF KENT
EARL OF GLOUCESTER
EDGAR, *son to Gloucester*
EDMUND, *bastard son to Gloucester*
CURAN, *a courtier*

OSWALD, *steward to Goneril*
OLD MAN, *tenant to Gloucester*
DOCTOR
FOOL
GONERIL
REGAN } *daughters to Lear*
CORDELIA
Gentleman, Herald, Captains, Knights of Lear's train,
    Messengers, Soldiers, Attendants, Servants

King Lear

Enter Kent, Gloucester, and Edmund

KENT. I thought the king had more affected the Duke of Albany than Cornwall.

GLOUCESTER. It did always seem so to us; but now, in the division of the kingdom, it appears not which of the dukes he values most, for equalities are so weighed that curiosity in neither can make choice of either's moiety.

KENT. Is not this your son, my lord?

GLOUCESTER. His breeding, sir, hath been at my charge. I have so often blushed to acknowledge him that now I am brazed to 't.

KENT. I cannot conceive you.

GLOUCESTER. Sir, this young fellow's mother could; whereupon she grew round-wombed, and had indeed, sir, a son for her cradle ere she had a husband for her bed. Do you smell a fault?

KENT. I cannot wish the fault undone, the issue of it being so proper.

GLOUCESTER. But I have a son, sir, by order of law, some year elder than this, who yet is no dearer in my account. Though this knave came something saucily to the world before he was sent for, yet was his mother fair; there was good sport at his making, and the whoreson must be acknowledged. Do you know this noble gentleman, Edmund?

EDMUND. No, my lord.

GLOUCESTER. My lord of Kent. Remember him hereafter as my honourable friend.

EDMUND. My services to your lordship.

KENT. I must love you, and sue to know you better.

EDMUND. Sir, I shall study deserving.

GLOUCESTER. He hath been out nine years, and away he shall again. [*a sennet sounded*] The king is coming.

Enter one bearing a coronet. Enter King Lear, Cornwall, Albany, Goneril, Regan, Cordelia, and attendants

LEAR. Attend the lords of France and Burgundy, Gloucester.

GLOUCESTER. I shall, my liege.
He goes out, attended by Edmund

LEAR. Meantime we shall express our darker purpose.
Give me the map there. Know that we have divided
In three our kingdom; and 'tis our fast intent
To shake all cares and business from our age,
Conferring them on younger strengths while we
Unburdened crawl toward death. Our son of Cornwall,
And you, our no less loving son of Albany,
We have this hour a constant will to publish
Our daughters' several dowers, that future strife
May be prevented now. The princes, France and Burgundy,
Great rivals in our youngest daughter's love,
Long in our court have made their amorous sojourn,
And here are to be answered. Tell me, my daughters
(Since now we will divest us both of rule,
Interest of territory, cares of state),
Which of you shall we say doth love us most,
That we our largest bounty may extend
Where nature doth with merit challenge. Goneril,
Our eldest-born, speak first.

GONERIL. Sir, I love you more than word can wield the matter;
Dearer than eyesight, space and liberty;
Beyond what can be valued rich or rare;
No less than life with grace, health, beauty, honour;
As much as child e'er loved, or father found:
A love that makes breath poor, and speech unable.
Beyond all manner of "so much" I love you.

CORDELIA [*aside*]. What shall Cordelia speak? Love, and be silent.

LEAR. Of all these bounds, even from this line to this,
With shadowy forests and with champaigns riched,
With plenteous rivers and wide-skirted meads,
We make thee lady. To thine and Albany's issues
Be this perpetual. What says our second daughter,
Our dearest Regan, wife of Cornwall?

REGAN. I am made of that self metal as my sister,
And prize me at her worth. In my true heart
I find she names my very deed of love:
Only she comes too short, that I profess
Myself an enemy to all other joys
Which the most precious spirit of sense possesses,
And find I am alone felicitate
In your dear Highness' love.

CORDELIA [*aside*].   Then poor Cordelia!
And yet not so, since I am sure my love's
More ponderous than my tongue.

LEAR. To thee and thine, hereditary ever,
Remain this ample third of our fair kingdom,
No less in space, validity, and pleasure
Than that conferred on Goneril. Now, our joy,
Although our last and least, to whose young love
The vines of France and milk of Burgundy
Strive to be interested, what can you say to draw
A third more opulent than your sisters? Speak.

CORDELIA. Nothing, my lord.

LEAR. Nothing?

CORDELIA. Nothing.

LEAR. Nothing will come of nothing; speak again.

CORDELIA. Unhappy that I am, I cannot heave
My heart into my mouth. I love your Majesty
According to my bond, no more nor less.

LEAR. How, how, Cordelia? Mend your speech a little,
Lest you may mar your fortunes.

CORDELIA.   Good my lord,
You have begot me, bred me, loved me. I
Return those duties back as are right fit,
Obey you, love you, and most honour you.
Why have my sisters husbands, if they say
They love you all? Haply, when I shall wed,
That lord whose hand must take my plight shall carry
Half my love with him, half my care and duty.
Sure I shall never marry like my sisters,
To love my father all.

LEAR. But goes thy heart with this?
CORDELIA.   Ay, my good lord.
LEAR. So young, and so untender?
CORDELIA. So young, my lord, and true.
LEAR. Let it be so; thy truth then be thy dower!
  For, by the sacred radiance of the sun,
  The mysteries of Hecate and the night,   110
  By all the operation of the orbs
  From whom we do exist and cease to be,
  Here I disclaim all my paternal care,
  Propinquity and property of blood,
  And as a stranger to my heart and me
  Hold thee from this for ever. The barbarous
    Scythian,
  Or he that makes his generation messes
  To gorge his appetite, shall to my bosom
  Be as well neighboured, pitied, and relieved,
  As thou my sometime daughter.
KENT.   Good my liege— 120
LEAR. Peace, Kent!
  Come not between the dragon and his wrath.
  I loved her most, and thought to set my rest
  On her kind nursery. [to Cordelia] Hence, and avoid
    my sight!—
  So be my grave my peace as here I give
  Her father's heart from her. Call France! Who stirs?
  Call Burgundy! Cornwall and Albany,
  With my two daughters' dowers digest the third;
  Let pride, which she calls plainness, marry her.
  I do invest you jointly with my power,   130
  Pre-eminence, and all the large effects
  That troop with majesty. Ourself, by monthly
    course,
  With reservation of an hundred knights
  By you to be sustained, shall our abode
  Make with you by due turn. Only we shall retain
  The name and all th' addition to a king: the sway,
  Revenue, execution of the rest,
  Belovéd sons, be yours; which to confirm,
  This coronet part between you.
KENT.   Royal Lear,
  Whom I have ever honoured as my king,   140
  Loved as my father, as my master followed,
  As my great patron thought on in my prayers—
LEAR. The bow is bent and drawn; make from the
    shaft.
KENT. Let it fall rather, though the fork invade
  The region of my heart! Be Kent unmannerly
  When Lear is mad. What wouldst thou do, old man?
  Think'st thou that duty shall have dread to speak
  When power to flattery bows? To plainness
    honour's bound
  When majesty stoops to folly. Reserve thy state,
  And in thy best consideration check   150
  This hideous rashness. Answer my life my
    judgement,
  Thy youngest daughter does not love thee least,
  Nor are those empty-hearted whose low sounds
  Reverb no hollowness.
LEAR.   Kent, on thy life, no more!
KENT. My life I never held but as a pawn
  To wage against thine enemies; ne'er feared to lose
    it,
  Thy safety being motive.
LEAR.   Out of my sight!
KENT. See better, Lear, and let me still remain

  The true blank of thine eye.
LEAR. Now by Apollo—
KENT.   Now by Apollo, king,   160
  Thou swear'st thy gods in vain.
LEAR.   O vassal! miscreant!
               Laying his hand on his sword
ALBANY. } Dear sir, forbear!
CORNWALL. }
KENT. Kill thy physician, and the fee bestow
  Upon the foul disease. Revoke thy gift,
  Or, whilst I can vent clamour from my throat,
  I'll tell thee thou dost evil.
LEAR.   Hear me, recreant,
  On thine allegiance, hear me!
  That thou hast sought to make us break our vow—
  Which we durst never yet—and with strained pride
  To come betwixt our sentence and our power— 170
  Which nor our nature nor our place can bear,—
  Our potency made good, take thy reward.
  Five days we do allot thee for provision
  To shield thee from disasters of the world,
  And on the sixth to turn thy hated back
  Upon our kingdom. If, on the tenth day following,
  Thy banished trunk be found in our dominions,
  The moment is thy death. Away! By Jupiter,
  This shall not be revoked.
KENT. Fare thee well, king; sith thus thou wilt appear, 180
  Freedom lives hence and banishment is here.
  [to Cordelia] The gods to their dear shelter take thee,
    maid,
  That justly think'st and hast most rightly said.
  [to Goneril and Regan] And your large speeches may
    your deeds approve,
  That good effects may spring from words of love.
  Thus Kent, O princes, bids you all adieu;
  He'll shape his old course in a country new.
                      He goes

Flourish. Re-enter Gloucester, with France, Burgundy, and
Attendants

GLOUCESTER. Here's France and Burgundy, my noble
  lord.
LEAR. My lord of Burgundy,
  We first address toward you, who with this king 190
  Hath rivalled for our daughter. What in the least
  Will you require in present dower with her,
  Or cease your quest of love?
BURGUNDY.   Most royal majesty,
  I crave no more than hath your highness offered—
  Nor will you tender less?
LEAR.   Right noble Burgundy,
  When she was dear to us, we did hold her so;
  But now her price is fall'n. Sir, there she stands.
  If aught within that little seeming-substance,
  Or all of it, with our displeasure pieced,
  And nothing more, may fitly like your grace,   200
  She's there, and she is yours.
BURGUNDY.   I know no answer.
LEAR. Will you, with those infirmities she owes,
  Unfriended, new adopted to our hate,
  Dowered with our curse and strangered with our
    oath,
  Take her or leave her?
BURGUNDY.   Pardon me, royal sir.
  Election makes not up on such conditions.

LEAR. Then leave her, sir; for, by the power that made
  me,
  I tell you all her wealth. [*to France*] For you, great
    king,
  I would not from your love make such a stray
  To match you where I hate; therefore beseech you 210
  T' avert your liking a more worthier way
  Than on a wretch whom Nature is ashamed
  Almost t' acknowledge hers.
FRANCE.   This is most strange,
  That she whom even but now was your best object,
  The argument of your praise, balm of your age,
  The best, the dearest, should in this trice of time
  Commit a thing so monstrous to dismantle
  So many folds of favour. Sure her offence
  Must be of such unnatural degree
  That monsters it, or your-vouched affection   220
  Fall into taint; which to believe of her
  Must be a faith that reason without miracle
  Should never plant in me.
CORDELIA.   I yet beseech your majesty—
  If for I want that glib and oily art
  To speak and purpose not, since what I well intend,
  I'll do 't before I speak—that you make known
  It is no vicious blot, murder or foulness,
  No unchaste action or dishonoured step,
  That hath deprived me of your grace and favour;
  But even for want of that for which I am richer—   230
  A still-soliciting eye, and such a tongue
  That I am glad I have not, though not to have it
  Hath lost me in your liking.
LEAR.   Better thou
  Hadst not been born than not t' have pleased me
    better.
FRANCE. Is it but this—a tardiness in nature
  Which often leaves the history unspoke
  That it intends? My lord of Burgundy,
  What say you to the lady? Love's not love
  When it is mingled with regards that stands
  Aloof from th' entire point. Will you have her?   240
  She is herself a dowry.
BURGUNDY.   Royal king,
  Give but that portion which yourself proposed,
  And here I take Cordelia by the hand,
  Duchess of Burgundy.
LEAR. Nothing. I have sworn; I am firm.
BURGUNDY. I am sorry then you have so lost a father
  That you must lose a husband.
CORDELIA.   Peace be with Burgundy!
  Since that respect and fortunes are his love,
  I shall not be his wife.
FRANCE. Fairest Cordelia, that art most rich, being
    poor;   250
  Most choice, forsaken; and most loved, despised;
  Thee and thy virtues here I seize upon.
  Be it lawful I take up what's cast away.
  Gods, gods! 'Tis strange that from their cold'st
    neglect
  My love should kindle to inflamed respect.
  Thy dowerless daughter, king, thrown to my
    chance,
  Is queen of us, of ours, and our fair France.
  Not all the dukes of wat'rish Burgundy
  Can buy this unprized precious maid of me.
  Bid them farewell, Cordelia, though unkind;   260
  Thou losest here, a better where to find.

LEAR. Thou hast her, France; let her be thine, for we
  Have no such daughter, nor shall ever see
  That face of hers again. Therefore be gone
  Without our grace, our love, our benison.
  Come, noble Burgundy.

           Flourish. Lear, Burgundy, Cornwall,
                 Albany, Gloucester, and
                             attendants depart

FRANCE.   Bid farewell to your sisters.
CORDELIA. The jewels of our father, with washed eyes
  Cordelia leaves you, I know you what you are,
  And like a sister am most loath to call
  Your faults as they are named. Love well our father; 270
  To your professèd bosoms I commit him:
  But yet, alas, stood I within his grace,
  I would prefer him to a better place.
  So farewell to you both.
REGAN. Prescribe not us our duty.
GONERIL.   Let your study
  Be to content your lord, who hath received you
  At Fortune's alms. You have obedience scanted,
  And well are worth the want that you have wanted.
CORDELIA. Time shall unfold what plighted cunning
    hides,
  Who covert faults at last with shame derides.   280
  Well may you prosper.
FRANCE.   Come, my fair Cordelia.
                                    He leads her away
GONERIL. Sister, it is not little I have to say of what
  most nearly appertains to us both. I think our father
  will hence tonight.
REGAN. That's most certain, and with you; next month
  with us.
GONERIL. You see how full of changes his age is. The
  observation we have made of it hath not been little.
  He always loved our sister most, and with what poor
  judgement he hath now cast her off appears too   290
  grossly.
REGAN. 'Tis the infirmity of his age; yet he hath ever
  but slenderly known himself.
GONERIL. The best and soundest of his time hath been
  but rash; then must we look from his age to receive,
  not alone the imperfections of long-engraffed condition, but therewithal the unruly waywardness that
  infirm and choleric years bring with them.
REGAN. Such unconstant starts are we like to have from
  him as this of Kent's banishment.   300
GONERIL. There is further compliment of leave-taking
  between France and him. Pray you let us hit together. If our father carry authority with such disposition as he bears, this last surrender of his will but
  offend us.
REGAN. We shall further think of it.
GONERIL. We must do something, and i' th' heat.
                                             They go

           Scene 2: *The Earl of Gloucester's castle*

Enter Edmund, with a letter

EDMUND. Thou, Nature, art my goddess; to thy law
  My services are bound. Wherefore should I
  Stand in the plague of custom, and permit
  The curiosity of nations to deprive me,
  For that I am some twelve or fourteen moonshines
  Lag of a brother? Why bastard? wherefore base?
  When my dimensions are as well compact,

My mind as generous, and my shape as true,
As honest madam's issue? Why brand they us
With base? with baseness? bastardy? base, base?   10
Who, in the lusty stealth of Nature, take
More composition and fierce quality
Than doth, within a dull, stale, tiréd bed,
Go to th' creating a whole tribe of fops
Got 'tween a sleep and wake? Well then,
Legitimate Edgar, I must have your land.
Our father's love is to the bastard Edmund
As to th' legitimate. Fine word, 'legitimate'!
Well, my legitimate, if this letter speed,
And my invention thrive, Edmund the base   20
Shall top th' legitimate. I grow, I prosper.
Now, gods, stand up for bastards!

Enter Gloucester

GLOUCESTER. Kent banished thus? and France in choler
   parted?
And the king gone to-night? Prescribed his power?
Confined to exhibition? All this done
Upon the gad?—Edmund, how now? What news?
EDMUND. So please your lordship, none.
                     Putting the letter in his pocket
GLOUCESTER. Why so earnestly seek you to put up that
   letter?
EDMUND. I know no news, my lord.   30
GLOUCESTER. What paper were you reading?
EDMUND. Nothing, my lord.
GLOUCESTER. No? What needed then that terrible dis-
   patch of it into your pocket? The quality of nothing
   hath not such need to hide itself. Let's see. Come,
   if it be nothing, I shall not need spectacles.
EDMUND. I beseech you, sir, pardon me. It is a letter
   from my brother that I have not all o'er-read; and
   for so much as I have perused, I find it not fit for
   your o'erlooking.   40
GLOUCESTER. Give me the letter, sir.
EDMUND. I shall offend either to detain or give it. The
   contents, as in part I understand them, are to blame.
GLOUCESTER. Let's see, let's see.
EDMUND. I hope, for my brother's justification, he
   wrote this but as an essay or taste of my virtue.
GLOUCESTER [*reads*]. 'This policy and reverence of age
   makes the world bitter to the best of our times, keeps
   our fortunes from us till our oldness cannot relish
   them. I begin to find an idle and fond bondage in   50
   the oppression of aged tyranny, who sways, not as it
   hath power, but as it is suffered. Come to me, that
   of this I may speak more. If our father would sleep
   till I waked him, you should enjoy half his revenue
   for ever, and live the beloved of your brother,
                                                                              Edgar.'
Hum! Conspiracy? 'Sleep till I waked him, you
   should enjoy half his revenue.' My son Edgar! Had
   he a hand to write this? A heart and brain to breed
   it in? When came you to this? Who brought it?   60
EDMUND. It was not brought me, my lord: there's the
   cunning of it. I found it thrown in at the casement
   of my closet.
GLOUCESTER. You know the character to be your
   brother's?
EDMUND. If the matter were good, my lord, I durst
   swear it were his; but, in respect of that, I would fain
   think it were not.
GLOUCESTER. It is his.

EDMUND. It is his hand, my lord; but I hope his heart   70
   is not in the contents.
GLOUCESTER. Has he never before sounded you in this
   business?
EDMUND. Never, my lord. But I have heard him oft
   maintain it to be fit that, sons at perfect age, and
   fathers declined, the father should be as ward to the
   son, and the son manage his revenue.
GLOUCESTER. O villain, villain! His very opinion in
   the letter! Abhorred villain! Unnatural, detested,
   brutish villain! Worse than brutish! Go, sirrah, seek   80
   him. I'll apprehend him. Abominable villain! Where
   is he?
EDMUND. I do not well know, my lord. If it shall please
   you to suspend your indignation against my brother
   till you can derive from him better testimony of his
   intent, you should run a certain course; where, if you
   violently proceed against him, mistaking his purpose, it would make a great gap in your own
   honour, and shake in pieces the heart of his obedience. I dare pawn down my life for him that he hath   90
   writ this to feel my affection to your honour, and
   to no other pretence of danger.
GLOUCESTER. Think you so?
EDMUND. If your honour judge it meet, I will place
   you where you shall hear us confer of this and by
   an auricular assurance have your satisfaction, and
   that without any further delay than this very
   evening.
GLOUCESTER. He cannot be such a monster!
EDMUND. Nor is not, sure.   100
GLOUCESTER. To his father, that so tenderly and
   entirely loves him! Heaven and earth! Edmund, seek
   him out; wind me into him, I pray you; frame the
   business after your own wisdom. I would unstate
   myself to be in a due resolution.
EDMUND. I will seek him, sir, presently; convey the
   business as I shall find means, and acquaint you
   withal.
GLOUCESTER. These late eclipses in the sun and moon
   portend no good to us. Though the wisdom of   110
   nature can reason it thus and thus, yet nature finds
   itself scourged by the sequent effects. Love cools,
   friendship falls off, brothers divide. In cities, mutinies; in countries, discord; in palaces, treason; and the
   bond cracked 'twixt son and father. This villain of
   mine comes under the prediction; there's son against
   father: the king falls from bias of nature; there's
   father against child. We have seen the best of our
   time. Machinations, hollowness, treachery, and all
   ruinous disorders follow us disquietly to our graves.   120
   Find out this villain, Edmund; it shall lose thee
   nothing; do it carefully. And the noble and true-
   hearted Kent banished; his offence, honesty! 'Tis
   strange.   *He goes*
EDMUND. This is the excellent foppery of the world
   that when we are sick in fortune, often the surfeits
   of our own behaviour, we make guilty of our
   disasters the sun, the moon, and stars; as if we were
   villains on necessity, fools by heavenly compulsion,
   knaves, thieves, and treachers by spherical pre-   130
   dominance, drunkards, liars, and adulterers by an
   enforced obedience of planetary influence, and all
   that we are evil in by a divine thrusting on. An
   admirable evasion of whoremaster man, to lay his
   goatish disposition to the charge of a star! My father

compounded with my mother under the Dragon's tail, and my nativity was under Ursa Major, so that it follows I am rough and lecherous. Fut, I should have been that I am, had the maidenliest star in the firmament twinkled on my bastardizing. Edgar— 140

Enter Edgar

Pat! he comes, like the catastrophe of the old comedy. My cue is villainous melancholy, with a sigh like Tom o' Bedlam—O these eclipses do portend these divisions. [*humming sadly*] Fa, sol, la, me.

EDGAR. How now, brother Edmund? What serious contemplation are you in?

EDMUND. I am thinking, brother, of a prediction I read this other day, what should follow these eclipses.

EDGAR. Do you busy yourself with that?

EDMUND. I promise you, the effects he writes of 150 succeed unhappily, as of unnaturalness between the child and the parent, death, dearth, dissolutions of ancient amities, divisions in state, menaces and maledictions against king and nobles, needless diffidences, banishment of friends, dissipation of cohorts, nuptial breaches, and I know not what.

EDGAR. How long have you been a sectary astronomical?

EDMUND. When saw you my father last?

EDGAR. The night gone by. 160

EDMUND. Spake you with him?

EDGAR. Ay, two hours together.

EDMUND. Parted you in good terms? Found you no displeasure in him, by word nor countenance?

EDGAR. None at all.

EDMUND. Bethink yourself wherein you may have offended him; and at my entreaty forbear his presence until some little time hath qualified the heat of his displeasure, which at this instant so rageth in him that with the mischief of your person it would 170 scarcely allay.

EDGAR. Some villain hath done me wrong.

EDMUND. That's my fear. I pray you have a continent forbearance till the speed of his rage goes slower; and, as I say, retire with me to my lodging, from whence I will fitly bring you to hear my lord speak. Pray ye, go; there's my key. If you do stir abroad, go armed.

EDGAR. Armed, brother?

EDMUND. Brother, I advise you to the best. I am no 180 honest man if there be any good meaning toward you. I have told you what I have seen and heard— but faintly, nothing like the image and horror of it. Pray you, away!

EDGAR. Shall I hear from you anon?

EDMUND. I do serve you in this business.   *Edgar goes*
A credulous father! and a brother noble
Whose nature is so far from doing harms
That he suspects none; on whose foolish honesty
My practices ride easy! I see the business. 190
Let me, if not by birth, have lands by wit;
All with me's meet that I can fashion fit.   *He goes*

Scene 3: *The Duke of Albany's palace*

Enter Goneril and Oswald, her steward

GONERIL. Did my father strike my gentleman for chiding of his fool?

OSWALD. Ay, madam.

GONERIL. By day and night he wrongs me. Every hour
He flashes into one gross crime or other
That sets us all at odds. I'll not endure it.
His knights grow riotous, and himself upbraids us
On every trifle. When he returns from hunting
I will not speak with him: say I am sick.
If you come slack of former services, 10
You shall do well; the fault of it I'll answer.
                           Horns heard

OSWALD. He's coming, madam; I hear him.

GONERIL. Put on what weary negligence you please,
You and your fellows; I'd have it come to question.
If he distaste it, let him to my sister,
Whose mind and mine I know in that are one,
Not to be overruled. Idle old man,
That still would manage those authorities
That he hath given away! Now, by my life,
Old fools are babes again, and must be used 20
With checks as flatteries, when they are seen abused.
Remember what I have said.

OSWALD.   Well, madam.

GONERIL. And let his knights have colder looks among you;
What grows of it, no matter. Advise your fellows so.
I would breed from hence occasions, and I shall,
That I may speak. I'll write straight to my sister
To hold my very course. Prepare for dinner.
                             They go

Scene 4: *A hall in the same*

Enter Kent disguised

KENT. If but as well I other accents borrow,
That can my speech diffuse, my good intent
May carry through itself to that full issue
For which I razed my likeness. Now, banished Kent,
If thou canst serve where thou dost stand condemned,
So may it come thy master whom thou lov'st
Shall find thee full of labours.

Horns heard. Lear enters from hunting, with Knights and Attendants

LEAR. Let me not stay a jot for dinner; go get it ready.
                         Attendant goes out
How now! what art thou?

KENT. A man, sir. 10

LEAR. What dost thou profess? What would'st thou with us?

KENT. I do profess to be no less than I seem, to serve him truly that will put me in trust, to love him that is honest, to converse with him that is wise and says little, to fear judgement, to fight when I cannot choose, and to eat no fish.

LEAR. What art thou?

KENT. A very honest-hearted fellow, and as poor as the king. 20

LEAR. If thou be'st as poor for a subject as he's for a king, thou art poor enough. What would'st thou?

KENT. Service.

LEAR. Who would'st thou serve?

KENT. You.

LEAR. Dost thou know me, fellow?

KENT. No, sir; but you have that in your countenance which I would fain call master.

LEAR. What's that?
KENT. Authority.   30
LEAR. What services canst thou do?
KENT. I can keep honest counsel, ride, run, mar a
curious tale in telling it, and deliver a plain message
bluntly; that which ordinary men are fit for I am
qualified in, and best of me is diligence.
LEAR. How old art thou?
KENT. Not so young, sir, to love a woman for singing,
nor so old to dote on her for anything. I have years
on my back forty-eight.
LEAR. Follow me; thou shalt serve me. If I like thee   40
no worse after dinner I will not part from thee yet.
Dinner, ho! dinner! Where's my knave? my fool?
Go you and call my fool hither. *Attendant goes out*

Enter Oswald

You! you, sirrah! Where's my daughter?
OSWALD. So please you—   *Goes out*
LEAR. What says the fellow there? Call the clotpoll
back! [*Knight goes out*] Where's my fool? Ho! I think
the world's asleep. [*Knight returns*] How now?
Where's that mongrel?
KNIGHT. He says, my lord, your daughter is not well.   50
LEAR. Why came not the slave back to me when I
called him?
KNIGHT. Sir, he answered me in the roundest manner
he would not.
LEAR. He would not?
KNIGHT. My lord, I know not what the matter is,
but to my judgement your highness is not entertained with that ceremonious affection as you were
wont. There's a great abatement of kindness appears
as well in the general dependants as in the duke   60
himself also and your daughter.
LEAR. Ha! say'st thou so?
KNIGHT. I beseech you pardon me, my lord, if I be
mistaken, for my duty cannot be silent when I think
your highness wronged.
LEAR. Thou but rememb'rest me of mine own conception. I have perceived a most faint neglect of late,
which I have rather blamed as mine own jealous
curiosity than as a very pretence and purpose of unkindness; I will look further into't. But where's my   70
fool? I have not seen him this two days.
KNIGHT. Since my young lady's going into France, sir,
the fool hath much pined away.
LEAR. No more of that; I have noted it well. Go you
and tell my daughter I would speak with her. [*Attend-
dant goes out*] Go you, call hither my fool. [*Second
attendant goes out*]

Oswald returns

O you sir, you, come you hither, sir. Who am I, sir?
OSWALD. My lady's father.
LEAR. 'My lady's father', my lord's knave?
You whoreson dog, you slave, you cur!   80
OSWALD. I am none of these, my lord; I beseech your
pardon.
LEAR. Do you bandy looks with me, you rascal?
                                          Strikes him
OSWALD. I'll not be struken, my lord.
KENT. Nor tripped neither, you base football player.
                                      Tripping up his heels
LEAR. I thank thee, fellow. Thou serv'st me, and I'll
love thee.

KENT. Come, sir, arise, away! I'll teach you differences.
Away, away! If you will measure your lubber's
length again, tarry; but away! Go to; have you   90
wisdom? [*Oswald goes*] So.
LEAR. Now, my friendly knave, I thank thee. There's
earnest of thy service. [*giving money*]

Enter Fool

FOOL. Let me hire him too. Here's my coxcomb.
                                      Offers Kent his cap
LEAR. How now, my pretty knave? How dost thou?
FOOL. Sirrah, you were best take my coxcomb.
KENT. Why, fool?
FOOL. Why? For taking one's part that's out of favour.
Nay, an thou canst not smile as the wind sits, thou'lt
catch cold shortly. There, take my coxcomb! Why,   100
this fellow has banished two on's daughters, and did
the third a blessing against his will. If thou follow
him thou must needs wear my coxcomb. How now,
nuncle? Would I had two coxcombs and two
daughters!
LEAR. Why, my boy?
FOOL. If I gave them all my living, I'ld keep my cox-
combs myself. There's mine; beg another of thy
daughters.
LEAR. Take heed, sirrah—the whip.   110
FOOL. Truth's a dog must to kennel; he must be
whipped out, when the Lady's brach may stand by
th' fire and stink.
LEAR. A pestilent gall to me!
FOOL. Sirrah, I'll teach thee a speech.
LEAR. Do.
FOOL. Mark it, nuncle!
Have more than thou showest,
Speak less than thou knowest,
Lend less than thou owest,   120
Ride more than thou goest,
Learn more than thou trowest,
Set less than thou throwest;
Leave thy drink and thy whore,
And keep in-a-door,
And thou shalt have more
Than two tens to a score.
KENT. This is nothing, fool.
FOOL. Then 'tis like the breath of an unfeed lawyer—
you gave me nothing for't. Can you make no use of   130
nothing, nuncle?
LEAR. Why, no, boy; nothing can be made out of
nothing.
FOOL [*to Kent*]. Prithee tell him, so much the rent of
his land comes to. He will not believe a fool.
LEAR. A bitter fool!
FOOL. Dost thou know the difference, my boy, be-
tween a bitter fool and a sweet one?
LEAR. No, lad; teach me.
FOOL. That lord that counselled thee   140
To give away thy land,
Come place him here by me—
Do thou for him stand.
The sweet and bitter fool
Will presently appear:
The one in motley here,
The other found out—there!
LEAR. Dost thou call me fool, boy?
FOOL. All thy other titles thou hast given away; that
thou wast born with.   150

KENT. This is not altogether fool, my lord.

FOOL. No, faith, lords and great men·will not let me;
if I had a monopoly out, they would have part on't:
and ladies too, they will not let me have all the fool
to myself; they'll be snatching. Nuncle, give me an
egg, and I'll give thee two crowns.

LEAR. What two crowns shall they be?

FOOL. Why, after I have cut the egg i'th'middle and
eat up the meat, the two crowns of the egg. When
thou clovest thy crown i'th'middle and gav'st away 160
both parts, thou bor'st thine ass on thy back o'er the
dirt. Thou hadst little wit in thy bald crown when
thou gav'st thy golden one away. If I speak like
myself in this, let him be whipped that first finds it
so.

[singing] Fools had ne'er less grace in a year;
    For wise men are grown foppish,
    And know not how their wits to wear,
    Their manners are so apish.

LEAR. When were you wont to be so full of songs, 170
sirrah?

FOOL. I have used it, nuncle, e'er since thou mad'st thy
daughters thy mothers— for when thou gav'st them
the rod and putt'st down thine own breeches,
[singing] Then they for sudden joy did weep,
    And I for sorrow sung,
    That such a king should play bo-peep,
    And go the fools among.
Prithee, nuncle, keep a schoolmaster that can teach
thy fool to lie: I would fain learn to lie. 180

LEAR. An you lie, sirrah, we'll have you whipped.

FOOL. I marvel what kin thou and thy daughters are:
they'll have me whipped for speaking true, thou'lt
have me whipped for lying; and sometimes I am
whipped for holding my peace. I had rather be any
kind o' thing than a fool: and yet I would not be
thee, nuncle; thou hast pared thy wit o' both sides
and left nothing i'th' middle. Here comes one o' the
parings.

Enter Goneril

LEAR. How now, daughter? What makes that front- 190
let on? You are too much of late i'th'frown.

FOOL. Thou wast a pretty fellow when thou hadst no
need to care for her frowning; now thou art an O
without a figure. I am better than thou art now; I am
a fool, thou art nothing. [to Goneril] Yes, forsooth,
I will hold my tongue; so your face bids me, though
you say nothing.
    Mum, mum:
    He that keeps nor crust nor crumb,
    Weary of all, shall want some. 200
[pointing to Lear] That's a shelled peascod.

GONERIL. Not only, sir, this your all-licensed fool,
But other of your insolent retinue
Do hourly carp and quarrel, breaking forth
In rank and not-to-be-endured riots.
I had thought, by making this well known unto you,
To have found a safe redress; but now grow fearful,
By what yourself too late have spoke and done,
That you protect this course, and put it on
By your allowance; which if you should, the fault 210
Would not scape censure, nor the redresses sleep
Which, in the tender of a wholesome weal,
Might in their working do you that offence,
Which else were shame, that then necessity

Will call discreet proceeding.

FOOL. For you know, nuncle,
    The hedge-sparrow fed the cuckoo so long
    That it had it head bit off by it young.
So out went the candle, and we were left darkling.

LEAR. Are you our daughter? 220

GONERIL. I would you would make use of your good
    wisdom
(Whereof I know you are fraught) and put away
These dispositions which of late transport you
From what you rightly are.

FOOL. May not an ass know when the cart draws the
    horse?
        Whoop, Jug! I love thee.

LEAR. Does any here know me? This is not Lear.
Does Lear walk thus, speak thus? Where are his eyes?
Either his notion weakens, his discernings
Are lethargied—Ha! Waking? 'Tis not so? 230
Who is it that can tell me who I am?

FOOL. Lear's shadow!

LEAR. I would learn that; for by the marks
Of sovereignty, knowledge, and reason,
I should be false persuaded I had daughters.

FOOL. Which they will make an obedient father.

LEAR. Your name, fair gentlewoman?

GONERIL. This admiration, sir, is much o' th' savour
Of other your new pranks. I do beseech you
To understand my purposes aright. 240
As you are old and reverend, should be wise.
Here do you keep a hundred knights and squires—
Men so disordered, so debauched and bold,
That this our court, infected with their manners,
Shows like a riotous inn. Epicurism and lust
Makes it more like a tavern or a brothel
Than a graced palace. The shame itself doth speak
For instant remedy. Be then desired,
By her that else will take the thing she begs,
A little to disquantity your train; 250
And the remainders, that shall still depend,
To be such men as may besort your age,
Which know themselves and you.

LEAR.   Darkness and devils!
Saddle my horses; call my train together!
Degenerate bastard, I'll not trouble thee;
Yet have I left a daughter.

GONERIL. You strike my people, and your disordered
    rabble
Make servants of their betters.

Enter Albany

LEAR. Woe that too late repents!—O, are you come?
Is it your will? Speak, sir!—Prepare my horses. 260
Ingratitude, thou marble-hearted fiend,
More hideous when thou show'st thee in a child
Than the sea-monster!

ALBANY.   Pray, sir, be patient.

LEAR [to Goneril]. Detested kite, thou liest!
My train are men of choice and rarest parts,
That all particulars of duty know,
And in the most exact regard support
The worships of their name. O most small fault,
How ugly didst thou in Cordelia show,
Which, like an engine, wrenched my frame of
    nature 270
From the fixed place, drew from my heart all love,
And added to the gall. O Lear, Lear, Lear!

Beat at this gate that let thy folly in
Striking his head
And thy dear judgement out! Go, go, my people.
Knights and Kent go
ALBANY. My lord, I am guiltless, as I am ignorant
Of what hath moved you.
LEAR.   It may be so, my lord.
Hear, Nature; hear, dear goddess; hear!
Suspend thy purpose, if thou didst intend
To make this creature fruitful.
Into her womb convey sterility;   280
Dry up in her the organs of increase;
And from her derogate body never spring
A babe to honour her! If she must teem,
Create her child of spleen, that it may live
And be a thwart disnatured torment to her.
Let it stamp wrinkles in her brow of youth.
With cadent tears fret channels in her cheeks,
Turn all her mother's pains and benefits
To laughter and contempt, that she may feel
How sharper than a serpent's tooth it is   290
To have a thankless child! Away, away! *He goes*
ALBANY. Now, gods that we adore, whereof comes
this?
GONERIL. Never afflict yourself to know more of it,
But let his disposition have that scope
As dotage gives it.

Lear returns

LEAR. What, fifty of my followers at a clap?
Within a fortnight?
ALBANY.   What's the matter, sir?
LEAR. I'll tell thee. [*to Goneril*] Life and death!
I am ashamed
That thou hast power to shake my manhood thus;
That these hot tears, which break from me perforce,   300
Should make thee worth them. Blasts and fogs upon
thee!
Th'untented woundings of a father's curse
Pierce every sense about thee! Old fond eyes,
Beweep this cause again, I'll pluck ye out,
And cast you, with the waters that you loose,
To temper clay. Yea, is't come to this?
Ha! Let it be so. I have another daughter,
Who I am sure is kind and comfortable.
When she shall hear this of thee, with her nails
She'll flay thy wolvish visage. Thou shalt find   310
That I'll resume the shape which thou dost think
I have cast off for ever.   *He goes*
GONERIL.   Do you mark that?
ALBANY. I cannot be so partial, Goneril,
To the great love I bear you—
GONERIL. Pray you, content. What, Oswald, ho!
[*to the Fool*] You, sir, more knave than fool, after
your master!
FOOL. Nuncle Lear, nuncle Lear! Tarry; take the fool
with thee.
A fox, when one has caught her,
And such a daughter,   320
Should sure to the slaughter,
If my cap would buy a halter.
So the fool follows after.   *He goes*
GONERIL. This man hath had good counsel! A hundred
knights?
'Tis politic and safe to let him keep

At point a hundred knights; yes, that on every
dream,
Each buzz, each fancy, each complaint, dislike,
He may enguard his dotage with their powers,
And hold our lives in mercy. Oswald, I say!
ALBANY. Well, you may fear too far.
GONERIL.   Safer than trust too far.   330
Let me still take away the harms I fear,
Not fear still to be taken. I know his heart.
What he hath uttered I have writ my sister.
If she sustain him and his hundred knights,
When I have showed th'unfitness—

Enter Oswald

                                How now, Oswald?
What, have you writ that letter to my sister?
OSWALD. Ay, madam.
GONERIL. Take you some company, and away to
horse!
Inform her full of my particular fear,
And thereto add such reasons of your own   340
As may compact it more. Get you gone,
And hasten your return. [*Oswald goes*] No, no, my
lord,
This milky gentleness and course of yours
Though I condemn not, yet, under pardon,
You are much more attaxed for want of wisdom
Than praised for harmful mildness.
ALBANY. How far your eyes may pierce I cannot tell:
Striving to better, oft we mar what's well.
GONERIL. Nay, then—
ALBANY. Well, well; th'event.   *They go* 350

Scene 5: *Court before the same*

Enter Lear, Kent, and Fool

LEAR. Go you before to Cornwall with these letters.
Acquaint my daughter no further with anything
you know than comes from her demand out of the
letter. If your diligence be not speedy, I shall be there
afore you.
KENT. I will not sleep, my lord, till I have delivered
your letter.   *He goes*
FOOL. If a man's brains were in's heels, were't not in
danger of kibes?
LEAR. Ay, boy.   10
FOOL. Then I prithee be merry; thy wit shall not go
slip-shod.
LEAR. Ha, ha, ha!
FOOL. Shalt see thy other daughter will use thee
kindly; for, though she's as like this as a crab's like
an apple, yet I can tell what I can tell.
LEAR. What canst tell, boy?
FOOL. She will taste as like this as a crab does to a
crab. Thou canst tell why one's nose stands
i'th'middle on's face?   20
LEAR. No.
FOOL. Why, to keep one's eyes of either side's nose,
that what a man cannot smell out, he may spy into.
LEAR. I did her wrong.
FOOL. Canst tell how an oyster makes his shell?
LEAR. No.
FOOL. Nor I neither; but I can tell why a snail has a
house.
LEAR. Why?

FOOL. Why, to put's head in; not to give it away to his 30
daughters, and leave his horns without a case.

LEAR. I will forget my nature. So kind a father! Be my
horses ready?

FOOL. Thy asses are gone about 'em. The reason why
the seven stars are no moe than seven is a pretty
reason.

LEAR. Because they are not eight.

FOOL. Yes, indeed; thou would'st make a good fool.

LEAR. To take't again perforce! Monster Ingratitude!

FOOL. If thou wert my fool, nuncle, I'd have thee 40
beaten for being old before thy time.

LEAR. How's that?

FOOL. Thou should'st not have been old till thou hadst
been wise.

LEAR. O, let me not be mad, not mad, sweet heaven!
Keep me in temper; I would not be mad!

Enter Gentleman

How now! Are the horses ready?

GENTLEMAN. Ready, my lord.

LEAR. Come, boy.

FOOL. She that's a maid now, and laughs at my
departure, 50
Shall not be a maid long, unless things be cut shorter.
They go

ACT 2
Scene 1: *The castle of the Earl of Gloucester*

Enter Edmund and Curan, meeting

EDMUND. Save thee, Curan.

CURAN. And you, sir. I have been with your father,
and given him notice that the Duke of Cornwall
and Regan his Duchess will be here with him this
night.

EDMUND. How comes that?

CURAN. Nay, I know not. You have heard of the news
abroad, I mean the whispered ones, for they are yet
but ear-bussing arguments?

EDMUND. Not I. Pray you, what are they? 10

CURAN. Have you heard of no likely wars toward
'twixt the Dukes of Cornwall and Albany?

EDMUND. Not a word.

CURAN. You may do, then, in time. Fare you well, sir.
He goes

EDMUND. The Duke be here tonight? The better! best!
This weaves itself perforce into my business.
My father hath set guard to take my brother;
And I have one thing, of a queasy question,
Which I must act. Briefness and fortune, work!
Brother, a word! Descend! Brother, I say! 20

Enter Edgar

My father watches: O sir, fly this place!
Intelligence is given where you are hid.
You have now the good advantage of the night.
Have you not spoken 'gainst the Duke of Cornwall?
He's coming hither, now i'th'night, i'th' haste,
And Regan with him. Have you nothing said
Upon his party 'gainst the Duke of Albany?
Advise yourself.

EDGAR.   I am sure on't, not a word.

EDMUND. I hear my father coming. Pardon me,
In cunning I must draw my sword upon you. 30

Draw, seem to defend yourself; now quit you
well.—
Yield! Come before my father. Light, ho! Here!—
Fly, brother.—Torches, torches!   *Edgar goes*
So; farewell.
Some blood drawn on me would beget opinion
Of my more fierce endeavour. [*Wounds his arm*]
I have seen drunkards
Do more than this in sport—Father, father!
Stop, stop! No help?

Enter Gloucester, and servants with torches

GLOUCESTER.   Now, Edmund, where's the villain?

EDMUND. Here stood he in the dark, his sharp sword
out,
Mumbling of wicked charms, conjuring the moon
To stand auspicious mistress.

GLOUCESTER.   But where is he? 40

EDMUND. Look, sir, I bleed.

GLOUCESTER.   Where is the villain, Edmund?

EDMUND. Fled this way, sir, when by no means he
could—

GLOUCESTER. Pursue him, ho! Go after. [*Some servants
go*] By no means what?

EDMUND. Persuade me to the murder of your lordship.
But that I told him the revenging gods
'Gainst parricides did all the thunder bend,
Spoke with how manifold and strong a bond
The child was bound to th'father—sir, in fine,
Seeing how loathly opposite I stood
To his unnatural purpose, in fell motion 50
With his preparéd sword he charges home
My unprovided body, latched mine arm;
And when he saw my best alarumed spirits,
Bold in the quarrel's right, roused to th'encounter,
Or whether gasted by the noise I made,
Full suddenly he fled.

GLOUCESTER.   Let him fly far:
Not in this land shall he remain uncaught;
And found—dispatch. The noble Duke my master,
My worthy arch and patron, comes tonight.
By his authority I will proclaim it, 60
That he which finds him shall deserve our thanks,
Bringing the murderous coward to the stake;
He that conceals him, death.

EDMUND. When I dissuaded him from his intent,
And found him pight to do it, with curst speech
I threatened to discover him. He replied,
'Thou unpossessing bastard, dost thou think,
If I would stand against thee, would the reposal
Of any trust, virtue, or worth in thee
Make thy words faithed? No. What I should deny, 70
(As this I would—ay, though thou didst produce
My very character) I'd turn it all
To thy suggestion, plot, and damnéd practice;
And thou must make a dullard of the world,
If they not thought the profits of my death
Were very pregnant and potential spurs
To make thee seek it.'

GLOUCESTER.   O strange and fastened villain!
Would he deny his letter, said he? I never got him.
A tucket heard
Hark, the Duke's trumpets! I know not why he
comes.
All ports I'll bar; the villain shall not scape; 80
The Duke must grant me that. Besides, his picture

I will send far and near, that all the kingdom
May have due note of him; and of my land,
Loyal and natural boy, I'll work the means
To make thee capable.

Enter Cornwall, Regan, and attendants

CORNWALL. How now, my noble friend? Since I came
  hither,
Which I can call but now, I have heard strange news.
REGAN. If it be true, all vengeance comes too short
  Which can pursue th'offender. How dost, my lord?
GLOUCESTER. O madam, my old heart is cracked, it's
  cracked.   90
REGAN. What! Did my father's godson seek your life?
  He whom my father named, your Edgar?
GLOUCESTER. O lady, lady, shame would have it hid!
REGAN. Was he not companion with the riotous
  knights
  That tended upon my father?
GLOUCESTER. I know not, madam. 'Tis too bad, too
  bad!
EDMUND. Yes, madam; he was of that consort.
REGAN. No marvel, then, though he were ill affected.
  'Tis they have put him on the old man's death,
  To have th'expense and waste of his revenues.   100
  I have this present evening from my sister
  Been well informed of them, and with such cautions
  That, if they come to sojourn at my house,
  I'll not be there.
CORNWALL.   Nor I, assure thee, Regan.
  Edmund, I hear that you have shown your father
  A childlike office.
EDMUND.   It was my duty, sir.
GLOUCESTER. He did bewray his practice; and received
  This hurt you see, striving to apprehend him.
CORNWALL. Is he pursued?
GLOUCESTER.   Ay, my good lord.
CORNWALL. If he be taken, he shall never more   110
  Be feared of doing harm. Make your own purpose,
  How in my strength you please. For you, Edmund,
  Whose virtue and obedience doth this instant
  So much commend itself, you shall be ours.
  Natures of such deep trust we shall much need;
  You we first seize on.
EDMUND.   I shall serve you, sir,
  Truly, however else.
GLOUCESTER.   For him I thank your Grace.
CORNWALL. You know not why we came to visit you?
REGAN. Thus out of season, threading dark-eyed night: 120
  Occasions, noble Gloucester, of some prize,
  Wherein we must have use of your advice.
  Our father he hath writ, so hath our sister,
  Of differences, which I best thought it fit
  To answer from our home. The several messengers
  From hence attend dispatch. Our good old friend,
  Lay comforts to your bosom, and bestow
  Your needful counsel to our businesses,
  Which craves the instant use.
GLOUCESTER.   I serve you, madam.
  Your Graces are right welcome. *Flourish. They go*

Scene 2: *Before Gloucester's castle*

Enter Kent and Oswald, meeting

OSWALD. Good dawning to thee, friend. Art of this
  house?

KENT. Ay.
OSWALD. Where may we set our horses?
KENT. I'th'mire.
OSWALD. Prithee, if thou lov'st me, tell me.
KENT. I love thee not.
OSWALD. Why then, I care not for thee.
KENT. If I had thee in Lipsbury Pinfold, I would
  make thee care for me.
OSWALD. Why dost thou use me thus? I know thee
  not.   10
KENT. Fellow I know thee.
OSWALD. What dost thou know me for?
KENT. A knave, a rascal, an eater of broken meats;
  a base, proud, shallow, beggarly, three-suited,
  hundred-pound, filthy worsted-stocking knave; a
  lily-livered, action-taking, whoreson, glass-gazing,
  super-serviceable, finical rogue; one-trunk-inherit-
  ing slave; one that wouldst be a bawd in way of good
  service, and art nothing but the composition of a
  knave, beggar, coward, pandar, and the son and heir 20
  of a mongrel bitch: one whom I will beat into
  clamorous whining if thou deni'st the least syllable
  of thy addition.
OSWALD. Why, what a monstrous fellow art thou,
  thus to rail on one that is neither known of thee nor
  knows thee!
KENT. What a brazen-faced varlet art thou, to deny
  thou knowest me! Is it two days since I tripped up
  thy heels and beat thee before the king? Draw, you
  rogue; for, though it be night, yet the moon shines. 30
  I'll make a sop o' th' moonshine of you, you whoreson cullionly barber-monger. Draw!
                                        Drawing his sword
OSWALD. Away! I have nothing to do with thee.
KENT. Draw, you rascal! You come with letters against
  the king, and take Vanity the puppet's part against
  the royalty of her father. Draw, you rogue, or I'll so
  carbonado your shanks! Draw, you rascal! Come
  your ways!
OSWALD. Help, ho! murder! help!
KENT. Strike, you slave! Stand, rogue! Stand, you neat 40
  slave! Strike!   *Beating him*
OSWALD. Help, ho! murder, murder!

Enter Edmund, with his rapier drawn

EDMUND - How now? What's the matter? Part!
KENT. With you, goodman boy, if you please! Come,
  I'll flesh ye; come on, young master!

Enter Cornwall, Regan, Gloucester and servants

GLOUCESTER. Weapons? Arms? What is the matter
  here?
CORNWALL. Keep peace, upon your lives!
  He dies that strikes again. What is the matter?
REGAN. The messengers from our sister and the king!   50
CORNWALL. What is your difference? Speak.
OSWALD. I am scarce in breath, my lord.
KENT. No marvel, you have so bestirred your valour.
  You cowardly rascal, Nature disclaims in thee; a
  tailor made thee.
CORNWALL. Thou art a strange fellow; a tailor make
  a man?
KENT. A tailor, sir. A stone-cutter or a painter could
  not have made him so ill, though they had been but
  two years o'th'trade.   60
CORNWALL. Speak yet, how grew your quarrel?

OSWALD. This ancient ruffian, sir, whose life I have
  spared
  At suit of his grey beard—
KENT. Thou whoreson zed, thou unnecessary letter!
  My lord, if you will give me leave, I will tread this
  unbolted villain into mortar and daub the wall of a
  jakes with him. Spare my grey beard, you wagtail?
CORNWALL. Peace, sirrah!
  You beastly knave, know you no reverence?
KENT. Yes, sir; but anger hath a privilege.   70
CORNWALL. Why art thou angry?
KENT. That such a slave as this should wear a sword,
  Who wears no honesty. Such smiling rogues as
  these,
  Like rats, oft bite the holy cords atwain
  Which are too intrince t'unloose: smooth every
  passion
  That in the natures of their lords rebel,
  Bring oil to fire, snow to the colder moods;
  Renege, affirm, and turn their halcyon beaks
  With every gale and vary of their masters,
  Knowing nought (like dogs) but following.   80
  A plague upon your epileptic visage!
  Smile you my speeches, as I were a Fool?
  Goose, if I had you upon Sarum Plain,
  I'd drive ye cackling home to Camelot.
CORNWALL. What, art thou mad, old fellow?
GLOUCESTER. How fell you out? Say that.
KENT. No contraries hold more antipathy
  Than I and such a knave.
CORNWALL. Why dost thou call him knave? What is
  his fault?
KENT. His countenance likes me not.   90
CORNWALL. No more perchance does mine, nor his,
  nor hers.
KENT. Sirs, 'tis my occupation to be plain:
  I have seen better faces in my time
  Than stands on any shoulder that I see
  Before me at this instant.
CORNWALL.   This is some fellow,
  Who, having been praised for bluntness, doth affect
  A saucy roughness, and constrains the garb
  Quite from his nature. He cannot flatter, he!
  An honest mind and plain, he must speak truth!
  An they will take it, so; if not, he's plain.   100
  These kind of knaves I know which in this plainness
  Harbour more craft and more corrupter ends
  Than twenty silly-ducking observants
  That stretch their duties nicely.
KENT. Sir, in good faith, in sincere verity,
  Under th'allowance of your great aspect,
  Whose influence, like the wreath of radiant fire
  On flick'ring Phoebus' front—
CORNWALL.   What mean'st by this?
KENT. To go out of my dialect, which you
  discommend so much.
  I know, sir, I am no flatterer. He that beguiled you 110
  in a plain accent was a plain knave, which for my
  part I will not be, though I should win "your
  Displeasure" to entreat me to 't.
CORNWALL. What was th'offence you gave him?
OSWALD. I never gave him any.
  It pleased the king his master very late
  To strike at me upon his misconstruction,
  When he, compact, and flattering his displeasure,
  Tripped me behind: being down, insulted, railed,

And put upon him such a deal of man   120
That worthied him, got praises of the king
For him attempting who was self-subdued,
And, in the fleshment of this dread exploit,
Drew on me here again.
KENT.   None of these rogues and cowards
But Ajax is their fool.
CORNWALL.   Fetch forth the stocks!
You stubborn ancient knave, you reverend
  braggart,
We'll teach you!
KENT.   Sir, I am too old to learn.
Call not your stocks for me; I serve the king,
On whose employment I was sent to you.
You shall do small respect, show too bold malice 130
Against the grace and person of my master,
Stocking his messenger.
CORNWALL.   Fetch forth the stocks!
As I have life and honour, there shall he sit till noon.
REGAN. Till noon? Till night, my lord, and all night
  too.
KENT. Why, madam, if I were your father's dog,
  You should not use me so.
REGAN.   Sir, being his knave, I will.
CORNWALL. This is a fellow of the self-same colour
  Our sister speaks of. Come, bring away the stocks.
                                        Stocks brought out
GLOUCESTER. Let me beseech your Grace not to do so.
  His fault is much, and the good king his master   140
  Will check him for't. Your purposed low correction
  Is such as basest and contemnéd'st wretches
  For pilf'rings and most common trespasses
  Are punished with. The king must take it ill
  That he, so slightly valued in his messenger,
  Should have him thus restrained.
CORNWALL.   I'll answer that.
REGAN. My sister may receive it much more worse
  To have her gentleman abused, assaulted,
  For following her affairs. Put in his legs.
                                        Kent is put in the stocks
  [to Cornwall] Come my lord, away.   150
                                        All go in
                                except Gloucester and Kent
GLOUCESTER. I am sorry for thee, friend; 'tis the duke's
  pleasure,
  Whose disposition, all the world well knows,
  Will not be rubbed nor stopped. I'll entreat for thee.
KENT. Pray do not, sir. I have watched, and travelled
  hard.
  Some time I shall sleep out, the rest I'll whistle.
  A good man's fortune may grow out at heels.
  Give you good morrow!
GLOUCESTER. The duke's to blame in this; 'twill be ill
  taken.   He goes
KENT. Good king, that must approve the common
  saw,
  Thou out of heaven's benediction com'st   160
  To the warm sun!
  Approach, thou beacon to this under globe,
  That by thy comfortable beams I may
  Peruse this letter. Nothing almost sees miracles
  But misery. I know 'tis from Cordelia,
  Who hath most fortunately been informed
  Of my obscuréd course and shall find time....
  From this enormous state, seeking to give
  Losses their remedies. All weary and o'erwatched,

Take vantage, heavy eyes, not to behold   170
This shameful lodging.
Fortune, good night; smile once more; turn thy
wheel.   *Sleeps*

Scene 3: *The open country*

Enter Edgar

EDGAR. I heard myself proclaimed,
And by the happy hollow of a tree
Escaped the hunt. No port is free, no place
That guard and most unusual vigilance
Does not attend my taking. Whiles I may scape
I will preserve myself; and am bethought
To take the basest and most poorest shape
That ever penury in contempt of man
Brought near to beast. My face I'll grime with filth,
Blanket my loins, elf all my hairs in knots,   10
And with presented nakedness outface
The winds and persecutions of the sky.
The country gives me proof and precedent
Of Bedlam beggars who, with roaring voices,
Strike in their numbed and mortified bare arms
Pins, wooden pricks, nails, sprigs of rosemary;
And with this horrible object, from low farms,
Poor pelting villages, sheep-cotes, and mills,
Sometimes with lunatic bans, sometime with
prayers,
Enforce their charity. 'Poor Turlygod, poor Tom!'   20
That's something yet! Edgar I nothing am.   *He goes*

Scene 4: *Before Gloucester's castle. Kent in the stocks*

Enter Lear, Fool and Gentleman

LEAR. 'Tis strange that they should so depart from
home,
And not send back my messenger.
GENTLEMAN.   As I learned,
The night before there was no purpose in them
Of this remove.
KENT.   Hail to thee, noble master!
LEAR. Ha!
Mak'st thou this shame thy pastime?
KENT.   No, my lord.
FOOL. Ha, ha! He wears cruel garters. Horses are tied
by the heads, dogs and bears by th' neck, monkies
by th' loins, and men by th' legs. When a man's
over-lusty at legs, then he wears wooden nether-   10
stocks.
LEAR. What's he that hath so much thy place mistook
To set thee here?
KENT.   It is both he and she,
Your son and daughter.
LEAR. No.
KENT. Yes.
LEAR. No, I say.
KENT. I say yea.
LEAR. No, no, they would not.
KENT. Yes, yes, they have.   20
LEAR. By Jupiter, I swear no!
KENT. By Juno, I swear ay!
LEAR.   They durst not do 't,
They could not, would not do 't; 'tis worse than
murder
To do upon respect such violent outrage.
Resolve me with all modest haste which way

Thou mightst deserve or they impose this usage,
Coming from us.
KENT.   My lord, when at their home
I did commend your Highness' letters to them,
Ere I was risen from the place that showed
My duty kneeling, came there a reeking post,   30
Stewed in his haste, half breathless, panting forth
From Goneril his mistress salutations;
Delivered letters, spite of intermission,
Which presently they read: on whose contents
They summoned up their meiny, straight took
horse,
Commanded me to follow and attend
The leisure of their answer, gave me cold looks:
And meeting here the other messenger,
Whose welcome I perceived had poisoned mine—
Being the very fellow which of late   40
Displayed so saucily against your Highness—
Having more man than wit about me, drew.
He raised the house with loud and coward cries.
Your son and daughter found this trespass worth
The shame which here it suffers.
FOOL. Winter's not gone yet if the wild geese fly that
way.
    Fathers that wear rags
      Do make their children blind,
    But fathers that bear bags
      Shall see their children kind.   50
    Fortune, that arrant whore,
      Ne'er turns the key to th' poor.
But for all this thou shalt have as many dolours
from thy daughters as thou canst tell in a year.
LEAR. O, how this mother swells up toward my
heart!
Hysterica passio! Down, thou climbing sorrow
Thy element's below. Where is this daughter?
KENT. With the earl, sir, here within.
LEAR.   Follow me not; stay here.
                                        He goes
GENTLEMAN. Made you no more offence but what you
speak of?   60
KENT. None.
How chance the king comes with so small a
number?
FOOL. An thou hadst been set i'th'stocks for that
question, thou'dst well deserved it.
KENT. Why, fool?
FOOL. We'll set thee to school to an ant, to teach thee
there's no labouring i'th'winter. All that follow
their noses are led by their eyes but blind men, and
there's not a nose among twenty but can smell him   70
that's stinking. Let go thy hold when a great wheel
runs down a hill, lest it break thy neck with following; but the great one that goes upward, let him
draw thee after. When a wise man gives thee better
counsel, give me mine again. I would ha' none but
knaves use it, since a fool gives it.
    That sir which serves and seeks for gain
      And follows but for form,
    Will pack when it begins to rain
      And leave thee in the storm.   80
    But I will tarry; the Fool will stay
      And let the wise man fly.
    The knave turns fool that runs away;
      The Fool no knave, perdy.
KENT. Where learned you this, fool?

FOOL. Not i'th'stocks, fool!

Re-enter Lear, with Gloucester

LEAR. Deny to speak with me? They are sick, they are weary,
They have travelled all the night? Mere fetches; ay,
The images of revolt and flying off.
Fetch me a better answer.

GLOUCESTER.   My dear lord,   90
You know the fiery quality of the duke,
How unremovable and fixed he is
In his own course.

LEAR.   Vengeance! plague! death! confusion!
Fiery? What quality? Why, Gloucester, Gloucester,
I'ld speak with the Duke of Cornwall and his wife.

GLOUCESTER. Well, my good lord, I have informed them so.

LEAR. Informed them? Dost thou understand me, man?

GLOUCESTER. Ay, my good lord.

LEAR. The king would speak with Cornwall; the dear father
Would with his daughter speak, commands her service.   100
Are they informed of this? My breath and blood!
Fiery? the fiery duke? Tell the hot duke that—
No, but not yet; may be he is not well:
Infirmity doth still neglect all office
Whereto our health is bound. We are not ourselves
When nature, being oppressed, commands the mind
To suffer with the body. I'll forbear,
And am fall'n out with my more headier will
To take the indisposed and sickly fit
For the sound man. [*looking on Kent*] Death on my state! Wherefore   110
Should he sit here? This act persuades me
That this remotion of the duke and her
Is practice only. Give me my servant forth.
Go tell the duke and 's wife I'ld speak with them
Now, presently; bid them come forth and hear me,
Or at their chamber door I'll beat the drum
Till it cry sleep to death.

GLOUCESTER. I would have all well betwixt you.
                                   Goes

LEAR. O me, my heart! My rising heart! But down!

FOOL. Cry to it, nuncle, as the cockney did to the eels   120
when she put 'em i' th' paste alive. She knapped 'em
o'th' coxcombs with a stick and cried 'Down,
wantons, down!' 'Twas her brother that, in pure
kindness to his horse, buttered his hay.

Re-enter Gloucester, with Cornwall, Regan, and servants

LEAR. Good morrow to you both.

CORNWALL.   Hail to your Grace!
                       Kent here set at liberty

REGAN. I am glad to see your Highness.

LEAR. Regan, I think you are. I know what reason
I have to think so; if thou shouldst not be glad,
I would divorce me from thy mother's tomb,
Sepulchring an adultress. [*to Kent*] O, are you free?   130
Some other time for that.—Beloved Regan,
Thy sister's naught. O Regan, she hath tied
Sharp-toothed unkindness, like a vulture, here.
                       Points to his heart
I can scarce speak to thee; thou'lt not believe
With how depraved a quality—O Regan!

REGAN. I pray you, sir, take patience. I have hope
You less know how to value her desert
Than she to scant her duty.

LEAR.   Say? How is that?

REGAN. I cannot think my sister in the least
Would fail her obligation. If, sir, perchance   140
She have restrained the riots of your followers,
'Tis on such ground, and to such wholesome end,
As clears her from all blame.

LEAR. My curses on her!

REGAN.   O sir, you are old;
Nature in you stands on the very verge
Of his confine. You should be ruled and led
By some discretion that discerns your state
Better than you yourself. Therefore I pray you
That to our sister you do make return;
Say you have wronged her.

LEAR.   Ask her forgiveness?   150
Do you but mark how this becomes the house!
'Dear daughter, I confess that I am old: *Kneeling*
Age is unnecessary; on my knees I beg
That you'll vouchsafe me raiment, bed, and food!'

REGAN. Good sir, no more; these are unsightly tricks.
Return you to my sister.

LEAR [*rising*].   Never, Regan!
She hath abated me of half my train,
Looked black upon me, struck me with her tongue
Most serpent-like upon the very heart.
All the stored vengeances of heaven fall   160
On her ingrateful top. Strike her young bones,
You taking airs, with lameness!

CORNWALL.   Fie, sir, fie!

LEAR. You nimble lightnings, dart your blinding flames
Into her scornful eyes! Infect her beauty,
You fen-sucked fogs, drawn by the pow'rful sun
To fall and blister her!

REGAN.   O the blest gods!
So will you wish on me when the rash mood—

LEAR. No, Regan, thou shalt never have my curse.
Thy tender-hefted nature shall not give
Thee o'er to harshness. Her eyes are fierce; but thine   170
Do comfort and not burn. 'Tis not in thee
To grudge my pleasures, to cut off my train,
To bandy hasty words, to scant my sizes,
And in conclusion to oppose the bolt
Against my coming in. Thou better know'st
The offices of nature, bond of childhood,
Effects of courtesy, dues of gratitude:
Thy half o' th' kingdom hast thou not forgot,
Wherein I thee endowed.

REGAN.   Good sir, to th' purpose.

LEAR. Who put my man i' th' stocks?   *Tucket heard*

CORNWALL.   What trumpet's that?   180

REGAN. I know't—my sister's. This approves her letter,
That she would soon be here.

Enter Oswald

                           Is your lady come?

LEAR. This is a slave, whose easy-borrowed pride
Dwells in the sickly grace of her he follows.
Out, varlet, from my sight!

CORNWALL.   What means your Grace?

LEAR. Who stocked my servant? Regan, I have good hope

Thou didst not know on't.

Enter Goneril

Who comes here? O heavens,
If you do love old men, if your sweet sway
Allow obedience, if you yourselves are old,
Make it your cause; send down and take my part! 190
[*to Goneril*] Art not ashamed to look upon this
beard?
O Regan! will you take her by the hand?
GONERIL. Why not by th' hand, sir? How have I
offended?
All's not offence that indiscretion finds
And dotage terms so.
LEAR. O sides, you are too tough!
Will you yet hold? How came my man i' th' stocks?
CORNWALL. I set him there, sir; but his own disorders
Deserved much less advancement.
LEAR. You? Did you?
REGAN. I pray you, father, being weak, seem so.
If, till the expiration of your month, 200
You will return and sojourn with my sister,
Dismissing half your train, come then to me.
I am now from home, and out of that provision
Which shall be needful for your entertainment.
LEAR. Return to her? and fifty men dismissed?
No, rather I abjure all roofs, and choose
To wage against the enmity o' th' air,
To be a comrade with the wolf and owl—
Necessity's sharp pinch! Return with her?
Why, the hot-blooded France, that dowerless took 210
Our youngest born, I could as well be brought
To knee his throne, and squire-like, pension beg
To keep base life afoot. Return with her?
Persuade me rather to be slave and sumpter
To this detested groom. *Looking at Oswald*
GONERIL. At your choice, sir.
LEAR. I prithee, daughter, do not make me mad.
I will not trouble thee, my child; farewell:
We'll no more meet, no more see one another.
But yet thou art my flesh, my blood, my daughter—
Or rather a disease that's in my flesh, 220
Which I must needs call mine. Thou art a boil,
A plague-sore, or embosséd carbuncle
In my corrupted blood. But I'll not chide thee:
Let shame come when it will, I do not call it;
I do not bid the thunder-bearer shoot,
Nor tell tales of thee to high-judging Jove.
Mend when thou canst; be better at thy leisure:
I can be patient; I can stay with Regan,
I and my hundred knights.
REGAN. Not altogether so.
I looked not for you yet, nor am I provided 230
For your fit welcome. Give ear, sir, to my sister;
For those that mingle reason with your passion
Must be content to think you old, and so—
But she knows what she does.
LEAR. Is this well spoken?
REGAN. I dare avouch it, sir. What! fifty followers?
Is it not well? What should you need of more?
Yea, or so many, sith that both charge and danger
Speak 'gainst so great a number? How in one
house
Should many people, under two commands,
Hold amity? 'Tis hard, almost impossible. 240

GONERIL. Why might not you, my lord, receive
attendance
From those that she calls servants, or from mine?
REGAN. Why not, my lord? If then they chanced to
slack ye,
We could control them. If you will come to me
(For now I spy a danger), I entreat you
To bring but five and twenty: to no more
Will I give place or notice.
LEAR. I gave you all—
REGAN. And in good time you gave it.
LEAR. Made you my guardians, my depositaries,
But kept a reservation to be followed 250
With such a number. What! must I come to you
With five and twenty? Regan, said you so?
REGAN. And speak 't again, my lord; no more with
me.
LEAR. Those wicked creatures yet do look
well-favoured
When others are more wicked; not being the worst
Stands in some rank of praise. [*to Goneril*] I'll go with
thee,
Thy fifty yet doth double five and twenty,
And thou art twice her love.
GONERIL. Hear me, my lord.
What need you five and twenty, ten, or five,
To follow in a house where twice so many 260
Have a command to tend you?
REGAN. What need one?
LEAR. O reason not the need! Our basest beggars
Are in the poorest things superfluous.
Allow not nature more than nature needs,
Man's life is cheap as beast's. Thou art a lady;
If only to go warm were gorgeous,
Why, nature need not what thou gorgeous wear'st,
Which scarcely keeps thee warm. But for true
need—
You heavens, give me patience—patience I need!
You see me here, you gods, a poor old man, 270
As full of grief as age, wretched in both.
If it be you that stirs these daughters' hearts
Against their father, fool me not so much
To bear it tamely; touch me with noble anger,
And let not women's weapons, water drops,
Stain my man's cheeks. No, you unnatural hags,
I will have such revenges on you both
That all the world shall—I will do such things—
What they are yet I know not, but they shall be
The terrors of the earth! You think I'll weep; 280
No, I'll not weep:
I have full cause of weeping, [*storm heard approaching*]
but this heart
Shall break into a hundred thousand flaws
Or ere I'll weep. O Fool, I shall go mad!
He goes, the Fool, Gloucester,
and Kent following
CORNWALL. Let us withdraw; 'twill be a storm.
REGAN. This house is little: the old man and's people
Cannot be well bestowed.
GONERIL. 'Tis his own blame; hath put himself from
rest,
And must needs taste his folly.
REGAN. For his particular, I'll receive him gladly, 290
But not one follower.
GONERIL. So am I purposed.
Where is my lord of Gloucester?

CORNWALL. Followed the old man forth. [*Gloucester re-enters*] He is returned.

GLOUCESTER. The king is in high rage.

CORNWALL.   Whither is he going?

GLOUCESTER. He calls to horse, but will I know not whither.

CORNWALL. 'Tis best to give him way; he leads himself.

GONERIL. My lord, entreat him by no means to stay.

GLOUCESTER. Alack, the night comes on, and the bleak winds
Do sorely ruffle. For many miles about
There's scarce a bush.

REGAN.   O sir, to wilful men   300
The injuries that they themselves procure
Must be their schoolmasters. Shut up your doors;
He is attended with a desperate train,
And what they may incense him to, being apt
To have his ear abused, wisdom bids fear.

CORNWALL. Shut up your doors, my lord; 'tis a wild night:
My Regan counsels well. Come out o' th' storm.
                                        They go in

                    ACT 3
             Scene 1: *A heath*

A storm with thunder and lightning. Enter Kent and a Gentleman meeting

KENT. Who's there besides foul weather?

GENTLEMAN. One minded like the weather, most unquietly.

KENT. I know you. Where's the King?

GENTLEMAN. Contending with the fretful elements;
Bids the wind blow the earth into the sea,
Or swell the curléd waters 'bove the main,
That things might change or cease; tears his white hair,
Which the impetuous blasts with eyeless rage
Catch in their fury and make nothing of;
Strives in his little world of man to out-storm   10
The to-and-fro-conflicting wind and rain.
This night, wherein the cub-drawn bear would couch,
The lion and the belly-pinchéd wolf
Keep their fur dry, unbonneted he runs,
And bids what will take all.

KENT.   But who is with him?

GENTLEMAN. None but the Fool, who labours to outjest
His heart-struck injuries.

KENT.   Sir, I do know you,
And dare upon the warrant of my note
Commend a dear thing to you. There is division,   20
Although as yet the face of it is covered
With mutual cunning, 'twixt Albany and Cornwall,
Who have—as who have not, that their great stars
Throned and set high?—servants, who seem no less,
Which are to France the spies and speculations
Intelligent of our state. What hath been seen,
Either in snuffs and packings of the Dukes,
Or the hard rein which both of them hath borne
Against the old kind King; or something deeper,
Whereof perchance these are but furnishings....
But true it is from France there comes a power   30

Into this scattered kingdom, who already,
Wise in our negligence, have secret feet
In some of our best ports and are at point
To show their open banner. Now to you:
If on my credit you dare build so far
To make your speed to Dover, you shall find
Some that will thank you, making just report
Of how unnatural and bemadding sorrow
The King hath cause to plain.
I am a gentleman of blood and breeding,   40
And from some knowledge and assurance offer
This office to you.

GENTLEMAN. I will talk further with you.

KENT.   No, do not.
For confirmation that I am much more
Than my out-wall, open this purse and take
What it contains. If you shall see Cordelia
(As fear not but you shall), show her this ring,
And she will tell you who your fellow is
That yet you do not know. Fie on this storm!
I will go seek the King.   50

GENTLEMAN. Give me your hand. Have you no more to say?

KENT. Few words, but, to effect, more than all yet—
That when we have found the King (in which your pain
That way, I'll this) he that first lights on him
Holla the other.   *They go their separate ways*

          Scene 2: *Another part of the heath*

Storm still. Enter Lear with Fool

LEAR. Blow, winds, and crack your cheeks! rage! blow!
You cataracts and hurricanoes, spout
Till you have drenched our steeples, drowned the cocks!
You sulph'rous and thought-executing fires,
Vaunt-couriers of oak-cleaving thunderbolts,
Singe my white head! And thou, all-shaking thunder,
Strike flat the thick rotundity o'th'world,
Crack Nature's moulds, all germens spill at once
That make ingrateful man!

FOOL. O nuncle, court holy water in a dry house is   10
better than this rain-water out o' door. Good
nuncle, in; ask thy daughters blessing! Here's a night
pities neither wise men nor fools.

LEAR. Rumble thy bellyful! Spit, fire! spout, rain!
Nor rain, wind, thunder, fire are my daughters.
I tax not you, you elements, with unkindness;
I never gave you kingdom, called you children;
You owe me no subscription. Then let fall
Your horrible pleasure. Here I stand your slave,
A poor, infirm, weak, and despised old man: 20
But yet I call you servile ministers,
That will with two pernicious daughters join
Your high-engendered battles 'gainst a head
So old and white as this. O, ho! 'tis foul!

FOOL. He that has a house to put's head in has a good head-piece.
        The codpiece that will house
          Before the head has any,
        The head and he shall louse:
          So beggars marry many.   30
        The man that makes his toe

What he his heart should make
Shall of a corn cry woe,
And turn his sleep to wake.
For there was never yet fair woman but she made
mouths in a glass.

Enter Kent

LEAR. No, I will be the pattern of all patience;
I will say nothing.
KENT. Who's there?
FOOL. Marry, here's grace and a codpiece; that's a wise 40
man and a fool.
KENT. Alas, sir, are you here? Things that love night
Love not such nights as these. The wrathful skies
Gallow the very wanderers of the dark
And make them keep their caves. Since I was man,
Such sheets of fire, such bursts of horrid thunder,
Such groans of roaring wind and rain, I never
Remember to have heard. Man's nature cannot
carry
Th'affliction nor the fear.
LEAR.   Let the great gods,
That keep this dreadful pudder o'er our heads,   50
Find out their enemies now. Tremble, thou wretch
That hast within thee undivulgéd crimes
Unwhipped of justice. Hide thee, thou bloody hand,
Thou perjured, and thou simular of virtue
That art incestuous. Caitiff, to pieces shake,
That under covert and convenient seeming
Hast practised on man's life. Close pent-up guilts,
Rive your concealing continents, and cry
These dreadful summoners grace. I am a man
More sinned against than sinning.
KENT.   Alack, bare-headed? 60
Gracious my lord, hard by here is a hovel;
Some friendship will it lend you 'gainst the tempest:
Repose you there, while I to this hard house
(More harder than the stones whereof 'tis raised,
Which even but now, demanding after you,
Denied me to come in) return, and force
Their scanted courtesy.
LEAR.   My wits begin to turn.
Come on, my boy. How dost, my boy? Art cold?
I am cold myself. Where is this straw, my fellow?
The art of our necessities is strange,   70
And can make vile things precious. Come, your
hovel.
Poor fool and knave, I have one part in my heart
That's sorry yet for thee.
FOOL [*sings*].
He that has and a little tiny wit—
With heigh-ho, the wind and the rain—
Must make content with his fortunes fit,
Though the rain it raineth every day.
LEAR. True, boy. Come, bring us to this hovel.
                                    Lear and Kent go
FOOL. This is a brave night to cool a courtesan! I'll
speak a prophecy ere I go: 80
When priests are more in word than matter;
When brewers mar their malt with water;
When nobles are their tailors' tutors;
No heretics burned, but wenches' suitors;
Then shall the realm of Albion
Come to great confusion.
When every case in law is right;
No squire in debt nor no poor knight;

When slanders do not live in tongues,
Nor cutpurses come not to throngs;   90
When usurers tell their gold i'th'field,
And bawds and whores do churches build;
Then comes the time, who lives to see 't,
That going shall be used with feet.

This prophecy Merlin shall make, for I live before
his time.   *Goes*

Scene 3: *Gloucester's castle*

Enter Gloucester and Edmund, with lights

GLOUCESTER. Alack, alack, Edmund, I like not this unnatural dealing. When I desired their leave that I
might pity him, they took from me the use of mine
own house, charged me on pain of perpetual displeasure neither to speak of him, entreat for him, or
any way sustain him.
EDMUND. Most savage and unnatural!
GLOUCESTER. Go to; say you nothing. There is
division between the Dukes, and a worse matter
than that. I have received a letter this night—'tis 10
dangerous to be spoken—I have locked the letter in
my closet. These injuries the King now bears will
be revenged home. There is part of a power already
footed; we must incline to the King. I will look him
and privily relieve him; go you and maintain talk
with the Duke, that my charity be not of him perceived; if he ask for me, I am ill and gone to bed. If
I die for it (as no less is threat'ned me), the King, my
old master, must be relieved. There is strange things
toward, Edmund; pray you be careful.   *He goes* 20
EDMUND. This courtesy, forbid thee, shall the Duke
Instantly know, and of that letter too.
This seems a fair deserving, and must draw me
That which my father loses—no less than all.
The younger rises when the old doth fall.
                                    He goes

Scene 4: *The heath. Before a hovel Storm still*

Enter Lear, Kent, and Fool

KENT. Here is the place, my lord; good my lord, enter:
The tyranny of the open night 's too rough
For nature to endure.
LEAR.   Let me alone.
KENT. Good my lord, enter here.
LEAR.   Wilt break my heart?
KENT. I had rather break mine own. Good my lord,
enter.
LEAR. Thou think'st 'tis much that this contentious
storm
Invades us to the skin: so 'tis to thee;
But where the greater malady is fixed,
The lesser is scarce felt. Thou'dst shun a bear;
But if thy flight lay toward the roaring sea,   10
Thou'dst meet the bear i'th'mouth. When the
mind's free,
The body's delicate; this tempest in my mind
Doth from my senses take all feeling else
Save what beats there—filial ingratitude!
Is it not as this mouth should tear this hand
For lifting food to 't? But I will punish home!
No, I will weep no more. In such a night
To shut me out? Pour on; I will endure.

In such a night as this? O Regan, Goneril!
Your old kind father whose frank heart gave all!   20
O, that way madness lies; let me shun that!
No more of that.
KENT.   Good my lord, enter here.
LEAR. Prithee go in thyself, seek thine own ease;
This tempest will not give me leave to ponder
On things would hurt me more. But I'll go in.
[to the Fool] In, boy, go first. You houseless
poverty—
Nay, get thee in; I'll pray, and then I'll sleep—
                                                    Fool goes in
Poor naked wretches, whereso'er you are,
That bide the pelting of this pitiless storm,
How shall your houseless heads and unfed sides,   30
Your looped and windowed raggedness, defend you
From seasons such as these? O, I have ta'en
Too little care of this! Take physic, pomp;
Expose thyself to feel what wretches feel,
That thou mayst shake the superflux to them
And show the heavens more just.
EDGAR [within]. Fathom and half, fathom and half!
Poor Tom!   The Fool runs out from the hovel
FOOL. Come not in here, nuncle, here's a spirit.
Help me, help me!   40
KENT. Give me thy hand. Who's there?
FOOL. A spirit, a spirit! He says his name's poor Tom.
KENT. What art thou that dost grumble there
i'th'straw?
Come forth?

Enter Edgar, disguised as a madman, from the hovel

EDGAR. Away! The foul fiend follows me!
Through the sharp hawthorn blow the cold winds.
Humh! Go to thy bed and warm thee.
LEAR. Didst thou give all to thy daughters? And art
thou come to this?
EDGAR. Who gives anything to poor Tom? whom the   50
foul fiend hath led through fire and through flame,
through ford and whirlpool, o'er bog and quag-
mire; that hath laid knives under his pillow, and
halters in his pew; set ratsbane by his porridge; made
him proud of heart, to ride on a bay trotting horse
over four-inched bridges, to course his own shadow
for a traitor. Bless thy five wits! Tom's a-cold. O,
do de, do de, do de. Bless thee from whirlwinds,
star-blasting, and taking! Do poor Tom some
charity, whom the foul fiend vexes. There could I   60
have him now—and there—and there again—and
there!   Storm still
LEAR. What, has his daughters brought him to this
pass?
Couldst thou save nothing? Wouldst thou give 'em
all?
FOOL. Nay, he reserved a blanket; else we had been all
shamed.
LEAR. Now all the plagues that in the pendulous air
Hang fated o'er men's faults light on thy daughters!
KENT. He hath no daughters, sir.
LEAR. Death, traitor! Nothing could have subdued
nature   70
To such a lowness but his unkind daughters.
Is it the fashion that discarded fathers
Should have thus little mercy on their flesh?
Judicious punishment! 'Twas this flesh begot
Those pelican daughters.

EDGAR. Pillicock sat on Pillicock Hill.
Alow! alow, loo, loo!
FOOL. This cold night will turn us all to fools and
madmen.
EDGAR. Take heed o'th'foul fiend. Obey thy parents,   80
keep thy word justly, swear not, commit not with
man's sworn spouse, set not thy sweet heart on
proud array. Tom's a-cold.
LEAR. What hast thou been?
EDGAR. A servingman! proud in heart and mind; that
curled my hair, wore gloves in my cap; served the
lust of my mistress' heart, and did the act of darkness
with her; swore as many oaths as I spake words, and
broke them in the sweet face of heaven; one that
slept in the contriving of lust, and waked to do it.   90
Wine loved I deeply, dice dearly; and in woman
out-paramoured the Turk. False of heart, light of
ear, bloody of hand; hog in sloth, fox in stealth, wolf
in greediness, dog in madness, lion in prey. Let not
the creaking of shoes nor the rustling of silks betray
thy poor heart to woman. Keep thy foot out of
brothels, thy hand out of plackets, thy pen from
lenders' books, and defy the foul fiend.
Still through the hawthorn blows the cold wind,
Says suum, mun, hey nonny nonny.   100
Dolphin my boy, boy!—sessa! let him trot by.
                                                 Storm still
LEAR. Thou wert better in a grave than to answer
with thy uncovered body this extremity of the skies.
Is man no more than this? Consider him well. Thou
ow'st the worm no silk, the beast no hide, the sheep
no wool, the cat no perfume. Ha! Here's three on's
are sophisticated: thou art the thing itself. Unaccom-
modated man is no more but such a poor, bare,
forked animal as thou art. Off, off, you lendings!
Come, unbutton here!   *Strives to tear off his clothes* 110
FOOL. Prithee, nuncle, be contented; 'tis a naughty
night to swim in!

Sees Gloucester approaching with a torch

Now a little fire in a wild field were like an old
lecher's heart—a small spark, all the rest on's body
cold. Look, here comes a walking fire.
EDGAR. This is the foul Flibbertigibbet. He begins at
curfew, and walks till first cock. He gives the web
and the pin, squinies the eye, and makes the harelip;
mildews the white wheat, and hurts the poor
creature of earth.   120
S'Withold footed thrice the 'old:
He met the Nightmare and her nine fold;
Bid her alight
And her troth plight—
And aroint thee, witch, aroint thee!
KENT. How fares your grace?
LEAR. What's he?
KENT. Who's there? What is't you seek?
GLOUCESTER. What are you there? Your names?
EDGAR. Poor Tom, that eats the swimming frog, the   130
toad, the tadpole, the wall-newt and the water; that
in the fury of his heart, when the foul fiend rages,
eats cow-dung for sallets, swallows the old rat and
the ditch-dog, drinks the green mantle of the stand-
ing pool; who is whipped from tithing to tithing,
and stock-punished and imprisoned; who hath had
three suits to his back, six shirts to his body,

Horse to ride, and weapon to wear;
But mice and rats and such small deer
Have been Tom's food for seven long year.   140
Beware my follower. Peace, Smulkin; peace, thou
fiend!
GLOUCESTER. What, hath your Grace no better
company?
EDGAR. The Prince of Darkness is a gentleman!
Modo he's called, and Mahu.
GLOUCESTER. Our flesh and blood, my lord, is grown
so vile,
That it doth hate what gets it.
EDGAR. Poor Tom's a-cold.
GLOUCESTER. Go in with me; my duty cannot suffer
T' obey in all your daughters' hard commands.   150
Though their injunction be to bar my doors
And let this tyrannous night take hold upon you,
Yet have I ventured to come seek you out
And bring you where both fire and food is ready.
LEAR. First let me talk with this philosopher.
What is the cause of thunder?
KENT. Good my lord, take his offer; go into th' house.
LEAR. I'll talk a word with this same learned
Theban.
What is your study?
EDGAR. How to prevent the fiend and to kill vermin.   160
LEAR. Let me ask you one word in private.
KENT. Importune him once more to go, my lord;
His wits begin t' unsettle.
GLOUCESTER.   Canst thou blame him?
                                        Storm still
His daughters seek his death. Ah, that good Kent!
He said it would be thus, poor banished man!
Thou sayest the King grows mad; I'll tell thee,
friend,
I am almost mad myself. I had a son,
Now outlawed from my blood: he sought my life
But lately, very late: I loved him, friend,
No father his son dearer: true to tell thee,   170
The grief hath crazed my wits. What a night's this!
I do beseech your Grace—
LEAR.   O, cry you mercy, sir.
Noble philosopher, your company.
EDGAR. Tom's a-cold.
GLOUCESTER. In, fellow, there, into th' hovel; keep
thee warm.
LEAR. Come, let's in all.
KENT.   This way, my lord.
LEAR.   With him!
I will keep still with my philosopher.
KENT. Good my lord, soothe him; let him take the
fellow.
GLOUCESTER. Take him you on.
KENT. Sirrah, come on; go along with us.   180
LEAR. Come, good Athenian.
GLOUCESTER. No words, no words; hush!
EDGAR. Childe Roland to the dark tower came.
His word was still 'Fie, foh, and fum.
I smell the blood of a British man.'   *They go*

Scene 5: *Gloucester's castle*

Enter Cornwall and Edmund

CORNWALL. I will have my revenge ere I depart his
house.
EDMUND. How, my lord, I may be censured, that

nature thus gives way to loyalty, something fears me
to think of.
CORNWALL. I now perceive it was not altogether your
brother's evil disposition made him seek his death;
but a provoking merit, set awork by a reproveable
badness in himself.
EDMUND. How malicious is my fortune, that I must   10
repent to be just! This is the letter he spoke of, which
approves him an intelligent party to the advantages
of France. O heavens! that this treason were not—or
not I the detector!
CORNWALL. Go with me to the Duchess.
EDMUND. If the matter of this paper be certain, you
have mighty business in hand.
CORNWALL. True or false, it hath made thee Earl of
Gloucester. Seek out where thy father is, that he may
be ready for our apprehension.   20
EDMUND [*aside*]. If I find him comforting the King, it
will stuff his suspicion more fully. [*to Cornwall*] I
will persever in my course of loyalty, though the
conflict be sore between that and my blood.
CORNWALL. I will lay trust upon thee; and thou shalt
find a dearer father in my love.   *They leave*

Scene 6: *A room in a farmhouse adjoining Gloucester's
castle*

Enter Gloucester and Kent

GLOUCESTER. Here is better than the open air; take it
thankfully. I will piece out the comfort with what
addition I can: I will not be long from you.
KENT. All the power of his wits have given way to his
impatience. The gods reward your kindness!
                                        Gloucester goes out

Enter Lear, Edgar, and Fool

EDGAR. Frateretto calls me, and tells me Nero is an
angler in the lake of darkness. Pray, innocent, and
beware the foul fiend.
FOOL. Prithee, nuncle, tell me whether a madman be a
gentleman or a yeoman.   10
LEAR. A king, a king!
FOOL. No, he's a yeoman that has a gentleman to his
son; for he's a mad yeoman that sees his son a gentleman before him.
LEAR. To have a thousand with red burning spits
Come hizzing in upon 'em!
EDGAR. The foul fiend bites my back.
FOOL. He's mad that trusts in the tameness of a wolf,
a horse's health, a boy's love, or a whore's oath.
LEAR. It shall be done; I will arraign them straight.   20
[*to Edgar*] Come sit thou here, most learned justicer;
[*to the Fool*] Thou sapient sir, sit here. Now, you
she-foxes—
EDGAR. Look where he stands and glares! Want'st thou
eyes at trial, madam? [*sings*]
            Come o'er the burn, Bessy, to me.
FOOL [*sings*]   Her boat hath a leak,
                    And she must not speak
            Why she dares not come over to thee.
EDGAR. The foul fiend haunts poor Tom in the voice
of a nightingale. Hoppedance cries in Tom's belly   30
for two white herring. Croak not, black angel; I
have no food for thee.
KENT. How do you, sir? Stand you not so amazed.
Will you lie down and rest upon the cushions?

LEAR. I'll see their trial first. Bring in their evidence.
[*to Edgar*] Thou robéd man of justice, take thy
place;
[*to the Fool*] And thou, his yokefellow of equity,
Bench by his side. [*to Kent*] You are
o'th'commission;
Sit you too.
EDGAR. Let us deal justly. 40
Sleepest or wakest thou, jolly shepherd?
Thy sheep be in the corn;
And for one blast of thy minikin mouth
Thy sheep shall take no harm.
Purr the cat is gray.
LEAR. Arraign her first; 'tis Goneril. I here take my
oath before this honourable assembly, she kicked the
poor king, her father.
FOOL. Come hither, mistress; is your name Goneril?
LEAR. She cannot deny it. 50
FOOL. Cry you mercy, I took you for a jointed-stool.
LEAR. And here's another, whose warped looks
proclaim
What store her heart is made on. Stop her there!
Arms, arms, sword, fire! Corruption in the place!
False justicer, why hast thou let her scape?
EDGAR. Bless thy five wits!
KENT. O pity! Sir, where is the patience now
That you so oft have boasted to retain?
EDGAR. My tears begin to take his part so much
They mar my counterfeiting. 60
LEAR. The little dogs and all,
Tray, Blanche, and Sweetheart; see, they bark at me.
EDGAR. Tom will throw his head at them. Avaunt,
you curs!
Be thy mouth or black or white,
Tooth that poisons if it bite;
Mastiff, greyhound, mongrel grim,
Hound or spaniel, brach or lym,
Or bobtail tyke or trundle-tail,
Tom will make him weep and wail; 70
For, with throwing thus my head,
Dogs leaped the hatch, and all are fled.
Do, de, de, de. Sessa! Come, march to wakes and
fairs and market towns. Poor Tom, thy horn is dry.
LEAR. Then let them anatomize Regan; see what
breeds about her heart. Is there any cause in nature
that make these hard hearts? [*to Edgar*] You, sir, I
entertain for one of my hundred; only I do not like
the fashion of your garments. You will say they are
Persian; but let them be changed. 80
KENT. Now, good my lord, lie here and rest awhile.
LEAR. Make no noise, make no noise; draw the curtains. So, so; we'll go to supper i'th'morning.
FOOL. And I'll go to bed at noon.

Enter Gloucester

GLOUCESTER. Come hither, friend. Where is the King
my master?
KENT. Here, sir: but trouble him not; his wits are
gone.
GLOUCESTER. Good friend, I prithee take him in thy
arms.
I have o'erheard a plot of death upon him.
There is a litter ready; lay him in't,
And drive toward Dover, friend, where thou shalt
meet 90
Both welcome and protection. Take up thy master;

If thou should'st dally half an hour, his life,
With thine, and all that offer to defend him,
Stand in assuréd loss. Take up, take up,
And follow me, that will to some provision
Give thee quick conduct.
KENT. Oppresséd nature sleeps.
This rest might yet have balmed thy broken sinews,
Which, if convenience will not allow,
Stand in hard cure. [*to the Fool*] Come, help to
bear thy master;
Thou must not stay behind.
GLOUCESTER. Come, come, away! 100
*Gloucester, Kent, and the Fool
leave, carrying Lear*
EDGAR. When we our betters see bearing our woes,
We scarcely think our miseries our foes.
Who alone suffers, suffers most i'th'mind,
Leaving free things and happy shows behind.
But then the mind much sufferance doth o'erskip
When grief hath mates, and bearing fellowship.
How light and portable my pain seems now,
When that which makes me bend makes the King
bow.
He childed as I fathered! Tom, away!
Mark the high noises, and thyself bewray 110
When false opinion, whose wrong thoughts
defile thee,
In thy just proof repeals and reconciles thee.
What will hap more tonight, safe scape the King!
Lurk, lurk. *He goes*

Scene 7: Gloucester's castle

Enter Cornwall, Regan, Goneril, Edmund and Servants

CORNWALL [*to Goneril*]. Post speedily to my lord your
husband; show him this letter: the army of France is
landed. Seek out the traitor Gloucester.
REGAN. Hang him instantly.
GONERIL. Pluck out his eyes.
CORNWALL. Leave him to my displeasure. Edmund,
keep you our sister company. The revenges we are
bound to take upon your traitorous father are not fit
for your beholding. Advise the Duke, where you are
going, to a most festinate preparation: we are bound 10
to the like. Our posts shall be swift and intelligent
betwixt us. Farewell, dear sister; farewell, my Lord
of Gloucester.

Enter Oswald

How now? Where's the King?
OSWALD. My Lord of Gloucester hath conveyed him
hence.
Some five or six and thirty of his knights,
Hot questrists after him, met him at gate,
Who, with some other of the lord's dependants,
Are gone with him toward Dover, where they
boast
To have well-arméd friends.
CORNWALL. Get horses for your mistress. 20
GONERIL. Farewell, sweet lord, and sister.
CORNWALL. Edmund, farewell.
Goneril, Edmund, and Oswald go
Go seek the traitor Gloucester;
Pinion him like a thief, bring him before us.
Servants go

Though well we may not pass upon his life
Without the form of justice, yet our power
Shall do a court'sy to our wrath, which men
May blame, but not control.

Re-enter Servants, with Gloucester prisoner

                Who's there? The traitor?
REGAN. Ingrateful fox! 'tis he.
CORNWALL. Bind fast his corky arms.
GLOUCESTER. What means your Graces? Good my
    friends, consider   30
You are my guests. Do me no foul play, friends.
CORNWALL. Bind him, I say.   *Servants bind him*
REGAN.   Hard, hard. O filthy traitor!
GLOUCESTER. Unmerciful lady as you are, I'm none.
CORNWALL. To this chair bind him.   *They do so*
    Villain, thou shalt find—
                Regan plucks his beard
GLOUCESTER. By the kind gods, 'tis most ignobly done
To pluck me by the beard.
REGAN. So white, and such a traitor?
GLOUCESTER.   Naughty lady,
These hairs which thou dost ravish from my chin
Will quicken and accuse thee. I am your host:
With robbers' hands my hospitable favours   40
You should not ruffle thus. What will you do?
CORNWALL. Come, sir. What letters had you late
    from France?
REGAN. Be simple-answered, for we know the truth.
CORNWALL. And what confederacy have you with
    the traitors
Late footed in the kingdom?
REGAN.   To whose hands
You have sent the lunatic king ... Speak.
GLOUCESTER. I have a letter, guessingly set down,
Which came from one that's of a neutral heart,
And not from one opposed.
CORNWALL.   Cunning.
REGAN.   And false.
CORNWALL. Where hast thou sent the King?
GLOUCESTER.   To Dover. 50
REGAN. Wherefore to Dover? Wast thou not charged
    at peril—
CORNWALL. Wherefore to Dover? Let him answer
    that.
GLOUCESTER. I am tied to th' stake, and I must stand
    the course.
REGAN. Wherefore to Dover?
GLOUCESTER. Because I would not see thy cruel nails
Pluck out his poor old eyes, nor thy fierce sister
In his anointed flesh rash boarish fangs.
The sea, with such a storm as his loved head
In hell-black night endured, would have buoyed up,
And quenched the stelléd fires;   60
Yet, poor old heart, he holp the heavens to rain.
If wolves had at thy gate howled that dearn time,
Thou should'st have said 'Good porter, turn the
    key'.
All cruels else subscribe: but I shall see
The wingéd Vengeance overtake such children.
CORNWALL. See 't shalt thou never. Fellows, hold the
    chair.
Upon these eyes of thine I'll set my foot.
GLOUCESTER. He that will think to live till he be old,
Give me some help.... O cruel! O you gods!
REGAN. One side will mock another. Th'other too! 70

CORNWALL. If you see vengeance—
I SERVANT.   Hold your hand, my lord!
I have served you ever since I was a child,
But better service have I never done you
Than now to bid you hold.
REGAN.   How, now, you dog?
I SERVANT. If you did wear a beard upon your chin,
I'd shake it on this quarrel.
REGAN.   What do you mean?
CORNWALL. My villain?   *He unsheathes his sword*
I SERVANT [*drawing his weapon*]. Nay, then, come on,
and take the chance of anger.
REGAN [*to another Servant*]. Give me thy sword. A
    peasant stand up thus?
              She takes a sword and
              runs at him behind
I SERVANT. O, I am slain! My lord, you have one
    eye left   80
To see some mischief on him. O!   *He dies*
CORNWALL. Lest it see more, prevent it. Out, vile jelly!
Where is thy lustre now?
GLOUCESTER. All dark and comfortless! Where's my
    son Edmund?
Edmund, enkindle all the sparks of nature
To quit this horrid act.
REGAN.   Out, treacherous villain!
Thou call'st on him that hates thee. It was he
That made the overture of thy treasons to us,
Who is too good to pity thee.
GLOUCESTER. O, my follies! Then Edgar was abused. 90
Kind gods, forgive me that, and prosper him!
REGAN. Go thrust him out at gates, and let him smell
His way to Dover.   *They lead him out*
          How is 't, my lord? How look you?
CORNWALL. I have received a hurt. Follow me, lady.
Turn out that eyeless villain. Throw this slave
Upon the dunghill. Regan, I bleed apace.
Untimely comes this hurt. Give me your arm.
         He goes in, supported by Regan
2 SERVANT. I'll never care what wickedness I do,
If this man come to good.
3 SERVANT.   If she live long,
And in the end meet the old course of death,   100
Women will all turn monsters.
2 SERVANT. Let's follow the old earl, and get the
    bedlam
To lead him where he would; his roguish madness
Allows itself to anything.
3 SERVANT. Go thou; I'll fetch some flax and whites
    of eggs
To apply to his bleeding face. Now heaven help
    him!   *They go*

ACT 4
Scene 1: *The heath*

Enter Edgar

EDGAR. Yet better thus, and known to be contemned,
Than still contemned and ·flattered. To be worst,
The lowest and most dejected thing of Fortune,
Stands still in esperance, lives not in fear.
The lamentable change is from the best;
The worst returns to laughter. Welcome, then,
Thou unsubstantial air that I embrace:

The wretch that thou hast blown unto the worst
Owes nothing to thy blasts.

Enter Gloucester, led by an old man

                      But who comes here?
My father, poorly eyed! World, world, O world! 10
But that thy strange mutations make us hate thee,
Life would not yield to age.
OLD MAN.   O my good lord,
I have been your tenant, and your father's tenant,
These fourscore years.
GLOUCESTER. Away, get thee away! Good friend, be
    gone:
Thy comforts can do me no good at all;
Thee they may hurt.
OLD MAN.   You cannot see your way.
GLOUCESTER. I have no way, and therefore want no
    eyes;
I stumbled when I saw. Full oft 'tis seen
Our means secure us, and our mere defects 20
Prove our commodities. O dear son Edgar,
The food of thy abuséd father's wrath!
Might I but live to see thee in my touch,
I'd say I had eyes again.
OLD MAN.   How now? Who's there?
EDGAR [*aside*]. O gods! Who is't can say 'I am at the
    worst'?
I am worse than e'er I was.
OLD MAN.   'Tis poor mad Tom.
EDGAR [*aside*]. And worse I may be yet: the worst is not
So long as we can say 'This is the worst'.
OLD MAN. Fellow, where goest?
GLOUCESTER.   Is it a beggar-man?
OLD MAN. Madman, and beggar too. 30
GLOUCESTER. He has some reason, else he could not
    beg.
I' th' last night's storm I such a fellow saw,
Which made me think a man a worm. My son
Came then into my mind, and yet my mind
Was then scarce friends with him: I have heard
    more since.
As flies to wanton boys are we to th' gods;
They kill us for their sport.
EDGAR [*aside*].   How should this be?
Bad is the trade that must play fool to sorrow,
Ang'ring itself and others.—Bless thee, master!
GLOUCESTER. Is that the naked fellow?
OLD MAN.   Ay, my lord. 40
GLOUCESTER. Then prithee get thee away. If, for my
    sake,
Thou wilt o'ertake us hence a mile or twain
I' th' way toward Dover, do it for ancient love;
And bring some covering for this naked soul
Which I'll entreat to lead me.
OLD MAN.   Alack, sir, he is mad!
GLOUCESTER. 'Tis the time's plague when madmen
    lead the blind.
Do as I bid thee; or rather do thy pleasure:
Above the rest, be gone.
OLD MAN. I'll bring him the best 'parel that I have,
Come on't what will.   *He goes*
GLOUCESTER.   Sirrah, naked fellow! 50
EDGAR. Poor Tom's a-cold. [*aside*] I cannot daub it
    further.
GLOUCESTER. Come hither, fellow.

EDGAR [*aside*]. And yet I must. Bless thy sweet eyes,
    they bleed!
GLOUCESTER. Know'st thou the way to Dover?
EDGAR. Both stile and gate, horseway and footpath.
Poor Tom hath been sacred out of his good wits.
Bless thee, good man's son, from the foul fiend! Five
fiends have been in poor Tom at once: as Obidicut,
of lust; Hobbididence, prince of darkness; Mahu, of
stealing; Modo, of murder; Flibbertigibbet, of 60
mocking and mowing, who since possesses
chambermaids and waiting-women. So, bless thee,
master!
GLOUCESTER. Here, take this purse, thou whom the
    heavens' plagues
Have humbled to all strokes: that I am wretched
Makes thee the happier; Heavens, deal so still!
Let the superfluous and lust-dieted man,
That slaves your ordinance, that will not see
Because he does not feel, feel your power quickly;
So distribution should undo excess,   70
And each man have enough. Dost thou know
    Dover?
EDGAR. Ay, master.
GLOUCESTER. There is a cliff, whose high and bending
    head
Looks fearfully in the confinéd deep.
Bring me but to the very brim of it,
And I'll repair the misery thou dost bear
With something rich about me. From that place
I shall no leading need.
EDGAR.   Give me thy arm;
Poor Tom shall lead thee.   *They go*

     Scene 2: *Before the Duke of Albany's palace*

Enter Goneril and Edmund

GONERIL. Welcome, my lord. I marvel our mild
    husband
Not met us on the way.

Enter Oswald

                Now, where's your master?
OSWALD. Madam, within; but never man so changed.
I told him of the army that was landed;
He smiled at it: I told him you were coming;
His answer was, 'The worse'. Of Gloucester's
    treachery
And of the loyal service of his son
When I informed him, then he called me sot
And told me I had turned the wrong side out.
What most he should dislike seems pleasant to him; 10
What like, offensive.
GONERIL [*to Edmund*]. Then shall you go no further.
It is the cowish terror of his spirit,
That dares not undertake; he'll not feel wrongs
Which tie him to an answer. Our wishes on the
    way
May prove effects. Back, Edmund, to my brother;
Hasten his musters and conduct his powers:
I must change arms at home and give the distaff
Into my husband's hands. This trusty servant
Shall pass between us: ere long you are like to hear
(If you dare venture in your own behalf)   20
A mistress's command. Wear this [*giving a favour*].
    Spare speech;
Decline your head: this kiss, if it durst speak,

Would stretch thy spirits up into the air.
Conceive, and fare thee well.

EDMUND. Yours in the ranks of death!

GONERIL.   My most dear Gloucester!

Edmund goes

O, the difference of man and man!
To thee a woman's services are due;
A fool usurps my bed.

OSWALD.   Madam, here comes my lord.

He goes

Enter Albany

GONERIL. I have been worth the whistling.

ALBANY.   O Goneril,
You are not worth the dust which the rude wind 30
Blows in your face! I fear your disposition.
That nature which contemns it origin
Cannot be bordered certain in itself.
She that herself will sliver and disbranch
From her material sap, perforce must wither
And come to deadly use.

GONERIL. No more! The text is foolish.

ALBANY. Wisdom and goodness to the vile seem vile;
Filths savour but themselves. What have you done?
Tigers, not daughters, what have you performed? 40
A father, and a gracious agéd man,
Whose reverence even the head-lugged bear would
  lick,
Most barbarous, most degenerate, have you
  madded.
Could my good brother suffer you to do it?
A man, a prince, by him so benefited!
If that the heavens do not their visible spirits
Send quickly down to tame these vile offences,
It will come
Humanity must perforce prey on itself
Like monsters of the deep.

GONERIL.   Milk-livered man! 50
That bear'st a cheek for blows, a head for wrongs:
Who hast not in thy brows an eye discerning
Thine honour from thy suffering; that not know'st
Fools do those villains pity who are punished
Ere they have done their mischief. Where's thy
  drum?
France spreads his banners in our noiseless land,
With pluméd helm thy state begins to threat,
Whilst thou, a moral fool, sits still and cries
'Alack, why does he so?'

ALBANY.   See thyself, devil!
Proper deformity shows not in the fiend   60
So horrid as in woman.

GONERIL.   O vain fool!

ALBANY. Thou changéd and self-covered thing, for
  shame
Bemonster not thy feature! Were't my fitness
To let these hands obey my blood,
They are apt enough to dislocate and tear
Thy flesh and bones: howe'er thou art a fiend,
A woman's shape doth shield thee.

GONERIL. Marry, your manhood! mew!

Enter a Messenger

ALBANY. What news?

MESSENGER. O, my good lord, the Duke of Cornwall's
  dead,   70
Slain by his servant, going to put out

The other eye of Gloucester.

ALBANY.   Gloucester's eyes!

MESSENGER. A servant that he bred, thrilled with
  remorse,
Opposed against the act, bending his sword
To his great master; who, thereat enraged,
Flew on him, and amongst them felled him dead;
But not without that harmful stroke which since
Hath plucked him after.

ALBANY.   This shows you are above,
You justicers, that these our nether crimes
So speedily can venge! But, O poor Gloucester! 80
Lost he his other eye!

MESSENGER.   Both, both, my lord.
This letter, madam, craves a speedy answer;
'Tis from your sister.   *Presents a letter*

GONERIL [*aside*].   One way I like this well;
But being widow, and my Gloucester with her,
May all the building in my fancy pluck
Upon my hateful life. Another way
The news is not so tart.—I'll read, and answer.

She goes out

ALBANY. Where was his son when they did take his
  eyes?

MESSENGER. Come with my lady hither.

ALBANY.   He is not here.

MESSENGER. No, my good lord; I met him back again. 90

ALBANY. Knows he the wickedness?

MESSENGER. Ay, my good lord; 'twas he informed
  against him,
And quit the house on purpose, that their
  punishment
Might have the freer course.

ALBANY.   Gloucester, I live
To thank thee for the love thou show'dst the
  King,
And to revenge thine eyes. Come hither, friend;
Tell me what more thou know'st.   *They go*

Scene 3: The French camp near Dover

Enter Kent and a Gentleman

KENT. Why the King of France is so suddenly gone
  back know you no reason?

GENTLEMAN. Something he left imperfect in the state,
  which since his coming forth is thought of, which
  imports to the kingdom so much fear and danger
  that his personal return was most required and
  necessary.

KENT. Who hath he left behind him general?

GENTLEMAN. The Marshal of France, Monsieur La Far.

KENT. Did your letters pierce the queen to any 10
  demonstration of grief?

GENTLEMAN. Ay, sir; she took them, read them in my
  presence,
And now and then an ample tear trilled down
Her delicate cheek. It seemed she was a queen
Over her passion, who, most rebel-like,
Sought to be king o'er her.

KENT.   O, then it moved her.

GENTLEMAN. Not to a rage; patience and sorrow strove
Who should express her goodliest. You have seen
Sunshine and rain at once; her smiles and tears
Were like, a better way: those happy smilets   20
That played on her ripe lip seemed not to know
What guests were in her eyes, which parted thence

As pearls from diamonds dropped. In brief,
Sorrow would be a rarity most beloved
If all could so become it.
KENT.   Made she no verbal question?
GENTLEMAN. Faith, once or twice she heaved the name
    of 'father'
pantingly forth, as if it pressed her heart;
Cried 'Sisters, sisters! Shame of ladies! Sisters!
Kent! father! sisters! What, i'th'storm? i'th'night?
Let pity not believe it!' There she shook   30
The holy water from her heavenly eyes
That clamour moistened; then away she started
To deal with grief alone.
KENT.   It is the stars,
The stars above us, govern our conditions;
Else one self mate and make could not beget
Such different issues. You spoke not with her since?
GENTLEMAN. No.
KENT. Was this before the King returned?
GENTLEMAN.   No, since
KENT. Well, sir, the poor distressèd Lear's i'th'town,
Who sometime, in his better tune, remembers   40
What we are come about, and by no means
Will yield to see his daughter.
GENTLEMAN.   Why, good sir?
KENT. A sovereign shame so elbows him: his own
    unkindness,
That stripped her from his benediction, turned her
To foreign casualties, gave her dear rights
To his dog-hearted daughters—these things sting
His mind so venomously that burning shame
Detains him from Cordelia.
GENTLEMAN.   Alack, poor gentleman!
KENT. Of Albany's and Cornwall's powers you heard
    not?
GENTLEMAN. 'Tis so, they are afoot.   50
KENT. Well, sir, I'll bring you to our master Lear
And leave you to attend him. Some dear cause
Will in concealment wrap me up awhile;
When I am known aright, you shall not grieve
Lending me this acquaintance. I pray you go
Along with me.   They go

Scene 4: The same

Enter, with drum and colours, Cordelia, Doctor, and Soldiers

CORDELIA. Alack, 'tis he! Why, he was met even now
As mad as the vexed sea, singing aloud,
Crowned with rank fumiter and furrow-weeds,
With hardocks, hemlock, nettles, cuckoo-flowers,
Darnel, and all the idle weeds that grow
In our sustaining corn. A century send forth;
Search every acre in the high-grown field,
And bring him to our eye. [*an Officer goes*] What
    can man's wisdom
In the restoring his bereavèd sense?
He that helps him take all my outward worth.   10
DOCTOR. There is means, madam.
Our foster-nurse of nature is repose,
The which he lacks. That to provoke in him
Are many simples operative, whose power
Will close the eye of anguish.
CORDELIA.   All blest secrets,
All you unpublished virtues of the earth,
Spring with my tears! Be aidant and remediate

In the good man's distress!—Seek, seek for him,
Lest his ungoverned rage dissolve the life
That wants the means to lead it.

Enter Messenger

MESSENGER.   News, madam!   20
The British powers are marching hitherward.
CORDELIA. 'Tis known before; our preparation stands
In expectation of them. O dear father,
It is thy business that I go about!
Therefore great France
My mourning and importuned tears hath pitied.
No blown ambition doth our arms incite,
But love, dear love, and our aged father's right.
Soon may I hear and see him!   *They go*

Scene 5: Gloucester's castle

Enter Regan and Oswald

REGAN. But are my brother's powers set forth?
OSWALD.   Ay, madam.
REGAN. Himself in person there?
OSWALD.   Madam, with much ado.
Your sister is the better soldier.
REGAN. Lord Edmund spake not with your lord at
    home?
OSWALD. No, madam.
REGAN. What might import my sister's letter to him?
OSWALD. I know not, lady.
REGAN. Faith, he is posted hence on serious matter.
It was great ignorance, Gloucester's eyes being out,
To let him live: where he arrives he moves   10
All hearts against us. Edmund, I think, is gone,
In pity of his misery, to dispatch
His nighted life; moreover, to descry
The strength o'th'enemy.
OSWALD. I must needs after him, madam, with my
    letter.
REGAN. Our troops set forth tomorrow. Stay with us;
The ways are dangerous.
OSWALD.   I may not, madam;
My lady charged my duty in this business.
REGAN. Why should she write to Edmund? Might
    not you
Transport her purposes by word? Belike,   20
Some things, I know not what. I'll love thee
    much—
Let me unseal the letter.
OSWALD.   Madam, I had rather—
REGAN. I know your lady does not love her husband;
I am sure of that: and at her late being here
She gave strange oeillades and most speaking looks
To noble Edmund. I know you are of her bosom.
OSWALD. I, madam!
REGAN. I speak in understanding: you are: I know't;
Therefore I do advise you take this note.
My lord is dead; Edmund and I have talked,   30
And more convenient is he for my hand
Than for your lady's. You may gather more.
If you do find him, pray you give him this;
And when your mistress hears thus much from you,
I pray desire her call her wisdom to her.
So fare you well.
If you do chance to hear of that blind traitor,
Preferment falls on him that cuts him off.

OSWALD. Would I could meet him, madam! I should show
What party I do follow.
REGAN.   Fare thee well.   *They go* 40

Scene 6: *The Country near Dover*

Enter Gloucester, and Edgar dressed like a peasant

GLOUCESTER. When shall I come to th' top of that same hill?
EDGAR. You do climb up it now; look how we labour.
GLOUCESTER. Methinks the ground is even.
EDGAR.   Horrible steep.
Hark, do you hear the sea?
GLOUCESTER.   No, truly.
EDGAR. Why, then your other senses grow imperfect
By your eyes' anguish.
GLOUCESTER.   So may it be indeed.
Methinks thy voice is altered, and thou speak'st
In better phrase and matter than thou didst.
EDGAR. You're much deceived: in nothing am I changed
But in my garments.
GLOUCESTER.   Methinks you're better spoken. 10
EDGAR. Come on, sir, here's the place: stand still; how fearful
And dizzy 'tis to cast one's eyes so low!
The crows and choughs that wing the midway air
Show scarce so gross as beetles. Half way down
Hangs one that gathers samphire—dreadful trade!
Methinks he seems no bigger than his head.
The fishermen that walk upon the beach
Appear like mice: and yond tall anchoring bark
Diminished to her cock; her cock a buoy
Almost too small for sight. The murmuring surge, 20
That on th'unnumb'réd idle pebble chafes,
Cannot be heard so high. I'll look no more,
Lest my brain turn, and the deficient sight
Topple down headlong.
GLOUCESTER.   Set me where you stand.
EDGAR. Give me your hand. You are now within a foot
Of th'extreme verge. For all beneath the moon
Would I not leap upright.
GLOUCESTER.   Let go my hand.
Here, friend, 's another purse, in it a jewel
Well worth a poor man's taking. Fairies and gods
Prosper it with thee! Go thou further off: 30
Bid me farewell, and let me hear thee going.
EDGAR. Now fare ye well, good sir.
GLOUCESTER.   With all my heart!
EDGAR. Why I do trifle thus with his despair
Is done to cure it.
GLOUCESTER.   O you mighty gods!   *He kneels*
This world I do renounce, and in your sights
Shake patiently my great affliction off.
If I could bear it longer, and not fall
To quarrel with your great opposeless wills,
My snuff and loathéd part of nature should
Burn itself out. If Edgar live, O bless him!   40
Now, fellow, fare thee well.
EDGAR.   Gone, sir; farewell!
                    Gloucester falls forward, and
                                        swoons
[*aside*] And yet I know not how conceit may rob
The treasury of life when life itself

Yields to the theft. Had he been where he thought,
By this had thought been past. [*aloud*] Alive, or dead?
Ho, you sir! friend! hear you, sir! Speak!
[*aside*] Thus might he pass indeed: yet he revives.
[*aloud*] What are you, sir?
GLOUCESTER.   Away, and let me die.
EDGAR. Hadst thou been aught but gossamer, feathers, air,
(So many fathom down precipitating),   50
Thou'dst shivered like an egg: but thou dost breathe,
Hast heavy substance, bleed'st not, speak'st, art sound.
Ten masts at each make not the altitude
Which thou hast perpendicularly fell:
Thy life's a miracle. Speak yet again.
GLOUCESTER. But have I fall'n, or no?
EDGAR. From the dread summit of this chalky bourn.
Look up a-height; the shrill-gorged lark so far
Cannot be seen, or heard. Do but look up.
GLOUCESTER. Alack, I have no eyes.   60
Is wretchedness deprived that benefit
To end itself by death? 'Twas yet some comfort
When misery could beguile the tyrant's rage
And frustrate his proud will.
EDGAR.   Give me your arm.
Up; so. How is't? Feel you your legs? You stand.
GLOUCESTER. Too well, too well.
EDGAR.   This is above all strangeness.
Upon the crown o'th'cliff what thing was that
Which parted from you?
GLOUCESTER.   A poor unfortunate beggar.
EDGAR. As I stood here below methought his eyes
Were two full moons; he had a thousand noses,   70
Horns whelked and waved like the enridgéd sea.
It was some fiend. Therefore, thou happy father,
Think that the clearest gods, who make them honours
Of men's impossibilities, have preserved thee.
GLOUCESTER. I do remember now. Henceforth I'll bear
Affliction till it do cry out itself
'Enough, enough,' and die. That thing you speak of,
I took it for a man. Often 'twould say
'The fiend, the fiend',—he led me to that place.
EDGAR. Bear free and patient thoughts.

Enter Lear, crowned with wild flowers and nettles

                        But who comes here? 80
The safer sense will ne'er accommodate
His master thus.
LEAR. No, they cannot touch me for coining; I am the king himself.
EDGAR. O thou side-piercing sight!
LEAR. Nature's above art in that respect. There's your press-money. That fellow handles his bow like a crow-keeper: draw me a clothier's yard. Look, look, a mouse! Peace, peace; this piece of toasted cheese will do't. There's my gauntlet; I'll prove it on a 90 giant. Bring up the brown bills. O, well flown, bird; i'th'clout, i'th'clout: hewgh! Give the word.
EDGAR. Sweet marjoram.
LEAR. Pass.
GLOUCESTER. I know that voice.
LEAR. Ha! Goneril with a white beard? They flattered me like a dog, and told me I had the white hairs in my beard ere the black ones were there. To say 'ay'

and 'no' to everything that I said! 'Ay,' and 'no' too,
was no good divinity. When the rain came to wet 100
me once and the wind to make me chatter, when
the thunder would not peace at my bidding, there I
found 'em, there I smelt 'em out! Go to, they are not
men o' their words: they told me I was everything;
'tis a lie— I am not ague-proof.

GLOUCESTER. The trick of that voice I do well
remember:
Is't not the king?

LEAR.   Ay, every inch a king!
When I do stare, see how the subject quakes.
I pardon that man's life. What was thy cause?
Adultery?   110
Thou shalt not die. Die for adultery? No!
The wren goes to 't, and the small gilded fly
Does lecher in my sight.
Let copulation thrive: for Gloucester's bastard son
Was kinder to his father than my daughters
Got 'tween the lawful sheets.
To 't, luxury, pell-mell! for I lack soldiers.
Behold yond simp'ring dame
Whose face between her forks presages snow,
That minces virtue and does shake the head 120
To hear of pleasure's name;
The fitchew nor the soiléd horse goes to 't
With a more riotous appetite.
Down from the waist they are centaurs,
Though women all above.
But to the girdle do the gods inherit,
Beneath is all the fiend's.
There's hell, there's darkness, there is the sulphurous
pit;
Burning, scalding, stench, consumption: fie, fie, fie,
pah, pah!
Give me an ounce of civet; good apothecary, 130
sweeten my imagination: there's money for thee.

GLOUCESTER. O, let me kiss that hand!

LEAR. Let me wipe it first; it smells of mortality.

GLOUCESTER. O ruined piece of Nature! This great
world
Shall so wear out to naught. Dost thou know me?

LEAR. I remember thine eyes well enough. Dost thou
squiny at me?
No, do thy worst, blind Cupid; I'll not love.
Read thou this challenge; mark but the penning of
it.

GLOUCESTER. Were all thy letters suns, I could not
see.

EDGAR [aside]. I would not take this from report. It is, 140
And my heart breaks at it.

LEAR. Read.

GLOUCESTER. What! With the case of eyes?

LEAR. O ho, are you there with me? No eyes in your
head, nor no money in your purse? Your eyes are
in a heavy case, your purse in a light; yet you see
how this world goes.

GLOUCESTER. I see it feelingly.

LEAR. What! Art mad? A man may see how this world
goes with no eyes. Look with thine ears: see how 150
yond justice rails upon yond simple thief. Hark in
thine ear: change places and, handy-dandy, which is
the justice, which is the thief? Thou hast seen a
farmer's dog bark at a beggar?

GLOUCESTER. Ay, sir.

LEAR. And the creature run from the cur? there thou
mightst behold the great image of authority—a
dog's obeyed in office.
Thou rascal beadle, hold thy bloody hand!
Why dost thou lash that whore? Strip thy own back; 160
Thou hotly lusts to use her in that kind
For which thou whipp'st her. The usurer hangs the
cozener.
Through tattered clothes great vices do appear;
Robes and furred gowns hide all. Plate sin with
gold,
And the strong lance of justice hurtless breaks:
Arm it in rags, a pigmy's straw does pierce it.
None does offend, none, I say none. I'll able 'em;
Take that of me, my friend, who have the power
To seal th'accuser's lips. Get thee glass eyes
And, like a scurvy politician, seem   170
To see the things thou dost not. Now, now, now,
now!
Pull off my boots; harder, harder! So.

EDGAR. O, matter and impertinency mixed!
Reason in madness!

LEAR. If thou wilt weep my fortunes, take my eyes.
I know thee well enough; thy name is Gloucester.
Thou must be patient. We came crying hither;
Thou know'st the first time that we smell the air
We wawl and cry. I will preach to thee: mark!

GLOUCESTER. Alack, alack the day!   180

LEAR. When we are born, we cry that we are come
To this great stage of fools. This' a good block!
                          Taking off the crown
It were a delicate stratagem to shoe
A troop of horse with felt: I'll put't in proof,
And when I have stol'n upon these son-in-laws,
Then kill, kill, kill, kill, kill, kill!

Enter a Gentleman with attendants

GENTLEMAN. O, here he is: lay hand upon him. Sir,
Your most dear daughter—

LEAR. No rescue? What, a prisoner? I am even
The natural fool of Fortune. Use me well;   190
You shall have ransom. Let me have surgeons;
I am cut to th'brains.

GENTLEMAN.   You shall have anything.

LEAR. No seconds? All myself?
Why, this would make a man a man of salt,
To use his eyes for garden water-pots,
Ay, and laying autumn's dust. I will die bravely,
Like a smug bridegroom. What! I will be jovial.
Come, come, I am a king, masters, know you that?

GENTLEMAN. You are a royal one, and we obey you.

LEAR. Then there's life in't. Come, an you get it you 200
shall get it by running. Sa, sa, sa, sa.
                 He runs away; attendants follow

GENTLEMAN. A sight most pitiful in the meanest
wretch,
Past speaking of in a king! Thou hast one daughter
Who redeems nature from the general curse
Which twain have brought her to.

EDGAR. Hail, gentle sir!

GENTLEMAN.   Sir, speed you. What's your will?

EDGAR. Do you hear aught, sir, of a battle toward?

GENTLEMAN. Most sure, and vulgar: every one hears
that,
Which can distinguish sound.

EDGAR.   But, by your favour,
How near's the other army?   210

GENTLEMAN. Near, and on speedy foot: the main descry
Stands on the hourly thought.
EDGAR.   I thank you, sir:
that's all.
GENTLEMAN. Though that the queen on special cause is here,
Her army is moved on.
EDGAR.   I thank you, sir.
                                        Gentleman goes
GLOUCESTER. You ever-gentle gods, take my breath from me;
Let not my worser spirit tempt me again
To die before you please!
EDGAR.   Well pray you, father.
GLOUCESTER. Now, good sir, what are you?
EDGAR. A most poor man, made tame to Fortune's blows,
Who, by the art of known and feeling sorrows,   220
Am pregnant to good pity. Give me your hand;
I'll lead you to some biding.
GLOUCESTER.   Hearty thanks:
The bounty and the benison of Heaven
To boot, and boot!

Enter Oswald

OSWALD.   A proclaimed prize! Most happy!
That eyeless head of thine was first framed flesh
To raise my fortunes. Thou old unhappy traitor,
Briefly thyself remember; the sword is out
That must destroy thee.
GLOUCESTER.   Now let thy friendly hand
Put strength enough to't.   *Edgar interposes*
OSWALD.   Wherefore, bold peasant,
Dar'st thou support a published traitor? Hence,   230
Lest that th'infection of his fortune take
Like hold on thee. Let go his arm.
EDGAR. Chill not let go, zir, without vurther cagion.
OSWALD. Let go, slave, or thou di'st.
EDGAR. Good gentleman, go your gate, and let poor voke pass. An 'chud ha' bin zwaggered out of my life, 'twould not ha' bin zo long as 'tis by a vortnight. Nay, come not near th'old man; keep out, che vor' ye, or Ice try whither your costard or my ballow be the harder. Chill be plain with you.   240
OSWALD. Out, dunghill!   *They fight*
EDGAR. Chill pick your teeth, zir. Come; no matter vor your foins.   *Oswald falls*
OSWALD. Slave, thou hast slain me. Villain, take my purse:
If ever thou wilt thrive, bury my body,
And give the letters which thou find'st about me
To Edmund, Earl of Gloucester; seek him out
Upon the British party. O, untimely death! Death!
                                        He dies
EDGAR. I know thee well—a serviceable villain,
As duteous to the vices of thy mistress   250
As badness would desire.
GLOUCESTER.   What, is he dead?
EDGAR. Sit you down, father; rest you.
Let's see these pockets; the letters that he speaks of
May be my friends. He's dead; I am only sorry
He had no other deathsman. Let us see.
Leave, gentle wax; and, manners, blame us not:
To know our enemies' minds we rip their hearts;
Their papers is more lawful.   *Reads the letter*

'Let our reciprocal vows be rememb'red. You have many opportunities to cut him off: if your will want   260
not, time and place will be fruitfully offered. There is nothing done if he return the conqueror: then am I the prisoner, and his bed my gaol; from the loathed warmth whereof deliver me, and supply the place for your labour.
    Your (wife, so I would say) affectionate servant,
                                        Goneril.'
O indistinguished space of woman's will!
A plot upon her virtuous husband's life,
And the exchange my brother! Here in the sands   270
Thee I'll rake up, thou post unsanctified
Of murderous lechers; and in the mature time
With this ungracious paper strike the sight
Of the death-practised Duke. For him 'tis well
That of thy death and business I can tell.
GLOUCESTER. The King is mad; how stiff is my vile sense
That I stand up and have ingenious feeling
Of my huge sorrows! Better I were distract:
So should my thoughts be severed from my griefs,
And woes by wrong imaginations lose   280
The knowledge of themselves.   *Drum afar off*
EDGAR.   Give me your hand:
Far off methinks I hear the beaten drum.
Come, father, I'll bestow you with a friend.
                                        They go

Scene 7: *A tent in the French camp*

Enter Cordelia, Kent, Doctor and Gentleman

CORDELIA. O thou good Kent, how shall I live and work
To match thy goodness? My life will be too short,
And every measure fail me.
KENT. To be acknowledged, madam, is o'er-paid.
All my reports go with the modest truth;
Nor more, nor clipped, but so.
CORDELIA.   Be better suited:
These weeds are memories of those worser hours;
I prithee put them off.
KENT.   Pardon, dear madam;
Yet to be known shortens my made intent.
My boon I make it that you know me not   10
Till time, and I, think meet.
CORDELIA. Then be't so, my good lord. [*to the Doctor*]
How does the King?
DOCTOR. Madam, sleeps still.
CORDELIA. O you kind gods,
Cure this great breach in his abusèd nature!
Th'untuned and jarring senses, O, wind up
Of this child-changèd father!
DOCTOR.   So please your Majesty
That we may wake the King? He hath slept long.
CORDELIA. Be governed by your knowledge, and proceed
I'th'sway of your own will. Is he arrayed?   20
GENTLEMAN. Ay, madam: in the heaviness of sleep
We put fresh garments on him.
DOCTOR. Be by, good madam, when we do awake him;
I doubt not of his temperance.
CORDELIA.   Very well.

Enter Lear asleep in a chair carried by servants. Soft music

DOCTOR. Please you draw near. Louder the music
   there!
CORDELIA. O my dear father, restoration hang
   Thy medicine on my lips, and let this kiss
   Repair those violent harms that my two sisters
   Have in thy reverence made!
KENT.   Kind and dear princess!
CORDELIA. Had you not been their father, these white
   flakes   30
   Did challenge pity of them. Was this a face
   To be opposed against the warring winds?
   To stand against the deep dread-bolted thunder
   In the most terrible and nimble stroke
   Of quick cross lightning? To watch—poor perdu!—
   With this thin helm? Mine enemy's dog,
   Though he had bit me, should have stood that night
   Against my fire; and wast thou fain, poor father,
   To hovel thee with swine and rogues forlorn,
   In short and musty straw? Alack, alack!   40
   'Tis wonder that thy life and wits at once
   Had not concluded all. He wakes; speak to him.
DOCTOR. Madam, do you; 'tis fittest.
CORDELIA. How does my royal lord? How fares your
   Majesty?
LEAR. You do me wrong to take me out o'th'grave:
   Thou art a soul in bliss; but I am bound
   Upon a wheel of fire, that mine own tears
   Do scald like molten lead.
CORDELIA.   Sir, do you know me?
LEAR. You are a spirit, I know; when did you die?
CORDELIA. Still, still, far wide!   50
DOCTOR. He's scarce awake; let him alone awhile.
LEAR. Where have I been? Where am I? Fair daylight?
   I am mightily abused; I should e'en die with pity
   To see another thus. I know not what to say.
   I will not swear these are my hands: let's see;
   I feel this pin prick. Would I were assured
   Of my condition!
CORDELIA.   O, look upon me, sir,
   And hold your hand in benediction o'er me;
   No, sir, you must not kneel.
LEAR.   Pray do not mock me;
   I am a very foolish fond old man,   60
   Fourscore and upward, not an hour more nor less;
   And, to deal plainly,
   I fear I am not in my perfect mind.
   Methinks I should know you, and know this man,
   Yet I am doubtful: for I am mainly ignorant
   What place this is; and all the skill I have
   Remembers not these garments, nor I know not
   Where I did lodge last night. Do not laugh at me,
   For (as I am a man) I think this lady
   To be my child Cordelia.
CORDELIA.   And so I am: I am!   70
LEAR. Be your tears wet? Yes, faith: I pray weep not.
   If you have poison for me, I will drink it:
   I know you do not love me, for your sisters
   Have (as I do remember) done me wrong;
   You have some causes; they have not.
CORDELIA.   No cause, no cause.
LEAR. Am I in France?
KENT.   In your own kingdom, sir.
LEAR. Do not abuse me.
DOCTOR. Be comforted, good madam: the great rage,
   You see, is killed in him; and yet it is danger
   To make him even o'er the time he has lost.   80

Desire him to go in; trouble him no more
   Till further settling.
CORDELIA. Will't please your Highness walk?
LEAR. You must bear with me. Pray you now, forget
   and forgive; I am old and foolish.
                     All go but Kent and the Gentleman
GENTLEMAN. Holds it true, sir, that the Duke of Corn-
   wall was so slain?
KENT. Most certain, sir.
GENTLEMAN. Who is conductor of his people?
KENT. As 'tis said, the bastard son of Gloucester.   90
GENTLEMAN. They say Edgar, his banished son, is with
   the Earl of Kent in Germany.
KENT. Report is changeable. 'Tis time to look about;
   the powers of the kingdom approach apace.
GENTLEMAN. The arbitrement is like to be bloody.
   Fare you well, sir.   *Goes*
KENT. My point and period will be throughly
   wrought,
   Or well or ill, as this day's battle's fought.   *Goes*

ACT 5
Scene 1: *The British camp near Dover*

*Enter, with drum and colours, Edmund, Regan, officers,
and soldiers*

EDMUND. Know of the Duke if his last purpose hold,
   Or whether, since, he is advised by aught
   To change the course; he's full of alteration
   And self-reproving; bring his constant pleasure.
                           To an officer, who goes out
REGAN. Our sister's man is certainly miscarried.
EDMUND. 'Tis to be doubted, madam.
REGAN.   Now, sweet lord,
   You know the goodness I intend upon you.
   Tell me—but truly—but then speak the truth—
   Do you not love my sister?
EDMUND.   In honoured love.
REGAN. But have you never found my brother's way   10
   To the forfended place?
EDMUND.   That thought abuses you.
REGAN. I am doubtful that you have been conjunct
   And bosomed with her, as far as we call hers.
EDMUND. No, by mine honour, madam.
REGAN. I never shall endure her: dear my lord,
   Be not familiar with her.
EDMUND.   Fear me not.
   She and the Duke her husband!

Enter, with drum and colours, Albany, Goneril, soldiers

GONERIL [*aside*]. I had rather lose the battle than that
   sister
   Should loosen him and me.
ALBANY. Our very loving sister, well be-met.   20
   Sir, this I hear: the King is come to his daughter,
   With others whom the rigour of our state
   Forced to cry out. Where I could not be honest,
   I never yet was valiant: for this business,
   It touches us as France invades our land,
   Not bolds the King, with others whom, I fear,
   Most just and heavy causes make oppose.
EDMUND. Sir, you speak nobly.
REGAN.   Why is this reasoned?
GONERIL. Combine together 'gainst the enemy;
   For these domestic and particular broils   30

Are not the question here.
ALBANY.   Let's then determine
With th'ancient of war on our proceeding.
EDMUND. I shall attend you presently at your tent.
REGAN. Sister, you'll go with us?
GONERIL. No.
REGAN. 'Tis most convenient; pray go with us.
GONERIL [aside]. O ho, I know the riddle.—I will go.

As they are going out, enter Edgar disguised

EDGAR. If e'er your Grace had speech with man so
    poor,
  Hear me one word.
ALBANY.   I'll overtake you.
                    All but Albany and Edgar depart
                              Speak.
EDGAR. Before you fight the battle, ope this letter.   40
  If you have victory, let the trumpet sound
  For him that brought it: wretched though I seem,
  I can produce a champion that will prove
  What is avouchéd there. If you miscarry,
  Your business of the world hath so an end,
  And machination ceases. Fortune love you!
ALBANY. Stay till I have read the letter.
EDGAR.   I was forbid it.
  When time shall serve, let but the herald cry,
  And I'll appear again.
ALBANY.   Why, fare thee well;
  I will o'erlook thy paper.   *Edgar goes* 50

Edmund returns

EDMUND. The enemy's in view; draw up your powers.
  Here is the guess of their true strength and forces,
  By diligent discovery; [*hands a paper*] but your haste
  Is now urged on you.
ALBANY.   We will greet the time.
                                        He goes
EDMUND. To both these sisters have I sworn my
    love;
  Each jealous of the other, as the stung
  Are of the adder. Which of them shall I take?
  Both? One? Or neither? Neither can be enjoyed
  If both remain alive: to take the widow
  Exasperates, makes mad her sister Goneril;   60
  And hardly shall I carry out my side,
  Her husband being alive. Now then, we'll use
  His countenance for the battle, which being done,
  Let her who would be rid of him devise
  His speedy taking off. As for the mercy
  Which he intends to Lear and to Cordelia,
  The battle done, and they within our power,
  Shall never see his pardon: for my state
  Stands on me to defend, not to debate.   *He goes*

          Scene 2: *A field between the two camps*

*Alarum. Enter the French army, Cordelia leading Lear by
the hand, and pass by. Enter Edgar and Gloucester*

EDGAR. Here, father, take the shadow of this tree
  For your good host. Pray that the right may thrive..
  If ever I return to you again,
  I'll bring you comfort.
GLOUCESTER.   Grace go with you, sir!
                                        Edgar goes

*Alarum heard from the battlefield hard by, and later a
retreat. Enter Edgar*

EDGAR. Away, old man; give me thy hand, away!
  King Lear hath lost, he and his daughter ta'en.
  Give me thy hand; come on!
GLOUCESTER. No further, sir; a man may rot even here.
EDGAR. What, in ill thoughts again? men must endure
  Their going hence, even as their coming hither;   10
  Ripeness is all. Come on.
GLOUCESTER.   And that's true too.
                                        They go

          Scene 3: *The British camp near Dover*

*Enter in conquest with drum and colours, Edmund; Lear and
Cordelia as prisoners; soldiers, Captain*

EDMUND. Some officers take them away: good guard,
  Until their greater pleasures first be known
  That are to censure them.
CORDELIA.   We are not the first
  Who with best meaning have incurred the worst.
  For thee, oppresséd King, I am cast down;
  Myself could else out-frown false Fortune's frown.
  Shall we not see these daughters and these sisters?
LEAR. No, no, no, no! Come, let's away to prison:
  We two alone will sing like birds i'th'cage;
  When thou dost ask me blessing, I'll kneel down   10
  And ask of thee forgiveness. So we'll live,
  And pray, and sing, and tell old tales, and laugh
  At gilded butterflies, and hear poor rogues
  Talk of court news; and we'll talk with them too—
  Who loses and who wins, who's in, who's out—
  And take upon 's the mystery of things,
  As if we were God's spies; and we'll wear out,
  In a walled prison, packs and sects of great ones
  That ebb and flow by th'moon.
EDMUND.   Take them away.
LEAR. Upon such sacrifices, my Cordelia,   20
  The gods themselves throw incense. Have I caught
    thee?
  He that parts us shall bring a brand from heaven
  And fire us hence like foxes. Wipe thine eyes;
  The good-years shall devour them, flesh and fell,
  Ere they shall make us weep! We'll see 'em starved
    first.
  Come.   *Lear and Cordelia are led away
                              under guard*
EDMUND. Come hither, captain; hark.
  Take thou this note; [*giving a paper*] go follow them
    to prison.
  One step I have advanced thee; if thou dost
  As this instructs thee, thou dost make thy way   30
  To noble fortunes. Know thou this, that men
  Are as the time is: to be tender-minded
  Does not become a sword: thy great employment
  Will not bear question; either say thou'lt do't,
  Or thrive by other means.
CAPTAIN.   I'll do't, my lord.
EDMUND. About it; and write happy when thou'st
    done.
  Mark,—I say instantly; and carry it so
  As I have set it down.
CAPTAIN. I cannot draw a cart, nor eat dried oats;
  If it be man's work I'll do't.   *He goes* 40

Flourish. Enter Albany, Goneril, Regan, Soldiers

ALBANY. Sir, you have showed today your valiant
    strain,
  And Fortune led you well. You have the captives

Who were the opposites of this day's strife:
I do require them of you, so to use them
As we shall find their merits and our safety
May equally determine.

EDMUND.   Sir, I thought it fit
To send the old and miserable King
To some retention and appointed guard;
Whose age had charms in it, whose title more,
To pluck the common bosom on his side   50
And turn our impressed lances in our eyes
Which do command them. With him I sent the
    Queen,
My reason all the same; and they are ready
Tomorrow, or at further space, t'appear
Where you shall hold your session. At this time
We sweat and bleed: the friend hath lost his friend;
And the best quarrels, in the heat, are cursed
By those that feel their sharpness.
The question of Cordelia and her father
Requires a fitter place.

ALBANY.   Sir, by your patience,   60
I hold you but a subject of this war,
Not as a brother.

REGAN.   That's as we list to grace him.
Methinks our pleasure might have been demanded
Ere you had spoke so far. He led our powers,
Bore the commission of my place and person
The which immediacy may well stand up
And call itself your brother.

GONERIL.   Not so hot!
In his own grace he doth exalt himself
More than in your addition.

REGAN.   In my rights
By me invested, he compeers the best.   70

ALBANY. That were the most if he should husband you.

REGAN. Jesters do oft prove prophets.

GONERIL.   Holla, holla!
That eye that told you so looked but asquint.

REGAN. Lady, I am not well, else I should answer
From a full-flowing stomach. General,
Take thou my soldiers, prisoners, patrimony:
Dispose of them, of me; the walls are thine.
Witness the world that I create thee here
My lord and master.

GONERIL.   Mean you to enjoy him?

ALBANY. The let-alone lies not in your good will.   80

EDMUND. Nore in thine, lord.

ALBANY.   Half-blooded fellow, yes.

REGAN [to Edmund]. Let the drum strike; and prove my
    title thine.

ALBANY. Stay yet; hear reason. Edmund, I arrest thee
On capital treason, and, in thy attaint,
                          Pointing to Goneril
This gilded serpent. For your claim, fair sister,
I bar it in the interest of my wife;
'Tis she is sub-contracted to this lord,
And I, her husband, contradict your banns.
If you will marry, make your loves to me;
My lady is bespoke.

GONERIL.   An interlude!   90

ALBANY. Thou art armed, Gloucester: let the trumpet
    sound;
If none appear to prove upon thy person
Thy heinous, manifest, and many treasons,
There is my pledge! [*throwing down a glove*] I'll make
    it on thy heart,

Ere I taste bread, thou art in nothing less
Than I have here proclaimed thee.

REGAN.   Sick, O sick!

GONERIL [aside]. If not, I'll ne'er trust medicine.

EDMUND. There's my exchange! [*throwing down a
    glove*] What in the world he is
That names me traitor, villain-like he lies.
Call by the trumpet; he that dares approach,   100
On him, on you—who not?—I will maintain
My truth and honour firmly.

ALBANY. A herald, ho!

EDMUND.   A herald, ho, a herald!

ALBANY. Trust to thy single virtue; for thy soldiers,
All levied in my name, have in my name
Took their discharge.

REGAN.   My sickness grows upon me.

ALBANY. She is not well; convey her to my tent.
                          Regan is led away

Enter a Herald

Come hither, herald—Let the trumpet sound—
And read out this.   *A trumpet sounds*

HERALD [reads]. If any man of quality or degree within   110
    the lists of the army will maintain upon Edmund,
    supposed Earl of Gloucester, that he is a manifold
    traitor, let him appear by the third sound of the
    trumpet. He is bold in his defence.   *First trumpet*
Again!   *Second trumpet*
Again!   *Third trumpet*

An answering trumpet heard. Enter Edgar, in armour

ALBANY. Ask him his purposes—why he appears
Upon this call o'th'trumpet.

HERALD.   What are you?
Your name, your quality, and why you answer
This present summons?

EDGAR.   Know my name is lost;   120
By treason's tooth bare-gnawn and canker-bit:
Yet am I noble as the adversary
I come to cope.

ALBANY.   Which is that adversary?

EDGAR. What's he that speaks for Edmund, Earl of
    Gloucester?

EDMUND. Himself: what say'st thou to him?

EDGAR.   Draw thy sword,
That, if my speech offend a noble heart,
Thy arm may do thee justice; here is mine:
Behold, it is the privilege of mine honours,
My oath, and my profession. I protest,
Maugre thy strength, place, youth, and eminence,   130
Despite thy victor-sword and fire-new fortune,
Thy valour and thy heart, thou art a traitor,
False to thy gods, thy brother, and thy father,
Conspirant 'gainst this high illustrious prince,
And, from th'extremest upward of thy head
To the descent and dust below thy foot,
A most toad-spotted traitor. Say thou no,
This sword, this arm, and my best spirits are bent
To prove upon thy heart, whereto I speak,
Thou liest.

EDMUND.   In wisdom I should ask thy name;   140
But since thy outside looks so fair and warlike,
And that thy tongue some say of breeding breathes,
What safe and nicely I might well delay

By rule of knighthood, I disdain and spurn.
Back do I toss these treasons to thy head,
With the hell-hated lie o'erwhelm thy heart,
Which, for they yet glance by and scarcely bruise,
This sword of mine shall give them instant way
Where they shall rest for ever. Trumpets, speak!

Alarums. They fight. Edmund falls

ALBANY. Save him, save him!
GONERIL.   This is practice, Gloucester: 150
By th' law of war thou wast not bound to answer
An unknown opposite: thou art not vanquished,
But cozened and beguiled.
ALBANY.   Shut your mouth, dame,
Or with this paper shall I stop it.—Hold, sir.—
Thou worse than any name, read thine own evil.
No tearing, lady! I perceive you know it.
GONERIL. Say if I do—the laws are mine, not thine;
Who can arraign me for't?
ALBANY.   Most monstrous! O!
Know'st thou this paper?
GONERIL.   Ask me not what I know. *Goes*
ALBANY. Go after her: she's desperate; govern her. 160

Officer goes

EDMUND. What you have charged me with, that have
    I done,
And more, much more; the time will bring it out:
'Tis past, and so am I. But what art thou
That hast this fortune on me? If thou'rt noble,
I do forgive thee.
EDGAR.   Let's exchange charity.
I am no less in blood than thou art, Edmund;
If more, the more thou'st wronged me.
My name is Edgar, and thy father's son.
The gods are just, and of our pleasant vices
Make instruments to plague us: 170
The dark and vicious place where thee he got
Cost him his eyes.
EDMUND.   Thou'st spoken right, 'tis true.
The wheel is come full circle; I am here.
ALBANY [*to Edgar*]. Methought thy very gait did
    prophesy
A royal nobleness: I must embrace thee;
Let sorrow split my heart if ever I
Did hate thee or thy father.
EDGAR.   Worthy prince, I know't.
ALBANY. Where have you hid yourself?
How have you known the miseries of your father?
EDGAR. By nursing them, my lord. List a brief tale; 180
And when 'tis told, O that my heart would burst!
The bloody proclamation to escape
That followed me so near (O, our life's sweetness!
That we the pain of death would hourly die,
Rather than die at once!) taught me to shift
Into a madman's rags, t'assume a semblance
That very dogs disdained: and in this habit
Met I my father with his bleeding rings,
Their precious stones new lost; became his guide,
Led him, begged for him, saved him from despair; 190
Never (O fault!) revealed myself unto him
Until some half hour past, when I was armed.
Not sure, though hoping, of this good success,
I asked his blessing, and from first to last
Told him our pilgrimage. But his flawed heart
(Alack, too weak the conflict to support)
'Twixt two extremes of passion, joy and grief,
Burst smilingly.

EDMUND.   This speech of yours hath moved me,
And shall perchance do good: but speak you on;
You look as you had something more to say. 200
ALBANY. If there be more, more woeful, hold it in;
For I am almost ready to dissolve,
Hearing of this.
EDGAR.   This would have seemed a period
To such as love not sorrow; but another,
To amplify too much, would make much more,
And top extremity. Whilst I
Was big in clamour, came there in a man,
Who, having seen me in my worst estate,
Shunned my abhorred society; but then, finding
Who 'twas that so endured, with his strong arms 210
He fastened on my neck and bellowed out
As he'd burst heaven: threw him on my father;
Told the most piteous tale of Lear and him
That ever ear received, which in recounting
His grief grew puissant and the strings of life
Began to crack: twice then the trumpets sounded,
And there I left him tranced.
ALBANY.   But who was this?
EDGAR. Kent, sir, the banished Kent, who in disguise
Followed his enemy king and did him service
Improper for a slave. 220

Enter a Gentleman, with a bloody knife

GENTLEMAN. Help, help! O help!
EDGAR.   What kind of help?
ALBANY.   Speak, man!
EDGAR. What means this bloody knife?
GENTLEMAN.   'Tis hot, it smokes;
It came even from the heart of—O, she's dead!
ALBANY. Who dead? Speak, man!
GENTLEMAN. Your lady, sir, your lady: and her sister
By her is poisoned; she confesses it.
EDMUND. I was contracted to them both; all three
Now marry in an instant.
EDGAR.   Here comes Kent.

Enter Kent

ALBANY. Produce the bodies, be they alive or dead;

Gentleman goes

This judgement of the heavens, that makes us
    tremble, 230
Touches us not with pity. [*notices Kent*] O, is this he?
The time will not allow the compliment
Which very manners urges.
KENT.   I am come
To bid my king and master aye good night.
Is he not here?
ALBANY.   Great thing of us forgot!
Speak, Edmund; where's the king? and where's
    Cordelia?

The bodies of Goneril and Regan
are brought in

See'st thou this object, Kent?
KENT. Alack, why thus?
EDMUND.   Yet Edmund was beloved:
The one the other poisoned for my sake,
And after slew herself. 240
ALBANY. Even so. Cover their faces.
EDMUND. I pant for life. Some good I mean to do,
Despite of mine own nature. Quickly send
(Be brief in it) to th' castle, for my writ
Is on the life of Lear and on Cordelia.

Nay, send in time!

ALBANY.   Run, run, O run!

EDGAR. To who, my lord?—[to Edmund] Who has the
   office? Send
Thy token of reprieve.

EDMUND. Well thought on. Take my sword,
   Give it to the captain.

ALBANY.   Haste thee, for thy life!   250
                      Edgar hurries forth

EDMUND. He hath commission from thy wife and me
To hang Cordelia in the prison and
To lay the blame upon her own despair,
That she fordid herself.

ALBANY. The gods defend her!
   Bear him hence awhile.   *Edmund is borne off*

*Enter Lear with Cordelia in his arms, Edgar, Captain, and
others following*

LEAR. Howl, howl, howl! O, you are men of stones!
Had I your tongues and eyes, I'd use them so
That heaven's vault should crack! She's gone for
   ever.
I know when one is dead, and when one lives;   260
She's dead as earth. Lend me a looking-glass;
If that her breath will mist or stain the stone,
Why, then she lives.

KENT.   Is this the promised end?

EDGAR. Or image of that horror.

ALBANY.   Fall and cease!

LEAR. This feather stirs—she lives! If it be so,
It is a chance which does redeem all sorrows
That ever I have felt.

KENT [*kneeling*].   O my good master!

LEAR. Prithee away!

EDGAR.   'Tis noble Kent, your friend.

LEAR. A plague upon you, murderers, traitors all!
I might have saved her; now she's gone for ever!   270
Cordelia, Cordelia, stay a little!—Ha?
What is't thou say'st?—Her voice was ever soft,
Gentle and low, an excellent thing in woman—
I killed the slave that was a-hanging thee.

OFFICER. 'Tis true, my lords, he did.

LEAR.   Did I not, fellow?
I have seen the day, with my good biting falchion
I would have made them skip: I am old now,
And these same crosses spoil me. Who are you?
Mine eyes are not o' th' best; I'll tell you straight.

KENT. If Fortune brag of two she loved and hated,   280
One of them we behold.

LEAR. This is a dull sight. Are you not Kent?

KENT.   The same:
Your servant Kent. Where is your servant Caius?

LEAR. He's a good fellow, I can tell you that;
He'll strike, and quickly too. He's dead and rotten.

KENT. No, my good lord; I am the very man—

LEAR. I'll see that straight.

KENT. That from your first of difference and decay
Have followed your sad steps—

LEAR.   You are welcome hither.

KENT. Nor no man else. All's cheerless, dark, and
   deadly.   290
Your eldest daughters have fordone themselves,
And desperately are dead.

LEAR.   Ay, so I think.

ALBANY. He knows not what he says, and vain is it
That we present us to him.

EDGAR.   Very bootless.

Enter Captain

CAPTAIN. Edmund is dead, my lord.

ALBANY.   That's but a trifle here.
You lords and noble friends, know our intent:
What comfort to this great decay may come
Shall be applied. For us, we will resign,
During the life of this old majesty,
To him our absolute power; [to Edgar and Kent] to
   you your rights,   300
With boot and such addition as your honours
Have more than merited. All friends shall taste
The wages of their virtue, and all foes
The cup of their deservings. O see, see!

LEAR. And my poor fool is hanged! No, no, no life!
Why should a dog, a horse, a rat have life,
And thou no breath at all? Thou'lt come no more,
Never, never, never, never, never!
Pray you, undo this button. Thank you, sir.
Do you see this? Look on her! Look—her lips!   310
Look there, look there!

EDGAR.   He faints! My lord my lord!

KENT. Break, heart! I prithee break.

EDGAR.   Look up, my lord.

KENT. Vex not his ghost: O, let him pass; he hates him,
That would upon the rack of this tough world
Stretch him out longer.   *Lear dies*

EDGAR.   He is gone indeed.

KENT. The wonder is he hath endured so long;
He but usurped his life.

ALBANY. Bear them from hence. Our present business
Is general woe. [to Kent and Edgar] Friends of my
   soul, you twain
Rule in this realm, and the gored state sustain.   320

KENT. I have a journey, sir, shortly to go:
My master calls me; I must not say no.

EDGAR. The weight of this sad time we must obey;
Speak what we feel, not what we ought to say.
The oldest hath borne most: we that are young
Shall never see so much, nor live so long.
               *The bodies are borne out, all
               follow with a dead march*

Othello

The scene: Venice; Cyprus

CHARACTERS IN THE PLAY

DUKE OF VENICE
BRABANTIO, *a senator, father to Desdemona*
Other Senators
GRATIANO, *brother to Brabantio*
LODOVICO, *kinsman to Brabantio*
OTHELLO, *a noble Moor in the service of the Venetian state*
CASSIO, *his lieutenant*
IAGO, *his ancient*

RODERIGO, *a Venetian gentleman*
MONTANO, *Othello's predecessor as governor of Cyprus*
Clown, servant to Othello
DESDEMONA, *daughter to Brabantio and wife to Othello*
EMILIA, *wife to Iago*
BIANCA, *mistress to Cassio*
*Sailor, Messenger, Herald, Officers, Gentlemen,
    Musicians, and Attendants*

Othello

ACT 1

Scene 1: *Venice. A street*

Enter Roderigo and Iago

RODERIGO. Tush, never tell me; I take it much
  unkindly
  That thou, Iago, who hast had my purse
  As if the strings were thine, shouldst know of this.
IAGO. 'Sblood, but you'll not hear me.
  If ever I did dream of such a matter,
  Abhor me.
RODERIGO. Thou told'st me thou didst hold him in thy
  hate.
IAGO. Despise me if I do not. Three great ones of the
  city,
  In personal suit to make me his lieutenant,
  Off-capped to him; and, by the faith of man,   10
  I know my price: I am worth no worse a place.
  But he, as loving his own pride and purposes,
  Evades them with a bombast circumstance
  Horribly stuffed with epithets of war;
  And, in conclusion,
  Nonsuits my mediators: for, 'Certes,' says he,
  'I have already chose my officer.'
  And what was he?
  Forsooth, a great arithmetician,
  One Michael Cassio, a Florentine,   20
  A fellow almost damned in a fair wife,
  That never set a squadron in the field,
  Nor the division of a battle knows
  More than a spinster—unless the bookish theoric,
  Wherein the togéd consuls can propose
  As masterly as he; mere prattle without practice
  Is all his soldiership. But he, sir, had th'election;
  And I, of whom his eyes had seen the proof
  At Rhodes, at Cyprus, and on other grounds
  Christian and heathen, must be be-lee'd and calmed   30
  By debitor-and-creditor: this counter-caster,
  He, in good time, must his lieutenant be,
  And I—God bless the mark!—his Moorship's
  ancient.
RODERIGO. By heaven, I rather would have been his
  hangman.
IAGO. Why, there's no remedy: 'tis the curse of service;
  Preferment goes by letter and affection,
  And not by old gradation, where each second
  Stood heir to th'first. Now, sir, be judge yourself
  Whether I in any just term am affined
  To love the Moor.
RODERIGO.   I would not follow him then.   40
IAGO. O, sir, content you.
  I follow him to serve my turn upon him.
  We cannot all be masters, nor all masters
  Cannot be truly followed. You shall mark
  Many a duteous and knee-crooking knave
  That, doting on his own obsequious bondage,
  Wears out his time, much like his master's ass,
  For nought but provender, and, when he's old,
  cashiered.
  Whip me such honest knaves. Others there are
  Who, trimmed in forms and visages of duty,   50
  Keep yet their hearts attending on themselves;
  And, throwing but shows of service on their lords,
  Do well thrive by them; and, when they've lined
  their coats,
  Do themselves homage. These fellows have some
  soul,
  And such a one do I profess myself:
  For, sir,
  It is as sure as you are Roderigo,
  Were I the Moor, I would not be Iago;
  In following him, I follow but myself;
  Heaven is my judge, not I for love and duty,   60
  But seeming so, for my peculiar end;
  For when my outward action doth demonstrate
  The native act and figure of my heart
  In compliment extern, 'tis not long after
  But I will wear my heart upon my sleeve
  For daws to peck at—I am not what I am.
RODERIGO. What a full fortune does the thick-lips owe,
  If he can carry't thus!
IAGO.   Call up her father,
  Rouse him, make after him, poison his delight,
  Proclaim him in the streets, incense her kinsmen,   70
  And, though he in a fertile climate dwell,
  Plague him with flies; though that his joy be joy,
  Yet throw such changes of vexation on't
  As it may lose some colour.
RODERIGO. Here is her father's house; I'll call aloud.
IAGO. Do; with like timorous accent and dire yell
  As when, by night and negligence, the fire
  Is spied in populous cities.
RODERIGO. What, ho, Brabantio! Signior Brabantio,
  ho!
IAGO. Awake! what, ho, Brabantio! thieves! thieves!
  thieves!   80
  Look to your house, your daughter, and your bags!
  Thieves! thieves!

Brabantio appears above, at a window

BRABANTIO. What is the reason of this terrible
  summons?
  What is the matter there?
RODERIGO. Signior, is all your family within?
IAGO. Are your doors locked?
BRABANTIO.   Why, wherefore ask you this?
IAGO. 'Zounds, sir, you're robbed; for shame, put on
  your gown;
  Your heart is burst; you have lost half your soul;
  Even now, now, very now, an old black ram
  Is tupping your white ewe. Arise, arise;   90
  Awake the snorting citizens with the bell,
  Or else the devil will make a grandsire of you.
  Arise, I say.
BRABANTIO.   What, have you lost your wits?
RODERIGO. Most reverend signior, do you know my
  voice?
BRABANTIO. Not I; what are you?
RODERIGO. My name is Roderigo.
BRABANTIO.   The worser welcome:

I have charged thee not to haunt about my doors;
In honest plainness thou hast heard me say
My daughter is not for thee; and now, in madness,
Being full of supper and distempering draughts,   100
Upon malicious knavery dost thou come
To start my quiet.
RODERIGO. Sir, sir, sir—
BRABANTIO.   But thou must needs be sure
My spirit and my place have in them power
To make this bitter to thee.
RODERIGO.   Patience, good sir.
BRABANTIO. What tell'st thou me of robbing? This is
    Venice:
My house is not a grange.
RODERIGO.   Most grave Brabantio,
In simple and pure soul I come to you.
IAGO. 'Zounds, sir, you are one of those that will not
    serve God, if the devil bid you. Because we come to   110
    do you service and you think we are ruffians, you'll
    have your daughter covered with a Barbary horse;
    you'll have your nephews neigh to you; you'll have
    coursers for cousins, and jennets for germans.
BRABANTIO. What profane wretch art thou?
IAGO. I am one, sir, that comes to tell you your
    daughter and the Moor are now making the beast
    with two backs.
BRABANTIO. Thou art a villain.
IAGO.   You are a senator.
BRABANTIO. This thou shalt answer; I know thee,
    Roderigo.   120
RODERIGO. Sir, I will answer anything. But I beseech
    you,
If't be your pleasure and most wise consent,
As partly I find it is, that your fair daughter,
At this odd-even and dull watch o' th'night,
Transported with no worse nor better guard
But with a knave of common hire, a gondolier,
To the gross clasps of a lascivious Moor—
If this be known to you, and your allowance,
We then have done you bold and saucy wrong;
But if you know not this, my manners tell me   130
We have your wrong rebuke. Do not believe
That, from the sense of all civility,
I thus would play and trifle with your reverence.
Your daughter, if you have not given her leave,
I say again, hath made a gross revolt,
Tying her duty, beauty, wit, and fortunes
In an extravagant and wheeling stranger
Of here and everywhere. Straight satisfy yourself.
If she be in her chamber or your house,
Let loose on me the justice of the state   140
For thus deluding you.
BRABANTIO.   Strike on the tinder, ho!
Give me a taper! call up all my people!
This accident is not unlike my dream;
Belief of it oppresses me already.
Light, I say! light!   *He goes in*
IAGO.   Farewell, for I must leave you:
It seems not meet nor wholesome to my place
To be produced—as, if I stay, I shall—
Against the Moor; for I do know the state,
However this may gall him with some check,
Cannot with safety cast him; for he's embarked   150
With such loud reason to the Cyprus wars,
Which even now stand in act, that, for their souls,
Another of his fathom they have none

To lead their business: in which regard,
Though I do hate him as I do hell-pains,
Yet, for necessity of present life,
I must show out a flag and sign of love,
Which is indeed but sign. That you shall surely find
    him,
Lead to the Sagittary the raiséd search,
And there will I be with him. So farewell.   160
                                        He goes

Enter, below, Brabantio, and Servants with torches

BRABANTIO. It is too true an evil: gone she is;
And what's to come of my despiséd time
Is nought but bitterness. Now, Roderigo,
Where didst thou see her? O unhappy girl!
With the Moor, say'st thou? Who would be a
    father!
How didst thou know 'twas she? O, she deceives me
Past thought! What said she to you? Get more
    tapers.
Raise all my kindred. Are they married, think you?
RODERIGO. Truly, I think they are.
BRABANTIO. O heaven! How got she out? O treason
    of the blood!   170
Fathers, from hence trust not your daughters' minds
By what you see them act! Is there not charms
By which the property of youth and maidhood
May be abused? Have you not read, Roderigo,
Of some such thing?
RODERIGO.   Yes, sir, I have indeed.
BRABANTIO. Call up my brother. O, that you had had
    her!
Some one way, some another. Do you know
Where we may apprehend her and the Moor?
RODERIGO. I think I can discover him, if you please
To get good guard and go along with me.   180
BRABANTIO. Pray you, lead on. At every house I'll call;
I may command at most. Get weapons, ho!
And raise some special officers of night.
On, good Roderigo; I'll deserve your pains.
                                        They go

Scene 2: *Another street*

Enter Othello, Iago, and Attendants with torches

IAGO. Though in the trade of war I have slain men,
Yet do I hold it very stuff o'th'conscience
To do no contrived murder. I lack iniquity
Sometimes to do me service. Nine or ten times
I had thought t'have jerked him here under the ribs.
OTHELLO. 'Tis better as it is.
IAGO.   Nay, but he prated,
And spoke such scurvy and provoking terms
Against your honour
That, with the little godliness I have,
I did full hard forbear him. But I pray, sir,   10
Are you fast married? For be sure of this,
That the magnifico is much beloved,
And hath in his effect a voice potential
As double as the duke's. He will divorce you,
Or put upon you what restraint and grievance
The law, with all his might to enforce it on,
Will give him cable.
OTHELLO.   Let him do his spite;
My services which I have done the signiory
Shall out-tongue his complaints. 'Tis yet to know—

Which, when I know that boasting is an honour,   20
I shall promulgate—I fetch my life and being
From men of royal siege; and my demerits
May speak unbonneted to as proud a fortune
As this that I have reached. For know, Iago,
But that I love the gentle Desdemona,
I would not my unhouséd free condition
Put into circumscription and confine
For the sea's worth. But look what lights come
   yond!
IAGO. Those are the raiséd father and his friends.
   You were best go in.
OTHELLO.   Not I; I must be found.   30
My parts, my title, and my perfect soul,
Shall manifest me rightly. Is it they?
IAGO. By Janus, I think no.

Enter Cassio, and certain Officers with torches

OTHELLO. The servants of the duke, and my lieutenant!
   The goodness of the night upon you, friends!
   What is the news?
CASSIO.   The duke does greet you, general,
And he requires your haste-post-haste appearance
Even on the instant.
OTHELLO.   What is the matter, think you?
CASSIO. Something from Cyprus, as I may divine.
It is a business of some heat: the galleys   40
Have sent a dozen sequent messengers
This very night at one another's heels;
And many of the consuls, raised and met,
Are at the duke's already. You have been hotly
   called for;
When, being not at your lodging to be found,
The senate hath sent about three several quests
To search you out.
OTHELLO.   'Tis well I am found by you.
I will but spend a word here in the house,
And go with you.   *He goes in*
CASSIO.   Ancient, what makes he here?
IAGO. Faith, he tonight hath boarded a land carack;   50
If it prove lawful prize, he's made for ever.
CASSIO. I do not understand.
IAGO.   He's married.
CASSIO.   To who?

Re-enter Othello

IAGO. Marry, to—Come, captain, will you go?
OTHELLO.   Have with you.
CASSIO. Here comes another troop to seek for you.
IAGO. It is Brabantio. General, be advised;
   He comes to bad intent.

*Enter Brabantio, Roderigo, and Officers with torches and
weapons*

OTHELLO.   Holla! stand there!
RODERIGO. Signior, it is the Moor.
                    Down with him, thief!
                    They draw on both sides
IAGO. You, Roderigo! come sir, I am for you.
OTHELLO. Keep up your bright swords, for the dew
   will rust them.
   Good signior, you shall more command with years   60
   Than with your weapons.
BRABANTIO. O thou foul thief, where hast thou stowed
   my daughter?
Damned as thou art, thou hast enchanted her:

For I'll refer me to all things of sense,
If she in chains of magic were not bound,
Whether a maid so tender, fair, and happy,
So opposite to marriage that she shunned
The wealthy curléd darlings of our nation,
Would ever have, t'incur a general mock,
Run from her guardage to the sooty bosom   70
Of such a thing as thou—to fear, not to delight.
Judge me the world, if 'tis not gross in sense
That thou hast practised on her with foul charms,
Abused her delicate youth with drugs or minerals
That weaken motion: I'll have't disputed on;
'Tis probable and palpable to thinking.
I therefore apprehend and do attach thee
For an abuser of the world, a practiser
Of arts inhibited and out of warrant.
Lay hold upon him. If he do resist,   80
Subdue him at his peril.
OTHELLO.   Hold your hands,
Both you of my inclining and the rest:
Were it my cue to fight, I should have known it
Without a prompter. Where will you that I go
To answer this your charge?
BRABANTIO.   To prison, till fit time
Of law and course of direct session
Call thee to answer.
OTHELLO.   What if I do obey?
How may the duke be therewith satisfied,
Whose messengers are here about my side,
Upon some present business of the state   90
To bring me to him?
1 OFFICER.   'Tis true, most worthy signior;
The duke's in council, and your noble self,
I am sure, is sent for.
BRABANTIO.   How! the duke in council!
In this time of the night! Bring him away.
Mine's not an idle cause: the duke himself,
Or any of my brothers of the state,
Cannot but feel this wrong as 'twere their own;
For if such actions may have passage free,
Bond-slaves and pagans shall our statesmen be.
                                   They go

Scene 3: *A council-chamber*

The Duke and Senators sitting at a table; Officers attending

DUKE. There is no composition in these news
   That gives them credit.
1 SENATOR.   Indeed they are disproportioned:
   My letters say a hundred and seven galleys.
DUKE. And mine, a hundred and forty.
2 SENATOR.   And mine, two hundred;
But though they jump not on a just account—
As in these cases where the aim reports
'Tis oft with difference—yet do they all confirm
A Turkish fleet, and bearing up to Cyprus.
DUKE. Nay, it is possible enough to judgement;
   I do not so secure me in the error,   10
   But the main article I do approve
   In fearful sense.
SAILOR [*without*]. What, ho! what, ho! what, ho!
1 OFFICER. A messenger from the galleys.

Enter Sailor

DUKE.   Now, what's the business?
SAILOR. The Turkish preparation makes for Rhodes;

So was I bid report here to the state
By Signior Angelo.
DUKE. How say you by this change?
1 SENATOR.   This cannot be,
By no assay of reason; 'tis a pageant
To keep us in false gaze. When we consider
Th'importancy of Cyprus to the Turk,   20
And let ourselves again but understand
That, as it more concerns the Turk than Rhodes,
So may he with more facile question bear it,
For that it stands not in such warlike brace,
But altogether lacks th'abilities
That Rhodes is dressed in—if we make thought of
this,
We must not think the Turk is so unskilful
To leave that latest which concerns him first,
Neglecting an attempt of ease and gain
To wake and wage a danger profitless.   30
DUKE. Nay, in all confidence, he's not for Rhodes.
1 OFFICER. Here is more news.

Enter a Messenger

MESSENGER. The Ottomites, reverend and gracious,
Steering with due course toward the isle of Rhodes,
Have there injointed with an after fleet.
1 SENATOR. Ay, so I thought. How many, as you
guess?
MESSENGER. Of thirty sail; and now they do re-stem
Their backward course, bearing with frank
appearance
Their purposes toward Cyprus. Signior Montano,
Your trusty and most valiant servitor,   40
With his free duty recommends you thus,
And prays you to relieve him.
DUKE. 'Tis certain then for Cyprus.
Marcus Luccicos, is not he in town?
1 SENATOR. He's now in Florence.
DUKE. Write from us to him; post-post-haste dispatch.
1 SENATOR. Here comes Brabantio and the valiant
Moor.

Enter Brabantio, Othello, Iago, Roderigo, and Officers

DUKE. Valiant Othello, we must straight employ you
Against the general enemy Ottoman.
[*to Brabantio*] I did not see you; welcome, gentle
signior;   50
We lacked your counsel and your help tonight.
BRABANTIO. So did I yours. Good your grace, pardon
me:
Neither my place nor aught I heard of business
Hath raised me from my bed, nor doth the general
care
Take hold on me; for my particular grief
Is of so flood-gate and o'erbearing nature
That it engluts and swallows other sorrows,
And yet is still itself.
DUKE.   Why, what's the matter?
BRABANTIO. My daughter! O, my daughter!
ALL.   Dead?
BRABANTIO.   Ay, to me:
She is abused, stolen from me and corrupted   60
By spells and medicines bought of mountebanks;
For nature so preposterously to err,
Being not deficient, blind, or lame of sense,
Sans witchcraft could not.
DUKE. Whoe'er he be that in this foul proceeding

Hath thus beguiled your daughter of herself,
And you of her, the bloody book of law
You shall yourself read in the bitter letter
After your own sense, yea, though our proper son
Stood in your action.
BRABANTIO.   Humbly I thank your grace. 70
Here is the man: this Moor, whom now, it seems,
Your special mandate for the state affairs
Hath hither brought.
ALL.   We are very sorry for't.
DUKE [*to Othello*]. What in your own part can you say
to this?
BRABANTIO. Nothing, but this is so.
OTHELLO. Most potent, grave, and reverend signiors,
My very noble and approved good masters,
That I have ta'en away this old man's daughter,
It is most true; true, I have married her:
The very head and front of my offending   80
Hath this extent, no more. Rude am I in my speech,
And little blest with the soft phrase of peace:
For since these arms of mine had seven years' pith
Till now some nine moons wasted, they have used
Their dearest action in the tented field;
And little of this great world can I speak
More than pertains to feats of broil and battle;
And therefore little shall I grace my cause
In speaking for myself. Yet, by your patience,
I will a round unvarnished tale deliver   90
Of my whole course of love: what drugs, what
charms,
What conjuration, and what mighty magic—
For such proceedings I am charged withal—
I won his daughter.
BRABANTIO.   A maiden never bold;
Of spirit so still and quiet that her motion
Blushed at herself; and she—in spite of nature,
Of years, of country, credit, everything—
To fall in love with what she feared to look on!
It is a judgement maimed and most imperfect
That will confess perfection so could err   100
Against all rules of nature, and must be driven
To find out practices of cunning hell
Why this should be. I therefore vouch again
That with some mixtures powerful o'er the blood,
Or with some dram conjured to this effect,
He wrought upon her.
DUKE.   To vouch this is no proof,
Without more wider and more overt test
Than these thin habits and poor likelihoods
Of modern seeming do prefer against him.
1 SENATOR. But, Othello, speak: 110
Did you by indirect and forcéd courses
Subdue and poison this young maid's affections?
Or came it by request and such fair question
As soul to soul affordeth?
OTHELLO.   I beseech you,
Send for the lady to the Sagittary,
And let her speak of me before her father;
If you do find me foul in her report,
The trust, the office I do hold of you,
Not only take away, but let your sentence
Even fall upon my life.
DUKE.   Fetch Desdemona hither.   120
OTHELLO. Ancient, conduct them; you best know the
place.   *Iago departs with attendants*
And till she come, as truly as to heaven

I do confess the vices of my blood,
So justly to your grave ears I'll present
How I did thrive in this fair lady's love,
And she in mine.
DUKE. Say it, Othello.
OTHELLO. Her father loved me, oft invited me,
Still questioned me the story of my life
From year to year—the battles, sieges, fortunes,   130
That I have passed.
I ran it through, even from my boyish days
To th'very moment that he bade me tell it:
Wherein I spake of most disastrous chances,
Of moving accidents by flood and field,
Of hair-breadth scapes i'th'imminent deadly breach,
Of being taken by the insolent foe,
And sold to slavery; of my redemption thence,
And portance in my travels' history:
Wherein of antres vast and deserts idle,   140
Rough quarries, rocks, and hills whose heads touch
      heaven,
It was my hint to speak—such was the process;
And of the Cannibals that each other eat,
The Anthropophagi, and men whose heads
Do grow beneath their shoulders. This to hear
Would Desdemona seriously incline;
But still the house affairs would draw her thence,
Which ever as she could with haste dispatch
She'ld come again, and with a greedy ear
Devour up my discourse; which I observing,   150
Took once a pliant hour, and found good means
To draw from her a prayer of earnest heart
That I would all my pilgrimage dilate,
Whereof by parcels she had something heard,
But not intentively. I did consent,
And often did beguile her of her tears
When I did speak of some distressful stroke
That my youth suffered. My story being done,
She gave me for my pains a world of sighs:
She swore, in faith 'twas strange, 'twas passing
      strange;   160
'Twas pitiful, 'twas wondrous pitiful;
She wished she had not heard it, yet she wished
That heaven had made her such a man; she
      thanked me,
And bade me, if I had a friend that loved her,
I should but teach him how to tell my story,
And that would woo her. Upon this hint I spake;
She loved me for the dangers I had passed,
And I loved her that she did pity them.
This only is the witchcraft I have used.
Here comes the lady; let her witness it.   170

Enter Desdemona, Iago, and Attendants

DUKE. I think this tale would win my daughter too.
      Good Brabantio,
Take up this mangled matter at the best:
Men do their broken weapons rather use
Than their bare hands.
BRABANTIO.   I pray you, hear her speak.
If she confess that she was half the wooer,
Destruction on my head, if my bad blame
Light on the man! Come hither, gentle mistress:
Do you perceive in all this company
Where most you owe obedience?
DESDEMONA.   My noble father,   180
I do perceive here a divided duty.

To you I am bound for life and education;
My life and education both do learn me
How to respect you. You are the lord of duty;
I am hitherto your daughter. But here's my
      husband;
And so much duty as my mother showed
To you, preferring you before her father,
So much I challenge that I may profess
Due to the Moor my lord.
BRABANTIO.   God bu'y! I've done.
Please it your grace, on to the state affairs.   190
I had rather to adopt a child than get it.
Come hither, Moor:
I here do give thee that with all my heart,
Which, but thou hast already, with all my heart
I would keep from thee. For your sake, jewel,
I am glad at soul I have no other child;
For thy escape would teach me tyranny,
To hang clogs on them. I have done, my Lord.
DUKE. Let me speak like yourself, and lay a sentence
Which, as a grise or step, may help these lovers   200
Into your favour.
When remedies are past, the griefs are ended
By seeing the worst, which late on hopes depended.
To mourn a mischief that is past and gone
Is the next way to draw new mischief on.
What cannot be preserved when Fortune takes,
Patience her injury a mockery makes.
The robbed that smiles steals something from the
      thief;
He robs himself that spends a bootless grief.
BRABANTIO. So let the Turk of Cyprus us beguile,   210
We lose it not so long as we can smile.
He bears the sentence well that nothing bears
But the free comfort which from thence he hears;
But he bears both the sentence and the sorrow
That to pay grief must of poor patience borrow.
These sentences, to sugar or to gall,
Being strong on both sides, are equivocal.
But words are words: I never yet did hear
That the bruised heart was piecèd through the ear.
I humbly beseech you, proceed to th'affairs of state.   220
DUKE. The Turk with a most mighty preparation
makes for Cyprus. Othello, the fortitude of the place
is best known to you; and though we have there a
substitute of most allowed sufficiency, yet opinion,
a sovereign mistress of effects, throws a more safer
voice on you: you must therefore be content to
slubber the gloss of your new fortunes with this
more stubborn and boisterous expedition.
OTHELLO. The tyrant Custom, most grave senators,
Hath made the flinty and steel couch of war   230
My thrice-driven bed of down. I do agnize
A natural and prompt alacrity
I find in hardness; and do undertake
These present wars against the Ottomites.
Most humbly therefore bending to your state,
I crave fit disposition for my wife,
Due reference of place and exhibition,
With such accommodation and besort
As levels with her breeding.
DUKE.   Why, if you please,
Be't at her father's.
BRABANTIO.   I'll not have it so.   240
OTHELLO. Nor I.
DESDEMONA.   Nor I; I would not there reside,

To put my father in impatient thoughts
By being in his eye. Most gracious duke,
To my unfolding lend your prosperous ear,
And let me find a charter in your voice
T'assist my simpleness.

DUKE. What would you, Desdemona?

DESDEMONA. That I did love the Moor to live with
  him,
My downright violence and scorn of fortunes
May trumpet to the world. My heart's subdued   250
Even to the very quality of my lord.
I saw Othello's visage in his mind,
And to his honours and his valiant parts
Did I my soul and fortunes consecrate.
So that, dear lords, if I be left behind,
A moth of peace and he go to the war,
The rights for why I love him are bereft me,
And I a heavy interim shall support
By his dear absence. Let me go with him.

OTHELLO. Let her have your voice.   260
Vouch with me, heaven, I therefore beg it not
To please the palate of my appetite;
Nor to comply with heat and young affects
In my distinct and proper satisfaction;
But to be free and bounteous to her mind.
And heaven defend your good souls that you think
I will your serious and great business scant
For she is with me. No, when light-winged toys
Of feathered Cupid seel with wanton dullness
My speculative and officed instruments,   270
That my disports corrupt and taint my business,
Let housewives make a skillet of my helm,
And all indign and base adversities
Make head against my estimation!

DUKE. Be it as you shall privately determine,
Either for her stay or going; th'affair cries haste,
And speed must answer it.

I SENATOR. You must away tonight.

OTHELLO.   With all my heart.

DUKE. At nine i'th'morning here we'll meet again.
Othello, leave some officer behind,   280
And he shall our commission bring to you;
With such things else of quality and respect
As doth import you.

OTHELLO.   So please your grace, my ancient:
A man he is of honesty and trust;
To his conveyance I assign my wife,
With what else needful your good grace shall think
To be sent after me.

DUKE.   Let it be so.
Good night to everyone. [to Brabantio] And,
  noble signior,
If virtue no delighted beauty lack,
Your son-in-law is far more fair than black.   290

I SENATOR. Adieu, brave Moor; use Desdemona well.

BRABANTIO. Look to her, Moor, if thou hast eyes to
  see:
She has deceived her father, and may thee.

OTHELLO. My life upon her faith!
                    Duke, Senators, Officers, etc.
                             depart
           Honest Iago,
My Desdemona must I leave to thee;
I prithee, let thy wife attend on her,
And bring them after in the best advantage.
Come, Desdemona, I have but an hour

Of love, of worldly matter and direction,
To spend with thee: we must obey the time.   300
           Othello and Desdemona go out

RODERIGO. Iago!

IAGO. What say'st thou, noble heart?

RODERIGO. What will I do, think'st thou?

IAGO. Why, go to bed and sleep.

RODERIGO. I will incontinently drown myself.

IAGO. If thou dost, I shall never love thee after. Why,
thou silly gentleman!

RODERIGO. It is silliness to live when to live is torment;
and then have we a prescription to die when death
is our physician.   310

IAGO. O villanous! I have looked upon the world for
four times seven years; and since I could distinguish
betwixt a benefit and an injury, I never found a man
that knew how to love himself. Ere I would say I
would drown myself for the love of a guinea-hen, I
would change my humanity with a baboon.

RODERIGO. What should I do? I confess it is my shame
to be so fond, but it is not in my virtue to amend it.

IAGO. Virtue! a fig! 'tis in ourselves that we are thus
or thus. Our bodies are gardens, to the which our   320
wills are gardeners; so that if we will plant nettles
or sow lettuce, set hyssop and weed up tine, supply
it with one gender of herbs or distract it with many,
either to have it sterile with idleness or manured
with industry—why, the power and corrigible
authority of this lies in our wills. If the beam of our
lives had not one scale of reason to poise another
of sensuality, the blood and baseness of our natures
would conduct us to most preposterous conclusions.
But we have reason to cool our raging motions, our   330
carnal stings, our unbitted lusts; whereof I take this,
that you call love, to be a set or scion.

RODERIGO. It cannot be.

IAGO. It is merely a lust of the blood and a permission
of the will. Come, be a man. Drown thyself! Drown
cats and blind puppies. I have professed me thy
friend, and I confess me knit to thy deserving with
cables of perdurable toughness. I could never better
stead thee than now. Put money in thy purse;
follow thou these wars; defeat thy favour with an   340
usurped beard. I say, put money in thy purse. It
cannot be that Desdemona should long continue her
love to the Moor—put money in thy purse—nor he
his to her: it was a violent commencement, and thou
shalt see an answerable sequestration—put but
money in thy purse. These Moors are changeable in
their wills—fill thy purse with money. The food
that to him now is as luscious as locusts, shall be
to him shortly as bitter as coloquintida. She must
change for youth: when she is sated with his body,   350
she will find the error of her choice. Therefore put
money in thy purse. If thou wilt needs damn thyself,
do it a more delicate way than drowning. Make all
the money thou canst. If sanctimony and a frail vow
betwixt an erring barbarian and a supersubtle
Venetian be not too hard for my wits and all the
tribe of hell, thou shalt enjoy her; therefore make
money. A pox of drowning thyself! 'Tis clean out of
the way. Seek thou rather to be hanged in compassing thy joy than to be drowned and go without   360
her.

RODERIGO. Wilt thou be fast to my hopes, if I depend
on the issue?

IAGO. Thou art sure of me. Go, make money. I have
  told thee often, and I re-tell thee again and again,
  I hate the Moor. My cause is hearted; thine hath no
  less reason. Let us be conjunctive in our revenge
  against him. If thou canst cuckold him, thou dost
  thyself a pleasure, me a sport. There are many events
  in the womb of time, which will be delivered.   370
  Traverse! go; provide thy money. We will have
  more of this tomorrow. Adieu.
RODERIGO. Where shall we meet i'th'morning?
IAGO. At my lodging.
RODERIGO. I'll be with thee betimes.
IAGO. Go to; farewell. Do you hear, Roderigo?
RODERIGO. What say you?
IAGO. No more of drowning, do you hear?
RODERIGO. I am changed.
IAGO. Go to; farewell. Put money enough in your   380
  purse.
RODERIGO. I'll sell all my land.   *Goes*
IAGO. Thus do I ever make my fool my purse;
  For I mine own gained knowledge should profane
  If I would time expend with such a snipe
  But for my sport and profit. I hate the Moor;
  And it is thought abroad that 'twixt my sheets
  He's done my office. I know not if't be true;
  Yet I, for mere suspicion in that kind,
  Will do as if for surety. He holds me well;   390
  The better shall my purpose work on him.
  Cassio's a proper man: let me see now;
  To get his place, and to plume up my will
  In double knavery. How? How? Let's see:
  After some time to abuse Othello's ear
  That he is too familiar with his wife;
  He hath a person and a smooth dispose
  To be suspected—framed to make women false.
  The Moor is of a free and open nature
  That thinks men honest that but seem to be so,   400
  And will as tenderly be led by th'nose
  As asses are.
  I have't. It is engendered. Hell and night
  Must bring this monstrous birth to the world's light.
                          Goes

ACT 2

Scene 1: *A sea-port in Cyprus. An open place near*
the quay

Enter Montano and two Gentlemen

MONTANO. What from the cape can you discern at sea?
1 GENTLEMAN. Nothing at all: it is a high-wrought
  flood;
  I cannot 'twixt the heaven and the main
  Descry a sail.
MONTANO. Methinks the wind hath spoke aloud at
  land;
  A fuller blast ne'er shook our battlements.
  If it hath ruffianed so upon the sea,
  What ribs of oak, when mountains melt on them,
  Can hold the mortise? What shall we hear of this?
2 GENTLEMAN. A segregation of the Turkish fleet: 10
  For do but stand upon the foaming shore,
  The chidden billow seems to pelt the clouds;
  The wind-shaked surge, with high and monstrous
  mane,
  Seems to cast water on the burning Bear,
  And quench the guards of th'ever-fixéd pole.

  I never did like molestation view
  On the enchaféd flood.
MONTANO.   If that the Turkish fleet
  Be not ensheltered and embayed, they are drowned;
  It is impossible they bear it out.

Enter a third Gentleman

3 GENTLEMAN. News, lads! our wars are done: 20
  The desperate tempest hath so banged the Turks
  That their designment halts. A noble ship of Venice
  Hath seen a grievous wreck and sufferance
  On most part of their fleet.
MONTANO. How! is this true?
3 GENTLEMAN.   The ship is here put in,
  A Veronesa; Michael Cassio,
  Lieutenant to the warlike Moor Othello,
  Is come on shore; the Moor himself at sea,
  And is in full commission here for Cyprus.
MONTANO. I am glad on't; 'tis a worthy governor.   30
3 GENTLEMAN. But this same Cassio, though he speak
  of comfort
  Touching the Turkish loss, yet he looks sadly,
  And prays the Moor be safe; for they were parted
  With foul and violent tempest.
MONTANO.   Pray heaven he be;
  For I have served him, and the man commands
  Like a full soldier. Let's to the sea-side, ho!
  As well to see the vessel that's come in
  As to throw out our eyes for brave Othello,
  Even till we make the main and th'aerial blue
  An indistinct regard.
3 GENTLEMAN.   Come, let's do so;   40
  For every minute is expectancy
  Of more arrivance.

Enter Cassio

CASSIO. Thanks you, the valiant of this warlike isle,
  That so approve the Moor! O, let the heavens
  Give him defence against the elements,
  For I have lost him on a dangerous sea.
MONTANO. Is he well shipped?
CASSIO. His bark is stoutly timbered, and his pilot
  Of very expert and approved allowance;
  Therefore my hopes, not forfeited to death,   50
  Stand in bold cure.
            [*a cry heard*]: 'A sail, a sail, a sail!'

Enter a fourth Gentleman

CASSIO. What noise?
4 GENTLEMAN. The town is empty; on the brow
  o'th'sea
  Stand ranks of people, and they cry 'A sail!'
CASSIO. My hopes do shape him for the Governor.
                          Guns heard
2 GENTLEMAN. They do discharge their shot of
  courtesy:
  Our friends at least.
CASSIO.   I pray you, sir, go forth,
  And give us truth who 'tis that is arrived.
2 GENTLEMAN. I shall.   *Goes*
MONTANO. But, good lieutenant, is your general
  wived?   60
CASSIO. Most fortunately: he hath achieved a maid
  That paragons description and wild fame;
  One that excels the quirks of blazoning pens,
  And in th'essential vesture of creation
  Does tire the ingener.

Re-enter second Gentleman

How now! who has put in?

2 GENTLEMAN. 'Tis one Iago, ancient to the general.

CASSIO. He's had most favourable and happy speed:
Tempests themselves, high seas, and howling winds,
The guttered rocks, and congregated sands,
Traitors insteeped to clog the guiltless keel,   70
As having sense of beauty, do omit
Their mortal natures, letting go safely by
The divine Desdemona.

MONTANO.   What is she?

CASSIO. She that I spake of, our great captain's captain,
Left in the conduct of the bold Iago;
Whose footing here anticipates our thoughts
A se'nnight's speed. Great Jove, Othello guard,
And swell his sail with thine own powerful breath,
That he may bless this bay with his tall ship,
Make love's quick pants in Desdemona's arms,   80
Give renewed fire to our extinct spirits,
And bring all Cyprus comfort.

Enter Desdemona, Emilia, Iago, Roderigo, and Attendants

O, behold,
The riches of the ship is come on shore!
You men of Cyprus, let her have your knees.
Hail to thee, lady! and the grace of heaven,
Before, behind thee, and on every hand,
Enwheel thee round!

DESDEMONA.   I thank you, valiant Cassio.
What tidings can you tell me of my lord?

CASSIO. He is not yet arrived; nor know I aught
But that he's well and will be shortly here.   90

DESDEMONA. O, but I fear—How lost you company?

CASSIO. The great contention of the sea and skies
Parted our fellowship. But, hark! a sail!

[*a cry heard*], 'A sail, a sail!', [*and then guns*]

2 GENTLEMAN. They give their greeting to the citadel:
This likewise is a friend.

CASSIO.   See for the news.

Gentleman goes

Good ancient, you are welcome. [*to Emilia*]
Welcome, mistress.
Let it not gall your patience, good Iago,
That I extend my manners; 'tis my breeding
That gives me this bold show of courtesy.

Kisses her

IAGO. Sir, would she give you so much of her lips   100
As of her tongue she oft bestows on me,
You'd have enough.

DESDEMONA. Alas, she has no speech.

IAGO.   In faith, too much;
I find it still when I have list to sleep.
Marry, before your ladyship, I grant,
She puts her tongue a little in her heart
And chides with thinking.

EMILIA. You have little cause to say so.

IAGO. Come on, come on; you are pictures out of
doors, bells in your parlours, wild-cats in your   110
kitchens; saints in your injuries, devils being
offended; players in your housewifery, and hussies
in your beds.

DESDEMONA. O, fie upon thee, slanderer!

IAGO. Nay, it is true, or else I am a Turk:
You rise to play, and go to bed to work.

EMILIA. You shall not write my praise.

IAGO.   No, let me not.

DESDEMONA. What wouldst thou write of me, if thou
shouldst praise me?

IAGO. O gentle lady, do not put me to't;   120
For I am nothing if not critical.

DESDEMONA. Come on, assay—There's one gone to
the harbour?

IAGO. Ay, madam.

DESDEMONA [*aside*]. I am not merry; but I do beguile
The thing I am by seeming otherwise.
[*aloud*] Come, how wouldst thou praise me?

IAGO. I am about it; but indeed my invention comes
from my pate as birdlime does from frieze—it
plucks out brains and all. But my muse labours, and
thus she is delivered.
If she be fair and wise, fairness and wit,
The one's for use, the other useth it.

DESDEMONA. Well praised! How if she be black and
witty?

IAGO. If she be black, and thereto have a wit,   130
She'll find a white that shall her blackness hit.

DESDEMONA. Worse and worse.

EMILIA. How if fair and foolish?

IAGO. She never yet was foolish that was fair;
For even her folly helped her to an heir.

DESDEMONA. These are old fond paradoxes to make
fools laugh i'th'alehouse. What miserable praise hast   140
thou for her that's foul and foolish?

IAGO. There's none so foul, and foolish thereunto,
But does foul pranks which fair and wise
ones do.

DESDEMONA. O heavy ignorance! thou praisest the
worst best. But what praise couldst thou bestow on
a deserving woman indeed—one that in the
authority of her merit did justly put on the vouch
of very malice itself?

IAGO. She that was ever fair, and never proud,
Had tongue at will, and yet was never loud,   150
Never lacked gold, and yet went never gay,
Fled from her wish, and yet said 'Now
I may';
She that, being angered, her revenge
being nigh,
Bade her wrong stay, and her displeasure fly;
She that in wisdom never was so frail
To change the cod's head for the
salmon's tail;
She that could think, and ne'er disclose
her mind,
See suitors following, and not look behind;
She was a wight, if ever such wight were—

DESDEMONA. To do what?   160

IAGO. To suckle fools and chronicle small beer.

DESDEMONA. O most lame and impotent conclusion!
Do not learn of him, Emilia, though he be thy
husband. How say you, Cassio? Is he not a most
profane and liberal counsellor?

CASSIO. He speaks home, madam. You may relish him
more in the soldier than in the scholar.

IAGO [*aside*]. He takes her by the palm. Ay, well said,
whisper. With as little a web as this will I ensnare as
great a fly as Cassio. Ay, smile upon her, do; I will   170
gyve thee in thine own courtship. You say true:
'tis so, indeed. If such tricks as these strip you out
of your lieutenantry, it had been better you had not

kissed your three fingers so oft, which now again
you are most apt to play the sir in. Very good;
well kissed! an excellent courtesy! 'tis so, indeed, Yet
again your fingers to your lips? Would they were
clyster-pipes for your sake! *Trumpets within*
[aloud] The Moor! I know his trumpet.
CASSIO.   'Tis truly so.
DESDEMONA. Let's meet him and receive him.
CASSIO.   Lo where he comes! 180

Enter Othello and Attendants

OTHELLO. O my fair warrior!
DESDEMONA.   My dear Othello!
OTHELLO. It gives me wonder great as my content
To see you here before me. O my soul's joy!
If after every tempest come such calms,
May the winds blow till they have wakened death!
And let the labouring bark climb hills of seas
Olympus-high and duck again as low
As hell's from heaven! If it were now to die,
'Twere now to be most happy; for I fear,
My soul hath her content so absolute
That not another comfort like to this
Succeeds in unknown fate.
DESDEMONA.   The heavens forbid
But that our loves and comforts should increase,
Even as our days do grow!   .
OTHELLO.   Amen to that, sweet powers!
I cannot speak enough of this content:
It stops me here; it is too much of joy.
And this, and this, the greatest discords be
                                        They kiss
That e'er our hearts shall make!
IAGO *[aside]*. O, you are well tuned now! But I'll set
down the pegs that make this music, as honest as 200
I am.
OTHELLO. Come, let's to the castle.
News, friends: our wars are done; the Turks are
  drowned.
How does my old acquaintance of this isle?
Honey, you shall be well desired in Cyprus;
I have found great love amongst them. O my sweet,
I prattle out of fashion, and I dote
In mine own comfort. I prithee, good Iago,
Go to the bay, and disembark my coffers;
Bring thou the master to the citadel;   210
He is a good one, and his worthiness
Does challenge much respect. Come, Desdemona,
Once more well met at Cyprus.

                        All but Iago and Roderigo depart
IAGO. Do thou meet me presently at the harbour.
Come hither. If thou be'st valiant—as they say base
men being in love have then a nobility in their
natures more than is native to them—list me. The
lieutenant tonight watches on the court of guard.
First, I must tell thee this: Desdemona is directly
in love with him.   220
RODERIGO. With him! why, 'tis not possible.
IAGO. Lay thy finger thus, and let thy soul be instructed. Mark me with what violence she first loved
the Moor but for bragging and telling her fantastical
lies. And will she love him still for prating?—let not
thy discreet heart think it. Her eye must be fed; and
what delight shall she have to look on the devil?
When the blood is made dull with the act of sport,
there should be—again to inflame it and to give

satiety a fresh appetite—loveliness in favour, 230
sympathy in years, manners, and beauties; all which
the Moor is defective in. Now, for want of these
required conveniencies, her delicate tenderness will
find itself abused, begin to heave the gorge, disrelish
and abhor the Moor. Very nature will instruct her
in it and compel her to some second choice.
Now, sir, this granted—as it is a most pregnant and
unforced position—who stands so eminent in the
degree of this fortune as Cassio does?—a knave very
voluble; no further conscionable than in putting on 240
the mere form of civil and humane seeming, for the
better compassing of his salt and most hidden loose
affection. Why, none; why, none—a slipper and
subtle knave; a finder-out of occasions; that has an
eye can stamp and counterfeit advantages, though
true advantage never present itself; a devilish knave!
Besides, the knave is handsome, young, and hath all
those requisites in him that folly and green minds
look after; a pestilent complete knave; and the
woman hath found him already.   250
RODERIGO. I cannot believe that in her; she's full of
most blest condition.
IAGO. Blest fig's-end! The wine she drinks is made of
grapes. If she had been blest, she would never have
loved the Moor. Blest pudding! Didst thou not see
her paddle with the palm of his hand? Didst not
mark that?
RODERIGO. Yes, that I did; but that was but courtesy.
IAGO. Lechery, by this hand; an index and obscure
prologue to the history of lust and foul thoughts. 260
They met so near with their lips that their breaths
embraced together—villanous thoughts, Roderigo!
When these mutualities so marshal the way, hard at
hand comes the master and main exercise, th'incorporate conclusion. Pish! But, sir, be you ruled
by me. I have brought you from Venice. Watch you
tonight; for the command, I'll lay't upon you.
Cassio knows you not; I'll not be far from you. Do
you find some occasion to anger Cassio, either by
speaking too loud or tainting his discipline, or from 270
what other course you please which the time shall
more favourably minister.
RODERIGO. Well.
IAGO. Sir, he's rash and very sudden in choler, and
haply may strike at you—provoke him that he may;
for even out of that will I cause these of Cyprus
to mutiny, whose qualification shall come into no
true taste again but by the displanting of Cassio.
So shall you have a shorter journey to your desires
by the means I shall then have to prefer them, and 280
the impediment most profitably removed, without
the which there were no expectation of our
prosperity.
RODERIGO. I will do this, if you can bring it to any
opportunity.
IAGO. I warrant thee. Meet me by and by at the
citadel. I must fetch his necessaries ashore. Farewell.
RODERIGO. Adieu.   *Goes*
IAGO. That Cassio loves her, I do well believe't;
That she loves him, 'tis apt and of great credit.   290
The Moor, howbeit that I endure him not,
Is of a constant, loving, noble nature;
And I dare think he'll prove to Desdemona
A most dear husband. Now, I do love her too,
Not out of absolute lust—though peradventure

I stand accountant for as great a sin—
But partly led to diet my revenge
For that I do suspect the lusty Moor
Hath leaped into my seat, the thought whereof
Doth like a poisonous mineral gnaw my inwards;   300
And nothing can or shall content my soul
Till I am evened with him, wife for wife;
Or failing so, yet that I put the Moor
At least into a jealousy so strong
That judgement cannot cure. Which thing to do,
If this poor trash of Venice, whom I leash
For his quick hunting, stand the putting on,
I'll have our Michael Cassio on the hip,
Abuse him to the Moor in the rank garb—
For I fear Cassio with my night-cap too—   310
Make the Moor thank me, love me, and reward me,
For making him egregiously an ass,
And practising upon his peace and quiet
Even to madness. 'Tis here, but yet confused;
Knavery's plain face is never seen till used.   *Goes*

Scene 2: *A street*

Enter a Herald with a proclamation; people following

HERALD. It is Othello's pleasure, our noble and valiant
general, that, upon certain tidings now arrived importing the mere perdition of the Turkish fleet,
every man put himself into triumph; some to dance,
some to make bonfires, each man to what sport and
revels his addiction leads him: for, besides these
beneficial news, it is the celebration of his nuptial.
So much was his pleasure should be proclaimed.
All offices are open, and there is full liberty of feasting from this present hour of five till the bell have   10
told eleven. Heaven bless the isle of Cyprus and our
noble general Othello!   *He moves on*

Scene 3: *A hall in the citadel*

Enter Othello, Desdemona, Cassio, and Attendants

OTHELLO. Good Michael, look you to the guard
  tonight.
Let's teach ourselves that honourable stop,
Not to outsport discretion.
CASSIO. Iago hath direction what to do;
But notwithstanding with my personal eye
Will I look to't.
OTHELLO.   Iago is most honest.
Michael, good night; tomorrow with your earliest
Let me have speech with you. Come, my dear love,
The purchase made, the fruits are to ensue;
That profit's yet to come 'tween me and you.   10
Good night.
                          Othello, Desdemona, and
                          Attendants depart

Enter Iago

CASSIO. Welcome, Iago; we must to the watch.
IAGO. Not this hour, lieutenant; 'tis not yet ten
o'clock. Our general cast us thus early for the love
of his Desdemona; who let us not therefore blame:
he hath not yet made wanton the night with her, and
she is sport for Jove.
CASSIO. She's a most exquisite lady.
IAGO. And, I'll warrant her, full of game.
CASSIO. Indeed she's a most fresh and delicate creature.   20

IAGO. What an eye she has! methinks it sounds a parley
to provocation.
CASSIO. An inviting eye; and yet methinks right
modest.
IAGO. And when she speaks, is it not an alarum to love?
CASSIO. She is indeed perfection.
IAGO. Well, happiness to their sheets! Come, lieutenant, I have a stoup of wine; and here without
are a brace of Cyprus gallants that would fain have
a measure to the health of black Othello.   30
CASSIO. Not tonight, good Iago; I have very poor and
unhappy brains for drinking. I could well wish
courtesy would invent some other custom of entertainment.
IAGO. O, they are our friends—but one cup; I'll drink
for you.
CASSIO. I have drunk but one cup tonight, and that
was craftily qualified too, and behold what innova-
tion it makes here. I am unfortunate in the infirmity
and dare not task my weakness with any more.   40
IAGO. What, man! 'Tis a night of revels; the gallants
desire it.
CASSIO. Where are they?
IAGO. Here at the door; I pray you, call them in.
CASSIO. I'll do't; but it dislikes me.   *Goes*
IAGO. If I can fasten but one cup upon him,
With that which he hath drunk tonight already,
He'll be as full of quarrel and offence
As my young mistress' dog. Now my sick fool
  Roderigo,
Whom love hath turned almost the wrong side out,   50
To Desdemona hath tonight caroused
Potations pottle-deep; and he's to watch.
Three else of Cyprus, noble swelling spirits,
That hold their honours in a wary distance,
The very elements of this warlike isle,
Have I tonight flustered with flowing cups;
And they watch too. Now, 'mongst this flock of
  drunkards,
Am I to put our Cassio in some action
That may offend the isle. But here they come;
If consequence do but approve my dream,   60
My boat sails freely, both with wind and stream.

Re-enter Cassio; with him Montano and Gentlemen;
Servants following with wine

CASSIO. 'Fore God, they have given me a rouse
already.
MONTANO. Good faith, a little one; not past a pint, as
I am a soldier.
IAGO. Some wine, ho!
  [*sings*] And let me the canakin clink, clink;
           And let me the canakin clink;
             A soldier's a man;
             O, man's life's but a span;   70
           Why, then, let a soldier drink.
Some wine, boys!
CASSIO. 'Fore God, an excellent song.
IAGO. I learned it in England, where indeed they are
most potent in potting; your Dane, your German,
and your swag-bellied Hollander—Drink, ho!—are
nothing to your English.
CASSIO. Is your Englishman so exquisite in his
drinking?
IAGO. Why, he drinks you with facility your Dane   80
dead drunk; he sweats not to overthrow your

Almain; he gives your Hollander a vomit ere the
next pottle can be filled.
CASSIO. To the health of our general!
MONTANO. I am for it, lieutenant, and I'll do you
justice.
IAGO. O sweet England!
  [sings] King Stephen was and-a worthy peer,
       His breeches cost him but a crown;
       He held them sixpence all too dear,   90
         With that he called the tailor lown.

       He was a wight of high renown,
       And thou art but of low degree;
       'Tis pride that pulls the country down;
         Then take thy auld cloak about thee.
Some wine, ho!
CASSIO. Why, this is a more exquisite song than the
other.
IAGO. Will you hear't again?
CASSIO. No; for I hold him to be unworthy of his place   100
that does those things. Well, God's above all; and
there be souls must be saved, and there be souls must
not be saved.
IAGO. It's true, good lieutenant.
CASSIO. For mine own part—no offence to the
general, nor any man of quality—I hope to be saved.
IAGO. And so do I too, lieutenant.
CASSIO. Ay, but, by your leave, not before me; the
lieutenant is to be saved before the ancient. Let's
have no more of this; let's to our affairs. God forgive   110
us our sins! Gentlemen, let's look to our business.
Do not think, gentlemen, I am drunk; this is my
ancient; this is my right hand, and this is my left
hand. I am not drunk now: I can stand well enough,
and I speak well enough.
ALL. Excellent well.
CASSIO. Why, very well then; you must not think then
that I am drunk.   *Goes out*
MONTANO. To th'platform, masters; come, let's set the
watch.   120
IAGO. You see this fellow that is gone before:
  He is a soldier fit to stand by Caesar
  And give direction; and do but see his vice—
  'Tis to his virtue a just equinox,
  The one as long as th'other. 'Tis pity of him.
  I fear the trust Othello puts him in,
  On some odd time of his infirmity,
  Will shake this island.
MONTANO.   But is he often thus?
IAGO. 'Tis evermore the prologue to his sleep:
  He'll watch the horologe a double set,   130
  If drink rock not his cradle.
MONTANO.   It were well
  The general were put in mind of it.
  Perhaps he sees it not, or his good nature
  Prizes the virtue that appears in Cassio,
  And looks not on his evil: is not this true?

Enter Roderigo

IAGO [aside]. How, now, Roderigo!
  I pray you, after the lieutenant; go.   *Roderigo goes*
MONTANO. And 'tis great pity that the noble Moor
  Should hazard such a place as his own second
  With one of an ingraft infirmity: 140
  It were an honest action to say
  So to the Moor.

IAGO.   Not I, for this fair island:
  I do love Cassio well, and would do much
  To cure him of this evil.[*a cry within*], 'Help! Help!'
                       But hark! what noise?

Re-enter Cassio, pursuing Roderigo

CASSIO. 'Zounds, you rogue, you rascal!
MONTANO. What's the matter, lieutenant?
CASSIO. A knave teach me my duty! I'll beat the knave
  Into a twiggen bottle.
RODERIGO.   Beat me!
CASSIO.   Dost prate, rogue?
                              Striking Roderigo
MONTANO. Nay, good lieutenant; pray sir, hold your
  hand.
CASSIO. Let go, sir, or I'll knock you o'er the mazard. 150
MONTANO. Come, come, you're drunk.
CASSIO. Drunk!   *They fight*
IAGO [aside]. Away, I say; go out and cry a mutiny.
                                  Roderigo goes
  [*aloud*] Nay, good lieutenant! God's will, gentlemen!
  Help, ho!—lieutenant—sir—Montano—sir—
  Help, masters!—Here's a goodly watch indeed!
                              A bell rings
  Who's that that rings the bell?—Diablo, ho!
  The town will rise. God's will, lieutenant, hold;
  You will be shamed for ever.

Re-enter Othello and Attendants

OTHELLO. What is the matter here?
MONTANO.   'Zounds, I bleed still. 160
  I am hurt to th'death. He dies.
                          Assailing Cassio again
OTHELLO.   Hold, for your lives!
IAGO. Hold, ho! Lieutenant—sir—Montano—
  gentlemen—
  Have you forgot all sense of place and duty?
  The general speaks to you; hold, hold, for shame!
OTHELLO. Why, how now, ho! from whence ariseth
  this?
  Are we turned Turks, and to ourselves do that
  Which heaven hath forbid the Ottomites?
  For Christian shame, put by this barbarous brawl.
  He that stirs next to carve for his own rage
  Holds his soul light; he dies upon his motion.   170
  Silence that dreadful bell; it frights the isle
  From her propriety. What is the matter, masters?
  Honest Iago, that look'st dead with grieving,
  Speak who began this; on thy love, I charge thee.
IAGO. I do not know. Friends all but now, even now,
  In quarter and in terms like bride and groom
  Divesting them for bed; and then, but now,
  As if some planet had unwitted men,
  Swords out, and tilting one at other's breast,
  In opposition bloody. I cannot speak   180
  Any beginning to this peevish odds;
  And would in action glorious I had lost
  Those legs that brought me to a part of it!
OTHELLO. How comes it, Michael, you are thus
  forgot?
CASSIO. I pray you, pardon me; I cannot speak.
OTHELLO. Worthy Montano, you were wont be civil;
  The gravity and stillness of your youth
  The world hath noted, and your name is great
  In mouths of wisest censure: what's the matter
  That you unlace your reputation thus,   190

And spend your rich opinion for the name
Of a night-brawler? give me answer to it.
MONTANO. Worthy Othello, I am hurt to danger;
  Your officer, Iago, can inform you—
  While I spare speech, which something now offends
  me—
  Of all that I do know; nor know I aught
  By me that's said or done amiss this night—
  Unless self-charity be sometimes a vice,
  And to defend ourselves it be a sin
  When violence assails us.
OTHELLO.   Now, by heaven,   200
  My blood begins my safer guides to rule,
  And passion, having my best judgement collied,
  Assays to lead the way. If I once stir,
  Or do but lift this arm, the best of you
  Shall sink in my rebuke. Give me to know
  How this foul rout began, who set it on,
  And he that is approved in this offence,
  Though he had twinned with me, both at a birth,
  Shall lose me. What! in a town of war,
  Yet wild, the people's hearts brimful of fear,   210
  To manage private and domestic quarrel,
  In night, and on the court and guard of safety!
  'Tis monstrous. Iago, who began't?
MONTANO. If partially affined, or leagued in office,
  Thou dost deliver more or less than truth,
  Thou art no soldier.
IAGO.   Touch me not so near;
  I had rather have this tongue cut from my mouth
  Than it should do offence to Michael Cassio;
  Yet, I persuade myself, to speak the truth
  Shall nothing wrong him. This it is, general.   220
  Montano and myself being in speech,
  There comes a fellow crying out for help,
  And Cassio following with determined sword
  To execute upon him. Sir, this gentleman
  Steps in to Cassio and entreats his pause;
  Myself the crying fellow did pursue,
  Lest by his clamour—as it so fell out—
  The town might fall in fright; he, swift of foot,
  Outran my purpose; and I returned the rather
  For that I heard the clink and fall of swords,   230
  And Cassio high in oath; which till tonight
  I ne'er might say before. When I came back—
  For this was brief—I found them close together
  At blow and thrust; even as again they were
  When you yourself did part them.
  More of this matter can I not report;
  But men are men; the best sometimes forget.
  Though Cassio did some little wrong to him,
  As men in rage strike those that wish them best,
  Yet surely Cassio, I believe, received   240
  From him that fled some strange indignity,
  Which patiencē could not pass.
OTHELLO.   I know, Iago,
  Thy honesty and love doth mince this matter,
  Making it light to Cassio. Cassio, I love thee;
  But never more be officer of mine.

Re-enter Desdemona, attended

  Look if my gentle love be not raised up!
  I'll make thee an example.
DESDEMONA.   What's the matter?
OTHELLO. All's well, dear sweeting; come away to
  bed.

Sir, for your hurts, myself will be your surgeon.
                        They lead Montano away
Iago, look with care about the town,   250
And silence those whom this vile brawl distracted.
Come, Desdemona: 'tis the soldiers' life
To have their balmy slumbers waked with strife.
                        All but Iago and Cassio depart
IAGO. What, are you hurt, lieutenant?
CASSIO. Ay, past all surgery.
IAGO. Marry, heaven forbid!
CASSIO. Reputation, reputation, reputation! O, I have
  lost my reputation! I have lost the immortal part of
  myself, and what remains is bestial. My reputation,
  Iago, my reputation!   260
IAGO. As I am an honest man, I thought you had
  received some bodily wound; there is more sense in
  that than in reputation. Reputation is an idle and
  most false imposition; oft got without merit and lost
  without deserving. You have lost no reputation at
  all, unless you repute yourself such a loser. What,
  man! there are ways to recover the general again.
  You are but now cast in his mood, a punishment
  more in policy than in malice; even so as one would
  beat his offenceless dog to affright an imperious lion.   270
  Sue to him again, and he's yours.
CASSIO. I will rather sue to be despised than to deceive
  so good a commander with so light, so drunken,
  and so indiscreet an officer. Drunk! and speak
  parrot! and squabble! swagger! swear! and discourse
  fustian with one's own shadow! O thou invisible
  spirit of wine, if thou hast no name to be known
  by, let us call thee devil!
IAGO. What was he that you followed with your
  sword? What had he done to you?   280
CASSIO. I know not.
IAGO. Is't possible?
CASSIO. I remember a mass of things, but nothing
  distinctly; a quarrel, but nothing wherefore. O, that
  men should put an enemy in their mouths to steal
  away their brains! that we should, with joy,
  pleasance, revel and applause, transform ourselves
  into beasts!
IAGO. Why, but you are now well enough. How
  came you thus recovered?   290
CASSIO. It hath pleased the devil drunkenness to give
  place to the devil wrath: one unperfectness shows
  me another, to make me frankly despise myself.
IAGO. Come, you are too severe a moraller. As the
  time, the place, and the condition of this country
  stands, I could heartily wish this had not befallen;
  but since it is as it is, mend it for your own good.
CASSIO. I will ask him for my place again; he shall tell
  me I am a drunkard! Had I as many mouths as
  Hydra, such an answer would stop them all. To be   300
  now a sensible man, by and by a fool, and presently
  a beast! O strange! Every inordinate cup is unblest,
  and the ingredience is a devil.
IAGO. Come, come, wine is a good familiar creature,
  if it be well used; exclaim no more against it. And,
  good lieutenant, I think you think I love you.
CASSIO. I have well approved it, sir. I drunk!
IAGO. You or any man living may be drunk at a time.
  I'll tell you what you shall do. Our general's wife is
  now the general: I may say so in this respect, for that 310
  he hath devoted and given up himself to the contemplation, mark and denotement of her parts and

graces. Confess yourself freely to her; importune her
help to put you in your place again. She is of so
free, so kind, so apt, so blessed a disposition, she
holds it a vice in her goodness not to do more than
she is requested. This broken joint between you and
her husband entreat her to splinter; and, my fortunes
against any lay worth naming, this crack of your
love shall grow stronger than it was before.   320
CASSIO. You advise me well.
IAGO. I protest, in the sincerity of love and honest
    kindness.
CASSIO. I think it freely; and betimes in the morning
    I will beseech the virtuous Desdemona to undertake
    for me. I am desperate of my fortunes if they check
    me here.
IAGO. You are in the right. Good night, lieutenant;
    I must to the watch.
CASSIO. Good night, honest Iago.   Goes 330
IAGO. And what's he then that says I play the villain,
    When this advice I give is free and honest,
    Probal to thinking, and indeed the course
    To win the Moor again? For 'tis most easy
    Th'inclining Desdemona to subdue
    In any honest suit. She's framed as fruitful
    As the free elements. And then for her
    To win the Moor, were't to renounce his baptism,
    All seals and symbols of redeeméd sin,
    His soul is so enfettered to her love   340
    That she may make, unmake, do what she list,
    Even as her appetite shall play the god
    With his weak function. How am I then a villain
    To counsel Cassio to this parallel course,
    Directly to his good? Divinity of hell!
    When devils will the blackest sins put on,
    They do suggest at first with heavenly shows,
    As I do now; for while this honest fool
    Plies Desdemona to repair his fortunes,
    And she for him pleads strongly to the Moor,   350
    I'll pour this pestilence into his ear,
    That she repeals him for her body's lust;
    And by how much she strives to do him good,
    She shall undo her credit with the Moor.
    So will I turn her virtue into pitch,
    And out of her own goodness make the net
    That shall enmesh them all.

Enter Roderigo

                            How now, Roderigo!
RODERIGO. I do follow here in the chase, not like a
    hound that hunts, but one that fills up the cry. My
    money is almost spent; I have been tonight exceed-   360
    ingly well cudgelled; and I think the issue will be,
    I shall have so much experience for my pains; and so,
    with no money at all and a little more wit, return
    again to Venice.
IAGO. How poor are they that have not patience!
    What wound did ever heal but by degrees?
    Thou know'st we work by wit and not by
    witchcraft,
    And wit depends on dilatory time.
    Does't not go well? Cassio hath beaten thee,
    And thou by that small hurt hast cashiered Cassio.   370
    Though other things grow fair against the sun,
    Yet fruits that blossom first will first be ripe.
    Content thyself awhile. By th'mass, 'tis morning;
    Pleasure and action make the hours seem short.

Retire thee; go where thou art billeted.
Away, I say; thou shalt know more hereafter.
Nay, get thee gone.   Roderigo goes
                    Two things are to be done:
My wife must move for Cassio to her mistress—
I'll set her on—
Myself the while to draw the Moor apart,   380
And bring him jump when he may Cassio find
Soliciting his wife. Ay, that's the way;
Dull not device by coldness and delay.   Goes

ACT 3
Scene 1: *The citadel. Outside Othello's lodging*

Enter Cassio and some Musicians

CASSIO. Masters, play here; I will content your pains;
    Something that's brief; and bid 'Good morrow,
    general'.   *Music*

Enter Clown

CLOWN. Why, masters, have your instruments been in
    Naples, that they speak i'th'nose thus?
1 MUSICIAN. How, sir, how?
CLOWN. Are these, I pray you, wind instruments?
1 MUSICIAN. Ay, marry, are they, sir.
CLOWN. O, thereby hangs a tail.
1 MUSICIAN. Whereby hangs a tale, sir?
CLOWN. Marry, sir, by many a wind instrument that   10
    I know. But, masters, here's money for you; and the
    general so likes your music, that he desires you, for
    love's sake, to make no more noise with it.
1 MUSICIAN. Well, sir, we will not.
CLOWN. If you have any music that may not be heard,
    to't again; but, as they say, to hear music the general
    does not greatly care.
1 MUSICIAN. We have none such, sir.
CLOWN. Then put up your pipes in your bag, for I'll
    away. Go; vanish into air; away!   *Musicians go* 20
CASSIO. Dost thou hear, my honest friend?
CLOWN. No, I hear not your honest friend; I hear you.
CASSIO. Prithee, keep up thy quillets. There's a poor
    piece of gold for thee: if the gentlewoman that
    attends the general's wife be stirring, tell her there's
    one Cassio entreats her a little favour of speech. Wilt
    thou do this?
CLOWN. She is stirring, sir; if she will stir hither, I
    shall seem to notify unto her.
CASSIO. Do, good my friend.   *Clown goes*

Enter Iago

                    In happy time, Iago.   30
IAGO. You have not been abed then?
CASSIO. Why, no; the day had broke before we parted.
    I have made bold, Iago,
    To send in to your wife: my suit to her
    Is that she will to virtuous Desdemona
    Procure me some access.
IAGO.   I'll send her to you presently;
    And I'll devise a mean to draw the Moor
    Out of the way, that your converse and business
    May be more free.
CASSIO. I humbly thank you for't. [*Iago goes*] I never
    knew   40
    A Florentine more kind and honest.

Enter Emilia

EMILIA. Good morrow, good lieutenant: I am sorry
For your displeasure; but all will sure be well.
The general and his wife are talking of it,
And she speaks for you stoutly. The Moor replies
That he you hurt is of great fame in Cyprus
And great affinity, and that in wholesome wisdom
He might not but refuse you; but he protests he
  loves you,
And needs no other suitor but his liking
To take the safest occasion by the front   50
To bring you in again.
CASSIO.   Yet, I beseech you,
If you think fit, or that it may be done,
Give me advantage of some brief discourse
With Desdemon alone.
EMILIA.   Pray you, come in;
I will bestow you where you shall have time
To speak your bosom freely.
CASSIO   I am much bound to you.   *They go*

Scene 2: *A room in the citadel*

Enter Othello, Iago, and Gentlemen

OTHELLO. These letters give, Iago, to the pilot,
And by him do my duties to the senate.
That done, I will be walking on the works;
Repair there to me.
IAGO.   Well, my good lord, I'll do't.   *Goes*
OTHELLO. This fortification, gentlemen, shall we see't?
GENTLEMEN. We'll wait upon your lordship. *They go*

Scene 3: *Before the citadel*

Enter Desdemona, Cassio, and Emilia

DESDEMONA. Be thou assured, good Cassio, I will do
All my abilities in thy behalf.
EMILIA. Good madam, do; I warrant it grieves my
  husband
As if the case were his.
DESDEMONA. O, that's an honest fellow. Do not doubt,
  Cassio,
But I will have my lord and you again
As friendly as you were.
CASSIO.   Bounteous madam,
Whatever shall become of Michael Cassio,
He's never anything but your true servant.
DESDEMONA. I know't; I thank you. You do love my
  lord;   10
You have known him long; and be you well assured
He shall in strangeness stand no farther off
Than in a politic distance.
CASSIO.   Ay, but, lady,
That policy may either last so long,
Or feed upon such nice and waterish diet,
Or breed itself so out of circumstance,
That, I being absent, and my place supplied,
My general will forget my love and service.
DESDEMONA. Do not doubt that: before Emilia here
I give thee warrant of thy place. Assure thee,   20
If I do vow a friendship, I'll perform it
To the last article. My lord shall never rest:
I'll watch him tame, and talk him out of patience;
His bed shall seem a school, his board a shrift;
I'll intermingle everything he does
With Cassio's suit. Therefore be merry, Cassio;
For thy solicitor shall rather die

Than give thy cause away.

Enter Othello and Iago, at a distance

EMILIA. Madam, here comes my lord.
CASSIO. Madam, I'll take my leave.   30
DESDEMONA. Why, stay, and hear me speak.
CASSIO. Madam, not now: I am very ill at ease,
Unfit for mine own purposes.
DESDEMONA. Well, do your discretion.   *Cassio goes*
IAGO. Ha! I like not that.
OTHELLO. What dost thou say?
IAGO. Nothing, my lord; or if—I know not what.
OTHELLO. Was not that Cassio parted from my wife?
IAGO. Cassio, my lord! No, sure, I cannot think it,
That he would steal away so guilty-like,   40
Seeing you coming.
OTHELLO.   I do believe 'twas he.
DESDEMONA. How now, my lord!
I have been talking with a suitor here,
A man that languishes in your displeasure.
OTHELLO. Who is't you mean?
DESDEMONA. Why, your lieutenant, Cassio. Good
  my lord,
If I have any grace or power to move you,
His present reconciliation take;
For if he be not one that truly loves you,
That errs in ignorance and not in cunning,   50
I have no judgement in an honest face.
I prithee, call him back.
OTHELLO.   Went he hence now?
DESDEMONA. Ay, sooth; so humbled,
That he hath left part of his grief with me
To suffer with him. Good love, call him back.
OTHELLO. Not now, sweet Desdemon; some other
  time.
DESDEMONA. But shall't be shortly?
OTHELLO.   The sooner, sweet, for you.
DESDEMONA. Shall't be tonight at supper?
OTHELLO.   No, not tonight.
DESDEMONA. Tomorrow dinner then?
OTHELLO.   I shall not dine at home:
I meet the captains at the citadel.   60
DESDEMONA. Why then, tomorrow night; or Tuesday
  morn;
On Tuesday noon, or night; On Wednesday morn.
I prithee, name the time; but let it not
Exceed three days. In faith, he's penitent;
And yet his trespass, in our common reason—
Save that, they say, the wars must make example
Out of their best—is not almost a fault
T'incur a private check. When shall he come?
Tell me, Othello. I wonder in my soul
What you would ask me that I should deny,   70
Or stand so mammering on. What! Michael Cassio,
That came a-wooing with you, and so many a time,
When I have spoke of you dispraisingly,
Hath ta'en your part—to have so much to do
To bring him in! Trust me, I could do much—
OTHELLO. Prithee, no more. Let him come when he
  will;
I will deny thee nothing.
DESDEMONA.   Why, this is not a boon;
'Tis as I should entreat you wear your gloves,
Or feed on nourishing dishes, or keep you warm,
Or sue to you to do peculiar profit   80
To your own person. Nay, when I have a suit

Wherein I mean to touch your love indeed,
It shall be full of poise and difficult weight,
And fearful to be granted.
OTHELLO.   I will deny thee nothing.
Whereon, I do beseech thee, grant me this,
To leave me but a little to myself.
DESDEMONA. Shall I deny you? no; farewell, my lord.
OTHELLO. Farewell, my Desdemona, I'll come
straight.
DESDEMONA. Emilia, come. Be as your fancies teach
you;
Whate'er you be, I am obedient.   90
                    Desdemona and Emilia go
OTHELLO. Excellent wretch! Perdition catch my soul
But I do love thee; and when I love thee not
Chaos is come again.
IAGO.   My noble lord—
OTHELLO. What dost thou say, Iago?
IAGO.   Did Michael Cassio,
When you wooed my lady, know of your love?
OTHELLO. He did, from first to last. Why dost thou
ask?
IAGO. But for a satisfaction of my thought;
No further harm.
OTHELLO.   Why of thy thought, Iago?
IAGO. I did not think he had been acquainted with her.
OTHELLO. O, yes, and went between us very oft.   100
IAGO. Indeed!
OTHELLO. Indeed? ay, indeed. Discern'st thou aught
in that?
Is he not honest?
IAGO. Honest, my lord?
OTHELLO. Honest? ay, honest.
IAGO. My lord, for aught I know.
OTHELLO. What dost thou think?
IAGO. Think, my lord?
OTHELLO. Think, my lord! Alas, thou echo'st me,
As if there were some monster in thy thought   110
Too hideous to be shown. Thou dost mean some-
thing:
I heard thee say even now, thou likedst not that,
When Cassio left my wife. What didst not like?
And when I told thee he was of my counsel
In my whole course of wooing, thou criedst
'Indeed!'
And didst contract and purse thy brow together,
As if thou then hadst shut up in thy brain
Some horrible conceit. If thou dost love me,
Show me thy thought.
IAGO. My lord, you know I love you.
OTHELLO.   I think thou dost;   120
And for I know thou'rt full of love, and honest,
And weigh'st thy words before thou giv'st them
breath,
Therefore these stops of thine fright me the more:
For such things in a false disloyal knave
Are tricks of custom; but in a man that's just
They're close dilations, working from the heart
That passion cannot rule.
IAGO.   For Michael Cassio,
I dare be sworn I think that he is honest.
OTHELLO. I think so too.
IAGO.   Men should be what they seem;
Or those that be not, would they might seem none!   130
OTHELLO. Certain, men should be what they seem.
IAGO. Why then, I think Cassio's an honest man.

OTHELLO. Nay, yet there's more in this.
I prithee, speak to me as to thy thinkings,
As thou dost ruminate, and give thy worst of
thoughts
The worst of words.
IAGO.   Good my lord, pardon me:
Though I am bound to every act of duty,
I am not bound to that all slaves are free to.
Utter my thoughts! Why, say they are vile and
false—
As where's that palace whereinto foul things   140
Sometimes intrude not? who has a breast so pure,
But some uncleanly apprehensions
Keep leets and law-days, and in session sit
With meditations lawful?
OTHELLO. Thou dost conspire against thy friend, Iago,
If thou but think'st him wronged and mak'st his ear
A stranger to thy thoughts.
IAGO.   I do beseech you—
Though I perchance am vicious in my guess,
As, I confess, it is my nature's plague
To spy into abuses, and oft my jealousy   150
Shapes faults that are not—that your wisdom then,
From one that so imperfectly conceits,
Would take no notice, nor build yourself a trouble
Out of his scattering and unsure observance.
It were not for your quiet nor your good,
Nor for my manhood, honesty, or wisdom,
To let you know my thoughts.
OTHELLO.   What dost thou mean?
IAGO. Good name in man and woman, dear my lord,
Is the immediate jewel of their souls:
Who steals my purse steals trash—'tis something,
nothing;   160
'Twas mine, 'tis his, and has been slave to thousands;
But he that filches from me my good name
Robs me of that which not enriches him
And makes me poor indeed.
OTHELLO.   I'll know thy thoughts!
IAGO. You cannot, if my heart were in your hand;
Nor shall not, while 'tis in my custody.
OTHELLO. Ha!
IAGO.   O, beware, my lord, of jealousy;
It is the green-eyed monster, which doth mock
The meat it feeds on: that cuckold lives in bliss
Who, certain of his fate, loves not his wronger;   170
But, O, what damnéd minutes tells he o'er
Who dotes, yet doubts, suspects, yet fondly loves!
OTHELLO. O misery!
IAGO. Poor and content is rich, and rich enough;
But riches fineless is as poor as winter
To him that ever fears he shall be poor.
Good heaven the souls of all my tribe defend
From jealousy!
OTHELLO.   Why, why is this?
Think'st thou I'ld make a life of jealousy,
To follow still the changes of the moon   180
With fresh suspicions? No; to be once in doubt
Is once resolved. Exchange me for a goat,
When I shall turn the business of my soul
To such exsufflicate and blown surmise
Matching thy inference. 'Tis not to make me
jealous
To say my wife is fair, loves company,
Is free of speech, sings, plays and dances well;
Where virtue is, these are more virtuous;

Nor from mine own weak merits will I draw
The smallest fear or doubt of her revolt;   190
For she had eyes and chose me. No, Iago:
I'll see before I doubt; when I doubt, prove;
And on the proof, there is no more but this,
Away at once with love or jealousy!

IAGO. I am glad of it; for now I shall have reason
To show the love and duty that I bear you
With franker spirit. Therefore, as I am bound,
Receive it from me. I speak not yet of proof.
Look to your wife; observe her well with Cassio;
Wear your eye thus not jealous nor secure: 200
I would not have your free and noble nature
Out of self-bounty be abused. Look to't:
I know our country disposition well;
In Venice they do let heaven see the pranks
They dare not show their husbands; their best
      conscience
Is not to leave't undone, but keep't unknown.

OTHELLO. Dost thou say so?

IAGO. She did deceive her father, marrying you;
And when she seemed to shake and fear your looks,
She loved them most.

OTHELLO.   And so she did.

IAGO.   Why then,   210
She that so young could give out such a
      seeming,
To seel her father's eyes up close as oak,
He thought 'twas witchcraft—but I am much to
      blame;
I humbly do beseech you of your pardon
For too much loving you.

OTHELLO.   I am bound to thee for ever.

IAGO. I see this hath a little dashed your spirits.

OTHELLO. Not a jot, not a jot.

IAGO.   In faith, I fear it has.
I hope you will consider what is spoke
Comes from my love. But I do see you're moved.
I am to pray you not to strain my speech   220
To grosser issues nor to larger reach
Than to suspicion.

OTHELLO. I will not.

IAGO.   Should you do so, my lord,
My speech should fall into such vile success
As my thought aimed not at. Cassio's my worthy
      friend—
My lord, I see you're moved.

OTHELLO.   No, not much moved:
I do not think but Desdemona's honest.

IAGO. Long live she so! and long live you to think so!

OTHELLO. And yet, how nature erring from itself—

IAGO. Ay, there's the point: as—to be bold with you— 230
Not to affect many proposed matches
Of her own clime, complexion, and degree,
Whereto we see in all things nature tends—
Foh! one may smell, in such, a will most rank,
Foul disproportion, thoughts unnatural.
But pardon me: I do not in position
Distinctly speak of her; though I may fear
Her will, recoiling to her better judgement,
May fall to match you with her country forms,
And happily repent.

OTHELLO.   Farewell, farewell.   240
If more thou dost perceive, let me know more;
Set on thy wife to observe. Leave me, Iago.

IAGO [going]. My lord, I take my leave.

OTHELLO. Why did I marry? This honest creature
      doubtless
Sees and knows more, much more, than he unfolds.

IAGO [returning]. My lord, I would I might entreat
      your honour
To scan this thing no further. Leave it to time:
Although 'tis fit that Cassio have his place—
For sure he fills it up with great ability—
Yet if you please to hold him off awhile,
You shall by that perceive him and his means;   250
Note if your lady strain his entertainment
With any strong or vehement importunity—
Much will be seen in that. In the mean time,
Let me be thought too busy in my fears—
As worthy cause I have to fear I am—
And hold her free, I do beseech your honour.

OTHELLO. Fear not my government.

IAGO. I once more take my leave.   Goes

OTHELLO. This fellow's of exceeding honesty,   260
And knows all qualities, with a learnèd spirit,
Of human dealings. If I do prove her haggard,
Though that her jesses were my dear heart-strings,
I'ld whistle her off and let her down the wind
To prey at fortune. Haply, for I am black
And have not those soft parts of conversation
That chamberers have, or for I am declined
Into the vale of years—yet that's not much—
She's gone; I am abused, and my relief
Must be to loathe her. O curse of marriage,   270
That we can call these delicate creatures ours,
And not their appetites! I had rather be a toad,
And live upon the vapour of a dungeon,
Than keep a corner in the thing I love
For others' uses. Yet, 'tis the plague of great ones;
Prerogatived are they less than the base;
'Tis destiny unshunnable, like death:
Even then this forkèd plague is fated to us
When we do quicken. Look where she comes:

Re-enter Desdemona and Emilia

If she be false, O, then heaven mocks itself!   280
I'll not believe't.

DESDEMONA.   How now, my dear Othello!
Your dinner, and the generous islanders
By you invited, do attend your presence.

OTHELLO. I am to blame.

DESDEMONA.   Why do you speak so faintly?
Are you not well?

OTHELLO. I have a pain upon my forehead here.

DESDEMONA. Faith, that's with watching; 'twill away
      again:
Let me but bind it hard, within this hour
It will be well.

OTHELLO.   Your napkin is too little;
      *He puts the handkerchief from
      him; and she drops it*
Let it alone. Come, I'll go in with you.   290

DESDEMONA. I am very sorry that you are not well.
                     Othello and Desdemona go

EMILIA. I am glad I've found this napkin:
This was her first remembrance from the Moor;
My wayward husband hath a hundred times
Wooed me to steal it; but she so loves the token,
For he conjured her she should ever keep it,
That she reserves it evermore about her
To kiss and talk to. I'll have the work ta'en out,

And give't Iago. What he will do with it
Heaven knows, not I: 300
I nothing but to please his fantasy.

Re-enter Iago

IAGO. How now! What do you here alone?
EMILIA. Do not you chide; I have a thing for you.
IAGO. A thing for me? it is a common thing—
EMILIA. Ha!
IAGO. To have a foolish wife.
EMILIA. O, is that all? What will you give me now
  For that same handkerchief?
IAGO.   What handkerchief?
EMILIA. What handkerchief!
  Why, that the Moor first gave to Desdemona;   310
  That which so often you did bid me steal.
IAGO. Hast stole it from her?
EMILIA. No, faith; she let it drop by negligence,
  And, to th'advantage, I being here took't up.
  Look, here it is.
IAGO.   A good wench; give it me.
EMILIA. What will you do with't, that you've been so
  earnest
  To have me filch it?
IAGO [*snatching it*].   Why, what's that to you?
EMILIA. If't be not for some purpose of import,
  Give't me again. Poor lady, she'll run mad
  When she shall lack it.   320
IAGO. Be not acknown on't; I have use for it.
  Go, leave me.   *Emilia goes*
  I will in Cassio's lodging lose this napkin,
  And let him find it. Trifles light as air
  Are to the jealous confirmations strong
  As proofs of Holy Writ: this may do something.
  The Moor already changes with my poison:
  Dangerous conceits are in their natures poisons
  Which at the first are scarce found to distaste
  But, with a little act upon the blood,   330
  Burn like the mines of sulphur.

Re-enter Othello

                                    I did say so:
  Look where he comes! Not poppy, nor
    mandragora,
  Nor all the drowsy syrups of the world,
  Shall ever medicine thee to that sweet sleep
  Which thou owedst yesterday.
OTHELLO.   Ha! Ha! false to me?
IAGO. Why, how now, general! no more of that.
OTHELLO. Avaunt! be gone! thou hast set me on the
  rack:
  I swear 'tis better to be much abused
  Than but to know't a little.
IAGO.   How now, my lord!
OTHELLO. What sense had I of her stolen hours of lust? 340
  I saw't not, thought it not, it harmed not me:
  I slept the next night well, fed well, was merry;
  I found not Cassio's kisses on her lips.
  He that is robbed, not wanting what is stolen,
  Let him not know't, and he's not robbed at all.
IAGO. I am sorry to hear this.
OTHELLO. I had been happy, if the general camp,
  Pioneers and all, had tasted her sweet body,
  So I had nothing known. O, now for ever
  Farewell the tranquil mind! farewell content!   350
  Farewell the pluméd troops, and the big wars
  That make ambition virtue—O, farewell!
  Farewell the neighing steed and the shrill trump,
  The spirit-stirring drum, th'ear-piercing fife,
  The royal banner, and all quality,
  Pride, pomp, and circumstance, of glorious war!
  And, O you mortal engines, whose rude throats
  Th'immortal Jove's dread clamours counterfeit,
  Farewell! Othello's occupation's gone!
IAGO. Is't possible, my lord?   360
OTHELLO. Villain, be sure thou prove my love a
  whore;
  Be sure of it; give me the ocular proof;
                                    Takes him by the throat
  Or, by the worth of mine eternal soul,
  Thou hadst been better have been born a dog
  Than answer my waked wrath!
IAGO.   Is't come to this?
OTHELLO. Make me to see't; or, at the least, so prove it,
  That the probation bear no hinge nor loop
  To hang a doubt on; or woe upon thy life!
IAGO. My noble lord—
OTHELLO. If thou dost slander her and torture me,   370
  Never pray more; abandon all remorse;
  On horror's head horrors accumulate;
  Do deeds to make heaven weep, all earth amazed;
  For nothing canst thou to damnation add
  Greater than that.
IAGO.   O grace! O heaven forgive me!
  Are you a man? have you a soul, or sense?
  God bu'y you; take mine office. O wretched fool,
  That liv'st to make thine honesty a vice!
  O monstrous world! Take note, take note, O world,
  To be direct and honest is not safe.   380
  I thank you for this profit, and from hence
  I'll love no friend sith love breeds such offence.
OTHELLO. Nay, stay; thou shouldst be honest.
IAGO. I should be wise; for honesty's a fool,
  And loses that it works for.
OTHELLO.   By the world,
  I think my wife be honest, and think she is not;
  I think that thou art just, and think thou art not:
  I'll have some proof. Her name, that was as fresh
  As Dian's visage, is now begrimed and black
  As mine own face. If there be cords, or knives,   390
  Poison, or fire, or suffocating streams,
  I'll not endure it. Would I were satisfied!
IAGO. I see, sir, you are eaten up with passion:
  I do repent me that I put it to you.
  You would be satisfied?
OTHELLO.   Would! nay, and will.
IAGO. And may; but how? how satisfied, my lord?
  Would you, the supervisor, grossly gape on—
  Behold her topped?
OTHELLO.   Death and damnation! O!
IAGO. It were a tedious difficulty, I think,
  To bring them to that prospect: damn them then,   400
  If ever mortal eyes do see them bolster
  More than their own! What then? how then?
  What shall I say? Where's satisfaction?
  It is impossible you should see this,
  Were they as prime as goats, as hot as monkeys,
  As salt as wolves in pride, and fools as gross
  As ignorance made drunk. But yet, I say,
  If imputation and strong circumstance,
  Which lead directly to the door of truth,
  Will give you satisfaction, you might have't.   410

OTHELLO. Give me a living reason she's disloyal.
IAGO. I do not like the office;
But sith I am entered in this cause so far,
Pricked to't by foolish honesty and love,
I will go on. I lay with Cassio lately,
And being troubled with a raging tooth,
I could not sleep.
There are a kind of men so loose of soul,
That in their sleeps will mutter their affairs:
One of this kind is Cassio.   420
In sleep I heard him say 'Sweet Desdemona,
Let us be wary, let us hide our loves';
And then, sir, would he gripe and wring my hand,
Cry 'O sweet creature!' and then kiss me hard,
As if he plucked up kisses by the roots,
That grew upon my lips; then laid his leg
Over my thigh, and sighed, and kissed, and then
Cried 'Cursèd fate that gave thee to the Moor!'
OTHELLO. O monstrous! monstrous!
IAGO.   Nay, this was but his dream.
OTHELLO. But this denoted a foregone conclusion: 430
'Tis a shrewd doubt, though it be but a dream.
IAGO. And this may help to thicken other proofs
That do demonstrate thinly.
OTHELLO.   I'll tear her all to pieces.
IAGO. Nay, but be wise: yet we see nothing done;
She may be honest yet. Tell me but this:
Have you not sometimes seen a handkerchief
Spotted with strawberries in your wife's hand?
OTHELLO. I gave her such a one; 'twas my first gift.
IAGO. I know not that; but such a handkerchief—
I am sure it was your wife's—did I today   440
See Cassio wipe his beard with.
OTHELLO.   If it be that—
IAGO. If it be that, or any that was hers,
It speaks against her with the other proofs.
OTHELLO. O, that the slave had forty thousand lives!
One is too poor, too weak for my revenge.
Now do I see 'tis true. Look: here, Iago,
All my fond love thus do I blow to heaven—
'Tis gone.
Arise, black vengeance, from thy hollow cell!
Yield up, O love, thy crown and hearted throne   450
To tyrannous hate! Swell, bosom, with thy fraught,
For 'tis of aspics' tongues!
IAGO.   Yet be content.
OTHELLO. O, blood, blood, blood!
IAGO. Patience, I say; your mind perhaps may change.
OTHELLO. Never, Iago: like to the Pontic sea,
Whose icy current and compulsive course
Ne'er feels retiring ebb, but keeps due on
To the Propontic and the Hellespont;
Even so my bloody thoughts, with violent pace,
Shall ne'er look back, ne'er ebb to humble love,   460
Till that a capable and wide revenge
Swallow them up. Now, by yond marble heaven,
In the due reverence of a sacred vow   *Kneels*
I here engage my words.
IAGO.   Do not rise yet.   *Kneels*
Witness you ever-burning lights above,
You elements that clip us round about,
Witness that here Iago doth give up
The execution of his wit, hands, heart,
To wronged Othello's service! Let him command,
And to obey shall be without remorse,   470
What bloody business ever.   *They rise*

OTHELLO.   I greet thy love,
Not with vain thanks, but with acceptance
bounteous,
And will upon the instant put thee to't:
Within these three days let me hear thee say
That Cassio's not alive.
IAGO.   My friend is dead;
'Tis done at your request. But let her live.
OTHELLO. Damn her, lewd minx! O, damn her!
damn her!
Come, go with me apart; I will withdraw,
To furnish me with some swift means of death
For the fair devil. Now art thou my lieutenant.   480
IAGO. I am your own for ever.   *They go*

Scene 4: *The same*

Enter Desdemona, Emilia, and Clown

DESDEMONA. Do you know, sirrah, where Lieutenant
Cassio lies?
CLOWN. I dare not say he lies anywhere.
DESDEMONA. Why, man?
CLOWN. He's a soldier; and for one to say a soldier
lies, is stabbing.
DESDEMONA. Go to: where lodges he?
CLOWN. To tell you where he lodges, is to tell you
where I lie.
DESDEMONA. Can anything be made of this?   10
CLOWN. I know not where he lodges; and for me to
devise a lodging, and say he lies here or he lies there,
were to lie in mine own throat.
DESDEMONA. Can you inquire him out, and be edified
by report?
CLOWN. I will catechize the world for him: that is,
make questions and by them answer.
DESDEMONA. Seek him; bid him come hither. Tell him
. I have moved my lord on his behalf, and hope all
will be well.   20
CLOWN. To do this is within the compass of man's wit,
and therefore I will attempt the doing it.   *Goes*
DESDEMONA. Where should I lose that handkerchief,
Emilia?
EMILIA. I know not, madam.
DESDEMONA. Believe me, I had rather lose my purse
Full of crusadoes; and but my noble Moor
Is true of mind and made of no such baseness
As jealous creatures are, it were enough
To put him to ill thinking.
EMILIA.   Is he not jealous?
DESDEMONA. Who, he! I think the sun where he was
born   30
Drew all such humours from him.
EMILIA.   Look where he comes!
DESDEMONA. I will not leave him now till Cassio
Be called to him.

Enter Othello

                            How is't with you, my lord?
OTHELLO. Well, my good lady.[*aside*] O, hardness to
dissemble!
How do you, Desdemona?
DESDEMONA.   Well, my good lord.
OTHELLO. Give me your hand: this hand is moist, my
lady.
DESDEMONA. It yet hath felt no age nor known no
sorrow.

OTHELLO. This argues fruitfulness and liberal heart:
Hot, hot, and moist. This hand of yours requires
A sequester from liberty, fasting and prayer,   40
Much castigation, exercise devout;
For there's a young and sweating devil here
That commonly rebels. 'Tis a good hand,
A frank one.
DESDEMONA.   You may, indeed, say so;
For 'twas that hand that gave away my heart.
OTHELLO. A liberal hand: the hearts of old gave hands;
But our new heraldry is hands, not hearts.
DESDEMONA. I cannot speak of this. Come now, your
promise.
OTHELLO. What promise, chuck?
DESDEMONA. I have sent to bid Cassio come speak with
you.   50
OTHELLO. I have a salt and sorry rheum offends me;
Lend my thy handkerchief.
DESDEMONA. Here, my lord.
OTHELLO. That which I gave you.
DESDEMONA. I have it not about me.
OTHELLO. Not?
DESDEMONA. No, indeed, my lord.
OTHELLO. That's a fault. That handkerchief
Did an Egyptian to my mother give;
She was a charmer, and could almost read   60
The thoughts of people: she told her, while she
kept it
'Twould make her amiable and subdue my father
Entirely to her love; but if she lost it
Or made a gift of it, my father's eye
Should hold her loathéd and his spirits should hunt
After new fancies. She dying gave it me,
And bid me, when my fate would have me wive,
To give it her. I did so; and take heed on't:
Make it a darling like your precious eye;
To lose't or give't away were such perdition   70
As nothing else could match.
DESDEMONA.   Is't possible?
OTHELLO. 'Tis true. There's magic in the web of it:
A sibyl, that had numbered in the world
The sun to course two hundred compasses,
In her prophetic fury sewed the work;
The worms were hallowed that did breed the silk;
And it was dyed in mummy which the skilful
Conserved of maidens' hearts.
DESDEMONA.   Indeed! is't true?
OTHELLO. Most veritable; therefore look to't well.
DESDEMONA. Then would to God that I had never
seen't!   80
OTHELLO. Ha! wherefore?
DESDEMONA. Why do you speak so startingly and rash?
OTHELLO. Is't lost? is't gone? speak, is it out o'th'way?
DESDEMONA. Heaven bless us!
OTHELLO. Say you?
DESDEMONA. It is not lost; but what an if it were?
OTHELLO. How!
DESDEMONA. I say it is not lost.
OTHELLO. Fetch't; let me see't.
DESDEMONA. Why, so I can, sir, but I will not now.   90
This is a trick to put me from my suit:
Pray you, let Cassio be received again.
OTHELLO. Fetch me the handkerchief: my mind
misgives.
DESDEMONA. Come, come;
You'll never meet a more sufficient man.

OTHELLO. The handkerchief!
DESDEMONA.   I pray, talk me of Cassio.
OTHELLO. The handkerchief!
DESDEMONA.   A man that all his time
Hath founded his good fortunes on your love,
Shared dangers with you—
OTHELLO. The handkerchief!   100
DESDEMONA. In sooth, you are to blame.
OTHELLO. Away!   He goes
EMILIA. Is not this man jealous?
DESDEMONA. I ne'er saw this before.
Sure there's some wonder in this handkerchief:
I am most unhappy in the loss of it.
EMILIA. 'Tis not a year or two shows us a man:
They are all but stomachs and we all but food;
They eat us hungerly, and when they are full
They belch us. Look you, Cassio and my husband. 110

Enter Cassio and Iago

IAGO. There is no other way: 'tis she must do't;
And, lo, the happiness! go and importune her.
DESDEMONA. How now, good Cassio! what's the news
with you?
CASSIO. Madam, my former suit: I do beseech you
That, by your virtuous means, I may again
Exist and be a member of his love
Whom I with all the office of my heart
Entirely honour. I would not be delayed:
If my offence be of such mortal kind
That nor my service past nor present sorrow,   120
Nor purposed merit in futurity,
Can ransom me into his love again,
But to know so must be my benefit;
So shall I clothe me in a forced content
And shut myself up in some other course
To fortune's alms.
DESDEMONA.   Alas, thrice-gentle Cassio!
My advocation is not now in tune;
My lord is not my lord, nor should I know him
Were he in favour as in humour altered.
So help me every spirit sanctified,   130
As I have spoken for you all my best
And stood within the blank of his displeasure
For my free speech! You must awhile be patient:
What I can do I will; and more I will
Than for myself I dare—let that suffice you.
IAGO. Is my lord angry?
EMILIA.   He went hence but now,
And certainly in strange unquietness.
IAGO. Can he be angry? I have seen the cannon
When it hath blown his ranks into the air
And, like the devil, from his very arm   140
Puffed his own brother; and is he angry?
Something of moment then: I will go meet him;
There's matter in't indeed if he be angry.
DESDEMONA. I prithee, do so.   *Iago goes*
                       Something sure of state,
Either from Venice, or some unhatched practice
Made demonstrable here in Cyprus to him,
Hath puddled his clear spirit; and in such cases
Men's natures wrangle with inferior things,
Though great ones are their object. 'Tis even so;
For let our finger ache, and it indues   150
Our other healthful members to a sense
Of pain. Nay, we must think men are not gods,
Nor of them look for such observancy

As fits the bridal. Beshrew me much, Emilia,
I was, unhandsome warrior as I am,
Arraigning his unkindness with my soul;
But now I find I had suborned the witness,
And he's indicted falsely.

EMILIA. Pray heaven it be state matters, as you think,
And no conception nor no jealous toy   160
Concerning you.

DESDEMONA. Alas the day, I never gave him cause!

EMILIA. But jealous souls will not be answered so;
They are not ever jealous for the cause,
But jealous for they're jealous: 'tis a monster
Begot upon itself, born on itself.

DESDEMONA. Heaven keep that monster from
Othello's mind!

EMILIA. Lady, amen.

DESDEMONA. I will go seek him. Cassio, walk
hereabout:
If I do find him fit, I'll move your suit,   170
And seek to effect it to my uttermost.

CASSIO. I humbly thank your ladyship.

                    Desdemona and Emilia depart

Enter Bianca

BIANCA. 'Save you, friend Cassio!

CASSIO.   What make you from home?
How is it with you, my most fair Bianca?
In faith, sweet love, I was coming to your house.

BIANCA. And I was going to your lodging, Cassio.
What, keep a week away? seven days and nights?
Eight score eight hours? and lovers' absent hours,
More tedious than the dial eight score times?
O weary reckoning!

CASSIO.   Pardon me, Bianca: 180
I have this while with leaden thoughts been pressed;
But I shall in a more continuate time
Strike off this score of absence. Sweet Bianca,
                    Giving Desdemona's handkerchief
Take me this work out.

BIANCA.   O Cassio, whence came this?
This is some token from a newer friend:
To the felt absence now I feel a cause;
Is't come to this? Well, well.

CASSIO.   Go to, woman!
Throw your vile guesses in the devil's teeth,
From whence you have them. You are jealous now
That this is from some mistress, some remembrance: 190
No, by my faith, Bianca.

BIANCA.   Why, whose is it?

CASSIO. I know not neither. I found it in my
chamber.
I like the work well. Ere it be demanded—
As like enough it will—I'd have it copied:
Take it, and do't; and leave me for this time.

BIANCA. Leave you! wherefore?

CASSIO. I do attend here on the general;
And think it no addition, nor my wish,
To have him see me womaned.

BIANCA.   Why, I pray you?

CASSIO. Not that I love you not.

BIANCA.   But that you do not love me. 200
I pray you, bring me on the way a little;
And say if I shall see you soon at night.

CASSIO. 'Tis but a little way that I can bring you,
For I attend here; but I'll see you soon.

BIANCA. 'Tis very good; I must be circumstanced.
                                        They go

                            ACT 4
                    Scene 1: *The same*

Enter Othello and Iago

IAGO. Will you think so?

OTHELLO.   Think so, Iago!

IAGO.   What,
To kiss in private?

OTHELLO.   An unauthorised kiss.

IAGO. Or to be naked with her friend in bed
An hour or more, not meaning any harm?

OTHELLO. Naked in bed, Iago, and not mean harm!
It is hypocrisy against the devil:
They that mean virtuously and yet do so,
The devil their virtue tempts and they tempt
heaven.

IAGO. So they do nothing, 'tis a venial slip:
But if I give my wife a handkerchief—   10

OTHELLO. What then?

IAGO. Why, then, 'tis hers, my lord; and being hers,
She may, I think, bestow't on any man.

OTHELLO. She is protectress of her honour too:
May she give that?

IAGO. Her honour is an essence that's not seen;
They have it very oft that have it not:
But for the handkerchief—

OTHELLO. By heaven, I would most gladly have
forgot it.
Thou said'st—O, it comes o'er my memory,   20
As doth the raven o'er the infected house,
Boding to all—he had my handkerchief.

IAGO. Ay, what of that?

OTHELLO.   That's not so good now.

IAGO.   What
If I had said I had seen him do you wrong?
Or heard him say—as knaves be such abroad,
Who having, by their own importunate suit,
Or voluntary dotage of some mistress,
Convincéd or supplied them, cannot choose
But they must blab—

OTHELLO.   Hath he said anything?

IAGO. He hath, my lord; but, be you well assured, 30
No more than he'll unswear.

OTHELLO.   What hath he said?

IAGO. Faith, that he did—I know not what he did.

OTHELLO. What? what?

IAGO. Lie—

OTHELLO. With her?

IAGO.   With her, on her; what you will.

OTHELLO. Lie with her! lie on her!—We say lie on her,
when they belie her.—Lie with her! 'Zounds, that's
fulsome!   Handkerchief—confessions—handkerchief! To confess and be hanged for his labour; first,
to be hanged; and then to confess. I tremble at it.
Nature would not invest herself in such shadowing 40
passion without some instruction. It is not words
that shakes me thus. Pish! Noses, ears, and lips. Is't
possible?—Confess?—Handkerchief?—O devil!
                                        Falls in a trance

IAGO. Work on,
My medicine, work! Thus credulous fools are
caught;

And many worthy and chaste dames even thus,
All guiltless, meet reproach. What, ho! my lord!
My lord, I say! Othello!

Enter Cassio

How now, Cassio!
CASSIO. What's the matter?
IAGO. My lord is fallen into an epilepsy.   50
This is his second fit; he had one yesterday.
CASSIO. Rub him about the temples.
IAGO.   No, forbear;
The lethargy must have his quiet course;
If not, he foams at mouth, and by and by
Breaks out to savage madness. Look, he stirs.
Do you withdraw yourself a little while.
He will recover straight; when he is gone,
I would on great occasion speak with you.
                                    Cassio goes
How is it, general? have you not hurt your head?
OTHELLO. Dost thou mock me?
IAGO.   I mock you! no, by heaven. 60
Would you would bear your fortune like a man!
OTHELLO. A hornéd man's a monster and a beast.
IAGO. There's many a beast then in a populous city,
And many a civil monster.
OTHELLO. Did he confess it?
IAGO.   Good sir, be a man:
Think every bearded fellow that's but yoked
May draw with you. There's millions now alive
That nightly lie in those unproper beds
Which they dare swear peculiar; your case is better.
O, 'tis the spite of hell, the fiend's arch-mock, 70
To lip a wanton in a secure couch,
And to suppose her chaste! No, let me know;
And knowing what I am, know what she shall be.
OTHELLO. O, thou art wise; 'tis certain.
IAGO.   Stand you awhile apart;
Confine yourself but in a patient list.
Whilst you were here o'erwhelméd with your
       grief—
A passion most unsuiting such a man—
Cassio came hither; I shifted him away,
And laid good scuse upon your ecstasy;
Bade him anon return and speak with me;   80
The which he promised. Do but encave yourself,
And mark the fleers, the gibes, and notable scorns,
That dwell in every region of his face;
For I will make him tell the tale anew,
Where, how, how oft, how long ago and when
He hath and is again to cope your wife.
I say, but mark his gestures. Marry, patience;
Or I shall say you're all in all a spleen,
And nothing of a man.
OTHELLO.   Dost thou hear, Iago?
I will be found most cunning in my patience;   90
But—dost thou hear?—most bloody.
IAGO.   That's not amiss;
But yet keep time in all. Will you withdraw?
                                Othello retires
Now will I question Cassio of Bianca,
A hussy that by selling her desires
Buys herself bread and clothes: it is a creature
That dotes on Cassio; as 'tis the strumpet's plague
To beguile many and be beguiled by one.
He, when he hears of her, cannot refrain
From the excess of laughter. Here he comes.

Re-enter Cassio

As he shall smile, Othello shall go mad;   100
And his unbookish jealousy must construe
Poor Cassio's smiles, gestures, and light behaviours,
Quite in the wrong. How do you now, lieutenant?
CASSIO. The worser that you give me the addition
Whose want even kills me.
IAGO. Ply Desdemona well, and you are sure on't.
Now, if this suit lay in Bianca's power,
How quickly should you speed!
CASSIO.   Alas, poor caitiff!
OTHELLO. Look how he laughs already!
IAGO. I never knew a woman love man so.   110
CASSIO. Alas, poor rogue! I think, in faith, she loves
me.
OTHELLO. Now he denies it faintly, and laughs it out.
IAGO. Do you hear, Cassio?
OTHELLO. Now he importunes him to tell it o'er.
Go to; well said, well said.
IAGO. She gives it out that you shall marry her.
Do you intend it?
CASSIO, Ha, ha, ha!
OTHELLO. Do you triumph, Roman? do you triumph?
CASSIO. I marry her! what, a customer! I prithee, bear 120
some charity to my wit; do not think it so unwhole-
some. Ha, ha, ha!
OTHELLO. So, so, so, so; they laugh that win.
IAGO. Faith, the cry goes that you marry her.
CASSIO. Prithee, say true.
IAGO. I am a very villain else.
OTHELLO. Have you scored me? Well.
CASSIO. This is the monkey's own giving out: she is
persuaded I will marry her, out of her own love and
flattery, not out of my promise.   130
OTHELLO. Iago beckons me; now he begins the story.
CASSIO. She was here even now; she haunts me in
every place. I was the other day talking on the sea-
bank with certain Venetians; and thither comes the
bauble, and, by this hand, falls me thus about my
neck—
OTHELLO. Crying 'O dear Cassio!' as it were: his
gesture imports it.
CASSIO. So hangs, and lolls, and weeps upon me; so
shakes, and pulls me: ha, ha, ha!   140
OTHELLO. Now he tells how she plucked him to my
chamber. O, I see that nose of yours, but not that
dog I shall throw it to.
CASSIO. Well, I must leave her company.
IAGO. Before me! look where she comes!
CASSIO. 'Tis such another fitchew! marry, a perfumed
one.

Enter Bianca

What do you mean by this haunting of me?
BIANCA. Let the devil and his dam haunt you! What
did you mean by that same handkerchief you gave   150
me even now? I was a fine fool to take it. I must
take out the work? A likely piece of work that you
should find it in your chamber and not know who
left it there! This is some minx's token, and I must
take out the work? There; give it your hobby-horse.
Wheresoever you had it, I'll take out no work on't.
CASSIO. How now, my sweet Bianca! how now! how
now!
OTHELLO. By heaven, that should be my handkerchief!

BIANCA. An you'll come to supper tonight, you may; 160
an you will not, come when you are next prepared
for. *Goes*

IAGO. After her, after her.

CASSIO. Faith, I must; she'll rail in the street else.

IAGO. Will you sup there?

CASSIO. Faith, I intend so.

IAGO. Well, I may chance to see you; for I would very
fain speak with you.

CASSIO. Prithee, come; will you?

IAGO. Go to; say no more. *Cassio goes* 170

OTHELLO [*comes forward*]. How shall I murder him,
Iago?

IAGO. Did you perceive how he laughed at his vice?

OTHELLO. O Iago!

IAGO. And did you see the handkerchief?

OTHELLO. Was that mine?

IAGO. Yours, by this hand—and to see how he prizes
the foolish woman your wife! She gave it him, and
he hath given it his whore.

OTHELLO. I would have him nine years a-killing. A 180
fine woman! a fair woman! a sweet woman!

IAGO. Nay, you must forget that.

OTHELLO. Ay, let her rot, and perish, and be damned
tonight; for she shall not live. No, my heart is turned
to stone: I strike it, and it hurts my hand. O, the
world hath not a sweeter creature: she might lie by
an emperor's side and command him tasks.

IAGO. Nay, that's not your way.

OTHELLO. Hang her! I do but say what she is: so
delicate with her needle, an admirable musician— 190
O, she will sing the savageness out of a bear—of so
high and plenteous wit and invention—

IAGO. She's the worse for all this.

OTHELLO. O, a thousand, thousand times—and then,
of so gentle a condition!

IAGO. Ay, too gentle.

OTHELLO. Nay, that's certain; but yet the pity of it,
Iago! O Iago, the pity of it, Iago!

IAGO. If you be so fond over her iniquity, give her
patent to offend; for, if it touch not you, it comes 200
near nobody.

OTHELLO. I will chop her into messes—cuckold me!

IAGO. O, 'tis foul in her.

OTHELLO. With mine officer!

IAGO. That's fouler.

OTHELLO. Get me some poison, Iago—this night. I'll
not expostulate with her, lest her body and beauty
unprovide my mind again—this night, Iago.

IAGO. Do it not with poison: strangle her in her bed,
even the bed she hath contaminated. 210

OTHELLO. Good, good: the justice of it pleases; very
good.

IAGO. And for Cassio, let me be his undertaker: you
shall hear more by midnight.

OTHELLO. Excellent good. [*a trumpet sounds*] What
trumpet is that same?

IAGO. I warrant, something from Venice.

Enter Lodovico, Desdemona, and Attendants

'Tis Lodovico!
This comes from the Duke; and see, your wife is
with him.

LODOVICO. God save you, worthy general!

OTHELLO. With all my heart, sir.

LODOVICO. The Duke and senators of Venice greet
you. *Gives him a letter*

OTHELLO. I kiss the instrument of their pleasures. 220
Opens and reads

DESDEMONA. And what's the news, good cousin
Lodovico?

IAGO. I am very glad to see you, signior;
Welcome to Cyprus.

LODOVICO. I thank you. How does Lieutenant Cassio?

IAGO. Lives, sir.

DESDEMONA. Cousin, there's fallen between him and
my lord
An unkind breach; but you shall make all well.

OTHELLO. Are you sure of that?

DESDEMONA. My lord?

OTHELLO [*reads*]. 'This fail you not to do, as you
will—' 230

LODOVICO. He did not call; he's busy in the paper.
Is there division 'twixt my lord and Cassio?

DESDEMONA. A most unhappy one; I would do much
T'atone them, for the love I bear to Cassio.

OTHELLO. Fire and brimstone!

DESDEMONA. My lord?

OTHELLO. Are you wise?

DESDEMONA. What, is he angry?

LODOVICO. May be the letter moved him;
For, as I think, they do command him home,
Deputing Cassio in his government. 240

DESDEMONA. By my troth, I am glad on't.

OTHELLO. Indeed!

DESDEMONA. My lord?

OTHELLO. I am glad to see you mad.

DESDEMONA. Why, sweet Othello!

OTHELLO. Devil! *Striking her*

DESDEMONA. I have not deserved this.

LODOVICO. My lord, this would not be believed in
Venice,
Though I should swear I saw't. 'Tis very much.
Make her amends; she weeps.

OTHELLO. O devil, devil!
If that the earth could teem with woman's tears,
Each drop she falls would prove a crocodile.
Out of my sight!

DESDEMONA. I will not stay to offend you. *Going* 250

LODOVICO. Truly, an obedient lady.
I do beseech your lordship, call her back.

OTHELLO. Mistress!

DESDEMONA. My lord?

OTHELLO. What would you with her, sir?

LODOVICO. Who, I, my lord?

OTHELLO. Ay; you did wish that I would make her
turn.
Sir, she can turn and turn, and yet go on
And turn again; and she can weep, sir, weep;
And she's obedient, as you say, obedient,
Very obedient. Proceed you in your tears.— 260
Concerning this, sir,—O well-painted passion!—
I am commanded home.—Get you away;
I'll send for you anon.—Sir, I obey the mandate,
And will return to Venice.—Hence, avaunt!—
Desdemona goes
Cassio shall have my place. And, sir, tonight,
I do entreat that we may sup together.
You are welcome, sir, to Cyprus.—Goats and
monkeys! *He goes*

LODOVICO. Is this the noble Moor whom our full
    senate
    Call all in all sufficient? Is this the nature
    Whom passion could not shake? whose solid virtue 270
    The shot of accident nor dart of chance
    Could neither graze nor pierce?
IAGO.   He is much changed.
LODOVICO. Are his wits safe? is he not light of brain?
IAGO. He's that he is. I may not breathe my censure
    What he might be; if what he might he is not,
    I would to heaven he were!
LODOVICO.   What, strike his wife!
IAGO. Faith, that was not so well; yet would I knew
    That stroke would prove the worst!
LODOVICO.   Is it his use?
    Or did the letters work upon his blood,
    And new-create this fault?
IAGO.   Alas, alas!   280
    It is not honesty in me to speak
    What I have seen and known. You shall observe
      him,
    And his own courses will denote him so
    That I may save my speech; do but go after,
    And mark how he continues.
LODOVICO. I am sorry that I am deceived in him.
                                          They go

Scene 2: A room in the citadel

Enter Othello and Emilia

OTHELLO. You have seen nothing, then?
EMILIA. Nor ever heard, nor ever did suspect.
OTHELLO. Yes, you have seen Cassio and she together.
EMILIA. But then I saw no harm, and then I heard
    Each syllable that breath made up between them.
OTHELLO. What, did they never whisper?
EMILIA.   Never, my lord.
OTHELLO. Nor send you out o'th'way?
EMILIA. Never.
OTHELLO. To fetch her fan, her gloves, her mask, nor
    nothing?
EMILIA. Never, my lord.   10
OTHELLO. That's strange.
EMILIA. I durst, my lord, to wager she is honest,
    Lay down my soul at stake. If you think other,
    Remove your thought: it doth abuse your bosom.
    If any wretch have put this in your head,
    Let heaven requite it with the serpent's curse!
    For if she be not honest, chaste, and true,
    There's no man happy: the purest of their wives
    Is foul as slander.
OTHELLO.   Bid her come hither; go. *Emilia goes*
    She says enough; yet she's a simple bawd   20
    That cannot say as much. This is a subtle whore,
    A closet lock and key of villanous secrets;
    And yet she'll kneel and pray; I have seen her do't.

Enter Desdemona with Emilia

DESDEMONA. My lord, what is your will?
OTHELLO.   Pray, chuck, come hither.
DESDEMONA. What is your pleasure?
OTHELLO.   Let me see your eyes;
    Look in my face.
DESDEMONA.   What horrible fancy's this?
OTHELLO [*to Emilia*]. Some of your function, mistress:
    Leave procreants alone and shut the door;
    Cough, or cry hem, if anybody come—

Your mystery, your mystery; nay, dispatch.   30
                                  Emilia goes out
DESDEMONA. Upon my knees, what doth your speech
    import?
    I understand a fury in your words,
    But not the words.
OTHELLO. Why, what art thou?
DESDEMONA. Your wife, my lord; your true and loyal
    wife.
OTHELLO. Come, swear it, damn thyself;
    Lest, being like one of heaven, the devils themselves
    Should fear to seize thee. Therefore be double-
    damned:
    Swear thou art honest.
DESDEMONA.   Heaven doth truly know it.
OTHELLO. Heaven truly knows that thou art false as
    hell.   40
DESDEMONA. To whom, my lord? with whom? how
    am I false?
OTHELLO. Ah, Desdemon! Away! away! away!
DESDEMONA. Alas the heavy day! Why do you weep?
    Am I the motive of these tears, my lord?
    If haply you my father do suspect
    An instrument of this your calling back,
    Lay not your blame on me; if you have lost him,
    Why, I have lost him too.
OTHELLO.   Had it pleased heaven
    To try me with affliction; had they rained
    All kind of sores and shames on my bare head,   50
    Steeped me in poverty to the very lips,
    Given to captivity me and my utmost hopes,
    I should have found in some place of my soul
    A drop of patience; but, alas, to make me
    A fixèd figure for the time of scorn
    To point his slow unmoving finger at!
    Yet could I bear that too; well, very well;
    But there, where I have garnered up my heart,
    Where either I must live or bear no life,
    The fountain from the which my current runs,   60
    Or else dries up—to be discarded thence!
    Or keep it as a cistern for foul toads
    To knot and gender in! Turn thy complexion there,
    Patience, thou young and rose-lipped cherubin,
    Ay, there, look grim as hell!
DESDEMONA. I hope my noble lord esteems me honest.
OTHELLO. O, ay; as summer flies are in the shambles,
    That quicken even with blowing. O thou weed,
    Who art so lovely fair and smell'st so sweet
    That the sense aches at thee, would thou hadst ne'er
    been born!   70
DESDEMONA. Alas, what ignorant sin have I
    committed?
OTHELLO. Was this fair paper, this most goodly book,
    Made to write 'whore' upon? What committed!
    Committed! O thou public commoner!
    I should make very forges of my cheeks,
    That would to cinders burn up modesty,
    Did I but speak thy deeds. What committed!
    Heaven stops the nose at it, and the moon winks;
    The bawdy wind, that kisses all it meets,
    Is hushed within the hollow mine of earth,   80
    And will not hear it. What committed!
    Impudent strumpet!
DESDEMONA.   By heaven, you do me wrong.
OTHELLO. Are not you a strumpet?
DESDEMONA.   No, as I am a Christian.

If to preserve this vessel for my lord
From any other foul unlawful touch
Be not to be a strumpet, I am none.
OTHELLO. What, not a whore?
DESDEMONA.   No, as I shall be saved.
OTHELLO. Is't possible?
DESDEMONA. O, heaven forgive us!
OTHELLO.   I cry you mercy then:
I took you for that cunning whore of Venice   90
That married with Othello. [raising his voice] You,
mistress,
That have the office opposite to Saint Peter,
And keep the gate of hell!

Re-enter Emilia

You, you, ay, you!
We've done our course; there's money for your
pains:
I pray you, turn the key, and keep our counsel.
                                                              Goes
EMILIA. Alas, what does this gentleman conceive?
How do you, madam? how do you, my good lady?
DESDEMONA. Faith, half asleep.
EMILIA. Good madam, what's the matter with my
lord?
DESDEMONA. With who?   100
EMILIA. Why, with my lord, madam.
DESDEMONA. Who is thy lord?
EMILIA.   He that is yours, sweet lady.
DESDEMONA. I have none: do not talk to me, Emilia;
I cannot weep, nor answers have I none
But what should go by water. Prithee, tonight
Lay on my bed my wedding sheets—remember;
And call thy husband hither.
EMILIA.   Here's a change indeed! *Goes*
DESDEMONA. 'Tis meet I should be used so, very meet.
How have I been behaved, that he might stick
The small'st opinion on my least misuse?   110

Re-enter Emilia with Iago

IAGO. What is your pleasure, madam? How is't with
you?
DESDEMONA. I cannot tell. Those that do teach young
babes
Do it with gentle means and easy tasks:
He might have chid me so; for, in good faith,
I am a child to chiding.
IAGO.   What's the matter, lady?
EMILIA. Alas, Iago, my lord hath so bewhored her.
Thrown such despite and heavy terms upon her,
As true heart cannot bear.
DESDEMONA. Am I that name, Iago?
IAGO.   What name, fair lady?
DESDEMONA. Such as she said my lord did say I was. 120
EMILIA. He called her whore: a beggar in his drink
Could not have laid such terms upon his callet.
IAGO. Why did he so?
DESDEMONA. I do not know; I am sure I am none
such.
IAGO. Do not weep, do not weep. Alas the day!
EMILIA. Hath she forsook so many noble matches,
Her father, and her country, and her friends,
To be called whore? Would it not make one weep?
DESDEMONA. It is my wretched fortune.
IAGO.   Beshrew him for't!
How comes this trick upon him!

DESDEMONA.   Nay, heaven doth know. 130
EMILIA. I will be hanged, if some eternal villain,
Some busy and insinuating rogue,
Some cogging, cozening slave, to get some office,
Have not devised this slander; I'll be hanged else.
IAGO. Fie, there is no such man; it is impossible.
DESDEMONA. If any such there be, heaven pardon him!
EMILIA. A halter pardon him! and hell gnaw his bones!
Why should he call her whore? who keeps her
company?
What place? what time? what form? what
likelihood?
The Moor's abused by some most villanous knave, 140
Some base notorious knave, some scurvy fellow.
O heaven, that such companions thou'ldst unfold,
And put in every honest hand a whip
To lash the rascals naked through the world
Even from the east to th'west!
IAGO.   Speak within door.
EMILIA. O, fie upon them! Some such squire he was
That turned your wit the seamy side without,
And made you to suspect me with the Moor.
IAGO. You are a fool; go to.
DESDEMONA.   Alas, Iago,
What shall I do to win my lord again?   150
Good friend, go to him; for, by this light of heaven,
I know not how I lost him. Here I kneel:
If e'er my will did trespass 'gainst his love
Either in discourse of thought or actual deed,
Or that mine eyes, mine ears, or any sense,
Delighted them in any other form,
Or that I do not yet, and ever did,
And ever will, though he do shake me off
To beggarly divorcement, love him dearly,
Comfort forswear me! Unkindness may do much;   160
And his unkindness may defeat my life,
But never taint my love. I cannot say 'whore':
It does abhor me now I speak the word;
To do the act that might the addition earn
Not the world's mass of vanity could make me.
IAGO. I pray you, be content; 'tis but his humour:
The business of the state does him offence,
And he does chide with you.
DESDEMONA.   If 'twere no other!
IAGO. 'Tis but so, I warrant.   *Trumpets sound*
Hark how these instruments summon to supper!   170
The messengers of Venice stay the meat:
Go in, and weep not; all things shall be well.
                                    Desdemona and Emilia go

Enter Roderigo

How now, Roderigo!
RODERIGO. I do not find that thou deal'st justly with
me.
IAGO. What in the contrary?
RODERIGO. Every day thou daff'st me with some
device, Iago; and rather, as it seems to me now,
keep'st from me all conveniency than suppliest me
with the least advantage of hope. I will indeed no   180
longer endure it; nor am I yet persuaded to put up
in peace what already I have foolishly suffered.
IAGO. Will you hear me, Roderigo?
RODERIGO. Faith, I have heard too much; for your
words and performances are no kin together.
IAGO. You charge me most unjustly.
RODERIGO. With nought but truth. I have wasted

myself out of my means. The jewels you have had
from me to deliver to Desdemona would half have
corrupted a votarist. You have told me she hath   190
received them and returned me expectations and
comforts of sudden respect and acquaintance; but I
find none.

IAGO. Well; go to; very well.

RODERIGO. Very well! go to! I cannot go to, man; nor
'tis not very well. By this hand, I think 'tis very
scurvy, and begin to find myself fopped in it.

IAGO. Very well.

RODERIGO. I tell you 'tis not very well. I will make
myself known to Desdemona. If she will return me   200
my jewels, I will give over my suit and repent my
unlawful solicitation; if not, assure yourself I will
seek satisfaction of you.

IAGO. You have said now.

RODERIGO. Ay, and said nothing but what I protest
intendment of doing.

IAGO. Why, now I see there's mettle in thee; and even
from this instant do build on thee a better opinion
than ever before. Give me thy hand, Roderigo: thou
hast taken against me a most just exception; but yet, 210
I protest, I have dealt most directly in thy affair.

RODERIGO. It hath not appeared.

IAGO. I grant indeed it hath not appeared, and your
suspicion is not without wit and judgement. But,
Roderigo, if thou hast that in thee indeed, which I
have greater reason to believe now than ever—I
mean purpose, courage, and valour—this night
show it: if thou the next night following enjoy not
Desdemona, take me from this world with
treachery and devise engines for my life.   220

RODERIGO. Well, what is it? is it within reason and
compass?

IAGO. Sir, there is especial commission come from
Venice to depute Cassio in Othello's place.

RODERIGO. Is that true? why then, Othello and
Desdemona return again to Venice.

IAGO. O, no; he goes into Mauritania, and takes away
with him the fair Desdemona, unless his abode be
lingered here by some accident: wherein none can be
so determinate as the removing of Cassio.   230

RODERIGO. How do you mean removing of him?

IAGO. Why, by making him uncapable of Othello's
place; knocking out his brains.

RODERIGO. And that you would have me do?

IAGO. Ay, if you dare do yourself a profit and a right.
He sups tonight with a harlotry, and thither will I
go to him: he knows not yet of his honourable
fortune. If you will watch his going thence, which
I will fashion to fall out between twelve and one,
you may take him at your pleasure. I will be near   240
to second your attempt, and he shall fall between us.
Come, stand not amazed at it, but go along with me;
I will show you such a necessity in his death that
you shall think yourself bound to put it on him. It
is now high supper-time, and the night grows to
waste. About it.

RODERIGO. I will hear further reason for this.

IAGO. And you shall be satisfied.   *They go*

Scene 3: *Another room in the citadel*

Enter Othello, Lodovico, Desdemona, Emilia,
and Attendants

LODOVICO. I do beseech you, sir, trouble yourself no
further.

OTHELLO. O, pardon me; 'twill do me good to walk.

LODOVICO. Madam, good night; I humbly thank your
ladyship.

DESDEMONA. Your honour is most welcome.

OTHELLO.   Will you walk, sir?
O, Desdemona!

DESDEMONA. My lord?

OTHELLO. Get you to bed on th'instant; I will be
returned forthwith. Dismiss your attendant there:
look't be done.   10

DESDEMONA. I will, my lord.
                    Othello, Lodovico, and Attendants go

EMILIA. How goes it now? he looks gentler than he did.

DESDEMONA. He says he will return incontinent:
He hath commanded me to go to bed,
And bade me to dismiss you.

EMILIA.   Dismiss me!

DESDEMONA. It was his bidding; therefore, good
Emilia,
Give me my nightly wearing, and adieu:
We must not now displease him.

EMILIA. I would you had never seen him!

DESDEMONA. So would not I: my love doth so approve
him,   20
That even his stubbornness, his checks, his frowns—
Prithee, unpin me—have grace and favour in them.

EMILIA. I have laid those sheets you bade me on the
bed.

DESDEMONA. All's one. Good faith, how foolish are
our minds!
If I do die before thee, prithee, shroud me
In one of those same sheets.

EMILIA.   Come, come, you talk.

DESDEMONA. My mother had a maid called Barbara.
She was in love; and he she loved proved mad
And did forsake her. She had a song of 'willow'—
An old thing 'twas, but it expressed her fortune,   30
And she died singing it. That song tonight
Will not go from my mind. I have much to do
But to go hang my head all at one side
And sing it like poor Barbara. Prithee, dispatch.

EMILIA. Shall I go fetch your night-gown?

DESDEMONA.   No, unpin me here.
This Lodovico is a proper man.

EMILIA. A very handsome man.

DESDEMONA. He speaks well.

EMILIA. I know a lady in Venice would have walked
barefoot to Palestine for a touch of his nether lip.   40

DESDEMONA [*sings*].
The poor soul sat sighing by a sycamore tree,
    Sing all a green willow;
Her hand on her bosom, her head on her knee,
    Sing willow, willow, willow:
The fresh streams ran by her, and murmured
    her moans;
    Sing willow, willow, willow;
Her salt tears fell from her, and softened
    the stones—
Lay by these—
    Sing willow, willow, willow;
Prithee, hie thee; he'll come anon—   50
    Sing all a green willow must be my garland.
Let nobody blame him; his scorn I approve—
Nay, that's not next. Hark! who is't that knocks?

EMILIA. It's the wind.

DESDEMONA [*sings*]

> I called my love false love; but what said he then?
> Sing willow, willow, willow;
> If I court moe women, you'll couch with moe men.

So, get thee gone; good night. Mine eyes do itch;
Does that bode weeping?

EMILIA.   'Tis neither here nor there.

DESDEMONA. I have heard it said so. O, these men, these men!

Dost thou in conscience think—tell me, Emilia—   60
That there be women do abuse their husbands
In such gross kind?

EMILIA.   There be some such, no question.

DESDEMONA. Wouldst thou do such a deed for all the world?

EMILIA. Why, would not you?

DESDEMONA.   No, by this heavenly light!

EMILIA. Nor I neither by this heavenly light: I might do't as well i'th'dark.

DESDEMONA. Wouldst thou do such a deed for all the world?

EMILIA. The world's a huge thing: it is a great prize   70
for a small vice.

DESDEMONA. In troth, I think thou wouldst not.

EMILIA. In troth, I think I should; and undo't when
I had done't. Marry, I would not do such a thing for
a joint-ring, nor for measures of lawn, nor for
gowns, petticoats, nor caps, nor any petty exhibition. But for all the whole world—ud's pity, who
would not make her husband a cuckold to make him
a monarch? I should venture purgatory for't.

DESDEMONA. Beshrew me, if I would do such a wrong   80
for the whole world.

EMILIA. Why, the wrong is but a wrong i'th'world;
and having the world for your labour, 'tis a wrong
in your own world, and you might quickly make
it right.

DESDEMONA. I do not think there is any such woman.

EMILIA. Yes, a dozen; and as many to th'vantage as
would store the world they played for.
But I do think it is their husbands' faults
If wives do fall. Say that they slack their duties   90
And pour our treasures into foreign laps,
Or else break out in peevish jealousies,
Throwing restraint upon us; or say they strike us,
Or scant our former having in despite—
Why, we have galls, and though we have some grace,
Yet have we some revenge. Let husbands know
Their wives have sense like them: they see, and smell,
And have their palates both for sweet and sour,
As husbands have. What is it that they do
When they change us for others? Is it sport?   100
I think it is. And doth affection breed it?
I think it doth. Is't frailty that thus errs?
It is so too. And have not we affections,
Desires for sport, and frailty, as men have?
Then let them use us well: else let them know,
The ills we do, their ills instruct us so.

DESDEMONA. Good night, good night.   *Emilia goes*
                                        Heaven me such uses send,
Not to pick bad from bad, but by bad mend!   *Goes*

ACT 5
Scene 1: *A street*

Enter Iago and Roderigo

IAGO. Here, stand behind this bulk; straight will he come.
Wear thy good rapier bare, and put it home;
Quick, quick; fear nothing; I'll be at thy elbow.
It makes us, or it mars us; think on that,
And fix most firm thy resolution.

RODERIGO. Be near at hand; I may miscarry in't.

IAGO. Here, at thy hand. Be bold, and take thy stand.
                                                        Retires

RODERIGO. I have no great devotion to the deed;
And yet he hath given me satisfying reasons.
'Tis but a man gone. Forth, my sword: he dies.   10

IAGO. I have rubbed this young quat almost to the sense,
And he grows angry. Now, whether he kill Cassio,
Or Cassio him, or each do kill the other,
Every way makes my gain: live Roderigo,
He calls me to a restitution large
Of gold and jewels that I bobbed from him,
As gifts to Desdemona—
It must not be; if Cassio do remain,
He hath a daily beauty in his life
That makes me ugly; and besides, the Moor   20
May unfold me to him—there stand I in much peril.
No, he must die. Be't so. I hear him coming.

Enter Cassio

RODERIGO. I know his gait; 'tis he. Villain, thou diest!
                                        Makes a pass at Cassio

CASSIO. That thrust had been mine enemy indeed,
But that my coat is better than thou think'st.
I will make proof of thine.
                                Draws, and wounds Roderigo

RODERIGO.   O, I am slain!
                    *Iago from behind strikes at Cassio's
                                legs, and hurries off*

CASSIO. I am maimed for ever. Help, ho! murder! murder!
                                                        Falls

Enter Othello

OTHELLO. The voice of Cassio: Iago keeps his word.

RODERIGO. O, villain that I am!

OTHELLO.   It is even so.

CASSIO. O, help, ho! light! a surgeon!   30

OTHELLO. 'Tis he. O brave Iago, honest and just,
That hast such noble sense of thy friend's wrong!
Thou teachest me: minion, your dear lies dead,
And your unblest fate hies. Strumpet, I come!
Forth of my heart, those charms, thine eyes, are blotted!
Thy bed lust-stained shall with lust's blood be spotted.   *He goes*

Enter Lodovico and Gratiano

CASSIO. What, ho! no watch? no passage?
murder! murder!

GRATIANO. 'Tis some mischance; the voice is very direful.

CASSIO. O, help!

LODOVICO. Hark!   40

RODERIGO. O wretched villain!

LODOVICO. Two or three groan. It is a heavy night;
These may be counterfeits: let's think't unsafe

To come in to the cry without more help.
>*They stand aside*

RODERIGO. Nobody come? then shall I bleed to death.
LODOVICO. Hark!

Re-enter Iago, with a light

GRATIANO. Here's one comes in his shirt, with light
   and weapons.
IAGO. Who's there? whose noise is this that cries on
   murder?
LODOVICO. We do not know.
IAGO.   Did not you hear a cry?
CASSIO. Here, here! for heaven's sake, help me!
IAGO.   What's the matter?   50
GRATIANO. This is Othello's ancient, as I take it.
LODOVICO. The same indeed; a very valiant fellow.
IAGO. What are you here that cry so grievously?
CASSIO. Iago? O, I am spoiled, undone by villains!
   Give me some help.
IAGO. O me, lieutenant! what villains have done this?
CASSIO. I think that one of them is hereabout,
   And cannot make away.
IAGO.   O treacherous villains!
   What are you there? [*spies Lodovico and Gratiano*].
   Come in and give some help.
RODERIGO. O, help me here!   60
CASSIO. That's one of them.
IAGO.   O murderous slave! O villain!
>*Stabs Roderigo*
RODERIGO. O damned Iago! O inhuman dog!
IAGO. Kill men i'th'dark! Where be these bloody
   thieves?
   How silent is this town! Ho! murder! murder!
>*Lodovico and Gratiano come forward*
   What may you be? are you of good or evil?
LODOVICO. As you shall prove us, praise us.
IAGO. Signior Lodovico?
LODOVICO. He, sir.
IAGO. I cry you mercy. Here's Cassio hurt by villains.
GRATIANO. Cassio!   70
IAGO. How is't, brother?
CASSIO. My leg is cut in two.
IAGO.   Marry, heaven forbid!
   Light, gentlemen: I'll bind it with my shirt.

Enter Bianca

BIANCA. What is the matter, ho? who is't that cried?
IAGO. Who is't that cried!
BIANCA. O my dear Cassio! my sweet Cassio! O
   Cassio, Cassio, Cassio!
IAGO. O notable strumpet! Cassio, may you suspect
   Who they should be that have thus mangled you?
CASSIO. No.   80
GRATIANO. I am sorry to find you thus: I have been
   to seek you.
IAGO. Lend me a garter. So. O, for a chair,
   To bear him easily hence!
BIANCA. Alas, he faints! O Cassio, Cassio, Cassio!
IAGO. Gentlemen all, I do suspect this trash
   To be a party in this injury.
   Patience awhile, good Cassio. Come, come;
   Lend me a light. Know we this face or no?
   Alas, my friend and my dear countryman
   Roderigo? No—yes, sure; 'tis Roderigo.   90
GRATIANO. What, of Venice?
IAGO. Even he, sir. Did you know him?

GRATIANO.   Know him! ay.
IAGO. Signior Gratiano? I cry your gentle pardon:
   These bloody accidents must excuse my manners,
   That so neglected you.
GRATIANO.   I am glad to see you.
IAGO. How do you, Cassio? O, a chair, a chair!
GRATIANO. Roderigo!
IAGO. He, he, 'tis he. [*a chair brought*] O, that's well
   said; the chair.
   Some good man bear him carefully from hence;   100
   I'll fetch the general's surgeon. [*to Bianca*] For you,
   mistress,
   Save you your labour. He that lies slain here, Cassio,
   Was my dear friend: what malice was between you?
CASSIO. None in the world; nor do I know the man.
IAGO [*to Bianca*]. What, look you pale? O, bear him
   out o'th'air.
>*Cassio is borne in, and the*
>*body of Roderigo removed*
   Stay you, good gentlemen. Look you pale, mistress?
   Do you perceive the gastness of her eye?
   Nay, if you stare, we shall hear more anon.
   Behold her well; I pray you, look upon her:
   Do you see, gentlemen? nay, guiltiness will speak,
   Though tongues were out of use.   110

Enter Emilia

EMILIA. 'Las, what's the matter? what's the matter,
   husband?
IAGO. Cassio hath here been set on in the dark
   By Roderigo, and fellows that are scaped:
   He's almost slain, and Roderigo dead.
EMILIA. Alas, good gentleman! alas, good Cassio!
IAGO. This is the fruits of whoring. Prithee, Emilia,
   Go know of Cassio where he supped tonight.
   What, do you shake at that?
BIANCA. He supped at my house; but I therefore shake
   not.
IAGO. O, did he so? I charge you, go with me.   120
EMILIA. O, fie upon thee, strumpet!
BIANCA. I am no strumpet; but of life as honest
   As you that thus abuse me.
EMILIA.   As I! foh! fie upon thee!
IAGO. Kind gentlemen, let's see poor Cassio dressed.
   Come, mistress, you must tell's another tale.
   Emilia, run you to the citadel,
   And tell my lord and lady what hath happed.
   Will you go on afore? [*aside*] This is the night
   That either makes me or fordoes me quite.   *They go*

Scene 2: *A chamber in the citadel; Desdemona asleep*
>*in her bed*

Enter Othello with a light; he locks the door

OTHELLO. It is the cause, it is the cause, my soul.
   Let me not name it to you, you chaste stars!
   It is the cause. Yet I'll not shed her blood,
   Nor scar that whiter skin of hers than snow
   And smooth as monumental alabaster—
   Yet she must die, else she'll betray more men.
   Put out the light, and then put out the light:
   If I quench thee, thou flaming minister,
   I can again thy former light restore
   Should I repent me; but once put out thy light,   10
   Thou cunning'st pattern of excelling nature,

I know not where is that Promethean heat
That can thy light relume.   *Sets down the taper*
                    When I have plucked the rose,
I cannot give it vital growth again,
It needs must wither: I'll smell it on the tree.
                                        Kisses her
O balmy breath, that dost almost persuade
Justice to break her sword! One more, one more.
Be thus when thou art dead, and I will kill thee,
And love thee after. One more, and that's the last.
So sweet was ne'er so fatal. I must weep,   20
But they are cruel tears; this sorrow's heavenly:
It strikes where it doth love. She wakes.
DESDEMONA. Who's there? Othello?
OTHELLO. Ay, Desdemona.
DESDEMONA. Will you come to bed, my lord?
OTHELLO. Have you prayed tonight, Desdemona?
DESDEMONA.   Ay, my lord.
OTHELLO. If you bethink yourself of any crime
Unreconciled as yet to heaven and grace,
Solicit for it straight.
DESDEMONA. Alack, my lord, what may you mean by
that?   30
OTHELLO. Well, do it, and be brief; I will walk by:
I would not kill thy unpreparéd spirit;
No—heaven forfend!—I would not kill thy soul.
DESDEMONA. Talk you of killing?
OTHELLO. Ay, I do.
DESDEMONA. Then heaven have mercy on me!
OTHELLO. Amen, with all my heart!
DESDEMONA. If you say so, I hope you will not kill me.
OTHELLO. Hum!
DESDEMONA. And yet I fear you; for you're fatal then   40
When your eyes roll so. Why I should fear I know
not,
Since guiltiness I know not; but yet I feel I fear.
OTHELLO. Think on thy sins.
DESDEMONA.   They are loves I bear to you.
OTHELLO. Ay, and for that thou diest.
DESDEMONA. That death's unnatural that kills for
loving.
Alas, why gnaw you so your nether lip?
Some bloody passion shakes your very frame:
These are portents; but yet I hope, I hope,
They do not point on me.
OTHELLO.   Peace, and be still!
DESDEMONA. I will so. What's the matter?   50
OTHELLO. That handkerchief which I so loved and
gave thee,
Thou gav'st to Cassio.
DESDEMONA.   No, by my life and soul!
Send for the man, and ask him.
OTHELLO.   Sweet soul, take heed,
Take heed of perjury: thou art on thy death-bed.
DESDEMONA. Ay, but not yet to die.
OTHELLO.   Yes, presently:
Therefore confess thee freely of thy sin;
For to deny each article with oath
Cannot remove nor choke the strong conception
That I do groan withal. Thou art to die.
DESDEMONA. O Lord have mercy on me!
OTHELLO.   I say, amen.   60
DESDEMONA. And have you mercy too! I never did
Offend you in my life; never loved Cassio
But with such general warranty of heaven
As I might love. I never gave him token.

OTHELLO. By heaven, I saw my handkerchief in's
hand.
O perjured woman! thou dost stone my heart,
And mak'st me call what I intend to do
A murder, which I thought a sacrifice.
I saw the handkerchief.
DESDEMONA.   He found it then;
I never gave it him. Send for him hither: 70
Let him confess a truth.
OTHELLO.   He hath confessed.
DESDEMONA. What, my lord?
OTHELLO. That he hath used thee.
DESDEMONA.   How? unlawfully?
OTHELLO. Ay.
DESDEMONA. He will not say so.
OTHELLO.   No, his mouth is stopped;
Honest Iago hath ta'en order for't.
DESDEMONA. O, my fear interprets! what, is he dead?
OTHELLO. Had all his hairs been lives, my great
revenge
Had stomach for them all.
DESDEMONA. Alas, he is betrayed, and I undone!   80
OTHELLO. Out, strumpet! weep'st thou for him to my
face?
DESDEMONA. O, banish me, my lord, but kill me not!
OTHELLO. Down, strumpet!
DESDEMONA. Kill me tomorrow; let me live tonight!
OTHELLO. Nay, if you strive—
DESDEMONA. But half an hour!
OTHELLO.   Being done, there is no pause.
DESDEMONA. But while I say one prayer!
OTHELLO.   It is too late.   *He smothers her*
EMILIA [*at the door without*]. My lord, my lord!
what, ho! my lord, my lord!
OTHELLO. What noise is this?—Not dead? not yet quite
dead?
I that am cruel am yet merciful;   90
I would not have thee linger in thy pain.
So, so.
EMILIA [*without*].   What, ho! my lord, my lord!
OTHELLO.   Who's there?
EMILIA [*without*]. O, good my lord, I'ld speak a word
with you!
OTHELLO. Yes: 'tis Emilia.—By and by.—She's dead.
'Tis like she comes to speak of Cassio's death;
The noise was high. Ha! no more moving?
Still as the grave. Shall she come in? were't good?
I think she stirs again. No. What's best to do?
If she come in, she'll sure speak to my wife—
My wife! my wife! what wife? I have no wife.   100
O, insupportable! O heavy hour!
Methinks it should be now a huge eclipse
Of sun and moon, and that th'affrighted globe
Should yawn at alteration.
EMILIA [*without*].   I do beseech
That I may speak with you. O, good my lord!
OTHELLO. I had forgot thee: O, come in, Emilia.
Soft; by and by. Let me the curtains draw.
Where art thou?   *Unlocks the door*

Enter Emilia

                    What's the matter with thee now?
EMILIA. O, my good lord, yonder's foul murder done!
OTHELLO. What, now?   110
EMILIA. But now, my lord.
OTHELLO. It is the very error of the moon;

She comes more nearer earth than she was wont
And makes men mad.
EMILIA. Cassio, my lord, hath killed a young Venetian
Called Roderigo.
OTHELLO.   Roderigo killed!
And Cassio killed!
EMILIA.   No, Cassio is not killed.
OTHELLO. Not Cassio killed! then murder's out of
  tune,
And sweet revenge grows harsh.
DESDEMONA. O, falsely, falsely murdered!
EMILIA.   Alas, what cry is that? 120
OTHELLO. That! what?
EMILIA. Out, and alas! that was my lady's voice.
                           She draws back the curtain
Help! help, ho! help! O lady, speak again!
Sweet Desdemona! O sweet mistress, speak!
DESDEMONA. A guiltless death I die.
EMILIA. O, who hath done this deed?
DESDEMONA. Nobody: I myself. Farewell;
Commend me to my kind lord: O, farewell! *Dies*
OTHELLO. Why, how should she be murdered?
EMILIA.   Alas, who knows?
OTHELLO. You heard her say herself, it was not I.   130
EMILIA. She said so: I must needs report the truth.
OTHELLO. She's like a liar gone to burning hell:
'Twas I that killed her.
EMILIA.   O, the more angel she,
And you the blacker devil!
OTHELLO. She turned to folly, and she was a whore.
EMILIA. Thou dost belie her, and thou art a devil.
OTHELLO. She was false as water.
EMILIA.   Thou art rash as fire to say
That she was false: O, she was heavenly true!
OTHELLO. Cassio did top her: ask thy husband else;
O, I were damned beneath all depth in hell   140
But that I did proceed upon just grounds
To this extremity. Thy husband knew it all.
EMILIA. My husband!
OTHELLO. Thy husband.
EMILIA. That she was false to wedlock?
OTHELLO. Ay, with Cassio. Nay, had she been true,
If heaven would make me such another world
Of one entire and perfect chrysolite,
I'ld not have sold her for it.
EMILIA. My husband!
OTHELLO. Ay, 'twas he that told me on her first; 150
An honest man he is, and hates the slime
That sticks on filthy deeds.
EMILIA.   My husband!
OTHELLO. What needs this iterance, woman? I say thy
  husband.
EMILIA. O mistress, villany hath made mocks with
  love!
My husband say that she was false!
OTHELLO.   He, woman:
I say thy husband; dost understand the word?
My friend, thy husband, honest, honest Iago.
EMILIA. If he say so, may his pernicious soul
Rot half a grain a day! He lies to th'heart.
She was too fond of her most filthy bargain.   160
OTHELLO. Ha!
EMILIA. Do thy worst:
This deed of thine is no more worthy heaven
Than thou wast worthy her.
OTHELLO.   Peace, you were best.

EMILIA. Thou hast not·half that power to do me harm
As I have to be hurt. O gull! O dolt!
As ignorant as dirt! thou hast done a deed—
I care not for thy sword; I'll make thee known,
Though I lost twenty lives. Help! help, ho! help!
The Moor hath killed my mistress! Murder! murder! 170

Enter Montano, Gratiano, Iago, and others

MONTANO. What is the matter? How now, general!
EMILIA. O, are you come, Iago? You have done well,
That men must lay their murders on your neck.
GRATIANO. What is the matter?
EMILIA. Disprove this villain, if thou be'st a man:
He says thou told'st him that his wife was false.
I know thou didst not, thou'rt not such a villain.
Speak, for my heart is full.
IAGO. I told him what I thought, and told no more
Than what he found himself was apt and true.   180
EMILIA. But did you ever tell him she was false?
IAGO. I did.
EMILIA. You told a lie, an odious, damnèd lie;
Upon my soul, a lie, a wicked lie!
She false with Cassio! Did you say with Cassio?
IAGO. With Cassio, mistress. Go to, charm your
  tongue.
EMILIA. I will not charm my tongue; I am bound to
  speak:
My mistress here lies murdered in her bed—
ALL. O heavens forfend!
EMILIA. And your reports have set the murder on.   190
OTHELLO. Nay, stare not, masters: it is true indeed.
GRATIANO. 'Tis a strange truth.
MONTANO. O monstrous act!
EMILIA.   Villany, villany, villany!
I think upon't; I think—I smell't: O villany!
I thought so then; I'll kill myself for grief:
O villany, villany!
IAGO. What, are you mad? I charge you, get you
  home.
EMILIA. Good gentlemen, let me have leave to speak:
'Tis proper I obey him, but not now.
Perchance, Iago, I will ne'er go home.   200
OTHELLO. O! O! O!   *Falls on the bed*
EMILIA.   Nay, lay thee down and roar;
For thou hast killed the sweetest innocent
That e'er did lift up eye.
OTHELLO [*rising*].   O, she was foul!
I scarce did know you, uncle. There lies your niece,
Whose breath indeed these hands have newly
  stopped.
I know this act shows horrible and grim.
GRATIANO. Poor Desdemon! I am glad thy father's
  dead.
Thy match was mortal to him, and pure grief
Shore his old thread in twain. Did he live now,
This sight would make him do a desperate turn,   210
Yea, curse his better angel from his side,
And fall to reprobance.
OTHELLO. 'Tis pitiful; but yet Iago knows
That she with Cassio hath the act of shame
A thousand times committed. Cassio confessed it;
And she did gratify his amorous works
With that recognizance and pledge of love
Which I first gave her—I saw it in his hand:
It was a handkerchief, an antique token
My father gave my mother.   220

EMILIA. O God! O heavenly God!

IAGO. 'Zounds! hold your peace.

EMILIA.   'Twill out, 'twill out. I peace!
No, I will speak as liberal as the north;
Let heaven and men and devils, let them all,
All, all, cry shame against me, yet I'll speak.

IAGO. Be wise, and get you home.

EMILIA.   I will not.

Iago offers to stab her

GRATIANO.   Fie!
Your sword upon a woman!

EMILIA. O thou dull Moor! that handkerchief thou
  speak'st of
I found by fortune, and did give my husband;
For often with a solemn earnestness,   230
More than indeed belonged to such a trifle,
He begged of me to steal it.

IAGO.   Villanous whore!

EMILIA. She give it Cassio! no, alas, I found it,
And I did give't my husband.

IAGO.   Filth, thou liest!

EMILIA. By heaven, I do not, I do not, gentlemen.
O murderous coxcomb! what should such a fool
Do with so good a wife?

OTHELLO.   Are there no stones in heaven
But what serve for the thunder? Precious villain!

*He runs at Iago, but Montano
disarms him; in the confusion,
Iago stabs Emilia from behind
and escapes*

GRATIANO. The woman falls; sure, he hath killed his
  wife.

EMILIA. Ay, ay. O, lay me by my mistress' side.   240

GRATIANO. He's gone, but his wife's killed.

MONTANO. 'Tis a notorious villain. Take you this
  weapon,
Which I have here recovered from the Moor.
Come, guard the door without; let him not pass,
But kill him rather. I'll after that same villain,
For 'tis a damnéd slave.

*All but Othello and Emilia
depart*

OTHELLO.   I am not valiant neither,
But every puny whipster gets my sword.
But why should honour outlive honesty?
Let it go all.

EMILIA.   What did thy song bode, lady?
Hark, canst thou hear me? I will play the swan,   250
And die in music. [*singing*] Willow, willow, willow.
Moor, she was chaste; she loved thee, cruel Moor;
So come my soul to bliss, as I speak true;
So speaking as I think, alas, I die.   *Dies*

OTHELLO. I have another weapon in this chamber:
It was a sword of Spain, the ice brook's temper—
O, here it is. Uncle, I must come forth.

GRATIANO [*at the door*]. If thou attempt it, it will cost
  thee dear:
Thou hast no weapon, and perforce must suffer.

OTHELLO. Look in upon me then, and speak with me,   260
Or, naked as I am, I will assault thee.

Re-enter Gratiano

GRATIANO. What is the matter?

OTHELLO.   Behold, I have a weapon
A better never did itself sustain
Upon a soldier's thigh. I have seen the day

That with this little arm and this good sword
I have made my way through more impediments
Than twenty times your stop—but, O vain boast!
Who can control his fate?—'tis not so now.
Be not afraid, though you do see me weaponed:
Here is my journey's end, here is my butt   270
And very sea-mark of my utmost sail.
Do you go back dismayed? 'tis a lost fear:
Man but a rush against Othello's breast,
And he retires. Where should Othello go?
Now, [*he turns to the bed*] how dost thou look now?
  O ill-starred wench!
Pale as thy smock! When we shall meet at compt,
This look of thine will hurl my soul from heaven,
And fiends will snatch at it. Cold, cold, my girl!
Even like thy chastity.
O curséd, curséd slave! Whip me, ye devils,   280
From the possession of this heavenly sight!
Blow me about in winds! roast me in sulphur!
Wash me in steep-down gulfs of liquid fire!
O Desdemon! dead Desdemon! dead! O! O!

*Enter Lodovico, Montano, Cassio carried in a chair, and
Officers with Iago, prisoner*

LODOVICO. Where is this rash and most unfortunate
  man?

OTHELLO. That's he that was Othello: here I am.

LODOVICO. Where is that viper? Bring the villain
  forth.

OTHELLO. I look down towards his feet: but that's a
  fable;
If that thou be'st a devil, I cannot kill thee.

Wounds Iago

LODOVICO. Wrench his sword from him.

IAGO.   I bleed, sir, but not killed.   290

OTHELLO. I am not sorry neither: I'ld have thee live;
For, in my sense, 'tis happiness to die.

LODOVICO. O thou Othello, that wert once so good,
Fallen in the practice of a damnéd slave
What shall be said to thee?

OTHELLO.   Why, anything:
An honourable murderer, if you will;
For nought did I in hate, but all in honour.

LODOVICO. This wretch hath part confessed his
  villany.
Did you and he consent in Cassio's death?

OTHELLO. Ay.   300

CASSIO. Dear general, I never gave you cause.

OTHELLO. I do believe it, and I ask your pardon.
Will you, I pray, demand that demi-devil
Why he hath thus ensnared my soul and body?

IAGO. Demand me nothing: what you know, you
  know;
From this time forth I never will speak word.

LODOVICO. What, not to pray?

GRATIANO.   Torments will ope your lips.

OTHELLO. Well, thou dost best.

LODOVICO. Sir, you shall understand what hath
  befallen,
Which, as I think, you know not. Here is a letter,   310
Found in the pocket of the slain Roderigo,
And here another: the one of them imports
The death of Cassio to be undertook
By Roderigo.

OTHELLO. O villain!

CASSIO.   Most heathenish and most gross!

LODOVICO. Now here's another discontented paper,
  Found in his pocket too: and this, it seems,
  Roderigo meant t'have sent this damnéd villain;
  But that, belike, Iago in the nick
  Came in and satisfied him.
OTHELLO.   O the pernicious caitiff! 320
  How came you, Cassio, by that handkerchief
  That was my wife's?
CASSIO.   I found it in my chamber:
  And he himself confessed but even now
  That there he dropped it for a special purpose
  Which wrought to his desire.
OTHELLO.   O fool! fool! fool!
CASSIO. There is besides, in Roderigo's letter,
  How he upbraids Iago that he made him
  Brave me upon the watch; whereon it came
  That I was cast; and even but now he spake—
  After long seeming dead—Iago hurt him, 330
  Iago set him on.
LODOVICO. You must forsake this room, and go with
  us;
  Your power and your command is taken off,
  And Cassio rules in Cyprus. For this slave,
  If there be any cunning cruelty
  That can torment him much and hold him long,
  It shall be his. You shall close prisoner rest,
  Till that the nature of your fault be known
  To the Venetian state. Come, bring away.
OTHELLO. Soft you; a word or two before you go. 340
  I have done the state some service, and they know't.
  No more of that. I pray you, in your letters,
  When you shall these unlucky deeds relate,
  Speak of me as I am; nothing extenuate,
  Nor set down aught in malice. Then must you
  speak

Of one that loved not wisely but too well;
Of one not easily jealous but, being wrought,
Perplexed in the extreme; of one whose hand,
Like the base Indian, threw a pearl away
Richer than all his tribe; of one whose subdued eyes, 350
Albeit unuséd to the melting mood,
Drop tears as fast as the Arabian trees
Their medicinable gum—Set you down this;
And say besides, that in Aleppo once,
Where a malignant and a turbaned Turk
Beat a Venetian and traduced the state,
I took by th'throat the circumciséd dog
And smote him:—thus.   *He stabs himself*
LODOVICO. O bloody period!
GRATIANO.   All that's spoke is marred.
OTHELLO. I kissed thee ere I killed thee: no way but
  this, 360
  Killing myself, to die upon a kiss.
              Falls on the bed, and dies
CASSIO. This did I fear, but thought he had no weapon;
  For he was great of heart.
LODOVICO [*to Iago*].   O Spartan dog,
  More fell than anguish, hunger, or the sea!
  Look on the tragic loading of this bed—
  This is thy work. The object poisons sight;
  Let it be hid. [*they draw the curtains*] Gratiano,
    keep the house,
  And seize upon the fortunes of the Moor,
  For they succeed on you. To you, lord governor,
  Remains the censure of this hellish villain, 370
  The time, the place, the torture: O, enforce it!
  Myself will straight aboard, and to the state
  This heavy act with heavy heart relate.   *They go*

Antony
and Cleopatra

The scene: the Roman Empire

CHARACTERS IN THE PLAY

ANTONY
OCTAVIUS CÆSAR } *triumvirs*
LEPIDUS

SEXTUS POMPEIUS

DOMITIUS ENOBARBUS
VENTIDIUS
EROS
SCARUS
DERCETUS   } *friends to Antony*
DEMETRIUS
PHILO

MÆCENAS
AGRIPPA
DOLABELLA
PROCULEIUS } *friends to Cæsar*
THIDIAS
GALLUS

MENAS
MENECRATES } *friends to Sextus Pompeius*
VARRIUS

TAURUS, *lieutenant-general to Cæsar*
CANIDIUS, *lieutenant-general to Antony*
SILIUS, *an officer in Ventidius' army*
A Schoolmaster, *ambassador from Antony to Cæsar*
ALEXAS
MARDIAN, *a eunuch* } *attendants on Cleopatra*
SELEUCUS
DIOMEDES
A Soothsayer
A Clown
CLEOPATRA, *queen of Egypt*
OCTAVIA, *sister to Cæsar, and wife to Antony*
CHARMIAN } *attendants on Cleopatra*
IRAS
Officers, soldiers, messengers, and other attendants

Anthony and Cleopatra

ACT 1

Scene 1: *Alexandria. A room in Cleopatra's palace*

Enter Demetrius and Philo

PHILO. Nay, but this dotage of our general's
O'erflows the measure: those his goodly eyes,
That o'er the files and musters of the war
Have glowed like plated Mars—now bend, now turn,
The office and devotion of their view
Upon a tawny front: his captain's heart,
Which in the scuffles of great fights hath burst
The buckles on his breast, reneges all temper,
And is become the bellows and the fan
To cool a gipsy's lust.

Flourish. Enter Antony, Cleopatra, her ladies, the train, with eunuchs fanning her

Look where they come: 10
Take but good note, and you shall see in him
The triple pillar of the world transformed
Into a strumpet's fool. Behold and see.
CLEOPATRA. If it be love indeed, tell me how much.
ANTONY. There's beggary in the love that can be reckoned.
CLEOPATRA. I'll set a bourn how far to be beloved.
ANTONY. Then must thou needs find out new heaven, new earth.

Enter an Attendant

ATTENDANT. News, my good lord, from Rome.
ANTONY.   Grates me! the sum.
CLEOPATRA. Nay, hear them, Antony:
Fulvia perchance is angry; or, who knows   20
If the scarce-bearded Cæsar have not sent
His powerful mandate to you, 'Do this, or this;
Take in that kingdom, and enfranchise that;
Perform't, or else we damn thee.'
ANTONY.   How, my love?
CLEOPATRA. Perchance? nay, and most like:
You must not stay here longer, your dismission
Is come from Cæsar; therefore hear it, Antony.
Where's Fulvia's process? Cæsar's I would say? both?
Call in the messengers. As I am Egypt's queen,
Thou blushest, Antony, and that blood of thine   30
Is Cæsar's homager: else so thy cheek pays shame
When shrill-tongued Fulvia scolds. The messengers!
ANTONY. Let Rome in Tiber melt, and the wide arch
Of the ranged empire fall! Here is my space.
Kingdoms are clay: our dungy earth alike
Feeds beast as man: the nobleness of life
Is to do thus; when such a mutual pair   *Embracing*
And such a twain can do't, in which I bind,
On pain of punishment, the world to weet
We stand up peerless.
CLEOPATRA.   Excellent falsehood!   40
Why did he marry Fulvia, and not love her?
I'll seem the fool I am not; Antony
Will be himself.
ANTONY.   But stirred by Cleopatra.

Now, for the love of Love and her soft hours,
Let's not confound the time with conference harsh:
There's not a minute of our lives should stretch
Without some pleasure new. What sport to-night?
CLEOPATRA. Hear the ambassadors.
ANTONY.   Fie, wrangling queen!
Whom every thing becomes, to chide, to laugh,
To weep; whose every passion fully strives   50
To make itself, in thee, fair and admired!
No messenger but thine, and all alone
To-night we'll wander through the streets and note
The qualities of people. Come, my queen;
Last night you did desire it. [*to the Attendant*] Speak not to us.

*Antony and Cleopatra depart
with their train*

DEMETRIUS. Is Cæsar with Antonius prized so slight?
PHILO. Sir, sometimes, when he is not Antony,
He comes too short of that great property
Which still should go with Antony.
DEMETRIUS.   I am full sorry
That he approves the common liar, who   60
Thus speaks of him at Rome: but I will hope
Of better deeds to-morrow. Rest you happy!
They go

Scene 2: *The same*

Enter Enobarbus, three other Romans, a Soothsayer, Cleopatra's attendants Charmian, Iras, Mardian the Eunuch, and Alexas

CHARMIAN. Lord Alexas, sweet Alexas, most any thing
Alexas, almost most absolute Alexas, where's the
soothsayer that you praised so to th'queen? O, that
I knew this husband, which, you say, must charge
his horns with garlands!
ALEXAS. Soothsayer!
SOOTHSAYER. Your will?
CHARMIAN. Is this the man? Is't you, sir, that know
things?
SOOTHSAYER. In Nature's infinite book of secrecy
A little I can read.
ALEXAS.   Show him your hand.   10
ENOBARBUS [*to a servant*]. Bring in the banquet
quickly; wine enough
Cleopatra's health to drink.
CHARMIAN. Good sir, give me good fortune.
SOOTHSAYER. I make not, but foresee.
CHARMIAN. Pray then, foresee me one.
SOOTHSAYER. You shall be yet far fairer than you are.
CHARMIAN. He means in flesh.
IRAS. No, you shall paint when you are old.
CHARMIAN. Wrinkles forbid!
ALEXAS. Vex not his prescience, be attentive.   20
CHARMIAN. Hush!
SOOTHSAYER. You shall be more beloving than beloved.
CHARMIAN. I had rather heat my liver with drinking.
ALEXAS. Nay, hear him.
CHARMIAN. Good now, some excellent fortune! Let

me be married to three kings in a forenoon, and
widow them all: let me have a child at fifty, to
whom Herod of Jewry may do homage: find me to
marry me with Octavius Cæsar, and companion me 30
with my mistress.

SOOTHSAYER. You shall outlive the lady whom you
serve.

CHARMIAN. O excellent! I love long life better than
figs.

SOOTHSAYER. You have seen and proved a fairer
former fortune
Than that which is to approach.

CHARMIAN. Then belike my children shall have no
names: prithee, how many boys and wenches must
I have?   40

SOOTHSAYER. If every of your wishes had a womb,
And fertile every wish, a million.

CHARMIAN. Out, fool! I forgive thee for a witch.

ALEXAS. You think none but your sheets are privy to
your wishes.

CHARMIAN. Nay, come, tell Iras hers.

ALEXAS. We'll know all our fortunes.

ENOBARBUS. Mine and most of our fortunes to-night
shall be—drunk to bed.

IRAS. There's a palm presages chastity, if nothing else. 50

CHARMIAN. E'en as the o'erflowing Nilus presageth
famine.

IRAS. Go, you wild bedfellow, you cannot soothsay.

CHARMIAN. Nay, if an oily palm be not a fruitful
prognostication, I cannot scratch mine ear. Prithee,
tell her but a worky-day fortune.

SOOTHSAYER. Your fortunes are alike.

IRAS. But how, but how? give me particulars.

SOOTHSAYER. I have said.

IRAS. Am I not an inch of fortune better than she? 60

CHARMIAN. Well, if you were but an inch of fortune
better than I . . . where would you choose it?

IRAS. Not in my husband's nose.

CHARMIAN. Our worser thoughts heavens mend!
Alexas—come, his fortune, his fortune! O, let him
marry a woman that cannot go, sweet Isis, I beseech
thee! and let her die too, and give him a worse! and
let worse follow worse, till the worst of all follow
him laughing to his grave, fifty-fold a cuckold!
Good Isis, hear me this prayer, though thou deny 70
me a matter of more weight; good Isis, I beseech
thee!

IRAS. Amen, dear goddess, hear that prayer of thy
people! For, as it is a heart-breaking to see a handsome man loose-witted, so it is a deadly sorrow to
behold a foul knave uncuckolded: therefore, dear
Isis, keep decorum, and fortune him accordingly!

CHARMIAN. Amen.

ALEXAS. Lo, now, if it lay in their hands to make me
a cuckold, they would make themselves whores but 80
they'ld do't!

ENOBARBUS. Hush! here comes Antony.

Enter Cleopatra

CHARMIAN.   Not he, the queen.
CLEOPATRA. Saw you my lord?
ENOBARBUS. No, lady.
CLEOPATRA. Was he not here?
CHARMIAN. No, madam.
CLEOPATRA. He was disposed to mirth, but on the
sudden

A Roman thought hath struck him. Enobarbus!
ENOBARBUS. Madam?
CLEOPATRA. Seek him, and bring him hither.   *He goes*
Where's Alexas?   90
ALEXAS. Here, at your service. My lord approaches.

Enter Antony with a Messenger and Attendants

CLEOPATRA. We will not look upon him: go with us.
                                              They leave
MESSENGER. Fulvia thy wife first came into the field.
ANTONY. Against my brother Lucius?
MESSENGER. Ay:
But soon that war had end, and the time's state
Made friends of them, jointing their force 'gainst
Cæsar,
Whose better issue in the war from Italy
Upon the first encounter drave them.
ANTONY.   Well, what worst?
MESSENGER. The nature of bad news infects the teller. 100
ANTONY. When it concerns the fool or coward. On!
Things that are past are done. With me, 'tis thus—
Who tells me true, though in his tale lie death,
I hear him as he flattered.
MESSENGER.   Labienus—
This is stiff news—hath with his Parthian force
Extended Asia from Euphrates,
His conquering banner shook from Syria
To Lydia and to Ionia,
Whilst—
ANTONY. Antony, thou wouldst say—
MESSENGER.   O, my lord!
ANTONY. Speak to me home, mince not the general
tongue,   110
Name Cleopatra as she is called in Rome;
Rail thou in Fulvia's phrase, and taunt my faults
With such full license as both truth and malice
Have power to utter. O, then we bring forth weeds
When our quick minds lie still, and our ills told us
Is as our earing. Fare thee well awhile.
MESSENGER. At your noble pleasure.   *He goes*
ANTONY. From Sicyon, ho, the news! Speak there!
1 ATTENDANT. The man from Sicyon, is there such
an one?
2 ATTENDANT. He stays upon your will.
ANTONY.   Let him appear. 120
These strong Egyptian fetters I must break,
Or lose myself in dotage.

Enter another Messenger, with a letter

                              What are you?
2 MESSENGER. Fulvia thy wife is dead.
ANTONY.   Where died she?
2 MESSENGER. In Sicyon:
Her length of sickness, with what else more serious
Importeth thee to know, this bears.   *Gives a letter*
ANTONY.   Forbear me.
                    Messenger and Attendants withdraw
There's a great spirit gone! Thus did I desire it:
What our contempts doth often hurl from us,
We wish it ours again; the present pleasure,
By revolution lowering, does become   130
The opposite of itself: she's good, being gone;
The hand could pluck her back that shoved her on.
I must from this enchanting queen break off:
Ten thousand harms, more than the ills I know,
My idleness doth hatch. Ho, now! Enobarbus!

Enobarbus returns

ENOBARBUS. What's your pleasure, sir?

ANTONY. I must with haste from hence.

ENOBARBUS. Why then we kill all our women. We see
how mortal an unkindness is to them; if they suffer
our departure death's the word. 140

ANTONY. I must be gone.

ENOBARBUS. Under a compelling occasion let women
die. It were pity to cast them away for nothing,
though between them and a great cause they should
be esteemed nothing. Cleopatra, catching but the
least noise of this, dies instantly; I have seen her die
twenty times upon far poorer moment: I do think
there is mettle in death, which commits some loving
act upon her, she hath such a celerity in dying.

ANTONY. She is cunning past man's thought. 150

ENOBARBUS. Alack, sir, no; her passions are made of
nothing but the finest part of pure love. We cannot
call her winds and waters sighs and tears; they are
greater storms and tempests than almanacs can
report. This cannot be cunning in her; if it be, she
makes a shower of rain as well as Jove.

ANTONY. Would I had never seen her!

ENOBARBUS. O, sir, you had then left unseen a wonderful piece of work, which not to have been blest
withal would have discredited your travel. 160

ANTONY. Fulvia is dead.

ENOBARBUS. Sir?

ANTONY. Fulvia is dead.

ENOBARBUS. Fulvia!

ANTONY. Dead.

ENOBARBUS. Why, sir, give the gods a thankful sacrifice. When it pleaseth their deities to take the wife
of a man from him, it shows to man the tailors of
the earth; comforting therein, that when old robes
are worn out there are members to make new. If 170
there were no more women but Fulvia, then had
you indeed a cut, and the case to be lamented: this
grief is crowned with consolation; your old smock
brings forth a new petticoat: and indeed the tears
live in an onion that should water this sorrow.

ANTONY. The business she hath broachéd in the state
Cannot endure my absence.

ENOBARBUS. And the business you have broached here
cannot be without you; especially that of Cleopatra's, which wholly depends on your abode. 180

ANTONY. No more light answers. Let our officers
Have notice what we purpose. I shall break
The cause of our expedience to the queen,
And get her leave to part. For not alone
The death of Fulvia, with more urgent touches,
Do strongly speak to us, but the letters too
Of many our contriving friends in Rome
Petition us at home: Sextus Pompeius
Hath given the dare to Cæsar and commands
The empire of the sea: our slippery people, 190
Whose love is never linked to the deserver
Till his deserts are past, begin to throw
Pompey the Great and all his dignities
Upon his son; who, high in name and power,
Higher than both in blood and life, stands up
For the main soldier: whose quality, going on,
The sides o'th'world may danger. Much is breeding,
Which, like the courser's hair, hath yet but life
And not a serpent's poison. Say, our pleasure,

To such whose place is under us, requires 200
Our quick remove from hence.

ENOBARBUS. I shall do't. *They go*

Scene 3

Enter Cleopatra, Charmian, Iras, and Alexas

CLEOPATRA. Where is he?

CHARMIAN. I did not see him since.

CLEOPATRA. See where he is, who's with him, what
he does:
I did not send you: if you find him sad,
Say I am dancing; if in mirth, report
That I am sudden sick. Quick, and return.
Alexas goes

CHARMIAN. Madam, methinks, if you did love him
dearly,
You do not hold the method to enforce
The like from him.

CLEOPATRA. What should I do, I do not?

CHARMIAN. In each thing give him way, cross him
in nothing.

CLEOPATRA. Thou teachest like a fool: the way to
lose him. 10

CHARMIAN. Tempt him not so too far; iwis, forbear:
In time we hate that which we often fear.

Antony enters

But here comes Antony.

CLEOPATRA. I am sick and sullen.

ANTONY. I am sorry to give breathing to my
purpose—

CLEOPATRA. Help me away, dear Charmian, I shall fall.
It cannot be thus long, the sides of nature
Will not sustain it.

ANTONY. Now, my dearest queen—

CLEOPATRA. Pray you, stand farther from me.

ANTONY. What's the matter?

CLEOPATRA. I know, by that same eye, there's some
good news.
What, says the married woman you may go? 20
Would she had never given you leave to come!
Let her not say 'tis I that keep you here.
I have no power upon you; hers you are.

ANTONY. The gods best know—

CLEOPATRA. O, never was there queen
So mightily betrayed! yet at the first
I saw the treasons planted.

ANTONY. Cleopatra—

CLEOPATRA. Why should I think you can be mine
and true
(Though you in swearing shake the thronéd gods),
Who have been false to Fulvia! Riotous madness,
To be entangled with those mouth-made vows, 30
Which break themselves in swearing!

ANTONY. Most sweet queen—

CLEOPATRA. Nay, pray you, seek no colour for
your going,
But bid farewell, and go: when you sued staying,
Then was the time for words: no going then;
Eternity was in our lips and eyes,
Bliss in our brows' bent; none our parts so poor
But was a race of heaven: they are so still,
Or thou, the greatest soldier of the world,
Art turned the greatest liar.

ANTONY. How now, lady!

CLEOPATRA. I would I had thy inches; thou
  shouldst know   40
  There were a heart in Egypt.
ANTONY.   Hear me, queen:
  The strong necessity of time commands
  Our services awhile; but my full heart
  Remains in use with you. Our Italy
  Shines o'er with civil swords: Sextus Pompeius
  Makes his approaches to the port of Rome:
  Equality of two domestic powers
  Breed scrupulous faction: the hated, grown to
    strength,
  Are newly grown to love: the condemned Pompey,
  Rich in his father's honour, creeps apace   50
  Into the hearts of such as have not thrived
  Upon the present state, whose numbers threaten;
  And quietness grown sick of rest would purge
  By any desperate change. My more particular,
  And that which most with you should safe my
    going,
  Is Fulvia's death.
CLEOPATRA. Though age from folly could not give
  me freedom,
  It does from childishness: can Fulvia die?
ANTONY. She's dead, my queen.
  Look here, and at thy sovereign leisure read   60
  The garboils she awaked: at the last, best,
  See when and where she died.
CLEOPATRA.   O most false love!
  Where be the sacred vials thou shouldst fill
  With sorrowful water? Now I see, I see,
  In Fulvia's death, how mine received shall be.
ANTONY. Quarrel no more, but be prepared to know
  The purposes I bear; which are, or cease,
  As you shall give th'advice. By the fire
  That quickens Nilus' slime, I go from hence
  Thy soldier, servant, making peace or war   70
  As thou affects.
CLEOPATRA.   Cut my lace, Charmian, come;
  But let it be—I am quickly ill, and well—
  So Antony loves.
ANTONY.   My precious queen, forbear;
  And give true evidence to his love, which stands
  An honourable trial.
CLEOPATRA.   So Fulvia told me.
  I prithee, turn aside and weep for her,
  Then bid adieu to me, and say the tears
  Belong to Egypt: good now, play one scene
  Of excellent dissembling, and let it look
  Like perfect honour.
ANTONY.   You'll heat my blood: no more.   80
CLEOPATRA. You can do better yet; but this is meetly.
ANTONY. Now, by my sword
CLEOPATRA.   And target. Still he mends;
  But this is not the best. Look, prithee, Charmian,
  How this Herculean Roman does become
  The carriage of his chafe.
ANTONY. I'll leave you, lady.
CLEOPATRA.   Courteous lord, one word.
  Sir, you and I must part, but that's not it:
  Sir, you and I have loved, but there's not it:
  That you know well: something it is I would:
  O, my oblivion is a very Antony,   90
  And I am all forgotten.
ANTONY.   But that your royalty
  Holds idleness your subject, I should take you

For idleness itself.
CLEOPATRA.   'Tis sweating labour
  To bear such idleness so near the heart
  As Cleopatra this. But, sir, forgive me,
  Since my becomings kill me when they do not
  Eye well to you. Your honour calls you hence;
  Therefore be deaf to my unpitied folly,
  And all the gods go with you! Upon your sword
  Sit laurel victory! and smooth success   100
  Be strewed before your feet!
ANTONY.   Let us go. Come;
  Our separation so abides and flies,
  That thou, residing here, goes yet with me,
  And I, hence fleeing, here remain with thee.
  Away!   *They go*

Scene 4: *Rome. Cæsar's house*

*Enter Octavius Cæsar, reading a letter, Lepidus, and their
train*

CÆSAR. You may see, Lepidus, and henceforth know,
  It is not Cæsar's natural vice to hate
  Our great competitor. From Alexandria
  This is the news: he fishes, drinks and wastes
  The lamps of night in revel: is not more manlike
  Than Cleopatra, nor the queen of Ptolemy
  More womanly than he: hardly gave audience, or
  Vouchsafed to think he had partners: you shall find
    there
  A man who is the abstract of all faults
  That all men follow.
LEPIDUS.   I must not think there are   10
  Evils enow to darken all his goodness:
  His faults in him seem as the spots of heaven,
  More fiery by night's blackness, hereditary
  Rather than purchased, what he cannot change
  Than what he chooses.
CÆSAR. You are too indulgent. Let's grant it is not
  Amiss to tumble on the bed of Ptolemy,
  To give a kingdom for a mirth, to sit
  And keep the turn of tippling with a slave,
  To reel the streets at noon and stand the buffet   20
  With knaves that smell of sweat: say this
    becomes him—
  As his composure must be rare indeed
  Whom these things cannot blemish—yet must
    Antony
  No way excuse his foils, when we do bear
  So great weight in his lightness. If he filled
  His vacancy with his voluptuousness,
  Full surfeits and the dryness of his bones
  Call on him for't: but to confound such time
  That drums him from his sport and speaks as loud
  As his own state and ours—'tis to be chid   30
  As we rate boys, who, being mature in knowledge,
  Pawn their experience to their present pleasure,
  And so rebel to judgement.

Enter a Messenger

LEPIDUS.   Here's more news.
MESSENGER. Thy biddings have been done, and
  every hour,
  Most noble Cæsar, shalt thou have report
  How 'tis abroad. Pompey is strong at sea,
  And it appears he is beloved of those
  That only have feared Cæsar: to the fleets

The discontents repair, and men's reports
Give him much wronged.
CÆSAR.   I should have known no less: 40
It hath been taught us from the primal state,
That he which is was wished until he were;
And the ebbed man, ne'er loved till ne'er worth
    love,
Comes deared by being lacked. This common body,
Like to a vagabond flag upon the stream,
Goes to and back, lackeying the varying tide,
To rot itself with motion.
MESSENGER.   Cæsar, I bring thee word,
Menecrates and Menas, famous pirates,
Make the sea serve them, which they ear and wound
With keels of every kind: many hot inroads 50
They make in Italy; the borders maritime
Lack blood to think on't, and flush youth revolt:
No vessel can peep forth, but 'tis as soon
Taken as seen; for Pompey's name strikes more
Than could his war resisted.
CÆSAR.   Antony,
Leave thy lascivious wassails. When thou once
Wast beaten from Modena, where thou slew'st
Hirtius and Pansa, consuls, at thy heel
Did famine follow, whom thou fought'st against
(Though daintily brought up) with patience more 60
Than savages could suffer: thou didst drink
The stale of horses and the gilded puddle
Which beasts would cough at: thy palate then did
    deign
The roughest berry on the rudest hedge;
Yea, like the stag, when snow the pasture sheets,
The barks of trees thou browsed. On the Alps
It is reported thou didst eat strange flesh,
Which some did die to look on: and all this—
It wounds thine honour that I speak it now—
Was borne so like a soldier that thy cheek 70
So much as lanked not.
LEPIDUS.   'Tis pity of him.
CÆSAR. Let his shames quickly
Drive him to Rome. 'Tis time we twain
Did show ourselves i'th'field, and to that end
Assemble we immediate council. Pompey
Thrives in our idleness.
LEPIDUS.   To-morrow, Cæsar,
I shall be furnished to inform you rightly
Both what by sea and land I can be able
To front this present time.
CÆSAR.   Till which encounter,
It is my business too. Farewell. 80
LEPIDUS. Farewell, my lord: what you shall know
    meantime
Of stirs abroad, I shall beseech you, sir,
To let me be partaker.
CÆSAR.   Doubt not, sir;
I knew it for my bond.   *They go*

Scene 5: *Alexandria. Cleopatra's palace*

Enter Cleopatra, Charmian, Iras, and Mardian

CLEOPATRA. Charmian!
CHARMIAN. Madam?
CLEOPATRA. Ha, ha!
Give me to drink mandragora.
CHARMIAN.   Why, madam?

CLEOPATRA. That I might sleep out this great gap of
    time
My Antony is away.
CHARMIAN.   You think of him too much.
CLEOPATRA. O, 'tis treason!
CHARMIAN.   Madam, I trust not so.
CLEOPATRA. Thou, eunuch Mardian!
MARDIAN.   What's your highness' pleasure?
CLEOPATRA. Not now to hear thee sing; I take
    no pleasure
In aught an eunuch has: 'tis well for thee, 10
That, being unseminared, thy freer thoughts
May not fly forth of Egypt. Hast thou affections?
MARDIAN. Yes, gracious madam.
CLEOPATRA. Indeed?
MARDIAN. Not in deed, madam, for I can do nothing
But what indeed is honest to be done:
Yet have I fierce affections, and think
What Venus did with Mars.
CLEOPATRA.   O Charmian,
Where think'st thou he is now? Stands he, or sits
    he?
Or does he walk? or is he on his horse? 20
O happy horse, to bear the weight of Antony!
Do bravely, horse! for wot'st thou whom thou
    mov'st?
The demi-Atlas of this earth, the arm
And burgonet of men. He's speaking now,
Or murmuring 'Where's my serpent of old Nile?'
For so he calls me: now I feed myself
With most delicious poison. Think on me,
That am with Phœbus' amorous pinches black
And wrinkled deep in time? Broad-fronted Cæsar,
When thou wast here above the ground, I was 30
A morsel for a monarch: and great Pompey
Would stand and make his eyes grow in my brow;
There would he anchor his aspéct and die
With looking on his life.

Enter Alexas from Antony

ALEXAS.   Sovereign of Egypt, hail!
CLEOPATRA. How much unlike art thou Mark Antony!
Yet, coming from him, that great med'cine hath
With his tinct gilded thee.
How goes it with my brave Mark Antony?
ALEXAS. Last thing he did, dear queen,
He kissed—the last of many doubled kisses— 40
This orient pearl. His speech sticks in my heart.
CLEOPATRA. Mine ear must pluck it thence.
ALEXAS.   'Good friend,' quoth he,
'Say, the firm Roman to great Egypt sends
This treasure of an oyster; at whose foot,
To mend the petty present, I will piece
Her opulent throne with kingdoms; all the east,
Say thou, shall call her mistress.' So he nodded,
And soberly did mount an arm-gaunt steed,
Who neighed so high, that what I would have spoke
Was beastly dumbed by him.
CLEOPATRA.   What was he, sad or merry? 50
ALEXAS. Like to the time o'th'year between the
    extremes
Of hot and cold, he was nor sad nor merry.
CLEOPATRA. O well divided disposition! Note him,
Note him, good Charmian, 'tis the man; but note
    him:
He was not sad, for he would shine on those

That make their looks by his; he was not merry,
Which seemed to tell them his remembrance lay
In Egypt with his joy; but between both.
O heavenly mingle! Be'st thou sad or merry,
The violence of either thee becomes,   60
So does it no man else. Met'st thou my posts?
ALEXAS. Ay, madam, twenty several messengers:
Why do you send so thick?
CLEOPATRA.   Who's born that day
When I forget to send to Antony,
Shall die a beggar. Ink and paper, Charmian.
Welcome, my good Alexas. Did I, Charmian,
Ever love Cæsar so?
CHARMIAN.   O that brave Cæsar!
CLEOPATRA. Be choked with such another emphasis!
Say, the brave Antony.
CHARMIAN.   The valiant Cæsar!
CLEOPATRA. By Isis, I will give thee bloody teeth,   70
If thou with Cæsar paragon again
My man of men.
CHARMIAN.   By your most gracious pardon,
I sing but after you.
CLEOPATRA.   My salad days,
When I was green in judgement, cold in blood,
To say as I said then. But come, away,
Get me ink and paper.
He shall have every day a several greeting,
Or I'll unpeople Egypt.   *They go*

ACT 2

Scene 1: *Messina. Pompey's house*

Enter Pompey, Menecrates, and Menas, in warlike manner

POMPEY. If the great gods be just, they shall assist
The deeds of justest men.
MENAS.   Know, worthy Pompey,
That what they do delay, they not deny.
POMPEY. Whiles we are suitors to their throne, decays
The thing we sue for.
MENAS.   We, ignorant of ourselves,
Beg often our own harms, which the wise powers
Deny us for our good; so find we profit
By losing of our prayers.
POMPEY.   I shall do well:
The people love me, and the sea is mine;
My powers are crescent, and my auguring hope   10
Says it will come to th'full. Mark Antony
In Egypt sits at dinner, and will make
No wars without doors: Cæsar gets money where
He loses hearts: Lepidus flatters both,
Of both is flattered, but he neither loves,
Not either cares for him.
MENAS.   Cæsar and Lepidus.
Are in the field: a mighty strength they carry.
POMPEY. Where have you this? 'tis false.
MENAS.   From Silvius, sir.
POMPEY. He dreams: I know they are in Rome
      together,
Looking for Antony. But all the charms of love, 20
Salt Cleopatra, soften thy waned lip!
Let witchcraft join with beauty, lust with both!
Tie up the libertine in a field of feasts,
Keep his brain fuming; Epicurean cooks
Sharpen with cloyless sauce his appetite;

That sleep and feeding may prorogue his honour
Even till a Lethe'd dulness—

Enter Varrius

                            How now, Varrius!
VARRIUS. This is most certain that I shall deliver:
Mark Antony is every hour in Rome
Expected: since he went from Egypt 'tis   30
A space for farther travel.
POMPEY.   I could have given less matter
A better ear. Menas, I did not think
This amorous surfeiter would have donned his helm
For such a petty war: his soldiership
Is twice the other twain: but let us rear
The higher our opinion, that our stirring
Can from the lap of Egypt's widow pluck
The ne'er-lust-wearied Antony.
MENAS.   I cannot hope
Cæsar and Antony shall well greet together:
His wife that's dead did trespasses to Cæsar;   40
His brother warred upon him, although I think
Not moved by Antony.
POMPEY.   I know not, Menas,
How lesser enmities may give way to greater.
Were't not that we stand up against them all,
'Twere pregnant they should square between
      themselves;
For they have entertainéd cause enough
To draw their swords: but how the fear of us
May cement their divisions and bind up
The petty difference, we yet not know.
Be't as our gods will have't! It only stands   50
Our lives upon to use our strongest hands.
Come, Menas.   *They go*

Scene 2: *Rome. The house of Lepidus*

Enter Enobarbus and Lepidus

LEPIDUS. Good Enobarbus, 'tis a worthy deed,
And shall become you well, to entreat your captain
To soft and gentle speech.
ENOBARBUS.   I shall entreat him
To answer like himself: if Cæsar move him,
Let Antony look over Cæsar's head,
And speak as loud as Mars. By Jupiter,
Were I wearer of Antonio's beard,
I would not shave't to-day.
LEPIDUS.   'Tis not a time
For private stomaching.
ENOBARBUS.   Every time
Serves for the matter that is then born in't.   10
LEPIDUS. But small to greater matters must give way.
ENOBARBUS. Not if the small come first.
LEPIDUS.   Your speech is passion:
But, pray you, stir no embers up. Here comes
The noble Antony.

Antony and Ventidius enter

ENOBARBUS.   And yonder, Cæsar.

Cæsar, Mæcenas, and Agrippa enter

ANTONY. If we compose well here, to Parthia:
Hark, Ventidius.
CÆSAR.   I do not know,
Mæcenas; ask Agrippa.
LEPIDUS.   Noble friends,

That which combined us was most great, and
  let not
A leaner action rend us. What's amiss,
May it be gently heard: when we debate   20
Our trivial difference loud, we do commit
Murder in healing wounds: then, noble partners,
The rather for I earnestly beseech,
Touch you the sourest points with sweetest terms,
Nor curstness grow to th'matter.

ANTONY.   'Tis spoken well.
Were we before our armies and to fight,
I should do thus.   *Flourish*

CÆSAR. Welcome to Rome.

ANTONY.   Thank you.

CÆSAR.   Sit.

ANTONY.   Sit, sir.

CÆSAR.   Nay, then.

ANTONY. I learn, you take things ill which are not so;
Or being, concern you not.

CÆSAR.   I must be laughed at,   30
If, or for nothing or a little, I
Should say myself offended, and with you
Chiefly i'th'world; more laughed at, that I should
Once name you derogately, when to sound your
  name
It not concerned me.

ANTONY.   My being in Egypt, Cæsar,
What was't to you?

CÆSAR. No more than my residing here at Rome
Might be to you in Egypt: yet, if you there
Did practise on my state, your being in Egypt
Might be my question.

ANTONY.   How intend you, practised?   40

CÆSAR. You may be pleased to catch at mine intent
By what did here befall me. Your wife and brother
Made wars upon me, and their contestation
Was then for you, you were the word of war.

ANTONY. You do mistake your business; my brother
  never
Did urge me in his act; I did inquire it,
And have my learning from some true reports
That drew their swords with you. Did he not rather
Discredit my authority with yours,
And make the wars alike against my stomach,   50
Having alike your cause? Of this my letters
Before did satisfy you. If you'll patch a quarrel,
As matter whole you have to make it with,
It must not be with this.

CÆSAR.   You praise yourself.
By laying defects of judgement to me, but
You patched up your excuses.

ANTONY.   Not so, not so;
I know you could not lack, I am certain on't,
Very necessity of this thought, that I,
Your partner in the cause 'gainst which he fought,
Could not with grateful eyes attend those wars   60
Which fronted mine own peace. As for my wife,
I would you had her spirit in such another:
The third o'th'world is yours, which with a snaffle
You may pace easy, but not such a wife—

ENOBARBUS. Would we had all such wives, that the
men might go to wars with the women!

ANTONY. —So much incurbable; her garboils, Cæsar,
Made out of her impatience (which not wanted
Shrewdness of policy too), I grieving grant
Did you too much disquiet: for that you must   70

But say, I could not help it.

CÆSAR.   I wrote to you.
When rioting in Alexandria you
Did pocket up my letters, and with taunts
Did gibe my missive out of audience.

ANTONY.   Sir,
He fell upon me, ere admitted, then:
Three kings I had newly feasted and did want
Of what I was i'th'morning: but next day
I told him of myself, which was as much
As to have asked him pardon. Let this fellow
Be nothing of our strife; if we contend,   80
Out of our question wipe him.

CÆSAR.   You have broken
The article of your oath, which you shall never
Have tongue to charge me with.

LEPIDUS.   Soft, Cæsar!

ANTONY. No, Lepidus, let him speak:
The honour is sacred which he talks on now,
Supposing that I lacked it. But on, Cæsar;
The article of my oath—

CÆSAR. To lend me arms and aid when I required
  them;
The which you both denied.

ANTONY.   Neglected rather,
And then when poisoned hours had bound me up   90
From mine own knowledge. As nearly as I may,
I'll play the penitent to you: but mine honesty
Shall not make poor my greatness, nor my power
Work without it. Truth is that Fulvia,
To have me out of Egypt, made wars here;
For which myself, the ignorant motive, do
So far ask pardon as befits mine honour
To stoop in such a case.

LEPIDUS.   'Tis noble spoken.

MÆCENAS. If it might please you, to enforce no further
The griefs between ye: to forget them quite   100
Were to remember that the present need
Speaks to atone you.

LEPIDUS.   Worthily spoken, Mæcenas.

ENOBARBUS. Or, if you borrow one another's love for
the instant, you may, when you hear no more
words of Pompey, return it again: you shall have
time to wrangle in when you have nothing else to do.

ANTONY. Thou art a soldier only: speak no more.

ENOBARBUS. That truth should be silent I had
almost forgot.

ANTONY. You wrong this presence; therefore speak
no more.

ENOBARBUS. Go to, then; your considerate stone.   110

CÆSAR. I do not much dislike the matter, but
The manner of his speech; for't cannot be
We shall remain in friendship, our conditions
So differing in their acts. Yet, if I knew
What hoop should hold us staunch from edge
  to edge
O'th'world, I would pursue it.

AGRIPPA.   Give me leave, Cæsar.

CÆSAR. Speak, Agrippa.

AGRIPPA. Thou hast a sister by the mother's side,
Admired Octavia: great Mark Antony
Is now a widower.

CÆSAR.   Say not so, Agrippa: 120
If Cleopatra heard you, your reproof
Were well deserved of rashness.

ANTONY. I am not married, Cæsar: let me hear

Agrippa further speak.

AGRIPPA. To hold you in perpetual amity,
To make you brothers, and to knit your hearts
With an unslipping knot, take Antony
Octavia to his wife; whose beauty claims
No worse a husband than the best of men;
Whose virtue and whose general graces speak   130
That which none else can utter. By this marriage
All little jealousies which now seem great,
And all great fears which now import their dangers,
Would then be nothing: truths would be tales,
Where now half tales be truths: her love to both
Would each to other and all loves to both
Draw after her. Pardon what I have spoke,
For 'tis a studied, not a present thought,
By duty ruminated.

ANTONY.   Will Cæsar speak?

CÆSAR. Not till he hears how Antony is touched   140
With what is spoken already.

ANTONY.   What power is in Agrippa,
If I would say, 'Agrippa, be it so,'
To make this good?

CÆSAR.   The power of Cæsar, and
His power unto Octavia.

ANTONY.   May I never
(To this good purpose, that so fairly shows)
Dream of impediment! Let me have thy hand:
Further this act of grace; and from this hour
The heart of brothers govern in our loves
And sway our great designs!

CÆSAR.   There's my hand.
A sister I bequeath you, whom no brother   150
Did ever love so dearly: let her live
To join our kingdoms and our hearts—and never
Fly off our loves again!

LEPIDUS.   Happily, amen!

ANTONY. I did not think to draw my sword
'gainst Pompey;
For he hath laid strange courtesies and great
Of late upon me. I must thank him only,
Lest my remembrance suffer ill report;
At heel of that, defy him.

LEPIDUS.   Time calls upon's:
Of us must Pompey presently be sought,
Or else he seeks out us.

ANTONY.   Where lies he?   160

CÆSAR. About the Mount Misenum.

ANTONY.   What is his strength
By land?

CÆSAR.   Great and increasing: but by sea
He is an absolute master.

ANTONY.   So is the fame.
Would we had spoke together! Haste we for it:
Yet, ere we put ourselves in arms, dispatch we
The business we have talked of.

CÆSAR.   With most gladness;
And do invite you to my sister's view,
Whither straight I'll lead you.

ANTONY.   Let us, Lepidus,
Not lack your company.

LEPIDUS.   Noble Antony,
Not sickness should detain me.   170

           Flourish. Cæsar, Antony, and
           Lepidus go out together

MÆCENAS. Welcome from Egypt, sir.

ENOBARBUS. Half the heart of Cæsar, worthy Mæce-

nas! My honourable friend, Agrippa!

AGRIPPA. Good Enobarbus!

MÆCENAS. We have cause to be glad that matters are
so well digested. You stayed well by't in Egypt.

ENOBARBUS. Ay, sir; we did sleep day out of countenance, and made the night light with drinking.

MÆCENAS. Eight wild-boars roasted whole at a breakfast, and but twelve persons there; is this true?   180

ENOBARBUS. This was but as a fly by an eagle: we had
much more monstrous matter of feast, which
worthily deserved noting.

MÆCENAS. She's a most triumphant lady, if report be
square to her.

ENOBARBUS. When she first met Mark Antony, she
pursed up his heart, upon the river of Cydnus.

AGRIPPA. There she appeared indeed; or my reporter
devised well for her.

ENOBARBUS. I will tell you.   190
The barge she sat in, like a burnisht throne
Burned on the water: the poop was beaten gold;
Purple the sails, and so perfumèd that
The winds were love-sick with them; the oars
   were silver,
Which to the tune of flutes kept stroke and made
The water which they beat to follow faster,
As amorous of their strokes. For her own person,
It beggared all description, she did lie
In her pavilion, cloth-of-gold, of tissue,
O'er-picturing that Venus where we see   200
The fancy outwork nature: on each side her
Stood pretty dimpled boys, like smiling Cupids,
With divers-coloured fans, whose wind did seem
To glow the delicate cheeks which they did cool,
And what they undid did.

AGRIPPA.   O, rare for Antony!

ENOBARBUS. Her gentlewomen, like the Nereides,
So many mermaids, tended her i'th'eyes,
And made their bends adornings: at the helm
A seeming mermaid steers: the silken tackle
Swell with the touches of those flower-soft hands,   210
That yarely frame the office. From the barge
A strange invisible perfume hits the sense
Of the adjacent wharfs. The city cast
Her people out upon her; and Antony,
Enthroned i'th'market-place, did sit alone,
Whistling to th'air; which, but for vacancy,
Had gone to gaze on Cleopatra too,
And made a gap in nature.

AGRIPPA.   Rare Egyptian!

ENOBARBUS. Upon her landing, Antony sent to her,
Invited her to supper: she replied,   220
It should be better he became her guest;
Which she entreated: our courteous Antony,
Whom ne'er the word of 'No' woman heard speak,
Being barbered ten times o'er, goes to the feast,
And, for his ordinary, pays his heart
For what his eyes eat only.

AGRIPPA.   Royal wench!
She made great Cæsar lay his sword to bed:
He ploughed her, and she cropped.

ENOBARBUS.   I saw her once
Hop forty paces through the public street;
And having lost her breath, she spoke, and panted,   230
That she did make defect perfection,
And, breathless, power breathe forth.

MÆCENAS. Now Antony must leave her utterly.

ENOBARBUS. Never; he will not:
Age cannot wither her, nor custom stale
Her infinite variety: other women cloy
The appetites they feed, but she makes hungry
Where most she satisfies: for vilest things
Become themselves in her, that the holy priests
Bless her when she is riggish.   240
MÆCENAS. If beauty, wisdom, modesty, can settle
The heart of Antony, Octavia is
A blessed lottery to him.
AGRIPPA.   Let us go.
Good Enobarbus, make yourself my guest
Whilst you abide here.
ENOBARBUS.   Humbly, sir, I thank you.
                          They go

Scene 3: *The same. Cæsar's house*

Enter Antony, Cæsar, and Octavia between them

ANTONY. The world and my great office will
     sometimes
Divide me from your bosom.
OCTAVIA.   All which time
Before the gods my knee shall bow in prayers
To them for you.
ANTONY.   Good night, sir. My Octavia,
Read not my blemishes in the world's report:
I have not kept my square, but that to come
Shall all be done by th'rule. Good night, dear lady.
OCTAVIA. Good night, sir.
CÆSAR. Good night.   *He leads his sister away*

Enter Soothsayer

ANTONY. Now, sirrah; you do wish yourself in Egypt? 10
SOOTHSAYER. Would I had never come from thence,
nor you hither!
ANTONY. If you can, you reason?
SOOTHSAYER. I see it in my motion, have it not in my
tongue: but yet hie you to Egypt again.
ANTONY. Say to me, whose fortunes shall rise higher,
Cæsar's or mine?
SOOTHSAYER. Cæsar's.
Therefore, O Antony, stay not by his side.
Thy demon, that thy spirit which keeps thee, is   20
Noble, courageous, high, unmatchable,
Where Cæsar's is not. But near him thy angel
Becomes a fear; as being o'erpowered. Therefore
Make space enough between you.
ANTONY.   Speak this no more.
SOOTHSAYER. To none but thee: no more but when
to thee.
If thou dost play with him at any game,
Thou art sure to lose; and, of that natural luck,
He beats thee 'gainst the odds: thy lustre thickens,
When he shines by: I say again, thy spirit
Is all afraid to govern thee near him,   30
But he away, 'tis noble.
ANTONY.   Get thee gone:
Say to Ventidius I would speak with him.
He shall to Parthia. [*Soothsayer goes*] Be it art or hap,
He hath spoken true: the very dicé obey him,
And in our sports my better cunning faints
Under his chance: if we draw lots, he speeds;
His cocks do win the battle still of mine
When it is all to nought, and his quails ever
Beat mine, inhooped, at odds. I will to Egypt: 40

And though I make this marriage for my peace,
I'th'East my pleasure lies.

Enter Ventidius

                O, come, Ventidius,
You must to Parthia: your commission's ready;
Follow me, and receive't.   *They go*

Scene 4: *The same. A street*

Enter Lepidus, Mæcenas, and Agrippa

LEPIDUS. Trouble yourselves no further: pray you,
     hasten
Your generals after.
AGRIPPA.   Sir, Mark Antony
Will e'en but kiss Octavia, and we'll follow.
LEPIDUS. Till I shall see you in your soldier's dress,
Which will become you both, farewell.
MÆCENAS.   We shall,
As I conceive the journey, be at th'Mount
Before you, Lepidus.
LEPIDUS.   Your way is shorter;
My purposes do draw me much about:
You'll win two days upon me.
MÆCENAS. }
AGRIPPA. }   Sir, good success!
LEPIDUS. Farewell.   *They go* 10

Scene 5: *Alexandria. Cleopatra's palace*

Enter Cleopatra, Charmian, Iras, and Alexas

CLEOPATRA. Give me some music; music, moody food
Of us that trade in love.
ALL.   The music, ho!

Enter Mardian the Eunuch

CLEOPATRA. Let it alone, let's to billiards: come,
Charmian.
CHARMIAN. My arm is sore; best play with Mardian.
CLEOPATRA. As well a woman with an eunuch played
As with a woman. Come, you'll play with me, sir?
MARDIAN. As well as I can, madam.
CLEOPATRA. And when good will is showed, though't
come too short,
The actor may plead pardon. i'll none now,
Give me mine angle, we'll to th'river: there,   10
My music playing far off, I will betray
Tawny-finned fishes; my bended hook shall pierce
Their slimy jaws, and as I draw them up,
I'll think them every one an Antony,
And say 'Ah, ha! you're caught.'
CHARMIAN.   'Twas merry when
You wagered on your angling; when your diver
Did hang a salt-fish on his hook, which he
With fervency drew up.
CLEOPATRA.   That time—O times!—
I laughed him out of patience; and that night
I laughed him into patience; and next morn,   20
Ere the ninth hour, I drunk him to his bed;
Then put my tires and mantles on him, whilst
I wore his sword Philippan.

Enter a Messenger

                O, from Italy!
Rain thou thy fruitful tidings in mine ears,
That long time have been barren.
MESSENGER.   Madam, madam,—

CLEOPATRA. Antonio's dead! If thou say so, villain,
Thou kill'st thy mistress: but well and free,
If thou so yield him, there is gold, and here
My bluest veins to kiss: a hand that kings
Have lipped, and trembled kissing.
MESSENGER. First, madam, he is well.   30
CLEOPATRA.   Why, there's more gold.
But, sirrah, mark, we use
To say the dead are well: bring it to that,
The gold I give thee well I melt and pour
Down thy ill-uttering throat.
MESSENGER. Good madam, hear me.
CLEOPATRA.   Well, go to, I will;
But there's no goodness in thy face. If Antony
Be free and healthful—so tart a favour
To trumpet such good tidings! If not well,
Thou shouldst come like a Fury crowned with
    snakes,   40
Not like a formal man.
MESSENGER.   Will't please you hear me?
CLEOPATRA. I have a mind to strike thee ere thou
    speak'st:
Yet, if thou say Antony lives, is well,
Or friends with Cæsar, or not captive to him,
I'll set thee in a shower of gold, and hail
Rich pearls upon thee.
MESSENGER.   Madam, he's well.
CLEOPATRA.   Well said.
MESSENGER. And friends with Cæsar.
CLEOPATRA.   Thou'rt an honest man.
MESSENGER. Cæsar and he are greater friends than
    ever.
CLEOPATRA. Make thee a fortune from me.
MESSENGER.   But yet, madam,—
CLEOPATRA. I do not like 'But yet,' it does allay   50
The good precedence; fie upon 'But yet'?
'But yet' is as a gaoler to bring forth
Some monstrous malefactor. Prithee, friend,
Pour out the pack of matter to mine ear,
The good and bad together: he's friends with
    Cæsar,
In state of health, thou say'st, and thou say'st, free.
MESSENGER. Free, madam! no; I made no such report:
He's bound unto Octavia.
CLEOPATRA.   For what good turn?
MESSENGER. For the best turn i'th'bed.
CLEOPATRA.   I am pale, Charmian.
MESSENGER. Madam, he's married to Octavia.   60
CLEOPATRA. The most infectious pestilence upon thee!
                    Strikes him down
MESSENGER. Good madam, patience.
CLEOPATRA.   What say you?
    [*strikes him again*] Hence,
Horrible villain! or I'll spurn thine eyes
Like balls before me; I'll unhair thy head,
                    She hales him up and down
Thou shalt be whipped with wire, and stewed in
    brine,
Smarting in ling'ring pickle.
MESSENGER.   Gracious madam,
I that do bring the news made not the match.
CLEOPATRA. Say 'tis not so, a province I will give thee,
And make thy fortunes proud: the blow thou hadst
Shall make thy peace for moving me to rage,   70
And I will boot thee with what gift beside
Thy modesty can beg.

MESSENGER.   He's married, madam.
CLEOPATRA. Rogue, thou hast lived too long.
                    Draws a knife
MESSENGER.   Nay, then I'll run.
What mean you, madam? I have made no fault.
                    Goes
CHARMIAN. Good madam, keep yourself within
    yourself.
The man is innocent.
CLEOPATRA. Some innocents 'scape not the
    thunderbolt.
Melt Egypt into Nile! and kindly creatures
Turn all to serpents! Call the slave again:
Though I am mad, I will not bite him. Call!   80
CHARMIAN. He is afeard to come.
CLEOPATRA.   I will not hurt him.
                    Charmian goes
These hands do lack nobility, that they strike
A meaner than myself; since I myself
Have given myself the cause.

Charmian returns with the Messenger

                    Come hither, sir.
Though it be honest, it is never good
To bring bad news: give to a gracious message
An host of tongues, but let ill tidings tell
Themselves when they be felt.
MESSENGER.   I have done my duty.
CLEOPATRA. Is he married?
I cannot hate thee worser than I do,   90
If thou again say 'Yes.'
MESSENGER.   He's married, madam.
CLEOPATRA. The gods confound thee! dost thou hold
    there still?
MESSENGER. Should I lie, madam?
CLEOPATRA.   O, I would thou didst,
So half my Egypt were submerged and made
A cistern for scaled snakes! Go, get thee hence:
Hadst thou Narcissus in thy face, to me
Thou wouldst appear most ugly. He is married?
MESSENGER. I crave your highness' pardon.
CLEOPATRA.   He is married?
MESSENGER. Take no offence that I would not offend
    you:
To punish me for what you make me do   100
Seems much unequal: he's married to Octavia.
CLEOPATRA. O, that his fault should make a knave
    of thee,
Thou art not what thou'rt sure of! Get thee hence:
The merchandise which thou hast brought from
    Rome
Are all too dear for me: lie they upon thy hand,
And be undone by 'em!   *He goes*
CHARMIAN.   Good your highness, patience.
CLEOPATRA. In praising Antony, I have dispraised
    Cæsar.
CHARMIAN. Many times, madam.
CLEOPATRA.   I am paid for't now.
Lead me from hence;
I faint, O Iras, Charmian: 'tis no matter.   110
Go to the fellow, good Alexas; bid him
Report the feature of Octavia: her years,
Her inclination, let him not leave out
The colour of her hair. Bring me word quickly.
                    Alexas goes
Let him for ever go! let him not—Charmian—

Though he be painted one way like a Gorgon,
The other way's a Mars. [to Mardian] Bid you Alexas
Bring me word how tall she is. Pity me, Charmian,
But do not speak to me. Lead me to my chamber.
                                                          They go

Scene 6: *Near Misenum; the sea in the distance*

*Flourish. Enter Pompey and Menas from one side, with
drum and trumpet: at another, Cæsar, Antony, Lepidus,
Enobarbus, Mæcenas, Agrippa, with soldiers marching*

POMPEY. Your hostages I have, so have you mine;
And we shall talk before we fight.
CÆSAR.   Most meet
That first we come to words; and therefore have we
Our written purposes before us sent;
Which, if thou hast considered, let us know
If 'twill tie up thy discontented sword
And carry back to Sicily much tall youth
That else must perish here.
POMPEY.   To you all three,
The senators alone of this great world,
Chief factors for the gods: I do not know   10
Wherefore my father should revengers want,
Having a son and friends, since Julius Cæsar,
Who at Philippi the good Brutus ghosted,
There saw you labouring for him. What was't
That moved pale Cassius to conspire, and what
Made the all-honoured honest Roman, Brutus,
With the armed rest, courtiers of beauteous
      freedom,
To drench the Capitol, but that they would
Have one man but a man? And that is it
Hath made me rig my navy, at whose burthen   20
The angered ocean foams; with which I meant
To scourge th'ingratitude that despiteful Rome
Cast on my noble father.
CÆSAR.   Take your time.
ANTONY. Thou canst not fear us, Pompey with thy
      sails;
We'll speak with thee at sea: at land, thou know'st
How much we do o'ercount thee.
POMPEY.   At land indeed
Thou dost o'ercount me of my father's house:
But since the cuckoo builds not for himself,
Remain in't as thou mayst.
LEPIDUS.   Be pleased to tell us—
For this is from the present—how you take   30
The offers we have sent you.
CÆSAR.   There's the point.
ANTONY. Which do not be entreated to, but weigh
What it is worth embraced.
CÆSAR.   And what may follow,
To try a larger fortune.
POMPEY.   You have made me offer
Of Sicily, Sardinia; and I must
Rid all the sea of pirates; then, to send
Measures of wheat to Rome; this 'greed upon,
To part with unhacked edges and bear back
Our targes undinted.
CÆSAR.   ⎫
ANTONY.   ⎬   That's our offer.
LEPIDUS.   ⎭
POMPEY.   ⎭   Know then,
I came before you here a man prepared   40
To take this offer: but Mark Antony

Put me to some impatience: though I lose
The praise of it by telling, you must know,
When Cæsar and your brother were at blows,
Your mother came to Sicily and did find
Her welcome friendly.
ANTONY.   I have heard it, Pompey,
And am well studied for a liberal thanks
Which I do owe you.
POMPEY.   Let me have your hand:
I did not think, sir, to have met you here.
ANTONY. The beds i'th'east are soft; and thanks to you, 50
That called me timelier than my purpose hither;
For I have gained by't.
CÆSAR.   Since I saw you last.
There's a change upon you.
POMPEY.   Well, I know not
What counts harsh Fortune casts upon my face,
But in my bosom shall she never come,
To make my heart her vassal.
LEPIDUS.   Well met here.
POMPEY. I hope so, Lepidus. Thus we are agreed:
I crave our composition may be written
And sealed between us.
CÆSAR.   That's the next to do.
POMPEY. We'll feast each other ere we part, and let's 60
Draw lots who shall begin.
ANTONY.   That will I, Pompey.
POMPEY. No, Antony, take the lot:
But, first or last, your fine Egyptian cookery
Shall have the fame. I have heard that Julius Cæsar—
Grew fat with feasting there.
ANTONY.   You have heard much.
POMPEY. I have fair meanings, sir.
ANTONY.   And fair words to them.
POMPEY. Then so much have I heard:
And I have heard, Apollodorus carried—
ENOBARBUS. No more of that: he did so.
POMPEY.   What, I pray you?
ENOBARBUS. A certain queen to Cæsar in a mattress. 70
POMPEY. I know thee now, how far'st thou, soldier?
ENOBARBUS.   Well,
And well am like to do, for I perceive
Four feasts are toward.
POMPEY.   Let me shake thy hand.
I never hated thee: I have seen thee fight,
When I have envied thy behaviour.
ENOBARBUS.   Sir,
I never loved you much, but I ha'praised ye
When you have well deserved ten times as much
As I have said you did.
POMPEY.   Enjoy thy plainness,
It nothing ill becomes thee.
Aboard my galley I invite you all: 80
Will you lead, lords?
CÆSAR.   ⎫
ANTONY.   ⎬   Show's the way, sir.
LEPIDUS.'   ⎭
POMPEY.   Come.
                              *They go; Menas and
                                  Enobarbus remain*

MENAS [*aside*]. Thy father, Pompey, would ne'er have
      made this treaty. [*to Enobarbus*] You and I have
      known, sir.
ENOBARBUS. At sea, I think.
MENAS. We have, sir.
ENOBARBUS. You have done well by water.

MENAS. And you by land.

ENOBARBUS. I will praise any man that will praise me; though it cannot be denied what I have done by land.

MENAS. Nor what I have done by water.

ENOBARBUS. Yes, something you can deny for your own safety: you have been a great thief by sea.

MENAS. And you by land.

ENOBARBUS. There I deny my land service. But give me your hand, Menas: if our eyes had authority, here they might take two thieves kissing.

MENAS. All men's faces are true, whatsome'er their hands are.

ENOBARBUS. But there is never a fair woman has a true face.

MENAS. No slander, they steal hearts.

ENOBARBUS. We came hither to fight with you.

MENAS. For my part, I am sorry it is turned to a drinking. Pompey doth this day laugh away his fortune.

ENOBARBUS. If he do, sure he cannot weep't back again.

MENAS. You've said, sir. We looked not for Mark Antony here: pray you, is he married to Cleopatra?

ENOBARBUS. Cæsar's sister is called Octavia.

MENAS. True, sir; she was the wife of Caius Marcellus.

ENOBARBUS. But she is now the wife of Marcus Antonius.

MENAS. Pray ye, sir?

ENOBARBUS. 'Tis true.

MENAS. Then is Cæsar and he for ever knit together.

ENOBARBUS. If I were bound to divine of this unity, I would not prophesy so.

MENAS. I think the policy of that purpose made more in the marriage than the love of the parties.

ENOBARBUS. I think so too. But you shall find, the band that seems to tie their friendship together will be the very strangler of their amity: Octavia is of a holy, cold, and still conversation.

MENAS. Who would not have his wife so?

ENOBARBUS. Not he that himself is not so; which is Mark Antony. He will to his Egyptian dish again: then shall the sighs of Octavia blow the fire up in Cæsar, and, as I said before, that which is the strength of their amity shall prove the immediate author of their variance. Antony will use his affection where it is: he married but his occasion here.

MENAS. And thus it may. Come, sir, will you aboard? I have a health for you.

ENOBARBUS. I shall take it, sir: we have used our throats in Egypt.

MENAS. Come, let's away.   *They follow the others*

Scene 7: *The deck of Pompey's galley, off Misenum*

Music plays. Enter two or three Servants, with a banquet

1 SERVANT. Here they'll be, man. Some o'their plants are ill-rooted already; the least wind i'th'world will blow them down.

2 SERVANT. Lepidus is high-coloured.

1 SERVANT. They have made him drink alms-drink.

2 SERVANT. As they pinch one another by the disposition, he cries out 'No more'; reconciles them to his entreaty and himself to th'drink.

1 SERVANT. But it raises the greater war between him and his discretion.

2 SERVANT. Why, this it is to have a name in great men's fellowship: I had as lief have a reed that will do me no service as a partisan I could not heave.

1 SERVANT. To be called into a huge sphere, and not to be seen to move in't, are the holes where eyes should be, which pitifully disaster the cheeks.

A sennet sounded. Cæsar, Antony, Pompey, Lepidus, Agrippa, Mæcenas, Enobarbus, Menas, with other captains, come up on deck; Pompey assists Lepidus.

ANTONY [*to Cæsar*]. Thus do they, sir; they take the flow o'th'Nile
By certain scales i'th'pyramid; they know,
By th'height, the lowness, or the means, if dearth
Or foison follow: the higher Nilus swells,
The more it promises: as it ebbs, the seedsman
Upon the slime and ooze scatters his grain,
And't shortly comes to harvest.

LEPIDUS. You've strange serpents there?

ANTONY. Ay, Lepidus.

LEPIDUS. Your serpent of Egypt is bred now of your mud by the operation of your sun: so is your crocodile.

ANTONY. They are so.

POMPEY. Sit—and some wine! A health to Lepidus!

LEPIDUS. I am not so well as I should be, but I'll ne'er out.

ENOBARBUS. Not till you have slept; I fear me you'll be in till then.

LEPIDUS. Nay, certainly, I have heard the Ptolemies' pyramises are very goodly things; without contradiction, I have heard that.

MENAS [*aside*]. Pompey, a word.

POMPEY [*aside*].   Say in mine ear, what is't?

MENAS [*whispers in's ear*]. Forsake thy seat, I do beseech thee, captain,
And hear me speak a word.

POMPEY [*aside*].   Forbear me till anon.—
[*calls*] This wine for Lepidus!

LEPIDUS. What manner o'thing is your crocodile?

ANTONY. It is shaped, sir, like itself, and it is as broad as it hath breadth: it is just so high as it is, and moves with it own organs: it lives by that which nourisheth it, and the elements once out of it, it transmigrates.

LEPIDUS. What colour is it of?

ANTONY. Of it own colour too.

LEPIDUS. 'Tis a strange serpent.

ANTONY. 'Tis so, and the tears of it are wet.

CÆSAR. Will this description satisfy him?

ANTONY. With the health that Pompey gives him, else he is a very epicure.   *Menas whispers again*

POMPEY [*aside*]. Go hang, sir, hang! Tell me of that! away! Do as I bid you. [*aloud*] Where's this cup I called for?

MENAS [*aside*]. If for the sake of merit thou wilt hear me,
Rise from thy stool.

POMPEY [*aside*]. I think thou'rt mad. The matter?
Rises, and walks aside

MENAS. I have ever held my cap off to thy fortunes.

POMPEY. Thou hast served me with much faith. What's else to say?
Be jolly, lords.

ANTONY.   These quick-sands, Lepidus,
Keep off them, for you sink.

MENAS. Wilt thou be lord of all the world?
POMPEY.   What say'st thou?
MENAS. Wilt thou be lord of the whole world?
    That's twice.
POMPEY. How should that be?
MENAS.   But entertain it,
    And, though thou think me poor, I am the man
    Will give thee all the world.
POMPEY.   Hast thou drunk well?
MENAS. No, Pompey, I have kept me from the cup. 70
    Thou art, if thou dar'st be, the earthly Jove:
    Whate'er the ocean pales, or sky inclips,
    Is thine, if thou wilt ha't.
POMPEY.   Show me which way.
MENAS. These three world-sharers, these competitors,
    Are in thy vessel: let me cut the cable;
    And, when we are put off, fall to their throats:
    All then is thine.
POMPEY.   Ah, this thou shouldst have done,
    And not have spoke on't! In me 'tis villany;
    In thee't had been good service. Thou must know,
    'Tis not my profit that does lead mine honour;   80
    Mine honour, it. Repent that e'er thy tongue
    Hath so betrayed thine act: being done unknown,
    I should have found it afterwards well done,
    But must condemn it now. Desist, and drink.
MENAS [to himself]. For this
    I'll never follow thy palled fortunes more.
    Who seeks, and will not take when once 'tis offered,
    Shall never find it more.
POMPEY.   This health to Lepidus!
ANTONY. Bear him ashore. I'll pledge it for him,
    Pompey.
ENOBARBUS. Here's to thee, Menas!
MENAS.   Enobarbus, welcome! 90
POMPEY. Fill till the cup be hid.
ENOBARBUS. There's a strong fellow, Menas.
    Pointing to the attendant who carries off Lepidus
MENAS. Why?
ENOBARBUS. A' bears the third part of the world, man;
    see'st not?
MENAS. The third part then is drunk: would it were all,
    That it might go on wheels!
ENOBARBUS. Drink thou; increase the reels.
MENAS. Come.
POMPEY. This is not yet an Alexandrian feast.
ANTONY. It ripens towards it. Strike the vessels, ho! 100
    Here's to Cæsar!
CÆSAR.   I could well forbear't.
    It's monstrous labour, when I wash my brain
    And it grows fouler.
ANTONY.   Be a child o'th'time.
CÆSAR. Possess it, I'll make answer:
    But I had rather fast from all, four days,
    Than drink so much in one.
ENOBARBUS [to Antony].   Ha, my brave emperor!
    Shall we dance now the Egyptian Bacchanals,
    And celebrate our drink?
POMPEY.   Let's ha't, good soldier.
ANTONY. Come, let's all take hands,
    Till that the conquering wine hath steeped our sense 110
    In soft and delicate Lethe.
ENOBARBUS.   All take hands.
    Make battery to our ears with the loud music:
    The while I'll place you: then the boy shall sing;
    The holding every man shall bear as loud

As his strong sides can volley.
         Music plays. Enobarbus places
                   them hand in hand

THE SONG

    Come, thou monarch of the vine,
    Plumpy Bacchus with pink eyne!
    In thy fats our cares be drowned,
    With thy grapes our hairs be crowned.
    Cup us, till the world go round,   120
    Cups us, till the world go round!
CÆSAR. What would you more? Pompey, good night.
    Good brother,
    Let me request you off: our graver business
    Frowns at this levity. Gentle lords, let's part;
    You see we have burnt our cheeks: strong Enobarb
    Is weaker than the wine; and mine own tongue
    Splits what it speaks: the wild disguise hath almost
    Anticked us all. What needs more words?
    Good night.
    Good Antony, your hand.
POMPEY.   I'll try you on the shore.
ANTONY. And shall, sir: give's your hand.
POMPEY.   O Antony, 130
    You have my father's house—But, what? we are
    friends.
    Come down into the boat.   *They go down*
ENOBARBUS.   Take heed you fall not.
           Enobarbus and Menas remain
    Menas, I'll not on shore.
MENAS.   No, to my cabin.
    These drums! these trumpets, flutes! what!
    Let Neptune hear we bid a loud farewell
    To these great fellows: sound and be hanged, sound
    out!
         Musicians sound a flourish, with drums
ENOBARBUS. Hoo! says a'. There's my cap.
MENAS. Hoo! Noble captain, come.   *They go below*

ACT 3
Scene 1: *A plain in Syria*

*Enter Ventidius as it were in triumph, the dead body of
Pacorus borne before him; with Silius, and other Romans,
officers, and soldiers*

VENTIDIUS. Now, darting Parthia, art thou struck,
    and now
    Pleased fortune does of Marcus Crassus' death
    Make me revenger. Bear the king's son's body
    Before our army. Thy Pacorus, Orodes,
    Pays this for Marcus Crassus.
SILIUS.   Noble Ventidius,
    Whilst yet with Parthian blood thy sword is warm,
    The fugitive Parthians follow; spur through Media,
    Mesopotamia, and the shelters whither
    The routed fly: so thy grand captain Antony
    Shall set thee on triumphant chariots and   10
    Put garlands on thy head.
VENTIDIUS.   O Silius, Silius,
    I have done enough: a lower place, note well,
    May make too great an act; for learn this, Silius,
    Better to leave undone than by our deed
    Acquire too high a fame when him we serve's away.
    Cæsar and Antony have ever won
    More in their officer than person: Sossius,

One of my place in Syria, his lieutenant,
For quick accumulation of renown,
Which he achieved by th'minute, lost his favour.   20
Who does i'th'wars more than his captain can
Becomes his captain's captain: and ambition,
The soldier's virtue, rather makes choice of loss
Than gain which darkens him.
I could do more to do Antonius good
But 'twould offend him, and in his offence
Should my performance perish.
SILIUS.   Thou hast, Ventidius, that
Without the which a soldier and his sword
Grants scarce distinction. Thou wilt write to
    Antony?
VENTIDIUS. I'll humbly signify what in his name,   30
That magical word of war, we have effected;
How, with his banners and his well-paid ranks,
The ne'er-yet-beaten horse of Parthia
We have jaded out o'th'field.
SILIUS.   Where is he now?
VENTIDIUS. He purposeth to Athens: whither, with
    what haste
The weight we must convey with's will permit,
We shall appear before him. On, there; pass along!
                                        They go forward

Scene 2: *Rome. An antechamber in Cæsar's house*

Enter Agrippa at one door, Enobarbus at another

AGRIPPA. What, are the brothers parted?
ENOBARBUS. They have dispatched with Pompey; he
    is gone;
The other three are sealing. Octavia weeps
To part from Rome; Cæsar is sad, and Lepidus
Since Pompey's feast, as Menas says, is troubled
With the greensickness.
AGRIPPA.   'Tis a noble Lepidus.
ENOBARBUS. A very fine one: O, how he loves Cæsar!
AGRIPPA. Nay, but how dearly he adores Mark
    Antony!
ENOBARBUS. Cæsar? Why, he's the Jupiter of men.
AGRIPPA. What's Antony? The god of Jupiter.
ENOBARBUS. Spake you of Cæsar? How! the nonpareil!   10
AGRIPPA. O Antony! O thou Arabian bird!
ENOBARBUS. Would you praise Cæsar, say 'Cæsar': go
    no further.
AGRIPPA. Indeed, he plied them both with excellent
    praises.
ENOBARBUS. But he loves Cæsar best; yet he loves
    Antony:
Hoo! hearts, tongues, figures, scribes, bards, poets,
    cannot
Think, speak, cast, write, sing, number—hoo!—
His love to Antony. But as for Cæsar,
Kneel down, kneel down, and wonder.
AGRIPPA.   Both he loves.
ENOBARBUS. They are his shards, and he their beetle.
    [*trumpet within*] So!   20
This is to horse. Adieu, noble Agrippa.
AGRIPPA. Good fortune, worthy soldier, and farewell.

Enter Cæsar, Antony, Lepidus, and Octavia

ANTONY. No further, sir.
CÆSAR. You take from me a great part of myself;
Use me well in't. Sister, prove such a wife
As my thoughts make thee, and as my farthest band

Shall pass on thy approof. Most noble Antony,
Let not the piece of virtue which is set
Betwixt us as the cement of our love,
To keep it builded, be the ram to batter   30
The fortress of it; for better might we
Have loved without this means, if on both parts
This be not cherished.
ANTONY.   Make me not offended.
In your distrust.
CÆSAR.   I have said.
ANTONY.   You shall not find,
Though you be therein curious, the least cause
For what you seem to fear: so, the gods keep you,
And makes the hearts of Romans serve your ends!
We will here part.
CÆSAR. Farewell, my dearest sister, fare thee well:
The elements be kind to thee, and make   40
Thy spirits all of comfort! fare thee well.
OCTAVIA. My noble brother!
ANTONY. The April's in her eyes: it is love's spring,
And these the showers to bring it on. Be cheerful.
OCTAVIA. Sir, look well to my husband's house, and—
CÆSAR.   What,
    Octavia?
OCTAVIA.   I'll tell you in your ear.
ANTONY. Her tongue will not obey her heart, nor can
Her heart inform her tongue—the swan's down-
    feather,
That stands upon the swell at full of tide
And neither way inclines.   50
ENOBARBUS [*aside to Agrippa*]. Will Cæsar weep?
AGRIPPA [*aside*].   He has a cloud in's face.
ENOBARBUS [*aside*]. He were the worse for that, were
    he a horse;
So is he, being a man.
AGRIPPA [*aside*].   Why, Enobarbus,
When Antony found Julius Cæsar dead,
He cried almost to roaring; and he wept
When at Philippi he found Brutus slain.
ENOBARBUS. That year indeed he was troubled with
    a rheum;
What willingly he did confound he wailed,
Believe't, till I wept too.
CÆSAR.   No, sweet Octavia,
You shall hear from me still; the time shall not   60
Out-go my thinking on you.
ANTONY.   Come, sir come;
I'll wrestle with you in my strength of love:
Look, here I have you; thus I let you go,
And give you to the gods.
CÆSAR.   Adieu; be happy!
LEPIDUS. Let all the number of the stars give light
To thy fair way!
CÆSAR.   Farewell, farewell!   *Kisses Octavia*
ANTONY.   Farewell!
                              Trumpets sound; they go

Scene 3: *Alexandria. Cleopatra's palace*

Enter Cleopatra, Charmian, Iras, and Alexas

CLEOPATRA. Where is the fellow?
ALEXAS.   Half afeard to come.
CLEOPATRA. Go to, go to.

Enter the Messenger as before

                        Come hither, sir.

ALEXAS.   Good majesty,
Herod of Jewry dare not look upon you
But when you are well pleased.
CLEOPATRA.   That Herod's head
I'll have: but how, when Antony is gone
Through whom I might command it? Come thou
near.
MESSENGER. Most gracious majesty,—
CLEOPATRA.   Didst thou behold
Octavia?
MESSENGER. Ay, dread queen.
CLEOPATRA.   Where?
MESSENGER.   Madam, in Rome.
I looked her in the face, and saw her led
Between her brother and Mark Antony.   10
CLEOPATRA. Is she as tall as me?
MESSENGER.   She is not, madam.
CLEOPATRA. Didst hear her speak? is she shrill-tongued
or low?
MESSENGER. Madam, I heard her speak; she is
low-voiced.
CLEOPATRA. That's not so good: he cannot like her
long.
CHARMIAN. Like her! O Isis! 'tis impossible.
CLEOPATRA. I think so, Charmian: dull of tongue
and dwarfish.
What majesty is in her gait? Remember,
If e'er thou look'dst on majesty.
MESSENGER.   She creeps:
Her motion and her station are as one;
She shows a body rather than a life,   20
A statue than a breather.
CLEOPATRA.   Is this certain?
MESSENGER. Or I have no observance.
CHARMIAN.   Three in Egypt
Cannot make better note.
CLEOPATRA.   He's very knowing;
I do perceive't: there's nothing in her yet:
The fellow has good judgement.
CHARMIAN.   Excellent.
CLEOPATRA. Guess at her years, I prithee.
MESSENGER.   Madam,
She was a widow—
CLEOPATRA.   Widow! Charmian, hark.
MESSENGER. And I do think she's thirty.
CLEOPATRA. Bear'st thou her face in mind? is't long
or round?
MESSENGER. Round, even to faultiness.   30
CLEOPATRA. For the most part, too, they are foolish
that are so.
Her hair, what colour?
MESSENGER.   Brown, madam: and her forehead
As low as she would wish it.
CLEOPATRA.   There's gold for thee.
Thou must not take my former sharpness ill:
I will employ thee back again; I find thee
Most fit for business: go make thee ready;
Our letters are prepared.   He goes
CHARMIAN.   A proper man.
CLEOPATRA. Indeed, he is so: I repent me much
That so I harried him. Why, methinks, by him,
This creature's no such thing.
CHARMIAN.   Nothing, madam.   40
CLEOPATRA. The man hath seen some majesty, and
should know.
CHARMIAN. Hath he seen majesty? Isis else defend,

And serving you so long!
CLEOPATRA. I have one thing more to ask him yet,
good Charmian:
But 'tis no matter, thou shalt bring him to me
Where I will write. All may be well enough.
CHARMIAN. I warrant you, madam.   They go

Scene 4: *Athens. A Room in Antony's house*

Enter Antony and Octavia

ANTONY. Nay, nay, Octavia, not only that,
That were excusable, that and thousands more
Of semblable import, but he hath waged
New wars 'gainst Pompey, made his will and read it
To public ear,
Spoke scantly of me, when perforce he could not
But pay me terms of honour, cold and sickly
He vented them, most narrow measure lent me,
When the best hint was given him he not took't,
Or did it from his teeth.
OCTAVIA.   O my good lord,   10
Believe not all, or if you must believe,
Stomach not all. A more unhappy lady,
If this division chance, ne'er stood between,
Praying for both parts:
The good gods will mock me presently,
When I shall pray, 'O, bless my lord and husband!'
Undo that prayer, by crying out as loud,
'O, bless my brother!' Husband win, win brother,
Prays, and destroys the prayer—no midway
'Twixt these extremes at all.
ANTONY.   Gentle Octavia,   20
Let your best love draw to that point which seeks
Best to preserve it: if I lose mine honour,
I lose myself: better I were not yours
Than yours so branchless. But, as you requested,
Yourself shall go between's: the mean time, lady,
I'll raise the preparation of a war
Shall stain your brother: make your soonest haste;
So your desires are yours.
OCTAVIA.   Thanks to my lord.
The Jove of Power make me most weak, most weak,
Your reconciler! Wars 'twixt you twain would be 30
As if the world should cleave, and that slain men
Should solder up the rift.
ANTONY. When it appears to you where this begins,
Turn your displeasure that way; for our faults
Can never be so equal, that your love
Can equally move with them. Provide your going;
Choose your own company, and command what
cost
Your heart has mind to.   They go

Scene 5: *The same. Another room*

Enter Enobarbus and Eros, meeting

ENOBARBUS. How now, friend Eros!
EROS. There's strange news come, sir.
ENOBARBUS. What, man?
EROS. Cæsar and Lepidus have made wars upon
Pompey.
ENOBARBUS. This is old: what is the success?
EROS. Cæsar having made use of him in the wars
'gainst Pompey presently denied him rivality,
would not let him partake in the glory of the
action, and not resting here accuses him of letters 10

he had formerly wrote to Pompey; upon his own
appeal, seizes him: so the poor third is up, till death
enlarge his confine.

ENOBARBUS. Then, world, thou hast a pair of chaps,
no more;
And throw between them all the food thou hast,
They'll grind the one the other. Where's Antony?

EROS. He's walking in the garden—thus, and spurns
The rush that lies before him, cries 'Fool Lepidus!'
And threats the throat of that his officer
That murdered Pompey.

ENOBARBUS.   Our great navy's rigged.   20

EROS. For Italy and Cæsar. More, Domitius;
My lord desires you presently: my news
I might have told hereafter.

ENOBARBUS.   'Twill be naught:
But let it be. Bring me to Antony.

EROS. Come, sir.   They go

Scene 6: *Rome. Cæsar's house*

Enter Cæsar, Agrippa, and Mæcenas

CÆSAR. Contemning Rome, he has done all this,
and more,
In Alexandria: here's the manner of't:
I'th'market-place, on a tribunal silvered
Cleopatra and himself in chairs of gold
Were publicly enthroned: at the feet sat
Cæsarion, whom they call my father's son,
And all the unlawful issue that their lust
Since then hath made between them. Unto her
He gave the stablishment of Egypt; made her
Of lower Syria, Cyprus, Lydia,   10
Absolute queen.

MÆCENAS.   This in the public eye?

CÆSAR. I'th'common show-place, where they
exercise.
His sons he there proclaimed the kings of kings:
Great Media, Parthia and Armenia,
He gave to Alexander; to Ptolemy he assigned
Syria, Cilicia and Phœnicia: she
In th'habiliments of the goddess Isis
That day appeared, and oft before gave audience,
As 'tis reported, so.

MÆCENAS.   Let Rome be thus
Informed.

AGRIPPA. Who, queasy with his insolence   20
Already, will their good thoughts call from him.

CÆSAR. The people know it, and have now received
His accusations.

AGRIPPA.   Who does he accuse?

CÆSAR. Cæsar, and that having in Sicily
Sextus Pompeius spoiled we had not rated him
His part o'th'isle: then does he say, he lent me
Some shipping unrestored: lastly, he frets
That Lepidus of the triumvirate
Should be deposed; and, being, that we detain
All his revenue.

AGRIPPA.   Sir, this should be answered.   30

CÆSAR. 'Tis done already, and the messenger gone.
I have told him, Lepidus was grown too cruel,
That he his high authority abused
And did deserve his change: for what I have
conquered,
I grant him part; but then, in his Armenia
And other of his conquered kingdoms, I

Demand the like.

MÆCENAS.   He'll never yield to that.

CÆSAR. Nor must not then be yielded to in this.

Enter Octavia, with her train

OCTAVIA. Hail, Cæsar, and my lord! hail, most dear
Cæsar!

CÆSAR. That ever I should call thee castaway!   40

OCTAVIA. You have not called me so, nor have you
cause.

CÆSAR. Why have you stol'n upon us thus? You
come not
Like Cæsar's sister: the wife of Antony
Should have an army for an usher, and
The neighs of horse to tell of her approach
Long ere she did appear; the trees by th'way
Should have borne men, and expectation fainted,
Longing for what it had not; nay, the dust
Should have ascended to the roof of heaven,
Raised by your populous troops: but you are come   50
A market-maid to Rome, and have prevented
The ostentation of our love, which, left unshown,
Is often left unloved: we should have met you
By sea and land, supplying every stage
With an augmented greeting.

OCTAVIA.   Good my lord,
To come thus was I not constrained, but did it
On my free will. My lord, Mark Antony,
Hearing that you prepared for war, acquainted
My grievéd ear withal; whereon, I begged
His pardon for return.

CÆSAR.   Which soon he granted,   60
Being an abstract 'tween his lust and him.

OCTAVIA. Do not say so, my lord.

CÆSAR.   I have eyes upon him,
And his affairs come to me on the wind.
Where is he now?

OCTAVIA.   My lord, in Athens.

CÆSAR. No, my most wrongéd sister, Cleopatra
Hath nodded him to her. He hath given his empire
Up to a whore, who now are levying
The kings o'th'earth for war: he hath assembled
Bocchus the king of Libya, Archelaus
Of Cappadocia, Philadelphos king   70
Of Paphlagonia, the Thracian king Adallas,
King Manchus of Arabia, King of Pont,
Herod of Jewry, Mithridates king
Of Comagene, Polemon and Amyntas
The kings of Mede and Lycaonia,
With a more larger list of sceptres.

OCTAVIA.   Ay me, most wretched,
That have my heart parted betwixt two friends
That do afflict each other!

CÆSAR.   Welcome hither:
Your letters did withhold our breaking forth,
Till we perceived both how you were wrong led   80
And we in negligent danger. Cheer your heart:
Be you not troubled with the time, which drives
O'er your content these strong necessities,
But let determined things to destiny
Hold unbewailed their way. Welcome to Rome;
Nothing more dear to me. You are abused
Beyond the mark of thought: and the high gods,
To do you justice, make his ministers
Of us and those that love you. Best of comfort,
And ever welcome to us.

AGRIPPA.　　　　　　Welcome, lady.　　90
MÆCENAS. Welcome, dear madam.
Each heart in Rome does love and pity you:
Only th'adulterous Antony, most large
In his abominations, turns you off;
And gives his potent regiment to a trull,
That noises it against us.
OCTAVIA.　　　　　　Is it so, sir?
CÆSAR. Most certain. Sister, welcome: pray you,
Be ever known to patience: my dear'st sister!

　　　　　　　　　　　　　　He leads her out

Scene 7: *Actium*

Enter Cleopatra and Enobarbus

CLEOPATRA. I will be even with thee, doubt it not.
ENOBARBUS. But why, why, why?
CLEOPATRA. Thou hast forspoke my being in these
　　wars,
And say'st it is not fit.
ENOBARBUS.　　　　　Well, is it, is it?
CLEOPATRA. Is't not denounced against us? Why
　　should not we
Be there in person?
ENOBARBUS [*aside*]. Well, I could reply:
If we should serve with horse and mares together,
The horse were merely lost; the mares would bear
A soldier and his horse.
CLEOPATRA.　　　　　What is't you say?
ENOBARBUS. Your presence needs must puzzle
　　Antony;　　　　　　　　　　　　　　10
Take from his heart, take from his brain, from's
　　time,
What should not then be spared. He is already
Traduced for levity, and 'tis said in Rome
That Photinus, an eunuch, and your maids
Manage this war.
CLEOPATRA.　　　　　Sink Rome, and their tongues rot
That speak against us! A charge we bear i'th'war,
And, as the president of my kingdom, will
Appear there for a man. Speak not against it,
I will not stay behind.
ENOBARBUS.　　　　　Nay, I have done.
Here comes the emperor.

Enter Antony and Canidius

ANTONY.　　　　　Is it not strange, Canidius,　20
That from Tarentum and Brundusium
He could so quickly cut the Ionian sea,
And take in Toryne? You have heard on't, sweet?
CLEOPATRA. Celerity is never more admired
Than by the negligent.
ANTONY.　　　　　A good rebuke,
Which might have well becomed the best of men,
To taunt at slackness. Canidius, we
Will fight with him by sea.
CLEOPATRA.　　　　　By sea! what else?
CANIDIUS. Why will my lord do so?
ANTONY.　　　　　For that he dares us to't.
ENOBARBUS. So hath my lord dared him to single fight.　30
CANIDIUS. Ay, and to wage this battle at Pharsalia,
Where Cæsar fought with Pompey: but these offers,
Which serve not for his vantage, he shakes off,
And so should you.
ENOBARBUS.　　　　　Your ships are not well manned,
Your mariners are muleters, reapers, people

Ingrossed by swift impress; in Cæsar's fleet
Are those that often have 'gainst Pompey fought:
Their ships are yare, yours heavy: no disgrace
Shall fall you for refusing him at sea,
Being prepared for land.
ANTONY.　　　　　By sea, by sea.　　40
ENOBARBUS. Most worthy sir, you therein throw away
The absolute soldiership you have by land,
Distract your army, which doth most consist
Of war-marked footmen, leave unexecuted
Your own renownéd knowledge, quite forgo
The way which promises assurance, and
Give up yourself merely to chance and hazard
From firm security.
ANTONY.　　　　　I'll fight at sea.
CLEOPATRA. I have sixty sails, Cæsar none better.
ANTONY. Our overplus of shipping will we burn;　50
And, with the rest full-manned, from th'head of
　　Actium
Beat th'approaching Cæsar. But if we fail,
We then can do't at land.

Enter a Messenger

　　　　　　　　　　　　　　Thy business?
MESSENGER. The news is true, my lord; he is descried;
Cæsar has taken Toryne.
ANTONY. Can he be there? in person 'tis impossible;
Strange that his power should be. Canidius,
Our nineteen legions thou shalt hold by land,
And our twelve thousand horse. We'll to our ship:
Away, my Thetis!

Enter a Soldier

　　　　　　　　　How now, worthy soldier?　60
SOLDIER. O noble emperor, do not fight by sea;
Trust not to rotten planks. Do you misdoubt
This sword and these my wounds? Let th'Egyptians
And the Phœnicians go a-ducking: we
Have used to conquer standing on the earth
And fighting foot to foot.
ANTONY.　　　　　Well, well, away!

　　　　　　　　He goes with Cleopatra,
　　　　　　　　　Enobarbus following

SOLDIER. By Hercules, I think I am i'th'right.
CANIDIUS. Soldier, thou art: but his whole action
　　grows
Not in the power on't: so our leader's led,
And we are women's men.
SOLDIER.　　　　　You keep by land　70
The legions and the horse whole, do you not?
CANIDIUS. Marcus Octavius, Marcus Justeius,
Publicola and Cælius, are for sea:
But we keep whole by land. This speed of Cæsar's
Carries beyond belief.
SOLDIER.　　　　　While he was yet in Rome,
His power went out in such distractions as
Beguiled all spies.
CANIDIUS.　　　　　Who's his lieutenant, hear you?
SOLDIER. They say, one Taurus.
CANIDIUS.　　　　　Well I know the man.

Enter a Messenger

MESSENGER. The emperor calls Canidius.
CANIDIUS. With news the time's in labour, and
　　throes forth　　　　　　　　　　　　80
Each minute some.　　　　　　*They go*

Scene 8

Enter Cæsar, and Taurus, with his army, marching

CÆSAR. Taurus!

TAURUS. My lord?

CÆSAR. Strike not by land, keep whole, provoke
        not battle
    Till we have done at sea. Do not exceed
    The prescript of this scroll: our fortune lies
    Upon this jump.   *They go*

Scene 9

Enter Antony and Enobarbus

ANTONY. Set we our squadrons on yond side o'th'hill,
    In eye of Cæsar's battle; from which place
    We may the number of the ships behold,
    And so proceed accordingly.   *They go*

Scene 10

*Canidius marcheth with his land army one way and
Taurus, the lieutenant of Cæsar, the other way. After
    their going in, is heard the noise of a sea-fight.*

Alarum. Enter Enobarbus

ENOBARBUS. Naught, naught, all naught! I can behold
        no longer:
    Th'Antoniad, the Egyptian admiral,
    With all their sixty, fly and turn the rudder:
    To see't mine eyes are blasted.

Enter Scarus

SCARUS.   Gods and goddesses,
    All the whole synod of them!

ENOBARBUS.   What's thy passion?

SCARUS. The greater cantle of the world is lost
    With very ignorance. We have kissed away
    Kingdoms and provinces.

ENOBARBUS.   How appears the fight?

SCARUS. On our side like the tokened pestilence,
    Where death is sure. Yon ribald-rid nag of Egypt— 10
    Whom leprosy o'ertake!—i'th'midst o'th'fight,
    When vantage like a pair of twins appeared,
    Both as the same, or rather ours the elder—
    The breese upon her, like a cow in June!—
    Hoists sails and flies.

ENOBARBUS. That I beheld:
    Mine eyes did sicken at the sight, and could not
    Endure a further view.

SCARUS.   She once being luffed,
    The noble ruin of her magic, Antony,
    Claps on his sea-wing, and (like a doting mallard), 20
    Leaving the fight in height, flies after her:
    I never saw an action of such shame;
    Experience, manhood, honour, ne'er before
    Did violate so itself.

ENOBARBUS.   Alack, alack!

Enter Canidius

CANIDIUS. Our fortune on the sea is out of breath,
    And sinks most lamentably. Had our general
    Been what he knew himself, it had gone well:
    O, he has given example for our flight
    Most grossly by his own!

ENOBARBUS.   Ay, are you thereabouts?
    Why then good night indeed.   30

CANIDIUS. Toward Peloponnesus are they fled.

SCARUS. 'Tis easy to't; and there I will attend
    What further comes.

CANIDIUS.   To Cæsar will I render
    My legions and my horse: six kings already
    Show me the way of yielding.

ENOBARBUS.   I'll yet follow
    The wounded chance of Antony, though my reason
    Sits in the wind against me.   *They go*

Scene 11: *Alexandria. Cleopatra's palace*

Enter Antony with Attendants

ANTONY. Hark! the land bids me tread no more
        upon't—
    It is ashamed to bear me. Friends, come hither:
    I am so lated in the world that I
    Have lost my way for ever. I have a ship
    Laden with gold, take that, divide it; fly,
    And make your peace with Cæsar.

ALL.   Fly! not we.

ANTONY. I have fled myself, and have instructed
        cowards
    To run and show their shoulders. Friends, be gone;
    I have myself resolved upon a course
    Which has no need of you. Be gone.   10
    My treasure's in the harbour, take it. O,
    I followed that I blush to look upon:
    My very hairs do mutiny, for the white
    Reprove the brown for rashness, and they them
    For fear and doting. Friends, be gone: you shall
    Have letters from me to some friends that will
    Sweep your way for you. Pray you, look not sad,
    Nor make replies of loathness; take the hint
    Which my despair proclaims; let that be left
    Which leaves itself: to the sea-side straightway: 20
    I will possess you of that ship and treasure.
    Leave me, I pray, a little: pray you now,
    Nay, do so; for indeed I have lost command,
    Therefore I pray you: I'll see you by and by.

                                            Sits down

Enter Cleopatra led by Charmian and Eros; Iras following

EROS. Nay, gentle madam, to him, comfort him.

IRAS. Do, most dear queen.

CHARMIAN. Do! why, what else?

CLEOPATRA. Let me sit down. O Juno!

ANTONY. No, no, no, no, no.

EROS. See you here, sir?   30

ANTONY. O fie, fie, fie!

CHARMIAN. Madam!

IRAS. Madam, O good empress!

EROS. Sir, sir!

ANTONY. Yes, my lord, yes; he at Philippi kept
    His sword e'en like a dancer; while I struck
    The lean and wrinkled Cassius; and 'twas I
    That the mad Brutus ended: he alone
    Dealt on lieutenantry and no practice had
    In the brave squares of war: yet now: no matter.   40

CLEOPATRA. Ah! stand by.

EROS. The queen, my lord, the queen.

IRAS. Go to him, madam, speak to him,
    He is unqualified with very shame.

CLEOPATRA. Well then, sustain me: O!

EROS. Most noble sir, arise, the queen approaches:
    Her head's declined, and death will seize her, but
    Your comfort makes the rescue.

ANTONY. I have offended reputation,
A most unnoble swerving.

EROS.   Sir, the queen.   50

ANTONY. O, whither hast thou led me, Egypt? See,
How I convey my shame out of thine eyes
By looking back what I have left behind
Stroyed in dishonour.

CLEOPATRA.   O my lord, my lord
Forgive my fearful sails! I little thought
You would have followed.

ANTONY.   Egypt, thou knew'st too well
My heart was to thy rudder tied by th'strings,
And thou shouldst tow me after: o'er my spirit
Thy full supremacy thou knew'st, and that
Thy beck might from the bidding of the gods   60
Command me.

CLEOPATRA.   O, my pardon!

ANTONY.   Now I must
To the young man send humble treaties, dodge
And palter in the shifts of lowness; who
With half the bulk o'th'world played as I pleased,
Making and marring fortunes. You did know
How much you were my conqueror, and that
My sword, made weak by my affection, would
Obey it on all cause.

CLEOPATRA.   Pardon, pardon!

ANTONY. Fall not a tear, I say; one of them rates
All that is won and lost: give me a kiss;   70
Even this repays me.
We sent our schoolmaster; is a' come back?
Love, I am full of lead.
Some wine, within there, and our viands!
    Fortune knows
We scorn her most when most she offers blows.
                                They go in

Scene 12: *Egypt. Cæsar's camp*

Enter Cæsar, Agrippa, Dolabella, Thidias, with others

CÆSAR. Let him appear that's come from Antony.
Know you him?

DOLABELLA.   Cæsar, 'tis his schoolmaster—
An argument that he is plucked, when hither
He sends so poor a pinion of his wing,
Which had superfluous kings for messengers
Not many moons gone by.

Enter a Schoolmaster, as ambassador from Antony

CÆSAR.   Approach, and speak.

SCHOOLMASTER. Such as I am, I come from Antony:
I was of late as petty to his ends
As is the morn-dew on the myrtle-leaf
To his grand sea.

CÆSAR.   Be't so: declare thine office.   10

SCHOOLMASTER. Lord of his fortunes he salutes thee,
    and
Requires to live in Egypt, which not granted,
He lessens his requests, and to thee sues
To let him breathe between the heavens and earth,
A private man in Athens: this for him.
Next, Cleopatra does confess thy greatness,
Submits her to thy might, and of thee craves
The circle of the Ptolemies for her heirs,
Now hazarded to thy grace.

CÆSAR.   For Antony,
I have no ears to his request. The queen   20

Of audience nor desire shall fail, so she
From Egypt drive her all-disgracéd friend,
Or take his life there: this if she perform,
She shall not sue unheard. So to them both.

SCHOOLMASTER. Fortune pursue thee.

CÆSAR.   Bring him through the bands.
                        The Schoolmaster goes
[*to Thidias*] To try thy eloquence, now 'tis time:
    dispatch;
From Antony win Cleopatra: promise,
And in our name, what she requires; add more,
As thine invention offers. Women are not
In their best fortunes strong, but want will perjure   30
The ne'er-touched vestal. Try thy cunning, Thidias;
Make thine own edict for thy pains, which we
Will answer as a law.

THIDIAS.   Cæsar, I go.

CÆSAR. Observe how Antony becomes his flaw,
And what thou think'st his very action speaks
In every power that moves.

THIDIAS.   Cæsar, I shall.   *They go*

Scene 13: *Alexandria. Cleopatra's palace*

Enter Cleopatra, Enobarbus, Charmian, and Iras

CLEOPATRA. What shall we do, Enobarbus?

ENOBARBUS.   Think, and die.

CLEOPATRA. Is Antony or we in fault for this?

ENOBARBUS. Antony only, that would make his will
Lord of his reason. What though you fled
From that great face of war, whose several ranges
Frighted each other, why should he follow?
The itch of his affection should not then
Have nicked his captainship at such a point,
When half to half the world opposed, he being
The meréd question: 'twas a shame no less   10
Than was his loss, to course your flying flags
And leave his navy gazing.

CLEOPATRA.   Prithee, peace.

Enter Antony, with the Schoolmaster

ANTONY. Is that his answer?

SCHOOLMASTER. Ay, my lord.

ANTONY. The queen shall then have courtesy, so she
Will yield us up.

SCHOOLMASTER.   He says so.

ANTONY.   Let her know't.
To the boy Cæsar send this grizzled head,
And he will fill thy wishes to the brim
With principalities.

CLEOPATRA.   That head, my lord?

ANTONY. To him again! tell him he wears the rose   20
Of youth upon him; from which the world should
    note
Something particular: his coin, ships, legions,
May be a coward's, whose ministers would prevail
Under the service of a child as soon
As i'th'command of Cæsar. I dare him therefore
To lay his gay comparisons apart
And answer me declined, sword against sword,
Ourselves alone: I'll write it: follow me.
                He goes, attended by the Schoolmaster

ENOBARBUS [*aside*]. Yes, like enough, high battled
    Cæsar will
Unstate his happiness and be staged to th'show   30
Against a sworder! I see men's judgements are

A parcel of their fortunes, and things outward
Do draw the inward quality after them,
To suffer all alike. That he should dream,
Knowing all measures, the full Cæsar will
Answer his emptiness! Cæsar, thou hast subdued
His judgement too.

Enter a Servant

SERVANT.   A messenger from Cæsar.
CLEOPATRA. What, no more ceremony? See, my
women,
Against the blown rose may they stop their nose
That kneeled unto the buds. Admit him, sir.   40
                              The Servant goes
ENOBARBUS [*aside*]. Mine honesty and I begin to
square.
The loyalty well held to fools does make
Our faith mere folly: yet he that can endure
To follow with allegiance a fall'n lord
Does conquer him that did his master conquer,
And earns a place i'th'story.

Enter Thidias

CLEOPATRA.   Cæsar's will?
THIDIAS. Hear it apart.
CLEOPATRA.   None but friends: say boldly.
THIDIAS. So, haply, are they friends to Antony.
ENOBARBUS. He needs as many, sir, as Cæsar has,
Or needs not us. If Cæsar please, our master   50
Will leap to be his friend: for us, you know,
Whose he is we are, and that is Cæsar's.
THIDIAS.   So.
Thus then, thou most renowned, Cæsar entreats
Not to consider in what case thou stand'st
Further than he is Cæsar.
CLEOPATRA.   Go on: right royal.
THIDIAS. He knows that you embraced not Antony
As you did love, but as you feared him.
CLEOPATRA.   O!
THIDIAS. The scars upon your honour therefore he
Does pity as constrainéd blemishes,
Not as deserved.
CLEOPATRA.   He is a god and knows   60
What is most right: mine honour was not yielded,
But conquered merely.
ENOBARBUS [*aside*].   To be sure of that,
I will ask Antony. Sir, sir, thou art so leaky
That we must leave thee to thy sinking, for
Thy dearest quit thee.
                              He goes out
THIDIAS.   Shall I say to Cæsar
What you require of him? for he partly begs
To be desired to give. It much would please him,
That of his fortunes you should make a staff
To lean upon. But it would warm his spirits,
To hear from me you had left Antony,   70
And put yourself under his shroud,
The universal landlord.
CLEOPATRA.   What's your name?
THIDIAS. My name is Thidias.
CLEOPATRA.   Most kind messenger,
Say to great Cæsar this: in deputation
I kiss his conqu'ring hand: tell him, I am prompt
To lay my crown at's feet, and there to kneel:
Tell him, from his all-obeying breath I hear
The doom of Egypt.
THIDIAS.   'Tis your noblest course.
Wisdom and fortune combating together,

If that the former dare but what it can,   80
No chance may shake it. Give me grace to lay
My duty on your hand.
CLEOPATRA.   Your Cæsar's father oft
(When he hath mused of taking kingdoms in)
Bestowed his lips on that unworthy place,
As it rained kisses.

Re-enter Antony and Enobarbus

ANTONY.   Favours, by Jove that thunders!
What art thou, fellow?
THIDIAS.   One that but performs
The bidding of the fullest man and worthiest
To have command obeyed.
ENOBARBUS [*aside*].   You will be whipped.
ANTONY [*shouts*]. Approach, there! [*to Cleopatra*] Ah,
you kite! [*pause*] Now, gods and devils!
Authority melts from me. Of late when I cried 'Ho!' 90
Like boys unto a muss, kings would start forth,
And cry 'Your will?'

Enter Attendants in haste

                    Have you no ears?
I am Antony yet. Take hence this Jack, and whip
him.
ENOBARBUS. 'Tis better playing with a lion's whelp
Than with an old one dying.
ANTONY.   Moon and stars!
Whip him! Were't twenty of the greatest tributaries
That do acknowledge Cæsar, should I find them
So saucy with the hand of she here—what's her name
Since she was Cleopatra? Whip him, fellows,
Till like a boy you see him cringe his face,   100
And whine aloud for mercy. Take him hence.
THIDIAS. Mark Antony—
ANTONY.   Tug him away: being whipped,
Bring him again. This Jack of Cæsar's shall
Bear us an errand to him,
                    Attendants take Thidias out
You were half blasted ere I knew you … Ha!
Have I my pillow left unpressed in Rome,
Forborne the getting of a lawful race,
And by a gem of women, to be abused
By one that looks on feeders?
CLEOPATRA.   Good my lord—
ANTONY. You have been a boggler ever: 110
But when we in our viciousness grow hard—
O misery on't!—the wise gods seel our eyes,
In our own filth drop our clear judgements, make us
Adore our errors, laugh at's while we strut
To our confusion.
CLEOPATRA.   O, is't come to this?
ANTONY. I found you as a morsel cold upon
Dead Cæsar's trencher; nay, you were a fragment
Of Gnæus Pompey's; besides what hotter hours,
Unregistered in vulgar fame, you have
Luxuriously picked out: for I am sure,   120
Though you can guess what temperance should be,
You know not what it is.
CLEOPATRA.   Wherefore is this?
ANTONY. To let a fellow that will take rewards
And say 'God quit you!' be familiar with
My playfellow, your hand, this kingly seal
And plighter of high hearts! O, that I were
Upon the hill of Basan, to outroar
The hornéd herd! for I have savage cause;
And to proclaim it civilly, were like

A haltered neck which does the hangman thank
For being yare about him.

Re-enter Attendants with Thidias

                                Is he whipped?
1 ATTENDANT. Soundly, my lord.
ANTONY.   Cried he? and begged a' pardon?
1 ATTENDANT. He did ask favour.
ANTONY. If that thy father live, let him repent
Thou wast not made his daughter; and be thou sorry
To follow Cæsar in his triumph, since
Thou hast been whipped for following him:
   henceforth
The white hand of a lady fever thee,
Shake thou to look on't. Get thee back to Cæsar,
Tell him thy entertainment: look thou say
He makes me angry with him. For he seems
Proud and disdainful, harping on what I am,
Not what he knew I was. He makes me angry,
And at this time most easy 'tis to do't:
When my good stars that were my former guides
Have empty left their orbs and shot their fires
Into th'abysm of hell. If he mislike
My speech and what is done, tell him he has
Hipparchus, my enfranchéd bondman, whom
He may at pleasure whip, or hang, or torture,
As he shall like, to quit me. Urge it thou:
Hence with thy stripes, be gone!   *Thidias goes*
CLEOPATRA. Have you done yet?
ANTONY.   Alack, our terrene moon
Is now eclipsed, and it portends alone
The fall of Antony.
CLEOPATRA.   I must stay his time.
ANTONY. To flatter Cæsar, would you mingle eyes
With one that ties his points?
CLEOPATRA.   Not know me yet?
ANTONY. Cold-hearted toward me?
CLEOPATRA.   Ah, dear, if I be so,
From my cold heart let heaven engender hail,
And poison it in the course, and the first stone
Drop in my neck: as it determines, so
Dissolve my life! the next Cæsarion smite!
Till by degrees the memory of my womb,
Together with my brave Egyptians all,
By the discandying of this pelleted storm
Lie graveless, till the flies and gnats of Nile
Have buried them for prey!
ANTONY.   I am satisfied.
Cæsar sets down in Alexandria, where
I will oppose his fate. Our force by land
Hath nobly held, our severed navy too
Have knit again, and fleet, threat'ning most sea-like.
Where hast thou been, my heart? Dost thou hear,
   lady?
If from the field I shall return once more
To kiss these lips, I will appear in blood;
I and my sword will earn our chronicle.
There's hope in't yet.
CLEOPATRA. That's my brave lord!
ANTONY. I will be treble-sinewed, hearted, breathed,
And fight maliciously: for when mine hours
Were nice and lucky, men did ransom lives
Of me for jests; but now I'll set my teeth,
And send to darkness all that stop me. Come,
Let's have one other gaudy night: call to me
All my sad captains; fill our bowls once more:

Let's mock the midnight bell.
CLEOPATRA.   It is my birth-day,
I had thought t'have held it poor. But since my lord
Is Antony again, I will be Cleopatra.
ANTONY. We will yet do well.
CLEOPATRA. Call all his noble captains to my lord.
ANTONY. Do so, we'll speak to them, and to-night
   I'll force
The wine peep through their scars. Come on,
   my queen;
There's sap in't yet. The next time I do fight
I'll make death love me; for I will contend
Even with his pestilent scythe.   *They go*
ENOBARBUS. Now he'll outstare the lightning. To
   be furious
Is to be frighted out of fear, and in that mood
The dove will peck the estridge; and I see still
A diminution in our captain's brain
Restores his heart: when valour preys on reason,
It eats the sword it fights with. I will seek
Some way to leave him.   *He follows*

ACT 4

Scene 1: *Before Alexandria*

Enter Cæsar, Agrippa, and Mæcenas, with his army;
Cæsar reading a letter

CÆSAR. He calls me boy, and chides as he had power
To beat me out of Egypt; my messenger
He hath whipped with rods; dares me to personal
   combat,
Cæsar to Antony. Let the old ruffian know
I have many other ways to die; meantime
Laugh at his challenge.
MÆCENAS.   Cæsar must think,
When one so great begins to rage, he's hunted
Even to falling. Give him no breath, but now
Make boot of his distraction. Never anger
Make good guard for itself.
CÆSAR.   Let our best heads
Know that to-morrow the last of many battles
We mean to fight. Within our files there are,
Of those that served Mark Antony but late,
Enough to fetch him in. See it done:
And feast the army; we have store to do't,
And they have earned the waste. Poor Antony!
    They go

Scene 2: *Alexandria. Cleopatra's palace*

Enter Antony, Cleopatra, Enobarbus, Charmian, Iras,
Alexas, with others

ANTONY. He will not fight with me, Domitius?
ENOBARBUS.   No.
ANTONY. Why should he not?
ENOBARBUS. He thinks, being twenty times of better
   fortune,
He is twenty men to one.
ANTONY.   To-morrow, soldier,
By sea and land I'll fight: or I will live,
Or bathe my dying honour in the blood
Shall make it live again. Woo't thou fight well?
ENOBARBUS. I'll strike, and cry 'Take all.'
ANTONY.   Well said. Come on:
Call forth my household servants: let's to-night
Be bounteous at our meal.

Enter three or four Servitors

ANTONY.   Give me thy hand,
Thou has been rightly honest, so hast thou,
Thou, and thou, and thou: you have served me well,
And kings have been your fellows.

CLEOPATRA.   What means this?

ENOBARBUS. 'Tis one of those odd tricks which
     sorrow shoots
Out of the mind.

ANTONY.   And thou art honest too.
I wish I could be made so many men,
And all of you clapped up together in
An Antony, that I might do you service
So good as you have done.

ALL.   The gods forbid!

ANTONY. Well, my good fellows, wait on me
     to-night:
Scant not my cups, and make as much of me
As when mine empire was your fellow too
And suffered my command.

CLEOPATRA.   What does he mean?

ENOBARBUS. To make his followers weep.

ANTONY.   Tend me to-night;
May be it is the period of your duty;
Haply you shall not see me more, or if,
A mangled shadow. Perchance to-morrow
You'll serve another master. I look on you
As one that takes his leave. Mine honest friends,
I turn you not away; but, like a master
Married to your good service, stay till death:
Tend me to-night two hours, I ask no more,
And the gods yield you for't!

ENOBARBUS.   What mean you, sir,
To give them this discomfort? Look, they weep,
And I, an ass, am onion-eyed: for shame,
Transform us not to women.

ANTONY.   Ho, ho, ho!
Now the witch take me, if I meant it thus!
Grace grow where those drops fall! My hearty
     friends,
You take me in too dolorous a sense;
For I spake to you for your comfort, did desire you
To burn this night with torches: know, my hearts,
I hope well of to-morrow, and will lead you
Where rather I'll expect victorious life
Than death and honour. Let's to supper, come,
And drown consideration.   *They go*

Scene 3: The same. A platform before the palace

Enter a company of Soldiers

1 SOLDIER. Brother, good night: to-morrow is the day.

2 SOLDIER. It will determine one way: fare you well.
     Heard you of nothing strange about the streets?

1 SOLDIER. Nothing: what news?

2 SOLDIER. Belike 'tis but a rumour. Good night to
     you.

1 SOLDIER. Well, sir, good night.

They meet other Soldiers

2 SOLDIER. Soldiers, have careful watch.

3 SOLDIER. And you. Good night, good night.

They place themselves in every corner of the platform

4 SOLDIER. Here we: and if to-morrow

Our navy thrive, I have an absolute hope
Our landmen will stand up.

3 SOLDIER.   'Tis a brave army,
And full of purpose

                 Strange music is heard below

4 SOLDIER.   Peace! what noise?

1 SOLDIER.   List, list!

2 SOLDIER. Hark!

1 SOLDIER.   Music i'th'air.

3 SOLDIER.   Under the earth.

4 SOLDIER. It signs well, does it not?

3 SOLDIER.   No.

1 SOLDIER.   Peace, I say!
What should this mean?

2 SOLDIER. 'Tis the god Hercules, whom Antony
     loved,
Now leaves him.

1 SOLDIER.   Walk, let's see if other watchmen
Do hear what we do.

2 SOLDIER.   How now, masters!

ALL [*speaking together*].   How now!
How now! Do you hear this?

1 SOLDIER.   Ay, is't not strange?

3 SOLDIER. Do you hear, masters? do you hear?

1 SOLDIER. Follow the noise so far as we have quarter;
Let's see how it will give off.

ALL.   Content. 'Tis strange.
                       They move off

Scene 4: Cleopatra's palace

Enter Antony and Cleopatra, Charmian and others attending

ANTONY. Eros! mine armour, Eros!

CLEOPATRA.   Sleep a little.

ANTONY. No, my chuck. Eros, come; mine armour,
Eros!

Enter Eros with armour

Come, good fellow, put thine iron on.
If fortune be not ours to-day, it is
Because we brave her: come.

CLEOPATRA.   Nay, I'll help too.
What's this for?

ANTONY.   Ah, let be, let be! thou art
The armourer of my heart: false, false: this, this.

CLEOPATRA. Sooth, la, I'll help: thus it must be.

ANTONY.   Well, well,
We shall thrive now. Seest thou, my good fellow?
Go put on thy defences.

EROS.   Briefly, sir.

CLEOPATRA. Is not this buckled well?

ANTONY.   Rarely, rarely:
He that unbuckles this, till we do please
To daff't for our repose, shall hear a storm.
Thou fumblest, Eros; and my queen's a squire
More tight at this than thou: dispatch. O love,
That thou couldst see my wars to-day, and knew'st
The royal occupation! thou shouldst see
A workman in't.

Enter an armed Soldier

         Good morrow to thee, welcome,
Thou look'st like him that knows a warlike charge:
To business that we love we rise betime,
And to go to't with delight.

SOLDIER.   A thousand, sir.

Early though't be, have on their riveted trim,
And at the port expect you.
> *Shout. Trumpets flourish*

Enter Captains and Soldiers

CAPTAIN. The morn is fair. Good morrow, general.
ALL. Good morrow, general.
ANTONY.   'Tis well blown, lads:
This morning, like the spirit of a youth
That means to be of note, begins betimes.
So, so; come, give me that: this way—well said!
Fare thee well, dame; whate'er becomes of me,
This is a soldier's kiss: rebukeable   30
And worthy shameful check it were, to stand
On more mechanic compliment. I'll leave thee
Now like a man of steel. You that will fight,
Follow me close; I'll bring you to't. Adieu.
> *They go, leaving Cleopatra and*
> *Charmian behind*

CHARMIAN. Please you, retire to your chamber?
CLEOPATRA.   Lead me.
He goes forth gallantly. That he and Cæsar might
Determine this great war in single fight!
Then Antony—but now—Well, on.   *They go*

Scene 5: *Before Alexandria*

Trumpets sound. Enter Antony and Eros; a Soldier meeting
them

SOLDIER. The gods make this a happy day to Antony!
ANTONY. Would thou and those thy scars had once
    prevailed
To make me fight at land!
SOLDIER.   Hadst thou done so,
The kings that have revolted and the soldier
That has this morning left thee would have still
Followed thy heels.
ANTONY.   Who's gone this morning?
SOLDIER.   Who!
One ever near thee: call for Enobarbus,
He shall not hear thee, or from Cæsar's camp
Say 'I am none of thine.'
ANTONY.   What sayest thou?
SOLDIER.   Sir,
He is with Cæsar.
EROS.   Sir, his chests and treasure   10
He has not with him.
ANTONY.   Is he gone?
SOLDIER.   Most certain.
ANTONY. Go, Eros, send his treasure after; do it;
Detain no jot, I charge thee: write to him—
I will subscribe—gentle adieus and greetings;
Say that I wish he never find more cause
To change a master. O, my fortunes have
Corrupted honest men! Dispatch. Enobarbus!
> *They go*

Scene 6

Flourish. Enter Cæsar with Agrippa, Enobarbus, and others

CÆSAR. Go forth, Agrippa, and begin the fight:
Our will is Antony be took alive;
Make it so known.
AGRILLA. Cæsar, I shall.   *Goes*
CÆSAR. The time of universal peace is near:

Prove this a prosp'rous day, the three-nooked world
Shall bear the olive freely.

Enter a Messenger

MESSENGER.   Antony
Is come into the field.
CÆSAR.   Go charge Agrippa
Plant those that have revolted in the vant,
That Antony may seem to spend his fury   10
Upon himself.   *All but Enobarbus go*
ENOBARBUS. Alexas did revolt, and went to Jewry on
Affairs of Antony; there did dissuade
Great Herod to incline himself to Cæsar
And leave his master Antony: for this pains
Cæsar hath hanged him. Canidius and the rest
That fell away have entertainment, but
No honourable trust. I have done ill,
Of which I do accuse myself so sorely
That I will joy no more.

Enter a Soldier of Cæsar's

SOLDIER.   Enobarbus, Antony   20
Hath after thee sent all thy treasure, with
His bounty overplus. The messenger
Came on my guard, and at thy tent is now
Unloading of his mules.
ENOBARBUS.   I give it you.
SOLDIER. Mock not, Enobarbus,
I tell you true: 't were best you safed the bringer
Out of the host; I must attend mine office,
Or would have done't myself. Your emperor
Continues still a Jove.   *He goes*
ENOBARBUS. I am alone the villain of the earth,   30
And feel I am so most. O Antony,
Thou mine of bounty, how wouldst thou have paid
My better service, when my turpitude
Thou dost so crown with gold! This blows my
    heart:
If swift thought break it not, a swifter mean
Shall outstrike thought: but thought will do't, I feel.
I fight against thee! No, I will go seek
Some ditch wherein to die; the foul'st best fits
My latter part of life.   *He goes*

Scene 7

Alarum. Drums and trumpets. Enter Agrippa and others

AGRIPPA. Retire, we have engaged ourselves too far:
Cæsar himself has work, and our oppression
Exceeds what we expected.   *They go*

Alarums. Enter Antony, and Scarus wounded

SCARUS. O my brave emperor, this is fought indeed!
Had we done so at first, we had droven them home
With clouts about their heads.
ANTONY.   Thou bleed'st apace.
SCARUS. I had a wound here that was like a 't',
But now 'tis made an 'h'.   *Retreat sounded afar off*
ANTONY.   They do retire.
SCARUS. We'll beat 'em into bench-holes. I have yet
Room for six scotches more   10

Enter Eros

EROS. They are beaten, sir, and our advantage serves
For a fair victory.

SCARUS. Let us score their backs
And snatch 'em up, as we take hares, behind:
'Tis sport to maul a runner.
ANTONY. I will reward thee
Once for thy sprightly comfort, and ten-fold
For thy good valour. Come thee on.
SCARUS. I'll half after.
They go forward

Scene 8

Alarum. Antony returns with Scarus and his army, march-
ing as from victory, with drums and trumpets

ANTONY. We have beat him to his camp: run one
before,
And let the queen know of our gests. To-morrow,
Before the sun shall see's, we'll spill the blood
That has to-day escaped. I thank you all,
For doughty-handed are you, and have fought
Not as you served the cause, but as't had been
Each man's like mine; you have shown all Hectors.
Enter the city, clip your wives, your friends,
Tell them your feats, whilst they·with joyful tears
Wash the congealment from your wounds and kiss 10
The honoured gashes whole.

Enter Cleopatra, attended

[*to Scarus*] Give me thy hand;
To this great Fairy I'll commend thy acts,
Make her thanks bless thee. O thou day o'th'world,
Chain mine armed neck; leap thou, attire and all,
Through proof of harness to my heart, and there
Ride on the pants triumphing!
CLEOPATRA. Lord of lords!
O infinite virtue, comest thou smiling from
The world's great snare uncaught?
ANTONY. My nightingale,
We have beat them to their beds. What, girl!
though grey
Do something mingle with our younger brown,
yet ha'we 20
A brain that nourishes our nerves and can
Get goal for goal of youth. Behold this man;
Commend unto his lips thy favouring hand:
Kiss it, my warrior: he hath fought to-day
As if a god in hate of mankind had
Destroyed in such a shape.
CLEOPATRA. I'll give thee, friend,
An armour all of gold; it was a king's.
ANTONY. He has deserved it, were it carbuncled
Like holy Phœbus' ear. Give me thy hand.
Through Alexandria make a jolly march, 30
Bear our hacked targets like the men that owe them.
Had our great palace the capacity
To camp this host, we all would sup together.
And drink carouses to the next day's fate,
Which promises royal peril. Trumpeters,
With brazen din blast you the city's ear;
Make mingle with our rattling tabourines;
That heaven and earth may strike their sounds
together,
Applauding our approach. *They go*

Scene 9

Enter a centurion and his company; Enobarbus follows

CENT. If we be not relieved within this hour,

We must return to th'court of guard: the night
Is shiny, and they say we shall embattle
By th'second hour i'th'morn.
1 WATCH. This last day was
A shrewd one to's.
ENOBARBUS. O, bear me witness, night,—
2 WATCH. What man is this?
1 WATCH. Stand close, and list him.
They go aside
ENOBARBUS. Be witness to me, O thou blessed moon.
When men revolted shall upon record
Bear hateful memory, poor Enobarbus did
Before thy face repent!
CENT. Enobarbus!
2 WATCH. Peace! 10
Hark further.
ENOBARBUS. O sovereign mistress of true melancholy,
The poisonous damp of night disponge upon me,
That life, a very rebel to my will,
May hang no longer on me: throw my heart
Against the flint and hardness of my fault;
Which, being dried with grief, will break to
powder,
And finish all foul thoughts. O Antony,
Nobler than my revolt is infamous,
Forgive me in thine own particular, 20
But let the world rank me in register
A master-leaver and a fugitive:
O Antony! O Antony! *Dies*
1 WATCH. Let's speak to him.
CENT. Let's hear him, for the things he speaks
May concern Cæsar.
2 WATCH. Let's do so. But he sleeps.
CENT. Swoons rather; for so bad a prayer as his
Was never yet for sleep.
1 WATCH. Go we to him.
2 WATCH. Awake, sir, awake, speak to us.
1 WATCH. Hear you, sir?
CENT. The hand of death hath raught him.
Drums afar off
Hark! the drums demurely wake the sleepers. 30
Let's bear him to th'court of guard: he is of note.
Our hour is fully out.
2 WATCH. Come on, then; he may recover yet.
They carry off the body

Scene 10

Enter Antony and Scarus, with their army

ANTONY. Their preparation is to-day by sea,
We please them not by land.
SCARUS. For both, my lord.
ANTONY. I would they'ld fight i'th'fire or i'th'air;
We'ld fight there too. But this it is, our foot
Upon the hills adjoining to the city
Shall stay with us—Order for sea is given;
They have put forth the haven—
Where their appointment we may best discover,
And look on their endeavour. *They go forward*

Scene 11

Enter Cæsar and his army

CÆSAR. But being charged, we will be still by land,
Which as I take't we shall, for his best force
Is forth to man his galleys. To the vales,

And hold our best advantage.

They march off

Scene 12: *Hills adjoining to Alexandria*

Enter Antony and Scarus

ANTONY. Yet they are not joined: where yond pine
    does stand,
  I shall discover all: I'll bring thee word
  Straight, how 'tis like to go.   *He goes up*

Alarum afar off, as at a sea-fight

SCARUS.   Swallows have built
  In Cleopatra's sails their nests: the augurers
  Say they know not, they cannot tell; look grimly
  And dare not speak their knowledge. Antony
  Is valiant, and dejected, and by starts
  His fretted fortunes give him hope, and fear,
  Of what he has, and has not.

Antony returns

ANTONY.   All is lost!
  This foul Egyptian hath betrayéd me: 10
  My fleet hath yielded to the foe, and yonder
  They cast their caps up and carouse together
  Like friends long lost. Triple-turned whore! 'tis thou
  Hast sold me to this novice, and my heart
  Makes only wars on thee. Bid them all fly!
  For when I am revenged upon my charm,
  I have done all. Bid them all fly, begone!

Scarus goes

  O sun, thy uprise shall I see no more:
  Fortune and Antony part here, even here
  Do we shake hands! All come to this? The hearts   20
  That spanieled me at heels, to whom I gave
  Their wishes, do discandy, melt their sweets
  On blossoming Cæsar; and this pine is barked,
  That overtopped them all. Betrayed I am.
  O this false soul of Egypt! this grave charm—
  Whose eye becked forth my wars and called them
    home,
  Whose bosom was my crownet, my chief end—
  Like a right gispy hath at fast and loose
  Beguiled me to the very heart of loss.
  What, Eros, Eros!

Enter Cleopatra

                  Ah, thou spell! Avaunt!   30
CLEOPATRA. Why is my lord enraged against his love?
ANTONY. Vanish, or I shall give thee thy deserving,
  And blemish Cæsar's triumph. Let him take thee,
  And hoist thee up to the shouting plebeians:
  Follow his chariot, like the greatest spot
  Of all thy sex: most monster-like, be shown
  For poor'st diminutives, for dolts, and let
  Patient Octavia plough thy visage up
  With her preparéd nails.   *She goes*
                        'Tis well thou'rt gone,
  If it be well to live; but better 'twere   40
  Thou fell'st into my fury, for one death
  Might have prevented many. Eros, ho!
  The shirt of Nessus is upon me: teach me,
  Alcides, thou mine ancestor, thy rage:
  Let me lodge Lichas on the horns o'th'moon,
  And with those hands that grasped the heaviest club
  Subdue my worthiest self ... The witch shall die.

To the young Roman boy she hath sold me, and
    I fall
  Under this plot: she dies for't. Eros, ho!
                                    He goes

Scene 13: *Alexandria. Cleopatra's palace*

Enter Cleopatra, Charmian, Iras, Mardian

CLEOPATRA. Help me, my women! O, he's more mad
  Than Telamon for his shield; the boar of Thessaly
  Was never so embossed.
CHARMIAN.   To th'monument!
  There lock yourself, and send him word you are
    dead.
  The soul and body rive not more in parting
  Than greatness going off.
CLEOPATRA.   To th'monument!
  Mardian, go tell him I have slain myself;
  Say that the last I spoke was 'Antony,'
  And word it, prithee, piteously. Hence, Mardian,
  And bring me how he takes my death. To
    th'monument!   10
                                    They go

Scene 14

Enter Antony and Eros

ANTONY. Eros, thou yet behold'st me?
EROS.   Ay, noble lord.
ANTONY. Sometimes we see a cloud that's dragonish,
  A vapour sometimes like a bear or lion,
  A towered citadel, a pendent rock,
  A forkéd mountain, or blue promontory
  With trees upon't, that nod unto the world
  And mock our eyes with air: thou hast seen these
    signs;
  They are black Vesper's pageants.
EROS.   Ay, my lord.
ANTONY. That which is now a horse, even with a
    thought
  The rack dislimns, and makes it indistinct   10
  As water is in water.
EROS.   It does, my lord.
ANTONY. My good knave Eros, now thy captain is
  Even such a body: here I am Antony,
  Yet cannot hold this visible shape, my knave.
  I made these wars for Egypt, and the queen—
  Whose heart I thought I had, for she had mine,
  Which, whilst it was mine, had annexed unto't
  A million moe, now lost—she, Eros, has
  Packed cards with Cæsar, and false-played my glory
  Unto an enemy's triumph.   20
  Nay, weep not, gentle Eros, there is left us
  Ourselves to end ourselves.

Enter Mardian

                        O, thy vile lady!
  She has robbed me of my sword.
MARDIAN.   No, Antony,
  My mistress loved thee and her fortunes mingled
  With thine entirely.
ANTONY.   Hence, saucy eunuch, peace!
  She hath betrayed me, and shall die the death.
MARDIAN. Death of one person can be paid but once,
  And that she has discharged. What thou wouldst do
  Is done unto thy hand: the last she spake

Was 'Antony! most noble Antony!'
Then in the midst a tearing groan did break
The name of Antony; it was divided
Between her heart and lips: she rendered life,
Thy name so buried in her.
ANTONY.   Dead then?
MARDIAN.   Dead.
ANTONY. Unarm, Eros, the long day's task is done,
  And we must sleep. [to Mardian] That thou depart'st
    hence safe,
  Does pay thy labour richly; go. [Mardian goes] Off,
    pluck off!
  The seven-fold shield of Ajax cannot keep
  This battery from my heart. O, cleave, my sides!
  Heart, once be stronger than thy continent,   40
  Crack thy frail case! Apace, Eros, apace!
  No more a soldier: bruiséd pieces, go;
  You have been nobly borne. From me awhile.
                                          Eros goes
  I will o'ertake thee, Cleopatra, and
  Weep for my pardon. So it must be, for now
  All length is torture: since the torch is out,
  Lie down and stray no farther: now all labour
  Mars what it does; yea, very force entangles
  Itself with strength: seal then, and all is done.
  Eros!—I come, my queen. Eros!—Stay for me.   50
  Where souls do couch on flowers, we'll hand
    in hand,
  And with our sprightly port make the ghosts gaze:
  Dido and her Aeneas shall want troops,
  And all the haunt be ours. Come, Eros, Eros!

Eros returns

EROS. What would my lord?
ANTONY.   Since Cleopatra died
  I have lived in such dishonour that the gods
  Detest my baseness. I, that with my sword
  Quartered the world, and o'er green Neptune's back
  With ships made cities, condemn myself to lack
  The courage of a woman—less noble mind   60
  Than she which by her death our Caesar tells
  'I am conqueror of myself.' Thou art sworn, Eros,
  That, when the exigent should come (which now
  Is come indeed) when I should see behind me
  Th'inevitable prosecution of
  Disgrace and horror, that, on my command,
  Thou then wouldst kill me. Do't, the time is come:
  Thou strik'st not me, 'tis Caesar thou defeat'st.
  Put colour in thy cheek.
EROS.   The gods withhold me!
  Shall I do that which all the Parthian darts,   70
  Though enemy, lost aim and could not?
ANTONY.   Eros,
  Wouldst thou be windowed in great Rome, and see
  Thy master thus with pleached arms, bending down
  His corrigible neck, his face subdued
  To penetrative shame; whilst the wheeled seat
  Of fortunate Caesar, drawn before him, branded
  His baseness that ensued?
EROS.   I would not see't.
ANTONY. Come, then; for with a wound I must
  be cured.
  Draw that thy honest sword, which thou hast worn
  Most useful for thy country.
EROS.   O, sir, pardon me!   80

ANTONY. When I did make thee free, swor'st thou   30
    not then
  To do this when I bade thee? Do it at once;
  Or thy precedent services are all
  But accidents unpurposed. Draw, and come.
EROS. Turn from me then that noble countenance,
  Wherein the worship of the whole world lies.
ANTONY [turns]. Lo thee!
EROS. My sword is drawn.
ANTONY.   Then let it do at once
  The thing why thou hast drawn it.
EROS.   My dear master,
  My captain, and my emperor, let me say,   90
  Before I strike this bloody stroke, farewell.
ANTONY. 'Tis said, man—and farewell.
EROS. Farewell, great chief. Shall I strike now?
ANTONY.   Now, Eros.
EROS. Why, there then: thus I do escape the sorrow
  Of Antony's death.   *Kills himself*
ANTONY.   Thrice-nobler than myself!
  Thou teachest me, O valiant Eros, what
  I should and thou couldst not. My queen and Eros
  Have by their brave instruction got upon me
  A nobleness in record: but I will be
  A bridegroom in my death, and run into't   100
  As to a lover's bed. Come then; and, Eros,
  Thy master dies thy scholar: to do thus
                              Falling on his sword
  I learned of thee. How! not dead? not dead?
  The guard, ho! O, dispatch me!

Enter Dercetus and Guard

1 GUARD.   What's the noise?
ANTONY. I have done my work ill, friends: O, make
    an end
  Of what I have begun.
2 GUARD.   The star is fall'n.
1 GUARD. And time is at his period.
ALL.   Alas, and woe!
ANTONY. Let him that loves me strike me dead.
1 GUARD.   Not I.   110
2 GUARD. Nor I.
3 GUARD. Nor any one.   *They fly*
DERCETUS. Thy death and fortunes bid thy followers
    fly.
  This sword but shown to Caesar, with this tidings,
  Shall enter me with him.

Diomedes enters

DIOMEDES. Where's Antony?
DERCETUS.   There, Diomed, there.
DIOMEDES.   Lives he?
  Wilt thou not answer, man?   *Dercetus goes*
ANTONY. Art thou there, Diomed? Draw thy sword,
    and give me
  Sufficing strokes for death.
DIOMEDES.   Most absolute lord,
  My mistress Cleopatra sent me to thee.
ANTONY. When did she send thee?
DIOMEDES.   Now, my lord.
ANTONY.   Where is she?
DIOMEDES. Locked in her monument. She had a
    prophesying fear   120
  Of what hath come to pass: for when she saw—
  Which never shall be found—you did suspect
  She had disposed with Caesar, and that your rage

Would not be purged, she sent you word she
    was dead;
But, fearing since how it might work, hath sent
Me to proclaim the truth, and I am come,
I dread, too late.
ANTONY. Too late, good Diomed: call my guard,
    I prithee.
DIOMEDES. What, ho, the emperor's guard! The guard,
    what, ho!
Come, your lord calls.   130

Enter four or five of the Guard of Antony

ANTONY. Bear me, good friends, where Cleopatra
    bides,
'Tis the last service that I shall command you.
1 GUARD. Woe, woe are we, sir, you may not live
    to wear
All your true followers out.
ALL.   Most heavy day!
ANTONY. Nay, good my fellows, do not please sharp
    fate
To grace it with your sorrows: bid that welcome
Which comes to punish us, and we punish it
Seeming to bear it lightly. Take me up.
I have led you oft, carry me now, good friends,
And have my thanks for all.   140
          They bear him away on his shield

Scene 15: *Alexandria. Cleopatra's monument*

Cleopatra, Charmian, Iras and maids come out upon the roof

CLEOPATRA. O Charmian, I will never go from hence.
CHARMIAN. Be comforted, dear madam.
CLEOPATRA.   No, I will not:
All strange and terrible events are welcome,
But comforts we despise; our size of sorrow,
Proportioned to our cause, must be as great
As that which makes it.

Enter Diomedes below

            How now! is he dead?
DIOMEDES. His death's upon him, but not dead.
Look out o'th'other side your monument;
His guard have brought him thither.

Enter Antony, borne by the Guard

CLEOPATRA.   O sun,
Burn the great sphere thou mov'st in! darkling stand 10
The varying shore o'th'world. O Antony,
Antony, Antony! Help, Charmian, help, Iras, help;
Help, friends below, let's draw him hither.
ANTONY.   Peace!
Not Cæsar's valour hath o'erthrown Antony,
But Antony's hath triumphed on itself.
CLEOPATRA. So it should be, that none but Anthony
Should conquer Antony, but woe 'tis so!
ANTONY. I am dying, Egypt, dying; only
I here importune death awhile, until
Of many thousand kisses the poor last   20
I lay upon thy lips.
CLEOPATRA.   I dare not, dear,
Dear my lord, pardon: I dare not open,
Lest I be taken. Not th'imperious show
Of the full-fortuned Cæsar ever shall
Be brooched with me, if knife, drugs, serpents, have
Edge, string, or operation. I am safe:

Your wife Octavia, with her modest eyes
And still conclusion, shall acquire no honour
Demurring upon me. But come, come, Antony—
Help me, my women—we must draw thee up;   30
Assist, good friends.
ANTONY.   O, quick, or I am gone.
CLEOPATRA. Here's sport indeed! How heavy weighs
    my lord!
Our strength is all gone into heaviness;
That makes the weight. Had I great Juno's power,
The strong-winged Mercury should fetch thee up
And set thee by Jove's side. Yet come a little—
Wishers were ever fools—O, come, come, come;
      They heave Antony aloft to Cleopatra
And welcome, welcome! Die when thou hast lived,
Quicken with kissing: had my lips that power,
Thus would I wear them out.
ALL.   Ah, heavy sight.   40
ANTONY. I am dying, Egypt, dying.
Give me some wine, and let me speak a little.
CLEOPATRA. No, let me speak, and let me rail so high,
That the false huswife Fortune break her wheel,
Provoked by my offence.
ANTONY.   One word, sweet queen.
Of Cæsar seek your honour, with your safety. O!
CLEOPATRA. They do not go together.
ANTONY.   Gentle, hear me:
None about Cæsar trust but Proculeius.
CLEOPATRA. My resolution and my hands I'll trust;
None about Cæsar.   50
ANTONY. The miserable change now at my end
Lament nor sorrow at: but please your thoughts
In feeding them with those my former fortunes
Wherein I lived ... the greatest prince o'th'world,
The noblest ... and do now not basely die,
Not cowardly put off my helmet to
My countryman ... a Roman by a Roman
Valiantly vanquished. Now my spirit is going,
I can no more.
CLEOPATRA.   Noblest of men, woo't die?
Hast thou no care of me? shall I abide   60
In this dull world, which in thy absence is
No better than a sty? O, see, my women ...
                      Antony dies
The crown o'th'earth doth melt. My lord!
O, withered is the garland of the war,
The soldier's pole is fall'n: young boys and girls
Are level now with men: the odds is gone,
And there is nothing left remarkable
Beneath the visiting moon.
CHARMIAN.   O, quietness, lady!
                    Cleopatra faints
IRAS. She's dead too, our sovereign.
CHARMIAN.   Lady!
IRAS.   Madam!
CHARMIAN. O madam, madam, madam!   70
IRAS. Royal Egypt, Empress!
CHARMIAN. Peace, peace, Iras!
CLEOPATRA. No more but e'en a woman, and
    commanded
By such poor passion as the maid that milks
And does the meanest chares. It were for me
To throw my sceptre at the injurious gods,
To tell them that this world did equal theirs
Till they had stol'n our jewel. All's but naught;
Patience is sottish, and impatience does

Become a dog that's mad: then is it sin
To rush into the secret house of death,
Ere death dare come to us? How do you, women?
What, what! good cheer! Why, how now,
　　Charmian!
My noble girls! Ah, women, women, look,
Our lamp is spent, it's out! Good sirs, take heart:
We'll bury him; and then, what's brave, what's
　　noble,
Let's do it after the high Roman fashion,
And make death proud to take us. Come, away.
This case of that huge spirit now is cold:
Ah, women, women! Come, we have no friend　90
But resolution and the briefest end.
　　　　They go, bearing off Antony's body

ACT 5

Scene 1: *Alexandria. Cæsar's camp*

Enter Cæsar, with Agrippa, Dolabella, Mæcenas, Gallus,
Proculeius, and his council of war

CÆSAR. Go to him, Dolabella, bid him yield;
　　Being so frustrate, tell him he mocks
　　The pauses that he makes.
DOLABELLA. 　　　　Cæsar, I shall. 　*He goes*

Enter Dercetus, with the sword of Antony

CÆSAR. Wherefore is that? and what art thou that
　　darest
　　Appear thus to us?
DERCETUS. 　　　I am called Dercetus.
　　Mark Antony I served, who best was worthy
　　Best to be served: whilst he stood up and spoke,
　　He was my master, and I wore my life
　　To spend upon his haters. If thou please
　　To take me to thee, as I was to him　　　10
　　I'll be to Cæsar; if thou pleasest not,
　　I yield thee up my life.
CÆSAR. 　　　　What is't thou say'st?
DERCETUS. I say, O Cæsar, Antony is dead.
CÆSAR. The breaking of so great a thing should make
　　A greater crack: the round world
　　Should have shook lions into civil streets,
　　And citizens to their dens. The death of Antony
　　Is not a single doom; in that name lay
　　A moiety of the world.
DERCETUS. 　　　　He is dead, Cæsar,
　　Not by a public minister of justice,　　　20
　　Nor by a hirèd knife; but that self hand
　　Which writ his honour in the acts it did,
　　Hath, with the courage which the heart did lend it,
　　Splitted the heart. This is his sword;
　　I robbed his wound of it; behold it stained
　　With his most noble blood.
CÆSAR. 　　　　Look you sad, friends?
　　The gods rebuke me, but it is tidings
　　To wash the eyes of kings.
AGRIPPA. 　　　And strange it is
　　That nature must compel us to lament
　　Our most persisted deeds.
MÆCENAS. 　　　His taints and honours　30
　　Waged equal with him.
AGRIPPA. 　　　A rarer spirit never
　　Did steer humanity: but you, gods, will give us
　　Some faults to make us men. Cæsar is touched.

MÆCENAS. When such a spacious mirror's set before
　　him,
　　He needs must see himself.
CÆSAR. 　　　O Antony!
　　I have followed thee to this. But we do lance
　　Diseases in our bodies: I must perforce
　　Have shown to thee such a declining day,
　　Or look on thine; we could not stall together
　　In the whole world. But yet let me lament　40
　　With tears as sovereign as the blood of hearts,
　　That thou, my brother, my competitor
　　In top of all design, my mate in empire
　　Friend and companion in the front of war,
　　The arm of mine own body, and the heart
　　Where mine his thoughts did kindle, that our stars
　　Unreconciliable should divide
　　Our equalness to this. Hear me, good friends—

Enter an Egyptian

　　But I will tell you at some meeter season.
　　The business of this man looks out of him;　50
　　We'll hear him what he says. Whence are you?
EGYPTIAN. A poor Egyptian, yet the queen my
　　mistress,
　　Confined in all she has, her monument,
　　Of thy intents desires instruction,
　　That she preparédly may frame herself
　　To th'way she's forced to.
CÆSAR. 　　　Bid her have good heart:
　　She soon shall know of us, by some of ours,
　　How honourable and how kindly we
　　Determine for her; for Cæsar cannot live
　　To be ungentle.
EGYPTIAN. 　　So the gods preserve thee!　60
　　　　　　　　He departs
CÆSAR. Come hither, Proculeius. Go and say,
　　We purpose her no shame: give her what comforts
　　The quality of her passion shall require;
　　Lest in her greatness by some mortal stroke
　　She do defeat us. For her life in Rome
　　Would be eternal in our triumph: go,
　　And with your speediest bring us to what she says
　　And how you find of her.
PROCULEIUS. 　　　Cæsar, I shall. 　*He goes*
CÆSAR. Gallus, go you along. (*Gallus also goes*]
　　Where's Dolabella,
　　To second Proculeius?
ALL. 　　　　Dolabella!　　　70
CÆSAR. Let him alone; for I remember now
　　How he's employed: he shall in time be ready.
　　Go with me to my tent, where you shall see
　　How hardly I was drawn into this war,
　　How calm and gentle I proceeded still
　　In all my writings. Go with me, and see
　　What I can show in this. 　　　*They go*

Scene 2: *Alexandria. The monument*

Enter Cleopatra, Charmian, Iras and Mardian seen within
through the bars of the gate

CLEOPATRA. My desolation does begin to make
　　A better life. 'Tis paltry to be Cæsar;
　　Not being Fortune, he's but Fortune's knave,
　　A minister of her will: and it is great
　　To do that thing that ends all other deeds;
　　Which shackles accidents and bolts up change;

Which sleeps, and never palates more the dung,
The beggar's nurse and Cæsar's.

Enter Proculeius. As he speaks with Cleopatra through the
bars, Gallus and soldiers enter, unseen by those within,
mount to the top with ladders, and go down into the
monument

PROCULEIUS. Cæsar sends greeting to the Queen of
   Egypt,
   And bids thee study on what fair demands   10
   Thou mean'st to have him grant thee.
CLEOPATRA.   What's thy name?
PROCULEIUS. My name is Proculeius.
CLEOPATRA.   Antony
   Did tell me of you, bade me trust you, but
   I do not greatly care to be deceived,
   That have no use for trusting. If your master
   Would have a queen his beggar, you must tell him,
   That majesty, to keep decorum, must
   No less beg than a kingdom: if he please
   To give me conquered Egypt for my son,
   He gives me so much of mine own as I   20
   Will kneel to him with thanks.
PROCULEIUS.   Be of good cheer;
   You're fall'n into a princely hand, fear nothing.
   Make your full reference freely to my lord,
   Who is so full of grace that it flows over
   On all that need. Let me report to him
   Your sweet dependence, and you shall find
   A conqueror that will pray in aid for kindness,
   Where he for grace is kneeled to.
CLEOPATRA.   Pray you, tell him
   I am his fortune's vassal, and I send him
   The greatness he has got. I hourly learn   30
   A doctrine of obedience, and would gladly
   Look him i'th'face.
PROCULEIUS.   This I'll report, dear lady.
   Have comfort, for I know your plight is pitied
   Of him that caused it.

The doors are suddenly flung open, showing Gallus and
soldiers standing behind Cleopatra and her women

GALLUS. You see how easily she may be surprised.
   Guard her till Cæsar come.   *He goes*
IRAS. Royal queen!
CHARMIAN. O Cleopatra! thou art taken, queen!
CLEOPATRA. Quick, quick, good hands.
                     Drawing a dagger
PROCULEIUS.   Hold, worthy lady, hold:
                  Seizes and disarms her
   Do not yourself such wrong, who are in this   40
   Relieved, but not betrayed.
CLEOPATRA.   What, of death too,
   That rids our dogs of languish?
PROCULEIUS.   Cleopatra,
   Do not abuse my master's bounty by
   Th'undoing of yourself: let the world see
   His nobleness well acted, which your death
   Will never let come forth.
CLEOPATRA.   Where art thou, death?
   Come hither, come! come, come, and take a queen
   Worth many babes and beggars!
PROCULEIUS.   O, temperance, lady!
CLEOPATRA. Sir, I will eat no meat, I'll not drink, sir—
   If idle talk will once be necessary—   50
   I'll not sleep neither. This mortal house I'll ruin,

Do Cæsar what he can. Know, sir, that I
Will not wait pinioned at your master's court,
Nor once be chastised with the sober eye
Of dull Octavia. Shall they hoist me up
And show me to the shouting varletry
Of censuring Rome? Rather a ditch in Egypt
Be gentle grave unto me! rather on Nilus' mud
Lay me stark nak'd, and let the water-flies
Blow me into abhorring! rather make   60
My country's high pyramides my gibbet,
And hang me up in chains!
PROCULEIUS.   You do extend
These thoughts of horror further than you shall
Find cause in Cæsar.

Enter Dolabella

DOLABELLA.   Proculeius,
   What thou hast done thy master Cæsar knows,
   And he hath sent for thee: for the queen,
   I'll take her to my guard.
PROCULEIUS.   So, Dolabella,
   It shall content me best: be gentle to her.
   [*to Cleopatra*] To Cæsar I will speak what you
     shall please,
   If you'll employ me to him.
CLEOPATRA.   Say, I would die.   70
                     Proculeius goes
DOLABELLA. Most noble Empress, you have heard
   of me?
CLEOPATRA. I cannot tell.
DOLABELLA.   Assuredly you know me.
CLEOPATRA. No matter, sir, what I have heard or
   known.
   You laugh when boys or women tell their dreams;
   Is't not your trick?
DOLABELLA.   I understand not, madam.
CLEOPATRA. I dreamed there was an Emperor Antony.
   O, such another sleep, that I might see
   But such another man!
DOLABELLA.   If it might please ye—
CLEOPATRA. His face was as the heavens, and therein
   stuck
   A sun and moon, which kept their course and
   lighted   80
   The little O, the earth.
DOLABELLA.   Most sovereign creature—
CLEOPATRA. His legs bestrid the ocean, his reared arm
   Crested the world: his voice was propertied
   As all the tunéd spheres, and that to friends;
   But when he meant to quail and shake the orb,
   He was as rattling thunder. For his bounty,
   There was no winter in't; an autumn 'twas
   That grew the more by reaping: his delights
   Were dolphin-like, they showed his back above
   The element they lived in: in his livery   90
   Walked crowns and crownets; realms and islands
   were
   As plates dropped from his pocket.
DOLABELLA.   Cleopatra—
CLEOPATRA. Think you there was, or might be, such
   a man
   As this I dreamed of?
DOLABELLA.   Gentle madam, no.
CLEOPATRA. You lie, up to the hearing of the gods.
   But if there be, or ever were, one such,
   It's past the size of dreaming: nature wants stuff

To vie strange forms with Fancy, yet 'timagine
An Antony were Nature's piece 'gainst Fancy,
Condemning shadows quite.
DOLABELLA.   Hear me, good madam. 100
Your loss is as yourself, great; and you bear it
As answering to the weight: would I might never
O'ertake pursued success, but I do feel,
By the rebound of yours, a grief that smites
My very heart at root.
CLEOPATRA.   I thank you, sir.
Know you what Cæsar means to do with me?
DOLABELLA. I am loath to tell you what I would
  you knew.
CLEOPATRA. Nay, pray you, sir,—
DOLABELLA.   Though he be honourable,—
CLEOPATRA. He'll lead me then in triumph?
DOLABELLA. Madam, he will, I know't.   Flourish
[Shouting heard]   Make way there! Cæsar! 110

Enter Cæsar, Gallus, Proculeius, Mæcenas, and others of
his train

CÆSAR. Which is the Queen of Egypt?
DOLABELLA. It is the Emperor, madam.
                              Cleopatra kneels
CÆSAR. Arise, you shall not kneel:
I pray you, rise, rise, Egypt.
CLEOPATRA.   Sir, the gods
Will have it thus; my master and my lord
I must obey.
CÆSAR.   Take to you no hard thoughts:
The record of what injuries you did us,
Though written in our flesh, we shall remember
As things but done by chance.
CLEOPATRA.   Sole sir o'th'world,
I cannot project mine own cause so well   120
To make it clear, but do confess I have
Been laden with like frailties which before
Have often shamed our sex.
CÆSAR.   Cleopatra, know,
We will extenuate rather than enforce:
If you apply yourself to our intents,
Which towards you are most gentle, you shall find
A benefit in this change; but if you seek
To lay on me a cruelty by taking
Antony's course, you shall bereave yourself
Of my good purposes and put your children   130
To that destruction which I'll guard them from
If thereon you rely. I'll take my leave.
CLEOPATRA. And may, through all the world: 'tis
  yours; and we,
Your scrutcheons and your signs of conquest, shall
Hang in what place you please. Here, my good lord.
                              She proffers a paper
CÆSAR. You shall advise me in all for Cleopatra.
CLEOPATRA. This is the brief of money, plate and
  jewels,
I am possessed of: 'tis exactly valued,
Not petty things admitted. Where's Seleucus?

Seleucus comes forward

SELEUCUS. Here, madam.   140
CLEOPATRA. This is my treasurer. Let him speak,
  my lord,
Upon his peril, that I have reserved
To myself nothing. Speak the truth, Seleucus.
SELEUCUS. Madam,

I had rather seal my lips than to my peril
Speak that which is not.
CLEOPATRA.   What have I kept back?
SELEUCUS. Enough to purchase what you have
  made known.
CÆSAR. Nay, blush not, Cleopatra, I approve
Your wisdom in the deed.
CLEOPATRA.   See, Cæsar! O, behold,
How pomp is followed! mine will now be yours, 150
And, should we shift estates, yours would be mine.
The ingratitude of this Seleucus does
Even make me wild. O slave, of no more trust
Than love that's hired! What, goest thou back?
  thou shalt
Go back, I warrant thee; but I'll catch thine eyes,
Though they had wings: slave, soulless villain, dog!
O rarely base!
CÆSAR.   Good queen, let us entreat you.
CLEOPATRA. O Cæsar, what a wounding shame is this,
That thou, vouchsafing here to visit me,
Doing the honour of thy lordliness   160
To one so meek, that mine own servant should
Parcel the sum of my disgraces by
Addition of his envy! Say, good Cæsar,
That I some lady trifles have reserved,
Immoment toys, things of such dignity
As we greet modern friends withal; and say,
Some nobler token I have kept apart
For Livia and Octavia, to induce
Their mediation; must I be unfolded
With one that I have bred? The gods! it smites me 170
Beneath the fall I have. [to Seleucus] Prithee, go
  hence;
Or I shall show the cinders of my spirits
Through th'ashes of my chance: wert thou a man,
Thou wouldst have mercy on me.
CÆSAR.   Forbear Seleucus
                              Seleucus goes
CLEOPATRA. Be it known, that we, the greatest, are
  misthought
For things that others do, and when we fall,
We answer others' merits in our name,
Are therefore to be pitied.
CÆSAR.   Cleopatra,
Not what you have reserved, nor what
  acknowledged,
Put we i'th'roll of conquest: still be't yours,   180
Bestow it at your pleasure, and believe
Cæsar's no merchant, to make price with you
Of things that merchants sold. Therefore be
  cheered;
Make not your thoughts your prisons: no, dear
  queen;
For we intend so to dispose you as
Yourself shall give us counsel. Feed, and sleep:
Our care and pity is so much upon you
That we remain your friend; and so, adieu.
CLEOPATRA. My master, and my lord!
CÆSAR.   Not so. Adieu.
                      Flourish. Cæsar and his train depart
CLEOPATRA. He words me, girls, he words me, that
  I should not   190
Be noble to myself: but, hark thee, Charmian.
                                        Whispers
IRAS. Finish, good lady, the bright day is done,
And we are for the dark.

CLEOPATRA.   Hie thee again,
I have spoke already, and it is provided,
Go put it to the haste.
CHARMIAN.   Madam, I will.

Re-enter Dolabella

DOLABELLA. Where's the queen?
CHARMIAN [*going*].   Behold, sir.
CLEOPATRA.   Dolabella?
DOLABELLA. Madam, as thereto sworn by your
    command
(Which my love makes religion to obey),
I tell you this: Cæsar through Syria
Intends his journey, and within three days   200
You with your children will he send before.
Make your best use of this: I have performed
Your pleasure and my promise.
CLEOPATRA.   Dolabella.
I shall remain your debtor.
DOLABELLA.   I your servant.
Adieu, good queen; I must attend on Cæsar.
CLEOPATRA. Farewell, and thanks.   *He goes*
            Now, Iras, what think'st thou?
Thou, an Egyptian puppet, shalt be shown
In Rome, as well as I: mechanic slaves
With greasy aprons, rules and hammers, shall
Uplift us to the view: in their thick breaths,   210
Rank of gross diet, shall we be enclouded
And forced to drink their vapour.
IRAS.   The gods forbid!
CLEOPATRA. Nay, 'tis most certain, Iras: saucy lictors
Will catch at us like strumpets, and scald rhymers
Ballad us out o'tune: the quick comedians
Extemporally will stage us and present
Our Alexandrian revels; Antony
Shall be brought drunken forth, and I shall see
Some squeaking Cleopatra boy my greatness
I'th'posture of a whore.
IRAS.   O the good gods!   220
CLEOPATRA. Nay, that's certain.
IRAS. I'll never see't! for I am sure my nails
Are stronger than mine eyes.
CLEOPATRA.   Why, that's the way
To fool their preparations, and to conquer
Their most absurd intents.

Charmian returns

            Now, Charmian!
Show me, my women, like a queen: go fetch
My best attires. I am again for Cydnus,
To meet Mark Antony. Sirrah Iras, go.
Now, noble Charmian, we'll dispatch indeed,
And when thou hast done this chare I'll give thee
    leave   230
To play till doomsday. Bring our crown and all.
            Iras goes. Loud voices heard
Wherefore's this noise?

Enter a Guardsman

GUARDSMAN.   Here is a rural fellow
That will not be denied your highness' presence.
He brings you figs.
CLEOPATRA. Let him come in.   *Guardsman goes*
            What poor an instrument
May do a noble deed! he brings me liberty.
My resolution's placed, and I have nothing

Of woman in me: now from head to foot
I am marble-constant; now the fleeting moon
No planet is of mine.

Guardsman returns with Clown, bringing in a basket

GUARDSMAN.   This is the man.   240
CLEOPATRA. Avoid, and leave him.   *He goes*
Hast thou the pretty worm of Nilus there,
That kills and pains not?
CLOWN. Truly, I have him: but I would not be the
party that should desire you to touch him, for his
biting is immortal; those that do die of it do seldom
or never recover.
CLEOPATRA. Remember'st thou any that have died   250
on't?
CLOWN. Very many, men and women too. I heard of
one of them no longer than yesterday—a very
honest woman, but something given to lie, as a
woman should not do but in the way of honesty—
how she died of the biting of it, what pain she
felt. Truly, she makes a very good report
o'th'worm; but he that will believe all that they say,
shall never be saved by half that they do: but this
is most falliable, the worm's an odd worm.
CLEOPATRA. Get thee hence; farewell.
CLOWN. I wish you all joy of the worm.   260
            Setting down the basket
CLEOPATRA. Farewell.
CLOWN. You must think this, look you, that the worm
will do his kind.
CLEOPATRA. Ay, ay; farewell.
CLOWN. Look you, the worm is not to be trusted
but in the keeping of wise people: for indeed there
is no goodness in the worm.
CLEOPATRA. Take thou no care, it shall be heeded.
CLOWN. Very good: give it nothing, I pray you, for it
is not worth the feeding.   270
CLEOPATRA. Will it eat me?
CLOWN. You must not think I am so simple but I
know the devil himself will not eat a woman: I
know that a woman is a dish for the gods, if the
devil dress her not. But, truly, these same whoreson
devils do the gods great harm in their women; for in
every ten that they make, the devils mar five.
CLEOPATRA. Well, get thee gone; farewell.
CLOWN. Yes, forsooth: I wish you joy o'th'worm.
            Goes

Re-enter Iras with a robe, crown, etc.

CLEOPATRA. Give me my robe, put on my crown,
    I have   280
Immortal longings in me. Now no more
The juice of Egypt's grape shall moist this lip.
Yare, yare, good Iras; quick. Methinks I hear
Antony call; I see him rouse himself
To praise my noble act; I hear him mock
The luck of Cæsar, which the gods give men
To excuse their after wrath. Husband, I come:
Now to that name my courage prove my title!
I am fire and air; my other elements
I give to baser life. So, have you done?   290
Come then and take the last warmth of my lips.
Farewell, kind Charmian, Iras, long farewell.
            Kisses them. Iras falls and dies
Have I the aspic in my lips? Dost fall?
If thou and nature can so gently part,

The stroke of death is as a lover's pinch,
Which hurts, and is desired. Dost thou lie still?
If thus thou vanishest, thou tell'st the world
It is not worth leave-taking.
CHARMIAN. Dissolve, thick cloud, and rain, that I
    may say
The gods themselves do weep!
CLEOPATRA.   This proves me base: 300
If she first meet the curléd Antony,
He'll make demand of her, and spend that kiss
Which is my heaven to have. Come, thou mortal
    wretch,
        To an asp, which she applies to her breast
With thy sharp teeth this knot intrinsicate
Of life at once untie: poor venomous fool,
Be angry, and dispatch. O, couldst thou speak,
That I might hear thee call great Cæsar ass,
Unpolicied!
CHARMIAN. O eastern star!
CLEOPATRA.   Peace, peace!
Dost thou not see my baby at my breast,
That sucks the nurse asleep?
CHARMIAN.   O, break! O, break! 310
CLEOPATRA. As sweet as balm, as soft as air, as gentle—
O Antony!—Nay, I will take thee too:
        Applying another asp to her arm
What should I stay—   *Dies*
CHARMIAN. In this wild world? So, fare thee well!
Now boast thee, death, in thy possession lies
A lass unparalleled. Downy windows, close;
And golden Phœbus never be beheld
Of eyes again so royal! Your crown's awry,
I'll mend it, and then play—

Enter the Guard, rustling in

1 GUARD. Where's the queen?
CHARMIAN.   Speak softly, wake her not. 320
1 GUARD. Cæsar hath sent—
CHARMIAN   Too slow a messenger.
                  Applies an asp
O, come apace, dispatch, I partly feel thee.
1 GUARD. Approach, ho! All's not well: Cæsar's
    beguiled.
2 GUARD. There's Dolabella sent from Cæsar; call him.
1 GUARD. What work is here! Charmian, is this
    well done?
CHARMIAN. It is well done, and fitting for a princess
Descended of so many royal kings.
Ah, soldier!   *Charmian dies*

Re-enter Dolabella

DOLABELLA. How goes it here?
2 GUARD.   All dead.
DOLABELLA.   Cæsar, thy thoughts
Touch their effects in this: thyself art coming 330
To see performed the dreaded act which thou
So sought'st to hinder.
[*shouts heard*] A way there, a way for Cæsar!

Enter Cæsar and all his train, marching

DOLABELLA. O sir, you are too sure an augurer;
That you did fear is done.
CÆSAR.   Bravest at the last,
She levelled at our purposes, and being royal
Took her own way. The manner of their deaths?
I do not see them bleed.
DOLABELLA.   Who was last with them?
1 GUARD. A simple countryman, that brought her figs:
This was his basket.
CÆSAR.   Poisoned then.
1 GUARD.   O Cæsar, 340
This Charmian lived but now, she stood and spake:
I found her trimming up the diadem
On her dead mistress; tremblingly she stood,
And on the sudden dropped.
CÆSAR.   O noble weakness!
If they had swallowed poison, 'twould appear
By external swelling: but she looks like sleep,
As she would catch another Antony
In her strong toil of grace.
DOLABELLA.   Here, on her breast,
There is a vent of blood, and something blown.
The like is on her arm. 350
1 GUARD. This is an aspic's trail, and these fig-leaves
Have slime upon them, such as th'aspic leaves
Upon the caves of Nile.
CÆSAR.   Most probable
That so she died; for her physician tells me
She hath pursued conclusions infinite
Of easy ways to die. Take up her bed,
And bear her women from the monument.
She shall be buried by her Antony.
No grave upon the earth shall clip in it
A pair so famous. High events as these 360
Strike those that make them; and their story is
No less in pity than his glory which
Brought them to be lamented. Our army shall
In solemn show attend this funeral,
And then to Rome. Come, Dolabella, see
High order in this great solemnity.
    They go; the soldiers bearing off the dead bodies

Cymbeline

The scene: Britain and Rome

CHARACTERS IN THE PLAY

CYMBELINE, *king of Britain*
CLOTEN, *son to the Queen by a former husband*
POSTHUMUS LEONATUS, *a gentleman, husband to Imogen*
BELARIUS, *a banished lord, disguised under the name of*
  Morgan
GUIDERIUS } *sons to Cymbeline, disguised under the names*
ARVIRAGUS } *of Polydore and Cadwal, supposed sons to*
  Morgan
PHILARIO, *friend to Posthumus* } *Italians*
JACHIMO, *friend to Philario*
CAIUS LUCIUS, *general of the Roman forces*
PISANIO, *servant to Posthumus*
CORNELIUS, *a physician*

A Roman Captain
Two British Captains
A Frenchman, *friend to Philario*
Two Lords of Cymbeline's court
Two Gentlemen of the same
Two Gaolers
QUEEN, *wife to Cymbeline*
IMOGEN, *daughter to Cymbeline by a former queen*
HELEN, *a lady attending on Imogen*
Lords, Ladies, Roman Senators, Tribunes, a Soothsayer,
  a Dutchman, a Spaniard, Musicians, Officers,
  Captains, Soldiers, Messengers, and other Attendants,
  Apparitions

Cymbeline

ACT 1

Scene 1: *Britain. The garden of Cymbeline's palace*

Enter two Gentlemen

1 GENTLEMAN. You do not meet a man but frowns.
   Our bloods
No more obey the heavens than our courtiers
Still seem as does the king.
2 GENTLEMAN.   But what's the matter?
1 GENTLEMAN. His daughter, and the heir of's
   kingdom, whom
He purposed to his wife's sole son—a widow
That late he married—hath referred herself
Unto a poor but worthy gentleman. She's wedded;
Her husband banished; she imprisoned. All
Is outward sorrow, though I think the king
Be touched at very heart.
2 GENTLEMAN.   None but the king?   10
1 GENTLEMAN. He that hath lost her too. So is the
   queen,
That most desired the match. But not a courtier,
Although they wear their faces to the bent
Of the king's looks, hath a heart that is not
Glad of the thing they scowl at.
2 GENTLEMAN.   And why so?
1 GENTLEMAN. He that hath missed the princess is a
   thing
Too bad for bad report; and he that hath her—
I mean, that married her, alack, good man!
And therefore banished—is a creature such
As, to seek through the regions of the earth   20
For one his like, there would be something failing
In him that should compare. I do not think
So fair an outward and such stuff within
Endows a man but he.
2 GENTLEMAN.   You speak him far.
1 GENTLEMAN. I do extend him, sir, within himself,
Crush him together, rather than unfold
His measure duly.
2 GENTLEMAN.   What's his name and birth?
1 GENTLEMAN. I cannot delve him to the root. His
   father
Was called Sicilius, who did join his honour
Against the Romans with Cassibelan,   30
But had his titles by Tenantius, whom
He served with glory and admired success,
So gained the sur-addition Leonatus;
And had, besides this gentleman in question,
Two other sons, who in the wars o'th'time
Died with their swords in hand; for which their
   father,
Then old and fond of issue, took such sorrow
That he quit being; and his gentle lady,
Big of this gentleman, our theme, deceased
As he was born. The king he takes the babe   40
To his protection, calls him Posthumus Leonatus,
Breeds him and makes him of his bed-chamber,
Puts to him all the learnings that his time
Could make him the receiver of, which he took
As we do air, fast as 'twas minist'red,

And in's spring became a harvest; lived in court—
Which rare it is to do—most praised, most loved;
A sample to the youngest, to th'more mature
A glass that feated them, and to the graver
A child that guided dotards. To his mistress,   50
For whom he now is banished, her own price
Proclaims how she esteemed him; and his virtue
By her election may be truly read,
What kind of man he is.
2 GENTLEMAN.   I honour him
Even out of your report. But pray you tell me,
Is she sole child to th'king?
1 GENTLEMAN.   His only child.
He had two sons—if this be worth your hearing,
Mark it—the eldest of them at three years old,
I'th'swathing clothes the other, from their nursery
Were stol'n, and to this hour no guess in knowledge   60
Which way they went.
2 GENTLEMAN.   How long is this ago?
1 GENTLEMAN. Some twenty years.
2 GENTLEMAN. That a king's children should be so
   conveyed,
So slackly guarded, and the search so slow
That could not trace them!
1 GENTLEMAN.   Howsoe'er 'tis strange,
Or that the negligence may well be laughed at,
Yet is it true, sir.
2 GENTLEMAN.   I do well believe you.
1 GENTLEMAN. We must forbear. Here comes the
   gentleman,
The queen and princess.   *They go*

Enter the Queen, Posthumus and Imogen

QUEEN. No, be assured you shall not find me,
   daughter,   70
After the slander of most stepmothers,
Evil-eyed unto you. You're my prisoner, but
Your gaoler shall deliver you the keys
That lock up your restraint. For you, Posthumus,
So soon as I can win th'offended king,
I will be known your advocate. Marry, yet
The fire of rage is in him, and 'twere good
You leaned unto his sentence with what patience
Your wisdom may inform you.
POSTHUMUS.   Please your highness,
I will from hence to-day.
QUEEN.   You know the peril.   80
I'll fetch a turn about the garden, pitying
The pangs of barred affections, though the king
Hath charged you should not speak together.
       She goes
IMOGEN.   O
Dissembling courtesy! How fine this tyrant
Can tickle where she wounds! My dearest husband,
I something fear my father's wrath, but nothing—
Always reserved my holy duty—what
His rage can do on me. You must be gone,
And I shall here abide the hourly shot
Of angry eyes, not comforted to live,   90
But that there is this jewel in the world

That I may see again.

POSTHUMUS.   My queen, my mistress:
O lady, weep no more, lest I give cause
To be suspected of more tenderness
Than doth become a man. I will remain
The loyal'st husband that did e'er plight troth.
My residence in Rome at one Philario's,
Who to my father was a friend, to me
Known but by letter; thither write, my queen,
And with mine eyes I'll drink the words you send,   100
Though ink be made of gall.

Re-enter Queen

QUEEN.   Be brief, I pray you.
If the king come, I shall incur I know not
How much of his displeasure. [*aside*] Yet I'll move
him
To walk this way. I never do him wrong
But he does buy my injuries, to be friends;
Pays dear for my offences.   *She goes*
POSTHUMUS.   Should we be taking leave
As long a term as yet we have to live,
The loathness to depart would grow. Adieu!
IMOGEN. Nay, stay a little.
Were you but riding forth to air yourself,   110
Such parting were too petty. Look here, love:
This diamond was my mother's; take it, heart;   .
But keep it till you woo another wife,
When Imogen is dead.
POSTHUMUS.   How, how? another?
You gentle gods, give me but this I have,
And cere up my embracements from a next
With bonds of death. [*putting on the ring.*] Remain,
remain thou here
While sense can keep it on. And, sweetest, fairest,
As I my poor self did exchange for you
To your so infinite loss, so in our trifles   120
I still win of you. For my sake wear this;
It is a manacle of love; I'll place it
Upon this fairest prisoner.
                    Putting a bracelet on her arm
IMOGEN.   O the gods!
When shall we see again?

Enter Cymbeline and Lords

POSTHUMUS.   Alack, the king!
CYMBELINE. Thou basest thing, avoid hence, from my
sight!
If after this command thou fraught the court
With thy unworthiness, thou diest. Away!
Thou'rt poison to my blood.
POSTHUMUS.   The gods protect you,
And bless the good remainders of the court.
I am gone.   *He goes*
IMOGEN.   There cannot be a pinch in death   130
More sharp than this is.
CYMBELINE.   O disloyal thing,
That shouldst repair my youth, thou heap'st
A year's age on me.
IMOGEN.   ..   I beseech you, sir,
Harm not yourself with your vexation.
I am senseless of your wrath; a touch more rare
Subdues all pangs, all fears.
CYMBELINE.   Past grace? obedience?
IMOGEN. Past hope, and in despair; that way past grace.

CYMBELINE. That mightst have had the sole son of my
queen!
IMOGEN. O blesséd, that I might not; I chose an eagle,
And did avoid a puttock.   140
CYMBELINE. Thou took'st a beggar, wouldst have
made my throne
A seat for baseness.
IMOGEN.   No, I rather added
A lustre to it.
CYMBELINE. O thou vile one!
IMOGEN.   Sir,
It is your fault that I have loved Posthumus:
You bred him as my playfellow, and he is
A man worth any woman; overbuys me
Almost the sum he pays.
CYMBELINE.   What, art thou mad?
IMOGEN. Almost, sir. Heaven restore me! Would I
were
A neat-herd's daughter, and my Leonatus
Our neighbour shepherd's son!

Re-enter Queen

CYMBELINE.   Thou foolish thing!   150
[*to the Queen*] They were again together; you have
done
Not after our command. Away with her,
And pen her up.
QUEEN.   Beseech your patience. Peace,
Dear lady daughter, peace! Sweet sovereign,
Leave us to ourselves, and make yourself some
comfort
Out of your best advice.
CYMBELINE.   Nay, let her languish
A drop of blood a day; and, being aged,
Die of this folly.   *Cymbeline and lords go*

Enter Pisanio

QUEEN.   Fie, you must give way.
Here is your servant. How now, sir? What news?
PISANIO. My lord your son drew on my master.
QUEEN.   Ha?   160
No harm, I trust, is done?
PISANIO.   There might have been,
But that my master rather played than fought,
And had no help of anger; they were parted
By gentlemen at hand.
QUEEN.   I am very glad on't.
IMOGEN. Your son's my father's friend; he takes his
part
To draw upon an exile. O brave sir!
I would they were in Afric both together;
Myself by with a needle, that I might prick
The goer-back. Why came you from your master?
PISANIO. On his command. He would not suffer me   170
To bring him to the haven; left these notes
Of what commands I should be subject to
When't pleased you to employ me.
QUEEN.   This hath been
Your faithful servant. I dare lay mine honour
He will remain so.
PISANIO.   I humbly thank your highness.
QUEEN. Pray walk awhile.
IMOGEN. About some half-hour hence, pray you speak
with me.
You shall at least go see my lord aboard.
For this time leave me.   *They go*

Scene 2: *The same. A public place*

Enter Cloten and two Lords

1 LORD. Sir, I would advise you to shift a shirt; the violence of action hath made you reek as a sacrifice. Where air comes out, air comes in; there's none abroad so wholesome as that you vent.

CLOTEN. If my shirt were bloody, then to shift it. Have I hurt him?

2 LORD. No, faith; not so much as his patience.

1 LORD. Hurt him? his body's a passable carcass, if he be not hurt. It is a throughfare for steel, if it be not hurt.

2 LORD. His steel was in debt; it went o'th'backside the town.

CLOTEN. The villain would not stand me.

2 LORD. No, but he fled forward still, toward your face.

1 LORD. Stand you? You have land enough of your own; but he added to your having, gave you some ground.

2 LORD. As many inches as you have oceans. Puppies!

CLOTEN. I would they had not come between us.

2 LORD. So would I, till you had measured how long a fool you were upon the ground.

CLOTEN. And that she should love this fellow, and refuse me!

2 LORD. If it be a sin to make a true election, she is damned.

1 LORD. Sir, as I told you always, her beauty and her brain go not together. She's a good sign, but I have seen small reflection of her wit.

2 LORD. She shines not upon fools, lest the reflection should hurt her.

CLOTEN. Come, I'll to my chamber. Would there had been some hurt done!

2 LORD. I wish not so; unless it had been the fall of an ass, which is no great hurt.

CLOTEN. You'll go with us?

1 LORD. I'll attend your lordship.

CLOTEN. Nay, come, let's go together.

2 LORD. Well, my lord.   *They go*

Scene 3: *A room in Cymbeline's palace*

Enter Imogen and Pisanio

IMOGEN. I would thou grew'st unto the shores o'th'haven,
And questionedst every sail; if he should write
And I not have it, 'twere a paper lost
As offered mercy is. What was the last
That he spake to thee?

PISANIO.   It was his queen, his queen!

IMOGEN. Then waved his handkerchief?

PISANIO.   And kissed it, madam.

IMOGEN. Senseless linen, happier therein than I!
And that was all?

PISANIO.   No, madam; for so long
As he could make me with this eye or ear
Distinguish him from the others, he did keep
The deck, with glove, or hat, or handkerchief,
Still waving, as the fits and stirs of's mind
Could best express how slow his soul sailed on,
How swift his ship.

IMOGEN.   Thou shouldst have made him
As little as a crow, or less, ere left

To after-eye him.

PISANIO.   Madam, so I did.

IMOGEN. I would have broke mine eye-strings, cracked them but
To look upon him, till the diminution
Of space had pointed him sharp as my needle;
Nay, followed him till he had melted from
The smallness of a gnat to air; and then
Have turned mine eye, and wept. But, good Pisanio,
When shall we hear from him?

PISANIO.   Be assured, madam,
With his next vantage.

IMOGEN. I did not take my leave of him, but had
Most pretty things to say. Ere I could tell him
How I would think on him at certain hours
Such thoughts and such; or I could make him swear
The shes of Italy should not betray
Mine interest and his honour; or have charged him,
At the sixth hour of morn, at noon, at midnight,
T'encounter me with orisons, for then
I am in heaven for him; or ere I could
Give him that parting kiss which I had set
Betwixt two charming words, comes in my father,
And like the tyrannous breathing of the north
Shakes all our buds from growing.

Enter a Lady

LADY.   The queen, madam,
Desires your highness' company.

IMOGEN. Those things I bid you do, get them dispatched.
I will attend the queen.

PISANIO.   Madam, I shall.   *They go*

Scene 4: *Rome. Philario's house*

Enter Philario, Jachimo, a Frenchman, a Dutchman, and a Spaniard

JACHIMO. Believe it, sir, I have seen him in Britain; he was then of a crescent note, expected to prove so worthy as since he hath been allowed the name of. But I could then have looked on him without the help of admiration, though the catalogue of his endowments had been tabled by his side, and I to peruse him by items.

PHILARIO. You speak of him when he was less furnished than now he is with that which makes him both without and within.

FRENCHMAN. I have seen him in France; we had very many there could behold the sun with as firm eyes as he.

JACHIMO. This matter of marrying his king's daughter, wherein he must be weighed rather by her value than his own, words him, I doubt not, a great deal from the matter.

FRENCHMAN. And then his banishment.

JACHIMO. Ay, and the approbation of those that weep this lamentable divorce under her colours are wonderfully to extend him, be it but to fortify her judgement, which else an easy battery might lay flat, for taking a beggar without less quality. But how comes it he is to sojourn with you? how creeps acquaintance?

PHILARIO. His father and I were soldiers together, to

whom I have been often bound for no less than my life.

Enter Posthumus

Here comes the Briton. Let him be so entertained amongst you as suits with gentlemen of your knowing to a stranger of his quality. I beseech you all be better known to this gentleman, whom I commend to you as a noble friend of mine. How worthy he is I will leave to appear hereafter, rather than story him in his own hearing.

FRENCHMAN. Sir, we have known together in Orleans.

POSTHUMUS. Since when I have been debtor to you for courtesies which I will be ever to pay and yet pay still.

FRENCHMAN. Sir, you o'er-rate my poor kindness; I was glad I did atone my countryman and you; it had been pity you should have been put together, with so mortal a purpose as then each bore, upon importance of so slight and trivial a nature.

POSTHUMUS. By your pardon, sir, I was then a young traveller; rather shunned to go even with what I heard than in my every action to be guided by others' experiences; but upon my mended judgement—if I offend not to say it is mended—my quarrel was not altogether slight.

FRENCHMAN. Faith, yes, to be put to the arbitrement of swords, and by such two that would by all likelihood have confounded one the other, or have fall'n both.

JACHIMO. Can we with manners ask what was the difference?

FRENCHMAN. Safely, I think; 'twas a contention in public, which may without contradiction suffer the report. It was much like an argument that fell out last night, where each of us fell in praise of our country mistresses; this gentleman at that time vouching—and upon warrant of bloody affirmation —his to be more fair, virtuous, wise, chaste, constant, qualified, and less attemptable than any the rarest of our ladies in France.

JACHIMO. That lady is not now living; or this gentleman's opinion, by this, worn out.

POSTHUMUS. She holds her virtue still, and I my mind.

JACHIMO. You must not so far prefer her 'fore ours of Italy.

POSTHUMUS. Being so far provoked as I was in France, I would abate her nothing, though I profess myself her adorer, not her friend.

JACHIMO. As fair and as good—a kind of hand-in-hand comparison—had been something too fair and too good for any lady in Britain. If she went before others I have seen, as that diamond of yours outlustres many I have beheld, I could not but believe she excelled many; but I have not seen the most precious diamond that is, nor you the lady.

POSTHUMUS. I praised her as I rated her: so do I my stone.

JACHIMO. What do you esteem it at?

POSTHUMUS. More than the world enjoys.

JACHIMO. Either your unparagoned mistress is dead, or she's outprized by a trifle.

POSTHUMUS. You are mistaken: the one may be sold or given, or if there were wealth enough for the purchase, or merit for the gift; the other is not a thing for sale, and only the gift of the gods.

JACHIMO. Which the gods have given you?

POSTHUMUS. Which by their graces I will keep.

JACHIMO. You may wear her in title yours; but you know strange fowl light upon neighbouring ponds. Your ring may be stol'n too, so your brace of unprizable estimations, the one is but frail and the other casual; a cunning thief, or a that way accomplished courtier, would hazard the winning both of first and last.

POSTHUMUS. Your Italy contains none so accomplished a courtier to convince the honour of my mistress, if in the holding or loss of that you term her frail. I do nothing doubt you have store of thieves; notwithstanding, I fear not my ring.

PHILARIO. Let us leave here, gentlemen.

POSTHUMUS. Sir, with all my heart. This worthy signior, I thank him, makes no stranger of me; we are familiar at first.

JACHIMO. With five times so much conversation, I should get ground of your fair mistress; make her go back even to the yielding, had I admittance, and opportunity to friend.

POSTHUMUS. No, no.

JACHIMO. I dare thereupon pawn the moiety of my estate to your ring, which in my opinion o'ervalues it something. But I make my wager rather against your confidence than her reputation; and to bar your offence herein too, I durst attempt it against any lady in the world.

POSTHUMUS. You are a great deal abused in too bold a persuasion, and I doubt not you sustain what you're worthy of by your attempt.

JACHIMO. What's that?

POSTHUMUS. A repulse; though your attempt, as you call it, deserve more—a punishment too.

PHILARIO. Gentlemen, enough of this. It came in too suddenly; let it die as it was born, and I pray you be better acquainted.

JACHIMO. Would I had put my estate and my neighbour's on th'approbation of what I have spoke—

POSTHUMUS. What lady would you choose to assail?

JACHIMO. Yours, whom in constancy you think stands so safe. I will lay you ten thousand ducats to your ring that, commend me to the court where your lady is, with no more advantage than the opportunity of a second conference, and I will bring from thence that honour of hers which you imagine so reserved.

POSTHUMUS. I will wage against your gold, gold to it. My ring I hold dear as my finger; 'tis part of it.

JACHIMO. You are a friend, and therein the wiser. If you buy lady's flesh at a million a dram, you cannot preserve it from tainting; but I see you have some religion in you, that you fear.

POSTHUMUS. This is but a custom in your tongue; you bear a graver purpose, I hope.

JACHIMO. I am the master of my speeches, and would undergo what's spoken, I swear.

POSTHUMUS. Will you? I shall but lend my diamond till your return. Let there be covenants drawn between's. My mistress exceeds in goodness the hugeness of your unworthy thinking. I dare you to this match: here's my ring.

PHILARIO. I will have it no lay.

JACHIMO. By the gods, it is one. If I bring you no sufficient testimony that I have enjoyed the dearest

bodily part of your mistress, my ten thousand ducats
are yours; so is your diamond too. If I come off, and
leave her in such honour as you have trust in, she
your jewel, this your jewel, and my gold are yours 160
—provided I have your commendation for my
more free entertainment.

POSTHUMUS. I embrace these conditions; let us have
articles betwixt us. Only, thus far you shall answer:
if you make your voyage upon her, and give me
directly to understand you have prevailed, I am no
further your enemy; she is not worth our debate. If
she remain unseduced, you not making it appear
otherwise, for your ill opinion and th'assault you
have made to her chastity, you shall answer me with 170
your sword.

JACHIMO. Your hand—a covenant. We will have these
things set down by lawful counsel, and straight
away for Britain, lest the bargain should catch cold
and starve. I will fetch my gold, and have our two
wagers recorded.

POSTHUMUS. Agreed.   *Posthumus and Jachimo go*

FRENCHMAN. Will this hold, think you?

PHILARIO. Signior Jachimo will not from it. Pray let
us follow 'em.   *They go* 180

Scene 5: *Britain. A room in Cymbeline's palace*

Enter Queen, Ladies, and Cornelius

QUEEN. Whiles yet the dew's on ground, gather those
      flowers;
Make haste. Who has the note of them?

I LADY.   I, madam.

QUEEN. Dispatch.   *Ladies go*
Now, master doctor, have you brought those drugs?

CORNELIUS. Pleaseth your highness, ay. Here they are,
      madam.   *Presenting a small box*
But I beseech your grace, without offence—
My conscience bids me ask—wherefore you have
Commanded of me these most poisonous
      compounds,
Which are the movers of a languishing death,
But though slow, deadly.

QUEEN.   I wonder, doctor,   10
Thou ask'st me such a question. Have I not been
Thy pupil long? Hast thou not learned me how
To make perfumes? distil? preserve? yea, so
That our great king himself doth woo me oft
For my confections? Having thus far proceeded—
Unless thou think'st me devilish—is't not meet
That I did amplify my judgement in
Other conclusions? I will try the forces
Of these thy compounds on such creatures as
We count not worth the hanging—but none
      human—   20
To try the vigour of them and apply
Allayments to their act, and by them gather
Their several virtues and effects.

CORNELIUS.   Your highness
Shall from this practice but make hard your heart;
Besides, the seeing these effects will be
Both noisome and infectious.

QUEEN.   O, content thee.

Enter Pisanio

[*aside*] Here comes a flattering rascal; upon him
Will I first work. He's factor for his master,

And enemy to my son. [*aloud*] How now, Pisanio?
Doctor, your service for this time is ended;   30
Take your own way.

CORNELIUS [*aside*].   I do suspect you, madam;
But you shall do no harm.

QUEEN [*to Pisanio*].   Hark thee, a word.

CORNELIUS [*aside*]. I do not like her. She doth think she
      has
Strange ling'ring poisons. I do know her spirit,
And will not trust one of her malice with
A drug of such damned nature. Those she has
Will stupefy and dull the sense awhile,
Which first perchance she'll prove on cats and dogs,
Then afterward up higher; but there is
No danger in what show of death it makes,   40
More than the locking up the spirits a time,
To be more fresh, reviving. She is fooled
With a most false effect; and I the truer
So to be false with her.

QUEEN.   No further service, doctor,
Until I send for thee.

CORNELIUS.   I humbly take my leave.
                                        Goes

QUEEN. Weeps she still, say'st thou? Dost thou think
      in time
She will not quench, and let instructions enter
Where folly now possesses? Do thou work.
When thou shalt bring me word she loves my son,
I'll tell thee on the instant thou art then   50
As great as is thy master; greater, for
His fortunes all lie speechless, and his name
Is at last gasp. Return he cannot, nor
Continue where he is. To shift his being
Is to exchange one misery with another,
And every day that comes comes to decay
A day's work in him. What shalt thou expect
To be depender on a thing that leans,
Who cannot be new built, nor has no friends
So much as but to prop him? [*the Queen drops the box:
      Pisanio takes it up*] Thou tak'st up   60
Thou know'st not what; but take it for thy labour:
It is a thing I made, which hath the king
Five times redeemed from death. I do not know
What is more cordial. Nay, I prithee take it;
It is an earnest of a further good
That I mean to thee. Tell thy mistress how
The case stands with her; do't as from thyself.
Think what a chance thou changest on; but think
Thou hast thy mistress still; to boot, my son,
Who shall take notice of thee. I'll move the king   70
To any shape of thy preferment, such
As thou'lt desire; and then myself, I chiefly,
That set thee on to this desert, am bound
To load thy merit richly. Call my women.
Think on my words.   *Pisanio goes*
                  A sly and constant knave;
Not to be shaked; the agent for his master,
And the remembrancer of her to hold
The hand-fast to her lord. I have given him that
Which, if he take, shall quite unpeople her
Of liegers for her sweet; and which she after,   80
Except she bend her humour, shall be assured
To taste of too.

Re-enter Pisanio with Ladies

              So, so; well done, well done.

The violets, cowslips, and the primroses,
Bear to my closet. Fare thee well, Pisanio;
Think on my words.   *Queen and ladies go*
PISANIO.   And shall do.
But when to my good lord I prove untrue,
I'll choke myself—there's all I'll do for you.
                                        Goes

Scene 6: *The same. Another room in the palace*

Enter Imogen alone

IMOGEN. A father cruel and a step-dame false,
A foolish suitor to a wedded lady
That hath her husband banished. O, that husband,
My supreme crown of grief, and those repeated
Vexations of it! Had I been thief-stol'n,
As my two brothers, happy; but most miserable
Is the desire that's glorious. Blest be those,
How mean soe'er, that have their honest wills,
Which seasons comfort. Who may this be? Fie!

Enter Pisanio and Jachimo

PISANIO. Madam, a noble gentleman of Rome,   10
Comes from my lord with letters.
JACHIMO.   Change you, madam?
The worthy Leonatus is in safety,
And greets your highness dearly. *Presents a letter*
IMOGEN.   Thanks, good sir;
You're kindly welcome.
JACHIMO. All of her that is out of door most rich!
If she be furnished with a mind so rare,
She is alone th'Arabian bird, and I
Have lost the wager. Boldness be my friend;
Arm me audacity from head to foot;
Or, like the Parthian, I shall flying fight;   20
Rather, directly fly.
IMOGEN [*reads*]. 'He is one of the noblest note, to
whose kindnesses I am most infinitely tied. Reflect
upon him accordingly, as you value your trust—
                              LEONATUS.'
So far I read aloud.
But even the very middle of my heart
Is warmed by th'rest, and takes it thankfully.
You are as welcome, worthy sir, as I
Have words to bid you, and shall find it so
In all that I can do.
JACHIMO.   Thanks, fairest lady.   30
What, are men mad? Hath nature given them eyes
To see this vaulted arch and the rich crop
Of sea and land, which can distinguish 'twixt
The fiery orbs above and the twinned stones
Upon the numbered beach, and can we not
Partition make with spectacles so precious
'Twixt fair and foul?
IMOGEN.   What makes your admiration?
JACHIMO. It cannot be i'th'eye—for apes and
          monkeys,
'Twixt two such shes, would chatter this way and
Contemn with mows the other; nor
          i'th'judgement—   40
For idiots in this case of favour would
Be wisely definite; nor i'th'appetite—
Sluttery, to such neat excellence opposed,
Should make desire vomit emptiness,
Not so allured to feed.
IMOGEN. What is the matter, trow?

JACHIMO.   The cloyéd will,
That satiate yet unsatisfied desire, that tub
Both filled and running, ravening first the lamb,
Longs after for the garbage.
IMOGEN.   What, dear sir,
Thus raps you? Are you well?
JACHIMO.   Thanks, madam, well.   50
[*to Pisanio*] Beseech you sir,
Desire my man's abode where I did leave him:
He's strange and peevish.
PISANIO.   I was going, sir,
To give him welcome.   *Goes*
IMOGEN. Continues well my lord? His health, beseech
you?
JACHIMO. Well, madam.
IMOGEN. Is he disposed to mirth? I hope he is.
JACHIMO. Exceeding pleasant; none a stranger there
So merry and so gamesome: he is called
The Briton reveller.
IMOGEN.   When he was here   60
He did incline to sadness, and oft-times
Not knowing why.
JACHIMO.   I never saw him sad.
There is a Frenchman his companion, one
An eminent monsieur, that, it seems, much loves
A Gallian girl at home. He furnaces
The thick sighs from him; whiles the jolly Briton—
Your lord, I mean—laughs from's free lungs, cries,
          'O,
Can my sides hold, to think that man, who knows
By history, report, or his own proof,
What woman is, yea, what she cannot choose   70
But must be, will's free hours languish for
Assuréd bondage?'
IMOGEN.   Will my lord say so?
JACHIMO. Ay, madam; with his eyes in flood with
          laughter.
It is a recreation to be by
And hear him mock the Frenchman. But heavens
          know
Some men are much to blame.
IMOGEN.   Not he, I hope.
JACHIMO. Not he; but yet heaven's bounty towards
          him might
Be used more thankfully. In himself 'tis much;
In you, which I account his, beyond all talents.
Whilst I am bound to wonder, I am bound   80
To pity too.
IMOGEN.   What do you pity, sir?
JACHIMO. Two creatures heartily.
IMOGEN.   Am I one, sir?
You look on me: what wreck discern you in me
Deserves your pity?
JACHIMO.   Lamentable! What,
To hide me from the radiant sun, and solace
I'th'dungeon by a snuff?
IMOGEN.   I pray you, sir,
Deliver with more openness your answers
To my demands. Why do you pity me?
JACHIMO. That others do,
I was about to say, enjoy your——But   90
It is an office of the gods to venge it,
Not mine to speak on't.
IMOGEN.   You seem to know
Something of me, or what concerns me; pray you
Since doubting things go ill often hurts more

Than to be sure they do; for certainties
Either are past remedies, or, timely knowing,
The remedy then born—discover to me
What both you spur and stop.
JACHIMO.   Had I this cheek
To bathe my lips upon; this hand, whose touch,
Whose every touch, would force the feeler's soul   100
To th'oath of loyalty; this object, which
Takes prisoner the wild motion of mine eye,
Fixing it only here; should I, damned then,
Slaver with lips as common as the stairs
That mount the Capitol; join gripes with hands
Made hard with hourly falsehood—falsehood as
With labour; then by-peeping in an eye
Base and illustrous as the smoky light
That's fed with stinking tallow—it were fit
That all the plagues of hell should at one time   110
Encounter such revolt.
IMOGEN.   My lord, I fear,
Has forgot Britain.
JACHIMO.   And himself. Not I
Inclined to this intelligence pronounce
The beggary of his change, but 'tis your graces
That from my mutest conscience to my tongue
Charms this report out.
IMOGEN.   Let me hear no more.
JACHIMO. O dearest soul, your cause doth strike my
          heart
With pity that doth make me sick. A lady
So fair, and fastened to an empery
Would make the great'st king double, to be
          partnered   120
With tomboys hired with that self exhibition
Which your own coffers yield; with diseased
          ventures
That play with all infirmities for gold
Which rottenness can lend nature; such boiled stuff
As well might poison poison. Be revenged,
Or she that bore you was no queen, and you
Recoil from your great stock.
IMOGEN.   Revenged?
How should I be revenged? If this be true—   130
As I have such a heart that both mine ears
Must not in haste abuse—if it be true,
How should I be revenged?
JACHIMO.   Should he make me
Live like Diana's priest betwixt cold sheets,
Whiles he is vaulting variable ramps,
In your despite, upon your purse—revenge it.
I dedicate myself to your sweet pleasure,
More noble than that runagate to your bed,
And will continue fast to your affection,
Still close as sure.
IMOGEN.   What ho, Pisanio!
JACHIMO. Let me my service tender on your lips.
IMOGEN. Away, I do condemn mine ears that have   140
So long attended thee. If thou wert honourable,
Thou wouldst have told this tale for virtue, not
For such an end thou seek'st, as base as strange.
Thou wrong'st a gentleman who is as far
From thy report as thou from honour, and
Solicits here a lady that disdains
Thee and the devil alike. What ho, Pisanio!
The king my father shall be made acquainted
Of thy assault. If he shall think it fit
A saucy stranger in his court to mart   150

As in a Romish stew, and to expound
His beastly mind to us, he hath a court
He little cares for and a daughter who
He not respects at all. What ho, Pisanio!
JACHIMO. O happy Leonatus! I may say,
The credit that thy lady hath of thee
Deserves thy trust, and thy most perfect goodness
Her assured credit. Blesséd live you long,
A lady to the worthiest sir that ever
Country called his; and you his mistress, only   160
For the most worthiest fit. Give me your pardon.
I have spoke this to know if your affiance
Were deeply rooted, and shall make your lord
That which he is new o'er; and he is one
The truest mannered, such a holy witch
That he enchants societies into him;
Half all men's hearts are his.
IMOGEN.   You make amends.
JACHIMO. He sits 'mongst men like a descended god;
He hath a kind of honour sets him off,
More than a mortal seeming. Be not angry,   170
Most mighty princess, that I have adventured
To try your taking of a false report, which hath
Honoured with confirmation your great judgement
In the election of a sir so rare,
Which you know cannot err. The love I bear him
Made me to fan you thus, but the gods made you,
Unlike all others, chaffless. Pray your pardon.
IMOGEN. All's well, sir: take my power i'th'court for
          yours.
JACHIMO. My humble thanks. I had almost forgot
T'entreat your grace but in a small request,   180
And yet of moment too, for it concerns
Your lord; myself and other noble friends
Are partners in the business.
IMOGEN.   Pray what is't?
JACHIMO. Some dozen Romans of us, and your lord—
The best feather of our wing—have mingled sums
To buy a present for the emperor;
Which I, the factor for the rest, have done
In France. 'Tis plate of rare device, and jewels
Of rich and exquisite form, their values great;
And I am something curious, being strange,   190
To have them in safe stowage. May it please you
To take them in protection?
IMOGEN.   Willingly;
And pawn mine honour for their safety; since
My lord hath interest in them, I will keep them
In my bedchamber.
JACHIMO.   They are in a trunk,
Attended by my men. I will make bold
To send them to you, only for this night;
I must aboard to-morrow.
IMOGEN.   O, no, no.
JACHIMO. Yes, I beseech; or I shall short my word
By length'ning my return. From Gallia   200
I crossed the seas on purpose and on promise
To see your grace.
IMOGEN.   I thank you for your pains;
But not away to-morrow!
JACHIMO.   O, I must, madam.
Therefore I shall beseech you, if you please
To greet your lord with writing, do't to-night.
I have outstood my time, which is material
To th'tender of our present.
IMOGEN.   I will write.

Send your trunk to me; it shall safe be kept
And truly yielded you. You're very welcome.

They go

ACT 2
Scene 1: *Britain. Before Cymbeline's palace*

Enter Cloten and two Lords

CLOTEN. Was there ever man had such luck? when I
kissed the jack upon an upcast, to be hit away! I
had a hundred pound on't; and then a whoreson
jackanapes must take me up for swearing, as if I
borrowed mine oaths of him, and might not spend
them at my pleasure.

I LORD. What got he by that? You have broke his pate
with your bowl.

2 LORD [*aside*]. If his wit had been like him that broke
it, it would have run all out.   10

CLOTEN. When a gentleman is disposed to swear, it is
not for any standers-by to curtail his oaths, ha?

2 LORD. No, my lord; [*aside*] nor crop the ears of them.

CLOTEN. Whoreson dog! I give him satisfaction?
Would he had been one of my rank!

2 LORD [*aside*]. To have smelt like a fool.

CLOTEN. I am not vexed more at any thing in th'earth.
A pox on't! I had rather not be so noble as I am; they
dare not fight with me, because of the queen my
mother. Every jack-slave hath his bellyful of fight-   20
ing, and I must go up and down like a cock that
nobody can match.

2 LORD [*aside*]. You are cock and capon too; and you
crow cock with your comb on.

CLOTEN. Sayest thou?

2 LORD. It is not fit your lordship should undertake
every companion that you give offence to.

CLOTEN. No, I know that; but it is fit I should commit
offence to my inferiors.

2 LORD. Ay, it is fit for your lordship only.   30

CLOTEN. Why, so I say.

I LORD. Did you hear of a stranger that's come to
court to-night?

CLOTEN. A stranger, and I not know on't?

2 LORD [*aside*]. He's a strange fellow himself, and
knows it not.

I LORD. There's an Italian come, and, 'tis thought, one
of Leonatus' friends.

CLOTEN. Leonatus? a banished rascal; and he's another,
whatsoever he be. Who told you of this stranger?   40

I LORD. One of your lordship's pages.

CLOTEN. Is it fit I went to look upon him? is there no
derogation in't?

2 LORD. You cannot derogate, my lord.

CLOTEN. Not easily, I think.

2 LORD [*aside*]. You are a fool granted; therefore your
issues, being foolish, do not derogate.

CLOTEN. Come, I'll go see this Italian. What I have
lost to-day at bowls I'll win to-night of him. Come,
go.   50

2 LORD. I'll attend your lordship.

Cloten and 1 Lord go

That such a crafty devil as is his mother
Should yield the world this ass! a woman that
Bears all down with her brain; and this her son
Cannot take two from twenty, for his heart,
And leave eighteen. Alas, poor princess,

Thou divine Imogen, what thou endur'st,
Betwixt a father by thy step-dame governed,
A mother hourly coining plots, a wooer
More hateful than the foul expulsion is   60
Of thy dear husband, than that horrid act
Of the divorce he'ld make. The heavens hold firm
The walls of thy dear honour; keep unshaked
That temple, thy fair mind, that thou mayst stand
T'enjoy thy banished lord and this great land!

Goes

Scene 2: *Imogen's bedchamber in Cymbeline's palace: a trunk in one corner of it*

Imogen in bed, reading; a Lady attending

IMOGEN. Who's there? my woman Helen?
LADY.   Please you, madam.
IMOGEN. What hour is it?
LADY.   Almost midnight, madam.
IMOGEN. I have read three hours then. Mine eyes are
weak;
Fold down the leaf where I have left; to bed.
Take not away the taper, leave it burning;
And if thou canst awake by four o'th'clock,
I prithee call me. Sleep hath seized me wholly.

Lady goes

To your protection I commend me, gods.
From fairies and the tempters of the night
Guard me, beseech ye.   10

Sleeps. Jachimo comes from the trunk

JACHIMO. The crickets sing, and man's o'er-laboured
sense
Repairs itself by rest. Our Tarquin thus
Did softly press the rushes ere he wakened
The chastity he wounded. Cytherea,
How bravely thou becomest thy bed! fresh lily,
And whiter than the sheets! That I might touch,
But kiss, one kiss! Rubies unparagoned,
How dearly they do't! 'Tis her breathing that
Perfumes the chamber thus. The flame o'th'taper
Bows toward her and would under-peep her lids   20
To see th'enclosèd lights, now canopied
Under these windows, white and azure-laced
With blue of heaven's own tinct. But my design—
To note the chamber. I will write all down:
Such and such pictures; there the window; such
Th'adornment of her bed; the arras, figures,
Why, such and such; and the contents o'th'story.
Ah, but some natural notes about her body
Above ten thousand meaner movables
Would testify, t'enrich mine inventory.   30
O sleep, thou ape of death, lie dull upon her,
And be her sense but as a monument,
Thus in a chapel lying. Come off, come off;

Taking off her bracelet

As slippery as the Gordian knot was hard.
'Tis mine; and this will witness outwardly,
As strongly as the conscience does within,
To th'madding of her lord. On her left breast
A mole cinque-spotted, like the crimson drops
I'th'bottom of a cowslip. Here's a voucher,
Stronger than ever law could make; this secret   40
Will force him think I have picked the lock and ta'en
The treasure of her honour. No more. To what end?
Why should I write this down that's riveted,
Screwed to my memory? She hath been reading late

The tale of Tereus; here the leaf's turned down
Where Philomel gave up. I have enough;
To th'trunk again, and shut the spring of it.
Swift, swift, you dragons of the night, that dawning
May bare the raven's eye! I lodge in fear;
Though this a heavenly angel, hell is here.   50
                                    Clock strikes

One, two, three. Time, time!
                        Goes into the trunk

Scene 3: *An ante-chamber adjoining Imogen's apartments*

Enter Cloten and Lords

1 LORD. Your lordship is the most patient man in loss,
the most coldest that ever turned up ace.
CLOTEN. It would make any man cold to lose.
1 LORD. But not every man patient after the noble
temper of your lordship. You are most hot and
furious when you win.
CLOTEN. Winning will put any man into courage. If I
could get this foolish Imogen, I should have gold
enough. It's almost morning, is't not?
1 LORD. Day, my lord.   10
CLOTEN. I would this music would come. I am advised
to give her music o' mornings; they say it will
penetrate.

Enter Musicians

Come on, tune. If you can penetrate her with your
fingering, so; we'll try with tongue too. If none will
do, let her remain; but I'll never give o'er. First, a
very excellent good-conceited thing; after, a
wonderful sweet air, with admirable rich words to
it; and then let her consider.

                    SONG
Hark, hark, the lark at heaven's gate sings,   20
    And Phoebus 'gins arise,
His steeds to water at those springs
    On chaliced flowers that lies;
And winking Mary-buds begin
    To ope their golden eyes;
With every thing that pretty is,
    My lady sweet, arise;
    Arise, arise!

CLOTEN. So, get you gone. If this penetrate, I will
consider your music the better; if it do not, it is a   30
vice in her ears, which horse-hairs and calf's-guts,
nor the voice of unpaved eunuch to boot, can never
amend.   *Musicians go*

Enter Cymbeline and Queen

2 LORD. Here comes the king.
CLOTEN. I am glad I was up so late, for that's the
reason I was up so early. He cannot choose but take
this service I have done fatherly. Good morrow to
your majesty and to my gracious mother.
CYMBELINE. Attend you here the door of our stern
daughter? Will she not forth?   40
CLOTEN. I have assailed her with musics, but she
vouchsafes no notice.
CYMBELINE. The exile of her minion is too new;
She hath not yet forgot him. Some more time
Must wear the print of his remembrance out,
And then she's yours.
QUEEN.   You are most bound to th'king,

Who lets go by no vantages that may
Prefer you to his daughter. Frame yourself
To orderly solicits, and be friended
With aptness of the season; make denials   50
Increase your services; so seem as if
You were inspired to do those duties which
You tender to her; that you in all obey her,
Save when command to your dismission tends,
And therein you are senseless.
CLOTEN.   Senseless? not so.

Enter a Messenger

MESSENGER. So like you, sir, ambassadors from Rome;
The one is Caius Lucius.
CYMBELINE.   A worthy fellow,
Albeit he comes on angry purpose now;
But that's no fault of his. We must receive him
According to the honour of his sender;   60
And towards himself, his goodness forespent on us,
We must extend our notice. Our dear son,
When you have given good morning to your
    mistress,
Attend the queen and us; we shall have need
T'employ you towards this Roman. Come, our
    queen.   *All but Cloten go*
CLOTEN. If she be up, I'll speak with her; if not,
Let her lie still and dream. By your leave, ho!
                                        Knocks

I know her women are about her; what
If I do line one of their hands? 'Tis gold
Which buys admittance—oft it doth—yea, and
    makes   70
Diana's rangers false themselves, yield up
Their deer to th'stand o'th'stealer; and 'tis gold
Which makes the true man killed and saves the thief;
Nay, sometime hangs both thief and true man. What
Can it not do and undo? I will make
One of her women lawyer to me, for
I yet not understand the case myself.
By your leave.   *Knocks*

Enter a Lady

LADY. Who's there that knocks?
CLOTEN.   A gentleman.
LADY.   No more?
CLOTEN. Yes, and a gentlewoman's son.
LADY.   That's more   80
Than some whose tailors are as dear as yours
Can justly boast of. What's your lordship's pleasure?
CLOTEN. Your lady's person; is she ready?
LADY.   Ay,
To keep her chamber.
CLOTEN.   There is gold for you;
Sell me your good report.
LADY. How, my good name? or to report of you
What I shall think is good? The princess.
                                    Lady goes

Enter Imogen

CLOTEN. Good morrow, fairest sister. Your sweet
    hand.
IMOGEN. Good morrow, sir. You lay out too much
    pains
For purchasing but trouble. The thanks I give   90
Is telling you that I am poor of thanks,

And scarce can spare them.
CLOTEN.   Still I swear I love you.
IMOGEN. If you but said so, 'twere as deep with me.
If you swear still, your recompense is still
That I regard it not.
CLOTEN.   This is no answer.
IMOGEN. But that you shall not say I yield being silent,
I would not speak. I pray you, spare me. Faith,
I shall unfold equal discourtesy
To your best kindness; one of your great knowing
Should learn, being taught, forbearance.   100
CLOTEN. To leave you in your madness, 'twere my sin.
I will not.
IMOGEN. Fools are not mad folks.
CLOTEN.   Do you call me fool?
IMOGEN. As I am mad, I do.
If you'll be patient, I'll no more be mad;
That cures us both. I am much sorry, sir,
You put me to forget a lady's manners
By being so verbal; and learn now for all
That I, which know my heart, do here pronounce
By th'very truth of it, I care not for you,   110
And am so near the lack of charity
To accuse myself I hate you; which I had rather
You felt than make't my boast.
CLOTEN.   You sin against
Obedience, which you owe your father. For
The contract you pretend with that base wretch,
One bred of alms and fostered with cold dishes,
With scraps o'th'court, it is no contract, none.
And though it be allowed in meaner parties—
Yet who than he more mean?—to knit their souls,
On whom there is no more dependency   120
But brats and beggary, in self-figured knot;
Yet you are curbed from that enlargement by
The consequence o'th'crown, and must not foil
The precious note of it with a base slave,
A hilding for a livery, a squire's cloth,
A pantler—not so eminent.
IMOGEN.   Profane fellow,
Wert thou the son of Jupiter, and no more
But what thou art besides, thou wert too base
To be his groom; thou wert dignified enough,
Even to the point of envy, if 'twere made   130
Comparative for your virtues, to be styled
The under-hangman of his kingdom, and hated
For being preferred so well.
CLOTEN.   The south fog rot him!
IMOGEN. He never can meet more mischance than
     come
To be but named of thee. His meanest garment
That ever hath but clipped his body is dearer
In my respect than all the hairs above thee,
Were they all made such men. How now, Pisanio!

Enter Pisanio

CLOTEN. 'His garment'! Now the devil—
IMOGEN. To Dorothy my woman hie thee presently.   140
CLOTEN. 'His garment'!
IMOGEN.   I am sprited with a fool,
Frighted, and ang'red worse. Go bid my woman
Search for a jewel that too casually
Hath left mine arm. It was thy master's. 'Shrew me
If I would lose it for a revenue
Of any king's in Europe! I do think
I saw't this morning; confident I am

Last night 'twas on mine arm; I kissed it.
I hope it be not gone to tell my lord
That I kiss aught but he.
PISANIO.   'Twill not be lost.   150
IMOGEN. I hope so; go and search.   *Pisanio goes*
CLOTEN.   You have abused me.
'His meanest garment'!
IMOGEN.   Ay, I said so, sir.
If you will make't an action, call witness to't.
CLOTEN. I will inform your father.
IMOGEN.   Your mother too.
She's my good lady, and will conceive, I hope,
But the worst of me. So I leave you, sir,
To th'worse of discontent.   *Goes*
CLOTEN.   I'll be revenged.
'His meanest garment'! Well.   *Goes*

Scene 4: *Rome. Philario's house*

Enter Posthumus and Philario

POSTHUMUS. Fear it not, sir; I would I were so sure
To win the king as I am bold her honour
Will remain hers.
PHILARIO.   What means do you make to him?
POSTHUMUS. Not any; but abide the change of time,
Quake in the present winter's state, and wish
That warmer days would come. In these fear'd
     hopes,
I barely gratify your love; they failing,
I must die much your debtor.
PHILARIO. Your very goodness and your company
O'erpays all I can do. By this, your king   10
Hath heard of great Augustus. Caius Lucius
Will do's commission throughly. And I think
He'll grant the tribute, send th'arrearages,
Or look upon our Romans, whose remembrance
Is yet fresh in their grief.
POSTHUMUS.   I do believe,
Statist though I am none, nor like to be,
That this will prove a war; and you shall hear
The legions now in Gallia sooner landed
In our not-fearing Britain than have tidings
Of any penny tribute paid. Our countrymen   20
Are men more ordered than when Julius Caesar
Smiled at their lack of skill, but found their courage
Worthy his frowning at. Their discipline,
Now mingled with their courage, will make known
To their approvers they are people such
That mend upon the world.

Enter Jachimo

PHILARIO.   See, Jachimo!
POSTHUMUS. The swiftest harts have posted you by
     land,
And winds of all the corners kissed your sails,
To make your vessel nimble.
PHILARIO.   Welcome, sir.
POSTHUMUS. I hope the briefness of your answer made   30
The speediness of your return.
JACHIMO.   Your lady
Is one the fairest that I have looked upon—
POSTHUMUS. And therewithal the best, or let her
     beauty
Look through a casement to allure false hearts,
And be false with them.
JACHIMO.   Here are letters for you.

POSTHUMUS. Their tenour good, I trust.

JACHIMO.   'Tis very like.

PHILARIO. Was Caius Lucius in the Briton court
When you were there?

JACHIMO.   He was expected then,
But not approached.

POSTHUMUS.   All is well yet.
Sparkles this stone as it was wont, or is't not   40
Too dull for your good wearing?

JACHIMO.   If I have lost it,
I should have lost the worth of it in gold.
I'll make a journey twice as far t'enjóy
A second night of such sweet shortness which
Was mine in Britain; for the ring is won.

POSTHUMUS. The stone's too hard to come by.

JACHIMO.   Not a whit,
Your lady being so easy.

POSTHUMUS.   Make not, sir,
Your loss your sport. I hope you know that we
Must not continue friends.

JACHIMO.   Good sir, we must,
If you keep covenant. Had I not brought   50
The knowledge of your mistress home, I grant
We were to question farther; but I now
Profess myself the winner of her honour,
Together with your ring; and not the wronger
Of her or you, having proceeded but
By both your wills.

POSTHUMUS.   If you can make't apparent
That you have tasted her in bed, my hand
And ring is yours. If not, the foul opinion
You had of her pure honour gains or loses
Your sword or mine, or masterless leaves both   60
To who shall find them.

JACHIMO.   Sir, my circumstances,
Being so near the truth as I will make them,
Must first induce you to believe; whose strength
I will confirm with oath; which I doubt not
You'll give me leave to spare, when you shall find
You need it not.

POSTHUMUS.   Proceed.

JACHIMO.   First, her bedchamber—
Where I confess I slept not, but profess
Had that was well worth watching—it was hanged
With tapestry of silk and silver; the story
Proud Cleopatra when she met her Roman,   70
And Cydnus swelled above the banks, or for
The press of boats or pride; a piece of work
So bravely done, so rich, that it did strive
In workmanship and value; which I wondered
Could be so rarely and exactly wrought,
Since the true life was out on't.

POSTHUMUS.   This is true;
And this you might have heard of here, by me
Or by some other.

JACHIMO.   More particulars
Must justify my knowledge.

POSTHUMUS.   So they must,
Or do your honour injury.

JACHIMO.   The chimney   80
Is south the chamber, and the chimney-piece
Chaste Dian bathing. Never saw I figures
So likely to report themselves; the cutter
Was as another nature; dumb, outwent her,
Motion and breath left out.

POSTHUMUS.   This is a thing

Which you might from relation likewise reap,
Being, as it is, much spoke of.

JACHIMO.   The roof o'th'chamber
With golden cherubins is fretted; her andirons—
I had forgot them—were two winking Cupids
Of silver, each on one foot standing, nicely   90
Depending on their brands.

POSTHUMUS.   This is her honour!
Let it be granted you have seen all this—and praise
Be given to your remembrance—the description
Of what is in her chamber nothing saves
The wager you have laid.

JACHIMO.   Then, if you can
                         Showing the bracelet
Be pale, I beg but leave to air this jewel. See!
And now 'tis up again; it must be married
To that your diamond; I'll keep them.

POSTHUMUS.   Jove!
Once more let me behold it. Is it that
Which I left with her?

JACHIMO.   Sir, I thank her, that.   100
She stripped it from her arm; I see her yet;
Her pretty action did outsell her gift,
And yet enriched it too. She gave it me
And said she prized it once.

POSTHUMUS.   May be she plucked it off
To send it me.

JACHIMO.   She writes so to you, doth she?

POSTHUMUS. O, no, no, no, 'tis true! Here, take this
too;   *Gives the ring*
It is a basilisk unto mine eye,
Kills me to look on't. Let there be no honour
Where there is beauty; truth where semblance; love
Where there's another man. The vows of women   110
Of no more bondage be to where they are made
Than they are to their virtues, which is nothing.
O, above measure false!

PHILARIO.   Have patience, sir,
And take your ring again; 'tis not yet won.
It may be probable she lost it, or
Who knows if one her women, being corrupted,
Hath stol'n it from her?

POSTHUMUS.   Very true;
And so I hope he came by't. Back my ring;
Render to me some corporal sign about her
More evident than this; for this was stol'n.   120

JACHIMO. By Jupiter, I had it from her arm.

POSTHUMUS. Hark you, he swears; by Jupiter he
swears.
'Tis true, nay, keep the ring, 'tis true. I am sure
She would not lose it. Her attendants are
All sworn and honourable. They induced to steal it?
And by a stranger? No, he hath enjoyed her.
The cognizance of her incontinency
Is this. She hath bought the name of whore thus
dearly.
There, take thy hire; and all the fiends of hell
Divide themselves between you!

PHILARIO.   Sir, be patient;   130
This is not strong enough to be believed
Of one persuaded well of.

POSTHUMUS.   Never talk on't;
She hath been colted by him.

JACHIMO.   If you seek
For further satisfying, under her breast—
Worthy the pressing—lies a mole, right proud

Of that most delicate lodging. By my life,
I kissed it, and it gave me present hunger
To feed again, though full. You do remember
This stain upon her?

POSTHUMUS.   Ay, and it doth confirm
Another stain, as big as hell can hold,   140
Were there no more but it.

JACHIMO.   Will you hear more?

POSTHUMUS. Spare your arithmetic; never count the
    turns.
Once, and a million!

JACHIMO.   I'll be sworn.

POSTHUMUS.   No swearing.
If you will swear you have not done't, you lie;
And I will kill thee if thou dost deny
Thou'st made me cuckold.

JACHIMO.   I'll deny nothing.

POSTHUMUS. O that I had her here to tear her
    limb-meal!
I will go there and do't i'th'court, before
Her father. I'll do something.   *Goes*

PHILARIO.   Quite besides
The government of patience! You have won.   150
Let's follow him and pervert the present wrath
He hath against himself.

JACHIMO.   With all my heart.
                           They go

Scene 5

Re-enter Posthumus

POSTHUMUS. Is there no way for men to be, but
    women
Must be half-workers? We are all bastards,
And that most venerable man which I
Did call my father was I know not where
When I was stamped. Some coiner with his tools
Made me a counterfeit; yet my mother seemed
The Dian of that time; so doth my wife
The nonpareil of this. O, vengeance, vengeance!
Me of my lawful pleasure she restrained,
And prayed me oft forbearance; did it with   10
A pudency so rosy, the sweet view on't
Might well have warmed old Saturn; that I thought
    her
As chaste as unsunned snow. O, all the devils!
This yellow Jachimo in an hour—was't not?—
Or less—at first? Perchance he spoke not, but
Like a full-acorned boar, a German one,
Cried 'O!' and mounted; found no opposition
But what he looked for should oppose and she
Should from encounter guard. Could I find out
The woman's part in me—for there's no motion   20
That tends to vice in man but I affirm
It is the woman's part; be it lying, note it,
The woman's; flattering, hers; deceiving, hers;
Lust and rank thoughts, hers, hers; revenges, hers;
Ambitions, covetings, change of prides, disdain,
Nice longing, slanders, mutability,
All faults that man may name, nay, that hell knows,
Why, hers, in part or all, but rather all;
For even to vice
They are not constant, but are changing still   30
One vice but of a minute old for one
Not half so old as that. I'll write against them,
Detest them, curse them; yet 'tis greater skill

In a true hate, to pray they have their will:
The very devils cannot plague them better.
                               Goes

ACT 3

Scene 1: *Britain. A hall in Cymbeline's palace*

*Enter in state, Cymbeline, Queen, Cloten, and Lords at
one door, and at another, Caius Lucius and attendants*

CYMBELINE. Now say, what would Augustus Cæsar
    with us?

LUCIUS. When Julius Cæsar, whose remembrance yet
Lives in men's eyes, and will to ears and tongues
Be theme and hearing ever, was in this Britain,
And conquered it, Cassibelan, thine uncle,
Famous in Cæsar's praises no whit less
Than in his feats deserving it, for him
And his succession granted Rome a tribute,
Yearly three thousand pounds, which by thee lately
Is left untendered.

QUEEN.   And, to kill the marvel,   10
Shall be so ever.

CLOTEN.   There be many Cæsars
Ere such another Julius. Britain's a world
By itself, and we will nothing pay
For wearing our own noses.

QUEEN.   That opportunity
Which then they had to take from's, to resume
We have again. Remember, sir, my liege,
The kings your ancestors, together with
The natural bravery of your isle, which stands
As Neptune's park, ribbed and paled in
With rocks unscalable and roaring waters,   20
With sands that will not bear your enemies' boats,
But suck them up to th'topmast. A kind of conquest
Cæsar made here, but made not here his brag
Of 'Came, and saw, and overcame'. With shame—
The first that ever touched him—he was carried
From off our coast, twice beaten; and his shipping,
Poor ignorant baubles, on our terrible seas,
Like egg-shells moved upon their surges, cracked
As easily 'gainst our rocks; for joy whereof
The famed Cassibelan, who was once at point—   30
O giglot fortune!—to master Cæsar's sword,
Made Lud's town with rejoicing fires bright,
And Britons strut with courage.

CLOTEN. Come, there's no more tribute to be paid.
Our kingdom is stronger than it was at that time;
and, as I said, there is no moe such Cæsars. Other
of them may have crooked noses, but to owe such
straight arms, none.

CYMBELINE. Son, let your mother end.

CLOTEN. We have yet many among us can gripe as   40
hard as Cassibelan. I do not say I am one; but I have
a hand. Why tribute? why should we pay tribute?
If Cæsar can hide the sun from us with a blanket,
or put the moon in his pocket, we will pay him
tribute for light; else, sir, no more tribute, pray you
now.

CYMBELINE. You must know,
Till the injurious Romans did extort
This tribute from us, we were free. Cæsar's
    ambition,
Which swelled so much that it did almost stretch   50
The sides o'th'world, against all colour here

Did put the yoke upon's; which to shake off
Becomes a warlike people, whom we reckon
Ourselves to be. We do say then to Cæsar,
Our ancestor was that Mulmutius which
Ordained our laws, whose use the sword of Cæsar
Hath too much mangled; whose repair and franchise
Shall, by the power we hold, be our good deed,
Though Rome be therefore angry. Mulmutius
  made our laws,
Who was the first of Britain which did put   60
His brows within a golden crown, and called
Himself a king.
LUCIUS.   I am sorry, Cymbeline,
That I am to pronounce Augustus Cæsar—
Cæsar, that hath moe kings his servants than
Thyself domestic officers—thine enemy
Receive it from me, then: war and confusion
In Cæsar's name pronounce I 'gainst thee. Look
For fury not to be resisted. Thus defied,
I thank thee for myself.
CYMBELINE.   Thou art welcome, Caius.
Thy Cæsar knighted me; my youth I spent   70
Much under him; of him I gathered honour;
Which he to seek of me again, perforce,
Behoves me keep at utterance. I am perfect
That the Pannonians and Dalmatians for
Their liberties are now in arms, a precedent
Which not to read would show the Britons cold;
So Cæsar shall not find them.
LUCIUS.   Let proof speak.
CLOTEN. His majesty bids you welcome. Make pas-
time with us a day or two, or longer. If you seek us
afterwards in other terms, you shall find us in our 80
salt-water girdle. If you beat us out of it, it is yours,
if you fall in the adventure, our crows shall fare the
better for you; and there's an end.
LUCIUS. So, sir.
CYMBELINE. I know your master's pleasure, and he
  mine.
All the remain is 'Welcome'.   *They go*

Scene 2

Enter Pisanio, reading of a letter

PISANIO. How? of adultery? Wherefore write you not
What monster's her accuser? Leonatus,
O master, what a strange infection
Is fall'n into thy ear! What false Italian,
As poisonous tongued as handed, hath prevailed
On thy too ready hearing? Disloyal? No.
She's punished for her truth, and undergoes,
More goddess-like than wife-like, such assaults
As would take in some virtue. O my master,
Thy mind to her is now as low as were   10
Thy fortunes. How? that I should murder her?
Upon the love and truth and vows which I
Have made to thy command? I, her? her blood?
If it be so to do good service, never
Let me be counted serviceable. How look I,
That I should seem to lack humanity
So much as this fact comes to? [*reading*] 'Do't. The
  letter
That I have sent her, by her own command
Shall give thee opportunity.' O damned paper,
Black as the ink that's on thee! Senseless bauble,   20
Art thou a fedary for this act, and look'st

So virgin-like without? Lo, here she comes.

Enter Imogen

I am ignorant in what I am commanded.
IMOGEN. How now, Pisanio!
PISANIO. Madam, here is a letter from my lord.
IMOGEN. Who, thy lord? that is my lord Leonatus?
O, learned indeed were that astronomer
That knew the stars as I his characters;
He'ld lay the future open. You good gods,
Let what is here contained relish of love,   30
Of my lord's health, of his content—yet not
That we two are asunder; let that grieve him.
Some griefs are medicinable; that is one of them,
For it doth physic love—of his content
All but in that. Good wax, thy leave. Blest be
You bees that make these locks of counsel! Lovers
And men in dangerous bonds pray not alike;
Though forfeiters you cast in prison, yet
You clasp young Cupid's tables. Good news, gods!
[*reads*] 'Justice, and your father's wrath, should he 40
take me in his dominion, could not be so cruel to me,
as you, O the dearest of creatures, would even renew
me with your eyes. Take notice that I am in
Cambria, at Milford Haven. What your own love
will out of this advise you, follow. So he wishes you
all happiness, that remains loyal to his vow, and your
increasing in love   LEONATUS POSTHUMUS.'
O, for a horse with wings! Hear'st thou, Pisanio?
He is at Milford Haven. Read, and tell me
How far 'tis thither. If one of mean affairs   50
May plod it in a week, why may not I
Glide thither in a day? Then, true Pisanio,
Who long'st like me to see thy lord, who long'st—
O let me bate—but not like me—yet long'st,
But in a fainter kind—O, not like me,
For mine's beyond beyond; say, and speak thick—
Love's counsellor should fill the bores of hearing,
To th'smothering of the sense—how far it is
To this same blessèd Milford. And by th'way
Tell me how Wales was made so happy as   60
T'inherit such a haven. But first of all,
How we may steal from hence; and for the gap
That we shall make in time from our hence-going
And our return, to excuse—but first, how get hence.
Why should excuse be born or ere begot?
We'll talk of that hereafter. Prithee speak,
How many score of miles may we well ride
'Twixt hour and hour?
PISANIO.   One score 'twixt sun and sun,
Madam, 's enough for you, and too much too.
IMOGEN. Why, one that rode to's execution, man,   70
Could never go so slow. I have heard of riding
  wagers
Where horses have been nimbler than the sands
That run i'th'clock's behalf. But this is fool'ry.
Go bid my woman feign a sickness, say
She'll home to her father; and provide me presently
A riding-suit, no costlier than would fit
A franklin's housewife.
PISANIO.   Madam, you're best consider.
IMOGEN. I see before me, man. Nor here, nor here,
Nor what ensues, but have a fog in them,
That I cannot look through. Away, I prithee;   80
Do as I bid thee. There's no more to say;
Accessible is none but Milford way.   *They go*

Scene 3: *Wales: a mountainous country with a cave*

Enter Belarius, Guiderius, and Arviragus

BELARIUS. A goodly day not to keep house with such
  Whose roof's as low as ours. Stoop, boys; this gate
  Instructs you how t'adore the heavens, and bows
    you
  To a morning's holy office. The gates of monarchs
  Are arched so high that giants may jet through
  And keep their impious turbans on, without
  Good morrow to the sun. Hail, thou fair heaven!
  We house i'th'rock, yet use thee not so hardly
  As prouder livers do.
GUIDERIUS.   Hail, heaven!
ARVIRAGUS.   Hail, heaven!
BELARIUS. Now for our mountain sport. Up to yond
  hill,   10
  Your legs are young; I'll tread these flats. Consider,
  When you above perceive me like a crow,
  That it is place which lessens and sets off;
  And you may then revolve what tales I have told
    you
  Of courts, of princes, of the tricks in war;
  This service is not service, so being done,
  But being so allowed. To apprehend thus
  Draws us a profit from all things we see;
  And often to our comfort shall we find
  The sharded beetle in a safer hold   20
  Than is the full-winged eagle. O, this life
  Is nobler than attending for a check,
  Richer than doing nothing for a bauble,
  Prouder than rustling in unpaid-for silk;
  Such gain the cap of him that makes them fine,
  Yet keeps his book uncrossed. No life to ours.
GUIDERIUS. Out of your proof you speak; we, poor
  unfledged,
  Have never winged from view o'th'nest, nor know
    not
  What air's from home. Haply this life is best,
  If quiet life be best; sweeter to you   30
  That have a sharper known; well corresponding
  With your stiff age; but unto us it is
  A cell of ignorance, travelling abed,
  A prison, or a debtor that not dares
  To stride a limit.
ARVIRAGUS.   What should we speak of
  When we are old as you? when we shall hear
  The rain and wind beat dark December, how
  In this our pinching cave shall we discourse
  The freezing hours away? We have seen nothing;
  We are beastly-subtle as the fox for prey,   40
  Like warlike as the wolf for what we eat;
  Our valour is to chase what flies; our cage
  We make a choir, as doth the prisoned bird,
  And sing our bondage freely.
BELARIUS.   How you speak!
  Did you but know the city's usuries,
  And felt them knowingly; the art o'th'court,
  As hard to leave as keep, whose top to climb
  Is certain falling, or so slipp'ry that
  The fear's as bad as falling; the toil o'th'war,
  A pain that only seems to seek out danger   50
  I'th'name of fame and honour, which dies
    i'th'search
  And hath as oft a sland'rous epitaph
  As record of fair act; nay, many times,

Doth ill deserve by doing well; what's worse,
Must curtsy at the censure. O, boys, this story
The world may read in me; my body's marked
With Roman swords, and my report was once
First with the best of note. Cymbeline loved me;
And when a soldier was the theme, my name
Was not far off. Then was I as a tree   60
Whose boughs did bend with fruit; but in one night
A storm, or robbery, call it what you will,
Shook down my mellow hangings, nay, my leaves,
And left me bare to weather.
GUIDERIUS.   Uncertain favour!
BELARIUS. My fault being nothing, as I have told you
  oft,
  But that two villains, whose false oaths prevailed
  Before my perfect honour, swore to Cymbeline
  I was confederate with the Romans. So
  Followed my banishment, and this twenty years
  This rock and these demesnes have been my world, 70
  Where I have lived at honest freedom, paid
  More pious debts to heaven than in all
  The fore-end of my time. But up to th'mountains!
  This is not hunters' language. He that strikes
  The venison first shall be the lord o'th'feast;
  To him the other two shall minister;
  And we will fear no poison, which attends
  In place of greater state. I'll meet you in the valleys.
                   Guiderius and Arviragus go
  How hard it is to hide the sparks of nature!
  These boys know little they are sons to th'king, 80
  Nor Cymbeline dreams that they are alive.
  They think they are mine; and though trained up
    thus meanly,
  I'th'cave wherein they bow, their thoughts do hit
  The roofs of palaces, and nature prompts them
  In simple and low things to prince it much
  Beyond the trick of others. This Polydore,
  The heir of Cymbeline and Britain, who
  The king his father called Guiderius—Jove!
  When on my three-foot stool I sit and tell
  The warlike feats I have done, his spirits fly out 90
  Into my story; say 'Thus mine enemy fell,
  And thus I set my foot on's neck', even then
  The princely blood flows in his cheek, he sweats,
  Strains his young nerves, and puts himself in posture
  That acts my words. The younger brother, Cadwal,
  Once Arviragus, in as like a figure
  Strikes life into my speech and shows much more
  His own conceiving. Hark, the game is roused!
  O Cymbeline, heaven and my conscience knows
  Thou didst unjustly banish me; whereon,   100
  At three and two years old, I stole these babes,
  Thinking to bar thee of succession as
  Thou reft'st me of my lands. Euriphile,
  Thou wast their nurse; they took thee for their
    mother,
  And every day do honour to her grave.
  Myself, Belarius, that am Morgan called,
  They take for natural father. The game is up.
                           Goes

Scene 4: *Country near Milford Haven*

Enter Pisanio and Imogen

IMOGEN. Thou told'st me, when we came from horse,
  the place

Was near at hand. Ne'er longed my mother so
To see me first as I have now. Pisanio, man,
Where is Posthumus? What is in thy mind,
That makes thee stare thus? Wherefore breaks that
    sigh
From th'inward of thee? One but painted thus
Would be interpreted a thing perplexed
Beyond self-explication. Put thyself
Into a haviour of less fear, ere wildness
Vanquish my staider senses. What's the matter?   10
Why tender'st thou that paper to me with
A look untender? If't be summer news,
Smile to't before; if winterly, thou need'st
But keep that countenance still. My husband's hand?
That drug-damned Italy hath out-craftied him,
And he's at some hard point. Speak, man; thy
    tongue
May take off some extremity, which to read
Would be even mortal to me.

PISANIO.   Please you read,
And you shall find me, wretched man, a thing
The most disdained of fortune.   20

IMOGEN [reads]. 'Thy mistress, Pisanio, hath played the
strumpet in my bed; the testimonies whereof lie
bleeding in me. I speak not out of weak surmises, but
from proof as strong as my grief and as certain as I
expect my revenge. That part thou, Pisanio, must
act for me, if thy faith be not tainted with the breach
of hers. Let thine own hands take away her life; I
shall give thee opportunity at Milford Haven. She
hath my letter for the purpose; where, if thou fear
to strike, and to make me certain it is done, thou 30
art the pandar to her dishonour, and equally to me
disloyal.'

PISANIO. What shall I need to draw my sword? the
    paper
Hath cut her throat already. No, 'tis slander,
Whose edge is sharper than the sword, whose
    tongue
Outvenoms all the worms of Nile, whose breath
Rides on the posting winds and doth belie
All corners of the world. Kings, queens, and states,
Maids, matrons, nay, the secrets of the grave
This viperous slander enters. What cheer, madam? 40

IMOGEN. False to his bed? What is it to be false?
To lie in watch there, and to think on him?
To weep 'twixt clock and clock? if sleep charge
    nature,
To break it with a fearful dream of him,
And cry myself awake? that's false to's bed, is it?

PISANIO. Alas, good lady!

IMOGEN. I false? Thy conscience witness. Jachimo,
Thou didst accuse him of incontinency;
Thou then look'dst like a villain; now, methinks,
Thy favour's good enough. Some jay of Italy,   50
Whose mother was her painting, hath betrayed him.
Poor I am stale, a garment out of fashion;
And, for I am richer than to hang by th'walls,
I must be ripped. To pieces with me! O,
Men's vows are women's traitors! All good
    seeming,
By thy revolt, O husband, shall be thought
Put on for villainy; not born where't grows,
But worn a bait for ladies.

PISANIO.   Good madam, hear me.

IMOGEN. True honest men being heard like false Æneas

Were in his time thought false; and Sinon's weeping 60
Did scandal many a holy tear, took pity
From most true wretchedness. So thou, Posthumus,
Wilt lay the leaven on all proper men;
Goodly and gallant shall be false and perjured
From thy great fail. Come, fellow, be thou honest;
Do thou thy master's bidding. When thou see'st
    him,
A little witness my obedience. Look,
I draw the sword myself; take it, and hit
The innocent mansion of my love, my heart.
Fear not; 'tis empty of all things but grief;   70
Thy master is not there, who was indeed
The riches of it. Do his bidding; strike.
Thou mayst be valiant in a better cause,
But now thou seem'st a coward.

PISANIO.   Hence, vile instrument!
Thou shalt not damn my hand.

IMOGEN.   Why, I must die;
And if I do not by thy hand, thou art
No servant of thy master's. Against self-slaughter
There is a prohibition so divine
That cravens my weak hand. Come, here's my
    heart:
Something's afore't. Soft, soft! we'll no defence; 80
Obedient as the scabbard. What is here?
The scriptures of the loyal Leonatus,
All turned to heresy? Away, away,
Corrupters of my faith! you shall no more
Be stomachers to my heart. Thus may poor fools
Believe false teachers; though those that are betrayed
Do feel the treason sharply, yet the traitor
Stands in worse case of woe. And thou, Posthumus,
That didst set up
My disobedience 'gainst the king my father,   90
And make me put into contempt the suits
Of princely fellows, shalt hereafter find
It is no act of common passage, but
A strain of rareness; and I grieve myself
To think, when thou shalt be disedged by her
That now thou tirest on, how thy memory
Will then be panged by me. Prithee, dispatch;
The lamb entreats the butcher. Where's thy knife?
Thou art too slow to do thy master's bidding
When I desire it too.

PISANIO.   O gracious lady,   100
Since I received command to do this business
I have not slept one wink.

IMOGEN.   Do't, and to bed then.

PISANIO. I'll wake mine eye-balls out first.

IMOGEN.   Wherefore then
Didst undertake it? Why hast thou abused
So many miles with a pretence? this place?
Mine action, and thine own? our horses' labour?
The time inviting thee? the perturbed court,
For my being absent? whereunto I never
Purpose return. Why hast thou gone so far,
To be unbent when thou hast ta'en thy stand,   110
Th'elected deer before thee?

PISANIO.   But to win time
To lose so bad employment; in the which
I have considered of a course. Good lady,
Hear me with patience.

IMOGEN.   Talk thy tongue weary; speak.
I have heard I am a strumpet, and mine ear,
Therein false struck, can take no greater wound,

Nor tent to bottom that. But speak.

PISANIO.   Then, madam,
I thought you would not back again.

IMOGEN.   Most like,
Bringing me here to kill me.

PISANIO.   Not so, neither;
But if I were as wise as honest, then   120
My purpose would prove well. It cannot be
But that my master is abused. Some villain,
Ay, and singular in his art, hath done you both
This cursèd injury.

IMOGEN. Some Roman courtezan.

PISANIO.   No, on my life.
I'll give but notice you are dead, and send him
Some bloody sign of it; for 'tis commanded
I should do so. You shall be missed at court,
And that will well confirm it.

IMOGEN.   Why, good fellow,
What shall I do the while? where bide? how live?   130
Or in my life what comfort, when I am
Dead to my husband?

PISANIO.   If you'll back to th'court—

IMOGEN. No court, no father, nor no more ado
With that harsh, feeble, noble, simple nothing,
That Cloten, whose love-suit hath been to me
As fearful as a siege.

PISANIO.   If not at court,
Then not in Britain must you bide.

IMOGEN.   Where then?
Hath Britain all the sun that shines? Day, night,
Are they not but in Britain? I'th'world's volume
Our Britain seems as of it, but not in't;   140
In a great pool a swan's nest. Prithee think
There's livers out of Britain.

PISANIO.   I am most glad
You think of other place. Th'ambassador,
Lucius the Roman, comes to Milford Haven
To-morrow. Now if you could wear a mind
Dark as your fortune is, and but disguise
That which t'appear itself must not yet be
But by self-danger, you should tread a course
Pretty and full of view; yea, haply, near
The residence of Posthumus; so nigh, at least,   150
That though his actions were not visible, yet
Report should render him hourly to your ear
As truly as he moves.

IMOGEN.   O, for such means,
Though peril to my modesty, not death on't,
I would adventure.

PISANIO.   Well then, here's the point:
You must forget to be a woman; change
Command into obedience; fear and niceness—
The handmaids of all women, or, more truly,
Woman it pretty self—into a waggish courage,
Ready in gibes, quick-answered, saucy and   160
As quarrelous as the weasel. Nay, you must
Forget that rarest treasure of your cheek,
Exposing it—but, O, the harder heart!
Alack, no remedy!—to the greedy touch
Of common-kissing Titan, and forget
Your laboursome and dainty trims, wherein
You made great Juno angry.

IMOGEN.   Nay, be brief.
I see into thy end, and am almost
A man already.

PISANIO.   First, make yourself but like one.

Forethinking this, I have already fit—   170
'Tis in my cloak-bag—doublet, hat, hose, all
That answer to them. Would you, in their serving,
And with what imitation you can borrow
From youth of such a season, 'fore noble Lucius
Present yourself, desire his service, tell him
Wherein you're happy—which will make him
    know
If that his head have ear in music—, doubtless
With joy he will embrace you; for he's honourable,
And, doubling that, most holy, Your means
    abroad—
You have me, rich; and I will never fail   180
Beginning nor supplyment.

IMOGEN.   Thou art all the comfort
The gods will diet me with. Prithee away;
There's more to be considered; but we'll even
All that good time will give us. This attempt
I am soldier to, and will abide it with
A prince's courage. Away, I prithee.

PISANIO. Well, madam, we must take a short farewell,
Lest, being missed, I be suspected of
Your carriage from the court. My noble mistress,
Here is a box—I had it from the queen—   190
What's in't is precious; if you are sick at sea,
Or stomach-qualmed at land, a dram of this
Will drive away distemper. To some shade,
And fit you to your manhood; may the gods
Direct you to the best!

IMOGEN.   Amen. I thank thee.
They go in opposite directions

Scene 5: *A room in Cymbeline's palace*

Enter Cymbeline, Queen, Cloten, Lucius, and Lords

CYMBELINE. Thus far, and so farewell.

LUCIUS.   Thanks, royal sir.
My emperor hath wrote I must from hence;
And am right sorry that I must report ye
My master's enemy.

CYMBELINE.   Our subjects, sir,
Will not endure his yoke; and for ourself
To show less sovereignty than they, must needs
Appear unkinglike.

LUCIUS.   So, sir. I desire of you
A conduct over land to Milford Haven.
Madam, all joy befall your grace, and you.

CYMBELINE. My lords, you are appointed for that
    office;   10
The due of honour in no point omit.
So farewell, noble Lucius.

LUCIUS.   Your hand, my lord.

CLOTEN. Receive it friendly; but from this time forth
I wear it as your enemy.

LUCIUS.   Sir, the event
Is yet to name the winner. Fare you well.

CYMBELINE. Leave not the worthy Lucius, good my
    lords,
Till he hath crossed the Severn. Happiness!
Lucius and lords go

QUEEN. He goes hence frowning; but it honours us
That we have given him cause.

CLOTEN.   'Tis all the better;
Your valiant Britons have their wishes in it.   20

CYMBELINE. Lucius hath wrote already to the emperor
How it goes here. It fits us therefore ripely

Our chariots and our horsemen be in readiness.
The powers that he already hath in Gallia
Will soon be drawn to head, from whence he moves
His war for Britain.
QUEEN.   'Tis not sleepy business,
But must be looked to speedily and strongly.
CYMBELINE. Our expectation that it would be thus
Hath made us forward. But, my gentle queen,
Where is our daughter? She hath not appeared   30
Before the Roman, nor to us hath tendered
The duty of the day. She looks us like
A thing more made of malice than of duty;
We have noted it. Call her before us, for
We have been too slight in sufferance.
                                    An attendant goes
QUEEN.   Royal sir,
Since the exile of Posthumus, most retired
Hath her life been; the cure whereof, my lord,
'Tis time must do. Beseech your majesty,
Forbear sharp speeches to her. She's a lady
So tender of rebukes that words are strokes,   40
And strokes death to her.

Re-enter Attendant

CYMBELINE.   Where is she, sir? How
Can her contempt be answered?
ATTENDANT.   Please you, sir,
Her chambers are all locked, and there's no answer
That will be given to th'loud'st of noise we make.
QUEEN. My lord, when last I went to visit her,
She prayed me to excuse her keeping close;
Whereto constrained by her infirmity
She should that duty leave unpaid to you,
Which daily she was bound to proffer. This
She wished me to make known; but our great court 50
Made me to blame in memory.
CYMBELINE.   Her doors locked?
Not seen of late? Grant, heavens, that which I fear
Prove false!   *Goes*
QUEEN. Son, I say, follow the king.
CLOTEN. That man of hers, Pisanio, her old servant,
I have not seen these two days.
QUEEN.   Go, look after.
                                    Cloten goes
Pisanio, thou that stand'st so for Posthumus!
He hath a drug of mine. I pray his absence
Proceed by swallowing that; for he believes
It is a thing most precious. But for her,   60
Where is she gone? Haply despair hath seized her;
Or, winged with fervour of her love, she's flown
To her desired Posthumus. Gone she is
To death or to dishonour, and my end
Can make good use of either. She being down,
I have the placing of the British crown.

Re-enter Cloten

How now, my son?
CLOTEN.   'Tis certain she is fled.
Go in and cheer the king; he rages, none
Dare come about him.
QUEEN.   All the better. May
This night forestall him of the coming day!   70
                                              Goes
CLOTEN. I love and hate her. For she's fair and royal,
And that she hath all courtly parts more exquisite
Than lady, ladies, woman—from every one

The best she hath, and she, of all compounded,
Outsells them all—I love her therefore; but
Disdaining me and throwing favours on
The low Posthumus slanders so her judgement
That what's else rare is choked; and in that point
I will conclude to hate her, nay, indeed,
To be revenged upon her. For when fools   80
Shall—

Enter Pisanio

                Who is here? What, are you packing, sirrah?
Come hither. Ah, you precious pandar! Villain,
Where is thy lady? In a word, or else
Thou art straightway with the fiends.
PISANIO.   O, good my lord!
CLOTEN. Where is thy lady? or, by Jupiter,
I will not ask again. Close villain,
I'll have this secret from thy heart, or rip
Thy heart to find it. Is she with Posthumus?
From whose so many weights of baseness cannot
A dram of worth be drawn.
PISANIO.   Alas, my lord,   90
How can she be with him? When was she missed?
He is in Rome.
CLOTEN.   Where is she, sir? Come nearer.
No farther halting; satisfy me home
What is become of her.
PISANIO. O, my all-worthy lord!
CLOTEN.   All-worthy villain,
Discover where thy mistress is at once,
At the next word; no more of 'worthy lord'!
Speak, or thy silence on the instant is
Thy condemnation and thy death.
PISANIO.   Then, sir,
This paper is the history of my knowledge   100
Touching her flight.   *Presenting a letter*
CLOTEN.   Let's see't. I will pursue her
Even to Augustus' throne.
PISANIO [*aside*].   Or this or perish.
She's far enough, and what he learns by this
May prove his travel, not her danger.
CLOTEN.   Hum!
PISANIO [*aside*]. I'll write to my lord she's dead. O
Imogen,
Safe mayst thou wander, safe return again!
CLOTEN. Sirrah, is this letter true?
PISANIO. Sir, as I think.
CLOTEN. It is Posthumus' hand; I know't. Sirrah, if 110
thou wouldst not be a villain, but do me true service,
undergo those employments wherein I should have
cause to use thee with a serious industry—that is,
what villainy soe'er I bid thee do, to perform it
directly and truly—I would think thee an honest
man; thou shouldst neither want my means for thy
relief, nor my voice for thy preferment.
PISANIO. Well, my good lord.
CLOTEN. Wilt thou serve me? for since patiently and
constantly thou hast stuck to the bare fortune of that
beggar Posthumus, thou canst not in the course of   120
gratitude but be a diligent follower of mine. Wilt
thou serve me?
PISANIO. Sir, I will.
CLOTEN. Give me thy hand; here's my purse. Hast any
of thy late master's garments in thy possession?
PISANIO. I have, my lord, at my lodging the same suit
he wore when he took leave of my lady and mistress.

CLOTEN. The first service thou dost me, fetch that suit
hither. Let it be thy first service; go.
PISANIO. I shall, my lord. *Goes* 130
CLOTEN. Meet thee at Milford Haven! I forgot to ask
him one thing; I'll remember't anon. Even there,
thou villain Posthumus, will I kill thee. I would these
garments were come. She said upon a time—the
bitterness of it I now belch from my heart—that she
held the very garment of Posthumus in more respect
than my noble and natural person, together with the
adornment of my qualities. With that suit upon my
back will I ravish her; first kill him, and in her eyes;
there shall she see my valour, which will then be a 140
torment to her contempt. He on the ground, my
speech of insultment ended on his dead body, and
when my lust hath dined—which, as I say, to vex
her I will execute in the clothes that she so praised—
to the court I'll knock her back, foot her home again.
She hath despised me rejoicingly, and I'll be merry
in my revenge.

Re-enter Pisanio, with the clothes

Be those the garments?
PISANIO. Ay, my noble lord.
CLOTEN. How long is't since she went to Milford 150
Haven?
PISANIO. She can scarce be there yet.
CLOTEN. Bring this apparel to my chamber; that is the
second thing that I have commanded thee. The third
is that thou wilt be a voluntary mute to my design.
Be but duteous and true, preferment shall tender
itself to thee. My revenge is now at Milford; would
I had wings to follow it! Come, and be true.
Goes
PISANIO. Thou bid'st me to my loss; for, true to thee
Were to prove false, which I will never be 160
To him that is most true. To Milford go,
And find not her whom thou pursuedst. Flow, flow,
You heavenly blessings, on her. This fool's speed
Be crossed with slowness; labour be his meed.
Goes

Scene 6: *Wales: before the cave of Belarius*

Enter Imogen alone, in boy's clothes

IMOGEN. I see a man's life is a tedious one.
I have tired myself, and for two nights together
Have made the ground my bed. I should be sick,
But that my resolution helps me. Milford,
When from the mountain-top Pisanio showed thee,
Thou wast within a ken. O Jove, I think
Foundations fly the wretched: such, I mean,
Where they should be relieved. Two beggars told
me
I could not miss my way. Will poor folks lie,
That have afflictions on them, knowing 'tis 10
A punishment or trial? Yes; no wonder,
When rich ones scarce tell true. To lapse in fulness
Is sorer than to lie for need; and falsehood
Is worse in kings than beggars. My dear lord,
Thou art one o'th'false ones. Now I think on thee
My hunger's gone; but even before, I was
At point to sink for food. But what is this?
Here is a path to't; 'tis some savage hold.
I were best not call; I dare not call; yet famine,
Ere clean it o'erthrow nature, makes it valiant. 20

Plenty and peace breeds cowards; hardness ever
Of hardiness is mother. Ho! who's here?
If any thing that's civil, speak; if savage,
Take or lend. Ho! no answer? then I'll enter.
Best draw my sword; and if mine enemy
But fear the sword like me, he'll scarcely look on't.
Such a foe, good heavens! *Goes into the cave*

Enter Belarius, Guiderius, and Arviragus

BELARIUS. You, Polydore, have proved best
woodman and
Are master of the feast. Cadwal and I
Will play the cook and servant; 'tis our match. 30
The sweat of industry would dry and die
But for the end it works to. Come, our stomachs
Will make what's homely savoury; weariness
Can snore upon the flint, when resty sloth
Finds the down pillow hard. Now peace be here,
Poor house, that keep'st thyself.
GUIDERIUS. I am throughly weary.
ARVIRAGUS. I am weak with toil, yet strong in
appetite.
GUIDERIUS. There is cold meat i'th'cave; we'll browse
on that
Whilst what we have killed be cooked.
BELARIUS [*looking into the cave*]. Stay, come not in.
But that it eats our victuals, I should think 40
Here were a fairy.
GUIDERIUS. What's the matter, sir?
BELARIUS. By Jupiter, an angel; or, if not,
An earthly paragon. Behold divineness
No elder than a boy.

Imogen comes from the cave

IMOGEN. Good masters, harm me not.
Before I entered here I called, and thought
To have begged or bought what I have took. Good
troth,
I have stol'n nought; nor would not though I had
found
Gold strewed i'th'floor. Here's money for my meat.
I would have left it on the board so soon 50
As I had made my meal, and parted
With prayers for the provider.
GUIDERIUS. Money, youth?
ARVIRAGUS. All gold and silver rather turn to dirt,
As 'tis no better reckoned but of those
Who worship dirty gods.
IMOGEN. I see you're angry.
Know, if you kill me for my fault, I should
Have died had I not made it.
BELARIUS. Whither bound?
IMOGEN. To Milford Haven.
BELARIUS. What's your name?
IMOGEN. Fidele, sir. I have a kinsman who 60
Is bound for Italy; he embarked at Milford;
To whom being going, almost spent with hunger,
I am fall'n in this offence.
BELARIUS. Prithee, fair youth,
Think us no churls, nor measure our good minds
By this rude place we live in. Well encountered.
'Tis almost night; you shall have better cheer
Ere you depart, and thanks to stay and eat it.
Boys, bid him welcome.
GUIDERIUS. Were you a woman, youth,
I should woo hard but be your groom in honesty;

I bid for you as I'ld buy.
ARVIRAGUS.   I'll make't my comfort   70
He is a man, I'll love him as my brother:
And such a welcome as I'ld give to him
After long absence, such is yours. Most welcome.
Be sprightly, for you fall 'mongst friends.
IMOGEN.   'Mongst friends?
—If brothers. [aside] Would it had been so that they
Had been my father's sons! then had my prize
Been less, and so more equal ballasting
To thee, Posthumus.
BELARIUS.   He wrings at some distress.
GUIDERIUS. Would I could free't!
ARVIRAGUS.   Or I; whate'er it be,
What pain it cost, what danger! Gods!
BELARIUS.   Hark, boys.   80
                                                            Whispering
IMOGEN. Great men
That had a court no bigger than this cave,
That did attend themselves, and had the virtue
Which their own conscience sealed them, laying by
That nothing-gift of differing multitudes,
Could not outpeer these twain. Pardon me, gods,
I'ld change my sex to be companion with them,
Since Leonatus' false.
BELARIUS.   It shall be so.
Boys, we'll go dress our hunt. Fair youth, come in;
Discourse is heavy, fasting; when we have supped,   90
We'll mannerly demand thee of thy story,
So far as thou wilt speak it.
GUIDERIUS.   Pray draw near.
ARVIRAGUS. The night to th'owl and morn to th'lark
less welcome.
IMOGEN. Thanks, sir.
ARVIRAGUS. I pray draw near.   They go

Scene 7: Rome. A public place

Enter two Roman Senators and Tribunes

1 SENATOR. This is the tenour of the emperor's writ:
That since the common men are now in action
'Gainst the Pannonians and Dalmatians,
And that the legions now in Gallia are
Full weak to undertake our wars against
The fall'n-off Britons, that we do incite
The gentry to this business. He creates
Lucius proconsul; and to you the tribunes,
For this immediate levy, he commends
His absolute commission. Long live Cæsar!   10
1 TRIBUNE. Is Lucius general of the forces?
2 SENATOR.   Ay.
1 TRIBUNE. Remaining now in Gallia?
1 SENATOR.   With those legions
Which I have spoke of, whereunto your levy
Must be supplyant. The words of your commission
Will tie you to the numbers and the time
Of their dispatch.
1 TRIBUNE.   We will discharge our duty.
                                                            They go

ACT 4
Scene 1: Wales: near the cave of Belarius

Enter Cloten alone

CLOTEN. I am near to th'place where they should meet,
if Pisanio have mapped it truly. How fit his garments serve me! Why should his mistress, who was
made by him that made the tailor, not be fit too? the
rather—saving reverence of the word—for 'tis said a
woman's fitness comes by fits. Therein I must play
the workman. I dare speak it to myself, for it is not
vain-glory for a man and his glass to confer in his
own chamber; I mean, the lines of my body are as
well drawn as his; no less young, more strong, not   10
beneath him in fortunes, beyond him in the advantage of the time, above him in birth, alike conversant in general services, and more remarkable in
single oppositions; yet this imperceiverant thing
loves him in my despite. What mortality is! Posthumus, thy head, which now is growing upon thy
shoulders, shall within this hour be off; thy mistress
enforced; thy garments cut to pieces before her face;
and all this done, spurn her home to her father, who
may haply be a little angry for my so rough usage;   20
but my mother, having power of his testiness, shall
turn all into my commendations. My horse is tied
up safe; out, sword, and to a sore purpose! Fortune
put them into my hand. This is the very description
of their meeting-place; and the fellow dares not
deceive me.   Goes

Scene 2: Before the cave of Belarius

Enter Belarius, Guiderius, Arviragus, and Imogen from the
cave

BELARIUS [to Imogen]. You are not well. Remain here
in the cave;
We'll come to you after hunting.
ARVIRAGUS [to Imogen].   Brother, stay here.
Are we not brothers?
IMOGEN.   So man and man should be;
But clay and clay differs in dignity,
Whose dust is both alike. I am very sick.
GUIDERIUS. Go you to hunting; I'll abide with him.
IMOGEN. So sick I am not, yet I am not well;
But not so citizen a wanton as
To seem to die ere sick. So please you, leave me;
Stick to your journal course: the breach of custom   10
Is breach of all. I am ill, but your being by me
Cannot amend me. Society is no comfort
To one not sociable. I am not very sick,
Since I can reason of it. Pray you trust me here:
I'll rob none but myself; and let me die,
Stealing so poorly.
GUIDERIUS.   I love thee, I have spoke it,
How much the quantity, the weight as much,
As I do love my father.
BELARIUS.   What? how, how?
ARVIRAGUS. If it be sin to say so, sir, I yoke me
In my good brother's fault. I know not why   20
I love this youth, and I have heard you say,
Love's reason's without reason. The bier at door,
And a demand who is't shall die, I'ld say
'My father, not this youth'.
BELARIUS [aside].   O noble strain!
O worthiness of nature, breed of greatness!
"Cowards father cowards and base things sire base;
Nature hath meal and bran, contempt and grace."
I'm not their father; yet who this should be
Doth miracle itself, loved before me.

[to Guiderius and Arviragus] 'Tis the ninth hour
      o'th'morn.
ARVIRAGUS.   Brother, farewell.   30
IMOGEN. I wish ye sport.
ARVIRAGUS.   You health. [to Belarius] So
      please you, sir.
IMOGEN [aside]. These are kind creatures. Gods, what
      lies I have heard!
Our courtiers say all's savage but at court.
Experience, O, thou disprovest report!
Th'imperious seas breeds monsters; for the dish
Poor tributary rivers as sweet fish.
I am sick still, heart-sick. Pisanio,
I'll now taste of thy drug.   Swallows some
GUIDERIUS.   I could not stir him.
He said he was gentle, but unfortunate;
Dishonestly afflicted, but yet honest.   40
ARVIRAGUS. Thus did he answer me; yet said hereafter
      I might know more.
BELARIUS.   To th'field, to th'field.
We'll leave you for this time; go in and rest.
ARVIRAGUS. We'll not be long away.
BELARIUS.   Pray be not sick,
For you must be our housewife.
IMOGEN.   Well or ill,
I am bound to you.
BELARIUS.   And shalt be ever.
                                Imogen goes into the cave
This youth, howe'er distress'd, appears he hath had
Good ancestors.
ARVIRAGUS.   How angel-like he sings!
GUIDERIUS. But his neat cookery! he cut our roots in
      characters;
And sauced our broths, as Juno had been sick,   50
And he her dieter.
ARVIRAGUS.   Nobly he yokes
A smiling with a sigh, as if the sigh
Was that it was for not being such a smile;
The smile mocking the sigh that it would fly
From so divine a temple to commix
With winds that sailors rail at.
GUIDERIUS.   I do note
That grief and patience, rooted in him both,
Mingle their spurs together.
ARVIRAGUS.   Grow patience,
And let the stinking elder, grief, untwine
His perishing root with the increasing vine.   60
BELARIUS. It is great morning. Come away. Who's
      there?

Enter Cloten

CLOTEN. I cannot find those runagates; that villain
Hath mocked me. I am faint.
BELARIUS.   'Those runagates'?
Means he not us? I partly know him; 'tis
Cloten, the son o'th'queen. I fear some ambush.
I saw him not these many years, and yet
I know 'tis he. We are held as outlaws. Hence!
GUIDERIUS. He is but one; you and my brother search
What companies are near; pray you, away;
Let me alone with him.   *Belarius and Arviragus go*
CLOTEN.   Soft, what are you   70
That fly me thus? some villain mountaineers?
I have heard of such. What slave art thou?
GUIDERIUS.   A thing
More slavish did I ne'er than answering

A slave without a knock.
CLOTEN.   Thou art a robber,
A law-breaker, a villain. Yield thee, thief.
GUIDERIUS. To who? to thee? What art thou? Have
      not I
An arm as big as thine, a heart as big?
Thy words, I grant, are bigger; for I wear not
My dagger in my mouth. Say what thou art,
Why I should yield to thee.
CLOTEN.   Thou villain base,   80
Know'st me not by my clothes?
GUIDERIUS.   No, nor thy tailor, rascal,
Who is thy grandfather. He made those clothes,
Which, as it seems, make thee.
CLOTEN.   Thou precious varlet,
My tailor made them not.
GUIDERIUS.   Hence then, and thank
The man that gave them thee. Thou art some fool;
I am loath to beat thee.
CLOTEN.   Thou injurious thief,
Hear but my name, and tremble.
GUIDERIUS.   What's thy name?
CLOTEN. Cloten, thou villain.
GUIDERIUS. Cloten, thou double villain, be thy name,
I cannot tremble at it: were it Toad, or Adder,
      Spider,   90
'Twould move me sooner.
CLOTEN.   To thy further fear,
Nay, to thy mere confusion, thou shalt know
I am son to th'queen.
GUIDERIUS.   I am sorry for't; not seeming
So worthy as thy birth.
CLOTEN.   Art not afeard?
GUIDERIUS. Those that I reverence, those I fear, the
      wise.
At fools I laugh, not fear them.
CLOTEN.   Die the death.
When I have slain thee with my proper hand,
I'll follow those that even now fled hence,
And on the gates of Lud's town set your heads.
Yield, rustic mountaineer.   *They go out fighting* 100

Re-enter Belarius and Arviragus

BELARIUS. No company's abroad?
ARVIRAGUS. None in the world; you did mistake him,
      sure.
BELARIUS. I cannot tell; long is it since I saw him,
But time hath nothing blurred those lines of favour
Which then he wore; the snatches in his voice,
And burst of speaking, were as his; I am absolute
'Twas very Cloten.
ARVIRAGUS.   In this place we left them;
I wish my brother make good time with him,
You say he is so fell.
BELARIUS.   Being scarce made up,
I mean to man, he had not apprehension   110
Of roaring terrors; for defect of judgement
Is oft the cease of fear.

Re-enter Guiderius with Cloten's head

                      But see, thy brother.
GUIDERIUS. This Cloten was a fool, an empty purse;
There was no money in't. Not Hercules
Could have knocked out his brains, for he had none.
Yet I not doing this, the fool had borne
My head as I do his.

BELARIUS.　　　　　　　　What hast thou done?
GUIDERIUS. I am perfect what: cut off one Cloten's
　　head,
　Son to the queen, after his own report,
　Who called me traitor, mountaineer, and swore　　120
　With his own single hand he'ld take us in,
　Displace our heads where—thank the gods—they
　　grow,
　And set them on Lud's town.
BELARIUS.　　　　　　　We are all undone.
GUIDERIUS. Why, worthy father, what have we to lose
　But that he swore to take, our lives? The law
　Protects not us; then why should we be tender
　To let an arrogant piece of flesh threat us,
　Play judge and executioner all himself,
　For we do fear the law? What company
　Discover you abroad?
BELARIUS.　　　　　　　No single soul　　130
　Can we set eye on; but in all safe reason
　He must have some attendants. Though his humour
　Was nothing but mutation, ay, and that
　From one bad thing to worse, not frenzy, not
　Absolute madness could so far have raved,
　To bring him here alone. Although perhaps
　It may be heard at court that such as we
　Cave here, hunt here, are outlaws, and in time
　May make some stronger head, the which he
　　hearing—
　As it is like him—might break out, and swear　　140
　He'ld fetch us in; yet is't not probable
　To come alone, either he so undertaking,
　Or they so suffering. Then on good ground we fear,
　If we do fear this body hath a tail
　More perilous than the head.
ARVIRAGUS.　　　　　　　Let ordinance
　Come as the gods foresay it; howsoe'er,
　My brother hath done well.
BELARIUS.　　　　　　　I had no mind
　To hunt this day. The boy Fidele's sickness
　Did make my way long forth.
GUIDERIUS.　　　　　　　With his own sword,
　Which he did wave against my throat, I have ta'en　　150
　His head from him. I'll throw't into the creek
　Behind our rock, and let it to the sea,
　And tell the fishes he's the queen's son, Cloten.
　That's all I reck.　　　　　　　Goes
BELARIUS.　　　　　I fear 'twill be revenged.
　Would, Polydore, thou hadst not done't, though
　　valour
　Becomes thee well enough.
ARVIRAGUS.　　　　　　Would I had done't,
　So the revenge alone pursued me. Polydore,
　I love thee brotherly, but envy much
　Thou hast robbed me of this deed. I would revenges
　That possible strength might meet would seek us
　　through　　160
　And put us to our answer.
BELARIUS.　　　　　　　Well, 'tis done.
　We'll hunt no more to-day, nor seek for danger
　'Where there's no profit. I prithee to our rock;
　You and Fidele play the cooks; I'll stay
　Till hasty Polydore return, and bring him
　To dinner presently.
ARVIRAGUS.　　　　　　Poor sick Fidele,
　I'll willingly to him. To gain his colour
　I'ld let a parish of such Clotens blood,

　And praise myself for charity.　　　　　Goes
BELARIUS.　　　　　　　O thou goddess,
　Thou divine Nature, how thyself thou blazon'st　　170
　In these two princely boys! They are as gentle
　As zephyrs blowing below the violet,
　Not wagging his sweet head; and yet as rough,
　Their royal blood enchafed, as the rud'st wind
　That by the top doth take the mountain pine
　And make him stoop to th'vale. 'Tis wonder
　That an invisible instinct should frame them
　To royalty unlearned, honour untaught,
　Civility not seen from other, valour
　That wildly grows in them, but yields a crop　　180
　As if it had been sowed. Yet still it's strange
　What Cloten's being here to us portends,
　Or what his death will bring us.

Re-enter Guiderius

GUIDERIUS.　　　　　　Where's my brother?
　I have sent Cloten's clotpoll down the stream,
　In embassy to his mother; his body's hostage
　For his return.　　　　　　　Solemn music
BELARIUS.　　　My ingenious instrument!
　Hark, Polydore, it sounds. But what occasion
　Hath Cadwal now to give it motion? Hark!
GUIDERIUS. Is he at home?
BELARIUS.　　　　He went hence even now.
GUIDERIUS. What does he mean? Since death of my
　　dear'st mother　　190
　It did not speak before. All solemn things
　Should answer solemn accidents. The matter?
　Triumphs for nothing and lamenting toys
　Is jollity for apes and grief for boys.
　Is Cadwal mad?

*Re-enter Arviragus with Imogen, dead, bearing her in his
arms*

BELARIUS.　　　　　Look, here he comes,
　And brings the dire occasion in his arms
　Of what we blame him for.
ARVIRAGUS.　　　　　The bird is dead
　That we have made so much on. I had rather
　Have skipped from sixteen years of age to sixty,
　To have turned my leaping time into a crutch,　　200
　Than have seen this.
GUIDERIUS.　　　　O sweetest, fairest lilly!
　My brother wears thee not the one half so well
　As when thou grew'st thyself.
BELARIUS.　　　　　O melancholy!
　Who ever yet could sound thy bottom? find
　The ooze, to show what coast thy sluggish crare
　Might easiliest harbour in? Thou blessed thing,
　Jove knows what man thou mightst have made;
　　but I,
　Thou diedst, a most rare boy, of melancholy.
　How found you him?
ARVIRAGUS.　　　　　Stark, as you see;
　Thus smiling, as some fly had tickled slumber,　　210
　Not as death's dart being laughed at; his right cheek
　Reposing on a cushion.
GUIDERIUS.　　　　　Where?
ARVIRAGUS.　　　　　O'th'floor,
　His arms thus leagued; I thought he slept, and put
　My clouted brogues from off my feet, whose
　　rudeness
　Answered my steps too loud.

GUIDERIUS. Why, he but sleeps.
If he be gone, he'll make his grave a bed;
With female fairies will his tomb be haunted,
And worms will not come to thee.
ARVIRAGUS. With fairest flowers,
Whilst summer lasts, and I live here, Fidele,
I'll sweeten thy sad grave. Thou shalt not lack   220
The flower that's like thy face, pale primrose, nor
The azured harebell, like thy veins; no, nor
The leaf of eglantine, whom not to slander,
Out-sweet'ned not thy breath. The ruddock would
With charitable bill—O bill sore shaming
Those rich-left heirs that let their fathers lie
Without a monument!—bring thee all this;
Yea, and furred moss besides, when flowers are
none,
To winter-ground thy corse.
GUIDERIUS. Prithee have done,
And do not play in wench-like words with that   230
Which is so serious. Let us bury him,
And not protract with admiration what
Is now due debt. To th'grave.
ARVIRAGUS. Say, where shall's lay him?
GUIDERIUS. By good Euriphile, our mother.
ARVIRAGUS. Be't so;
And let us, Polydore, though now our voices
Have got the mannish crack, sing him to th'ground,
As once our mother; use like note and words,
Save that 'Euriphile' must be 'Fidele'.
GUIDERIUS. Cadwal,
I cannot sing. I'll weep, and word it with thee;   240
For notes of sorrow out of tune are worse
Than priests and fanes that lie.
ARVIRAGUS. We'll speak it then.
BELARIUS. Great griefs, I see, medicine the less; for
Cloten
Is quite forgot. He was a queen's son, boys;
And though he came our enemy, remember
He was paid for that; though mean and mighty
rotting
Together have one dust, yet reverence,
That angel of the world, doth make distinction
Of place 'tween high and low. Our foe was princely,
And though you took his life as being our foe,   250
Yet bury him as a prince.
GUIDERIUS. Pray you fetch him hither.
Thersites' body is as good as Ajax'
When neither are alive.
ARVIRAGUS. If you'll go fetch him,
We'll say our song the whilst. Brother, begin.
Belarius goes
GUIDERIUS. Nay, Cadwal, we must lay his head to
th'east;
My father hath a reason for it.
ARVIRAGUS. 'Tis true.
GUIDERIUS. Come on then and remove him.
ARVIRAGUS. So. Begin.

SONG

GUIDERIUS.
    Fear no more the heat o'th'sun,
      Nor the furious winter's rages;
    Thou thy worldly task hast done,   260
      Home art gone and ta'en thy wages.
    Golden lads and girls all must,
    As chimney-sweepers, come to dust.

ARVIRAGUS.
    Fear no more the frown o'th'great;
      Thou art past the tyrant's stroke;
    Care no more to clothe and eat;
      To thee the reed is as the oak.
    The sceptre, learning, physic, must
    All follow this and come to dust.

GUIDERIUS. Fear no more the lightning flash,   270
ARVIRAGUS.   Nor th'all-dreaded thunder-stone;
GUIDERIUS. Fear not slander, censure rash;
ARVIRAGUS. Thou hast finished joy and moan.
BOTH.   All lovers young, all lovers must
    Consign to thee and come to dust.

GUIDERIUS. No exorciser harm thee!
ARVIRAGUS. Nor no witchcraft charm thee!
GUIDERIUS. Ghost unlaid forbear thee!
ARVIRAGUS. Nothing ill come near thee!
BOTH.   Quiet consummation have;   280
    And renownéd be thy grave!

Re-enter Belarius with the body of Cloten

GUIDERIUS. We have done our obsequies. Come, lay
him down.
BELARIUS. Here's a few flowers, but 'bout midnight
more:
The herbs that have on them cold dew o'th'night
Are strewings fitt'st for graves. Upon their faces.
You were as flowers, now wither'd; even so
These herblets shall, which we upon you strew.
Come on, away; apart upon our knees.
The ground that gave them first has them again.
Their pleasures here are past, so is their pain.   290
Belarius, Guiderius and Arviragus go
IMOGEN [*awaking*]. Yes, sir, to Milford Haven; which
is the way?—
I thank you. By yond bush? Pray, how far thither?
'Ods pittikins, can it be six mile yet?
I have gone all night. Faith, I'll lie down and sleep.
But, soft, no bedfellow! O gods and goddesses!
Seeing the body of Cloten
These flowers are like the pleasures of the world;
This bloody man, the care on't, I hope I dream;
For so I thought I was a cave-keeper,
And cook to honest creatures. But 'tis not so;
'Twas but a bolt of nothing, shot at nothing,   300
Which the brain makes of fumes. Our very eyes
Are sometimes like our judgements, blind. Good
faith,
I tremble still with fear; but if there be
Yet left in heaven as small a drop of pity
As a wren's eye, feared gods, a part of it!
The dream's here still; even when I wake, it is
Without me, as within me; not imagined, felt.
A headless man? The garments of Posthumus?
I know the shape of's leg; this is his hand;
His foot Mercurial; his Martial thigh;   310
The brawns of Hercules; but his Jovial face—
Murder in heaven? How? 'Tis gone. Pisanio,
All curses madded Hecuba gave the Greeks,
And mine to boot, be darted on thee! Thou,
Conspired with that irregulous devil, Cloten,
Hath here cut off my lord. To write and read
Be henceforth treacherous! Damned Pisanio
Hath with his forgéd letters—damned Pisanio—
From this most bravest vessel of the world

Struck the main-top. O Posthumus, alas,   320
Where is thy head? where's that? Ay me! where's
    that?
Pisanio might have killed thee at the heart,
And left this head on. How should this be? Pisanio?
'Tis he and Cloten; malice and lucre in them
Have laid this woe here. O, 'tis pregnant, pregnant!
The drug he gave me, which he said was precious
And cordial to me, have I not found it
Murd'rous to th'senses? That confirms it home.
This is Pisanio's deed, and Cloten's. O!
Give colour to my pale cheek with thy blood,   330
That we the horrider may seem to those
Which chance to find us. O, my lord, my lord!
                                        Falls on the body

*Enter Lucius, a Captain and other Officers, and a Sooth-
sayer*

CAPTAIN. To them the legions garrisoned in Gallia
After your will have crossed the sea, attending
You here at Milford Haven with your ships.
They are here in readiness.
LUCIUS.   But what from Rome?
CAPTAIN. The senate hath stirred up the confiners
And gentlemen of Italy, most willing spirits
That promise noble service; and they come
Under the conduct of bold Jachimo,   340
Siena's brother.
LUCIUS.   When expect you them?
CAPTAIN. With the next benefit o'th'wind.
LUCIUS.   This forwardness
Makes our hopes fair. Command our present
    numbers
Be mustered; bid the captains look to't. Now, sir,
What have you dreamed of late of this war's
    purpose?
SOOTHSAYER. Last night the very gods showed me a
    vision—
I fast and prayed for their intelligence—thus:
I saw Jove's bird, the Roman eagle, winged
From the spongy south to this part of the west,
There vanished in the sunbeams; which portends,   350
Unless my sins abuse my divination,
Success to th'Roman host.
LUCIUS.   Dream often so,
And never false. Soft, ho, what trunk is here
Without his top? The ruin speaks that sometime
It was a worthy building. How? a page?
Or dead or sleeping on him? But dead rather;
For nature doth abhor to make his bed
With the defunct, or sleep upon the dead.
Let's see the boy's face.
CAPTAIN.   He's alive, my lord.
LUCIUS. He'll then instruct us of this body. Young
    one,   360
Inform us of thy fortunes, for it seems
They crave to be demanded. Who is this
Thou makest thy bloody pillow? Or who was he
That, otherwise than noble nature did,
Hath altered that good picture? What's thy interest
In this sad wreck? How came't? Who is't?
What art thou?
IMOGEN.   I am nothing; or if not,
Nothing to be were better. This was my master,
A very valiant Briton and a good,
That here by mountaineers lies slain. Alas,   370

There is no more such masters. I may wander
From east to occident; cry out for service;
Try many, all good; serve truly; never
Find such another master.
LUCIUS.   'Lack, good youth,
Thou mov'st no less with thy complaining than
Thy master in bleeding. Say his name, good friend.
IMOGEN. Richard du Champ. [*aside*] If I do lie, and do
No harm by it, though the gods hear, I hope
They'll pardon it. [*to Lucius*] Say you, sir?
LUCIUS. Thy name?   380
IMOGEN. Fidele, sir.
LUCIUS. Thou dost approve thyself the very same:
Thy name fits well thy faith, thy faith thy name.
Wilt take thy chance with me? I will not say
Thou shalt be so well mastered, but be sure,
No less beloved. The Roman emperor's letters
Sent by a consul to me should not sooner
Than thine own worth prefer thee. Go with me.
IMOGEN. I'll follow, sir. But first, an't please the gods,
I'll hide my master from the flies, as deep   390
As these poor pickaxes can dig; and when
With wild wood-leaves and weeds I ha' strewed his
    grave
And on it said a century of prayers,
Such as I can, twice o'er, I'll weep and sigh,
And leaving so his service, follow you,
So please you entertain me.
LUCIUS.   Ay, good youth,
And rather father thee than master thee.
My friends,
The boy hath taught us manly duties; let us
Find out the prettiest daisied plot we can,   400
And make him with our pikes and partisans
A grave. Come, arm him. Boy, he is preferred
By thee to us, and he shall be interred
As soldiers can. Be cheerful; wipe thine eyes.
Some falls are means the happier to arise.
                                            They go

Scene 3: *A room in Cymbeline's palace*

Enter Cymbeline, Lords, Pisanio, and attendants

CYMBELINE. Again; and bring me word how 'tis with
    her.   *An attendant goes*
A fever with the absence of her son;
A madness, of which her life's in danger. Heavens,
How deeply you at once do touch me! Imogen,
The great part of my comfort, gone; my queen
Upon a desperate bed, and in a time
When fearful wars point at me; her son gone,
So needful for this present. It strikes me past
The hope of comfort. But for thee, fellow,
Who needs must know of her departure and   10
Dost seem so ignorant, we'll enforce it from thee
By a sharp torture.
PISANIO.   Sir, my life is yours;
I humbly set it at your will; but for my mistress,
I know nothing where she remains, why gone,
Nor when she purposes return. Beseech your
    highness,
Hold me your loyal servant.
I LORD.   Good my liege,
The day that she was missing he was here;
I dare be bound he's true and shall perform
All parts of his subjection loyally. For Cloten,

There wants no diligence in seeking him,   20
And will no doubt be found.
CYMBELINE.   The time is troublesome.
[to Pisanio] We'll slip you for a season, but our
  jealousy
Does yet depend.
I LORD.   So please your majesty,
The Roman legions, all from Gallia drawn,
Are landed on your coast, with a supply
Of Roman gentlemen by the senate sent.
CYMBELINE. Now for the counsel of my son and queen!
I am amazed with matter.
I LORD.   Good my liege,
Your preparation can affront no less
Than what you hear of. Come more, for more
  you're ready.
The want is but to put those powers in motion   30
That long to move.
CYMBELINE.   I thank you. Let's withdraw,
And meet the time as it seeks us. We fear not
What can from Italy annoy us, but
We grieve at chances here. Away!
                                          All but Pisanio go
PISANIO. I heard no letter from my master since
I wrote him Imogen was slain. 'Tis strange.
Nor hear I from my mistress, who did promise
To yield me often tidings. Neither know I
What is betid to Cloten, but remain   40
Perplexed in all. The heavens still must work.
Wherein I am false I am honest; not true, to be true.
These present wars shall find I love my country,
Even to the note o'th'king, or I'll fall in them.
All other doubts, by time let them be cleared.
Fortune brings in some boats that are not steered.
                                                      Goes

Scene 4: *Wales: Before the cave of Belarius*

Enter Belarius, Guiderius, and Arviragus

GUIDERIUS. The noise is round about us.
BELARIUS.   Let us from it.
ARVIRAGUS. What pleasure, sir, find we in life, to
  lock it
From action and adventure?
GUIDERIUS.   Nay, what hope
Have we in hiding us? This way the Romans
Must or for Britons slay us or receive us
For barbarous and unnatural revolts
During their use, and slay us after.
BELARIUS.   Sons,
We'll higher to the mountains; there secure us.
To the king's party there's no going. Newness
Of Cloten's death—we being not known, not
  mustered   10
Among the bands—may drive us to a render
Where we have lived, and so extort from's that
Which we have done, whose answer would be death
Drawn on with torture.
GUIDERIUS.   This is, sir, a doubt
In such a time nothing becoming you,
Nor satisfying us.
ARVIRAGUS.   It is not likely
That when they hear the Roman horses neigh,
Behold their quartered fires, have both their eyes
And ears so cloyed importantly as now,
That they will waste their time upon our note,   20
To know from whence we are.
BELARIUS.   O, I am known
Of many in the army. Many years,
Though Cloten then but young, you see, not wore
  him
From my remembrance. And besides, the king
Hath not deserved my service nor your loves,
Who find in my exile the want of breeding,
The certainty of this hard life; aye hopeless
To have the courtesy your cradle promised,
But to be still hot summer's tanlings and
The shrinking slaves of winter.
GUIDERIUS.   Than be so   30
Better to cease to be. Pray, sir, to th'army.
I and my brother are not known; yourself
So out of thought, and thereto so o'ergrown,
Cannot be questioned.
ARVIRAGUS.   By this sun that shines
I'll thither. What thing is't that I never
Did see man die, scarce ever looked on blood,
But that of coward hares, hot goats, and venison,
Never bestrid a horse, save one that had
A rider like myself, who ne'er wore rowel
Nor iron on his heel! I am ashamed   40
To look upon the holy sun, to have
The benefit of his blest beams, remaining
So long a poor unknown.
GUIDERIUS.   By heavens, I'll go;
If you will bless me sir, and give me leave,
I'll take the better care; but if you will not,
The hazard therefore due fall on me by
The hands of Romans!
ARVIRAGUS.   So say I; amen.
BELARIUS. No reason I, since of your lives you set
So slight a valuation, should reserve
My cracked one to more care. Have with you, boys!   50
If in your country wars you chance to die,
That is my bed too, lads, and there I'll lie.
Lead, lead. [aside] The time seems long; their blood
  thinks scorn
Till it fly out and show them princes born.
                                                   They go

ACT 5

Scene 1: *Britain. The Roman camp*

Enter Posthumus alone, with a bloody handkerchief

POSTHUMUS. Yea, bloody cloth, I'll keep thee; for I
  wished
Thou shouldst be coloured thus. You married ones,
If each of you should take this course, how many
Must murder wives much better than themselves
For wrying but a little! O Pisanio,
Every good servant does not all commands;
No bond but to do just ones. Gods, if you
Should have ta'en vengeance on my faults, I never
Had lived to put on this; so had you saved
The noble Imogen to repent, and struck   10
Me, wretch, more worth your vengeance. But
  alack,
You snatch some hence for little faults; that's love,
To have them fall no more; you some permit
To second ills with ills, each elder worse,
And make them dread it, to the doers' thrift.
But Imogen is your own; do your best wills,

And make me blest to obey. I am brought hither
Among th'Italian gentry, and to fight
Against my lady's kingdom. 'Tis enough
That, Britain, I have killed thy mistress; peace,   20
I'll give no wound to thee. Therefore, good heavens,
Hear patiently my purpose. I'll disrobe me
Of these Italian weeds, and suit myself
As does a Briton peasant. So I'll fight
Against the part I come with; so I'll die
For thee, O Imogen, even for whom my life
Is every breath a death; and thus, unknown,
Pitied nor hated, to the face of peril
Myself I'll dedicate. Let me make men know
More valour in me than my habits show.   30
Gods, put the strength o'th'Leonati in me.
To shame the guise o'th'world, I will begin
The fashion—less without and more within.
                                                     Goes

Scene 2: *Field of battle between the British and Roman
                        camps*

*Enter from one side, Lucius, Jachimo, and the Roman
Army; from the other side, the British Army; Leonatus
Posthumus following, like a poor soldier. They march over
and go out. Then enter again, in skirmish, Jachimo and
Posthumus: he vanquisheth and disarmeth Jachimo, and then
leaves him*

JACHIMO. The heaviness and guilt within my bosom
Takes off my manhood. I have belied a lady,
The princess of this country, and the air on't
Revengingly enfeebles me; or could this carl,
A very drudge of nature's, have subdued me
In my profession? Knighthoods and honours borne
As I wear mine are titles but of scorn.
If that thy gentry, Britain, go before
This lout as he exceeds our lords, the odds
Is that we scarce are men and you are gods.   10
                                                     Goes

*The battle continues; the Britons fly; Cymbeline is taken:
then enter, to his rescue, Belarius, Guiderius and Arviragus*

BELARIUS. Stand, stand, we have the advantage of the
          ground;
The lane is guarded; nothing routs us but
The villainy of our fears.

GUIDERIUS   }
AND ARVIRAGUS.   }   Stand, stand, and fight.

*Re-enter Posthumus, and seconds the Britons: they rescue
Cymbeline and go out. Then re-enter Lucius, Jachimo, with
Imogen*

LUCIUS. Away, boy, from the troops, and save thyself;
For friends kill friends, and the disorder's such
As war were hoodwinked.
JACHIMO.   'Tis their fresh supplies.
LUCIUS. It is a day turned strangely; or betimes
Let's reinforce, or fly.   *They go*

Scene 3: *Another part of the field*

Enter Posthumus and a British Lord

LORD. Cam'st thou from where they made the stand?
POSTHUMUS.   I did;
Though you, it seems, come from the fliers?
LORD.   I did.

POSTHUMUS. No blame be to you, sir; for all was lost,
But that the heavens fought. The king himself
Of his wings destitute, the army broken,
And but the backs of Britons seen, all flying
Through a strait lane; the enemy full-hearted,
Lolling the tongue with slaught'ring, having work
More plentiful than tools to do't, struck down
Some mortally, some slightly touched, some falling   10
Merely through fear, that the strait pass was
          dammed
With dead men hurt behind, and cowards living
To die with length'ned shame.
LORD.   Where was this lane?
POSTHUMUS. Close by the battle, ditched, and walled
          with turf;
Which gave advantage to an ancient soldier,
An honest one, I warrant, who deserved
So long a breeding as his white beard came to,
In doing this for's country. Athwart the lane
He, with two striplings—lads more like to run
The country base than to commit such slaughter;   20
With faces fit for masks, or rather fairer
Than those for preservation cased, or shame—
Made good the passage; cried to those that fled,
'Our Britain's harts die flying, not our men:
To darkness fleet souls that fly backwards. Stand,
Or we are Romans, and will give you that
Like beasts which you shun beastly, and may save
But to look back in frown. Stand, stand'. These
          three,
Three thousand confident, in act as many—
For three performers are the file when all   30
The rest do nothing—with this word 'Stand, stand',
Accommodated by the place, more charming
With their own nobleness, which could have turned
A distaff to a lance, gilded pale looks;
Part shame, part spirit renewed, that some, turned
          coward
But by example—O, a sin in war,
Damned in the first beginners!—'gan to look
The way that they did and to grin like lions
Upon the pikes o'th'hunters. Then began
A stop i'th'chaser, a retire; anon   40
A rout, confusion thick; forthwith they fly
Chickens, the way which they stooped eagles;
          slaves,
The strides they victors made; and now our
          cowards,
Like fragments in hard voyages, became
The life o'th'need. Having found the back-door
          open
Of the unguarded hearts, heavens, how they
          wound!
Some slain before, some dying, some their friends
O'er-borne i'th'former wave, ten chased by one,
Are now each one the slaughterman of twenty,
Those that would die or ere resist are grown   50
The mortal bugs o'th'field.
LORD.   This was strange chance:
A narrow lane, an old man, and two boys.
POSTHUMUS. Nay, do not wonder at it; you are made
Rather to wonder at the things you hear
Than to work any. Will you rhyme upon't,
And vent if for a mock'ry? Here is one:
'Two boys, an old man—twice a boy—a lane,
Preserved the Britons, was the Romans' bane.'

LORD. Nay, be not angry, sir.
POSTHUMUS.   'Lack, to what end?
Who dares not stand his foe, I'll be his friend;   60
For if he'll do as he is made to do,
I know he'll quickly fly my friendship too.
You have put me into rhyme.
LORD.   Farewell; you're angry.
                                 Goes
POSTHUMUS. Still going? This is a lord! O noble
    misery,
To be i'th'field, and ask 'what news?' of me!
To-day how many would have given their honours
To have saved their carcasses! took heel to do't,
And yet died too! I, in mine own woe charmed,
Could not find death where I did hear him groan,
Nor feel him where he struck. Being an ugly
    monster,   70
'Tis strange he hides him in fresh cups, soft beds,
Sweet words; or hath moe ministers than we
That draw his knives i'th'war. Well, I will find him;
For being now a favourer to the Briton,
No more a Briton, I have resumed again
The part I came in. Fight I will no more,
But yield me to the veriest hind that shall
Once touch my shoulder. Great the slaughter is
Here made by th'Roman; great the answer be
Britons must take. For me, my ransom's death;   80
On either side I come to spend my breath,
Which neither here I'll keep nor bear again,
    But end it by some means for Imogen.

Enter two British Captains and Soldiers

1 CAPTAIN. Great Jupiter be praised, Lucius is taken.
    'Tis thought the old man and his sons were angels.
2 CAPTAIN. There was a fourth man, in a silly habit,
    That gave th'affront with them.
1 CAPTAIN.   So 'tis reported;
But none of 'em can be found. Stand, who's there?
POSTHUMUS. A Roman,
Who had not now been drooping here if seconds   90
Had answered him.
2 CAPTAIN.   Lay hands on him; a dog!
A leg of Rome shall not return to tell
What crows have pecked them here. He brags his
    service
As if he were of note: bring him to th'king.

Enter Cymbeline, Belarius, Guiderius, Arviragus, Pisanio,
and Roman Captives. The Captains present Posthumus to
Cymbeline, who delivers him over to a Gaoler: then all go

Scene 4: A British prison

Enter Posthumus and two Gaolers

1 GAOLER. You shall not now be stol'n, you have locks
    upon you;
So graze as you find pasture.
2 GAOLER.   Ay, or a stomach.
                         The gaolers go
POSTHUMUS. Most welcome, bondage, for thou art a
    way,
I think, to liberty. Yet am I better
Than one that's sick o'th'gout, since he had rather
Groan so in perpetuity than be cured
By th'sure physician, death, who is the key

T'unbar these locks. My conscience, thou art
    fettered
More than my shanks and wrists. You good gods,
    give me
The penitent instrument to pick that bolt,   10
Then, free for ever. Is't enough I am sorry?
So children temporal fathers do appease;
Gods are more full of mercy. Must I repent,
I cannot do it better than in gyves,
Desired more than constrained. To satisfy,
If of my freedom 'tis the main part, take
No stricter render of me than my all.
I know you are more clement than vile men,
Who of their broken debtors take a third,
A sixth, a tenth, letting them thrive again   20
On their abatement; that's not my desire.
For Imogen's dear life take mine; and though
'Tis not so dear, yet 'tis a life; you coined it.
'Tween man and man they weigh not every stamp;
Though light, take pieces for the figure's sake;
You rather mine, being yours. And so, great
    powers,
If you will take this audit, take this life,
And cancel these cold bonds. O Imogen,
I'll speak to thee in silence.   *Sleeps*

Solemn music. Enter, as in an apparition, Sicilius Leonatus,
father to Posthumus, an old man, attired like a warrior;
leading in his hand an ancient matron, his wife and mother
to Posthumus, with music before them. Then, after other
music, follow the two young Leonati, brothers to Posthumus,
with wounds as they died in the wars. They circle
Posthumus round as he lies sleeping

SICILIUS.   No more, thou thunder-master, show   30
              Thy spite on mortal flies.
          With Mars fall out, with Juno chide,
              That thy adulteries
                Rates and revenges.
          Hath my poor boy done aught but well,
              Whose face I never saw?
          I died whilst in the womb he stayed
              Attending nature's law;
          Whose father then—as men report
              Thou orphans' father art—   40
          Thou shouldst have been, and shielded
            him
              From this earth-vexing smart.
MOTHER.   Lucina lent not me her aid,
              But took me in my throes,
          That from me was Posthumus ripped,
              Came crying 'mongst his foes,
              A thing of pity.
SICILIUS.   Great nature like his ancestry
              Moulded the stuff so fair
          That he deserved the praise o'th'world,   50
              As great Sicilius' heir.
1 BROTHER. When once he was mature for man,
              In Britain where was he
          That could stand up his parallel,
              Or fruitful object be
          In eye of Imogen, that best
              Could deem his dignity?
MOTHER.   With marriage wherefore was he
              mocked,
              To be exiled, and thrown
          From Leonati seat, and cast   60

           From her his dearest one,
             Sweet Imogen?
SICILIUS. Why did you suffer Jachimo,
           Slight thing of Italy,
      To taint his nobler heart and brain
           With needless jealousy,
             And to become the geck and scorn
           O'th'other's villainy?
2 BROTHER. For this from stiller seats we came,
           Our parents and us twain,   70
      That striking in our country's cause
           Fell bravely and were slain,
      Our fealty and Tenantius' right
           With honour to maintain.
1 BROTHER. Like hardiment Posthumus hath
           To Cymbeline performed.
      Then, Jupiter, thou king of gods,
           Why hast thou thus adjourned
      The graces for his merits due,
           Being all to dolours turned?   80
SICILIUS. Thy crystal window ope; look out;
           No longer exercise
      Upon a valiant race thy harsh
           And potent injuries.
MOTHER. Since, Jupiter, our son is good,
           Take off his miseries.
SICILIUS. Peep through thy marble mansion; help;
           Or we poor ghosts will cry
      To th'shining synod of the rest
           Against thy deity.   90
BOTH BROTHERS. Help, Jupiter, or we appeal,
           And from thy justice fly.

*Jupiter descends in thunder and lightning, sitting upon an
eagle; he throws a thunderbolt. The ghosts fall on their
knees*

JUPITER. No more, you petty spirits of region low,
      Offend our hearing; hush! How dare you
           ghosts
      Accuse the thunderer, whose bolt, you know,
           Sky-planted, batters all rebelling coasts?
      Poor shadows of Elysium, hence, and rest
           Upon your never-withering banks
             of flowers.
      Be not with mortal accidents oppressed;
           No care of yours it is; you know 'tis ours. 100
      Whom best I love I cross; to make my gift,
           The more delayed, delighted. Be content;
      Your low-laid son our godhead will uplift;
           His comforts thrive, his trials well are
             spent.
      Our Jovial star reigned at his birth, and in
           Our temple was he married. Rise,
             and fade.
      He shall be lord of lady Imogen,
           And happier much by his afflictior. made.
      This tablet lay upon his breast, wherein
           Our pleasure his full fortune doth confine; 110
      And so away; no farther with your din
           Express impatience, lest you stir up mine.
      Mount, eagle, to my palace crystalline.
                              Ascends
SICILIUS. He came in thunder; his celestial breath
  Was sulphurous to smell; the holy eagle
  Stooped, as to foot us. His ascension is
  More sweet than our blest fields. His royal bird

Prunes the immortal wing and cloys his beak,
  As when his god is pleased.
ALL.   Thanks, Jupiter.
SICILIUS. The marble pavement closes, he is entered 120
  His radiant roof. Away, and, to be blest,
  Let us with care perform his great behest.
                      The ghosts vanish
POSTHUMUS [*waking*]. Sleep, thou hast been a
      grandsire, and begot
  A father to me; and thou hast created
  A mother and two brothers. But, O scorn,
  Gone! they went hence so soon as they were born;
  And so I am awake. Poor wretches that depend
  On greatness' favour dream as I have done;
  Wake, and find nothing. But, alas, I swerve;
  Many dream not to find, neither deserve,   130
  And yet are steeped in favours; so am I,
  That have this golden chance, and know not why.
  What fairies haunt this ground? A book? O rare one,
  Be not, as is our fangled world, a garment
  Nobler than that it covers. Let thy effects
  So follow to be most unlike our courtiers,
  As good as promise.   *Reads*
  'When as a lion's whelp shall, to himself un-
known, without seeking find, and be embraced by
a piece of tender air, and when from a stately cedar 140
shall be lopped branches which, being dead many
years, shall after revive, be jointed to the old stock,
and freshly grow; then shall Posthumus end his
miseries, Britain be fortunate and flourish in peace
and plenty.'
  'Tis still a dream; or else such stuff as madmen
Tongue, and brain not; either both, or nothing,
Or senseless speaking, or a speaking such
As sense cannot untie. Be what it is,
The action of my life is like it, which   150
I'll keep, if but for sympathy.

Re-enter Gaolers

1 GAOLER. Come, sir, are you ready for death?
POSTHUMUS. Over-roasted rather; ready long ago.
1 GAOLER. Hanging is the word, sir; if you be ready
  for that you are well cooked.
POSTHUMUS. So, if I prove a good repast to the spectators, the dish pays the shot.
1 GAOLER. A heavy reckoning for you, sir. But the
  comfort is, you shall be called to no more payments,
  fear no more tavern bills, which are as often the 160
  sadness of parting, as the procuring of mirth. You
  come in faint for want of meat, depart reeling with
  too much drink; sorry that you have paid too much,
  and sorry that you are paid too much; purse and
  brain both empty: the brain the heavier for being
  too light, the purse too light, being drawn of
  heaviness. Of this contradiction you shall now be
  quit. O, the charity of a penny cord! it sums up
  thousands in a trice; you have no true debitor-and-
  creditor but it; of what's past, is, and to come, the 170
  discharge; your neck, sir, is pen, book, and counters;
  so the acquittance follows.
POSTHUMUS. I am merrier to die than thou art to live.
1 GAOLER. Indeed, sir, he that sleeps feels not the
  toothache; but a man that were to sleep your sleep,
  and a hangman to help him to bed, I think he
  would change places with his officer; for look you,
  sir, you know not which way you shall go.

POSTHUMUS. Yes indeed do I, fellow.

1 GAOLER. Your death has eyes in's head then; I have 180
not seen him so pictured. You must either be
directed by some that take upon them to know, or
take upon yourself that which I am sure you do not
know, or jump the after-inquiry on your own peril;
and how you shall speed in your journey's end, I
think you'll never return to tell on.

POSTHUMUS. I tell thee, fellow, there are none want
eyes to direct them the way I am going, but such
as wink and will not use them.

1 GAOLER. What an infinite mock is this, that a man 190
should have the best use of eyes to see the way of
blindness! I am sure hanging's the way of winking.

Enter a Messenger

MESSENGER. Knock off his manacles; bring your
prisoner to the king.

POSTHUMUS. Thou bringest good news, I am called to
be made free.

1 GAOLER. I'll be hanged then.

POSTHUMUS. Thou shalt be then freer than a gaoler;
no bolts for the dead.   *All but 1 Gaoler go*

1 GAOLER. Unless a man would marry a gallows and 200
beget young gibbets, I never saw one so prone. Yet,
on my conscience there are verier knaves desire to
live, for all he be a Roman; and there be some of
them too that die against their wills; so should I, if
I were one. I would we were all of one mind, and
one mind good. O, there were desolation of gaolers
and gallowses! I speak against my present profit, but
my wish hath a preferment in't.   *Goes*

Scene 5: *Cymbeline's tent*

Enter Cymbeline, Belarius, Guiderius, Arviragus, Pisanio,
Lords, Officers, and Attendants

CYMBELINE. Stand by my side, you whom the gods
have made
Preservers of my throne. Woe is my heart
That the poor soldier that so richly fought,
Whose rags shamed gilded arms, whose naked
breast
Stepped before targes of proof, cannot be found.
He shall be happy that can find him, if
Our grace can make him so.

BELARIUS.   I never saw
Such noble fury in so poor a thing;
Such precious deeds in one that promised nought
But beggary and poor looks.

CYMBELINE.   No tidings of him? 10

PISANIO. He hath been searched among the dead and
living,
But no trace of him.

CYMBELINE.   To my grief, I am
The heir of his reward; [*to Belarius, Guiderius, and*
Arviragus] which I will add
To you, the liver, heart, and brain of Britain,
By whom I grant she lives. 'Tis now the time
To ask of whence you are. Report it.

BELARIUS.   Sir,
In Cambria are we born, and gentlemen;
Further to boast were neither true nor modest,
Unless I add, we are honest.

CYMBELINE.   Bow your knees.
Arise my knights o'th'battle; I create you   20
Companions to our person, and will fit you
With dignities becoming your estates.

Enter Cornelius and Ladies

There's business in these faces. Why so sadly
Greet you our victory? you look like Romans,
And not o'th'court of Britain

CORNELIUS.   Hail, great king!
To sour your happiness, I must report
The queen is dead.

CYMBELINE.   Who worse than a physician
Would this report become? But I consider,
By medicine life may be prolonged, yet death
Will seize the doctor too. How ended she?   30

CORNELIUS. With horror, madly dying, like her life,
Which, being cruel to the world, concluded
Most cruel to herself. What she confessed
I will report, so please you; these her women
Can trip me if I err, who with wet cheeks
Were present when she finished.

CYMBELINE.   Prithee say.

CORNELIUS. First, she confessed she never loved you;
only
Affected greatness got by you, not you;
Married your royalty, was wife to your place;
Abhorred your person.

CYMBELINE.   She alone knew this;   40
And but she spoke it dying, I would not
Believe her lips in opening it. Proceed.

CORNELIUS. Your daughter whom she bore in hand to
love
With such integrity, she did confess
Was as a scorpion to her sight; whose life,
But that her flight prevented it, she had
Ta'en off by poison.

CYMBELINE.   O most delicate fiend!
Who is't can read a woman? Is there more?

CORNELIUS. More, sir, and worse. She did confess she
had
For you a mortal mineral, which, being took,   50
Should by the minute feed on life, and, ling'ring,
By inches waste you. In which time she purposed,
By watching, weeping, tendance, kissing, to
O'ercome you with her show; and in time,
When she had fitted you with her craft, to work
Her son into th'adoption of the crown;
But failing of her end by his strange absence,
Grew shameless-desperate; opened, in despite
Of heaven and men, her purposes; repented
The evils she hatched were not effected; so   60
Despairing died.

CYMBELINE.   Heard you all this, her women?

LADIES. We did, so please your highness.

CYMBELINE.   Mine eyes
Were not in fault, for she was beautiful;
Mine ears that heard her flattery, nor my heart
That thought her like her seeming. It had been
vicious
To have mistrusted her; yet, O my daughter,
That it was folly in me thou mayst say,
And prove it in thy feeling. Heaven mend all!

Enter Lucius, Jachimo, the Soothsayer, and other Roman
Prisoners, guarded; Posthumus behind, and Imogen

Thou com'st not, Caius, now for tribute; that
The Britons have razed out, though with the loss 70
Of many a bold one; whose kinsmen have made suit
That their good souls may be appeased with
  slaughter
Of you their captives, which ourself have granted;
So think of your estate.
LUCIUS. Consider, sir, the chance of war; the day
Was yours by accident; had it gone with us,
We should not, when the blood was cool, have
  threatened
Our prisoners with the sword. But since the gods
Will have it thus, that nothing but our lives
May be called ransom, let it come. Sufficeth 80
A Roman with a Roman's heart can suffer.
Augustus lives to think on't; and so much
For my peculiar care. This one thing only
I will entreat: my boy, a Briton born,
Let him be ransomed. Never master had
A page so kind, so duteous, diligent,
So tender over his occasions, true,
So feat, so nurse-like; let his virtue join
With my request, which I'll make bold your
  highness
Cannot deny; he hath done no Briton harm 90
Though he have served a Roman. Save him, sir,
And spare no blood beside.
CYMBELINE.   I have surely seen him.
His favour is familiar to me. Boy,
Thou hast looked thyself into my grace,
And art mine own. I know not why, wherefore,
To say, 'Live, boy'. Ne'er thank thy master; live;
And ask of Cymbeline what boon thou wilt,
Fitting my bounty and thy state, I'll give it;
Yea, though thou do demand a prisoner,
The noblest ta'en.
IMOGEN.   I humbly thank your highness. 100
LUCIUS. I do not bid thee beg my life, good lad,
And yet I know thou wilt.
IMOGEN.   No, no; alack,
There's other work in hand. I see a thing
Bitter to me as death; your life, good master,
Must shuffle for itself.
LUCIUS.   The boy disdains me,
He leaves me, scorns me. Briefly die their joys
That place them on the truth of girls and boys.
Why stands he so perplexed?
CYMBELINE.   What wouldst thou, boy?
I love thee more and more; think more and more
What's best to ask. Know'st him thou look'st on?
  speak,   110
Wilt have him live? Is he thy kin? thy friend?
IMOGEN. He is a Roman, no more kin to me
Than I to your highness; who, being born your
  vassal,
Am something nearer.
CYMBELINE.   Wherefore ey'st him so?
IMOGEN. I'll tell you, sir, in private, if you please
To give me hearing.
CYMBELINE.   Ay, with all my heart,
And lend my best attention. What's thy name?
IMOGEN. Fidele, sir.
CYMBELINE.   Thou'rt my good youth, my page;
I'll be thy master. Walk with me; speak freely.
                        Cymbeline and Imogen walk
                                            aside

BELARIUS. Is not this boy revived from death?
ARVIRAGUS.   One sand another 120
Not more resembles—that sweet rosy lad
Who died, and was Fidele. What think you?
GUIDERIUS. The same dead thing alive.
BELARIUS. Peace, peace, see further; he eyes us not;
  forbear;
Creatures may be alike; were't he, I am sure
He would have spoke to us.
GUIDERIUS.   But we saw him dead.
BELARIUS. Be silent; let's see further.
PISANIO [*aside*].   It is my mistress.
Since she is living, let the time run on
To good or bad.
                        Cymbeline and Imogen come
                                            forward
CYMBELINE.   Come, stand thou by our side;
Make thy demand aloud. [*to Jachimo*] Sir, step you
  forth;   130
Give answer to this boy, and do it freely,
Or, by our greatness and the grace of it,
Which is our honour, bitter torture shall
Winnow the truth from falsehood. On, speak to
  him.
IMOGEN. My boon is that this gentleman may render
Of whom he had this ring.
POSTHUMUS [*aside*].   What's that to him?
CYMBELINE. That diamond upon your finger, say
How came it yours?
JACHIMO. Thou'lt torture me to leave unspoken that
Which, to be spoke, would torture thee.
CYMBELINE.   How? me? 140
JACHIMO. I am glad to be constrained to utter that
Torments me to conceal. By villainy
I got this ring; 'twas Leonatus' jewel,
Whom thou didst banish; and—which more may
  grieve thee,
As it doth me—a nobler sir ne'er lived
'Twixt sky and ground. Wilt thou hear more, my
  lord?
CYMBELINE. All that belongs to this.
JACHIMO.   That paragon, thy daughter,
For whom my heart drops blood, and my false
  spirits
Quail to remember—Give me leave; I faint.
CYMBELINE. My daughter? what of her? Renew thy
  strength;   150
I had rather thou shouldst live while nature will
Than die ere I hear more. Strive, man, and speak.
JACHIMO. Upon a time—unhappy was the clock
That struck the hour!—it was in Rome—accursed
The mansion where!—'twas at a feast—O, would
Our viands had been poisoned, or at least
Those which I heaved to head!—the good
  Posthumus—
What should I say? he was too good to be
Where ill men were, and was the best of all
Amongst the rar'st of good ones—sitting sadly, 160
Hearing us praise our loves of Italy
For beauty that made barren the swelled boast
Of him that best could speak; for feature, laming
The shrine of Venus or straight-pight Minerva,
Postures beyond brief Nature; for condition,
A shop of all the qualities that man
Loves woman for; besides that hook of wiving,
Fairness which strikes the eye—

CYMBELINE.   I stand on fire.
  Come to the matter.
JACHIMO.   All too soon I shall,
  Unless thou wouldst grieve quickly. This
    Posthumus,   170
  Most like a noble lord in love and one
  That had a royal lover, took his hint,
  And not dispraising whom we praised—therein
  He was as calm as virtue—he began
  His mistress' picture; which by his tongue being
    made,
  And then a mind put in't, either our brags
  Were cracked of kitchen-trulls, or his description
  Proved us unspeaking sots.
CYMBELINE.   Nay, nay, to th'purpose.
JACHIMO. Your daughter's chastity—there it begins.
  He spake of her as Dian had hot dreams   180
  And she alone were cold; whereat I, wretch,
  Made scruple of his praise, and wagered with him
  Pieces of gold 'gainst this which then he wore
  Upon his honoured finger, to attain
  In suit the place of's bed and win this ring
  By hers and mine adultery. He, true knight,
  No lesser of her honour confident
  Than I did truly find her, stakes this ring;
  And would so, had it been a carbuncle
  Of Phœbus' wheel; and might so safely, had it   190
  Been all the worth of's car. Away to Britain
  Post I in this design. Well may you, sir,
  Remember me at court; where I was taught
  Of your chaste daughter the wide difference
  'Twixt amorous and villainous. Being thus
    quenched
  Of hope, not longing, mine Italian brain
  'Gan in your duller Britain operate
  Most vilely; for my vantage, excellent.
  And, to be brief, my practice so prevailed,
  That I returned with simular proof enough   200
  To make the noble Leonatus mad,
  By wounding his belief in her renown
  With tokens thus and thus; averring notes
  Of chamber-hanging, pictures, this her bracelet—
  O cunning, how I got it!—nay, some marks
  Of secret on her person, that he could not
  But think her bond of chastity quite cracked,
  I having ta'en the forfeit. Whereupon—
  Methinks I see him now—
POSTHUMUS [advancing].   Ay, so thou dost,
  Italian fiend! Ay me, most credulous fool,   210
  Egregious murderer, thief, any thing
  That's due to all the villains past, in being,
  To come! O, give me cord, or knife, or poison,
  Some upright justicer! Thou, king, send out
  For torturers ingenious: it is I
  That all th'abhorréd things o'th'earth amend
  By being worse than they. I am Posthumus,
  That killed thy daughter; villain-like, I lie;
  That caused a lesser villain than myself,
  A sacrilegious thief, to do't. The temple
  Of virtue was she; yea, and she herself.   220
  Spit, and throw stones, cast mire upon me, set
  The dogs o'th'street to bay me. Every villain
  Be called Posthumus Leonatus, and
  Be 'villain' less than 'twas! O Imogen!
  My queen, my life, my wife! O Imogen,
  Imogen, Imogen!

IMOGEN.   Peace, my lord; hear, hear.
POSTHUMUS. Shall's have a play of this? Thou scornful
    page,
  There lie thy part.   Strikes her: she falls
PISANIO.   O gentlemen, help!
  Mine and your mistress! O my lord Posthumus,   230
  You ne'er killed Imogen till now. Help, help!
  Mine honoured lady!
CYMBELINE.   Does the world go round?
POSTHUMUS. How comes these staggers on me?
PISANIO.   Wake, my mistress!
CYMBELINE. If this be so, the gods do mean to strike me
  To death with mortal joy.
PISANIO.   How fares my mistress?
IMOGEN. O, get thee from my sight;
  Thou gavest me poison. Dangerous fellow, hence!
  Breathe not where princes are.
CYMBELINE.   The tune of Imogen.
PISANIO. Lady,
  The gods throw stones of sulphur on me, if   240
  That box I gave you was not thought by me
  A precious thing; I had it from the queen.
CYMBELINE. New matter still.
IMOGEN.   It poisoned me.
CORNELIUS.   O gods!
  I left out one thing which the queen confessed,
  Which must approve thee honest: 'If Pisanio
  Have' said she 'given his mistress that confection
  Which I gave him for a cordial, she is served
  As I would serve a rat.'
CYMBELINE.   What's this, Cornelius?
CORNELIUS. The queen, sir, very oft importuned me
  To temper poisons for her, still pretending   250
  The satisfaction of her knowledge only
  In killing creatures vile, as cats and dogs,
  Of no esteem. I, dreading that her purpose
  Was of more danger, did compound for her
  A certain stuff which being ta'en would cease
  The present power of life, but in short time
  All offices of nature should again
  Do their due functions. Have you ta'en of it?
IMOGEN. Most like I did, for I was dead.
BELARIUS.   My boys,
  There was our error.
GUIDERIUS.   This is, sure, Fidele.   260
IMOGEN. Why did you throw your wedded lady from
    you?
  Think that you are upon a lock, and now
  Throw me again.   Embracing him
POSTHUMUS.   Hang there like fruit, my soul,
  Till the tree die!
CYMBELINE.   How now, my flesh? my child?
  What, mak'st thou me a dullard in this act?
  Wilt thou not speak to me?
IMOGEN [kneeling].   Your blessing, sir.
BELARIUS [to Guiderius and Arviragus]. Though you did
    love this youth, I blame ye not;
  You had a motive for't.
CYMBELINE.   My tears that fall
  Prove holy water on thee! Imogen,
  Thy mother's dead.
IMOGEN.   I am sorry for't, my lord.   270
CYMBELINE. O, she was naught; and long of her it was
  That we meet here so strangely; but her son
  Is gone, we know not how or where.
PISANIO.   My lord,

Now fear is from me, I'll speak troth. Lord Cloten,
Upon my lady's missing, came to me
With his sword drawn, foamed at the mouth, and
swore,
If I discovered not which way she was gone,
It was my instant death. By accident,
I had a feignéd letter of my master's
Then in my pocket, which directed him   280
To seek her on the mountains near to Milford;
Where, in a frenzy, in my master's garments,
Which he enforced from me, away he posts
With unchaste purpose, and with oath to violate
My lady's honour. What became of him
I further know not.
GUIDERIUS.   Let me end the story:.
I slew him there.
CYMBELINE.   Marry, the gods forfend!
I would not thy good deeds should from my lips
Pluck a hard sentence. Prithee, valiant youth,
Deny't again.
GUIDERIUS.   I have spoke it, and I did it.   290
CYMBELINE. He was a prince.
GUIDERIUS. A most incivil one. The wrongs he did me
Were nothing prince-like; for he did provoke me
With language that would make me spurn the sea,
If it could so roar to me. I cut off's head,
And am right glad he is not standing here
To tell this tale of mine.
CYMBELINE.   I am sorrow for thee.
By thine own tongue thou art condemned, and must
Endure our law. Thou'rt dead.
IMOGEN.   That headless man
I thought had been my lord.
CYMBELINE.   Bind the offender,   300
And take him from our presence.
BELARIUS.   Stay, sir king.
This man is better than the man he slew,
As well descended as thyself, and hath
More of thee merited than a band of Clotens
Had ever scar for. [to the guard] Let his arms alone;
They were not born for bondage.
CYMBELINE.   Why, old soldier:
Wilt thou undo the worth thou art unpaid for,
By tasting of our wrath? How of descent
As good as we?
ARVIRAGUS.   In that he spake too far.
CYMBELINE. And thou shalt die for't.
BELARIUS.   We will die all three   310
But I will prove that two on's are as good
As I have given out him. My sons, I must
For mine own part unfold a dangerous speech,
Though haply well for you.
ARVIRAGUS.   Your danger's ours.
GUIDERIUS. And our good his.
BELARIUS.   Have at it then; by leave,
Thou hadst, great king, a subject who
Was called Belarius.
CYMBELINE.   What of him? he is
A banished traitor.
BELARIUS.   He it is that hath
Assumed this age; indeed a banished man,
I know not how a traitor.
CYMBELINE.   Take him hence;   320
The whole world shall not save him.
BELARIUS.   Not too hot;
First pay me for the nursing of thy sons,

And let it be confiscate all, so soon
As I have received it.
CYMBELINE.   Nursing of my sons?
BELARIUS. I am too blunt and saucy: here's my knee.
Ere I arise I will prefer my sons,
Then spare not the old father. Mighty sir,
These two young gentlemen that call me father,
And think they are my sons, are none of mine;
They are the issue of your loins, my liege,   330
And blood of your begetting.
CYMBELINE.   How? my issue?
BELARIUS. So sure as you your father's. I, old Morgan,
Am that Belarius whom you sometime banished.
Your pleasure was my mere offence, my
punishment
Itself, and all my treason; that I suffered
Was all the harm I did. These gentle princes—
For such and so they are—these twenty years
Have I trained up; those arts they have as I
Could put into them. My breeding was, sir, as
Your highness knows. Their nurse, Euriphile,   340
Whom for the theft I wedded, stole these children
Upon my banishment; I moved her to't,
Having received the punishment before
For that which I did then. Beaten for loyalty
Excited me to treason. Their dear loss,
The more of you 'twas felt, the more it shaped
Unto my end of stealing them. But gracious sir,
Here are your sons again, and I must lose
Two of the sweet'st companions in the world.
The benediction of these covering heavens   350
Fall on their heads like dew! for they are worthy
To inlay heaven with stars.
CYMBELINE.   Thou weep'st, and speak'st.
The service that you three have done is more
Unlike than this thou tell'st. I lost my children;
If these be they, I know not how to wish
A pair of worthier sons.
BELARIUS.   Be pleased awhile.
This gentleman, whom I call Polydore,
Most worthy prince, as yours, is true Guiderius;
This gentleman, my Cadwal, Arviragus,
Your younger princely son; he, sir, was lapped   360
In a most curious mantle, wrought by th'hand
Of his queen mother, which for more probation
I can with ease produce.
CYMBELINE.   Guiderius had
Upon his neck a mole, a sanguine star;
It was a mark of wonder.
BELARIUS.   This is he,
Who hath upon him still that natural stamp.
It was wise nature's end in the donation,
To be his evidence now.
CYMBELINE.   O, what am I?
A mother to the birth of three? Ne'er mother
Rejoiced deliverance more. Blest pray you be,   370
That, after this strange starting from your orbs,
You may reign in them now! O Imogen,
Thou hast lost by this a kingdom.
IMOGEN.   No, my lord;
I have got two worlds by't. O my gentle brothers,
Have we thus met? O, never say hereafter
But I am truest speaker: you called me brother,
When I was but your sister; I you brothers,
When ye were so indeed.
CYMBELINE.   Did you e'er meet?

ARVIRAGUS. Ay, my good lord.

GUIDERIUS. And at first meeting loved,
Continued so until we thought he died. 380

CORNELIUS. By the queen's dram she swallowed.

CYMBELINE. O rare instinct!
When shall I hear all through? This fierce
abridgement
Hath to it circumstantial branches which
Distinction should be rich in. Where? how lived
you?
And when came you to serve our Roman captive?
How parted with your brothers? how first met
them?
Why fled you from the court? and whither? These,
And your three motives to the battle, with
I know not how much more, should be demanded,
And all the other by-dependences, 390
From chance to chance; but nor the time nor place
Will serve our long inter'gatories. See
Posthumus anchors upon Imogen;
And she, like harmless lightning, throws her eye
On him, her brothers, me, her master, hitting
Each object with a joy; the counterchange
Is severally in all. Let's quit this ground,
And smoke the temple with our sacrifices.
[to Belarius] Thou art my brother; so we'll hold thee
ever.

IMOGEN. You are my father too, and did relieve me 400
To see this gracious season.

CYMBELINE. All o'erjoyed,
Save these in bonds; let them be joyful too,
For they shall taste our comfort.

IMOGEN. My good master,
I will yet do you service.

LUCIUS. Happy be you!

CYMBELINE. The forlorn soldier that so nobly fought,
He would have well becomed this place and graced
The thankings of a king.

POSTHUMUS. I am, sir,
The soldier that did company these three
In poor beseeming; 'twas a fitment for
The purpose I then followed. That I was he, 410
Speak, Jachimo. I had you down, and might
Have made you finish.

JACHIMO [kneeling]. I am down again;
But now my heavy conscience sinks my knee,
As then your force did. Take that life, beseech you,
Which I so often owe; but your ring first,
And here the bracelet of the truest princess
That ever swore her faith.

POSTHUMUS. Kneel not to me.
The power that I have on you is to spare you;
The malice towards you to forgive you. Live,
And deal with others better.

CYMBELINE. Nobly doomed! 420
We'll learn our freeness of a son-in-law;
Pardon's the word to all.

ARVIRAGUS. You holp us, sir,
As you did mean indeed to be our brother;
Joyed are we that you are.

POSTHUMUS. Your servant, princes. Good my lord of
Rome,
Call forth your soothsayer. As I slept, methought
Great Jupiter, upon his eagle backed,
Appeared to me, with other spritely shows

Of mine own kindred. When I waked, I found
This label on my bosom; whose containing 430
Is so from sense in hardness that I can
Make no collection of it. Let him show
His skill in the construction.

LUCIUS. Philarmonus!

SOOTHSAYER. Here, my good lord.

LUCIUS. Read, and declare the meaning.

SOOTHSAYER [reads]. 'When as a lion's whelp shall, to
himself unknown, without seeking find, and be
embraced by a piece of tender air; and when from a
stately cedar shall be lopped branches which, being
dead many years, shall after revive, be jointed to the
old stock, and freshly grow; then shall Posthumus 440
end his miseries, Britain be fortunate and flourish in
peace and plenty.'
Thou, Leonatus, art the lion's whelp;
The fit and apt construction of thy name,
Being Leo-natus, doth import so much.
[to Cymbeline] The piece of tender air, thy virtuous
daughter,
Which we call 'mollis aer'; and 'mollis aer'
We term it 'mulier'; [to Posthumus] which 'mulier'
I divine
Is this most constant wife; who even now,
Answering the letter of the oracle, 450
Unknown to you, unsought, were clipped about
With this most tender air.

CYMBELINE. This hath some seeming.

SOOTHSAYER. The lofty cedar, royal Cymbeline,
Personates thee; and thy lopped branches point
Thy two sons forth, who, by Belarius stol'n,
For many years thought dead, are now revived,
To the majestic cedar joined, whose issue
Promises Britain peace and plenty.

CYMBELINE. Well;
My peace we will begin. And, Caius Lucius,
Although the victor, we submit to Cæsar 460
And to the Roman empire, promising
To pay our wonted tribute, from the which
We were dissuaded by our wicked queen,
Whom heavens in justice both on her and hers
Have laid most heavy hand.

SOOTHSAYER. The fingers of the powers above do tune
The harmony of this peace. The vision,
Which I made known to Lucius ere the stroke
Of this yet scarce-cold battle, at this instant
Is full accomplished; for the Roman eagle, 470
From south to west on wing soaring aloft,
Lessened herself, and in the beams o'th'sun
So vanished; which foreshowed our princely eagle,
Th'imperial Cæsar, should again unite
His favour with the radiant Cymbeline,
Which shines here in the west.

CYMBELINE. Laud we the gods,
And let our crookéd smokes climb to their nostrils
From our blest altars. Publish we this peace
To all our subjects. Set we forward; let
A Roman and a British ensign wave 480
Friendly together; so through Lud's town march,
And in the temple of great Jupiter
Our peace we'll ratify; seal it with feasts.
Set on there. Never was a war did cease,
Ere bloody hands were washed, with such a peace.
They go

Pericles, Prince of Tyre

The scene: dispersedly in various countries

CHARACTERS IN THE PLAY

ANTIOCHUS, *King of Antioch*
PERICLES, *Prince of Tyre*
HELICANUS
ESCANES } *two lords of Tyre*
SIMONIDES, *King of Pentapolis*
CLEON, *Governor of Tharsus*
LYSIMACHUS, *Governor of Mytilene*
CERIMON, *a lord of Ephesus*
THALIARD, *a lord of Antioch*
PHILEMON, *servant to Cerimon*
LEONINE, *servant to Dionyza*
Marshal

A Pandar
BOULT, *his servant*
The daughter of Antiochus
DIONYZA, *wife to Cleon*
THAISA, *daughter to Simonides*
MARINA, *daughter to Pericles and Thaisa*
LYCHORIDA, *nurse to Marina*
A Bawd
Lords, Knights, Gentlemen, Sailors, Pirates, Fishermen,
   and Messengers
DIANA
GOWER, *as Chorus*

Pericles, Prince of Tyre

ACT 1

Prologue: *Before the palace of Antioch, with heads
displayed above the entrance*

Enter Gower, as Chorus

GOWER. To sing a song that old was sung,
From ashes ancient Gower is come,
Assuming man's infirmities,
To glad your ear and please your eyes.
It hath been sung at festivals,
On ember-eves and holy ales;
And lords and ladies in their lives
Have read it for restoratives;
The purchase is to make men glorious;
Et bonum quo antiquius, eo melius.　　　　10
If you, born in these latter times
When wit's more ripe, accept my rhymes,
And that to hear an old man sing
May to your wishes pleasure bring,
I life would wish, and that I might
Waste it for you like taper-light.
This Antioch, then; Antiochus the great
Built up this city for his chiefest seat,
The fairest in all Syria:
I tell you what mine authors say:　　　　20
This king unto him took a fere,
Who died and left a female heir,
So buxom, blithe and full of face
As heaven had lent her all his grace;
With whom the father liking took,
And her to incest did provoke.
Bad child, worse father, to entice his own
To evil should be done by none.
But custom what they did begin
Made with long use account no sin.　　　　30
The beauty of this sinful dame
Made many princes thither frame,
To seek her as a bed-fellow,
In marriage-pleasures play-fellow;
Which to prevent he made a law,
To keep her still and men in awe,
That whoso asked her for his wife,
His riddle told not, lost his life.
So for her many a wight did die,
As yon grim looks do testify.　　　　40
What now ensues, to the judgement of your eye
I give my cause, who best can justify.　　*He goes*

Scene 1

Enter Antiochus, Prince Pericles and followers

ANTIOCHUS. Young Prince of Tyre, you have at large
received
The danger of the task you undertake.
PERICLES. I have, Antiochus, and, with a soul
Embold'ned with the glory of her praise,
Think death no hazard in this enterprise.
ANTIOCHUS. Bring in our daughter, clothéd like a
bride,

For the embracements even of Jove himself;
At whose conception, till Lucina reigned,
Nature this dowry gave: to glad her presence,
The senate-house of planets all did sit,　　　　10
To knit in her their best perfections.

Music. Enter Antiochus' Daughter

PERICLES. See where she comes, apparelled like the
spring,
Graces her subjects, and her thoughts the king
Of every virtue gives renown to men!
Her face the book of praises, where is read
Nothing but curious pleasures, as from thence
Sorrow were ever razed, and testy wrath
Could never be her mild companion.
You gods that made me man and sway in love,
That have inflamed desire in my breast　　　　20
To taste the fruit of yon celestial tree
Or die in the adventure, be my helps,
As I am son and servant to your will,
To compass such a boundless happiness!
ANTIOCHUS. Prince Pericles—
PERICLES. That would be son to great Antiochus.
ANTIOCHUS. Before thee stands this fair Hesperides,
With golden fruit, but dangerous to be touched;
For death-like dragons here affright thee hard.
Her face, like heaven, enticeth thee to view　　　　30
Her countless glory, which desert must gain;
And which without desert because thine eye
Presumes to reach, all the whole heap must die.
Yon sometimes famous princes, like thyself,
Drawn by report, advent'rous by desire,
Tell thee, with speechless tongues and semblance
pale,
That without covering save yon field of stars,
Here they stand martyrs, slain in Cupid's wars;
And with dead cheeks advise thee to desist
For going on death's net, whom none resist.　　　　40
PERICLES. Antiochus, I thank thee, who hath taught
My frail mortality to know itself,
And by those fearful objects to prepare
This body, like to them, to what I must;
For death remembered should be like a mirror,
Who tells us life's but breath, to trust it error.
I'll make my will then, and, as sick men do,
Who know the world, see heaven, but feeling woe
Gripe not at earthly joys as erst they did,
So I bequeath a happy peace to you　　　　50
And all good men, as every prince should do;
My riches to the earth from whence they came;
But my unspotted fire of love to you.
　　　　　　　　　　　　To the princess
Thus ready for the way of life or death,
I wait the sharpest blow, Antiochus.
ANTIOCHUS. Scorning advice, read the conclusion
then:
Which read and not expounded, 'tis decreed,
As these before thee thou thyself shalt bleed.
DAUGHTER. Of all 'sayed yet, mayst thou prove
prosperous!

Of all 'sayed yet, I wish thee happiness!
PERICLES. Like a bold champion I assume the lists,
  Nor ask advice of any other thought
  But faithfulness and courage.

He reads the riddle

'I am no viper, yet I feed
  On mother's flesh that did me breed.
  I sought a husband, in which labour
  I found that kindness from a father.
  He's father, son, and husband mild;
  I mother, wife, and yet his child.
  How this may be, and yet in two,
  As you will live, resolve it you.'

[*aside*] Sharp physic is the last: but, O you powers
That gives heaven countless eyes to view men's acts,
Why cloud they not their sights perpetually,
If this be true, which makes me pale to read it?
Fair glass of light, I loved you, and could still,
Were not this glorious casket stored with ill.
But I must tell you, now my thoughts revolt;
For he's no man on whom perfections wait
That, knowing sin within, will touch the gate.
You are a fair viol and your sense the strings,
Who, fingered to make man his lawful music,
Would draw heaven down and all the gods to hearken,
But being played upon before your time,
Hell only danceth at so harsh a chime.
Good sooth, I care not for you.
ANTIOCHUS. Prince Pericles, touch not, upon thy life,
  For that's an article within our law,
  As dangerous as the rest. Your time's expired:
  Either expound now or receive your sentence.
PERICLES. Great king,
Few love to hear the sins they love to act;
'Twould braid yourself too near for me to tell it.
Who has a book of all that monarchs do,
He's more secure to keep it shut than shown;
For vice repeated is like the wand'ring wind,
Blows dust in others' eyes, to spread itself;
And yet the end of all is bought thus dear,
The breath is gone, and the sore eyes see clear
To stop the air would hurt them. The blind mole casts
Copped hills towards heaven, to tell the earth is thronged
By man's oppression; and the poor worm doth die for't.
Kings are earth's gods; in vice their law's their will;
And if Jove stray, who dares say Jove doth ill?
It is enough you know; and it is fit,
What being more known grows worse, to smother it.
All love the womb that their first being bred,
Then give my tongue like leave to love my head.
ANTIOCHUS [*aside*]. Heaven, that I had thy head! He has
  found the meaning
But I will gloze with him. [*aloud*] Young prince of Tyre,
  Though by the tenour of our strict edict,
  Your exposition misinterpreting,
  We might proceed to cancel of your days;
  Yet hope, succeeding from so fair a tree
  As your fair self, doth tune us otherwise.
  Forty days longer we do respite you;

If by which time our secret be undone,
This mercy shows we'll joy in such a son;
And until then your entertain shall be
As doth befit our honour and your worth.

All but Pericles go

PERICLES. How courtesy would seem to cover sin,
When what is done is like an hypocrite,
The which is good in nothing but in sight!
If it be true that I interpret false,
Then were it certain you were not so bad
As with foul incest to abuse your soul;
Where now you're both a father and a son,
By your uncomely claspings with your child,
Which pleasures fits a husband, not a father;
And she an eater of her mother's flesh,
By the defiling of her parents' bed;
And both like serpents are, who though they feed
On sweetest flowers, yet they poison breed.
Antioch, farewell! for wisdom sees, those men
Blush not in actions blacker than the night,
Will shun no course to keep them from the light.
One sin, I know, another doth provoke;
Murder's as near to lust as flame to smoke.
Poison and treason are the hands of sin,
Ay, and the targets, to put off the shame.
Then, lest my life be cropped to keep you clear,
By flight I'll shun the danger which I fear.   *He goes*

Re-enter Antiochus

ANTIOCHUS. He hath found the meaning,
  For which we mean to have his head.
  He must not live to trumpet forth my infamy,
  Nor tell the world Antiochus doth sin
  In such a loathed manner;
  And therefore instantly this prince must die;
  For by his fall my honour must keep high.
  Who attends us there?

Enter Thaliard

THALIARD. Doth your highness call?
ANTIOCHUS. Thaliard, you are of our chamber, Thaliard,
  And our mind partakes her private actions
  To your secrecy; and for your faithfulness
  We will advance you, Thaliard.
  Behold, here's poison, and here's gold;
  We hate the prince of Tyre, and thou must kill him:
  It fits thee not to ask the reason why;
  Because we bid it. Say, is it done?
THALIARD. My lord, 'tis done.
ANTIOCHUS.   Enough.

Enter a Messenger

Let your breath cool yourself, telling your haste.
MESSENGER. My lord, prince Pericles is fled.   *He goes*
ANTIOCHUS. As thou wilt live, fly after; and like an
  arrow shot from a well experienced archer hits the
  mark his eye doth level at, so thou never return
  unless thou say 'Prince Pericles is dead.'
THALIARD. My lord, if I can get him within my pistol's
  length, I'll make him sure enough: so, farewell to
  your highness.
ANTIOCHUS. Thaliard, adieu! [*Thaliard goes*] Till
  Pericles be dead,
  My heart can lend no succour to my head.

He goes

Scene 2: *Tyre. A room in the palace*

Enter Pericles

PERICLES [*to lords without*]. Let none disturb us. Why
    should this change of thoughts.
The sad companion, dull-eyed melancholy,
Be my so used a guest as not an hour
In the day's glorious walk, or peaceful night,
The tomb where grief should sleep, can breed me
    quiet?
Here pleasures court mine eyes, and mine eyes
    shun them,
And danger, which I feared, is at Antioch,
Whose arm seems far too short to hit me here;
Yet neither pleasure's art can joy my spirits,
Nor yet the other's distance comfort me.   10
Then it is thus: the passions of the mind,
That have their first conception by misdread,
Have after-nourishment and life by care;
And what was first but fear what might be done,
Grows elder now and cares it be not done.
And so with me: the great Antiochus,
'Gainst whom I am too little to contend,
Since he's so great can make his will his act,
Will think me speaking, though I swear to silence;
Nor boots it me to say I honour him,   20
If he suspect I may dishonour him.
And what may make him blush in being known,
He'll stop the course by which it might be known;
With hostile forces he'll o'erspread the land,
And with th'ostent of war will look so huge,
Amazement shall drive courage from the state,
Our men be vanquished ere they do resist,
And subjects punished that ne'er thought offence:
Which care of them, not pity of myself,
Who am no more but as the tops of trees   30
Which fence the roots they grow by and defend
    them,
Makes both my body pine and soul to languish,
And punish that before that he would punish.

Enter Helicanus, with other Lords

FIRST LORD. Joy and all comfort in your sacred breast!
SECOND LORD. And keep your mind, till you return to
    us,
Peaceful and comfortable!
HELICANUS. Peace, peace, and give experience tongue.
They do abuse the king that flatter him:
For flattery is the bellows blows up sin;
The thing the which is flattered, but a spark,   40
To which that blast gives heat and stronger glowing;
Whereas reproof, obedient and in order,
Fits kings, as they are men, for they may err.
When Signior Soothe here does proclaim a peace,
He flatters you, makes war upon your life.
Prince, pardon me, or strike me, if you please;
                              Kneeling
I cannot be much lower than my knees.
PERICLES. All leave us else; but let your cares o'erlook
What shipping and what lading's in our haven,
And then return to us. [*the lords go*] Helicanus, thou 50
Hast movéd us: what seest thou in our looks?
HELICANUS. An angry brow, dread lord.
PERICLES. If there be such a dart in princes' frowns,
How durst thy tongue move anger to our face?
HELICANUS. How dares the plants look up to heaven,

From whence they have their nourishment?
PERICLES. Thou knowest I have power to take thy life
    from thee.
HELICANUS. I have ground the axe myself;
Do but you strike the blow.
PERICLES. Rise, prithee, rise; sit down; thou art no
    flatterer;   60
I thank thee for't; and heaven forbid
That kings should let their ears hear their faults hid!
Fit counsellor and servant for a prince,
Who by thy wisdom makes a prince thy servant,
What wouldst thou have me do?
HELICANUS.   To bear with patience
Such griefs as you do lay upon yourself.
PERICLES. Thou speak'st like a physician, Helicanus,
That ministers a potion unto me
That thou wouldst tremble to receive thyself.
Attend me then: I went to Antioch,   70
Where as thou know'st against the face of death
I sought the purchase of a glorious beauty,
From whence an issue I might propagate,
Are arms to princes and bring joys to subjects.
Her face was to mine eye beyond all wonder;
The rest—hark in thine ear—as black as incest;
Which by my knowledge found, the sinful father
Seemed not to strike, but smooth; but thou know'st
    this,
'Tis time to fear when tyrants seems to kiss.
Which fear so grew in me, I hither fled,   80
Under the covering of a careful night,
Who seemed my good protector; and, being here,
Bethought me what was past, what might succeed.
I knew him tyrannous; and tyrants' fears
Decrease not, but grow faster than the years;
And should he doubt, as 'tis no doubt he doth,
That I should open to the list'ning air
How many worthy princes' bloods were shed,
To keep his bed of blackness un-laid-ope,
To lop that doubt, he'll fill this land with arms,   90
And make pretence of wrong that I have done him;
When all, for mine, if I may call offence,
Must feel war's blow, who spares not innocence:
Which love to all, of which thyself art one,
Who now reprovedst me for't,—
HELICANUS.   Alas, sir!
PERICLES. Drew sleep out of mine eyes, blood from my
    cheeks,
Musings into my mind, with thousand doubts
How I might stop this tempest ere it came;
And finding little comfort to relieve them,
I thought it princely charity to grieve them.   100
HELICANUS. Well, my lord, since you have given me
    leave to speak,
Freely will I speak. Antiochus you fear,
And justly, too, I think you fear the tyrant
Who either by public war or private treason
Will take away your life.
Therefore, my lord, go travel for a while,
Till that his rage and anger be forgot,
Or till the Destinies do cut his thread of life.
Your rule direct to any; if to me,
Day serves not light more faithful than I'll be.   110
PERICLES. I do not doubt thy faith;
But should he wrong my liberties in my absence?
HELICANUS. We'll mingle our bloods together in the
    earth,

From whence we had our being and our birth.

PERICLES. Tyre, I now look from thee then, and to
    Tharsus
Intend my travel, where I'll hear from thee;
And by whose letters I'll dispose myself.
The care I had and have of subjects' good
On thee I lay, whose wisdom's strength can bear it.
I'll take thy word for faith, not ask thine oath: 120
Who shuns not to break one will crack them both.
But in our orbs we'll live so round and safe,
That time of both this truth shall ne'er convince,
Thou show'dst a subject's shine, I a true prince'.
                                 They go

Scene 3: *Tyre. An ante-chamber in the palace*

Enter Thaliard solus

THALIARD. So, this is Tyre, and this the court. Here
    must I kill King Pericles; and if I do it not, I am sure
    to be hanged at home: 'tis dangerous. Well, I per-
    ceive he was a wise fellow and had good discretion,
    that, being bid to ask what he would of the king,
    desired he might know none of his secrets: now do I
    see he had some reason for't; for if a king bid a man
    be a villain, he's bound by the indenture of his oath
    to be one. Husht! here comes the lords of Tyre.

Enter Helicanus, Escanes, with other Lords

HELICANUS. You shall not need, my fellow peers of
    Tyre,
Further to question of your king's departure.   10
His sealed commission left in trust with me
Does speak sufficiently he's gone to travel.
THALIARD [*aside*]. How? the king gone?
HELICANUS. If further yet you will be satisfied,
Why, as it were unlicensed of your loves,
He would depart, I'll give some light unto you.
Being at Antioch—
THALIARD [*aside*].   What from Antioch?
HELICANUS. Royal Antiochus—on what cause I know
    not—
Took some displeasure at him; at least he judged so; 20
And doubting lest that he had erred or sinned,
To show his sorrow, he'ld correct himself;
So puts himself unto the shipman's toil,
With whom each minute threatens life or death.
THALIARD [*aside*]. Well, I perceive I shall not be hanged
    now, although I would;
But since he's gone, the king's ears it must please;
He scaped the land, to perish at the seas.
I'll present myself. Peace to the lords of Tyre!
HELICANUS. Lord Thaliard from Antiochus is
    welcome.
THALIARD. From him I come   30
With message unto princely Pericles;
But since my landing I have understood
Your lord has betook himself to unknown travels,
My message must return from whence it came.
HELICANUS. We have no reason to desire it,
Commended to our master, not to us;
Yet, ere you shall depart, this we desire,
As friends to Antioch, we may feast in Tyre.
                                 They go

Scene 4: *Tharsus. A room in the Governor's house*

*Enter Cleon the Governor of Tharsus, with his wife
Dionyza and others*

CLEON. My Dionyza, shall we rest us here,
And by relating tales of others' griefs,
See if 'twill teach us to forget our own?
DIONYZA. That were to blow at fire in hope to
    quench it;
For who digs hills because they do aspire
Throws down one mountain to cast up a higher.
O my distresséd lord, even such our griefs are;
Here they are but felt, and seen with mischief's eyes,
But like to groves, being topped, they higher rise.
CLEON. O Dionyza,   10
Who wanteth food, and will not say he wants it,
Or can conceal his hunger till he famish?
Our tongues and sorrows to sound deep
Our woes into the air; our eyes to weep,
Till tongues fetch breath that may proclaim them
    louder;
That, if heaven slumber while their creatures want,
They may awake their helps to comfort them.
I'll then discourse our woes, felt several years,
And wanting breath to speak help me with tears.
DIONYZA. I'll do my best, sir.   20
CLEON. This Tharsus, o'er which I have the
    government,
A city on whom plenty held full hand,
For riches strewed herself even in her streets;
Whose towers bore heads so high they kissed the
    clouds,
And strangers ne'er beheld but wond'red at;
Whose men and dames so jetted and adorned,
Like one another's glass to trim them by;
Their tables were stored full, to glad the sight,
And not so much to feed on as delight;
All poverty was scorned, and pride so great,   30
The name of help grew odious to repeat.
DIONYZA. O, 'tis too true.
CLEON. But see what heaven can do by this our
    change:
Those mouths, who but of late earth, sea and air
Were all too little to content and please,
Although they gave their creatures in abundance,
As houses are defiled for want of use,
They are now starved for want of exercise,
Those palates who, not yet two summers younger,
Must have inventions to delight the taste,   40
Would now be glad of bread, and beg for it;
Those mothers who, to nuzzle up their babes,
Thought nought too curious, are ready now
To eat those little darlings whom they loved.
So sharp are hunger's teeth, that man and wife
Draw lots who first shall die to lengthen life.
Here stands a lord, and there a lady weeping;
Here many sink, yet those which see them fall
Have scarce strength left to give them burial.
Is not this true?   50
DIONYZA. Our cheeks and hollow eyes do witness it.
CLEON. O, let those cities that of plenty's cup
And her prosperities so largely taste,
With their superfluous riots, hear these tears!
The misery of Tharsus may be theirs.

LORD. Where's the lord governor?

CLEON. Here.
  Speak out thy sorrows which thou bring'st in haste,
  For comfort is too far for us to expect.

LORD. We have descried, upon our neighbouring
    shore,   60
  A portly sail of ships make hitherward.

CLEON. I thought as much.
  One sorrow never comes but brings an heir,
  That may succeed as his inheritor;
  And so in ours: some neighbouring nation,
  Taking advantage of our misery,
  Hath stuffed the hollow vessels with their power,
  To beat us down, the which are down already,
  And make a conquest of unhappy men,
  Whereas no glory's got to overcome.   70

LORD. That's the least fear; for, by the semblance
  Of their white flags displayed, they bring us peace,
  And come to us as favourers, not as foes.

CLEON. Thou speak'st like him's untutored to repeat:
  Who makes the fairest show means most deceit.
  But bring they what they will, what need we fear?
  On ground's the lowest, and we are half way there.
  Go tell their general we attend him here,
  To know for what he comes and whence he comes
  And what he craves.   80

LORD. I go, my lord.   *He goes*

CLEON. Welcome is peace, if he on peace consist;
  If wars, we are unable to resist.

Enter Pericles with Attendants

PERICLES. Lord governor, for so we hear you are,
  Let not our ships and number of our men
  Be like a beacon fired t'amaze your eyes.
  We have heard your miseries as far as Tyre,
  And seen the desolation of your streets;
  Nor come we to add sorrow to your tears,
  But to relieve them of their heavy load;   90
  And these our ships, you happily may think
  Are like the Trojan horse was stuffed within
  With bloody veins expecting overthrow,
  Are stored with corn to make your needy bread,
  And give them life whom hunger starved half dead.

ALL. The gods of Greece protect you!
  And we'll pray for you.

PERICLES.   Arise, I pray you, rise;
  We do not look for reverence, but for love
  And harbourage for ourself, our ships and men.

CLEON. The which when any shall not gratify,   100
  Or pay you with unthankfulness in thought,
  Be it our wives, our children, or ourselves,
  The curse of heaven and men succeed their evils!
  Till when,—the which I hope shall ne'er be seen—
  Your grace is welcome to our town and us.

PERICLES. Which welcome we'll accept; feast here
    awhile,
  Until our stars that frown lend us a smile.
                       They go

ACT 2
Prologue

Enter Gower

GOWER. Here have you seen a mighty king
  His child, I wis, to incest bring;
  A better prince and benign lord
  Prove awful both in deed and word.

Be quiet then as men should be,
Till he hath passed necessity.
I'll show you those in trouble's reign
Losing a mite, a mountain gain.
The good in conversation,
To whom I give my benison,   10
Is still at Tharsus, where each man
Thinks all is writ he speken can;
And, to remember what he does,
Build his statue to make him glorious.
But tidings to the contrary
Are brought your eyes; what need speak I?

Dumb Show

*Enter, at one door, Pericles, talking with Cleon; all the
train with them. Enter, at another door, a Gentleman, with
a letter to Pericles; Pericles shows the letter to Cleon,
Pericles gives the Messenger a reward, and knights him.
Exit Pericles at one door, and Cleon at another*

Good Helicane, that stayed at home,
Not to eat honey like a drone
From others' labours; for though he strive
To killen bad, keep good alive;   20
And to fulfil his prince' desire,
Sends word of all that haps in Tyre:
How Thaliard came full bent with sin
And had intent to murder him;
And that in Tharsus was not best
Longer for him to make his rest.
He, doing so, put forth to seas,
Where when men been, there's seldom ease;
For now the wind begins to blow;
Thunder above and deeps below   30
Makes such unquiet that the ship
Should house him safe is wrecked and split;
And he, good prince, having all lost,
By waves from coast to coast is tossed.
All perishen of man, of pelf,
Ne aught escapened but himself;
Till fortune, tired with doing bad,
Threw him ashore, to give him glad.
And here he comes. What shall be next,
Pardon old Gower,—this 'longs the text.   *He goes* 40

Scene 1: *Pentapolis. An open place by the sea-side*

Enter Pericles, wet

PERICLES. Yet cease your ire, you angry stars of heaven!
  Wind, rain, and thunder, remember, earthly man
  Is but a substance that must yield to you;
  And I, as fits my nature, do obey you.
  Alas, the seas hath cast me on the rocks,
  Washed me from shore to shore, and left me breath
  Nothing to think on but ensuing death.
  Let it suffice the greatness of your powers
  To have bereft a prince of all his fortunes;
  And having thrown him from your wat'ry grave,   10
  Here to have death in peace is all he'll crave.

Enter three Fishermen

1 FISHERMAN. What, ho, Pilch!

2 FISHERMAN. Ha, come and bring away the nets!

1 FISHERMAN. What, Patchbreech, I say!

3 FISHERMAN. What say you, master?

1 FISHERMAN. Look how thou stirrest now! come away, or I'll fetch thee with a wanion.

3 FISHERMAN. Faith, master, I am thinking of the poor men that were cast away before us even now.

1 FISHERMAN. Alas, poor souls, it grieved my heart to 20 hear what pitiful cries they made to us to help them, when, well-a-day, we could scarce help ourselves.

3 FISHERMAN. Nay, master, said not I as much when I saw the porpoise, how he bounced and tumbled? they say they're half fish, half flesh: a plague on them, they ne'er come but I look to be washed. Master, I marvel how the fishes live in the sea.

1 FISHERMAN. Why, as men do a-land: the great ones eat up the little ones. I can compare our rich misers to nothing so fitly as to a whale; a' plays and tumbles, 30 driving the poor fry before him, and at last devours them all at a mouthful: such whales have I heard on a'th'land, who never leave gaping till they ha' swallowed the whole parish, church, steeple, bells, and all.

PERICLES [aside]. A pretty moral.

3 FISHERMAN. But, master, if I had been the sexton, I would have been that day in the belfry.

2 FISHERMAN. Why, man?

3 FISHERMAN. Because he should have swallowed me 40 too; and when I had been in his belly, I would have kept such a jangling of the bells, that he should never have left till he cast bells, steeple, church, and parish, up again. But if the good King Simonides were of my mind,—

PERICLES [aside]. Simonides?

3 FISHERMAN. We would purge the land of these drones, that rob the bee of her honey.

PERICLES [aside]. How from the finny subject of the sea
These fishers tell the infirmities of men;   50
And from their wat'ry empire recollect
All that may men approve or men detect!
Peace be at your labour, honest fishermen.

2 FISHERMAN. Honest! good fellow, what's that? If it be a day fits you, search out of the calendar, and nobody look after it.

PERICLES. May see the sea hath cast upon your coast—

2 FISHERMAN. What a drunken knave was the sea to cast thee in our way!

PERICLES. A man whom both the waters and the wind, 60
In that vast tennis-court, hath made the ball
For them to play upon, entreats you pity him;
He asks of you, that never used to beg.

1 FISHERMAN. No, friend, cannot you beg? Here's them in our country of Greece gets more with begging than we can do with working.

2 FISHERMAN. Canst thou catch any fishes then?

PERICLES. I never practised it.

2 FISHERMAN. Nay, then thou wilt starve, sure; for here's nothing to be got now-a-days, unless thou 70 canst fish for't.

PERICLES. What I have been I have forgot to know;
But what I am, want teaches me to think on:
A man thronged up with cold; my veins are chill,
And have no more of life than may suffice
To give my tongue that heat to ask your help;
Which if you shall refuse, when I am dead,
For that I am a man, pray you see me buried.

1 FISHERMAN. Die quoth-a? Now gods forbid't, an I have a gown here; come, put it on; keep thee warm. 80

Now, afore me, a handsome fellow! Come, thou shalt go home, and we'll have flesh for holidays, fish for fasting-days, and moreo'er puddings and flap-jacks, and thou shalt be welcome.

PERICLES. I thank you, sir.

2 FISHERMAN. Hark you, my friend; you said you could not beg.

PERICLES. I did but crave.

2 FISHERMAN. But crave? Then I'll turn craver too, and so I shall 'scape whipping.   90

PERICLES. Why, are your beggars whipped then?

2 FISHERMAN. O, not all, my friend, not all; for if all your beggars were whipped, I would wish no better office than to be beadle. But, master, I'll go draw up the net.   He goes with 3 Fisherman

PERICLES [aside]. How well this honest mirth becomes their labour!

1 FISHERMAN. Hark you, sir, do you know where ye are?

PERICLES. Not well.

1 FISHERMAN. Why, I'll tell you: this is called Penta- 100 polis, and our king the good Simonides.

PERICLES. The good Simonides, do you call him?

1 FISHERMAN. Ay, sir; and he deserves so to be called for his peaceable reign and good government.

PERICLES. He is a happy king, since he gains from his subjects the name of good by his government. How far is his court distant from this shore?

1 FISHERMAN. Marry, sir, half a day's journey; and I'll tell you, he hath a fair daughter, and to-morrow 110 is her birthday; and there are princes and knights come from all parts of the world to joust and tourney for her love.

PERICLES. Were my fortunes equal to my desires,
I could wish to make one there.

1 FISHERMAN. O, sir, things must be as they may; and what a man cannot get, he may lawfully deal for his wife's soul.

Enter the two Fishermen, drawing up a net

2 FISHERMAN. Help, master, help! here's a fish hangs in the net, like a poor man's right in the law; 'twill 120 hardly come out. Ha! bots on't, 'tis come at last, and 'tis turned to a rusty armour.

PERICLES. An armour, friends! I pray you, let me see it.

Thanks, Fortune, yet, that after all thy crosses
Thou givest me somewhat to repair myself;
And though it was mine own, part of my heritage,
Which my dead father did bequeath to me,
With this strict charge, even as he left his life,
'Keep it, my Pericles; it hath been a shield
'Twixt me and death:'—and pointed to this brace— 130
'For that it saved me, keep it; in like necessity—
The which the gods protect thee from!—may
defend thee.'
It kept where I kept, I so dearly loved it;
Till the rough seas, that spares not any man,
Took it in rage, though calmed have given't again:
I thank thee for't: my shipwreck now's no ill,
Since I have here my father gave in his will.

1 FISHERMAN. What mean you, sir?

PERICLES. To beg of you, kind friends, this coat of worth,
For it was sometime target to a king;   140
I know it by this mark, He loved me dearly,

And for his sake I wish the having of it;
And that you'ld guide me to your sovereign's court,
Where with it I may appear a gentleman;
And if that ever my low fortunes better,
I'll pay your bounties; till then rest your debtor.

I FISHERMAN. Why, wilt thou tourney for the lady?

PERICLES. I'll show the virtue I have borne in arms.

I FISHERMAN. Why, d'ye take it, and the gods give
thee good on't! 150

2 FISHERMAN. Ay, but hark you, my friend; 'twas we
that made up this garment through the rough seams
of the waters: there are certain condolements, certain vails. I hope, sir, if you thrive, you'll remember
from whence you had it.

PERICLES. Believe't, I will.
By your furtherance I am clothed in steel;
And spite of all the rapture of the sea
This jewel holds his building on my arm.
Unto thy value I will mount myself 160
Upon a courser, whose delightful steps
Shall make the gazer joy to see him tread.
Only, my friends, I yet am unprovided
Of a pair of bases.

2 FISHERMAN. We'll sure provide: thou shalt have my
best gown to make thee a pair; and I'll bring thee
to the court myself.

PERICLES. Then honour be but equal to my will,
This day I'll rise, or else add ill to ill. *They go*

Scene 2: *The same. A public way or platform leading to
the lists. A pavilion by the side of it for the reception of
the King, Princess, Lords, etc.*

Enter Simonides, Thaisa, Lords, and Attendants

SIMONIDES. Are the knights ready to begin the
triumph?

I LORD. They are, my liege,
And stay your coming to present themselves.

SIMONIDES. Return them, we are ready; and our
daughter,
In honour of whose birth these triumphs are,
Sits here, like Beauty's child, whom Nature gat
For men to see and seeing wonder at.
A Lord goes

THAISA. It pleaseth you, my royal father, to express
My commendations great, whose merit's less.

SIMONIDES. It's fit it should be so; for princes are 10
A model which heaven makes like to itself:
As jewels lose their glory if neglected,
So princes their renowns if not respected.
'Tis now your honour, daughter, to entertain
The labour of each knight in his device.

THAISA. Which, to preserve mine honour, I'll
perform.

*The first Knight passes by, and
his Squire presents his shield to
the Princess*

SIMONIDES. Who is the first that doth prefer himself?

THAISA. A knight of Sparta, my renowned father;
And the device he bears upon his shield
Is a black Ethiop reaching at the sun; 20
The word, 'Lux tua vit mihi.'

SIMONIDES. He loves you well that holds his life of you.
The second Knight passes
Who is the second that presents himself?

THAISA. A prince of Macedon, my royal father;

And the device he bears upon his shield
Is an arméd knight that's conquered by a lady;
The motto thus, in Spanish, 'Piu per dolcera que per
força.' *The third Knight passes*

SIMONIDES. And who the third?

THAISA. The third of Antioch:
And his device, a wreath of chivalry;
The word, 'Me pompae provexit apex.' 30
The fourth Knight passes

SIMONIDES. What is the fourth?

THAISA. A burning torch that's turnéd upside down;
The word, 'Qui me alit, me extinguit.'

SIMONIDES. Which shows that beauty hath his power
at will,
Which can as well inflame as it can kill.
The fifth Knight passes

THAISA. The fifth, an hand environéd with clouds,
Holding out gold that's by the touchstone tried;
The motto thus, 'Sic spectanda fides.'
The sixth Knight, Pericles, passes

SIMONIDES. And what's
The sixth and last, the which the knight himself 40
With such a graceful courtesy delivered?

THAISA. He seems to be a stranger; but his present is
A withered branch, that's only green at top;
The motto, 'In hac spe vivo.'

SIMONIDES. A pretty moral;
From the dejected state wherein he is,
He hopes by you his fortunes yet may flourish.

I LORD. He had need mean better than his outward
show
Can any way speak in his just commend;
For by his rusty outside he appears 50
To have practised more the whipstock than the
lance.

2 LORD. He well may be a stranger, for he comes
To an honoured triumph strangely furnishéd.

3 LORD. And on set purpose let his armour rust
Until this day, to scour it in the dust.

SIMONIDES. Opinion's but a fool, that makes us scan
The outward habit by the inward man.
But stay, the knights are coming; we will withdraw
Into the gallery. *They go*

Great shouts heard from the lists, and cries of 'The
mean knight'

Scene 3: *The same. A hall of state: a banquet prepared*

*Enter Simonides, Thaisa, Lords, Knights, and Attendants,
from tilting*

SIMONIDES. Knights,
To say you're welcome were superfluous.
To place upon the volume of your deeds,
As in a title-page, your worth in arms,
Were more than you expect, or more than's fit,
Since every worth in show commends itself.
Prepare for mirth, for mirth becomes a feast.
You are princes and my guests.

THAISA. But you, my knight and guest;
To whom this wreath of victory I give, 10
And crown you king of this day's happiness.

PERICLES. 'Tis more by fortune, lady, than my merit.

SIMONIDES. Call it by what you will, the day is yours;
And here, I hope, is none that envies it.
In framing artists, art hath thus decreed,

To make some good, but others to exceed;
And you are her laboured scholar. Come, queen
  o'th'feast—
For, daughter, so you are— here take your place:
Marshal the rest as they deserve their grace.
KNIGHTS. We are honoured much by good Simonides. 20
SIMONIDES. Your presence glads our days: honour we
  love;
For who hates honour hates the gods above.
MARSHAL. Sir, yonder is your place.
PERICLES.   Some other is more fit.
1 KNIGHT. Contend not, sir; for we are gentlemen
Have neither in our hearts nor outward eyes
Envied the great nor shall the low despise.
PERICLES. You are right courteous knights.
SIMONIDES.   Sit, sir, sit.
  [aside] By Jove, I wonder, that is king of thoughts,
These cates resist me, he not thought upon.
THAISA [aside]. By Juno, that is queen of marriage, 30
All viands that I eat do seem unsavoury,
Wishing him my meat.—Sure he's a gallant
  gentleman.
SIMONIDES. He's but a country gentleman; has done no
  more
Than other knights have done; has broken a staff
Or so; so let it pass.
THAISA [aside]. To me he seems like diamond to glass.
PERICLES [aside]. Yon king's to me like to my father's
  picture,
Which tells me in that glory once he was;
Had princes sit, like stars, about his throne,
And he the sun, for them to reverence;
None that beheld him but, like lesser lights, 40
Did vail their crowns to his supremacy;
Where now his son's a glow-worm in the night,
The which hath fire in darkness, none in light:
Whereby I see that Time's the king of men;
He's both their parent, and he is their grave,
And gives them what he will, not what they crave.
SIMONIDES. What, are you merry, knights?
KNIGHTS. Who can be other in this royal presence?
SIMONIDES. Here, with a cup that's stored unto the
  brim,—
As you do love, fill to your mistress' lips,— 50
We drink this health to you.
KNIGHTS.   We thank your grace.
SIMONIDES. Yet pause awhile:
Yon knight doth sit too melancholy,
As if the entertainment in our court
Had not a show might countervail his worth.
Note it not you, Thaisa?
THAISA. What is't to me, my father?
SIMONIDES. O, attend, my daughter:
Princes, in this, should live like gods above, 60
Who freely give to every one that come
To honour them;
And princes not doing so are like to gnats,
Which make a sound, but killed are wond'red at.
Therefore to make his entrance more sweet,
Here, say we drink this standing-bowl of wine to
  him.
THAISA. Alas, my father, it befits not me
Unto a stranger knight to be so bold:
He may my proffer take for an offence,
Since men take women's gifts for impudence. 70
SIMONIDES. How?

Do as I bid you, or you'll move me else.
THAISA [aside]. Now, by the gods, he could not please
  me better.
SIMONIDES. And furthermore tell him, we desire to
  know of him,
Of whence he is, his name and parentage.
THAISA. The king my father, sir, has drunk to you.
PERICLES. I thank him.
THAISA. Wishing it so much blood unto your life.
PERICLES. I thank both him and you, and pledge him
  freely.
THAISA. And further he desires to know of you   80
Of whence you are, your name and parentage.
PERICLES. A gentleman of Tyre; my name, Pericles;
My education been in arts and arms;
Who, looking for adventures in the world,
Was by the rough seas reft of ships and men,
And after shipwreck driven upon this shore.
THAISA. He thanks your grace; names himself Pericles,
A gentleman of Tyre,
Who only by misfortune of the seas
Bereft of ships and men, cast on this shore. 90
SIMONIDES. Now, by the gods, I pity his misfortune,
And will awake him from his melancholy.
Come, gentlemen, we sit too long on trifles,
And waste the time, which looks for other revels.
Even in your armours, as you are addressed,
Will well become a soldier's dance.
I will not have excuse with saying this:
Loud music is too harsh for ladies' heads,
Since they love men in arms as well as beds.

The Knights dance

So, this was well asked, 'twas so well performed. 100
Come, sir, here's a lady that wants breathing too;
And I have heard, you knights of Tyre
Are excellent in making ladies trip,
And that their measures are as excellent.
PERICLES. In those that practise them they are, my
  lord.
SIMONIDES. O, that's as much as you would be denied
Of your fair courtesy.

The knights and Ladies dance

                    Unclasp, unclasp:
Thanks, gentlemen, to all; all have done well,
[to Pericles] But you the best. Pages and lights
  conduct
These knights unto their several lodgings! Yours, sir, 110
We have given order should be next our own.
PERICLES. I am at your grace's pleasure.
SIMONIDES. Princes, it is too late to talk of love,
And that's the mark I know you level at.
Therefore each one betake him to his rest;
To-morrow all for speeding do their best.

                         They go

Scene 4: Tyre. A room in the Governor's house

Enter Helicanus and Escanes

HELICANUS. No, Escanes, know this of me,
Antiochus from incest lived not free;
For which,
The most high gods not minding longer to
Withhold the vengeance that they had in store,
Due to this heinous capital offence,

Even in the height and pride of all his glory,
When he was seated in a chariot
Of an inestimable value, and
His daughter with him, a fire from heaven came,   10
And shrivelled up their bodies, even to loathing;
For they so stunk,
That all those eyes adored them ere their fall
Scorn now their hand should give them burial.
ESCANES. 'Twas very strange.
HELICANUS. And yet but justice; for though this king
    were great,
His greatness was no guard to bar heaven's shaft,
But sin had his reward.
ESCANES.   'Tis very true.

Enter two or three Lords

1 LORD. See, not a man in private conference
    Or council has respect with him but he.   20
2 LORD. It shall no longer grieve without reproof.
3 LORD. And cursed be he that will not second it.
1 LORD. Follow me then. Lord Helicane, a word.
HELICANUS. With me? and welcome; happy day, my
    lords.
1 LORD. Know that our griefs are risen to the top,
    And now at length they overflow their banks.
HELICANUS. Your griefs! for what? wrong not the
    prince you love.
1 LORD. Wrong not yourself, then, noble Helicane;
    But if the prince do live, let us salute him,
    Or know what ground's made happy by his breath.   30
    If in the world he live, we'll seek him out;
    If in his grave he rest, we'll find him there;
    And be resolved he lives to govern us,
    Or dead, gives cause to mourn his funeral,
    And leaves us to our free election.
2 LORD. Whose death's indeed the strongest in our
    censure;
    And knowing this: kingdoms without a head,
    Like goodly buildings left without a roof
    Soon fall to ruin, your noble self,
    That best know how to rule and how to reign,   40
    We thus submit unto—our sovereign.
ALL. Live, noble Helicane!
HELICANUS. For Honour's cause, forbear your
    suffrages.
    If that you love Prince Pericles, forbear.
    Take I your wish, I leap into the seas,
    Where's hourly trouble for a minute's ease.
    A twelvemonth longer, let me entreat you
    To forbear the absence of your king;
    If in which time expired he not return,
    I shall with agéd patience bear your yoke.   50
    But if I cannot win you to this love,
    Go search like nobles, like noble subjects,
    And in your search spend your adventurous worth;
    Whom if you find and win unto return,
    You shall like diamonds sit about his crown.
1 LORD. To wisdom he's a fool that will not yield;
    And since Lord Helicane enjoineth us,
    We with our travels will endeavour it.
HELICANUS. Then you love us, we you, and we'll
    clasp hands:
    When peers thus knit, a kingdom ever stands.   60
                                                They go

Scene 5: *Pentapolis. A room in the palace*

*Enter the King, Simonides, reading of a letter, at one door:
the Knights meet him*

1 KNIGHT. Good morrow to the good Simonides.
SIMONIDES. Knights, from my daughter this I let you
    know,
    That for this twelvemonth she'll not undertake
    A married life.
    Her reason to herself is only known,
    Which from her by no means can I get.
2 KNIGHT. May we not have access to her, my lord?
SIMONIDES. Faith, by no means; she hath so strictly
    Tied her to her chamber, that 'tis impossible.
    One twelve moons more she'll wear Diana's livery;   10
    This by the eye of Cynthia hath she vowed,
    And on her virgin honour will not break it.
3 KNIGHT. Loath to bid farewell, we take our leaves.
                                        The Knights go
SIMONIDES. So,
    They are well dispatched; now to my daughter's
    letter:
    She tells me here, she'll wed the stranger knight,
    Or never more to view nor day nor light.
    'Tis well, mistress; your choice agrees with mine;
    I like that well; nay, how absolute she's in't,
    Not minding whether I dislike or no!   20
    Well, I do commend her choice;
    And will no longer have it be delayed.
    Soft, here he comes: I must dissemble it.

Enter Pericles

PERICLES. All fortune to the good Simonides!
SIMONIDES. To you as much: sir, I am beholding to
    you
    For your sweet music this last night. I do
    Protest my ears were never better fed
    With such delightful pleasing harmony.
PERICLES. It is your grace's pleasure to commend;
    Not my desert.
SIMONIDES.   Sir, you are music's master.   30
PERICLES. The worst of all her scholars, my good lord.
SIMONIDES. Let me ask you one thing:
    What do you think of my daughter, sir?
PERICLES. A most virtuous princess.
SIMONIDES. And she is fair too, is she not?
PERICLES. As a fair day in summer, wondrous fair.
SIMONIDES. Sir, my daughter thinks very well of you;
    Ay, so well, that you must be her master,
    And she will be your scholar: therefore look to it.
PERICLES. I am unworthy for her schoolmaster.   40
SIMONIDES. She thinks not so; peruse this writing else.
PERICLES [*aside*]. What's here?
    A letter, that she loves the knight of Tyre!
    'Tis the king's subtlety to have my life.
    [*aloud*] O, seek not to entrap me, gracious lord,
    A stranger and distresséd gentleman,
    That never aimed so high to love your daughter,
    But bent all offices to honour her.
SIMONIDES. Thou hast bewitched my daughter, and
    thou art
    A villain.
PERICLES.   By the gods, I have not.   50
    Never did thought of mine levy offence;
    Nor never did my actions yet commence
    A deed might gain her love or your displeasure.

SIMONIDES. Traitor, thou liest.

PERICLES.   Traitor!

SIMONIDES.   Ay, traitor.

PERICLES. Even in his throat—unless it be the king—
    That calls me traitor, I return the lie.

SIMONIDES [aside]. Now, by the gods, I do applaud his
    courage.

PERICLES. My actions are as noble as my thoughts,
    That never relished of a base descent.
    I came unto your court for honour's cause,   60
    And not to be a rebel to your state;
    And he that otherwise accounts of me,
    This sword shall prove he's honour's enemy.

SIMONIDES. No?
    Here comes my daughter, she can witness it.

Enter Thaisa

PERICLES. Then, as you are as virtuous as fair,
    Resolve your angry father, if my tongue
    Did e'er solicit, or my hand subscribe
    To any syllable that made love to you.

THAISA. Why, sir, say if you had, who takes offence 70
    At that would make me glad?

SIMONIDES. Yea, mistress, are you so peremptory?
    [aside] I am glad on't with all my heart.—
    I'll tame you; I'll bring you in subjection.
    Will you, not having my consent,
    Bestow your love and your affections
    Upon a stranger? [aside] who, for aught I know,
    May be, nor can I think the contrary,
    As great in blood as I myself.
    Therefore hear you, mistress; either frame   80
    Your will to mine—and you, sir, hear you,
    Either be ruled by me, or I will make you—
    Man and wife.
    Nay, come, your hands and lips must seal it too;
    And being joined, I'll thus your hopes destroy;
    And for a further grief,—God give you joy!
    What, are you both pleased?

THAISA.   Yes, if you love me, sir.

PERICLES. Even as my life my blood that fosters it.

SIMONIDES. What, are you both agreed?

BOTH. Yes, if't please your majesty.   90

SIMONIDES. It pleaseth me so well, that I will see you
    wed;
    And then, with what haste you can, get you to bed.
                       They go

ACT 3
Prologue

Enter Gower

GOWER. Now sleep y-slackéd hath the rout;
    No din but snores the house about,
    Made louder by the o'er-fed breast
    Of this most pompous marriage-feast.
    The cat, with eyne of burning coal,
    Now couches 'fore the mouse's hole;
    And crickets at the oven's mouth
    Sing the blither for their drouth.
    Hymen hath brought the bride to bed,
    Where by the loss of maidenhead
    A babe is moulded. Be attent,   10
    And time that is so briefly spent
    With your fine fancies quaintly eche.
    What's dark in show I'll plain with speech.

Dumb Show

*Enter Pericles and Simonides at one door, with attendants;
a Messenger meets them, kneels, and gives Pericles a letter;
Pericles shows it Simonides; the Lords kneel to him. Then
enter Thaisa with child, with Lychorida, a nurse; the
King shows her the letter; she rejoices; she and Pericles take
leave of her father, and depart with Lychorida and their
attendants. Then Simonides and the rest go*

    By many a dern and painful perch
    Of Pericles the careful search,
    By the four opposing coigns
    Which the world together joins,
    Is made with all due diligence
    That horse and sail and high expense   20
    Can stead the quest. At last from Tyre,
    Fame answering the most strange inquire,
    To th'court of King Simonides
    Are letters brought, the tenour these:
    Antiochus and his daughter dead,
    The men of Tyrus on the head
    Of Helicanus would set on
    The crown of Tyre, but he will none.
    The mutiny he there hastes t'appease;
    Says to 'em, if King Pericles   30
    Come not home in twice six moons,
    He, obedient to their dooms,
    Will take the crown. The sum of this,
    Brought hither to Pentapolis,
    Y-ravishéd the regions round,
    And every one with claps can sound,
    'Our heir-apparent is a king!
    Who dreamed, who thought of such a thing?'
    Brief, he must hence depart to Tyre.
    His queen with child makes her desire—   40
    Which who shall cross?—along to go.
    Omit we all their dole and woe.
    Lychorida, her nurse, she takes,
    And so to sea; their vessel shakes
    On Neptune's billow; half the flood
    Hath their keel cut; but fortune's mood
    Varies again; the grisléd north
    Disgorges such a tempest forth,
    That, as a duck for life that dives,
    So up and down the poor ship drives.   50
    The lady shrieks and well-a-near
    Does fall in travail with her fear;
    And what ensues in this fell storm
    Shall for itself itself perform.
    I nill relate, action may
    Conveniently the rest convey;
    Which might not what by me is told.
    In your imagination hold
    This stage the ship, upon whose deck
    The sea-tossed Pericles appears to speak.   *He goes* 60

Scene 1

Enter Pericles, a-shipboard

PERICLES. The god of this great vast, rebuke these
    surges,
    Which wash both heaven and hell; and thou that
    hast
    Upon the winds command, bind them in brass,

Having called them from the deep! O, still
Thy deaf'ning dreadful thunders; gently quench
Thy nimble sulphurous flashes! O, how, Lychorida,
How does my queen? Thou stormest venomously;
Wilt thou spit all thyself? The seaman's whistle
Is as a whisper in the ears of death,
Unheard. Lychorida!—Lucina, O   10
Divinest patroness and midwife gentle
To those that cry by night, convey thy deity
Aboard our dancing boat; make swift the pangs
Of my queen's travails! Now, Lychorida!

Enter Lychorida, with an Infant

LYCHORIDA. Here is a thing too young for such a place,
  Who, if it had conceit, would die, as I
  Am like to do; take in your arms this piece
  Of your dead queen.
PERICLES.   How? how, Lychorida?
LYCHORIDA. Patience, good sir; do not assist the storm.
  Here's all that is left living of your queen,   20
  A little daughter: for the sake of it,
  Be manly, and take comfort.
PERICLES.   O you gods!
  Why do you make us love your goodly gifts,
  And snatch them straight away? We here below
  Recall not what we give, and therein may
  Use honour with you.
LYCHORIDA.   Patience, good sir,
  Even for this charge.
PERICLES.   Now, mild may be thy life!
  For a more blusterous birth had never babe;
  Quiet and gentle thy conditions! for
  Thou art the rudeliest welcome to this world   30
  That e'er was princess' child. Happy what follows!
  Thou hast as chiding a nativity
  As fire, air, water, earth and heaven can make,
  To herald thee from the womb.
  Even at the first thy loss is more than can
  Thy portage quit, with all thou canst find here.
  Now, the good gods throw their best eyes upon't!

Enter two Sailors

1 SAILOR. What courage, sir? God save you!
PERICLES. Courage enough: I do not fear the flaw;
  It hath done to me the worst. Yet, for the love   40
  Of this poor infant, this fresh-new seafarer,
  I would it would be quiet.
1 SAILOR. Slack the bolins there! Thou wilt not, wilt
  thou? Blow, and split thyself.
2 SAILOR. But sea-room, an the brine and cloudy
  billow kiss the moon, I care not.
1 SAILOR. Sir, your queen must overboard; the sea
  works high, the wind is loud, and will not lie till the
  ship be cleared of the dead.
PERICLES. That's your superstition.   50
1 SAILOR. Pardon us, sir; with us at sea it hath been
  still observed; and we are strong in custom. Therefore briefly yield her; for she must overboard
  straight.
PERICLES. As you think meet. Most wretched queen!
LYCHORIDA. Here she lies, sir.
PERICLES. A terrible childbed hast thou had, my dear;
  No light, no fire: th'unfriendly elements
  Forgot thee utterly; nor have I time
  To give thee hallowed to thy grave, but straight   60
  Must cast thee, scarcely coffined, in the ooze;

Where, for a monument upon thy bones,
And e'er-remaining lamps, the belching whale   3.2
And humming water must o'erwhelm thy corpse,
Lying with simple shells. O Lychorida,
Bid Nestor bring me spices, ink and paper,
My casket and my jewels; and bid Nicander
Bring me the satin coffer; lay the babe
Upon the pillow; hie thee, whiles I say
A priestly farewell to her; suddenly, woman.   70
                       Lychorida goes
2 SAILOR. Sir, we have a chest beneath the hatches,
  Caulked and bituméd ready.
PERICLES. I thank thee. Mariner, say what coast is this?
2 SAILOR. We are near Tharsus.
PERICLES. Thither, gentle mariner,
  Alter thy course from Tyre. When canst thou reach
  it?
2 SAILOR. By break of day, if the wind cease.
PERICLES. O, make for Tharsus!
  There will I visit Cleon, for the babe
  Cannot hold out to Tyrus; there I'll leave it   80
  At careful nursing. Go thy ways, good mariner:
  I'll bring the body presently.   *They go*

Scene 2: Ephesus. A room in Cerimon's house

*Enter Lord Cerimon with a Servant, and persons who have
been shipwrecked*

CERIMON. Philemon, ho!

Enter Philemon

PHILEMON. Doth my lord call?
CERIMON. Get fire and meat for these poor men:
  'T'as been a turbulent and stormy night.
SERVANT. I have been in many; but such a night as this,
  Till now, I ne'er enduréd.
CERIMON. Your master will be dead ere you return;
  There's nothing can be minist'red to nature
  That can recover him. Give this to the pothecary,
  And tell me how it works.   *All but Cerimon go*

Enter two Gentlemen

1 GENTLEMAN.   Good morrow.   10
2 GENTLEMAN. Good morrow to your lordship.
CERIMON.   Gentlemen,
  Why do you stir so early?
1 GENTLEMAN. Sir,
  Our lodgings, standing bleak upon the sea,
  Shook as the earth did quake;
  The very principals did seem to rend
  And all to topple; pure surprise and fear
  Made me to quit the house.
2 GENTLEMAN. That is the cause we trouble you so
  early;
  'Tis not our husbandry.
CERIMON.   O, you say well.   20
1 GENTLEMAN. But I much marvel that your lordship,
  having
  Rich tire about you, should at these early hours
  Shake off the golden slumber of repose.
  'Tis most strange,
  Nature should be so conversant with pain,
  Being thereto not compelled.
CERIMON.   I held it ever,
  Virtue and cunning were endowments greater
  Than nobleness and riches: careless heirs

May the two latter darken and expend,
But immortality attends the former,   30
Making a man a god. 'Tis known, I ever
Have studied physic, though which secret art,
By turning o'er authorities, I have,
Together with my practice, made familiar
To me and to my aid the blest infusions
That dwells in vegetives, in metals, stones;
And I can speak of the disturbances
That nature works, and of her cures; which doth
  give me
A more content in course of true delight
Than to be thirsty after tottering honour,   40
Or tie my treasure up in silken bags,
To please the fool and death.
2 GENTLEMAN. Your honour has through Ephesus
  poured forth
Your charity, and hundreds call themselves
Your creatures, who by you have been restored;
And not your knowledge, your personal pain, but
  even
Your purse, still open, hath built Lord Cerimon
Such strong renown as time shall never [raze].

Enter two or three with a chest

1 SERVANT. So; lift there.
CERIMON. What's that?   50
1 SERVANT. Sir,
Even now did the sea toss up on our shore
This chest: 'tis of some wreck.
CERIMON. Set't down, let's look upon't.
2 GENTLEMAN. 'Tis like a coffin, sir.
CERIMON.   Whate'er it be,
'Tis wondrous heavy. Wrench it open straight.
If the sea's stomach be o'ercharged with gold,
'Tis a good constraint of fortune it belches upon us.
2 GENTLEMAN. 'Tis so, my lord.
CERIMON. How close 'tis caulked and bitumed! Did 60
  the sea cast it up?
1 SERVANT. I never saw so huge a billow, sir, as tossed
  it up on shore.
CERIMON. Wrench it open: soft! it smells most sweetly
  in my sense.
2 GENTLEMAN. A delicate odour.
CERIMON. As ever hit my nostril. So, up with it.
O you most potent gods! what's here? a corse!
2 GENTLEMAN. Most strange!
CERIMON. Shrouded in cloth of state; balmed and en- 70
  treasured with full bags of spices! A passport too!
Apollo, perfect me in the characters!
                             Reads from a scroll
  'Here I give to understand,
  If e'er this coffin drives a-land,
  I, King Pericles, have lost
  This queen, worth all our mundane cost.
  Who finds her, give her burying;
  She was the daughter of a king.
  Besides this treasure for a fee,
  The gods requite his charity!'   80
If thou livest, Pericles, thou hast a heart
That even cracks for woe! This chanced to-night.
2 GENTLEMAN. Most likely, sir.
CERIMON.   Nay, certainly to-night;
For look how fresh she looks! They were too rough
That threw her in the sea. Make a fire within.
Fetch hither all my boxes in my closet.

Death may usurp on nature many hours,
And yet the fire of life kindle again
The o'erpressed spirits. I heard of an Egyptian
That had nine hours lien dead,   90
Who was by good appliance recoveréd.

Enter one with napkins and fire

Well said, well said; the fire and cloths.
The still and woful music that we have,
Cause it to sound, beseech you.
The vial once more; how thou stirr'st, thou block!
The music there! I pray you, give her air.
Gentlemen,
This queen will live; nature awakes; a warmth
Breathes out of her; she hath not been entranced
Above five hours; see how she 'gins to blow   100
Into life's flower again!
1 GENTLEMAN.   The heavens,
Through you, increase our wonder, and set up
Your fame for ever.
CERIMON.   She is alive; behold,
Her eyelids, cases to those heavenly jewels
Which Pericles hath lost, begin to part
Their fringes of bright gold; the diamonds
Of a most praiséd water doth appear
To make the world twice rich. Live,
And make us weep to hear your fate, fair creature,
Rare as you seem to be.   *She moves*
THAISA.   O dear Diana,   110
Where am I? Where's my lord? What world is this?
2 GENTLEMAN. Is not this strange?
1 GENTLEMAN. Most rare.
CERIMON. Hush, my gentle neighbours!
Lend me your hands; to the next chamber bear her.
Get linen: now this matter must be looked to,
For her relapse is mortal. Come, come;
And Æsculapius guide us!   *They carry her away*

Scene 3: *Tharsus. A room in the Governor's house*

*Enter Pericles, Cleon, Dionyza, and Lychorida with
Marina in her arms*

PERICLES. Most honoured Cleon, I must needs be gone;
My twelve months are expired, and Tyrus stands
In a litigious peace. You, and your lady,
Take from my heart all thankfulness! The gods
Make up the rest upon you!
CLEON.   Your shafts of fortune,
Though they hurt you mortally, yet glance
Full woundingly on us.
DIONYZA.   O your sweet queen!
That the strict fates had pleased you had brought
  her hither,
To have blessed mine eyes with her!
PERICLES.   We cannot but obey
The powers above us. Could I rage and roar   10
As doth the sea she lies in, yet the end
Must be as 'tis. My gentle babe Marina,
Whom, for she was born at sea, I have named so,
  here
I charge your charity withal, leaving her
The infant of your care; beseeching you
To give her princely training, that she may
Be mannered as she is born.
CLEON.   Fear not, my lord, but think
Your grace, that fed my country with your corn,

For which the people's prayers still fall upon you,
Must in your child be thought on. If neglection   20
Should therein make me vile, the common body,
By you relieved, would force me to my duty.
But if to that my nature need a spur,
The gods revenge it upon me and mine,
To the end of generation!

PERICLES.   I believe you;
Your honour and your goodness teach me to't,
Without your vows. Till she be married, madam,
By bright Diana, whom we honour all,
Unscissored shall this hair of mine remain,
Though I show ill in't. So I take my leave.   30
Good madam, make me blessèd in your care
In bringing up my child.

DIONYZA.   I have one myself,
Who shall not be more dear to my respect
Than yours, my lord.

PERICLES.   Madam, my thanks and prayers.

CLEON. We'll bring your grace e'en to the edge
    o'th'shore,
Then give you up to the masked Neptune and
The gentlest winds of heaven.

PERICLES.   I will embrace
Your offer. Come, dearest madam. O, no tears,
Lychorida, no tears;
Look to your little mistress, on whose grace   40
You may depend hereafter. Come, my lord.
                                   They go

Scene 4: *Ephesus. A room in Cerimon's house*

Enter Cerimon and Thaisa

CERIMON. Madam, this letter, and some certain jewels,
Lay with you in your coffer; which are at your
    command.
Know you the character?

THAISA.   It is my lord's.
That I was shipped at sea, I well remember,
Even on my eaning time; but whether there
Delivered, by the holy gods,
I cannot rightly say. But since King Pericles,
My wedded lord, I ne'er shall see again,
A vestal livery will I take me to,
And never more have joy.   10

CERIMON. Madam, if this you purpose as ye speak,
Diana's temple is not distant far,
Where you may abide till your date expire.
Moreover, if you please, a niece of mine
Shall there attend you.

THAISA. My recompense is thanks, that's all;
Yet my good will is great, though the gift small.
                                   They go

ACT 4
Prologue

Enter Gower

GOWER. Imagine Pericles arrived at Tyre,
Welcomed and settlèd to his own desire.
His woeful queen we leave at Ephesus,
Unto Diana there 's a votaress.
Now to Marina bend your mind,
Whom our fast-growing scene must find
At Tharsus, and by Cleon trained
In music's letters; who hath gained

Of education all the grace,
Which makes her both the heart and place   10
Of general wonder. But, alack,
That monster envy, oft the wrack
Of earnèd praise, Marina's life
Seeks to take off by treason's knife,
And in this kind:—our Cleon hath
One daughter, and a full grown wench,
Even ripe for marriage rite; this maid
Hight Philoten; and it is said
For certain in our story, she
Would ever with Marina be;   20
Be't when she weaved the sleided silk
With fingers long, small, white as milk;
Or when she would with sharp neele wound
The cambric, which she made more sound
By hurting it; or when to th'lute
She sung, and made the night-bird mute,
That still records with moan; or when
She would with rich and constant pen
Vail to her mistress Dian; still
This Philoten contends in skill   30
With absolute Marina: so
With dove of Paphos might the crow
Vie feathers white. Marina gets
All praises, which are paid as debts,
And not as given. This so darks
In Philoten all graceful marks,
That Cleon's wife, with envy rare
A present murderer does prepare
For good Marina, that her daughter
Might stand peerless by this slaughter.   40
The sooner her vile thoughts to stead,
Lychorida, our nurse, is dead;
And cursèd Dionyza hath
The pregnant instrument of wrath
Prest for this blow. The unborn event
I do commend to your content;
Only I carried wingèd time
Post on the lame feet of my rhyme;
Which never could I so convey,
Unless your thoughts went on my way.   50
Dionyza does appear,
With Leonine, a murderer.   *He goes*

Scene 1: *Tharsus. An open place near the sea-shore*

Enter Dionyza with Leonine

DIONYZA. Thy oath remember; thou hast sworn to
    do't.
'Tis but a blow, which never shall be known.
Thou canst not do a thing in the world so soon,
To yield thee so much profit. Let not conscience,
Which is but cold, in flaming, thy love bosom,
Inflame too nicely; nor let pity, which
Even women have cast off, melt thee, but be
A soldier to thy purpose.

LEONINE. I will do't; but yet she is a goodly creature.

DIONYZA. The fitter then the gods should have her.   10
Here she comes weeping for her only mistress'
    death.
Thou art resolved?

LEONINE. I am resolved.

Enter Marina, with a basket of flowers

MARINA. No, I will rob Tellus of her weed,
　　To strew thy green with flowers; the yellows, blues,
　　The purple violets, and marigolds,
　　Shall, as a carpet, hang upon thy grave,
　　While summer-days doth last. Ay me! poor maid,
　　Born in a tempest when my mother died,
　　This world to me is as a lasting storm,   20
　　Whirring me from my friends.
DIONYZA. How now, Marina! why do you keep
　　　alone?
　　How chance my daughter is not with you?
　　Do not consume your blood with sorrowing:
　　Have you a nurse of me! Lord, how your favour's
　　Changéd with this unprofitable woe!
　　Come, give me your flowers, ere the sea mar it.
　　Walk with Leonine; the air is quick there,
　　And it pierces and sharpens the stomach.
　　Come, Leonine, take her by the arm, walk with her. 30
MARINA. No, I pray you; I'll not bereave you of your
　　servant.
DIONYZA. Come, come;
　　I love the king your father and yourself
　　With more than foreign heart. We every day
　　Expect him here: when he shall come, and find
　　Our paragon to all reports thus blasted,
　　He will repent the breadth of his great voyage;
　　Blame both my lord and me, that we have taken
　　No care to your best courses. Go, I pray you,   40
　　Walk, and be cheerful once again; resume
　　That excellent complexion, which did steal
　　The eyes of young and old. Care not for me;
　　I can go home alone.
MARINA.　　　　　　　Well, I will go;
　　But yet I have no desire to it.
DIONYZA. Come, come, I know 'tis good for you.
　　Walk half an hour, Leonine, at the least.
　　Remember what I have said.
LEONINE.　　　　　　　I warrant you, madam.
DIONYZA. I'll leave you, my sweet lady, for a while.
　　Pray, walk softly, do not heat your blood.   50
　　What! I must have care of you.
MARINA.　　　　　　　My thanks, sweet madam.
　　　　　　　　　　　　　　　　　　Dionyza goes
　　Is this wind westerly that blows?
LEONINE.　　　　　　　South-west.
MARINA. When I was born, the wind was north.
LEONINE.　　　　　　　Was't so?
MARINA. My father, as nurse said, did never fear,
　　But cried 'Good seamen!' to the sailors, galling
　　His kingly hands, haling ropes;
　　And, clasping to the mast, endured a sea
　　That almost burst the deck.
LEONINE. When was this?
MARINA. When I was born.   60
　　Never was waves nor wind more violent;
　　And from the ladder-tackle washes off
　　A canvas-climber. 'Ha!' says one, 'wolt out?'
　　And with a dropping industry they skip
　　From stem to stern; the boatswain whistles, and
　　The master calls and trebles their confusion.
LEONINE. Come, say your prayers.
MARINA. What mean you?
LEONINE. If you require a little space for prayer,
　　I grant it. Pray; but be not tedious,   70
　　For the gods are quick of ear, and I am sworn
　　To do my work with haste.

MARINA.　　　　　　　Why will you kill me?
LEONINE. To satisfy my lady.
MARINA. Why would she have me killed?
　　Now, as I can remember, by my troth,
　　I never did her hurt in all my life.
　　I never spake bad word, nor did ill turn
　　To any living creature; believe me, la,
　　I never killed a mouse, nor hurt a fly,
　　Nor trod upon a worm against my will,
　　But I wept for't. How have I offended,   80
　　Wherein my death might yield her any profit,
　　Or my life imply her any danger?
LEONINE. My commission
　　Is not to reason of the deed, but do't.
MARINA. You will not do't for all the world, I hope.
　　You are well-favoured, and your looks foreshow
　　You have a gentle heart. I saw you lately,
　　When you caught hurt in parting two that fought.
　　Good sooth, it showed well in you. Do so now.   90
　　Your lady seeks my life; come you between.
　　And save poor me, the weaker.
LEONINE.　　　　　　　I am sworn,
　　And will dispatch.　　　　　　　He seizes her

Enter Pirates

1 PIRATE. Hold, villain!　　　　　Leonine runs away
2 PIRATE. A prize! a prize!
3 PIRATE. Half-part, mates, half-part. Come let's
　　have her aboard suddenly.　　They carry off Marina

Re-enter Leonine

LEONINE. These roguing thieves serve the great pirate
　　Valdes;
　　And they have seized Marina. Let her go;
　　There's no hope she will return. I'll swear she's dead, 100
　　And thrown into the sea. But I'll see further.
　　Perhaps they will but please themselves upon her,
　　Not carry her abroad. If she remain,
　　Whom they have ravished must by me be slain.
　　　　　　　　　　　　　　　　　　He goes

Scene 2: Mytilene. A room in a brothel

Enter Pandar, Bawd, and Boult

PANDAR. Boult!
BOULT. Sir?
PANDAR. Search the market narrowly; Mytilene is full
　　of gallants. We lost too much money this mart by
　　being too wenchless.
BAWD. We were never so much out of creatures. We
　　have but poor three, and they can do no more than
　　they can do; and with continual action are even as
　　good as rotten.
PANDAR. Therefore let's have fresh ones, whate'er we 10
　　pay for them. If there be not a conscience to be used
　　in every trade, we shall never prosper.
BAWD. Thou sayest true: 'tis not our bringing up of
　　poor bastards—as, I think, I have brought up some
　　eleven—
BOULT. Ay, to eleven; and brought them down again.
　　But shall I search the market?
BAWD. What else, man? The stuff we have, a strong
　　wind will blow it to pieces, they are so pitifully
　　sodden.   20
PANDAR. Thou sayest true; they're too unwholesome,

o' conscience. The poor Transylvanian is dead, that lay with the little baggage.

BOULT. Ay, she quickly pooped him; she made him roast-meat for worms. But I'll go search the market.   *He goes*

PANDAR. Three or four thousand chequins were as pretty a proportion to live quietly, and so give over.

BAWD. Why to give over, I pray you? is it a shame to get when we are old?

PANDAR. O, our credit comes not in like the com- 30 modity, nor the commodity wages not with the danger: therefore, if in our youths we could pick up some pretty estate, 'twere not amiss to keep our door hatched. Besides, the sore terms we stand upon with the gods will be strong with us for giving o'er.

BAWD. Come, other sorts offend as well as we.

PANDAR. As well as we? ay, and better too; we offend worse. Neither is our profession any trade; it's no calling. But here comes Boult.

Re-enter Boult, with the Pirates and Marina

BOULT. Come your ways, my masters; you say she's a 40 virgin?

I PIRATE. O, sir, we doubt it not.

BOULT. Master, I have gone through for this piece you see. If you like her, so; if not, I have lost my earnest.

BAWD. Boult, has she any qualities?

BOULT. She has a good face, speaks well, and has excellent good clothes; there's no farther necessity of qualities can make her be refused.

BAWD. What's her price, Boult?

BOULT. It cannot be bated one doit of a thousand 50 pieces.

PANDAR. Well, follow me, my masters, you shall have your money presently. Wife, take her in; instruct her what she has to do, that she may not be raw in her entertainment.   *Pandar and Pirates go*

BAWD. Boult, take you the marks of her, the colour of her hair, complexion, height, her age, with warrant of her virginity; and cry 'He that will give most shall have her first.' Such a maidenhead were no cheap thing, if men were as they have been. Get 60 this done as I command you.

BOULT. Performance shall follow.   *He goes*

MARINA. Alack that Leonine was so slack, so slow! He should have struck, not spoke; or that these pirates, Not enough barbarous, had not o'erboard Thrown me to seek my mother!

BAWD. Why lament you, pretty one?

MARINA. That I am pretty.

BAWD. Come, the gods have done their part in you.

MARINA. I accuse them not. 70

BAWD. You are light into my hands, where you are like to live.

MARINA. The more my fault, To 'scape his hands where I was like to die.

BAWD. Ay, and you shall live in pleasure.

MARINA. No.

BAWD. Yes, indeed shall you, and taste gentlemen of all fashions. You shall fare well; you shall have the difference of all complexions. What do you stop your ears? 80

MARINA. Are you a woman?

BAWD. What would you have me be, an I be not a woman?

MARINA. An honest woman, or not a woman.

BAWD. Marry, whip the gosling: I think I shall have 4.2 something to do with you. Come, you're a young foolish sapling, and must be bowed as I would have you.

MARINA. The gods defend me!

BAWD. If it please the gods to defend you by men, 90 then men must comfort you, men must feed you, men stir you up. Boult's returned.

Re-enter Boult

Now, sir, hast thou cried her through the market?

BOULT. I have cried her almost to the number of her hairs; I have drawn her picture with my voice.

BAWD. And I prithee tell me, how dost thou find the inclination of the people, especially of the younger sort?

BOULT. Faith, they listened to me as they would have 100 hearkened to their father's testament. There was a Spaniard's mouth wat'red, and he went to bed to her very description.

BAWD. We shall have him here to-morrow with his best ruff on.

BOULT. To-night, to-night. But, mistress, do you know the French knight that cowers i'the hams?

BAWD. Who, Monsieur Veroles?

BOULT. Ay, he: he offered to cut a caper at the pro- clamation; but he made a groan at it, and swore he 110 would see her to-morrow.

BAWD. Well, well; as for him, he brought his disease hither: here he does but repair it. I know he will come in our shadow, to scatter his crowns in the sun.

BOULT. Well, if we had of every nation a traveller, we should lodge them with this sign.

BAWD. Pray you, come hither awhile. You have fortunes coming upon you. Mark me: you must seem to do that fearfully which you commit willingly, despise profit where you have most gain. To weep that you live as ye do makes pity in 120 your lovers: seldom but that pity begets you a good opinion, and that opinion a mere profit.

MARINA. I understand you not.

BOULT. O, take her home, mistress, take her home; these blushes of hers must be quenched with some present practice.

BAWD. Thou sayest true, i'faith, so they must; for your bride goes to that with shame which is her way to go with warrant.

BOULT. Faith, some do, and some do not. But, 130 mistress, if I have bargained for the joint—

BAWD. Thou mayest cut a morsel off the spit.

BOULT. I may so?

BAWD. Who should deny it? Come, young one, I like the manner of your garments well.

BOULT. Ay, by my faith, they shall not be changed yet.

BAWD. Boult, spend thou that in the town; report what a sojourner we have; you'll lose nothing by custom. When nature framed this piece, she meant 140 thee a good turn; therefore say what a paragon she is, and thou hast the harvest out of thine own report.

BOULT. I warrant you, mistress, thunder shall not so awake the beds of eels as my giving out her beauty stir up the lewdly inclined. I'll bring home some to-night.

BAWD. Come your ways; follow me.

MARINA. If fires be hot, knives sharp, or waters deep,
  Untied I still my virgin knot will keep.
  Diana, aid my purpose!   150
BAWD. What have we to do with Diana? Pray you,
  will you go with us?   *They go*

Scene 3: *Tharsus. A room in the Governor's house*

Enter Cleon and Dionyza

DIONYZA. Why are you foolish? Can it be undone?
CLEON. O Dionyza, such a piece of slaughter
  The sun and moon ne'er looked upon!
DIONYZA. I think you'll turn a child again.
CLEON. Were I chief lord of all this spacious world,
  I'ld give it to undo the deed. A lady,
  Much less in blood than virtue, yet a princess
  To equal any single crown o'th'earth
  I'th'justice of compare! O villain Leonine!
  Whom thou hast pois'ned too.   10
  If thou hadst drunk to him, 't had been a kindness
  Becoming well thy fact. What canst thou say
  When noble Pericles shall demand his child?
DIONYZA. That she is dead. Nurses are not the fates.
  To foster is not ever to preserve.
  She died at night; I'll say so. Who can cross it?
  Unless you play the pious innocent,
  And for an honest attribute cry out
  'She died by foul play.'
CLEON.   O, go to. Well, well.
  Of all the faults beneath the heavens, the gods   20
  Do like this worst.
DIONYZA.   Be one of those that thinks
  The petty wrens of Tharsus will fly hence
  And open this to Pericles. I do shame
  To think of what a noble strain you are
  And of how coward a spirit.
CLEON.   To such proceeding
  Who ever but his approbation added,
  Though not his prime consent, he did not flow
  From honourable sources.
DIONYZA.   Be it so, then.
  Yet none does know, but you, how she came dead,
  Nor none can know, Leonine being gone.   30
  She did distain my child, and stood between
  Her and her fortunes; none would look on her,
  But cast their gazes on Marina's face;
  Whilst ours was blurted at, and held a malkin,
  Not worth the time of day. It pierced me thorough;
  And though you call my course unnatural,
  You not your child well loving, yet I find
  It greets me as an enterprise of kindness
  Performed to your sole daughter.
CLEON.   Heavens forgive it!
DIONYZA. And as for Pericles, what should he say?   40
  We wept after her hearse, and yet we mourn.
  Her monument
  Is almost finished, and her epitaphs
  In glitt'ring golden characters express
  A general praise to her, and care in us
  At whose expense 'tis done.
CLEON.   Thou art like the harpy,
  Which, to betray, dost, with thine angel's face,
  Seize with thine eagle's talents.
DIONYZA. Ye're like one that superstitiously
  Do swear to th'gods that winter kills the flies: 50
  But yet I know you'll do as I advise.   *They go*

Scene 4

Enter Gower, before the monument of Marina at Tharsus

GOWER. Thus time we waste, and longest leagues
    make short;
  Sail seas in cockles, have and wish but for't;
  Making, to take imagination,
  From bourn to bourn, region to region.
  By you being pardoned, we commit no crime
  To use one language in each several clime
  Where our scene seems to live. I do beseech you
  To learn of me, who stand i'th'gaps to teach you
  The stages of our story. Pericles
  Is now again thwarting the wayward seas,   10
  Attended on by many a lord and knight,
  To see his daughter, all his life's delight.
  Old Helicanus goes along. Behind
  Is left to govern it, you bear in mind,
  Old Escanes, whom Helicanus late
  Advanced in time to great and high estate.
  Well-sailing ships and bounteous winds have
    brought
  This king to Tharsus—think his pilot thought;
  So with his steerage shall your thoughts go on—
  To fetch his daughter home, who first is gone.   20
  Like motes and shadows see them move awhile;
  Your ears unto your eyes I'll reconcile.

Dumb Show

Enter Pericles at one door, with all his train; Cleon and Dionyza at the other. Cleon shows Pericles the tomb; whereat Pericles makes lamentation, puts on sackcloth, and in a mighty passion departs. Then Cleon, Dionyza, and the rest go also

  See how belief may suffer by foul show!
  This borrowed passion stands for true-owed woe;
  And Pericles, in sorrow all devoured,
  With sighs shot through and biggest tears
    o'ershowered,
  Leaves Tharsus and again embarks. He swears
  Never to wash his face, nor cut his hairs.
  He puts on sackcloth, and to sea. He bears
  A tempest, which his mortal vessel tears,   30
  And yet he rides it out. Now please you wit
  The epitaph is for Marina writ
  By wicked Dionyza.
        Reads the inscription on Marina's monument
  'The fairest, sweet'st and best, lies here,
  Who withered in her spring of year.
  She was of Tyrus the king's daughter,
  On whom foul death hath made this slaughter;
  Marina was she called; and at her birth,
  Thetis, being proud, swallowed some part
    o'th'earth.
  Therefore the earth, fearing to be o'erflowed,   40
  Hath Thetis' birth-child on the heavens bestowed;
  Wherefore she does, and swears she'll never stint,
  Make raging battery upon shores of flint.'

  No visor does become black villainy
  So well as soft and tender flattery.
  Let Pericles believe his daughter's dead,
  And bear his courses to be orderéd
  By Lady Fortune; while our scene must play
  His daughter's woe and heavy well-a-day
  In her unholy service. Patience, then,   50
  And think you now are all in Mytilen.   *He goes*

Scene 5: *Mytilene. A street before the brothel*

Enter two Gentlemen from the brothel

1 GENTLEMAN. Did you ever hear the like?

2 GENTLEMAN. No, nor never shall do in such a place as this, she being once gone.

1 GENTLEMAN. But to have divinity preached there! did you ever dream of such a thing?

2 GENTLEMAN. No, no. Come, I am for no more bawdy-houses; shall's go hear the vestals sing?

1 GENTLEMAN. I'll do any thing now that is virtuous; but I am out of the road of rutting for ever.

They go

Scene 6: *The same. A room in the brothel*

Enter Pandar, Bawd, and Boult

PANDAR. Well, I had rather than twice the worth of her she had ne'er come here.

BAWD. Fie, fie upon her! she's able to freeze the god Priapus, and undo a whole generation. We must either get her ravished or be rid of her. When she should do for clients her fitment and do me the kindness of our profession, she has me her quirks, her reasons, her master-reasons, her prayers, her knees; that she would make a puritan of the devil, if he should cheapen a kiss of her.

BOULT. Faith, I must ravish her, or she'll disfurnish us of all our cavalleria and make our swearers priests.   10

PANDAR. Now, the pox upon her green-sickness for me!

BAWD. Faith, there's no way to be rid on't but by the way to the pox. Here comes the Lord Lysimachus disguised.

BOULT. We should have both lord and lown, if the peevish baggage would but give way to customers.

Enter Lysimachus

LYSIMACHUS. How now! How a dozen of virginities?   20

BAWD. Now, the gods to-bless your honour!

BOULT. I am glad to see your honour in good health.

LYSIMACHUS. You may so; 'tis the better for you that your resorters stand upon sound legs. How now, wholesome iniquity, have you that a man may deal withal, and defy the surgeon?

BAWD. We have here one, sir, if she would—but there never came her like in Mytilene.

LYSIMACHUS. If she'ld do the deed of darkness, thou wouldst say.   30

BAWD. Your honour knows what 'tis to say well enough.

LYSIMACHUS. Well, call forth, call forth.

BOULT. For flesh and blood, sir, white and red, you shall see a rose; and she were a rose indeed, if she had but—

LYSIMACHUS. What, prithee?

BOULT. O, sir, I can be modest.

LYSIMACHUS. That dignifies the renown of a bawd, no less than it gives a good report to a number to be   40 chaste.   *Boult goes*

BAWD. Here comes that which grows to the stalk; never plucked yet, I can assure you.

Re-enter Boult with Marina

Is she not a fair creature?

LYSIMACHUS. Faith, she would serve after a long   4.6 voyage at sea. Well, there's for you: leave us.

BAWD. I beseech your honour, give me leave a word, and I'll have done presently.

LYSIMACHUS. I beseech you, do.

BAWD [*to Marina*]. First, I would have you note, this   50 is an honourable man.

MARINA. I desire to find him so, that I may worthily note him.

BAWD. Next, he's the governor of this country, and a man whom I am bound to.

MARINA. If he govern the country, you are bound to him indeed; but how honourable he is in that, I know not.

BAWD. Pray you, without any more virginal fencing, will you use him kindly? He will line your apron   60 with gold.

MARINA. What he will do graciously, I will thankfully receive.

LYSIMACHUS. Ha' you done?

BAWD. My lord, she's not paced yet; you must take some pains to work her to your manage. Come, we will leave his honour and her together. Go thy ways.

Bawd, Pandar, and Boult depart

LYSIMACHUS. Now, pretty one, how long have you been at this trade?

MARINA. What trade, sir?   70

LYSIMACHUS. Why, I cannot name't but I shall offend.

MARINA. I cannot be offended with my trade. Please you to name it.

LYSIMACHUS. How long have you been of this profession?

MARINA. E'er since I can remember.

LYSIMACHUS. Did you go to't so young? Were you a gamester at five or at seven?

MARINA. Earlier too, sir, if now I be one.

LYSIMACHUS. Why, the house you dwell in proclaims   80 you to be a creature of sale.

MARINA. Do you know this house to be a place of such resort, and will come into't? I hear say you're of honourable parts and are the governor of this place.

LYSIMACHUS. Why, hath your principal made known unto you who I am?

MARINA. Who is my principal?

LYSIMACHUS. Why, your herb-woman; she that sets seeds and roots of shame and iniquity. O, you have   90 heard something of my power, and so stand aloof for more serious wooing. But I protest to thee, pretty one, my authority shall not see thee, or else look friendly upon thee. Come, bring me to some private place. Come, come.

MARINA. If you were born to honour, show it now; If put upon you, make the judgement good That thought you worthy of it.

LYSIMACHUS. How's this? How's this? Some more; be sage.

MARINA.   For me

That am a maid, though most ungentle fortune   100 Have placed me in this sty, where, since I came, Diseases have been sold dearer than physic— That the gods Would set me free from this unhallowed place, Though they did change me to the meanest bird That flies i'th'purer air!

LYSIMACHUS. I did not think thou couldst have spoke
    so well;
Ne'er dreamed thou couldst.
Had I brought hither a corrupted mind,
Thy speech had altered it. Hold, here's gold for   110
    thee:
Persever in that clear way thou goest,
And the gods strengthen thee!
MARINA.   The good gods preserve you!
LYSIMACHUS. For me, be you thoughten
That I came with no ill intent; for to me
The very doors and windows savour vilely.
Fare thee well. Thou art a piece of virtue, and
I doubt not but thy training hath been noble.
Hold, here's more gold for thee.
A curse upon him, die he like a thief,
That robs thee of thy goodness! If thou dost   120
Hear from me, it shall be for thy good.

Re-enter Boult

BOULT. I beseech your honour, one piece for me.
LYSIMACHUS. Avaunt, thou damned door-keeper!
Your house, but for this virgin that doth prop it,
Would sink, and overwhelm you. Away! *He goes*
BOULT. How's this? We must take another course
with you. If your peevish chastity, which is not
worth a breakfast in the cheapest country under the
cope, shall undo a whole household, let me be
gelded like a spaniel. Come your ways.   130
MARINA. Whither would you have me?
BOULT. I must have your maidenhead taken off, or the
common hangman shall execute it. Come your
ways. We'll have no more gentlemen driven away.
Come your ways, I say.

Re-enter Bawd and Pandar

BAWD. How now! what's the matter?
BOULT. Worse and worse, mistress; she has here
spoken holy words to the Lord Lysimachus.
BAWD. O abominable!
BOULT. She makes our profession as it were to stink   140
afore the face of the gods.
BAWD. Marry, hang her up for ever!
BOULT. The nobleman would have dealt with her like
a nobleman, and she sent him away as cold as a
snowball, saying his prayers too.
BAWD. Boult, take her away; use her at thy pleasure.
Crack the glass of her virginity, and make the rest
malleable.
BOULT. An if she were a thornier piece of ground than
she is, she shall be ploughed.   150
MARINA. Hark, hark, you gods!
BAWD. She conjures: away with her! Would she had
never come within my doors! Marry, hang you!
She's born to undo us. Will you not go the way of
womenkind? Marry, come up, my dish of chastity
with rosemary and bays! *The Bawd and Pandar go*
BOULT. Come, mistress; come your ways with me.
MARINA. Whither wilt thou have me?
BOULT. To take from you the jewel you hold so dear.
MARINA. Prithee, tell me one thing first.   160
BOULT. Come now, your one thing.
MARINA. What canst thou wish thine enemy to be?
BOULT. Why, I could wish him to be my master, or
rather, my mistress.
MARINA. Neither of these are so bad as thou art,

Since they do better thee in their command.
Thou hold'st a place, for which the pained'st fiend
Of hell would not in reputation change.
Thou art the damnéd door-keeper to every
Coistrel that comes inquiring for his Tib;   170
To the choleric fisting of every rogue
Thy ear is liable; thy food is such
As hath been belched on by infected lungs.
BOULT. What would you have me do? go to the wars,
would you? where a man may serve seven years for
the loss of a leg, and have not money enough in the
end to buy him a wooden one?
MARINA. Do any thing
But this thou doest. Empty old receptacles,
Or common shores, of filth;   180
Serve by indenture to the common hangman.
Any of these ways are yet better than this;
For what thou professest, a baboon, could he speak,
Would own a name too dear. That the gods
Would safely deliver me from this place!
Here, here's gold for thee.
If that thy master would gain by me,
Proclaim that I can sing, weave, sew, and dance,
With other virtues, which I'll keep from boast;
And I will undertake all these to teach.   190
I doubt not but this populous city will
Yield many scholars.
BOULT. But can you teach all this you speak of?
MARINA. Prove that I cannot, take me home again,
And prostitute me to the basest groom
That doth frequent your house.
BOULT. Well, I will see what I can do for thee; if I
can place thee, I will.
MARINA. But amongst honest women.
BOULT. Faith, my acquaintance lies little amongst   200
them. But since my master and mistress hath bought
you, there's no going but by their consent; therefore
I will make them acquainted with your purpose, and
I doubt not but I shall find them tractable enough.
Come, I'll do for thee what I can; come your ways.
                                                        They go

ACT 5
Prologue

Enter Gower

GOWER. Marina thus the brothel 'scapes, and chances
Into an honest house, our story says.
She sings like one immortal, and she dances
As goddess-like to her admiréd lays;
Deep clerks she dumbs, and with her neele composes
Nature's own shape, of bud, bird, branch, or berry,
That even her art sisters the natural roses;
Her inkle, silk, twin with the rubied cherry;
That pupils lacks she none of noble race,
Who pour their bounty on her, and her gain   10
She gives the curséd bawd. Here we her place;
And to her father turn our thoughts again,
Where we left him on the sea. We there him lost;
Whence, driven before the winds, he is arrived
Here where his daughter dwells; and on this coast
Suppose him now at anchor; the city strived
God Neptune's annual feast to keep; from whence
Lysimachus our Tyrian ship espies,
His banners sable, trimmed with rich expense;
And to him in his barge with fervour hies.   20

In your supposing once more put your sight;
Of heavy Pericles, think this his bark;
Where what is done in action, more, if might,
Shall be discovered, please you sit and hark.
                                        He goes

*Scene 1: On board Pericle's ship, off Mytilene. A pavilion
on deck, with a curtain before it; Pericles within, reclining
on a couch. A barge lies beside the Tyrian vessel*

*Enter two Sailors, one belonging to the Tyrian vessel, the
other to the barge; to them Helicanus*

TYRIAN SAILOR [*to the Sailor of Mytilene*]. Where is
    Lord Helicanus? he can resolve you.
    O, here he is.
    Sir, there is a barge put off from Mytilene,
    And in it is Lysimachus the governor,
    Who craves to come aboard. What is your will?
HELICANUS. That he have his. Call up some gentlemen.
TYRIAN SAILOR. Ho, gentlemen! my lord calls.

Enter two or three Gentlemen

I GENTLEMAN. Doth your lordship call?
HELICANUS. Gentlemen, there is some of worth would
    come aboard;
    I pray, greet him fairly.   10
                *The Gentlemen and the two Sailors
                descend, and go on board the barge*

*Enter from thence, Lysimachus, and Lords; with the Gentle-
men and the two Sailors*

TYRIAN SAILOR. Sir,
    This is the man that can, in aught you would,
    Resolve you.
LYSIMACHUS. Hail, reverend sir! the gods preserve you!
HELICANUS. And you, sir, to outlive the age I am,
    And die as I would do.
LYSIMACHUS.   You wish me well.
    Being on shore, honouring of Neptune's triumphs,
    Seeing this goodly vessel ride before us,
    I made to it, to know of whence you are.
HELICANUS. First, what is your place?   20
LYSIMACHUS. I am the governor of this place you
    lie before.
HELICANUS. Sir,
    Our vessel is of Tyre, in it the king;
    A man who for this three months hath not spoken
    To any one, nor taken sustenance
    But to prorogue his grief.
LYSIMACHUS. Upon what ground is his
    distemperature?
HELICANUS. 'Twould be too tedious to repeat;
    But the main grief springs from the loss
    Of a belovéd daughter and a wife.   30
LYSIMACHUS. May we not see him?
HELICANUS. You may;
    But bootless is your sight; he will not speak
    To any.
LYSIMACHUS. Yet let me obtain my wish.
HELICANUS. Behold him. [*Pericles discovered*] This was
    a goodly person,
    Till the disaster that, one mortal night,
    Drove him to this.
LYSIMACHUS. Sir king, all hail! the gods preserve you!
    Hail, royal sir!

HELICANUS. It is in vain; he will not speak to you.   40
I LORD. Sir,
    We have a maid in Mytilene, I durst wager,
    Would win some words of him.
LYSIMACHUS.   'Tis well bethought.
    She, questionless, with her sweet harmony
    And other chosen attractions, would allure,
    And make a batt'ry through his deafened ports,
    Which now are midway stopped.
    She is all happy as the fairest of all,
    And with her fellow maids is now upon
    The leafy shelter that abuts against   50
    The island's side.   *Whispers a Lord, who goes off
                                in the barge of Lysimachus*
HELICANUS. Sure, all effectless; yet nothing we'll omit
    That bears recovery's name. But, since your
    kindness
    We have stretched thus far, let us beseech you
    That for our gold we may provision have,
    Wherein we are not destitute for want,
    But weary for the staleness.
LYSIMACHUS.   O, sir, a courtesy
    Which if we should deny, the most just gods
    For every graff would send a caterpillar,
    And so inflict our province. Yet once more   60
    Let me entreat to know at large the cause
    Of your king's sorrow.
HELICANUS. Sit, sir, I will recount it to you.
    But see, I am prevented.

*The Lord returns in the barge with Marina and one of her
attendants*

LYSIMACHUS. O, here's the lady that I sent for.
    Welcome, fair one!—It's not a goodly presence?
HELICANUS. She's a gallant lady.
LYSIMACHUS. She's such a one, that, were I well assured
    Came of a gentle kind and noble stock,
    I'ld wish no better choice, and think me rarely wed.   70
    Fair one, all goodness that consists in beauty,
    Expect even here, where is a kingly patient,
    If that thy prosperous and artificial feat
    Can draw him but to answer thee in aught,
    Thy sacred physic shall receive such pay
    As thy desires can wish.
MARINA.   Sir, I will use
    My utmost skill in his recovery, provided
    That none but I and my companion maid
    Be suffered to come near him.
LYSIMACHUS.   Come, let us leave her;
    And the gods make her prosperous!   80

They withdraw; Marina sings

LYSIMACHUS. Marked he your music?
MARINA.   No, nor looked on us.
LYSIMACHUS. See, she will speak to him.
MARINA. Hail, sir! my lord, lend ear.
PERICLES. Hum, ha!   *Roughly repulses her*
MARINA. I am a maid,
    My lord, that ne'er before invited eyes,
    But have been gazed on like a comet; she speaks,
    My lord, that, may be, hath endured a grief
    Might equal yours, if both were justly weighed.
    Though wayward fortune did malign my state,   90
    My derivation was from ancestors
    Who stood equivalent with mighty kings;
    But time hath rooted out my parentage,

And to the world and awkward casualties
Bound me in servitude. [aside] I will desist;
But there is something glows upon my cheek,
And whispers in mine ear 'Go not till he speak.'
PERICLES. My fortunes—parentage—good
  parentage—
To equal mine— was it not thus? what say you?
MARINA. I said, my lord, if you did know my
  parentage,
You would not do me violence.
PERICLES. I do think so. Pray you, turn your eyes upon
  me.
You're like something that—What
  countrywoman?
Here of these shores?
MARINA.   No, nor of any shores;
Yet I was mortally brought forth, and am
No other than I appear.
PERICLES. I am great with woe, and shall deliver
  weeping.
My dearest wife was like this maid,
And such a one my daughter might have been:
My queen's square brows; her stature to an inch;
As wand-like straight, as silver-voiced;
Her eyes as jewel-like and cased as richly;
In pace another Juno;
Who starves the ears she feeds, and makes them
  hungry,
The more she gives them speech. Where do you
  live?
MARINA. Where I am but a stranger: from the deck
You may discern the place.
PERICLES.   Where were you bred?
And how achieved you these endowments, which
You make more rich to owe?
MARINA. If I
Should tell my history, it would seem like lies
Disdained in the reporting.
PERICLES.   Prithee, speak.
Falseness cannot come from thee; for thou look'st
Modest as Justice, and thou seem'st a palace
For the crowned Truth to dwell in. I will believe
  thee,
And make my senses credit thy relation
To points that seem impossible; for thou look'st
Like one I loved indeed. What were thy friends?
Didst thou not say, when I did push thee back—
Which was when I perceived thee—that thou cam'st
From good descending?
MARINA.   So indeed I did.
PERICLES. Report thy parentage. I think thou said'st
Thou hadst been tossed from wrong to injury,
And that thou thoughts' thy griefs might equal
  mine,
If both were opened.
MARINA.   Some such thing I said,
And said no more but what my thoughts
Did warrant me was likely.
PERICLES.   Tell thy story;
If thine considered prove the thousandth part
Of my endurance, thou art a man, and I
Have suffered like a girl; yet thou dost look
Like Patience gazing on kings' graves and smiling
Extremity out of act. What were thy friends?
How lost thou them? Thy name, my most kind
  virgin?

Recount, I do beseech thee: come, sit by me.
MARINA. My name is Marina.
PERICLES.   O, I am mocked,
And thou by some incensèd god sent hither
To make the world laugh at me.
MARINA.   Patience, good sir,
Or here I'll cease.
PERICLES.   Nay, I'll be patient.
Thou little know'st how thou dost startle me,
To call thyself Marina.
MARINA.   The name
Was given me by one that had some power,
My father, and a king.
PERICLES.   How, a king's daughter?
And called Marina?
MARINA.   You said you would believe me;
But, not to be a troubler of your peace,
I will end here.
PERICLES.   But are you flesh and blood?
Have you a working pulse, and are no fairy?
Motion as well? Speak on. Where were you born?
And wherefore called Marina?
MARINA.   Called Marina
For I was born at sea.
PERICLES.   At sea! what mother?
MARINA. My mother was the daughter of a king;
Who died the minute I was born,
As my good nurse Lychorida hath oft
Delivered weeping.
PERICLES.   O, stop there a little!—
This is the rarest dream that e'er dulled sleep
Did mock sad fools withal: this cannot be
My daughter—buried!—Well, where were you
  bred?
I'll hear you more, to th'bottom of your story,
And never interrupt you.
MARINA. You scorn; believe me, 'twere best I did give
  o'er.
PERICLES. I will believe you by the syllable
Of what you shall deliver. Yet, give me leave:
How came you in these parts? where were you bred?
MARINA. The king my father did in Tharsus leave me;
Till cruel Cleon, with his wicked wife,
Did seek to murder me;
And having wooed a villain to attempt it,
Who having drawn to do't,
A crew of pirates came and rescued me;
Brought me to Mytilene. But, good sir,
Whither will you have me? Why do you weep? It
  may be,
You think me an impostor: no, good faith;
I am the daughter to King Pericles,
If good King Pericles be.
PERICLES. Ho, Helicanus!
HELICANUS. Calls my lord?
PERICLES. Thou art a grave and noble counsellor,
Most wise in general. Tell me, if thou canst,
What this maid is, or what is like to be,
That thus hath made me weep?
HELICANUS.   I know not;
But here's the regent, sir, of Mytilene
Speaks nobly of her.
LYSIMACHUS.   She never would tell
Her parentage; being demanded that,
She would sit still and weep.
PERICLES. O Helicanus, strike me, honoured sir;

Give me a gash, put me to present pain;
Lest this great sea of joys rushing upon me
O'erbear the shores of my mortality,
And drown me with their sweetness. O, come
    hither,
Thou that beget'st him that did thee beget;
Thou that wast born at sea, buried at Tharsus,   200
And found at sea again! O Helicanus,
Down on thy knees; thank the holy gods as loud
As thunder threatens us: this is Marina.
What was thy mother's name? tell me but that,
For truth can never be confirmed enough,
Though doubts did ever sleep.
MARINA. First, sir, I pray,
    What is your title?
PERICLES. I am Pericles of Tyre: but tell me now
My drowned queen's name, as in the rest you said   210
Thou hast been godlike perfect, the heir of
    kingdoms,
And another life to Pericles thy father.
MARINA. Is it no more to be your daughter than
To say my mother's name was Thaisa?
Thaisa was my mother, who did end
The minute I began.
PERICLES. Now, blessing on thee! rise; thou art my
    child.
Give me fresh garments, mine own Helicanus.
She is not dead at Tharsus, as she should have been,
By savage Cleon; she shall tell thee all;
When thou shalt kneel, and justify in knowledge
She is thy very princess. Who is this?
HELICANUS. Sir, 'tis the governor of Mytilene,
Who, hearing of your melancholy state,
Did come to see you.
PERICLES. I embrace you.
Give me my robes. I am wild in my beholding.
O heavens bless my girl! But, hark, what music?
Tell Helicanus, my Marina, tell him
O'er, point by point, for yet he seems to doubt,   230
How sure you are my daughter. But, what music?
HELICANUS. My lord, I hear none.
PERICLES. None?
The music of the spheres! List, my Marina.
LYSIMACHUS. It is not good to cross him; give him
    way.
PERICLES. Rarest sounds! Do ye not hear?
LYSIMACHUS.   Music, my lord?
PERICLES. I hear most heavenly music.
It nips me unto list'ning, and thick slumber
Hangs upon mine eyes: let me rest.   *He sleeps*
LYSIMACHUS. A pillow for his head: so leave him all.   240
Well, my companion friends,
If this but answer to my just belief,
I'll well remember you.   *All but Pericles go*

Diana appears to Pericles in a vision

DIANA. My temple stands in Ephesus: hie thee thither,
And do upon mine altar sacrifice.
There, when my maiden priests are met together,
Before the people all,
Reveal how thou at sea didst lose thy wife.
To mourn thy crosses, with thy daughter's, call,
And give them repetition to the life.   250
Perform my bidding, or thou livest in woe;
Do't, and be happy; by my silver bow!
Awake, and tell thy dream.   *Disappears*

PERICLES. Celestial Dian, goddess argentine,
I will obey thee. Helicanus!

Re-enter Helicanus, Lysimachus, and Marina

HELICANUS.   Sir?
PERICLES. My purpose was for Tharsus, there to strike
The inhospitable Cleon; but I am
For other service first: toward Ephesus
Turn our blown sails; eftsoons I'll tell thee why.
[*to Lysimachus*] Shall we refresh us, sir, upon your
    shore,   260
And give you gold for such provision
As our intents will need?
LYSIMACHUS. Sir,
With all my heart; and, when you come ashore,
I have another suit.
PERICLES.   You shall prevail,
Were it to woo my daughter; for it seems
You have been noble towards her.
LYSIMACHUS.   Sir, lend me your arm.
PERICLES. Come, my Marina.   *They go*

Scene 2: *The temple of Diana at Ephesus; Thaisa standing
near the altar, as high priestess; a number of Virgins on each
side; Cerimon and other Inhabitants of Ephesus attending*

Enter Gower

GOWER. Now our sands are almost run;
More a little, and then dumb.
This, my last boon, give me,
For such kindness must relieve me,
That you aptly will suppose
What pageantry, what feats, what shows,
What minstrelsy and pretty din,
The regent made in Mytilin,
To greet the king. So he thrived,
That he is promised to be wived   10
To fair Marina; but in no wise
Till he had done his sacrifice,
As dian bade: whereto being bound,
The interim, pray you, all confound.
In feathered briefness sails are filled,
And wishes fall out as they're willed.
At Ephesus, the temple see,
Our king and all his company.
That he can hither come so soon,
Is by your fancies' thankful doom.   *He goes*   20

Scene 3

*Enter Pericles, with his train; Lysimachus, Helicanus, and
Marina*

PERICLES. Hail, Dian! to perform thy just command,
I here confess myself the king of Tyre;
Who, frighted from my country, did wed
At Pentapolis the fair Thaisa.
At sea in childbed died she, but brought forth
A maid-child called Marina; who, O goddess,
Wears yet thy silver livery. She at Tharsus
Was nursed with Cleon; who at fourteen years
He sought to murder; but her better stars
Brought her to Mytilene; 'gainst whose shore   10
Riding, her fortunes brought the maid aboard us,
Where, by her own most clear remembrance, she
Made known herself my daughter.

THAISA.   Voice and favour!
You are, you are—O royal Pericles!—   *Faints*
PERICLES. What means the nun? she dies! help,
gentlemen!
CERIMON. Noble sir,
If you have told Diana's altar true,
This is your wife.
PERICLES.   Reverend appearer, no;
I threw her overboard with these very arms.
CERIMON. Upon this coast, I warrant you.
PERICLES.   'Tis most certain. 20
CERIMON. Look to the lady. O, she's but overjoyed.
Early one blustering morn this lady was
Thrown upon this shore. I oped the coffin,
Found there rich jewels; recovered her, and placed
her
Here in Diana's temple.
PERICLES.   May we see them?
CERIMON. Great sir, they shall be brought you to my
house,
Whither I invite you. Look, Thaisa is
Recoveréd.
THAISA. O, let me look!
If he be none of mine, my sanctity   30
Will to my sense bend no licentious ear,
But curb it, spite of seeing. O, my lord,
Are you not Pericles? Like him you spake,
Like him you are. Did you not name a tempest,
A birth, and death?
PERICLES.   The voice of dead Thaisa!
THAISA. That Thaisa am I,
Supposéd dead and drowned.
PERICLES. Immortal Dian!
THAISA.   Now I know you better.
When we with tears parted Pentapolis,
The king my father gave you such a ring.   40
                                    Shows a ring
PERICLES. This, this: no more, you gods! your present
kindness
Makes my past miseries sports. You shall do well,
That on the touching of her lips I may
Melt, and no more be seen. O, come, be buried
A second time within these arms.
MARINA.   My heart
Leaps to be gone into my mother's bosom.
                                    Kneels to Thaisa
PERICLES. Look who kneels here, flesh of thy flesh,
Thaisa;
Thy burden at the sea, and called Marina
For she was yielded there.
THAISA.   Blest, and mine own!
HELICANUS. Hail, madam, and my queen!
THAISA.   I know you not. 50
PERICLES. You have heard me say, when I did fly
from Tyre,
I left behind an ancient substitute.
Can you remember what I called the man?
I have named him oft.
THAISA.   'Twas Helicanus, then.

PERICLES. Still confirmation.
Embrace him, dear Thaisa; this is he.
Now do I long to hear how you were found;
How possibly preserved; and who to thank,
Besides the gods, for this great miracle.
THAISA. Lord Cerimon, my lord; this man,   60
Through whom the gods have shown their power;
that can
From first to last resolve you.
PERICLES.   Reverend sir,
The gods can have no mortal officer
More like a god than you. Will you deliver
How this dead queen re-lives?
CERIMON.   I will, my lord.
Beseech you first, go with me to my house,
Where shall be shown you all was found with her;
How she came placed here in the temple;
No needful thing omitted.
PERICLES.   Pure Dian,
I bless thee for thy vision, and will offer   70
Nightly oblations to thee. Thaisa,
This prince, the fair betrothéd of your daughter,
Shall marry her at Pentapolis. And now,
This ornament
Makes me look dismal will I clip to form;
And what this fourteen years no razor touched,
To grace thy marriage-day, I'll beautify.
THAISA. Lord Cerimon hath letters of good credit;
Sir, my father's dead.
PER. Heavens make a star of him! Yet there, my
queen,   80
We'll celebrate their nuptials, and ourselves
Will in that kingdom spend our following days.
Our son and daughter shall in Tyrus reign.
Lord Cerimon, we do our longing stay
To hear the rest untold: sir, lead's the way.
                                    They go

Enter Gower

GOWER. In Antiochus and his daughter you have heard
Of monstrous lust the due and just reward.
In Pericles, his queen and daughter, seen,
Although assailed with fortune fierce and keen,
Virtue preserved from fell destruction's blast,   90
Led on by heaven and crowned with joy at last.
In Helicanus may you well descry
A figure of truth, of faith, of loyalty.
In reverend Cerimon there well appears
The worth that learnéd charity aye wears.
For wicked Cleon and his wife, when fame
Had spread their curséd deed to th'honoured name
Of Pericles, to rage the city turn,
That him and his they in his palace burn;
The gods for murder seeméd so content   100
To punish, although not done, but meant.
So, on your patience evermore attending,
New joy wait on you! Here our play has ending.
                                    He goes

The Poems

Venus and Andonis

Vilia miretur vulgus; mihi flavus Apollo
Pocula Castalia plena ministret aqua

TO THE

RIGHT HONOURABLE HENRY WRIOTHESLEY,

EARL OF SOUTHAMPTON, AND BARON OF TITCHFIELD

Right Honourable,

I know not how I shall offend in dedicating my unpolished lines to your lordship, nor how the world will censure me for choosing so strong a prop to support so weak a burden: only, if your honour seem but pleased, I account my self highly praised, and vow to take advantage of all idle hours, till I have honoured you with some graver labour. But if the first heir of my invention prove deformed, I shall be sorry it had so noble a godfather, and never after ear so barren a land, for fear it yield me still so bad a harvest. I leave it to your honourable survey, and your honour to your heart's content; which I wish may always answer your own wish, and the world's hopeful expectations.

Your honour's in all duty,
William Shakespeare

EVEN as the sun with purple-coloured face
Had ta'en his last leave of the weeping morn,
Rose-cheeked Adonis hied him to the chase;
Hunting he loved, but love he laughed to scorn.
　Sick-thoughted Venus makes amain unto him, 5
　And like a bold-faced suitor 'gins to woo him.

'Thrice fairer than myself,' thus she began,
'The field's chief flower, sweet above compare,
Stain to all nymphs, more lovely than a man,
More white and red than doves or roses are; 10
　Nature that made thee with herself at strife
　Saith that the world hath ending with thy life.

'Vouchsafe, thou wonder, to alight thy steed,
And rein his proud head to the saddle-bow;
If thou wilt deign this favour, for thy meed 15
A thousand honey secrets shalt thou know.
　Here come and sit, where never serpent hisses,
　And being set, I'll smother thee with kisses;

'And yet not cloy thy lips with loathed saiety,
But rather famish them amid their plenty, 20
Making them red and pale with fresh variety;
Ten kisses short as one, one long as twenty.
　A summer's day will seem an hour but short,
　Being wasted in such time-beguiling sport.'

With this she seizeth on his sweating palm, 25
The precedent of pith and livelihood,
And, trembling in her passion, calls it balm,
Earth's sovereign salve to do a goddess good.
　Being so enraged, desire doth lend her force
　Courageously to pluck him from his horse. 30

Over one arm the lusty courser's rein,
Under her other was the tender boy,
Who blushed and pouted in a dull disdain,
With leaden appetite, unapt to toy;
　She red and hot as coals of glowing fire, 35
　He red for shame, but frosty in desire.

The studded bridle on a ragged bough
Nimbly she fastens—O, how quick is love!
The steed is stalled up, and even now
To tie the rider she begins to prove. 40
　Backward she pushed him, as she would be thrust,
　And governed him in strength, though not in lust.

So soon was she along as he was down,
Each leaning on their elbows and their hips;
Now doth she stroke his cheek, now doth he frown, 45
And 'gins to chide, but soon she stops his lips,
　And kissing speaks, with lustful language broken,
　'If thou wilt chide, thy lips shall never open.'

He burns with bashful shame; she with her tears
Doth quench the maiden burning of his cheeks; 50
Then with her windy sighs and golden hairs
To fan and blow them dry again she seeks.
　He saith she is immodest, blames her miss;
　What follows more she murders with a kiss.

Even as an empty eagle, sharp by fast, 55
Tires with her beak on feathers, flesh and bone,
Shaking her wings, devouring all in haste,
Till either gorge be stuffed or prey be gone;
　Even so she kissed his brow, his cheek, his chin,
　And where she ends she doth anew begin. 60

Forced to content, but never to obey,
Panting he lies and breatheth in her face;
She feedeth on the steam as on a prey,
And calls it heavenly moisture, air of grace,
   Wishing her cheeks were gardens full of flowers, 65
   So they were dewed with such distilling showers.

Look how a bird lies tangled in a net,
So fast'ned in her arms Adonis lies;
Pure shame and awed resistance made him fret,
Which bred more beauty in his angry eyes. 70
   Rain added to a river that is rank
   Perforce will force it overflow the bank.

Still she entreats, and prettily entreats,
For to a pretty ear she tunes her tale;
Still is he sullen, still he lours and frets, 75
'Twixt crimson shame and anger ashy-pale;
   Being red, she loves him best, and being white,
   Her best is bettered with a more delight.

Look how he can, she cannot choose but love;
And by her fair immortal hand she swears 80
From his soft bosom never to remove
Till he take truce with her contending tears,
   Which long have rained, making her cheeks all wet;
   And one sweet kiss shall pay this countless debt.

Upon this promise did he raise his chin, 85
Like a dive-dapper peering through a wave,
Who, being looked on, ducks as quickly in;
So offers he to give what she did crave;
   But when her lips were ready for his pay,
   He winks, and turns his lips another way. 90

Never did passenger in summer's heat
More thirst for drink than she for this good turn.
Her help she sees, but help she cannot get;
She bathes in water, yet her fire must burn.
   'O, pity,' 'gan she cry. 'flint-hearted boy! 95
   'Tis but a kiss I beg; why art thou coy?

'I have been wooed, as I entreat thee now,
Even by the stern and direful god of war,
Whose sinewy neck in battle ne'er did bow,
Who conquers where he comes in every jar; 100
   Yet hath he been my captive and my slave,
   And begged for that which thou unasked shalt have.

'Over my altars hath he hung his lance,
His batt'red shield, his uncontrollèd crest,
And for my sake hath learned to sport and dance, 105
To toy, to wanton, dally, smile and jest,
   Scorning his churlish drum and ensign red,
   Making my arms his field, his tent my bed.

'Thus he that overruled I overswayèd,
Leading him prisoner in a red-rose chain; 110
Strong-tempered steel his stronger strength obeyèd,
Yet was he servile to my coy disdain.
   O, be not proud, nor brag not of thy might,
   For mast'ring her that foiled the god of fight!

'Touch but my lips with those fair lips of thine— 115
Though mine be not so fair, yet are they red—
The kiss shall be thine own as well as mine.
What see'st thou in the ground? hold up thy head;
   Look in mine eyeballs, there thy beauty lies;
   Then why not lips on lips, since eyes in eyes? 120

'Art thou ashamed to kiss? then wink again,
And I will wink; so shall the day seem night.
Love keeps his revels where there are but twain;
Be bold to play, our sport is not in sight.
   These blue-veined violets whereon we lean 125
   Never can blab, nor know not what we mean.

'The tender spring upon thy tempting lip
Shews thee unripe; yet mayst thou well be tasted;
Make use of time, let not advantage slip;
Beauty within itself should not be wasted. 130
   Fair flowers that are not gath'red in their prime
   Rot and consume themselves in little time.

'Were I hard-favoured, foul, or wrinkled-old,
Ill-nurtured, crooked, churlish, harsh in voice,
O'erworn, despisèd, rheumatic and cold, 135
Thick-sighted, barren, lean, and lacking juice,
   Then mightst thou pause, for then I were not for
     thee;
   But having no defects, why dost abhor me?

'Thou canst not see one wrinkle in my brow;
Mine eyes are grey and bright and quick in turning; 140
My beauty as the spring doth yearly grow,
My flesh is soft and plump, my marrow burning;
   My smooth moist hand, were it with thy hand felt,
   Would in thy palm dissolve, or seem to melt.

'Bid me discourse, I will enchant thine ear, 145
Or, like a fairy, trip upon the green,
Or, like a nymph, with long dishevellèd hair,
Dance on the sands, and yet no footing seen.
   Love is a spirit all compact of fire,
   Not gross to sink, but light, and will aspire. 150

'Witness this primrose bank whereon I lie;
These forceless flowers like sturdy trees support me;
Two strengthless doves will draw me through the sky
From morn till night, even where I list to sport me.
   Is love so light, sweet boy, and may it be 155
   That thou should think it heavy unto thee?

'Is thine own heart to thine own face affected?
Can thy right hand seize love upon thy left?
Then woo thyself, be of thyself rejected,
Steal thine own freedom, and complain on theft. 160
   Narcissus so himself himself forsook,
   And died to kiss his shadow in the brook.

'Torches are made to light, jewels to wear,
Dainties to taste, fresh beauty for the use,
Herbs for their smell, and sappy plants to bear; 165
Things growing to themselves are growth's abuse.
   Seeds spring from seeds and beauty breedeth beauty;
   Thou wast begot; to get it is thy duty.

'Upon the earth's increase why shouldst thou feed,
Unless the earth with thy increase be fed?   170
By law of nature thou art bound to breed,
That thine may live when thou thyself art dead;
  And so in spite of death thou dost survive,
  In that thy likeness still is left alive.'

By this, the love-sick queen began to sweat,   175
For where they lay the shadow had forsook them,
And Titan, tiréd in the mid-day heat,
With burning eye did hotly overlook them,
  Wishing Adonis had his team to guide,
  So he were like him, and by Venus' side.   180

And now Adonis, with a lazy sprite,
And with a heavy, dark, disliking eye,
His louring brows o'erwhelming his fair sight,
Like misty vapours when they blot the sky,
  Souring his cheeks, cries 'Fie, no more of love! 185
  The sun doth burn my face; I must remove.'

'Ay me,' quoth Venus, 'young, and so unkind!
What bare excuses mak'st thou to be gone!
I'll sigh celestial breath, whose gentle wind   190
Shall cool the heat of this descending sun;
  I'll make a shadow for thee of my hairs;
  If they burn too, I'll quench them with my tears.

'The sun that shines from heaven shines but warm,
And lo, I lie between that sun and thee;   195
The heat I have from thence doth little harm;
Thine eye darts forth the fire that burneth me;
  And were I not immortal, life were done
  Between this heavenly and earthly sun.

'Art thou obdurate, flinty, hard as steel?   200
Nay, more than flint, for stone at rain relenteth.
Art thou a woman's son, and canst not feel
What 'tis to love, how want of love tormenteth?
  O, had thy mother borne so hard a mind,
  She had not brought forth thee, but died unkind. 205

'What am I that thou shouldst contemn me this?
Or what great danger dwells upon my suit?
What were thy lips the worse for one poor kiss?
Speak, fair; but speak fair words, or else be mute.
  Give me one kiss, I'll give it thee again,   210
  And one for int'rest, if thou wilt have twain.

'Fie, lifeless picture, cold and senseless stone,
Well painted idol, image dull and dead,
Statue contenting but the eye alone,
Thing like a man, but of no woman bred!   215
  Thou art no man, though of a man's complexion,
  For men will kiss even by their own direction.'

This said, impatience chokes her pleading tongue,
And swelling passion doth provoke a pause;
Red cheeks and fiery eyes blaze forth her wrong;   220
Being judge in love, she cannot right her cause;
  And now she weeps, and now she fain would speak,
  And now her sobs do her intendments break.

Sometimes she shakes her head, and then his hand,
Now gazeth she on him, now on the ground;   225
Sometime her arms infold him like a band;
She would, he will not in her arms be bound;
  And when from thence he struggles to be gone,
  She locks her lily fingers one in one.

'Fondling,' she saith, 'since I have hemmed thee here 230
Within the circuit of this ivory pale,
I'll be a park, and thou shalt be my deer;
Feed where thou wilt, on mountain or in dale;
  Graze on my lips, and if those hills be dry,
  Stray lower, where the pleasant fountains lie.   235

'Within this limit is relief enough,
Sweet bottom-grass and high delightful plain,
Round rising hillocks, brakes obscure and rough,
To shelter thee from tempest and from rain:
  Then be my deer, since I am such a park;   240
  No dog shall rouse thee, though a thousand bark.'

At this Adonis smiles as in disdain,
That in each cheek appears a pretty dimple.
Love made those hollows, if himself were slain,
He might be buried in a tomb so simple;   245
  Foreknowing well, if there he came to lie,
  Why, there Love lived, and there he could not die.

These lovely caves, these round enchanting pits,
Opened their mouths to swallow Venus' liking.
Being mad before, how doth she now for wits?   250
Struck dead at first, what needs a second striking?
  Poor queen of love, in thine own law forlorn,
  To love a cheek that smiles at thee in scorn!

Now which way shall she turn? what shall she say?
Her words are done, her woes the more increasing;   255
The time is spent, her object will away,
And from her twining arms doth urge releasing.
  'Pity,' she cries, 'some favour, some remorse!'
  Away he springs, and hasteth to his horse.

But lo, from forth a copse that neighbours by,   260
A breeding jennet, lusty, young and proud,
Adonis' trampling courser doth espy,
And forth she rushes, snorts and neighs aloud.
  The strong-necked steed, being tied unto a tree,
  Breaketh his rein and to her straight goes he.   265

Imperiously he leaps, he neighs, he bounds,
And now his woven girths he breaks asunder;
The bearing earth with his hard hoof he wounds,
Whose hollow womb resounds like heaven's thunder;
  The iron bit he crusheth 'tween his teeth,   270
  Controlling what he was controlléd with.

His ears up-pricked; his braided hanging mane
Upon his compassed crest now stand on end;
His nostrils drink the air, and forth again,
As from a furnace, vapours doth he send;   275
  His eye, which scornfully glisters like fire,
  Shows his hot courage and his high desire.

Sometime he trots, as if he told the steps,
With gentle majesty and modest pride;
Anon he rears upright, curvets and leaps,   280
As who should say 'Lo, thus my strength is tried,
    And this I do to captivate the eye
    Of the fair breeder that is standing by.'

What recketh he his rider's angry stir,
His flattering 'Holla' or his 'Stand, I say'?   285
What cares he now for curb or pricking spur?
For rich caparisons or trappings gay?
    He sees his love, and nothing else he sees,
    For nothing else with his proud sight agrees.

Look when a painter would surpass the life   290
In limning out a well-proportionéd steed,
His art with nature's workmanship at strife,
As if the dead the living should exceed;
    So did this horse excel a common one
    In shape, in courage, colour, pace and bone.   295

Round-hoofed, short-jointed, fetlocks shag and long,
Broad breast, full eye, small head and nostril wide,
High crest, short ears, straight legs and passing strong,
Thin mane, thick tail, broad buttock, tender hide;
    Look what a horse should have he did not lack, 300
    Save a proud rider on so proud a back.

Sometime he scuds far off, and there he stares;
Anon he starts at stirring of a feather;
To bid the wind a base he now prepares,
And whe'er he run or fly they know not whether;   305
    For through his mane and tail the high wind sings,
    Fanning the hairs, who wave like feath'red wings.

He looks upon his love and neighs unto her;
She answers him as if she knew his mind;
Being proud, as females are, to see him woo her,   310
She puts on outward strangeness, seems unkind,
    Spurns at his love and scorns the heat he feels,
    Beating his kind embracements with her heels.

Then, like a melancholy malcontent,
He vails his tail, that, like a falling plume,   315
Cool shadow to his melting buttock lent;
He stamps, and bites the poor flies in his fume.
    His love, perceiving how he was enraged,
    Grew kinder, and his fury was assuaged.

His testy master goeth about to take him,   320
When, lo, the unbacked breeder, full of fear,
Jealous of catching, swiftly doth forsake him,
With her the horse, and left Adonis there.
    As they were mad, unto the wood they hie them,
    Out-stripping crows that strive to over-fly them. 325

All swoln with chafing, down Adonis sits,
Banning his boist'rous and unruly beast;
And now the happy season once more fits
That love-sick Love by pleading may be blest;
    For lovers say the heart hath treble wrong   330
    When it is barred the aidance of the tongue.

An oven that is stopped, or river stayed,
Burneth more hotly, swelleth with more rage;
So of concealéd sorrow may be said,
Free vent of words love's fire doth assuage;   335
    But when the heart's attorney once is mute,
    The client breaks, as desperate in his suit.

He sees her coming, and begins to glow,
Even as a dying coal revives with wind,
And with his bonnet hides his angry brow,   340
Looks on the dull earth with disturbéd mind,
    Taking no notice that she is so nigh,
    For all askance he holds her in his eye.

O, what a sight it was, wistly to view
How she came stealing to the wayward boy!   345
To note the fighting conflict of her hue,
How white and red each other did destroy!
    But now her cheek was pale, and by and by
    It flashed forth fire, as lightning from the sky.

Now was she just before him as he sat,   350
And like a lowly lover down she kneels;
With one fair hand she heaveth up his hat,
Her other tender hand his fair cheek feels;
    His tend'rer cheek receives her soft hand's print
    As apt as new-fall'n snow takes any dint.   355

O, what a war of looks was then between them,
Her eyes petitioners to his eyes suing!
His eyes saw her eyes as they had not seen them;
Her eyes wooed still, his eyes disdained the wooing;
    And all this dumb play had his acts made plain   360
    With tears which chorus-like her eyes did rain.

Full gently now she takes him by the hand,
A lily prisoned in a gaol of snow,
Or ivory in an alabaster band;
So white a friend engirts so white a foe: 365
    This beauteous combat, wilful and unwilling,
    Showed like two silver doves that sit a-billing.

Once more the engine of her thoughts began:
'O fairest mover on this mortal round,
Would thou wert as I am, and I a man,   370
My heart all whole as thine, thy heart my wound;
    For one sweet look thy help I would assure thee,
    Though nothing but my body's bane would cure
        thee.'

'Give me my hand,' saith he; 'why dost thou feel it?'
'Give me my heart,' saith she, 'and thou shalt have it; 375
O, give it me, lest thy hard heart do steel it,
And being steeled, soft sighs can never grave it;
    Then love's deep groans I never shall regard,
    Because Adonis' heart hath made mine hard.'

'For shame,' he cries, 'let go, and let me go;   380
My day's delight is past, my horse is gone,
And 'tis your fault I am bereft him so.
I pray you hence, and leave me here alone;
    For all my mind, my thought, my busy care,
    Is how to get my palfrey from the mare.'   385

Thus she replies: 'Thy palfrey, as he should,
Welcomes the warm approach of sweet desire.
Affection is a coal that must be cooled;
Else, suffered, it will set the heart on fire.
    The sea hath bounds, but deep desire hath none,   390
    Therefore no marvel though thy horse be gone.

'How like a jade he stood tied to the tree,
Servilely mastered with a leathern rein!
But when he saw his love, his youth's fair fee,
He held such petty bondage in disdain,   395
    Throwing the base thong from his bending crest,
    Enfranchising his mouth, his back, his breast.

'Who sees his true-love in her naked bed,
Teaching the sheets a whiter hue than white,
But, when his glutton eye so full hath fed,   400
His other agents aim at like delight?
    Who is so faint that dares not be so bold
    To touch the fire, the weather being cold?

'Let me excuse thy courser, gentle boy;
And learn of him, I heartily beseech thee,   405
To take advantage on presented joy;
Though I were dumb, yet his proceedings teach thee.
    O, learn to love; the lesson is but plain,
    And once made perfect, never lost again.'

'I know not love,' quoth he, 'nor will not know it,   410
Unless it be a boar, and then I chase it.
'Tis much to borrow, and I will not owe it.
My love to love is love but to disgrace it;
    For I have heard it is a life in death,
    That laughs, and weeps, and all but with a breath.   415

'Who wears a garment shapeless and unfinished?
Who plucks the bud before one leaf put forth?
If springing things be any jot diminished,
They wither in their prime, prove nothing worth.
    The colt that's backed and burdened being young   420
    Loseth his pride, and never waxeth strong.

'You hurt my hand with wringing; let us part,
And leave this idle theme, this bootless chat;
Remove your siege from my unyielding heart;
To love's alarms it will not ope the gate.   425
    Dismiss your vows, your feignéd tears, your flatt'ry;
    For where a heart is hard they make no batt'ry.'

'What, canst thou talk?' quoth she, 'hast thou a tongue?
O, would thou hadst not, or I had no hearing!
Thy mermaid's voice hath done me double wrong;   430
I had my load before, now pressed with bearing:
    Melodious discord, heavenly tune harsh sounding,
    Ears' deep-sweet music, and heart's deep-sore
      wounding.

'Had I no eyes but ears, my ears would love
That inward beauty and invisible;   435
Or were I deaf, thy outward parts would move
Each part in me that were but sensible.
    Though neither eyes nor ears, to hear nor see,
    Yet should I be in love by touching thee.

'Say that the sense of feeling were bereft me,   440
And that I could not see, nor hear, nor touch,
And nothing but the very smell were left me,
Yet would my love to thee be still as much;
    For from the stillitory of thy face excelling
    Comes breath perfumed, that breedeth love by   445
      smelling.

'But O, what banquet wert thou to the taste,
Being nurse and feeder of the other four!
Would they not wish the feast might ever last,
And bid Suspicion double-lock the door,
    Lest Jealousy, that sour unwelcome guest,   450
    Should by his stealing in disturb the feast?'

Once more the ruby-coloured portal opened,
Which to his speech did honey passage yield;
Like a red morn, that ever yet betokened
Wrack to the seaman, tempest to the field,   455
    Sorrow to shepherds, woe unto the birds,
    Gusts and foul flaws to herdmen and to herds.

This ill presage advisedly she marketh.
Even as the wind is hushed before it raineth,
Or as the wolf doth grin before he barketh,   460
Or as the berry breaks before it staineth,
    Or like the deadly bullet of a gun,
    His meaning struck her ere his words begun.

And at his look she flatly falleth down,
For looks kill love, and love by looks reviveth;   465
A smile recures the wounding of a frown.
But blesséd bankrupt that by loss so thriveth!
    The silly boy, believing she is dead,
    Claps her pale cheek, till clapping makes it red;

And all amazed brake off his late intent,   470
For sharply he did think to reprehend her,
Which cunning love did wittily prevent.
Fair fall the wit that can so well defend her!
    For on the grass she lies as she were slain,
    Till his breath breatheth life in her again.   475

He wrings her nose, he strikes her on the cheeks,
He bends her fingers, holds her pulses hard,
He chafes her lips, a thousand ways he seeks
To mend the hurt that his unkindness marred;
    He kisses her; and she, by her good will,   480
    Will never rise, so he will kiss her still.

The night of sorrow now is turned to day:
Her two blue windows faintly she upheaveth,
Like the fair sun, when in his fresh array
He cheers the morn, and all the earth relieveth;   485
    And as the bright san glorifies the sky,
    So is her face illumined with her eye;

Whose beams upon his hairless face are fixed,
As if from thence they borrowéd all their shine.
Were never four such lamps together mixed,   490
Had not his clouded with his brow's repine;
    But hers, which through the crystal tears gave light,
    Shone like the moon in water seen by night.

'O, where am I?' quoth she; 'in earth or heaven,
Or in the ocean drenched, or in the fire? 495
What hour is this? or morn or weary even?
Do I delight to die, or life desire?
    But now I lived, and life was death's annoy;
    But now I died, and death was lively joy.

'O, thou didst kill me: kill me once again. 500
Thy eyes' shrewd tutor, that hard heart of thine,
Hath taught them scornful tricks, and such disdain
That they have murd'red this poor heart of mine;
    And these mine eyes, true leaders to their queen,
    But for thy piteous lips no more had seen. 505

'Long may they kiss each other, for this cure!
O, never let their crimson liveries wear!
And as they last, their verdure still endure
To drive infection from the dangerous year!
    That the star-gazers, having writ on death, 510
    May say, the plague is banished by thy breath.

'Pure lips, sweet seals in my soft lips imprinted,
What bargains may I make, still to be sealing?
To sell myself I can be well contented,
So thou wilt buy, and pay, and use good dealing; 515
    Which purchase if thou make, for fear of slips
    Set thy seal manual on my wax-red lips.

'A thousand kisses buys my heart from me;
And pay them at thy leisure, one by one.
What is ten hundred touches unto thee? 520
Are they not quickly told and quickly gone?
    Say for non-payment that the debt should double,
    Is twenty hundred kisses such a trouble?'

'Fair queen,' quoth he, 'if any love you owe me,
Measure my strangeness with my unripe years; 525
Before I know myself, seek not to know me;
No fisher but the ungrown fry forbears.
    The mellow plum doth fall, the green sticks fast,
    Or being early plucked is sour to taste.

'Look, the world's comforter, with weary gait, 530
His day's hot task hath ended in the west;
The owl, night's herald, shrieks 'tis very late;
The sheep are gone to fold, birds to their nest;
    And coal-black clouds that shadow heaven's light
    Do summon us to part, and bid good night. 535

'Now let me say "Good night", and so say you;
If you will say so, you shall have a kiss.'
'Good night', quoth she; and, ere he says 'Adieu',
The honey fee of parting tend'red is:
    Her arms do lend his neck a sweet embrace; 540
    Incorporate then they seem; face grows to face.

Till breathless he disjoined, and backward drew
The heavenly moisture, that sweet coral mouth,
Whose precious taste her thirsty lips well knew,
Whereon they surfeit, yet complain on drouth. 545
    He with her plenty pressed, she faint with dearth,
    Their lips together glued, fall to the earth.

Now quick desire hath caught the yielding prey,
And glutton-like she feeds, yet never filleth;
Her lips are conquerors, his lips obey, 550
Paying what ransom the insulter willeth;
    Whose vulture thought doth pitch the price so high
    That she will draw his lips' rich treasure dry.

And having felt the sweetness of the spoil,
With blindfold fury she begins to forage; 555
Her face doth reek and smoke, her blood doth boil,
And careless lust stirs up a desperate courage,
    Planting oblivion, beating reason back,
    Forgetting shame's pure blush and honour's wrack.

Hot, faint and weary, with her hard embracing, 560
Like a wild bird being tamed with too much handling,
Or as the fleet-foot roe that's tired with chasing,
Or like the froward infant stilled with dandling,
    He now obeys and now no more resisteth,
    While she takes all she can, not all she listeth. 565

What wax so frozen but dissolves with temp'ring,
And yields at last to every light impression?
Things out of hope are compass'd oft with vent'ring,
Chiefly in love, whose leave exceeds commission:
    Affection faints not like a pale-face coward, 570
    But then woos best when most his choice is froward.

When he did frown, O, had she then gave over,
Such nectar from his lips she had not sucked.
Foul words and frowns must not repel a lover;
What though the rose have prickles, yet 'tis plucked. 575
    Were beauty under twenty locks kept fast,
    Yet love breaks through, and picks them all at last.

For pity now she can no more detain him;
The poor fool prays her that he may depart.
She is resolved no longer to restrain him; 580
Bids him farewell, and look well to her heart,
    The which by Cupid's bow she doth protest
    He carries thence incagéd in his breast.

'Sweet boy,' she says, 'this night I'll waste in sorrow,
For my sick heart commands mine eyes to watch. 585
Tell me, love's master, shall we meet to-morrow?
Say, shall we? shall we? wilt thou make the match?'
    He tells her, no; to-morrow he intends
    To hunt the boar with certain of his friends.

'The boar!' quoth she: whereat a sudden pale, 590
Like lawn being spread upon the blushing rose,
Usurps her cheek; she trembles at his tale,
And on his neck her yoking arms she throws.
    She sinketh down, still hanging by his neck,
    He on her belly falls, she on her back. 595

Now is she in the very lists of love,
Her champion mounted for the hot encounter.
All is imaginary she doth prove;
He will not manage her, although he mount her;
    That worse than Tantalus' is her annoy, 600
    To clip Elysium and to lack her joy.

Even so poor birds, deceived with painted grapes,
Do surfeit by the eye and pine the maw;
Even so she languisheth in her mishaps
As those poor birds that helpless berries saw.   605
  The warm effects which she in him finds missing
  She seeks to kindly with continual kissing.

But all in vain, good queen, it will not be.
She hath assayed as much as may be proved;
Her pleading hath deserved a greater fee;   610
She's Love, she loves, and yet she is not loved.
  'Fie, fie,' he says, 'you crush me; let me go;
  You have no reason to withhold me so.'

'Thou hadst been gone,' quoth she, 'sweet boy, ere this,
But that thou told'st me thou wouldst hunt the boar. 615
O, be advised: thou know'st not what it is
With javelin's point a churlish swine to gore,
  Whose tushes never sheathed he whetteth still,
  Like to a mortal butcher bent to kill.

'On his bow-back he hath a battle set   620
Of bristly pikes that ever threat his foes;
His eyes like glow-worms shine when he doth fret;
His snout digs sepulchres where'er he goes;
  Being moved, he strikes whate'er is in his way,
  And whom he strikes his crookéd tushes slay.   625

'His brawny sides, with hairy bristles arméd,
Are better proof than thy spear's point can enter;
His short thick neck cannot be easily harméd;
Being ireful, on the lion he will venter:
  The thorny brambles and embracing bushes,   630
  As fearful of him, part; through whom he rushes.

'Alas, he nought esteems that face of thine,
To which Love's eyes pays tributary gazes;
Nor thy soft hands, sweet lips and crystal eyne,
Whose full perfection all the world amazes;   635
  But having thee at vantage—wondrous dread!—
  Would root these beauties as he roots the mead.

'O, let him keep his loathsome cabin still;
Beauty hath nought to do with such foul fiends.
Come not within his danger by thy will;   640
They that thrive well take counsel of their friends.
  When thou didst name the boar, not to dissemble,
  I feared thy fortune, and my joints did tremble.

'Didst thou not mark my face? was it not white?
Saws't thou not signs of fear lurk in mine eye?   645
Grew I not faint? and fell I not downright?
Within my bosom, whereon thou dost lie,
  My boding heart pants, beats, and takes no rest,
  But, like an earthquake, shakes thee on my breast.

'For where Love reigns, disturbing Jealousy   650
Doth call himself Affection's sentinel;
Gives false alarms, suggesteth mutiny,
And in a peaceful hour doth cry "Kill, kill!"
  Distemp'ring gentle Love in his desire,
  As air and water do abate the fire.   655

'This sour informer, this bate-breeding spy,
This canker that eats up Love's tender spring,
This carry-tale, dissentious Jealousy,
That sometime true news, sometime false doth bring,
  Knocks at my heart, and whispers in mine ear   660
  That if I love thee I thy death should fear;

'And more than so, presenteth to mine eye
The picture of an angry chafing boar
Under whose sharp fangs on his back doth lie
An image like thyself, all stained with gore;   665
  Whose blood upon the fresh flowers being shed
  Doth make them droop with grief and hang the
    head.

'What should I do, seeing thee so indeed,
That tremble at th'imagination?
The thought of it doth make my faint heart bleed,   670
And fear doth teach it divination:
  I prophesy thy death, my living sorrow,
  If thou encounter with the boar to-morrow.

'But if thou needs wilt hunt, be ruled by me;
Uncouple at the timorous flying hare,   675
Or at the fox which lives by subtlety,
Or at the roe which no encounter dare.
  Pursue these fearful creatures o'er the downs,
  And on thy well-breathed horse keep with thy
    hounds.

'And when thou hast on foot the purblind hare,   680
Mark the poor wretch, to overshoot his troubles,
How he outruns the wind, and with what care
He cranks and crosses with a thousand doubles.
  The many musits through the which he goes
  Are like a labyrinth to amaze his foes.   685

'Sometime he runs among a flock of sheep,
To make the cunning hounds mistake their smell,
And sometime where earth-delving conies keep,
To stop the loud pursuers in their yell;
  And sometime sorteth with a herd of deer.   690
  Danger deviseth shifts; wit waits on fear.

'For there his smell with others being mingled,
The hot scent-snuffing hounds are driven to doubt,
Ceasing their clamorous cry till they have singled
With much ado the cold fault cleanly out.   695
  Then do they spend their mouths; Echo replies,
  As if another chase were in the skies.

'By this, poor Wat, far off upon a hill,
Stands on his hinder legs with list'ning ear,
To hearken if his foes pursue him still;   700
Anon their loud alarums he doth hear;
  And now his grief may be comparéd well
  To one sore sick that hears the passing-bell.

'Then shalt thou see the dew-bedabbled wretch
Turn, and return, indenting with the way;   705
Each envious brier his weary legs do scratch,
Each shadow makes him stop, each murmur stay;
  For misery is trodden on by many,
  And being low never relieved by any.

'Lie quietly and hear a little more; 710
Nay, do not struggle, for thou shalt not rise.
To make thee hate the hunting of the boar,
Unlike myself thou hear'st me moralize,
  Applying this to that, and so to so;
  For love can comment upon every woe. 715

'Where did I leave?' 'No matter where,' quoth he;
'Leave me, and then the story aptly ends.
The night is spent.' 'Why, what of that?' quoth she.
'I am', quoth he, 'expected of my friends;
  And now 'tis dark, and going I shall fall.' 720
  'In night', quoth she, 'desire sees best of all.

'But if thou fall, O, then imagine this,
The earth, in love with thee, thy footing trips,
And all is but to rob thee of a kiss.
Rich preys make true men thieves; so do thy lips 725
  Make modest Dian cloudy and forlorn,
  Lest she should steal a kiss, and die forsworn.

'Now of this dark night I perceive the reason:
Cynthia for shame obscures her silver shine,
Till forging Nature be condemned of treason, 730
For stealing moulds from heaven that were divine,
  Wherein she framed thee, in high heaven's despite,
  To shame the sun by day and her by night.

'And therefore hath she bribed the Destinies
To cross the curious workmanship of Nature, 735
To mingle beauty with infirmities
And pure perfection with impure defeature,
  Making it subject to the tyranny
  Of mad mischances and much misery;

'As burning fevers, agues pale and faint, 740
Life-poisoning pestilence and frenzies wood,
The marrow-eating sickness whose attaint
Disorder breeds by heating of the blood,
  Surfeits, imposthumes, grief and damned despair,
  Swear Nature's death for framing thee so fair. 745

'And not the least of all these maladies
But in one minute's fight brings beauty under.
Both favour, savour, hue and qualities,
Whereat th'impartial gazer late did wonder,
  Are on the sudden wasted, thawed and done, 750
  As mountain snow melts with the midday sun.

'Therefore, despite of fruitless chastity,
Love-lacking vestals and self-loving nuns,
That on the earth would breed a scarcity
And barren dearth of daughters and of sons, 755
  Be prodigal: the lamp that burns by night
  Dries up his oil to lend the world his light.

'What is thy body but a swallowing grave,
Seeming to bury that posterity
Which by the rights of time thou needs must have, 760
If thou destroy them not in dark obscurity?
  If so, the world will hold thee in disdain,
  Sith in thy pride so fair a hope is slain.

'So in thyself thyself art made away;
A mischief worse than civil home-bred strife, 765
Or theirs whose desperate hands themselves do slay,
Or butcher sire that reaves his son of life.
  Foul cank'ring rust the hidden treasure frets,
  But gold that's put to use more gold begets.'

'Nay, then,' quoth Adon, 'you will fall again 770
Into your idle over-handled theme;
The kiss I gave you is bestowed in vain,
And all in vain you strive against the stream;
  For, by this black-faced night, desire's foul nurse,
  Your treatise makes me like you worse and worse. 775

'If love have lent you twenty thousand tongues,
And every tongue more moving than your own,
Bewitching like the wanton mermaid's songs,
Yet from mine ear the tempting tune is blown;
  For know, my heart stands armèd in mine ear, 780
  And will not let a false sound enter there,

'Lest the deceiving harmony should run
Into the quiet closure of my breast;
And then my little heart were quite undone,
In his bedchamber to be barred of rest. 785
  No, lady, no; my heart longs not to groan,
  But soundly sleeps, while now it sleeps alone.

'What have you urged that I cannot reprove?
The path is smooth that leadeth on to danger;
I hate not love, but your device in love 790
That lends embracements unto every stranger.
  You do it for increase: O strange excuse,
  When reason is the bawd to lust's abuse!

'Call it not love, for Love to heaven is fled
Since sweating Lust on earth usurped his name; 795
Under whose simple semblance he hath fed
Upon fresh beauty, blotting it with blame;
  Which the hot tyrant stains and soon bereaves,
  As caterpillars do the tender leaves.

'Love comforteth like sunshine after rain, 800
But Lust's effect is tempest after sun;
Love's gentle spring doth always fresh remain,
Lust's winter comes ere summer half be done;
  Love surfeits not, Lust like a glutton dies;
  Love is all truth, Lust full of forgèd lies. 805

'More I could tell, but more I dare not say;
The text is old, the orator too green.
Therefore, in sadness, now I will away;
My face is full of shame, my heart of teen:
  Mine ears that to your wanton talk attended 810
  Do burn themselves for having so offended.'

With this, he breaketh from the sweet embrace
Of those fair arms which bound him to her breast,
And homeward through the dark lawnd runs apace;
Leaves Love upon her back deeply distressed. 815
  Look how a bright star shooteth from the sky,
  So glides he in the night from Venus' eye;

Which after him she darts, as one on shore
Gazing upon a late-embarkéd friend,
Till the wild waves will have him seen no more,   320
Whose ridges with the meeting clouds contend;
    So did the merciless and pitchy night
    Fold in the object that did feed her sight.

Whereat amazed as one that unaware
Hath dropped a precious jewel in the flood,   825
Or 'stonished as night-wand'rers often are,
Their light blown out in some mistrustful wood;
    Even so confounded in the dark she lay,
    Having lost the fair discovery of her way.

And now she beats her heart, whereat it groans,   830
That all the neighbour caves, as seeming troubled,
Make verbal repetition of her moans;
Passion on passion deeply is redoubled:
    'Ay me!' she cries, and twenty times, 'Woe, woe!'
    And twenty echoes twenty times cry so.   835

She, marking them, begins a wailing note,
And sings extemporally a woeful ditty;
How love makes young men thrall, and old men dote;
How love is wise in folly, foolish witty:
    Her heavy anthem still concludes in woe,   840
    And still the choir of echoes answer so.

Her song was tedious, and outwore the night,
For lovers' hours are long, though seeming short;
If pleased themselves, others, they think, delight
In such-like circumstance, with such-like sport.   845
    Their copious stories, oftentimes begun,
    End without audience, and are never done.

For who hath she to spend the night withal
But idle sounds resembling parasites,
Like shrill-tongued tapsters answering every call,   850
Soothing the humour of fantastic wits?
    She says ''Tis so'; they answer all ''Tis so';
    And would say after her, if she said 'No'.

Lo, here the gentle lark, weary of rest,
From his moist cabinet mounts up on high,   855
And wakes the morning, from whose silver breast
The sun ariseth in his majesty;
    Who doth the world so gloriously behold
    That cedar-tops and hills seem burnished gold.

Venus salutes him with this fair good-morrow: 860
'O thou clear god, and patron of all light,
From whom each lamp and shining star doth borrow
The beauteous influence that makes him bright,
    There lives a son that sucked an earthly mother
    May lend thee light, as thou dost lend to other.'   865

This said, she hasteth to a myrtle grove,
Musing the morning is so much o'erworn,
And yet she hears no tidings of her love;
She hearkens for his hounds and for his horn.
    Anon she hears them chant it lustily,   870
    And all in haste she coasteth to the cry.

And as she runs, the bushes in the way
Some catch her by the neck, some kiss her face,
Some twind about her thigh to make her stay;
She wildly breaketh from their strict embrace,   875
    Like a milch doe, whose swelling dugs do ache,
    Hasting to feed her fawn hid in some brake.

By this she hears the hounds are at a bay;
Whereat she starts, like one that spies an adder
Wreathed up in fatal folds just in his way,   880
The fear whereof doth make him shake and shudder;
    Even so the timorous yelping of the hounds
    Appals her senses and her spirit confounds.

For now she knows it is no gentle chase,
But the blunt boar, rough bear, or lion proud,   885
Because the cry remaineth in one place,
Where fearfully the dogs exclaim aloud.
    Finding their enemy to be so curst,
    They all strain court'sy who shall cope him first.

This dismal cry rings sadly in her ear,   890
Through which it enters to surprise her heart;
Who, overcome by doubt and bloodless fear,
With cold-pale weakness numbs each feeling part;
    Like soldiers, when their captain once doth yield,
    They basely fly and dare not stay the field.   895

Thus stands she in a trembling ecstasy;
Till, cheering up her senses all dismayed,
She tells them 'tis a causeless fantasy,
And childish error, that they are afraid;
    Bids them leave quaking, bids them fear no more;   900
    And with that word she spied the hunted boar,

Whose frothy mouth, bepainted all with red,
Like milk and blood being mingled both together,
A second fear through all her sinews spread,
Which madly hurries her she knows not whither: 905
    This way she runs, and now she will no further,
    But back retires to rate the boar for murther.

A thousand spleens bear her a thousand ways;
She treads the path that she untreads again;
Her more than haste is mated with delays,   910
Like the proceedings of a drunken brain,
    Full of respects, yet nought at all respecting,
    In hand with all things, nought at all effecting.

Here kennelled in a brake she finds a hound,
And asks the weary caitiff for his master;   915
And there another licking of his wound,
'Gainst venomed sores the only sovereign plaster;
    And here she meets another sadly scowling,
    To whom she speaks, and he replies with howling.

When he hath ceased his ill-resounding noise,   920
Another flap-mouthed mourner, black and grim,
Against the welkin volleys out his voice,
Another and another answer him,
    Clapping their proud tails to the ground below,
    Shaking their scratched ears, bleeding as they go.   925

Look how the world's poor people are amazéd
At apparitions, signs and prodigies,
Whereon with fearful eyes they long have gazéd,
Infusing them with dreadful prophecies;
   So she at these sad signs draws up her breath,   930
   And, sighing it again, exclaims on Death.

'Hard-favoured tyrant, ugly, meagre, lean,
Hateful divorce of love'—thus chides she Death—
'Grim-grinning ghost, earth's worm, what dost thou
   mean
To stifle beauty and to steal his breath   935
   Who when he lived, his breath and beauty set
   Gloss on the rose, smell to the violet?

'If he be dead—O no, it cannot be,
Seeing his beauty, thou shouldst strike at it—
O yes, it may; thou hast no eyes to see,   940
But hatefully at random dost thou hit.
   Thy mark is feeble age; but thy false dart
   Mistakes that aim, and cleaves an infant's heart.

'Hadst thou but bid beware, then he had spoke,
And, hearing him, thy power had lost his power.   945
The Destinies will curse thee for this stroke;
They bid thee crop a weed, thou pluck'st a flower.
   Love's golden arrow at him should have fled,
   And not Death's ebon dart, to strike him dead.

'Dost thou drink tears, that thou provokest such
   weeping?   950
What may a heavy groan advantage thee?
Why hast thou cast into eternal sleeping
Those eyes that taught all other eyes to see?
   Now Nature cares not for thy mortal vigour,
   Since her best work is ruined with thy rigour.'   955

Here overcome as one full of despair,
She vailed her eyelids, who, like sluices, stopped
The crystal tide that from her two cheeks fair
In the sweet channel of her bosom dropped;
   But through the flood-gates breaks the silver rain,   960
   And with his strong course opens them again.

O, how her eyes and tears did lend and borrow!
Her eye seen in the tears, tears in her eye;
Both crystals, where they viewed each other's sorrow,
Sorrow that friendly sighs sought still to dry;   965
   But like a stormy day, now wind, now rain,
   Sighs dry her cheeks, tears make them wet again.

Variable passions throng her constant woe,
As striving who should best become her grief;
All entertained, each passion labours so   970
That every present sorrow seemeth chief,
   But none is best. Then join they all together,
   Like many clouds consulting for foul weather.

By this, far off she hears some huntsman holla;
A nurse's song ne'er pleased her babe so well.   975
The dire imagination she did follow
This sound of hope doth labour to expel;
   For now reviving joy bids her rejoice,
   And flatters her it is Adonis' voice.

Whereat her tears began to turn their tide,   980
Being prisoned in her eye like pearls in glass;
Yet sometimes falls an orient drop beside,
Which her cheek melts, as scorning it should pass
   To wash the foul face of the sluttish ground,
   Who is but drunken when she seemeth drowned.   985

O hard-believing love, how strange it seems
Not to believe, and yet too credulous!
Thy weal and woe are both of them extremes;
Despair, and hope makes thee ridiculous:
   The one doth flatter thee in thoughts unlikely,   990
   In likely thoughts the other kills thee quickly.

Now she unweaves the web that she hath wrought;
Adonis lives, and Death is not to blame;
It was not she that called him all to nought.
Now she adds honours to his hateful name;   995
   She clepes him king of graves, and grave for kings,
   Imperious supreme of all mortal things.

'No, no,' quoth she, 'sweet Death, I did but jest;
Yet pardon me, I felt a kind of fear
When as I met the boar, that bloody beast,   1000
Which knows no pity, but is still severe.
   Then, gentle shadow—truth I must confess—
   I railed on thee, fearing my love's decease.

''Tis not my fault: the boar provoked my tongue;
Be wreaked on him, invisible commander;   1005
'Tis he, foul creature, that hath done thee wrong;
I did but act, he's author of thy slander.
   Grief hath two tongues, and never woman yet
   Could rule them both without ten women's wit.'

Thus, hoping that Adonis is alive,   1010
Her rash suspect she doth extenuate;
And that his beauty may the better thrive,
With Death she humbly doth insinuate;
   Tells him of trophies, statues, tombs, and stories
   His victories, his triumphs and his glories.   1015

'O Jove,' quoth she, 'how much a fool was I
To be of such a weak and silly mind
To wail his death who lives and must not die
Till mutual overthrow of mortal kind!
   For he being dead, with him is Beauty slain,   1020
   And, Beauty dead, black Chaos comes again.

'Fie, fie, fond love, thou art as full of fear
As one with treasure laden, hemmed with thieves;
Trifles unwitnesséd with eye or ear
Thy coward heart with false bethinking grieves.'   1025
   Even at this word she hears a merry horn,
   Whereat she leaps that was but late forlorn.

As falcons to the lure, away she flies;
The grass stoops not, she treads on it so light;
And in her haste unfortunately spies   1030
The foul boar's conquest on her fair delight;
   Which seen, her eyes, as murd'red with the view,
   Like stars ashamed of day, themselves withdrew;

Or as the snail, whose tender horns being hit,
Shrinks backward in his shelly cave with pain, 1035
And there all smoth'red up in shade doth sit,
Long after fearing to creep forth again;
  So at his bloody view her eyes are fled
  Into the deep-dark cabins of her head;

Where they resign their office and their light 1040
To the disposing of her troubled brain;
Who bids them still consort with ugly night,
And never wound the heart with looks again;
  Who, like a king perplexéd in his throne,
  By their suggestion gives a deadly groan, 1045

Whereat each tributary subject quakes;
As when the wind, imprisoned in the ground,
Struggling for passage, earth's foundation shakes,
Which with cold terror doth men's minds confound.
  This mutiny each part doth so surprise, 1050
  That from their dark beds once more leap her eyes;

And being opened, threw unwilling light
Upon the wide wound that the boar had trenched
In his soft flank; whose wonted lily white
With purple tears that his wound wept was drenched: 1055
  No flower was nigh, no grass, herb, leaf or weed,
  But stole his blood and seemed with him to bleed.

This solemn sympathy poor Venus noteth;
Over one shoulder doth she hang her head;
Dumbly she passions, franticly she doteth; 1060
She thinks he could not die, he is not dead.
  Her voice is stopped, her joints forget to bow;
  Her eyes are mad that they have wept till now.

Upon his hurt she looks so steadfastly
That her sight dazzling makes the wound seem three; 1065
And then she reprehends her mangling eye
That makes more gashes where no breach should be:
  His face seems twain, each several limb is doubled;
  For oft the eye mistakes, the brain being troubled.

'My tongue cannot express my grief for one, 1070
And yet,' quoth she, 'behold two Adons dead!
My sighs are blown away, my salt tears gone,
Mine eyes are turned to fire, my heart to lead;
  Heavy heart's lead, melt at mine eyes' red fire!
  So shall I die by drops of hot desire. 1075

'Alas, poor world, what treasure hast thou lost!
What face remains alive that's worth the viewing?
Whose tongue is music now? what canst thou boast
Of things long since, or any thing ensuing?
  The flowers are sweet, their colours fresh and trim; 1080
  But true sweet beauty lived and died with him.

'Bonnet nor veil henceforth no creature wear;
Nor sun nor wind will ever strive to kiss you.
Having no fair to lose, you need not fear;
The sun doth scorn you, and the wind doth hiss you. 1085
  But when Adonis lived, sun and sharp air
  Lurked like two thieves to rob him of his fair;

'And therefore would he put his bonnet on,
Under whose brim the gaudy sun would peep;
The wind would blow it off, and, being gone, 1090
Play with his locks. Then would Adonis weep;
  And straight, in pity of his tender years,
  They both would strive who first should dry his
    tears.

'To see his face the lion walked along
Behind some hedge, because he would not fear him; 1095
To recreate himself when he hath sung,
The tiger would be tame and gently hear him;
  If he had spoke, the wolf would leave his prey,
  And never fright the silly lamb that day.

'When he beheld his shadow in the brook, 1100
The fishes spread on it their golden gills;
When he was by, the birds such pleasure took
That some would sing, some other in their bills
  Would bring him mulberries and ripe-red cherries;
  He fed them with his sight, they him with berries. 1105

'But this foul, grim, and urchin-snouted boar,
Whose downward eye still looketh for a grave,
Ne'er saw the beauteous livery that he wore;
Witness the entertainment that he gave.
  If he did see his face, why then I know 1110
  He thought to kiss him, and hath killed him so.

''Tis true, 'tis true; thus was Adonis slain:
He ran upon the boar with his sharp spear,
Who did not whet his teeth at him again,
But by a kiss thought to persuade him there; 1115
  And nuzzling in his flank, the loving swine
  Sheathed unaware the tusk in his soft groin.

'Had I been toothed like him, I must confess,
With kissing him I should have killed him first;
But he is dead, and never did he bless 1120
My youth with his; the more am I accurst.'
  With this, she falleth in the place she stood,
  And stains her face with his congealéd blood.

She looks upon his lips, and they are pale;
She takes him by the hand, and that is cold; 1125
She whispers in his ears a heavy tale,
As if they heard the woeful words she told;
  She lifts the coffer-lids that close his eyes,
  Where, lo, two lamps, burnt out, in darkness lies;

Two glasses, where herself herself beheld 1130
A thousand times, and now no more, reflect;
Their virtue lost wherein they late excelled,
And every beauty robbed of his effect.
  'Wonder of time,' quoth she, 'this is my spite,
  That, thou being dead, the day should yet be light. 1135

'Since thou art dead, lo, here I prophesy
Sorrow on love hereafter shall attend;
It shall be waited on with jealousy,
Find sweet beginning but unsavoury end;
  Ne'er settled equally, but high or low, 1140
  That all love's pleasure shall not match his woe.

'It shall be fickle, false and full of fraud;
Bud, and be blasted, in a breathing while;
The bottom poison, and the top o'erstrawed
With sweets that shall the truest sight beguile; 1145
 The strongest body shall it make most weak,
 Strike the wise dumb, and teach the fool to speak.

'It shall be sparing, and too full of riot,
Teaching decrepit age to tread the measures;
The staring ruffian shall it keep in quiet, 1150
Pluck down the rich, enrich the poor with treasures;
 It shall be raging-mad, and silly-mild,
 Make the young old, the old become a child.

'It shall suspect where is no cause of fear;
It shall not fear where it should most mistrust; 1155
It shall be merciful and too severe,
And most deceiving when it seems most just;
 Perverse it shall be where it shows most toward,
 Put fear to valour, courage to the coward.

'It shall be cause of war and dire events, 1160
And set dissension 'twixt the son and sire;
Subject and servile to all discontents,
As dry combustious matter is to fire.
 Sith in his prime death doth my love destroy,
 They that love best their loves shall not enjoy.' 1165

By this the boy that by her side lay killed
Was melted like a vapour from her sight,
And in his blood that on the ground lay spilled
A purple flower sprung up, chequ'red with white,
 Resembling well his pale checks, and the blood 1170
 Which in round drops upon their whiteness stood.

She bows her head the new-sprung flower to smell,
Comparing it to her Adonis' breath;
And says within her bosom it shall dwell,
Since he himself is reft from her by death; 1175
 She crops the stalk, and in the breach appears
 Green-dropping sap, which she compares to tears.

'Poor flower,' quoth she, 'this was thy father's guise—
Sweet issue of a more sweet-smelling sire—
For every little grief to wet his eyes. 1180
To grow unto himself was his desire,
 And so 'tis thine; but know, it is as good
 To wither in my breast as in his blood.

'Here was thy father's bed, here in my breast;
Thou art the next of blood, and 'tis thy right. 1185
Lo, in this hollow cradle take thy rest;
My throbbing heart shall rock thee day and night;
 There shall not be one minute in an hour
 Wherein I will not kiss my sweet love's flower.'

Thus weary of the world, away she hies, 1190
And yokes her silver doves, by whose swift aid
Their mistress, mounted, through the empty skies
In her light chariot quickly is conveyed,
 Holding their course to Paphos, where their queen
 Means to immure herself and not be seen. 1195

The Rape of Lucrece

TO THE
RIGHT HONOURABLE
HENRY WRIOTHESLEY,
EARL OF SOUTHAMPTON, AND BARON
OF TITCHFIELD

The love I dedicate to your lordship is without end: whereof this pamphlet, without beginning is but a superfluous moiety. The warrant I have of your honourable disposition, not the worth of my untutored lines, make it assured of acceptance. What I have done is yours; what I have to do is yours; being part in all I have, devoted yours. Were my worth greater, my duty would show greater; meantime, as it is, it is bound to your lordship, to whom I wish long life still lengthened with all happiness.

> Your lordship's in all duty,
> William Shakespeare

THE ARGUMENT

Lucius Tarquinius, for his excessive pride surnamed Superbus, after he had caused his own father-in-law Servius Tullius to be cruelly murdered, and, contrary to the Roman laws and customs, not requiring or staying for the people's suffrages, had possessed himself of the kingdom, went accompanied with his sons and other noblemen of Rome, to besiege Ardea. During which siege the principal men of the army meeting one evening at the tent of Sextus Tarquinius, the king's son, in their discourses after supper every one commended the virtues of his own wife; among whom Collatinus extolled the incomparable chastity of his wife Lucretia. In that pleasant humour they all posted to Rome; and intending, by their secret and sudden arrival, to make trial of that which every one had before avouched, only Collatinus finds his wife, though it were late in the night, spinning amongst her maids: the other ladies were all found dancing and revelling, or in several disports. Whereupon the noblemen yielded Collatinus the victory, and his wife the fame. At that time Sextus Tarquinius being inflamed with Lucrece' beauty, yet smothering his passions for the present, departed with the rest back to the camp; from whence he shortly after privily withdrew himself, and was, according to his estate, royally entertained and lodged by Lucrece at Collatium. The same night he treacherously stealeth into her chamber, violently ravished her, and early in the morning speedeth away. Lucrece, in this lamentable plight, hastily dispatcheth messengers, one to Rome for her father, another to the camp for Collatine. They came, the one accompanied with Junius Brutus, the other with Publius Valerius; and finding Lucrece attired in mourning habit, demanded the cause of her sorrow. She, first taking an oath of them for her revenge, revealed the actor and whole manner of his dealing, and withal suddenly stabbed herself. Which done, with one consent they all vowed to root out the whole hated family of the Tarquins; and bearing the dead body to Rome, Brutus acquainted the people with the doer and manner of the vile deed, with a bitter invective against the tyranny of the king: wherewith the people were so moved, that with one consent and a general acclamation the Tarquins were all exiled, and the state government changed from kings to consuls.

From the besiegéd Ardea all in post,
Borne by the trustless wings of false desire,
Lust-breathéd Tarquin leaves the Roman host,
And to Collatium bears the lightless fire
Which, in pale embers hid, lurks to aspire   5
    And girdle with embracing flames the waist
    Of Collatine's fair love, Lucrece the chaste.

Haply that name of chaste unhapp'ly set
This bateless edge on his keen appetite;
When Collatine unwisely did not let   10
To praise the clear unmatchéd red and white
Which triumphed in that sky of his delight,
    Where mortal stars, as bright as heaven's beauties,
    With pure aspects did him peculiar duties.

For he the night before, in Tarquin's tent,   15
Unlocked the treasure of his happy state;
What priceless wealth the heavens had him lent
In the possession of his beauteous mate;
Reck'ning his fortune at such high-proud rate
    That kings might be espouséd to more fame,   20
    But king nor peer to such a peerless dame.

O happiness enjoyed but of a few!
And, if possessed, as soon decayed and done
As is the morning silver-melting dew
Against the golden splendour of the sun!   25
An expired date, cancelled ere well begun:
    Honour and beauty, in the owner's arms,
    Are weakly fortressed from a world of harms.

Beauty itself doth of itself persuade
The eyes of men without an orator;   30
What needeth then apology be made,
To set forth that which is so singular?
Or why is Collatine the publisher
    Of that rich jewel he should keep unknown
    From thievish ears, because it is his own?   35

Perchance his boast of Lucrece' sov'reignty
Suggested this proud issue of a king;
For by our ears our hearts oft tainted be.
Perchance that envy of so rich a thing,
Braving compare, disdainfully did sting   40
    His high-pitched thoughts, that meaner men should
        vaunt
    That golden hap which their superiors want.

But some untimely thought did instigate
His all too timeless speed, if none of those.
His honour, his affairs, his friends, his state,   45
Neglected all, with swift intent he goes
To quench the coal which in his liver glows.
    O rash-false heat, wrapped in repentant cold,
    Thy hasty spring still blasts, and ne'er grows old!

When at Collatium this false lord arrivéd,   50
Well was he welcomed by the Roman dame,
Within whose face beauty and virtue strivéd
Which of them both should underprop her fame:
When virtue bragged, beauty would blush for shame;
    When beauty boasted blushes, in despite   55
    Virtue would stain that o'er with silver white.

But beauty, in that white entituléd,
From Venus' doves doth challenge that fair field;
Then virtue claims from beauty beauty's red,
Which virtue gave the golden age to gild   60
Their silver cheeks, and called it then their shield;
    Teaching them thus to use it in the fight,
    When shame assailed, the red should fence the white.

This heraldry in Lucrece' face was seen,
Argued by beauty's red and virtue's white;   65
Of either's colour was the other queen,
Proving from world's minority their right;
Yet their ambition makes them still to fight,
    The sovereignty of either being so great
    That oft they interchange each other's seat.   70

This silent war of lilies and of roses
Which Tarquin viewed in her fair face's field,
In their pure ranks his traitor eye encloses;
Where, lest between them both it should be killed,
The coward captive vanquishéd doth yield   75
    To those two armies that would let him go
    Rather than triumph in so false a foe.

Now thinks he that her husband's shallow tongue,
The niggard prodigal that praised her so,
In that high task hath done her beauty wrong,   80
Which far exceeds his barren skill to show;
Therefore that praise which Collatine doth owe
    Enchanted Tarquin answers with surmise,
    In silent wonder of still-gazing eyes.

This earthly saint, adored by this devil,   85
Little suspecteth the false worshipper;
"For unstained thoughts do seldom dream on evil;
"Birds never limed no secret bushes fear.
So guiltless she securely gives good cheer
    And reverend welcome to her princely guest,   90
    Whose inward ill no outward harm expressed;

For that he coloured with his high estate,
Hiding base sin in pleats of majesty;
That nothing in him seemed inordinate,
Save sometime too much wonder of his eye,   95
Which, having all, all could not satisfy;
    But, poorly rich, so wanteth in his store
    That cloyed with much he pineth still for more.

But she, that never coped with stranger eyes,
Could pick no meaning from their parling looks,   100
Nor read the subtle-shining secrecies
Writ in the glassy margents of such books.
She touched no unknown baits, nor feared no hooks;
    Nor could she moralize his wanton sight,
    More than his eyes were opened to the light.   105

He stories to her ears her husband's fame,
Won in the fields of fruitful Italy;
And decks with praises Collatine's high name,
Made glorious by his manly chivalry
With bruiséd arms and wreaths of victory.   110
    Her joy with heaved-up hand she doth express,
    And wordless so greets heaven for his success.

Far from the purpose of his coming thither,
He makes excuses for his being there.
No cloudy show of stormy blust'ring weather   115
Doth yet in his fair welkin once appear;
Till sable Night, mother of dread and fear,
  Upon the world dim darkness doth display,
  And in her vaulty prison stows the day.

For then is Tarquin brought unto his bed,   120
Intending weariness with heavy sprite;
For after supper long he questionéd
With modest Lucrece, and wore out the night.
Now leaden slumber with life's strength doth fight;
And every one to rest himself betakes,   125
  Save thieves and cares and troubled minds that
  wakes.

As one of which doth Tarquin lie revolving
The sundry dangers of his will's obtaining;
Yet ever to obtain his will resolving,
Though weak-built hopes persuade him to abstaining;   130
Despair to gain doth traffic oft for gaining,
  And when great treasure is the meed proposéd,
  Though death be adjunct, there's no death supposéd.

Those that much covet are with gain so fond
That what they have not, that which they possess,   135
They scatter and unloose it from their bond,
And so, by hoping more, they have but less;
Or, gaining more, the profit of excess
  Is but to surfeit, and such griefs sustain
  That they prove bankrupt in this poor-rich gain.   140

The aim of all is but to nurse the life
With honour, wealth and ease, in waning age;
And in this aim there is such thwarting strife
That one for all or all for one we gage:
As life for honour in fell battle's rage;   145
  Honour for wealth; and oft that wealth doth cost
  The death of all, and all together lost.

So that in vent'ring ill we leave to be
The things we are for that which we expect;
And this ambitious foul infirmity,   150
In having much, torments us with defect
Of that we have; so then we do neglect
  The thing we have, and, all for want of wit,
  Make something nothing by augmenting it.

Such hazard now must doting Tarquin make,   155
Pawning his honour to obtain his lust;
And for himself himself he must forsake:
Then where is truth, if there be no self-trust?
When shall he think to find a stranger just
  When he himself himself confounds, betrays   160
  To sland'rous tongues and wretched hateful days?

Now stole upon the time the dead of night,
When heavy sleep had closed up mortal eyes;
No comfortable star did lend his light,
No noise but owls' and wolves' death-boding cries;   165
Now serves the season that they may surprise
  The silly lambs. Pure thoughts are dead and still,
  While lust and murder wakes to stain and kill.

And now this lustful lord, leaped from his bed,
Throwing his mantle rudely o'er his arm,   170
Is madly tossed between desire and dread;
Th'one sweetly flatters, th'other feareth harm;
But honest fear, bewitched with lust's foul charm,
  Doth too too oft betake him to retire,
  Beaten away by brain-sick rude desire.   175

His falchion on a flint he softly smiteth,
That from the cold stone sparks of fire do fly,
Whereat a waxen torch forthwith he lighteth,
Which must be lode-star to his lustful eye;
And to the flame thus speaks advisedly: 180
  'As from this cold flint I enforced this fire,
  So Lucrece must I force to my desire.'

Here pale with fear he doth premeditate
The dangers of his loathsome enterprise,
And in his inward mind he doth debate   185
What following sorrow may on this arise;
Then, looking scornfully, he doth despise
  His naked armour of still-slaughteréd lust,
  And justly thus controls his thoughts unjust:

'Fair torch, burn out thy light, and lend it not   190
To darken her whose light excelleth thine;
And die, unhalloweéd thoughts, before you blot
With your uncleanness that which is divine;
Offer incense to so pure a shrine;
  Let fair humanity abhor the deed   195
  That spots and stains love's modest snow-white
  weed.

'O shame to knighthood and to shining arms!
O foul dishonour to my household's grave!
O impious act, including all foul harms!
A martial man to be soft fancy's slave!   200
True valour still a true respect should have;
  Then my digression is so vile, so base,
  That it will live engraven in my face.

'Yea, though I die, the scandal will survive,
And be an eye-sore in my golden coat;   205
Some loathsome dash the herald will contrive,
To cipher me how fondly I did dote;
That my posterity, shamed with the note,
  Shall curse my bones, and hold it for no sin
  To wish that I their father had not been.   210

'What win I, if I gain the thing I seek?
A dream, a breath, a froth of fleeting joy.
Who buys a minute's mirth to wail a week?
Or sells eternity to get a toy?
For one sweet grape who will the vine destroy?   215
  Or what fond beggar, but to touch the crown,
  Would with the sceptre straight be strucken down?

'If Collatinus dream of my intent,
Will he not wake, and in a desp'rate rage
Post hither, this vile purpose to prevent?—   220
This siege that hath engirt his marriage,
This blur to youth, this sorrow to the sage,
  This dying virtue, this surviving shame,
  Whose crime will bear an ever-during blame.

'O what excuse can my invention make, 225
When thou shalt charge me with so black a deed?
Will not my tongue be mute, my frail joints shake,
Mine eyes forego their light, my false heart bleed?
The guilt being great, the fear doth still exceed; 230
  And extreme fear can neither fight nor fly,
  But coward-like with trembling terror die.

'Had Collatinus killed my son or sire,
Or lain in ambush to betray my life,
Or were he not my dear friend, this desire
Might have excuse to work upon his wife, 235
As in revenge or quittal of such strife;
  But as he is my kinsman, my dear friend,
  The shame and fault finds no excuse nor end.

'Shameful it is—ay, if the fact be known;
Hateful it is—there is no hate in loving; 240
I'll beg her love—but she is not her own;
The worst is but denial and reproving.
My will is strong, past reason's weak removing.—
  Who fears a sentence or an old man's saw
  Shall by a painted cloth be kept in awe.' 245

Thus graceless holds he disputation
'Tween frozen conscience and hot-burning will,
And with good thoughts makes dispensation,
Urging the worser sense for vantage still;
Which in a moment doth confound and kill 250
  All pure effects, and doth so far proceed
  That what is vile shows like a virtuous deed.

Quoth he, 'She took me kindly by the hand,
And gazed for tidings in my eager eyes,
Fearing some hard news from the warlike band 255
Where her belovéd Collatinus lies.
O how her fear did make her colour rise!
  First red as roses that on lawn we lay,
  Then white as lawn, the roses took away.

'And how her hand, in my hand being locked, 260
Forced it to tremble with her loyal fear!
Which struck her sad, and then it faster rocked
Until her husband's welfare she did hear;
Whereat she smiléd with so sweet a cheer
  That had Narcissus seen her as she stood 265
  Self-love had never drowned him in the flood.

'Why hunt I then for colour or excuses?
All orators are dumb when beauty pleadeth;
Poor wretches have remorse in poor abuses;
Love thrives not in the heart that shadows dreadeth; 270
Affection is my captain, and he leadeth;
  And when his gaudy banner is displayed,
  The coward fights and will not be dismayed.

'Then childish fear avaunt! debating die!
Respect and reason wait on wrinkled age! 275
My heart shall never countermand mine eye;
Sad pause and deep regard beseems the sage;
My part is youth, and beats these from the stage:
  Desire my pilot is, beauty my prize;
  Then who fears sinking where such treasure lies?' 280

As corn o'ergrown by weeds, so heedful fear
Is almost choked by unresisted lust.
Away he steals with open list'ning ear,
Full of foul hope and full of fond mistrust;
Both which, as servitors to the unjust, 285
  So cross him with their opposite persuasion
  That now he vows a league and now invasion.

Within his thought her heavenly image sits,
And in the selfsame seat sits Collatine.
That eye which looks on her confounds his wits; 290
That eye which him beholds, as more divine,
Unto a view so false will not incline;
  But with a pure appeal seeks to the heart,
  Which once corrupted takes the worser part;

And therein heartens up his servile powers, 295
Who, flatt'red by their leader's jocund show,
Stuff up his lust, as minutes fill up hours;
And as their captain, so their pride doth grow,
Paying more slavish tribute than they owe.
  By reprobate desire thus madly led, 300
  The Roman lord marcheth to Lucrece' bed.

The locks between her chamber and his will,
Each one by him enforced, retires his ward;
But, as they open, they all rate his ill,
Which drives the creeping thief to some regard. 305
The threshold grates the door to have him heard;
  Night-wand'ring weasels shriek to see him there;
  They fright him, yet he still pursues his fear.

As each unwilling portal yields him way,
Through little vents and crannies of the place 310
The wind wars with his torch to make him stay,
And blows the smoke of it into his face,
Extinguishing his conduct in this case;
  But his hot heart, which fond desire doth scorch,
  Puffs forth another wind that fires the torch; 315

And being lighted, by the light he spies
Lucretia's glove, wherein her needle sticks;
He takes it from the rushes where it lies,
And griping it, the needle his finger pricks,
As who should say 'This glove to wanton tricks 320
  Is not inured. Return again in haste;
  Thou see'st our mistress' ornaments are chaste.'

But all these poor forbiddings could not stay him;
He in the worst sense consters their denial:
The doors, the wind, the glove, that did delay him, 325
He takes for accidental things of trial;
Or as those bars which stop the hourly dial,
  Who with a ling'ring stay his course doth let,
  Till every minute pays the hour his debt.

'So, so,' quoth he, 'these lets attend the time, 330
Like little frosts that sometime threat the spring,
To add a more rejoicing to the prime,
And give the sneapéd birds more cause to sing.
Pain pays the income of each precious thing;
  Huge rocks, high winds, strong pirates, shelves and
    sands 335
  The merchant fears, ere rich at home he lands.'

Now is he come unto the chamber door
That shuts him from the heaven of his thought,
Which with a yielding latch, and with no more,
Hath barred him from the blessèd thing he sought.   340
So from himself impiety hath wrought,
   That for his prey to pray he doth begin,
   As if the heavens should countenance his sin.

But in the midst of his unfruitful prayer,
Having solicited th'eternal power   345
That his foul thoughts might compass his fair fair,
And they would stand auspicious to the hour,
Even there he starts; quoth he 'I must deflower:
   The powers to whom I pray abhor this fact;
   How can they then assist me in the act?   350

'Then Love and Fortune be my gods, my guide!
My will is backed with resolution.
Thoughts are but dreams till their effects be tried;
The blackest sin is cleared with absolution;
Against love's fire fear's frost hath dissolution.   355
   The eye of heaven is out, and misty night
   Covers the shame that follows sweet delight.'

This said, his guilty hand plucked up the latch,
And with his knee the door he opens wide.
The dove sleeps fast that this night-owl will catch. 360
Thus treason works ere traitors be espied.
Who sees the lurking serpent steps aside;
   But she, sound sleeping, fearing no such thing,
   Lies at the mercy of his mortal sting.

Into the chamber wickedly he stalks   365
And gazeth on her yet unstainèd bed.
The curtains being close, about he walks,
Rolling his greedy eyeballs in his head.
By their high treason is his heart misled,
   Which gives the watch-word to his hand full soon 370
   To draw the cloud that hides the silver moon.

Look as the fair and fiery-pointed sun,
Rushing from forth a cloud, bereaves our sight;
Even so, the curtain drawn, his eyes begun
To wink, being blinded with a greater light;   375
Whether it is that she reflects so bright
   That dazzleth them, or else some shame supposèd,
   But blind they are, and keep themselves enclosèd.

O, had they in that darksome prison died!
Then had they seen the period of their ill;   380
Then Collatine again, by Lucrece' side,
In his clear bed might have reposèd still;
But they must ope, this blessèd league to kill;
   And holy-thoughted Lucrece to their sight
   Must sell her joy, her life, her world's delight. 385

Her lily hand her rosy cheek lies under,
Coz'ning the pillow of a lawful kiss;
Who, therefore angry, seems to part in sunder,
Swelling on either side to want his bliss;
Between whose hills her head entombèd is;   390
   Where, like a virtuous monument, she lies,
   To be admired of lewd unhallowèd eyes.

Without the bed her other fair hand was,
On the green coverlet; whose perfect white
Showed like an April daisy on the grass,   395
With pearly sweat resembling dew of night.
Her eyes, like marigolds, had sheathed their light,
   And canopied in darkness sweetly lay,
   Till they might open to adorn the day.

Her hair, like golden threads, played with her breath— 400
O modest wantons! wanton modesty!—
Showing life's triumph in the map of death,
And death's dim look in life's mortality:
Each in her sleep themselves so beautify
   As if between them twain there were no strife,   405
   But that life lived in death and death in life.

Her breasts, like ivory globes circled with blue,
A pair of maiden worlds unconquerèd,
Save of their lord no bearing yoke they knew,
And him by oath they truly honourèd.   410
These worlds in Tarquin new ambition bred,
   Who like a foul usurper went about
   From this fair throne to heave the owner out.

What could he see but mightily he noted?
What did he note but strongly he desirèd?   415
What he beheld, on that he firmly doted,
And in his will his wilful eye he tirèd.
With more than admiration he admirèd
   Her azure veins, her alabaster skin,
   Her coral lips, her snow-white dimpled chin.   420

As the grim lion fawneth o'er his prey,
Sharp hunger by the conquest satisfied,
So o'er this sleeping soul doth Tarquin stay,
His rage of lust by gazing qualified;
Slacked, not suppressed; for standing by her side,   425
   His eye, which late this mutiny restrains,
   Unto a greater uproar tempts his veins;

And they, like straggling slaves for pillage fighting,
Obdurate vassals fell exploits effecting,
In bloody death and ravishment delighting,   430
Nor children's tears nor mothers' groans respecting,
Swell in their pride, the onset still expecting.
   Anon his beating heart, alarum striking,
   Gives the hot charge, and bids them do their liking.

His drumming heart cheers up his burning eye,   435
His eye commends the leading to his hand;
His hand, as proud of such a dignity,
Smoking with pride, marched on to make his stand
On her bare breast, the heart of all her land;
   Whose ranks of blue veins as his hand did scale, 440
   Left their round turrets destitute and pale.

They, must'ring to the quiet cabinet
Where their dear governess and lady lies,
Do tell her she is dreadfully beset,
And fright her with confusion of their cries.   445
She, much amazed, breaks ope her locked-up eyes,
   Who, peeping forth this tumult to behold,
   Are by his flaming torch dimmed and controlled.

Imagine her as one in dead of night
From forth dull sleep by dreadful fancy waking,⠀⠀450
That thinks she hath beheld some ghastly sprite,
Whose grim aspect sets every joint a-shaking;
What terror 'tis! but she, in worser taking,
⠀⠀From sleep disturbèd, heedfully doth view
⠀⠀The sight which makes supposèd terror true.⠀⠀455

Wrapped and confounded in a thousand fears,
Like to a new-killed bird she trembling lies;
She dares not look; yet, winking, there appears
Quick-shifting antics, ugly in her eyes.
"Such shadows are the weak brain's forgeries,⠀⠀460
⠀⠀Who, angry that the eyes fly from their lights,
⠀⠀In darkness daunts them with more dreadful sights.

His hand that yet remains upon her breast—
Rude ram, to batter such an ivory wall!—
May feel her heart, poor citizen, distressed,⠀⠀465
Wounding itself to death, rise up and fall,
Beating her bulk, that his hand shakes withal.
⠀⠀This moves in him more rage and lesser pity,
⠀⠀To make the breach and enter this sweet city.

First like a trumpet doth his tongue begin⠀⠀470
To sound a parley to his heartless foe,
Who o'er the white sheet peers her whiter chin,
The reason of this rash alarm to know,
Which he by dumb demeanour seeks to show;
⠀⠀But she with vehement prayers urgeth still⠀⠀475
⠀⠀Under what colour he commits this ill.

Thus he replies: 'The colour in thy face,
That even for anger makes the lily pale
And the red rose blush at her own disgrace,
Shall plead for me and tell my loving tale.⠀⠀480
Under that colour am I come to scale
⠀⠀Thy never-conquerèd fort. The fault is thine,
⠀⠀For those thine eyes betray thee unto mine.

'Thus I forestall thee, if thou mean to chide:
Thy beauty hath ensnared thee to this night,⠀⠀485
Where thou with patience must my will abide,
My will that marks thee for my earth's delight,
Which I to conquer sought with all my might;
⠀⠀But as reproof and reason beat it dead,
⠀⠀By thy bright beauty was it newly bred.⠀⠀490

'I see what crosses my attempt will bring;
I know what thorns the growing rose defends;
I think the honey guarded with a sting;
All this beforehand counsel comprehends;⠀⠀495
But will is deaf and hears no heedful friends;
⠀⠀Only he hath an eye to gaze on beauty,
⠀⠀And dotes on what he looks, 'gainst law or duty.

'I have debated, even in my soul,
What wrong, what shame, what sorrow I shall breed;
But nothing can affection's course control,⠀⠀500
Or stop the headlong fury of his speed.
I know repentant tears ensue the deed,
⠀⠀Reproach, disdain and deadly enmity;
⠀⠀Yet strive I to embrace mine infamy.'

This said, he shakes aloft his Roman blade,⠀⠀505
Which, like a falcon tow'ring in the skies,
Coucheth the fowl below with his wings' shade,
Whose crooked beak threats if he mount he dies.
So under his insulting falchion lies
⠀⠀Harmless Lucretia, marking what he tells⠀⠀510
⠀⠀With trembling fear, as fowl hear falcons' bells.

'Lucrece,' quoth he, 'this night I must enjoy thee.
If thou deny, then force must work my way,
For in thy bed I purpose to destroy thee;
That done, some worthless slave of thine I'll slay,⠀⠀515
To kill thine honour with thy life's decay;
⠀⠀And in thy dead arms do I mean to place him,
⠀⠀Swearing I slew him, seeing thee embrace him.

'So thy surviving husband shall remain
The scornful mark of every open eye;⠀⠀520
Thy kinsmen hang their heads at this disdain,
Thy issue blurred with nameless bastardy;
And thou, the author of their obloquy,
⠀⠀Shalt have thy trespass cited up in rhymes
⠀⠀And sung by children in succeeding times.⠀⠀525

'But if thou yield, I rest thy secret friend:
The fault unknown is as a thought unacted;
"A little harm done to a great good end
For lawful policy remains enacted.
"The poisonous simple sometime is compacted⠀⠀530
⠀⠀In a pure compound; being so applied,
⠀⠀His venom in effect is purified.

'Then, for thy husband and thy children's sake,
Tender my suit; bequeath not to their lot
The shame that from them no device can take,⠀⠀535
The blemish that will never be forgot;
Worse than a slavish wipe or birth-hour's blot;
⠀⠀For marks descried in men's nativity
⠀⠀Are nature's faults, not their own infamy.'

Here with a cockatrice' dead-killing eye⠀⠀540
He rouseth up himself, and makes a pause;
While she, the picture of pure piety,
Like a white hind under the gripe's sharp claws,
Pleads in a wilderness where are no laws
⠀⠀To the rough beast that knows no gentle right,⠀⠀545
⠀⠀Nor aught obeys but his foul appetite.

But when a black-faced cloud the world doth threat,
In his dim mist th'aspiring mountains hiding,
From earth's dark womb some gentle gust doth get,
Which blows these pitchy vapours from their biding,⠀⠀550
Hind'ring their present fall by this dividing;
⠀⠀So his unhallowèd haste her words delays,
⠀⠀And moody Pluto winks while Orpheus plays.

Yet, foul night-waking cat, he doth but dally,
While in his hold-fast foot the weak mouse panteth;⠀⠀555
Her sad behaviour feeds his vulture folly,
A swallowing gulf that even in plenty wanteth;
His ear her prayers admits, but his heart granteth
⠀⠀No penetrable entrance to her plaining.
⠀⠀"Tears harden lust, though marble wear with
⠀⠀⠀⠀raining.⠀⠀560

Her pity-pleading eyes are sadly fixéd
In the remórseless wrinkles of his face;
Her modest eloquence with sighs is mixéd,
Which to her oratory adds more grace.
  She puts the period often from his place,   565
    And midst the sentence so her accent breaks
    That twice she doth begin ere once she speaks.

She conjures him by high almighty Jove,
By knighthood, gentry, and sweet friendship's oath,
By her untimely tears, her husband's love,   570
By holy human law and common troth,
By heaven and earth, and all the power of both,
  That to his borrowéd bed he make retire,
    And stoop to honour, not to foul desire.

Quoth she: 'Reward not hospitality   575
With such black payment as thou hast pretended;
Mud not the fountain that gave drink to thee;
Mar not the thing that cannot be amended;
End thy ill aim before thy shoot be ended.
  He is no woodman that doth bend his bow   580
    To strike a poor unseasonable doe.

'My husband is thy friend—for his sake spare me;
Thyself art mighty—for thine own sake leave me;
Myself a weakling—do not then ensnare me;
Thou look'st not like deceit—do not deceive me.   585
My sighs like whirlwinds labour hence to heave thee.
  If ever man were moved with woman's moans,
    Be movéd with my tears, my sighs, my groans;

'All which together, like a troubled ocean,
Beat at thy rocky and wrack-threat'ning heart,   590
To soften it with their continual motion;
For stones dissolved to water do convert.
  O, if no harder than a stone thou art,
    Melt at my tears, and be compassionate!
    Soft pity enters at an iron gate.   595

'In Tarquin's likeness I did entertain thee;
Hast thou put on his shape to do him shame?
To all the host of heaven I complain me
Thou wrong'st his honour, wound'st his princely
    name.
Thou art not what thou seem'st; and if the same,   600
  Thou seem'st not what thou art, a god, a king;
    For kings, like gods should govern every thing.

'How will thy shame be seeded in thine age,
When thus thy vices bud before thy spring?
If in thy hope thou dar'st do such outrage,   605
What dar'st thou not when once thou art a king?
O, be rememb'red, no outrageous thing
  From vassal actors can be wiped away;
    Then kings' misdeeds cannot be hid in clay.

'This deed will make thee only loved for fear,   610
But happy monarchs still are feared for love;
With foul offenders thou perforce must bear,
When they in thee like offences prove.
If but for fear of this, thy will remove;
  For princes are the glass, the school, the book,   615
    Where subjects' eyes do learn, do read, do look.

'And wilt thou be the school where Lust shall learn?
Must he in thee read lectures of such shame?
Wilt thou be glass wherein it shall discern
Authority for sin, warrant for blame,   620
To privilege dishonour in thy name?
  Thou back'st reproach against long-living laud,
    And mak'st fair reputation but a bawd.

'Hast thou command? by him that gave it thee,
From a pure heart command thy rebel will;   625
Draw not thy sword to guard iniquity,
For it was lent thee all that brood to kill.
Thy princely office how canst thou fulfil,
  When patterned by thy fault foul sin may say
    He learned to sin, and thou didst teach the way? 630

'Think but how vile a spectacle it were
To view thy present trespass in another.
Men's faults do seldom to themselves appear;
Their own transgressions partially they smother;
This guilt would seem death-worthy in thy brother.   635
  O, how are they wrapped in with infamies
    That from their own misdeeds askance their eyes!

'To thee, to thee, my heaved-up hands, appeal,
Not to seducing lust, thy rash relier;
I sue for exiled majesty's repeal;   640
Let him return, and flatt'ring thoughts retire.
His true respect will prison false desire,
  And wipe the dim mist from thy doting eyne,
    That thou shalt see thy state and pity mine.'

'Have done,' quoth he, 'my uncontrolléd tide   645
Turns not, but swells the higher by this let.
Small lights are soon blown out, huge fires abide,
And with the wind in greater fury fret.
The petty streams that pay a daily debt
  To their salt sovereign, with their fresh falls' haste 650
    Add to his flow, but alter not his taste.'

'Thou art', quoth she, 'a sea, a sovereign king;
And, lo, there falls into thy boundless flood
Black lust, dishonour, shame, misgoverning,
Who seek to stain the ocean of thy blood.   655
If all these petty ills shall change thy good;
  Thy sea within a puddle's womb is hearséd,
    And not the puddle in thy sea disperséd.

'So shall these slaves be king, and thou their slave;
Thou nobly base, they basely dignified;   660
Thou their fair life, and they thy fouler grave;
Thou loathéd in their shame, they in their pride.
The lesser thing should not the greater hide;
  The cedar stoops not to the base shrub's foot,
    But low shrubs wither at the cedar's root.   665

'So let thy thoughts, low vassals to thy state'—
'No more,' quoth he; 'by heaven, I will not hear thee.
Yield to my love; if not, enforcéd hate,
Instead of love's coy touch, shall rudely tear thee;
That done, despitefully I mean to bear thee   670
  Unto the base bed of some rescal groom,
    To be thy partner in this shameful doom.'

This said, he sets his foot upon the light,
For light and lust are deadly enemies;
Shame folded up in blind concealing night, 675
When most unseen, then most doth tyrannize.
The wolf hath seized his prey, the poor lamb cries,
  Till with her own white fleece her voice controlled
  Entombs her outcry in her lips' sweet fold;

For with the nightly linen that she wears 680
He pens her piteous clamours in her head,
Cooling his hot face in the chastest tears
That ever modest eyes with sorrow shed.
O, that prone lust should stain so pure a bed!
  The spots whereof could weeping purify, 685
  Her tears should drop on them perpetually.

But she hath lost a dearer thing than life,
And he hath won what he would lose again.
This forcéd league doth force a further strife;
This momentary joy breeds months of pain; 690
This hot desire converts to cold disdain;
  Pure Chastity is rifled of her store,
  And Lust, the thief, far poorer than before.

Look as the full-fed hound or gorgéd hawk,
Unapt for tender smell or speedy flight, 695
Make slow pursuit, or altogether balk
The prey wherein by nature they delight,
So surfeit-taking Tarquin fares this night:
  His taste delicious, in digestion souring,
  Devours his will, that lived by foul devouring. 700

O, deeper sin than bottomless conceit
Can comprehend in still imagination!
Drunken Desire must vomit his receipt,
Ere he can see his own abomination.
While Lust is in his pride, no exclamation 705
  Can curb his heat or rein his rash desire,
  Till, like a jade, Self-will himself doth tire.

And then with lank and lean discoloured cheek,
With heavy eye, knit brow, and strengthless pace,
Feeble Desire, all recreant, poor and meek, 710
Like to a bankrupt beggar wails his case:
The flesh being proud, Desire doth fight with Grace,
  For there it revels, and when that decays
  The guilty rebel for remission prays.

So fares it with this faultful lord of Rome, 715
Who this accomplishment so hotly chaséd;
For now against himself he sounds this doom,
That through the length of times he stands disgracéd;
Besides, his soul's fair temple is defacéd,
  To whose weak ruins muster troops of cares, 720
  To ask the spotted princess how she fares.

She says her subjects with foul insurrection
Have battered down her consecrated wall,
And by their mortal fault brought in subjection
Her immortality, and made her thrall 725
To living death and pain perpetual;
  Which in her prescience she controlléd still,
  But her foresight could not forestall their will.

Ev'n in this thought through the dark night he stealeth,
A captive victor that hath lost in gain; 730
Bearing away the wound that nothing healeth,
The scar that will, despite of cure, remain;
Leaving his spoil perplexed in greater pain.
  She bears the load of lust he left behind,
  And he the burden of a guilty mind. 735

He like a thievish dog creeps sadly thence;
She like a wearied lamb lies panting there;
He scowls, and hates himself for his offence;
She, desperate, with her nails her flesh doth tear;
He faintly flies, sweating with guilty fear; 740
  She stays, exclaiming on the direful night;
  He runs, and chides his vanished, loathed delight.

He thence departs a heavy convertite;
She there remains a hopeless castaway;
He in his speed looks for the morning light; 745
She prays she never may behold the day.
'For day', quoth she, 'night's scapes doth open lay,
  And my true eyes have never practised how
  To cloak offences with a cunning brow.

'They think not but that every eye can see 750
The same disgrace which they themselves behold;
And therefore would they still in darkness be,
To have their unseen sin remain untold;
For they their guilt with weeping will unfold,
  And grave, like water that doth eat in steel, 755
  Upon my cheeks what helpless shame I feel.'

Here she exclaims against repose and rest,
And bids her eyes hereafter still be blind.
She wakes her heart by beating on her breast,
And bids it leap from thence, where it may find 760
Some purer chest to close so pure a mind.
  Frantic with grief thus breathes she forth her spite
  Against the unseen secrecy of night:

'O comfort-killing Night, image of hell!
Dim register and notary of shame! 765
Black stage for tragedies and murders fell!
Vast sin-concealing chaos! nurse of blame!
Blind muffled bawd! dark harbour for defame!
  Grim cave of death! whisp'ring conspirator
  With close-tongued treason and the ravisher! 770

'O hateful, vaporous and foggy Night!
Since thou art guilty of my cureless crime,
Muster thy mists to meet the eastern light,
Make war against proportioned course of time;
Or if thou wilt permit the sun to climb 775
  His wonted height, yet ere he go to bed,
  Knit poisonous clouds about his golden head.

'With rotten damps ravish the morning air;
Let their exhaled unwholesome breaths make sick
The life of purity, the supreme fair, 780
Ere he arrive his weary noon-tide prick;
And let thy musty vapours march so thick
  That in their smoky ranks his smoth'red light
  May set at noon and make perpetual night.

'Were Tarquin Night, as he is but Night's child,   785
The silver-shining queen he would distain;
Her twinkling handmaids too, by him defiled,
Through Night's black bosom should not peep again;
So should I have co-partners in my pain;
    And fellowship in woe doth woe assuage,   790
    As palmers' chat makes short their pilgrimage.

'Where now I have no one to blush with me,
To cross their arms and hang their heads with mine,
To mask their brows and hide their infamy;
But I alone alone must sit and pine,   795
Seasoning the earth with show'rs of silver brine,
    Mingling my talk with tears, my grief with groans,
    Poor wasting monuments of lasting moans.

'O Night, thou furnace of foul-reeking smoke,
Let not the jealous Day behold that face   800
Which underneath thy black all-hiding cloak
Immodestly lies martyred with disgrace!
Keep still possession of thy gloomy place,
    That all the faults which in thy reign are made
    May likewise be sepulchred in thy shade!   805

'Make me not object to the tell-tale Day.
The light will show, charactered in my brow,
The story of sweet chastity's decay,
The impious breach of holy wedlock vow;
Yea, the illiterate, that know not how   810
    To cipher what is writ in learnéd books,
    Will quote my loathsome trespass in my looks.

'The nurse, to still her child, will tell my story,
And fright her crying babe with Tarquin's name;
The orator, to deck his oratory,   815
Will couple my reproach to Tarquin's shame;
Feast-finding minstrels, tuning my defame,
    Will tie the hearers to attend each line,
    How Tarquin wrongéd me, I Collatine.

'Let my good name, that senseless reputation,   820
For Collatine's dear love be kept unspotted;
If that be made a theme for disputation,
The branches of another root are rotted,
And undeserved reproach to him allotted
    That is as clear from this attaint of mine   825
    As I ere this was pure to Collatine.

'O unseen shame! invisible disgrace!
O unfelt sore! crest-wounding, private scar!
Reproach is stamped in Collatinus' face,
And Tarquin's eye may read the mot afar,   830
"How he in peace is wounded, not in war.
    "Alas, how many bear such shameful blows,
    Which not themselves, but he that gives them
        knows!

'If, Collatine, thine honour lay in me,
From me by strong assault it is bereft.   835
My honey lost, and I, a drone-like bee,
Have no perfection of my summer left,
But robbed and ransacked by injurious theft.
    In thy weak hive a wand'ring wasp hath crept,
    And sucked the honey which thy chaste bee kept.   840

'Yet am I guilty of thy honour's wrack;
Yet for thy honour did I entertain him;
Coming from thee, I could not put him back,
For it had been dishonour to disdain him;
Besides, of weariness he did complain him,   845
    And talked of virtue: O unlooked-for evil,
    When virtue is profaned in such a devil!

'Why should the worm intrude the maiden bud?
Or hateful cuckoos hatch in sparrows' nests?
Or toads infect fair founts with venom mud?   850
Or tyrant folly lurk in gentle breasts?
Or kings be breakers of their own behests?
    "But no perfection is so absolute
    That some impurity doth not pollute.

'The agéd man that coffers up his gold   855
Is plagued with cramps and gouts and painful fits,
And scarce hath eyes his treasure to behold,
But like still-pining Tantalus he sits,
And useless barns the harvest of his wits,
    Having no other pleasure of his gain   860
    But torment that it cannot cure his pain.

'So then he hath it when he cannot use it,
And leaves it to be mast'red by his young;
Who in their pride do presently abuse it.
Their father was too weak, and they strong,   865
To hold their curséd-blesséd fortune long.
    "The sweets we wish for turn to loathéd sours
    "Even in the moment that we call them ours.

'Unruly blasts wait on the tender spring;
Unwholesome weeds take root with precious flowers: 870
The adder hisses where the sweet birds sing;
What virtue breeds iniquity devours.
We have no good that we can say is ours
    But ill-annexéd Opportunity
    Or kills his life or else his quality.   875

'O Opportunity, thy guilt is great!
'Tis thou that execut'st the traitor's treason;
Thou sets the wolf where he the lamb may get;
Whoever plots the sin, thou point'st the season;
'Tis thou that spurn'st at right, at law, at reason;   880
    And in thy shady cell, where none may spy him,
    Sits Sin, to seize the souls that wander by him.

'Thou mak'st the vestal violate her oath;
Thou blow'st the fire when temperance is thawed;
Thou smother'st honesty, thou murd'rest troth;   885
Thou foul abettor! thou notorious bawd!
Thou plantest scandal and displacest laud.
    Thou ravisher, thou traitor, thou false thief,
    Thy honey turns to gall, thy joy to grief!

'Thy secret pleasure turns to open shame,   890
Thy private feasting to a public fast,
Thy smoothing titles to a ragged name,
Thy sugared tongue to bitter wormwood taste;
Thy violent vanities can never last.
    How comes it then, vile Opportunity,   895
    Being so bad, such numbers seek for thee?

'When wilt thou be the humble suppliant's friend,
And bring him where his suit may be obtainéd?
When wilt thou sort an hour great strifes to end?
Or free that soul which wretchedness hath chainéd? 900
Give physic to the sick, ease to the painéd?
    The poor, lame, blind, halt, creep, cry out for thee;
    But they ne'er meet with Opportunity.

'The patient dies while the physician sleeps;
The orphan pines while the oppressor feeds; 905
Justice is feasting while the widow weeps;
Advice is sporting while infection breeds;
Thou grant'st no time for charitable deeds;
    Wrath, envy, treason, rape, and murder's rages,
    Thy heinous hours wait on them as their pages. 910

'When Truth and Virtue have to do with thee,
A thousand crosses keep them from thy aid;
They buy thy help, but Sin ne'er gives a fee;
He gratis comes, and thou art well appaid
As well to hear as grant what he hath said. 915
    My Collatine would else have come to me
    When Tarquin did, but he was stayed by thee.

'Guilty thou art of murder and of theft,
Guilty of perjury and subornation,
Guilty of treason, forgery and shift, 920
Guilty of incest, that abomination;
An accessary by thine inclination
    To all sins past and all that are to come,
    From the creation to the general doom.

'Misshapen Time, copesmate of ugly Night, 925
Swift subtle post, carrier of grisly care,
Eater of youth, false slave to false delight,
Base watch of woes, sin's pack-horse, virtue's snare;
Thou nursest all and murd'rest all that are.
    O, hear me then, injurious, shifting Time! 930
    Be guilty of my death, since of my crime.

'Why hath thy servant Opportunity
Betrayed the hours thou gavest me to repose,
Cancelled my fortunes and enchainéd me
To endless date of never-ending woes? 935
Time's office is to fine the hate of foes,
    To eat up errors by opinion bred,
    Not spend the dowry of a lawful bed.

'Time's glory is to calm contending kings,
To unmask falsehood and bring truth to light, 940
To stamp the seal of time in agéd things,
To wake the morn and sentinel the night,
To wrong the wronger till he render right,
    To ruinate proud buildings with thy hours
    And smear with dust their glitt'ring golden towers; 945

'To fill with worm-holes stately monuments,
To feed oblivion with decay of things,
To blot old books and alter their contents,
To pluck the quills from ancient ravens' wings,
To dry the old oak's sap and cherish springs, 950
    To spoil antiquities of hammered steel
    And turn the giddy round of Fortune's wheel;

'To show the beldam daughters of her daughter,
To make the child a man, the man a child,
To slay the tiger that doth live by slaughter, 955
To tame the unicorn and lion wild,
To mock the subtle in themselves beguiled,
    To cheer the ploughman with increased crops,
    And waste huge stones with little water-drops.

'Why work'st thou mischief in thy pilgrimage, 960
Unless thou couldst return to make amends?
One poor retiring minute in an age
Would purchase thee a thousand thousand friends,
Lending him wit that to bad debtors lends.
    O, this dread night, wouldst thou one hour come
        back, 965
    I could prevent this storm and shun thy wrack!

'Thou ceaseless lackey to eternity,
With some mischance cross Tarquin in his flight;
Devise extremes beyond extremity,
To make him curse this curséd crimeful night; 970
Let ghastly shadows his lewd eyes affright,
    And the dire thought of his committed evil
    Shape every bush a hideous shapeless devil.

'Disturb his hours of rest with restless trances,
Afflict him in his bed with bedrid groans; 975
Let there bechance him pitiful mischances,
To make him moan, but pity not his moans.
Stone him with hard'ned hearts, harder than stones;
    And let mild women to him lose their mildness,
    Wilder to him than tigers in their wildness. 980

'Let him have time to tear his curléd hair,
Let him have time against himself to rave,
Let him have time of time's help to despair,
Let him have time to live a loathed slave,
Let him have time a beggar's orts to crave, 985
    And time to see one that by alms doth live
    Disdain to him disdainéd scraps to give.

'Let him have time to see his friends his foes,
And merry fools to mock at him resort;
Let him have time to mark how slow time goes 990
In time of sorrow, and how swift and short
His time of folly and his time of sport;
    And ever let his unrecalling crime
    Have time to wail th'abusing of his time.

'O Time, thou tutor both to good and bad, 995
Teach me to curse him that thou taught'st this ill!
At his own shadow let the thief run mad,
Himself himself seek every hour to kill!
Such wretched hands such wretched blood should spill;
    For who so base would such an office have 1000
    As sland'rous deathsman to so base a slave?

'The baser is he, coming from a king,
To shame his hope with deeds degenerate.
The mightier man, the mightier is the thing
That makes him honoured or begets him hate; 1005
For greatest scandal waits on greatest state.
    The moon being clouded presently is missed,
    But little stars may hide them when they list.

'The crow may bathe his coal-black wings in mire
And unperceived fly with the filth away;   1010
But if the like the snow-white swan desire,
The stain upon his silver down will stay.
Poor grooms are sightless night, kings glorious day.
  Gnats are unnoted wheresoe'er they fly,
  But eagles gazed upon with every eye.   1015

'Out, idle words, servants to shallow fools!
Unprofitable sounds, weak arbitrators!
Busy yourselves in skill-contending schools;
Debate where leisure serves with dull debaters;
To trembling clients be you mediators.   1020
  For me, I force not argument a straw,
  Since that my case is past the help of law.

'In vain I rail at Opportunity,
At Time, at Tarquin, and uncheerful Night;
In vain I cavil with mine infamy,   1025
In vain I spurn at my confirmed despite:
This helpless smoke of words doth me no right.
  The remedy indeed to do me good
  Is to let forth my foul-defiléd blood.

'Poor hand, why quiver'st thou at this decree?   1030
Honour thyself to rid me of this shame;
For if I die, my honour lives in thee,
But if I live, thou livest in my defame.
Since thou couldst not defend thy loyal dame
  And wast afeard to scratch her wicked foe,   1035
  Kill both thyself and her for yielding so.'

This said, from her betumbled couch she starteth,
To find some desp'rate instrument of death.
But this no slaughterhouse no tool imparteth
To make more vent for passage of her breath,   1040
Which, thronging through her lips, so vanisheth
  As smoke from Etna that in air consumes,
  Or that which from dischargéd cannon fumes.

'In vain,' quoth she, 'I live, and seek in vain
Some happy mean to end a hapless life.   1045
I feared by Tarquin's falchion to be slain,
Yet for the selfsame purpose seek a knife;
But when I feared I was a loyal wife;
  So am I now—O no, that cannot be;
  Of that true type hath Tarquin rifled me.   1050

'O, that is gone for which I sought to live,
And therefore now I need not fear to die.
To clear this spot by death, at least I give
A badge of fame to slander's livery,
A dying life to living infamy.   1055
  Poor helpless help, the treasure stol'n away,
  To burn the guiltless casket where it lay!

'Well, well, dear Collatine, thou shalt not know
The stainéd taste of violated troth;
I will not wrong thy true affection so,   1060
To flatter thee with an infringéd oath;
This bastard graff shall never come to growth;
  He shall not boast who did thy stock pollute
  That thou art doting father of his fruit.

'Nor shall he smile at thee in secret thought,   1065
Nor laugh with his companions at thy state;
But thou shalt know thy int'rest was not bought
Basely with gold, but stol'n from forth thy gate.
For me, I am the mistress of my fate,
  And with my trespass never will dispense,   1070
  Till life to death acquit my forced offence.

'I will not poison thee with my attaint,
Nor fold my fault in cleanly-coined excuses;
My sable ground of sin I will not paint
To hide the truth of this false night's abuses.   1075
My tongue shall utter all; mine eyes, like sluices,
  As from a mountain-spring that feeds a dale,
  Shall gush pure streams to purge my impure tale.'

By this, lamenting Philomel had ended
The well-tuned warble of her nightly sorrow,   1080
And solemn night with slow sad gait descended
To ugly hell; when lo, the blushing morrow
Lends light to all fair eyes that light will borrow;
  But cloudy Lucrece shames herself to see,
  And therefore still in night would cloist'red be.   1085

Revealing day through every cranny spies,
And seems to point her out where she sits weeping;
To whom she sobbing speaks: 'O eye of eyes,
Why pry'st thou through my window? leave thy
      peeping;
Mock with thy tickling beams eyes that are sleeping;   1090
  Brand not my forehead with thy piercing light,
  For day hath nought to do what's done by night.'

Thus cavils she with every thing she sees.
True grief is fond and testy as a child,
Who wayward once, his mood with nought agrees.   1095
Old woes, not infant sorrows, bear them mild;
Continuance tames the one; the other wild,
  Like an unpractised swimmer plunging still
  With too much labour drowns for want of skill.

So she, deep-drenchéd in a sea of care,   1100
Holds disputation with each thing she views,
And to herself all sorrow doth compare;
No object but her passion's strength renews,
And as one shifts, another straight ensues.
  Sometime her grief is dumb and hath no words;   1105
  Sometime 'tis mad and too much talk affords.

The little birds that tune their morning's joy
Make her moans mad with their sweet melody;
"For mirth doth search the bottom of annoy;
"Sad souls are slain in merry company;   1110
"Grief best is pleased with grief's society
  True sorrow then is feelingly sufficed
  When with like semblance it is sympathized.

" 'Tis double death to drown in ken of shore;
"He ten times pines that pines beholding food;   1115
"To see the salve doth make the wound ache more;
"Great grief grieves most at that would do it good;
"Deep woes roll forward like a gentle flood,
  Who, being stopped, the bounding banks o'erflows;
  Grief dallied with nor law nor limit knows.   1120

'You mocking birds,' quoth she, 'your tunes entomb
Within your hollow-swelling featheréd breasts,
And in my hearing be you mute and dumb.
My restless discord loves no stops nor rests;
    "A woeful hostess brooks not merry guests.   1125
        Relish your nimble notes to pleasing ears;
        "Distress likes dumps when time is kept with
            tears.

'Come, Philomel, that sing'st of ravishment,
Make thy sad grove in my dishevelled hair.
As the dank earth weeps at thy languishment,   1130
So I at each sad strain will strain a tear,
And with deep groans the diapason bear;
    For burden-wise I'll hum on Tarquin still,
    While thou on Tereus descants better skill.

'And whiles against a thorn thou bear'st thy part   1135
To keep thy sharp woes waking, wretched I,
To imitate thee well, against my heart
Will fix a sharp knife to affright mine eye;
Who, if it wink, shall thereon fall and die.
    These means, as frets upon an instrument,   1140
    Shall tune our heart-strings to true languishment.

'And for, poor bird, thou sing'st not in the day,
As shaming any eye should thee behold,
Some dark deep desert, seated from the way,
That knows not parching heat nor freezing cold,   1145
Will we find out; and there we will unfold
    To creatures stern sad tunes, to change their kinds.
    Since men prove beasts, let beasts bear gentle minds.'

As the poor frighted deer, that stands at gaze,
Wildly determining which way to fly,   1150
Or one encompassed with a winding maze
That cannot tread the way out readily;
So with herself is she in mutiny,
    To live or die which of the twain were better,
    When life is shamed and death reproach's debtor. 1155

'To kill myself,' quoth she, 'alack, what were it,
But with my body my poor soul's pollution?
They that lose half with greater patience bear it
Than they whose whole is swallowed in confusion.
That mother tries a merciless conclusion   1160
    Who, having two sweet babes, when death takes
        one,
    Will slay the other and be nurse to none.

'My body or my soul, which was the dearer,
When the one pure, the other made divine?
Whose love of either to myself was nearer,   1165
When both were kept for heaven and Collatine?
Ay me! the bark pilled from the lofty pine,
    His leaves will wither and his sap decay;
    So must my soul, her bark being pilled away.

'Her house is sacked, her quiet interrupted,   1170
Her mansion battered by the enemy;
Her sacred temple spotted, spoiled, corrupted,
Grossly engirt with daring infamy;
Then let it not be called impiety,
    If in this blemished fort I make some hole   1175
    Through which I may convey this troubled soul.

'Yet die I will not till my Collatine
Have heard the cause of my untimely death,
That he may vow, in that sad hour of mine,
Revenge on him that made me stop my breath.   1180
My stainéd blood to Tarquin I'll bequeath,
    Which by him tainted shall for him be spent,
    And as his due writ in my testament.

'My honour I'll bequeath unto the knife
That wounds my body so dishonouréd.   1185
'Tis honour to deprive dishonoured life;
The one will live, the other being dead.
So of shame's ashes shall my fame be bred;
    For in my death I murder shameful scorn.
    My shame so dead, mine honour is new born.   1190

'Dear lord of that dear jewel I have lost,
What legacy shall I bequeath to thee?
My resolution, love, shall be thy boast,
By whose example thou revenged mayst be.
How Tarquin must be used, read it in me: 1195
    Myself, thy friend, will kill myself, thy foe,
    And, for my sake, serve thou false Tarquin so.

'This brief abridgement of my will I make:
My soul and body to the skies and ground;
My resolution, husband, do thou take;   1200
Mine honour be the knife's that makes my wound;
My shame be his that did my fame confound;
    And all my fame that lives disburséd be
    To those that live and think no shame of me.

'Thou, Collatine, shalt oversee this will;   1205
How was I overseen that thou shalt see it!
My blood shall wash the slander of mine ill;
My life's foul deed, my life's fair end shall free it.
Faint not, faint heart, but stoutly say "So be it".
    Yield to my hand; my hand shall conquer thee;   1210
    Thou dead, both die and both shall victors be.'

This plot of death when sadly she had laid,
And wiped the brinish pearl from her bright eyes,
With untuned tongue she hoarsely calls her maid,
Whose swift obedience to her mistress hies;   1215
    "For fleet-winged duty with thought's feathers flies.
    Poor Lucrece' cheeks unto her maid seem so
    As winter meads when sun doth melt their snow.

Her mistress she doth give demure good-morrow
With soft slow tongue, true mark of modesty,   1220
And sorts a sad look to her lady's sorrow,
For why her face wore sorrow's livery,
But durst not ask of her audaciously
    Why her two suns were cloud-eclipséd so,
    Nor why her fair cheeks over-washed with woe.   1225

But as the earth doth weep, the sun being set,
Each flower moist'ned like a melting eye,
Even so the maid with swelling drops 'gan wet
Her circled eyne, enforced by sympathy
Of those fair suns set in her mistress' sky,   1230
    Who in a salt-waved ocean quench their light,
    Which makes the maid weep like the dewy night.

A pretty while these pretty creatures stand,
Like ivory conduits coral cisterns filling.
One justly weeps; the other takes in hand   1235
No cause but company of her drops spilling:
Their gentle sex to weep are often willing,
    Grieving themselves to guess at others' smarts,
    And then they drown their eyes or break their
      hearts.

For men have marble, women waxen, minds,   1240
And therefore are they formed as marble will;
The weak oppressed, th'impression of strange kinds
Is formed in them by force, by fraud, or skill.
Then call them not the authors of their ill,
    No more than wax shall be accounted evil   1245
Wherein is stamped the semblance of a devil.

Their smoothness, like a goodly champaign plain,
Lays open all the little worms that creep;
In men, as in a rough-grown grove, remain
Cave-keeping evils that obscurely sleep.   1250
Through crystal walls each little mote will peep.
    Though men can cover crimes with bold stern
      looks,
    Poor women's faces are their own faults' books.

No man inveigh against the witheréd flower,
But chide rough winter that the flower hath killed.   1255
Not that devoured, but that which doth devour,
Is worthy blame. O, let it not be hild
Poor women's faults that they are so fulfilled
    With men's abuses: those proud lords to blame
    Make weak-made women tenants to their shame.   1260

The precedent whereof in Lucrece view,
Assailed by night with circumstances strong
Of present death, and shame that might ensue
By that her death, to do her husband wrong.
Such danger to resistance did belong,   1265
    That dying fear through all her body spread;
    And who cannot abuse a body dead?

By this, mild patience bid fair Lucrece speak
To the poor counterfeit of her complaining.
'My girl,' quoth she, 'on what occasion break   1270
Those tears from thee that down thy cheeks are
    raining?
If thou dost weep for grief of my sustaining,
    Know, gentle wench, it small avails my mood;
    If tears could help, mine own would do me good.

'But tell me, girl, when went'—and there she stayed 1275
Till after a deep groan—'Tarquin from hence?'
'Madam, ere I was up,' replied the maid,
'The more to blame my sluggard negligence.
Yet with the fault I thus far can dispense:
    Myself was stirring ere the break of day,   1280
    And ere I rose was Tarquin gone away.

'But, lady, if your maid may be so bold,
She would request to know your heaviness.'
'O, peace!' quoth Lucrece: 'if it should be told,
The repetition cannot make it less,   1285
For more it is than I can well express;
    And that deep torture may be called a hell
    When more is felt than one hath power to tell.

'Go, get me hither paper, ink and pen;
Yet save that labour, for I have them here.   1290
What should I say? One of my husband's men
Bid thou be ready by and by to bear
A letter to my lord, my love, my dear.
    Bid him with speed prepare to carry it;
    The cause craves haste and it will soon be writ.'   1295

Her maid is gone, and she prepares to write,
First hovering o'er the paper with her quill.
Conceit and grief an eager combat fight;
What wit sets down is blotted straight with will;
This is too curious-good, this blunt and ill: 1300
    Much like a press of people at a door,
    Throng her inventions, which shall go before.

At last she thus begins: 'Thou worthy lord
Of that unworthy wife that greeteth thee,
Health to thy person! next vouchsafe t'afford—   1305
If ever, love, thy Lucrece thou wilt see—
Some present speed to come and visit me.
    So I commend me, from our house in grief;
    My woes are tedious, though my words are brief.'

Here folds she up the tenor of her woe,   1310
Her certain sorrow writ uncertainly.
By this short schedule Collatine may know
Her grief, but not her grief's true quality;
She dares not thereof make discovery,
    Lest he should hold it her own gross abuse,   1315
    Ere she with blood had stained her stained excuse.

Besides, the life and feeling of her passion
She hoards, to spend when he is by to hear her,
When sighs and groans and tears may grace the fashion
Of her disgrace, the better so to clear her   1320
From that suspicion which the world might bear her.
    To shun this blot, she would not blot the letter
    With words, till action might become them better.

To see sad sights moves more than hear them told;
For then the eye interprets to the ear   1325
The heavy motion that it doth behold,
When every part a part of woe doth bear.
'Tis but a part of sorrow that we hear:
    Deep sounds make lesser noise than shallow fords,
    And sorrow ebbs, being blown with wind of words. 1330

Her letter now is sealed and on it writ
'At Ardea to my lord with more than haste.'
The post attends, and she delivers it,
Charging the sour-faced groom to hie as fast
As lagging fowls before the northern blast.   1335
    Speed more than speed but dull and slow she deems:
    Extremity still urgeth such extremes.

The homely villain curtsies to her low,
And blushing on her, with a steadfast eye
Receives the scroll without or yea or no,   1340
And forth with bashful innocence doth hie.
But they whose guilt within their bosoms lie
    Imagine every eye beholds their blame;
    For Lucrece thought he blushed to see her shame:

When, silly groom, God wot, it was defect   1345
Of spirit, life and bold audacity.
Such harmless creatures have a true respect
To talk in deeds, while others saucily
Promise more speed but do it leisurely.
  Even so this pattern of the worn-out age   1350
  Pawned honest looks, but laid no words to gage.

His kindled duty kindled her mistrust,
That two red fires in both their faces blazéd;
She thought he blushed, as knowing Tarquin's lust,
And blushing with him, wistly on him gazéd;   1355
Her earnest eye did make him more amazéd;
  The more she saw the blood his cheeks replenish,
  The more she thought he spied in her some blemish.

But long she thinks till he return again,
And yet the duteous vassal scarce is gone.   1360
The weary time she cannot entertain,
For now 'tis stale to sigh, to weep and groan;
So woe hath wearied woe, moan tiréd moan,
  That she her plaints a little while doth stay,
  Pausing for means to mourn some newer way.   1365

At last she calls to mind where hangs a piece
Of skilful painting, made for Priam's Troy,
Before the which is drawn the power of Greece,
For Helen's rape the city to destroy,
Threat'ning cloud-kissing Ilion with annoy;   1370
  Which the conceited painter drew so proud
  As heaven, it seemed, to kiss the turrets bowed.

A thousand lamentable objects there,
In scorn of nature, art gave lifeless life:
Many a dry drop seemed a weeping tear,   1375
Shed for the slaught'red husband by the wife;
The red blood reeked, to show the painter's strife;
  And dying eyes gleamed forth their ashy lights,
  Like dying coals burnt out in tedious nights.

There might you see the labouring pioneer   1380
Begrimed with sweat and smearéd all with dust;
And from the towers of Troy there would appear
The very eyes of men through loop-holes thrust,
Gazing upon the Greeks with little lust.
  Such sweet observance in this work was had   1385
  That one might see those far-off eyes look sad.

In great commanders grace and majesty
You might behold, triumphing in their faces;
In youth, quick bearing and dexterity;
And here and there the painter interlaces   1390
Pale cowards marching on with trembling paces,
  Which heartless peasants did so well resemble
  That one would swear he saw them quake
    and tremble.

In Ajax and Ulysses, O what art
Of physiognomy might one behold!   1395
The face of either ciphered either's heart;
Their face their manners most expressly told:
In Ajax's eyes blunt rage and rigour rolled;
  But the mild glance that sly Ulysses lent
  Showed deep regard and smiling government.   1400

There pleading might you see grave Nestor stand,
As 'twere encouraging the Greeks to fight,
Making such sober action with his hand
That it beguiled attention, charmed the sight.
In speech, it seemed, his beard all silver white   1405
  Wagged up and down, and from his lips did fly
  Thin winding breath which purled up to the sky.

About him were a press of gaping faces,
Which seemed to swallow up his sound advice,
All jointly list'ning, but with several graces,   1410
As if some mermaid did their ears entice,
Some high, some low, the painter was so nice;
  The scalps of many, almost hid behind,
  To jump up higher seemed, to mock the mind.

Here one man's hand leaned on another's head,   1415
His nose being shadowéd by his neighbour's ear;
Here one being thronged bears back, all boll'n and red;
Another smothered seems to pelt and swear;
And in their rage such signs of rage they bear
  As, but for loss of Nestor's golden words,   1420
  It seemed they would debate with angry swords.

For much imaginary work was there;
Conceit deceitful, so compact, so kind,
That for Achilles' image stood his spear
Griped in an arméd hand; himself behind   1425
Was left unseen, save to the eye of mind:
  A hand, a foot, a face, a leg, a head,
  Stood for the whole to be imaginéd.

And from the walls of strong-besiegéd Troy
When their brave hope, bold Hector, marched to field, 1430
Stood many Trojan mothers sharing joy
To see their youthful sons bright weapons wield;
And to their hope they such odd action yield
  That through their light joy seeméd to appear,
  Like bright things stained, a kind of heavy fear.   1435

And from the strand of Dardan where they fought
To Simois' reedy banks the red blood ran,
Whose waves to imitate the battle sought
With swelling ridges; and their ranks began
To break upon the galléd shore, and than   1440
  Retire again, till meeting greater ranks
  They join and shoot their foam at Simois' banks.

To this well-painted piece is Lucrece come,
To find a face where all distress is stelled.
Many she sees where cares have carvéd some,   1445
But none where all distress and dolour dwelled,
Till she despairing Hecuba beheld,
  Staring on Priam's wounds with her old eyes,
  Which bleeding under Pyrrhus' proud foot lies.

In her the painter had anatomized   1450
Time's ruin, beauty's wrack, and grim care's reign;
Her cheeks with chaps and wrinkles were disguised;
Of what she was no semblance did remain:
Her blue blood changed to black in every vein,
  Wanting the spring that those shrunk pipes had fed, 1455
  Showed life imprisoned in a body dead.

On this sad shadow Lucrece spends her eyes,
And shapes her sorrow to the beldam's woes,
Who nothing wants to answer her but cries,
And bitter words to ban her cruel foes: 1460
The painter was no god to lend her those;
  And therefore Lucrece swears he did her wrong,
  To give her so much grief and not a tongue.

'Poor instrument', quoth she, 'without a sound,
I'll tune thy woes with my lamenting tongue,   1465
And drop sweet balm in Priam's painted wound,
And rail on Pyrrhus that hath done him wrong,
And with my tears quench Troy that burns so long,
  And with my knife scratch out the angry eyes
  Of all the Greeks that are thine enemies.   1470

'Show me the strumpet that began this stir,
That with my nails her beauty I may tear.
Thy heat of lust, fond Paris, did incur
This load of wrath that burning Troy doth bear.
Thy eye kindled the fire that burneth here;   1475
  And here in Troy, for trespass of thine eye,
  The sire, the son, the dame and daughter die.

'Why should the private pleasure of some one
Become the public plague of many moe?
Let sin, alone committed, light alone   1480
Upon his head that hath transgresséd so;
Let guiltless souls be freed from guilty woe.
  For one's offence why should so many fall,
  To plague a private sin in general?

'Lo, here weeps Hecuba, here Priam dies,   1485
Here manly Hector faints, here Troilus swounds,
Here friend by friend in bloody channel lies,
And friend to friend gives unadvof séd wounds,
And one man's lust these many lives confounds.
  Had doting Priam checked his son's desire,   1490
  Troy had been bright with fame and not with fire.'

Here feelingly she weeps Troy's painted woes;
For sorrow, like a heavy-hanging bell
Once set on ringing, with his own weight goes;
Then little strength rings out the dolefull knell;   1495
So Lucrece, set a-work, sad tales doth tell
  To pencilled pensiveness and coloured sorrow;
  She lends them words, and she their looks
    doth borrow.

She throws her eyes about the painting round,
And who she finds forlorn she doth lament.   1500
At last she sees a wretched image bound
That piteous looks to Phrygian shepherds lent;
His face, though full of cares, yet showed content;
  Onward to Troy with the blunt swains he goes,
  So mild that Patience seemed to scorn his woes.   1505

In him the painter laboured with his skill
To hide deceit and give the harmless show
An humble gait, calm looks, eyes wailing still,
A brow unbent that seemed to welcome woe;
Cheeks neither red nor pale, but mingled so   1510
  That blushing red no guilty instance gave,
  Nor ashy pale the fear that false hearts have.

But, like a constant and confirméd devil,
He entertained a show so seeming just,
And therein so ensconced his secret evil,   1515
That jealousy itself could not mistrust
False creeping craft and perjury should thrust
  Into so bright a day such black-faced storms,
  Or blot with hell-born sin such saint-like forms.

The well-skilled workman this mild image drew   1520
For perjured Sinon, whose enchanting story
The credulous old Priam after slew;
Whose words, like wildfire, burnt the shining glory
Of rich-built Ilion, that the skies were sorry,
  And little stars shot from their fixéd places,   1525
  When their glass fell wherein they viewed their
    faces.

This picture she advisedly perused,
And chid the painter for his wondrous skill,
Saying, some shape in Sinon's was abused;
So fair a form lodged not a mind so ill;   1530
And still on him she gazed, and gazing still
  Such signs of truth in his plain face she spied
  That she concludes the picture was belied.

'It cannot be', quoth she, 'that so much guile'—
She would have said 'can lurk in such a look';   1535
But Tarquin's shape came in her mind the while,
And from her tongue 'can lurk' from 'cannot' took;
'It cannot be' she in that sense forsook,
  And turned it thus, 'It cannot be, I find,
  But such a face should bear a wicked mind;   1540

'For even as subtle Sinon here is painted,
So sober-sad, so weary and so mild,
As if with grief or travail he had fainted,
To me came Tarquin arméd to beguild
With outward honesty, but yet defiled   1545
  With inward vice. As Priam him did cherish,
  So did I Tarquin; so my Troy did perish.

'Look, look, how list'ning Priam wets his eyes,
To see those borrowéd tears that Sinon sheds.
Priam, why art thou old and yet not wise?   1550
For every tear he falls a Trojan bleeds;
His eye drops fire, no water thence proceeds;
  Those round clear pearls of his that move thy pity
  Are balls of quenchless fire to burn thy city.

'Such devils steal effects from lightless hell;   1555
For Sinon in his fire doth quake with cold,
And in that cold hot-burning fire doth dwell;
These contraries such unity do hold
Only to flatter fools and make them bold;
  So Priam's trust false Sinon's tears doth flatter   1560
  That he finds means to burn his Troy with water.'

Here, all enraged, such passion her assails,
That patience is quite beaten from her breast.
She tears the senseless Sinon with her nails,
Comparing him to that unhappy guest   1565
Whose deed hath made herself herself detest.
  At last she smilingly with this gives o'er:
  'Fool, fool!' quoth she, 'his wounds will not be sore.'

Thus ebbs and flows the current of her sorrow,
And time doth weary time with her complaining. 1570
She looks for night, and then she longs for morrow,
And both she thinks too long with her remaining.
Short time seems long in sorrow's sharp sustaining;
　　Though woe be heavy, yet it seldom sleeps,
　　And they that watch see time how slow it creeps. 1575

Which all this time hath overslipped her thought
That she with painted images hath spent,
Being from the feeling of her own grief brought
By deep surmise of others' detriment,
Losing her woes in shows of discontent. 1580
　　It easeth some, though none it ever curéd,
　　To think their dolour others have enduréd.

But now the mindful messenger come back
Brings home his lord and other company;
Who finds his Lucrece clad in mourning black, 1585
And round about her tear-distainéd eye
Blue circles streamed, like rainbows in the sky.
　　These water-galls in her dim element
　　Foretell new storms to those already spent.

Which when her sad-beholding husband saw, 1590
Amazedly in her sad face he stares:
Her eyes, though sod in tears, looked red and raw,
Her lively colour killed with deadly cares.
He hath no power to ask her how she fares;
　　Both stood, like old acquaintance in a trance, 1595
　　Met far from home, wond'ring each other's chance.

At last he takes her by the bloodless hand,
And thus begins: 'What uncouth ill event
Hath thee befall'n, that thou dost trembling stand?
Sweet love, what spite hath thy fair colour spent? 1600
Why art thou thus attired in discontent?
　　Unmask, dear dear, this moody heaviness,
　　And tell thy grief, that we may give redress.'

Three times with sighs she gives her sorrow fire
Ere once she can discharge one word of woe; 1605
At length addressed to answer his desire,
She modestly prepares to let them know
Her honour is ta'en prisoner by the foe;
　　While Collatine and his consorted lords
　　With sad attention long to hear her words. 1610

And now this pale swan in her wat'ry nest
Begins the sad dirge of her certain ending.
'Few words', quoth she, 'shall fit the trespass best,
Where no excuse can give the fault amending:
In me moe woes than words are now depending; 1615
　　And my laments would be drawn out too long,
　　To tell them all with one poor tiréd tongue.

'Then be this all the task it hath to say:
Dear husband, in the interest of thy bed
A stranger came, and on that pillow lay 1620
Where thou wast wont to rest thy weary head;
And what wrong else may be imaginéd
　　By foul enforcement might be done to me,
　　From that, alas, thy Lucrece is not free.

'For in the dreadful dead of dark midnight, 1625
With shining falchion in my chamber came
A creeping creature with a flaming light,
And softly cried "Awake, thou Roman dame,
And entertain my love; else lasting shame
　　On thee and thine this night I will inflict, 1630
　　If thou my love's desire do contradict.

' "For some hard-favoured groom of thine," quoth he,
"Unless thou yoke thy liking to my will,
I'll murder straight, and then I'll slaughter thee,
And swear I found you where you did fulfil 1635
The loathsome act of lust, and so did kill
　　The lechers in their deed: this act will be
　　My fame, and thy perpetual infamy."

'With this, I did begin to start and cry,
And then against my heart he set his sword, 1640
Swearing, unless I took all patiently,
I should not live to speak another word;
So should my shame still rest upon record,
　　And never be forgot in mighty Rome
　　Th'adulterate death of Lucrece and her groom. 1645

'Mine enemy was strong, my poor self weak,
And far the weaker with so strong a fear.
My bloody judge forbade my tongue to speak;
No rightful plea might plead for justice there.
His scarlet lust came evidence to swear 1650
　　That my poor beauty had purloined his eyes,
　　And when the judge is robbed, the prisoner dies.

'O, teach me how to make mine own excuse!
Or, at the least, this refuge let me find:
Though my gross blood be stained with this abuse, 1655
Immaculate and spotless is my mind;
That was not forced; that never was inclined
　　To accessary yieldings, but still pure
　　Doth in her poisoned closet yet endure.'

Lo, here, the hopeless merchant of this loss, 1660
With head declined, and voice damned up with woe,
With sad-set eyes and wreathéd arms across,
From lips new waxen pale begins to blow
The grief away that stops his answer so;
　　But, wretched as he is, he strives in vain; 1665
　　What he breathes out his breath drinks up again.

As through an arch the violent roaring tide
Outruns the eye that doth behold his haste,
Yet in the eddy boundeth in his pride
Back to the strait that forced him on so fast, 1670
In rage sent out, recalled in rage, being past;
　　Even so his sighs, his sorrows, make a saw,
　　To push grief on and back the same grief draw.

Which speechless woe of his poor she attendeth
And his untimely frenzy thus awaketh: 1675
'Dear lord, thy sorrow to my sorrow lendeth
Another power; no flood by raining slaketh.
My woe too sensible thy passion maketh
　　More feeling-painful. Let it then suffice
　　To drown one woe, one pair of weeping eyes. 1680

'And for my sake, when I might charm thee so,
For she that was thy Lucrece, now attend me:
Be suddenly revengéd on my foe,
Thine, mine, his own; suppose thou dost defend me
From what is past. The help that thou shalt lend me 1685
   Comes all too late, yet let the traitor die;
   "For sparing justice feeds iniquity.

'But ere I name him, you fair lords', quoth she,
Speaking to those that came with Collatine,
'Shall plight your honourable faiths to me,   1690
With swift pursuit to venge this wrong of mine;
For 'tis a meritorious fair design
   To chase injustice with revengeful arms:
   Knights, by their oaths, should right poor
      ladies' harms.'

At this request, with noble disposition   1695
Each present lord began to promise aid,
As bound in knighthood to her imposition,
Longing to hear the hateful foe bewrayed.
But she, that yet her sad task hath not said,
   The protestation stops. 'O, speak,' quoth she,   1700
   'How may this forcéd stain be wiped from me?

'What is the quality of my offence,
Being constrained with dreadful circumstance?
May my pure mind with the foul act dispense,
My low-declinéd honour to advance?   1705
May any terms acquit me from this chance?
   The poisonéd fountain clears itself again;
   And why not I from this compelléd stain?'

With this, they all at once began to say,
Her body's stain her mind untainted clears;   1710
While with a joyless smile she turns away
The face, that map which deep impression bears
Of hard misfortune, carved in it with tears.
   'No, no,' quoth she, 'no dame hereafter living
   By my excuse shall claim excuse's giving.'   1715

Here with a sigh, as if her heart would break,
She throws forth Tarquin's name: 'He, he,' she says,
But more than 'he' her poor tongue could not speak;
Till after many accents and delays,
Untimely breathings, sick and short assays,   1720
   She utters this: 'He, he, fair lords, 'tis he,
   That guides this hand to give this wound to me.'

Even here she sheathéd in her harmless breast
A harmful knife, that thence her soul unsheathéd:
That blow did bail it from the deep unrest   1725
Of that polluted prison where it breathéd.
Her contrite sighs unto the clouds bequeathéd
   Her wingéd sprite and through her wounds doth fly
   Life's lasting date from cancelled destiny.

Stone-still, astonished with this deadly deed,   1730
Stood Collatine and all his lordly crew;
Till Lucrece' father, that beholds her bleed,
Himself on her self-slaught'red body threw;
And from the purple fountain Brutus drew
   The murd'rous knife, and, as it left the place,   1735
   Her blood, in poor revenge, held it in chase;

And bubbling from her breast, it·doth divide
In two slow rivers, that the crimson blood
Circles her body in on every side,
Who like a late-sacked island vastly stood   1740
Bare and unpeopled in this fearful flood.
   Some of her blood still pure and red remained,
   And some looked black, and that false
      Tarquin stained.

About the mourning and congealéd face
Of that black blood a wat'ry rigol goes,   1745
Which seems to weep upon the tainted place;
And ever since, as pitying Lucrece' woes,
Corrupted blood some watery token shows;
   And blood untainted still doth red abide,
   Blushing at that which is so putrified.   1750

'Daughter, dear daughter,' old Lucretius cries,
'That life was mine which thou hast here deprivéd.
If in the child the father's image lies,
Where shall I live now Lucrece is unlivéd?
Thou wast not to this end from me derivéd.   1755
   If children predecease progenitors,
   We are their offspring, and they none of ours.

'Poor broken glass, I often did behold
In thy sweet semblance my old age new born;
But now that fair fresh mirror, dim and old,   1760
Shows me a bare-boned death by time outworn;
O, from thy cheeks my image thou hast torn,
   And shivered all the beauty of my glass,
   That I no more can see what once I was.

'O time, cease thou thy course and last no longer,   1765
If they surcease to be that should survive.
Shall rotten death make conquest of the stronger,
And leave the falt'ring feeble souls alive?
The old bees die, the young possess their hive.
   Then live, sweet Lucrece, live again, and see   1770
   Thy father die, and not thy father thee.'

By this, starts Collatine as from a dream,
And bids Lucretius give his sorrow place;
And then in key-cold Lucrece' bleeding stream
He falls, and bathes the pale fear in his face,   1775
And counterfeits to die with her a space;
   Till manly shame bids him possess his breath,
   And live to be revengéd on her death.

The deep vexation of his inward soul
Hath served a dumb arrest upon his tongue;   1780
Who, mad that sorrow should his use control
Or keep him from heart-easing words so long,
Begins to talk; but through his lips do throng
   Weak words, so thick come in his poor heart's aid
   That no man could distinguish what he said.   1785

Yet sometime 'Tarquin' was pronouncéd plain,
But through his teeth, as if the name he tore.
This windy tempest, till it blow up rain,
Held back his sorrow's tide, to make it more;
At last it rains, and busy winds give o'er;   1790
   Then son and father weep with equal strife
   Who should weep most, for daughter or for
      wife.

The one doth call her his, the other his,
Yet neither may possess the claim they lay.
The father says 'She's mine'. 'O, mine she is,'   1795
Replies her husband: 'do not take away
My sorrow's interest; let no mourner say
    He weeps for her, for she was only mine,
    And only must be wailed by Collatine.'

'O,' quoth Lucretius, 'I did give that life   1800
Which she too early and too late hath spilled.'
'Woe, woe,' quoth Collatine, 'she was my wife;
I owed her, and 'tis mine that she hath killed.'
'My daughter' and 'my wife' with clamours filled
    The dispersed air, who, holding Lucrece' life,   1805
    Answered their cries, 'my daughter' and 'my
        wife'.

Brutus, who plucked the knife from Lucrece' side,
Seeing such emulation in their woe,
Began to clothe his wit in state and pride,
Burying in Lucrece' wound his folly's show.   1810
He with the Romans was esteemed so
    As silly jeering idiots are with kings,
    For sportive words and utt'ring foolish things.

But now he throws that shallow habit by
Wherein deep policy did him disguise,   1815
And armed his long-hid wits advisedly
To check the tears in Collatinus' eyes.
'Thou wrongèd lord of Rome,' quoth he, 'arise;
    Let my unsounded self, supposed a fool,
    Now set thy long-experienced wit to school.   1820

'Why, Collatine, is woe the cure for woe?
Do wounds help wounds, or grief help grievous
        deeds?
Is it revenge to give thyself a blow
For his foul act by whom thy fair wife bleeds?
Such childish humour from weak minds proceeds.   1825
    Thy wretched wife mistook the matter so
    To slay herself, that should have slain her foe.

'Courageous Roman, do not steep thy heart
In such relenting dew of lamentations,
But kneel with me and help to bear thy part   1830
To rouse our Roman gods with invocations
That they will suffer these abominations,
    Since Rome herself in them doth stand disgracéd,
    By our strong arms from forth her fair streets
        chaséd.

'Now by the Capitol that we adore,   1835
And by this chaste blood so unjustly stainéd,
By heaven's fair sun that breeds the fat earth's store,
By all our country rights in Rome maintainéd,
And by chaste Lucrece' soul that late complainéd
    Her wrongs to us, and by this bloody knife,   1840
    We will revenge the death of this true wife.'

This said, he struck his hand upon his breast,
And kissed the fatal knife to end his vow,
And to his protestation urged the rest,
Who, wond'ring at him, did his words allow;   1845
Then jointly to the ground their knees they bow,
    And that deep vow which Brutus made before
    He doth again repeat, and that they swore.

When they had sworn to this adviséd doom,
They did conclude to bear dead Lucrece thence,   1850
To show her bleeding body thorough Rome,
And so to publish Tarquin's foul offence;
Which being done with speedy diligence,
    The Romans plausible did give consent
    To Tarquin's everlasting banishment.   1855

The Passionate Pilgrim

1

When my love swears that she is made of truth,
I do believe her, though I know she lies,
That she might think me some untutored youth,
Unskilful in the world's false forgeries.
Thus vainly thinking that she thinks me young,   5
Although I know my years be past the best,
I smiling credit her false-speaking tongue,
Outfacing faults in love with love's ill rest.
But wherefore says my love that she is young?
And wherefore say not I that I am old?   10
O, love's best habit's in a soothing tongue,
And age in love loves not to have years told.
   Therefore I'll lie with love, and love with me,
   Since that our faults in love thus smothered be.

2

Two loves I have, of comfort and despair,
That like two spirits do suggest me still;
My better angle is a man right fair,
My worser spirit a woman coloured ill.
To win me soon to hell, my female evil   5
Tempteth my better angel from my side,
And would corrupt my saint to be a devil,
Wooing his purity with her fair pride.
And whether that my angle be turned fiend,
Suspect I may, yet not directly tell;   10
For being both to me, both to each friend,
I guess one angel in another's hell.
   The truth I shall not know, but live in doubt,
   Till my bad angel fire my good one out.

3

Did not the heavenly rhetoric of thine eye,
'Gainst whom the world could not hold argument,
Persuade my heart to this false perjury?
Vows for thee broke deserve not punishment.
A woman I forswore; but I will prove,   5
Thou being a goddess, I forswore not thee:
My vow was earthly, thou a heavenly love;
Thy grace being gained cures all disgrace in me.
My vow was breath, and breath a vapour is;
Then, thou fair sun, that on this earth doth shine,   10
Exhal'st this vapour vow; in thee it is:
If broken, then it is no fault of mine.
   If by me broke, what fool is not so wise
   To break an oath, to win a paradise?

4

Sweet Cytherea, sitting by a brook
With young Adonis, lovely, fresh and green,
Did court the lad with many a lovely look,
Such looks as none could look but beauty's queen.
She told him stories to delight his ear;   5
She showed him favours to allure his eye;
To win his heart, she touched him here and there;
Touches so soft still conquer chastity.

But whether unripe years did want conceit,
Or he refused to take her figuréd proffer,   10
The tender nibbler would not touch the bait,
But smile and jest at every gentle offer:
   Then fell she on her back, fair queen, and toward:
   He rose and ran away; ah, fool too froward.

5

If love make me forsworn, how shall I swear to love?
O never faith could hold, if not to beauty vowéd:
Though to myself forsworn, to thee I'll constant
    prove;
Those thoughts, to me like oaks, to thee like
    osiers bowéd.
Study his bias leaves, and makes his book thine eyes, 5
Where all those pleasures live that art can comprehend.
If knowledge be the mark, to know thee shall suffice;
Well learnéd is that tongue that well can thee
    commend.
All ignorant that soul that sees thee without wonder;
Which is to me some praise, that I thy parts admire.   10
Thine eye Jove's lightning seems, thy voice his
    dreadful thunder,
Which, not to anger bent, is music and sweet fire.
   Celestial as thou art, O do not love that wrong,
   To sing heaven's praise with such an earthly tongue.

6

Scarce had the sun dried up the dewy morn,
And scarce the herd gone to the hedge for shade,
When Cytherea, all in love forlorn,
A longing tarriance for Adonis made
Under an osier growing by a brook,   5
A brook where Adon used to cool his spleen.
Hot was the day; she hotter that did look
For his approach, that often there had been.
Anon he comes, and throws his mantle by,
And stood stark naked on the brook's green brim: 10
The sun looked on the world with glorious eye,
Yet not so wistly as this queen on him.
   He, spying her, bounced in whereas he stood;
   'O Jove,' quoth she, 'why was not I a flood!'

7

Fair is my love, but not so fair as fickle;
Mild as a dove, but neither true nor trusty;
Brighter than glass, and yet, as glass is, brittle;
Softer than wax, and yet as iron rusty;
   A lily pale, with damask dye to grace her;   5
   None fairer, nor none falser to deface her.

Her lips to mine how often hath she joinéd,
Between each kiss her oaths of true love swearing!
How many tales to please me hath she coinéd,
Dreading my love, the loss thereof still fearing!   10
   Yet in the midst of all her pure protestings
   Her faith, her oaths, her tears, and all were jestings.

She burned with love, as straw with fire flameth;
She burned out love, as soon as straw out-burneth;
She framed the love, and yet she foiled the framing; 15
She bade love last, and yet she fell a-turning.
 Was this a lover, or a lecher whether?
 Bad in the best, though excellent in neither.

8

If music and sweet poetry agree,
As they must needs, the sister and the brother,
Then must the love be great 'twixt thee and me,
Because thou lov'st the one and I the other.
Dowland to thee is dear, whose heavenly touch 5
Upon the lute doth ravish human sense;
Spenser to me, whose deep conceit is such
As passing all conceit needs no defence.
Thou lov'st to hear the sweet melodious sound
That Phoebus' lute, the queen of music, makes; 10
And I in deep delight am chiefly drowned
When as himself to singing he betakes.
 One god is god of both, as poets feign;
 One knight loves both, and both in thee remain.

9

Fair was the morn, when the fair queen of love,
 . . . . . .
Paler for sorrow than her milk-white dove,
For Adon's sake, a youngster proud and wild,
Her stand she takes upon a steep-up hill, 5
Anon Adonis comes with horn and hounds;
She, silly queen, with more than love's good will,
Forbade the boy he should not pass those grounds.
'Once', quoth she, 'did I see a fair sweet youth
Here in these brakes deep-wounded with a boar, 10
Deep in the thigh, a spectacle of ruth!
See, in my thigh,' quoth she, 'here was the sore.'
 She showéd hers; he saw more wounds than one,
 And blushing fled, and left her all alone.

10

Sweet rose, fair flower, untimely plucked, soon vaded,
Plucked in the bud and vaded in the spring!
Bright orient pearl, alack, too timely shaded!
Fair creature, killed too soon by death's sharp sting!
Like a green plum that hangs upon a tree, 5
And falls through wind before the fall should be.

I weep for thee and yet no cause I have;
For why thou left'st me nothing in thy will.
And yet thou left'st me more than I did crave,
For why I cravéd nothing of thee still: 10
 O yes, dear friend, I pardon crave of thee,
 Thy discontent thou didst bequeath to me.

11

Venus with young Adonis sitting by her
Under a myrtle shade began to woo him;
She told the youngling how god Mars did try her,
And as he fell to her, so fell she to him.
'Even thus', quoth she, 'the warlike god embraced me', 5
And then she clipped Adonis in her arms;
'Even thus', quoth she, 'the warlike god unlaced me',
As if the boy should use like loving charms;
'Even thus', quoth she, 'he seizéd on my lips',

And with her lips on his did act the seizure;
And as she fetchéd breath, away he skips,
And would not take her meaning nor her pleasure.
 Ah, that I had my lady at this bay,
 To kiss and clip me till I run away!

12

Crabbéd age and youth cannot live together:
Youth is full of pleasance, age is full of care;
Youth like summer morn, age like winter weather;
Youth like summer brave, age like winter bare.
Youth is full of sport, age's breath is short; 5
 Youth is nimble, age is lame;
Youth is hot and bold, age is weak and cold;
 Youth is wild and age is tame.
Age, I do abhor thee; youth, I do adore thee;
 O, my love, my love is young! 10
Age, I do defy thee. O, sweet shepherd, hie thee,
 For methinks thou stay too long.

13

Beauty is but a vain and doubtful good,
A shining gloss that vadeth suddenly,
A flower that dies when first it 'gins to bud,
A brittle glass that's broken presently;
 A doubtful good, a gloss, a glass, a flower, 5
 Lost, vaded, broken, dead within an hour.

And as goods lost are seld or never found,
As vaded gloss no rubbing will refresh,
As flowers dead lie witheréd on the ground,
As broken glass no cement can redress: 10
 So beauty blemished once, for ever lost,
 In spite of physic, painting, pain and cost.

14

Good night, good rest: ah, neither be my share;
She bade good night that kept my rest away;
And daffed me to a cabin hanged with care,
To descant on the doubts of my decay.
 'Farewell,' quoth she, 'and come again to-morrow'; 5
 Fare well I could not, for I supped with sorrow.

Yet at my parting sweetly did she smile,
In scorn or friendship nill I conster whether;
'T may be, she joyed to jest at my exile,
'T may be, again to make me wander thither: 10
 'Wander', a word for shadows like myself,
 As take the pain, but cannot pluck the pelf.

Lord, how mine eyes throw gazes to the east!
My heart doth charge the watch; the morning rise
Doth cite each moving sense from idle rest, 15
Not daring trust the office of mine eyes.
 While Philomela sings, I sit and mark,
 And wish her lays were tunéd like the lark.

For she doth welcome daylight with her ditty,
And drives away dark dreaming night: 20
The night so packed, I post unto my pretty;
Heart hath his hope and eyes their wishéd sight;
 Sorrow changed to solace and solace mixed
  with sorrow;
 For why, she sighed, and bade me come to-morrow.

Were I with her, the night would post too soon,   25
But now are minutes added to the hours;
To spite me now, each minute seems a moon;
Yet not for me, shine sun to succour flowers!
 Pack night, peep day; good day, of night now
  borrow;
 Short night, to-night, and length thyself
  to-morrow.   30

15

It was a lording's daughter, the fairest one of three,
That likéd of her master as well as well might be,
Till looking on an Englishman, the fairest that eye
 could see,
 Her fancy fell a-turning.
Long was the combat doubtful that love with love
 did fight,   5
To leave the master loveless, or kill the gallant knight;
To put in practice either, alas, it was a spite
 Unto the silly damsel!
But one must be refuséd; more mickle was the pain
That nothing could be uséd to turn them both to gain,   10
For of the two the trusty knight was wounded
 with disdain:
 Alas, she could not help it!
Thus art with arms contending was victor of the day,
Which by a gift of learning did bear the maid away:
Then, lullaby, the learnéd man hath got the lady gay;   15
 For now my song is ended.

16

On a day, alack the day!
Love, whose month was ever May,
Spied a blossom passing fair,
Playing in the wanton air.
Through the velvet leaves the wind   5
All unseen 'gan passage find,
That the lover, sick to death,
Wished himself the heaven's breath,
'Air', quoth he, 'thy cheeks may blow;
Air, would I might triumph so!   10
But, alas! my hand hath sworn
Ne'er to pluck thee from thy thorn;
Vow, alack! for youth unmeet,
Youth, so apt to pluck a sweet.
Thou for whom Jove would swear   15
Juno but an Ethiope were;
And deny himself for Jove,
Turning mortal for thy love.'

17

My flocks feed not, my ewes breed not,
My rams speed not, all is amiss;
Love is dying, faith's defying,
Heart's denying, causer of this.
All my merry jigs are quite forgot,   5
All my lady's love is lost, God wot;
Where her faith was firmly fixed in love,
There a nay is placed without remove.
 One silly cross wrought all my loss;
 O frowning Fortune, curséd fickle dame!   10
 For now I see inconstancy
 More in women than in men remain.

In black mourn I, all fears scorn I,
Love hath forlorn me, living in thrall:
Heart is bleeding, all help needing,
O cruel speeding, fraughted with gall.   15
My shepherd's pipe can sound no deal;
My wether's bell rings doleful knell;
My curtal dog that wont to have played,
Plays not at all, but seems afraid;   20
 My sighs so deep procures to weep,
 In howling wise, to see my doleful plight.
 How sighs resound through heartless ground,
 Like a thousand vanquished men in bloody fight!

Clear wells spring not, sweet birds sing not,   25
Green plants bring not forth their dye;
Herds stand weeping, flocks all sleeping,
Nymphs back peeping fearfully.
All our pleasure known to us poor swains,
All our merry meetings on the plains,   30
All our evening sport from us is fled,
All our love is lost, for Love is dead.
 Farewell, sweet lass, thy like ne'er was
 For a sweet content, the cause of all my moan:
 Poor Corydon must live alone;   35
 Other help for him I see that there is none.

18

When as thine eye hath chose the dame,
And stalled the deer that thou shouldst strike,
Let reason rule things worthy blame,
As well as fancy, partial might;
 Take counsel of some wiser head,   5
 Neither too young nor yet unwed.

And when thou com'st thy tale to tell,
Smooth not thy tongue with filéd talk,
Lest she some subtle practice smell—
A cripple soon can find a halt—   10
 But plainly say thou lov'st her well,
 And set thy person forth to sell.

And to her will frame all thy ways;
Spare not to spend, and chiefly there
Where thy desert may merit praise,   15
By ringing in thy lady's ear:
 The strongest castle, tower and town,
 The golden bullet beats it down.

Serve always with assuréd trust,
And in thy suit be humble true;   20
Unless thy lady prove unjust,
Press never thou to choose anew:
 When time shall serve, be thou not slack
 To proffer, though she put thee back.

What though her frowning brows be bent,   25
Her cloudy looks will calm ere night,
And then too late she will repent
That thus dissembled her delight;
 And twice desire, ere it be day,
 That which with scorn she put away.   30

What though she strive to try her strength,
And ban and brawl, and say thee nay,
Her feeble force will yield at length,

When craft hath taught her thus to say:
'Had women been so strong as men, 35
In faith, you had not had it then,'

The wiles and guiles that women work,
Dissembled with an outward show,
The tricks and toys that in them lurk,
The cock that treads them shall not know. 40
Have you not heard it said full oft,
A woman's nay doth stand for nought?

Think women still to strive with men,
To sin and never for to saint:
There is no heaven, by holy then, 45
When time with age shall them attaint.
Were kisses all the joys in bed,
One woman would another wed.

But, soft, enough, too much I fear,
Lest that my mistress hear my song; 50
She will not stick to round me on th'ear,
To teach my tongue to be so long,
Yet will she blush, here be it said,
To hear her secrets so bewrayed.

19

Live with me, and be my love,
And we will all the pleasures prove
That hills and valleys, dales and fields,
And all the craggy mountains yield.

There will we sit upon the rocks, 5
And see the shepherds feed their flocks,
By shallow rivers, by whose falls
Melodious birds sing madrigals.

There will I make thee a bed of roses,
With a thousand fragrant posies, 10
A cap of flowers, and a kirtle
Embroider'd all with leaves of myrtle.

A belt of straw and ivy buds,
With coral clasps and amber studs;
And if these pleasures may thee move, 15
Then live with me and be my love.

LOVE'S ANSWER

If that the world and love were young,
And truth in every shepherd's tongue,
These pretty pleasures might me move
To live with thee and be thy love. 20

20

As it fell upon a day
In the merry month of May,
Sitting in a pleasant shade
Which a grove of myrtles made,
Beasts did leap and birds did sing, 5
Trees did grow and plants did spring;
Every thing did banish moan,
Save the nightingale alone:
She, poor bird, as all forlorn,
Leaned her breast up-till a thorn, 10
And there sung the dolefull'st ditty,
That to hear it was great pity:
'Fie, fie, fie', now would she cry;
'Tereu, Tereu!' by and by;
That to hear her so complain, 15
Scarce I could from tears refrain;
For her griefs so lively shown
Made me think upon mine own.
Ah, thought I, thou mourn'st in vain!
None takes pity on thy pain: 20
Senseless trees they cannot hear thee;
Ruthless beasts they will not cheer thee:
King Pandion he is dead;
All thy friends are lapped in lead;
All thy fellow birds do sing, 25
Careless of thy sorrowing.
Whilst as fickle Fortune smiled,
Thou and I were both beguiled.
    Every one that flatters thee
Is no friend in misery. 30
Words are easy, like the wind;
Faithful friends are hard to find:
Every man will be thy friend
Whilst thou hast wherewith to spend;
But if store of crowns be scant, 35
No man will supply thy want.
If that one be prodigal,
Bountiful they will him call,
And with such-like flattering,
'Pity but he were a king'; 40
If he be addict to vice,
Quickly him they will entice;
If to women he be bent,
They have at commandment.
But if Fortune once do frown, 45
Then farewell his great renown;
They that fawned on him before
Use his company no more.
He that is thy friend indeed,
He will help thee in thy need: 50
If thou sorrow, he will weep;
If thou wake, he cannot sleep;
Thus of every grief in heart
He with thee doth bear a part.
These are certain signs to know 55
Faithful friend from flatt'ring foe.

The Phoenix and the Turtle

Let the bird of loudest lay,
On the sole Arabian tree,
Herald sad and trumpet be,
To whose sound chaste wings obey.

But thou shrieking harbinger,   5
Foul precurrer of the fiend,
Augur of the fever's end,
To this troop come thou not near!

From this session interdict
Every fowl of tyrant wing,   10
Save the eagle, feath'red king:
Keep the obsequy so strict.

Let the priest in surplice white,
That defunctive music can,
Be the death-divining swan,   15
Lest the requiem lack his right.

And thou treble-dated crow,
That thy sable gender mak'st
With the breath thou giv'st and tak'st,
'Mongst our mourners shalt thou go.   20

Here the anthem doth commence:
Love and constancy is dead;
Phoenix and the turtle fled
In a mutual flame from hence.

So they loved, as love in twain   25
Had the essence but in one;
Two distincts, division none:
Number there in love was slain.

Hearts remote, yet not asunder;
Distance, and no space was seen   30
'Twixt this turtle and his queen:
But in them it were a wonder.

So between them love did shine,
That the turtle saw his right
Flaming in the phoenix' sight;   35
Either was the other's mine.

Property was thus appalléd,
That the self was not the same;
Single nature's double name
Neither two nor one was calléd.   40

Reason, in itself confounded,
Saw division grow together,
To themselves yet either neither,
Simple were so well compounded;

That it cried, How true a twain   45
Seemeth this concordant one!
Love hath reason, reason none,
If what parts can so remain.

Whereupon it made this threne
To the phoenix and the dove,   50
Co-supremes and stars of love,
As chorus to their tragic scene.

THRENOS

Beauty, truth, and rarity,
Grace in all simplicity,   55
Here enclosed, in cinders lie.

Death is now the phoenix' nest;
And the turtle's loyal breast
To eternity doth rest.

Leaving no posterity,
'Twas not their infirmity,   60
It was married chastity.

Truth may seem, but cannot be;
Beauty brag, but 'tis not she;
Truth and beauty buried be.

To this urn let those repair   65
That are either true or fair;
For these dead birds sigh a prayer.

A Lover's Complaint

From off a hill whose concave womb reworded
A plaintful story from a sist'ring vale,
My spirits t'attend this double voice accorded,
And down I laid to list the sad-tuned tale,
Ere long espied a fickle maid full pale,   5
Tearing of papers, breaking rings atwain,
Storming her world with sorrow's wind and rain.

Upon her head a platted hive of straw,
Which fortified her visage from the sun,
Whereon the thought might think sometime it saw   10
The carcase of a beauty spent and done.
Time had not scythéd all that youth begun,
Nor youth all quit, but spite of heaven's fell rage
Some beauty peeped through lattice of seared age.

Oft did she heave her napkin to her eyne,   15
Which on it had conceited characters,
Laund'ring the silken figures in the brine
That seasonéd woe had pelleted in tears,
And often reading what contents it bears;
As often shrieking undistinguished woe,   20
In clamours of all size, both high and low.

Sometimes her levelled eyes their carriage ride,
As they did batt'ry to the spheres intend;
Sometime diverted their poor balls are tied
To th'orbéd earth; sometimes they do extend   25
Their view right on; anon their gazes lend
To every place at once, and nowhere fixed,
The mind and sight distractedly commixed.

Her hair, nor loose nor tied in formal plat,
Proclaimed in her a careless hand of pride;   30
For some, untucked, descended her sheaved hat,
Hanging her pale and pinéd cheek beside;
Some in her threaden fillet still did bide,
And, true to bondage, would not break from
          thence,
Though slackly braided in loose negligence.   35

A thousand favours from a maund she drew
Of amber, crystal, and of beaded jet,
Which one by one she in a river threw,
Upon whose weeping margent she was set;
Like usury applying wet to wet,   40
Or monarchs' hands that lets not bounty fall
Where want cries some, but where excess begs all.

Of folded schedules had she many a one,
Which she perused, sighed, tore, and gave the flood;
Cracked many a ring of posied gold and bone,   45
Bidding them find their sepulchres in mud;
Found yet moe letters sadly penned in blood,
With sleided silk feat and affectedly
Enswathed and sealed to curious secrecy.

These often bathed she in her fluxive eyes,   50
And often kissed, and often 'gan to tear;
Cried, 'O false blood, thou register of lies,
What unapprovéd witness dost thou bear!
Ink would have seemed more black and damnéd here!
This said, in top of rage the lines she rents,   55
Big discontents so breaking their contents.

A reverend man that grazed his cattle nigh,
Sometime a blusterer that the ruffle knew
Of court, of city, and had let go by
The swiftest hours observéd as they flew,   60
Towards this afflicted fancy fastly drew;
And, privileged by age, desires to know
In brief the grounds and motives of her woe.

So slides he down upon his grainéd bat,
And comely distant sits he by her side;   65
When he again desires her, being sat,
Her grievance with his hearing to divide.
If that from him there may be aught applied
Which may her suffering ecstasy assuage,
'Tis promised in the charity of age.   70

'Father,' she says, 'though in me you behold
The injury of many a blasting hour,
Let it not tell your judgement I am old:
Not age, but sorrow, over me hath power.
I might as yet have been a spreading flower,   75
Fresh to myself, if I had self-applied
Love to myself, and to no love beside.

'But woe is me! too early I attended
A youthful suit—it was to gain my grace—
O, one by nature's outwards so commended   80
That maidens' eyes stuck over all his face.
Love lacked a dwelling and made him her place;
And when in his fair parts she did abide,
She was new lodged and newly deified.

'His browny locks did hang in crookéd curls;   85
And every light occasion of the wind
Upon his lips their silken parcels hurls.
What's sweet to do, to do will aptly find:
Each eye that saw him did enchant the mind;
For on his visage was in little drawn   90
What largeness thinks in Paradise was sawn.

'Small show of man was yet upon his chin;
His phoenix down began but to appear,
Like unshorn velvet, on that termless skin,
Whose bare out-bragged the web it seemed to wear; 95
Yet showed his visage by that cost more dear;
And nice affections wavering stood in doubt
If best were as it was, or best without.

'His qualities were beauteous as his form,
For maiden-tongued he was, and thereof free;   100
Yet if men moved him, was he such a storm
As oft 'twixt May and April is to see,
When winds breathe sweet, unruly though they be.
His rudeness so with his authorized youth
Did livery falseness in a pride of truth.   105

'Well could he ride, and often men would say,
"That horse his mettle from his rider takes:
Proud of subjection, noble by the sway,
What rounds, what bounds, what course, what stop
    he makes!"
And controversy hence a question takes,   110
Whether the horse by him became his deed,
Or he his manage by th'well-doing steed.

'But quickly on this side the verdict went:
His real habitude gave life and grace
To appertainings and to ornament,   115
Accomplished in himself, not in his case,
All aids, themselves made fairer by their place,
Came for additions; yet their purposed trim
Pierced not his grace, but were all graced by him.

'So on the tip of his subduing tongue   120
All kind of arguments and question deep,
All replication prompt, and reason strong,
For his advantage still did wake and sleep.
To make the weeper laugh, the laugher weep,
He had the dialect and different skill,   125
Catching all passions in his craft of will,

'That he did in the general bosom reign
Of young, of old, and sexes both enchanted,
To dwell with him in thoughts, or to remain
In personal duty, following where he haunted.   130
Consents bewitched, ere he desire, have granted,
And dialogued for him what he would say,
Asked their own wills, and made their wills obey.

'Many there were that did his picture get,
To serve their eyes, and in it put their mind;   135
Like fools that in th'imagination set
The goodly objects which abroad they find
Of lands and mansions, theirs in thought assigned;
And labouring in moe pleasures to bestow them
Than the true gouty landlord which doth owe them. 140

'So many have, that never touched his hand,
Sweetly supposed them mistress of his heart.
My woeful self, that did in freedom stand,
And was my own fee-simple, not in part,
What with his art in youth, and youth in art,   145
Threw my affections in his charméd power
Reserved the stalk and gave him all my flower.

'Yet did I not, as some my equals did,
Demand of him, nor being desiréd yielded;
Finding myself in honour so forbid,   150
With safest distance I mine honour shielded.
Experience for me many bulwarks builded
Of proofs new-bleeding, which remained the foil
Of this false jewel, and his amorous spoil.

'But ah, who ever shunned by precedent   155
The destined ill she must herself assay?
Or forced examples, 'gainst her own content,
To put the by-past perils in her way?
Counsel may stop awhile what will not stay;
For when we rage, advice is often seen   160
By blunting us to make our wills more keen.

'Nor gives it satisfaction to our blood
That we must curb it upon others' proof,
To be forbod the sweets that seems so good
For fear of harms that preach in our behoof.   165
O appetite, from judgement stand aloof!
The one a palate hath that needs will taste,
Though Reason weep, and cry it is thy last.

'For further I could say this man's untrue,
And knew the patterns of his foul beguiling;   170
Heard where his plants in others' orchards grew;
Saw how deceits were gilded in his smiling;
Knew vows were ever brokers to defiling;
Thought characters and words merely but art,
And bastards of his foul adulterate heart.   175

'And long upon these terms I held my city,
Till thus he 'gan besiege me: "Gentle maid,
Have of my suffering youth some feeling pity,
And be not of my holy vows afraid.
That's to ye sworn to none was ever said;   180
For feasts of love I have been called unto,
Till now did ne'er invite nor never woo.

'"All my offences that abroad you see
Are errors of the blood, none of the mind;
Love made them not; with acture they may be,   185
Where neither party is nor true nor kind.
They sought their shame that so their shame did find;
And so much less of shame in me remains
By how much of me their reproach contains.

'"Among the many that mine eyes have seen,   190
Not one whose flame my heart so much as warméd,
Or my affection put to th'smallest teen,
Or any of my leisures ever charméd.
Harm have I done to them, but ne'er was harméd;
Kept hearts in liveries, but mine own was free,   195
And reigned commanding in his monarchy.

'"Look here what tributes wounded fancies sent me,
Of paléd pearls and rubies red as blood;
Figuring that they their passions likewise lent me
Of grief and blushes, aptly understood   200
In bloodless white and the encrimsoned mood—
Effects of terror and dear modesty,
Encamped in hearts, but fighting outwardly.

'"And, lo, behold these talents of their hair,
With twisted metal amorously empleached,   205
I have receiv'd from many a several fair,
Their kind acceptance weepingly beseeched,
With the annexions of fair gems enriched,
And deep-brained sonnets that did amplify
Each stone's dear nature, worth, and quality.   210

'"The diamond? why, 'twas beautiful and hard,
Whereto his invised properties did tend;
The deep-green em'rald, in whose fresh regard
Weak sights their sickly radiance do amend;
The heaven-hued sapphire and the opal blend   215
With objects manifold; each several stone,
With wit well blazoned, smiled, or made some moan.

'"Lo, all these trophies of affections hot,
Of pensived and subdued desires the tender,
Nature hath charged me that I hoard them not,   220
But yield them up where I myself must render—
That is, to you, my origin and ender;
For these, of force, must your oblations be,
Since I their altar, you enpatron me.

'"O then advance of yours that phraseless hand   225
Whose white weighs down the airy scale of praise;
Take all these similes to your own command,
Hallowéd with sighs that burning lungs did raise;
What me your minister for you obeys
Works under you; and to your audit comes   230
Their distract parcels in combinéd sums.

'"Lo, this device was sent me from a nun,
Or sister sanctified, of holiest note,
Which late her noble suit in court did shun,
Whose rarest havings made the blossoms dote;   235
For she was sought by spirits of richest coat,
But kept cold distance, and did thence remove
To spend her living in eternal love.

'"But, O my sweet, what labour is't to leave
The thing we have not, mast'ring what not strives,   240
Playing the place which did no form receive,
Playing patient sports in unconstrainéd gyves!
She that her fame so to herself contrives,
The scars of battle scapeth by the flight,
And makes her absence valiant, not her might.   245

'"O pardon me in that my boast is true!
The accident which brought me to her eye
Upon the moment did her force subdue,
And now she would the cagéd cloister fly.
Religious love put out religion's eye,   250
Not to be tempted, would she be immuréd,
And now to tempt all liberty procuréd.

'"How mighty then you are, O hear me tell!
The broken bosoms that to me belong
Have emptied all their fountains in my well,   255
And mine I pour your ocean all among.
I strong o'er them, and you o'er me being strong,
Must for your victory us all congest,
As compound love to physic your cold breast.

'"My parts had pow'r to charm a sacred nun,   260
Who, disciplined, ay, dieted in grace,
Believed her eyes when they t'assail begun,
All vows and consecrations giving place,
O most potential love, vow, bond, nor space,
In thee hath neither sting, knot, nor confine,   265
For thou art all, and all things else are thine.

'"When thou impressest, what are precepts worth
Of stale example? When thou wilt inflame,
How coldly those impediments stand forth,
Of wealth, of filial fear, law, kindred, fame!   270
Love's arms are peace, 'gainst rule, 'gainst sense,
          'gainst shame.
And sweetens, in the suff'ring pangs it bears,
The aloes of all forces, shocks and fears.

'"Now all these hearts that do on mine depend,
Feeling it break, with bleeding groans they pine,   275
And supplicant their sighs to your extend,
To leave the batt'ry that you make 'gainst mine,
Lending soft audience to my sweet design,
And credent soul to that strong-bonded oath,
That shall prefer and undertake my troth."   280

'This said, his wat'ry eyes he did dismount,
Whose sights till then were levelled on my face;
Each cheek a river running from a fount
With brinish current downward flowed apace.
O, how the channel to the stream gave grace!   285
Who glazed with crystal gate the glowing roses
That flame through water which their hue encloses.

'O father, what a hell of witchcraft lies
In the small orb of one particular tear!
But with the inundation of the eyes   290
What rocky heart to water will not wear?
What breast so cold that is not warméd here?
O cleft effect! cold modesty, hot wrath,
Both fire from hence and chill extincture hath.

'For lo, his passion, but an art of craft,   295
Even there resolved my reason into tears;
There my white stole of chastity I daffed,
Shook off my sober guards and civil fears;
Appear to him as he to me appears,
All melting; though our drops this diff'rence bore: 300
His poisoned me, and mine did him restore.

'In him a plenitude of subtle matter,
Applied to cautels, all strange forms receives,
Of burning blushes or of weeping water,
Or swooning paleness; and he takes and leaves,   305
In either's aptness, as it best deceives,
To blush at speeches rank, to weep at woes,
Or to turn white and swoon at tragic shows;

'That not a heart which in his level came
Could scape the hail of his all-hurting aim,   310
Showing fair nature is both kind and tame;
And, veiled in them, did win whom he would maim.
Against the thing he sought he would exclaim;
When he most burned in heart-wished luxury,
He preached pure maid and praised cold chastity.   315

'Thus merely with the garment of a Grace
The naked and concealéd fiend he covered,
That th'unexperient gave the tempter place,
Which, like a cherubin, above them hovered.
Who, young and simple, would not be so lovered?   320
Ay me, I fell, and yet do question make
What I should do again for such a sake.

'O, that infected moisture of his eye,
O, that false fire which in his cheek so glowéd,
O, that forced thunder from his heart did fly,   325
O, that sad breath his spongy lungs bestowéd,
O, all that borrowéd motion, seeming owéd,
Would yet again betray the fore-betrayed,
And new pervert a reconciléd maid.'

The Sonnets

TO. THE. ONLIE. BEGETTER. OF.
THESE. INSUING. SONNETS.
MR. W. H. ALL. HAPPINESSE.
AND. THAT. ETERNITIE.
PROMISED.
BY.
OUR. EVER-LIVING. POET.
WISHETH.
THE. WELL-WISHING.
ADVENTURER. IN.
SETTING.
FORTH.

T.T.

The Sonnets

1

From fairest creatures we desire increase,
That thereby beauty's rose might never die,
But as the riper should by time decease,
His tender heir might bear his memory:
But thou contracted to thine own bright eyes,   5
Feed'st thy light's flame with self-substantial fuel,
Making a famine where abundance lies,
Thy self thy foe, to thy sweet self too cruel:
Thou that art now the world's fresh ornament,
And only herald to the gaudy spring,   10
Within thine own bud buriest thy content,
And tender churl mak'st waste in niggarding:
  Pity the world, or else this glutton be,
  To eat the world's due, by the grave and thee.

2

When forty winters shall besiege thy brow,
And dig deep trenches in thy beauty's field,
Thy youth's proud livery so gazed on now,
Will be a tattered weed of small worth held:
Then being asked, where all thy beauty lies,   5
Where all the treasure of thy lusty days;
To say within thine own deep sunken eyes,
Were an all-eating shame, and thriftless praise.
How much more praise deserved thy beauty's use,
If thou couldst answer 'This fair child of mine   10
Shall sum my count, and make my old excuse'
Proving his beauty by succession thine.
  This were to be new made when thou art old,
  And see thy blood warm when thou feel'st it cold.

3

Look in thy glass and tell the face thou viewest,
Now is the time that face should form another,
Whose fresh repair if now thou not renewest,
Thou dost beguile the world, unbless some mother.
For where is she so fair whose uneared womb   5
Disdains the tillage of thy husbandry?
Or who is he so fond will be the tomb,
Of his self-love to stop posterity?
Thou art thy mother's glass and she in thee
Calls back the lovely April of her prime,   10
So thou through windows of thine age shalt see,
Despite of wrinkles this thy golden time.
  But if thou live remembered not to be,
  Die single and thine image dies with thee.

4

Unthrifty loveliness why dost thou spend,
Upon thy self thy beauty's legacy?
Nature's bequest gives nothing but doth lend,
And being frank she lends to those are free:
Then beauteous niggard why dost thou abuse,   5
The bounteous largess given thee to give?
Profitless usurer why dost thou use
So great a sum of sums yet canst not live?
For having traffic with thy self alone,
Thou of thy self thy sweet self dost deceive,   10
Then how when nature calls thee to be gone,
What acceptable audit canst thou leave?
  Thy unused beauty must be tombed with thee,
  Which uséd lives th' executor to be.

5

Those hours .that with gentle work did frame
The lovely gaze where every eye doth dwell
Will play the tyrants to the very same,
And that unfair which fairly doth excel:
For never-resting time leads summer on   5
To hideous winter and confounds him there,
Sap checked with frost and lusty leaves quite gone,
Beauty o'er-snowed and bareness every where:
Then were not summer's distillation left
A liquid prisoner pent in walls of glass,   10
Beauty's effect with beauty were bereft,
Nor it nor no remembrance what it was.
  But flowers distilled though they with winter meet,
  Leese but their show, their substance still lives sweet.

6

Then let not winter's raggéd hand deface,
In thee thy summer ere thou be distilled:
Make sweet some vial; treasure thou some place,
With beauty's treasure ere it be self-killed:
That use is not forbidden usury,   5
Which happies those that pay the willing loan;
That's for thy self to breed another thee,
Or ten times happier be it ten for one,
Ten times thy self were happier than thou art,
If ten of thine ten times refigured thee: 10
Then what could death do if thou shouldst depart,
Leaving thee living in posterity?
  Be not self-willed for thou art much too fair,
  To be death's conquest and make worms thine heir.

7

Lo in the orient when the gracious light
Lifts up his burning head, each under eye
Doth homage to his new-appearing sight,
Serving with looks his sacred majesty,
And having climbed the steep-up heavenly hill,   5
Resembling strong youth in his middle age,
Yet mortal looks adore his beauty still,
Attending on his golden pilgrimage:
But when from highmost pitch with weary car,
Like feeble age he reeleth from the day,   10
The eyes (fore duteous) now converted are
From his low tract and look another way:
    So thou, thy self out-going in thy noon:
    Unlooked on diest unless thou get a son.

8

Music to hear, why hear'st thou music sadly?
Sweets with sweets war not, joy.delights in joy:
Why lov'st thou that which thou receiv'st not gladly,
Or else receiv'st with pleasure thine annoy?
If the true concord of well-tunéd sounds,   5
By unions married do offend thine ear,
They do but sweetly chide thee, who confounds
In singleness the parts that thou shouldst bear.
Mark how one string sweet husband to another,
Strikes each in each by mutual ordering;   10
Resembling sire, and child, and happy mother,
Who all in one, one pleasing note do sing:
    Whose speechless song being many, seeming one,
    Sings this to thee, 'Thou single wilt prove none'.

9

Is it for fear to wet a widow's eye,
That thou consum'st thy self in single life?
Ah, if thou issueless shalt hap to die,
The world will wail thee like a makeless wife,
The world will be thy widow and still weep,   5
That thou no form of thee hast left behind,
When every private widow well may keep,
By children's eyes, her husband's shape in mind:
Look what an unthrift in the world doth spend
Shifts but his place, for still the world enjoys it;   10
But beauty's waste hath in the world an end,
And kept unused the user so destroys it:
    No love toward others in that bosom sits
    That on himself such murd'rous shame commits.

10

For shame deny that thou bear'st love to any
Who for thy self art so unprovident.
Grant if thou wilt, thou art beloved of many,
But that thou none lov'st is most evident:
For thou art so possessed with murd'rous hate,   5
That 'gainst thy self thou stick'st not to conspire,
Seeking that beauteous roof to ruinate
Which to repair should be thy chief desire:
O change thy thought, that I may change my mind,
Shall hate be fairer lodged than gentle love?   10
Be as thy presence is gracious and kind,
Or to thy self at least kind-hearted prove,
    Make thee another self for love of me,
    That beauty still may live in thine or thee.

11

As fast as thou shalt wane so fast thou grow'st,
In one of thine, from that which thou departest,
And that fresh blood which youngly thou bestow'st,
Thou mayst call thine, when thou from youth
    convertest,
Herein lives wisdom, beauty, and increase,   5
Without this folly, age, and cold decay,
If all were minded so, the times should cease,
And threescore year would make the world away:
Let those whom nature hath not made for store,
Harsh, featureless, and rude, barrenly perish: 10
Look whom she best endowed, she gave thee more;
Which bounteous gift thou shouldst in bounty cherish:
    She carved thee for her seal, and meant thereby,
    Thou shouldst print more, not let that copy die.

12

When I do count the clock that tells the time,
And see the brave day sunk in hideous night,
When I behold the violet past prime,
And sable curls all silvered o'er with white:
When lofty trees I see barren of leaves,   5
Which erst from heat did canopy the herd
And summer's green all girded up in sheaves,
Borne on the bier with white and bristly beard:
Then of thy beauty do I question make
That thou among the wastes of time must go,   10
Since sweets and beauties do themselves forsake,
And die as fast as they see others grow,
    And nothing 'gainst Time's scythe can make defence
    Save breed to brave him, when he takes thee hence.

13

O that you were your self, but love you are
No longer yours, than you your self here live,
Against this coming end you should prepare,
And your sweet semblance to some other give.
So should that beauty which you hold in lease   5
Find no determination, then you were
Your self again after your self's decease,
When your sweet issue your sweet form should bear.
Who lets so fair a house fall to decay,
Which husbandry in honour might uphold,   10
Against the stormy gusts of winter's day
And barren rage of death's eternal cold?
    O none but unthrifts, dear my love you know,
    You had a father, let your son say so.

14

Not from the stars do I my judgement pluck,
And yet methinks I have astronomy,
But not to tell of good, or evil luck,
Of plagues, of dearths, or seasons' quality,
Nor can I fortune to brief minutes tell;   5
Pointing to each his thunder, rain and wind,
Or say with princes if it shall go well
By oft predict that I in heaven find.
But from thine eyes my knowledge I derive,
And constant stars in them I read such art   10
As truth and beauty shall together thrive
If from thy self, to store thou wouldst convert:
    Or else of thee this I prognosticate,
    Thy end is truth's and beauty's doom and date.

15

When I consider every thing that grows
Holds in perfection but a little moment.
That this huge stage presenteth nought but shows
Whereon the stars in secret influence comment.
When I perceive that men as plants increase,   5
Cheered and checked even by the self-same sky:
Vaunt in their youthful sap, at height decrease,
And wear their brave state out of memory.
Then the conceit of this inconstant stay,
Sets you most rich in youth before my sight,   10
Where wasteful time debateth with decay
To change your day of youth to sullied night,
    And all in war with Time for love of you,
    As he takes from you, I engraft you new.

16

But wherefore do not you a mightier way
Make war upon this bloody tyrant Time?
And fortify your self in your decay
With means more blessed than my barren rhyme?
Now stand you on the top of happy hours,   5
And many maiden gardens yet unset,
With virtuous wish would bear you living flowers,
Much liker than your painted counterfeit:
So should the lines of life that life repair
Which this (Time's pencil) or my pupil pen   10
Neither in inward worth nor outward fair
Can make you live your self in eyes of men.
    To give away your self, keeps your self still,
    And you must live drawn by your own sweet skill.

17

Who will believe my verse in time to come
If it were filled with your most high deserts?
Though yet heaven knows it is but as a tomb
Which hides your life, and shows not half your parts:
If I could write the beauty of your eyes,   5
And in fresh numbers number all your graces,
The age to come would say this poet lies,
Such heavenly touches ne'er touched earthly faces.
So should my papers (yellowed with their age)
Be scorned, like old men of less truth than tongue,   10
And your true rights be termed a poet's rage,
And stretchéd metre of an antique song.
    But were some child of yours alive that time,
    You should live twice in it, and in my rhyme.

18

Shall I compare thee to a summer's day?
Thou art more lovely and more temperate:
Rough winds do shake the darling buds of May,
And summer's lease hath all too short a date:
Sometime too hot the eye of heaven shines,   5
And often is his gold complexion dimmed,
And every fair from fair sometime declines,
By chance, or nature's changing course untrimmed:
But thy eternal summer shall not fade,
Nor lose possession of that fair thou ow'st,   10
Nor shall death brag thou wand'rest in his shade,
When in eternal lines to time thou grow'st,
    So long as men can breathe or eyes can see,
    So long lives this, and this gives life to thee.

19

Devouring Time blunt thou the lion's paws,
And make the earth devour her own sweet brood,
Pluck the keen teeth from the fierce tiger's jaws,
And burn the long-lived phœnix in her blood,
Make glad and sorry seasons as thou fleet'st,   5
And do whate'er thou wilt swift-footed Time
To the wide world and all her fading sweets:
But I forbid thee one most heinous crime,
O carve not with thy hours my love's fair brow,
Nor draw no lines there with thine antique pen,   10
Him in thy course untainted do allow,
For beauty's pattern to succeeding men.
    Yet do thy worst old Time: despite thy wrong,
    My love shall in my verse ever live young.

20

A woman's face with nature's own hand painted,
Hast thou the master mistress of my passion,
A woman's gentle heart but not acquainted
With shifting change as is false women's fashion,
An eye more bright than theirs, less false in rolling: 5
Gilding the object whereupon it gazeth,
A man in hue all hues in his controlling,
Which steals men's eyes and women's souls amazeth.
And for a woman wert thou first created,
Till nature as she wrought thee fell a-doting,   10
And by addition me of thee defeated,
By adding one thing to my purpose nothing.
    But since she pricked thee out for women's pleasure,
    Mine be thy love and thy love's use their treasure.

21

So is it not with me as with that muse,
Stirred by a painted beauty to his verse,
Who heaven it self for ornament doth use,
And every fair with his fair doth rehearse,
Making a couplement of proud compare   5
With sun and moon, with earth and sea's rich gems:
With April's first-born flowers and all things rare,
That heaven's air in this huge rondure hems.
O let me true in love but truly write,
And then believe me, my love is as fair,   10
As any mother's child, though not so bright
As those gold candles fixed in heaven's air:
    Let them say more that like of hearsay well,
    I will not praise that purpose not to sell.

22

My glass shall not persuade me I am old,
So long as youth and thou are of one date,
But when in thee time's furrows I behold,
Then look I death my days should expiate.
For all that beauty that doth cover thee,   5
Is but the seemly raiment of my heart,
Which in thy breast doth live, as thine in me,
How can I then be elder than thou art?
O therefore love be of thyself so wary,
As I not for my self, but for thee will,   10
Bearing thy heart which I will keep so chary
As tender nurse her babe from faring ill.
    Presume not on thy heart when mine is slain,
    Thou gav'st me thine not to give back again.

23

As an unperfect actor on the stage,
Who with his fear is put beside his part,
Or some fierce thing replete with too much rage,
Whose strength's abundance weakens his own heart;
So I for fear of trust, forget to say,   5
The perfect ceremony of love's rite,
And in mine own love's strength seem to decay,
O'ercharged with burthen of mine own love's might:
O let my looks be then the eloquence,
And dumb presagers of my speaking breast,   10
Who plead for love, and look for recompense,
More than that tongue that more hath more expressed.
    O learn to read what silent love hath writ,
    To hear with eyes belongs to love's fine wit.

24

Mine eye hath played the painter and hath stelled,
Thy beauty's form in table of my heart,
My body is the frame wherein 'tis held,
And perspective it is best painter's art.
For through the painter must you see his skill,   5
To find where your true image pictured lies,
Which in my bosom's shop is hanging still,
That hath his windows glazéd with thine eyes:
Now see what good turns eyes for eyes have done,
Mine eyes have drawn thy shape, and thine for me   10
Are windows to my breast, where-through the sun
Delights to peep, to gaze therein on thee;
    Yet eyes this cunning want to grace their art,
    They draw but what they see, know not the heart.

25

Let those who are in favour with their stars,
Of public honour and proud titles boast,
Whilst I whom fortune of such triumph bars
Unlooked for joy in that I honour most;
Great princes' favourites their fair leaves spread,   5
But as the marigold at the sun's eye,
And in themselves their pride lies buriéd,
For at a frown they in their glory die.
The painful warrior famouséd for fight,
After a thousand victories once foiled,   10
Is from the book of honour razéd quite,
And all the rest forgot for which he toiled:
    Then happy I that love and am beloved
    Where I may not remove nor be removed.

26

Lord of my love, to whom in vassalage
Thy merit hath my duty strongly knit;
To thee I send this written embassage
To witness duty, not to show my wit.
Duty so great, which wit so poor as mine   5
May make seem bare, in wanting words to show it;
But that I hope some good conceit of thine
In thy soul's thought (all naked) will bestow it:
Till whatsoever star that guides my moving,
Points on me graciously with fair aspect,   10
And puts apparel on my tattered loving,
To show me worthy of thy sweet respect,
    Then may I dare to boast how I do love thee,
    Till then, not show my head where thou mayst
      prove me.

27

Weary with toil, I haste me to my bed,
The dear respose for limbs with travel tired,
But then begins a journey in my head
To work my mind, when body's work's expired.
For then my thoughts (from far where I abide)   5
Intend a zealous pilgrimage to thee,
And keep my drooping eyelids open wide,
Looking on darkness which the blind do see.
Save that my soul's imaginary sight
Presents thy shadow to my sightless view,   10
Which like a jewel (hung in ghastly night)
Makes black night beauteous, and her old face new.
    Lo thus by day my limbs, by night my mind,
    For thee, and for my self, no quiet find.

28

How can I then return in happy plight
That am debarred the benefit of rest?
When day's oppression is not eased by night,
But day by night and night by day oppressed.
And each (though enemies to either's reign)   5
Do in consent shake hands to torture me,
The one by toil, the other to complain
How far I toil, still farther off from thee.
I tell the day to please him thou art bright,
And dost him grace when clouds do blot the heaven: 10
So flatter I the swart-complexioned night,
When sparkling stars twire not thou gild'st the even.
    But day doth daily draw my sorrows longer,
    And night doth nightly make grief's length seem
      stronger

29

When in disgrace with Fortune and men's eyes,
I all alone beweep my outcast state,
And trouble deaf heaven with my bootless cries,
And look upon my self and curse my fate,
Wishing me like to one more rich in hope,   5
Featured like him, like him with friends possessed,
Desiring this man's art, and that man's scope,
With what I most enjoy contented least,
Yet in these thoughts my self almost despising,
Haply I think on thee, and then my state,   10
(Like to the lark at break of day arising
From sullen earth) sings hymns at heaven's gate,
    For thy sweet love remembered such wealth brings,
    That then I scorn to change my state with kings.

30

When to the sessions of sweet silent thought,
I summon up remembrance of things past,
I sigh the lack of many a thing I sought,
And with old woes new wail my dear time's waste:
Then can I drown an eye (unused to flow)   5
For precious friends hid in death's dateless night,
And weep afresh love's long since cancelled woe,
And moan th' expense of many a vanished sight.
Then can I grieve at grievances foregone,
And heavily from woe to woe tell o'er   10
The sad account of fore-bemoanéd moan,
Which I new pay as if not paid before.
    But if the while I think on thee (dear friend)
    All losses are restored, and sorrows end.

31

Thy bosom is endearéd with all hearts,
Which I by lacking have supposéd dead,
And there reigns love and all love's loving parts,
And all those friends which I thought buriéd.
How many a holy and obsequious tear   5
Hath dear religious love stol'n from mine eye,
As interest of the dead, which now appear,
But things removed that hidden in thee lie.
Thou art the grave where buried love doth live,
Hung with the trophies of my lovers gone,   10
Who all their parts of me to thee did give,
That due of many, now is thine alone.
    Their images I loved, I view in thee,
    And thou (all they) hast all the all of me.

32

If thou survive my well-contented day,
When that churl death my bones with dust shall cover
And shalt by fortune once more re-survey
These poor rude lines of thy deceaséd lover:
Compare them with the bett'ring of the time,   5
And though they be outstripped by every pen,
Reserve them for my love, not for their rhyme,
Exceeded by the height of happier men.
O then vouchsafe me but this loving thought,
'Had my friend's Muse grown with this growing age,   10
A dearer birth than this his love had brought
To march in ranks of better equipage:
    But since he died and poets better prove,
    Theirs for their style I'll read, his for his love'.

33

Full many a glorious morning have I seen,
Flatter the mountain tops with sovereign eye,
Kissing with golden face the meadows green;
Gilding pale streams with heavenly alchemy:
Anon permit the basest clouds to ride,   5
With ugly rack on his celestial face,
And from the forlorn world his visage hide
Stealing unseen to west with this disgrace:
Even so my sun one early morn did shine,
With all triumphant splendour on my brow,   10
But out alack, he was but one hour mine,
The region cloud hath masked him from me now.
    Yet him for this, my love no whit disdaineth,
    Suns of the world may stain, when heaven's
        sun staineth.

34

Why didst thou promise such a beauteous day,
And make me travel forth without my cloak,
To let base clouds o'ertake me in my way,
Hiding thy brav'ry in their rotten smoke?
'Tis not enough that through the cloud thou break,   5
To dry the rain on my storm-beaten face,
For no man well of such a salve can speak,
That heals the wound, and cures not the disgrace:
Nor can thy shame give physic to my grief,
Though thou repent, yet I have still the loss,   10
Th' offender's sorrow lends but weak relief
To him that bears the strong offence's cross.
    Ah but those tears are pearl which thy love sheds,
    And they are rich, and ransom all ill deeds.

35

No more be grieved at that which thou hast done,
Roses have thorns, and silver fountains mud,
Clouds and eclipses stain both moon and sun,
And loathsome canker lives in sweetest bud.
All men make faults, and even I in this,   5
Authorizing thy trespass with compare,
My self corrupting salving thy amiss,
Excusing thy sins more than thy sins are:
For to thy sensual fault I bring in sense,
Thy adverse party is thy advocate,   10
And 'gainst my self a lawful plea commence:
Such civil war is in my love and hate,
    That I an accessary needs must be,
    To that sweet thief which sourly robs from me.

36

Let me confess that we two must be twain,
Although our undivided loves are one:
So shall those blots that do with me remain,
Without thy help, by me be borne alone.
In our two loves there is but one respect,   5
Though in our lives a separable spite,
Which though it alter not love's sole effect,
Yet doth it steal sweet hours from love's delight.
I may not evermore acknowledge thee,
Lest my bewailéd guilt should do thee shame,   10
Nor thou with public kindness honour me,
Unless thou take that honour from thy name:
    But do not so, I love thee in such sort,
    As thou being mine, mine is thy good report.

37

As a decrepit father takes delight,
To see his active child do deeds of youth,
So I, made lame by Fortune's dearest spite
Take all my comfort of thy worth and truth.
For whether beauty, birth, or wealth, or wit,   5
Or any of these all, or all, or more
Entitled in thy parts, do crownéd sit,
I make my love engrafted to this store:
So then I am not lame, poor, nor despised,
Whilst that this shadow doth such substance give,   10
That I in thy abundance am sufficed,
And by a part of all thy glory live:
    Look what is best, that best I wish in thee,
    This wish I have, then ten times happy me.

38

How can my muse want subject to invent
While thou dost breathe that pour'st into my verse,
Thine own sweet argument, too excellent,
For every vulgar paper to rehearse?
O give thy self the thanks if aught in me,   5
Worthy perusal stand against thy sight,
For who's so dumb that cannot write to thee,
When thou thy self dost give invention light?
Be thou the tenth Muse, ten times more in worth
Than those old nine which rhymers invocate,   10
And he that calls on thee, let him bring forth
Eternal numbers to outlive long date.
    If my slight muse do please these curious days,
    The pain be mine, but thine shall be the praise.

39

O how thy worth with manners may I sing,
When thou art all the better part of me?
What can mine own praise to mine own self bring:
And what is't but mine own when I praise thee?   5
Even for this, let us divided live,
And our dear love lose name of single one,
That by this separation I may give:
That due to thee which thou deserv'st alone:
O absence what a torment wouldst thou prove,
Were it not thy sour leisure gave sweet leave,   10
To entertain the time with thoughts of love,
Which time and thoughts so sweetly doth deceive.
    And that thou teachest how to make one twain,
    By praising him here who doth hence remain.

40

Take all my loves, my love, yea take them all,
What hast thou then more than thou hadst before?
No love, my love, that thou mayst true love call,
All mine was thine, before thou hadst this more:
Then if for my love, thou my love receivest,   5
I cannot blame thee, for my love thou usest,
But yet be blamed, if thou thy self deceivest
By wilful taste of what thy self refusest.
I do forgive thy robbery gentle thief
Although thou steal thee all my poverty: 10
And yet love knows it is a greater grief
To bear love's wrong, than hate's known injury.
    Lascivious grace, in whom all ill well shows,
    Kill me with spites yet we must not be foes.

41

Those pretty wrongs that liberty commits,
When I am sometime absent from thy heart,
Thy beauty, and thy years full well befits,
For still temptation follows where thou art.
Gentle thou art, and therefore to be won,   5
Beauteous thou art, therefore to be assailed.
And when a woman woos, what woman's son,
Will sourly leave her till he have prevailed?
Ay me, but yet thou mightst my seat forbear,
And chide thy beauty, and thy straying youth,   10
Who lead thee in their riot even there
Where thou art forced to break a twofold truth:
    Hers by thy beauty tempting her to thee,
    Thine by thy beauty being false to me.

42

That thou hast her it is not all my grief,
And yet it may be said I loved her dearly,
That she hath thee is of my wailing chief,
A loss in love that touches me more nearly.
Loving offenders thus I will excuse ye,   5
Thou dost love her, because thou know'st I love her,
And for my sake even so doth she abuse me,
Suff'ring my friend for my sake to approve her.
If I lose thee, my loss is my love's gain,
And losing her, my friend hath found that loss,   10
Both find each other, and I lose both twain,
And both for my sake lay on me this cross,
    But here's the joy, my friend and I are one,
    Sweet flattery, then she loves but me alone.

43

When most I wink then do mine eyes best see,
For all the day they view things unrespected,
But when I sleep, in dreams they look on thee,
And darkly bright, are bright in dark directed.
Then thou whose shadow shadows doth make bright,   5
How would thy shadow's form, form happy show,
To the clear day with thy much clearer light,
When to unseeing eyes thy shade shines so!
How would (I say) mine eyes be blessèd made,
By looking on thee in the living day,   10
When in dead night thy fair imperfect shade,
Through heavy sleep on sightless eyes doth stay!
    All days are nights to see till I see thee,
    And nights bright days when dreams do show thee
    me.

44

If the dull substance of my flesh were thought,
Injurious distance should not stop my way,
For then despite of space I would be brought,
From limits far remote, where thou dost stay,
No matter then although my foot did stand   5
Upon the farthest earth removed from thee,
For nimble thought can jump both sea and land,
As soon as think the place where he would be.
But ah, thought kills me that I am not thought
To leap large lengths of miles when thou art gone,   10
But that so much of earth and water wrought,
I must attend, time's leisure with my moan.
    Receiving nought by elements so slow,
    But heavy tears, badges of either's woe.

45

The other two, slight air, and purging fire,
Are both with thee, wherever I abide,
The first my thought, the other my desire,
These present-absent with swift motion slide.
For when these quicker elements are gone   5
In tender embassy of love to thee,
My life being made of four, with two alone,
Sinks down to death, oppressed with melancholy.
Until life's composition be recured,
By those swift messengers returned from thee,   10
Who even but now come back again assured,
Of thy fair health, recounting it to me.
    This told, I joy, but then no longer glad,
    I send them back again and straight grow sad.

46

Mine eye and heart are at a mortal war,
How to divide the conquest of thy sight,
Mine eye, my heart thy picture's sight would bar,
My heart, mine eye the freedom of that right,
My heart doth plead that thou in him dost lie,   5
(A closet never pierced with crystal eyes)
But the defendant doth that plea deny,
And says in him thy fair appearance lies.
To side this title is impanellèd
A quest of thoughts, all tenants to the heart,   10
And by their verdict is determinèd
The clear eye's moiety, and the dear heart's part.
    As thus, mine eye's due is thy outward part,
    And my heart's right, thy inward love of heart.

47

Betwixt mine eye and heart a league is took,
And each doth good turns now unto the other,
When that mine eye is famished for a look,
Or heart in love with sighs himself doth smother;
With my love's picture then my eye doth feast,   5
And to the painted banquet bids my heart:
Another time mine eye is my heart's guest,
And in his thoughts of love doth share a part.
So either by thy picture or my love,
Thy self away, art present still with me,   10
For thou not farther than my thoughts canst move,
And I am still with them, and they with thee.
   Or if they sleep, thy picture in my sight
   Awakes my heart, to heart's and eye's delight.

48

How careful was I when I took my way,
Each trifle under truest bars to thrust,
That to my use it might unusèd stay
From hands of falsehood, in sure wards of trust!
But thou, to whom my jewels trifles are,   5
Most worthy comfort, now my greatest grief,
Thou best of dearest, and mine only care,
Art left the prey of every vulgar thief.
Thee have I not locked up in any chest,
Save where thou art not, though I feel thou art,   10
Within the gentle closure of my breast,
From whence at pleasure thou mayst come and part,
   And even thence thou wilt be stol'n I fear,
   For truth proves thievish for a prize so dear.

49

Against that time (if ever that time come)
When I shall see thee frown on my defects,
When as thy love hath cast his utmost sum,
Called to that audit by advised respects,
Against that time when thou shalt strangely pass,   5
And scarcely greet me with that sun thine eye,
When love converted from the thing it was
Shall reasons find of settled gravity;
Against that time do I ensconce me here
Within the knowledge of mine own desert,   10
And this my hand, against my self uprear,
To guard the lawful reasons on thy part,
   To leave poor me, thou hast the strength of laws,
   Since why to love, I can allege no cause.

50

How heavy do I journey on the way,
When what I seek (my weary travel's end)
Doth teach that ease and that repose to say
'Thus far the miles are measured from thy friend.'
The beast that bears me, tirèd with my woe,   5
Plods dully on, to bear that weight in me,
As if by some instinct the wretch did know
His rider loved not speed being made from thee:
The bloody spur cannot provoke him on,
That sometimes anger thrusts into his hide,   10
Which heavily he answers with a groan,
More sharp to me than spurring to his side,
   For that same groan doth put this in my mind,
   My grief lies onward and my joy behind.

51

Thus can my love excuse the slow offence,
Of my dull bearer, when from thee I speed,
From where thou art, why should I haste me thence?
Till I return of posting is no need.
O what excuse will my poor beast then find,   5
When swift extremity can seem but slow?
Then should I spur though mounted on the wind,
In wingèd speed no motion shall I know,
Then can no horse with my desire keep pace,
Therefore desire (of perfect'st love being made)   10
Shall neigh (no dull flesh) in his fiery race,
But love, for love, thus shall excuse my jade,
   Since from thee going, he went wilful-slow,
   Towards thee I'll run, and give him leave to go.

52

So am I as the rich whose blessèd key,
Can bring him to his sweet up-lockèd treasure,
The which he will not every hour survey,
For blunting the fine point of seldom pleasure.
Therefore are feasts so solemn and so rare,   5
Since seldom coming in that long year set,
Like stones of worth they thinly placed are,
Or captain jewels in the carcanet.
So is the time that keeps you as my chest,
Or as the wardrobe which the robe doth hide,   10
To make some special instant special-blest,
By new unfolding his imprisoned pride.
   Blessèd are you whose worthiness gives scope,
   Being had to triumph, being lacked to hope.

53

What is your substance, whereof are you made,
That millions of strange shadows on you tend?
Since every one, hath every one, one shade,
And you but one, can every shadow lend:
Describe Adonis and the counterfeit,   5
Is poorly imitated after you,
On Helen's cheek all art of beauty set,
And you in Grecian tires are painted new:
Speak of the spring, and foison of the year,
The one doth shadow of your beauty show,   10
The other as your bounty doth appear,
And you in every blessèd shape we know.
   In all external grace you have some part,
   But you like none, none you for constant heart.

54

O how much more doth beauty beauteous seem,
By that sweet ornament which truth doth give!
The rose looks fair, but fairer we it deem
For that sweet odour, which doth in it live:
The canker blooms have full as deep a dye,   5
As the perfumèd tincture of the roses,
Hang on such thorns, and play as wantonly,
When summer's breath their maskèd buds discloses:
But for their virtue only is their show,
They live unwooed, and unrespected fade,   10
Die to themselves. Sweet roses do not so,
Of their sweet deaths, are sweetest odours made:
   And so of you, beauteous and lovely youth,
   When that shall vade, by verse distills your truth.

55

Not marble, nor the gilded monuments
Of princes shall outlive this powerful rhyme,
But you shall shine more bright in these contents
Than unswept stone, besmeared with sluttish time.
When wasteful war shall statues overturn,   5
And broils root out the work of masonry,
Nor Mars his sword, nor war's quick fire shall burn:
The living record of your memory.
'Gainst death, and all-oblivious enmity
Shall you pace forth, your praise shall still find room, 10
Even in the eyes of all posterity
That wear this world out to the ending doom.
  So till the judgment that your self arise,
  You live in this, and dwell in lovers' eyes.

56

Sweet love renew thy force, be it not said
Thy edge should blunter be than appetite,
Which but to-day by feeding is allayed,
To-morrow sharpened in his former might.
So love be thou, although to-day thou fill   5
Thy hungry eyes, even till they wink with fulness,
To-morrow see again, and do not kill
The spirit of love, with a perpetual dulness:
Let this sad interim like the ocean be
Which parts the shore, where two contracted new, 10
Come daily to the banks, that when they see:
Return of love, more blest may be the view.
  Or call it winter, which being full of care,
  Makes summer's welcome, thrice more wished,
    more rare.

57

Being your slave what should I do but tend,
Upon the hours, and times of your desire?
I have no precious time at all to spend;
Nor services to do till you require.
Nor dare I chide the world-without-end hour,   5
Whilst I (my sovereign) watch the clock for you,
Nor think the bitterness of absence sour,
When you have bid your servant once adieu.
Nor dare I question with my jealous thought,
Where you may be, or your affairs suppose, 10
But like a sad slave stay and think of nought
Save where you are, how happy you make those.
  So true a fool is love, that in your will,
  (Though you do any thing) he thinks no ill.

58

That god forbid, that made me first your slave,
I should in thought control your times of pleasure,
Or at your hand th' account of hours to crave,
Being your vassal bound to stay your leisure.
O let me suffer (being at your beck)   5
Th' imprisoned absence of your liberty,
And patience tame to sufferance bide each check,
Without accusing you of injury.
Be where you list, your charter is so strong,
That you your self may privilege your time 10
To what you will, to you it doth belong,
Your self to pardon of self-doing crime.
  I am to wait, though waiting so be hell,
  Not blame your pleasure be it ill or well.

59

If there be nothing new, but that which is,
Hath been before, how are our brains beguiled,
Which labouring for invention bear amiss
The second burthen of a former child!
O that record could with a backward look,   5
Even of five hundred courses of the sun,
Show me your image in some antique book,
Since mind at first in character was done.
That I might see what the old world could say,
To this composéd wonder of your frame, 10
Whether we are mended, or whether better they,
Or whether revolution be the same.
  O sure I am the wits of former days,
  To subjects worse have given admiring praise.

60

Like as the waves make towards the pebbled shore,
So do our minutes hasten to their end,
Each changing place with that which goes before,
In sequent toil all forwards do contend.
Nativity once in the main of light,   5
Crawls to maturity, wherewith being crowned,
Crookéd eclipses 'gainst his glory fight,
And Time that gave, doth now his gift confound.
Time doth transfix the flourish set on youth,
And delves the parallels in beauty's brow, 10
Feeds on the rarities of nature's truth,
And nothing stands but for his scythe to mow.
  And yet to times in hope, my verse shall stand
  Praising thy worth, despite his cruel hand.

61

Is it thy will, thy image should keep open
My heavy eyelids to the weary night?
Dost thou desire my slumbers should be broken,
While shadows like to thee do mock my sight?
Is it thy spirit that thou send'st from thee   5
So far from home into my deeds to pry,
To find out shames and idle hours in me,
The scope and tenure of thy jealousy?
O no, thy love though much, is not so great,
It is my love that keeps mine eye awake, 10
Mine own true love that doth my rest defeat,
To play the watchman ever for thy sake.
  For thee watch I, whilst thou dost wake elsewhere,
  From me far off, with others all too near.

62

Sin of self-love possesseth all mine eye,
And all my soul, and all my every part;
And for this sin there is no remedy,
It is so grounded inward in my heart.
Methinks no face so gracious is as mine,   5
No shape so true, no truth of such account,
And for my self mine own worth do define,
As I all other in all worths surmount.
But when my glass shows me my self indeed
Beated and chopt with tanned antiquity, 10
Mine own self-love quite contrary I read:
Self, so self-loving were iniquity.
  'Tis thee (my self) that for my self I praise,
  Painting my age with beauty of thy days.

63

Against my love shall be as I am now
With Time's injurious hand crushed and o'erworn,
When hours have drained his blood and filled his brow
With lines and wrinkles, when his youthful morn
Hath travelled on to age's steepy night,   5
And all those beauties whereof now he's king
Are vanishing, or vanished out of sight,
Stealing away the treasure of his spring:
For such a time do I now fortify
Against confounding age's cruel knife,   10
That he shall never cut from memory
My sweet love's beauty, though my lover's life.
  His beauty shall in these black lines be seen,
  And they shall live, and he in them still green.

64

When I have seen by Time's fell hand defaced
The rich-proud cost of outworn buried age,
When sometime lofty towers I see down-rased,
And brass eternal slave to mortal rage.
When I have seen the hungry ocean gain   5
Advantage on the kingdom of the shore,
And the firm soil win of the watery main,
Increasing store with loss, and loss with store.
When I have seen such interchange of state,
Or state it self confounded, to decay,   10
Ruin hath taught me thus to ruminate
That Time will come and take my love away.
  This thought is as a death which cannot choose
  But weep to have, that which it fears to lose.

65

Since brass, nor stone, nor earth, nor boundless sea,
But sad mortality o'ersways their power,
How with this rage shall beauty hold a plea,
Whose action is no stronger than a flower?
O how shall summer's honey breath hold out,   5
Against the wrackful siege of batt'ring days,
When rocks impregnable are not so stout,
Nor gates of steel so strong but time decays?
O fearful meditation, where alack,
Shall Time's best jewel from Time's chest lie hid?   10
Or what strong hand can hold his swift foot back,
Or who his spoil of beauty can forbid?
  O none, unless this miracle have might,
  That in black ink my love may still shine bright.

66

Tired with all these for restful death I cry,
As to behold desert a beggar born,
And needy nothing trimmed in jollity,
And purest faith unhappily forsworn,
And gilded honour shamefully misplaced,   5
And maiden virtue rudely strumpeted,
And right perfection wrongfully disgraced,
And strength by limping sway disabled,
And art made tongue-tied by authority,
And folly (doctor-like) controlling skill,   10
And simple truth miscalled simplicity,
And captive good attending captain ill.
  Tired with all these, from these would I be gone,
  Save that to die, I leave my love alone.

67

Ah wherefore with infection should he live,
And with his presence grace impiety,
That sin by him advantage should achieve,
And lace it self with his society?
Why should false painting imitate his cheek,   5
And steal dead seeming of his living hue?
Why should poor beauty indirectly seek,
Roses of shadow, since his rose is true?
Why should he live, now nature bankrupt is,
Beggared of blood to blush through lively veins,   10
For she hath no exchequer now but his,
And proud of many, lives upon his gains?
  O him she stores, to show what wealth she had,
  In days long since, before these last so bad.

68

Thus is his cheek the map of days outworn,
When beauty lived and died as flowers do now,
Before these bastard signs of fair were born,
Or durst inhabit on a living brow:
Before the golden tresses of the dead,   5
The right of sepulchres, were shorn away,
To live a second life on second head,
Ere beauty's dead fleece made another gay:
In him those holy antique hours are seen,
Without all ornament, it self and true,   10
Making no summer of another's green,
Robbing no old to dress his beauty new,
  And him as for a map doth Nature store,
  To show false Art what beauty was of yore.

69

Those parts of thee that the world's eye doth view,
Want nothing that the thought of hearts can mend:
All tongues (the voice of souls) give thee that due,
Uttering bare truth, even so as foes commend.
Thy outward thus with outward praise is crowned,   5
But those same tongues that give thee so thine own,
In other accents do this praise confound
By seeing farther than the eye hath shown.
They look into the beauty of thy mind,
And that in guess they measure by thy deeds,   10
Then churls their thoughts (although their eyes
    were kind)
To thy fair flower add the rank smell of weeds:
  But why thy odour matcheth not thy show,
  The soil is this, that thou dost common grow.

70

That thou art blamed shall not be thy defect,
For slander's mark was ever yet the fair,
The ornament of beauty is suspect,
A crow that flies in heaven's sweetest air.
So thou be good, slander doth but approve,   5
Thy worth the greater being wooed of time,
For canker vice the sweetest buds doth love,
And thou present'st a pure unstained prime.
Thou hast passed by the ambush of young days,
Either not assailed, or victor being charged,   10
Yet this thy praise cannot be so thy praise,
To tie up envy, evermore enlarged,
  If some suspect of ill masked not thy show,
  Then thou alone kingdoms of hearts shouldst owe.

71

No longer mourn for me when I am dead,
Than you shall hear the surly sullen bell
Give warning to the world that I am fled
From this vile world with vilest worms to dwell:
Nay if you read this line, remember not,
The hand that writ it, for I love you so,
That I in your sweet thoughts would be forgot,
If thinking on me then should make you woe.
O if (I say) you look upon this verse,
When I (perhaps) compounded am with clay,
Do not so much as my poor name rehearse;
But let your love even with my life decay.
    Lest the wise world should look into your moan,
    And mock you with me after I am gone.

72

O lest the world should task you to recite,
What merit lived in me that you should love
After my death (dear love) forget me quite,
For you in me can nothing worthy prove.
Unless you would devise some virtuous lie,
To do more for me than mine own desert,
And hang more praise upon deceased I,
Than niggard truth would willingly impart:
O lest your true love may seem false in this,
That you for love speak well of me untrue,
My name be buried where my body is,
And live no more to shame nor me, nor you.
    For I am shamed by that which I bring forth,
    And so should you, to love things nothing worth.

73

That time of year thou mayst in me behold,
When yellow leaves, or none, or few do hang
Upon those boughs which shake against the cold,
Bare ruined choirs, where late the sweet birds sang.
In me thou seest the twilight of such day,
As after sunset fadeth in the west,
Which by and by black night doth take away,
Death's second self that seals up all in rest.
In me thou seest the glowing of such fire,
That on the ashes of his youth doth lie,
As the death-bed, whereon it must expire,
Consumed with that which it was nourished by.
    This thou perceiv'st, which makes thy love more
        strong,
    To love that well, which thou must leave ere long.

74

But be contented when that fell arrest,
Without all bail shall carry me away,
My life hath in this line some interest,
Which for memorial still with thee shall stay.
When thou reviewest this, thou dost review,
The very part was consecrate to thee,
The earth can have but earth, which is his due,
My spirit is thine the better part of me,
So then thou hast but lost the dregs of life,
The prey of worms, my body being dead,
The coward conquest of a wretch's knife,
Too base of thee to be rememberéd,
    The worth of that, is that which it contains,
    And that is this, and this with thee remains.

75

So are you to my thoughts as food to life,
Or as sweet-seasoned showers are to the ground;
And for the peace of you I hold such strife
As 'twixt a miser and his wealth is found.
Now proud as an enjoyer, and anon
Doubting the filching age will steal his treasure,
Now counting best to be with you alone,
Then bettered that the world may see my pleasure,
Sometime all full with feasting on your sight,
And by and by clean starvéd for a look,
Possessing or pursuing no delight
Save what is had, or must from you be took.
    Thus do I pine and surfeit day by day,
    Or gluttoning on all, or all away.

76

Why is my verse so barren of new pride?
So far from variation or quick change?
Why with the time do I not glance aside
To new-found methods, and to compounds strange?
Why write I still all one, ever the same,
And keep invention in a noted weed,
That every word doth almost tell my name,
Showing their birth, and where they did proceed?
O know sweet love I always write of you,
And you and love are still my argument:
So all my best is dressing old words new,
Spending again what is already spent:
    For as the sun is daily new and old,
    So is my love still telling what is told.

77

Thy glass will show thee how thy beauties wear,
Thy dial how thy precious minutes waste,
These vacant leaves thy mind's imprint will bear,
And of this book, this learning mayst thou taste.
The wrinkles which thy glass will truly show,
Of mouthéd graves will give thee memory,
Thou by thy dial's shady stealth mayst know,
Time's thievish progress to eternity.
Look what thy memory cannot contain,
Commit to these waste blanks, and thou shalt find
Those children nursed, delivered from thy brain,
To take a new acquaintance of thy mind.
    These offices, so oft as thou wilt look,
    Shall profit thee, and much enrich thy book.

78

So oft have I invoked thee for my muse,
And found such fair assistance in my verse,
As every alien pen hath got my use,
And under thee their poesy disperse.
Thine eyes, that taught the dumb on high to sing,
And heavy ignorance aloft to fly,
Have added feathers to the learnéd's wing,
And given grace a double majesty.
Yet be most proud of that which I compile,
Whose influence is thine, and born of thee,
In others' works thou dost but mend the style,
And arts with thy sweet graces gracéd be.
    But thou art all my art, and dost advance
    As high as learning, my rude ignorance.

79

Whilst I alone did call upon thy aid,
My verse alone had all thy gentle grace,
But now my gracious numbers are decayed,
And my sick muse doth give an other place.
I grant (sweet love) thy lovely argument   5
Deserves the travail of a worthier pen,
Yet what of thee thy poet doth invent,
He robs thee of, and pays it thee again,
He lends thee virtue, and he stole that word,
From thy behaviour, beauty doth he give   10
And found it in thy cheek: he can afford
No praise to thee, but what in thee doth live.
   Then thank him not for that which he doth say,
   Since what he owes thee, thou thy self dost pay.

80

O how I faint when I of you do write,
Knowing a better spirit doth use your name,
And in the praise thereof spends all his might,
To make me tongue-tied speaking of your fame.
But since your worth (wide as the ocean is)   5
The humble as the proudest sail doth bear,
My saucy bark (inferior far to his)
On your broad main doth wilfully appear.
Your shallowest help will hold me up afloat,
Whilst he upon your soundless deep doth ride,   10
Or (being wrecked) I am a worthless boat,
He of tall building, and of goodly pride.
   Then if he thrive and I be cast away,
   The worst was this, my love was my decay.

81

Or I shall live your epitaph to make,
Or you survive when I in earth am rotten,
From hence your memory death cannot take,
Although in me each part will be forgotten.
Your name from hence immortal life shall have,   5
Though I (once gone) to all the world must die,
The earth can yield me but a common grave,
When you entombéd in men's eyes shall lie,
Your monument shall be my gentle verse,
Which eyes not yet created shall o'er-read,   10
And tongues to be, your being shall rehearse,
When all the breathers of this world are dead,
   You still shall live (such virtue hath my pen)
   Where breath most breathes, even in the mouths
      of men.

82

I grant thou wert not married to my muse,
And therefore mayst without attaint o'erlook
The dedicated words which writers use
Of their fair subject, blessing every book.
Thou art as fair in knowledge as in hue,   5
Finding thy worth a limit past my praise,
And therefore art enforced to seek anew,
Some fresher stamp of the time-bettering days.
And do so love, yet when they have devised,
What strainéd touches rhetoric can lend,   10
Thou truly fair, wert truly sympathized,
In true plain words, by thy true-telling friend.
   And their gross painting might be better used,
   Where cheeks need blood, in thee it is abused.

83

I never saw that you did painting need,
And therefore to your fair no painting set,
I found (or thought I found) you did exceed,
That barren tender of a poet's debt:
And therefore have I slept in your report,   5
That you your self being extant well might show,
How far a modern quill doth come too short,
Speaking of worth, what worth in you doth grow.
This silence for my sin you did impute,
Which shall be most my glory being dumb,   10
For I impair not beauty being mute,
When others would give life, and bring a tomb.
   There lives more life in one of your fair eyes,
   Than both your poets can in praise devise.

84

Who is it that says most, which can say more,
Than this rich praise, that you alone, are you?
In whose confine immuréd is the store,
Which should example where your equal grew.
Lean penury within that pen doth dwell,   5
That to his subject lends not some small glory,
But he that writes of you, if he can tell,
That you are you, so dignifies his story.
Let him but copy what in you is writ,
Not making worse what nature made so clear,   10
And such a counterpart shall fame his wit,
Making his style admiréd every where.
   You to your beauteous blessings add a curse,
   Being fond on praise, which makes your praises
      worse.

85

My tongue-tied muse in manners holds her still,
While comments of your praise richly compiled,
Reserve their character with golden quill,
And precious phrase by all the Muses filed.
I think good thoughts, whilst other write good words,   5
And like unlettered clerk still cry Amen,
To every hymn that able spirit affords,
In polished form of well refinéd pen.
Hearing you praised, I say 'tis so, 'tis true,
And to the most of praise add something more,   10
But that is in my thought, whose love to you
(Though words come hindmost) holds his rank before,
   Then others, for the breath of words respect,
   Me for my dumb thoughts, speaking in effect.

86

Was it the proud full sail of his great verse,
Bound for the prize of (all too precious) you,
That did my ripe thoughts in my brain inhearse,
Making their tomb the womb wherein they grew?
Was it his spirit, by spirits taught to write,   5
Above a mortal pitch, that struck me dead?
No, neither he, nor his compeers by night
Giving him aid, my verse astonishéd.
He nor that affable familiar ghost
Which nightly gulls him with intelligence,   10
As victors of my silence cannot boast,
I was not sick of any fear from thence.
   But when your countenance filled up his line,
   Then lacked I matter, that enfeebled mine.

87

Farewell! thou art too dear for my possessing,
And like enough thou know'st thy estimate,
The charter of thy worth gives thee releasing:
My bonds in thee are all determinate.
For how do I hold thee but by thy granting, 5
And for that riches where is my deserving?
The cause of this fair gift in me is wanting,
And so my patent back again is swerving.
Thy self thou gav'st, thy own worth then not
    knowing,
Or me to whom thou gav'st it, else mistaking, 10
So thy great gift upon misprision growing,
Comes home again, on better judgment making.
    Thus have I had thee as a dream doth flatter,
    In sleep a king, but waking no such matter.

88

When thou shalt be disposed to set me light,
And place my merit in the eye of scorn,
Upon thy side, against my self I'll fight,
And prove thee virtuous, though thou art forsworn:
With mine own weakness being best acquainted, 5
Upon thy part I can set down a story
Of faults concealed, wherein I am attainted:
That thou in losing me, shalt win much glory:
And I by this will be a gainer too,
For bending all my loving thoughts on thee, 10
The injuries that to my self I do,
Doing thee vantage, double-vantage me.
    Such is my love, to thee I so belong,
    That for thy right, my self will bear all wrong.

89

Say that thou didst forsake me for some fault,
And I will comment upon that offence,
Speak of my lameness, and I straight will halt:
Against thy reasons making no defence.
Thou canst not (love) disgrace me half so ill, 5
To set a form upon desiréd change,
As I'll my self disgrace, knowing thy will,
I will acquaintance strangle and look strange:
Be absent from thy walks and in my tongue,
Thy sweet belovéd name no more shall dwell, 10
Lest I (too much profane) should do it wrong:
And haply of our old acquaintance tell.
    For thee, against my self I'll vow debate,
    For I must ne'er love him whom thou dost hate.

90

Then hate me when thou wilt, if ever, now,
Now while the world is bent my deeds to cross,
Join with the spite of fortune, make me bow,
And do not drop in for an after-loss:
Ah do not, when my heart hath 'scaped this sorrow, 5
Come in the rearward of a conquered woe,
Give not a windy night a rainy morrow,
To linger out a purposed overthrow.
If thou wilt leave me, do not leave me last,
When other petty griefs have done their spite, 10
But in the onset come, so shall I taste
At first the very worst of fortune's might.
    And other strains of woe, which now seem woe,
    Compared with loss of thee, will not seem so.

91

Some glory in their birth, some in their skill,
Some in their wealth, some in their body's force,
Some in their garments though new-fangled ill:
Some in their hawks and hounds, some in their horse.
And every humour hath his adjunct pleasure, 5
Wherein it finds a joy above the rest,
But these particulars are not my measure,
All these I better in one general best.
Thy love is better than high birth to me,
Richer than wealth, prouder than garments' costs, 10
Of more delight than hawks and horses be:
And having thee, of all men's pride I boast.
    Wretched in this alone, that thou mayst take,
    All this away, and me most wretched make.

92

But do thy worst to steal thy self away,
For term of life thou art assuréd mine,
And life no longer than thy love will stay,
For it depends upon that love of thine.
Then need I not to fear the worst of wrongs, 5
When in the least of them my life hath end,
I see, a better state to me belongs
Than that, which on thy humour doth depend.
Thou canst not vex me with inconstant mind,
Since that my life on thy revolt doth lie, 10
O what a happy title do I find,
Happy to have thy love, happy to die!
    But what's so blesséd-fair that fears no blot?
    Thou mayst be false, and yet I know it not.

93

So shall I live, supposing thou art true,
Like a deceivéd husband, so love's face,
May still seem love to me, though altered new:
Thy looks with me, thy heart in other place.
For there can live no hatred in thine eye, 5
Therefore in that I cannot know thy change,
In many's looks, the false heart's history
Is writ in moods and frowns and wrinkles strange.
But heaven in thy creation did decree,
That in thy face sweet love should ever dwell, 10
Whate'er thy thoughts, or thy heart's workings be,
Thy looks should nothing thence, but sweetness tell.
    How like Eve's apple doth thy beauty grow,
    If thy sweet virtue answer not thy show.

94

They that have power to hurt, and will do none,
That do not do the thing, they most do show,
Who moving others, are themselves as stone,
Unmovéd, cold, and to temptation slow:
They rightly do inherit heaven's graces, 5
And husband nature's riches from expense,
They are the lords and owners of their faces,
Others, but stewards of their excellence:
The summer's flower is to the summer sweet,
Though to it self, it only live and die, 10
But if that flower with base infection meet,
The basest weed outbraves his dignity:
    For sweetest things turn sourest by their deeds,
    Lilies that fester, smell far worse than weeds.

95

How sweet and lovely dost thou make the shame,
Which like a canker in the fragrant rose,
Doth spot the beauty of thy budding name!
O in what sweets dost thou thy sins enclose!
That tongue that tells the story of thy days,　5
(Making lascivious comments on thy sport)
Cannot dispraise, but in a kind of praise,
Naming thy name, blesses an ill report.
O what a mansion have those vices got,
Which for their habitation chose out thee,　10
Where beauty's veil doth cover every blot,
And all things turns to fair, that eyes can see!
　　Take heed (dear heart) of this large privilege,
　　The hardest knife ill-used doth lose his edge.

96

Some say thy fault is youth, some wantonness,
Some say thy grace is youth and gentle sport,
Both grace and faults are loved of more and less:
Thou mak'st faults graces, that to thee resort:
As on the finger of a thronèd queen,　5
The basest jewel will be well esteemed:
So are those errors that in thee are seen,
To truths translated, and for true things deemed.
How many lambs might the stern wolf betray,
If like a lamb he could his looks translate!　10
How many gazers mightst thou lead away,
If thou wouldst use the strength of all thy state!
　　But do not so, I love thee in such sort,
　　As thou being mine, mine is thy good report.

97

How like a winter hath my absence been
From thee, the pleasure of the fleeting year!
What freezings have I felt, what dark days seen!
What old December's bareness everywhere!
And yet this time removed was summer's time,　5
The teeming autumn big with rich increase,
Bearing the wanton burden of the prime,
Like widowed wombs after their lords' decease:
Yet this abundant issue seemed to me
But hope of orphans, and unfathered fruit,　10
For summer and his pleasures wait on thee,
And thou away, the very birds are mute.
　　Or if they sing, 'tis with so dull a cheer,
　　That leaves look pale, dreading the winter's near.

98

From you have I been absent in the spring,
When proud-pied April (dressed in all his trim)
Hath put a spirit of youth in every thing:
That heavy Saturn laughed and leaped with him.
Yet nor the lays of birds, nor the sweet smell　5
Of different flowers in odour and in hue,
Could make me any summer's story tell:
Or from their proud lap pluck them where they grew:
Nor did I wonder at the lily's white,
Nor praise the deep vermilion in the rose,　10
They were but sweet, but figures of delight:
Drawn after you, you pattern of all those.
　　Yet seemed it winter still, and you away,
　　As with your shadow I with these did play.

99

The forward violet thus did I chide,
Sweet thief, whence didst thou steal thy sweet that
　　smells,
If not from my love's breath? The purple pride
Which on thy soft cheek for complexion dwells,
In my love's veins thou hast too grossly dyed.　5
The lily I condemnèd for thy hand,
And buds of marjoram had stol'n thy hair,
The roses fearfully on thorns did stand,
One blushing shame, another white despair:
A third nor red, nor white, had stol'n of both,　10
And to his robbery had annexed thy breath,
But for his theft in pride of all his growth
A vengeful canker eat him up to death.
　　More flowers I noted, yet I none could see,
　　But sweet, or colour it had stol'n from thee.

100

Where art thou Muse that thou forget'st so long,
To speak of that which gives thee all thy might?
Spend'st thou thy fury on some worthless song,
Darkening thy power to lend base subjects light?
Return forgetful Muse, and straight redeem,　5
In gentle numbers time so idly spent,
Sing to the ear that doth thy lays esteem,
And gives thy pen both skill and argument.
Rise resty Muse, my love's sweet face survey,
If time have any wrinkle graven there,　10
If any, be a satire to decay,
And make time's spoils despisèd everywhere.
　　Give my love fame faster than Time wastes life,
　　So thou prevent'st his scythe, and crookèd knife.

101

O truant Muse what shall be thy amends,
For thy neglect of truth in beauty dyed?
Both truth and beauty on my love depends:
So dost thou too, and therein dignified:
Make answer Muse, wilt thou not haply say,　5
'Truth needs no colour with his colour fixed,
Beauty no pencil, beauty's truth to lay:
But best is best, if never intermixed?
Because he needs no praise, wilt thou be dumb?
Excuse not silence so, for't lies in thee,　10
To make him much outlive a gilded tomb:
And to be praised of ages yet to be.
　　Then do thy office Muse, I teach thee how,
　　To make him seem long hence, as he shows now.

102

My love is strengthened though more weak in
　　seeming,
I love not less, though less the show appear,
That love is merchandized, whose rich esteeming,
The owner's tongue doth publish every where.
Our love was new, and then but in the spring,　5
When I was wont to greet it with my lays,
As Philomel in summer's front doth sing,
And stops her pipe in growth of riper days:
Not that the summer is less pleasant now
Than when her mournful hymns did hush the night,　10
But that wild music burthens every bough,
And sweets grown common lose their dear delight.
　　Therefore like her, I sometime hold my tongue:
　　Because I would not dull you with my song.

103

Alack what poverty my muse brings forth,
That having such a scope to show her pride,
The argument all bare is of more worth
Than when it hath my added praise beside.
O blame me not if I no more can write!   5
Look in your glass and there appears a face,
That over-goes my blunt invention quite,
Dulling my lines, and doing me disgrace.
Were it not sinful then striving to mend,
To mar the subject that before was well?   10
For to no other pass my verses tend,
Than of your graces and your gifts to tell.
    And more, much more than in my verse can sit,
    Your own glass shows you, when you look in it.

104

To me fair friend you never can be old,
For as you were when first your eye I eyed,
Such seems your beauty still: three winters cold,
Have from the forests shook three summers' pride,
Three beauteous springs to yellow autumn turned,   5
In process of the seasons have I seen,
Three April perfumes in three hot Junes burned,
Since first I saw you fresh which yet are green.
Ah yet doth beauty like a dial hand,
Steal from his figure, and no pace perceived,   10
So your sweet hue, which methinks still doth stand
Hath motion, and mine eye may be deceived.
    For fear of which, hear this thou age unbred,
    Ere you were born was beauty's summer dead.

105

Let not my love be called idolatry,
Nor my belovéd as an idol show,
Since all alike my songs and praises be
To one, of one, still such, and ever so.
Kind is my love to-day, to-morrow kind,   5
Still constant in a wondrous excellence,
Therefore my verse to constancy confined,
One thing expressing, leaves out difference.
Fair, kind, and true, is all my argument,
Fair, kind, and true, varying to other words,   10
And in this change is my invention spent,
Three themes in one, which wondrous scope affords.
    Fair, kind, and true, have often lived alone.
    Which three till now, never kept seat in one.

106

When in the chronicle of wasted time,
I see descriptions of the fairest wights,
And beauty making beautiful old rhyme,
In praise of ladies dead, and lovely knights,
Then in the blazon of sweet beauty's best,   5
Of hand, of foot; of lip, of eye, of brow,
I see their antique pen would have expressed,
Even such a beauty as you master now.
So all their praises are but prophecies
Of this our time, all you prefiguring,   10
And for they looked but with divining eyes,
They had not skill enough your worth to sing:
    For we which now behold these present days,
    Have eyes to wonder, but lack tongues to praise.

107

Not mine own fears, nor the prophetic soul,
Of the wide world, dreaming on things to come,
Can yet the lease of my true love control,
Supposed as forfeit to a confined doom.
The mortal moon hath her eclipse endured,   5
And the sad augurs mock their own presage,
Incertainties now crown themselves assured,
And peace proclaims olives of endless age.
Now with the drops of this most balmy time,
My love looks fresh, and death to me subscribes,   10
Since spite of him I'll live in this poor rhyme,
While he insults o'er dull and speechless tribes.
    And thou in this shalt find thy monument,
    When tyrants' crests and tombs of brass are spent.

108

What's in the brain that ink may character,
Which hath not figured to thee my true spirit,
What's new to speak, what now to register,
That may express my love, or thy dear merit?
Nothing sweet boy, but yet like prayers divine,   5
I must each day say o'er the very same,
Counting no old thing old, thou mine, I thine,
Even as when first I hallowed thy fair name.
So that eternal love in love's fresh case,
Weighs not the dust and injury of age,   10
Nor gives to necessary wrinkles place,
But makes antiquity for aye his page,
    Finding the first conceit of love there bred,
    Where time and outward form would show it dead.

109

O never say that I was false of heart,
Though absence seemed my flame to qualify,
As easy might I from my self depart,
As from my soul which in thy breast doth lie:
That is my home of love, if I have ranged,   5
Like him that travels I return again,
Just to the time, not with the time exchanged,
So that my self bring water for my stain,
Never believe though in my nature reigned,
All frailties that besiege all kinds of blood,   10
That it could so preposterously be stained,
To leave for nothing all thy sum of good:
    For nothing this wide universe I call,
    Save thou my rose, in it thou art my all.

110

Alas 'tis true, I have gone here and there,
And made my self a motley to the view,
Gored mine own thoughts, sold cheap what is most
    dear,
Made old offences of affections new.
Most true it is, that I have looked on truth   5
Askance and strangely: but by all above,
These blenches gave my heart another youth,
And worse essays proved thee my best of love.
Now all is done, have what shall have no end,
Mine appetite I never more will grind   10
On newer proof, to try an older friend,
A god in love, to whom I am confined.
    Then give me welcome, next my heaven the best,
    Even to thy pure and most most loving breast.

III

O for my sake do you with Fortune chide,
The guilty goddess of my harmful deeds,
That did not better for my life provide,
Than public means which public manners breeds.
Thence comes it that my name receives a brand,   5
And almost thence my nature is subdued
To what it works in, like the dyer's hand:
Pity me then, and wish I were renewed,
Whilst like a willing patient I will drink,
Potions of eisel 'gainst my strong infection,   10
No bitterness that I will bitter think,
Nor double penance to correct correction.
   Pity me then dear friend, and I assure ye,
   Even that your pity is enough to cure me.

112

Your love and pity doth th' impression fill,
Which vulgar scandal stamped upon my brow,
For what care I who calls me well or ill,
So you o'er-green my bad, my good allow?
You are my all the world, and I must strive,   5
To know my shames and praises from your tongue,
None else to me, nor I to none alive,
That my steeled sense or changes right or wrong.
In so profound abysm I throw all care
Of others' voices, that my adder's sense,   10
To critic and to flatterer stopped are:
Mark how with my neglect I do dispense.
   You are so strongly in my purpose bred,
   That all the world besides methinks are dead.

113

Since I left you, mine eye is in my mind,
And that which governs me to go about,
Doth part his function, and is partly blind,
Seems seeing, but effectually is out:
For it no form delivers to the heart   5
Of bird, of flower, or shape which it doth latch,
Of his quick objects hath the mind no part,
Nor his own vision holds what it doth catch:
For if it see the rud'st or gentlest sight,
The most sweet favour or deformed'st creature,   10
The mountain, or the sea, the day, or night:
The crow, or dove, it shapes them to your feature.
   Incapable of more, replete with you,
   My most true mind thus maketh mine untrue.

114

Or whether doth my mind being crowned with you
Drink up the monarch's plague this flattery?
Or whether shall I say mine eye saith true,
And that your love taught it this alchemy?
To make of monsters, and things indigest,   5
Such cherubins as your sweet self resemble,
Creating every bad a perfect best
As fast as objects to his beams assemble:
O 'tis the first, 'tis flattery in my seeing,
And my great mind most kingly drinks it up,   10
Mine eye well knows what with his gust is 'greeing,
And to his palate doth prepare the cup.
   If it be poisoned, 'tis the lesser sin,
   That mine eye loves it and doth first begin.

115

Those lines that I before have writ do lie,
Even those that said I could not love you dearer,
Yet then my judgment knew no reason why,
My most full flame should afterwards burn clearer,
But reckoning time, whose millioned accidents   5
Creep in 'twixt vows, and change decrees of kings,
Tan sacred beauty, blunt the sharp'st intents,
Divert strong minds to the course of alt'ring things:
Alas why fearing of time's tyranny,
Might I not then say 'Now I love you best,'   10
When I was certain o'er incertainty,
Crowning the present, doubting of the rest?
   Love is a babe, then might I not say so
   To give full growth to that which still doth grow.

116

Let me not to the marriage of true minds
Admit impediments, love is not love
Which alters when it alteration finds,
Or bends with the remover to remove.
O no, it is an ever-fixèd mark   5
That looks on tempests and is never shaken;
It is the star to every wand'ring bark,
Whose worth's unknown, although his height be
   taken.
Love's not Time's fool, though rosy lips and cheeks
Within his bending sickle's compass come,   10
Love alters not with his brief hours and weeks,
But bears it out even to the edge of doom:
   If this be error and upon me proved,
   I never writ, nor no man ever loved.

117

Accuse me thus, that I have scanted all,
Wherein I should your great deserts repay,
Forgot upon your dearest love to call,
Whereto all bonds do tie me day by day,
That I have frequent been with unknown minds,   5
And given to time your own dear-purchased right,
That I have hoisted sail to all the winds
Which should transport me farthest from your sight.
Book both my wilfulness and errors down,
And on just proof surmise, accumulate,   10
Bring me within the level of your frown,
But shoot not at me in your wakened hate:
   Since my appeal says I did strive to prove
   The constancy and virtue of your love.

118

Like as to make our appetite more keen
With eager compounds we our palate urge,
As to prevent our maladies unseen,
We sicken to shun sickness when we purge.
Even so being full of your ne'er-cloying sweetness,   5
To bitter sauces did I frame my feeding;
And sick of welfare found a kind of meetness,
To be diseased ere that there was true needing.
Thus policy in love t' anticipate
The ills that were not, grew to faults assured,   10
And brought to medicine a healthful state
Which rank of goodness would by ill be cured.
   But thence I learn and find the lesson true,
   Drugs poison him that so feil sick of you.

119

What potions have I drunk of Siren tears
Distilled from limbecks foul as hell within,
Applying fears to hopes, and hopes to fears,
Still losing when I saw my self to win!
What wretched errors hath my heart committed,   5
Whilst it hath thought it self so blessèd never!
How have mine eyes out of their spheres been fitted
In the distraction of this madding fever!
O benefit of ill, now I find true
That better is, by evil still made better.   10
And ruined love when it is built anew
Grows fairer than at first, more strong, far greater.
  So I return rebuked to my content,
  And gain by ills thrice more than I have spent.

120

That you were once unkind befriends me now,
And for that sorrow, which I then did feel,
Needs must I under my transgression bow,
Unless my nerves were brass or hammered steel.
For if you were by my unkindness shaken   5
As I by yours, y'have passed a hell of time,
And I a tyrant have no leisure taken
To weigh how once I suffered in your crime.
O that our night of woe might have remembered
My deepest sense, how hard true sorrow hits,   10
And soon to you, as you to me then tendered
The humble salve, which wounded bosoms fits!
  But that your trespass now becomes a fee,
  Mine ransoms yours, and yours must ransom me.

121

'Tis better to be vile than vile esteemed,
When not to be, receives reproach of being,
And the just pleasure lost, which is so deemed,
Not by our feeling, but by others' seeing.
For why should others' false adulterate eyes   5
Give salutation to my sportive blood?
Or on my frailties why are frailer spies,
Which in their wills count bad what I think good?
No, I am that I am, and they that level
At my abuses, reckon up their own,   10
I may be straight though they themselves be bevel;
By their rank thoughts, my deeds must not be shown
  Unless this general evil they maintain,
  All men are bad and in their badness reign.

122

Thy gift, thy tables, are within my brain
Full charactered with lasting memory,
Which shall above that idle rank remain
Beyond all date even to eternity.
Or at the least, so long as brain and heart   5
Have faculty by nature to subsist,
Till each to razed oblivion yield his part
Of thee, thy record never can be missed:
That poor retention could not so much hold,
Nor need I tallies thy dear love to score,   10
Therefore to give them from me was I bold,
To trust those tables that receive thee more:
  To keep an adjunct to remember thee
  Were to import forgetfulness in me.

123

No! Time, thou shalt not boast that I do change,
Thy pyramids built up with newer might
To me are nothing novel, nothing strange,
They are but dressings of a former sight:
Our dates are brief, and therefore we admire,   5
What thou dost foist upon us that is old,
And rather make them born to our desire,
Than think that we before have heard them told:
Thy registers and thee I both defy,
Not wond'ring at the present, nor the past,   10
For thy records, and what we see doth lie,
Made more or less by thy continual haste:
  This I do vow and this shall ever be,
  I will be true despite thy scythe and thee.

124

If my dear love were but the child of state,
It might for Fortune's bastard be unfathered,
As subject to time's love or to time's hate,
Weeds among weeds, or flowers with flowers
    gathered.
No it was builded far from accident,   5
It suffers not in smiling pomp, nor falls
Under the blow of thrallèd discontent,
Whereto th' inviting time our fashion calls:
It fears not policy that heretic,
Which works on leases of short-numbered hours,   10
But all alone stands hugely politic,
That it nor grows with heat, nor drowns with showers.
  To this I witness call the fools of time,
  Which die for goodness, who have lived for crime.

125

Were't aught to me I bore the canopy,
With my extern the outward honouring,
Or laid great bases for eternity,
Which proves more short than waste or ruining?
Have I not seen dwellers on form and favour   5
Lose all, and more by paying too much rent
For compound sweet; forgoing simple savour,
Pitiful thrivers in their gazing spent?
No, let me be obsequious in thy heart,
And take thou my oblation, poor but free,   10
Which is not mixed with seconds, knows no art,
But mutual render, only me for thee.
  Hence, thou suborned informer, a true soul
  When most impeached, stands least in thy control.

126

O thou my lovely boy who in thy power,
Dost hold Time's fickle glass his fickle hour:
Who hast by waning grown, and therein show'st,
Thy lovers withering, as thy sweet self grow'st.
If Nature (sovereign mistress over wrack)   5
As thou goest onwards still will pluck thee back,
She keeps thee to this purpose, that her skill
May time disgrace, and wretched minutes kill.
Yet fear her O thou minion of her pleasure,
She may detain, but not still keep her treasure!   10
  Her audit (though delayed) answered must be,
  And her quietus is to render thee.

127

In the old age black was not counted fair,
Or if it were it bore not beauty's name:
But now is black beauty's successive heir,
And beauty slandered with a bastard shame,
For since each hand hath put on nature's power, 5
Fairing the foul with art's false borrowed face,
Sweet beauty hath no name no holy bower,
But is profaned, if not lives in disgrace.
Therefore my mistress' eyes are raven black,
Her eyes so suited, and they mourners seem, 10
At such who not born fair no beauty lack,
Slandering creation with a false esteem,
 Yet so they mourn becoming of their woe,
 That every tongue says beauty should look so.

128

How oft when thou, my music, music play'st,
Upon that blessèd wood whose motion sounds
With thy sweet fingers when thou gently sway'st
The wiry concord that mine ear confounds,
Do I envy those jacks that nimble leap, 5
To kiss the tender inward of thy hand,
Whilst my poor lips which should that harvest reap,
At the wood's boldness by thee blushing stand.
To be so tickled they would change their state
And situation with those dancing chips, 10
O'er whom thy fingers walk with gentle gait,
Making dead wood more blest than living lips,
 Since saucy jacks so happy are in this,
 Give them thy fingers, me thy lips to kiss.

129

Th' expense of spirit in a waste of shame
Is lust in action, and till action, lust
Is perjured, murd'rous, bloody full of blame,
Savage, extreme, rude, cruel, not to trust,
Enjoyed no sooner but despised straight, 5
Past reason hunted, and no sooner had
Past reason hated as a swallowed bait,
On purpose laid to make the taker mad.
Mad in pursuit and in possession so,
Had, having, and in quest, to have extreme, 10
A bliss in proof and proved, a very woe,
Before a joy proposed behind a dream.
 All this the world well knows yet none knows well,
 To shun the heaven that leads men to this hell.

130

My mistress' eyes are nothing like the sun,
Coral is far more red, than her lips red,
If snow be white, why then her breasts are dun:
If hairs be wires, black wires grow on her head:
I have seen roses damasked, red and white, 5
But no such roses see I in her cheeks,
And in some perfumes is there more delight,
Than in the breath that from my mistress reeks.
I love to hear her speak, yet well I know,
That music hath a far more pleasing sound: 10
I grant I never saw a goddess go,
My mistress when she walks treads on the ground.
 And yet by heaven I think my love as rare,
 As any she belied with false compare.

131

Thou art as tyrannous, so as thou art,
As those whose beauties proudly make them cruel;
For well thou know'st to my dear doting heart
Thou art the fairest and most precious jewel.
Yet in good faith some say that thee behold, 5
Thy face hath not the power to make love groan;
To say they err, I dare not be so bold,
Although I swear it to my self alone.
And to be sure that is not false I swear,
A thousand groans but thinking on thy face, 10
One on another's neck do witness bear
Thy black is fairest in my judgment's place.
 In nothing art thou black save in thy deeds,
 And thence this slander as I think proceeds.

132

Thine eyes I love, and they as pitying me,
Knowing thy heart torment me with disdain,
Have put on black, and loving mourners be,
Looking with pretty ruth upon my pain.
And truly not the morning sun of heaven 5
Better becomes the grey cheeks of the east,
Nor that full star that ushers in the even
Doth half that glory to the sober west
As those two mourning eyes become thy face:
O let it then as well beseem thy heart 10
To mourn for me since mourning doth thee grace,
And suit thy pity like in every part.
 Then will I swear beauty herself is black,
 And all they foul that thy complexion lack.

133

Beshrew that heart that makes my heart to groan
For that deep wound it gives my friend and me;
Is't not enough to torture me alone,
But slave to slavery my sweet'st friend must be?
Me from my self thy cruel eye hath taken, 5
And my next self thou harder hast engrossed,
Of him, my self, and thee I am forsaken,
A torment thrice three-fold thus to be crossed:
Prison my heart in thy steel bosom's ward,
But then my friend's heart let my poor heart bail, 10
Whoe'er keeps me, let my heart be his guard,
Thou canst not then use rigour in my gaol.
 And yet thou wilt, for I being pent in thee,
 Perforce am thine and all that is in me.

134

So now I have confessed that he is thine,
And I my self am mortgaged to thy will,
My self I'll forfeit, so that other mine,
Thou wilt restore to be my comfort still:
But thou wilt not, nor he will not be free, 5
For thou art covetous, and he is kind,
He learned but surety-like to write for me,
Under that bond that him as fast doth bind.
The statute of thy beauty thou wilt take,
Thou usurer that put'st forth all to use, 10
And sue a friend, came debtor for my sake,
So him I lose through my unkind abuse.
 Him have I lost, thou hast both him and me,
 He pays the whole, and yet am I not free.

135

Whoever hath her wish, thou hast thy will,
And 'Will' to boot, and 'Will' in over-plus,
More than enough am I that vex thee still,
To thy sweet will making addition thus.
Wilt thou whose will is large and spacious,   5
Not once vouchsafe to hide my will in thine?
Shall will in others seem right gracious,
And in my will no fair acceptance shine?
The sea all water, yet receives rain still,
And in abundance addeth to his store,   10
So thou being rich in will add to thy will
One will of mine to make thy large will more.
    Let no unkind, no fair beseechers kill,
    Think all but one, and me in that one 'Will.'

136

If thy soul check thee that I come so near,
Swear to thy blind soul that I was thy 'Will',
And will thy soul knows is admitted there,
Thus far for love, my love-suit sweet fulfil.
'Will', will fulfil the treasure of thy love,   5
Ay, fill it full with wills, and my will one,
In things of great receipt with ease we prove,
Among a number one is reckoned none.
Then in the number let me pass untold,
Though in thy store's account I one must be,   10
For nothing hold me, so it please thee hold,
That nothing me, a something sweet to thee.
    Make but my name thy love, and love that still,
    And then thou lov'st me for my name is Will.

137

Thou blind fool Love, what dost thou to mine eyes,
That they behold and see not what they see?
They know what beauty is, see where it lies,
Yet what the best is, take the worst to be.
If eyes corrupt by over-partial looks,   5
Be anchored in the bay where all men ride,
Why of eyes' falsehood hast thou forgèd hooks,
Whereto the judgment of my heart is tied?
Why should my heart think that a several plot,
Which my heart knows the wide world's common
    place?   10
Or mine eyes seeing this, say this is not
To put fair truth upon so foul a face?
    In things right true my heart and eyes have erred,
    And to this false plague are they now transferred.

138

When my love swears that she is made of truth,
I do believe her though I know she lies,
That she might think me some untutored youth,
Unlearnèd in the world's false subtleties.
Thus vainly thinking that she thinks me young,   5
Although she knows my days are past the best,
Simply I credit her false-speaking tongue,
On both sides thus is simple truth suppressed:
But wherefore says she not she is unjust?
And wherefore say not I that I am old?   10
O love's best habit is in seeming trust,
And age in love, loves not to have years told.
    Therefore I lie with her, and she with me,
    And in our faults by lies we flattered be.

139

O call not me to justify the wrong,
That thy unkindness lays upon my heart,
Wound me not with thine eye but with thy tongue,
Use power with power, and slay me not by art,
Tell me thou lov'st elsewhere; but in my sight,   5
Dear heart forbear to glance thine eye aside,
What need'st thou wound with cunning when thy
    might
Is more than my o'erpressed defence can bide?
Let me excuse thee, ah my love well knows,
Her pretty looks have been mine enemies,   10
And therefore from my face she turns my foes,
That they elsewhere might dart their injuries:
    Yet do not so, but since I am near slain,
    Kill me outright with looks, and rid my pain.

140

Be wise as thou art cruel, do not press
My tongue-tied patience with too much disdain:
Lest sorrow lend me words and words express,
The manner of my pity-wanting pain.
If I might teach thee wit better it were,   5
Though not to love, yet love to tell me so,
As testy sick men when their deaths be near,
No news but health from their physicians know.
For if I should despair I should grow mad,
And in my madness might speak ill of thee,   10
Now this ill-wresting world is grown so bad,
Mad slanderers by mad ears believèd be.
    That I may not be so, nor thou belied,
    Bear thine eyes straight, though thy proud heart go
    wide.

141

In faith I do not love thee with mine eyes,
For they in thee a thousand errors note,
But 'tis my heart that loves what they despise,
Who in despite of view is pleased to dote.
Nor are mine ears with thy tongue's tune delighted,   5
Nor tender feeling to base touches prone,
Nor taste, nor smell, desire to be invited
To any sensual feast with thee alone:
But my five wits, nor my five senses can
Dissuade one foolish heart from serving thee,   10
Who leaves unswayed the likeness of a man,
Thy proud heart's slave and vassal wretch to be:
    Only my plague thus far I count my gain,
    That she that makes me sin, awards me pain.

142

Love is my sin, and thy dear virtue hate,
Hate of my sin, grounded on sinful loving,
O but with mine, compare thou thine own state,
And thou shalt find it merits not reproving,
Or if it do, not from those lips of thine,   5
That have profaned their scarlet ornaments,
And sealed false bonds of love as oft as mine,
Robbed others' beds' revenues of their rents.
Be it lawful I love thee as thou lov'st those,
Whom thine eyes woo as mine importune thee,   10
Root pity in thy heart that when it grows,
Thy pity may deserve to pitied be.
    If thou dost seek to have what thou dost hide,
    By self-example mayst thou be denied.

143

Lo as a careful huswife runs to catch,
One of her feathered creatures broke away,
Sets down her babe and makes all swift dispatch
In pursuit of the thing she would have stay:
Whilst her neglected child holds her in chase,   5
Cries to catch her whose busy care is bent,
To follow that which flies before her face:
Not prizing her poor infant's discontent;
So run'st thou after that which flies from thee,
Whilst I thy babe chase thee afar behind,   10
But if thou catch thy hope turn back to me:
And play the mother's part, kiss me, be kind.
  So will I pray that thou mayst have thy Will,
  If thou turn back and my loud crying still.

144

Two loves I have of comfort and despair,
Which like two spirits do suggest me still,
The better angel is a man right fair:
The worser spirit a woman coloured ill.
To win me soon to hell my female evil,   5
Tempteth my better angel from my side,
And would corrupt my saint to be a devil:
Wooing his purity with her foul pride.
And whether that my angel be turned fiend,
Suspect I may, yet not directly tell,   10
But being both from me both to each friend,
I guess one angel in another's hell.
  Yet this shall I ne'er know but live in doubt,
  Till my bad angel fire my good one out.

145

Those lips that Love's own hand did make,
Breathed forth the sound that said 'I hate',
To me that languished for her sake:
But when she saw my woeful state,
Straight in her heart did mercy come,   5
Chiding that tongue that ever sweet,
Was used in giving gentle doom:
And taught it thus anew to greet:
'I hate' she altered with an end,
That followed it as gentle day,   10
Doth follow night who like a fiend
From heaven to hell is flown away.
  'I hate', from hate away she threw,
  And saved my life saying 'not you'.

146

Poor soul the centre of my sinful earth,
My sinful earth these rebel powers array,
Why dost thou pine within and suffer dearth
Painting thy outward walls so costly gay?
Why so large cost having so short a lease,   5
Dost thou upon thy fading mansion spend?
Shall worms inheritors of this excess
Eat up thy charge? is this thy body's end?
Then soul live thou upon thy servant's loss,
And let that pine to aggravate thy store;   10
Buy terms divine in selling hours of dross;
Within be fed, without be rich no more,
  So shall thou feed on death, that feeds on men,
  And death once dead, there's no more dying then.

147

My love is as a fever longing still,
For that which longer nurseth the disease,
Feeding on that which doth preserve the ill,
Th' uncertain sickly appetite to please:
My reason the physician to my love,   5
Angry that his prescriptions are not kept
Hath left me, and I desperate now approve,
Desire is death, which physic did except.
Past cure I am, now reason is past care,
And frantic-mad with evermore unrest,   10
My thoughts and my discourse as mad men's are,
At random from the truth vainly expressed.
  For I have sworn thee fair, and thought thee bright,
  Who art as black as hell, as dark as night.

148

O me! what eyes hath love put in my head,
Which have no correspondence with true sight,
Or if they have, where is my judgment fled,
That censures falsely what they see aright?
If that be fair whereon my false eyes dote,   5
What means the world to say it is not so?
If it be not, then love doth well denote,
Love's eye is not so true as all men's: no,
How can it? O how can love's eye be true,
That is so vexed with watching and with tears?   10
No marvel then though I mistake my view,
The sun it self sees not, till heaven clears.
  O cunning love, with tears thou keep'st me blind,
  Lest eyes well-seeing thy foul faults should find.

149

Canst thou O cruel, say I love thee not,
When I against my self with thee partake?
Do I not think on thee when I forgot
Am of my self, all-tyrant, for thy sake?
Who hateth thee that I do call my friend,   5
On whom frown'st thou that I do fawn upon,
Nay if thou lour'st on me do I not spend
Revenge upon my self with present moan?
What merit do I in my self respect,
That is so proud thy service to despise,   10
When all my best doth worship thy defect,
Commanded by the motion of thine eyes?
  But love hate on for now I know thy mind,
  Those that can see thou lov'st, and I am blind.

150

O from what power hast thou this powerful might,
With insufficiency my heart to sway,
To make me give the lie to my true sight,
And swear that brightness doth not grace the day?
Whence hast thou this becoming of things ill,   5
That in the very refuse of thy deeds,
There is such strength and warrantise of skill,
That in my mind thy worst all best exceeds?
Who taught thee how to make me love thee more,
The more I hear and see just cause of hate?   10
O though I love what others do abhor,
With others thou shouldst not abhor my state.
  If thy unworthiness raised love in me,
  More worthy I to be beloved of thee.

151

Love is too young to know what conscience is,
Yet who knows not conscience is born of love?
Then gentle cheater urge not my amiss,
Lest guilty of my faults thy sweet self prove.
For thou betraying me, I do betray   5
My nobler part to my gross body's treason,
My soul doth tell my body that he may,
Triumph in love, flesh stays no farther reason,
But rising at thy name doth point out thee,
As his triumphant prize, proud of this pride,   10
He is contented thy poor drudge to be,
To stand in thy affairs, fall by thy side.
   No want of conscience hold it that I call,
   Her love, for whose dear love I rise and fall.

152

In loving thee thou know'st I am forsworn,
But thou art twice forsworn to me love swearing,
In act thy bed-vow broke and new faith torn,
In vowing new hate after new love bearing,
But why of two oaths' breach do I accuse thee,   5
When I break twenty? I am perjured most,
For all my vows are oaths but to misuse thee:
And all my honest faith in thee is lost.
For I have sworn deep oaths of thy deep kindness:
Oaths of thy love, thy truth, thy constancy,   10
And to enlighten thee gave eyes to blindness,
Or made them swear against the thing they see.
   For I have sworn thee fair: more perjured I,
   To swear against the truth so foul a lie.

153

Cupid laid by his brand and fell asleep,
A maid of Dian's this advantage found,
And his love-kindling fire did quickly steep
In a cold valley-fountain of that ground:
Which borrowed from this holy fire of Love,   5
A dateless lively heat still to endure,
And grew a seeting bath which yet men prove,
Against strange maladies a sovereign cure:
But at my mistress' eye Love's brand new-fired,
The boy for trial needs would touch my breast,   10
I sick withal the help of bath desired,
And thither hied a sad distempered guest.
   But found no cure, the bath for my help lies,
   Where Cupid got new fire; my mistress' eyes.

154

The little Love-god lying once asleep,
Laid by his side his heart-inflaming brand,
Whilst many nymphs that vowed chaste life to keep,
Came tripping by, but in her maiden hand,
The fairest votary took up that fire,   5
Which many legions of true hearts had warmed,
And so the general of hot desire,
Was sleeping by a virgin hand disarmed.
This brand she quenchéd in a cool well by,
Which from Love's fire took heat perpetual,   10
Growing a bath and healthful remedy,
For men diseased, but I my mistress' thrall,
   Came there for cure and this by that I prove,
   Love's fire heats water, water cools not love.

Glossary

ABATE, omit, except, blunt

ABATEMENT, depreciation, reduction

ABHOMINABLE, a frequent 16th–17th cent. spelling, inhuman

ABIDE, sojourn, for a while only

ABILITY, strength

ABLE, suitable, appropriate

ABLE (for), a match for

ABODE, (i) delay; (ii) presage

ABORTIVE, unnatural, at once untimely and monstrous

ABRIDGEMENT, (i) a short or shortened play for an evening's entertainment at court; (ii) that which cut's one short

ABROACH, on foot

ABROGATE SCURRILITY, cut out indecency

ABRUPTION, breaking off (in speech)

ABSEY BOOK, a primer, ABC book

ABSTRACT, (i) epitome; (ii) abridgement (of distance), a short cut

ABSYRTUS, brother of Medea, murdered and cut into pieces by her to delay her father's pursuit on her flight from Colchos to Jason

ABUSE, (i) deceive; (ii) misuse, maltreat

ABY, pay the penalty for

ACADEME, a philosophical school or association of students

ACCIDENT, incident

ACCITE, summon

ACCOMMODATIONS, comforts, conveniences

ACCOMPT (beyond), unprecedented

ACCORD, concord, harmony

ACCORDINGLY, in proportion

ACCOST, nautical term (to coast) then coming into fashion, meaning greet politely

ACE, throw of one at dice

ACHERON, one of the rivers of Hades

ACHILLES' SPEAR, Telephus, Priam's son-in-law, wounded by Achilles, was cured by rust scraped from the spear

ACQUITTANCE, written acknowledgement of debt

ACROSS, expression from the tilt yard implying a jest or sally has missed its mark

ACT, activity, the life of action

ACTAEON, was transformed into a stag with horns and pursued by his own hounds—the classical prototype of the Elizabethan cuckold

AD UNGUEM, Lat. at the fingers' ends

ADAMANT, fabulous rock or stone to which were ascribed properties of the diamond and of the loadstone or magnet

ADDITION, title, style of address

ADDRESS, ready, equip, prepare

ADHERE, cohere

ADMIRAL, flagship

ADMIRATION, wonder, marvel; notes of —, notes of exclamation

ADONIS' GARDENS, orig. beds of plants surrounding images of Adonis, their rapid withering being the usual point of the allusion

ADOPTIOUS, assumed, adopted (a coinage of Shakespeare's)

ADVANCE, (i) raise, lift up; (ii) reveal

ADVENTURE, accident, chance

ADVERTISE, (i) instruct, inform; (ii) warn

ADVICE, prudence, forethought; 'upon more —', 'on further consideration'

ADVISE, consider, reflect, take care

AEACIDES, descendants of Aeacus, e.g. Ajax

AEDILE, the Tribunes were allowed two aediles to arrest and execute and to carry out other civil duties

AERY, (i) nest of a bird of prey; (ii) a brood of young eagles

AESCULAPIUS, god of medicine, son of Apollo

AESOP, the reputed fabulist, said to have been a hunch-backed Phygian slave

AFFECT, (sb) passion, desire; (vb) resort to

AFFECTED, (i) in love; (ii) attacked by disease

AFFECTION, disposition, inclination

AFFRAY, startle

AFFRONT, confront

AFFY, betroth

AFTER-SUPPER, rather a dessert at the end of supper than a rere- or second supper late at night

AGAIN, in consequence

AGAINST THE HAIR, against the grain, derived from stroking an animal the wrong way

AGAMEMNON, chief leader of the Greeks against Troy

AGATE, very diminutive person, in allusion to small figures, cut in agate, used as seals

AGENOR, father of Europa

AGGRAVATE, exaggerate; '— his style', give him a new title.

AGLET-BABY, small figure forming tag of a point or lace

AGNIZE, acknowledge

AGONY, agony of death, death throes

AGOOD, in good earnest

A-HOLD, A-HAULED, hauled right into the wind so as to reset canvas

AIM, 'aim better at me', think better of me

AIM AT, guess at, hint at

AJAX, son of Telamon, who in a fit of madness at Ulysses being awarded the arms of Achilles, slew a flock of sheep, thinking them his enemies

ALARUM, trumpet call to arms

ALBION, Britain

ALCIDES, name of Hercules as grandson of Alcaeus

ALE, 'go to the ale with a Christian', a reference to Church-ale, a parish festival

ALECTO, one of the Furies

ALL-AMORT, sick to death, dejected

ALLA NOSTRA CASA BEN VENUTO, welcome to our house

ALLHALLOWMASS, All Saints' Day, November 1st

ALLICHOLY, melancholy

ALLOTTERY, assignment of a share

ALLOW, prove, approve, permit by authority

ALLUSION, jest, allegory, riddle

ALLY, kinsman

ALMAIN, German

ALMS, an act of charity

ALMS-BASKET, in which broken meats from the tables of the wealthy were collected for distribution among the poor

ALONE, peerless, unique

ALTERING, changing physical processes for the bad (by disease) or for the good (by medicine)

ALTHAEA, wife of king of Calydon. Informed by the Fates at the birth of her son Meleager that he would die when a brand on the fire was consumed, she snatched it from the hearth, later to burn it after Meleager slew his brothers

AMAIN, at full speed

AMAIMON, a mighty devil

AMAZE, confuse, bewilder

AMBLE, a favourite Elizabethan pace

AMES-ACE, i.e. ambs-ace, the lowest possible throw at dice, the double ace

ANATOMIZE, (i) dissect (surg.); (ii) lay open minutely, expose

ANATOMY, (i) skeleton; (ii) a corpse for dissection

ANCHISES, father of Aeneas, who carried him from burning Troy

ANCIENT, ensign, standard-bearer

ANCIENTRY, antique style, old people

ANCUS MARCIUS, legendary fourth king of Rome

AN-END, perpetually

ANGEL, gold coin, value c. 50p, another name for the noble

ANGLE, hook

ANSWER, (i) discharge a debt; (ii) reply to a charge, hence charge

ANSWER (sb), return hit in fencing

ANTHEM, song of grief or mourning

ANTHROPOPHAGINIAN, man-eater

ANTIATES, people of Antium, in Latium, chief city of the Volsces

ANTIC, (i) buffoon, clown, fool; (ii) pageant, masque; (adj.) quaint, grotesque, fantastic

APE-BEARER, one who carries a monkey about for exhibition, a strolling buffoon

APPARENT, obvious, evident, open

APPEACH, turn informer, accuse

APPEAL (sb), impeachment of treason which the accuser is prepared to prove by combat

APPELLANT (sb and adj.) challenger, accusing

APPENDIX, jocularly, one who follows behind

APPERTAINMENT, prerogative

APPLE-JOHN, ripened about St John's Day (midsummer) and eaten two years later when shrivelled and wrinkled

APPLIANCES, medical applications

APPOINT, ordain, devote (a person or thing)

APPOINTMENT, (i) engagement, business; (ii) equipment

APPREHEND, seize a point

APPREHENSION, quickness of wit

APPROBATION, credit, proof

APPROOF, confirmed reputation

APPROPRIATION, special attribute

APPROVE, (i) test, try; (ii) confirm, prove

APPURTENANCE, adjunct

APRICOCK, obs. form of 'apricot'.

AQUA-VITAE, ardent spirits

AQUILON, the north or north-north-east wind

ARABIAN BIRD, the phoenix, q.v.

ARAISE, raise from the dead

ARBITREMENT, scrutiny

ARGAL, a perversion of 'ergo'

ARGIER, old form of Algiers

ARGOSY, 'merchant vessel of largest size and burden' (OED)

ARGUMENT, (i) theme of conversation, of contention, esp. for jest or scorn; (ii) proof, evidence

ARGUS, of the hundred eyes, set by Juno as guard over Io, to prevent Jupiter making love to her

ARION, the Greek musician who, threatened with death on board ship, threw himself into the sea, and was saved by a dolphin who had heard his lute-playing

ARMADO, a fleet of warships

ARMIGERO, an armiger, an esquire

ARMIPOTENT, mighty in arms

ARMS CROSSED, hold down sorrow

ARRAS, tapestry wall-hanging

ARREST, seize as security

ART, learning, science, magic, the skill or power learning bestows

ARTERIES ('the nimble spirits in the'), refers to old medical notion that arteries were the channel, not only of blood, but also of the vital 'spirits'

ARTHUR'S SHOW, 'The Ancient Order of Prince Arthur and his knightly Armory' gave an annual exhibition of archery at Mile End

ARTIFICIAL, skilled in art, q.v.

ARTIST, man of skill or learning, a physician

ASCANIUS, son of Aeneas

ASHER HOUSE, a residence of the Bishop of Winchester near Hampton Court. Asher is now Esher

ASKANCE, scornful, sidelong glance

ASPECT, (i) a glance; (ii) the favourable or unfavourable influence of a planet according to the old astrologers; (iii) appearance

ASPERSION, dew, shower

ASSAY, (i) attempt; (ii) learn by experience

ASSINEGO, young ass, fool

ASSUME, (i) take to oneself formally the insignia of office or symbol of vocation (OED); (ii) put or take on garb, aspect or character. Term in demonology for devils disguising themselves as some dead person

ASSURED, betrothed

ASTRAEA, goddess of Justice, who lived among men in the Golden Age and thereafter deserted earth for heaven

ASTRINGER, austringer, falconer, keeper of goshawks

ATE, goddess of mischief and bloodshed; 'more Ates'—more instigation

ATOMIES, motes, specks of dust in a sunbeam

ATONE, unite, reconcile

ATTACHED, seized, arrested

ATTAINDER, (i) 'in — of', condemned to; (ii) dishonouring stain

ATTENTIVE, observant

ATTORNEY (vb), perform at second hand

ATTORNEYED, employed as attorney or agent

ATTORNEY-GENERAL, legal representative acting under a general power of attorney

AUGURER, augur, member of Roman priestly college whose duty was to study auguries

AURORA, goddess of the dawn

AURORA'S HARBINGER, Venus Phosphor, the morning star

AUSTERELY, with self-restraint

AUTHENTIC, (i) of established credit; (ii) legally qualified or authorised

AVAIL, be profitable, of use

AVES, acclamations

AVOID, depart, quit

AWFUL, commanding respect

BACKARE!, stand back!

BACK-FRIEND, lit. a pretended or false friend

BACK-TRICK, uncertain, perhaps a caper backwards in dancing, a reverse in the galliard

BADGE, hallmark, lit. the mark worn by retainers

BAFFLE, (i) subject to public disgrace or infamy; (ii) dupe, hoodwink

BAILIFF, 'officer of justice under a sheriff who executes writs and processes, distrains and arrests; warrant officer, poursuivant or catchpole' (OED)

BAILLEZ, bring

BALDRIC, belt or girdle, usually leather, richly ornamented, used to support sword or bugle

BALK, omit, neglect

BALK LOGIC, chop logic

BALM, annoint with fragrant liquid

BALSAMUM, balm

BANBURY CHEESE, a very thin cheese

BAND, (i) bond, for debt; (ii) a leash to tie up a dog

BANDETTO, earliest Eng. form of bandit

BANDY, to strike ball to and fro at tennis; to give and take recriminations

BANKROUT, bankrupt

BANNER, properly 'banderole', fringed silk flag on a trumpet

BANQUET, dessert of fruit and wine served some time after supper

BAR IN LAW, plea which effectually prevents an action or claim

BARBARISM, ignorance

BARBARY COCK-PIGEON, fancy variety of pigeon

BARBASON, a prince of devils

BARBED, of a horse, armed with a barb, a protective covering for flanks and breast

BARE, shave

BARFUL, full of difficulties

BARGAIN (sell a), make a fool of

BARGULUS, a pirate who fought against Philip of Macedon

BARK ON TREE (sure as), the union of bark and tree was commonly taken as symbol of married state

BARM, yeast

BARN, bairn, child

BARNACLE, kind of wild goose

BARREN, dull-witted

BARTHOLOMEW BOAR-PIG, young porker fattened for sale at Bartholomew Fair on 24th August

BASE, boys' game, in which a player who leaves his base is chased and if caught is made prisoner

BASES, two-part embroidered mantle worn by knights on horse-back

BASIMECU, contemptuous term for Frenchman, from Fr. 'baisez mon cul'

BASKET-HILT, lit. a hilt of steel plates curved like a basket, but often an epithet for a poor swordsman

BASS-VIOL, violoncello

BASTA, enough

BASTARD, (i) brown or white sweet Spanish wine; (ii) the product of the artificial crossing of two different stocks

BASTED ON, tacked or sewn on loosely

BASTINADO, beating or cudgelling, esp. on the soles of the feet

BATE, (i) deduct; (ii) blunt; (iii) except; (iv) depress, reduce in weight; (v) flutter the wings impatiently

BAT-FOWLING, (i) killing birds by holding a lantern close to their roost and knocking down the victims as they blunder against the light; (ii) gulling a simpleton

BATLER, wooden club for beating clothes in wash

BATTLE, army, large armed force

BAUBLE, a fool's stick, ending in a fool's head

BAUBLING, trifling, toylike

BAWCOCK, fine fellow, colloquial term of endearment, from Fr. 'beau coq'

BAY, chorus of barking hounds in conflict with an animal, hence the animal's last stand

BAYNARD'S CASTLE, on the N. bank of the Thames, close to present Blackfriar's Br., once the house of Richard, Duke of York

BEAD, (i) a minute object; (ii) a prayer

BEADLE, parish constable, authorised to whip petty offenders

BEADSMAN, one who tells beads or prays for another

BEAGLE, lit. a small hound, also used contemptuously of a woman

BEAK, prow

BEAR, (i) carry off, win; (ii) 'bear a hand', treat in a certain way; (iii) 'bear hard', bear ill will to; (iv) 'bear it', conduct oneself; (v) 'bear with you', endure; (vi) 'bear in hand', delude or abuse with false pretences

BEAR'ARD, bear-herd, bear-ward

BEAR-BAITING, one of the most popular Eng. sports of the time, the bear was tied by a long chain to a stake in a ring and set upon by mastiffs

BEAR-HERD, one who leads a bear about the country for exhibition

BEARING-CLOTH, christening robe

BEAT, flap the wings

BEAVER, helmet, face-guard or visor of helmet

BEDLAM, corr. of Bethlehem Hospital for the insane, hence also a lunatic

BED-SWERVER, one unfaithful in marriage

BEETLE, (sb) heavy hammer or mallet; (vb) overhang

BEFORE ME, (i) in my presence; (ii) upon my soul

BEG, petition the court of wards for the custody of a minor, heiress, or idiot, as feudal superior

BELDAM, grandam

BELLMAN, watchman who called the hours

BELL-WETHER, ram with a bell at its neck to lead the flock

BE-METE, measure

BEMOIL, befoul

BEN VENUTO, welcome

BENCH, raise to official dignity

BENCHER, member of Roman senate, a senator

BENEDICITE, 'Bless you', exclamation of surprise, or salutation

BENT, lit. the extent to which a bow may be bent, hence the limit of capacity or endurance

BERGOMASK, dance of clowns or rustics, from Bergamo, Venice

BERMOOTHES, the Bermudas. On 29th July 1609 the *Sea Adventure*, carrying colonists to Virginia, was wrecked on the Bermudas

BESHREW, mischief take

BESONIAN, lit. raw, needy recruit, hence beggar or rascal

BESTOW, confer as a gift; '— oneself', acquit oneself, bear oneself

BESTRAUGHT, distracted, out of one's mind

BETEEM, grant, vouchsafe, pour

BETIME, betide

BETWEEN THIS AND HIS HEAD, a common phrase of the time

BEVIS, Saxon knight, of Southampton, hero of early Eng. metrical romance *Sir B. of Hampton*

BEVY, technical term for covey of quail or lapwing

BIAS, natural tendency or leaning, from the lead in one side of a bowl which makes it turn

BIBLE BABBLE, idle prating

BIDDY, fowl, chicken

BIDE UPON, dwell upon, insist upon

BIGGEN, or biggin, nightcap

BILBO, finely tempered sword of Bilbao manufacture

BILBOE, kind of stocks used on board ship

BILL, (i) long wooden-handled weapon, with blade or axe-shaped head; (ii) advertisement

BILLETS, logs of wood for fuel

BILLS (set up), posted up advertisements, i.e. issued a general challenge

BIRDBOLT, blunt, wooden-headed heavy arrow, used for shooting small birds from a short distance

BITUME, make watertight with bitumen

BLACK MONDAY, Easter Monday

BLANK, the white spot in the centre of the target

BLAZON, description, lit. interpretation of armorial bearings

BLENCH, swerve, start aside

BLENT, blended, mingled

BLOCK, (i) mould for a hat, hence fashion, style; (ii) blockhead, simpleton; (iii) stump for chopping

BLOOD (in), in full vigour, a hunting phrase

BLOODS, gallant fellows

BLOODY, blood-thirsty

BLOW (vb), (i) blow upon, puff out; (ii) make to blossom, i.e. blush

BLUE-CAPS, blue-bonnets, a term of contempt for the Scots

BLUE-EYED, (i) with blue-eyelids, a sign of pregnancy; (ii) with dark circles around the eye from excessive weeping or sleeplessness

BLUNT, (i) rude, unceremonious; (ii) not to be sharpened

BOAR OF THESSALY, sent by Artemis to ravage Calydon, brought to bay and slain by Meleager and Atalanta

BOARD, (i) accost, address; (ii) board a ship

BOB, lit. (i) trick deception; (ii) sharp rap or blow with fist, combining the two meanings a taunt or bitter jest

BODGES, clumsy phrases

BODKIN, long jewelled pin, with engraved or modelled top, for ladies' hair

BOGGLE, shy like a startled horse, take alarm

BOHEMIAN TARTAR, *v.* Hungarian

BOIL, seethe

BOILED-BRAINS, hot-headed youth

BOLD (be), be assured

BOLD-BEATING, prob. misprint for 'bowl-beating', i.e. pot-thumping

BOLIN, early form of 'bowline', a rope from the weather side of square sail to the bow

BOLT, (sb) sieve, strainer; (vb) sift

BOMBARD, large leather vessel containing liquor

BOMBAST, cotton-wool for padding or stuffing

BONA ROBA, high class courtesan, fr. It. 'Buona roba', good stuff

BONA TERRA, MALA GENS, Lat. a good land, a bad people

BOND, (i) signed contract; (ii) fetter

BONNY, often had sense of fine size, big

BOOK (without), from memory, by heart

BOOKS (in your), in favour with you

BOOR, husbandman, peasant

BOOT, (i) 'Grace to boot', Heaven help me; (ii) recompense

BOOT-HOSE, overstocking which covers the leg like a jackboot

BOOTS, 'Give me not the boots', don't make game of me

BOREAS, the north wind

BOSOM, desires or intimate thoughts

BOTCH UP, put together or stitch together clumsily

BOTCHER, repairing tailor; bungling workman

BOTS, horse disease caused by worms

BOTTLE, bundle of hay or straw, the feed prescribed for a horse by Elizabethan horse-keepers

BOTTOM, (i) core of the skein upon which wool was wound; (ii) dell, valley

BOUGHT AND SOLD, in modern slang 'sold'

BOUND, indentured under contract of service

BOUNDS (of feed), limits within which one had rights of pasturage, prob. in respect of common land

BOURN, boundary, landmark, stream

BOUT, round, turn

BOW, yoke for oxen

BOWHAND, *v.* wide

BOY, term of abuse or contempt

BOY (to her), a hunting cry

BRABBLE, brawl

BRACH, bitch

BRAID, of doubtful meaning and origin, possibly loose, lascivious

BRAINFORD, Brentford

BRANCHED, figured

BRAVELY, (i) with a light heart; (ii) at a high rate or value

BRAWL, the most ancient type of figure dancing

BREACH (of the sea), lit. where the waves break, the surf

BREAK, break faith, disband

BREAK A COMPARISON, metaphor from 'breaking a lance' at tilting

BREAK UP, (i) open a letter (break the wax); (ii) cut up, dismember (fowl or deer)

BREAK WITH, reveal, divulge

BREAKING GULF, the waves

BREAK-NECK, downfall, destruction

BREAST, voice for singing

BREATH, speech, utterance

BREATHE, take exercise

BREATHED, in training, with a good wind

BREATHER, living being, creature

BRED OUT, exhausted, degenerated

BREECHING SCHOLAR, schoolboy liable to be whipped

BRIAREUS, in Gr. mythology a monster with a hundred arms

BRIBED-DUCK, stolen deer

BRIEF, (i) list, summary; (ii) legal document

BROACH, let blood, lit. 'tap'

BROCK, badger, stinker

BROKE, act as procurer

BROKE CROSS, it was dishonourable for a tilter to have his lance broken cross-wise instead of length-wise against an opponent's shield

BROKEN, gap-toothed

BROKER, pander, go-between

BROOCH, ornament, often worn in the hat

BROW, (i) countenance; (ii) 'strike at the brow':— strike at the brow antler, i.e. aim for the lowest part of the stag's horn, the right mark for the archer

BROWN BILL, painted brown halberd, used by watchmen

BROWNIST, lit. follower of Robt. Browne, a founder of Independency, hence an extreme type of puritan

BRUISE, crush

BRUIT, noise, report

BUBUKLE, pimple, a confusion of 'bubo' abscess and 'carbuncle'

BUCK, (i) male deer, stag; (ii) dirty linen to be steeped in alkaline lye as the first process in buck-washing or bleaching

BUCKLE IN, encompass, limit

BUCKLERS (give the), yield, admit defeat

BUCKLERSBURY, London street for grocers and apothecaries, whose shops were full of herbs in 'simple time'

BUDGET, leather wallet or pouch

BUFF, stout leather, made of ox-hide, oiled, with a characteristic fuzzy surface and a dull whitish-yellow colour, used for the attire of sergeants, bum-bailiffs and soldiers

BUG, bogey, bugbear

BUGLE, ornamental tube-shaped bead-work, a black, glass bead

BULLY, (sb) gallant (a term of endearment)

BUM-BAILY, petty sheriff's officer who could arrest for theft

BUNCH OF GRAPES, the name of a room in an ale-house

BUR, (i) prickly seed-vessel; (ii) anything that produced a choking sensation in the throat

BURDEN, part for the bass singer

BURGONET, a kind of helmet

BURN DAYLIGHT, waste time

BURNING ZONE, the belt between the tropics of Cancer and Capricorn in the celestial sphere

BURST, smash

BURTHEN, accompaniment to a song, bass part, refrain

BUSH, lit. 'a branch or bunch of ivy', perhaps as a plant sacred to Bacchus, hung up as a vintner's sign, and hence the tavern sign

BUTCHERY, slaughterhouse, shambles

BUTTERY-BAR, ledge at the door of the buttery, hatch on which to rest tankards, etc.

BUTT-SHAFT, an unbarbed arrow used at the butts

BUZZ, (i) buzz of a bee; (ii) rumour, scandal

BUZZARD, inferior kind of hawk, unteachable by falconer, hence a type of stupidity; moth, cockchafer

BY ABOUT, concerning

BY'R LAKIN, vulgar form of 'By our Lady'

CABALLERO, Sp. gallant, good fellow

CABBAGE, cabbagehead, hence fool

CACODEMON, evil spirit

CADDIS, worsted yarn; '— ribbon', worsted tape from which garters were made

CADE, barrel of six score herrings

CADWALLADER, last British king, killed A.D. 635

CAELUM, Lat. sky

CAGE OF RUSHES, a 'cage' was a lock-up for petty male-factors, a cage of rushes would be a flimsy prison

CAITIFF, basely wretched

CAKE OF ROSES, or rose-cake, preparation of rose petals in the form of a cake and used as perfume

CALENDAR, register

CALF, dolt, ass

CALIVER, light musket

CALLET, a scold

CAMBRIA, Wales

CAMBYSES, son of Cyrus, King of Persia

CAMOMILE, creeping plant often covering paths of Elizabethan gardens

CANARY, (sb) (i) lively Spanish dance; (ii) sweet wine from the Canaries; (vb) to move the feet as in the canary

CANDIDATUS, candidate for office in Rome, lit. one clothed in white

CANDIED, frozen

CANDLE-CASE, receptacle for candle ends

CANDLE-HOLDER, an attendant who lighted others in a ceremony at night

CANDLE-MINE, tallow magazine

CANDLE-WASTER, book-worm, who burns the midnight oil

CANKER, the dog-rose

CANKER-BLOSSOM, a worm that cankers a blossom

CANKERED, (i) of weapons, rusted, corroded through disuse; (ii) of persons, malignant

CANTLE, segment of a sphere

CANTON, variant of 'canzon', a song

CANZONET, a short song

CAPABLE, (i) impressionable, intelligent; (ii) of marriageable age

CAPARISON, lit. ornamental trappings of a horse, hence outfit

CAPER, lit. a goat's leap, as a dancing movement it consisted of beating the feet in the air

CAPILET, a name for a horse

CAPITOL, temple of Jupiter on Capitoline Hill

CAPOCCHIA, It. simpleton

CAPON, (i) lit. a castrated cock, often signified a dull fool; (ii) a billet-doux

CAPRICCIO, It. caprice

CAPTIOUS, (i) fallacious, deceptive; (ii) receptive

CARACT, or 'charact', a mark, sign or symbol

CARBONADOED, stashed or stored, like a piece of meat for broiling

CARBUNCLE, red precious stone

CARCANET, 'ornamental collar or necklace, usually of gold or studded with jewels' (OED)

CARCASS OF A BUTT, a leaky old tub of a vessel

CARD OF TEN, card with ten pips

CARDECUE, Fr. 'quart d'écu', a silver coin worth about 7½p

CARD-MAKER, a card was an instrument with iron teeth for combing out wool fibres by hand

CARDUUS BENEDICTUS, the blessed thistle, a popular medicinal remedy of the time

CAREER, gallop or charge in the lists of a tournament; 'passed the —', ran away

CAREFUL, full of care

CARET, Lat. it is missing

CARL, churl

CAROL, orig. a ring dance with a song, hence any kind of song sung at festival times

CARP, (i) fresh-water, pond-bred fish; (ii) talkative person

CARPET, tapestry used for window-seats, bed-valances, etc.

CARPET-MONGER, CARPET-KNIGHT, contemptuous terms for one whose prowess belongs rather to the boudoir than the battle-field

CARRACK, galleon, lit. heavy-armed merchantman

CARRIAGE, (i) behaviour, line of action; (ii) demeanour

CARRION, putrefying, like a skeleton from which the flesh has rotted away

CARRY, (i) conquer, gain the prize; (ii) manage, carry out; '— coals', submit tamely to insult

CART, 'to cart with', bawds and harlots were punished by public exposure and whipping in a cart drawn through the streets

CARVE, (i) show great courtesy and affability; (ii) make advances by signalling in a peculiar way with the fingers—'a digitary ogle'

CASE, (sb) (i) cause, suit; (ii) condition; (iii) technical term for skin of fox or other vermin, mask; (vb) skin, strip (term in venery)

CASHIER, (i) discard; (ii) cheat, rob

CASSIBELAN, uncle of Cymbeline, the Latin Cassivelaunus, leader of resistance in Britain to Caesar's second invasion

CASSOCK, long loose cloak worn by musketeers and others in 16th and 17th cent.

CAST, (i) cast-off, discarded; (ii) put into a state or category of

CATAIAN, cheat, lit. an inhabitant of Cathay

CAT-A-MOUNTAIN, CAT O'MOUNTAIN, wild cat

CATAPLASM, plaster, poultice

CATASTROPHE, lit. the denouement of a play, hence a conclusion of any kind, the tail end

CATE, dainty, delicacy

CATER-COUSIN, 'scarce —', hardly on speaking terms

CATERPILLAR, rapacious person, extortioner

CATO, the elder, 234–149 B.C., famous after the 3rd Punic War for his 'delenda est Carthago'

CAUDLE, warm drink of thin gruel and wine, sweetened and spiced, for sick persons, especially women in childbirth

CAUSE, (i) 'first and second cause', reasons according to the laws of the duello for accepting or refusing a challenge; the laws of the duello in general; (ii) sickness, disease

CAUTEL, deceit, craft

CAVALERY, Cavaliero, form of address meaning 'gallant, gentleman'

CAVETO, Lat. caution (imp. of 'caveo', beware)

CENSER, a perforated fumigator

CENSORINUS, MARTIUS C., of the family of Coriolanus, but not his ancestor, censor c. 265 B.C.

CENSURE, judge, estimate (but not necessarily unfavourably)

CENTRE, lit. the centre of the earth, in Ptolemaic astronomy the centre of the universe, and so, figuratively, man's soul

CENTURY, a division of the Roman army, orig. a hundred men, commanded by a centurion

CERECLOTH, winding sheet

CESSE, archaic form of 'cease'

CHAFE, (i) irritate, vex; (ii) excite, heat

CHALLENGE, lay claim to, demand as a right

CHAM (the great), emperor of China (Cham:—Khan)

CHAMBERLAIN, male servant for bedchambers

CHAMPIAN, variant of 'champaign'

CHAMPION, (sb) one who fights for a cause in single combat; (vb) oppose in a 'wager of battle'

CHANCE, opportunity, possibility of good or bad fortune

CHANTRY, private chapel endowed for maintenance of one or more priests to sing daily mass for the souls of the departed

CHAPELESS, without the chape, the metal plate of the scabbard covering the point of the sword

CHAPMEN, merchants

CHARACTER, (sb) hidden meaning; (vb) engrave

CHARACTERY, symbolical writing

CHARGE, (sb) burden, load, hence importance, value; (ii) load, as the cannon with shot; load with arguments

CHARGEFUL, expensive

CHARINESS, scrupulous integrity

CHARLES' (orig. Charlemagne's) WAIN, the Great Bear constellation

CHARNECO, type of port wine named after village near Lisbon

CHASE, (sb) hunted animal, quarry; (vb) harass

CHEAPEN, make a bid for

CHEAT, (i) something stolen, theft; (ii) a thievish trick

CHEATER, escheator, an official of the Exchequer and because of opportunity for fraud, fig. a sharper

CHECK, a hawking term

CHEER, countenance, face; cheerly—blithely

CHEESE, the Welshman's love of cheese was a popular subject of jest at this time

CHEQUIN (It. zecchino), gold coin of Italy and Turkey worth about 35–50p

CHEERY-PIT, children's game of throwing cherry stones into a small pit or hole

CHEVERIL, lit. of kid leather, and therefore easily stretched, hence pliable, elastic

CHEWET, jackdaw, chatterbox

CHIDING, brawling or angry noise, esp. of hounds

CHILDE, title, in ballads and romances, of youth of noble birth, lit. one not yet knighted

CHILDING, breeding, fruitful, pregnant

CHIRRAH! Hail!

CHOICE, special value, estimation

CHOIR (vb), make music

CHOLLER, jowl

CHOPFT, chapped

CHOPINE, cork-soled shoe worn in Italy and Spain

CHORUS, Presenter or Prologue, to make plain the action

CHOUGH, jackdaw, chattern

CHISTENDOM, christian name

CHRISTOM CHILD, corr. of 'chrisom child', one who, dying within a month of birth, was buried in its chrisom cloth or christening robe

CHRYSOLITE, name of various golden-coloured gems

CHUCK, (i) familiar name of endearment applied to close relatives and dear friends; (ii) chicken

CICATRICE, lit. the scar of a wound, hence a scar-like mark

CIMMERIAN, 'black man', from Cimmerians in Homer, on whose land the sun never shone

CINQUE-PACE, a galliard of five steps

CIRCUMSTANCE, (i) evidence, argument; (ii) condition; (iii) circumlocution

CITE WITNESS, legal term, to call witnesses

CITTERN-HEAD, referring to the grotesquely carved head of the cittern, a common, wire-stringed instrument

CIVET, musk-smelling perfume, from the secretions of the civet cat, much used by gentry at that time

CIVIL, (i) grave, solemn; (ii) civilised, refined; (iii) becoming, seemly

CLACK-DISH, or clap-dish, lidded wooden dish, carried and clacked by beggars

CLAMMER, or clamber, tech. term of bell-ringing, to increase the strokes preparatory to stopping altogether, hence to stop from noise, to silence

CLAP, strike hands in token of a bargain

CLAP INTO, enter upon anything with alacrity and briskness, strike up

CLAP O' TH' SHOULDER, arrest

CLAPPER-CLAW (vb), maul, thrash

CLAP UP, fix up hastily, concoct hurriedly

CLAW, (vb) (i) scratch; (ii) tickle, fawn upon, flatter

CLEAN-TIMBERED, well built

CLEAR, (adj.) serene, innocent; (vb) purify, acquit, free from guilt

CLEAVE, (i) split or hit (the pin in the centre of the target); (ii) grasp

CLEFT, two-fold

CLEPE, call, name

CLERESTORY, orig. the upper part of the nave, with windows clear of the roof of the aisle, hence any large window high in the wall

CLERKLY, (i) like a scholar; (ii) smartly

CLEW, ball of thread or yarn

CLIMATE, (sb) clime, region; (vb) reside

CLINQUANT, glittering with gold or silver

CLIPT, (i) abbreviated; (ii) embraced

CLODPOLE, numskull, thickhead

CLOG, encumberance

CLOSE, (adj.) secluded, secret; (adv.) still!

CLOSE-STOOL, commode

CLOTHARIUS, prob. Clotaire, son of Clovis, early Merovingian king

CLOUD, (i) mask, veil; (ii) sully, defame

CLOUT, the mark in archery

CLUBS!, cry to summon aid to stop a brawl

CLYSTER-PIPE, tube for injecting an enema

COARSELY, meanly, slightingly

COCKATRICE, fabulous reptile, also called a basilisk, half-cock, half-serpent, supposed to be able to kill by its breath or look

COCKLE, darnel, tares

COCKLE-HAT, hat with cockle or scallop shell, as a sign of the wearer having been at the shrine of St James of Compostella in Spain

COCKNEY, spoilt child, pampered darling

COCK'S PASSION, corr. of oath 'God's Passion'

COCYTUS, one of the rivers of Hades

CODLING, immature or half-grown apple

CODPIECE, part of male hose or breeches made indelicately conspicuous in Shakespeare's time

CODS, (i) pods; (ii) testicles

COFFER, lit. strong box, hence a person's wealth

COG, cheat, at dice play

COGNIZANCE, term in heraldry for device or emblem worn by retainers, generally a distinctive badge

COIL, tumult, fuss, bother

COLDBRAND, a Danish giant defeated by Guy of Warwick

COLD, without power to move or influence (OED)

COLD SCENT, weak or faint scent in hunting

COLDLY, calmly, coolly

COLLIED, begrimed, murky

COLLOP, lit. a cut off the joint of meat, hence 'a chip off the old block'

COLLUSION, 'trick or ambiguity in words or reasoning' (OED)

COLOQUINTIDA, colocynth or bitter apple, which furnished an intensely bitter purgative

COLOSSUS, gigantic statue of Apollo which bestrode the harbour at Rhodes

COLOUR, pretext

COLOURING, (i) dyeing; (ii) giving a specious appearance

COLOURABLE COLOURS, plausible pretexts

COLOURS (fear no), fear no foe, have no fear

COLT, (i) a young horse; (ii) a lascivious male; (iii) a young or inexperienced person

COMBINATE, betrothed, affianced

COMBINED, tied, bound

COME AWAY, come here, come along

COME NEAR, begin to understand

COME OFF, pay up

COMEDIAN, stage player

COMES OFF WELL, turns out well

COME UPON, attack

COMFECT, 'Count Comfect', Count Sugar-plum

COMFORTABLE, of good comfort, cheerful, lending moral or spiritual support

COMFORTING, in legal sense abetting, countenancing

COMING-IN, (sb) allowance

COMMENDATIONS, rememberances

COMMODITY, (i) advantages, privileges; (ii) goods. The sale of commodities ('brown paper and old ginger', i.e. worthless rubbish) was a fictitious device adopted by usurers to circumvent the law and bleed their victims

COMMON ('make a common of'), make free of, take liberties with

COMMONER, prostitute

COMPACT, (sb) plot, conspiracy; (adj.) composed, made up of

COMPANION, fellow (contemptuous)

COMPASS, get possession of

COMPASSED, cut so as to fall in a circle

COMPETENT, legally admissible

COMPETITOR, partner, confederate

COMPLEMENT, formal civility; 'compliment' is a French word not anglicised before the end of the 17th cent.

COMPLETE, fully equipped, accomplished, consummate

COMPLEXION, (i) colour of skin, appearance; (ii) temperament, nature. Old medical theory said the complexion or composition of a man's body was made up of four humours or fluids, and if the proportion was disturbed disease would follow

COMPOSITION, the sum agreed upon

COMPROMISE, come to terms, settle differences

COMPT, reckoning

COMPTIBLE, lit. countable, liable to give account, and so liable to answer to, sensitive to

CON, commit to memory, learn one's part as actor

CON THANKS, offer thanks, acknowledge gratitude

CONCAVE, hollow

CONCEIT, (sb) (i) understanding, wit; (ii) imagination, fancy; (iii) ingenious or witty notion; (vb) form notions, entertain ideas

CONCEIVE, understand

CONCERN, engage the attention, affect with care, cause trouble

CONCOLINEL, meaning obscure, prob. title or opening word of a song

CONCUPY, concupiscence

CONDIGN, well-merited, worthy

CONDITION, character, characteristic; 'best conditioned':—best tempered

CONDOLE, grieve, lament

CONDUCT, (sb) (i) leadership, command; (ii) escort, safe conduct

CONDUIT, fountain

CONFEDERACY, conspiracy

CONFERENCE, conversation, talk (less formal and more general than its modern meaning)

CONFINES (sb) region, territory

CONFIRMED, unmoved, resolute

CONFOUND, ruin, destroy

CONFUTE, (i) render futile; (ii) silence in argument

CONGEE WITH, take leave of

CONGRUENT, fitting, agreeable

CONJECTURE, suspicion, evil surmise

CONJURER, lit. one who deals with devils or spirits

CONSIDER, remunerate, 'tip'

CONSISTORY, meeting of college of cardinals

CONSONANCY, consistency

CONSONANT, nonentity (a consonant being unable to stand alone like a vowel)

CONSORT, company, generally of musicians

CONSTABLE, LORD HIGH, principal officer in royal households of France and England

CONSTANT, resolute, self-possessed, (of a colour) uniform; 'constant question':—formally conducted discussion

CONSTELLATION, the configuration of 'stars' (planets) as supposed to have influence on men esp. at birth, hence disposition or character as determined by 'one's stars'

CONSTER, old form of 'construe'

CONSTRINGE, compress

CONTAGIOUS, catchy, catching (like a disease)

CONTAIN, retain, keep in one's possession or under one's control

CONTEMPTIBLE, scornful, contemptuous

CONTINENT, total sum; 'continents', the banks which should contain them

CONTINENT CANNON, variously explained as the law enjoining continence and the law contained in the edict

CONTINUE, contain, be continent

CONTINUER, horse with a good wind and staying power

CONTRIVE, spend or pass the time

CONTRIVER, schemer, plotter

CON TUTTO IL CUORE BEN TROVATO, with all my heart well met

CONVENTED, summoned

CONVERTITE, convert to a religious faith or way of life

CONVEYANCE, sleight of hand, dexterity

CONVEYED HIMSELF, passed himself off

CONVOY, means of transport, conveyance

CONY-CATCH (vb) cheat, swindle; cony (rabbit) was the dupe

COOLING CARD, 'apparently a term of some unknown game applied figuratively or punningly to anything that "cools" a person's passion or enthusiasm' (OED)

COPATAIN HAT, sugar-loaf hat

COPE, (i) strike, encounter; (ii) buy, barter, give in exchange for; (iii) debate with

COPHETUA, African king, known only in the ballad King Cophetua and the Beggarmaid

COPPER, ? false coin, perhaps referring to the newly introduced copper farthings

COPULATIVE, orig. a grammatical term, but also 'one about to be or desirous of being married'

COPY (of our conference), agenda, subject matter

CORAGIO!, Courage!

CORAM, quorum; Justices of Quorum or Coram sat on the bench at County Sessions

CORANTO, a lively dance

CORDELION, Coeur de Lion

CORDIAL, restoring, reviving

CORIN and Phillida, traditional names of lovers in pastoral poetry

CORINTH, Gr. town notorious in ancient times for its prostitutes; 'Corinthian', a gay dog

COMORANT, glutinous

CORNER-CAP, a symbol of authority to Elizabethans; three- or four-cornered cap worn by divines and members of the universities

CORNET, company of cavalry, from its standard, a horn-shaped pennon

CORNUTO, horned cuckold

COROLLARY, supernumerary

CORPORALL, champion. 'Corporal of the field' was 'a superior officer of the army in the 16th and 17th cent., who acted as assistant ... to the sergeant-major' (OED); there were four to each regiment

COST, extravagance, display

COSTARD, head (lit. a large apple)

COT-QUEAN, man who meddled with matters properly a house-wife's concern

COTSALL, the Cotswolds, a favourite resort for coursing matches

COUCH (lance), lower in order to attack

COUNSEL, resolution; 'in —', in private

COUNT OF, reckon with, attend to

COUNTENANCE, confidence of mien, hypocrisy, worldly credit

COUNTER, (sb) token coin used for arithmetical calculations; (adv.) opposite (to the trail taken by the game). The Counter was also a debtors' prison

COUNTERCHECK, rebuke or rebuff in retaliation

COUNTER-GATE, gate of the debtors' prison, notorious for its smell

COUNTERMAIDS (the passage of), forbids entry

COUNTERPOINT, counterpane

COUNTY, count, earl

COUPLE A GORGE, Fr. 'couper la gorge', cut the throat

COUPLEMENT, couple

COURSES, two small sails attached to the lower yards of a ship

COUSIN, any collateral relative more distant than brother or sister; 'cousin-german', first cousin

COUT, colt

COVENT, old form of 'Convent' (cf. Covent Garden)

COVER, (i) lay the cloth; (ii) cover the head

COVERED GOBLET, an empty goblet. Goblets were usually fitted with ornamental covers removed when in use

COVERT'ST, most secret

COWL-STAFF, stout pole passed through the handles of a cowl (lit. water-tub) so that it could be hoisted by two men

COX MY PASSION!, variant of 'Cock's passion' q.v.

COXCOMB, fool's cap

COY (vb), pat, caress

COYSTRILL, base fellow, originally a groom

COZ, cousin, used of any close relationship

COZEN, cheat; 'cozenage', fraud, imposture

COZIER, cobbler

CRAB, (i) crab apple; (ii) cross-grained

CRACK, (sb) (i) flaw, defect; (ii) pert boy; (vb) boast, make explosive sound

CRACK-HEMP, gallows bird

CRAMPS, rheumatic pains esp. of old people

CRANTS, garland, usually of white paper, hung in church on occasion of young girl's funeral

CRAVEN, a cock that 'cried creak' or acknowledged defeat

CRAZED, unsound, flawed

CREDIBLE, trustworthy

CREEK, winding narrow passage

CRESSET, iron basket on a pole, in which pitched rope, etc. was burnt for illumination

CREST, (i) helmet; (ii) ridge of neck of horse

CRISP, rippled; 'crisped', closely, stiffly curled

CRISPIN CRISPIAN, 25th October. SS Crispinus and Crispianus (brothers) were martyred at Soissons c. A.D. 287

CRITIC, fault-finder, jeerer

CRONE, withered old woman

CROSS, (i) thwart; (ii) sign with the cross in blessing; (iii) coin, with cross stamped on it

CROSS-GARTERED, wearing the garters above and below the knee so as to be crossed at the back

CROTCHET, (i) note in music; (ii) silly notion

CROW, 'pluck a crow together', proverb, to settle accounts, to pick a bone together

CROWFLOWER, buttercup

CROWN IMPERIAL, the cultivated fritillary

CROWNER, coroner

CROWNET, coronet

CRUPPER, leather strap which passes in a loop from the saddle round the horse's tail to keep the saddle from slipping

CRY, a pack of hounds

CRY AIM, applaud (archery term)

CRY OUT ON, denounce

CUCKOO-BUDS, unexplained; marsh marigold, buttercup and cowslip have all been suggested

CUCULLUS NON FACIT MONACHUM, a hood does not make a monk

CUE, v. part

CULL, choose, select

CULLION, base fellow, lit. testicle

CULVERIN, small cannon

CUM PRIVILEGIO AD IMPRIMENDUM SOLUM, with the privilege of sole printing

CURFEW BELL, orig. bell rung in evening to indicate 'domestic fires out' (Fr. 'couvre feu') but also a bell rung at three or four in the morning

CURIOUS, (i) particular; (ii) requiring care and attention

CURIOUS-KNOTTED, quaintly designed or laid out

CURSITORY, wandering, cursory

CURST, ill-tempered, shrewish, vicious

CURTAL, horse with its tail cut short

CURTAL-DOG, dog with a docked tail of no service in the chase

CURTLE-AXE, heavy sword for cutting or slashing

CURTSY, (i) bow (of any kind); (ii) a trifle

CURVET, manège term for a special type of horse leap

CUSHES, armour for the thighs

CUSTALORUM, a contraction of 'custos rotulorum', the keeper of the rolls

CUSTARD-COFFIN, custard pie

CUSTOM, trade

CUSTOMER, common woman, prostitute

CUT, lit. cart-horse, hence a term of abuse

CUT AND LONG TAIL, horses or dogs of all sorts

CUTS, ornamental slashes in a garment

CYCLOPS, race of one-eyed giants in Homer

CYDNUS, river in Cilicia on which Anthony first saw Cleopatra

CYNTHIA, the moon personified as a goddess

CYPRESS, (i) cypress tree; (ii) piece of black lawn used as kerchief as sign of mourning

CYMBELINE, name only derived from Cimobellinus, king of most of Britain c. 12 B.C. to c. A.D. 43

CYTHEREA, Venus, the name derived from Cythera in Cypress, one of the chief places of her worship

DAEDALUS, v. Icarus

DALLY WITH, linger lovingly over

DAFF, put off, thrust aside

DAMASK, the colour of the damask-rose, i.e. blush-colour

DAMON, a faithful friend (referring to the classical story of Damon and Pythias)

DANCE BAREFOOT, the elder unmarried sister was supposed to dance bare-foot at the wedding of a younger, hence 'to remain unmarried'

DANCING-HORSE, a well-known performing horse

DAPHNE, a nymph, who, fleeing from Apollo's importunities, was changed into a laurel at her own wish

DARDAN, Trojan

DARKLING, in the dark

DARNEL, could be tares or the common poppy

DARRAIGN, dispose in battle array

DATCHET-MEAD, between Windsor Little Park and the Thames

DANGER (within his), in his power, at his mercy

DAUBERY, false show

DAY-BED, sofa, prob. introduced towards the end of the 16th cent. and regarded by old-fashioned folk as luxurious if not wicked

DAZZLING, becoming dim or dazzled

DEAD, DEADLY, pale, death-like, mortal

DEALER, 'plain dealer' is one devoid of wit or conceit

DEAR, grievous, dire, sore

DEAREST, best

DEATH'S FACE, a skull; 'death-tokens', plague spots

DEBATE, contention

DEBILE, weak

DEBONAIR, gentle, meek

DEBOSHED, old form of 'debauched'

DECEIVABLE, deceptive

DECK, pack of cards; 'above deck', above board; poop deck in the stern of a vessel

DECK (vb), adorn, as with jewels

DECLINE, incline

DEEP-VOW (Master), a lover

DEFAULT (in the), at a need

DEFEATURE, disfigurement

DEFY, reject, disdain, disown

DELIVER, declare, make known, discover

DELIVERANCE, manner of speech, speech

DEMI-CANON, large gun with 6½ inch bore

DENAY, variant of 'deny'

DENIER, very small French coin

DENUNCIATION, formal announcement

DEPART WITHAL, part with, surrender

DEPOSE, examine on oath

DERACINATE, root up

DERIVE, inherit, bring down upon

DESCANT, (sb) variations; (vb) (i) warble; (ii) comment at length

DESPITE ('in the despite of'), in contempt of

DESTINIES, the Fates, Clotho, Lachesis and Atropos, who spin and weave the thread of life

DETERMINATE, intended, determined upon

DETESTED, abjured, renounced by oath

DEUCALION, the Noah of classical mythology, son of Prometheus

DEUCE-ACE, low throw at dice, two and one

DEVICE, a play or masque written for private presentation, an invention, ingenuity

DEWLAP, pendulous fold of skin on throat

DEXTER, heraldic term, right

DEY, woman, dairy woman

DIAL, may refer to watch, pocket sun-dial or mariner's compass

DIANA, goddess of the moon and chastity

DIAPASON, a bass in direct concord in octaves with the air

DIBBLE, tool for making holes for planting seeds

DICK, fellow, a term of contempt

DICKON, familiar form of Dick, Richard

DICTYNNA, a recondite name for the moon

DIDO, queen of Carthage, who slew herself when deserted by Aeneas

DIET, (sb) board and lodging, regimen; (vb) pay off after a day's work

DIFACIANT LAUDIS SUMMA SIT ISTA TUAE! The gods grant this may be the height of thy glory

DIFFERENCE, 'alteration or addition to a coat of arms to distinguish a junior member or branch of a family' (NED)

DIFFUSED, generally interpreted as 'disorderly' but could mean 'dispersed'

DIGEST, assimilate, amalgamate

DIGNITY, (i) worth; (ii) grandeur

DIGRESS, transgress, deviate

DILATED, extended

DILDO, lit. the phallus, a word often found in ballad refrains

DILEMMA, alternative course of action, difficulty to be faced

DILUCULO SURGERE SALUBERRIMUM EST, to get up early at dawn is most healthy

DIMENSION, bodily parts, proportions

DIOMEDE, one of the Greek leaders at Troy, who with Odysseus entered the Trojan camp and stole the horses of the King of Thrace

DIRECTION-GIVER, one who directs the archer's aim

DIS, Pluto, god of the underworld

DISABLE, disparage, belittle

DISBENCH, cause to leave seat, usually of Inns of Court membership

DISCANDY, melt, liquify

DISCARD, dismiss, discharge

DISCASE, undress

DISCHARGE, (sb) performance, a theatrical term; (vb) to pay (a debt), get rid of

DISCIPLINE, instruction

DISCOMFORTABLE, destroying comfort or happiness

DISCONTENTING, displeasing

DISCOURSE, reason, thought

DISCOVER, reveal by drawing aside a curtain

DISCOVERY, (i) disclosure; (ii) exploration

DISCRETION, discrimination

DISGRACIOUS, displeasing, out of favour

DISHONEST, (i) discreditable; (ii) immodest, unchaste

DISLIKEN, disguise

DISME, dime, tenth part, tithe

DISMOUNT, remove something from that on which it is mounted, e.g. a cannon from its carriage or a gem from its setting

DISPARK, convert to other purposes land where game is preserved

DISPOSED, in a jocund mood, inclined to mirth

DISPUTABLE, disputatious

DISPUTE, reason about, discuss

DISSOLVE, (i) break faith or troth, discharge; (ii) melt

DISTANCE, v. fencing

DISTEMPER, render unhealthy

DISTEMPERATURE, climatic inclemency or unwholesomeness. The word 'temperature' at this time comprised all atmospheric conditions

DISTINCTLY, separately

DISTRACTED, torn asunder, divided

DITTY, 'the words of a song as distinguished from its music or tune' (NED)

DIVERTED BLOOD. Technical medical language: old doctors claimed to be able to 'divert' the course of the humours or the blood by medicinal means

DIVINITY, divination

DIZY, could be 'dicey', given to dice, but 'dizy' was a common form of 'dizzy', giddy or foolish

DOCTRINE, science, knowledge

DOG ('to be a dog at'), to be expert

DOG-APE, a dog-faced baboon

DOG-DAYS, hottest period of the year, 13th July to 15th August, when Sirius, the Dog-star, rises nearly at the same time as the sun

DOIT, small Dutch coin, half an English farthing

DOLE, portion sparingly doled out

DOLLAR, the German thaler

DOLPHIN, (i) the Dauphin; (ii) sea mammal

DOMINEER, swagger, feast uproariously

DOMINICAL, the red letter denoting Sundays in the old almanacs

DOTAGE, doting, infatuation

DOTER, fond lover

DOUBLET-AND-HOSE, the male attire of the time

DOUBLE-TONGUE (i) deceitful tongue; (ii) alluding to the leathern tongue on the inside of a mask, held in the mouth to keep it in place

DOUBTFUL, dreadful

DOUGH ('my cake is dough'), I have failed

DOWAGER, widow with a dowage or jointure charged upon an estate

DOWER, one who gives a dowry to a bride

DOWLAS, coarse linen

DOWLE, a filament of a feather

DOWSABEL, Eng. form of 'Dulcibella' 'applied generically to a sweetheart' (OED)

DOXY, a beggar's mistress

DRAB, harlot

DRACHMA, Gr. silver coin, worth about 3½p

DRAFF, hog's wash

DRAM, 1/16th oz avoir. 1/8th oz fluid, hence a very small quantity

DRAUGHT, cesspool, sewer

DRAW DRY-FOOT, track game by mere scent of the footprint

DRAWN IN, taken in, cheated

DRESSINGS, ceremonial attire

DRIBBLING DART, an arrow falling feebly and so unable to pierce a corselet

DRIFT, plot, intention

DRIVE, drift

DROLLERY, puppet-show, comic picture

DROP FORTH, bring forth

DROP-HEIR, an heir who is gradually pining away

DRUM, drummer

DRUM (John or Tom), 'Tom Drum's entertainment': —a rough reception; many references in Elizabethan literature, probably to a tale now lost

DRUMBLE, loiter, be sluggish

DRY, (i) dull, stupid; (ii) thirsty; (iii) mean; (iv) lacking in amorousness

DRY BASTE, DRY BEAT, beat severely

DRY BRAIN. In the physiology of the day a dry brain accompanied slowness of apprehension

DRY HAND, a sign of old age; a moist hand was a supposed sign of lasciviousness

DUCAT, Spanish gold coin

DUELLO, the art of duelling; its code and practice

DULL, blunt

DUMB-SHOW, silent performance of part of a play to explain briefly events between the acts and to foreshadow what is to follow

DUMP, plaintive melody or song

DURANCE, (i) imprisonment; (ii) a stout kind of cloth, probably buff q.v.

DUTCH DISH, the German (Dutch) fondness for greasy cooking was apparently known at that time

DUTY, curtsy, due, reward

EAGLE-SIGHTED, able to gaze upon the sun

EANLING, newly born lamb

EAR (vb), plough

EARNEST, money paid as an instalment

EARNEST-GAPING, eagerly gazing, longing intensely

ECHE (vb), add to, lengthen

EDWARD SHOVEL-BOARDS, old broad shillings of Edward VI, worn smooth by age and use, and so convenient for the game of shovel-board or shove-groat

EFFIGY, likeness, portrait

EFTEST, possibly a misprint for 'estest':—pleasantest

EGALL, equal

EGLANTINE, the sweet briar

EGRESS AND REGRESS, legal term meaning right of entry esp. into harbours and waterways

EIGHT AND SIX, alternate lines of eight and six syllables, a common ballad metre

EISEL, vinegar

ELD, antiquity, old age

ELDER-GUN, popgun

ELEMENT (i) sky, firmament; (ii) sphere of life or comprehension.

ELEMENTS (the four), air, earth, fire and water, out of which, according to the old philosophy, everything, including man, was composed

ELEVEN AND TWENTY LONG, just the right length

ELL, 1¼ yards

ELVISH-MARKED, marked by malign fairies at birth

ELYSIUM, place of abode after death of those favoured by the gods

EMBLAZE, proclaim as a heraldic device

EMBOSS, drive a hunted animal to extremity; -ed, (i) swollen, tumid; (ii) played out, dead beat

EMBOWEL, disembowel

EMPALE, hem in

EMPERY, absolute dominion, territory under an absolute ruler

EMPIRIC, quack

EMPLOYMENT, business

EMULATION, ambition, jealous rivalry

ENCELADUS, one of the Titans who warred against the Olympian gods

ENCHANTINGLY, as under the influence of a charm

ENCOUNTER, external behaviour

ENDING ANTHEM, requiem

ENDS (old), tags, quotations

ENEW, lit. 'in eau', drive the quarry into covert or water

ENFORCED, violated

ENGAGE, pledge

ENGLUTTED, swallowed up

ENGROSS, buy up wholesale, monopolise.

ENJOINED (penitents), persons upon whom penance has been imposed by their spiritual adviser

ENRAGED, mad

ENSCONCE, conceal. lit. shelter within a fortification

ENTER, entry, theatrical term

ENTERTAIN, (i) engage in battle; (ii) treat, take into one's service

ENTERTAINMENT, reception, service

ENTRANCE, entrance fee

ENVIOUS, spiteful, hateful

EPHESIAN, boon companion

EPICURISM, 'conformity to the supposed principles of Epicurus' (OED), hence sensuality or gluttony

EPITHETON, descriptive term, orig. form of 'epithet'

EQUINOCTIAL, prob. means the celestial equator

EQUIPAGE, usually camp-followers' pickings or stolen goods, but 'in equipage':— step by step, therefore in instalments

ERCLES, Hercules

EREBUS, the classical hell

EREWHILE, a little while back

ERINGOES, candied roots of sea-holly, considered provocative

ERNE, grieve

ESCAPES OF WIT. OED explains as 'sallies' but Shakespeare seems to mean the little falsehoods a witty person allows himself in conversation

ETHIOPEAN, could refer to 'Ethiop's martial', a metallic compound known to the old chemists

ESTATE, (vb) bestow as an estate upon; (sb) class, rank; 'on all estates', on all sorts of person

ESTEEM, (i) value of a property; (ii) reputation of a man

ET BONUM QUO ANTIQUIUS EO MELIUS, the more ancient a good thing is the better

EVEN, (adj.) plain, easy, impartial; (vb) accomplish, carry out; tally, balance

EVENTS ('to his events'), to the issue of his affair

EVERLASTING, 'material used in 16th and 17th cent. for the dress of sergeants and catchpoles, app. identical with durance' (OED)

EVITATE, avoid

EXAMINE, test, question closely

EXCEPT, (i) find fault with; (ii) leave out of account

EXCREMENT, any outgrowth of the body, e.g. hair

EXERCISE, (i) religious observance, sermon; (ii) (in pl.) athletic field sports, military exercises

EXHALE, draw forth

EXHIBITION, maintenance allowance

EXORCIST, strictly one who expels spirits, but commonly used at the time as one who conjures or summons up spirits

EXPEDIENT, expeditious, prompt

EXPLICATION, explanation

EXPRESSURE, expression

EXTEMPORAL, extempore, without thought or trouble

EXTENT, seizure of lands in execution of a writ, sequestration

EXTORT, torture

EXTRACT, distil, extract quintessence

EXTREME, hyperbole

EYAS-MUSKET, young male sparrow-hawk; the musket was the smallest of the breed but a good hawk

EYE, spot of colour; 'be in eye', be within range

EYE-GLASS, the crystalline lens of the eye

EYNE, old plural of 'eyes'

FABLE, falsehood

FACE, (i) trim with braid or other material; (ii) bully; 'face it with a card of two', put a bold face on it

FACILITY, fluency

FACING, (i) trimming; (ii) browbeating

FACINOROUS, infamous, abominably wicked

FACT, crime

FACTION, dissension, factious quarrel

FACTOR, commercial agent

FADGE, (i) fit, be suitable; (ii) turn out, succeed

FADING, 'the refrain of a popular song of indecent character' (OED)

FAIR, fine; 'fair-faced', a specious deceiver; 'Fair fall!', good luck to!

FAIRING, lit. a present bought at a fair, hence any complimentary gift

FAITOR, rogue

FALCHION, single-edged sword

FALCON, female hawk

FALL, (sb) decline, decadence; (vb) let fall

FALLOW, brownish-yellow

FALSE GALLOP, a canter

FALSELY, treacherously

FALSING, deceiving, defrauding

FAMILIAR, (i) familiar spirit; (ii) intimate friend

FANATICAL, frantic, extravagant

FANCY, (sb) (i) love, affectation; (ii) imagination, fantasy; (iii) inclination, baseless supposition; (vb) fall in love

FANCY-MONGER, one who deals in love

FANE, temple

FANG, (sb) grip; (vb) seize

FANTASY, extravagant fancy, imagination

FARBOROUGH, mispronunciation of 'Tharborough', third borough, a petty constable

FARCE (vb), stuff, cram full, metaphorically pad out with pompous phrases

FARDEL, bundle

FARM (vb), lease the right of taxing to the highest bidder for a fixed cash payment

FARRE, old comparative of 'fair'

FARTHINGALE, hooped skirt, extending behind but not in front of the body

FASHIONS, the farcy, or farcin, a horse disease resembling glanders

FAST AND LOOSE, old cheating game, esp. with gypsies

FAST MY WIFE, 'handfasting' or betrothal, which was considered valid without religious ceremony

FAT, (i) gross, nauseating; (ii) slow-witted, dull

FATED, fateful, controlling man's destiny

FATHER (vb), (i) beget; (ii) act like a father;

FAULT, check caused by failure of scent

FAUSTE, PRECOR, etc., 'I pray thee, Faustus ...', opening words of Mantuan's first eclogue

FAVOUR (sb), (i) leave, leniency; (ii) face, countenance; (iii) lit. good will, so something given or worn as mark of affection or goodwill

FEAR, (sb) doubt; (vb) frighten, be afraid of

FEATFULLY, gracefully

FEATURE, limb, shape, part of the body

FEDARY, accomplice, confederate

FEE'D, employed

FEEDER, shepherd, servant

FEEDING, lit. feeding ground for sheep, hence landed property

FEEL (his meaning), perceive, sense

FEELINGLY, to the purpose, exactly

FEE-SIMPLE, in absolute possession

FEEZE, lit. frighten off, hence to flog. Pot-house term often meaning 'settle the hash of'

FELL, (adj.) angry, cruel; (sb) hide of an animal with wool or hair

FENCING TERMS. Distance: regulation interval between fencers; foin, veney, stoccado (stock) and punto: different kinds of hit or thrust; reverse; punto reverso, or back-handed thrust; montant, or montanto: upright blow

FESTINATELY, quickly

FETCH IN, take in, cheat

FETCH OFF, do for, kill

FIA, mispronunciation of 'via' *q.v.*

FICO, Italian for fig

FIELD, (i) 'surface of an escutcheon' (OED); (ii) field of battle, battle

FIERCE, ardent, excessive

FIGHTS, canvas screens to conceal men on shipboard before going into action

FIGURES, (i) astrological figures; (ii) waxen figures for purposes of enchantment; (iii) phantasms

FILE, lit. 'row of persons' used by Shakespeare for any collection of individuals. (i) roll, list; (ii) rank, line of soldiers; (iii) file for letters

FILED, polished

FILL-HORSE, cart-horse; the 'fills' were the shafts

FIND, (i) find out; (ii) unmask

FINE, (adj.) subtle; (vb) (i) bring to an end; (ii) punish

FINE AND RECOVERY, a legal procedure by which entailed property might be converted into fee-simple

FINGER, play upon a stringed instrument

FIRE-DRAKE, man with a fiery nose

FIRE-NEW, brand new

FIREWORK, pyrotechnical display, very popular at this time

FIRST AND SECOND CAUSE, technical excuses to escape a duel

FISH-WHOLE, thoroughly sound and healthy

FISNAMY, old form of 'physiognomy', face

FISTULA, long sinuous pipe-like ulcer with a narrow orifice

FIT, (adj.) apt, to the point; (vb) supply

FITCHEW, polecat

FIVES, vives, or avives, a swelling of the parotid glands in horses

FIXTURE, poise, tread

FIXURE, stability

FLAMEN, ancient Roman priest, devoted to the service of a particular god

FLAP-DRAGON, a burning raisin or plum floating alight in liquor and swallowed by topers

FLASK, a soldier's powderhorn

FLAT-LONG, with the flat of the sword

FLATNESS, completeness

FLATTER UP, pamper, coddle

FLATTERY, charm, palliation

FLAUNTS, ostentatious finery

FLAW, (i) sudden squall of wind; (ii) flakes or sparks of fire

FLAX-WENCH, female flax worker, type of coarse woman

FLEDGE, obs. form of 'fledged'

FLEER, grin

FLEET, (sbs) prison of the Star Chamber and Chancery Courts; (vb) while away the time

FLESH, (i) sate, gratify; (ii) inure to bloodshed

FLEWS, the large chops of a deep-mouthed hound

FLIGHT, (i) carrying power; (ii) special light arrows for long distance target-shooting

FLORENTIUS, Sir Florent, character in Gower's *Confessio Amantis*

FLOTE, fleet, also interpreted as 'the sea'

FLOURISH, varnish, embellishment

FLOUT, jeer, mock

FLOW, melt, stream down

FLOWER-DE-LUCE, fleur de lys, iris

FLUX, (i) continuous stream; (ii) discharge from the body

FLYING AT THE BROOK, hawking for water-fowl

FOH, exclamation of disgust

FOIN, fencing term

FOISON, plenty

FOLLOW, attend upon, wait

FOND, eager, glad, foolish

FOOL, Shakespeare often uses 'fool' as a term of endearment

FOOTBOY, boy attendant

FOOTCLOTH, richly ornamented covering for a horse

FOOTING, (i) foothold; (ii) establishment

FOOTMAN, foot soldier

FOPPERY, dupery, deceit, folly

FOR THE LORD'S SAKE, the cry of prisoners, through the grate, beseeching passers-by to place alms or food in the basket hung outside the window, esp. associated with Ludgate gaol

FORCE, (i) enforce; (ii) attach importance to

FORCED, far-fetched, strained

FORDONE, tired out

FORE-PAST, already passed, previous

FORFEITS IN A BARBER'S SHOP, teeth, which after extraction were hung up on a lute string in the barber's shops of the day. Barbers were also dentists

FORFEITURE, penalty for non-payment on required date

FORGERY, invention (not in a bad sense)

FORKED HEADS. Arrows were of two sorts, one with the points looking backwards and called the broad-headed or swallow-tail, the other with the points stretching forward and called the fork-headed or barbed

FORM, (i) order, orderly performance; (ii) excellence, proficiency

FORMAL, (i) normal, sane; (ii) punctilious, ceremonious

FORSAKE, refuse, abandon

FORTED, fortified

FORTHRIGHTS AND MEANDERS, paths straight and winding

FORTUNA DE LA GUERRA, the fortune of war

FOUL, (i) ugly, unpleasant; (ii) dirty; (iii) evil, vile

FOUNDERED, gone lame

FRAME, the action of framing, creation

FRAMPOLD, crusty, disagreeable

FRANCISCO, a Frenchman

FRANK, liberal, generous, free

FRANKLIN, yeoman

FRAUGHT, FRAUGHTAGE, cargo

FREE, (i) untainted by disease, free from care; (ii) unattached to a lover; (iii) generous; (iv) innocent; (v) gracious, willing

FREESTONE-COLOURED, with the dirty white or grey colour of limestone

FRENCH CROWN, (i) the 'écu', a French gold coin; (ii) the baldness caused by the 'French disease', i.e. syphilis

FRESH, hungry or thirsty

FRESHES, FRESHETS, streams of fresh water

FRET, (i) chequer; (ii) wear, fray; (iii) of merchandise, to deteriorate through moth, decay, etc.

FRETS, rings of gut or bars of wood to regulate the fingering on a lute

FRIEND, (i) sweetheart; (ii) relative, ancestor

FRIENDSHIP, favour, friendly aid

FRIEZE, a coarse cloth with a nap

FRIPPERY, old clothes shop

FRONT, (i) forehead; (ii) opening period

FROTH AND LIME, give short measure by frothing the ale too much, and mitigating the sourness of ale or wine by doctoring with lime

FRUSH, smash, batter

FULSOME, rank

FUME, 'noxious vapour supposed formerly to rise to the brain from the stomach' chiefly as the result of intoxication (OED)

FURNISH, equip

FURNITURE, outfit, trappings

FURRED GOWN. Most contemporary descriptions of usurers refer to 'fox fur' and 'budge' (lambskin)

FURRED PACK, bundle, borne on pedlar's back and covered with skin with hair outward

FUSTIAN, coarse cloth of cotton or flax, hence worthless, rubbishy

GABERDINE, cloak, long coat, worn loose or girdled, with long sleeves

GAGE, pledge, bind with formal promise

GALEN, Claudius Galenus (A.D. 131–?200), celebrated Greek physician whose medical writings remained authoritative in Europe for more than a thousand years

GALL, (i) a raw or sore place; (ii) bile, bitterness of spirit

GALLIA, GALLIAN, France, French

GALLIARD, quick, lively dance in triple time

GALLIASS, heavy, low-built vessel, larger than a galley

GALLIMAUFRY, medley, promiscuity

GALLOWAY, nag, small Scottish horse

GALLOWGLASS, heavy-armed Irish foot-soldier

GALLOWS, gallows-bird, one fit for hanging

GAMESTER, (i) athlete, gambler, adventurer; (ii) merry frolicsome person; (iii) lewd person, male or female

GAMUT, the musical scale or its lowest note

GAPING PIG, pig's head, mouth open, prepared for the table

GARBOIL, disturbance, brawl

GARGANTUA, Rabelais' voracious giant, with a mouth so large he swallowed five pilgrims with their staves in a salad

GARNISH, outfit, garment

GARTER, Garter King at Arms, the chief herald

GASKINS, short for galligaskins, wide hose

GAUD, toy, trinket

GAUDY, festive

GEAR, (i) dress; (ii) purpose, business

GELDED, mutilated, depreciated in value (of landed property)

GEMINY, pair

GENERALLY, completely

GENERATION, offspring

GENEROUS, noble, highborn

GENIUS, tutelary spirit, guardian spirit

GENTILITY, politeness, good manners

GENTLE, lit. well-born, hence gracious, kind

GEORGE, jewel, on which is a figure of St George, pendant to a collar, which is part of the insignia of the Garter

GERMAN, closely akin

GERMAN CLOCK, 'one of elaborate construction, often containing automatic figures of persons or animals' (OED)

GEST, the stage of a royal progress or journey, hence the time allotted for such a stage or halt

GESTURE, bearing, manner

GIB, cat

GIDDILY, lightly, carelessly

GIG, a whipping top

GIGLOTS, a lewd woman

GILDED, flushed, made drunken

GILLYVOR, clove-scented pink

GILT, 'a gilt nutmeg', i.e. 'endored' or glazed with the yoke of an egg, used for spicing ale or wine, a common lover's gift at that time

GIMMALED, 'consisting of two similar parts hinged together' (OED)

GIMMOR, joint or hinge in clockwork

GING, old form of 'gang'

GIRD, biting remark

GIRDLE (turn his), so as to bring his dagger, generally worn behind the right hip, round to his right hand

GIVE, consider, set down as

GIVE AIM, act as direction giver, q.v.

GIVE HORNS, make a husband a cuckold

GLANCE, cast reflection on, allude to

GLANDERS, a contagious horse disease

GLASS, hourglass

GLEAN, glean corn, cut off stragglers in battle

GLIB, geld, castrate

GLIMPSE, flash, transient brightness

GLOZE, (sb) pretence, disguise; (vb) make glosses, comment

GNAT, an insignificant creature that flutters about a light

GO ABOUT TO, intend to

GO TO!, Come! Come!

GO TO THE WORLD, get married

GO UNDER, go under the name of, appear to be

GOD BUY YOU, the Elizabethan half-way house between 'God be with you' and the modern 'good-bye'

GOD-DIG-YOU-DEN, God give you good even

GOD 'ILD YOU, God yield you (when 'yield':—reward, repay)

GOD'S A GOOD MAN, proverb, 'the world is as God made it, and all is for the best'

GOD'S BLESSING ON YOUR BEARD!, may you have sense more fitting a grey beard!

GOGS-WOUNS, by God's wounds, a common oath

GOLDEN LETTER, v. dominical

GOLGOTHA, graveyard, charnel-house

GOOD, well to do

GOOD DEED, indeed, in sooth

GOOD EVEN AND TWENTY, good day and plenty of them, even being any time after noon

GOOD-DEN, God give you good even

GOOD-JER (or 'Good-year'), not explained, possibly 'What the good-year':—'What the devil'

GOOD WORD, kindness

GOODLY, gracious, benign

GOOSE, tailor's smoothing iron

GOOSE OF WINCHESTER, one affected by VD, known as Winchester goose. The Southwark stews were formerly under the control of the Bishop of Winchester

GORDIAN KNOT, tied by Gordian, king of Phrygia, cut by Alexander the Great

GORDOBUC, mythical British king, hero of Sackville and Norton's *Gordobuc*

GOSLING, greenhorn, inexperienced person

GOSSIP, lit. sponsor to a child, so friend (esp. female) invited to attend a birth or act as god-parent, hence 'talkative person'

GOTTEN IN DRINK, cowards were credited with this origin

GOT-'UDGE-ME, God judge me

GOURD AND FULLAM, species of false dice

GOVERN, GOVERNMENT, 'regulate an instrument by means of its stops'

GRACE, (i) sense of duty; (ii) grace of God, i.e. redemption; (iii) favour; (iv) that which wins favour, reputation; (v) that which adorns

GRAFF, archaic variant of graft

GRAIN (in grain), indelible, ineradicable, short for 'dyed in grain':—fast dyed

GRAINED, furrowed, lined

GRANGE, lonely country house

GRASS (long for grass), long for freedom

GRATED, worried, pestered

GRAVEL, story

GRAVEL-BLIND, a jocular link between 'sand-blind' (partially blind) and 'stone-blind'

GRAVELLED, perplexed, non-plussed

GRAYMALKIN, or Grimalkin (lit. little grey Mall or Mary), common name for a cat

GREASILY, indecently, smuttily

GREAT CHAMBER, large reception room, a new feature in wealthy houses of the time

GREEK (sb) (i) cunning or wily person, cheat, sharper; (ii) a merry fellow, buffoon

GREEN GOOSE, a young goose, lit. one hatched in the autumn, green-fed in spring and sold in May

GREEN SICKNESS, a type of anaemia affecting young women

GREEN-SLEEVES (the tune of), an amorous ballad tune, associated somehow with harlotry

GRIFFIN, fabulous monster with the head of an eagle and body of a lion

GRISE, a step

GRISLY, terrible to behold

GRIZZLE, a sprinkling of grey hairs

GROAT, fourpenny piece

GROSS, obvious, palpable; 'by gross', wholesale

GROUND, basis, fundamental principle; lowest note

GROUNDLING, spectator who paid a penny to stand on the floor of the playhouse, hence an uncritical or unrefined auditor

GROW, accrue

GROW TO A POINT, come to the point

GROW UPON, (i) increase, grow up, so as to become more troublesome; (ii) take liberties with, presume upon

GUARDS, (i) ornamental borders, trimming or facings; (ii) two stars of Lesser Bear constellation pointing to Pole Star

GUIDON, standard, used by generals or kings

GUILED, treacherous, endowed with guile

GULES, heraldic name for red

GULL, trick

GUNSTONE, cannon ball

GURNET, gurnard, marine fish

GUST, taste, catch the flavour of

GUY OF WARWICK, famed in romance as the slayer of the Danish giant, Colbrand

HA?, eh?

HACK, appears to mean 'take to the road as a high-wayman', or, of a female, 'to become a harlot', but NED gives 'to ride on the road, as distinguished from cross-country or military riding'

HACKNEY, (i) a horse kept for hire; (ii) a prostitute

HADE LAND, unploughed strip between two portions of field used as boundary or means of access

HAGGARD, hawk which has moulted at least once before being caught and is therefore much more difficult to train; a wild hawk

HALBERD, 15th and 16th cent. weapon, combination of spear and battleaxe

HALYCON, bird supposed by the ancients to charm the waves to a calm, while breeding in a nest floating on the sea about the time of the winter solstice; 'halcyon days' were fourteen days of calm at this season

HALF ('your half'), your wife

HALF-BLOODED, of good family by virtue of one parent only

HALF-CAN, larger than the 'pot', which it had put out of fashion among topers

HALF-CHECKED BIT, one with the bridle attached half way up the cheek, giving inadequate leverage

HALF-CHEEK, profile

HALFPENNY PURSE, minuted purse, halfpennies being tiny silver coins at that time

HAMMER OF (vb), deliberate earnestly, turn over in one's mind

HAND (vb), deal with, handle

HAND (at any), in any case

HAND-FAST, under arrest

HANDS (at two), at close quarters in conflict

HANDS (man of one's hands), man of vigour and courage

HANDY-DANDY, child's game where an object is passed from hand to hand behind one's back whilst another guesses as to which hand it is in

HANGMAN, fit for the hangman, rascal

HANNIBAL, blunder, common at the time, for 'cannibal'

HAPPILY, haply

HAPPY MAN BE HIS DOLE, prov.:—may his dole (i.e. lot) be that of a happy man

HARBINGER, orig. one who provides or procures lodgings, hence forerunner, esp. of royal household

HARD, with an uneasy pace

HARD-FAVOURED, ugly

HAREBELL, wild hyacinth

HARE-FINDER, one 'whose business is to find or espy a hare in form' before coursing (NED), hence a very mild sort of huntsman

HARLOT, orig. vagabond, rascal (of either sex), generally used in reference to fornication; (adj.), lewd

HATCH (sit down at the), keep silence

HATCHES, movable planks forming a deck

HAUD CREDO, Lat. I do not believe it

HAUNTED, frequented

HAUTBOY, oboe

HAVE WITH YOU!, Here's for you!

HAVE WITH YOU, let's go together

HAVING, property, possession

HAVIOUR, appearance

HAVOC, merciless slaughter; 'cry havoc':—cry 'no quarter'

HAWK, (i) mattock or pick-axe; (ii) falcon

HAWK FOR THE BUSH, short-winged hawk for quarry such as pheasant, rabbit, etc. in woodland country

HAWKING, keen as a hawk's

HAY, 'country dance having a winding or serpentine motion, or being of the nature of a reel' (OED)

HEADBOROUGH, 'parish officer identical in function with petty constable' (NED)

HEADED, come to a head, like a boil

HEADSTALL, part of the bridle which surrounds the horse's head

HEAR, do you hear?, listen

HEARKEN, lie in wait

HEARSED, coffined

HEART-BURNED, suffering from heart-burn

HEART OF ELDER, of pith, as contrasted with 'heart of oak'

HEAVENS (for the), in heaven's name

HEAVY, stupid with grief

HEBONA, an imaginary poison, associated with henbane

HIC ET UBIQUE, here and everywhere

HECATE (the triple), the goddess was Diana on earth, Phoebe in the heavens and Hecate in the underworld, guardian of all witches

HECTOR, Trojan hero of the Iliad, regarded by Elizabethans as the type of blustering braggart

HECUBA, Hector's mother, wife of Priam, king of Troy

HEDGE-PRIEST, unlearned priest in minor orders

HEED, that which one heeds or attends to

HEEL (on the), at the end

HEELS ('light o' love with your heels'), light-heeled, i.e. unchaste, loose

HEFT, heaving, retching

HELEN, (i) in classical mythology the most beautiful woman of her time, wife of Menelaus, carried off to Troy by Paris, whence arose the Trojan wars; (ii) St Helena, mother of Constantine, reputed to have discovered the true cross buried on Calvary, led there by a vision

HELL, a debtors' prison; the name was originally given to part of the law courts at Westminster, used as a prison for the King's debtors

HELLESPONT, the Dardanelles

HELP, cure

HEMPEN HOME-SPUN, 'home-spun cloth made of hemp, hence one clad in such cloth, one of rustic or coarse manners' (OED)

HEMPSEED, tiny boy destined for the gallows

HEN, a chicken-hearted person

HENCHMAN, 'a squire or page to a prince or great man, who walked or rode beside him' (OED)

HENT, take possession of

HERALDRY, rank, precedence

HERB OF GRACE, or herb-grace, the old name for rue

HERCULES, Lat. name for Greek mythological hero Heracles, famed for supernormal strength

HERMES, Mercury, who invented the pipe, and with it lulled to sleep Argus of the hundred eyes

HERO, in classical mythology, a priestess of Aphrodite at Sestos on the European side of the Hellespont, loved by Leander, who swam to her at night from Abydos on the opposite shore; when he was drowned she threw herself into the waters

HEROD OF JEWRY, a type of outrageous audacity

HEY-HO, 'utterance apparently of nautical origin and marking the rhythm of movement in heaving and hauling; often used in the burdens of songs, with various emotional expression according to the intonation' (NED)

HICK AND HACK, copulate

HID-FOX, the child who hides in the Elizabethan game of hide-and-seek

HIGH AND LOW, false dice, loaded so as to cast high and low numbers at will

HIGH-CROSS, the cross in the centre of the town

HIGH-DAY, old form of 'hey-day', holiday

HIGH-PROOF, capable of enduring the severest tests

HIGH STEWARD, LORD, official in charge of coronation ceremony or presiding at a peer's trial

HIGH-STOMACHED, haughty

HIGHT, is called

HILDING, jade, baggage, good-for-nothing

HIND, (i) stag; (ii) peasant; (iii) farm servant

HINT, occasion

HIP (to have upon), a wrestling metaphor

HIPPED, lame in the hip

HIREN, Irene, mistress of Sultan Mahomet II, and later beheaded by him

HOB, NOB, variant of 'hab, nab':—'have it, have it not', i.e. come what may

HOBBY-HORSE, (i) figure in a morris dance 'formed by a man inside a frame with the head and tail of a horse, and with trappings reaching to the ground and hiding the actor, who prance and cavorted about' (Sh. Eng.) 'The hobby-horse is forgot' is generally supposed to be a quotation from some ballad satirizing Puritan opposition to morris-dancing; (ii) a prostitute

HOBOY, oboe

HOBGOBLIN, 'Hob' was a variant of Robert or Robin, hence 'Hobgoblin' was equivalent to Robin Goodfellow

HODGE-PUDDING, a large sausage of boar's or hog's meat, still a dainty in the west of England

HOLD, OR CUT BOWSTRINGS, archer's expression, not yet satisfactorily explained; possibly 'come rain, hail or shine' or 'keep your promises or give up the play'

HOLD IT UP, HOLD OUT, keep it up, persist

HOLDING, consistency, coherence

HOLE MADE IN ONE'S COAT, proverbial, hole in one's reputation; 'find a hole', catch one out

HOLIDAME (by my), by my Holy Dame, i.e. Our Lady

HOLLAND, fine linen fabric, first made in Holland

HOLLOW ('thy bones are hollow'), a supposed result of venereal disease

HOLY BREAD, 'the (ordinary unleavened) bread blessed after the Eucharist, and distributed to those who had not communicated' (NED)

HOLY-ROOD DAY, 14th September

HOLY-THISTLE, v. Carduus Benedictus

HOME (adv.), completely, effectively, back again to its right place

HOMELY, rude, uncomely

HONEST, chaste

HONEYDEW, 'sweet sticky substance formed on stems of leaves and plants' (OED)

HONEY-STALKS, stalks of clover flowers

HONORIFICABILITUDINITATIBUS, a jest of the medieval schools, supposed to be the longest word known; the nominative is a real word meaning 'the state of being loaded with honours'

HOODMAN, the blind man in 'hoodman-blind' or 'blind-man's-buff'

HOODWINK, cover up, a hawking term

HOOKING, 'hookers' were a species of rogue who 'carried with them a staff of five or six feet long, in which ... a little hole ... an iron hook, and with the same they will pluck ... quickly anything' through windows left open at night

HOOP, shout with astonishment

HORN-BOOK, a spelling primer, 'framed in wood, and covered with a thin plate of transparent horn'

HORN-MAD, mad with rage like a bull

HORNPIPE, a wind instrument, said to have been so called from bell and mouthpiece being made of horn

HORSE (vb), set one thing upon another, suggesting a jogging motion, and perhaps also the sense of 'covering' (the mare by the stallion)

HOST (vb), lodge, put up

HOSTILIUS, legendary third king of Rome

HOT BACKS, HOT-BACKED, lustful

HOT-HOUSE, a bathing house with hot baths

HOUSE-KEEPING, hospitality

HOVEL-POST, post used in the making of a stack of corn

HOW?, Well, what about it?

HOW NOW, exclamation of surprise, greeting, or simulated anger

HOX, hamstring

HOY, small vessel for short coastal jorneys

HULL (vb), drift with sails furled

HUMBLE, kind, civil

HUMILITY, humanity

HUMOROUS, moody, fanciful

HUMOUR, (sb) disposition, inclination, caprice; (vb) adapt oneself

HUNDRED MERRY TALES, a coarse jest book published in 1526

HUNGARIAN, in reference to discarded and cashiered soldiers from Hungary

HUNTER, dog for hunting

HURLY, tumult

HURRICANO, waterspout

HURTLING, noise of an encounter, collision or battle

HUSBAND, (sb) housekeeper; (vb) manage economically

HUSBANDRY, administration of the household

HUSHT, variant of 'hush', 'whist', etc., not a word

HYBLA, town in Sicily, famous for its honey

HYDRA, mythical nine-headed beast, slain by Hercules

HYEN, hyena

HYMENAEUS, Hymen, god of marriage, hence the wedding ceremony

HYPERION, god of the sun, the sun

HYRCANIA, land south of Caspian Sea, proverbial for wildness and savagery; 'Hyrcanian beast', the tiger

HYSSOP, aromatic herb, formerly much used in medicine

ICARUS, Daedalus made wings for himself and his son, Icarus, to fly from the labyrinth of Crete. He escaped, but Icarus flew too high, the sun melted the wax in his wings and he fell to the sea

IDEA, mental image

IDES, 13th or 15th day of the month (15th in March) in the Roman calendar

IDLE, foolish, cracked, delirious

I'FECKS, in faith

IGNOMY, old form of 'ignominy'

ILL, (i) savage, (ii) miserable

ILL-FAVOUREDLY, in an ugly fashion

ILLUSTRATE, illustrious

IMAGE, representative

IMBRUE, lit. 'stain with blood', hence pierce so as to cause blood

IMITARI, Lat. to copy

IMMEDIATELY, exactly, precisely

IMMODEST, excessive, immoderate

IMP, (sb) lit. sapling, scion (without any connection with evil), hence, youngster; (vb) falconry term, to engraft feathers in the wing of a bird to restore or improve flight, hence, enlarge

IMPARTIAL, taking no part, indifferent

IMPATIENT, angry

IMPAWN, give as a hostage

IMPEACH, (sb) accusation, charge; (vb) discredit, cast imputation upon, call in question

IMPETTICOAT (vb), pocket, in reference to fool's long coat

IMPORTANCE, import

IMPORTANT, urgent, importunate, not to be withstood

IMPOSE, IMPOSITION, injunction

IMPOSTUME, abscess

IMPRESE, for It. 'impresa', heraldic device imposed on a shield, with an attached motto

IMPRESSURE, impression

IMPUGN, dispute validity of a statement or line of action

IN, involved

IN CAPITE, held directly from the Crown

INCARNADINE, lit. make the colour of flesh, turn blood-red

INCENSE, instigate

INCIDENCY, incident

INCISION, (i) blood-letting; (ii) engrafting

INCLINING, partiality, favouritism

INCONSIDERATE, thoughtless, brainless

INCONTINENT, (i) straightway; (ii) unchaste

INCONY, delicious, rare, pretty

INDIFFERENT, (adj.) (i) impartial; (ii) ordinary, usual, correct; (adv.) tolerably, fairly

INCREASE, crops, vegetable products

INDIRECT, wrong, unjust

INDUCEMENT, instigation, influence

INFAMONIZE, defame

INFLUENCE, i.e. of a star in the astrological sense

INFORMAL, foolish, crazy

INFUSED WITH, inspired with

INGENEROUS, dastardly

INHERIT, possess, own

INHIBITED, forbidden

INJURIOUS, insulting

INKLE, a kind of linen tape

INLAND, belonging to the districts near the capital as opposed to the remote wilder parts

INLY, intimate, heartfelt

INN (vb), gather in grain, Harvest

INNOCENT, imbecile

INQUISITIVE, seeking to know or to find

INSANIA, madness

INSCULPED, engraved

INSINUATE, ingratiate oneself with, wheedle, insert

INSISTURE, steady continuance

INSTALMENT, seat in which a Knight of the Garter was installed

INSTANCE, illustration, example, argument

INSULT, triumph in an insolent fashion

INTEEMABLE, incapable of being emptied, inexhaustible

INTELLIGENCING, playing the spy

INTELLIGISNE, DOMINE?, do you understand, sir?

INTEND, pretend, offer

INTENDMENT, intention, project

INTENT, destination

INTER'GATORY, legal expression:—a question formally put or to be put to an accused person or witness

INTERIM, something done during an interval, respite

INTERLUDE, short play, generally for performance in a great banqueting hall

INTERMISSION, rest during work

INTERPRET, expound the meaning of a puppet show

INTIMATION, generally glossed as 'suggestion', but probably means 'interruption'

INTOLERABLE, excessive

INVENTION, artistic or literary faculty

INVITIS NUBIBUS, despite the clouds

INWARD, secret, privy, intimate

IRIS, goddess who appeared as the rainbow, the rainbow

IRK, distress, pain

ISIS, Egyptian goddess representing the moon and the female productive forces of nature

ITHACA, Aegean island, home of Ulysses

IWIS, certainly

JACK, (i) knave; (ii) serving man; (iii) leather drinking vessel; (iv) Jack o' Lantern or Will o' the Wisp

JACK-A-LENT, dressed-up puppet for boys to throw at in Lent

JACK-AN-APES, lit. monkey, but also 'satyr', a kind of ape

JADE, (sb) vicious, or ill-conditioned mare or woman; (vb) fool, play tricks with

JANGLING, altercation, wrangling

JANUS, Roman god with two faces

JAR, tick of the clock

JAYS, symbolical of loose women

JEALOUSY, suspicion, anxiety

JENNET, small Spanish horse

JEPHTHAH, a Judge of Israel who sacrificed his daughter in fulfilment of a foolish vow

JERKS OF INVENTION, sallies of wit

JERUSALEM CHAMBER, at West front of Westminster Abbey, now used as Chapter House

JESSES, narrow strips of soft leather, silk or other material, fastened to the legs of a trained hawk and connected to the falconer's wrist

JEST, masque, pageant

JET, strut, like a turkey

JEW, probably a playful diminutive of 'juvenal'

JEW'S EYE, proverbial expression for something valued lightly

JIG, (sb) (i) rapid lively dance time; (ii) farce or entertainment of singing and dancing performed after a play

JILL, (i) servant maid; (ii) gill, metal drinking vessel holding ½ pint

JOAN, a generic term for a country witch

JOCKEY, familiar form of Jack, John

JOINED STOOL, JOINT-STOOL, wooden stool, fitted by a joiner as opposed to one of cruder make

JOLLITY, 'pleasure, enjoyment, esp. sexual' (OED)

JOLLY, arrogant, overbearing

JOWL (vb), to dash or knock (two heads) together

JUGGLER, deceiver, trickster

JUMP, agree, coincide, tally

JUNO, wife of Jupiter, queen of the gods

JUST, just so, exactly so, cf. 'quite' today

JUSTIFY, prove, confirm

JUVENAL, a young fellow, from 'juvenile'

KECKSY, hemlock or cow parsnip

KEECH, lump of animal fat

KEEL, to cool a hot or boiling liquid by adding something cold

KEEP, inhabit, keep to

KEEPER, guardian angel

KENDAL GREEN, coarse green cloth worn only by labourers

KENNEL, gutter, channel

KERN, Irish foot soldier

KERSEY, stout coarse English cloth

KIBE, ulcerated chilblain on the heel

KICKSHAW, (Fr. quelquechose), orig. a fancy dish in cookery, a 'something French', hence a trifle, a gewgaw

KICKY-WICKY, jocular or ludicrous term for a wife, which suggests a humerous formation after the pattern of 'kicksy-whinsy', a whim or erratic fancy

KILL, subdue

KILL-HOLE, or kiln-hole, a small building or hovel containing a surface for drying grain, etc. or making malt

KILL THE HEART, utterly discourage

KIND, (sb) (i) sex; (ii) nature, character; (adj.) natural

KINDLY (adj. and adv.), natural (as belonging to a father), fittingly, by all means

KINDLE, give birth to, esp. hares, rabbits

KINDNESS, natural instinct

KISSING-COMFITS, perfumed sugar-plums, used by women to sweeten the breath

KITCHENED, entertained in the kitchen

KITE, falcon

KNACK, (i) sweetmeat, pastry; (ii) trifle, trinket; (iii) deceitful or crafty contrivance

KNAP, bite with a crackling sound

KNOT, band, company

KNOT-GRASS, well known weed, 'polygonum aviculare', an infusion of which was supposed to stunt the growth

KNOWINGLY, with knowledge to justify one's opinion

LABEL, lit. to add to a document a 'label' or strip of parchment with supplementary matter, hence to add a codicil

LACEDAEMON, Sparta

LACED-MUTTON, cant term for a courtesan; 'laced' possibly refers to a slashed bodice, with a pun on 'lace':—to make incisions in the breast of a bird before cooking

LADY-SMOCK, generally interpreted as cuckoo-flower, which however, is pale lilac, not 'silver-white'; we suggest 'stitchwort', the whitest of all spring flowers

LADY WALLED ABOUT WITH DIAMONDS, piece of jewellery much affected at the time, in the form of brooch or pendant; the figure might be an allegorical nude or a portrait

LA FIN COURONNE LES OEUVRES, the end crowns the works

LAM-DAMN, thrash to death

LAMPASS, a disease in which the roof of the horse's mouth swells and prevents mastication

LAND-SERVICE, (i) military service; (ii) a meal

LANDS (narrow), possibly the strips into which the fields were divided under the old agricultural system

LANTHORN, (i) lighthouse, or windowed turret on the roof of a hall; (ii) a lantern

LAPLAND SORCERERS, Lapps and Finns were said to have a reputation for sorcery

LAPSE, (sb) fall, ruin; (vb) apprehend, arrest

LAPWING, peewit, plover

LARGE, broad, loose, liberal, copious

LAROON, thief

LATCH, moisten

LATTEN, tin

LAUGHTER, a sitting of eggs

LAUND, glade

LAUS DEO, BONE, INTELLIGO, God be praised, my good friend, understand

LAVOLT, lavolta, 'a lively dance for two, consisting a good deal in high and active bounds' (OED)

LAY, exorcise or calm (a disturbed spirit)

LEAD APES IN HELL, the fate of old maids, since they could not lead children into heaven

LEADEN SWORD, imitation sword, stage property

LEAGUER, camp

LEASING, lying

LEAVE, oart with, lose

LEAVE OFF, give up as incurable

LEAVENED AND PREPARED CHOICE, 'a choice not hasty but considerate'

LECTURE, lesson

LEDA'S DAUGHTER, Helen of Troy

LEER, (i) face, complexion; (ii) ogle

LEET, a court held by the Lord of the Manor

LEGE, DOMINE, Lat. read, sir

LEIGER, resident ambassador

LEMON STUCK WITH CLOVES, for spicing ale

LENTEN, meagre, feeble; 'Lenten pie', properly pie containing no meat, and so fit for consumption in Lent

L'ENVOY, short stanza at the end of a poem, often defining its points, e.g. as in the Sonnets

LET, permit to remain, leave behind

LET ME ALONE, rely on me to

LETHE, river of Hades; 'lethe'd', oblivious

LETTERS-PATENT, an open letter from a Sovereign conferring some right, privilege or title

LEVEL, LEVEL AT, aim, guess at

LEWD, vile, worthless

LIBBARD, properly a leopard, but 'libbard' and 'lion' were synonymous terms in respect of the royal coat of arms

LIBERAL, loose in talk, gross, too free

LIBERTY, unrestrained action, licence

LICENCE, liberty of action (not licentiousness)

LICHAS, servant of Hercules who unwittingly brought him the Nessus shirt

LICTOR, Roman functionary who walked before the magistrates carrying the fasces

LIE, lodge, sojourn

LIE BY, (i) dwell near; (ii) take a mistress

LIE DROWNING THE WASHING OF TEN TIDES, i.e. worse than the fate of captured pirates, who were fastened to the shore, near Wapping Old Stairs, at low water mark, until three tides has passed over them

LIEGER, resident ambassador

LIEU, 'in lieu of', as a payment for, in acknowledgement of

LIFE IS A SHUTTLE, cf. Job, vii, 6 'my days are swifter than a weaver's shuttle'

LIGHT, (i) wanton, loose; (ii) slightly built, active, nimble

LIGHT O' LOVE, the tune, but not the words, of this dance song has survived

LIKELY, comely

LIKENESS, seeming, hypocrisy

LIMBEC, alembic, distilling vessel

LIMBER, limp, flabby

LIMBO PATRUM, Lat. 'limbus patrum', the place between heaven and hell where the righteous who died before Christ waited

LIME, to catch with bird-lime (a glutinous substance smeared on twigs to take small birds)

LIMIT, allotted time, prescribed period

LINE, (i) delineate, sketch; (ii) line, as a dog a bitch; (iii) the equator

LING (old), salted ling, commonly eaten in Lent

LINK, torch, the material of burnt torches, used for blacking

LINSEY-WOOLSEY, lit. coarse material, part wool, part flax. Hence neither one thing or the other, a medley, nonsense

LINSTOCK, staff to hold the gunner's lighted match

LION THAT HOLDS HIS POLL-AXE, traditional representation of Alexander's arms

LIQUOR, grease, oil

LIST, LISTS, selvage of cloth, border-edge, hence limits, bounds

LITTLE (in), in miniature

LIVE (of a vessel in a storm), escape destruction, remain afloat

LIVELIHOOD, animation

LIVELY, lifelike

LIVER, formerly considered the seat of the passions

LIVERY, dress, distinctive garb worn by retainers of a great lord

LIVING (sb), property, landed estate

LOACH, small fresh water pike

LOB, clown, lout, lubber

LOCKRAM, loosely woven hempen fabric

LODE-STAR, the star which shows the 'lode' or way and upon which the sailor's gaze and hopes are fixed

LOFTY, sublime, (or possibly) haughty

LOGGATS, a game rather like ninepins

LONG OF, along of, owing to

LONG PURPLE, early purple orchis, *orchis mascula*

'LONGING, belonging

LONGLY, for a long while

LOOSE, (adj.) random, not serious; (sb) 'at his very loose':—at the very last moment; (vb) turn loose (for breeding)

LOOSE OF QUESTION (in the), in the freedom of conversation

LORD HAVE MERCY UPON US, slogan written on the door of a plague-ridden house

LORD'S TOKENS, marks or spots which appeared on the patient at the last stage of the plague

LOSE, orig.:—to ruin, hence to ruin in estimation

LOSS, perdition, destruction

LOUD, windy, stormy

LOUSY, contemptible, of no importance

LOVE, appraise, set a value on

LOVE-IN-IDLENESS, (i) the heartsease, the pansy; (ii) love without serious intention

LOVE-SPRINGS, 'springs', the first tender shoots of a plant or tree

LOVES (of all), a phrase of strong entreaty

LOWER CHAIR. 'Every house had formerly ... what was called a 'low chair', designed for the ease of sick people, and, occasionally, occupied by lazy ones' (Steevens)

LOW-SPIRITED, base

LOZEL, or losel, good-for-nothing

LUBBER, over-grown, loutish fellow

LUCE, (i) pike (fresh-water); (ii) cod, hake (salt-water)

LUCIFER, properly the Morning Star, then the Devil

LUCINA, name given to Juno (she who brings light) as presiding over childbirth

LUD'S TOWN, London, from Lud, legendary British king and Cymbeline's grandfather in legends

LUGGAGE, military baggage, camp followers' pickings

LUMPISH, low-spirited

LUNES, tantrums, fits of lunacy

LUPERCAL, the Lupercalia, ancient fertility festival in honour of Pan

LURCH, pilfer

LURE, leather frame, decked with feathers and garnished with pieces of meat, which the falconer carried in his hand

LUSTY, gay, bright

LUTE, stringed instrument associated with love and serenades

LUXURY, lust, lasciviousness

LYM, bloodhound

MACE, spice consisting of the dried outer covering of the nutmeg

MACULATION, stain of impurity

MADONNA, mistress, my lady

MAGGOT-PIE, magpie

MAGNIFICENT, vainglorious, arrogant

MAGNIFICO, Venetian grandee

MAID, the young of skate or other fish

MAIL, wallet, budget

MAIL UP (a hawk), wrap her up in a cloth so that she cannot stir or struggle

MAIN-COURSE, mainsail

MAINTAIN, defend

MAKE (the door), shut, close, bar

MAKE (up), piece together, make good

MAKING, build, make, personal appearance

MALAPERT, impudent

MALIGNANCY, baleful or virulent character. The term is both medical and astrological

MALKIN, untidy female esp. servant, slut

MALLECHO, from Sp. 'malhecho', misdeed, iniquity

MALMSEY, a strong sweet wine

MALT-HORSE, a clumsy kind of horse used by malsters, a heavy stupid person

MALT-WORM, drunkard, lit. malt-weevil

MOMMET, doll, puppet; orig. 'mawmet' (Mahomet)

MAMMOCK, tear into fragments

MAN (a hawk), to accustom the bird to the presence of man, to tame

MANAGE, control, wield, a short gallop at full speed in a riding school

MANAKAN, or manikin, an artist's lay figure

MANDRAKE, poisonous plant, fabled to shriek when uprooted

MANKIND, infuriated, mad

MANNER (taken with the), more properly 'taken with the mainour', i.e. in the act

MANNERS, (i) polite behaviour; (ii) the older sense of moral character

MANTLE, of liquids, to become covered with a coating or scum

MANTUAN, i.e. Battista Spagnuoli of Mantua (d. 1576), whose *Ecologues* became a school text-book throughout Europe

MANUAL SEAL, authorised warrant

MANU CITA, with swift hand

MAP, epitome, embodiment

MARCH-CHICK, precocious youngster

MARGENT, margin of a page, the commentary or illuminated border in such a margin

MARK, (i) two nobles or about 65p, a sum of
money, not a coin; (ii) target, butt, anything at
which aim is taken; (iii) 'God bless the mark',
exclamatory phrase by way of apology for
some horrible, disgusting or profane mention

MARKET (ended the), an allusion to the proverb
'three women and a goose make a market'

MARL, clay

MARRY, orig. the name of the Virgin Mary, then
indeed, to be sure

MARRY TRAP, Dr Johnson interpreted it as 'an
exclamation of insult, when a man was caught
in his own stratagem'

MARS, Roman god of war

MARSHAL, officer in a palace or nobleman's house
charged with the arrangement of ceremonies and
presentation of guests

MARSHALSEA, debtors' prison in Southwark

MART, traffic

MARTLEMAS, referring to the slaughter of beasts, etc.
on St Martin's Day (11th November) for salting
and winter consumption

MARTLET, house-martin

MASQUING, stuff, cheap material fit only for masques
or amateur theatricals

MATCH (sb), bargain

MATED, amazed, confounded

MATERIAL, (i) stocked with notions; (ii) gross, carnal

MATTER, topics for discussion or conversation

MAUGRE, in spite of

MAUND, woven basket with handles

MAZES (in the green) labyrinths marked out on the
grass and kept fresh by the tread of boys' feet

MEACOCK, tame timid, milksop

MEALED, spotted stained, moled

MEAN, (adj.) moderate, mild; (sb) (i) tenor part;
(ii) opportunity; (iii) sum of money; (vb) (i) moan,
lament for the dead; (ii) lodge a formal complaint

MEASURE, a stately dance, moderation

MEASURABLE, meet, competent

MECHANICAL (sb), artisan, mechanic

MEDAL, metal disc, bearing a figure or inscription
and used as a charm or trinket

MEDDLE WITH, mingle with, engage in conflict

MEDEA, v. Absyrtus

MEDLAR, eaten when decayed to a soft pulpy state

MEET, keep an appointment; 'be meet with', be
quits with

MEHERCLE!, By Hercules!

MEINY, body of retainers

MEND, (i) make amends; (ii) improve, grow more
perfect

MENELAUS, Helen's husband, brother of Agamemnon

MERCATANTE, It. merchant

MERCURY, in Latin mythology the messenger of the
gods, whose feet were shod with winged sandals

MERE, complete, absolute; 'upon his mere request',
solely because he asked me

MERELY, as a matter of fact, nothing but

MERIT, (i) payment for service done; (ii) (theol.)
works

MEROPS' SON. Phaeton was the son of Phoebus and
Clymene, wife of Merops

MESS, lit. a party of four seated at the same table and
feeding from the same dish; dish

METE AT, aim at

METEOR, was any aerial phenomenon, e.g. the
aurora borealis

METHEGLINS, Welsh mead, spiced with honey

METHOD, conduct

METTLE, courage, disposition, vital energy

MEW, cage up, a falconry term. Lit. mew was the
cage where the hawk was kept during moulting
or mewing

MEWL, mew like a cat

MIDDLE EARTH (man of), mortal

MIGHT, 'takes it in might, not merit', values it for
the effort expended rather than the skill shown

MILL SIXPENCE, newly-introduced machine-made coin
with hard edges to replace the crudely hammered
coins

MILO, or Milon, famous athlete of Crotona of
6th cent. B.C., said to have carried a bull on his
shoulders

MIMIC, buffoon, burlesque player, contemptuous
term for actors in general

MINIME, by no means

MINIMUS, a creature of the smallest size

MINOS, mythical king of Crete, creator of the
labyrinth

MINOTAUR, monster, half man, half bull, kept in the
labyrinth of Minos

MINSTRELSY, domestic or court entertainers, not
necessarily musicians

MI PERDONATO, pardon me

MISANTHROPOS, Gr. man-hater

MISCARRY, come to harm

MISCONSTER, misjudge

MISPRISION, (i) misapprehension; (ii) mistake of
identity

MISPRIZE, despise, mistake, fail to appreciate

MISSGRAFFED, ill-grafted together, badly matched

MISSINGLY, with a sense of loss or distress

MISTAKEN, MISTOOK, taken to the wrong person,
miscarried

MISUSE, abuse, revile, misrepresent

MO, MOE, more in number

MOCKED, (i) deceived; (ii) ridiculed

MODEL, the technical term for an architect's or a
builder's plan

MODERN, commonplace, trite

MODESTY, self-restraint, moderation

MOIETY, share, portion; lit. half

MOME, blockhead, dolt

MOMENTANY, very common alternative to
'momentary' at this time

MONARCHO, a mad, but harmless Italian, suffering
from megalomania, who haunted Elizabeth's
court some time before 1580

MONGING, trafficking

MONMOUTH CAP, round, brimless, high-crowned hat
worn by sailors and soldiers

MONTANT, v. fencing

MONTH'S MIND, a strong inclination (orig. a mass
said a month after the death of a person)

MONUMENT, portent

MOONISH, changeable, fickle

MOONSHINE IN THE WATER, appearance without
reality, foolishness

MOPING, bewildered

MORAL, secret meaning

MORALISE, interpret, expound, esp. moral sentiments

MORISCO, Morris dancer

MORRIS DANCE, rustic dance, sometimes associated with May or Whitsun games, in which Robin Hood and Maid Marian figured

MORRIS-PIKE, a formidable kind of pike, said to be of Moorish origin

MORTAL, (i) subject to death; (ii) mortally foolish

MORTAL-BREATHING, i.e. like a mortal, breathing (and yet like a saint)

MORTIFIED, dead to the pressures of the world, a theological expression

MORTIFYING, death-causing. Sighs and groans were supposed to drain the blood

MORT O' TH' DEER, hunting call at the death of the deer

MOSE IN THE CHINE, suffer from glanders

MOTH, mote

MOTION, (i) puppet-show; 'this sensible warm motion', the body, conceived as a puppet; 'a motion generative', a puppet of the masculine gender; (ii) 'we in your motion turn, and you may move us' refers to the motions of the heavenly spheres in the old astronomy, i.e. woman is a planet, set in the sphere, man; (iii) inward prompting or impulse, emotion

MOTLEY. There were two sorts of fool: the motley fool and the fool in the yellow petticoat, the former being the superior intellectually, the latter being the 'natural' or idiot

MOUNTANTO, montanto, v. fencing

MOUNTEBANK (vb), win, like a quack at a fair, by tricking simpletons

MOUNTED, set up in position

MOUSE, a playful term of endearment

MUCH UPON THIS, 'TIS,:—That's about the size of it

MULMUTIUS, king of Britain, hero of a lost play of 1599

MUMBUDGET, probably derived from some children's game

MUMMY, (i) a pulpy substance or mass; (ii) a common drug, orig. made from Egyptian mummies

MURDERING PIECE, small cannon loaded with shrapnel

MURRION, a cattle disease, usu. spelt 'murrain'

MUSCADEL, sweet wine, commonly drunk by bridal party at conclusion of wedding

MUSE, marvel at

MUSSEL-SHELL, empty fool

MUTTON AND PORRIDGE, i.e. mutton-broth, with perhaps a side-glance at 'mutton' a loose woman

MUTTON ON FRIDAYS, 'mutton', a courtesan

MUTUAL, common to more than two

MYRMIDONS, Thessalian warriors brought to Troy by Achilles

MYSTERY, craft, trade

NAIL, (i) cloth measure of 2¼ in; (ii) 'blow one's nail', wait patiently while one has nothing to do, not 'warm one's hands' as generally interpreted

NAMELESS, inexpressible

NAPKIN, handkerchief

NARCISSUS, the youth who fell in love with his own reflection and killed himself in despair

NATIVE, nature

NATURAL, (i) idiot; (ii) not unnatural; 'natural philosopher', scientist, esp. physicist

NATURE, (i) natural affection between relatives; (ii) natural order of things; (iii) goddess, personifying the forces that create the phenomena of the material world; (iv) human nature, human race; (v) character, disposition; (vi) bodily constitution, vital functions

NAUGHT, (i) worthless, useless; (ii) 'be naught', keep quiet, make yourself scarce

NAUGHTY, wicked, worthless, good-for-naught

NAYWARD, denial

NAY-WORD, pass-word, watch-word, proverb

NEAF, fist

NEAPOLITAN BONEACHE,:—syphilis, supposed to have originated in Naples

NEAR-LEGGED BEFORE, standing with fore-legs close together and back legs wide apart

NEAT'S TONGUE, cured or dried ox-tongue

NEB, break

NEELE, needle

NEEZE, variant of sneeze

NEMEAN LION, fierce lion killed by Hercules

NEMESIS, 'goddess of retribution or vengeance, hence one who avenges or punishes' (OED)

NEPTUNE, god of the sea, hence the sea

NEREIDES, sea nymphs, daughters of Nereus

NERVES, sinews

NESSUS, the centaur whose poisoned shirt caused Hercules such agony

NESTOR, aged counsellor of the Greeks before Troy, hence the type of old age

NEW-FANGLED, carried away by novelty, giddy-pated

NEW MADE (man), man regenerate

NICE, modest, fastidious, refined

NICELY, ingeniously

NICK (out of all), beyond all computations

NICKNAME (vb) call by incorrect or improper name

NICK'S HIM LIKE A FOOL, 'Fools, undoubtedly, were shaved and nicked in a particular manner'

NIESS, or nyas, a young hawk in the aerie

NIGHT-CROW, 'bird supposed to croak or cry at night and to be of evil omen, probably an owl or night-jar' (OED)

NIGHT-GOWN, generally silk or satin faced with fur and fulfilling the purpose of a dressing-gown. Night-gowns proper were not introduced until mid-16th cent.

NIGHT-RULE, revels

NINE-MEN'S MORRIS, or Merels, a game for two players or parties, each of whom had the same number of pebbles, discs, pegs or pins. It was known as Nine Men's, Fivepenny or Three Men's Morris according to the number of men used. Not unlike hopscotch

NINE WORTHIES, traditionally Hector, Alexander, Julius Caesar, Joshua, David, Judas Maccabeus, Arthur, Charlemagne and Guy of Warwick or Godfrey of Bouillon. The list varies, but elsewhere Hercules and Pompey are not included

NINNY, 'pied ninny', referring to the jester's motley

NIOBE, in Greek mythology, the daughter of Tantalus who wept unceasingly for her children, slain by the gods, and was turned into a pillar of stone which continued to weep

NIT, lit. the egg of a louse, hence a very small insect or fly

NOBLE, a gold coin worth about 35p

NODDY, simpleton; (adj.) foolish

NOLL, noddle, head, jocular or contemptuous

NON-COME, taken by some as a nonsensical abbreviation of 'non compos', but perhaps intended as a substitute for 'non-plus'

NONSUIT, legal term, bring about the voluntary withdrawal of the plaintiff

NOOK-SHOTTEN, highly indented

NO POINT, a phrase from the French:—not at all

NORTH POLE, the pole star, symbol of constant determination

NOTE, (i) of music; (ii) stigma, mark of disgrace; 'out of my note', not in my list

NOTORIOUS, disgraceful, shameful

NO-VERBS, usually interpreted as 'words which do not exist', but possibly:—naywords, q.v.

NOVI HOMINEM TANQUAM TE, I know the man as well as I know you (from Lyly's *Grammar*)

NOVUM, a dice game, properly 'novem quinque', from its two main throws of nine and five

NUMA, legendary second king of Rome

NUMBERS RATIFIED, metrically correct verse

NUNNERY, a cant word for a house of ill fame

NURSE, housekeeper

NUTHOOK, catchpole, constable. 'Nutcrackers' was likewise a cant term for the pillory

NYM (vb), steal, filch

O, (plural Oes), a small circle or spot, spangle

O LORD, SIR, a common exclamation:—surely

OAK, oak leaves, actually the symbolic prize of a soldier, who had rescued another captured in battle, but also 'garland', an emblem of victory

OBLIGED FAITH, faith bound by contract

OBSCENELY, occasionally used deliberately as if connected with 'seen' and meaning 'openly, so as to be seen'

OBSEQUIOUS, zealous, dutiful

OBSERVANCE, respectful attention

OBSERVATION, observance

OBSTRUCTION, cessation of the vital functions, stoppage

OCCASION, events as they fall out, 'an opportunity of attacking, fault-finding, giving or taking offence' (OED)

ODDS, superiority, advantage

ODE, ditty, applied to lyrical verse in general at this time

OD'S LIFELINGS, perversion of oath 'God's life'

OD'S NOUNS, perversion of 'God's wounds'

OEILLADES, sheep's eyes, amorous glances

O'ER-LOOKED, i.e. with the evil eye

O'ERPARTED, having too difficult a part, or too many parts to play

O'ER-RAUGHT, over-reached, cheated

O'ERSHOT, wide of the mark

O'ERWEEN, to be arrogant or presumptuous

OFFENCE, displeasure, annoyance

OFFICER, sheriff's officer, catchpole

OLD, (i) coll.—plentiful, great; (ii) of long practice and experience, also (slang) clever, knowing; (iii) stale, worn out

OLIVER AND ROLAND, two chief knights of Charlemagne, commonly pitted against each other for martial exploits, hence the types of ideal knighthood

OLYMPUS, home of the gods in Greek mythology; type of high mountain

OMIT, disregard

OMNE BENE, Lat. all is well

ONCE, (i) ''tis once', once for all, in short; (ii) ever, at any time

OPEN, give tongue, like a hound

OPINION, self-conceit, reputation

OPPOSITE, (sb) opponent; (adj.) contradictory, obstructive, hostile

OPPUGNANCY, conflict

ORANGE-TAWNY, deep or dark yellow

ORBS UPON THE GREEN, fairy rings

ORCHARD, garden

ORDINARY, either 'commonplace', 'vulgar' or belonging to an ordinary (eating house)

ORGAN, feature, any part of the body

ORGULOUS, proud

ORIENT PEARL, a pearl from the Indian seas, more beautiful than those found in European mussels, hence a brilliant or precious pearl, esp. lustrous or shining

ORPHEUS, mythical lyre-player, son of the Muse, Calliope

ORTS, left-over scraps of food

OSIER, made of willow twigs

OSTENT, show, display

OTHERGATES, in other fashion

OTTOMITES, Ottoman Turks

OUNCE, lynx

OUPH, elf, lit. 'elf's child, changeling'

OUSEL, blackbird

OUT, out of pocket; 'out o' th' way', beside the point, gone astray

OUTSWEAR, footwear

OVERFLOWN, overwhelmed (as by a flood)

OVERPEER, tower over

OVER-SHOES, OVER-BOOTS, phrases expressing reckless continuance in a course already begun

OVER-TOPPING, v. trash

OVERTURE, declaration

OVERWATCH, sit up late at night

OVER-WEATHERED, worn by exposure to the weather

OWE (adj. and vb), own

OX, 'to make an ox of one', to make one out a fool

OYES, i.e. 'oyez', the crier's call

PACK, plot, conspiracy, gang of rascals; 'packed with', in conspiracy with

PADDOCK, toad

PAGEANT, movable scaffold on which open-air scenes were enacted or tableaux displayed in the miracle plays and civic shows

PAIN, (i) labour, toil, trouble; (ii) penalty

PAINFUL, pains-taking

PAINTED, feigning, specious, fictitious

PAINTED CLOTH, cloth or canvas, used as wall hangings or room partitions and painted in oil. The Worthies (q.v.) was a favourite subject

PAIR OF SHEARS, 'there went but a pair of shears between us', we are all of a piece

PAIR OF STAIRS, flight of stairs ('pair':—set)

PALABRAS, probably meaning 'pocas plabras' ('few words'), a Sp. phrase current at the time

PALFREY, saddle horse for ordinary riding

PALTER, play fast and loose

PANCAKE, fritter, flapjack

PANNONIANS, inhabitants of present-day Hungary

PANTALOON, orig. stock figure of It. comic stage, representing Venice; a dotard, old fool

PANTHEON, temple to all the gods, erected in Rome, 27 B.C.

PANTLER, servant in charge of the pantry

PARAGON (vb), compare as equals

PARCEL, (sb) constituent, part, lot, set; (vb) commercial term, enumerate by items

PARCEL-BAWD, partly a bawd (and partly a tapster)

PARIS-BALL, tennis ball

PARISH GARDEN, Paris Garden, a bear garden on Bankside, near the Globe Theatre

PARITOR, officer of the bishop's court who carries out citations

PARK, 'over park, over pale':—over enclosed private property, 'park' being an enclosure for game, and 'pale' any fenced piece of ground

PALMER, 'pilgrim returned from the Holy Land, in sign of which he carried a palm branch or leaf, often simply a pilgrim' (OED)

PARLE, negotiation or conference under truce

PARLOUS, syncopate form of 'perilous'

PART, (i) a player's 'part' comprised all his speeches written out on strips of paper. It included cues, the final words of speeches preceding his own and serving as signals to come in'; (ii) allotted portion, lot in life; (iii) wealth, rank; (iv) office duty, function

PART (vb), depart

PARTHIANS, warlike people to the S.E. of the Caspian Sea, famed for shooting arrows behind them when taking flight, hence Parthian shot

PART-COATED, in motley

PARTICULAR (sb), individual, personal concern

PARTISAN, (i) party adherent; (ii) long-shafted spear with broad head

PARTITION, (i) wall; (ii) section of learned book

PARTLET (Dame), used as the proper name of the hen in 'Reynard the Fox'

PASH, dial. word for 'head'

PASS, accomplish, execute, enact, settle (business)

PASS UPON, impose upon, make a fool of

PASSADO, from Sp. passada:—forward thrust with the sword, advancing the foot at the same time

PASSAGE, act, course, procedure

PASSANT, (i) excellently; (ii) heraldic term, of a beast, walking and looking to the dexter side with one forepaw raised

PASSES, tricks, devices

PASSION, (sb) bodily disorder, suffering, any powerful feeling either of mirth or sorrow; (vb) to be affected with deep feeling, grieve (obs)

PAT (adv.), just right

PATCH, fool, derived from fool's garb

PATEN, the small dish used with the chalice in the celebration of Holy Communion

PATENT, privilege

PATHETICAL, moving

PAUCA PALLABRIS (Palabras), PAUCA VERBA, few words, almost:—not a word

PAVED BED, probably refers to the method of burial in prison

PAVED FOUNTAIN, clear fountain with pebbly bottom

PAVILION, tent for a champion at a tournament

PAWN, stake, wager

PAX. For the kiss of peace given at mass in the early church there was substituted in the 13th cent. the practice of passing a tablet, called a 'pax', depicting the crucifixion, to the communicants to kiss

PAY, beat, punish, give an opponent his deserts; 'pay home', fully repay

PEACH, impeach, bring to trial

PEAKING, sneaking, prying

PEAL, a salvo of ordinance

PEARLS, cataracts

PEAT, spoiled child

PECK, a round vessel used as a peck measure

PEDANT, schoolmaster (without any necessary implication of contempt)

PEDASCULE, a word coined from 'pedant'

PEER, to be seen peeping through

PEEVISH, senseless, silly, morose

PEISE, the weights used in winding a clock

PELION, lofty range of mountains in Thessaly

PELL-MELL, lit. 'confusedly, without keeping ranks', and so headlong, recklessly

PELTING, paltry, petty

PENCIL, paint brush for a lady's toilet

PENELOPE, wife of Ulysses

PENNYWORTH, lit. a bargain; 'fit ... with a pennyworth', take revenge upon him

PENSIONERS, the gentlemen pensioners or royal bodyguard

PENTECOST, Whitsuntide

PEPIN (King), first of Carlovingian kings, father of Charlemagne, d. A.D. 768

PERDURABLY, everlastingly

PERDY, verily indeed (lit. by God par dieu)

PEREGRINATE, foreign fashioned. This 'singular and choice' epithet may be intended to suggest the astrological term 'peregrine' used of a planet out of its appropriate position in the Zodiac.

PERFECT, certain, assured

PERGE, Lat. proceed

PERIOD, goal

PERJURE, perjurer. Perjurers were punished at this time by being publicly exhibited with a paper on head or breast setting forth their guilt

PERPEND, ponder, consider, attend to

PERSPECTIVE, some kind of stereoscope

PERT, lively, sprightly

PETAR, petard, mortar, small engine of war to blow up walls, etc.

PETITION (that prays well for peace), the authorised form of grace concluded with 'God save our Queen and Realm and send us peace in Christ'

PETTITOES, trotters

PETRACH, 14th cent. It. poet who wrote famous love sonnets

PHAETHON, the type of youthful presumption. Son of Helios, drove the sun's chariot for a day but lost control and was struck down by a thunderbolt from Jupiter

PHANTASIME, fantastic being

PHARAMOND, semi-mythical Frankish ruler of the early 5th cent.

PHEAZAR, vizier

PHIBBUS, Phoebus, the sun god

PHILEMON. Ovid tells the story of Jupiter and Mercury visiting the old couple Baucis and Philemon in their cottage, the roof whereof was thatched

PHILIP AND JACOB, the festival of SS Philip and James, 1st May

PHILLIDA, v. Corin

PHILOMEL, Athenian maid, outraged by her brother-in-law, cut out her own tongue

PHILOMELE, classical for the nightingale

PHILOSOPHER, person learned in any science, including demonology. 'Philosopher's Stone', the goal of alchemy, which would turn all metals to gold and give immortality to those who drank it

PHOEBUS, the sun god in Greek mythology

PHOENIX, fabulous Arabian bird which was reborn out of its own ashes

PHRYGIAN, of Phrygia, the part of Asia Minor in which Troy was situated

PHRYGIAN TURK, v. Hungarian

PIA MATER, brain, lit. a membrane enclosing it

PICKED, fastidious

PICKT-HATCH, 'your manor of Pickthatch', a disreputable quarter of London

PIECE, work of art

PIECE UP, make up

PIKE, a detachable spike for thrusting at the enemy in the centre of the buckler

PILCH, outer garment of skin or leather

PILE, the downy nap on velvet or other fabrics (cf. three-pile); 'piled':—pilled or peeled, i.e. hairless, bald; 'piled for a French velvet' refers to the baldness consequent upon the 'French disease' (cf. French crown)

PILLICOCK, term of endearment for young boy

PIN, (sb) 'peg, nail or stud fixed in the centre of a target; (vb) 'pins the wenches on his sleeve', flaunts their dependence on him

PIN AND WEB, disease of the eye, probably characterised by a spot or excrescence like a pin's head and a film covering the general surface

PINCH, to reduce to straits (in argument), to put in a tight place

PINFOLD, pound for stray cattle

PINNACE, (i) light vessel, often in attendance on a larger one; (ii) go-between, bawd

PIONED AND TWILLED, 'pioned':—probably dug and sloped like a glacis, and 'twilled':—platted like a hurdle

PIONEER, soldier armed with spade or pick-axe to dig trenches, etc., the lowest of the camp

PIRE, peer, examine closely

PISSING-CONDUIT, popular name of a conduit or fountain at the west end of Cheapside

PITCH, lit. height, so excellence of any kind

PITCH A TOIL, set a snare

PITTANCE, scanty meal; orig. a sum of money left to a religious house to provide additional allowance of food, wine, etc. at a festival or anniversary

PLACE (sb), official position; 'place where':—fit place, right spot; 'take place', take effect, succeed, find acceptance

PLACES, texts, extracts, short passages from books, topics or subjects of discourse

PLACKET, petticoat, or a slit in the same

PLAIN-SONG. Term orig. applied to simple ecclesiastical chants, usually in a minor key. Apt to a metaphor drawn from the cuckoo's monotonous song in a minor third

PLANCHED, made of board or planks

PLANETARY, astrological notion, caused by the influence of a planet

PLANT, set up, furnish, esp. in connection with new colonies

PLANTAIN. The application of a plantain leaf as the popular remedy for bruises and wounds is constantly referred to in Elizabethan literature

PLANTATION, colonisation

PLASH, pool

PLAUSIVE, pleasing, gracious, popular

PLAY THE MEN, pipe all hands

PLEA, that which is claimed

PLEACHED, fenced, bordered, or over-arched with intertwisted boughs and twigs

PLEAD A NEW STATE, v. state

PLEASANT, jocular, facetious merry

PLEASE-MAN, ? officious parasite

PLUMMET, (i) a woollen fabric; (ii) plummet-line, for fathoming

PLUTO, god of Hades

PLUTUS, god of gold, and therefore of alchemists

POCKET UP, conceal (political slang)

POINT, (sb) (i) summit; (ii) matters in discussion; (iii) lace attaching hose to doublet; (iv) 'stand upon points', bother about trifles; 'point-devise' (adj.) extremely precise, perfectly correct; (vb) direct; 'point upon', astrological term, direct a malign influence on

POKING STICK, or putting stick, of iron, steel or brass, heated and used for starched ruffs

POLE, probably the long staff used by thieves on the Border

POLITIC, cunning, scheming, intrigue

POLL, the number of soldiers in the muster

POLL-CLIFT, pruned

POMANDER, scent ball hung about the neck

POMEWATER, large juicy kind of apple, popular in the 16th cent. but now forgotten

POMGARNET, pomegranate

POMPEY'S PORCH, portico of the theatre built by Pompey in 55 B.C.

POMPION, pumpkin, 'often applied in contempt to a big man' (OED)

PONTIC SEA, the Black Sea

POOR-JOHN, salted hake

POPERIN PEAR, variety of pear from Poperinghe in Flanders

POPINJAY, parrot, chattering overdressed coxcomb

PORPENTINE, porcupine

PORT, gate, grand or expensive style of living

POSITION, arrangement, disposition

POSSESSED, (i) informed, instructed; (ii) possessed by the devil

POSSET, 'drink composed of hot milk curdled with ale, wine, etc., formerly used as delicacy or remedy' (OED)

POST, (sb) stock, courier, messenger; (vb) ride as quickly as possible

POSY, a short motto, originally a line of verse inscribed on a knife as a heraldic motto

POTATOES, i.e. the 'batata' or sweet potato, considered provocative

POTTLE, two quarts

POUNCET-BOX, small perfume box with perforated lid

POWDERED, salted, pickled

PRACTICE, plot, conspiracy

PRAEMUNIRE, statute limiting the power of the Pope in England

PRAETOR, Roman magistrate, subordinate to consul, elected annually

PRAISE, appraise, i.e. sip; 'praise in departing', proverbial expression:—wait till the end before praising

PRANK, adorn, not in any disparaging sense

PRAT, PRATS, buttocks

PREACHMENT, 'obtrusive or wearisome discourse' (OED)

PREAMBULATE, go on before

PRECEPTIAL, composed of precepts

PRECINCT, a place under someone's control or rule

PRECISE, puritanical; 'precisian', puritan

PRE-CONTRACT, formal betrothal, which in Shakespeare's day was considered a legally valid marriage without religious ceremony (cf. Fast my wife)

PREDOMINATE. An astrological term: a predominant star was one in the ascendant, i.e. in that degree of the Zodiac which at any given moment is just rising above the horizon

PREFER, recommend, select for consideration

PREGNANT, resourceful, teeming with devices

PREMISES, stipulations

PREPARATIONS, accomplishments

PREPOSTEROUS, highly improper, perverse

PRESENT, represent; act or perform a part

PRESENTATION, semblance

PRESENTLY, at once, immediately

PRESS TO DEATH, reference to 'peine fort et dure', a torture laying heavy weights upon the victim's chest until he confessed

PRESS-MONEY, initial payment given to a man on his being 'pressed' into military service

PREST, ready

PRESTER JOHN. Fabulous Christian king of vast wealth and power who was supposed to live in Asia. In the 16th cent. the name was applied to the King of Abyssinia, whose title 'Prestigian' was easily deflected and altered to Prester John.

PRETENCE, intention, design

PRETTY AND, pretty (adv.), quite, very

PREVENT, forestall, anticipate

PREYFUL, killing much prey

PRIAPUS, classical god of fertility

PRICK, spot in the centre of the target, pin

PRICKET, a buck in its second year

PRIME, (i) springtime; (ii) the choisest quality of youth

PRIMERO, a popular card game

PRINCIPALITY, a spiritual being of high rank

PRISCIAN, late Latin grammarian fl. A.D. 525

PRIVATE (sb), privacy

PRIVILEGE, protection, lit. right of immunity

PRIZE, match contest; 'prizer', prize fighter

PRIZE (vb), reckon

PROCESS, story

PROCLAMATION, open declaration. 'Give him a better proclamation':—Show him to be a better man than you have declared

PRODITOR, traitor

PROFACE, formula of welcome in eating or drinking

PROFIT, progress in learning

PROGNE, sister of Philomel (q.v.) in revenge for whose violation she killed her son and fed her husband the flesh

PROLIXIOUS, superfluous, tedious

PROLONG, postpone

PROMETHEAN FIRE, fire of heaven, such as Prometheus stole (Greek mythology)

PROOF, trial, experiment; 'to the proof', so armed as to be invulnerable

PROPER, (i) own, peculiar to, belonging distinctively to; (ii) handsome, goodly

PROPERTY, (sb) particular quality; (vb) (i) make a tool of, use for one's own ends; (ii) take possession of; (iii) treat like a theatrical property

PROPONTIC SEA, Sea of Marmora

PROPOSE, converse, discuss, usually interpreted as 'purpose'

PROPORTION, (i) metrical form; (ii) portion, dowry

PROPRIETY, individuality, personal identity

PROTESTATION, solemn declaration

PROTEUS, the 'old man of the sea', who escaped by assuming a variety of shapes

PROUD, hot-blooded, lascivious, sensually excited

PRUNE, dress up, trim

PSALTERY, ancient and medieval stringed instrument

PUCELLE, maid; the French title adopted for Joan of Arc

PUDDINGS, guts of an animal, sausages and entrails stuffed with meat (cf. hodge-pudding)

PUKE, vomit

PUKE-STOCKINGS, cheap stockings of dyed cloth

PULPIT, platform, Rostra (erected for orations in the Roman Forum)

PUMPION, pumpkin

PUNK, harlot

PUNTO, v. fencing

PUNY, lit. junior, hence young and inexperienced

PUR, the name of the knave in the card game 'post and pair'

PURCHASE (after so many years'), the price of land reckoned in terms of its annual rent or return; 'purchased', acquired (legal term)

PURE (adv.), purely, entirely

PURGATION, (i) laxative; (ii) cleansing from guilt or suspicion

PURLIEU, a piece of land on the fringe of a forest

PURPLE-IN-GRAIN, fast-dyed purple or scarlet

PURSENT, present, represent

PUSH, pish!

PUSH-PIN, 'a child's game in which each player pushes or fillips his pin with the object of crossing that of another player' (OED)

PUT DOWN, (i) take down, snub, make a fool of; (ii) make incapable with drink; 'put off', baffle, repulse; 'put on', lay on (as a blow), pass off, force something upon one

PUTTER-OUT OF FIVE TO ONE, one who gambles on the risks of travel

PUTTING ON, incitement, pressing forward

PUTTOCK, kite, basest of hawk kind

PYRAMUS, lover of Thisbe

PYRRHUS, son of Achilles, instrumental in the capture of Troy

PYTHAGORAS, Greek philosopher who preached the doctrine of the transmigration of souls

QUAIL, slacken, become feeble
QUAINT, (i) ingenious, knowing; (ii) dainty
QUALIFIED, possessed of qualities
QUALIFY, abate, soften, moderate
QUALITY, (i) rank, business, social position; (ii) trait, human characteristic
QUALM, sudden feeling of faintness or sickness
QUANTITY, fragment
QUATCH-BUTTOCK, probably 'quatch':—quat, i.e. fat
QUEAN, hussy
QUEASY, squeamish
QUELL, destroy, kill
QUERN, hand-mill for grinding corn
QUESTANT, a Shakespearian coinage from 'quest' = (of hunting dogs) to search for game
QUESTION, discussion, debate, conversation; 'in question', of doubtful quality
QUEST, 'run with these false and most contrarious quests', a hunting metaphor, a quest being the cry of the hound upon the scent
QUICK, keen, vigorous (of the appetite)
QUICK RECREATION, lively sport
QUILL, pipe, reference to the shrill note of the wren
QUILLET, subtlety, verbal nicety
QUINTAIN, wooden figure at which to tilt
QUINTESSENCE, the 'fifth essence' of ancient and medieval philosophers supposed to be latent in all things, its extraction being one of the great objects of alchemy
QUIP, retort, sarcastic remark
QUIRK, quibbling argument, conceit, caprice. Orig. probably a 'sudden flourish or twist in writing or drawing'
QUIT, (i) absolve, acquit; (ii) pay one back; (iii) requite with reward
QUITTANCE, discharge from debt, receipt
QUOIT, tight-fitting cap
QUOTE, (i) refer to by citing page or chapter of book; (ii) observe, note; 'quoted', well-known, notorious
QUOTIDIAN, continuous fever or ague

RACE, herd, stud
RACK, strain, exaggerate, examine under torture, tear to pieces
RAG, worthless creature, a farthing
RAMPALLIAN, riotous strumpet
RAMPING, fierce, fr. heraldic term 'rampant'
RANGE, (i) fly wide — of a falcon; (ii) prove inconstant — of a woman
RANKLE, cause festering wound, breed corruption
RANKNESS, luxuriousness of growth
RAPIER, long, pointed sword for thrusting
RASCAL, RABBLE, often used collectively for the young inferior deer of a herd, but also in the sense of a deer who would neither fight nor run
RATE, (sb) style, mode of living; (vb) value
RATIONAL HIND, intelligent rustic
RATTLES, bladders with dried peas or beans inside
RAUGHT, reached
RAVIN DOWN, gulp down
RAWLY LEFT, unprovided for
RAYED, soiled, befouled
RAZE, erase, blot out; 'razure', obliteration
REASON, talk, hold conversation

REAVE, rob by force
REBATE, make dull, blunt
REBATO, stiff collar, in use c. 1590-1650
REBEL (vb), lust
RECEIVING, understanding, perception
RECHEAT, the sound for calling hounds together
RECKONING, keeping accounts
RECOLLECTED, lit. collected together, hence studied, far-fetched
RECOMFORTURE, consolation
RECORD, (sb) recollection; (vb) sing, warble
RECORDATION, reminder
RECORDER, vertical flute with whistle mouthpiece, its tone being soft and mournful
RECOUNTMENT, recital, relation
RECOVER, get hold of, obtain
RECREANT (sb and adj.), one who yields in combat, hence cowardly, craven
RECTOR, ruler, governor
RED DOMINICAL, v. Dominical
REDTIME TE CAPTUM QUAM QUEAS MINIMO, free yourself from captivity at the lowest ransom you may
RED-LATTICE, of the ale-house, red lattice windows being commonly found in ale-houses
RED-PLAGUE, bubonic plague
REECHY, smoky, dirty
REED-VOICE, a reedy or squeaking voice
REEK, rise like vapour; the word did not become offensive until the 19th cent.
REFELLED, repelled, refused to admit my plea
REGISTER, catalogue
REGREETS, salutations
REHEARSE, mention, formally recite
RELICS, mementoes, souvenirs, 'the sights'
RELISH, (sb) taste, trace, hint; (vb) make pleasant to the palate
REMAINDER, interest in an estate coming into effect on the death of the legatee
REMEMBRANCER, legal term, one employed to remember
REMONSTRANCE, usually explained as demonstration, manifestation
REMORSE, pity, compassion
REMOVE, departure from one place to another
RENDER, report, represent, describe
REPEAL, recall from exile
REPORT, legal term:—formal account of a case argued and determined in court
REPROVE, disprove
RERE-MOUSE, bat
RESERVE (vb), keep for oneself
RESIDENCE, continuance in a course of action
RESOLVE, set the mind at rest
RESPECT, reputation, regard; 'in my respect', as far as I am concerned; 'without respect', without reference to other things
RESPECTIVE, careful, regardful
RESPICE FINEM, a common jest, respect your end
REST (to set up one's), to be resolved, determined. Derived from primero, a card game, in which 'the rest' was the reserved stakes; originally meant to risk one's all, hence do one's utmost
RESTRAIN, forbid, prohibit, draw tight
RETENTION, medical term, the body's power to retain its proper contents, hence metaphorically stability or consistency

RETROGRADE (star), one apparently 'moving contrary to the order of the signs of the Zodiac or from East to West' (OED)

REVEL, take part in a noisy festivity, make one of a party of masquers

REVERBERATE (adj.), reverberating

REVERSE, *v.* fencing

REVERSION, 'the return of an estate to the donor or grantor or his heirs after the expiration of the grant' (OED); expectation

REVERTED, revolted

REVOLT, sudden revulsion of mind or feeling, generally in reference to passion

REVOLVE, consider

RHENISH, white Rhein wine such as hock or Moselle

RHEUM, catarrh; 'rheumatic diseases', diseases affecting the 'rheum' including catarrhs and colds of all kinds

RHODOPE, (Rhodopsis), Greek courtesan, reputed builder of the third pyramid

RIALTO, the Exchange in Venice

RIB, enclose

RID, destroy, discharge

RIDDLE-LIKE, mysteriously

RIGHT, straight; 'the right', the real, genuine

RIGOL, ring, circle

RINGLET, circular dance, fairy ring

RING-CARRIER, go-between

RINGWOOD, popular Elizabethan name for a hound

RIPE, ready, prepared

ROAD, roadstead

ROARERS, roisterers

RONYON, a term of abuse, scabby, mangy

ROOD, the Cross on which Christ was crucified

ROPE'S END, (i) commonly used as an instrument of punishment; (ii) a halter or hangman's noose

ROSCIUS, famous Roman comedian (d. 62 B.C.), supposed by Elizabethans to have been a tragic actor

ROSE, The Red Rose, the Duke of Buckingham's Manor, from 1561 became Merchant Taylor's School

ROSEMARY, used at both weddings and funerals as a symbol of remembrance

ROTE (by rote), from memory

ROTH, obs. spelling of 'ruth', calamity, grief

ROUGH, violent

ROUND (adj.), (i) spherical; (ii) severe, plain-spoken; 'roundly', outspokenly

ROUND, ROUNDEL, (i) simplest form of country dance in which the dancers from a circle; (ii) a roundabout course

ROYAL, coin worth about 50p

ROYNISH, scurvy, base

RUB, 'The Rub is any object or impediment which diverts the bowl from its course. It is a feature that lends itself to punning and metaphorical application (Sh. Eng.)

RUB THE ELBOW, to express pleasurable satisfaction

RUDDOCK, robin red-breast

RUDESBY, boisterous, unmannerly fellow

RUFF, or ruffle, 'the loose turned-over portion or flap of a top-boot' (OED)

RUIN, refuse, rubbish

RULE, conduct, behaviour

RUN, (i) flee in battle; (ii) make water

RUNAGATE, (i) deserter; (ii) runaway, vagabond

RUSSET, red, or sometimes grey

RUTH, pity

SACK, general name for white Spanish or Canary wines; 'burnt sack', a hot drink of sack and sugar

SACKBUT, brass trumpet, with slide like a trombone

SACKERSON, a famous bear at Paris Garden in Shakespeare's day

SADNESS, seriousness, soberness

SAFFRON, orange-red colouring matter used in confectionery, liqueurs, etc.

SAGGITARY, centaur

ST NICHOLAS, the patron saint of scholars

SALE-WORK, ready-made goods

SALT RHEUM, a running cold

SALVE, (i) ointment; (ii) salutation

SALVED, lit. anointed, hence palliated, softened

SANCTUARY, church or other sacred place where, by law, immunity from arrest was secured

SAND-BLIND, partially blind

SANDED, sandy-coloured

SATIS QUOD SUFFICIT, enough is as good as a feast

SATURN, planet and god, though of as cold, sluggish and gloomy

SAUCE THEM, make it hot for them

SAUCY, wanton, lascivious, presumptuous

SAVE YOUR REVERENCE, *v.* Sir Reverence

SAW, discourse

SAY, cloth resembling serge

SCAB, a scurvy fellow

SCALED, weighed in the balance, tested

SCALL, i.e. 'scald', scabby

SCAMBLING, roistering, contentious

SCAMELS, ? seamels, i.e. gulls

SCANDALLED, infamous

SCANT (vb), limit, restrict, cut short

SCAPE, escapade, breach of chastity

SCARFED, decked with streamers

SCATHE, harm

SCHOOL, university

SCHOOL OF NIGHT, if text not corrupt probably denotes a coterie of the day to which Raleigh, Harriot and Chapman belonged, dabbling in astronomy and unorthodox religious opinion

SCIATICA, supposedly a symptom of venereal disease

SCIENCE, profound knowledge

SCONCE, (i) a head; (ii) small fort; (iii) a protective screen

SCOPE, (i) room to move in; (ii) license; (iii) liberty

SCORE, (i) to keep count by notches or marks on stick or pot; (ii) obtain drink or goods on credit

SCOTCH JIG, lively round dance for a large number of people

SCOUT, lie in wait

SCRUBBED, undersized, insignificant

SCRUPLE, (i) apothecary's weight (20 grains), a minute portion; (ii) doubt, objection

SCUT, short tail of hare or deer

SEA-COAL, coal brought by sea from Newcastle, as opposed to charcoal

SEALED (in approbation), stamped with the official seal guaranteeing authenticity i.e. hall-marked

SEAL UP, make up one's mind

SEARCH, probe a wound, as with a surgeon's knife

SEASON, (i) mix something with food to make it more palatable, hence temper, alleviate; (ii) preserve by salting, embalm

SEASON (sb), occasion, opportunity; 'of the season', in the rutting season

SEA-WATER GREEN, colour associated with courtesy

SECRET, remedy or prescription known to doctors only

SECTARY ASTRONOMICAL, student of astronomy

SECTS, classes, ranks

SECURITY, legal security, e.g. signing a bond for a friend

SEEDNESS, the sowing of seed

SEEMING, hypocrisy

SEESE, Welsh pronunciation of 'cheese' *q.v.*

SEIZE UPON, take possession of

SEMBLATIVE, resembling, a Shakespearian coinage

SEMIRAMIS, mythical Assyrian queen, wife of Ninus, proverbial for her sexual licence

SENNET, trumpet or cornet fanfare for ceremonial entries and exits

SENSE, (i) desire; (ii) perception; (iii) reason; 'in all sense', on every account; 'sense of sense', the apprehension of the senses

SENSIBLY, with emotion

SENTENCES, saws, aphorisms, maxims

SENTENTIOUS, full of pithy sayings

SEQUESTERD, excommunicated, cut off from one's fellows

SERE, dry, dull, withered

SERGEANT, an officer whose duty it is to summon persons to appear before a court. 'Sergeant of the Band', is, strictly speaking, the commander of a company of soldiers

SERPIGO, general term for creeping or spreading skin disease

SERVANT, one devoted to the service of a lady, who was not pledged by accepting it

SERVE ONE'S TURN, (i) be of service to; (ii) satisfy sexually

SERVER, attendant at meal 'who superintended the arrangement of the table, seating and tasting and serving of the dishes' (OED)

SERVICE, (i) military service; (ii) food served up at table

SERVITOR, attendant

SESSA!, meaning doubtful, possibly an exclamation of encouragement, formerly a cry of triumph at a hit in fencing

SET (vb), set to music, put down; 'set against', oppose; 'set down', lay siege; 'set forth', (i) extol; (ii) carve up at table; 'set the world on wheels', let things go slide, enjoy oneself

SET (adj.), deliberate, not spontaneous

SETEBOS, mentioned in Eden's *History of Travel* (1577) as a deity or devil of the Patagonians

SHADOWED, shaded, umbrated (heraldic term)

SHAFT OR BOLT ON'T (make a), proverbial:—do one thing or another. A shaft was an arrow for the long-bow, a bolt a shorter one for the cross-bow; if the wood was too short for the one it would do for the other

SHAKE UP, rate soundly, abuse violently

SHARP, famished

SHEARMAN, one who cuts the superfluous nap in cloth-making

SHEEP-BITING, shifty, sneaking

SHEER-ALE, meaning doubtful, either thin or small ale, or undiluted ale

SHELVY, made of shelves or sandbanks

SHENT, rated, scolded

SHERIFF'S POST, Posts painted in two colours were formerly set up at the side of the door of a mayor, sheriff or other magistrate as a sign of office

SHIFT OUT OF, change out of (one suit of clothes for another)

SHIP-TIRE, head-dress, shaped like a ship, or having a ship-like ornament

SHOG, move off (slang)

SHOP, the organ of generation

SHORE, limit

SHORT KNIFE AND A THRONG, the cut-purse's requisites

SHOT, tavern reckoning

SHOTTEN (of a herring), one that has shed its roe, hence emaciated, good-for-nothing

SHOULDER-CLAPPER, an officer who arrests an offender

SHOULDER-SHOTTEN, with a dislocated shoulder

SHOVEL-BOARDS, *v.* Edward Shovel-boards

SHREWISHLY, sharply, ill-temperedly

SHREWD, (i) shrewish, sharp, keen-witted; (ii) mischievous, malicious; 'a shrewd turn', a nasty trick

SHRIEVE, old form of sheriff

SHRIFT, hearing of confession and giving of absolution thereafter

SHRINE, image of a saint or god

SHRIVE, 'shrive you a thousand idle pranks', I will call you to confession and make you tell your tricks; 'shriver', father confessor

SHROW, variant of shrew

SHUFFLE OFF, get rid of or evade something in a perfunctory manner

SHY, reserved

SYBIL, generic name of ancient Italian prophetesses, e.g. Sibylla, the Sybil of Cumae, to whom Apollo granted that her years should be as many of the grains in a handful of sand

SICILS, 'the Sicils', Naples and Sicily

SICLES, old form of shekels

SIDES, thighs, loins

SIEGE, seat, stool, excrement

SIGHT (in), conspicuously

SIGN, token, badge or device for identification

SIGNIFICANT, token

SIGNORY, domain, estate; 'signories', states of Northern Italy

SILLY, helpless, innocent

SIMPLE, poor, wretched, pitiful

SIMPLES, ingredients in medicine, not necessarily herbs, but later identified with that sense

SIMPLICITY, folly, silliness, harmlessness

SINCE, 'since night', a night ago

SINEWS, nerves

SINGLE, (i) poor, weak; (ii) unbroken

SINGLE BOND, meaning doubtful, either (i) an unconditional bond, or (ii) a bond without the names of the sureties attached

SINGLED, separated

SINISTER, (i) discourteous; (ii) heraldic term, left

SINK-A-PACE, or cinque -pace, a galliard of five steps

SINON, Greek warrior who induced the Trojans to allow into Troy the wooden horse

SIR, title prefixed to Christian names of persons, esp. priests or ministers, who had not graduated. The plural could be used of either sex

SIR REVERENCE, a corruption of 'save-reverence', an apology for mentioning an unpleasant fact; often used as euphemism for dung

SIRRAH, form of address to inferiors, esp. servants

SISTERING, neighbouring

SIT AT, live at

SKILL, knowledge, science

SKIN BETWEEN HIS BROWS. The phrase is always used with emphasising force after 'as honest as', 'as true as', etc. Possibly takes its origin from the practice of branding criminals between their brows

SKIPPER, light-brained, skipping fellow

SLEIDED, divided into filaments

SLICE, generally taken as referring to Banbury cheese (q.v.) but may be the hawking term for mute

'SLIGHT, an oath, God's light

SLIPS (in the), on the leash

SLIPS OF PROLIXITY, lapses into tediousness

SLOPS, wide, loose breeches, trunk hose

SLOW, heavy

SLUBBER, perform in a slovenly manner

SMACK, savour of, be strongly suggestive of

SMALL, the part of the leg below the calf

SMOCK, women's undergarment, shift, chemise

SMOKE, (sb), exhalation, so metaphorically verbiage, idle words; (vb) smell out, suspect

SMOTHER, the dense smoke of a flameless fire

SMUG, trim, neat

SNATCH, quibble, captious comment

SNEAPING, nipping

SNECK UP (or snick up), go and be hanged

SNIP, a snatch

SNIPT-TAFFETA, slashed silk

SNUFF (in), (i) in need of snuffing; (ii) in a rage; 'take in snuff', take offence

SOB, rest given to a horse to recover its wind

SOD, past part. of 'seethe' = boil to a decoction

SOFTLY-SPRIGHTED, a polite way of saying he was a coward

SO-HO, view halloo in hare-coursing

SOJOURN TO, travel to

SOLA!, hallo!

SOLACE, provide amusement

SOLEMN, ceremonial

SOLON, statesman of Athens (c. 640–558 B.C.), famous for his new constitution for Athens

SONNET, used loosely for any short poem of an amatory character

SONTIES, saints, dim. of 'sont', old form of 'saint'

SOON AT, betimes, near (of time)

SOPHISTER, cunning, cavilling disputer

SOPHY, Shah of Persia

SORE, severe, harsh

SORE, SOREL, bucks in respectively their fourth, third, year

SORT, (sb) (i) rank; (ii) set, crew; (iii) manner, method; 'in sort', in company, assembled together; (vb) (i) associate with; (ii) select; (iii) ordain, dispose

SOT, fool, drunkard

SOW, scatter, sprinkle

SPAN-COUNTER, a boys' game with counters or coins

SPAVIN, swelling of joint in horses

SPECIALTY, 'special contract, obligation or bond, expressed in an instrument under seal' (OED)

SPECTACLES, organs of vision

SPED, finished, done for

SPELL BACKWARD, misrepresent, distort

SPERR, fasten with bar or bolt, secure

SPHERE, one of the 'concentric transparent hollow globes imagined by the old astronomers as revolving round the earth and respectively carrying with them the several heavenly bodies' (OED)

SPIRITS, 'the nimble spirits in the arteries', v. arteries; 'faculties of perception' (OED)

SPITAL, lazar-house, a low class of hospital esp. for the leprous and the syphilitic

SPLAY, geld, castrate

SPLEEN, outburst, sudden access of passion, sport; the spleen was the seat of laughter as well as of anger

SPLIT (to make all), i.e. with agony or laughter

SPOILED, undone, ruined

SPOON-MEAT, lit. food prepared for infants, so dainties, delicacies

SPOTTED, wicked, morally stained

SPRAG, mispronunciation of 'sprack', brisk, alert

SPRIGHTFULLY, with great spirit

SPRING, beginning

SPRINGHALT, affection of hind legs of horse, causing muscles to contract spasmodically

SPRUCE, dandified, affected

SPUR, ask questions

SQUAND'RING, stray, straggling, lavishly distributed

SQUARE, (sb) (i) carpenter's set square; (ii) quarrel; (vb) frame or adjust something according to some standard or principle; also possibly 'strut, swagger'; 'squarer', a contentious or quarrelsome person

SQUASH, the unripe pod of a pea

STAFF, stave, verse, stanza

STAGGERS, a disease in horses accompanied by giddiness

STAIRS (keep below), remain a servant

STALE, (i) decoy, lure; (ii) dupe, laughing stock, lover or mistress whose devotion is turned into ridicule for the amusement of a rival; (iii) urine of cattle; (iv) harlot, common fellow

STALK, STALKING-HORSE, alludes to fowling with a stalking-horse, i.e. an old horse or ox, or an imitation of same, behind which the fowler lurks

STALL, keep, a metaphor from the stable

STALLION, ? dial. variant of 'staniel', a kestrel hawk, useless for falconry

STAND (a special), a sheltered position or covert for shooting at game

STAND TO, fall to; 'stand upon', concern

STANDARD, (i) standard-bearer; (ii) conduit

STANZE, STANZO, old and new forms of 'stanza'

STAPLE, the fibre of wool from which the yarn is spun

STAR-CHAMBER MATTER, the King's Council, sitting in the Star Chamber, exercised jurisdiction with regard to such offences as riots, slanders and libels, or even criticisms of magistrates. In 1590 a deer-stealing case was before it

STAR-CROSSED, thwarted by adverse influence of the planets

STARE, SWAGGER, behave in overbearing manner

STARKLY, stiffly, rigidly

STARRED, astrologically fated

STARS, a person's fortune or destiny viewed as determined by the stars

START, alarm, startle, swerve aside like a horse

STATE, (i) pose, deportment; (ii) dignity; (iii) property, estate; (iv) order, civil discipline; 'plead a new state', a term of rhetoric, with 'state':—the point in question or debate between contending parties

STATUTE-CAPS, prentice caps, woollen caps, decreed by the City of London to be worn by apprentices

STAY THANKSGIVING, wait for the grace at the end

STEAD UP, take another person's place

STEEP UP, precipitous, perpendicular

STEW, brothel; 'stewed prunes', a common term for prostitutes, from the 'stews'

STICK, fix, pin (like an ornament)

STICKLER-LIKE, like an umpire

STIGMATICAL, crooked, deformed

STILL, always, for ever

STILL SWINE EATS ALL THE DRAFF, prov.—the quiet sow eats all the hog's wash or refuse

STING, carnal impulse, sexual appetite

STOCCADO, v. fencing

STOCK, stocking, dowry

STOCK-FISH, dried cod, beaten before boiling

STOMACH, (i) courage; (ii) appetite

STOMACHER, ornamented chest garment worn by women

STONE-BOW, crossbow from which small stones or pellets were shot in fowling

STONES, testicles

STOOP, in falconry, fly to the lure

STOP, (i) obstruction, hindrance; (ii) pause, sudden check of a horse in the career; (iii) a fret on a lute; 'stopped', stuffed, deaf

STORY, dupe, laughing stock

STOUP, lit. a measure for liquor (2 quarts), hence a vessel for wine

STOVER, coarse grass

STRAIGHT, at once

STRAIN, (i) disposition, tendency; (ii) painful feeling

STRANGE, distant, unfriendly, severe

STRAPPADO, torture by disjointing the limbs

STRATAGEM, deed of violence

STRAY, cause to stray or wander

STREAK, smear

STRICTURE, strictness, severity of life

STRIFE, endeavour

STRIKE, astrological term; planets 'in opposition' were supposed to blast or strike objects beneath them. Cf. modern 'moon-struck'

STROSSERS, trousers

STUCK, (adj.) fastened; (sb) thrust, lunge, in fencing

STUDY, meditate, ponder

STYGIAN, of the Styx, the river of Hades across which the dead were ferried by Charon

SUBMISSION, confession

SUBORNATION, procuring or inciting one to crime

SUBSCRIBE FOR, undertake on behalf of

SUBSTANTIAL, 'your reason was not substantial why' i.e. your reason does not prove why

SUCCEEDING, consequences

SUCCESSION UPON, the line of heirs is never extinct

SUCK OUR BREATH, connected with old folk lore idea that the breath of man was his soul

SUDDENLY, immediately

SUE LIVERY, institute a suit for delivery or surrender of lands in the hands of the feudal suzerain until the heir could prove he was of age

SUFFERANCE, distress

SUFFICIENT, substantial, well-to-do

SUFFICIENCY, qualifications, ability

SUGGEST, prompt, tempt

SUIT, wooing, courtship; 'in all suits', in all respects; 'out of all suit', surpassingly; 'suited', (i) in accord; (ii) clothed in several suits

SUITOR, possibly:—shooter

SULLENS, morbid state of sullenness

SULPHUROUS, of lighting

SULTAN SOLYMAN, Solyman the Magnificent, Sultan of Turkey 1490–1566

SUN, 'get the sun of', get on the sunward side of an enemy so the sun shines in his eyes

SUN-BURNT. Elizabethan ladies were very careful to keep the sun from their complexions

SUN-EXPELLING MASK, much worn by ladies of quality when riding

SUP, provide supper for

SUPERSCRIPT, superscription, address

SUPPLANT, root out, pull out

SUPPLY, furnish with an occupant, fill

SUPPORTANCE, assistance; 'for the supportance of':— for the sake of

SUPPOSES, suppositions

SURECARD, winning card, hence a person bound to succeed

SUR-REINED, over-ridden, lit. over-reined

SUSTAINING GARMENTS, their clothes keep them afloat

SUTLER, one who sells supplies to the army, a camp-follower, not an officer

SUUM CUIQUE, to each his own

SWABBER, a sailor who had to see the ship was kept neat and clean

SWASHING, swaggering, dashing

SWAY, (i) control, in the astrological sense; (ii) determine opinion, influence judgement

SWAYED IN THE BACK, with a sunken back-bone

SWEAR OUT, forswear, abjure

SWEAT, 'a febrile disease characterised by profuse sweating, of which highly and rapidly fatal epidemics occurred in the 15th and 16th cents'

SWEET AND TWENTY, very sweet. The words 'and twenty' are used as an intensive

SWEET MOUTH, 'she has a sweet mouth', she is wanton, lecherous

SWINGE, (i) beat; (ii) have sexual intercourse

SWITZERS, Swiss mercenaries

SYLLA, Elizabethan spelling for L. Cornelius Sulla, Roman dictator

SYMPATHIZED, affected all alike

TABLE, (i) tablet for memoranda; (ii) in palmistry, the quadrangular space formed by the four principle lines on the palm of the hand; (iii) a board or flat surface on which a picture was painted, hence the picture itself; (iv) back-gammon board; 'table-book', note-book

TABOR, small drum, used generally with a pipe, traditional instruments of stage clown

TABOURINE, military drum

TACKLINGS, rigging

TAFFETA, thin silken stuff of lustrous appearance from which masks and vizards were made

TAILOR, the cry on a sudden fall backwards, with reference to the tailor's squatting position

TAKE, bewitch; 'take a button-hole lower', help undress, take down a peg; 'take off', relieve on of; 'take up', scold, reconcile

TALE, talk, remark

TALK APACE, chatter

TALENT, orig. a weight in Greece and Rome, then the value of this in gold or silver

TALL, sturdy

TALLENT, common 16th cent. form of 'talon'

TALLY, wooden stick marked with notches, to record a score, q.v.

TAMED, broached (like a flask)

TANG, clang, utter like a bell

TANTALUS, in Greek mythology, punished in Hades for his sin by having his thirst and hunger tormented by water receding when he is about to drink and fruit always eluding his grasp, hence tantalize

TARPEIAN ROCK, on the Capitoline Hill in Rome, from which traitors were hurled to their death

TARQUIN, Tarquinius Superbus, the younger of the two kings of this name, the violator of Lucrece in Shakespeare's poem

TARRE ON, incite

TARRIANCE, waiting

TARTAR-LIMBO, WORSE THAN HELL. Limbo:—hell, though also:—prison. 'Tartar' is a common abbreviation for Tartarus, hell

TASK (vb), impose a task upon, give a lesson to

TASTE, make trial of, hence (i) make use of; (ii) test

TAWDRY LACE, woman's silk lace or neck-tie, named after St Audrey (St Etheldreda)

TAWNY, dark-skinned, tanned

TAX, (sb) censure, blame; (vb) (i) task, make demands on; (ii) accuse; (iii) traduce, censure

TAXATION, satire, censure; lit. assessment of dues, hence imposition

TEAR A CAT, play the part of roistering hero

TEEN, sorrow, trouble

TELAMON, Ajax, son of Telamon, classical type of madman

TELL, count

TELLUS, the earth

TEMPER, concoct, compound, mix

TEMPERANCE, temperature. A puritan name

TEMPLE, not uncommonly used for church in 16th and 17th cents

TEMPORIZE WITH THE HOURS, put off the evil day

TEMPORARY, temporal

TENDER, have regard for, value

TENEMENT, land or real property held of another by any tenure

TENNIS BALLS, in Shakespeare's day made of white leather stuffed with hair

TENT, bed tester or canopy

TERCEL, male falcon

TERMAGENT, imaginary Muslim deity of turbulent character in the old morality plays

TERMINATIONS, definitions, expressions of opinion

TERMS, 'in terms of', in respect of

TESTER, sixpence; 'testerned', tipped with sixpence

TESTRIL, diminutive of 'tester'

TETTER, skin eruption

TEXT, to write in capitals, or in a text-hand, one of the more elaborate and formal scripts

THERSITES, scurrilous, deformed and ugly Greek warrior at the siege of Troy

THETIS, sea nymph, daughter of Nereus and mother of Achilles

THICK-PLEACHED, v. pleached

THIN-BELLY DOUBLET, doublet with unpadded lower part

THIRDBOROUGH, petty constable

THISBE, in classical mythology, maiden loved by Pyramus, a youth of Babylon

THISNE, or thissen, in this manner. Dialect word of north and midlands

THRASONICAL, boastful. Thraso is the braggart in Terence

THREE-PILE, the most expensive kind of velvet

THRIFT, (i) thriving, success; (ii) gain profit

THRILLING, piercing (with cold)

THROW, 'at this throw', on this occasion

THROW UPON, bestow

THRUM, tufted end of weaver's warp; 'thrummed hat', made of weavers' thrums, or possibly fringed with them to conceal the face

THUMP, imitation of the noise of a cannon

THUNDERSTONE, thunderbolt

TICKLE, (adj.) insecure, ticklish; (vb) (i) 'tickle' trout; (ii) flatter; (iii) ironical for punish or beat

TICK-TACK, a kind of backgammon

TIGHT, water-tight, sound; 'tightly', safely

TILLVALLY!, nonsense, fiddlesticks

TILTH, (i) tillage; (ii) fallow field

TIMBERED, v. clean-timbered

TIME, (i) favourable, propitious moment; (ii) with reference to the time of music; (iii) time of life, age; 'in good time', indeed!, forsooth!, well and good, just at the right moment; 'to the time', to eternity, for ever; 'timeless', untimely

TIME-PLEASER, time-server

TIMON, i.e. scorner of the world, esp. of women

TIPSTAFF, TIPSTAVES, officers whose staffs were tipped with silver and who took prisoners into custody; bailiffs

TIRED, (i) incorrigibly lazy; (ii) lit. 'attired', hence harnessed

TIRE ON, tear at, feed ravenously. Falconry term

TIRE-VALIANT, some kind of fanciful head-dress

TISICK, phthisic, consumptive

TITAN, Hyperion, the sun god, the sun

TITLE, what one is worth, lit. that to which one has a title

TOAZE, lit. count out (wool, etc.), hence elicit by close examination

TOIL, snare, net

TOLL, to get rid of, lit. to enter for sale on the toll book of a market

TONGS, rude musical instrument played with a key like the triangle

TOOTH, appetite

TOOTHPICKER. Tooth-picks, introduced from abroad, were much in request at the time

TOP, 'take the present time by the top', i.e. by the forelock

TOPGALLANT, platform for third section of mast above the deck

TOUCH, (i) sexual contact; (ii) hit or stroke in fencing; (iii) note, strain, lit. the fingering of a musical instrument; (iv) trait; (v) feeling, emotion of a subtle kind

TOUCH, TOUCHSTONE, hard basaltic stone upon which metal to be assayed was rubbed

TOUSE, tear

TOWER, falconry term to soar

TOY (sb), trifle

TRAIN, entice, lure

TRANSECT, prob. misprint of 'traject'

TRANSLATED, transformed

TRANSLATION OF, commentary upon

TRASH FOR OVER-TOPPING, a hunting phrase; 'trash':— check a hound by fastening a weight to its neck; 'over-topping':—out-stripping

TREATISE, story, discourse

TREBLE, make thrice as great

TREBLE HAUTBOY, smallest Elizabethan reed instrument

TRENCHER-KNIGHT, one who serves ladies at table

TRENCHER-MAN, glutton

TREY, throw of three at dice

TREY-TRIP, dice game probably depending on the throw of a three

TRIBUTARY, captive prince or chief who will pay tribute

TRICK, (i) device; (ii) particular habit, custom; (iii) characteristic expression of face or voice

TRICKSY, clever, full of devices

TRIFLE, trick of magic

TRIGON, astrological term: triple combination of hot and dry zodiacal signs, Aries, Leo and Saggitarius

TRIM, pretty, fine (generally ironical)

TRIP, trip in wrestling

TRIPLE, one of three, third

TRIPLEX, triple time in music

TRIUMPH, public festivity

TROLL-MY-DAMES, or Troll-madam, game for ladies, not unlike bagatelle

TROT, contemptuous epithet for an old woman

TROW, wonder

TROYAN, good fellow, boon companion

TRUCKLE-BED, small couch on castors

TRUE, honest

TRUNK SLEEVE, large wide sleeve

TRUST, conviction, belief

TRY WITH MAIN-COURSE, bring the ship close into the wind, with only the mainsail set

TUB. A reference to the treatment of venereal disease 'by a course of suffumigation with cinnabar in a meat-pickling vat' (Sh. Eng.)

TUCK, rapier

TUCKET, a flourish on a trumpet

TULLY, Cicero, Roman statesman and orator

TUMBLERS' HOOP, hoop garnished with ribbons, with which the tumbler did his tricks, and which he wore across his body

TUN-DISH, funnel

TUNE, humour, mood, temper

TUNEABLE, musical

TURK, (i) the Sultan of Turkey; (ii) the infidel

TURN, (i) be inconstant; (ii) shape or fashion a work of art, poem, tune or compliment

TURNED SPIT, the turn-spit was the lowest menial in the kitchen

TURN INTO, bring into

TURTLES, turtle-doves, proverbial for fidelity

TWICE-SOD SIMPLICITY, quintessence of stupidity

TWILLED, pioned

TWO AND THIRTY, A PIP OUT, not quite up to the mark. A jesting allusion, common at the time, to the card game 'one-and-thirty'

TWO OF THE FIRST, in heraldry, the first is the colour first mentioned in blazoning a coat of arms

TYPHON, mythical monster with tremendous voice, father of the Titans

TYRANNY, cruelty

UMBER, brown earth used as pigment

UNBANDED, without a hat band

UNBATED, unabated

UNBREATHED, unexercised; 'breathed':—in good wind

UNCASE, undress

UNCHARY (adv.), thriftlessly, carelessly

UNCIVIL, (i) disorderly, barbarous; (ii) impolite, discourteous

UNCONFIRMED, inexperienced

UNCOPE, unmuzzle

UNDERGO, take upon oneself

UNDERHAND, quiet, unobtrusive

UNDERTAKER, (i) one who takes up a challenge for another; (ii) contractor

UNDO, untie, release

UNEVEN, crooked

UNEXPRESSIVE, not to be expressed

UNFOLD, disclose, reveal

UNFOLDING STAR, the morning star

UNFURNISHED, unprovided with its fellow

UNGARTERED, the conventional sign of a love-lorn swain

UNHANDLED, not broken into

UNHATCHED, without dint or stain, i.e. never used in combat

UNKENNEL, unearth; kennel = fox's hole

UNMANNED, falconry term, unused to the presence of a man

UNPINKED. To pink leather was to ornament it by scalloping and punching out a pattern

UNPITIED, pitiless

UNPRIZABLE, of small account

UNQUESTIONABLE, taciturn, averse to conversation

UNRAKED, not banked up with ashes to keep the fire in all night

UNSEEMING, not seeming willingly

UNSHRUBBED, bare of bush or tree

UNSHUNNED, unshunnable, inevitable

UNSKILFULLY, without discernment

UNSTAUNCHED, not able to contain water

UNTAPIS, come out of cover or hiding

UNTOWARD, unmannerly

UNTREAD, retrace

UNTRUSSING, untying the points, unbuttoning

UNUM CITA, take one example

UNWEIGHING, thoughtless

UP AND DOWN, exactly, for all the world

UPSHOOT, archery term, the best shot up to any point in a contest

UPSHOT, the final shot in archery, and so the conclusion of the sport

UP-STARING, standing on end

UPSURPING, false

URCHINS, hedgehogs, or fiends in that form; 'urchin-shows', apparitions of urchins. The hedgehog was recognised as an emblem of the devil in Shakespeare's day

URINAL, physician's glass for testing the patient's water

URSA MAJOR, the Great Bear constellation

USE, interest, profit, benefit

USURP, ASSUME, supplant, misappropriate

UTIS (or utas), high jinks, lit. the octave of a festival

UTTER, (i) speak; (ii) offer for sale

UTTERANCE (to the), à l'outrance, to the last extremity

VAGRAM, a confusion of 'fragrant' and 'vagrant'

VAIL, (i) lower (nautical); (ii) do homage

VAILS, leavings of a feast

VAIN, false, silly

VALANCE, drapery hanging around frame of bedstead

VALENTINE, true-love token

VALIDITY, value, strength

VANTAGE, opportunity

VANTBRACE, defensive armour for forearm

VARA, (dial.) very

VARLETRY, mob, rabble

VARNISH, lend freshness to

VASSAL, abject creature

VAST OF NIGHT, the desolate hours of night when nature sleeps

VASTIDITY, immensity

VAWARD, vanward, forepart

VENDIBLE, 'a maid not vendible', an old maid past marriageable age, lit. past her market

VENETIA, VENETIA, CHI NON TI VEDE, NON TI PRETIA, a tag of Italian phrase found in several Elizabethan books:—Venice, Venice, who seeketh thee not, praiseth thee not

VENEW, VENEY, a thrust at fencing q.v.

VENGEANCE, mischief, harm

VENT (vb), lit. discharge, evacuate, hence utter; 'make vent of', talk of

VENTRICLE, of the brain, in medieval nomenclature the first and second were the seats of imagination and reason, and the third of memory

VENTURE, commercial speculation

VERDURE, freshness, vigour

VESTAL, priestess of Vesta in Rome, vowed to chastity

VEX, afflict, torment

VIA, adverb of encouragement, much used by commanders, and riders to their horses

VICE, comic character of the old moralities

VIDEO ET GAUDEO, I see and rejoice

VIDESNE QUIS VENIT, Do you see who comes

VIE, (i) to increase in number by addition or repetition; (ii) to hazard a sum at cards on the strength of one's hand

VILLAIN, slave, bondman, and ordinarily a rascal

VILLIAGO (fr. It. vigliacco, coward), vile or contemptible person

VIOL-DE-GAMBOYS, violoncello, bass viol

VIRGINALLING, lightly fingering, as if playing on the virginal

VIR SAPIT QUI PAUCA LOQUITUR, from Lyly's Grammar, That man is wise who speaketh few things or words

VIRTUE, essence; 'virtuous', of efficacious or powerful properties

VISITATION, affliction

VISITED, plague-stricken

VISITOR, one taking food

VISOR (or vizard), a mask

VIZAMENTS, advisements

VLOUTING-STOG, flouting-stock:—laughing-stock

VOICE, rumour, report

VOIDING LOBBY. Corridor or passage in which supplicants waited in hopes of admission to a lord's or a monarch's presence chamber

VOLABLE, quick

VOLQUESSEN, ancient country of the Velocasses, whose capital was Rouen

VOUCHER AND DOUBLE VOUCHER. Legal devices for recovery or converting estate entail into fee simple involving fictitious actions and the summoning (vouching) of men of straw to warrant titles which all parties wish invalidated, and which become invalidated by the vouchees defaulting

VULCAN, armourer of the gods, husband of Venus, cuckolded by Mars

VULGAR, public, common, well-known

WAFTAGE, passage by boat

WAINROPE, cart rope

WAIST, midship

WALLON, the part of the Netherlands bordering on France, its inhabitants Walloons

WAIT, attend upon

WAKE, a village feast

WANTON, rank-growing, out of hand

WARD, (i) generally explained as cell; (ii) bolts, lock, properly part of a lock; (iii) guard, 'come from thy ward':—come, off thy guard'

WARDER, staff or truncheon used to give signal for commencement or cessation of hostilities

WARDEN-PIE, a pie made of Warden pears or apples, called after the Cistercian Abbey at Warden, Bedfordshire

WARE, aware, cautious

WARE, BED OF, large bed 11 ft square, at Ware

WARP, cause to shrink or corrugate, go astray, deviate; 'warped':—crooked

WARRANTY, authorisation

WARRENER, rabbit-keeper

WASH, the barber's wash

WASHED AND SCOURED, knocked down and beaten

WASSAIL, revelry, carouse; 'wassail candle', a large candle to last the night of festivity

WATCH, keep a hawk awake

WATCHED, caught in the act

WATER-STANDING, perpetually filled with tears

WATERS FOR ALL, ready for anything

WAX, increase

WEAR, (sb) fashion; (vb) (i) be in the fashion; (ii) make weary

WEATHERCOCK, referring to a page's fantastic attire, a weathercock often having a pennon attached to it

WEEDS, dress, clothes

WEEK, 'in by the week':—trapped, caught. Lit. meaning unknown

WEEPING-RIPE, ready to weep

WEIGH, (i) be the same weight as; (ii) value at a certain rate

WELKIN, heaven

WELL-A-DAY!, Alas!

WELL-ADVISED, in one's right mind

WELL-DERIVED, well-born, well-descended

WELL-DIVULGED, well-received, of good report

WELL-ENTERED, thoroughly initiated, well trained

WELL-FAVOURED, gracious, beloved

WELL-FOUND, of tried merit

WELL-LIKING, in good condition, plump

WELL-SEEN, well taught

WELL TO LIVE, in capital health

WESTWARD-HO!, cry of Thames watermen leaving London, for Westminster

WEZAND, wind-pipe

WHALE BONE, WHITE AS, proverbial phrase, often found in early English poetry

WHAT TIME O' DAY?, when may that be?

WHELK, a pimple

WHEN? CAN YOU TELL?, a scornful expression to parry an impertinent question or request, similar in meaning to 'What next?'

WHIFFLER, officer who clears the way for a procession by flourishing a sword or a javelin

WHIRLS, metaphor from Fortune's wheel

WHILE-ERE, a while since

WHIRLIGIG, spinning contrivance, probably not a top but a cage upon a pivot for the punishment of thieves

WHITE, the white area at the centre of the target around the pin

WHITELY, pale

WHITING, bleaching

WHITSTERS, bleachers

WHOLE, solid

WIDE O' THE BOW HAND, wide of the mark. Lit. wide on the left or bowhand side of the target

WIDOW, to settle an estate (widowhood) upon a widow

WILDERNESS, wildness

WILL, intention, lust; 'by my will', intentionally

WILLOW, WILLOW GARLAND, the symbol of forlorn love

WIMPLED, muffled, blind-folded

WIND ABOUT, metaphor from stalking game—beat about the bush

WINDGALLS, disease of the fetlock in horses

WINDY SIDE, to the windward, so as to be able to escape easily

WINK, close the eyes, sleep, glimpse

WISH, commend

WIT-OLD (i) feeble witted; (ii) quibble on 'wittol', a contented cuckold

WOMAN OF THE WORLD, a married woman

WONT, is wont

WOOD, mad

WOODBINE, probably an error for 'bindweed'

WOODCOCK, the easiest bird to catch in a snare, hence a type of stupidity, a fool

WOODMAN, woman hunter

WOOLLEN (in the), between the blankets, without sheets

WOOLWARD, with woollen clothing next the skin

WORD, a pithy sentence; 'at a word', in short

WORKING, operation, effect, endeavour

WORLD (go to), get married

WORM, used as an expression of pity, esp. for those in love

WORT, sweet unfermented beer

WORTH, standing, authority, personal qualities; 'her worth, worth yours':—her personal qualities are worthy of your standing

WORTHY, excellence

WOT, pres. indic. of 'to wit', i.e. to know

WRACK, old form of 'wreck'

WRATH, wrathful; 'wrath of love', violent passion, ecstacy of love

WREATH (of chivalry), heraldic term, a chaplet of two different colours wound round each other and placed on top of a knight's helm

WREST, tuning key for certain wire-stringed instruments

WRING, writhe

WRITE, attain to: (i) 'to write man':—to reach man's estate; (ii) 'writ as little beard':—attained to as little beard

WRITE AGAINST, denounce

YARD, membrum virile

YARE, quick, ready, easily manageable (of a ship)

YCLIPED, called (deliberately archaic)

YEA AND NO (by), a puritan expletive

YEARS, 'in years', into wrinkles

YELLOWS, jaundice, generally of horses, but being a disease of the liver, formerly supposed to be the seat of the passions, also used for jealousy in man

YERK (of a horse), lash out with the heels, kick

YET, this word clearly had some comic significance, now lost

YOKE, couple; 'yoke-fellow', fellow worker

YOUNG, strong

YOUNGER, the younger son of the parable of the Prodigal Son, Luke xv, 12

YOUNG-EYES, with sight ever-young

YOUTH IN A BASKET, proverbial:—fortunate lover

ZANY, stage buffoon who initiated the tricks of the principal clown or fool

ZEALOUS, fervent

ZENITH, i.e. the height of my fortunes; an astrological term

ZEPHYR, mild, gentle breeze, the west wind

ZOUNDS, an oath, 'God's wounds'

ABBREVIATIONS

NED—The New English Dictionary

OED—Oxford English Dictionary

Sh. Eng.—Shakespeare's England

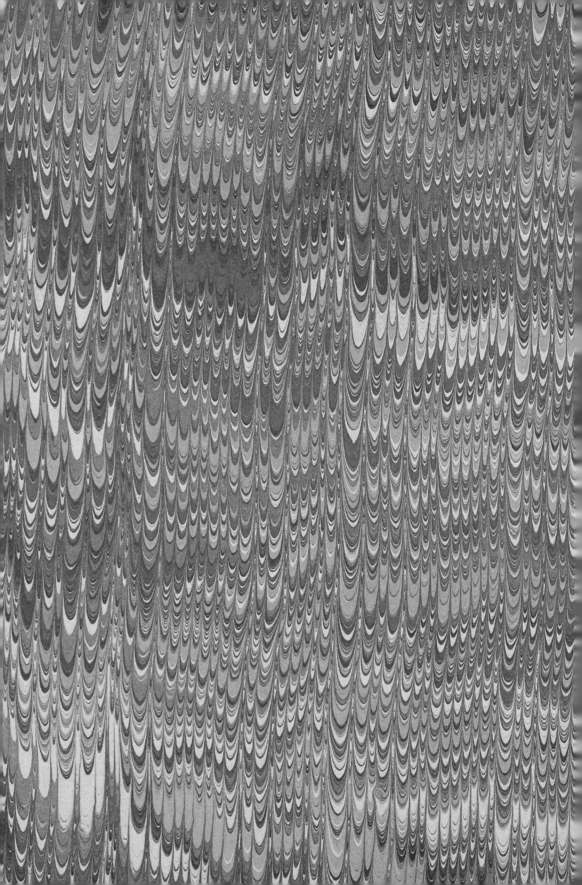